WHAT!!? NO APOCALYPSE?

—1000—

Angry crowds were yesterday demanding to know why they were still there. Furious at prophecies that said the world would come to an end on New Year's Day, AD1000, they took the law into their own hands and marched through the streets waving banners and shouting, "We want the end of the world to be nigh!"

Shake

In London, England, the official response was mixed.

"Off the record," said one cleric, "the Bible does mention an occurrence at the millennium. Something along the lines of 'Shake in thy clogs, this is the big one'. I think it's Revelations, but don't quote me."

Cover-up

Members of the action group "Apocalypse When?" are claiming there's been a **cover-up**. "We've been swindled!" said an AW spokes-peasant. "All we've heard for centuries is **'Watch it! The end of the world's coming! Best behave yourself, lads.'** And now what happens? Absolutely nothing, that's what! **It's a disgrace.**"

The "Apocalypse When?" office has been swamped with requests for information. "It's all been a plot to keep the workforce quiet," they insist. "All these years we've been meek and mild like the vicar told us, so we don't go to hell when the world ends. And for what? If you ask us, the establishment's in it up to the eyebrows."

Land

But it's not just the peasants who've been affected by

There's more of this to do, now the world hasn't ended!

Apocalypse fever. Wearing his AW sticker – "End not nigh? Ask me why!" – with pride, one distressed aristocrat moaned, "We've been ruined. Leases have been getting shorter for decades. On December 30 last year you couldn't rent anything for more than one day. It'll take ages for the market to recover."

Locked

Members of the All Soothsayers Brotherhood (ASB), who many hold responsible for the high level of expectation regarding the end of the world, were unavailable for comment. But we did manage to track down one seer, who spoke to us from behind an oak door with iron studs and ten locks.

"I'm beginning to think that we got the wrong millennium," admitted the shame-faced stargazer. "But look on the bright side. The weather's been bad lately, so there's every chance we're in the early stages of a spectacularly awful Apocalypse. My advice to the public is **Hang on to your tickets**!"

The Medieval Messenger

was written by
Fergus Fleming

designed by
Karen Tomlins

and edited by
Paul Dowswell

With thanks to Ruth Russell (design), Guy Smith (illustrations), and Christopher Smith (consultant).

The Medieval Messenger
ON OTHER PAGES

STRIKE A LIGHT!

Dark Ages over – it's official!

—1001—

So we're not a bunch of **uncivilized illiterate savages after all**! Ever since the Roman Empire fell to pieces six hundred years ago, historians have branded us a continent of brainless half-wits. But now the snooty scholars are playing a different tune. According to them we're back on the cultural map – with a vengeance.

Egghead

"Written records have a lot to do with it," admits one egghead monk. "Previously there were very few. These days almost every monastery worth its salt has a library."

So how does it feel to be civilized? "Fantastic!" says candlestick maker Baldwin Tubalard. "I can visit my cousin in Aquitaine now, and have a more than fifty percent chance of coming back alive – now that's what I call progress!"

How the two ages compare

DARK AGE 500–1000	MEDIEVAL AGE 1000–1450
Huts	Reach-for-the-sky cathedrals
Stupidity	Brains
Not much culture	Illuminations coming out of our ears
No money	Barrel-loads of it
Little trade	More trade than you can shake a mast at
Few written records	Manuscripts

Monks shamed

as hair ruse is rumbled

Bald Brother Etienne.

Monks who **plugged their lifestyle as a cure for baldness are in court today for making false claims.**

The trouble started when members of a French monastery lured thin-on-tops into their cloisters by promising to eliminate hair-loss problems. Novices soon found the "cure" was to have their heads shaved.

"I'd tried all the available treatments with no success," said Brother Etienne of Lyon. "When I heard of this offer it seemed too good to miss. Imagine my horror when I discovered I was going to be even balder than before."

But church leaders were quick to dismiss his claims. "This misguided individual is referring to the tonsure, a special trim in which the crown of the head is shaved as a gesture of humility. It so happens that this area of scalp also features in classic patterns of male baldness. The monasteries were quite within their rights to advertise it as a solution to hair-loss problems. Logically, if you're not meant to have any hair in that particular spot then its loss can't be a problem."

But the authorities are coming down on Etienne's side. A probe has been launched into monastery recruitment techniques. Meanwhile errant abbots are being advised to watch their step – **and their clippers.**

LET'S CALL IT RUSSIA!

KING VLAD IS NATION'S DAD!

—1003—

Vladimir, King of **Kiev, has decided to form a new nation.** Vlad is sick and tired of running a second-rate kingdom.

"World politics are going to change!" crowed the royal. "Nobody rated the Slavs in the past but now people are going to sit up and take notice. I'm going to build a superpower!"

Converted

Not half! Vlad has recently **married** his eighth wife, Princess Anna from Constantinople, and entered into an **alliance** with Anna's brother, Emperor Basil II. He's also **converted** himself and his subjects to Christianity, and has **conquered** pretty well everything immediately to the west of the Ural mountains.

New

The new state is to be called **Russia**. This comes from a Slav word *rus*, which is what the locals called **Vikings** who settled there in the eighth century. **And why not?**

"We're almost there. But our one big problem is writing," Vlad confided to the Messenger. "You lot in the West have it easy. You've got the Roman alphabet. Us? We've got the Cyrillic one."

Squashed

"Look at this – Д," he ranted. "Know what that is? It's a D. Yes, a D. Hard to believe isn't it? Now look at this. Ф. It's an F. Looks more like a squashed butterfly to me."

Saddled

"We've been saddled with it since that Greek missionary Saint Cyril came here in the 850s to try to convert us to Christianity. He's lucky we didn't boil him alive and feed his remains to the wolves. Still, people will get used to it in a few more centuries."

ENGLAND CRUMBLES AS NORMANS CONQUER

Military analysts attribute the Norman victory to their cross-stitching and chain-stitching skills. Their hemming was also very accomplished.

WILL WALLOPS HAZZA

—1066—

Luck wasn't on England's side when they met the chain-mail-clad Norman heavies at Hastings. Anglo-Saxon frontliners had been expecting a quick victory over the visitors. Instead they were shredded as the Norman offensive tore gaping holes in their outer field.

Past it

"It was October, and we were past our best," said an English axeman. "We should have cut them to pieces. But we'd already had a heavy season, what with rebellions here and there, and an invasion by the Norwegians. By the time we got to Hastings we had already peaked."

The Normans' masterful fighting left the Saxons in disarray. An early casualty was King Harold, who was stretchered off with an arrow in the eye.

"It's tough on Hazza," said his opposite number King William. "But he spent too much time on summer campaigns. You can't expect to come out top if you don't concentrate on the games that really matter."

Big plans

King William, who has already hinted that his new subjects can call him "The Conqueror", has big plans for England.

"First I'm going to build a large Tower in London," he said. "Then I'm going to see how much property people have got and then I'm going to tax them severely."

But first, William intends to commemorate his victory with a vivid depiction of his campaign against Harold. "We're calling it the Bayeux Tapestry," he told us. "Although between you and me, it's just a bit of embroidery."

RED TAPE RUNS WILD

—1086—

Paperwork – who needs it? That's the message from angry English land-owners as they struggle to meet the Domesday Book deadline.

"Nothing makes sense now that the Normans have taken over," moaned Lady Fotheringhay. Since her husband was killed at Hastings, Lady F. has single-handedly operated a farm in the village of Willybrook.

Fleece the rich

The Domesday Book is part of King William's new tax scheme to fleece the rich. Anyone who owns anything is being asked to fill in a questionnaire saying how many fields, houses, ducks, pigs, cows, sheep and servants they have. But for the weary Anglo aristocrats it's all too much.

Stumped

"I'm stumped," says Lady Fotheringhay. "Question Six

An anxious Lady Fotheringhay frets over her Domesday book forms.

asks whether my staff are freemen, bondservants, villeins, serfs or slaves. Well, really! How am I meant to know? **They all look the same to me.**"

ALL ABOARD THE INFIDEL EXPRESS!

Pope Urban says "Go for it!"

—1096—

The First Crusade is well underway having received official approval from the Pope. Lords from all over Western Europe are putting on their best helmets and heading for the Middle East. Their intention? To capture the holy city of Jerusalem and the holy land of Palestine, and teach the Muslim inhabitants (or *infidels*, as the crusaders call them) a lesson they'll never forget.

In the bag

The crusaders are doing well, thanks to a combination of their state-

Top notch gear gives our boys the edge.

Crusaders load up cargo boats in preparation for their three-year-long journey to Jerusalem.

of-the-art heavy cavalry and high-tech siege catapults.

"We've taken most major ports and are almost at Jerusalem," crowed breathless Belgian knight Fulk de Bulk. "I think we've got it in the bag."

Sacked

Not everyone's as happy as Fulk. Thousands of crusaders have died without getting anywhere near the Middle East. And thousands more have given up all hope of ever seeing Jerusalem. They've just sacked the nearest town beginning with J and gone home. **In fact some people are beginning to say it's all a waste of time.**

Sequel

Authorities are downplaying such suggestions. According to them the crusade has proved so **popular** that they are already planning several more.

"There is major sequel potential here," predicted Cardinal Goldwyn of Metro-Rome. "We foresee Second, Third and even Fourth Crusades. We've got a Children's Crusade in production and are looking at proposals for a People's Crusade. The public response has been tremendously enthusiastic."

The Messenger says: NOT IN THE MIDDLE EAST IT HASN'T!!

FRANK-LY CONFUSING

The Middle Easterners call crusaders "Franks". And the boys with crosses on their shirts are getting irritated.

"What a cheek! It's a bit over-familiar to be on first-name terms," says one indignant knight. "And if they must, why can't they get it right? Sure, lots of us are called Frank. But there are just as many who aren't. Some of us are Rons, some are Bills – I know at least five people called Bohemond – then there's Raymonds, Johns, Gregorys..."

Actually, says our linguistics correspondent, they call you *al-Faranj*. This sounds like "Franks" and is an Arabic word meaning *European*!

Next Week: IS YOUR BEST FRIEND AN INFIDEL?

Crusading opportunities

Jousting and jabbing and slicing and slashing – just four of the treats in store on our crusades!

CHILDREN'S CRUSADE

Are you between 8 and 12 with nothing to do this summer? Then join the Children's Crusade! Along our scenic route to the holy land of Palestine you will see new wildlife, camp out in strange places, and learn the ins and outs of foreign woodcraft.

Give us **your** time, and in return we guarantee that **you will almost certainly never return alive!**

HERMIT'S CRUSADE

Are you completely alone? Then join our crusade for the solitary gentleman. Travel without equipment, food or friends, and you will find many lovely spots in which to admire the tranquillity of the world. We particularly recommend the fine catacombs of the Middle East, in which you can be assured of eternal peace. Write enclosing stamped addressed parchment to

GOTCHA RECRUITMENT.

PET'S CRUSADE

Are you a pet? No, of course you're not – but you've probably got one or two. These little morsels can feel lonely when you're away fighting. So why not sign them up to our special Pet's Crusade? Call ARMY DINNERS now!

VILLAGE IDIOT'S CRUSADE

Are you an idiot? Yes? Then don't be ashamed to say so. Every village has one. **But here's your chance to look clever.** We're offering crusades at such cut-price rates they'll make your eyes cross!

PEOPLE'S CRUSADE

Are you a person? Yes? Then we want YOU to join our People's Crusade. No chain-mail, no horse, no chivalry. Just the gut determination to get a job done. You may not be able to do it, but who cares. All we want is people who are willing to try. Apply to NO FUTURE Enterprises.

JERUSALEM FALLS AS ARMY THUGS GO ON RAMPAGE

—1099—

Jerusalem has seen all kinds of visitors over the centuries. But none have been as ill-mannered as the crusaders. Having failed to pre-book, the mail-shirted louts simply turned up at the gate and demanded to be let in. When refused entry they took matters into their own hands and captured the town.

"We told them we were out of space, but they weren't taking No for an answer," said one dazed rep from the Jerusalem Tourist Board. "They just ran wild. I've never seen anything like it. The damage is enormous."

Trashed

"It is not a very good advertisement for Western civilization," agrees Adad Nirari, whose ten-room hotel, The Happy Haven, has been trashed from top to bottom. "I know we are supposed to have a tradition of hospitality, but this is going too far."

"Jerusalem is a holy city. Yet they strut around as if they own the place. They treat us Muslims like savages, whereas we're actually more civilized than they are. When they go back home they'll be taking our luxury goods like silks and spices with them, not to mention our ideas about medicine, astronomy and castle-building."

List

Angry Jerusalem hoteliers have drawn up a list of complaints against their uninvited conquerors. These include:

- **Breaking** down city walls
- **Storming** ramparts at all hours and **looting**
- Wholesale **slaughter** of Muslim and Jewish citizens
- Wading knee-deep through **blood** of enemies.

But crusader chiefs were unrepentant. "Admittedly, the boys were tired after a long campaign," said one crusader knight. "They've been on the road for three long years.

Now we've achieved our aim of capturing the holy city of Jerusalem we feel like letting off steam.

However, the locals will be pleased to hear that most of us will soon be going home. But a few of us are going to stay to set up a crusader kingdom here, with a king."

Crusader chiefs have confirmed this story and look set to announce that Baldwin, brother of crusader leader Geoffrey de Bouillon, is in line for the top job.

Crusaders letting off some steam in Jerusalem.

Spot the enemy in your midst with our 4-page pull-out special.

BECKET KICKS BUCKET

Thomas à Becket uttering his last words. ("Aaaaaaaagh," according to most witnesses.)

KING'S CURSES CAUSE CALAMITY AT CANTERBURY

— 1170 —

Thomas à Becket, the merchant's son from Merton, England, who became chancellor to King Henry II, and rose to even greater fame as archbishop of Canterbury, has been struck dead by four of the King's knights.

Serf-razing power

As chancellor, Becket, 52, had been a leading figure in Henry II's campaign to give more power to the monarchy and less to the church. A trusted adviser to the King, Becket also excelled himself as a soldier, razing castles to the ground and leading troops.

But things turned sour when Henry appointed his pal to the top job in the English church – archbishop of Canterbury. Becket immediately changed character, championing the church and its right to remain free from royal interference.

Henry raged and ranted as Thomas:
• Opposed the raising of taxes on the church.
• Banished some of Henry's top men from church premises.
• Upheld the right of villainous churchmen to be tried by their own soft-on-crime church courts, rather than by the King's flogging-and-hanging style government courts.

Henry launched a no-holds-barred campaign to ruin his former friend, and Becket fled to France, fearing for his life. But Henry agreed to allow him to come home when Becket, backed by the Pope, threatened the King with a no-excuses, no-money-back, one-way ticket to hell!

Bad temper

Becket returned to Canterbury in December 1170, but his quarrel with Henry was far from over. When he banished more of Henry's top men from church, the King snapped. Cursing and snarling, he let it be known that Thomas à Becket was obviously **tired of living**. So four of the King's knights sped down to Canterbury and slew him in his own cathedral.

But news of his death has made Canterbury a shrine to his followers, and already there are reports that Becket is to be made a saint. Henry, meanwhile, is overcome with remorse and plans to seek forgiveness from the Pope himself.

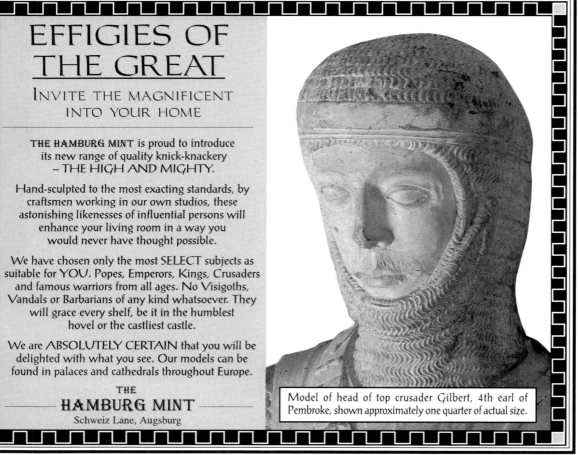

"GET OUT OF MY HEAD!"

Keyhole surgeon faces lockup

—1179—

Keyhole surgery? Angry patient Eldred Turnip is giving surgeons the length of his tongue. Having checked in for a trepanning operation – a routine procedure which involves drilling a hole in the skull to relieve headaches or bouts of madness – he came out with a gaping cavity the size of a saucer.

Latest thing

"They told me keyhole surgery was the latest thing," he told the Messenger. "But frankly I may as well have had it done by the local gravedigger. I mean, look at it."

Turnip is calling for revenge. "Six years in a dank dungeon would do" he told us.

Unfortunately for Eldred, although seers and sages predict that keys and keyholes will get smaller in the future, they're still extremely large and rather clumsy devices. Medical experts say Eldred should have avoided new-fangled hands-on surgery and stuck to the tried and trusted route of medicines and magic charms.

Mallet

"These so-called surgeons are just jumped-up barbers, or battlefield medics," said top physician Lancelot de Lozenge, "and expecting them to perform intricate operations is like asking a road-builder to fix your delicate gold bracelet with a great big mallet. Medicine has so much to offer I can't understand why Eldred took such drastic action."

Hands-on

Lozenge went on to tell the Messenger, "Therapeutic flowers and plants are available in great numbers, as are such health-giving foods as sugar and treacle. Why fix a bad head with painful surgery when a lotion of ginger and cinnamon will do the trick with much less fuss. Best of all get yourself touched by someone with healing powers. Kings are best, if you can get near enough to beg them to touch you, but a Jew or Muslim who has converted to Christianity also has the ability to cure all sorts of maladies by simply laying their hands on the patient."

Wrong signs

"Besides, these surgeons often perform their grisly chores at completely inappropriate times of the year. Anyone connected with medicine knows that you can only treat particular ailments at set astrological moments. I, for example, would only tend to a patient with bad headaches when the Moon is rising in Sagittarius. It's just asking for trouble to do it at any other time."

Trepanning – top treatment for headaches. Don't try this at home, kids!

PARISIANS UPSET AS KING PAVES STREETS

—1185—

Older residents are up in arms as Paris becomes Europe's first city to have paved streets. Ever since cobble-laying started last year, citizens have feared for their heritage. Now matters have come to a head.

"It makes my blood boil," says refuse collector Pierre Stinque. "Medieval cities are meant to be poky mazes, knee-deep in filth and so gloomy you can't see your nose in front of your face. Why do we have to be different from everyone else? It'll ruin the tourist trade for starters."

King Philip, the man behind the project, got hot and bothered when we asked him how this change would affect the leisure industry.

"What leisure?" he snarled. "We don't have any. We work hard here. Show me a holidaymaker and I'll show you a head on a stick. We need business. And business needs good streets."

Despite the promise of increased trade, locals are still unhappy.

"It won't stop here," says Pierre. "Paved streets are just the beginning. Before you know it there'll be boulevards everywhere letting in sunlight, vapours and God knows what. The people won't stand for it. One day there'll be a revolution. You mark my words."

Street cobblers in action. Local maidens have been advised to steer well clear of these lewd and outspoken workers, who are renowned for their baggy tights and all too visible bottoms.

"KING CARNAGE" DIES IN TENT

Genghis sparks bloodbath horror

—— **1227** ——

The mighty Mongol Empire is bidding a tearful farewell to cut-throat killing machine Genghis Khan. The warlord who tamed the Asian continent and still wanted more, has died.

Genghis, whose byword was "Join our horde and you'll never be bored", passed away in his tent *Dunpillagin'* pitched in the foothills of the Linbanshan mountains in China. His demise follows a long struggle against severe internal injuries. "He'd not been the same since he fell off his horse," said a royal insider.

He is best remembered for conquering half the world, and annihilating anyone who stood in his way.

Massacre

As news of his death spread through the empire, tributes poured in. "He certainly knew how to lay on a massacre," said a rival royal. "When it came to carnage Genghis was king."

Jog Ogudei, landlord of the Rack & Ruin, Genghis's local tavern, said, "Some people say he was too tough. But some-times you've got to be cruel to be kind. Those cities he razed – don't forget he gave those people the chance to surrender. You can't blame him for slaughtering them if they didn't take up his offer."

Put to sword

Genghis's body is currently being returned for burial at his headquarters in the Mongol capital of Karakorum.

The phrase "Put them to the sword" was never far from his lips, and soldiers in his funeral procession are making a special effort to show their respect by slaughtering anyone unfortunate enough to cross their path. "It's what he would have wanted," said a member of his entourage.

Genghis takes a tumble! The barbarian bigwig falls off his horse.

Rotten to the core... Is Genghis history's baddest apple?

The Mongols may have liked him, but no one else did. Some people even say Genghis was **worse** than fifth-century Slav madman Attila the Hun. So exactly who is the Baron of Barbarity, and Earl of Extermination?

Here on the Messenger we've compiled our own chart to answer that eternal question:

"Who is the baddest of the bad?"

Each category is awarded badness points from 1 to 10.

Messenger Messenger on the wall, Who is the Baddest of them all?	GENGHIS KHAN	POINTS OUT OF 10	ATTILA THE HUN	POINTS OUT OF 10
Nickname	"Conqueror of the world"	6	"Scourge of God"	10
Appearance	Gangly, feline, long beard, not particularly filthy.	4	Squat, scar-faced psychopath. Sinister moustache. Pointy hat. Absolutely filthy.	10
Character	Prone to acts of unspeakable violence. Cunning.	10	Cunning. Prone to acts of unspeakable violence.	10
Most barbaric exploits	Conquered half known world. Massacred entire cities. Used captives as human shields for army. Boiled enemy chiefs alive. Left mountain of human bones.	40*	Terrorized western Europe. Laid waste eastern Europe. Murdered brother. Invaded France because king refused to let him marry sister.	7
What his enemies said about him	He was sent by Satan to herald the end of the world.	10	He was sent by God to punish the world for its sins.	7
How he died	Long illness, following fall from horse.	0	Said to have been murdered in bed by his wife Ildeco.	10
TOTAL BADNESS POINTS	Congratulations, Genghis, the horse-loving nomad from the howling wastes of central Asia. You are HISTORY'S TOP TYRANT!	70	Bad luck Attila, you may have had the looks, you may even have had the table manners, but when it comes to sheer IN-YOUR-FACE BARBARITY you're second rate, mate.	54

*Messenger staff felt 10 points was insufficient for this category.

NO WAR IS COMPLETE WITHOUT

ELKHORN'S
SAFETY VISORS

How often have you had your nose chopped off and thought, "I could have avoided that if only I'd been wearing a decent visor."? Probably scores of times.

Elkhorn's Safety Visors come to the rescue. Buy from us and you'll never suffer that embarrassing problem again.

Elkhorn completes your all-over metal body protection. Our helmets suit all facial sizes and come with ready-made eyeholes AND breathing holes - perfect for those sultry crusader campaigns. No more stuffy battles when you're wearing an Elkhorn!

Will improve your fighting . The top-of-the-range "Barbarossa" includes a vicious tusk which is perfect for those in-your-face combat moments.

At Elkhorn we realize there's more to visors than mere fighting. They're a valuable social accessory - particularly at jousting tournaments. Have you noticed how the winning knight tilts his visor back in that devil-may-care way and comes forward to speak to his lady? How everybody loves it - particularly when the visor clangs down and traps his tongue! All our visors have friction bearings, so you'll never get that with an Elkhorn!

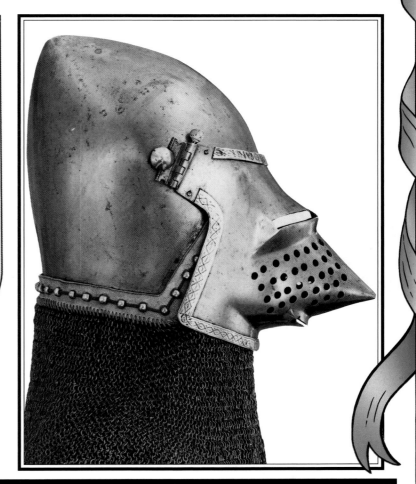

Battle-tested at Jerusalem, Antioch, Acre, Poitiers, Crécy, Agincourt, and many many more!!

NEW DEVELOPMENT FOR CRUSHED CITIZENS

London Bridge – the capital's hottest new address!!

1190

The Mayor of London is **stunned** and **shocked** about new developments on his best bridge. The Mayor has recently spent three weeks in a darkened bedroom recovering from a stomach-stretching 320 eels, eaten during a royal banquet. When he finally opened his curtains and looked out over the River Thames he saw that **London Bridge was covered in houses**.

Plank

The thunderstruck official finally mustered the strength to make a comment. "I'd noticed some people lurking around with hammers and planks," he told the Messenger, "but I thought they were from Public Works come to mend the gallows or something. Imagine my astonishment when I realized what was going on."

Sick

It seems that city dwellers are sick and tired of having to squeeze into every nook and cranny in the overcrowded area within the city walls. Commuters too are weary of dreadful travel conditions, and have opted for direct action.

"The roads are awful," one London Bridge dweller told us. "They're always congested. And nothing's ever spent on maintenance. I almost drowned in a pothole last winter. So a bunch of us got together and thought, here's a bit of empty space right by where we work. Why not develop it and save ourselves all that travel?"

Arch

The 19-arch site, long a hazard for Thames boatmen, has proved remarkably popular. A church has already been built on it, and prison authorities are planning a gatehouse where they can stick traitors' heads.

Redeveloped London Bridge, as seen from the prestigious Tower of London. The new properties are centrally located and convenient for river transportation.

GERMAN VICAR PANS GREEN MAN

1190

There I was, conducting a **perfectly ordinary evensong. Suddenly I had this eerie feeling. I turned around and saw this little green man staring at me. I was so shocked I fainted!"**

This report, from a **respectable German vicar**, is just one of thousands that are pouring in from all over Europe.

What's happening? Are we being invaded by **beings from another planet?**

NO! The Messenger can reveal that it's nothing more than an elaborate plot by church architects. Asked to brighten up our churches and bring them into the 13th century, the jolly japesters filled them with **ancient pagan symbols**.

Trade

Green Men, as they're known in the design trade, are carvings of faces or figures covered in **leaves**. Once upon a time they represented gods of nature. **But not any more**! According to Hans Hocke of the Gothenburg Church Architects Association they now portray "benign images which represent renewal and resurrection".

Next

Next time you're in church have a good look around. You're bound to find a Green Man somewhere – and

A Green Man, lurking in the roof of a church.

probably just where you're least expecting him!

Let us know how you get on. These cheery fellows are tucked away in all kinds of odd corners. We'll give five groats for the most outrageous Green Man location in Europe.

FRENCH PLAY DIRTY!

The route to victory was through a castle toilet.

BAD KING JOHN'S TOP TEN
TRIALS AND TORMENTS

—1216—

Was England's King John the worst monarch of the century? To celebrate the occasion of his death we've drawn up a chart of his top-tastic ten biggest flops and disasters...

❶ **1192** As a mere prince he **snatches** the English throne from brother King Richard who is off crusading. Beginning of era of extremely **high taxes.**

❷ **1193** John made to look **utterly stupid** by hunky underworld dreamboat Robin Hood, who runs rings around him in Nottinghamshire.

❸ **1194** Richard comes back from the crusades, and John has to give back the throne. (How demeaning!)

❹ **1199** Inherits throne again and promptly starts losing all England's foreign territories. (Quite useless!)

❺ **1214** His army is **defeated** by French at Battle of Bouvines, Flanders. Where is John at the time? Half a country away in Poitou "trying to organize a pincer movement". (So he says.)

❻ **1214 Raises taxes** 1,000 percent, making his nobles very irritated indeed. (Incredible folly.)

❼ **1215 Forced** by nobles to sign the **Magna Carta**, where he **gives away** enormous royal power and paves the way for democratic parliament. (Good for us. But for a king?...Eternal embarrassment.)

❽ **1215** French troops capture London. (**Will it never end**?)

❾ **1216** Catches **dysentery**. (Typically low and incompetent.)

❿ **1216** (again) **Dies**. Hurrah! But not before losing all his money, jewels, robes etc. in a marshy area of eastern England named the Wash. Known for ever after as "**the King who lost his clothes in the Wash**". (The final, wretched, unforgivable humiliation!)

Messenger comment: King John? – We say **MORE LIKE KING CONTEMPTIBLE!!!**

—1204—

Château Gaillard, England's strongest castle in France, **has fallen**. Built in 1190 by crusader hero King Richard the Lionheart, it includes the latest "tower and outer wall" castle-building technique, which Richard copied from his Muslim enemies.

"This castle is so well built," Rick used to boast, "that I could hold it if it was made of butter."

Weed

But Rick's successor, the ever-unpopular and weedy

King John, has let it **slip through his fingers**. After a seven-month siege, during which the castle was constantly mined and bombarded with crossbow fire, French soldiers crept through a toilet on the outer wall and captured the whole castle.

"We were caught with our pants down," admits one English knight.

Chortle

"This is going to change the face of Europe," chortled French king Philip. "For years the English have been laying claim to territories that belong to our lot.

From now on the English kings will have to content themselves with what they've got the other side of the Channel. After all, they can always have a go at invading Scotland."

Hanging

Military sources on both sides of the Channel agree that King John is a dolt. With Château Gaillard gone, the English kings have little hope of hanging on to territory in France, and that within a few decades they will have lost all their possessions in France.

England is on that island north of France, say the French, so the English ought to GET BACK THERE!

IT'S WAR! THREE YEARS LATE

—1340—

English troops crossing the Channel, on their way to do battle with France.

Edward III of England has decided he's the rightful king of France, but Philip of Valois, who actually IS the king of France, isn't going to go without making a SERIOUS FUSS about it!

Philip is also big pals with England's on-the-doorstep enemy Scotland, and Edward thinks Philip's about to invade England to help them! The result – France and England have officially opened the 100 Years War. **The trouble is it's taken three years to get started.**

"The original insults were exchanged as far back as 1337," admitted a French envoy. "But remember that 100 years of fighting takes some preparation. Both sides have had to **find** allies, **swap** additional insults, **raise** taxes, **train** armies, **invent** further insults and so on. **It's not a quick business.**"

Serious

Edward is taking the war so seriously he's issued a law commanding English peasants to stop playing football. Instead, they must polish up their skills with a bow and arrow. Anyone who disobeys faces public execution!

Rusty

Despite the long delay, hostilities started on a vigorous note with an unpleasant little campaign in the north of France, when Edward's troops rampaged around for five weeks, burning villages and destroying crops. Things have livened up with a sea battle on Midsummer's Day, just outside the port of Sluis, in Flanders. The English fleet defeated their opponents thanks to superior longbow skills. Quick-firing archers, stationed on wooden "castles" at either end of their ships, made short work of the opposition. But the French vowed they would make a comeback.

"Just a minor hiccup," smiled King Philip of France. "Our troops were rusty after all that hanging around, that's all. You wait. **We're only in the first year and there's another 99 to come.**"

General

This doesn't seem to have affected the general populace. As far as anyone can tell, England and France are both getting ready for more. "Don't stop now," seems to be the general opinion.

The Messenger says, "Watch this space!"

CRASH BANG WALLOP!
Calais comes a cropper

—1347—

After a siege lasting nearly a year, victorious English troops have been declared the owners of Calais. But angry citizens claim it was an unfair fight and are trying to have the decision overthrown. "We demand a re-siege!" stormed the Mayor of Calais. "The English cheated from start to finish. They have broken all the rules. **If this sort of thing continues it will ruin the good name of warfare.**"

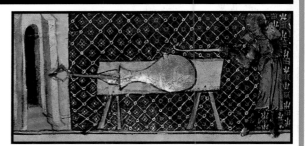

It looks like a vase, but it's far more dangerous.

Secret weapon

The French are hopping mad because the English have introduced a new weapon – gunpowder artillery.

"It's outrageous," said the Mayor. "We were expecting a standard siege, with ladders, heavy catapults, boiling oil, people starving slowly – you know, the usual kind of thing. But there was none of that. There I was, standing above the gate and having my midday laugh at the enemy, when there was this big bang and a cloud of smoke from the English lines.

I thought a stove had blown up or something, but then I heard a whooshing noise and next thing I knew there was a filthy big metal arrow sticking halfway through the gate. It shook me up I can tell you! And that's not all. The English have got TEN of these things."

Stop fussing

When questioned about their new weapon, the English were unrepentant.

"It fires arrows, so basically it's no different from a longbow," said the Bombardier-General. "The only difference is that the arrows are **bigger and nastier**, they **travel farther** and they **do more damage**."

He showed us one of these heavy iron weapons. As far as we could tell it looked harmless enough – unless you tried to pick it up!

"Appearances can be deceptive," he went on, tapping the cannon with his pointer. "It may look like a tipped-over vase. In fact it is a registered weapon of destruction. Now. Pay attention. What you do is fill the inside with gunpowder. Here! Then you stuff the arrow down the hole at the top. Here! Then you put a match to the hole at the other end. Here! And then you stand clear and cover your ears! "

Worse to come

When questioned by the Messenger, English diplomat Sir Castlemaine Faugh-ecks responded, "We feel the enemy is complaining about nothing. In a short while everyone will have artillery pieces like these. And they will be firing increasingly sophisticated missiles – such as stone and metal balls."

MYSTERY PLAGUE ROCKS EUROPE

We've been bad says bishop

——1349——

As yet another city fell victim to the "Black Death", church leaders were in general agreement about the cause of the mystery plague. "We've all been very bad, and God is punishing us," the Bishop of Rheims told his congregation.

Although some sages blamed the plague on the movement of the planets, there were few who went along with this view at Rheims Cathedral.

Black blotches

Doctors have told patients to be on the lookout for the following symptoms – terrible aches and pains, fever, insanity, headaches, peevishness, and bursting blisters which ooze black blood. Physicians have been unable to come up with a sure-fire cure for the plague but ten-year-old treacle and chopped-up grass snake is currently the most popular remedy. "I can't recommend it highly enough," said Jean le Bonne, a baker from Brittany, shortly before he died.

Meanwhile looting of affected areas seems to be a continuing problem. Some cities and towns are completely deserted, with their citizens either dying or fleeing into the countryside. "Looter looted my lute," said minstrel Jean de Chanson.

Doctors forecast the plague will last for three more years and kill a third of all Europeans.

The Bishop of Rheims explaining the cause of the plague to his congregation.

The plague. Bad news for man and beast.

Wat Tyler gets the wrong side of the Mayor of London.

WHAT'S WAT GOT? NOT A LOT, THAT'S WAT!

1381

Londoners had the time of their lives when Wat Tyler and his "Peasants' Revolt" came to town. "Two days of sheer enjoyment," said one critic. "It's rip-roaring entertainment for all the family."

Revolting peasants

It all began when Wat, a tiler from Kent, organized a rebellion to complain about taxes. He marched with 10,000 peasants to London and proceeded to give the locals the show of the century.

"It was a magnificent spectacle," said Tom Titmuss, who lives in a fifth floor apartment on London Bridge. "They ransacked all the wealthy households. Ho ho ho! You should have seen John of Gaunt's face when they threw everything he owned into the Thames."

Heads on sticks

"Then they upped the tempo. If they saw anyone they thought might be a taxman they cut off his head and stuck it on a stick! Great stuff! After that they started burning all the government buildings and opening all the prisons. I tell you, honestly, it was one of the best rebellions I've seen in my life."

Surprise

The climax of the two-day event came when Wat and his men presented their demands to 14-year-old King Richard II.

"We were considerably surprised," said His Majesty. "But naturally we seized a pen and moved our hand back and forth over a piece of paper to suggest that we were re-writing the law as he wanted. As one does, you know."

But it was Wat who got the biggest surprise, when the Mayor of London came up and stabbed him to death.

The rebels were then so confused that they asked the King what to do next. He told them to go home and they did what he said.

Contrived

"If I had any complaint about the rebellion, it was the ending," said Tom Titmuss. "I thought it was contrived and, frankly, rather implausible. But then that's so often the problem with real-life dramas isn't it? So many strands, so many different parts, all those crowd scenes. I mean, something's got to give hasn't it?

"Still, I thought it was a jolly good effort. **Ten out of ten!**"

Richard II. Wat got his goat.

ROYAL EXCLUSIVE

Longbow is best says Edward III

| Longbow – stone age? | Crossbow – too slow? |

Technology special

1347

Top monarch Edward III added fresh fuel to the longbow versus crossbow debate yesterday when he claimed, "Longbows are best". Speaking to posh pals at Glastonbury Tournament, he said, "Anyone who says these new crossbows are better is talking out of their hat. Only last year we thrashed the French fair and square with longbows at the battle of Crécy."

Stone age

Arms experts rallied to his support. "Longbows have a quicker rate of fire, and all weather capability," said one leading knight.

But crossbow bosses were undismayed. Robert de Courcey of Crossbow Deathblow Inc. refused to concede. "Get out of the stone age. Crossbows are 100% more accurate and have a much higher hit-to-kill ratio."

Bird breakthrough is bogus, says impatient patient

—— 1383 ——

P oorly patient Ron of Sallow, who doctors say is suffering from an imbalance of bodily humours, hit out yesterday at one of medicine's most recent and controversial techniques. Ron is disputing the accuracy of the so-called *Caladrius bird diagnosis* (C.B.D.) test.

In this procedure a Caladrius bird is placed in front of an ailing man to determine his chances of recovery. If the bird looks at him he will recover. If it looks away he will die.

" I just cawed to say I loathe you." Ron's bird turns him down.

Snuff

Ron's physician Jean de Tourniquet has refused him further treatment following a negative result, and patient Ron is getting more and more impatient! "I could tell at once that pesky bird didn't like me," fuming Ron told the Messenger.

Questioned about his health he went on, "It's my innards, they're not quite right. They ache a bit after I've eaten steamed pig fat and I get these blotches on my arms, but that doesn't mean I'm about to snuff it." Indeed, apart from a slight fever and an unpleasant rash Ron looked all right to us.

Rabbit

When we contacted Jean de Tourniquet he was quick to dismiss his patient's protests. "Ah, a tragic case," he told us, "and the C.B.D. test is never wrong. I've tried everything. A potion of rabbit droppings and mercury is an excellent remedy, but that doesn't seem to be working. I collected a couple of pints of blood from him, and that didn't work. Even a dose of wild lettuce and leeches hasn't cured him. Alas, we must wait for nature to take its course."

Right: Rattled Ron receives his daily dose of mercury and rabbit droppings.

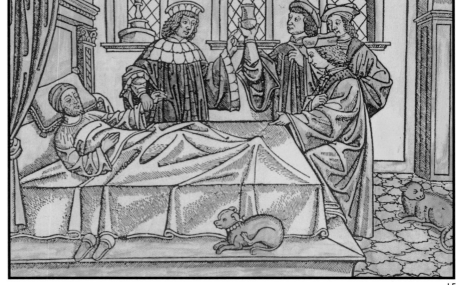

GO GOTHIC WITH
TOP-NOTCH
CONSTRUCTION

Is Your Attendance Falling?

Don't blame your sermons. More than likely it's your cathedral that needs revising. Look around. Do you see:
· Lurching spires? · Sagging pews? · Blocked transept?
· Puddles in the belfry?

Yes? Then call TOP-NOTCH CONSTRUCTION now! We have the answers to all your problems - and some you've never heard of.

Our architects are fully qualified masons who have spent years learning the secrets of their trade.

Whether you want a custom-made nave, a vestry refit or a complete gothic cathedral built from scratch, we'll supply you with accurate plans before you can say Evensong.

FLYING BUTTRESS

Build higher with this sure-fire support for sagging walls.

SPIRE

An absolute must! With one of these you're that little bit closer to heaven.

CLERESTORY

No, we don't know how to pronounce it either. But it lets in more light.

TOWER

Something to put a spire on. Or if a spire's that little bit too ostentatious, then something to put the bells in.

STAINED GLASS

The best in multichrome entertainment.

SAINTS

The congregation that never goes away. Good moral guidance for the rest of 'em too.

BELLS

Hear them chime. Carillons, peals, the lot. Also Dong, Dong, Dong, Dong.

TOMBS

Ultra-realistic pre-demise effigies of the departed. Legs crossed only if you've been on a crusade. Can also include dog under foot, wife by side, sword, packed-lunch etc.

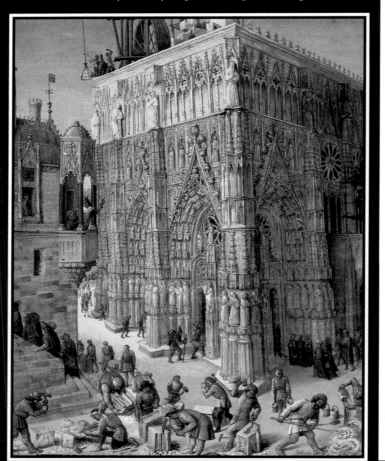

16

YOU AND YOUR STARS

with Patrick Thistle

The Messenger's own astrologer tells you what's in store...

Aquarius *January 21 to February 21*–
There will be no plague, no famine, no war, your teeth will not fall out and if you're a servant you will be thrashed no more than five times a day. Really! What a wonderful year!

Pisces *February 21 to March 21*–
All the portents suggest you will be taking a lot of baths this year. For heavens sake don't. Apart from the obvious dangers to your health, people will start to avoid you. Only do this on doctor's orders

Aries *March 21 to April 21*–
This looks like a dreadful year for you. Your sheep will die, your cows will go mad, your swine will keel over and your fowl will perish. Honestly, it's a really bad one. If I were you I'd give this year a miss and go straight on to the next one.

Taurus *April 21 to May 21* –
Those medicinal herbs you have been trying to grow for ages will start to pick up. Give the hyssop a lot of water in dry weather because it cures the colds which are going to afflict you in the winter. Did you cut back the marjoram hard last year? I hope so, because the new shoots are essential for the headaches which will plague you when you've recovered from the colds.

Gemini *May 21 to June 21* –
Well, Geminis are meant to be well-balanced people. But there's one who isn't. Yes, I'm talking about you, Edward I of England. You are a violent and miserable type who should be more careful about who you subjugate. The Scots will never forgive you. And stop building all those castles to frighten the Welsh.

Cancer *June 21 to July 21* –
Dig a big cellar and be prepared to hide there when Mongol hordes burn your house down. This precaution is a must for Cancerians who live in Hungary. The stars say that you will be ravaged, ransacked and ridiculed by a lot of rough types on horseback. So get digging now.

Leo *July 21 to August 21* –
Bad news for Cathars. Your austere Christian faith has been popular in France and Italy for a few years, but the established church doesn't like the way you're making it look corrupt and worldly. Expect an extremely violent reaction in the next few years (especially if you're reading this between 1200 and 1240).

Virgo *August 21 to September 21* –
You will make your usual pilgrimage to Compostela in Spain, you will eat your usual vast quantities of oysters when you get there, and this time, for once, YOU WILL NOT EAT A BAD ONE! Hurrah!

Libra *September 21 to October 21* –
Librans are harmonious, charming people who like to decorate their homes in pastel shades of brown. What a shame, then, that this year is going to be one of rich, exotic hues with gaudy clothes being imported from the East and garish stained-glass windows popping up everywhere. I advise you to stay indoors until the Gothic era has ended. Stock up with plenty of turnips!

Scorpio *October 21 to November 21* –
A rare configuration of stars suggests that Frederick Barbarossa, the Holy Roman Emperor, will drown one of you slowly in a wine barrel to see if he can detect any sign of your soul escaping. Condemned criminals should be especially cautious.

Sagittarius *November 21 to December 21* –
You will perform many feats of heroism with your trusty bow. But whatever you do, don't let it get too damp. This has led to many a poor performance in major battles.

Capricorn *December 21 to January 21* –
There is some uncertainty here. The planets are entering a particularly auspicious phase for Capricornians. They show every likelihood of prosperity and good fortune, particularly if your birthday is on the eighth. On the other hand, my birthday is on the eighth, and I'm having a rotten time. Astrology? Pah! Who needs it!

Messenger COMMENT

WE'VE NEVER HAD IT SO GOOD!

Remember how it used to be before we got medieval? Dark Ages, famine, backward farming practices, few towns and merchants, squabblesome populace, always being invaded by people in horned helmets. For goodness sake, **it was so bad we thought the world was going to end!** (__And what a joke that was, eh?__)

Now look at us! If we're not sitting pretty then I don't know what we're doing. More opportunities are open to us than ever before. We can:

Go on crusades   *Live in bigger towns*
Catch plague   *Catch more plague*
Build vast stone castles   *Wear fancy clothes*
Persecute religious minorities   *Put spices in our food*
Make pilgrimages   *Attend tournaments*

We couldn't do that in the Dark Ages, could we? **No Sir!** So what does this say for us? It says we're a go-ahead era, that's what! And if anybody wants to make jokes about "being Middle-Aged" __they'd better be wearing protection.__

What next?

__We took to the streets to ask our readers what they think the future holds__. There was one thing you all agreed on: the next Age is going to be called the **Renaissance**. Otherwise, your answers showed the intelligent variety we'd expect from Messenger readers. Here's a few of them:

"Plague! Lots more plague!"

"Bigger cities. Swankier palaces. Funnier clothes."

"Perspective. I foresee a far greater use of perspective in art. That, and a growth in interior design. Chapel ceilings will be particularly magnificent."

"Wars! Many more wars!"

"Seats of learning will be everywhere. Much more comfortable than these old stools."

"The use of telescopes to show that the earth orbits the sun."

"I think it will be the age of the potato, if they ever discover the country it grows in."

"Handwriting will be finished! So will parchment! It'll be printing and cheap, easy-to-read books made out of paper."

"There'll be more attempts to find a sea route to China. Who knows – they might even discover America if they go the wrong way."

"The end of the world will come in AD1500."

"No it won't."

Too many fast days equals a lot of baggy habits for Europe's monks.

FOOD IN THE FAST LANE

Monks are too thin! That's what leading abbots are saying as they introduce sweeping changes to monastery menus.

There are more than 200 foodless fast days (when monks don't eat for the good of their souls) on the Christian calendar – including Fridays and Lent. Hungry monks found they were only eating for a total of 23 weeks every year. The result? **A lot of baggy habits.**

Fast

Now new regulations say monks can eat anything they like on a fast day **so long as it's not meat.**

If that sounds boring, then think again. The ingenious cowlheads have come up with some mouth-watering recipes to tempt even the most jaded palate.

Tuck

Anything that lives in water has been classified as a FISH, so monks can tuck into such delicious dishes as fried frog with steamed turnip, and boiled beaver with hot buttered swede.

But some church chiefs are warning that relaxing the rules regarding clerical catering will lead to a waistline explosion, and **emaciated monks** will become **fat friars** before you can say **"A whole roast ox please, UNDERLINE ALL THE TRIMMINGS!"**

ARE YOU EATING A BALANCED DIET?

Frumpy and dumpy after all those Christmas parties?

Get back into shape with the Messenger diet.

Our expert nutritionists have drawn up an easy-to-follow menu to suit all pockets. This shows just what you should be eating at each meal.

	PEASANT	NOBLE
**BREAKFAST**	Rye bread Sliver of cheese	Eggs White bread Milk
**LUNCH**	Rye bread Sliver of cheese	Pastries Bit of cheese Spicy eels Fish cakes Sturgeon "The best roast that may be had." Oysters Venison Blancmange
**SUPPER**	Rye bread Sliver of cheese Cabbage* (Sundays only) *Omit if this causes wind and discomfort after meals. These are common symptoms of starvation and cabbage will make them worse.	As for lunch but add nibbles, aperitifs, hogsheads of wine and kegs of beer...

Property for sale

BIG CASTLE. Not yet stormed. Ramparts need some attention but otherwise OK. Three large living rooms and banqueting hall. Turret toilets empty on to peasants below. Delightful outlook. **Box 443**.

TOWN LOT. Derelict house and garden. Plague repossession. Looks fine from outside. Heaven knows what lies within. **Box 324**.

KRACK. Funny name, fantastic castle. Beautifully situated in Holy Land, with arrowslits, double walls, interior citadel and all-around protection. Built by crusaders but currently occupied by Muslim troops. Available to anyone with enough troops. **Box 657**.

HOLE. Well-placed hole set in dry bank on outskirts of pleasant village. Ditch within easy reach for washing, etc. Any reasonable offer. **Box 846**.

Lady Penelope's Q&A

HUNGRY FOR ADVICE? HERE'S FOOD FOR THOUGHT

HOLES

 I am told that I should supply trenchers at every meal. Why? I don't want people digging holes in the floor.

A. Don't be silly. Trenchers are what you put your guests' food on. They're thick slices of bread. And when they get too soggy you just throw them under the table for the dogs.

RUBBISH

 Our castle needs a new midden. Where can I get one?

As everyone knows, a midden is just another word for a scrapheap. You can buy them ready made, but the best way is to start your own. Simply choose a place downwind and put your kitchen scraps there. In a few months it'll be a perfectly acceptable pile of rotten food. Some people say you should move your midden at regular intervals to stop it from getting smelly. But I've found that my peasants will do the job for me. If I let them scrabble through it at regular intervals everything turns out smell-free and satisfactory.

SMOKE

 Dear Lady P. Our manor has a big hall. It's very nice and we eat there every day. But I've noticed that we spend mealtimes coughing and retching. Afterwards we smell strongly of smoke. What can I do?

Well, it sounds to me as if your hall is one of the old-fashioned types with a fireplace in the middle. What you need is one of the new hearths which fits into the wall and has a decent chimney to get rid of all that smoke. That'll deal with the coughing and the nasty smell. As for the retching, are you by any chance eating mud and grass? If so, stop it at once. The Dark Ages are over, you know!

CHEESY

 As a simple villein I live off rye bread and cheese. But sometimes I can't find cheese in the shops. Any answer to my dilemma?

There's a delightful dish called "False cheese on rye bread". What you do is take your usual slice of bread, put it on the table, and then pretend you have a piece of cheese to go with it. It brings out the rye taste to perfection. It has a quick preparation time and is very economical too!

PRONGS

 I've got this wonderful idea. When we sit down to dinner everyone just shovels it in with a spoon and a piece of bread. How unseemly! Why not have a metal implement with several prongs in order to carry morsels cleanly to your mouth?

 You're talking of something called a fork. They exist elsewhere but I'm afraid they haven't caught on in Europe. We're not that advanced. Besides, what would it do for a fellow's fighting reputation if he was caught using a sissy thing like that? Forget it, that's my advice.

FARMING NEWS

IT'S GOODBYE TO RIDGE-AND-FURROW!

Strip farming is to be axed as the landed gentry push through laws to change the face of farming.

For centuries peasants have farmed little strips of land about two paces wide. Nobody knows why. But this is how it's always been done. As a result, farms have become a higgledy-piggledy mess of ridges and furrows. The latest legislation intends to replace ridge-and-furrow with new units called "**fields**".

Delight

"The field is a delightfully simple concept," says one landowner. "What you do is clear the peasants off. Then till the place up, and plant hedges to divide the area into organized plots which will make **me** more **money**."

Not everyone is happy with this new concept. "Our traditional country way of life is disappearing," moaned peasant Cedric Sodd whose family has worked the same strip for ten generations. "I blame all you city folk, with your meddling and your weekend homes. I bet you people think strip farming's an adult game for landowners. How stupid can you get."

Headache

Other peasants are more optimistic. "Strip farming has been nothing but a headache," says Humbert of Oxley. "We

One of those new-style **FIELDS** – at the cutting edge of agricultural technology.

lie awake at night wondering whether we're tilling our own strip or someone else's. It's difficult remembering which one is yours. Nobody knows for sure. Life will be much easier and neater when we have a little square patch with a hedge around it."

Rhomboid

"You needn't stop with squares, either," enthused his friend Dogbert. "You could have rectangles, rhomboids, parallelograms, triangles – anything, in fact! It would give the landscape a lovely patchwork effect. Visually, the present system is incredibly monotonous. It's like looking at a vast pair of corduroy trousers."

And in the future people will stop and say, "Look at those little fields. How quaint! This is what we'd always imagined the countryside to be like!"

WHEY-HEY! WHAT'S ALL THIS THEN?

When it comes to whey, Europe is the world's TOP producer. In fact, farmers are producing so much of the stuff that they can hardly even <u>give it away</u>.

Lumps

"Well," said one farmer, "when you think about it, it's not surprising we can't get rid of it. Whey's the watery mixture with lumps in it, which is what's left over when you've finished making cheese. It's quite revolting. Who'd want to eat that?"

Fussy

Lady Muffet, a long-standing member of the Whey Marketing Board,

disagrees. "People are too fussy about their diets. In my day, everybody ate whey – if you were lucky you had some curds in it too. You could sit down on any old tuffet and just tuck in. But things were different then. I remember the country was full of spiders. Gosh they were a menace. They appeared from nowhere, wiggling their little legs and trying to sit down beside you. Some girls were frightened away. Me, I trod on them. They soon got the message."

Minority

Muffet is in the minority. With or without spiders, no one wants to eat whey nowadays.

Whey. Here's where it all begins...

FARMING NEWS

Planet of the sheep – "It's like a baa-d dream"

While shepherds amuse themselves, sheep plot to TAKE OVER THE WORLD.

Bleeting sweeps Europe

The human race is no longer in control. With **eight million** sheep roaming England alone – that's three sheep to every human – scared farmers are wondering if they've started something they can't stop.

It began low-key, with a few farmers moving their flocks around the country in search of better grazing. The result was so good that everybody got on the band-wagon. And now? **Gigantic flocks of sheep are moving up and down Europe eating everything in sight.**

Frantic

"There's nothing we can do," claimed a frantic shepherd. "Economically, there's no way we can compete against sheep. We don't grow wool or anything. What chance do we have? This is the end of human supremacy. In the very near future this planet will be run by sheep."

Bulky

We asked our agricultural specialist for his opinion, and he told us; "When you look at it, the sheep is far too bulky to become top dog. In an expanding-population scenario they would soon cover the landscape completely. Then they would die because there was no grass to eat.

My own feeling is that if there **is** any threat to humanity it will come from **rabbits.** They're small, unobtrusive and live underground. **By the time they're ready to take over we'll be totally unprepared.**"

OUCH! PIGS GET IT IN THE EAR

Runaway pigs – another hazard for city dwellers.

When little Prince Louis was riding through Paris the last thing he expected was to be knocked off his horse by a runaway pig. But that's what happened last month, leaving His Royal Highness with a fractured skull, and bacon as No.1 on the butcher's hit list. "That pig is sausages!" yelled Prince Lou from his sick bed.

The anguished royal has put a price on the head of every porker in town. And he's hired the public executioner to do the dirty work.

"It's a lot different from what I'm used to," admits "Max-the-Axe" de Slamm, whose nimble beheading technique has earned him the Chamois D'Or three years running. "Normally it's just a fellow on a block and you whack his head off. These pigs aren't half as easy. First you've got to catch them – and they're slippery little beggers I can tell you."

Necks

With Mad Max on the look-out, Parisian farmers are worried for their future.

"Contrary to popular belief, the town is quite a rural place," said one spokesman. "Almost everybody keeps some sort of livestock. Cows, sheep, chickens, pigs – you name it. Normally they're well behaved and nobody cares. Then you get one incident like this and everyone's breathing down our necks."

Capital cattle

Farmers have started moving their pigs around town to avoid capture. But Max is on top of things.

"I can hear 'em! Grunting and snorting! I wait around the corner of an alley. If there's the slightest snuffle I'm out there with my axe and **WHAM**! One curly-tail less!"

So far Max has caught two elderly pigs and three people with bad colds. WAY TO GO, MAX!

WHAT'S NEW AT THE SPANISH INQUISITION?

We meet the man in the know

b eretics galore!" smiled Senor X, the Inquisitor-General. "It's been absolutely frantic out there. We've got more than we can deal with! Already we're sending out for extra firewood. And our inquisitors are worked to the bone. So if any of your readers know how to crank a rack we'd be delighted to hear from them."

Senor X – being publicity shy, he refuses to reveal his real name – has been at the cutting edge of the Inquisition for years. His job – to seek out heretics, the greatest threat to a stable, ordered society since the Black Death.

It's a ghastly business. Inquisitor-General Senor X shows some heretics what happens if you step out of line.

Slippers

But when Messenger reporter Rosie de Jonqueville visited him at his home in Seville, he was wearing slippers and a casual tunic and was in an expansive mood.

So, we asked, exactly who **is** the Inquisition interested in interviewing?

"It's all to do with church regulations," he said, fiddling absent-mindedly with a thumbscrew. "If believers show the slightest sign of disagreeing with the sacred principles of the Catholic faith, that's heresy, and we inquisit them. This means we ask them a lot of searching questions about their faith. Granted, they're not easy questions. But we have some very simple physical tests for those who find the questions too complex. The point of it all is to get the accused to change his mind – or recant, as we inquisitors call it."

Pain

And what are those tests?

"Ho ho!" winked Senor X. "That would be telling, wouldn't it?"

Do those tests involve physical pain?

"Well, yes. I think that would be a fair assumption. But only for the best possible reasons, of course."

Such as being beaten on the feet? Burned at the stake?

"Well, perhaps now and then, and only as a last resort. You've obviously been listening to too many sensationalist town criers, young lady."

So what makes a heretic, we asked.

"Oh, anything. It doesn't really matter. Any slight deviation will do."

Foreign

Like being foreign?

"Absolutely! That's prime evidence. We devote a lot of our time to people who look different. After all, if you're from somewhere else there's no telling what nasty religious habits you might have picked up. And talking about habits, we've had endless trouble with the friars. These Dominicans and Franciscans! Always having to do things their own way. Really! They shouldn't question the authority of the church. They bring it on their own heads."

Harmless

Senor X looks perfectly harmless. **But while his tunic is stained with egg and gravy, his reputation is stained with blood.**

Does this worry him? "Oh no," he replied firmly. "Our aim is to enforce religious unity throughout Europe. There's only one faith – the Catholic faith – and **it's my job to make sure it stays that way.** If that means we have to torture people, and burn a couple of thousand at the stake, then **so be it.** It's worth all the trouble!"

Superstition special

HOW SUPERSTITIOUS ARE YOU?

Prof. "Omen" Tally de Raynjd gets to grips with what makes the world go around.

Life's a mystery isn't it? Things just happen out of the blue. Plague. Warfare. Famine. Dental decay. You name it. And we haven't the first idea what caused them.

But what do YOU think? I've drawn up a simple test so that you can tell whether you're one of the new-fangled scientific types or a straightforward believer in good old superstition.

Give it a go and see how YOU rate. It could change your life!

1. Walking down the street you notice someone up a ladder. Do you:
a) Walk under the ladder.
b) Walk around the ladder.
c) Kick the ladder down?

2. At a party you meet a man who introduces himself as a wizard. Do you:
a) Roll your eyes.
b) Put out two fingers in the sign of the evil eye.
c) Put out two fingers and poke him in the eyes?

3. You find you've got an unlucky 13 people sitting down to dinner. Do you:
a) Serve the spiced goat before it gets cold.
b) Find another guest.
c) Kill one of them?

4. A black cat crosses your path. Do you:
a) Think "That'll be Tibbins from next door."
b) Think "Oh! I'm going to have some good luck."
c) Strap the cat to the front of your shoe so you always have good luck?

5. An old woman comes up and says, "I can cure that wart on your nose." Do you:
a) Say "Thank you."
b) Tell the church authorities.
c) Burn her at the stake?

6. Accidentally you break a mirror. Do you:
a) Swear under your breath.
b) Look forward to seven years' bad luck.
c) Pretend someone else did it and tell them that if they don't take the blame they'll have seven years' bad luck starting right here and now?

7. You come across a wishing well. Do you:
a) Have a drink.
b) Throw in a coin and make a wish.
c) Storm the well, declare it your own, then take out all the money except for one small penny which you attach to a string and drop in and out to make multiple wishes?

8. You see a bright light streaking across the night sky. Do you:
a) Say, "Ah! It's a comet!"
b) Confess all your sins because the end is nigh.
c) Go on a drunken orgy of arson and looting because the end is nigh?

9. A calf is born with two heads. Do you:
a) Go, "Hmmm. Weird calf."
b) Predict certain calamity for your village.
c) Burn down the village to spare it from certain calamity?

SO HOW DID YOU DO?

If you scored mostly a's you are not at all superstitious. This means you are a scientifically-minded person and completely out of touch with society. You are missing out on a lot of exciting hopes and fears. I bet people think you're pretty odd. Actually, I'm surprised you haven't been dunked in the nearest pond to see if you're a witch.

If you scored mostly b's then you respect all the current superstitions and are a normal, honest-to-goodness, law-abiding citizen.

If you scored mostly c's then you are not only superstitious but brutal, loutish, bad tempered, violent, destructive and an out-and-out swine. <u>Congratulations! You're a perfect medieval specimen. Have you thought of going for high office?</u>

DON'T KILL THAT SPIDER!

A superstition is born

We like to think that superstitions are ancient things. Not a bit of it! Robert the Bruce, king of Scotland, came up with a brand new one only the other day.

Down

"I'd had a run of bad luck," he said. "I'd lost two battles to the English. They even executed three of my brothers. I was down and out. I didn't know what to do. Things were so bad I was even living in a cave. And I had to think up a new tactic. I was desperate!

Then I noticed a spider. It was crawling up the cave wall. It fell off once. It fell off twice. But on the third attempt it got there. And I thought, if a spider can do that, so can I!"

Thrashing

"So I rushed out and gave the English the biggest thrashing of their lives at a place called Bannockburn. They won't forget that in a hurry. They thought they owned Scotland. Now it looks like they're going to have to recognize we're an independent country. Pah! What a shower!"

Brave Bruce's victory has given us not one but TWO superstitions. "Don't kill a spider!" and "Third time lucky!"

Ticking

It's people like this who keep the world ticking over. Hooray for Bruce, says the Messenger. Let's have a lot more like him!

Robert the Bruce — third time lucky!

"MY QUARTERED ESCUTCHEON IS PURFLED AND HURTY!"

And whose wouldn't be?

Knowing the man behind the visor is so much easier with new style heraldry.

Relax. It's not some nasty medical condition. In normal language this means, "My shield has a gold rim and is divided into four sections with a pattern of blue dots."

What?

Don't laugh. It's all part of the latest craze sweeping every court in Europe – heraldry.

Who's who

It all started with the crusaders. Unable to tell who anyone was once he'd pulled down his visor, they came up with the idea of giving themselves individual emblems and painting them on their shields.

"It worked very well," said Raymond of Toulouse. "Before, we were just anonymous lumps of metal on horses. With the new system you could look at a knight's shield and say 'Ah! Three Rabbits Rampant! That'll be Fritz of Thuringia!'"

Stag Trippant

"Eventually, things got a bit out of hand. With more and more crusaders arriving in the Holy Land people started inventing all kinds of loopy emblems. You'd get things like a Stag Trippant (a prancing stag), or a Savage Affronté (a naked wildman with a beard). And then the enemy thought it was a good idea and started copying us. Frankly, it got very confusing, particularly in the bigger battles. But at least it brightened the place up."

Fretty Golpes

Now everyone's jumped on the bandwagon. A coat-of-arms is a must-have for every self-respecting knight, crusader or not. You can't get into a tournament without one.

And to make it extra exclusive they've invented this weird language that's half French and half English to go with it. Fretty Golpes? That's eight purple balls. Wolf Salient? A leaping wolf. Fessways Escarbuncles? A row of jewels. Lucy Gules? A red fish.

Terribly simple

We asked the man in charge of English heraldry why it had to be so complicated.

"No, no. It's not at all complicated," enthused Sable Basilisk. "Nor is it exclusive. Why, I bet there's a coat-of-arms for your paper. Let's look it up. Ah! Here we are. Messenger: a Pegasus, Current (ducally gorged and chained). There. What could be simpler?"

What indeed?

"I'M NOT DEAD!" INSISTS CORPSE

"Oh yes you are," says priest

Chantalle Lemon, a lace-maker from Flanders, was hopping mad when she learned yesterday that she was officially "dead".

The 23-year-old Assistant Darning Executive told us her story.

"I'd gone home to get a new darning mushroom when I suddenly fell asleep. After a little while I was awoken by a blanket being thrown over me. I stayed absolutely still because I thought it was a burglar, and I didn't want to disturb him in case he was violent. Then I felt myself being loaded on to a stretcher and carried out of the house.

I was taken to a place which was obviously a church. It smelled all musty, and there were people chanting in Latin. I stayed still out of respect until I realized they were reading prayers for the dead over me. At that I threw off the blanket and said, 'Here! What's going on?'

Castanets

Imagine my astonishment when the priest gave me a pair of castanets.

'What's this for?' I asked. 'Flamenco lessons?'

'No,' he said. 'You've got leprosy. You're now officially dead and we're going to take you to a leper colony where you can live with other official corpses. Whenever you come near us ordinary people you must rattle your castanets. Oh yes. And here's a pair of gloves because we don't want you touching us.'

Not a spot

Apparently someone had spotted a white spot on my hand, which is one of the first signs of leprosy. I pointed out that it was just a bit of lace fluff which had been caught between my fingers, but they took

Chantalle, yesterday.

absolutely no notice.

'Sic mortuus mundo, vivens iterum Deo,' said the priest. Roughly translated this means: God thinks you're alive but we don't.

Then he took me away to the leper colony. And that was that."

Medical review

Chantalle is pressing for a review but nobody will come near her in case they catch the dreaded disease.

"Sadly there is no cure for leprosy and none of us wants to risk it," said a medical spokesman.

MISTRESS MANNERS

The lady in the know offers her advice on all matters of etiquette

No blunder too bad! No faux pas too frightful! No gaffe too ghastly! Mistress Manners delves deep into her social treasure-chest and produces a gem to meet your every requirement.

Humble

Dear Mistress Manners,
I am a humble lad who works in my lord's kitchen. I perform all my duties with great care and humility. There is one problem, however. Come dinner I have to turn the spit above the central fireplace in the banqueting hall. This is a long, hot business. In fact it gets so hot that I long to throw off all my clothes and perform my chore stark naked. **Would this be acceptable in polite society?**
Andy Ladd, The Henhouse, Castle Keep, Northants.

Dear Master Ladd,
By all means. It is quite common to enter the finest banqueting hall and find the spit turner wearing nothing but his birthday suit. But when roasting some of the fattier animals, such as pig, you might like to wear an apron so that you don't get a sizzling great gob of lard just where you don't want it. OK?

Deep shame

Dear Mistress Manners,
I am deeply ashamed. I went last week to a public bathhouse. To my horror I emerged clean and fresh as a daisy. Now everybody shuns me because I do not smell like them, i.e. like an old midden. **What can I do to rectify this appalling gaffe?**
Name and address withheld by request.

Dear Peter Parsnip of 32 Castle Lane, Warwick,
You have been very improper indeed. As everybody knows, bath-houses are sinks of vice and iniquity, and while it is quite proper to indulge in vice and iniquity it is not done to flaunt the fact by being clean. What you must do is find the smelliest dungheap in town and roll in it. This will restore your normal, socially acceptable stink. In the future, avoid bathhouses at all costs. If you want to wash, may I recommend a thorough scouring with a mixture of mutton fat and wood ash. This is used by the majority of households and will allow you to smell like everyone else.

Wretched retch

Dear Mistress Manners,
I work and live in the basement of a very old and important castle. Normally my duties do not take me upstairs. But the other day I had some time on my hands and hearing that the castle was being attacked, I took the opportunity to make my first visit to the ramparts. It was very exciting strolling past all these busy bowmen, and nobody took any notice of me at all. But when I looked over the edge I was so overcome by vertigo that I lost my lunch all over the foreign gentlemen who were attacking us from below. Imagine my shame! **Can you tell me if there is an international sign of apology which I can make should such a dreadful thing happen again?**
Ron Cudlipp, Ye Olde Importante Castle, Hole.

Dear Ron,
The answer to your question is Yes. First stick out your tongue to get the gentlemen's attention. Then place your thumb against your nose and rapidly fan your fingers to and fro. This indicates that your actions were involuntary. They, in turn, will shake their fists to show that they understand. They may make certain other gestures involving one or sometimes two fingers, and perhaps also the forearm. But it is unnecessary to go into such social intricacies. The important thing, after these initial overtures, is to give them a small gift to say you are sorry. Oil is traditionally used. Don't bother with fancy bottles or wrapping paper. Simply boil it up in a cauldron and tip it over the edge. I guarantee that they will be visibly moved by your apology.

Half-gnawed

Dear Mistress Manners,
A query about dinner etiquette. When I'm eating I belch, I wipe my greasy fingers on my clothes, I throw half-gnawed bones over my shoulder, I pick my nose and suck my teeth noisily to get rid of all the leftovers stuck in them. For some reason nobody will speak to me. **Am I doing anything wrong?**
Ivo de Cologne, Chateau Sauvage, Savoy.

Dear Ivo,
Your demeanour at dinner is quite normal. Possibly your problem has financial roots. I'm sure that if you appeared at table with a large bag of coins and flung them around shouting, "There's plenty more where that came from," everyone would want to know you.

LETTER OF THE WEEK

Joust for fun

Dear Mistress Manners,
I am a princess who attends a lot of jousting tournaments. When the knight I like best goes out to fight, I like him to know I am rooting for him. **What is the proper way of doing this?**
Princess Ethel, The Turret, Middle-and-Legge.

Dear Princess Ethel,
Now, this is a most complicated subject. The usual way is to offer your knight a token which he can wear during the competition. This can be a handkerchief, a strip of cloth or a ribbon. Should you run short of these items you can give him almost anything else, provided it is your own personal property and not borrowed from another lady who doesn't like anyone.
***But be warned.** Such tokens are often worn on the knight's helmet, and it's not going to help his visibility – or your reputation – if he goes into competition with an ancient sock or some old underwear draped over his visor.*
Alternatively you can just jump up and down shouting, "KILL HIM! KILL HIM! YAAAY, COME ON THE BLUE KNIGHT!"

NEXT WEEK – COURTING SPECIAL

JUDGE SLAMS ROGUE PUBLISHER

MONK'S MONEY-MAKING MONASTERY SHAME

Thomas Minky, 36, ex-monk and self-confessed fraudster, hung his head in shame as Judge Roger de Floggem sentenced him to a life of silence in a Cistercian monastery.

"And think yourself lucky the Inquisition didn't get to you first," thundered the Judge as Minky was led from court.

Beasts

It all began with the new vogue for illuminated bestiaries. Marketed by monks as "pocket zoos", these hugely popular books show pictures of all known animals and are widely read throughout the continent. Money-minded Minky, who has been thrown out of several monasteries, decided to give them a new edge. Setting himself up as an independent publisher he used his illustrating skills to produce bestiaries like no other.

On-the-edge

"Usually we concentrate on rabbits, sheep, fish and the usual kiddie stuff," said one leading abbot. "But Minky took it to its limits. He played up the phoenixes, unicorns and all kinds of on-the-edge creatures. People bought his books like hot cakes. They thought it was fun."

But fun turned to fraud when Minky started to advertise these creatures locally, offering them as pets.

"They couldn't believe their luck," explained the abbot. "Minky would say, 'Young unicorns ready. Horns starting to grow', and he'd be flooded with cash. Of course, when the unicorn came it was just a foal with a lump on its head which got better in a week. The phoenix was nothing more than a singed chicken."

Rumbled

Minky's money-maker was rumbled when wildfowl breeder Jack "The Hen" McVitie sent off for some Barnacle Geese, which Minky claimed could be grown from a bush which sprouted from a barnacle. But when McVitie's barnacle failed to sprout he called trading officers who launched a full investigation into Minky's activities.

Eminent

"I've seen a fair few geese and ducks in my time," said one officer, "and in my considered and very eminent opinion Barnacle Geese come from *eggs* not barnacles."

Unfortunately, Minky had already sold over 200 barnacles to gullible customers, and when the news broke an angry crowd gathered outside his offices. The authorities were forced to take him into protective custody.

Serves him right

Following a three-hour trial, Judge Floggem passed sentence. "Thomas Minky, your publishing house is a disgrace. You have misled the public. You have sold them Talking Hedge-hogs and Fortune-telling Rabbits. You have even sold them Burn-and-Come-Again Phoenixes. In the case of the Barnacle Goose you have been particularly deceitful. You have brought disappointment to thousands of dissatisfied customers and are a menace to society. If I ever see you again you will be sent to the gallows and hung by the neck until you are dead."

Above – Minky is apprehended by a trading officer. Below – the infamous advert.

Parchment or paper – which is best?

Peter Pier, a respected dealer in antiquarian manuscripts, was horrified when he found he had been sold a dud. For years Pier had scoured local markets in search of an illustrated manuscipt of *Europe's Fighting Men*. When he found one he was delighted. But when he got it home he was less than happy.

"Would you believe it," he fumed. "What I thought was a perfectly good piece of **parchment** turned out to be nothing less than **paper**! It's outrageous! I warn all readers to be on the lookout."

Substances

The problem is that paper and parchment are both whitish substances on which you can write. To most people they look identical. But parchment is much sturdier and will last several lifetimes. Paper, on the other hand, is skimpy stuff which falls to pieces after a few years. So how do you pick the genuine article? We discussed the problem with parchment industry spokesman Maurice de Mouton.

Mashed and rolled

Mouton told us that paper was made of bits of cloth, which had been shredded, soaked, mashed and rolled. Parchment on the other hand was made of lamb's hide, finely scraped to a smooth finish. "Paper looks like parchment," he told us, " but it tears easily. It's **cheap**, it's **nasty**, and the only thing it's good for is **printing on**. However, we'll have to wait until the middle of the 15th century for that. I'd say there's no possible reason to use paper instead of parchment, unless you're a peasant who can only afford the cheapest materials. And if you are, what are you doing writing anyway – **you're supposed to be illiterate**."

TEMPUS FUGIT
"TIME FLIES"

Yes It Does *when you join the Troubadour Express. Here at TE we're in tune with the century. We're a book club with a difference – because we realize that most of you can't read. What we offer is the chance to become a literary lion without even having to turn a page. Choose any single cult classic from the list of titles below, and one of our select team of troubadours will visit your home to read or sing it to you. If you're not completely satisfied, just send him back to us and we will refund your money.*

KING ARTHUR

The tale of a plucky king whose Knights of the Round Table fight ceaselessly to defend England against foreign invaders. Taken from an original tale of a plucky Welsh king whose knights fight ceaselessly to defend their land against English invaders. Love, betrayal, heroism and magic. This one has it all. The most popular saga of the century.

ROMAN DE LA ROSE

Courtly love at its best. Who can resist this account of chivalric knights pining for their unattainable ladies? Cupid fires his bow and the impetuous heroes try to find the arrow. Do they succeed? Wait and see!

CANTERBURY TALES

A group of pilgrims are on their way to Canterbury. Where do they come from? What stories can they tell? Geoffrey Chaucer works his usual magic in this intimate peek into everyday English life. (You'll love the Wife of Bath's tale!)

DIVINE COMEDY

Wordsmith Dante Alighieri breaks new ground here. No laughs but plenty of excitement as he leads you on a voyage of self-exploration through hell, purgatory and paradise. Features beautiful heroine Beatrice – familiar to anyone who knows Dante's other works – plus the Italian super-hero and author, Virgil. Not to be missed under any circumstances.

PIERS PLOWMAN

A moral tale for the moral-minded. Piers, a hard-working peasant who eats brown bread and horse beans, is disgusted at the farm hands who spend their time drinking ale and singing "Hey Trolli-Lolli." See them get their comeuppance! A must for anyone interested in contemporary ethics.

MAGNA CARTA

A fascinating snippet from the archives. This historic document gives the full 63 clauses which enabled English barons to break free from tyrant King John. Listen to the rolling declarations: "No free man shall be taken or imprisoned, or stripped of his rights or possessions, or outlawed or exiled, or in any way ruined..." Stirring stuff! Our storytellers read the names of the barons who signed it with particular vim.

DECAMERON

Giovanni Boccaccio has excelled himself here. The Black Death is raging in Florence and a group of citizens have run for the hills. The result? One hundred of the very best short stories to be found anywhere. Will have you on the edge of your seat.

THE BIBLE

Settle down to a few Psalms with the world's best-selling book.

CAUTION. TE takes no responsibility for troubadours being drunk, mumbling, blind or dumb. Further, TE will not accept claims for any offensive material you may or may not hear during your aural feast. In addition, should the storyteller become abusive, refuse to leave, wreck your home and/or assault your kith, kin or chattels, TE reserves its liability to the 15.99 groats paid for each storytelling. AND we don't take forged coins. But if we accidentally accept yours, then we shall let you know about it IMMEDIATELY. Anything else? Oh yes. This has been printed in especially small print so that if you CAN read it you are obviously a very nosy serf who should know that you are automatically ineligible for any compensation rights which TE offers to the illiterate. So there.

NOW YOU SEE IT NOW YOU DON'T!

MIRACLE EYESIGHT INVENTION GETS THUMBS-DOWN

Roger "Egghead" Bacon has come up with yet another wacky gadget. The loopy English inventor shook financial institutions with his last suggestion: an enormous mirror which enemy countries could use to spy on each other. **Now he has gone one step further with a device to cure the partially sighted.**

V-shaped

"I haven't fine-tuned it yet," admitted raving Roger. "But the basic principle is you get two pieces of see-through stuff – glass would do excellently – then you cut them into convex shapes (that's bulging outwards from the sides to the middle, for the non-scientists among us), and hold them in front of your eyes. If you wanted to be really sophisticated you could join them with a V-shaped strip of metal and hang them on your nose. Just how they'd stay there, if you wanted to use them for reading, I don't know. But that's a minor wrinkle which can be ironed out at production stage."

Mixed reception

Financial experts responded coolly to news of Roger's invention.

"I don't envisage volume sales," said one medical

SPEC-TACULAR!!

An eminent scholar models Bacon's latest invention. But will the glass and metal " spectacles" catch on?

analyst from the Hello & Welcome Foundation. "I can see there might be a market for this in monasteries where they have to spend a lot of time peering at little words in dark rooms. But most people spend their time looking at big things – castles, towers, monasteries, endless vistas of ridge-and-furrow farmland and enormously fat lords, to give just a few examples. For the majority such a device would be completely useless."

However, Roger has strong support from the Royal Institute of Alchemists. The

President gave his whole-hearted backing to Bacon's new idea.

Water to gold

"Here at the Royal Institute of Alchemists we investigate everything, big and small. I foresee this invention will be invaluable to our research. Our current project is turning seawater into gold. This has received a lot of attention in recent months. Roger is one of our most eminent members and we fully intend to use his device to tell us if we have succeeded."

Bustling Bruges gets boost from new crane

The city of Bruges astonished the merchant world when it unveiled its revolutionary new crane. Running off a totally clean and renewable power source, it has been heralded as the way forward for all major trading ports.

"The mechanism is very simple," its operator explained. "There are two treadwheels. People get in them and walk on the spot. As the treadwheels turn, so the crane lifts the object."

Back to front

But workforce representatives are worried by this new mechanical device.

"This is all topsy-turvy," said one official. "If you took the people off the treadwheels and put them to work, they would do the job of loading and unloading cargoes just as efficiently as the crane."

Good eyeful

Port bosses dismissed such suggestions with an impatient shrug.

"How unimaginative. We foresee great things for this crane, particularly in the construction industry. Soon we will have gigantic versions of it, which will be able to lift much greater loads than mere humans.

Not only that, the operator will sit at the top, and as the people below turn the treadwheel he will be able to swivel the crane so that he can see in everybody's bedroom windows. And when the nights are dark, at Christmas say, you could put bright lights on the crane. That would really brighten the place up."

A crane. Did the inventor keep pet hamsters?

BUSINESS NEWS

MERCHANT EMPIRE IN MONOPOLY CONTROVERSY

Baltic business "bullies" claim

Business is booming for the Baltic-based Hanseatic League.

The Hanseatic League, long one of Europe's biggest trading organizations, has defied the rules by cornering the market in all produce from the Baltic.

The German-based league is an extraordinary success story, with trading posts as far apart as Bruges, London and Novgorod in Russia.

It started out as a confederation of north German towns and merchant associations, selling **pickled Baltic herrings**. From there it **expanded** its operations to include **wheat, timber** and **amber**. It received valuable strongarm backing from the powerful Teutonic Knights, a less-than-holy order who have been **creating mayhem** in Poland and Prussia under the guise of mounting a crusade.

Mint

Before long the league was so powerful that it **minted its own coins**, which became solid currency in every European state.

To begin with, the league did much useful work, protecting trade from pirates and robbers, building lighthouses, and training pilots to guide its ships through dangerous waters.

But not everyone likes the league. Foreign merchants have complained that they've used **bribes and loans** to win valuable European trading contracts, and **excluded** merchants outside their organization from trading in the areas they operate in.

Even more outrageously, when top Dane King Valdemar IV decided that Denmark wanted a slice of Baltic trade the league defeated their navy, crushed their army and took over Denmark. They only left when the Danes agreed that league merchants could do whatever they liked wherever they wanted. (All signed sealed and delivered in the 1370 Peace of Stralsund, fact fans!)

LOAVES IN NUMBER FIASCO

Bakers are furious at new legislation which says they must be honest. Instead of short-changing customers they are having to give them more than they asked for.

"The problem lies with bakers selling rolls in units of twelve," said a trading standards officer. "This means they can charge the same price whether the rolls are the size of a walnut or the size of footballs. We're introducing a new scheme whereby all rolls have to be a uniform weight. Officials will be touring the land making spot checks on suspect establishments. If they detect any knavery in the ovens they will levy a massive fine and throw the offender in a rat-infested cell."

But bakers claim this is unfair because most of them don't have any scales and have to go by guesswork. As a spokesman from Consolidated Buns, the bakers' guild, pointed out, this is leading to massive overproduction. "In many areas bakers live in fear for their lives. They're so scared they don't dare give customers 12 rolls any more. They give them 13, just in case they might be serving an inspector. This is disrupting the chain of production and baffling the population. It's an outrage."

A bakery yesterday. Support was not forthcoming from either the butchers or candlestick makers.

𝕸essenger PERSONAL

Looking for Master or Mistress Right? Then start right here!!

Please send all replies to the Messenger office quoting the appropriate reference. Ads accepted at two groats per word. Boxed ads 20 groats per line. Please allow at least 12 months for any reply.

🌹 **PRINCESS,** 26, brunette, own teeth, would like to meet prince or similar, castle-and-keep type, aged around 30. Must have excellent prospects. BZ/1208

🌹 **BALDING,** pockmarked dung merchant would like to meet tall, blonde goddess with view to marriage. No time wasters please. BZ/2085

🌹 **ME Fulk.** You Jane. Hairy-chested crusader seeks lissom lass to join him in life's jungle. BZ/2096

🌹 **JINGLE** my bells! Court jester wants silly soulmate for days of endless japes, jokes and jollity. Sense of fun essential. BZ/2078

🌹 **CHIVALRIC** squire seeks married princess to worship from afar. Quite harmless. DL/3890

🌹 **LONELY** king, recently deposed, would like to meet similar queen. All letters answered. BZ/1901

🌹 **PROFESSIONAL** knight seeks dishy damsel. My interests include fighting, arson, fighting, murder, fighting, warfare, battles, sieges, fighting, chainmail, fighting, weaponry, fighting, long walks and cozy evenings by the fire. What are yours? GQ/0001

🌹 **DESPERATELY** seeking Sibyl. Ex-monk Stephen seeks maiden to pamper and adore. Your portrait gets mine. FO/1242

🌹 **FOAMING AT MOUTH** Mongol-horde type guy, tired of looting and pillaging, seeks quiet Mrs. Mouse to snuggle up to in comfy little love nest. MH/149.

🌹 **WEALTHY** merchant (own fleet of trading vessels) seeks decorative lady for banquets and trade fairs. An ermine coat awaits! IC/498

🌹 **LOVE,** money, relationships – clairvoyant advises on all aspects of your life. No burners-at-the-stake, please. RC/365

MISCELLANEOUS

TYRANT seeks cowering populace. Impeccable qualifications – B.Sc. Tyranny, M.A. Mayhem, Hon. Fellow Genghis Khan School of Deportment. TM/134

FANCY a dose of viper pills, beaver kidneys or powdered clay? Druggist offers confidential treatment in your own home. Any area. Cleanliness and discretion assured and expected. BO/6579

BORED young mercenary looking for work. Major war preferred. But will accept good uprising. In fact, will do anything for money. TM/176

ARE you a dragon or other imaginary beast? College of Heralds has constant demand for unusual animals. Apply in writing in first instance. TP/2002

MAGNUS of Pomerania. Please send another letter. Your last was accidentally eaten in a famine. BZ/1166

IS there anybody out there? Map-maker, 32, financially secure, would like to hear from anything and anybody who lives beyond the known bounds of geography. OT/658.

The Messenger receives a huge amount of mail every day. Although we try very hard not to open the wrong letters, we cannot always promise not to do so. We therefore advise readers to mark their confidential replies with a large cross – or two crosses and a big arrow if they include material of a particularly embarrassing or in any way hilarious nature. Thank you.

SPOT THE DIFFERENCE

How observant are you? Test your prowess with these two pictures of merry dancing peasants.

Picture 1 shows them dancing to the sound of a skirling bagpipe. Picture 2 shows the same scene, but with a few subtle differences! There are ten in all. See if you can spot them!

Differences

1. Silhouette of supertanker on horizon. 2. Baseball cap on horizon instead of herd of sheep. 4. Shoal of fish instead of herd of sheep. 5. Poodle instead of mongrel begging dog. 6. Fifth dancer wearing denim jacket. 7. Fourth dancer wearing mini skirt and high heels. 8. Second dancer wearing personal stereo. 9. First dancer wearing running shoes. 10. Modern door has been added to backgroud building.

MAIL-ORDER CATALOGUE

As we approach the 50th season of the 100 Years War, BALDRICS is offering super-special goods at super-silly prices. Here are just a few of our crazy anniversary bargains.

PROTECTION

MACE. Not the spice but the genuine article. Muggers will run a mile when they see you. 1 DUCAT.

WOOLLIES

HOSE. A must for every peasant. Pre-grovelled for extra comfort. SIXPENCE.

MILITARY WARE

FULL METAL JACKET, trousers, shoes and gloves. Our stylish battle-dress looks as good in the pub as it does on the battlefield. Extra reinforcement at wrists and elbows to protect those valuable drinking joints. Helmet comes down to neck level, with closeable visor to shut out unwanted bar chatter. Perfect for a knight on the tiles! 7 DUCATS!

LATEST FASHIONS

CAPE AND COWL. Who would have thought it! At last a quality garment which combines practicality with anonymity. Made from best English wool, this head-to-toe outfit keeps the elements at bay while obscuring your identity from friend and foe alike. Watch expressions change from dread to delight as you fling back the hood to reveal that you are not the Angel of Death. 2 FLORINS.

HAIR CARE

SNOOD. Too much hair! This delightful hat comes with a bag attached. Just right for storing those excess tresses. ONLY 15 GROATS!

WINCH WARE

GET BACK IN THE SADDLE with a Williams winch.

Are you one of those knights who just can't get on his horse when he wants to! It's noisy, painful and embarrassing. AND IT ALWAYS HAPPENS WHEN YOU'RE IN A HURRY!

Williams Winches have designed a winch which is tailor-made for you. Just step into the loops and give your squire the signal. NO FUSS. NO PROBLEMS. As used by the flower of chivalry. ONLY 5 DUCATS.

EXCLUSIVE HEADWEAR

WIMPLE. A snood for the more mature lady. Completely covers the head, leaving only the face on view. No one need know how little hair you have. (Priory discounts available for nuns.) 10 GROATS!

With every order please add **3 groats** for ox-and-cartage.

QUALITY FOOTWEAR

SILLY SHOES. We don't know why no one has thought of good, leather boots. But until they do we shall continue to stock these pointy things. Shows off the one-toed foot to perfection. 9 FLORINS!

There is only one
BALDRICS
There is only one sale

Remember, with our unique, no-quibbles, groats-back guarantee, you can buy in confidence from BALDRICS.

PICTURE CREDITS. Ancient Art & Architecture Collection (cover t, m, 3t, 6b, 10b, 14br, 21t, 30tr); Bayerische Staatsbibliothek, Munich (28r); The Bridgeman Art Library (cover b l & r, 1, 2, 4 t & b,5b, 7t & b, 8bl, 12t, 13m, bl & r, 14t, 16, 18t, ml & r, 19t & b, 20l, 21b, 22, 23t & b, 24t & m, 25, 29b, 30tl & br, 31); British Library, London (26b); E.T. Archive (5t, 6t, 8br, 9, 10tl, 12m, 14bl 15l, 27, 29t); Giraudon, Paris (3b); Mary Evans Picture Library (cover tr, 8t, 28m). Credit is also due to the following archives & museums: Bibliothèque National, Paris (4t & b, 5b, 8bl & r, 14bl, 16, 19t, 22, 31); Bibliothèque Royale De Belgique, Brussels; (7b) Bodleian Library (11); British Library, London (cover bl, 1, 2, 12t, 13m & bl, 14t, 18ml & t, 19b, 20l, 21b, 24t & m, 25, 29b, 30br); British Museum (5t, 10tl); Christ Church, Oxford (12m); Hamburg Staatsarchiv (29t); Lambeth Palace, London (cover br, 23b); Musée Condé, Chantilly (18mr, 23t, 30tl); Prado, Madrid (7t); Seminaro Patriacale, Venice (13br); Tower Armouries (9); University Library, Heidelberg (27); Victoria & Albert Museum (6t). *Key: top – t. middle – m. bottom –b. left – l. right – r.* Every effort has been made to trace the copyright holders of material in this book. If any rights have been omitted, the publishers offer to rectify this in any subsequent editions following notification.

THE MGMT SOLUTION

Every 4LTR Press solution includes:

Heading Numbers Connect Print & eBook

Visually Engaging Textbook

Online Study Tools

Tear-out Review Cards

Interactive eBook

STUDENT RESOURCES:
- PowerPoint® Slides
- Videos
- Cases & Exercises
- E-Lectures
- KnowNOW!
- Self-Assessments
- Career Transitions
- Business Insights: Essentials
- Review Cards

Students sign in at **www.cengagebrain.com**

INSTRUCTOR RESOURCES:
- Instructor's Manual
- Test Bank
- PowerPoint® Slides
- Classroom Response Enabled Slides
- Instructor Prep Cards

Instructors sign in at **www.cengage.com/login**

"Both the printed book and digital add-ons were outstanding!!! Loved the book for the rich visual content and the easily understandable text."

– **Amit Bitnun**, Student, *Northeast Seneca College*

Engagement Tracker launches, giving faculty a window into student usage of digital tools.

AUGUST 2010

1 out of every 3 (1,400) schools has adopted a 4LTR Press solution.

4LTR Press adds eBooks in response to a 10% uptick in digital learning preferences.

NOVEMBER 2010

750,000 students are IN.

Third party research confirms that 4LTR Press digital solutions improve retention and outcomes.

IN 2011

60 unique solutions across multiple course areas validates the 4LTR Press concept.

CourseMate

Students access the 4LTR Press website at 4x's the industry average.

IN 2011

2,000

APRIL 2011

1 out of every 2 (2,000) schools has a 4LTR Press adoption.

AUGUST 2011

Over 1 million students are IN.

We're always evolving. Join the 4LTR Press In-Crowd on Facebook at www.facebook.com/4ltrpress

2012 AND BEYOND

SOUTH-WESTERN
CENGAGE Learning

MGMT6
Chuck Williams
Butler University

SVP, Learning Acquisitions & Solutions
Planning: Jack W. Calhoun

Editorial Director, Business & Economics:
Erin Joyner

Publisher: Mike Schenk

Executive Editor: Scott Person

Developmental Editor: John Choi,
B-books, Ltd.

VP 4LTR & Learning Solutions Strategy,
Institutional: Neil Marquardt

Senior Brand Manager: Robin LeFevre

Project Manager, 4LTR Press: Pierce Denny

Senior Marketing Development Manager:
Courtney Sheldon

Marketing Development Manager:
Jonathan Monahan

Production Director: Amy McGuire,
B-books, Ltd.

Sr. Content Project Manager:
Tamborah Moore

Media Editor: John Rich

Manufacturing Planner: Ron Montgomery

Production Service: B-books, Ltd.

Rights Acquisitions Specialist:
Deanna Ettinger

Photo Researcher: Charlotte Goldman

Text Permissions Researcher: Christina
Taylor, PreMediaGlobal

Sr. Art Director: Stacy Shirley

Internal Designer: Ke Design, Mason, OH

Cover Designer: Ke Design, Mason, OH

Cover Image: ©Thomas Barwick/Getty
Images/Iconica

For product information and technology assistance, contact us at
Cengage Learning Customer & Sales Support, 1-800-354-9706.

For permission to use material from this text or product,
submit all requests online at **www.cengage.com/permissions**.
Further permissions questions can be emailed to
permissionrequest@cengage.com.

Library of Congress Control Number: 2012955792

Student Edition ISBN-13: 978-1-285-09107-5
Student Edition ISBN-10: 1-285-09107-8

South-Western
5191 Natorp Boulevard
Mason, OH 45040
USA

Cengage Learning products are represented in Canada by Nelson Education, Ltd.

For your course and learning solutions, visit **www.cengage.com**. Purchase any of our products at your local college store or at our preferred online store **www.CengageBrain.com**.

Cover and Page i Photography Credits:
Inside Front Cover: © iStockphoto.com/sdominick; © iStockphoto.com/alexsl; © iStockphoto.com/A-Digit
Page i: © iStockphoto.com/CostinT; © iStockphoto.com/photovideostock; © iStockphoto.com/Leontura
Back Cover: © iStockphoto.com/René Mansi

Printed in the United States of America
1 2 3 4 5 6 7 17 16 15 14 13

Brief Contents

Contents

PART 2
Planning 86

PART 3
Organizing 176

PART 4
Leading 268

PART 5
Controlling 336

© iStockphoto.com/Joe Belanger

© iStockphoto.com/Andrew Dernie

THE IN-CROWD

Share your 4LTR Press story on Facebook at
www.facebook.com/4ltrpress for a chance to win.

To learn more about the In-Crowd opportunity 'like' us on Facebook.

1 Management

© Flying Colours Ltd/Digital Vision/Getty Images

LEARNING OUTCOMES

1-1 Describe what management is.

1-2 Explain the four functions of management.

1-3 Describe different kinds of managers.

1-4 Explain the major roles and subroles that managers perform in their jobs.

1-5 Explain what companies look for in managers.

1-6 Discuss the top mistakes that managers make in their jobs.

1-7 Describe the transition that employees go through when they are promoted to management.

1-8 Explain how and why companies can create competitive advantage through people.

CHECK OUT
STUDY TOOLS
AT THE END OF THIS CHAPTER.

© Monalyn Gracia/Corbis/Jupit

1-1 *Management Is . . .*

Management issues are fundamental to any organization: How do we plan to get things done, organize the company to be efficient and effective, lead and motivate employees, and put controls in place to make sure our plans are followed and our goals met? Good management is basic to starting a business, growing a business, and maintaining a business once it has achieved some measure of success.

To understand how important *good* management is, think about this mistake. To increase revenue, Bank of America (BoA) decided to charge account holders $5 per month for using debit cards to make purchases. Angry at having to pay $60 a year to access their own money, 300,000 customers signed an online petition protesting the policy, while another 21,000 pledged to close their accounts. Meanwhile, BoA's competitors tried to steal its customers by proudly advertising that they didn't charge fees or by canceling their plans for similar fees. The backlash against this highly unpopular move was so strong that BoA's stock dropped 3.5 percent the day after the fees were announced.[1]

Ah, bad managers and bad management. Is it any wonder that companies pay management consultants nearly $250 billion a year for advice on basic management issues such as how to lead people effectively, organize the company efficiently, and manage large-scale projects and processes?[2] This textbook will help you understand some of the basic issues that management consultants help companies resolve. (And it won't cost you billions of dollars.)

Many of today's managers got their start welding on the factory floor, clearing dishes off tables, helping customers fit a suit, or wiping up a spill in aisle 3. Similarly, lots of you will start at the bottom and work your way up. There's no better way to get to know your competition, your customers, and your business. But whether you begin your career at the entry level or as a supervisor, your job as a manager is not to do the work but to help others do theirs. **Management** is getting work done through others.

Vineet Nayar, CEO of IT services company **HCL Technologies**, doesn't see himself as the guy who has to do everything or have all the answers. Instead, he sees himself as "the guy who is obsessed with enabling employees to create value." Rather than coming up with solutions himself, Nayar creates opportunities for collaboration, for peer review, and for employees to give feedback on ideas and work processes. Says Nayar, "My job is to make sure everybody is enabled to do what they do well."[3]

Nayar's description of managerial responsibilities suggests that managers also have to be concerned with efficiency and effectiveness in the work process. **Efficiency** is getting work done with a minimum of effort, expense, or waste. UPS saves time (and makes money) by finding faster, more efficient ways to deliver packages, such as having its drivers walk at a quick 2.5 strides per second or using computers to design delivery routes with fewer left turns—it takes more time to cross traffic when turning left than it does when turning right. Likewise, UPS drivers have been trained to carry their truck keys on key rings that are always kept on their fingers. Why? To minimize time fumbling for the keys in their pocket before inserting them into the truck's ignition or door locks. Now, however, UPS

Management getting work done through others

Efficiency getting work done with a minimum of effort, expense, or waste

© Daniel Acker/Bloomberg via Getty Images

Effectiveness accomplishing tasks that help fulfill organizational objectives

is switching to keyless systems in which electronic key fobs are attached to drivers' belts. This allows drivers to start the engine and open the cargo hold with the quick touch of a button, saving each driver about 2 seconds per stop or about 6.5 minutes per day. David Abney, UPS's chief operating officer, concedes, "We're obsessive about efficiency."[4]

Efficiency alone, however, is not enough to ensure success. Managers must also strive for **effectiveness**, which is accomplishing tasks that help fulfill organizational objectives such as customer service and satisfaction. John F. Kennedy International Airport in New York City was notorious for crowded runways, resulting in delays that trapped passengers on idling airplanes with no access to food, water, or bathrooms (by law, passengers are required to stay in their seats until the plane is safely in the air). That changed, however, when the airport instituted a runway reservation system where each flight is assigned a takeoff time and no plane is allowed to leave the gate until its assigned time. How effective is the new system? Instead of forty planes queuing on the runway, now only six to eight planes wait in line for takeoff. And while flights delays are still common, passengers now experience them at the terminal, where they have access to food, bathrooms, and lounges. The airlines have also benefitted because they burn less fuel and save wear and tear on engines.[5]

1-2 *Management Functions*

Henri Fayol, who was a managing director (CEO) of a large steel company in the early 1900s, was one of the founders of the field of management. You'll learn more about Fayol and management's other key contributors when you read about the history of management in Chapter 2. Based on his twenty years of experience as a CEO, Fayol argued that "the success of an enterprise generally depends much more on the administrative ability of its leaders than on their technical ability."[6] A century later, Fayol's arguments still hold true. During a two-year study code-named Project Oxygen, Google analyzed performance reviews and feedback surveys to

identify the traits of its best managers. According to Laszlo Bock, Google's vice president for people operations, "We'd always believed that to be a manager, particularly on the engineering side, you need to be as deep or deeper a technical expert than the people who work for you. It turns out that that's absolutely the least important thing." What was most important? "Have a clear vision and strategy for the team." "Help your employees with career development." "Be productive and results-oriented." In short, Google found what Fayol observed, administrative ability, or management, is key to an organization's success.[7]

Managers need to perform five managerial functions in order to be successful, according to Fayol: planning, organizing, coordinating, commanding, and controlling.[8] Most management textbooks today have updated this list by dropping the coordinating function and referring to Fayol's commanding function as "leading." Fayol's management functions are thus known today in this updated form as planning, organizing, leading, and controlling. Studies indicate that managers who perform these management functions well are more successful, gaining promotions for themselves and profits for their companies. For example, the more time CEOs spend planning, the more profitable their companies are.[9] A twenty-five-year study at AT&T found that employees with better planning and decision-making skills were more likely to be promoted into management jobs, to be successful as managers, and to be promoted into upper levels of management.[10]

The evidence is clear. Managers serve their companies well when they plan, organize, lead, and control. So we've organized this textbook based on these functions of management, as shown in Exhibit 1.1.

*Now let's take a closer look at each of the management functions: **1-2a planning, 1-2b organizing, 1-2c leading,** and **1-2d controlling.***

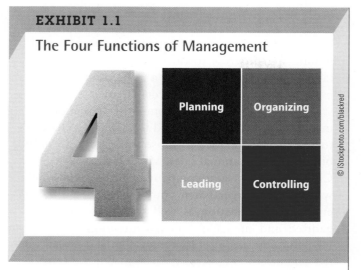
1-2a PLANNING

Planning involves determining organizational goals and a means for achieving them. As you'll learn in Chapter 5, planning is one of the best ways to improve performance. It encourages people to work harder, to work hard for extended periods, to engage in behaviors directly related to goal accomplishment, and to think of better ways to do their jobs. But most importantly, companies that plan have larger profits and faster growth than companies that don't plan.

For example, the question "What business are we in?" is at the heart of strategic planning. You'll learn about this in Chapter 6. If you can answer the question "What business are you in?" in two sentences or less, chances are you have a very clear plan for your business. But getting a clear plan is not so easy. Sometimes even very successful companies stray from their core business.

This happened when Cisco Systems, maker of the critical computer routers and switches that run the Internet and create high-speed networks in offices and homes, strayed from its core networking business by spending $34 billion acquiring or developing consumer products, such as Pure Digital, which made the once-popular Flip camera; Kiss Technology, which made networked DVD players; and Umi, a $600 videoconference service for homes that came with a $25 monthly charge for video access. Long-time CEO John Chambers has admitted that Cisco lost its focus and that going forward its priorities will be on its core business: "leadership in core routing, switching, and services; collaboration; data center virtualization and cloud; architectures; and video."[11] Accordingly, Cisco has now shut down its Flip, Kiss, and Umi divisions.

You'll learn more about planning in Chapter 5 on planning and decision making, Chapter 6 on organizational strategy, Chapter 7 on innovation and change, and Chapter 8 on global management.

1-2b ORGANIZING

Organizing is deciding where decisions will be made, who will do what jobs and tasks, and who will work for whom in the company. With 1,400 different computer systems; different labor unions representing pilots, flight attendants, and maintenance workers; and different ways of washing planes and boarding and feeding passengers; as well as different classes in the cabins (no first class on Continental), Continental Airlines and United Airlines faced an enormous organizing task to merge their two companies into the world's second-largest airline. Lori Gobillot, vice president of integration management, managed the reorganization by overseeing thirty-three teams that decided the fastest way to board passengers and which computer systems to use, United's or Continental's, for scheduling crews, routing planes, handling bags and cargo, or just basic accounting. Said Gobillot, "I tell them to be fact-based, and direct and objective, and keep the emotions out of it—and don't keep score. It's not important how many things come from United and how many come from Continental." The goal was to reduce annual expenses by $1.2 billion. Each decision matters, as reducing costs by as little a half-cent per mile could result in a $1 billion increase in annual profits for an industry that historically loses billions each year.[12]

You'll learn more about organizing in Chapter 9 on designing organizations, Chapter 10 on managing teams, Chapter 11 on managing human resources, and Chapter 12 on managing individuals and a diverse work force.

1-2c LEADING

Our third management function, **leading**, involves inspiring and motivating workers to work hard to achieve organizational goals. For Alan Mulally, CEO of Ford Motor Company, a critical part of keeping his employees motivated is to "communicate, communicate, communicate. Everyone has to know

Planning determining organizational goals and a means for achieving them

Organizing deciding where decisions will be made, who will do what jobs and tasks, and who will work for whom

Leading inspiring and motivating workers to work hard to achieve organizational goals

the plan, its status, and areas that need special attention." Accordingly, Mulally distributed a set of cards with Ford's mission on one side and the company's four most important goals on the other. He also hosts a Business Plan Review each week with his top executives to check on performance company-wide, which is tracked via 280 charts, each with the name and picture of the manager responsible. Mulally's leadership brought Ford back from the brink of bankruptcy. In a series of timely maneuvers and shrewd business deals, Mulally secured a $23.6 billion loan and then sold off several noncore brands to raise capital prior to the recession, which kept Ford sufficiently capitalized as the world economy slowed. And while General Motors and Chrysler were forced to seek government loans and eventually file for bankruptcy, Ford stayed afloat on its own, and by 2012 not only recovered the $30.1 billion it had lost from 2006 to 2008, but also posted three straight years of profits totaling $29.5 billion.[13]

You'll learn more about leading in Chapter 13 on motivation, Chapter 14 on leadership, and Chapter 15 on managing communication.

DOING THE RIGHT THING

One of the worst things you can do as a manager is micromanage—making every decision, watching over every employee, being involved in every single facet of the business. Sure, things might get done a little bit faster or more to your liking; however, experts on leadership and management agree that managers who try to control everything show an unwillingness to trust employees and that this attitude will eventually make subordinates complacent and less creative. According to Ira Bryck, of the University of Massachusetts's Family Business Center, frontline workers, not mangers, are best equipped to identify potential problems and come up with solutions. Instead of trying to solve every issue, Bryck says that managers should focus on giving employees goals and delegating them to work out the details necessary to meet those goals.

Source: C. Tuna, "Micromanagers Miss Bull's Eye," *Wall Street Journal*, November 3, 2008, accessed October 10, 2010, http://online.wsj.com/article/SB122566866580091589.html.

1-2d CONTROLLING

The last function of management, **controlling**, is monitoring progress toward goal achievement and taking corrective action when progress isn't being made. The basic control process involves setting standards to achieve goals, comparing actual performance to those standards, and then making changes to return performance to those standards. At $410 billion a year in annual sales, Mike Duke, Wal-Mart's CEO, runs the largest company in the world (which will be even larger when you read this). Duke, an engineer by education, is well known for being organized and meticulous in his attention to detail. He maintains a red folder—eight in all—for each of the executives who reports to him. On the outside of each folder, his assistant will write the executive's name and the time of Duke's next meeting with him. Each folder contains a set of goals, problems, and follow-up items related to that manager's responsibilities. For example, the folder for Brian Cornell, who runs Sam's Club, Wal-Mart's discount warehouse chain, contains recent sales figures, a question that Duke has regarding the strategy Sam's is using to purchase real estate for new locations, and an email from a Sam's Club member who wrote to Duke complaining that the Member's Mark facial tissue (a private brand sold by Sam's) gets stuck in the box and doesn't pull out easily. Regarding the tissue, Duke said, "Brian's team identified that as a real problem. And I said, 'Great, now that we've identified the problem, when are we going to solve it?' And I keep this in here until Brian tells me it's solved. It's a follow-up mechanism."[14]

You'll learn more about the control function in Chapter 16 on control, Chapter 17 on managing information, and Chapter 18 on managing service and manufacturing operations.

1-3 *Kinds of Managers*

Not all managerial jobs are the same. The demands and requirements placed on the CEO of Sony are significantly different from those placed on the manager of your local Wendy's restaurant.

As shown in Exhibit 1.2, there are four kinds of managers, each with different jobs and responsibilities: **1-3a top managers, 1-3b middle managers, 1-3c first-line managers,** *and* **1-3d team leaders.**

EXHIBIT 1.2

What the Four Kinds of Managers Do

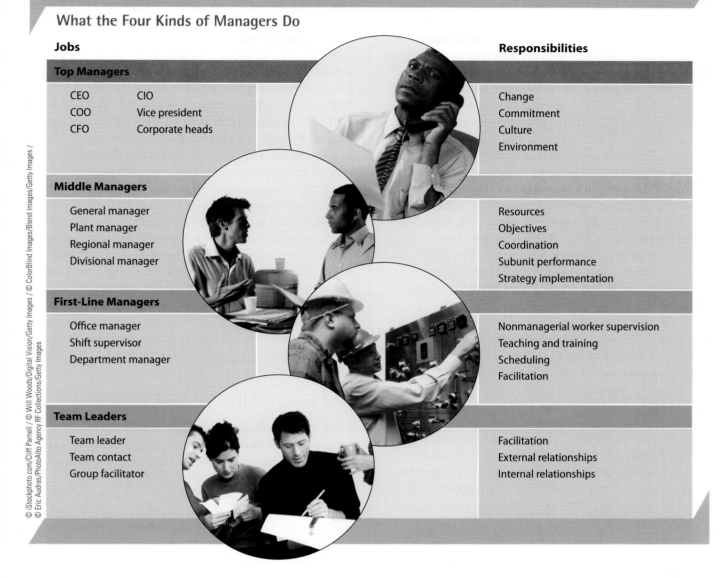

Jobs — **Responsibilities**

Top Managers

CEO	CIO
COO	Vice president
CFO	Corporate heads

Change
Commitment
Culture
Environment

Middle Managers

General manager
Plant manager
Regional manager
Divisional manager

Resources
Objectives
Coordination
Subunit performance
Strategy implementation

First-Line Managers

Office manager
Shift supervisor
Department manager

Nonmanagerial worker supervision
Teaching and training
Scheduling
Facilitation

Team Leaders

Team leader
Team contact
Group facilitator

Facilitation
External relationships
Internal relationships

1-3a TOP MANAGERS

Top managers hold positions like chief executive officer (CEO), chief operating officer (COO), chief financial officer (CFO), and chief information officer (CIO) and are responsible for the overall direction of the organization. Top managers have the following responsibilities.[15] First, they are responsible for creating a context for change. In fact, both Leo Apotheker, the former CEO of Hewlett Packard, and Carol Bartz, the former CEO of Yahoo!, were fired precisely because they had not moved fast enough to bring about significant changes in their companies.[16]

Indeed, in both Europe and the United States, 35 percent of all CEOs are eventually fired because of their inability to successfully change their companies.[17] Creating a context for change includes forming a long-range vision or mission for the company. As one CEO said, "The CEO has to think about the future more than anyone."[18] Once that vision or mission is set, the second responsibility of top managers is to develop employees' commitment to and ownership of the company's performance. That is, top managers are responsible for creating employee buy-in. Third, top managers must create a positive organizational culture through language and action. Top managers impart company values, strategies, and lessons through what they do and say to

Top managers executives responsible for the overall direction of the organization

Middle managers responsible for setting objectives consistent with top management's goals and for planning and implementing subunit strategies for achieving these objectives

First-line managers train and supervise the performance of nonmanagerial employees who are directly responsible for producing the company's products or services

others both inside and outside the company. Indeed, no matter what they communicate, it's critical for CEOs to send and reinforce clear, consistent messages.[19] A former *Fortune* 500 CEO said, "I tried to [use] exactly the same words every time so that I didn't produce a lot of, 'Last time you said this, this time you said that.' You've got to say the same thing over and over and over."[20] Likewise, it's important to actively manage internal organizational communication. Kimberly Till, CEO of Harris Interactive, a New York–based market research company, emphasizes the importance of frequent communication, saying, "I keep all the employees in the loop through weekly emails, town hall meetings and forums, video clips of big decisions and visits to the offices."[21]

Finally, top managers are responsible for monitoring their business environments. A. G. Lafley, former CEO of Procter & Gamble, believes that most people do not understand the CEO's responsibilities. Says Lafley, "Conventional wisdom suggests that the CEO was primarily a coach and a utility infielder, dropping in to solve [internal] problems where they crop up. In fact, however, the CEO has a very specific job that only he or she can do: Link the external world with the internal organization."[22] This means that top managers must closely monitor customer needs, competitors' moves, and long-term business, economic, and social trends.

1-3b MIDDLE MANAGERS

Middle managers hold positions like plant manager, regional manager, or divisional manager. They are responsible for setting objectives consistent with top management's goals and for planning and implementing subunit strategies for achieving those objectives.[23] One specific middle management responsibility is to plan and allocate resources to meet objectives.

A second major responsibility is to coordinate and link groups, departments, and divisions within a company. In February 2008, a tornado destroyed a **Caterpillar** plant in Oxford, Mississippi, the only plant in the company that produced a particular coupling required for many of Caterpillar's machines. The disaster threatened a worldwide production shutdown. Greg Folley, a middle manager in charge of the

parts division that included the plant, gave workers two weeks to restore production to pre-tornado levels. He said, "I was betting on people to get it done." He contacted new vendors, sent engineers from other Caterpillar locations to Mississippi to check quality, and set up distribution operations in another facility. Meanwhile, Kevin Kempa, the plant manager in Oxford, moved some employees to another plant, delivered new training to employees during the production hiatus, and oversaw reconstruction of the plant. The day before the two-week deadline, the Oxford plant was up and running and produced 8,000 parts.[24]

A third responsibility of middle management is to monitor and manage the performance of the subunits and individual managers who report to them. Finally, middle managers are also responsible for implementing the changes or strategies generated by top managers. Why? Because they're closer to the managers and employees who work on a daily basis with suppliers to effectively and efficiently deliver the company's product or service. In short, they're closer to the people who can best solve problems and implement solutions.

1-3c FIRST–LINE MANAGERS

First-line managers hold positions like office manager, shift supervisor, or department manager. The primary responsibility of first-line managers is to manage the performance of entry-level employees who are directly responsible for producing a company's goods and services. Thus, first-line managers are the only managers who don't supervise other managers. The responsibilities of first-line managers include monitoring, teaching, and short-term planning.

First-line managers encourage, monitor, and reward the performance of their workers. Jennifer Lepird is the human resources staffer on a team at **Intuit** that manages the acquisitions of companies that Intuit buys. When Intuit bought Paycycle, one of its competitors, Lepird stayed up all night putting together a spreadsheet that showed how the salary structure for Paycycle's managers and employees should be integrated with Intuit's. Her acquisition team manager, a first-line manager, sent her a thank you email and a gift certificate for several hundred dollars. Lepird was thrilled by her boss's reward, saying, "The fact that somebody took the time to recognize the effort made the long hours just melt away."[25]

First-line managers are also responsible for teaching entry-level employees how to do their jobs. They

also make detailed schedules and operating plans based on middle management's intermediate-range plans. By contrast to the long-term plans of top managers (three to five years out) and the intermediate plans of middle managers (six to eighteen months out), first-line managers engage in plans and actions that typically produce results within two weeks.[26] Consider the typical convenience store manager (e.g., 7-Eleven) who starts the day by driving past competitors' stores to inspect their gasoline prices and then checks the outside of his or her store for anything that might need maintenance, such as burned-out lights or signs, or restocking, like windshield washer fluid and paper towels. Then comes an inside check, where the manager determines what needs to be done for that day. (Are there enough donuts and coffee for breakfast or enough sandwiches for lunch?) Once the day is planned, the manager turns to weekend orders. After accounting for the weather (hot or cold) and the sales trends at the same time last year, the manager makes sure the store will have enough beer, soft drinks, and Sunday papers on hand. Finally, the manager looks seven to ten days ahead for hiring needs. Because of strict hiring procedures (basic math tests, drug tests, and background checks), it can take that long to hire new employees. Said one convenience store manager, "I have to continually interview, even if I am fully staffed."[27]

1-3d TEAM LEADERS

The fourth kind of manager is a team leader. This relatively new kind of management job developed as companies shifted to self-managing teams, which, by definition, have no formal supervisor. In traditional management hierarchies, first-line managers are responsible for the performance of nonmanagerial employees and have the authority to hire and fire workers, make job assignments, and control resources. In this new structure, the teams themselves perform nearly all of the functions performed by first-line managers under traditional hierarchies.[28]

Team leaders have a different set of responsibilities than traditional first-line managers.[29] **Team leaders** are primarily responsible for facilitating team activities toward accomplishing a goal. This doesn't mean team leaders are responsible for team performance. They aren't. The team is. Team leaders help their team members plan and schedule work, learn to solve problems, and work effectively with each other. Management consultant Franklin Jonath says, "The idea is for the team leader to be at the service of the group." It should be clear that the team members own the outcome. The leader is there to bring intellectual, emotional, and spiritual resources to the team. Through his or her actions, the leader should be able to show the others how to think about the work that they're doing in the context of their lives. It's a tall order, but the best teams have such leaders.[30]

Relationships among team members and between different teams are crucial to good team performance and must be well managed by team leaders, who are responsible for fostering good relationships and addressing problematic ones within their teams. Getting along with others is much more important in team structures because team members can't get work done without the help of teammates.

Peter Löscher, the CEO of the German conglomerate Siemens, argues that teamwork based on trust is

Team leaders managers responsible for facilitating team activities toward goal accomplishment

© Antenna/fStop/Jupiterimages

the foundation of business success. He says, "Business is about lining up a leadership team or a group of people and you rally them behind a cause or a certain direction. But the underlying strength is the trust within the team—so that you actually are no longer just playing individually at your best, but you're also trying to understand what you can do to make the team better."[31]

Team leaders are also responsible for managing external relationships. Team leaders act as the bridge or liaison between their teams and other teams, departments, and divisions in a company. For example, if a member of Team A complains about the quality of Team B's work, Team A's leader is responsible for solving the problem by initiating a meeting with Team B's leader. Together, these team leaders are responsible for getting members of both teams to work together to solve the problem. If it's done right, the problem is solved without involving company management or blaming members of the other team.[32]

So the team leader's job involves a different set of skills than traditional management jobs typically do. For example, a Hewlett-Packard ad for a team leader position says, "Job seeker must enjoy coaching, working with people, and bringing about improvement through hands-off guidance and leadership."[33] Team leaders who fail to understand how their roles are different from those of traditional managers often struggle in their jobs. A team leader at Texas Instruments said, "I didn't buy into teams, partly because there was no clear plan on what I was supposed to do. . . . I never let the operators [team members] do any scheduling or any ordering of parts because that was mine. I figured as long as I had that, I had a job."[34]

You will learn more about teams in Chapter 10.

1-4 *Managerial Roles*

Although all four types of managers engage in planning, organizing, leading, and controlling, if you were to follow them around during a typical day on the job, you would probably not use these terms to describe what they actually do. Rather, what you'd see are the various roles managers play. Professor Henry Mintzberg followed five American CEOs, shadowing each for a week and analyzing their mail, their conversations, and their actions. He concluded that managers fulfill three major roles while performing their jobs—interpersonal roles, informational roles, and decisional roles.[35]

In other words, managers talk to people, gather and give information, and make decisions. Furthermore, as shown in Exhibit 1.3, these three major roles can be subdivided into ten subroles. *Let's examine each major role—1-4a interpersonal, 1-4b informational, and 1-4c decisional roles—and their ten subroles.*

1-4a INTERPERSONAL ROLES

More than anything else, management jobs are people-intensive. Estimates vary with the level of management, but most managers spend between two-thirds and four-fifths of their time in face-to-face communication with others.[36] If you're a loner, or if you consider dealing with people a pain, then you may not be cut out for management work. In fulfilling the interpersonal role of management, managers perform three subroles: figurehead, leader, and liaison.

In the **figurehead role**, managers perform ceremonial duties like greeting company visitors, speaking at the opening of a new facility, or representing the

---

EXHIBIT 1.3

Mintzberg's Managerial Roles

Interpersonal Roles
- Figurehead
- Leader
- Liaison

Informational Roles
- Monitor
- Disseminator
- Spokesperson

Decisional Roles
- Entrepreneur
- Disturbance Handler
- Resource Allocator
- Negotiator

company at a community luncheon to support local charities. When NetJets, a fractional private jet ownership company, broke ground on a new 140,000-square-foot headquarters in Columbus, Ohio, its new CEO Jordan Hansell presided over the ceremony.[37]

In the **leader role**, managers motivate and encourage workers to accomplish organizational objectives. At **RedPeg Marketing**, cofounder Brad Nierenberg motivates his employees with company perks, such as a three-bedroom beach house that is available to all forty-eight employees for vacations, cold beer in the refrigerator, free breakfast at staff meetings, and trophies and awards for great performance. Once, after the company had met a critical goal, Nierenberg walked into the office with $38,000 in cash, or $1,000 each for his then thirty-eight employees. Said Nierenberg, "I thought, 'I've got to make a big deal out of this; I can't just put it in their checking account because that's not as fun.' I thought it would be cool for them to see $38,000 in cash."[38]

In the **liaison role**, managers deal with people outside their units. Studies consistently indicate that managers spend as much time with outsiders as they do with their own subordinates and their own bosses. When Mike Tannenbaum, general manager of the New York Jets, headed across town to the headquarters of J.P. Morgan Chase, he wasn't paying J.P. Morgan CEO Jamie Dimon a social call. Tannenbaum had scheduled the meeting to discuss J.P. Morgan's risk assessment and acquisition processes. The appointment with Dimon was part of a much broader initiative in which members from all levels of the Jets organization were encouraged to interact with professionals outside of their fields, such as firefighters, storm chasers, and bankers like Dimon, for the purpose of learning better management and decision-making processes. The Jets are also planning opportunities in the future for J.P. Morgan employees to visit their facilities. In this case, the liaison role operates in both directions, as managers are initiating interactions with outsiders and outsiders are coming to them.[39]

1-4b INFORMATIONAL ROLES

Not only do managers spend most of their time in face-to-face contact with others, they spend much of it obtaining and sharing information. Indeed, Mintzberg found that the managers in his study spent 40 percent of their time giving and getting information from others. In this regard, management can be viewed as gathering information by scanning the business environment and listening to others in face-to-face conversations, processing that information, and then sharing it with people both inside and outside the company. Mintzberg described three informational sub-roles: monitor, disseminator, and spokesperson.

In the **monitor role**, managers scan their environment for information, actively contact others for information, and, because of their personal contacts, receive a great deal of unsolicited information. Besides receiving firsthand information, managers monitor their environment by reading local newspapers and the *Wall Street Journal* to keep track of customers, competitors, and technological changes that may affect their businesses. Now, managers can also take advantage of electronic monitoring and distribution services that track the news wires (Associated Press, Reuters, and so on) for stories related to their businesses. These services deliver customized electronic newspapers that include only stories on topics the managers specify. Business Wire (http://www.businesswire.com) monitors and distributes daily news headlines from major industries (e.g., automotive, banking and financial, health, high tech).[40] CyberAlert (http://www.cyberalert.com) keeps round-the-clock track of new stories in categories chosen by each subscriber.[41] Another site, FNS NewsClips Online (http://fednewsmonitoring.com), provides subscribers with daily electronic news clips from more than 5,000 online news sites.[42]

Because of their numerous personal contacts and their access to subordinates, managers are often hubs for the distribution of critical information. In the **disseminator role**, managers share the information they have collected with their subordinates and others in the company. At **Telefónica O2**, a British-based telecommunications firm ranked as one of the best places to work in London, managers sit down twice a year with their employees to review a pocket-sized pamphlet outlining the company's goals and objectives. The discussions center around how the employees' personal development and growth plans can be linked to the company's goals.[43] Although there will never be a complete substitute for face-to-face dissemination of information, **Serena Software**, based in

Redwood City, California, uses Facebook to communicate worldwide with its 850 employees. On "Facebook Fridays," employees are given an hour, should they choose, to spend time using Facebook to communicate about themselves or learn about others in the company. Serena Software relies on Facebook so much for recruiting new employees and marketing its products that it has become the company's de facto intranet.⁴⁴ (You'll read more about intranets in Chapter 15 on communication.)

In contrast to the disseminator role, in which managers distribute information to employees inside the company, managers in the **spokesperson role** share information with people outside their departments and companies. One of the most common ways CEOs serve as spokespeople for their companies is at annual meetings with company shareholders or the board of directors. CEOs also serve as spokespeople to the media when their companies are involved in major news stories. During the most recent North American International Auto Show held in Detroit, Michigan, Fiat CEO Sergio Macchione announced that his company would be making a major investment in U.S. manufacturing by building an ultra-luxury Maserati SUV in one of its Chrysler-run Detroit factories (Fiat owns 54 percent of Chrysler). The ultra-luxury SUV, equipped with a Ferrari engine and designed to compete with offerings from Porsche and Audi, will be built at Chrysler's Jefferson North assembly plant and exported around the world.⁴⁵

1-4c DECISIONAL ROLES

Mintzberg found that obtaining and sharing information is not an end in itself. Obtaining and sharing information with people inside and outside the company is useful to managers because it helps them make good decisions. According to Mintzberg, managers engage in four decisional subroles: entrepreneur, disturbance handler, resource allocator, and negotiator.

In the **entrepreneur role**, managers adapt themselves, their subordinates, and their units to change. When Peter Löscher took over as CEO of Siemens, the German manufacturer had just been fined $2.5 billion for bribing government officials throughout the world to gain favor to win contracts. As a result, Löscher knew massive change was needed. He started by replacing the company's entire executive team and eventually replaced half of Siemens' middle managers. Then, he sold Siemens' best-performing units, mobile phones and information technology, and used the proceeds to invest in sustainable projects like solar energy, wind energy, and high-efficiency electricity grids, from which Siemens now derives $38 billion in sales annually. Today, 100,000 Siemens employees are so-called green-collar workers. Despite the turnaround, Löscher maintains an entrepreneurial mindset, saying, "Being good today means you have to be better tomorrow, and even better the day after tomorrow. The biggest risk is complacency."⁴⁶

A manager is responsible not only for providing direction and guidance to employees but also for making sure to create a work environment that allows them to be the best. Author and columnist Jeff Haden identifies nine things that managers often do that create an uncomfortable and unproductive work atmosphere.

1. Pressuring employees to attend social events. When your employees are with people from work, even at some party, it might just end up feeling like "work."
2. Asking an employee to do something that you've already asked someone else to do.
3. Pressuring employees to give to charity.
4. Not giving employees time to eat during mealtime hours.
5. Asking employees to do self-evaluations.
6. Asking employees to evaluate their coworkers.
7. Revealing too much information to employees.
8. Asking employees to make sure that you stay on course during meetings.
9. Asking employees to do something that you don't want to do.

Source: J. Haden, "9 Things You Should Never Ask Employees to Do," *Inc.com*, February 22, 2012, accessed February 25, 2012, http://www.inc.com/jeff-haden/9-things-you-should-never-ask-employees-to-do.html.

In the **disturbance handler role**, managers respond to pressures and problems so severe that they demand immediate attention and action. In early 2011, Sony's PlayStation Network, an online gaming platform, and Qriocity, a music streaming service, were hacked, leading to the theft of personal information from more than 77 million users and the complete shutdown of both services for twenty-three days. Howard Stringer, then Sony's CEO and president, apologized for the "inconvenience and concern caused by this attack," and promised to prevent anything similar from recurring. He also announced a $1 million insurance policy that would cover users who might be affected by identity theft because of the data breach. Further, he announced that users would be given a "Welcome Back" package consisting of one free month of service to make up for time lost because of the service outage.[47]

In the **resource allocator role**, managers decide who will get what resources and how many resources they will get. For years, Adobe's Flash software allowed web publishers to include animation, video, and other interactive elements in their websites. While Flash performed those functions effectively on personal computers, it did not work nearly as well on smartphones and tablet computers. Furthermore, with the development of HTML5, which provides built-in web coding for those functions, and the announcement from the late Steve Jobs, then Apple's CEO, that neither the iPhone nor iPad would support Flash, Adobe's leadership decided not to invest further resources in developing Flash for mobile devices. Instead, it will now devote more time and money into developing animation, video, and interactive tools for HTML5, which works on personal computers, smartphones, and tablets.[48] Danny Winokur, vice president and general manager of interactive development, said, "HTML5 is now universally supported on major mobile devices, in some cases exclusively. This makes HTML5 the best solution for creating and deploy-

ing content in the browser across mobile platforms."[49]

In the **negotiator role**, managers negotiate schedules, projects, goals, outcomes, resources, and employee raises. For example, after years of lawsuits, it only took two days for Roger Faxon, the new CEO of **EMI Group Ltd.**, which owns the rights to sell Beatles music, to negotiate a deal to make the legendary band's music available for sale at Apple's iTunes store. It had been long thought that the surviving band members, Paul McCartney and Ringo Starr, and the widows of deceased band members John Lennon and George Harrison, who have veto rights over how the music is distributed, would never permit digital downloads of the band's music. But, in the end, they agreed. Just two months after the agreement was negotiated, five million Beatles songs and two million Beatles albums had been sold and downloaded via iTunes.[50]

Disturbance handler role the decisional role managers play when they respond to severe problems that demand immediate action

Resource allocator role the decisional role managers play when they decide who gets what resources and in what amounts

Negotiator role the decisional role managers play when they negotiate schedules, projects, goals, outcomes, resources, and employee raises

1-5 *What Companies Look for in Managers*

I didn't have the slightest idea what my job was. I walked in giggling and laughing because I had been promoted and had no idea what

PlayStation Vita

Technical skills the specialized procedures, techniques, and knowledge required to get the job done

Human skills the ability to work well with others

Conceptual skills the ability to see the organization as a whole, understand how the different parts affect each other, and recognize how the company fits into or is affected by its environment

principles or style to be guided by. After the first day, I felt like I had run into a brick wall. (Sales Representative #1)

Suddenly, I found myself saying, boy, I can't be responsible for getting all that revenue. I don't have the time. Suddenly you've got to go from [taking care of] yourself and say now I'm the manager, and what does a manager do? It takes awhile thinking about it for it to really hit you . . . a manager gets things done through other people. That's a very, very hard transition to make. (Sales Representative #2)[51]

The preceding statements were made by two star sales representatives who, on the basis of their superior performance, were promoted to the position of sales manager. As their comments indicate, at first they did not feel confident about their ability to do their jobs as managers. Like most new managers, these sales managers suddenly realized that the knowledge, skills, and abilities that led to success early in their careers (and were probably responsible for their promotion into the ranks of management) would not necessarily help them succeed as managers. As sales representatives, they were responsible only for managing their own performance. But as sales managers, they were now directly responsible for supervising all of the sales representatives in their sales territories. Furthermore, they were now directly accountable for whether those sales representatives achieved their sales goals. If performance in nonmanagerial jobs doesn't necessarily prepare you for a managerial job, then what does it take to be a manager?

When companies look for employees who would be good managers, they look for individuals who have technical skills, human skills, conceptual skills, and the motivation to manage.[52] Exhibit 1.4 shows the relative importance of these four skills to the jobs of team leaders, first-line managers, middle managers, and top managers.

Technical skills are the specialized procedures, techniques, and knowledge required to get the job done. For the sales managers described above, technical skills involve the ability to find new sales prospects, develop accurate sales pitches based on customer needs, and close the sale. For a nurse supervisor, techni-

nical skills include being able to insert an IV or operate a crash cart if a patient goes into cardiac arrest.

Technical skills are most important for team leaders and lower-level managers because they supervise the workers who produce products or serve customers. Team leaders and first-line managers need technical knowledge and skills to train new employees and help employees solve problems. Technical knowledge and skills are also needed to troubleshoot problems that employees can't handle. Technical skills become less important as managers rise through the managerial ranks, but they are still important.

Human skills can be summarized as the ability to work well with others. Managers with human skills work effectively within groups, encourage others to express their thoughts and feelings, are sensitive to others' needs and viewpoints, and are good listeners and communicators. Human skills are equally important at all levels of management, from first-line supervisors to CEOs. However, because lower-level managers spend much of their time solving technical problems, upper-level managers may actually spend more time dealing directly with people. On average, first-line managers spend 57 percent of their time with people, but that percentage increases to 63 percent for middle managers and 78 percent for top managers.[53]

Conceptual skills are the ability to see the organization as a whole, to understand how the different parts of the company affect each other, and to

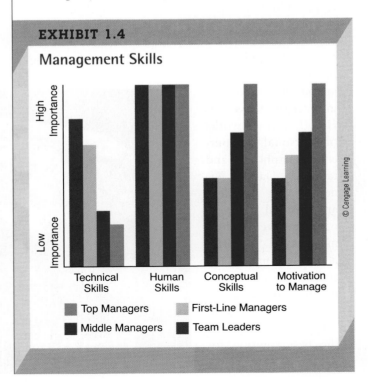

EXHIBIT 1.4

Management Skills

Technical Skills · Human Skills · Conceptual Skills · Motivation to Manage

■ Top Managers ■ Middle Managers ■ First-Line Managers ■ Team Leaders

© Cengage Learning

recognize how the company fits into or is affected by its external environment such as the local community, social and economic forces, customers, and the competition. Good managers have to be able to recognize, understand, and reconcile multiple complex problems and perspectives. In other words, managers have to be smart! In fact, intelligence makes so much difference for managerial performance that managers with above-average intelligence typically outperform managers of average intelligence by approximately 48 percent.[54] Clearly, companies need to be careful to promote smart workers into management. Conceptual skills increase in importance as managers rise through the management hierarchy.

Good management involves much more than intelligence, however. For example, making the department genius a manager can be disastrous if that genius lacks technical skills, human skills, or one other factor known as the motivation to manage. **Motivation to manage** is an assessment of how motivated employees are to interact with superiors, participate in competitive situations, behave assertively toward others, tell others what to do, reward good behavior and punish poor behavior, perform actions that are highly visible to others, and handle and organize administrative tasks. Managers typically have a stronger motivation to manage than their subordinates, and managers at higher levels usually have a stronger motivation to manage than managers at lower levels. Furthermore, managers with a stronger motivation to manage are promoted faster, are rated as better managers by their employees, and earn more money than managers with a weak motivation to manage.[55]

1-6 *Mistakes Managers Make*

Another way to understand what it takes to be a manager is to look at the mistakes managers make. In other words, we can learn just as much from what managers shouldn't do as from what they should do. Exhibit 1.5 lists the top ten mistakes managers make.

Several studies of U.S. and British managers have compared "arrivers," or managers who made it all the way to the top of their companies, with "derailers," or managers who were successful early in their careers but were knocked off the fast track by the time they reached the middle to upper levels of management.[56]

Motivation to manage an assessment of how enthusiastic employees are about managing the work of others

The researchers found that there were only a few differences between arrivers and derailers. For the most part, both groups were talented and both groups had weaknesses. But what distinguished derailers from arrivers was that derailers possessed two or more fatal flaws with respect to the way they managed people. Although arrivers were by no means perfect, they usually had no more than one fatal flaw or had found ways to minimize the effects of their flaws on the people with whom they worked.

The number-one mistake made by derailers was that they were insensitive to others by virtue of their abrasive, intimidating, and bullying management style. The authors of one study described a manager who walked into his subordinate's office and interrupted a meeting by saying, "I need to see you." When the subordinate tried to explain that he was not available because he was in the middle of a meeting, the manager barked, "I don't give a damn. I said I wanted to see you now."[57] Not surprisingly, only 25 percent of derailers were rated by others as being good with people, compared to 75 percent of arrivers.

The second mistake was that derailers were often cold, aloof, or arrogant. Although this sounds like insensitivity to others, it has more to do with derailed

EXHIBIT 1.5

Top Ten Mistakes Managers Make

1. Insensitive to others: abrasive, intimidating, bullying style
2. Cold, aloof, arrogant
3. Betray trust
4. Overly ambitious: thinking of next job, playing politics
5. Specific performance problems with the business
6. Overmanaging: unable to delegate or build a team
7. Unable to staff effectively
8. Unable to think strategically
9. Unable to adapt to boss with different style
10. Overdependent on advocate or mentor

Source: M. W. McCall, Jr., and M. M. Lombardo, "What Makes a Top Executive?" *Psychology Today*, February 1983, 26–31.

managers being so smart, so expert in their areas of knowledge, that they treated others with contempt because they weren't experts, too. For example, AT&T called in an industrial psychologist to counsel its vice president of human resources because she had been blamed for "ruffling too many feathers" at the company.[58] Interviews with the vice president's coworkers and subordinates revealed that they thought she was brilliant, was "smarter and faster than other people," "generates a lot of ideas," and "loves to deal with complex issues." Unfortunately, these smarts were accompanied by a cold, aloof, and arrogant management style. The people she worked with complained that she does "too much too fast," treats coworkers with "disdain," "impairs teamwork," "doesn't always show her warm side," and has "burned too many bridges."[59]

The third mistake made by derailers involved betraying a trust. Betraying a trust doesn't mean being dishonest. Instead, it means making others look bad by not doing what you said you would do when you said you would do it. That mistake, in itself, is not fatal because managers and their workers aren't machines. Tasks go undone in every company every single business day. There's always too much to do and not enough time, people, money, or resources to do it. The fatal betrayal of trust is failing to inform others when things will not be done on time. This failure to admit mistakes, quickly inform others of the mistakes, take responsibility for the mistakes, and then fix them without blaming others clearly distinguished the behavior of derailers from arrivers.

The fourth mistake was being overly political and ambitious. Managers who always have their eye on their next job rarely establish more than superficial re-lationships with peers and coworkers. In their haste to gain credit for successes that would be noticed by upper management, they make the fatal mistake of treating people as though they don't matter. An employee with an overly ambitious boss described him this way: "He treats employees coldly, even cruelly. He assigns blame without regard to responsibility, and takes all the credit for himself. I once had such a boss, and he gave me a new definition of shared risk: If something I did was successful, he took the credit. If it wasn't, I got the blame."[60]

The fatal mistakes of being unable to delegate, build a team, and staff effectively indicate that many derailed managers were unable to make the most basic transition to managerial work: to quit being hands-on doers and get work done through others. Two things go wrong when managers make these mistakes. First, when managers meddle in decisions that their subordinates should be making—when they can't stop being doers—they alienate the people who work for them. Rich Dowd, founder of Dowd Associates, an executive search firm, admits to constantly monitoring and interrupting employees because they weren't doing the job "in the way I saw fit, even when their work was outstanding." According to Richard Kilburg of Johns Hopkins University, when managers interfere with workers' decisions, "You . . . have a tendency to lose your most creative people. They're able to say, 'Screw this. I'm not staying here.'"[61] Indeed, one employee told Dowd that if he was going to do her job for her, she would quit. Second, because they are trying to do their subordinates' jobs in addition to their own, managers who fail to delegate will not have enough time to do much of anything well.

1-7 The Transition to Management: The First Year

In her book *Becoming a Manager: Mastery of a New Identity*, Harvard Business School professor Linda Hill followed the development of nineteen people in their first year as managers. Her study found that becoming a manager produced a profound psychological transition that changed the way these managers viewed themselves and others. As shown in Exhibit 1.6, the evolution of the managers' thoughts, expectations, and realities over the course of their

EXHIBIT 1.6

Stages in the Transition to Management

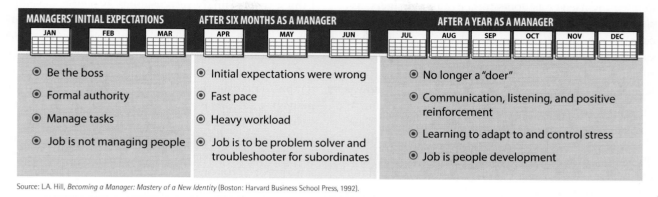

MANAGERS' INITIAL EXPECTATIONS			AFTER SIX MONTHS AS A MANAGER			AFTER A YEAR AS A MANAGER					
JAN	FEB	MAR	APR	MAY	JUN	JUL	AUG	SEP	OCT	NOV	DEC

MANAGERS' INITIAL EXPECTATIONS	AFTER SIX MONTHS AS A MANAGER	AFTER A YEAR AS A MANAGER
◉ Be the boss	◉ Initial expectations were wrong	◉ No longer a "doer"
◉ Formal authority	◉ Fast pace	◉ Communication, listening, and positive reinforcement
◉ Manage tasks	◉ Heavy workload	◉ Learning to adapt to and control stress
◉ Job is not managing people	◉ Job is to be problem solver and troubleshooter for subordinates	◉ Job is people development

Source: L.A. Hill, *Becoming a Manager: Mastery of a New Identity* (Boston: Harvard Business School Press, 1992).

first year in management reveals the magnitude of the changes they experienced.

Initially, the managers in Hill's study believed that their job was to exercise formal authority and to manage tasks—basically being the boss, telling others what to do, making decisions, and getting things done. One of the managers Hill interviewed said, "Being the manager means running my own office, using my ideas and thoughts." Another said, "[The office is] my baby. It's my job to make sure it works."[62] In fact, most of the new managers were attracted to management positions because they wanted to be in charge. Surprisingly, the new managers did not believe that their job was to manage people. The only aspects of people management mentioned by the new managers were hiring and firing.

After six months, most of the new managers had concluded that their initial expectations about managerial work were wrong. Management wasn't just about being the boss, making decisions, and telling others what to do. The first surprise was the fast pace and heavy workload involved. Said one of Hill's managers, "This job is much harder than you think. It is 40 to 50 percent more work than being a producer! Who would have ever guessed?" The pace of managerial work was

Top managers spend an average of nine minutes on a given task before having to switch to another.

startling, too. Another manager said, "You have eight or nine people looking for your time . . . coming into and out of your office all day long." A somewhat frustrated manager declared that management was "a job that never ended . . . a job you couldn't get your hands around."[63]

Informal descriptions like these are consistent with studies indicating that the average first-line manager spends no more than two minutes on a task before being interrupted by a request from a subordinate, a phone call, or an email. The pace is somewhat less hurried for top managers, who spend an average of approximately nine minutes on a task before having to switch to another. In practice, this means that supervisors may perform thirty different tasks per hour, while top managers perform seven different tasks per hour, with each task typically different from the one that preceded it. A manager described this frenetic level of activity by saying, "The only time you are in control is when you shut your door, and then I feel I am not doing the job I'm supposed to be doing, which is being with the people."[64]

The other major surprise after six months on the job was that the managers' expectations about what they should do as managers were very different from their subordinates' expectations. Initially, the managers defined their jobs as helping their subordinates perform their jobs well. For the managers, who still defined themselves as doers rather than managers, assisting their subordinates meant going out on sales calls or handling customer complaints. One manager said, "I like going out with the rep, who may need me to lend him my credibility as manager. I like the challenge, the joy in closing. I go out with the reps and we make the call and talk about the customer; it's fun."[65] But when the managers "assisted" in this way, their subordinates were resentful and viewed their help as interference. The subordinates wanted their managers to help them by solving problems that they couldn't solve. Once the managers realized this distinction, they embraced their role as problem-solver and troubleshooter. Thus, they could help without interfering with their subordinates' jobs.

After a year on the job, most of the managers thought of themselves as managers and no longer as doers. In making the transition, they finally realized that people management was the most important

MGMT ≠ BOSSY

part of their job. One of Hill's interviewees summarized the lesson that had taken him a year to learn by saying, "As many demands as managers have on their time, I think their primary responsibility is people development. Not production, but people development."[66] Another indication of how much their views had changed was that most of the managers now regretted the rather heavy-handed approach they had used in their early attempts to manage their subordinates. "I wasn't good at managing . . . , so I was bossy like a first-grade teacher." "Now I see that I started out as a drill sergeant. I was inflexible, just a lot of how-to's." By the end of the year, most of the managers had abandoned their authoritarian approach for one based on communication, listening, and positive reinforcement.

Finally, after beginning their year as managers in frustration, the managers came to feel comfortable with their subordinates, with the demands of their jobs, and with their emerging managerial styles. While being managers had made them acutely aware of their limitations and their need to develop as people, it also provided them with an unexpected reward of coaching and developing the people who worked for them. One manager said, "It gives me the best feeling to see somebody do something well after I have helped them. I get excited." Another stated, "I realize now that when I accepted the position of branch manager that it is truly an exciting vocation. It is truly awesome, even at this level; it can be terribly challenging and terribly exciting."[67]

1-8 Competitive Advantage through People

If you walk down the aisle of the business section in your local bookstore, you'll find hundreds of books that explain precisely what companies need to do to be successful. Unfortunately, the best-selling business books tend to be faddish, changing dramatically every few years. One thing that hasn't changed, though, is the importance of good people and good management: Companies can't succeed for long without them.

In his books *Competitive Advantage through People: Unleashing the Power of the Work Force* and *The Human Equation: Building Profits by Put-*

ting People First, Stanford University business professor Jeffrey Pfeffer contends that what separates top-performing companies from their competitors is the way they treat their work forces—in other words, their management style.[68]

Pfeffer found that managers in top-performing companies used ideas like employment security, selective hiring, self-managed teams and decentralization, high pay contingent on company performance, extensive training, reduced status distinctions (between managers and employees), and extensive sharing of financial information to achieve financial performance that, on average, was 40 percent higher than that of other companies. These ideas, which are explained in detail in Exhibit 1.7, help organizations develop work forces that are smarter, better trained, more motivated, and more committed than their competitors' work forces. And—as indicated by the phenomenal growth and return on investment earned by these companies—smarter, better trained, and more committed work forces provide superior products and service to customers. Such customers keep buying and, by telling others about their positive experiences, bring in new customers.

According to Pfeffer, companies that invest in their people will create long-lasting competitive advantages that are difficult for other companies to duplicate. Indeed, other studies clearly demonstrate that sound management practices can produce substantial advantages in four critical areas of organizational performance: sales revenues, profits, stock market returns, and customer satisfaction.

In terms of sales revenues and profits, a study of nearly 1,000 U.S. firms found that companies that use *just some* of the ideas shown in Exhibit 1.7 had $27,044 more sales per employee and $3,814 more profit per employee than companies that didn't. For a 100-person company, these differences amount to $2.7 million more in sales and nearly $400,000 more in annual profit! For a 1,000-person company, the

---

EXHIBIT 1.7

Competitive Advantage through People: Management Practices

1. Employment Security—Employment security is the ultimate form of commitment companies can make to their workers. Employees can innovate and increase company productivity without fearing the loss of their jobs.

2. Selective Hiring—If employees are the basis for a company's competitive advantage and those employees have employment security, then the company needs to aggressively recruit and selectively screen applicants in order to hire the most talented employees available.

3. Self-Managed Teams and Decentralization—Self-managed teams are responsible for their own hiring, purchasing, job assignments, and production. Self-managed teams can often produce enormous increases in productivity through increased employee commitment and creativity. Decentralization allows employees who are closest to (and most knowledgeable about) problems, production, and customers to make timely decisions. Decentralization increases employee satisfaction and commitment.

4. High Wages Contingent on Organizational Performance—High wages are needed to attract and retain talented workers and to indicate that the organization values its workers. Employees, like company founders, shareholders, and managers, need to share in the financial rewards when the company is successful. Why? Because employees who have a financial stake in their companies are more likely to take a long-run view of the business and think like business owners.

5. Training and Skill Development—Like a high-tech company that spends millions of dollars to upgrade computers or research and development labs, a company whose competitive advantage is based on its people must invest in the training and skill development of its people.

6. Reduction of Status Differences—A company should treat everyone, no matter what the job, as equal. There are no reserved parking spaces. Everyone eats in the same cafeteria and has similar benefits. The result: improved communication as employees focus on problems and solutions rather than on how they are less valued than managers.

7. Sharing Information—If employees are to make decisions that are good for the long-term health and success of the company, they need to be given information about costs, finances, productivity, development times, and strategies that was previously known only by company managers.

Source: J. Pfeffer, *The Human Equation: Building Profits by Putting People First* (Boston: Harvard Business School Press, 1996).

MGMT TRENDS

One company that knows how to invest in people is Salesforce.com, a cloud computing service based in San Francisco. When an employee, John Greene, was diagnosed with leukemia, employees throughout the company mobilized to look for a possible bone marrow donor. CEO Marc Benioff even posted details about Greene's case and how to donate marrow on his personal Twitter site. When Greene began receiving treatment, he found that some of the costs of therapy were not covered by his insurance. The company quickly picked up the bill so that he would not be burdened by extra medical expenses. Gillian Jenkins, an employee at Salesforce.com's offices in England, had a similar experience. She had to undergo treatments for myeloma that were not covered by insurance and would have cost her $54,000. The company not only paid the full bill but also told her that it would pay all of her costs if she wanted to come to the United States for treatment. By caring for people in this way, Salesforce.com produces a healthy, happy, motivated staff that is proud to give maximum efforts to see the company succeed.

Source: D. A. Kaplan, "Salesforces' Happy Workforce," *Fortune*, February 6, 2012, 101–112.

difference grows to $27 million more in sales and $4 million more in annual profit![69]

Another study that considers the effect of investing in people on company sales found that poorly performing companies were able to improve their average return on investment from 5.1 percent to 19.7 percent and increase sales by $94,000 per employee. They did this by adopting management techniques as simple as setting performance expectations (establishing goals, results, and schedules), coaching (informal, ongoing discussions between managers and subordinates about what is being done well and what could be done better), reviewing (annual, formal discussion about results), and rewarding employee performance (adjusting salaries and bonuses based on employee performance and results).[70] So, in addition to significantly improving the profitability of healthy companies, sound management practices can turn around failing companies.

To determine how investing in people affects stock market performance, researchers matched companies on *Fortune* magazine's list of "100 Best Companies to Work for in America" with companies that were similar in industry, size, and—this is key—operating performance. Both sets of companies were equally good performers; the key difference was how well they treated their employees. For both sets of companies, the researchers found that employee attitudes such as job satisfaction changed little from year to year. The people who worked for the "100 Best" companies were consistently much more satisfied with their jobs

and employers year after year than were employees in the matched companies. More importantly, those stable differences in employee attitudes were strongly related to differences in stock market performance. Over a one-year period, an investment in the "100 Best" would have resulted in an 82 percent cumulative stock return compared with just 37 percent for the matched companies.[71] This difference is remarkable given that both sets of companies were equally good performers at the beginning of the period.

Finally, research also indicates that managers have an important effect on customer satisfaction. Many people find this surprising. They don't understand how managers, who are largely responsible for what goes on inside the company, can affect what goes on outside the company. They wonder how managers, who often interact with customers under negative conditions (when customers are angry or dissatisfied), can actu-

ally improve customer satisfaction. It turns out that managers influence customer satisfaction through employee satisfaction. When employees are satisfied with their jobs, their bosses, and the companies they work for, they provide much better service to customers.[72] In turn, customers are more satisfied, too. Indeed, customers of companies on *Fortune*'s list of "100 Best," where employees are much more satisfied with their jobs and their companies, have much higher customer satisfaction scores than do customers of comparable companies that are not on *Fortune*'s list. Over an eight-year period, that difference in customer satisfaction also resulted in a 14 percent annual stock market return for the "100 Best" companies compared to a 6 percent return for the overall stock market.[73]

You will learn more about the service-profit chain in Chapter 18 on managing service and manufacturing operations.

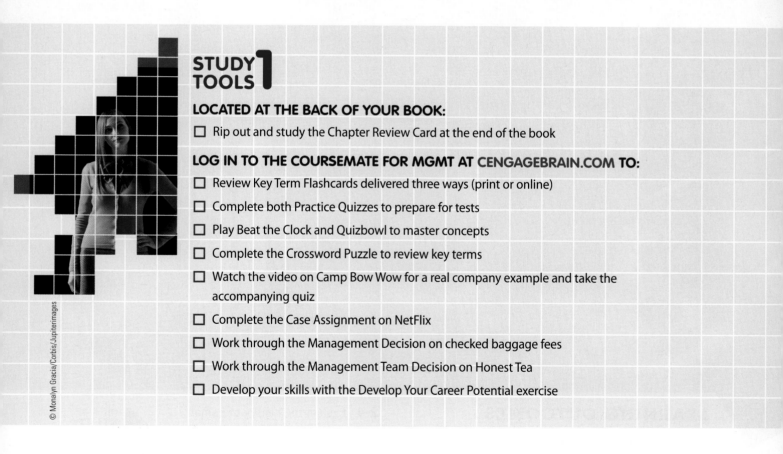

STUDY TOOLS 1

LOCATED AT THE BACK OF YOUR BOOK:

☐ Rip out and study the Chapter Review Card at the end of the book

LOG IN TO THE COURSEMATE FOR MGMT AT CENGAGEBRAIN.COM TO:

☐ Review Key Term Flashcards delivered three ways (print or online)

☐ Complete both Practice Quizzes to prepare for tests

☐ Play Beat the Clock and Quizbowl to master concepts

☐ Complete the Crossword Puzzle to review key terms

☐ Watch the video on Camp Bow Wow for a real company example and take the accompanying quiz

☐ Complete the Case Assignment on NetFlix

☐ Work through the Management Decision on checked baggage fees

☐ Work through the Management Team Decision on Honest Tea

☐ Develop your skills with the Develop Your Career Potential exercise

2 The History
of Management

LEARNING OUTCOMES

2-1 Explain the origins of management.

2-2 Explain the history of scientific management.

2-3 Discuss the history of bureaucratic and administrative management.

2-4 Explain the history of human relations management.

2-5 Discuss the history of operations, information, systems, and contingency management.

CHECK OUT
STUDY TOOLS
AT THE END OF
THIS CHAPTER.

2-1 *The Origins of Management*

Each day, managers are asked to solve challenging problems and are given only a limited amount of time, people, or resources. Yet it's still their responsibility to get things done on time and within budget. Tell today's managers to "reward workers for improved production or performance," "set specific goals to increase motivation," or "innovate to create and sustain a competitive advantage," and they'll respond, "Duh! Who doesn't know that?" A mere 125 years ago, however, business ideas and practices were so different that today's widely accepted management ideas would have been as self-evident as space travel, cell phones, and the Internet. In fact, management jobs and careers didn't exist 125 years ago, so management was not yet a field of study. Now, of course, managers and management are such an important part of the business world that it's hard to imagine organizations without them. So if there were no managers 125 years ago, but you can't walk down the hall today without bumping into one, where did management come from?

Although we can find the seeds of many of today's management ideas throughout history, not until the last two centuries did systematic changes in the nature of work and organizations create a compelling need for managers.

2-1a MANAGEMENT IDEAS AND PRACTICES THROUGHOUT HISTORY

Examples of management thought and practice can be found throughout history.[1] For example, the earliest recorded instance of information management dates to ancient Sumer (modern Iraq), *circa* 8000–3000 BCE. Sumerian businessmen used small clay tokens to calculate quantities of grain and livestock—and later, value-added goods like perfume or pottery—they owned and traded in temples and at city gates. Different shapes and sizes represented different types and quantities of goods. The tokens were also used to store data. They were kept in small clay envelopes, and the token shapes were impressed on the outside of the envelope to indicate what was inside. Eventually, someone figured out that it was easier to just write these symbols with a stylus on a tablet instead of using the tokens. In the end, the new technology of *writing* led to more efficient management of the business of Sumerian temples.[2]

A task as enormous as building the great pyramids in Egypt was bound to present practical problems that would lead to the development of management ideas. Egyptians recognized the need for planning, organizing, and controlling; for submitting written requests; and for consulting staff for advice before making decisions. The enormity of the task they faced is evident in the pyramid of King Khufu, which contains 2.3 million blocks of stone. Each block had to be quarried, cut to precise size and shape, cured (hardened in the sun), transported by boat for two to three days, moved to the construction site, numbered to identify where it would be placed, and then shaped and smoothed so that it would fit perfectly into place. It took 20,000 workers twenty-three years to complete this pyramid; more than 8,000 were needed just to quarry the stones and transport them. A typical quarry expedition might include 100 army officers, fifty government and religious officials, and 200 members of the king's court to lead the expedition; 130 stonemasons to cut the stones; and 5,000 soldiers, 800 barbarians, and

2,000 bond servants to load and unload the stones from the ships.[3]

Exhibit 2.1 shows how other management ideas and practices throughout history relate to the management functions we discuss in this textbook.

2-1b WHY WE NEED MANAGERS TODAY

Working from 8:00 a.m. to 5:00 p.m., coffee breaks, lunch hours, crushing rush hour traffic, and punching a time clock are things we associate with today's working world. Work hasn't always been this way, however. In fact, the design of jobs and organizations has changed dramatically over the last 500 years. For most of humankind's history, for example, people didn't commute to work.[4] Work usually occurred in homes or on farms. In 1720, almost 80 percent of the 5.5 million people in England lived and worked in the country. And as recently as 1870, two-thirds of Americans earned their living from agriculture. Even most of those who didn't earn their living from agriculture didn't commute to work. Blacksmiths, furniture makers, leather goods makers, and other skilled tradespeople or craftspeople who formed trade guilds (the historical predecessors of labor unions) in England as early as 1093 typically worked out of shops in or next to their homes.[5] Likewise, cottage workers worked with each other out of small homes that were often built in a semicircle. A family in each cottage would complete a different production step, and work passed from one cottage to the next until production was

---

EXHIBIT 2.1

Management Ideas and Practice throughout History

Time	Individual or Group	Planning	Organizing	Leading	Controlling	Contributions to Management Thought and Practice
5000 BCE	Sumerians				√	Written record keeping.
4000 BCE to 2000 BCE	Egyptians	√	√		√	Planning, organizing, and controlling to build the pyramids; submitting requests in writing; making decisions after consulting staff for advice.
1800 BCE	Hammurabi				√	Controls; using witnesses in legal cases.
600 BCE	Nebuchadnezzar		√	√		Wage incentives and production control.
500 BCE	Sun Tzu	√		√		Strategy; identifying and attacking opponents' weaknesses.
400 BCE	Xenophon	√	√	√	√	Management as separate art.
400 BCE	Cyrus		√	√	√	Human relations and motion study.
175	Cato		√			Job descriptions.
284	Diocletian		√			Delegation of authority.
900	al-Farabi			√		Leadership traits.
1100	Ghazali			√		Managerial traits.
1418	Barbarigo		√			Different organizational forms/structures.
1436	Venetians				√	Numbering, standardization, and interchangeability of parts.
1500	Sir Thomas More			√		Critique of poor management and leadership.
1525	Machiavelli		√	√		Cohesiveness, power, and leadership in organizations.

Source: C. S. George, Jr., *The History of Management Thought* (Englewood Cliffs, NJ: Prentice Hall, 1972).

© PhotoQuest/Archive Photos/Getty Images

dropped from 12.5 man-hours to just 93 minutes after switching to mass production.[7]

Second, instead of being performed in fields, homes, or small shops, jobs occurred in large, formal organizations where hundreds, if not thousands, of people worked under one roof.[8] In 1849, for example, **Chicago Harvester** (the predecessor of International Harvester) ran the largest factory in the United States with just 123 workers. Yet by 1913, Henry Ford employed 12,000 employees in his Highland Park, Michigan, factory alone. Because the number of people working in manufacturing quintupled from 1860 to 1890, and individual factories employed so many workers under one roof, companies now had a strong need for disciplinary rules to impose order and structure. For the first time, they needed managers who knew how to organize large groups, work with employees, and make good decisions.

complete. With small, self-organized work groups, no commute, no bosses, and no common building, there wasn't a strong need for management.

During the Industrial Revolution (1750–1900), however, jobs and organizations changed dramatically.[6] First, unskilled laborers running machines began to replace high-paid, skilled artisans. What made this possible? The availability of power (steam engines and, later, electricity) as well as numerous related inventions, including Darby's coke-smelting process and Cort's puddling and rolling process (both for making iron), as well as Hargreaves's spinning jenny and Arkwright's water frame (both for spinning cotton). Whereas artisans made entire goods by themselves by hand, this new production system was based on a division of labor: Each worker, interacting with machines, performed separate, highly specialized tasks that were but a small part of all the steps required to make manufactured goods. Mass production was born as rope- and chain-driven assembly lines moved work to stationary workers who concentrated on performing one small task over and over again. While workers focused on their singular tasks, managers were needed to coordinate the different parts of the production system and optimize its overall performance. Productivity skyrocketed at companies that understood this. At **Ford Motor Company**, where the assembly line was developed, the time required to assemble a car

2-2 *Scientific Management*

Before 1880, business educators taught only basic bookkeeping and secretarial skills, and no one published books or articles about management.[9] Today you can turn to dozens of academic journals (such as the Academy of Management's *Journal* or *Review*, *Administrative Science Quarterly*, the *Strategic Management Journal*, and the *Journal of Applied Psychology*), hundreds of business school and practitioner journals (such as *Harvard Business Review*, *MIT Sloan Management Review*, and the *Academy of Management Perspectives*), and thousands of books and articles if you have a question about management. In the next four sections, you will learn about some important contributors to the field of management and how their ideas shaped our current understanding of management theory and practice.

Bosses, who were hired by the company owner or founder, used to make decisions by the seat of their pants—haphazardly, without any systematic study,

Scientific management
thoroughly studying and testing different work methods to identify the best, most efficient way to complete a job

Soldiering when workers deliberately slow their pace or restrict their work output

Rate buster a group member whose work pace is significantly faster than the normal pace in his or her group

thought, or collection of information. If the bosses decided that workers should work twice as fast, little or no thought was given to worker motivation. If workers resisted, the bosses often resorted to physical beatings to get workers to work faster, harder, or longer. With no incentives for bosses and workers to cooperate with one another, both groups played the system by trying to take advantage of each other. Moreover, each worker did the same job in his or her own way with different methods and different tools. In short, there were no procedures to standardize operations, no standards by which to judge whether performance was good or bad, and no follow-up to determine if productivity or quality actually improved when changes were made.[10]

This all changed, however, with the advent of **scientific management**, which involved thorough study and testing of different work methods to identify the best, most efficient ways to complete a job.

Let's find out more about scientific management by learning about 2-2a Frederick W. Taylor, the father of scientific management; 2-2b Frank and Lillian Gilbreth and motion studies; and 2-2c Henry Gantt and his Gantt charts.

2-2α FATHER OF SCIENTIFIC MANAGEMENT: FREDERICK W. TAYLOR

Frederick W. Taylor (1856–1915), the father of scientific management, began his career as a worker at **Midvale Steel Company**. He was later promoted to patternmaker, supervisor, and then chief engineer. At Midvale, Taylor was deeply affected by his three-year struggle to get the men who worked for him to do, as he called it, "a fair day's work." Taylor, who had worked alongside the men as a coworker before becoming their boss, said, "We who were the workmen of that shop had the quantity output carefully agreed upon for everything that was turned out in the shop. We limited the output to about, I should think, one third of what we could very well have done." Taylor explained that, as soon as he became the boss, "the men who were working under me . . . knew that I was onto the whole game of **soldiering**, or deliberately restricting output."[11] When Taylor told his workers, "I have accepted a job under

the management of this company and I am on the other side of the fence . . . I am going to try to get a bigger output," the workers responded, "We warn you, Fred, if you try to bust any of these rates [a **rate buster** was someone who worked faster than the group] we will have you over the fence in six weeks."[12]

Over the next three years, Taylor tried everything he could think of to improve output. By doing the job himself, he showed workers that it was possible to produce more output. He hired new workers and trained them himself, hoping they would produce more. But "very heavy social pressure" from the other workers kept them from doing so. Pushed by Taylor, the workers began breaking their machines so that they couldn't produce. Taylor responded by fining them every time they broke a machine and for any violation of the rules, no matter how small, such as being late to work. Tensions became so severe that some of the workers threatened to shoot Taylor. Looking back at the situation, Taylor reflected, "It is a horrid life for any man to live, not to be able to look any workman in the face all day long without seeing hostility there and feeling that every man around one is his virtual enemy." He said, "I made up my mind either to get out of the business entirely and go into some other line of work, or to find some remedy for this unbearable condition."[13]

The remedy that Taylor eventually developed was scientific management. Taylor, who once described scientific management as "seventy-five percent science and twenty-five percent common sense," emphasized that the goal of scientific management was to use systematic study to find the "one best way" of doing each task. To do that, managers had to follow the four principles shown in Exhibit 2.2. The first principle was to "develop a science" for each element of work. Study it. Analyze it. Determine the "one best way" to do the work. For example, one of Taylor's controversial proposals at the time was to give rest breaks to factory workers doing physical labor. We take morning, lunch, and afternoon breaks for granted, but in Taylor's day, factory workers were expected to work without stopping.[14] When Taylor said that breaks would increase worker productivity, no one believed him. Nonetheless, through systematic experiments, he showed that workers receiving frequent rest breaks were able to greatly increase their daily output.

Second, managers had to scientifically select, train, teach, and develop workers to help them reach their full potential. Before Taylor, supervisors often hired on the basis of favoritism and nepotism. Who you knew was often more important than what you

MGMT TRENDS

How do you get employees and managers on the same page? According to Frederick Taylor, one of the best ways to align managers and employees was to use incentives. As Taylor wrote in *The Principles of Scientific Management*:

> In order to have any hope of obtaining the initiative of his workmen the manager must give some special incentive to his men beyond that which is given to the average of the trade. This incentive can be given in several different ways, as, for example, the hope of rapid promotion or advancement; higher wages, either in the form of generous piecework prices or of a premium or bonus of some kind for good and rapid work; shorter hours of labor; better surroundings and working conditions than are ordinarily given, etc., and, above all, this special incentive should be accompanied by that personal consideration for, and friendly contact with, his workmen which comes only from a genuine and kindly interest in the welfare of those under him. It is only by giving a special inducement or "incentive" of this kind that the employer can hope even approximately to get the "initiative" of his workmen.

Source: F. W. Taylor, The Principles of Scientific Management (New York: Harper, 1911).

could do. By contrast, Taylor instructed supervisors to hire "first-class" workers on the basis of their aptitude to do a job well. In one of the first applications of this principle, physical reaction times were used to select bicycle ball-bearing inspectors who had to be able to examine ball bearings as fast as they were produced on a production line. For similar reasons, Taylor also recommended that companies train and develop their workers—a rare practice at the time.

The third principle instructed managers to cooperate with employees to ensure that the scientific principles were actually implemented. Labor unrest was widespread at the time; the number of labor strikes against companies doubled between 1893 and 1904. As Taylor knew from personal experience, workers and management more often than not viewed each other as enemies. Taylor's advice ran contrary to the common wisdom of the day. He said, "The majority of these men believe that the fundamental interests of employees and employers are necessarily antagonistic. Scientific management, on the contrary, has for its very foundation the firm conviction that the true interests of the two are one and the same; that prosperity for the employer cannot exist through a long term of years unless it is accompanied by prosperity for the employee and vice versa; and that it is possible to give the workman what he most wants—high wages—and the employer what he wants—a low labor cost for his manufactures."[15]

The fourth principle of scientific management was to divide the work and the responsibility equally between management and workers. Prior to Taylor, workers alone were held responsible for productivity and performance. But, said Taylor, "Almost every act of the workman should be preceded by one or more preparatory acts of the management which enable him

---

EXHIBIT 2.2

Taylor's Four Principles of Scientific Management

First:	Develop a science for each element of a man's work, which replaces the old rule-of-thumb method.
Second:	Scientifically select and then train, teach, and develop the workman, whereas in the past he chose his own work and trained himself as best he could.
Third:	Heartily cooperate with the men so as to ensure all of the work being done is in accordance with the principles of the science that has been developed.
Fourth:	There is an almost equal division of the work and the responsibility between the management and the workmen. The management take over all the work for which they are better fitted than the workmen, while in the past almost all of the work and the greater part of the responsibility were thrown upon the men.

Source: F. W. Taylor, *The Principles of Scientific Management* (New York: Harper, 1911).

Motion study breaking each task or job into its separate motions and then eliminating those that are unnecessary or repetitive

Time study timing how long it takes good workers to complete each part of their jobs

to do his work better and quicker than he otherwise could. And each man should daily be taught by and receive the most friendly help from those who are over him, instead of being, at the one extreme, driven or coerced by his bosses, and at the other left to his own unaided devices."[16]

Above all, Taylor believed these principles could be used to determine a "fair day's work," that is, what an average worker could produce at a reasonable pace, day in and day out. Once that was determined, it was management's responsibility to pay workers fairly for that fair day's work. In essence, Taylor was trying to align management and employees so that what was good for employees was also good for management. In this way, he believed, workers and managers could avoid the conflicts he had experienced at Midvale Steel.

Although Taylor remains a controversial figure among some academics who believe that his ideas were bad for workers, his key ideas have stood the test of time.[17] These include using systematic analysis to identify the best methods; scientifically selecting, training, and developing workers; promoting cooperation between management and labor; developing standardized approaches and tools; setting specific tasks or goals and then rewarding workers with financial incentives; and giving workers shorter work hours and frequent breaks. In fact, his ideas are so well accepted and widely used that we take most of them for granted. As eminent management scholar Edwin Locke says, "The point is not, as is often claimed, that he was 'right in the context of his time,' but is now outdated, but that *most of his insights are still valid today*."[18]

2-2b MOTION STUDIES: FRANK AND LILLIAN GILBRETH

The husband and wife team of Frank and Lillian Gilbreth are best known for their use of motion studies to simplify work, but they also made significant contributions to the employment of disabled workers and to the field of industrial psychology. Like Frederick Taylor, their early experiences significantly shaped their interests and contributions to management.

Though admitted to MIT, Frank Gilbreth (1868–1924) began his career as an apprentice bricklayer. While learning the trade, he noticed the bricklayers using three different sets of motions—one to teach others how to lay bricks, a second to work at a slow pace,

and a third to work at a fast pace.[19] Wondering which was best, he studied the various approaches and began eliminating unnecessary motions. For example, by designing a stand that could be raised to waist height, he eliminated the need to bend over to pick up each brick. Turning to grab a brick was faster and easier than bending down. By having lower-paid workers place all the bricks with their most attractive side up, bricklayers didn't waste time turning a brick over to find it. By mixing a more consistent mortar, bricklayers no longer had to tap each brick numerous times to put it in the right position. Together, Gilbreth's improvements raised productivity from 120 to 350 bricks per hour and from 1,000 bricks to 2,700 bricks per day.

As a result of his experience with bricklaying, Gilbreth and his wife, Lillian, developed a long-term interest in using motion study to simplify work, improve productivity, and reduce the level of effort required to safely perform a job. Indeed, Frank Gilbreth said, "The greatest waste in the world comes from needless, ill-directed, and ineffective motions."[20] **Motion study** broke each task or job into separate motions and then eliminated those that were unnecessary or repetitive. Because many motions were completed very quickly, the Gilbreths used motion-picture films, then a relatively new technology, to analyze jobs. Most film cameras at that time were hand cranked and thus variable in their film speed, so Frank invented the micro chronometer, a large clock that could record time to 1/2,000th of a second. By placing the micro chronometer next to the worker in the camera's field of vision and attaching a flashing strobe light to the worker's hands to better identify the direction and sequence of key movements, the Gilbreths could use film to detect and precisely time even the slightest, fastest movements. Motion study typically yielded production increases of 25 to 300 percent.[21]

Frederick W. Taylor also strove to simplify work, but he did so by managing time rather than motion as the Gilbreths did.[22] Taylor developed time study to put an end to soldiering and to determine what could be considered a fair day's work. **Time study** worked by

© iStockphoto.com/melhi

timing how long it took a "first-class man" to complete each part of his job. A standard time was established after allowing for rest periods, and a worker's pay would increase or decrease depending on whether the worker exceeded or fell below that standard.

Lillian Gilbreth (1878–1972) was an important contributor to management in her own right. She was the first woman to receive a Ph.D. in industrial psychology as well as the first woman to become a member of the Society of Industrial Engineers and the American Society of Mechanical Engineers. When Frank died in 1924, she continued the work of their management consulting company (which they had shared for over a dozen years) on her own. Lillian, who was concerned with the human side of work, was one of the first contributors to industrial psychology, originating ways to improve office communication, incentive programs, job satisfaction, and management training. Her work also convinced the government to enact laws regarding workplace safety, ergonomics, and child labor.

2-2c CHARTS: HENRY GANTT

Henry Gantt (1861–1919) was first a protégé and then an associate of Frederick Taylor. Gantt is best known for the Gantt chart, but he also made significant contributions to management with respect to pay-for-performance plans and the training and development of workers. As shown in Exhibit 2.3, a **Gantt chart** visually indicates what tasks must be completed at which times in order to complete a project. It accomplishes this by showing time in various units on the x-axis and tasks on the y-axis. For example, Exhibit 2.3 shows that the following tasks must be completed by the following dates: In order to start construction on a new company headquarters by the week of November 18, the architectural firm must be selected by October 7, architectural planning done by November 4, permits obtained from the city by November 11, site preparation finished by November 18, and loans and financing finalized by November 18.

Though simple and straightforward, Gantt charts were revolutionary in the era of seat-of-the-pants management because of the detailed planning information they provided to managers. As Gantt wrote, "By using the graphical forms its [the Gantt chart's] value is very much increased, for the general appearance of the sheet is sufficient to tell how closely the schedule is being

Gantt chart a graphical chart that shows which tasks must be completed at which times in order to complete a project or task

---

EXHIBIT 2.3

Gantt Chart for Starting Construction on a New Headquarters

Tasks	Weeks	23 Sep to 29 Sep	30 Sep to 6 Oct	7 Oct to 13 Oct	14 Oct to 20 Oct	21 Oct to 27 Oct	28 Oct to 3 Nov	4 Nov to 10 Nov	11 Nov to 17 Nov	18 Nov to 25 Nov
Interview and select architectural firm		Architect by October 7								
Hold weekly planning meetings with architects				Planning with architects by November 4						
Obtain permits and approval from city							Permits & approval by November 11			
Begin preparing site for construction								Site preparation done by November 18		
Finalize loans and financing									Financing finalized by November 18	
Begin construction										Start building
Tasks	Weeks	23 Sep to 29 Sep	30 Sep to 6 Oct	7 Oct to 13 Oct	14 Oct to 20 Oct	21 Oct to 27 Oct	28 Oct to 3 Nov	4 Nov to 10 Nov	11 Nov to 17 Nov	18 Nov to 25 Nov

© Cengage Learning

Bureaucracy the exercise of
control on the basis of knowledge, expertise, or experience

lived up to; in other words, whether the plant is being run efficiently or not."[23] Gantt said, "Such sheets show at a glance where the delays occur, and indicate what must have our attention in order to keep up the proper output." The use of Gantt charts is so widespread today that nearly all project management software and computer spreadsheets have the capability to create charts that track and visually display the progress being made on a project.

Finally, Gantt, along with Taylor, was one of the first to strongly recommend that companies train and develop their workers.[24] In his work with companies, he found that workers achieved their best performance levels if they were trained first. At the time, however, supervisors were reluctant to teach workers what they knew for fear that they could lose their jobs to more knowledgeable workers. Gantt overcame the supervisors' resistance by rewarding them with bonuses for properly training all of their workers. Said Gantt, "This is the first recorded attempt to make it in the financial interest of the foreman to teach the individual worker, and the importance of it cannot be overestimated, for it changes the foreman from a driver of men to their friend and helper."[25] Gantt's approach to training was straightforward: "(1) a scientific investigation in detail of each piece of work, and the determination of the best method and the shortest time in which the work can be done. (2) A teacher capable of teaching the best method and the shortest time. (3) Reward for both teacher and pupil when the latter is successful."[26]

2-3 *Bureaucratic and Administrative Management*

The field of scientific management developed quickly in the United States between 1895 and 1920 and focused on improving the efficiency of manufacturing facilities and their workers. At about the same time, equally important ideas about bureaucratic and administrative management were developing in Europe. German sociologist Max Weber presented a new way to run entire organizations (bureaucratic management) in *The Theory of Social and Economic Organization*, published in 1922. Henri Fayol, an experienced French CEO, published

his ideas about how and what managers should do in their jobs (administrative management) in *General and Industrial Management* in 1916.

*Let's find out more about the contributions Weber and Fayol made to management by learning about **2-3a bureaucratic management** and **2-3b administrative management**.*

2-3a BUREAUCRATIC MANAGEMENT: MAX WEBER

Today, when we hear the term *bureaucracy*, we think of inefficiency and red tape, incompetence and ineffectiveness, and rigid administrators blindly enforcing nonsensical rules. When German sociologist Max Weber (1864–1920) first proposed the idea of bureaucratic organizations, however, these problems were associated with monarchies and patriarchies rather than bureaucracies. In monarchies, where kings, queens, sultans, and emperors ruled, and patriarchies, where a council of elders, wise men, or male heads of extended families ruled, the top leaders typically achieved their positions by virtue of birthright. For example, when the queen died, her oldest son became king regardless of his intelligence, experience, education, or desire. Likewise, promotion to prominent positions of authority in monarchies and patriarchies was based on who you knew (politics), who you were (heredity), or ancient rules and traditions.

It was against this historical background of monarchical and patriarchal rule that Weber proposed the then-new idea of bureaucracy. *Bureaucracy* comes from the French word *bureaucratie*. Since *bureau* means desk or office and *cratie* or *cracy* means to rule, *bureaucracy* literally means to rule from a desk or office. According to Weber, **bureaucracy** is "the exercise of control on the basis of knowledge."[27] Rather than ruling by virtue of favoritism or personal or family connections, people in a bureaucracy would lead by virtue of their rational-legal authority—in other words, their knowledge, expertise, or experience. Furthermore, the aim of bureaucracy is not to protect authority but to achieve an organization's goals in the most efficient way possible.

Exhibit 2.4 shows the seven elements that, according to Weber, characterize bureaucracies. First, instead of hiring people because of their family or political connections or personal loyalty, they should be hired because their technical training or education qualifies them to do the job well. Second, along the same lines, promotion within the company should no longer be based on who you know (politics) or who you are (heredity) but on your experience or achievements. And to further limit the influence of personal connections in the promotion process, *managers* rather than organizational owners should decide who gets promoted. Third, each position or job is part of a chain of command that clarifies who reports to whom throughout the organization. Those higher in the chain of command have the right, if they so choose, to give commands, take action, and make decisions concerning activities occurring anywhere below them in the chain. Unlike in many monarchies or patriarchies, however, those lower in the chain of command are protected by a grievance procedure that gives them the right to appeal the decisions of those in higher positions. Fourth, to increase efficiency and effectiveness, tasks and responsibilities should be separated and assigned to those best qualified to complete them. Authority is vested in these task-defined positions rather than in people, and the authority of each position is clearly defined in order to reduce confusion and conflict. If you move to a different job in a bureaucracy, your authority increases or decreases commensurate with the responsibilities of that job. Fifth, because of his strong distaste for favoritism, Weber believed that an organization's rules and procedures should apply to all members regardless of their position or status. Sixth, to ensure consistency and fairness over time and across different leaders and supervisors, all rules, procedures, and decisions should be recorded in writing. Finally, to reduce favoritism, "professional" managers rather than company owners should manage or supervise the organization.

EXHIBIT 2.4

Elements of Bureaucratic Organizations

Qualification-based hiring:	Employees are hired on the basis of their technical training or educational background.
Merit-based promotion:	Promotion is based on experience or achievement. Managers, not organizational owners, decide who is promoted.
Chain of command:	Each job occurs within a hierarchy, the chain of command, in which each position reports and is accountable to a higher position. A grievance procedure and a right to appeal protect people in lower positions.
Division of labor:	Tasks, responsibilities, and authority are clearly divided and defined.
Impartial application of rules and procedures:	Rules and procedures apply to all members of the organization and will be applied in an impartial manner, regardless of one's position or status.
Recorded in writing:	All administrative decisions, acts, rules, or procedures will be recorded in writing.
Managers separate from owners:	The owners of an organization should not manage or supervise the organization.

Source: M. Weber, *The Theory of Social and Economic Organization*, trans. A. Henderson and T. Parsons (New York: The Free Press, 1947), 329–334.

When viewed in historical context, Weber's ideas about bureaucracy represent a tremendous improvement in how organizations should be run. Fairness supplanted favoritism, the goal of efficiency replaced the goal of personal gain, and logical rules and procedures took the place of traditions or arbitrary decision making.

Today, however, after more than a century of experience, we recognize that bureaucracy has limitations as well. Weber called bureaucracy the "iron cage" and said, "Once fully established, bureaucracy is among those social structures which are the hardest to destroy."[28] In bureaucracies, managers are supposed to influence employee behavior by fairly rewarding or punishing employees for compliance or noncompliance with organizational policies, rules, and procedures. In reality, however, most employees would argue that bureaucratic managers emphasize punishment for noncompliance much more than rewards for compliance. Ironically, bureaucratic management was created to prevent just this type of managerial behavior.

2-3b ADMINISTRATIVE MANAGEMENT: HENRI FAYOL

Though his work was not translated and widely recognized in the United States until 1949, Frenchman Henri Fayol (1841–1925) was as important a contributor to the field of management as Frederick Taylor. Like Taylor and the Gilbreths, Fayol's work experience significantly shaped his thoughts and ideas about management. But, whereas Taylor's ideas changed companies from the shop floor up, Fayol's ideas were shaped by his experience as a managing director (CEO) and generally changed companies from the board of directors down.[29] Fayol is best known for developing five functions of managers and fourteen principles of management as well as for his belief that management can and should be taught to others.

The most formative events in Fayol's business career came during his twenty-plus years as the managing director (CEO) of Compagnie de Commentry-Fourchambault et Décazeville, commonly known as **Comambault**, a vertically integrated steel company that owned several coal and iron ore mines and employed 10,000 to 13,000 workers. Fayol was initially hired by the board of directors to shut down the "hopeless" steel company. The company was facing increased competition from English and German steel companies, which had lower costs, and from new steel mills in northern and eastern France, which were closer to major markets

and thus could avoid the large shipping costs incurred by Fayol's company, located in central France.[30] In the five years before Fayol became CEO, production had dropped more than 60 percent, from 38,000 to 15,000 annual metric tons. Comambault had exhausted a key supply of coal needed for steel production, had already shut down one steel mill, and was losing money at another.[31] The company had quit paying dividends to shareholders and had no cash to invest in new technology, such as blast furnaces, that could lower its costs and increase productivity.

So the board hired Fayol as CEO to quickly dissolve and liquidate the business. But, after "four months of reflection and study," he presented the board with a plan, backed by detailed facts and figures, to save the company.[32] With little to lose, the board agreed. Fayol then began the process of turning the company around by obtaining supplies of key resources such as coal and iron ore; using research to develop new steel alloy products; carefully selecting key subordinates in research, purchasing, manufacturing, and sales and then delegating responsibility to them; and cutting costs by moving the company to a better location closer to key markets.[33] Looking back ten years later, Fayol attributed his and the company's success to changes in management practices. He wrote, "When I assumed the responsibility for the restoration of Décazeville, I did not rely on my technical superiority. . . . I relied on my ability as an organizer [and my] skill in handling men."[34]

Based on his experience as a CEO, Fayol argued that "the success of an enterprise generally depends much more on the administrative ability of its leaders than on their technical ability."[35] And, as you learned in Chapter 1, Fayol argued that managers need to perform five managerial functions if they are to be successful: planning, organizing, coordinating, commanding, and controlling.[36] Because most management textbooks have dropped the coordinating function and now refer to Fayol's commanding function as "leading," these functions are widely known as planning (determining organizational goals and a means for achieving them), organizing (deciding where decisions will be made, who will do what jobs and tasks, and who will work for whom), leading (inspiring and motivating workers to work hard to achieve organizational goals), and controlling (monitoring progress toward goal achievement and taking corrective action when needed). In addition, according to Fayol, effective management is based on the fourteen principles in Exhibit 2.5.

EXHIBIT 2.5

Fayol's Fourteen Principles of Management

1   Division of work

Increase production by dividing work so that each worker completes smaller tasks or job elements.

2   Authority and responsibility

A manager's authority, which is the "right to give orders," should be commensurate with the manager's responsibility. However, organizations should enact controls to prevent managers from abusing their authority.

3   Discipline

Clearly defined rules and procedures are needed at all organizational levels to ensure order and proper behavior.

4   Unity of command

To avoid confusion and conflict, each employee should report to and receive orders from just one boss.

5   Unity of direction

One person and one plan should be used in deciding the activities to be carried out to accomplish each organizational objective.

6   Subordination of individual interests to the general interest

Employees must put the organization's interests and goals before their own.

7   Remuneration

Compensation should be fair and satisfactory to both the employees and the organization; that is, don't overpay or underpay employees.

8   Centralization

Avoid too much centralization or decentralization. Strike a balance depending on the circumstances and employees involved.

9   Scalar chain

From the top to the bottom of an organization, each position is part of a vertical chain of authority in which each worker reports to just one boss. For the sake of simplicity, communication outside normal work groups or departments should follow the vertical chain of authority.

10   Order

To avoid conflicts and confusion, order can be obtained by having a place for everyone and having everyone in his or her place; in other words, there should be no overlapping responsibilities.

11   Equity

Kind, fair, and just treatment for all will develop devotion and loyalty. This does not exclude discipline, if warranted, and consideration of the broader general interest of the organization.

12   Stability of tenure of personnel

Low turnover, meaning a stable work force with high tenure, benefits an organization by improving performance, lowering costs, and giving employees, especially managers, time to learn their jobs.

13   Initiative

Because it is a "great source of strength for business," managers should encourage the development of initiative, or the ability to develop and implement a plan, in others.

14   *Esprit de corps*

Develop a strong sense of morale and unity among workers that encourages coordination of efforts.

Sources: H. Fayol, *General and Industrial Management* (London: Pittman & Sons, 1949); M. Fells, "Fayol Stands the Test of Time," *Journal of Management History* 6 (2000): 345–360; C. Rodrigues, "Fayol's 14 Principles of Management Then and Now: A Framework for Managing Today's Organizations Effectively," *Management Decision* 39 (2001): 880–889.

Domination an approach to dealing with conflict in which one party satisfies its desires and objectives at the expense of the other party's desires and objectives

Compromise an approach to dealing with conflict in which both parties give up some of what they want in order to reach agreement on a plan to reduce or settle the conflict

Integrative conflict resolution an approach to dealing with conflict in which both parties indicate their preferences and then work together to find an alternative that meets the needs of both

2-4 *Human Relations Management*

As we have seen, scientific management focuses on improving efficiency; bureaucratic management focuses on using knowledge, fairness, and logical rules and procedures; and administrative management focuses on how and what managers should do in their jobs. The human relations approach to management focuses on *people*, particularly the psychological and social aspects of work. This approach to management sees people not as just extensions of machines but as valuable organizational resources in their own right. Human relations management holds that people's needs are important and that their efforts, motivation, and performance are affected by the work they do and their relationships with their bosses, coworkers, and work groups. In other words, efficiency alone is not enough. Organizational success also depends on treating workers well.

Let's find out more about human relations management by learning about 2-4a Mary Parker Follett's theories of constructive conflict and coordination, 2-4b Elton Mayo's Hawthorne Studies, and 2-4c Chester Barnard's theories of cooperation and acceptance of authority.

2-4a CONSTRUCTIVE CONFLICT AND COORDINATION: MARY PARKER FOLLETT

Mary Parker Follett (1868–1933) was a social worker with a degree in political science who, in her fifties, after twenty-five years of working with schools and non-profit organizations, began lecturing and writing about management and working extensively as a consultant for business and government leaders in the United States and Europe. Although her contributions were overlooked for decades, perhaps because she was a woman or perhaps because they were so different, many of today's "new" management ideas can clearly be traced to her work.

Follett believed that the best way to deal with conflict was not **domination**, where one side wins and the other loses, or **compromise**,

where each side gives up some of what it wants, but integration. Said Follett, "There is a way beginning now to be recognized at least, and even occasionally followed: when two desires are *integrated*, that means that a solution has been found in which both desires have found a place that neither side has had to sacrifice anything."[37] So, rather than one side dominating the other or both sides compromising, the point of **integrative conflict resolution** is to have both parties indicate their preferences and then work together to find an alternative that meets the needs of both. According to Follett, "Integration involves invention, and the clever thing is to recognize this, and not to let one's thinking stay within the boundaries of two alternatives which are mutually exclusive." Indeed, Follett's ideas about the positive use of conflict and an integrative approach to conflict resolution predate accepted thinking in the negotiation and conflict resolution literature by six decades (see the best-selling book *Getting to Yes: Negotiating Agreement without Giving In* by Roger Fisher, William Ury, and Bruce Patton).

Exhibit 2.6 summarizes Follett's contributions to management in her own words. She casts power as "with" rather than "over" others. Giving orders involves discussing instructions and dealing with resentment. Authority flows from job knowledge and experience rather than position. Leadership involves setting the tone for the team rather than being aggressive and dominating, which may be harmful. Coordination and control should be based on facts and information. In the end, Follett's contributions added significantly to our understanding of the human, social, and psychological sides of management. Peter Parker, the former chairman of the London School of Economics, said about Follett: "People

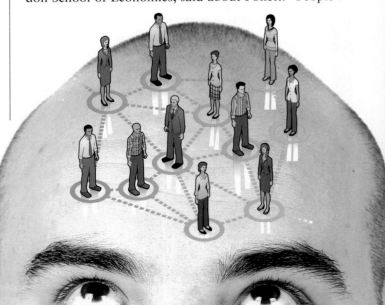

EXHIBIT 2.6

MARY PARKER FOLLETT SAYS . . .

On constructive conflict...

"As conflict—difference—is here in this world, as we cannot avoid it, we should, I think, use it to work for us. Instead of condemning it, we should set it to work for us."

On power...

"It seems to me that whereas power usually means power-over, the power of some person or group over some other person or group, it is possible to develop the conception of power-with, a jointly developed power, a co-active, not a coercive power."

On the giving of orders...

"An advantage of not exacting blind obedience, of discussing your instructions with your subordinates, is that if there is any resentment, any come-back, you get it out into the open, and when it is in the open you can deal with it."

On authority...

"Authority should go with knowledge and experience, that is where obedience is due, no matter whether it is up the line or down."

On leadership...

"Of the greatest importance is the ability to grasp a total situation. . . . Out of a welter of facts, experience, desires, aims, the leader must find the unifying thread. He must see a whole, not a mere kaleidoscope of pieces. . . . The higher up you go, the more ability you have to have of this kind."

On coordination...

"The most important thing to remember about unity is—that there is no such thing. There is only unifying. You cannot get unity and expect it to last a day—or five minutes. Every man in a business should be taking part in a certain process and that process is unifying."

On control...

"Central control is coming more and more to mean the co-relation of many controls rather than a superimposed control."

Source: M. Parker Follett, *Mary Parker Follett—Prophet of Management: A Celebration of Writings from the 1920s*, ed. P. Graham (Boston: Harvard Business School Press, 1995).

often puzzle about who is the father of management. I don't know who the father was, but I have no doubt about who was the mother."[38]

2-4b HAWTHORNE STUDIES: ELTON MAYO

Australian-born Elton Mayo (1880–1948) is best known for his role in the famous Hawthorne Studies at the **Western Electric Company**. The Hawthorne Studies were conducted in several stages between 1924 and 1932 at a Western Electric plant in Chicago. Although Mayo didn't join the studies until 1928, he played a significant role thereafter, writing about the results in his book *The Human Problems of an Industrial Civilization*.[39] The first stage of the Hawthorne Studies investigated the effects of lighting levels and incentives on employee productivity in the Relay Test Assembly Room, where workers took approximately a minute to put "together a coil, armature, contact springs, and insulators in a fixture and secure the parts by means of four machine screws."[40]

Two groups of six experienced female workers, five to do the work and one to supply needed parts, were separated from the main part of the factory by a ten-foot partition and placed at a standard work bench with the necessary parts and tools. Over the next five years, the experimenters introduced various levels and combinations of lighting, financial incentives, and rest pauses (work breaks) to study the effect on productivity. Curiously, however, production levels increased whether the experimenters increased or decreased the lighting, paid workers based on individual production or group production, or increased or decreased the number and length of rest pauses. In fact, Mayo and his fellow researchers were surprised that production steadily increased from 2,400 relays per day at the beginning of the study to 3,000 relays per day five years later. The question was: Why?

Mayo and his colleagues eventually concluded that two things accounted for the results. First, substantially more attention was paid to these workers than to workers in the rest of the plant. Mayo wrote, "Before every change of program [in the study], the group is consulted. Their comments are listened to and discussed; sometimes their objections are allowed to negate a suggestion. The group unquestionably develops a sense of participation in the critical determinations and becomes something of a social unit."[41]

For years, the "Hawthorne Effect" has been *incorrectly* defined as increasing productivity by paying more attention to workers.[42] But it is not simply about attention from management. The Hawthorne Effect cannot be understood without giving equal importance to the social units, which became intensely cohesive groups. Mayo said, "What actually happened was that six individuals became a team and the team gave itself wholeheartedly and spontaneously to cooperation in the experiment. The consequence was that they felt themselves to be participating freely and without afterthought, and were happy in the knowledge that they were working without coercion from above or limits from below."[43]

For the first time, human factors related to work were found to be more important than the physical conditions or design of the work. Together, the increased attention from management and the development of a cohesive work group led to significantly higher levels of job satisfaction and productivity. In short, the Hawthorne Studies found that workers' feelings and attitudes affected their work.

The next stage of the Hawthorne Studies was conducted in the Bank Wiring Room, where "the group consisted of nine wiremen, three solderers, and two inspectors. Each of these groups performed a specific task and collaborated with the other two in completion of each unit of equipment. The task consisted of setting up the banks of terminals side-by-side on frames, wiring the corresponding terminals from bank to bank, soldering the connections, and inspecting with a test set for short circuits or breaks in the wire. One solderman serviced the work of the three wireman."[44] While productivity increased in the Relay Test Assembly Room no matter what the researchers did, productivity dropped in the Bank Wiring Room. Again, the question was: Why?

Mayo and his colleagues found that the differences in performance were due to group dynamics. The workers in the Bank Wiring Room had been an existing work group for some time and had already developed strong negative norms that governed their behavior. For instance, despite a group financial incentive for production, the group members decided that they would wire only 6,000 to 6,600 connections a day (depending on the kind of equipment they were wiring), well below the production goal of 7,300 connections that management had set for them. Individual workers who worked at a faster pace were socially ostracized from the group or "binged" (hit on the arm) until they slowed their work pace. Thus, the group's behavior was reminiscent of the soldiering that Frederick Taylor had

DOING THE RIGHT THING

Building a Good Team

In the Hawthorne Studies, Elton Mayo revealed the importance of group dynamics and cohesion in the workplace. In trying to build cohesion, many modern managers turn to team-building exercises like trust falls, ropes courses, and scavenger hunts. And while these activities might be fun, they aren't particularly effective at building group cohesion and teaching workers how to work well together. When planning your department's annual retreat, skip the trust falls and get straight to work, focusing on helping the team discover how to produce great results. After all, it's only when teams work together to overcome serious obstacles that team members learn to count on each other.

Source: J. Haden. "6 Ways to Ruin a Company Offsite Meeting," Inc.com, February 21, 2012, accessed February 25, 2012, http://www.inc.com/jeff-haden/6-ways-to-ruin-a-company-offsite-meeting.html.

observed. Mayo concluded, "Work [was] done in accord with the group's conception of a day's work; this was exceeded by only one individual who was cordially disliked."[45]

In the end, the Hawthorne Studies demonstrated that the workplace was more complex than previously thought, that workers were not just extensions of machines, and that financial incentives weren't necessarily the most important motivator for workers. By highlighting the crucial role, positive or negative, that groups, group norms, and group behavior play at work, Mayo strengthened Mary Parker Follett's point about coordination—make just one change in an organization and others, some expected and some unexpected, will occur. Thanks to Mayo and his colleagues and their work on the Hawthorne Studies, managers better understood the effect that group social interactions, employee satisfaction, and attitudes had on individual and group performance.

2-4c COOPERATION AND ACCEPTANCE OF AUTHORITY: CHESTER BARNARD

Like Henri Fayol, Chester Barnard (1886–1961) had experiences as a top executive that shaped his views

of management. Barnard began his career in 1909 as an engineer and translator for AT&T, becoming a general manager at Pennsylvania Bell Telephone in 1922 and then president of **New Jersey Bell Telephone** in 1927.[46] Barnard's ideas, published in his classic book, *The Functions of the Executive*, influenced companies from the board of directors down. He is best known for his ideas about cooperation and the acceptance of authority.

Barnard proposed a comprehensive theory of cooperation in formal organizations. In fact, he defines an **organization** as a "system of consciously coordinated activities or forces of two or more persons."[47] In other words, organization occurs whenever two people work together for some purpose, whether it be classmates working together to complete a class project, Habitat for Humanity volunteers donating their time to build a house, or managers working with subordinates to reduce costs, improve quality, or increase sales. Why did Barnard place so much emphasis on cooperation? Because cooperation is *not* the normal state of affairs: "Failure to cooperate, failure of cooperation, failure of organization, disorganization, disintegration, destruction of organization—and reorganization—are characteristic facts of human history."[48]

According to Barnard, the extent to which people willingly cooperate in an organization depends on how workers perceive executive authority and whether they're willing to accept it. Many managerial requests or directives fall within a *zone of indifference* in which acceptance of managerial authority is automatic. For example, if your supervisor asks you for a copy of the monthly inventory report, and compiling and writing that report is part of your job, you think nothing of the request and automatically send it. In general, people will be indifferent to managerial directives or orders if they (1) are understood, (2) are consistent with the purpose of the organization, (3) are compatible with the people's personal interests, and (4) can actually be carried out by those people. Acceptance of managerial authority (i.e., cooperation) is not automatic, however. Ask people to do things contrary to the organization's purpose or to their own benefit and they'll put up a fight. While many people assume that managers have the authority to do whatever they want, Barnard, referring to the "fiction of superior authority," believed that workers ultimately grant managers their authority.

Organization a system of consciously coordinated activities or forces created by two or more people

2-5 *Operations, Information, Systems, and Contingency Management*

In this last section, we review four other significant historical approaches to management that have influenced how today's managers produce goods and services on a daily basis, gather and manage the information they need to understand their businesses and make good decisions, understand how the different parts of the company work together as a whole, and recognize when and where particular management practices are likely to work.

To better understand these ideas, let's learn about **2-5a operations management, 2-5b information management, 2-5c systems management,** *and* **2-5d contingency management.**

2-5a OPERATIONS MANAGEMENT

In Chapter 18, you will learn about *operations management*, which involves managing the daily production of goods and services. In general, operations management uses a quantitative or mathematical approach to find ways to increase productivity, improve quality, and manage or reduce costly inventories. The most commonly used operations management tools and methods are quality control, forecasting techniques, capacity planning, productivity measurement and improvement, linear programming, scheduling systems, inventory systems, work measurement techniques (similar to the Gilbreths' motion studies), project management (similar to Gantt's charts), and cost-benefit analysis.[49]

Since the 16th century, skilled craftspersons made the lock, stock, and barrel of a gun by hand. After each part was made, a skilled gun finisher assembled the parts into a complete gun. But the gun finisher did not simply screw the different parts of a gun together, as is done today. Instead, each handmade part required extensive finishing and adjusting so that it would fit together with the other handmade gun parts. Hand-fitting was necessary because, even when made by the same skilled craftspeople, no two parts were alike. In fact, gun finishers played a role similar to that of fine watchmakers who meticulously assembled expensive watches—without them, the product simply wouldn't work. Today, we would say that these parts were low quality because they varied so much from one part to another.

All this changed in 1791 when the U.S. government, worried about a possible war with France, ordered 40,000 muskets from private gun contractors. All but one contractor built handmade muskets assembled by skilled gun finishers who made sure that all the parts fit together. Thus, each musket was unique. If a part broke, a replacement part had to be handcrafted. But one contractor, Eli Whitney of New Haven, Connecticut (who is better known for his invention of the cotton gin) determined that if gun parts were made accurately enough, guns could be made with standardized, interchangeable parts. So he designed machine tools that allowed unskilled workers to make each gun part the same as the next. Said Whitney, "The tools which I contemplate to make are similar to an engraving on copper plate from which may be taken a great number of impressions perceptibly alike."[50] Years passed before Whitney delivered his 10,000 muskets to the U.S. government. But he demonstrated the superiority of interchangeable parts to President-elect Thomas Jefferson in 1801 by quickly and easily assembling complete muskets from randomly picked piles of musket parts. Today, because of Whitney's ideas, most products, from cars to toasters to space shuttles, are manufactured using standardized, interchangeable parts.

But even with this advance, manufacturers still could not produce a part unless they had seen or examined it firsthand. Thanks to Gaspard Monge, a Frenchman of modest beginnings, this soon changed. Monge's greatest achievement was his book *Descriptive Geometry.*[51] In it, he explained techniques for drawing three-dimensional objects on paper. For the first time, precise drawings permitted manufacturers to make standardized, interchangeable parts without first examining a prototype. Today, thanks to Monge, manufacturers rely on CAD (computer-aided design) and CAM (computer-aided manufacturing) to take three-dimensional designs straight from the computer to the factory floor.

Once standardized, interchangeable parts became the norm, and once parts could be made from design

drawings alone, manufacturers ran into a costly problem that they had never faced before: too much inventory. *Inventory* is the amount and number of raw materials, parts, and finished products that a company has in its possession. In fact, large factories were accumulating parts inventories sufficient for two to three months, much more than they needed on a daily basis to run their manufacturing operations. A solution to this problem was found in 1905 when the **Oldsmobile Motor Works** in Detroit burned down.[52] Management rented a new production facility to get production up and running as quickly as possible after the fire. But because the new facility was much smaller, there was no room to store large stockpiles of inventory (which the company couldn't afford anyway as it was short on funds). Therefore, the company made do with what it called "hand-to-mouth inventories," in which each production station had only enough parts on hand to do a short production run. Since all of its parts suppliers were close by, Oldsmobile could place orders in the morning and receive them in the afternoon (even without telephones), just as with today's computerized just-in-time inventory systems. So, contrary to common belief, just-in-time inventory systems were not invented by Japanese manufacturers. Instead, they were invented out of necessity a century ago because of a fire.

2-5b INFORMATION MANAGEMENT

For most of recorded history, information has been costly, difficult to obtain, and slow to spread. Because of the immense labor and time it took to hand-copy information, books, manuscripts, and written documents of any kind were rare and extremely expensive. Word of Joan of Arc's death in 1431 took eighteen months to travel from France across Europe to Constantinople (now Istanbul, Turkey).

Consequently, throughout history, organizations have pushed for and quickly adopted new information technologies that reduce the cost or increase the speed with which they can acquire, store, retrieve, or communicate information. The first technologies to truly revolutionize the business use of information were paper and the printing press. In the 14th century, water-powered machines were created to pulverize rags into pulp to make paper. Paper prices, which were

already lower than those of animal-skin parchments, dropped dramatically. Less than a half-century later, Johannes Gutenberg invented the printing press, which greatly reduced the cost and time needed to copy written information. In 15th-century Florence, Italy, a scribe would charge one florin (an Italian unit of money) to hand-copy one document page. By contrast, a printer would set up and print 1,025 copies of the same document for just three florins. Within fifty years of its invention, Gutenberg's printing press cut the cost of information by 99.8 percent!

What Gutenberg's printing press did for publishing, the manual typewriter did for daily communication. Before 1850, most business correspondence was written by hand and copied using the letter press. With the ink still wet, the letter would be placed into a tissue-paper book. A hand press would then be used to squeeze the book and copy the still-wet ink onto the tissue paper. By the 1870s, manual typewriters made it cheaper, easier, and faster to produce and copy business correspondence. Of course, in the 1980s, slightly more than a century later, typewriters were replaced by personal computers and word processing software with the same results.

Finally, businesses have always looked for information technologies that would speed access to timely information. The Medici family, which opened banks throughout Europe in the early 1400s, used post messengers to keep in contact with their more than forty branch managers. The post messengers, who predated the U.S. Postal Service Pony Express by 400 years, could travel ninety miles per day, twice what average riders could cover, because the Medicis were willing to pay for the expense of providing them with fresh horses. This need for timely information also led companies to quickly adopt the telegraph in the 1860s, the telephone in the 1880s, and, of course, Internet technologies in the last two decades.

2-5c SYSTEMS MANAGEMENT

Today's companies are much more complex than they used to be. They are larger and employ more people. They most likely manufacture, service, *and* finance what they sell, not only in their home markets but in foreign markets throughout the world, too. They also operate in complex, fast-changing, competitive, global environments that can quickly turn

System a set of interrelated elements or parts that function as a whole

Subsystems smaller systems that operate within the context of a larger system

Synergy when two or more subsystems working together can produce more than they can working apart

Closed systems systems that can sustain themselves without interacting with their environments

Open systems systems that can sustain themselves only by interacting with their environments, on which they depend for their survival

competitive advantages into competitive disadvantages. How, then, can managers make sense of this complexity, both within and outside their organizations?

One way to deal with organizational and environmental complexity is to take a systems view of organizations. The systems approach is derived from theoretical models in biology and social psychology developed in the 1950s and 1960s.[53] A **system** is a set of interrelated elements or parts that function as a whole. Rather than viewing one part of an organization as separate from the other parts, a systems approach encourages managers to complicate their thinking by looking for connections between the different parts of the organization. Indeed, one of the more important ideas in the systems approach to management is that organizational systems are composed of parts or **subsystems**, which are simply smaller systems within larger systems. Subsystems and their connections matter in systems theory because of the possibility for managers to create synergy. **Synergy** occurs when two or more subsystems working together can produce more than

they can working apart. In other words, synergy occurs when 1 + 1 = 3.

Systems can be open or closed. **Closed systems** can function without interacting with their environments. But nearly all organizations should be viewed as **open systems** that interact with their environments and depend on them for survival. Therefore, rather than viewing what goes on within the organization as separate from what goes on outside it, the systems approach encourages managers to look for connections between the different parts of the organization and the different parts of its environment. Exhibit 2.7 illustrates how the elements of systems management work together.

A systems view of organizations offers several advantages. First, it forces managers to view their organizations as part of and subject to the competitive, economic, social, technological, and legal/regulatory forces in their environments.[54] Second, it forces managers to be aware of how the environment affects specific parts of the organization. Third, because of the complexity and difficulty of trying to achieve synergies among different parts of the organization, the systems view encourages managers to focus on better communication and cooperation within the organization. Finally, it makes managers acutely aware that good internal management of the organization may not be enough to ensure survival. Survival also depends on making sure that the organization continues to satisfy critical environmental stakeholders such as

EXHIBIT 2.7

Systems View of Organizations

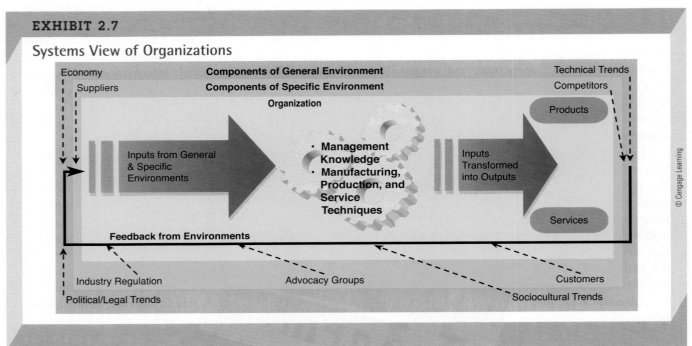

© Cengage Learning

shareholders, employees, customers, suppliers, governments, and local communities.

2-5d CONTINGENCY MANAGEMENT

Earlier, you learned that the goal of scientific management was to use systematic study to find the one best way of doing each task and then use that one best way everywhere. The problem, as you may have gathered from reading about the various approaches to management, is that no one in management seems to agree on what that one best way is. Furthermore, more than 100 years of management research has shown that there are clear boundaries or limitations to most management theories and practices. No management ideas or practices are universal. Although any theory or practice may work much of the time, none works all the time. How, then, is a manager to decide what theory to use? Well, it depends on the situation. The **contingency approach** to management clearly states that there are no universal management theories and that the most effective management theory or idea depends on the kinds of problems or situations that managers or organizations are facing at a particular time.[55] In short, the best way depends on the situation.

One of the practical implications of the contingency approach to management is that management is much harder than it looks. In fact, because of the clarity and obviousness of management theories (OK, most of them), students and workers often wrongly assume that a company's problems would be quickly and easily solved if management would take just a few simple steps. If this were true, few companies would have problems.

A second implication of the contingency approach is that managers need to look for key contingencies that differentiate today's situation or problems from yesterday's situation or problems. Moreover, it means that managers need to spend more time analyzing problems, situations, and employees before taking action to fix them. Finally, it means that as you read this text and learn about management ideas and practices, you need to pay particular attention to qualifying phrases such as "usually," "in these situations," "for this to work," and "under these circumstances." Doing so will help you identify the key contingencies that will help you become a better manager.

Contingency approach holds that there are no universal management theories and that the most effective management theory or idea depends on the kinds of problems or situations that managers are facing at a particular time and place

STUDY TOOLS 2

LOCATED AT THE BACK OF YOUR BOOK:

☐ Rip out and study the Chapter Review Card at the end of the book

LOG IN TO THE COURSEMATE FOR MGMT AT CENGAGEBRAIN.COM TO:

☐ Review Key Term Flashcards delivered three ways (print or online)

☐ Complete both Practice Quizzes to prepare for tests

☐ Play Beat the Clock and Quizbowl to master concepts

☐ Complete the Crossword Puzzle to review key terms

☐ Watch the video on Barcelona Restaurant Group for a real company example and take the accompanying quiz

☐ Complete the Case Assignment on ISG Steelton

☐ Work through the Management Decision on workplace discipline

☐ Work through the Management Team Decision on resolving conflicts

☐ Develop your skills with the Develop Your Career Potential exercise

3 Organizational
Environments and Culture

LEARNING OUTCOMES

3-1 Discuss how changing environments affect organizations.

3-2 Describe the four components of the general environment.

3-3 Explain the five components of the specific environment.

3-4 Describe the process that companies use to make sense of their changing environments.

3-5 Explain how organizational cultures are created and how they can help companies be successful.

CHECK OUT
STUDY TOOLS
AT THE END OF
THIS CHAPTER.

3-1 *Changing Environments*

This chapter examines the internal and external forces that affect business. We begin by explaining how the changes in external organizational environments affect the decisions and performance of a company. Next, we examine the two types of external organizational environment: the general environment that affects all organizations and the specific environment unique to each company. Then, we learn how managers make sense of their changing general and specific environments. The chapter finishes with a discussion of internal organizational environments by focusing on organizational culture. But first, let's see how the changes in external organizational environments affect the decisions and performance of a company.

External environments are the forces and events outside a company that have the potential to influence or affect it. Catastrophic floods in Thailand killed 600 people and created $45 billion in damage that shut production facilities of some of the best-known technology companies in the world for months. Apple's CEO, Tim Cook, stated at the time that he was "virtually certain there will be an overall industry shortage of disk drives." Indeed, Western Digital, one of the largest manufacturers of hard drives, produced just 28.5 million units following the flood, or half what it was planning. Hard drive shortages resulted in a 12 percent drop in worldwide sales of personal computers, which in turn reduced sales of Microsoft's Windows operating system, which is loaded onto new computers.[1]

Let's examine the three basic characteristics of changing external environments: 3-1a environmental change; 3-1b environmental complexity; 3-1c resource scarcity; and 3-1d the uncertainty that environmental change, complexity, and resource scarcity can create for organizational managers.

3-1a ENVIRONMENTAL CHANGE

Environmental change is the rate at which a company's general and specific environments change. In **stable environments**, the rate of environmental change is slow. Apart from occasional shortages due to drought or frost, the wholesale food distribution business—where dairy items, fresh produce, baked goods, poultry, fish, and meat are processed and delivered by trucks from warehouses to restaurants, grocers, and other retailers—changes little from year to year. Distributors take shipments from farmers, food manufacturers, and food importers, consolidate them at warehouses, and then distribute them to retailers. While recent adoption of global positioning satellite (GPS) systems and radio frequency identification (RFID) devices might be seen as "change," wholesale food distributors began using them because, like the trucks they bought to replace horse-drawn carriages in the early 1900s, GPS and RFID improved the core part of their business—getting the freshest food ingredients to customers as quickly and inexpensively as possible—which has not changed in over a century.[2]

External environments
all events outside a company that have the potential to influence or affect it

Environmental change
the rate at which a company's general and specific environments change

Stable environment an environment in which the rate of change is slow

While wholesale food distribution companies have stable environments, Research in Motion (RIM), which produces Blackberry smartphones, competes in an extremely dynamic external environment. In **dynamic environments**, the rate of environmental change is fast. RIM's competitors, such as Apple, Samsung, HTC, and Motorola, frequently updated models with innovative features and new technology. Over a three-year span, Apple released four different iPhone models, the 3G, the 3GS, the 4, and the 4S, each having significantly better features and functionality. For instance, the iPhone 4S has an 8 megapixel camera, can record in full high-definition video, and uses voice commands to send messages, schedule meetings, place phone calls, or dictate texts. Six months after the iPhone 4s was introduced, none of RIM's phones had any of these features.[3]

Although you might think that a company's external environment would be either stable or dynamic, research suggests that companies often experience both. According to **punctuated equilibrium theory**, companies go through long periods of stability (equilibrium) during which incremental changes occur, followed by short, complex periods of dynamic, fundamental change (revolutionary periods), finishing with a return to stability (new equilibrium).[4]

One example of punctuated equilibrium has affected the airline industry in the United States. Three times in the last thirty years, the U.S. airline industry has experienced revolutionary periods. The first, from mid-1979 to mid-1982, occurred immediately after airline deregulation in 1978. Prior to deregulation, the federal government controlled where airlines could fly, how much could be charged, when they could fly, and the number of flights they could have on a particular route. After deregulation, these choices were left to the airlines. The large financial losses during this period clearly indicate that the airlines had trouble adjusting to the intense competition that occurred after deregulation. By mid-1982, however, profits returned to the industry and held steady until mid-1989.

Then, after experiencing record growth and profits, U.S. airlines lost billions of dollars between 1989 and 1993 as the industry went through dramatic changes. Key expenses, including jet fuel and employee salaries, which had held steady for years, suddenly increased. Furthermore, revenues, which had grown steadily year after year, suddenly dropped because of dramatic changes in the airlines' customer base. Business travelers, who had typically paid full-price fares, comprised more than half of all passengers during the 1980s. However, by the late 1980s, the largest customer base had changed to leisure travelers, who wanted the cheapest flights they could get.[5] With expenses suddenly up and revenues suddenly down, the airlines responded to these changes in their business environment by laying off 5 to 10 percent of their workers, canceling orders for new planes, and eliminating unprofitable routes. Starting in 1993 and lasting till 1998, these changes helped the airline industry achieve profits far in excess of their historical levels. The industry began to stabilize, if not flourish, just as punctuated equilibrium theory predicts.[6]

The third revolutionary period for the U.S. airline industry began with the terrorist attacks of September 11, 2001, in which planes were used as missiles to bring down the World Trade Center towers and damage the Pentagon. The immediate effect was a 20 percent drop in scheduled flights, a 40 percent drop in passengers, and losses so large that the U.S. government approved a $15 billion bailout to keep the airlines in business. Heightened airport security also affected airports, the airlines themselves, and airline customers. Five years after the 9/11 attacks, United Airlines, U.S. Airways, Delta, and American Airlines had reduced staffing by 169,000 full-time jobs to cut costs after losing a combined $42 billion.[7] Due to their financially weaker position, the airlines restructured operations to take advantage of the combined effect of increased passenger travel, a sharply

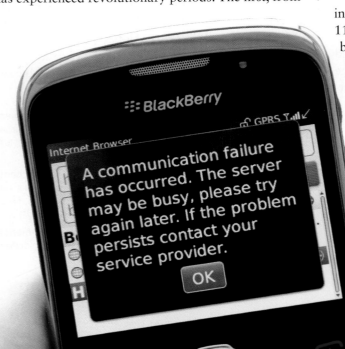

reduced cost structure, and a 23 percent reduction in the fleet to return their businesses to profitability.[8] But, just as the airlines were heading toward a more stable period of equilibrium in 2006 and 2007, the price of oil jumped dramatically, doubling, if not tripling, the price of jet fuel, which prompted the airlines to charge for luggage (to increase revenues and discourage heavy baggage) and cut flights using older, fuel-inefficient jets.

3-1b ENVIRONMENTAL COMPLEXITY

Environmental complexity refers to the number and the intensity of external factors in the environment that affect organizations. **Simple environments** have few environmental factors, whereas **complex environments** have many environmental factors. The dairy industry is an excellent example of a relatively simple external environment. Even accounting for decades-old advances in processing and automatic milking machines, milk is produced the same way today as it was 100 years ago. And although food manufacturers introduce dozens of new dairy-based products each year, U.S. milk production has grown a meager 1.25 percent per year over the last decade. In short, producing milk is a highly competitive but simple business that has experienced few environmental changes.[9]

At the other end of the spectrum, few industries find themselves in more complex environments today than the newspaper business. For a century, making money selling newspapers was relatively simple: sell subscriptions for daily home delivery, and then sell classified ads and retail ads to reach those subscribers. In today's digital age, however, that business model doesn't work when you can get instantaneous news online, usually for free. Thus, it's no surprise that newspaper advertising revenues have fallen for six straight years, including a 7.3 percent drop in 2011. Today, annual newspaper advertising revenues are $23.9 billion, or less than half 2005 levels of $49.4 billion.[10] As a result, the largest newspapers in the country are reporting staggering losses—nearly $40 million at the New York Times Company (publisher of the *New York Times*, *Boston Globe*, and several other regional papers) and $18.2 million at the Washington Post Company.[11]

3-1c RESOURCE SCARCITY

The third characteristic of external environments is resource scarcity. **Resource scarcity** is the abundance or shortage of critical organizational resources in an organization's external environment. China produces 95 percent of rare earth materials that are needed to make everything from wind turbines, to hybrid vehicles, to compact fluorescent light (CFL) bulbs. So when the Chinese government announced that it would cut exports by 72 percent, prices of products that use rare earth metals soared. For example, compact fluorescent light bulbs use the rare earth compound europium oxide, which according to General Electric (GE), one of the largest makers of fluorescent light bulbs, costs ten times what it did before China dramatically cut exports. As a result, the cost of a GE three-pack of 11-watt CFL bulbs, which provide as much light as 40-watt incandescent bulbs, has increased 37 percent to $15.88![12]

Simple   Complex

Uncertainty extent to which managers can understand or predict which environmental changes and trends will affect their businesses

General environment the economic, technological, sociocultural, and political trends that indirectly affect all organizations

Specific environment the customers, competitors, suppliers, industry regulations, and advocacy groups that are unique to an industry and directly affect how a company does business

3-1d UNCERTAINTY

As Exhibit 3.1 shows, environmental change, environmental complexity, and resource scarcity affect environmental **uncertainty**, which is how well managers can understand or predict the external changes and trends affecting their businesses. Starting at the left side of the figure, environmental uncertainty is lowest when environmental change and environmental complexity are at low levels and resource scarcity is small (i.e., resources are plentiful). In these environments, managers feel confident that they can understand, predict, and react to the external forces that affect their businesses. By contrast, the right side of the figure shows that environmental uncertainty is highest when environmental change and complexity are extensive and resource scarcity is a problem. In these environments, managers may not be confident that they can understand, predict, and handle the external forces affecting their businesses.

3-2 *General Environment*

As Exhibit 3.2 shows, two kinds of external environments influence organizations: the general environment and the specific environment. The **general environment** consists of the economy and the technological, sociocultural, and political/legal trends that indirectly affect *all* organizations. Changes in any sector of the general environment eventually affect most organizations. For example, when the Federal Reserve lowers its prime lending rate, most businesses benefit because banks and credit card companies often lower the interest rates they charge for loans. Consumers, who can then borrow money more cheaply, might borrow more to buy homes, cars, refrigerators, and large-screen plasma or LCD TVs.

Each organization also has a **specific environment** that is unique to that firm's industry and directly affects the way it conducts day-to-day business. Because of concerns with rising obesity, the U.S. Food and Drug Administration (FDA) now requires restaurants, bakeries, coffee shops, and grocery and convenience stores with twenty or more locations to post calorie count information on their menus. FDA deputy commissioner

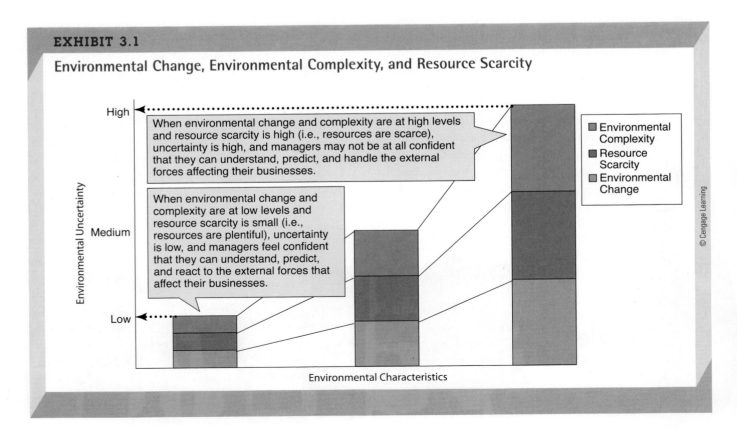

EXHIBIT 3.1

Environmental Change, Environmental Complexity, and Resource Scarcity

When environmental change and complexity are at high levels and resource scarcity is high (i.e., resources are scarce), uncertainty is high, and managers may not be at all confident that they can understand, predict, and handle the external forces affecting their businesses.

When environmental change and complexity are at low levels and resource scarcity is small (i.e., resources are plentiful), uncertainty is low, and managers feel confident that they can understand, predict, and react to the external forces that affect their businesses.

Environmental Uncertainty — High / Medium / Low

Environmental Characteristics

- Environmental Complexity
- Resource Scarcity
- Environmental Change

© Cengage Learning

Business confidence indices indices that show managers' level of confidence about future business growth

EXHIBIT 3.2

General and Specific Environments

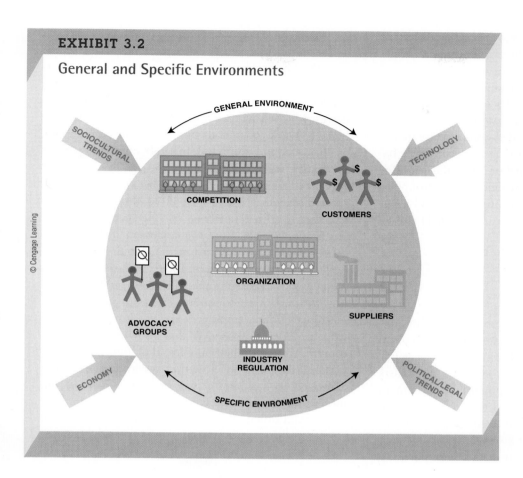

for foods, Mike Taylor, said, "We've got a huge obesity problem in this country and its due in part to excess calorie consumption outside the home. Consumers generally when you ask them say they would prefer to have that information." Restaurants with fewer than twenty locations, or places such as movie theaters or bowling alleys, whose primary business is not serving or selling food, are exempt from this regulation.[13]

The specific environment, which will be discussed in detail in Section 3.3 of this chapter, includes customers, competitors, suppliers, industry regulation, and advocacy groups.

*But first let's take a closer look at the four components of the general environment: **3-2a the economy** and **3-2b the technological, 3-2c sociocultural**, and **3-2d political/legal trends that indirectly affect all organizations**.*

3-2a ECONOMY

The current state of a country's economy affects virtually every organization doing business there. In general, in a growing economy, more people are working and wages are growing, and therefore consumers have relatively more money to spend. More products

are bought and sold in a growing economy than in a static or shrinking economy. Though an individual firm's sales will not necessarily increase, a growing economy does provide an environment favorable to business growth. In contrast, in a shrinking economy, consumers have less money to spend and relatively fewer products are bought and sold. Thus, a shrinking economy makes growth for individual businesses more difficult.

Because the economy influences basic business decisions, such as whether to hire more employees, expand production, or take out loans to purchase equipment, managers scan their economic environments for signs of significant change. Unfortunately, the economic statistics that managers rely on when making these decisions are notoriously poor predictors of *future* economic activity. A manager who decides to hire ten more employees because economic data suggest future growth could very well have to lay off those newly hired workers when the economic growth does not occur. In fact, a famous economic study found that at the beginning of a business quarter (a period of only three months), even the best economic forecasters could not accurately predict whether economic activity would grow or shrink *in that same quarter*![14]

Because economic statistics can be poor predictors, some managers try to predict future economic activity by keeping track of business confidence. **Business confidence indices** show how confident actual managers are about future business growth. For example, the Conference Board's CEO Confidence Index is a quarterly survey of 100 CEOS in large companies across a variety of different industries that examines attitudes regarding future growth in the economy or particular industries.[15] Another widely cited measure is the Small Business Research Board's Business Confidence

Technology the knowledge, tools, and techniques used to transform input into output

Index, which asks 500 small business owners and managers to express their optimism (or pessimism) about future business sales and prospects.[16] Managers often prefer business confidence indices to economic statistics because they know that other managers make business decisions that are in line with their expectations concerning the economy's future. So if the Conference Board or Small Business Research Board business confidence indices are dropping, a manager might decide against hiring new employees, increasing production, or taking out additional loans to expand the business.

3-2b TECHNOLOGICAL COMPONENT

Technology is the knowledge, tools, and techniques used to transform inputs (raw materials, information, and so on) into outputs (products and services). For example, the inputs of authors, editors, and artists (knowledge) and the use of equipment like computers and printing presses (technology) transformed paper, ink, and glue (raw materials) into this book (the finished product). In the case of a service company such as an airline, the technology consists of equipment, including airplanes, repair tools, and computers, as well as the knowledge of mechanics, ticketers, and flight crews. The output is the service of transporting people from one place to another.

Changes in technology can help companies provide better products or produce their products more efficiently. Although technological changes can benefit a business, they can also threaten it. Companies must embrace new technology and find effective ways to use it to improve their products and services or decrease costs. If they don't, they will lose out to those companies that do.

3-2c SOCIOCULTURAL COMPONENT

The sociocultural component of the general environment refers to the demographic characteristics, general behavior, attitudes, and beliefs of people in a particular society. Sociocultural changes and trends influence organizations in two important ways.

First, changes in demographic characteristics, such as the number of people with particular skills or the growth of or decline in the number of people with particular population characteristics (marital status, age, gender, ethnicity) affect how companies staff their businesses. Married women with children are much more likely to work today than they were four decades ago, as illustrated in Exhibit 3.3. In 1960, only 18.6 percent of women with children under the age of six and 39 percent of women with children between the ages of six and seventeen worked. By 2010, those percentages had risen to 61.6 percent and 76.7 percent, respectively.

Second, sociocultural changes in behavior, attitudes, and beliefs also affect the demand for a business's products and services. Today, with more married women with children in the work force, traffic congestion creating longer commutes, and both parents working longer hours, employees are much more likely to value products and services that allow them to recapture free time with their families, and families are deliberately selective about how they spend their free time. Thus, people—especially working mothers—use numerous services to help reduce the amount of time they spend doing chores and household management

© iStockphoto.com/camilla wisbauer

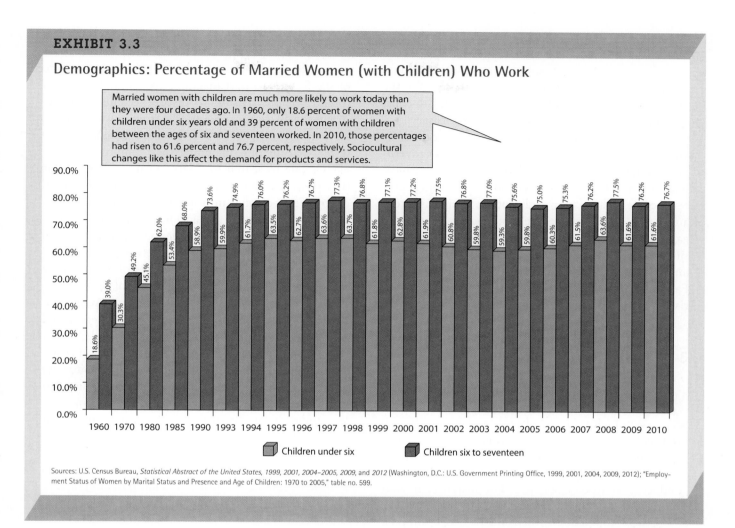

EXHIBIT 3.3

Demographics: Percentage of Married Women (with Children) Who Work

Married women with children are much more likely to work today than they were four decades ago. In 1960, only 18.6 percent of women with children under six years old and 39 percent of women with children between the ages of six and seventeen worked. In 2010, those percentages had risen to 61.6 percent and 76.7 percent, respectively. Sociocultural changes like this affect the demand for products and services.

Children under six Children six to seventeen

Sources: U.S. Census Bureau, *Statistical Abstract of the United States, 1999, 2001, 2004–2005, 2009,* and *2012* (Washington, D.C.: U.S. Government Printing Office, 1999, 2001, 2004, 2009, 2012); "Employment Status of Women by Marital Status and Presence and Age of Children: 1970 to 2005," table no. 599.

tasks. For example, at McGraw Wentworth, a provider of group healthcare benefits, employees can get their laundry picked up and returned on site. IT staffing firm Akraya provides employees with professional home cleaning services.[17]

3-2d POLITICAL/LEGAL COMPONENT

The political/legal component of the general environment includes the legislation, regulations, and court decisions that govern and regulate business behavior. New laws and regulations continue to impose additional responsibilities on companies. Unfortunately, many managers are unaware of these new responsibilities. For example, under the 1991 Civil Rights Act (http://www.eeoc.gov/policy/cra91 .html), if an employee is sexually harassed by anyone at work (a supervisor, a coworker, or even a customer), the company—not just the harasser—is

potentially liable for damages, attorneys' fees, and back pay.[18] Under the Family and Medical Leave Act (http://www.dol.gov/dol/topic/benefits-leave/fmla .htm), employees who have been on the job one year are guaranteed twelve weeks of unpaid leave per year to tend to their own illnesses or to their elderly parents, a newborn baby, or a newly adopted child. Employees are guaranteed the same job, pay, and benefits when they return to work.[19]

Many managers are also unaware of the potential legal risks associated with traditional managerial decisions about recruiting, hiring, and firing employees. Increasingly, businesses and managers are being sued for negligent hiring and supervision, defamation, invasion of privacy, emotional distress, fraud, and misrepresentation during employee recruitment.[20] More than 14,000 suits for wrongful termination (unfairly firing employees) are filed each year.[21] In fact, wrongful termination lawsuits increased by 77 percent during the 1990s.[22] One in four employers will at some point be sued for wrongful termination. It can cost $300,000 to settle such a case once it goes to court, but employers lose 70 percent of court cases, and the former employee is awarded, on average, $1 million or more.[23] On the other hand, employers who settle before going to court typically pay just $10,000 to $100,000 per case.[24]

Not everyone agrees that companies' legal risks are too severe. Indeed, many believe that the government should do more to regulate and restrict business behavior and that it should be easier for average citizens to sue dishonest or negligent corporations. From a managerial perspective, the best medicine against legal risk is prevention. As a manager, it is your responsibility to educate yourself about the laws, regulations, and potential lawsuits that could affect your business. Failure to do so may put you and your company at risk of sizable penalties, fines, or legal charges.

3-3 *Specific Environment*

As you just learned, changes in any sector of the general environment (economic, technological, sociocultural, and political/legal) eventually affect most organizations. Each organization also has a specific environment that is unique to that firm's industry and directly affects the way it conducts day-to-day business. For instance, if your customers decide to use another product, your main competitor cuts prices 10 percent, your best supplier can't deliver raw materials, federal regulators mandate reductions in pollutants in your industry, or environmental groups accuse your company of selling unsafe products, the impact from the specific environment on your business is immediate.

*Let's examine how the **3-3a customer, 3-3b competitor, 3-3c supplier, 3-3d industry regulation, and 3-3e advocacy group** components of the specific environment affect businesses.*

3-3a CUSTOMER COMPONENT

Customers purchase products and services. Companies cannot exist without customer support. Monitoring customers' changing wants and needs is critical to business success. There are two basic strategies for monitoring customers: reactive and proactive.

Reactive customer monitoring involves identifying and addressing customer trends and problems after they occur. One reactive strategy is to listen closely to customer complaints and respond to customer concerns. The online forums for Activision-Blizzard's

World of Warcraft (WoW), the most popular web-based role-playing game, are infamous for trolls—users who take advantage of the anonymous nature of the forums to post insulting and hateful messages for no obvious reason. To discourage this behavior, Activision-Blizzard announced forum posters would have to start using their real names. Forum users protested that anyone, including their employers, could use Google to search the WoW forum and see what they posted. Others worried that hackers might track down their personal information to steal their identity. Some even feared physical harm from other WoW players, who would now be able to identify and locate them. Finally, others felt that that using real names would undercut the fantasy elements of WoW. Three days after creating the policy, because of overwhelming complaints about the new policy, Activision-Blizzard reacted again by announcing that users would be allowed to use anonymous names after all.[25]

Companies that respond quickly to customer letters of complaint (i.e., reactive customer monitoring) are viewed much more favorably than companies that are slow to respond or never respond.[26] In particular, studies have shown that when a company sends a follow-up letter to thank the customer for writing, offers a sincere, specific response to the complaint (not a form letter, but an explanation of how the problem will be handled), and offers a small gift, coupons, or a refund to make up for the problem, customers are much more likely to purchase products or services again from that company.[27]

Proactive monitoring of customers means identifying and addressing customer needs, trends, and issues *before* they occur.

While it's commonly believed that attracting high rollers who bet huge amounts of money is the key to profitability in the gaming industry, Harrah's casinos determined that 80 percent of its revenues and 100 percent of its profits come from "low rollers," the 30 percent of its customers who only spend $100 to $500 per visit. Harrah's calls them "avid experience players" because of the regularity with which they gamble. The trick to attracting and keeping these customers is to identify and address their needs, which Harrah's does through its electronic Total Rewards program cards that these frequent gamblers insert into slot machines or hand to blackjack table attendants whenever they place a bet. Thanks to the data obtained from those cards, Harrah's can identify what different customers need to keep them coming back to Harrah's, rather than to other casinos. Linda Maranees, a regular customer, says, "Harrah's is savvy." Because she plays the

Summer Premiers

How do you gain more viewers in the hyper-competitive television market? Many cable companies have found that the answer is to take advantage of the season. Over-the-air broadcast networks (ABC, CBS, NBC, Fox) tend to premiere their best shows in the fall while showing reruns or lesser-known, newer shows in the summer. Cable networks are taking advantage by using the summer to debut new shows like *Rizzoli & Isles* on TNT and *Covert Affairs* on USA, and new episodes of popular shows like *Ice Road Truckers* on the History Channel. The strategy is a smashing success, as the ten largest cable networks have increased viewership by 5 percent from the previous year.

Source: B. Stelter, "With Summer, Big Cable Channels Keep Getting Bigger," *New York Times*, August 15, 2010, accessed December 15, 2010, http://www.nytimes.com/2010/08/16/business/media/16cable.html.

slot machines, Harrah's will offer her cash rewards—which she can then put into slot machines. By contrast, Harrah's figured out that Tina Montgomery will bet more or visit more often if offered a free or "comped" hotel room. Why? Because her husband, who doesn't gamble, "stays in the room" when she goes to the casino.[28] How well does this work? By identifying and meeting customers' needs, Harrah's now gets 43 percent of its customers' gambling business, compared to 36 percent before its Total Rewards program.[29]

3-3b COMPETITOR COMPONENT

Competitors are companies in the same industry that sell similar products or services to customers. Ford, Toyota, Honda, Nissan, Hyundai, and Kia all compete for automobile customers. NBC, ABC, CBS, and Fox (along with hundreds of cable channels) compete for TV viewers' attention. McDonald's, Burger King, Wendy's, Hardee's, Chick-fil-A, and a host of others compete for fast-food customers' dollars. Often the difference between business success and failure comes down to whether your company is doing a better job of satisfying customer wants and needs than the competition. Consequently, companies need to keep close track of what their competitors are doing. To do this, managers perform a **competitive analysis**, which involves deciding who your competitors are, anticipating competitors' moves, and determining competitors' strengths and weaknesses.

Surprisingly, managers often do a poor job of identifying potential competitors because they tend to focus on only two or three well-known competitors with similar goals and resources.[30]

Another mistake managers may make when analyzing the competition is to underestimate potential competitors' capabilities. When this happens, managers don't take the steps they should to continue to improve their products or services. The result can be significant decreases in both market share and profits. For nearly a decade, traditional phone companies ignored the threat to their business from VoIP (Voice over Internet Protocol). Early on, software products like Cool Talk, Internet Phone, and Web Phone made it possible to make inexpensive long-distance phone calls using VoIP. Aside from the software, the only requirements were an Internet service provider and a computer that had a sound card, speakers, and a microphone. The sound quality was only as good as AM radio, but people who were used to poor-quality sound on their cell phones didn't care because the calls were so much cheaper.[31]

The ultimate threat to the phone companies and cable companies comes from a VoIP product, the Ooma Telo. About the size of a small dinner plate, it plugs into your network router and then your phone. Plug in the power, and voila, at a onetime cost of roughly $200, you have phone service without a monthly phone bill.[32] With the average landline costing about $35 a month, Ooma pays for itself in just over six months and then saves nearly $900 in monthly phone bills in just the first three years of use. Ooma does charge about $40 to port your current phone number to your Ooma account. And, for just $10 a month for its Premier benefits, you get a second line or phone number, three-way conferencing, the ability to send voice mails to your email account, call screening, and much more. But, even at $10 a month, the total savings are still $300 per year. Even Vonage, which charges $25 to $35 a month for VoIP phone service and has been taking business away from the phone companies and cable companies, could lose business to Ooma.

3-3c SUPPLIER COMPONENT

Suppliers are companies that provide material, human, financial, and informational resources to other companies. U.S. Steel buys iron ore from suppliers to

Supplier dependence the degree to which a company relies on a supplier because of the importance of the supplier's product to the company and the difficulty of finding other sources of that product

Buyer dependence the degree to which a supplier relies on a buyer because of the importance of that buyer to the supplier and the difficulty of finding other buyers for its products

Opportunistic behavior a transaction in which one party in the relationship benefits at the expense of the other

Relationship behavior the establishment of mutually beneficial, long-term exchanges between buyers and suppliers

Industry regulation regulations and rules that govern the business practices and procedures of specific industries, businesses, and professions

make steel products. When IBM sells a mainframe computer, it also provides support staff, engineers, and other technical consultants to the company that bought the computer. If you're shopping for desks, chairs, and office supplies, chances are Office Depot will be glad to help your business open a revolving charge account to pay for your purchases. When a clothing manufacturer has spent $100,000 to purchase new high-pressure water drills to cut shirt and pants patterns to precise sizes, the water drill manufacturer, as part of the purchase, will usually train the workers to use the machinery.

A key factor influencing the impact and quality of the relationship between companies and their suppliers is how dependent they are on each other.[33] **Supplier dependence** is the degree to which a company relies on that supplier because of the importance of the supplier's product to the company and the difficulty of finding other sources for that product. **Buyer dependence** is the degree to which a supplier relies on a buyer because of the importance of that buyer to the supplier's sales and the difficulty of finding other buyers of its products. United Space Alliance (USA) is a company jointly created by Boeing and Lockheed Martin to provide space operations services. Its biggest and most important client (or buyer) was NASA's space shuttle program, for which it provided mission planning, training, engineering, maintenance, software development, launch and recovery, and flight operations. But when NASA terminated the Space Shuttle program in 2011, USA lost its primary buyer. With few other companies needing its services, USA Company announced that it would reduce its work force by nearly half. A few months later, it was revealed that senior executives at USA's parent companies instructed management to stop pursuing new contracts, fueling rumors that the company would soon be shut down completely.[34]

A high degree of buyer or seller dependence can lead to **opportunistic behavior**, in which one party

benefits at the expense of the other. Although opportunistic behavior between buyers and suppliers will never be completely eliminated, many companies believe that both buyers and suppliers can benefit by improving the buyer-supplier relationship.[35]

In contrast to opportunistic behavior, **relationship behavior** focuses on establishing a mutually beneficial, long-term relationship between buyers and suppliers.[36] Toyota is well known for developing positive long-term relationships with its key suppliers. Donald Esmond, who runs Toyota's U.S. division, says, "I think what they [suppliers] appreciate . . . is we don't go in and say, 'Reduce the costs by 6 percent; if you don't, somebody else is going to get the business.' We go in and say we want to come in and help you [figure out] where you can save costs so we can reduce our overall price. So it's a different approach."[37]

3-3d INDUSTRY REGULATION COMPONENT

Whereas the political/legal component of the general environment affects all businesses, the **industry regulation** component consists of regulations and rules that govern the practices and procedures of specific industries, businesses, and professions. For example, cigarette manufacturers are now required to place large warning labels on their products and advertisements. The labels contain graphic images of diseased lungs or a dead body, along with direct messages, such as "Smoking can kill you" and "Cigarettes cause cancer." The labels must cover half of the cigarette carton, both front and back, and 20 percent of the space of any advertisement. Forty other countries already require similar graphic warnings.[38]

Regulatory agencies affect businesses by creating and enforcing rules and regulations to protect consumers, workers, or society as a whole. For example, the U.S. Department of Agriculture and the Food and

Alan Pryke/Newspix/Rex Features via AP Images

FACTS

Federal Regulatory Agencies and Commissions

Consumer Product Safety Commission
Reduces risk of injuries and deaths associated with consumer products, sets product safety standards, enforces product recalls, and provides consumer education **http://www.cpsc.gov**

Department of Labor
Collects employment statistics and administers labor laws concerning safe working conditions, minimum hourly wages and overtime pay, employment discrimination, and unemployment insurance **http://www.dol.gov**

Environmental Protection Agency
Reduces and controls pollution through research, monitoring, standard setting, and enforcement activities **http://www.epa.gov**

Equal Employment Opportunity Commission
Promotes fair hiring and promotion practices **http://www.eeoc.gov**

Federal Communications Commission
Regulates interstate and international communications by radio, television, wire, satellite, and cable **http://www.fcc.gov**

Federal Reserve System
As nation's central bank, controls interest rates and money supply and monitors the U.S. banking system to produce a growing economy with stable prices **http://www.federalreserve.gov**

Federal Trade Commission
Restricts unfair methods of business competition and misleading advertising; enforces consumer protection laws **http://www.ftc.gov**

Food and Drug Administration
Protects nation's health by making sure food, drugs, and cosmetics are safe **http://www.fda.gov**

National Labor Relations Board
Monitors union elections and stops companies from engaging in unfair labor practices **http://www.nlrb.gov**

Occupational Safety and Health Administration
Saves lives, prevents injuries, and protects the health of workers **http://www.osha.gov**

Securities and Exchange Commission
Protects investors in the bond and stock markets, guarantees access to information on publicly traded securities, and regulates firms that sell securities or give investment advice **http://www.sec.gov**

Drug Administration regulate the safety of seafood (as well as meat and poultry) through the science-based Hazard Analysis and Critical Control Points program. Seafood processors are required to identify hazards (toxins, chemicals, pesticides, and decomposition) that could cause the fish they process to be unsafe. They must also establish critical control points to control hazards both inside and outside their fish-processing plants and then establish monitoring, corrective action, and verification procedures to certify that the fish they process is safe to consume.[39]

The nearly 100 federal agencies and regulatory commissions can affect almost any kind of business. For example, when product testers at The Coca-Cola Company discovered trace amounts of a fungicide in orange juice imported from Brazil, the Food and

Drug Administration temporarily banned importation of orange juice shipments so they could be tested for safety.[40]

3-3e ADVOCACY GROUPS

Advocacy groups are groups of concerned citizens who band together to try to influence the business practices of specific industries, businesses, and professions. The members of a group generally share the same point of view on a particular issue. For example, environmental advocacy groups might try

Advocacy groups
concerned citizens who band together to try to influence the business practices of specific industries, businesses, and professions

Public communications
an advocacy group tactic that relies on voluntary participation by the news media and the advertising industry to get the advocacy group's message out

Media advocacy an advocacy group tactic that involves framing issues as public issues; exposing questionable, exploitative, or unethical practices; and forcing media coverage by buying media time or creating controversy that is likely to receive extensive news coverage

Product boycott an advocacy group tactic that involves protesting a company's actions by persuading consumers not to purchase its product or service

to get manufacturers to reduce smokestack pollution emissions. Unlike the industry regulation component of the specific environment, advocacy groups cannot force organizations to change their practices. Nevertheless, they can use a number of techniques to try to influence companies, including public communications, media advocacy, web pages, blogs, and product boycotts.

The **public communications** approach relies on *voluntary* participation by the news media and the advertising industry to send out an advocacy group's message. For example, a public service campaign to encourage people to quit smoking ran the following ads in newspapers and magazines throughout Europe: a photo showing the foot of a young person with a toe

tag (indicating the person was dead), with the caption "Smokers die younger"; a picture showing clean lungs next to brown- and black-stained lungs, with the caption "Smoking causes fatal lung cancer"; and a photo of a baby in an intensive care unit hooked up to a respirator, with the caption "Smoking when pregnant harms your baby."[41]

Media advocacy is much more aggressive than the public communications approach. A **media advocacy** approach typically involves framing the group's concerns as public issues (affecting everyone); exposing questionable, exploitative, or unethical practices; and creating controversy that is likely to receive extensive news coverage.

A **product boycott** is a tactic in which an advocacy group actively tries to persuade consumers not to purchase a company's product or service. When an explosion on one of British Petroleum's (BP) oil rigs in April 2010 caused massive amounts of oil to leak into the Gulf of Mexico, many American consumers expressed outrage by boycotting BP gas. Protesters created "Boycott BP" websites and Facebook groups, staged protests at BP service stations, and distributed bumper stickers that said, "AnyoneButBP." Tyson Slocum, director of Public Citizen, an advocacy group, said, "These are symbolic acts taken by people who are outraged and frustrated. But this is a fitting response

DOING THE RIGHT THING

Those who expect bribes often hide behind jargon or slang.

The Language of Bribery

In many foreign countries, bribery is an accepted and even expected part of doing business, even though there are laws that are meant to prevent illegal gifts and payments. Because of these laws, those who expect bribes often hide behind jargon or slang so that they can disguise the true nature of the exchange of money. In Italy, for example, a bribe might be called a *spintarella*, "a little push," while it might be called *fakelaki*, "a little purse," in Greece. An offer of a bribe might often be described as something to eat or drink—a *pot-de-vin* ("glass of wine") in France, a *mordida* ("a bite") in Spain, or a *finjaan 'ahwa* ("a cup of coffee") in Syria. In Russia, someone might ask for a bribe by suggesting that "we need to come to agreement." So how can companies navigate this confusing jumble of foreign slang? James Tillen and Sonia Delman, of the international law firm Miller & Chevalier Chartered, give the following suggestions:

- Incorporate local dialects, slang, and customs into compliance policies and training programs.
- Use role-play exercises with locally relevant language and customs in anticorruption training sessions.
- Instruct employees to clarify any dubious payment requests.
- Include colloquial bribery terms as "red flags" in internal audit modules.

Source: J. G. Tillen and S. M. Delman, "A Bribe by Any Other Name," *Forbes.com*, May 28, 2010, accessed December 10, 2010, http://www.forbes.com/2010/05/28/bribery-slang-jargon-leadership-managing -compliance_2.html.

because, after all, BP over the years has spent millions promoting this image of being a green, environmentally friendly company. It was all for show. Boycotting their brand is the best way to counter that kind of charade."[42]

3-4 *Making Sense of Changing Environments*

In Chapter 1, you learned that managers are responsible for making sense of their business environments. As our discussions of the general and specific environments have indicated, however, making sense of business environments is not an easy task. *Because external environments can be dynamic, confusing, and complex, managers use a three-step process to make sense of the changes in their external environments: 3-4a environmental scanning, 3-4b interpreting environmental factors, and 3-4c acting on threats and opportunities.*

3-4a ENVIRONMENTAL SCANNING

Environmental scanning involves searching the environment for important events or issues that might affect an organization. Managers scan the environment to stay up-to-date on important factors in their industry. The American Hospital Association, for instance, publishes the "AHA Environmental Scan" annually to help hospital and health system managers understand the trends and market forces that have a "high probability of affecting the health-care field." In its latest report, it indicated that the single biggest threat to work force productivity in the United States was chronic diseases, noting that at least 80 percent of workers have one chronic condition. The report also states that over half of patients want to use email and Internet tools to communicate with their doctors, that nationwide physician shortages will double to nearly 63,000 fewer doctors than needed within five years, and that the availability of drugs may reach a critical level, as more than 240 prescription drugs were either in low supply or completely out of stock.[43]

Managers also scan their environments to reduce uncertainty. During Super Bowl XLVI, held in Indianapolis, Indiana, **Raidious**, a digital marketing agency, set up the Social Media Command Center, a downtown office filled with staffers monitoring what was being said about the event on Twitter, Facebook, Foursquare, and other social media sites. So, for example, if a number of people tweeted that the parking situation at a certain venue was terrible, Raidious would see the complaints and quickly send out staffers to resolve the situation.[44]

Organizational strategies also affect environmental scanning. In other words, managers pay close attention to trends and events that are directly related to their company's ability to compete in the marketplace.[45] Knights Apparel, a manufacturer of collegiate-licensed clothing based in South Carolina, recognized that its customers were increasingly concerned about buying clothes produced in "sweatshops" in developing countries where workers were paid as little as $100 per month. Instead of the legally required minimum wage of $147 a month, Knights's wages of $500 a month are based on the actual cost of living in the Dominican Republic. While costs have increased by

"Physician shortages will double to nearly 63,000 fewer doctors than needed within five years."

Cognitive maps graphic depictions of how managers believe environmental factors relate to possible organizational actions

20 percent, or eighty cents per T-shirt, the company has not increased its prices. CEO Joseph Bozich said, "We're pricing the product such that we're not asking the retailer or the consumer to sacrifice in order to support it."[46] Knights's hope is that this policy will make its product more desirable than those of its competitors, Nike and Adidas. Kellie A. McElhaney, a professor of corporate social responsibility at UC Berkeley said, "A lot of college students would much rather pay for a brand that shows workers are treated well." Knights has already received lucrative deals with Duke University, Barnes & Noble, and Follett's, a chain of college textbook stores.[47]

Finally, environmental scanning is important because it contributes to organizational performance. Environmental scanning helps managers detect environmental changes and problems before they become organizational crises.[48] Furthermore, companies whose CEOs do more environmental scanning have higher profits.[49] CEOs in better-performing firms scan their firms' environments more frequently and scan more key factors in their environments in more depth and detail than do CEOs in poorer-performing firms.[50]

3-4b INTERPRETING ENVIRONMENTAL FACTORS

After scanning, managers determine what environmental events and issues mean to the organization. Typically, managers view environmental events and issues as either threats or opportunities. When managers interpret environmental events as threats, they take steps to protect the company from further harm. Just five years ago, Finland-based Nokia made 49 percent of all smartphones sold worldwide. Though still the world's largest cell phone maker, its market share has shrunk to just 25 percent. This steep drop is due largely to competition from Apple's iPhone, as well as phones powered by Google's Android, both of which give users hundreds of thousands of applications and an easy-to-use touchscreen software interface that Nokia's Symbian operating system could not match. For that reason, and the $1.4 billion in costs it would save by no longer supporting Symbian, Nokia agreed to partner with Microsoft to produce phones using the Windows Phone operating system, which it hopes allows its phones to compete against iPhones and Androids.[51]

By contrast, when managers interpret environmental events as opportunities, they consider strategic alternatives for taking advantage of those events to improve company performance. Apple is known for recognizing opportunities and capitalizing on them. The market for high-end "smart" phones, full-featured mobile phones that also function as handheld personal computers, is growing roughly 2 percent per year. Because of opportunities in this market, Apple developed the iPhone. Then CEO Steve Jobs announced the release more than six months in advance to generate hype, stimulate demand, and dampen sales of competitors. The iPhone features a wider screen, intuitive touch-screen controls, and the ability to use faster Wi-Fi networks so that users can email, surf the web, and communicate with Bluetooth-enabled devices—plus, of course, download and play iTunes music. According to the most recent figures available, Apple sold more than 35 million of the iPhone 4s, in just six months. And, as of July 2011, just three years after opening the App Store, Apple announced that it had sold its 15 billionth app.[52]

3-4c ACTING ON THREATS AND OPPORTUNITIES

After scanning for information on environmental events and issues and interpreting them as threats or opportunities, managers have to decide how to respond to these environmental factors. Deciding what to do under conditions of uncertainty is always difficult. Managers can never be completely confident that they have all the information they need or that they correctly understand the information they have.

Because it is impossible to comprehend all the factors and changes, managers often rely on simplified models of external environments called cognitive maps. **Cognitive maps** summarize the perceived relationships between environmental factors and possible organizational actions. For example, the cognitive map shown in Exhibit 3.4 represents a small clothing-store owner's interpretation of her business environment. The map shows three kinds of variables. The first variables, shown as rectangles, are environmental factors, such as a Wal-Mart or a large mall twenty minutes away. The second variables, shown in ovals, are potential actions that the store owner might take, such as a low-cost strategy; a good-value, good-service strategy; or a "large selection of the latest fashions" strategy. The third variables, shown as trapezoids, are company strengths, such as low employee turnover, and weaknesses, such as small size.

The plus and minus signs on the map indicate whether the manager believes there is a positive or negative relationship between variables. For example, the manager believes that a low-cost strategy won't work because Wal-Mart and Target are nearby. Offering a large selection of the latest fashions would not work either—not with the small size of the store and that large nearby mall. However, the manager believes that a good-value, good-service strategy would lead to success and profits because of the store's low employee turnover, good knowledge of customers, reasonable selection of clothes at reasonable prices, and good location.

EXHIBIT 3.4

Cognitive Maps

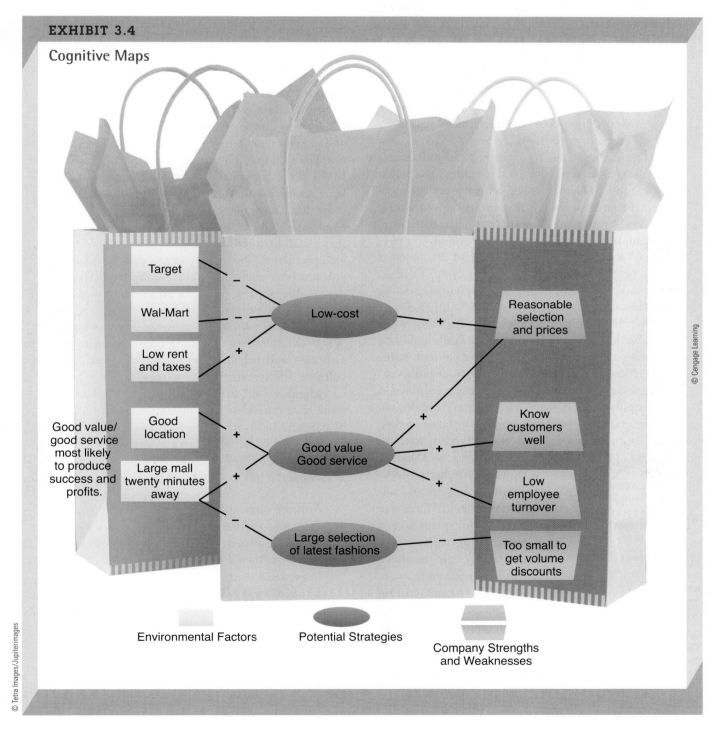

3-5 *Organizational Cultures: Creation, Success, and Change*

We have been looking at trends and events outside of companies that have the potential to affect them. By contrast, the **internal environment** consists of the trends and events *within* an organization that affect the management, employees, and **organizational culture**. Internal environments are important because they affect what people think, feel, and do at work. The key component in internal environments is organizational culture, or the set of key values, beliefs, and attitudes shared by members of the organization.

Under Armour, the sporting apparel and accessories maker, got its start two decades ago when founder and CEO Kevin Plank, a former college football player and special teams captain, sewed shorts and shirts himself in his grandmother's Baltimore, Maryland, basement. Today, Under Armour is a fast-growing—sales increased 38 percent in 2011—$1.5 billion company that competes with Nike, Reebok, and Adidas. One of the keys to its meteoric rise may be its "faster-stronger-better" internal culture. Plank says, "We as a company don't sleep much. We work harder. We have a commitment that I think would be exhausting to someone else." To sustain that hard-driving, competitive culture, Under Armour builds camaraderie and a team orientation among employees. New employees are given big welcome breakfasts. Staff members are treated to outdoor movie nights, tuition reimbursement, and discounted tickets to sporting events, and there is a club for working mothers that offers support and advice. Says Plank, "I manage the company much like a team. Coming out of school and starting the business, sales and marketing were offense, and manufacturing was defense, and finance and operations were like special teams. What I've come to find out is that when the company is the best, it's not that one team is playing and another team

is winning on the side, it's that everyone is on the field together."[53]

Let's take a closer look at **3-5a how organizational cultures are created and maintained, 3-5b the characteristics of successful organizational cultures,** *and* **3-5c how companies can accomplish the difficult task of changing organizational cultures.**

3-5a CREATION AND MAINTENANCE OF ORGANIZATIONAL CULTURES

A primary source of organizational culture is the company founder. Founders like Thomas J. Watson, Sr. (IBM), Sam Walton (Wal-Mart), and Bill Gates (Microsoft) create organizations in their own images and imprint them with their beliefs, attitudes, and values. For example, Thomas J. Watson proclaimed that IBM's three basic beliefs were the pursuit of excellence, customer service, and showing respect for the individual, meaning company employees. Microsoft employees share founder Bill Gates's determination to stay ahead of software competitors. Says a Microsoft vice president, "No matter how good your product, you are only eighteen months away from failure."[54] Although company founders are instrumental in the creation of organizational cultures, eventually founders retire, die, or choose to leave their companies. When the founders are gone, how are their values, attitudes, and beliefs sustained in the organizational culture? Answer: stories and heroes.

Members tell **organizational stories** to make sense of organizational events and changes and to emphasize culturally consistent assumptions, decisions, and actions.[55] At Wal-Mart, stories abound about founder Sam Walton's thriftiness as he strove to make Wal-Mart the low-cost retailer that it is today.

In those days, we would go on buying trips with Sam, and we'd all stay, as much as we could, in one room or two. I remember one time in Chicago when we stayed eight of us to a room. And the room wasn't very big to begin with. You might say we were on a pretty restricted budget. (Gary Reinboth, one of Wal-Mart's first store managers)[56]

When the founders are gone, how are their values, attitudes, and beliefs sustained in the organizational culture?

Sam Walton's thriftiness still permeates Wal-Mart today. Everyone, including top executives and the

---

Internal environment
the events and trends inside an organization that affect management, employees, and organizational culture

Organizational culture
the values, beliefs, and attitudes shared by organizational members

Organizational stories
stories told by organizational members to make sense of organizational events and changes and to emphasize culturally consistent assumptions, decisions, and actions

CEO, flies coach rather than business or first class. When employees travel on business, it's still the norm to share rooms (though two to a room, not eight!) at inexpensive motels like Motel 6 and Super 8 instead of Holiday Inns. Likewise, Wal-Mart will reimburse only up to $15 per meal on business travel, which is half to one third the reimbursement rate at similar-sized companies (remember, Wal-Mart is one of the largest companies in the world). At one of its annual meetings, former CEO Lee Scott reinforced Sam Walton's beliefs by exhorting Wal-Mart employees to bring back and use the free pencils and pens from their travels. Most people in the audience didn't think he was kidding, and he probably wasn't.[57]

A second way in which organizational culture is sustained is by recognizing and celebrating heroes. By definition, **organizational heroes** are organizational people admired for their qualities and achievements within the organization. After a late-October snowstorm in upstate New York resulted in a complete sellout of snow blowers, a Home Depot customer was still waiting for the snow blower he wanted to arrive a month later. After calling several stores and using Home Depot's website to search the inventory of every store in a fifty-mile radius, he emailed Home Depot's headquarters in Atlanta, Georgia, out of frustration, wanting to know when he could expect delivery at his local store. In turn, his local store manager called to tell him the snow blower he wanted was in stock at a Home Depot four hours away and that it would be shipped in a week. The next day, however, the store manager called back and said that the snow blower was ready for pickup. When he asked how that was possible, the manager responded that he had two of his store's employees drive four hours to the other store (and four hours back) so that he could have his machine sooner. Said the customer in response to this heroic effort, "I was already [a] pretty devoted Home Depot customer, but this guy just made me a loyal customer for life."[58]

3-5b SUCCESSFUL ORGANIZATIONAL CULTURES

Preliminary research shows that organizational culture is related to organizational success. As shown in Exhibit 3.5, cultures based on adaptability, involvement, a clear mission, and consistency can help companies achieve higher sales growth, return on assets, profits, quality, and employee satisfaction.[59]

Adaptability is the ability to notice and respond to changes in the organization's environment. Cultures

Organizational heroes people celebrated for their qualities and achievements within an organization

need to reinforce important values and behaviors, but a culture becomes dysfunctional if it prevents change. One of the surest ways to do that is to discourage open discussion and disagreement. In cultures that promote higher levels of *employee involvement* in decision making, employees feel a greater sense of ownership and responsibility. Employee involvement has been a hallmark of Genencor since its creation as a joint venture between Genentech and Corning in 1982. Genencor designs its human resources programs by regularly polling employees about which benefits they enjoy and which they would like the company to offer. Most dramatically, when Genencor built its headquarters, it gave its employees a say in the design. Scientists requested that the labs be placed along the building's exterior so they could receive natural light. "I've worked in labs without windows," says staff scientist Fiona Harding, "and seeing the sun makes the time spent in the lab much more pleasant." The building also features a "main street," where employees congregate to collaborate and interact throughout the day. CEO Jean-Jacques Bienaime believes that these employee-driven design features lead to a more stimulating workplace. "If you want employees to be productive,

EXHIBIT 3.5

Keys to an Organizational Culture That Fosters Success

Consistency

Clear Mission

Adaptability

Employee Involvement

© iStockphoto.com/Les Cunliffe

Company mission a company's purpose or reason for existing

Consistent organizational culture a company culture in which the company actively defines and teaches organizational values, beliefs, and attitudes

you have to create a nurturing environment and let them be creative," he says. Such a commitment to employee involvement in decision making is definitely paying off for the company. Its turnover rate was less than 4 percent (the national industry average is 18.5 percent), and its employees generate approximately $60,000 more revenue per employee than its largest competitor, Novozymes.[60]

Company mission is the business's purpose or reason for existing. In organizational cultures with a clear company mission, the organization's strategic purpose and direction are apparent to everyone in the company. When managers are uncertain about their business environments, the mission helps guide the discussions, decisions, and behavior of the people in the company. Novo Nordisk, a pharmaceutical company based in Denmark, has one clear goal: to cure diabetes. Everything it does as an organization—from research and innovation to marketing to its social responsibility—is geared toward revolutionizing the way diabetes is treated and prevented. Novo Nordisk's mission is about improving the lives of its customers.[61]

Culture Party Time

When two companies merge, there is always the risk that the culture of one company will clash with the other, making it miserable for people to work together. The success of a merger, then, often means that companies must be skilled at not only integrating operations like sales and manufacturing, but also at integrating two different cultures. When Southwest Airlines acquired AirTran, it took several steps to help AirTran employees quickly adjust to Southwest's casual, fun culture. Southwest sent a group of employees on a "One LUV" tour (Southwest's stock symbol is LUV) to major AirTran hubs. There they met with AirTran employees, answering whatever questions they had about what it was like to work at Southwest. The airline also assigned each AirTran employee a "wingmate" from Southwest who would help them adjust to working for a different company.

Source: K. Yamanouchi, "Southwest Spreads 'LUV' to AirTran," *Atlanta Journal-Constitution*, July 12, 2011, accessed February 26, 2012, http://www.ajc.com/business/southwest-spreads-luv-to-1012760.html.

Finally, in **consistent organizational cultures**, the company actively defines and teaches organizational values, beliefs, and attitudes. At Zappos, an online shoe retailer, maintaining a consistent organizational culture begins with the hiring process. One of the reasons Tony Hsieh, now CEO of Zappos.com, sold his start-up company, LinkExchange, was because "the company culture just went completely downhill."[62] As LinkExchange grew, managers hired people based on their skills alone and ignored the culture. As a result, the company was staffed by employees who weren't excited or passionate about the work they were doing. When Hsieh joined Zappos, he and his employees developed a list of ten core values (for instance, "Embrace and Drive Change" and "Be Passionate and Determined") that gave everyone at the company shared values and a common corporate language. Then, to avoid the mistakes he made at LinkExchange, Hsieh made sure that Zappos's culture played a significant role in hiring decisions. As a result, prospective hires go through two rounds of interviews. Says Hsieh, "The hiring manager and his or her team will interview for the standard fit within the team, relevant experience, technical ability and so on. But then our HR department does a separate set of interviews purely for culture fit. They actually have questions for each and every one of the core values."

Having a consistent or strong organizational culture doesn't guarantee good company performance. When core beliefs are widely shared and strongly held, it is very difficult to bring about needed change. Consequently, companies with strong cultures tend to perform poorly when they need to adapt to dramatic changes in their external environments. Their consistency sometimes prevents them from adapting to those changes.[63]

3-5c CHANGING ORGANIZATIONAL CULTURES

As shown in Exhibit 3.6, organizational cultures exist on three levels.[64] On the first, or surface, level are the reflections of an organization's culture that can be seen and observed, such as symbolic artifacts (for example, dress codes and office layouts) and workers' and managers' behaviors. Next, just below the surface, are the values and beliefs expressed by people in the company. You can't see these values and beliefs, but they become clear if you carefully listen to what people say and observe how decisions are made or explained. Finally, unconsciously held assumptions and

EXHIBIT 3.6

Three Levels of Organizational Culture

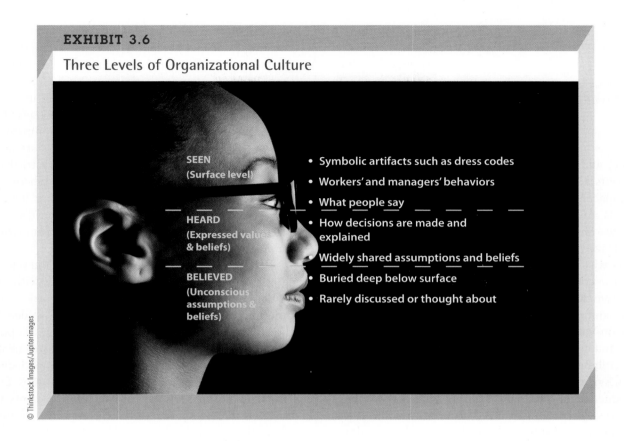

SEEN (Surface level)
- Symbolic artifacts such as dress codes
- Workers' and managers' behaviors
- What people say

HEARD (Expressed values & beliefs)
- How decisions are made and explained

Widely shared assumptions and beliefs

BELIEVED (Unconscious assumptions & beliefs)
- Buried deep below surface
- Rarely discussed or thought about

© Thinkstock Images/Jupiterimages

beliefs about the company are buried deep below the surface. These are the unwritten views and rules that are so strongly held and so widely shared that they are rarely discussed or even thought about unless someone attempts to change them or unknowingly violates them. Changing such assumptions and beliefs can be very difficult. Instead, managers should focus on the parts of the organizational culture they can control. These include observable surface-level items, such as workers' behaviors and symbolic artifacts, and expressed values and beliefs, which can be influenced through employee selection. Let's see how these can be used to change organizational cultures.

One way of changing a corporate culture is to use behavioral addition or behavioral substitution to establish new patterns of behavior among managers and employees. **Behavioral addition** is the process of having managers and employees perform a new behavior, while **behavioral substitution** is having managers and employees perform a new behavior in place of another behavior. The key in both instances is to choose behaviors that are central to and symbolic of the old culture you're changing and the new culture that you want to create. When Mike Ullman became the CEO of JCPenney, he thought the company's culture was stuck in the 19th century (when the company was started).

Employees called each other Mr. and Mrs., casual attire was unacceptable even on Fridays, and any elaborate decoration of office cubicles was reported to a team of office police charged with enforcing corporate décor guidelines. Ullman quickly determined that the company's stringent code of conduct was, among other things, keeping it from recruiting the talent it needed. Mike Theilmann, the human resources officer, drafted a list of what he called "quick hits," small changes that would have a big impact on the culture. The first of Theilmann's initiatives was a campaign titled "Just Call Me Mike," which he hoped would cure employees of the entrenched practice of calling executives and managers Mr. and Mrs. Three JCPenney officers are named Mike, along with nearly 400 other employees at headquarters. Theilmann created posters containing photos of the three executive Mikes along with a list of all the advantages of being on a first-name basis. Top of the list? "First names

Behavioral addition the process of having managers and employees perform new behaviors that are central to and symbolic of the new organizational culture that a company wants to create

Behavioral substitution the process of having managers and employees perform new behaviors central to the new organizational culture in place of behaviors that were central to the old organizational culture

Visible artifacts visible signs of an organization's culture, such as the office design and layout, company dress code, and company benefits and perks, like stock options, personal parking spaces, or the private company dining room

create a friendly place to shop and work."[65]

Another way in which managers can begin to change corporate culture is to change the **visible artifacts** of their old culture, such as the office design and layout, company dress code, and recipients (or nonrecipients) of company benefits and perks like stock options, personal parking spaces, or the private company dining room. In the 1990s, AOL was the dominant force among Internet service and content providers. So many people had AOL accounts that its well-known "You've Got Mail" alert was the title of a Hollywood movie. However, intense competition from high-speed Internet providers, two decades of bad decisions, and a costly merger with and then split from Time Warner reduced it to a Silicon Valley dinosaur. AOL is trying to shed that image and create a new culture that emphasizes creativity, collaboration, and innovation. Brad Garlinghouse, AOL's new president, said, "AOL wasn't building great products, and the brand was reflecting that. We have to expunge the ghosts of AOL and start fresh." A key component of AOL's culture change is the tear down and complete redesign of offices in Palo Alto, California. Whereas its old offices had drab halls, cubicles, and high walls that limited employee interactions, the newly redesigned office is an open design featuring a central space with glass-walled work rooms for team collaboration, round standalone rooms with opaque

glass for quiet work that requires privacy and concentration, and public spaces with pool, Ping-Pong, and foosball tables, couches and chairs with laptop stands, and a cafeteria that's open 24/7. Consistent with its culture change, AOL also took the unusual move of opening up its redesigned offices to seventy-five employees from twenty-five start-up companies, who work with and share ideas with AOL's staffers. CEO Tim Armstrong said, "We really have tried to make our offices into centers of creativity where we can invite other people to come in and work for us. The opportunity is to take some of the world's best entrepreneurs and technologists and have them work in a deeply engaging place."[66]

Cultures can also be changed by hiring and selecting people with values and beliefs consistent with the company's desired culture. *Selection* is the process of gathering information about job applicants to decide who should be offered a job. As discussed in Chapter 11 on human resources, most selection instruments measure whether job applicants have the knowledge, skills, and abilities needed to succeed in their jobs. But companies are increasingly testing job applicants to determine how they fit with the company's desired culture (i.e., values and beliefs). Management consultant Ram Charan says, "A poor job match is not only harmful to the individual but also to the company."[67] At Partners + Napier, an advertising agency, the three most important values are courage, ingenuity, and family. So how do these values carry over into the hiring process? According to CEO Sharon Napier, the ideal candidate is curious, willing to try new things and learn about the products the agency is working on. According to Napier, "If you don't really want to know how something works, if you don't read a lot, then you're not a very curious person. And in our business you really have to be. If I'm going to put you

Let Them Play!

Riley Gibson, the founder and CEO of Napkin Labs, a developer of crowdsourcing apps, believes that a start-up company is more likely to become an effective, productive company if there is a culture of play. It's not just that pool tables and go-karts give employees a fun atmosphere to be in but that a culture of play provides stimulation for innovation and creativity, relieves tension, raises morale, helps attract and retain top talent, and helps employees accept each other and be more open to different kinds of people. As Gibson says, "It's the companies that work hard to establish cultures of play that attract great people, continuously push the boundaries of innovation, and ultimately win."

Source: R. Gibson, "Let Your Employees Play!" *Inc.com*, February 14, 2012, accessed February 26, 2012, http://www.inc.com/riley-gibson/5-reasons-your-start-up-should -be-playing-more.html.

© Richard Levine/Alamy

on an account like Kodak, I want you to learn how to make a photo book . . . if you're not interested in digging in, then that'll say a lot about you."[68]

The second step is to ensure that applicants fit with the culture by using selection tests, instruments, and exercises to measure these values and beliefs in job applicants. (See Chapter 11 for a complete review of applicant and managerial selection.) **Menlo Innovations**, a software development company based in Ann Arbor, Michigan, was founded with the goal of creating the ultimate collaborative environment, one in which everyone works on everything together. In fact, most employees at Menlo work in pairs, sharing one computer as they work on projects collaboratively. The process of teaching this organizational value begins with the hiring process, with what the management team calls "extreme interviewing." Instead of the typical question-and-answer format, applicants are grouped into pairs, and each pair is given a task that reflects the kind of work that the company usually does. Each pair is given twenty minutes to complete the exercise, and then new pairs are formed and assigned another task. James Goebel, one of the company's co-founders, tells the applicants, "This is not about what's on your résumé. This is our best attempt to figure out [if] you are a good fit for our culture." Moreover, he lets applicants know, "This is not about getting the right answer. The thing you will be evaluated on is whether you bring out all the best qualities in your partner. Your job is to make the other applicant look as good as possible."[69]

Corporate cultures are very difficult to change. Consequently, there is no guarantee that any one approach—changing visible cultural artifacts, using behavioral substitution, or hiring people with values consistent with a company's desired culture—will change a company's organizational culture. The best results are obtained by combining these methods. Together, these are some of the best tools managers have for changing culture because they send the clear message to managers and employees that "the accepted way of doing things" has changed.

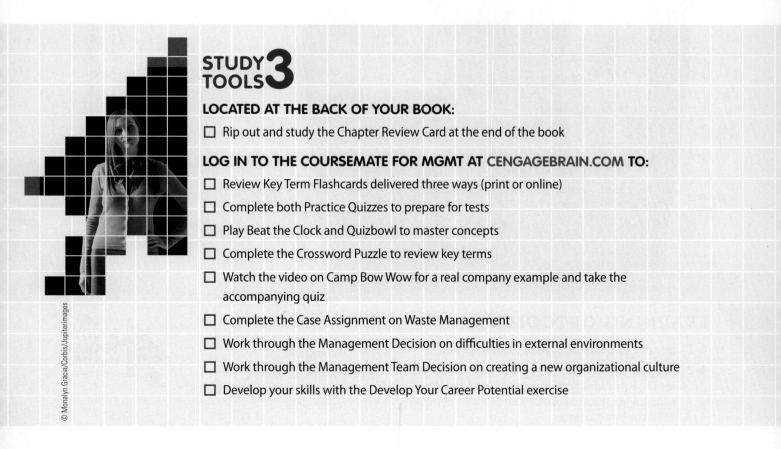

© Monalyn Gracia/Corbis/Jupiterimages

STUDY TOOLS 3

LOCATED AT THE BACK OF YOUR BOOK:

☐ Rip out and study the Chapter Review Card at the end of the book

LOG IN TO THE COURSEMATE FOR MGMT AT CENGAGEBRAIN.COM TO:

☐ Review Key Term Flashcards delivered three ways (print or online)

☐ Complete both Practice Quizzes to prepare for tests

☐ Play Beat the Clock and Quizbowl to master concepts

☐ Complete the Crossword Puzzle to review key terms

☐ Watch the video on Camp Bow Wow for a real company example and take the accompanying quiz

☐ Complete the Case Assignment on Waste Management

☐ Work through the Management Decision on difficulties in external environments

☐ Work through the Management Team Decision on creating a new organizational culture

☐ Develop your skills with the Develop Your Career Potential exercise

4 Ethics and
Social Responsibility

LEARNING OUTCOMES

4-1 Identify common kinds of workplace deviance.

4-2 Describe the U.S. Sentencing Commission Guidelines for Organizations and explain how they both encourage ethical behavior and punish unethical behavior by businesses.

4-3 Describe what influences ethical decision making.

4-4 Explain what practical steps managers can take to improve ethical decision making.

4-5 Explain to whom organizations are socially responsible.

4-6 Explain for what organizations are socially responsible.

4-7 Explain how organizations can choose to respond to societal demands for social responsibility.

4-8 Explain whether social responsibility hurts or helps an organization's economic performance.

CHECK OUT
STUDY TOOLS
AT THE END OF THIS CHAPTER.

4-1 *Workplace Deviance*

Today, it's not enough for companies to make a profit. We also expect managers to make a profit by doing the right things. Unfortunately, no matter what managers decide to do, someone or some group will be unhappy with the outcome. Managers don't have the luxury of choosing theoretically optimal, win-win solutions that are obviously desirable to everyone involved. In practice, solutions to ethical and social responsibility problems aren't optimal. Often, managers must be satisfied with a solution that just makes do or does the least harm. Rights and wrongs are rarely crystal clear to managers charged with doing the right thing. The business world is much messier than that.

Ethics is the set of moral principles or values that defines right and wrong for a person or group. Unfortunately, numerous studies have consistently produced distressing results about the state of ethics in today's business world. A Society of Human Resources Management survey found that only 27 percent of employees felt that their organization's leadership was ethical.[1] In a study of 1,324 randomly selected workers, managers, and executives across multiple industries, 48 percent of the respondents admitted to actually committing an unethical or illegal act in the past year! These acts included cheating on an expense account, discriminating against coworkers, forging signatures, paying or accepting kickbacks, and looking the other way when environmental laws were broken.[2]

Other studies contain good news. When people believe their work environment is ethical, they are six times more likely to stay with that company than if they believe they work in an unethical environment.[3] One study asked 570 white-collar workers which of twenty-eight qualities were important in company leaders. The results? Honesty (24 percent) and integrity/morals/ethics (16 percent) ranked by far the highest. (Caring/compassion was third at 7 percent.)[4] According to Eduardo Castro-Wright, vice chairman of Wal-Mart Stores, "There's nothing that destroys credibility more than not being able to look someone in the eye and have them know that they can trust you."[5] In short, much needs to be done to make workplaces more ethical, but—and this is very important—most managers and employees want this to happen.

Ethical behavior follows accepted principles of right and wrong. Depending on which study you look at, one-third to three-quarters of all employees admit that they have stolen from their employers, committed computer fraud, embezzled funds, vandalized company property, sabotaged company projects, faked injuries to receive workers' compensation benefits or insurance, or been "sick" from work when they weren't really sick. Experts estimate that unethical behaviors like these, which researchers call *workplace deviance*, may cost companies as much as $1 trillion a year, or roughly 7 percent of their revenues.[6]

Workplace deviance is unethical behavior that violates organizational norms about right and wrong. As Exhibit 4.1 on page 66 shows, workplace deviance can be categorized by how deviant the behavior is, from minor to serious, and by the target of the deviant behavior, either the organization or particular people in the workplace.[7]

Ethics the set of moral principles or values that defines right and wrong for a person or group

Ethical behavior behavior that conforms to a society's accepted principles of right and wrong

Workplace deviance unethical behavior that violates organizational norms about right and wrong

EXHIBIT 4.1

Types of Workplace Deviance

Organizational

Production Deviance
- ⊙ Leaving early
- ⊙ Taking excessive breaks
- ⊙ Intentionally working slowly
- ⊙ Wasting resources

Property Deviance
- ⊙ Sabotaging equipment
- ⊙ Accepting kickbacks
- ⊙ Lying about hours worked
- ⊙ Stealing from company

Minor ←————————→ **Serious**

Political Deviance
- ⊙ Showing favoritism
- ⊙ Gossiping about coworkers
- ⊙ Blaming coworkers
- ⊙ Competing nonbeneficially

Personal Aggression
- ⊙ Sexual harassment
- ⊙ Verbal abuse
- ⊙ Stealing from coworkers
- ⊙ Endangering coworkers

Interpersonal

Source: Republished with permission of Academy of Management, P.O. Box 3020, Briar Cliff Manor, NY, 10510-8020. "A Typology of Deviant Workplace Behaviors" (Figure), S. L. Robinson and R. J. Bennett. *Academy of Management Journal*, 1995, Vol. 38. Reproduced by permission of the publisher via Copyright Clearance Center, Inc.

brackets during the first two weeks of the tournament.[8] Lonnie Giamela, an attorney in Los Angeles, graduated from Georgetown University's law school. After Georgetown was eliminated from the recent tournament, he and his former law school classmates went on Facebook to chat about the game. Giamela noted, "Thirty different law offices across the country. At 800 bucks an hour, imagine the drain on law firms. . . "[9]

Property deviance is unethical behavior aimed at company property or products. Examples include sabotaging, stealing, or damaging equipment or products and overcharging for services and then pocketing the difference. Employee stealing is more widespread than you'd think. A survey of twenty-four large retailers employing 2.3 million workers found that one out of twenty-eight employees was caught stealing each year.[10] Likewise, 58 percent of office workers acknowledge taking company property for personal use, according to a survey conducted for Lawyers.com.[11]

Theft of company merchandise by employees, called **employee shrinkage**, is another common form of

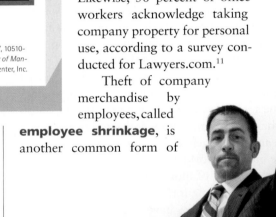

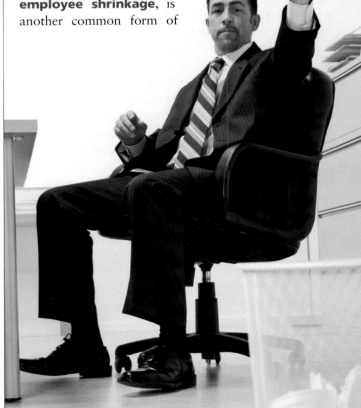

Company-related deviance can affect both tangible and intangible assets. One kind of workplace deviance, called **production deviance**, hurts the quality and quantity of work produced. Examples include leaving early, taking excessively long work breaks, intentionally working slower, or wasting resources. Every spring, employees fill out their tournament brackets for March Madness in hopes of winning office betting pools (which are technically illegal) for most accurately predicting which teams advance during the NCAA basketball tournament. Thanks to technology, employees can watch all of the games online or get updates via Twitter or special sports apps on their smartphones. Outplacement firm Challenger, Gray & Christmas estimates that employers will lose nearly 8.4 million work hours to employees who spend ninety minutes a day following their college teams or checking on their

Production deviance
unethical behavior that hurts the quality and quantity of work produced

Property deviance
unethical behavior aimed at the organization's property or products

Employee shrinkage
employee theft of company merchandise

property deviance. Employee shrinkage costs U.S. retailers more than $19.5 billion a year, and employees steal more merchandise (47 percent) than shoplifters (32 percent).[12] "Sweethearting" occurs when employees discount or don't ring up merchandise their family or friends bring to the cash register. In "dumpster diving," employees unload trucks, stash merchandise in a dumpster, and then retrieve it after work.[13]

Whereas production and property deviance harm companies, political deviance and personal aggression are unethical behaviors that hurt particular people within companies. **Political deviance** is using one's influence to harm others in the company. Examples include making decisions based on favoritism rather than performance, spreading rumors about coworkers, or blaming others for mistakes they didn't make. **Personal aggression** is hostile or aggressive behavior toward others. Examples include sexual harassment, verbal abuse, stealing from coworkers, or personally threatening coworkers. One of the fastest-growing kinds of personal aggression is workplace violence. More than 2 million Americans are victims of some form of workplace violence each year. According to a U.S. Bureau of Labor Statistics (BLS) survey of 7.4 million U.S. companies, 5.4 percent of all employees suffered an incident of workplace violence each year.[14] Between 525 and 1,000 people are actually killed at work each year.[15] For more information on workplace violence, see the BLS website, http://www.bls.gov/iif/osh_wpvs.htm.

4-2 *U.S. Sentencing Commission Guidelines for Organizations*

A male supervisor is sexually harassing female coworkers. A sales representative offers a $10,000 kickback to persuade an indecisive customer to do business with his company. A company president secretly meets with the CEO of her biggest competitor, and they agree not to compete in markets where the other has already established customers. Each of these behaviors is clearly unethical (and, in these cases, also illegal). Historically, if management was unaware of such activities, the company could not be held responsible for them. Since 1991, however, when the U.S. Sentencing Commission Guidelines for

Organizations were established, companies can be prosecuted and punished *even if management didn't know about the unethical behavior*. Penalties can be substantial, with maximum fines approaching a whopping $300 million.[16] An amendment made in 2004 outlines much stricter ethics training requirements and emphasizes creating a legal and ethical company culture.[17]

Let's examine **4-2a to whom the guidelines apply and what they cover** *and* **4-2b how, according to the guidelines, an organization can be punished for the unethical behavior of its managers and employees.**

4-2a WHO, WHAT, AND WHY?

Nearly all businesses are covered by the U.S. Sentencing Commission's guidelines. This includes nonprofits, partnerships, labor unions, unincorporated organizations and associations, incorporated organizations, and even pension funds, trusts, and joint stock companies. If your organization can be characterized as a business (remember, nonprofits count, too), then it is subject to the guidelines.[18]

The guidelines cover offenses defined by federal laws such as invasion of privacy, price fixing, fraud, customs violations, antitrust violations, civil rights violations, theft, money laundering, conflicts of interest, embezzlement, dealing in stolen goods, copyright infringements, extortion, and more. But it's not enough merely to stay within the law. The purpose of the guidelines is not just to punish companies *after* they or their employees break the law, but rather to encourage companies to take proactive steps that will discourage or prevent white-collar crime *before* it happens. The guidelines also give companies an incentive to cooperate with and disclose illegal activities to federal authorities.[19]

4-2b DETERMINING THE PUNISHMENT

The guidelines impose smaller fines on companies that take proactive steps to encourage ethical behavior or voluntarily disclose illegal activities to federal authorities. Essentially, the law uses a carrot-and-stick approach. The stick is the threat of heavy fines that can total millions of dollars. The carrot is a greatly reduced fine, but only if the company has started an effective compliance program (discussed below) to encourage

Political deviance using one's influence to harm others in the company

Personal aggression hostile or aggressive behavior toward others

EXHIBIT 4.2

Offense Levels, Base Fines, Culpability Scores, and Possible Total Fines under the U.S. Sentencing Commission Guidelines for Organizations

Offense Level	Base Fine	Culpability Scores 0.05	0.5	1.0	2.0	3.0	4.0
6 or less	$ 5,000	$ 250	$ 2,500	$ 5,000	$ 10,000	$ 15,000	$ 20,000
7	7,500	375	3,750	7,500	15,000	22,500	30,000
8	10,000	500	5,000	10,000	20,000	30,000	40,000
9	15,000	750	7,500	15,000	30,000	45,000	60,000
10	20,000	1,000	10,000	20,000	40,000	60,000	80,000
11	30,000	1,500	15,000	30,000	60,000	90,000	120,000
12	40,000	2,000	20,000	40,000	80,000	120,000	160,000
13	60,000	3,000	30,000	60,000	120,000	180,000	240,000
14	85,000	4,250	42,500	85,000	170,000	255,000	340,000
15	125,000	6,250	62,500	125,000	250,000	375,000	500,000
16	175,000	8,750	87,500	175,000	350,000	525,000	700,000
17	250,000	12,500	125,000	250,000	500,000	750,000	1,000,000
18	350,000	17,500	175,000	350,000	700,000	1,050,000	1,400,000
19	500,000	25,000	250,000	500,000	1,000,000	1,500,000	2,000,000
20	650,000	32,500	325,000	650,000	1,300,000	1,950,000	2,600,000
21	910,000	45,500	455,000	910,000	1,820,000	2,730,000	3,640,000
22	1,200,000	60,000	600,000	1,200,000	2,400,000	3,600,000	4,800,000
23	1,600,000	80,000	800,000	1,600,000	3,200,000	4,800,000	6,400,000
24	2,100,000	105,000	1,050,000	2,100,000	4,200,000	6,300,000	8,400,000
25	2,800,000	140,000	1,400,000	2,800,000	5,600,000	8,400,000	11,200,000
26	3,700,000	185,000	1,850,000	3,700,000	7,400,000	11,100,000	14,800,000
27	4,800,000	240,000	2,400,000	4,800,000	9,600,000	14,400,000	19,200,000
28	6,300,000	315,000	3,150,000	6,300,000	12,600,000	18,900,000	25,200,000
29	8,100,000	405,000	4,050,000	8,100,000	16,200,000	24,300,000	32,400,000
30	10,500,000	525,000	5,250,000	10,500,000	21,000,000	31,500,000	42,000,000
31	13,500,000	675,000	6,750,000	13,500,000	27,000,000	40,500,000	54,000,000
32	17,500,000	875,000	8,750,000	17,500,000	35,000,000	52,500,000	70,000,000
33	22,000,000	1,100,000	11,000,000	22,000,000	44,000,000	66,000,000	88,000,000
34	28,500,000	1,425,000	14,250,000	28,500,000	57,000,000	85,500,000	114,000,000
35	36,000,000	1,800,000	18,000,000	36,000,000	72,000,000	108,000,000	144,000,000
36	45,500,000	2,275,000	22,750,000	45,500,000	91,000,000	136,500,000	182,000,000
37	57,500,000	2,875,000	28,750,000	57,500,000	115,000,000	172,500,000	230,000,000
38 or more	72,500,000	3,625,000	36,250,000	72,500,000	145,000,000	217,500,000	290,000,000

Source: United States Sentencing Commission, *Guidelines Manual*, §3E1.1 (Nov. 2009), 509–531, accessed June 4, 2010, http://www.ussc.gov/2009guid/GL2009.pdf.

ethical behavior *before* the illegal activity occurs.[20] The method used to determine a company's punishment illustrates the importance of establishing a compliance program, as illustrated in Exhibit 4.2.

The first step is to compute the *base fine* by determining what *level of offense* has occurred. The level of the offense (i.e., its seriousness) varies depending on

the kind of crime, the loss incurred by the victims, and how much planning went into the crime. For example, simple fraud is a level 6 offense (there are thirty-eight levels in all). But if the victims of that fraud lost more than $5 million, that level 6 offense becomes a level 22 offense. Moreover, anything beyond minimal planning to commit the fraud results in an increase of two levels to a level 24 offense. How much difference would this make to a company? As Exhibit 4.2 shows, crimes at or below level 6 incur a base fine of $5,000, whereas the base fine for level 24 is $2.1 million, a difference of $2.095 million! The base fine for level 38, the top-level offense, is a hefty $72.5 million.

After assessing a *base fine*, the judge computes a culpability score, which is a way of assigning blame to the company. The culpability score can range from 0.05 to 4.0. The greater the corporate responsibility in conducting, encouraging, or sanctioning illegal or unethical activity, the higher the culpability score. A company that already has a compliance program and voluntarily reports the offense to authorities will incur a culpability score of 0.05. By contrast, a company whose management secretly plans, approves, and participates in illegal or unethical activity will receive the maximum score of 4.0.

The culpability score is critical because the total fine is computed by multiplying the base fine by the culpability score. Going back to our level 24 fraud offense, the left point of the upper arrow in Exhibit 4.2 shows that a company with a compliance program that turns itself in will be fined only $105,000 ($2,100,000 × 0.05). In contrast, a company that secretly planned, approved, and participated in illegal activity will be fined $8.4 million ($2,100,000 × 4.0), as shown by the right point of the upper arrow. The difference is even greater for level 38 offenses. As shown by the left point of the bottom arrow, a company with a compliance program and a 0.05 culpability score is fined only $3.625 million, whereas a company with the maximum 4.0 culpability score is fined a whopping $290 million, as indicated by the right point of the bottom arrow. These differences clearly show the importance of having a compliance program in place. Over the last decade, 1,494 companies have been charged under the U.S. Sentencing Guidelines. Seventy-six percent of those charged were fined, with the average fine exceeding $2 million. Company fines are on average twenty times larger now than before the implementation of the guidelines in 1991.[21]

Fortunately for companies that want to avoid paying these stiff fines, the U.S. Sentencing Guidelines clearly spell out the seven necessary components of an effective compliance program.[22] Exhibit 4.3 lists those components. Caremark International, a managed-care

EXHIBIT 4.3

Compliance Program Steps from the U.S. Sentencing Commission Guidelines for Organizations

Revise compliance program if required

7 **Improve** program after violations

1 **Establish** standards and procedures

2 **Assign** upper-level managers to be in charge

6 **Enforce** standards consistently and fairly

Delegate decision-making authority only to ethical employees 3

Train employees on standards and procedures

5

Encourage employees to report violations 4

Source: D. R. Dalton, M. B. Metzger, and J. W. Hill, "The 'New' U.S. Sentencing Commission Guidelines: A Wake-up Call for Corporate America," *Academy of Management Executive* 8 (1994): 7–16.

service provider in Delaware, pleaded guilty to criminal charges related to its physician contracts and improper patient referrals. When it was sued by shareholders for negligence and poor management, the Delaware court dismissed the case, ruling that the company's ethics compliance program, built on the components described in Exhibit 4.3, was a good-faith attempt to monitor employees and that the company did not knowingly allow illegal and unethical behavior to occur. The court went on to rule that a compliance program based on the U.S. Sentencing Guidelines was enough to shield the company from liability.[23]

4-3 Influences on Ethical Decision Making

On a cold morning in the midst of a winter storm, schools were closed and most people had decided to stay home from work.

Nevertheless, Richard Addessi had already showered, shaved, and dressed to go to work. He kissed his wife Joan goodbye, but before he could get to his car, he fell dead on the garage floor of a sudden heart attack. Addessi was four months short of his thirty-year anniversary with the company. Having begun work at IBM at the age of eighteen, he was just forty-eight years old.[24]

You're the vice president in charge of benefits at IBM. Given that he was only four months short of full retirement, do you award full retirement benefits to Richard Addessi's wife and daughters? If the answer is yes, they will receive his full retirement benefits of $1,800 a month and free lifetime medical coverage. If you say no, his widow and two daughters will receive only $340 a month. They will also have to pay $473 a month to continue their current medical coverage. As the VP in charge of benefits at IBM, what would be the ethical thing for you to do?

Although some ethical issues are easily solved, many do not have clearly right or wrong answers. But even though the answers are rarely clear, mangers do need to have a clear sense of *how* to arrive at an answer in order to manage this ethical ambiguity well.

The ethical answers that managers choose depend on **4-3a the ethical intensity of the decision,** *4-3b the* **moral development of the manager,** *and* **4-3c the ethical principles used to solve the problem.**

4-3a ETHICAL INTENSITY OF THE DECISION

Managers don't treat all ethical decisions the same. The manager who has to decide whether to deny or extend full benefits to Joan Addessi and her family is going to treat that decision much more seriously than the decision of how to deal with an assistant who has been taking paper home for personal use. These decisions differ in their **ethical intensity,** or the degree of concern people have about an ethical is-

sue. When addressing an issue of high ethical intensity, managers are more aware of the impact their decision will have on others. They are more likely to view the decision as an ethical or moral decision than as an economic decision. They are also more likely to worry about doing the right thing.

Six factors must be taken into account when determining the ethical intensity of an action, as shown in Exhibit 4.4. **Magnitude of consequences** is the total harm or benefit derived from an ethical decision. The more people who are harmed or the greater the harm to those people, the larger the consequences. **Social consensus** is agreement on whether behavior is bad or good. **Probability of effect** is the chance that something will happen that results in harm to others. If we combine these factors, we can see the effect they can have on ethical intensity. For example, if there is *clear agreement* (social consensus) that a managerial decision or action is *certain* (probability of effect) to have *large negative consequences* (magnitude of consequences) in some way, then people will be highly concerned about that managerial decision or action, and ethical intensity will be high.

Temporal immediacy is the time between an act and the consequences the act produces. Temporal immediacy is stronger if a manager has to lay off workers next week as opposed to three months from now. **Proximity of effect** is the social, psychological, cultural, or physical distance of a decision maker from those affected by his or her decisions. Thus, proximity of effect is greater when a manager lays off employees he knows than when he lays off employees that he doesn't know. Finally, whereas the magnitude of consequences is the total effect across all people, **concentration of effect** is how much an act affects the

© iStockphoto.com/Trevor Hunt

EXHIBIT 4.4 Six Factors That Contribute to Ethical Intensity

Magnitude of consequences

Social consensus

Probability of effect

Temporal immediacy

Proximity of effect

Concentration of effect

Source: Republished with permission of Academy of Management; P.O. Box 3020, Briar Cliff Manor, NY, 10510-8020. T.M. Jones, "Ethical Decision Making by Individuals in Organizations: An Issue Contingent Model," *Academy of Management Review* 16 (1991) 366–395; Reproduced by permission of the publisher via Copyright Clearance Center, Inc.

EXHIBIT 4.5

Kohlberg's Stages of Moral Development

Stage 1 Punishment and Obedience	Stage 2 Instrumental Exchange	Stage 3 Good Boy, Nice Girl	Stage 4 Law and Order	Stage 5 Social Contract	Stage 6 Universal Principle
Preconventional		Conventional		Postconventional	
Self-Interest		Societal Expectations		Internalized Principles	

© Cengage Learning

average person. Temporarily laying off 100 employees for ten months without pay has greater concentration of effect than temporarily laying off 1,000 employees for one month.

Which of these six factors has the most impact on ethical intensity? Studies indicate that managers are much more likely to view decisions as ethical issues when the magnitude of consequences (total harm) is high and there is a social consensus (agreement) that a behavior or action is bad.[25]

4-3b MORAL DEVELOPMENT

A friend of yours has given you the latest version of Microsoft Office. She stuffed the software disks in your backpack with a note saying that you should install it on your computer and get it back to her in a couple of days. You're tempted. No one would find out. Even if someone does, Microsoft probably isn't going to come after you. Microsoft goes after the big fish—companies that illegally copy and distribute software to their workers and pirates that illegally sell cheap unauthorized copies.[26] What are you going to do?

In part, according to psychologist Lawrence Kohlberg, your decision will be based on your level of moral development. Kohlberg identified three phases of moral development, with two stages in each phase (see Exhibit 4.5).[27] At the **preconventional level of moral development**, people decide based on selfish reasons. For example, if you are in Stage 1, the punishment and obedience stage, your primary concern will be to avoid trouble for yourself. So you won't copy the software, because you are afraid of being caught and punished. Yet, in Stage 2, the instrumental

exchange stage, you worry less about punishment and more about doing things that directly advance your wants and needs. So you copy the software.

People at the **conventional level of moral development** make decisions that conform to societal expectations. In other words, they look outside themselves to others for guidance on ethical issues. In Stage 3, the "good boy, nice girl" stage, you normally do what the other "good boys" and "nice girls" are doing. If everyone else is illegally copying software, you will, too. But if they aren't, you won't either.

Preconventional level of moral development the first level of moral development, in which people make decisions based on selfish reasons

Conventional level of moral development the second level of moral development, in which people make decisions that conform to societal expectations

Postconventional level of moral development

Conventional level of moral development

Preconventional level of moral development

© iStockphoto.com/Mike Kiev

Postconventional level of moral development the third level of moral development, in which people make decisions based on internalized principles

Principle of long-term self-interest an ethical principle that holds that you should never take any action that is not in your or your organization's long-term self-interest

In the law and order stage, Stage 4, you again look for external guidance and do whatever the law permits, so you won't copy the software.

People at the **postconventional level of moral development** use internalized ethical principles to solve ethical dilemmas. In Stage 5, the social contract stage, you will refuse to copy the software because, as a whole, society is better off when the rights of others—in this case, the rights of software authors and manufacturers—are not violated. In Stage 6, the universal principle stage, you might or might not copy the software, depending on your principles of right and wrong. Moreover, you will stick to your principles even if your decision conflicts with the law (Stage 4) or what others believe is best for society (Stage 5). For example, those with socialist or communist beliefs would probably choose to copy the software because they believe goods and services should be owned by society rather than by individuals and corporations.

Kohlberg believed that people would progress sequentially from earlier stages to later stages as they became more educated and mature. But only 20 percent of adults ever reach the postconventional stage of moral development, where internal principles guide their decisions. Most adults are in the conventional stage of moral development, in which they look outside themselves to others for guidance on ethical issues. This means that most people in the workplace look to and need leadership when it comes to ethical decision making.[28]

4-3c PRINCIPLES OF ETHICAL DECISION MAKING

Beyond an issue's ethical intensity and a manager's level of moral maturity, the particular ethical principles that managers use will also affect how they solve ethical dilemmas. Unfortunately, there is no one ideal principle to use in making ethical business decisions.

According to professor LaRue Hosmer, a number of different ethical principles can be used to make business decisions: long-term self-interest, personal virtue, religious injunctions, government requirements, utilitarian benefits, individual rights, and distributive justice.[29] All of these ethical principles encourage managers and employees to take others' interests into account when making ethical decisions. At the same time, however, these principles can lead to very different ethical actions, as we can see by using these principles to decide whether to award full benefits to Joan Addessi and her children.

According to the **principle of long-term self-interest**, you should never take any action that is not in your or your organization's long-term self-interest. Although this sounds as if the principle promotes

selfishness, it doesn't. What we do to maximize our long-term interests (save more, spend less, exercise every day, watch what we eat) is often very different from what we do to maximize short-term interests (max out our credit cards, be couch potatoes, eat whatever we want). At any given time, IBM has nearly 1,000 employees who are just months away from retirement. Thus, because of the costs involved, it serves IBM's long-term interest to pay full benefits only after employees have put in thirty full years.

The **principle of personal virtue** holds that you should never do anything that is not honest, open, and truthful and that you would not be glad to see reported in the newspapers or on TV. Using the principle of personal virtue, IBM might have quietly awarded Joan Addessi her husband's full benefits. Had it done so, it could have avoided the publication of an embarrassing *Wall Street Journal* article on this topic.

The **principle of religious injunctions** holds that you should never take an action that is unkind or that harms a sense of community, such as the positive feelings that come from working together to accomplish a commonly accepted goal. Using this principle, IBM would have been concerned foremost with compassion and kindness, and it would have awarded full benefits to Joan Addessi.

According to the **principle of government requirements**, the law represents the minimal moral standards of society, so you should never take any action that violates the law. Using this principle, IBM would deny full benefits to Joan Addessi because her husband did not work for the company for thirty years. Indeed, making exceptions would violate the federal Employee Retirement Income Security Act of 1974.

The **principle of utilitarian benefits** states that you should never take an action that does not result in greater good for society. In short, you should do whatever creates the greatest good for the greatest number. At first, this principle seems to suggest that IBM should award full benefits to Joan Addessi. If IBM did this with any regularity, however, the costs would be enormous, profits would shrink, and IBM would have to cut its stock dividend, harming countless shareholders, many of whom rely on IBM dividends for retirement income. In this case, the principle does not lead to a clear choice.

The **principle of individual rights** holds that you should never take an action that infringes on

others' agreed-upon rights. Using this principle, IBM would deny Joan Addessi full benefits. If it carefully followed the rules specified in its pension plan and granted Mrs. Addessi due process, meaning the right to appeal the decision, then IBM would not be violating her rights. In fact, it could be argued that providing full benefits to Mrs. Addessi would violate the rights of employees who had to wait thirty full years to receive full benefits.

Finally, under the **principle of distributive justice**, you should never take any action that harms the least fortunate among us in some way. This principle is designed to protect the poor, the uneducated, and the unemployed. Although Joan Addessi could probably find a job, it's unlikely that she could easily find one that would support her and her daughters in the manner to which they were accustomed after twenty years as a stay-at-home mom. Using the principle of distributive justice, IBM would award her full benefits.

So, what did IBM decide to do? Since Richard Addessi had not completed thirty full years with the company, IBM officials felt they had no choice but to give Joan Addessi and her two daughters the smaller, partial retirement benefits. Do you think IBM's decision was ethical? It's likely many of you don't. You may wonder how the company could be so heartless as to deny Richard Addessi's family the full benefits to which you believe they were entitled. Yet others might argue that IBM did the ethical thing by strictly following the rules laid out in its pension benefit plan. Indeed, an IBM spokesperson stated that making exceptions would violate the federal Employee Retirement Income Security Act of 1974. After all, being fair means applying the rules to everyone.

Principle of personal virtue an ethical principle that holds that you should never do anything that is not honest, open, and truthful and that you would not be glad to see reported in the newspapers or on TV

Principle of religious injunctions an ethical principle that holds that you should never take any action that is not kind and that does not build a sense of community

Principle of government requirements an ethical principle that holds that you should never take any action that violates the law, for the law represents the minimal moral standard

Principle of utilitarian benefits an ethical principle that holds that you should never take any action that does not result in greater good for society

Principle of individual rights an ethical principle that holds that you should never take any action that infringes on others' agreed-upon rights

Principle of distributive justice an ethical principle that holds that you should never take any action that harms the least fortunate among us: the poor, the uneducated, the unemployed

4-4 Practical Steps to Ethical Decision Making

Managers can encourage more ethical decision making in their organizations by **4-4a carefully selecting and hiring ethical employees, 4-4b establishing a specific code of ethics, 4-4c training employees to make ethical decisions,** and **4-4d creating an ethical climate.**

4-4a SELECTING AND HIRING ETHICAL EMPLOYEES

As an employer, how can you increase your chances of hiring honest employees, the kind who would return a wallet filled with money to its rightful owner? **Overt integrity tests** estimate job applicants' honesty by asking them directly what they think or feel about theft or about punishment of unethical behaviors.[30] For example, an employer might ask an applicant, "Would you ever consider buying something from somebody if you knew the person had stolen the item?" or "Don't most people steal from their companies?" Surprisingly, unethical people will usually answer "yes" to such questions, because they believe that the world is basically dishonest and that dishonest behavior is normal.[31]

Personality-based integrity tests indirectly estimate job applicants' honesty by measuring psychological traits such as dependability and conscientiousness. For example, prison inmates serving time for white-collar crimes (counterfeiting, embezzlement, and fraud) scored much lower than a comparison group of middle-level managers on scales measuring reliability, dependability, honesty, conscientiousness, and abiding by rules.[32] These results show that companies can selectively hire and promote people who will be more ethical.[33]

4-4b CODES OF ETHICS

Today, almost all large corporations have an ethics code in place. Even if a company has a code of ethics like this, two things must still happen if those codes are to encourage ethical decision making and behavior.[34] First, a company must communicate its code to others both inside and outside the company.

Second, in addition to having an ethics code with general guidelines like "do unto others as you would have others do unto you," management must also develop practical ethical standards and procedures specific to the company's line of business. Hershey's, the leading producer of chocolate and confectionary goods in North America, also does business in ninety countries. Visitors to Hershey's website can download the company's "Code of Ethical Business Conduct" in eight languages. The code sets specific ethical standards on topics ranging from treatment of coworkers, to protecting the environment, to maintenance of financial records. For example, the code states specifically, "If management, our auditors or government investigators request information or documentation from us, we must cooperate. This means we may not conceal, alter or destroy such information. Falsifying business records, destroying documents or lying to auditors, investigators or government officials is a serious offense." Likewise, Hershey's code states that information about competitors can only be obtained in legal and ethical ways and that it is wrong to attempt to pry confidential information from others. "If a coworker, customer or business partner has competitive information that they are required to keep confidential, we must not encourage them to disclose it."[35] Specific codes of ethics such as this make it much easier for employees to decide what to do when they want to do the right thing.

4-4c ETHICS TRAINING

In addition to establishing ethical standards for the company, managers must sponsor and be involved in ethics and compliance training in order to create an ethical company culture.[36] The first objective of ethics training is to develop employees' awareness of ethics.[37] This means helping employees recognize which issues are ethical issues and then avoiding rationalizing unethical behavior by thinking, "This isn't really illegal or immoral" or "No one will ever find out." Several companies have created board games to improve awareness of ethical issues.[38] Other ethics training tools, like the Kew Gardens Principles, examine how ethical decisions can be made in specific scenarios. The Kew Gardens Principles were based on the study of a murder in Kew Gardens, New York, in which witnesses to the attack

Overt integrity test a written test that estimates job applicants' honesty by directly asking them what they think or feel about theft or about punishment of unethical behaviors

Personality-based integrity test a written test that indirectly estimates job applicants' honesty by measuring psychological traits, such as dependability and conscientiousness

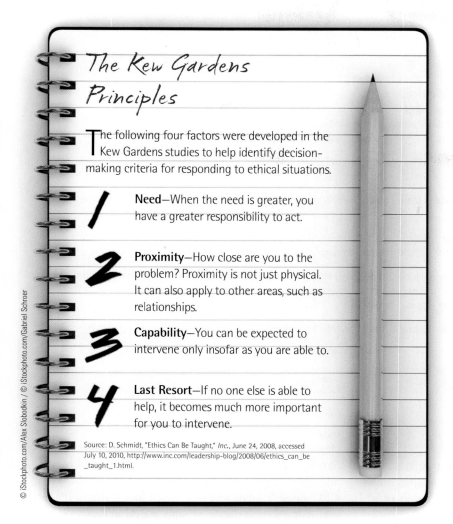

The Kew Gardens Principles

The following four factors were developed in the Kew Gardens studies to help identify decision-making criteria for responding to ethical situations.

1 **Need**—When the need is greater, you have a greater responsibility to act.

2 **Proximity**—How close are you to the problem? Proximity is not just physical. It can also apply to other areas, such as relationships.

3 **Capability**—You can be expected to intervene only insofar as you are able to.

4 **Last Resort**—If no one else is able to help, it becomes much more important for you to intervene.

Source: D. Schmidt, "Ethics Can Be Taught," *Inc.*, June 24, 2008, accessed July 10, 2010, http://www.inc.com/leadership-blog/2008/06/ethics_can_be_taught_1.html.

---

failed to intervene or seek help. Researchers developed a series of four decision-making factors that are used to help employees determine how they should respond to problems and ethical situations, even when the problems were not of their own doing (see box "The Kew Gardens Principles").[39] These decision-making factors can be applied to other scenarios as well. Specific company-related questions and scenarios make it easier for managers and employees to recognize and be aware of ethical issues and situations.

The second objective for ethics training programs is to achieve credibility with employees. Not surprisingly, employees can be highly suspicious of management's reasons for offering ethics training. Some companies have hurt the credibility of their ethics programs by having outside instructors and consultants conduct the classes.[40] Employees often complain that outside instructors and consultants are teaching theory that has nothing to do with their jobs and the practical dilemmas they actually face on a daily basis. CA Technologies made its ethics training practical and relevant by creating a

series of comical training videos with a fictional manager, Griffin Peabody, who is shown facing a series of ethics issues, such as conflicts of interest, competitive intelligence, workplace harassment, client expenses, and conduct outside of the workplace (search "Griffin Peabody" at YouTube.com). Chief ethics officer Joel Katz says, "It's easy for it [i.e., ethics training] to become a check-the-box exercise. We use Griffin's escapades to teach compliance lessons in a funny way." For instance, since CA Technologies acquires lots of companies—a common practice in technology industries—it's critical, and required by law, that its employees keep potential acquisitions confidential to prevent insider trading. Chief compliance officer Gary Brown says, "They think they can tell a friend, 'Guess what I was working on today.' They have to realize it is a much bigger problem." To reinforce this point, Griffin Peabody is visited by Securities and Exchange Commission investigators after publicly disclosing information about a company that is being acquired.[41]

Ethics training becomes even more credible when top managers teach the initial ethics classes to their subordinates who in turn teach their subordinates.[42] Michael Hoffman, executive director for the Center for Business Ethics at Bentley College, says that having managers teach ethics courses greatly reinforces the seriousness with which employees treat ethics in the workplace.[43] Unfortunately, though, 25 percent of large companies don't require top managers to attend, much less teach, ethics training.[44] The good news is that this scenario is changing thanks to the 2004 amendment to the Sentencing Guidelines. Indeed, a recent survey shows that board involvement in ethics and compliance programs jumped from 21 percent in 1987 to 96 percent in 2005.[45]

The third objective of ethics training is to teach employees a practical model of ethical decision making. A basic model should help them think about the consequences their choices will have on others and consider how they will choose between different solutions. Exhibit 4.6 on the next page presents a basic model of ethical decision making.

EXHIBIT 4.6

A Basic Model of Ethical Decision Making

1. **Identify the problem.** What makes it an ethical problem? Think in terms of rights, obligations, fairness, relationships, and integrity. How would you define the problem if you stood on the other side of the fence?

2. **Identify the constituents.** Who has been hurt? Who could be hurt? Who could be helped? Are they willing players, or are they victims? Can you negotiate with them?

3. **Diagnose the situation.** How did it happen in the first place? What could have prevented it? Is it going to get worse or better? Can the damage now be undone?

4. **Analyze your options.** Imagine the range of possibilities. Limit yourself to the two or three most manageable. What are the likely outcomes of each? What are the likely costs? Look to the company mission statement or code of ethics for guidance.

5. **Make your choice.** What is your intention in making this decision? How does it compare with the probable results? Can you discuss the problem with the affected parties before you act? Could you disclose without qualm your decision to your boss, the CEO, the board of directors, your family, or society as a whole?

6. **Act.** Do what you have to do. Don't be afraid to admit errors. Be as bold in confronting a problem as you were in causing it.

Source: L. A. Berger, "Train All Employees to Solve Ethical Dilemmas," *Best's Review—Life-Health Insurance Edition* 95 (1995): 70–80.

4-4d ETHICAL CLIMATE

Organizational culture is key to fostering ethical decision making. The 2009 National Business Ethics Survey reported that only 39 percent of employees who work at companies with a strong ethical culture (where core beliefs are widely shared and strongly held) have observed others engaging in unethical behavior, whereas 76 percent of those who work in organizations with weak ethical cultures (where core beliefs are not widely shared or strongly held) have observed others engage in unethical behavior. Employees in strong ethical cultures are also more likely to report violations, because they expect that management wants them reported and won't retaliate against them for doing so.[46]

The first step in establishing an ethical climate is for managers, especially top managers, to act ethically themselves. It's no surprise that in study after study, when researchers ask, "What is the most important influence on your ethical behavior at work?" the answer comes back, "My manager."

A second step in establishing an ethical climate is for top management to be active in and committed to the company ethics program.[47] Top managers who consistently talk about the importance of ethics and back up that talk by participating in their companies' ethics programs send the clear message that ethics matter. Business writer Dayton Fandray says, "You can have ethics offices and officers and training programs and reporting systems, but if the CEO doesn't seem to care, it's all just a sham. It's not surprising to find that the companies that really do care about ethics make a point of including senior management in all of their ethics and compliance programs."[48]

A third step is to put in place a reporting system that encourages managers and employees to report potential ethics violations. **Whistleblowing**, that is, reporting others' ethics violations, is a difficult step for most people to take.[49] Potential whistleblowers often fear that they, and not the ethics violators, will be punished.[50] Managers who have been interviewed about whistleblowing have said, "In every organization, someone's been screwed for standing up." "If anything, I figured that by taking a strong stand I might get myself in trouble. People might look at me as a goody two-shoes. Someone might try to force me out." An employee at Countrywide Financial Corporation, one of the biggest originators of subprime mortgage loans, was fired for uncovering numerous instances of wire, mail, and bank fraud among Countrywide employees. The fired employee also reported to federal officials that other employees who tried to speak up about the fraudulent activities were also fired. In a suit filed by the U.S. Department of Labor, Bank of America, which bought Countrywide, was ordered to

Whistleblowing reporting others' ethics violations to management or legal authorities

Social responsibility a business's obligation to pursue policies, make decisions, and take actions that benefit society

Shareholder model a view of social responsibility that holds that an organization's overriding goal should be profit maximization for the benefit of shareholders

pay a fine of $930,000 and reinstate the employee. David Michaels, an assistant secretary at the Department of Labor, said, "It's clear from our investigations that Bank of America used illegal retaliatory tactics against this employee. This employee showed great courage reporting potential fraud and standing up for the rights of other employees."[51]

The factor that does the most to discourage whistleblowers from reporting problems is lack of company action on their complaints.[52] Thus, the final step in developing an ethical climate is for management to fairly and consistently punish those who violate the company's code of ethics. Netflix immediately fired an employee at a Netflix call center who was caught stealing credit card information from the customers she was supposed to be helping. Netflix spokesperson Steve Swaswy said, "We do everything we can to safeguard our members' personal data and privacy, and when there's an issue like this we deal with it swiftly and decisively."[53] Amazingly, though, not all companies fire ethics violators. In fact, 8 percent of surveyed companies admit that they would promote top performers even if they violated ethical standards.[54]

4-5 *To Whom Are Organizations Socially Responsible?*

Social responsibility is a business's obligation to pursue policies, make decisions, and take actions that benefit society.[55] Unfortunately, because there are strong disagreements over to whom and for what in society organizations are responsible,

it can be difficult for managers to know what is or will be perceived as socially responsible corporate behavior. In a recent McKinsey & Company study of 1,144 top global executives, 79 percent predicted that at least some responsibility for dealing with future social and political issues would fall on corporations, but only 3 percent said they themselves do a good job of dealing with these issues.[56] So what should managers and corporations do to be socially responsible?

There are two perspectives regarding to whom organizations are socially responsible: the shareholder model and the stakeholder model. According to the late Nobel Prize–winning economist Milton Friedman, the only social responsibility that organizations have is to satisfy their owners, that is, company shareholders. This view—called the **shareholder model**—holds that the only social responsibility that businesses have is to maximize profits. By maximizing profit, the firm maximizes shareholder wealth and satisfaction. More specifically, as profits rise, the company stock owned by shareholders generally increases in value.

Friedman argued that it is socially irresponsible for companies to divert time, money, and attention from maximizing profits to social causes and charitable organizations. The first problem, he believed, is that organizations cannot act effectively as moral agents for all company shareholders. Although shareholders are likely to agree on investment issues concerning a company, it's highly unlikely that they have common views on what social causes a company should or should not support.

The second major problem, Friedman said, is that the time, money, and attention diverted to social causes undermine market efficiency.[57] In competitive markets, companies compete for raw materials, talented workers, customers, and investment funds. A company that spends money on social causes will have less money to purchase quality materials or to hire talented workers

Stakeholder model a theory of corporate responsibility that holds that management's most important responsibility, long-term survival, is achieved by satisfying the interests of multiple corporate stakeholders

Stakeholders persons or groups with a "stake," or legitimate interest, in a company's actions

who can produce a valuable product at a good price. If customers find the company's product less desirable, its sales and profits will fall. If profits fall, the company's stock price will decline, and the company will have difficulty attracting investment funds that could be used to fund long-term growth. In the end, Friedman argues, diverting the firm's money, time, and resources to social causes hurts customers, suppliers, employees, and shareholders. Russell Roberts, an economist at George Mason University, agrees, saying, "Doesn't it make more sense to have companies do what they do best, make good products at fair prices, and then let consumers use the savings for the charity of their choice?"[58]

By contrast, under the **stakeholder model**, management's most important responsibility is the firm's long-term survival (not just maximizing profits), which is achieved by satisfying the interests of multiple corporate stakeholders (not just shareholders).[59] **Stakeholders** are persons or groups with a legitimate interest in a company.[60] Since stakeholders are interested in and affected by the organization's actions, they have a "stake" in what those actions are. PepsiCo CEO Indra Nooyi says that because stakeholders are multifaceted, with different interests, a company operating under the stakeholder model has to redefine "profit." She says, "[we] have to make sure our new P & L (profit & loss statement) actually says revenue, less costs of goods sold, less costs to society—and that's your real profit."[61]

Stakeholder groups may try to influence the firm to act in their own interests. Exhibit 4.7 shows the various stakeholder groups that the organization must satisfy to assure its long-term survival. Being responsible to multiple stakeholders raises two basic questions. First, how does a company identify organizational stakeholders? Second, how does a company balance the needs of different stakeholders? Distinguishing

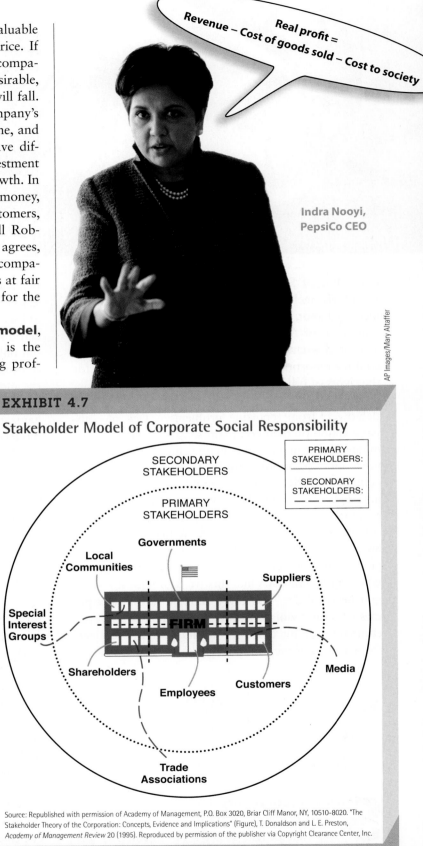

Real profit = Revenue – Cost of goods sold – Cost to society

Indra Nooyi, PepsiCo CEO

AP Images/Mary Altaffer

EXHIBIT 4.7

Stakeholder Model of Corporate Social Responsibility

PRIMARY STAKEHOLDERS:

SECONDARY STAKEHOLDERS: – – – –

SECONDARY STAKEHOLDERS

PRIMARY STAKEHOLDERS

Governments

Local Communities

Suppliers

Special Interest Groups

FIRM

Shareholders

Media

Employees

Customers

Trade Associations

Source: Republished with permission of Academy of Management, P.O. Box 3020, Briar Cliff Manor, NY, 10510-8020. "The Stakeholder Theory of the Corporation: Concepts, Evidence and Implications" (Figure), T. Donaldson and L. E. Preston, *Academy of Management Review* 20 (1995). Reproduced by permission of the publisher via Copyright Clearance Center, Inc.

between primary and secondary stakeholders can help answer these questions.[62]

Some stakeholders are more important to the firm's survival than others. **Primary stakeholders** are groups on which the organization depends for its long-term survival; they include shareholders, employees, customers, suppliers, governments, and local communities. When managers are struggling to balance the needs of different stakeholders, the stakeholder model suggests that the needs of primary stakeholders take precedence over the needs of secondary stakeholders. But among primary stakeholders, are some more important than others? According to the life-cycle theory of organizations, the answer is yes. In practice, the answer is also yes, as CEOs typically give somewhat higher priority to shareholders, employees, and customers than to suppliers, governments, and local communities, no matter what stage of the life cycle a company is in.[63] Addressing the concerns of primary stakeholders is important because if a stakeholder group becomes dissatisfied and terminates its relationship with the company, the company could be seriously harmed or go out of business.

Secondary stakeholders, such as the media and special interest groups, can influence or be influenced by the company. Unlike the primary stakeholders, however, they do not engage in regular transactions with the company and are not critical to its long-term survival. Meeting the needs of primary stakeholders is therefore usually more important than meeting the needs of secondary stakeholders. Nevertheless, secondary stakeholders are still important because they can affect public perceptions and opinions about socially responsible behavior.

For instance, PETA, People for the Ethical Treatment of Animals, is calling for a total boycott of Australia's $2.2 billion wool industry. With an aggressive ad campaign entitled, "Did your sweater cause a bloody butt?" PETA wants Australia's 55,000 sheep farmers to stop the practice of "mulesing," which it considers cruel. Mulesing removes skin folds from a sheep's rear end, usually without anesthesia, to prevent the animal from becoming infested with blow-fly eggs, which turn into flesh-eating maggots. PETA has convinced thirty leading fashion retailers, such as Benetton, Abercrombie & Fitch, Timberland, H&M, and Hugo Boss, to stop using Australian wool. PETA spokesperson Matt Prescott says, "Approaching companies with big names and deep pockets is the best way to drive change."[64] Craig Johnston, an Australian farmer with 6,000 merino sheep, says, "We don't

mules to be cruel, we do it because it's the best husbandry practice available. Once a sheep suffers flystrike you are at a loss to do anything."[65] Still, as a result of PETA's pressure, Australian Wool Innovation, the industry's trade group, is sponsoring research to develop alternatives to mulesing.[66]

So, to whom are organizations socially responsible? Many commentators, especially economists and financial analysts, continue to argue that organizations are responsible only to shareholders. Increasingly, however, top managers have come to believe that they and their companies must be socially responsible to their stakeholders. Today, surveys show that as many as 80 percent of top-level managers believe that it is unethical to focus just on shareholders. Twenty-nine states have changed their laws to allow company boards of directors to consider the needs of employees, creditors, suppliers, customers, and local communities, as well as those of shareholders.[67] Although there is not complete agreement, a majority of opinion makers would argue that companies must be socially responsible to their stakeholders.

4-6 For What Are Organizations Socially Responsible?

If organizations are to be socially responsible to stakeholders, what are they to be socially responsible *for*? Companies can best benefit their stakeholders by fulfilling their economic, legal, ethical, and discretionary responsibilities.[68] Economic and legal responsibilities are at the bottom of the pyramid because they play a larger part in a company's social responsibility than do ethical and discretionary responsibilities. However, the relative importance of these various responsibilities depends on society's expectations of corporate social responsibility at a particular point in time.[69] A century ago, society expected businesses to meet their economic and legal responsibilities and little else. Today, when society judges whether businesses are socially responsible, ethical and discretionary responsibilities are considerably more important than they used to be (see box "Doing the Right Thing").

Economic responsibility
a company's social responsibility to make a profit by producing a valued product or service

Legal responsibility a company's social responsibility to obey society's laws and regulations

Historically, **economic responsibility**, or making a profit by producing a product or service valued by society, has been a business's most basic social responsibility. Organizations that don't meet their financial and economic expectations come under tremendous pressure. For example, company boards are quick these days to fire CEOs. Typically, all it takes is two or three bad quarters in a row. Owen Van Natta, CEO of MySpace, was fired after just eight months on the job. When he started, MySpace had 64 percent of social networking traffic, compared to 29 percent for Facebook. When he was fired, Facebook had 68 percent and MySpace had 28 percent.[70] William Rollnick, who became acting chairman of Mattel after the company fired its previous CEO, says, "There's zero forgiveness. You screw up and you're dead."[71] On an annual basis, roughly 4 percent of the CEOs of large companies are fired each year.[72] Nearly one-third of all CEOs are eventually fired because of their inability to successfully change their companies.[73] In fact, CEOs are three times more likely to be fired today than they were two decades ago.

Legal responsibility is a company's social responsibility to obey society's laws and regulations as it tries to meet its economic responsibilities. For in-

AP Images/Matt Dunham

stance, companies award stock options so that managers and employees are rewarded when the company does well. Stock options give you the right to purchase shares of stock at a set price. Let's say that on June 1, the company awards you the right (or option) to buy 100 shares of stock, which, on that day, sell for $10 a share. If the stock price falls below $10, the options are worthless. But, if the stock price rises above $10, the options have value. Specifically, if the stock price rises to $15 a share, you can exercise your option by paying the company $1,000 (100 shares at $10 a share). But because the stock is selling for $15, you can sell your 100 shares for $1,500 and make $500. But what

DOING THE RIGHT THING

Almost every company, it seems, is bragging about how they care about the environment, whether it's car companies touting their fuel-efficient vehicles or computer makers talking about how they recycle electronic components. Most consumers, however, don't believe that companies are committed to being green. According to a Harris Interactive poll, just 16 percent of consumers believe that most companies are committed to improving the environment by practicing sustainable business or offering environmentally responsible products. Forty-eight percent of consumers believe that some companies are committed to that goal, while 24 percent believe that only a few companies are so committed. So what can managers do? Ron Loch, vice president for greentech and sustainability at Gibbs & Soell, says, "As long as companies are transparent in their communications and don't overstate the social and environmental impact of their efforts, they can avoid being painted with the greenwash brush. It gets back to the need of really taking inventory of what is happening throughout the organization and then weaving that into a compelling, credible and defensible narrative." So do the right thing—don't talk about being green just to get consumers' attention. Make sure that the message you send out to consumers reflects the social responsibility commitments that your company has made.

Source: M. Dolliver, "Thumbs Down on Corporate Green Efforts," Adweek.com, August 31, 2010, http://www.adweek.com/aw/content_display/news/client/e3i84260d4301c885f91b2cd8a712f323cf.

© iStockphoto.com/Juanmonino

if you could go back in time to, say, January 1 when the stock was selling for $5? You'd make $1,000 instead of $500. It would be unethical and illegal, however, to "backdate" your option to when the stock sold for a lower price. Doing so would illegally increase the value of your option. But that's exactly what the president and chief operating officer did at Monster Worldwide (which runs Monster.com). By improperly backdating his option, he earned an additional $24 million.[74] At Monster, however, backdating was condoned by the CEO, who routinely backdated options for members of the management team.[75]

Ethical responsibility is a company's social responsibility not to violate accepted principles of right and wrong when conducting its business. News Corporation, owned by billionaire Rupert Murdoch, which owns the *Wall Street Journal* and Fox News, is a global media company offering network programming, films, television shows, direct broadcast satellite television, and publishing, primarily in the United States, the United Kingdom, and Australia. News Corporation shut down *News of the World*, the best-selling Sunday newspaper in the UK, after it was discovered that its reporters tapped into voice mails in pursuit of stories, including those of murdered children, family members of war dead, and relatives of people killed in the 2005 London terrorist attacks. James Murdoch, News Corporation's then deputy chief operating officer who eventually resigned his position because of the scandal, said that the newspaper's reputation had been "sullied by behavior that was wrong." On the shutting down of the newspaper, he went on to say, "The *News of the World* is in the business of holding others to account. But it failed when it came to itself." Former reader Kandice Kameka said, "When I found out about the tapping with the murder victim I was just gobsmacked—I didn't want anything to do with it after that. They just have no respect for people."[76]

Discretionary responsibilities pertain to the social roles that businesses play in society beyond their economic, legal, and ethical responsibilities. After an earthquake and tsunami devastated the eastern coast of Japan, killing nearly 16,000 people, a number of companies took immediate action to provide aid and relief for survivors. Honda donated 300 million yen (about $3.7 million) to fund rescue operations and gave away 1,000 portable generators to those left without power. IKEA Japan gave away furniture and household items to 15,000 families living in temporary homes in the two regions most affected by the disaster. Meanwhile, SoftBank, a Japanese telecommunications and Internet company, announced that its CEO, Masayoshi Son, would be donating not only $120 million of his own money to relief funds but also his entire salary every year until his retirement.[77]

Carrying out discretionary responsibilities such as these is voluntary. Companies are not considered unethical if they don't perform them. Today, however, corporate stakeholders expect companies to do much more than in the past to meet their discretionary responsibilities.

4-7 Responses to Demands for Social Responsibility

Social responsiveness refers to a company's strategy to respond to stakeholders' economic, legal, ethical, or discretionary expectations concerning social responsibility. A social responsibility problem exists whenever company actions do not meet stakeholder expectations. One model of social responsiveness identifies four strategies for responding to social responsibility problems: reactive, defensive, accommodative, and proactive. These strategies differ in the extent to which the company is willing to act to meet or exceed society's expectations.

A company using a **reactive strategy** will do less than society expects. It may deny responsibility for a problem or fight any suggestions that the company should solve a problem. By contrast, a company using a **defensive strategy** would admit responsibility for a problem but would do the least required to meet societal expectations. Foxconn is a Taiwanese electronics manufacturing company that operates Chinese factories that produce 40 percent of the world's consumer electronic products. Over the last four

Ethical responsibility a company's social responsibility not to violate accepted principles of right and wrong when conducting its business

Discretionary responsibilities the social roles that a company fulfills beyond its economic, legal, and ethical responsibilities

Social responsiveness refers to a company's strategy to respond to stakeholders' economic, legal, ethical, or discretionary expectations concerning social responsibility

Reactive strategy a social responsiveness strategy in which a company does less than society expects

Defensive strategy a social responsiveness strategy in which a company admits responsibility for a problem but does the least required to meet societal expectations

years, at the Foxconn factories that make iPhones and iPads, eighteen employees attempted suicide, most by leaping to their deaths. After the eleventh suicide, the company placed suicide nets that reach twenty feet out around the perimeter of each building. An extensive *New York Times* investigation found that employees often worked seven days a week, were exposed to dangerous chemicals, and lived in crowded, company-supplied dorm rooms, some with as many as twenty people per three-bedroom apartment. However, Apple, which had been conducting audits of its suppliers' manufacturing facilities for many years, was slow to respond. A consultant with Business for Social Responsibility, a company Apple hired for advice on labor issues, said, "We've spent years telling Apple there are serious problems and recommending changes. They don't want to pre-empt problems, they just want to avoid embarrassments." A former Apple executive said, "If you see the same pattern of problems, year after year, that means the company's ignoring the issue rather than solving it. Noncompliance is tolerated, as long as the suppliers promise to try harder next time. If we meant business, core violations would disappear." After the *New York Times* story, Apple began working with the Fair Labor Association, a nonprofit organization that promotes and monitors safe working conditions. Four years after the problems began, following the Fair Labor Association's report, Apple and Foxconn agreed to increase pay, limit workers to a maximum of forty-nine hours a week, build more dormitories, and hire thousands of additional workers. [78]

A company using an **accommodative strategy** will accept responsibility for a problem and take a progressive approach by doing all that could be expected to solve the problem. Unilever, one of the world's largest consumer product companies, annually buys 1.5 million tons of palm oil to be used in margarine, ice cream, soap, and shampoo. Greenpeace protestors dressed as orangutans and climbed to the top of the company's headquarters in London to draw attention to the palm oil suppliers, who they claimed were destroying palm forests in Indonesia and Malaysia. Emulating an award-winning Dove soap commercial, "Evolution," Greenpeace then produced a short video entitled "Dove Onslaught(er)," which attributed the use of palm oil in Unilever's Dove soap to deforestation of palm forests (see both on YouTube.com). [79] Unilever accepted responsibility for the problem, stating, ". . . following a public challenge from Greenpeace, we formalized our commitment to draw all our palm oil from certified sustainable sources by 2015. We also agreed to support a moratorium on any further deforestation in South-East Asia." [80] Unilever also formed a coalition of fifty companies and nonprofits to influence palm oil growers, introduced resolutions at the Roundtable on Sustainable Palm Oil to encourage palm oil growers to change their foresting practices, began audits of its palm oil suppliers to make sure their practices were consistent with its new recommendations, and began working with Greenpeace and other groups to promote change in the industry.

Finally, a company using a **proactive strategy** will anticipate responsibility for a problem before it occurs, do more than expected to address the problem, and lead the industry in its approach. Two decades ago, Merck, a pharmaceutical company, began giving away its drug for river blindness, which thrives and spreads easily along fertile riverbanks in Africa and Latin America. River blindness affects 37 million people worldwide and could infect up to 100 million others. [81] Merck's drug program is the largest ongoing medical donation program in history. Since 1987, Merck has given away 530 million treatments at a cost of $3.75 billion. The World Health Organization now believes that, thanks to Merck's contributions, river blindness is on the verge of being completely eliminated in Africa. [82]

4-8 Social Responsibility and Economic Performance

One question that managers often ask is, "Does it pay to be socially responsible?" In previous editions of this textbook, the answer was "no," as early research indicated that there was not an inherent relationship between social responsibility and economic performance. [83] Recent research, however, leads to different conclusions. There is no trade-off between being socially responsible and economic performance. [84] And there is a small, positive relationship between being socially responsible and economic

A Really Green Car

The 2012 Fisker Karma is a plug-in hybrid vehicle that aims to combine luxurious design and exhilarating performance with environmental responsibility. Its primary "green" feature is the engine, which combines an electric motor with a traditional gas-powered motor. There are, however, numerous other aspects of the car that reflect sustainable design and production. The shimmer of the exterior, for example, comes from crushed up bits of recycled glass that are mixed into the paint. All of the interior fabric is made of recycled materials, and the wood paneling on its doors is made from fallen or rescued wood, such that no tree is ever cut down for material. The car's roof, meanwhile, is covered with solar panels that help power the accessories and recharge the battery.

Source: "Review: Fisker Karma, Sustainable Style," TheSmokingTire.com, February 6, 2012, accessed February 28, 2012, http://www.thesmokingtire.com/2012/review-fisker-karma-sustainable-style/.

© FABRICE COFFRINI/AFP/Getty Images

performance that strengthens with corporate reputation.[85] Let's explore what each of these results means.

First, there is no trade-off between being socially responsible and economic performance.[86] Being socially responsible usually won't make a business less profitable. What this suggests is that the costs of being socially responsible—and those costs can be high, especially early on—can be offset by a better product or corporate reputation, which results in stronger sales or higher profit margins. For example, Honda, which introduced the first hybrid car in North America, has long been an industry leader in fuel efficiency and environmentally friendly technology. So when it decided to enter the private plane market with the new HondaJet, it took the same approach, using lightweight composite materials, instead of metal alloys, in the plane's body and working closely with General Electric to design an efficient, lightweight, powerful engine, that when mounted—in a unique design—above the wings, further reduced fuel consumption. These features not only help the HondaJet use less fuel, but they also make the HondaJet lighter and faster than competitors. The unique engine and wing design gives it more interior space, reduces cabin noise, and makes it cheaper to operate. And, while it seats a pilot and just four passengers, the cost of flying the HondaJet will be no more expensive on a per-mile basis than the common Canadair CRJ-200 regional jet, which transports forty to fifty passengers. Honda believes that its socially responsible design is the key to making the HondaJet profitable.[87]

Second, it usually *does* pay to be socially responsible, and that relationship becomes stronger particularly when a company or its products have a strong reputation for social responsibility.[88] For example, GE, long one of the most admired and profitable corporations in the world, was one of the first and largest *Fortune* 500 companies to make a strategic commitment to providing environmentally friendly products and services. CEO Jeffrey Immelt wants GE to "develop and drive the technologies of the future that will protect and clean our environment."[89] Is Immelt doing this because of personal beliefs? He says no. "It's no great thrill for me to do this stuff . . . I never put it in right versus wrong terms." GE calls its strategy "ecoimagination," which it says is "helping to solve the world's biggest environmental challenges while driving profitable growth for GE." Says Immelt, "We invest in the basic strategies that we think are going to fit into [ecoimagination], but make money for our investors at the same time."[90] In just five years, GE has increased the number of ecoimagination products from seventeen to eighty. As a result, it now sells more than $17 billion of such products and services each year, with annual revenue growth increasing by double digits.[91]

Finally, even if there is generally a small positive relationship between social responsibility and economic performance that becomes stronger when a company or its products have a positive reputation for social responsibility, and even if there is no trade-off between being socially responsible and economic performance, there is no guarantee that socially responsible companies will be profitable. Simply put, socially responsible companies experience the same ups and downs in economic performance that traditional businesses do. A good example is Ben & Jerry's, the ice cream company. Ben & Jerry's is as famous for its commitment to social responsibility as it is for its super premium ice cream, as it donates 7.5 percent of its pretax profits to support AIDS patients, homeless people, and the environment.[92] As cofounder Ben Cohen says, "We see ourselves as somewhat of a social service agency and somewhat of an ice cream company."[93] But—and this is a big "but"—despite its outstanding reputation as a socially responsible company, Ben & Jerry's consistently had financial troubles after going public (selling shares of stock to the public) fifteen years ago. In fact, its financial problems became so severe that Cohen and fellow cofounder Jerry Greenfield sold the company to British-based Unilever.[94] Being socially responsible may be the right thing to do, and it is usually associated with increased profits, but it doesn't guarantee business success.

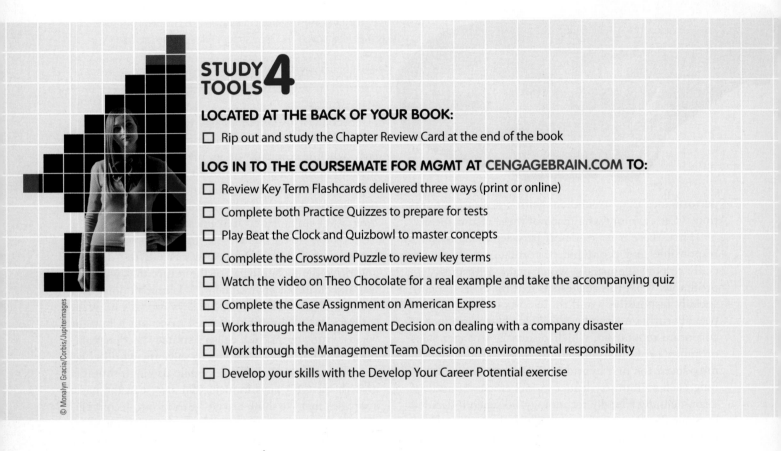

STUDY TOOLS 4

LOCATED AT THE BACK OF YOUR BOOK:

☐ Rip out and study the Chapter Review Card at the end of the book

LOG IN TO THE COURSEMATE FOR MGMT AT CENGAGEBRAIN.COM TO:

☐ Review Key Term Flashcards delivered three ways (print or online)

☐ Complete both Practice Quizzes to prepare for tests

☐ Play Beat the Clock and Quizbowl to master concepts

☐ Complete the Crossword Puzzle to review key terms

☐ Watch the video on Theo Chocolate for a real example and take the accompanying quiz

☐ Complete the Case Assignment on American Express

☐ Work through the Management Decision on dealing with a company disaster

☐ Work through the Management Team Decision on environmental responsibility

☐ Develop your skills with the Develop Your Career Potential exercise

© Monalyn Gracia/Corbis/Jupiterimages

The costs of being socially responsible can be offset by a better product or corporate reputation, which results in stronger sales or higher profit margins.

WHY CHOOSE?

Every 4LTR Press solution comes complete with a visually engaging textbook in addition to an interactive eBook. Go to CourseMate for MGMT to begin using the eBook. Access at **www.cengagebrain.com**

Complete the Speak Up survey in CourseMate at **www.cengagebrain.com**

 Follow us at www.facebook.com/4ltrpress

©iStockphoto/A-Digit | © Cengage Learning 2011

5 Planning and Decision Making

LEARNING OUTCOMES

5-1 Discuss the benefits and pitfalls of planning.

5-2 Describe how to make a plan that works.

5-3 Discuss how companies can use plans at all management levels, from top to bottom.

5-4 Explain the steps and limits to rational decision making.

5-5 Explain how group decisions and group decision-making techniques can improve decision making.

CHECK OUT **STUDY TOOLS** AT THE END OF THIS CHAPTER.

© 2006 LOOK Photography/Jupiterimages

© Mihalyn Gracia/Corbis/Jupiterimages

5-1 *Benefits and Pitfalls of Planning*

Even inexperienced managers know that planning and decision making are central parts of their jobs. Figure out what the problem is. Generate potential solutions or plans. Pick the best one. Make it work. Experienced managers, however, know how hard it really is to make good plans and decisions. One seasoned manager says: "I think the biggest surprises are the problems. Maybe I had never seen it before. Maybe I was protected by my management when I was in sales. Maybe I had delusions of grandeur, I don't know. I just know how disillusioning and frustrating it is to be hit with problems and conflicts all day and not be able to solve them very cleanly."[1]

Planning is choosing a goal and developing a method or strategy to achieve that goal. Having succeeded in the United States, where it is now the second-largest foreign carmaker, selling 1.1 million low-priced, high-quality, feature-rich cars per year, Hyundai and its Kia subsidiary are planning to expand in Europe. With a 5.1 percent share of the European market, it plans to expand sales by 25 percent to 500,000 cars per year by 2013. To accomplish the plan, Hyundai will introduce new models, like the i40, Veloster, and i30, all of which have been designed and styled specifically to suit European consumer tastes. The company will also add a third shift to its factory in the Czech Republic and expand annual production there by 100,000 cars. Stefan Bratzel, director of the Center of Automotive Management at the University of Applied Sciences in Bergisch Gladbach, Germany, says, "Hyundai is one of VW's most serious challengers. The mix of good value, quality, and design is a solid basis, and they've been getting more innovative every year."[2]

Are you one of those naturally organized people who always makes a daily to-do list, writes everything down so you won't forget, and never misses a deadline because you keep track of everything with your handy time-management notebook or iPhone or PC? Or are you one of those flexible, creative, go-with-the-flow people who dislikes planning and organizing because it restricts your freedom, energy, and performance? Some people are natural planners. They love it and can see only its benefits. Others dislike planning and can see only its disadvantages. It turns out that *both* views have real value.

*Planning has advantages and disadvantages. Let's learn about **5-1a the benefits** and **5-1b the pitfalls of planning**.*

5-1a BENEFITS OF PLANNING

Planning offers several important benefits: intensified effort, persistence, direction, and creation of task strategies.[3] First, managers and employees put forth greater effort when following a plan. Take two workers. Instruct one to "do your best" to increase production, and instruct the other to achieve a 2 percent increase in production each month. Research shows that the one with the specific plan will work harder.[4]

Second, planning leads to persistence, that is, working hard for long periods. In fact, planning encourages persistence even when there may be little chance of short-term success.[5] McDonald's founder Ray Kroc, a keen believer in the power of

> **Planning** choosing a goal and developing a strategy to achieve that goal

persistence, had this quotation from President Calvin Coolidge hung in all of his executives' offices: "Nothing in the world can take the place of persistence. Talent will not; nothing is more common than unsuccessful men with talent. Genius will not; unrewarded genius is almost a proverb. Education will not; the world is full of educated derelicts. Persistence and determination alone are omnipotent."[6]

The third benefit of planning is direction. Plans encourage managers and employees to direct their persistent efforts *toward* activities that help accomplish their goals and *away* from activities that don't.[7] The fourth benefit of planning is that it encourages the development of task strategies. In other words, planning not only encourages people to work hard for extended periods and to engage in behaviors directly related to goal accomplishment, it also encourages them to think of better ways to do their jobs. Finally, perhaps the most compelling benefit of planning is that it has been proved to work for both companies and individuals. On average, companies with plans have larger profits and grow much faster than companies that don't.[8] The same holds true for individual managers and employees: There is no better way to improve the performance of the people who work in a company than to have them set goals and develop strategies for achieving those goals.

5-1b PITFALLS OF PLANNING

Despite the significant benefits associated with planning, it is not a cure-all. Plans won't fix all organizational problems. In fact, many management authors and consultants believe that planning can harm companies in several ways.[9]

The first pitfall of planning is that it can impede change and prevent or slow needed adaptation. Sometimes companies become so committed to achieving the goals set forth in their plans, or on following the strategies and tactics spelled out in them, that they fail to see that their plans aren't working or that their goals need to change. For nearly a century, Kodak dominated the photography business, as it was world famous for its photo paper, its cameras, and especially its film. However, its commitment to film ultimately proved disastrous as its business turned digital. The tragic irony, of course, is that Kodak engineers invented digital photography in 1975 but didn't pursue the technology out of fear that it would destroy its highly profitable film business. So while other photo companies were busy remaking themselves for the digital age (Canon, for example, stopped selling its last film camera in 2004), Kodak still dedicated most of its resources to the film market, resulting in huge losses. Since 2003, Kodak has closed thirteen factories and laid off 47,000 employees at a cost of $3.4 billion. With a debt of $6.8 billion and losses in six of the past seven years, Kodak was forced to declare Chapter 11 bankruptcy. Don Strickland, a former Kodak vice president for digital imaging, said "Out of the bankruptcy proceedings, a much smaller company can emerge. But I really don't believe that there's going to be another Kodak moment."[10]

The second pitfall is that planning can create a false sense of certainty. Planners sometimes feel that they know exactly what the future holds for their competitors, their suppliers, and their companies. However, all plans are based on assumptions: "The price of gasoline will increase by 4 percent per year"; "Exports will continue to rise." For plans to work, the assumptions on which they are based must hold true. If the assumptions turn out to be false, then the plans based on them are likely to fail.

The third potential pitfall of planning is the detachment of planners. In theory, strategic planners and top-level managers are supposed to focus on the big picture and not concern themselves with the details of implementation (i.e., carrying out the plan). According to management professor Henry Mintzberg, detachment leads planners to plan for things they don't understand.[11] Plans are meant to be guidelines for action, not abstract theories. Consequently, planners need to be familiar with the daily details of their businesses if they are to produce plans that can work.

Andrew Cosslett, CEO of InterContinental Hotels in London, describes one of his earliest experiences working as a sales representative for Wall's Ice Cream, a subsidiary of

Unilever, which is based in London. Cosslett's supervisors passed to him a sales plan crafted by upper management that involved making sales calls on roughly six hundred shops. Speaking of the detachment of planners, Cosslett says, "The biggest thing I remember from those days . . . was how much of what comes out of corporate offices is of absolutely no purpose, and how far removed some people are from the front line. I was out there expected to sell this ice cream in the middle of winter in Liverpool. It was pretty tough, and I was in there trying to sell these two-pound ice cream cakes because head office said that's what we had to sell."[12]

5-2 *How to Make a Plan That Works*

Planning is a double-edged sword. If done right, planning brings about tremendous increases in individual and organizational performance. If planning is done wrong, however, it can have just the opposite effect and harm individual and organizational performance.

In this section, you will learn how to make a plan that works. As depicted in Exhibit 5.1, planning consists of 5-2a setting goals, 5-2b developing commitment to the goals, 5-2c developing effective action plans, 5-2d tracking progress toward goal achievement, and 5-2e maintaining flexibility in planning.

S.M.A.R.T. goals goals that are specific, measurable, attainable, realistic, and timely

5-2a SETTING GOALS

The first step in planning is to set goals. To direct behavior and increase effort, goals need to be specific and challenging.[13] For example, deciding to "increase sales this year" won't direct and energize workers as much as deciding to "increase North American sales by 4 percent in the next six months." Specific, challenging goals provide a target for which to aim and a standard against which to measure success.

One way of writing effective goals for yourself, your job, or your company is to use the S.M.A.R.T. guidelines. **S.M.A.R.T. goals** are **S**pecific, **M**easurable, **A**ttainable, **R**ealistic, and **T**imely.[14] Let's take a look at Honda's recently announced plan to lead the world in fuel efficiency in every vehicle class within three years to see how it measures up to the S.M.A.R.T. guidelines for goals.

First, is the goal *Specific*? Yes, Honda's plan does not state that the company will produce fuel-efficient cars but that every car it makes will lead its class in gas mileage. Is the goal *Measurable*? Again the answer is yes, since a class-by-class comparison of fuel efficiency with competitors will show whether Honda has achieved its goal. Whether the goal is *Attainable* or not depends on whether Honda is able to develop innovative engines that are more efficient than its competitors'. Honda plans to enhance its VTEC (Variable Valve Timing and Lift Electronic Control System) engine technology by minimizing friction within the engine

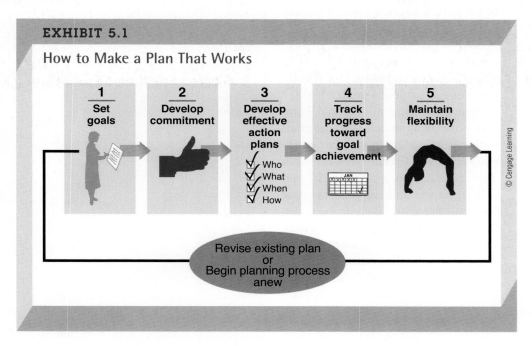

EXHIBIT 5.1

How to Make a Plan That Works

| 1 Set goals | 2 Develop commitment | 3 Develop effective action plans — Who, What, When, How | 4 Track progress toward goal achievement | 5 Maintain flexibility |

Revise existing plan or Begin planning process anew

© Cengage Learning

Goal commitment the determination to achieve a goal

Action plan a plan that lists the specific steps, people, resources, and time period needed to attain a goal

by reducing the number of belts (for example, an electric water pump will replace the standard belt-driven water pump). Less friction will, of course, result in better gas mileage. The goal is *Realistic,* given that Honda is using and significantly improving existing engine technologies rather than inventing brand-new ones. For example, in addition to less friction, Honda's more efficient hybrid (gas plus battery power) engines will be lighter, thanks to making the engine block thinner, and will use high-performing lithium-ion batteries that recharge fully within three hours. Finally, the goal is *Timely,* since Honda announced that it plans to achieve its goal in three years.[15]

5-2b DEVELOPING COMMITMENT TO GOALS

Just because a company sets a goal doesn't mean that people will try to accomplish it. If workers don't care about a goal, that goal won't encourage them to work harder or smarter. Thus, the second step in planning is to develop commitment to goals.[16]

Goal commitment is the determination to achieve a goal. Commitment to achieve a goal is not automatic. Managers and workers must choose to commit themselves to a goal. Edwin Locke, professor emeritus of management at the University of Maryland and the foremost expert on how, why, and when goals work, tells a story about an overweight friend who lost seventy-five pounds. Locke says, "I asked him how he did it, knowing how hard it was for most people to lose so much weight." His friend responded, "Actually, it was quite simple. I simply decided that I *really wanted* to do it."[17] Put another way, goal commitment is really wanting to achieve a goal.

So how can managers bring about goal commitment? The most popular approach is to set goals participatively. Rather than assigning goals to workers ("Johnson, you've got till Tuesday of next week to redesign the flux capacitor so it gives us 10 percent more output"), managers and employees choose goals together. The goals are more likely to be realistic and attainable if employees participate in setting them. Another technique for gaining commitment to a goal is to make the goal public. For example, college students who publicly communicated their semester grade goals ("This semester, I'm shooting for a 3.5") to significant others (usually a parent or sibling) were much more committed to achieving their grades than

those who did not. Still another way to increase goal commitment is to obtain top management's support. Top management can show support for a plan or program by providing funds, speaking publicly about the plan, or participating in the plan itself.

5-2c DEVELOPING EFFECTIVE ACTION PLANS

The third step in planning is to develop effective action plans. An **action plan** lists the specific steps (how), people (who), resources (what), and time period (when) for accomplishing a goal (see box "Don't Remind Me" below for an example of Ocean Spray's plan for marketing to baby boomers). Mozilla was created in 1998 to provide an alternative web browser to Microsoft's Internet Explorer, which had a 90 percent market share. Today, Mozilla's Firefox browser is found on 25 percent of computers but has less than a 1 percent share in the fastest-growing market, mobile computing. With no app for the iPhone or iPad and its Firefox browser for Android on just 4 percent of the 200 million Android devices being used by consumers, Mozilla risks becoming irrelevant. The first step in its detailed plan to strengthen its presence in mobile computing, the "how,"

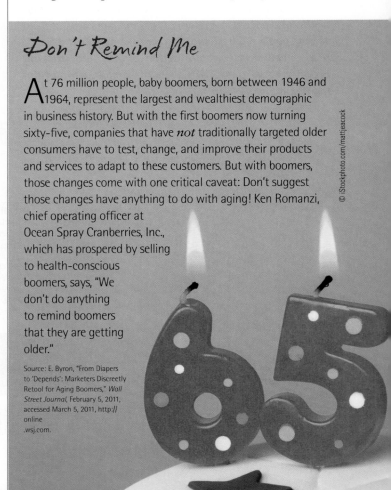

Don't Remind Me

At 76 million people, baby boomers, born between 1946 and 1964, represent the largest and wealthiest demographic in business history. But with the first boomers now turning sixty-five, companies that have *not* traditionally targeted older consumers have to test, change, and improve their products and services to adapt to these customers. But with boomers, those changes come with one critical caveat: Don't suggest those changes have anything to do with aging! Ken Romanzi, chief operating officer at Ocean Spray Cranberries, Inc., which has prospered by selling to health-conscious boomers, says, "We don't do anything to remind boomers that they are getting older."

Source: E. Byron, "From Diapers to 'Depends': Marketers Discreetly Retool for Aging Boomers," *Wall Street Journal,* February 5, 2011, accessed March 5, 2011, http://online.wsj.com.

© iStockphoto.com/mattjeacock

is to develop a new mobile browser for Android systems, which, unlike Apple's iOS operating system for iPhones and iPads, are built with commonly used Java programming. To do that, Mozilla is expanding its 20-engineer mobile software team, the "who," with significantly more resources, meaning the "what," by making its entire 250-person engineering team responsible for developing an Android browser. CEO Gary Kovacs says that the company is also on a "massive hiring spree" for mobile designers. Finally, Mozilla has established a time period, the "when," by announcing that it plans to reach agreements with phone makers by 2012 to make its Firefox Mobile a default browser on their phones.[18]

5-2d TRACKING PROGRESS

The fourth step in planning is to track progress toward goal achievement. There are two accepted methods

Proximal goals short-term goals or subgoals

Distal goals long-term or primary goals

of tracking progress. The first is to set proximal goals and distal goals. **Proximal goals** are short-term goals or subgoals, whereas **distal goals** are long-term or primary goals.[19]

The second method of tracking progress is to gather and provide performance feedback. Regular, frequent performance feedback allows workers and managers to track their progress toward goal achievement and make adjustments in effort, direction, and strategies.[20] Exhibit 5.2 shows the impact of feedback on safety behavior at a large bakery company with a worker safety record that was two-and-a-half times worse than the industry average. During the baseline period, workers in the wrapping department, who measure and mix ingredients, roll the bread dough, and put it into baking pans, performed their jobs

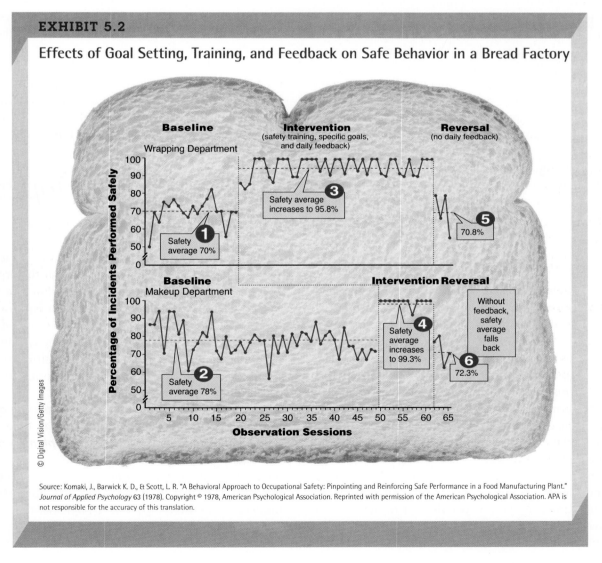

EXHIBIT 5.2

Effects of Goal Setting, Training, and Feedback on Safe Behavior in a Bread Factory

Source: Komaki, J., Barwick K. D., & Scott, L. R. "A Behavioral Approach to Occupational Safety: Pinpointing and Reinforcing Safe Performance in a Food Manufacturing Plant." *Journal of Applied Psychology* 63 (1978). Copyright © 1978, American Psychological Association. Reprinted with permission of the American Psychological Association. APA is not responsible for the accuracy of this translation.

© Digital Vision/Getty Images

safely about 70 percent of the time (see 1 in Exhibit 5.2). The baseline safety record for workers in the makeup department, who bag and seal baked bread and assemble, pack, and tape cardboard cartons for shipping, was somewhat better at 78 percent (see 2). The company then gave workers thirty minutes of safety training, set a goal of 90 percent safe behavior, and then provided daily feedback (such as a chart similar to Exhibit 5.2). Performance improved dramatically. During the intervention period, safely performed behaviors rose to an average of 95.8 percent for wrapping workers (see 3) and 99.3 percent for workers in the makeup department (see 4), and never fell below 83 percent. Thus, the combination of training, a challenging goal, and feedback led to a dramatic increase in performance. The importance of feedback alone can be seen in the reversal stage, when the company quit posting daily feedback on safe behavior. Without daily feedback, the percentage of safely performed behaviors returned to baseline levels—70.8 percent for the wrapping department (see 5) and 72.3 percent for the makeup department (see 6). For planning to be effective, workers need both a specific, challenging goal and regular feedback to track their progress. Indeed, additional research indicates that the effectiveness of goal setting can be doubled by the addition of feedback.[21]

5-2e MAINTAINING FLEXIBILITY

Because action plans are sometimes poorly conceived and goals sometimes turn out not to be achievable, the last step in developing an effective plan is to maintain flexibility. One method of maintaining flexibility while planning is to adopt an options-based approach.[22] The goal of **options-based planning** is to keep options open by making small, simultaneous investments in many alternative plans. Then, when one or a few of these plans emerge as likely winners, you invest even more in these plans while discontinuing or reducing investment in the others.

In part, options-based planning is the opposite of traditional planning. Whereas the purpose of an action plan is to commit people and resources to a particular course of action, the purpose of options-based planning is to leave those commitments open by maintaining **slack resources**—that is, a cushion of resources, such as extra time, people, money, or production capacity, that can be used to address and adapt to unanticipated changes, problems, or opportunities.[23] Holding options open gives you choices. And choices, combined with slack resources, give you flexibility. At the end of 2011, Google had assets totaling $52 billion and cash reserves of $44 billion. That huge cash reserve allowed it to strategically acquire companies, extending its reach into key markets. For example, Google expanded its ability to give users high-quality restaurant reviews by purchasing Zagat, a company that publishes well-respected restaurant review guides, for $151 million. In a separate deal, Google spent $700 million to buy travel search company ITA so that it could compete with travel sites like Expedia and Orbitz. Finally, Google paid $12.5 billion to buy Motorola Mobility, the division of Motorola that produces cell phones, so it could compete more directly with Apple's iPhone and iPad.[24]

So why keep so much cash on hand? Maintaining substantial cash helped Google keep its options open. And having options, combined with slack resources (i.e., that extra cash), equals flexibility, which is the options-based approach to planning.

5-3 *Planning from Top to Bottom*

Planning works best when the goals and action plans at the bottom and middle of the organization support the goals and action plans at the top of the organization. In other words, planning works best when everybody pulls in the same direction. Exhibit 5.3 illustrates this planning continuity, beginning at the top with a clear definition of the company purpose and ending at the bottom with the execution of operational plans.

*Let's see how **5-3a top managers create the organization's purpose statement and strategic objective, 5-3b middle managers develop tactical plans and use management by objectives to motivate employee efforts toward the overall purpose and strategic objective,** and **5-3c first-level managers use operational, single-use, and standing plans to implement the tactical plans.***

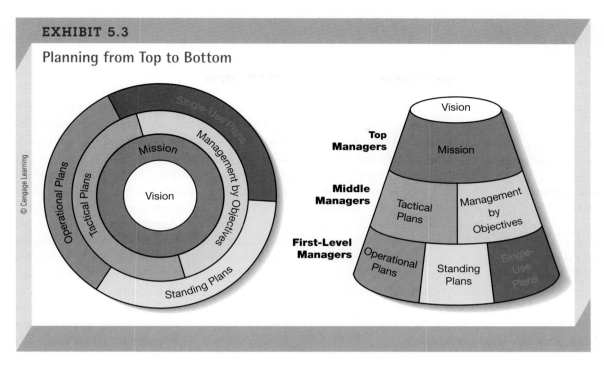

EXHIBIT 5.3

Planning from Top to Bottom

5-3a STARTING AT THE TOP

Top management is responsible for developing long-term **strategic plans** that make clear how the company will serve customers and position itself against competitors in the next two to five years. Keith R. McLoughlin, CEO of Electrolux, a Sweden-based appliance maker, has set a strategic goal to overtake its chief competitor, Whirlpool, and become the number one appliance company in the world. According to McLoughlin, the goal will be met by taking advantage of Electrolux's worldwide presence and distribution network. Says McLoughlin, "We're the only one that has the distribution and local market presence in over 150 countries. You have to know the local consumer, and we do that globally more than anyone." Consistent with its strategic goal of global growth, only 5 percent of its 50,920 employees are in Sweden, while 20 percent are in Brazil (one of its fastest-growing markets), 16 percent are in the United States, and 12 per-

"Our goal is to overtake Whirlpool and become the number one appliance company in the world!"

cent are in Italy. Electrolux's strategic plans for the United States are to expand in the high-end appliance market where, for example, it sells a $3,500 stainless steel range that boils water in ninety seconds. Growth in Asia and Latin America will come by spending up to $1.6 billion a year to strategically acquire appliance companies in each of those markets.[25]

Strategic planning begins with the creation of an organizational purpose. A **purpose statement**, which is often referred to as an organizational mission or vision, is a statement of a company's purpose or reason for existing.[26] Purpose statements should be brief—no more than two sentences. They should also be enduring, inspirational, clear, and consistent with widely shared company beliefs and values. An excellent example of a well-crafted purpose statement is that of Avon, the cosmetics company. It guides everyone in the organization and provides a focal point for the delivery of beauty

Strategic plans overall company plans that clarify how the company will serve customers and position itself against competitors over the next two to five years

Purpose statement a statement of a company's purpose or reason for existing

Strategic objective a more specific goal that unifies company-wide efforts, stretches and challenges the organization, and possesses a finish line and a time frame

Tactical plans plans created and implemented by middle managers that specify how the company will use resources, budgets, and people over the next six months to two years to accomplish specific goals within its mission

Management by objectives (MBO) a four-step process in which managers and employees discuss and select goals, develop tactical plans, and meet regularly to review progress toward goal accomplishment

products and services to the customers, women around the world. The purpose is the same whether Avon is selling lipstick to women in India, shampoo packets to women in the Amazon, or jewelry to women in the United States. Despite these regional differences in specific strategy, the overall goal—understanding the needs of women globally—does not change. Other examples of organizational purpose statements that have been particularly effective include Walt Disney Company's "to make people happy" and Schlage Lock Company's "to make the world more secure."[27]

The **strategic objective**, which flows from the purpose, is a more specific goal that unifies company-wide efforts, stretches and challenges the organization, and possesses a finish line and a time frame.[28] For example, in 1961, President John F. Kennedy established a strategic objective for **NASA** with this simple statement: "Achieving the goal, before this decade is out, of landing a man on the moon and returning him safely to earth."[29] NASA achieved this strategic objective on July 20, 1969, when astronaut Neil Armstrong walked on the moon. Once the strategic objective has been accomplished, a new one should be chosen. However, the new strategic objective must grow out of the organization's purpose, which does not change significantly over time. Consider, for example, NASA's hopes to accomplish its latest strategic goal, or what it calls its "exploration systems mission directorate," between 2015 and 2020. NASA's strategic goal is to "return to the moon where we will build a sustainable long-term human presence."[30] NASA further explains its strategic goal by saying, "As the space shuttle approaches retirement and the International Space Station nears completion, NASA is building the next fleet of vehicles to bring astronauts back to the moon, and possibly to Mars and beyond."

5-3b BENDING IN THE MIDDLE

Middle management is responsible for developing and carrying out tactical plans to accomplish the organization's strategic objective. **Tactical plans** specify how a company will use resources, budgets, and people to accomplish specific goals related to its strategic objective for the next five years. Whereas strategic plans and objectives are used to focus company efforts over the next two to five years, tactical plans and objectives are used to direct behavior, efforts, and attention over the next six months to two years. American Airlines, for example, has filed for Chapter 11 bankruptcy, from which it hopes to emerge with lower costs, reduced debt, a stronger balance sheet, and new strategic plans to ensure its long-term success. American's labor costs, the highest in the industry, represent 30 percent of total costs, compared to just 21 percent at Delta Air Lines and United/Continental, and place the company at a cost disadvantage estimated at $800 million a year in higher costs. Therefore, a key part of American's tactical plans (i.e., regarding resources, budgets, and people) for emerging successfully from bankruptcy include cutting 13,000 of 80,000 jobs, replacing retirement pensions with contribution-based retirement plans, and cutting health benefits for both current employees and retirees. American also plans to increase revenue by $1 billion through partnerships with other airlines and by making flight processes more efficient.[31]

Management by objectives is a management technique often used to develop and carry out tactical plans. **Management by objectives (MBO)** is a four-step process in which managers and their employees (1) discuss possible goals; (2) collectively select goals that are challenging, attainable, and consistent with the company's overall goals; (3) jointly develop tactical plans that lead to the accomplishment of tactical goals and objectives; and (4) meet regularly to review progress toward accomplishment of those goals. At **Kindermusik International**, a music education publisher, all fifty employees attend weekly one-hour meetings to review the company's weekly goals and financial results. Half-day review sessions are held each quarter to review results against quarterly and annual goals and to discuss how to cut costs and increase revenues. Because they regularly review and discuss goal progress, employees were sensitive to reducing costs, so they proposed replacing the company's five-day sales convention, which costs about $50,000, with a series of year-round virtual meetings with sales managers, sales representatives, and customers. CEO Michael Dougherty said, "If you'd asked me, I would have said, 'We've always done the convention.' But the folks who are closer to the event and closer to the customers know that there were other and better ways to achieve the same goal."[32]

5-3c FINISHING AT THE BOTTOM

Lower-level managers are responsible for developing and carrying out **operational plans**, which are the day-to-day plans for producing or delivering the organization's products and services. Operational plans direct the behavior, efforts, and priorities of operative employees for periods ranging from thirty days to six months. There are three kinds of operational plans: single-use plans, standing plans, and budgets.

Single-use plans deal with unique, one-time-only events. After a devastating earthquake and tsunami critically disabled a nuclear power plant, several Japanese electric companies warned that they might not be able to provide enough power for businesses and residents. The Japanese government then required heavy power users to cut their consumption by 15 percent, which required many businesses to enact conservation plans. Sony, for example, announced that it would encourage all workers to leave their offices by 5:00 p.m., one hour earlier than usual, and shut off the air conditioning promptly at 6:00 p.m. The company also decided to extend summer holidays at several factories in order to reduce power consumption. Komatsu, a manufacturer of heavy machinery, announced that it would close two stories of its ten-story headquarters building and give employees one day off per week. Nissan, meanwhile, installed power meters at its factories so that it could stop its operations when its daily power consumption target was exceeded.[33]

Unlike single-use plans that are created, carried out once, and then never used again, **standing plans** save managers time because once the plans are created, they can be used repeatedly to handle frequently recurring events. If you encounter a problem that you've seen before, someone in your company has probably written a standing plan that explains how to address it. Using this plan rather than reinventing the wheel will save you time. There are three kinds of standing plans: policies, procedures, and rules and regulations.

Policies indicate the general course of action that company managers should take in response to a particular event or situation. A well-written policy will also specify why the policy exists and what outcome the policy is intended to produce. By law, all U.S. companies are required to give their employees three unpaid months of maternity or paternity leave. However, Accenture, a leading consulting firm, gives new mothers eight weeks of paid leave, the option of reduced hours when they return to work, and up to forty hours of subsidized care for their babies in their homes or at a daycare center.[34]

Procedures are more specific than policies because they indicate the series of steps that should be taken in response to a particular event. A manufacturer's procedure for handling defective products might include the following steps.

- Step 1: Rejected material is locked in a secure area with "reject" documentation attached.

- Step 2: Material Review Board (MRB) identifies the defect and notes how far outside the standard the rejected products are.

- Step 3: MRB determines the disposition of the defective product as either scrap or rework.

- Step 4: Scrap is either discarded or recycled, and rework is sent back through the production line to be fixed.

- Step 5: If delays in delivery will result, MRB member notifies customer.[35]

Rules and regulations are even more specific than procedures because they specify what must happen or not happen. They describe precisely how a particular action should be performed. For instance, many companies have rules and regulations forbidding managers from writing job reference letters for employees who have worked at their firms because a negative reference may prompt a former employee to sue for defamation of character.[36]

After single-use plans and standing plans, budgets are the third kind of operational plan. **Budgeting** is quantitative planning because it forces managers to decide how to allocate available money to best

---

Operational plans day-to-day plans, developed and implemented by lower-level managers, for producing or delivering the organization's products and services over a thirty-day to six-month period

Single-use plans plans that cover unique, one-time-only events

Standing plans plans used repeatedly to handle frequently recurring events

Policies standing plans that indicate the general course of action that should be taken in response to a particular event or situation

Procedures standing plans that indicate the specific steps that should be taken in response to a particular event

Rules and regulations standing plans that describe how a particular action should be performed or what must happen or not happen in response to a particular event

Budgeting quantitative planning through which managers decide how to allocate available money to best accomplish company goals

accomplish company goals. According to Jan King, author of *Business Plans to Game Plans*, "Money sends a clear message about your priorities. Budgets act as a language for communicating your goals to others."

5-4 *Steps and Limits to Rational Decision Making*

Decision making is the process of choosing a solution from available alternatives.[37] **Rational decision making** is a systematic process in which managers define problems, evaluate alternatives, and choose optimal solutions that provide maximum benefits to their organizations. Thus, for example, if your department must purchase new computers, your boss expects you to define and analyze the computer-purchase problem and explore alternatives. Furthermore, your solution has to be optimal, because the

© iStockphoto.com/fredfroese

> **Money sends a clear message about your priorities. Budgets act as a language for communicating your goals to others.**

department is going to live with the computer equipment you recommend for the next three years.

*Let's learn more about each of these: **5-4a define the problem, 5-4b identify decision criteria, 5-4c weigh the criteria, 5-4d generate alternative courses of action, 5-4e evaluate each alternative,** and **5-4f compute the optimal decision.** Then we'll consider **5-4g limits to rational decision making.***

5-4a DEFINE THE PROBLEM

The first step in decision making is identifying and defining the problem. A **problem** exists when there is a gap between a desired state (what is wanted) and an existing state (the situation you are actually facing). For instance, women want to look good and be comfortable in properly fitted clothes. But since the garment industry's size standards are outdated (collected sixty years ago on a small group of Caucasian women in their 20s) or ignored, fit varies tremendously. A size 8 in one brand will be a size 10 in another. As a result, women who can't find well-fitting clothes leave stores without purchasing or are forced to buy poorly fitted clothes that are returned to the store or discarded after several wearings. Either way, the result is the same: Clothing manufacturers have a problem because dissatisfied customers won't buy their brands in the future.[38]

The presence of a gap between an existing state (such as selling clothes that should fit, but don't) and a desired state is no guarantee that managers will make decisions to solve problems. Three things must occur for this to happen.[39] First, managers have to be aware of the gap. They have to know there is a problem before they can begin solving it. For example, after noticing that people were spending more money on their pets, a new dog food company created an expensive, high-quality dog food. To emphasize its quality, the dog food was sold in cans and bags with gold labels, red letters, and detailed information about its benefits and nutrients. Yet the product did not sell very well, and the company went out of business in less than a year. Its founders didn't understand why. When they asked a manager at a competing dog food company what their biggest mistake had been, the answer was "Simple. You didn't have a picture of a dog on the package."[40] This problem would have been easy to solve if management had only been aware of it.

Being aware of a problem isn't enough to begin the decision-making process. Managers have to be motivated to reduce the gap between a desired and an existing state. For almost a decade, managers at Bor-

ders Books were aware of the gap between its struggling performance and the strong sales, market share, and profits it desired. Moreover, they knew that its poor performance resulted from not embracing online, electronic sales like its competitors Amazon, Barnes & Noble, and Netflix did. Amazingly, Borders actually outsourced its online presence to Amazon, strengthening its rival and weakening its own position. Why? So it could invest more money in its brick-and-mortar stores. In its 2000 annual report the company explained: "Our online investment will be channeled to support our in-store platform, while Borders.com [run by Amazon for Borders] will continue to be utilized as a convenience retail channel." And, instead of viewing online sales as a growth opportunity, Borders "targeted loss reduction as a major goal in this area." Likewise, Borders's e-book reader, the Kobo, was introduced almost four years after Amazon's Kindle and Barnes & Noble's Nook. Even though Borders's leadership was aware of these problems, it did not take action to resolve them until it was too late to save the failing company, which was liquidated and then closed.[41]

Finally, it's not enough to be aware of a problem and be motivated to solve it. Managers must also have the knowledge, skills, abilities, and resources to fix the problem.

5-4b IDENTIFY DECISION CRITERIA

Decision criteria are the standards used to guide judgments and decisions. Typically, the more criteria a potential solution meets, the better that solution will be.

Again, imagine that your boss asks for suggestions about purchasing new computers for the office. What general factors would be important when purchas-

ing computers? Reliability, price, warranty, on-site service, and compatibility with existing software, printers, and computers would all be important, but you must also consider the technical details. What specific capabilities would you want the office computers to have? Well, with technology changing so quickly, you'll probably want to buy computers with as much capability and flexibility as you can afford. Today, for the first time, laptops now account for over 50 percent of the market.[42] Business laptops come in four distinct model types. There are budget models that are good for routine office work but are usually saddled with a slower processor; workhorse models that are not lightweight but have all the features; slim models for traveling that usually require an external drive to read/write to a DVD/CD; and tablet models like Apple's iPad.[43] What will the users really need? Will they need to burn CDs and DVDs, or just read them? How much memory and hard drive space will the users need? Should you pay extra for durability, file encryption, larger screens, and extra-large batteries? Answering questions like these will help you identify the criteria that will guide the purchase of the new equipment.

5-4c WEIGH THE CRITERIA

After identifying decision criteria, the next step is deciding which criteria are more or less important. Although there are numerous mathematical models for weighing decision criteria, all require the decision maker to provide an initial ranking of the criteria. Some use **absolute comparisons**, in which each criterion is compared with a standard or ranked on its own merits. For example, *Consumer Reports* uses nine criteria when it rates and recommends new cars: predicted reliability, current owners' satisfaction, predicted depreciation (the price you could expect if you sold the car), ability to avoid an accident, fuel economy, crash protection, acceleration, ride, and front seat comfort.[44]

Different individuals will rank these criteria differently, depending on what they value or require in a car. Exhibit 5.4 on the next page shows the absolute weights that someone buying a car might use. Because these weights are absolute, each criterion is judged on its own importance, using a five-point scale, with 5 representing "critically important" and 1 representing

Decision criteria the standards used to guide judgments and decisions

Absolute comparisons a process in which each decision criterion is compared to a standard or ranked on its own merits

EXHIBIT 5.4

Absolute Weighting of Decision Criteria for a Car Purchase

5 critically important
4 important
3 somewhat important
2 not very important
1 completely unimportant

1. Predicted reliability	1	2	3	4	(5)
2. Owner satisfaction	1	(2)	3	4	5
3. Predicted depreciation	(1)	2	3	4	5
4. Avoiding accidents	1	2	3	(4)	5
5. Fuel economy	1	2	3	4	(5)
6. Crash protection	1	2	3	(4)	5
7. Acceleration	(1)	2	3	4	5
8. Ride	1	2	(3)	4	5
9. Front seat comfort	1	2	3	4	(5)

© Cengage Learning

"completely unimportant." In this instance, predicted reliability, fuel economy, and front seat comfort were rated most important, and acceleration and predicted depreciation were rated least important.

Another method uses **relative comparisons**, in which each criterion is compared directly with every other criterion.[45] Exhibit 5.5 shows six criteria that someone might use when buying a house. Moving down the first column of Exhibit 5.5, we see that the time of the daily commute has been rated less important (−1) than school system quality; more important (+1) than having an in-ground pool, a sun room, or a quiet street; and just as important as the house being brand new (0). Total weights, which are obtained by summing the scores in each column, indicate that the school system quality and

Relative comparisons a process in which each decision criterion is compared directly with every other criterion

daily commute are the most important factors to this home buyer, while an in-ground pool, sun room, and a quiet street are the least important. So with relative comparison, criteria are directly compared with each other.

5-4d GENERATE ALTERNATIVE COURSES OF ACTION

After identifying and weighting the criteria that will guide the decision-making process, the next step is to identify possible courses of action that could solve the problem. In general, at this step, the idea is to generate as many alternatives as possible. Let's assume that you're trying to select a city in Europe to be the location of a major office. After meeting with your staff, you generate a list of possible alternatives: Amsterdam, Netherlands; Barcelona or Madrid, Spain; Berlin, Frankfurt, or Munich, Germany; Brussels, Belgium; London, England; Paris, France; and Zurich, Switzerland.

5-4e EVALUATE EACH ALTERNATIVE

The next step is to systematically evaluate each alternative against each criterion. Because of the amount of information that must be collected, this step can take much longer and be much more expensive than other steps in the decision-making process. When selecting a European city for your office, you could contact economic development offices in each city, systematically interview businesspeople or executives who operate there, retrieve and use published govern-

EXHIBIT 5.5

Relative Comparison of Home Characteristics

HOME CHARACTERISTICS	L	SSQ	IP	SR	QS	NBH
Daily commute (L)		+1	−1	−1	−1	0
School system quality (SSQ)	−1		−1	−1	−1	−1
In-ground pool (IP)	+1	+1		0	0	+1
Sun room (SR)	+1	+1	0		0	0
Quiet street (QS)	+1	+1	0	0		0
Newly built house (NBH)	0	+1	−1	0	0	
Total weight	(+2)	(+5)	(−3)	(−2)	(−2)	(0)

© Cengage Learning

ment data on each location, or rely on published studies such as Cushman & Wakefield's *European Cities Monitor*, which conducts an annual survey of more than five hundred senior European executives who rate thirty-four European cities on twelve business-related criteria.[46]

No matter how you gather the information, once you have it, the key is to use that information systematically to evaluate each alternative against each criterion. Exhibit 5.6 shows how each of the ten cities on your staff's list fared with respect to each of the twelve criteria (higher scores are better), from qualified staff to freedom from pollution. Although London has the most qualified staff, the best access to markets and tele-

And the winner is … London. When all the weighted averages are calculated and compared, London is the best city in Europe for business.

communications, and is the easiest city to travel to and from, it is also one of the most polluted and expensive cities on the list. Paris offers excellent access to markets and clients, but if your staff is multilingual, Brussels may be a better choice.

5-4f COMPUTE THE OPTIMAL DECISION

The final step in the decision-making process is to compute the optimal decision by determining the optimal value of each alternative. This is done by multiplying the rating for each criterion (Step 5-4e) by the weight for that criterion (Step 5-4c), and then summing those scores for each alternative course of action that you generated

EXHIBIT 5.6

Criteria Ratings Used to Determine the Best Location for a New Office

Criteria Weights:	Access to Markets 0.60	Qualified staff 0.53	Telecom- munications 0.52	Travel to/from City 0.42	Cost & Value of Office Space 0.33	Cost of Staff 0.32	Available Office Space 0.25	Languages Spoken 0.21	Business Climate 0.20	Travel within City 0.20	Quality of Life 0.16	Freedom from pollution 0.16	Weighted Average	Ranking
Amsterdam	0.42	0.40	0.39	0.68	0.30	0.19	0.30	0.96	0.47	0.34	0.44	0.63	1.72	5
Barcelona	0.23	0.32	0.16	0.29	0.52	0.59	0.52	0.23	0.31	0.47	1.08	0.42	1.45	8
Berlin	0.44	0.39	0.41	0.35	0.78	0.40	0.79	0.50	0.34	0.78	0.38	0.29	1.85	4
Brussels	0.46	0.43	0.37	0.48	0.44	0.17	0.42	0.98	0.37	0.29	0.41	0.27	1.65	7
Dusseldorf	0.30	0.30	0.23	0.21	0.37	0.14	0.28	0.18	0.17	0.22	0.20	0.26	0.97	10
Frankfurt	0.68	0.57	0.70	1.17	0.38	0.11	0.44	0.57	0.38	0.35	0.17	0.18	2.16	3
London	1.50	1.36	1.27	1.79	0.27	0.10	0.42	1.48	0.55	1.26	0.46	0.15	4.03	1
Madrid	0.45	0.46	0.27	0.41	0.52	0.61	0.67	0.22	0.29	0.53	0.67	0.13	1.70	6
Munich	0.34	0.47	0.48	0.37	0.18	0.03	0.18	0.30	0.22	0.47	0.62	0.57	1.36	9
Paris	1.09	0.84	0.89	1.36	0.22	0.10	0.37	0.58	0.30	1.07	0.52	0.12	2.83	2

Source: "European Cities Monitor," Cushman & Wakefield, 2008, accessed May 20, 2009, http://www.cushwake.com/cwglobal/docviewer/2008_European_Cities_Monitor.pdf.

Maximize choosing the best alternative

Satisficing choosing a "good-enough" alternative

(Step 5-4d). For example, the five hundred executives participating in Cushman & Wakefield's survey of the best European cities for business rated the twelve decision criteria in terms of importance, as shown in the first row of Exhibit 5.6. Access to markets, qualified staff, telecommunications, and easy travel to and from the city were the four most important factors, while quality of life and freedom from pollution were the least important factors. To calculate the optimal value for Paris, the weight for each category is multiplied by its score in each category ($.53 \times .84$) in the qualified staff category, for example). Then all of these scores are added together to produce the optimal value, as follows:

$$(.60 \times 1.09) + (.53 \times .84) + (.52 \times .89) +$$
$$(.42 \times 1.36) + (.33 \times .22) + (.32 \times .10) +$$
$$(.25 \times .37) + (.21 \times .58) + (.20 \times .30) +$$
$$(.20 \times 1.07) + (.16 \times .52) + (.16 \times .12) = 2.83$$

Since London has a weighted average of 4.03 compared to 2.83 for Paris and 2.16 for Frankfurt (the cities with the next-best ratings), London clearly ranks as the best location for your company's new European office because of its large number of qualified staff; easy access to markets; outstanding ease of travel to, from, and within the city; excellent telecommunications; and top-notch business climate.

5-4g LIMITS TO RATIONAL DECISION MAKING

In general, managers who diligently complete all six steps of the rational decision-making model will make better decisions than those who don't. So, when they can, managers should try to follow the steps in the rational decision-making model, especially for big decisions with long-range consequences.

To make completely rational decisions, managers would have to operate in a perfect world with no real-world constraints. Of course, it never actually works like that in the real world. Managers face time and money constraints. They often don't have time to make extensive lists of decision criteria. And they often don't have the resources to test all possible solutions against all possible criteria.

In theory, fully rational decision makers **maximize** decisions by choosing the optimal solution. In practice, however, limited resources along with atten-

tion, memory, and expertise problems make it nearly impossible for managers to maximize decisions. Consequently, most managers don't maximize—they satisfice. Whereas maximizing is choosing the best alternative, **satisficing** is choosing a "good-enough" alternative. With twenty-four decision criteria, fifty alternative computers to choose from, two computer labs with hundreds of thousands of dollars of equipment, and unlimited time and money, the manager could test all alternatives against all decision criteria and choose the perfect computer. In reality, however, the manager's limited time, money, and expertise mean that only a few alternatives will be assessed against a few decision criteria. In practice, the manager will visit two or three computer or electronics stores, read a couple of recent computer reviews, and get bids from Dell, Lenovo, and Hewlett-Packard as well as some online superstores like CDW or PC Connection. The decision will be complete when the manager finds a good-enough laptop that meets a few decision criteria.

5-5 Using Groups to Improve Decision Making

According to a study reported in *Fortune* magazine, 91 percent of U.S. companies use teams and groups to solve specific problems (i.e., make decisions).[47] Why so many? Because when done properly, group decision making can lead to much better decisions than those typically made by individuals. In fact, numerous studies show that groups consistently outperform individuals on complex tasks.

Let's explore the **5-5a advantages and pitfalls of group decision making** *and see how the following group decision-making methods—* **5-5b structured conflict, 5-5c the nominal group technique, 5-5d the Delphi technique,** *and* **5-5e electronic brainstorming**—*can be used to improve decision making.*

5-5a ADVANTAGES AND PITFALLS OF GROUP DECISION MAKING

Groups can do a much better job than individuals in two important steps of the decision-making process: defining the problem and generating alternative solutions. Still, group decision making is subject to some pitfalls that can quickly erase these gains. One possible pitfall is groupthink. **Groupthink** occurs in highly cohesive groups when group members feel intense pressure to agree with each other so that the group can approve a proposed solution.[48] Because groupthink leads to consideration of a limited number of solutions and restricts discussion of any considered solutions, it usually results in poor decisions. Groupthink is most likely to occur under the following conditions:

- The group is insulated from others with different perspectives.
- The group leader begins by expressing a strong preference for a particular decision.
- The group has no established procedure for systematically defining problems and exploring alternatives.
- Group members have similar backgrounds and experiences.[49]

A second potential problem with group decision making is that it takes considerable time. Reconciling schedules so that group members can meet takes time. Furthermore, it's a rare group that consistently holds productive task-oriented meetings to effectively work through the decision process. Some of the most common complaints about meetings (and thus group decision making) are that the meeting's purpose is unclear, participants are unprepared, critical people are absent or late, conversation doesn't stay focused on the problem, and no one follows up on the decisions that were made. Teresa Taylor, the chief operations officer at Qwest, avoids many of these problems by opening every meeting with the question "Do we all know why we're here?" Surprisingly, she often finds that many people can't answer the question—they just show up to a meeting because they've been invited. Taylor will clarify the purpose of the meeting even further by asking, "Are we making decisions? Are you going to ask me for something at the end?" In doing so, she helps participants focus their attention. Once the purpose is identified, Taylor will even allow people to leave the meeting if they feel like they don't need to be there.[50]

Groupthink a barrier to good decision making caused by pressure within the group for members to agree with each other

---

I've Got You on Speakerphone

Conference calls are a great way to hold meetings. They are an easy way to get people to check in no matter where they are, but there are also many challenges for making them effective and efficient. It can be hard to hear what other people are saying. Callers may be watching television or surfing the Web instead of paying attention. Participants may not be used to talking on the phone with more than one person and can end up talking over each other. David Lavenda, vice president of Mainsoft, offers ten tips for effective conference calls.

1. Keep statements short and ask for frequent feedback.
2. Don't use slides if you can avoid it, since reading slides with text is boring, and you can't control what people are looking at.
3. If you must show slides, don't send them ahead of time.
4. Send out an agenda ahead of time and stick to it.
5. Use video if possible. Skype or webcams provide visual cues that help people stay engaged and on task.
6. Let the participants know if you are recording the call.
7. Start on time.
8. Make sure the moderator dials in early.
9. Don't dial in from a mobile phone.
10. Set limits on call duration.

Source: D. Lavenda, "10 Rules for Effective Conference Calls," *Fast Company*, May 26, 2010, accessed February 22, 2011, http://www.fastcompany.com/1651164/10-rules-for-effective -conference-calls.

© iStockphoto.com/Paul Vasarhelyi

C-type conflict (cognitive conflict) disagreement that focuses on problem- and issue-related differences of opinion

A-type conflict (affective conflict) disagreement that focuses on individuals or personal issues

A third possible pitfall to group decision making is that sometimes one or two people, perhaps the boss or a strong-willed, vocal group member, can dominate group discussions and limit the group's consideration of different problem definitions and alternative solutions. And, unlike individual decisions where people feel personally responsible for making a good choice, another potential problem is that group members may not feel accountable for the decisions made and actions taken by the group.

Although these pitfalls can lead to poor decision making, this doesn't mean that managers should avoid using groups to make decisions. When done properly, group decision making can lead to much better decisions. The pitfalls of group decision making are not inevitable. Managers can overcome most of them by using the various techniques described next (see box "I've Got You on Speakerphone" for tips on how to make conference calls more effective).

5-5b STRUCTURED CONFLICT

Most people view conflict negatively. Yet the right kind of conflict can lead to much better group decision making. **C-type conflict**, or "cognitive conflict," focuses on problem- and issue-related differences of opinion.[51] In c-type conflict, group members disagree because their different experiences and expertise lead them to view the problem and its potential solutions differently. C-type conflict is also characterized by a willingness to examine, compare, and reconcile those differences to produce the best possible solution. Alteon WebSystems, now a division of Nortel Networks, makes critical use of c-type conflict. Top manager Dominic Orr described Alteon's c-type conflict this way:

> *People arrive with a proposal or a solution—and with the facts to support it. After an idea is presented, we open the floor to objective, and often withering, critiques. And if the idea collapses under scrutiny, we move on to another: no hard feelings. We're judging the idea, not the person. At the same time, we don't really try to regulate emotions. Passionate conflict means that we're getting somewhere, not that the discussion is out of control. But one person does act as referee—by asking basic questions like "Is this good for the customer?" or "Does it keep our time-to-market advantage intact?" By focusing relentlessly on the facts, we're able to see the strengths and weaknesses of an idea clearly and quickly.*[52]

By contrast, **a-type conflict**, meaning "affective conflict," refers to the emotional reactions that can oc-

A-type conflict: When disagreements become personal rather than professional

cur when disagreements become personal rather than professional. A-type conflict often results in hostility, anger, resentment, distrust, cynicism, and apathy. Unlike c-type conflict, a-type conflict undermines team effectiveness by preventing teams from engaging in the activities characteristic of c-type conflict that are critical to team effectiveness. Examples of a-type conflict statements are "your idea," "our idea," "my department," "you don't know what you are talking about," or "you don't understand our situation." Rather than focusing on issues and ideas, these statements focus on individuals.[53]

The **devil's advocacy** approach can be used to create c-type conflict by assigning an individual or a subgroup the role of critic. The following five steps establish a devil's advocacy program:

1. Generate a potential solution.
2. Assign a devil's advocate to criticize and question the solution.
3. Present the critique of the potential solution to key decision makers.
4. Gather additional relevant information.
5. Decide whether to use, change, or not use the originally proposed solution.[54]

When properly used, the devil's advocacy approach introduces c-type conflict into the decision-making process. Contrary to the common belief that conflict is bad, studies show that these methods lead not only to less a-type conflict but also to improved decision quality and greater acceptance of decisions once they have been made.[55]

Another method of creating c-type conflict is **dialectical inquiry**, which creates c-type conflict by forcing decision makers to state the assumptions of a proposed solution (a thesis) and then generate a solution that is the opposite (antithesis) of the proposed solution. The following are the five steps of the dialectical inquiry process:

1. Generate a potential solution.
2. Identify the assumptions underlying the potential solution.
3. Generate a conflicting counterproposal based on the opposite assumptions.
4. Have advocates of each position present their arguments and engage in a debate in front of key decision makers.
5. Decide whether to use, change, or not use the originally proposed solution.

5-5c NOMINAL GROUP TECHNIQUE

Nominal means "in name only." Accordingly, the **nominal group technique** received its name because it begins with a quiet time in which group members independently write down as many problem definitions and alternative solutions as possible. In other words, the nominal group technique begins by having group members act as individuals. After the quiet time, the group leader asks each member to share one idea at a time with the group. As they are read aloud, ideas are posted on flip charts or wallboards for all to see. This step continues until all ideas have been shared. In the next step, the group discusses the advantages and disadvantages of the ideas. The nominal group technique closes with a second quiet time in which group members independently rank the ideas presented. Group members then read their rankings aloud, and the idea with the highest average rank is selected.[56]

The nominal group technique improves group decision making by decreasing a-type conflict. But it also restricts c-type conflict. Consequently, the nominal group technique typically produces poorer decisions than the devil's advocacy and dialectical inquiry approaches. Nonetheless, more than eighty studies have found that nominal groups produce better ideas than those produced by traditional groups.[57]

5-5d DELPHI TECHNIQUE

In the **Delphi technique**, the members of a panel of experts respond to questions and to each other until reaching agreement on an issue. The first step is to assemble a panel of experts. Unlike other approaches to group decision making, however, it isn't necessary to bring the panel members together in one place. Because the Delphi technique does not require the experts to leave their offices or disrupt their schedules, they are more likely to participate.

The second step is to create a questionnaire consisting of a series of open-ended questions for the group. In the third step, the group members' written responses are analyzed, summarized, and fed back to the group for reactions until the members reach agreement. Asking group members why they agree or disagree is important because it helps uncover their unstated assumptions and beliefs. Again, this process of summarizing panel feedback and obtaining reactions to that feedback continues until the panel members reach agreement.

5-5e ELECTRONIC BRAINSTORMING

Brainstorming, in which group members build on others' ideas, is a technique for generating a large number of alternative solutions. Brainstorming has four rules:

1. The more ideas, the better.
2. All ideas are acceptable, no matter how wild or crazy they might seem.
3. Other group members' ideas should be used to come up with even more ideas.
4. Criticism or evaluation of ideas is not allowed.

Although brainstorming is great fun and can help managers generate a large number of alternative solutions, it does have a number of disadvantages. Fortunately, **electronic brainstorming**, in which group members use computers to communicate and generate alternative solutions, overcomes the disadvantages associated with face-to-face brainstorming.[58]

The first disadvantage that electronic brainstorming overcomes is **production blocking**, which occurs when you have an idea but have to wait to share it because someone else is already presenting an idea to the group. During this short delay, you may

forget your idea or decide that it really wasn't worth sharing. Production blocking doesn't happen with electronic brainstorming. All group members are seated at computers, so everyone can type in ideas whenever they occur. There's no waiting your turn to be heard by the group.

The second disadvantage that electronic brainstorming overcomes is **evaluation apprehension**, that is, being afraid of what others will think of your ideas. With electronic brainstorming, all ideas are anonymous. When you type in an idea and hit the Enter key to share it with the group, group members see only the idea. Furthermore, many brainstorming software programs also protect anonymity by displaying ideas in random order. So if you laugh maniacally when you type "Cut top management's pay by 50 percent!" and then hit the Enter key, it won't show up immediately on everyone's screen. This makes it doubly difficult to determine who is responsible for which comments.

In the typical layout for electronic brainstorming, all participants sit in front of computers around a U-shaped table. This configuration allows them to see their computer screens, the other participants, a large main screen, and a meeting leader or facilitator. Step 1 in electronic brainstorming is to anonymously generate as many ideas as possible. Groups commonly generate one hundred ideas in a half-hour period. Step 2 is to edit the generated ideas, categorize them, and eliminate redundancies. Step 3 is to rank the categorized ideas in terms of quality. Step 4, the last step, has three parts: generate a series of action steps, decide the best order for accomplishing these steps, and identify who is responsible for each step. All four steps are accomplished with computers and electronic brainstorming software.[59]

Studies show that electronic brainstorming is much more productive than face-to-face brainstorming. Four-person electronic brainstorming groups produce 25 to 50 percent more ideas than four-person regular brainstorming groups, and twelve-person electronic brainstorming groups produce 200 percent more ideas than regu-

© iStockphoto.com/alengo

lar groups of the same size! In fact, because production blocking (having to wait your turn) is not a problem in electronic brainstorming, the number and quality of ideas generally increase with group size.[60]

Even though it works much better than traditional brainstorming, electronic brainstorming has disadvantages, too. An obvious problem is the expense of computers, networks, software, and other equipment. As these costs continue to drop, however, electronic brainstorming will become cheaper.

Another problem is that the anonymity of ideas may bother people who are used to having their ideas accepted by virtue of their position (i.e., the boss). On the other hand, one CEO said, "Because the process is anonymous, the sky's the limit in terms of what you can say, and as a result it is more thought-provoking. As a CEO, you'll probably discover things you might

Twelve-person electronic brainstorming groups produce 200 percent more ideas than regular groups of the same size!

not want to hear but need to be aware of."[61]

A third disadvantage is that outgoing individuals who are more comfortable expressing themselves verbally may find it difficult to express themselves in writing. Finally, the most obvious problem is that participants have to be able to type. Those who can't type, or who type slowly, may be easily frustrated and find themselves at a disadvantage compared to experienced typists. For example, one meeting facilitator was informed that an especially fast typist was pretending to be more than one person. Says the facilitator, "He'd type 'Oh, I agree' and then 'Ditto, ditto' or 'What a great idea,' all in quick succession, using different variations of uppercase and lowercase letters and punctuation. He tried to make it seem like a lot of people were concurring, but it was just him." Eventually, the person sitting next to him got suspicious and began watching his screen.[62]

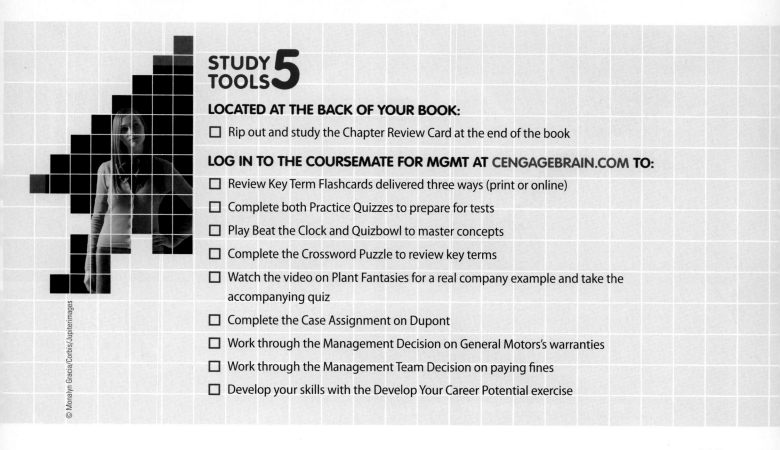

© Monalyn Gracia/Corbis/Jupiterimages

STUDY TOOLS 5

LOCATED AT THE BACK OF YOUR BOOK:

☐ Rip out and study the Chapter Review Card at the end of the book

LOG IN TO THE COURSEMATE FOR MGMT AT CENGAGEBRAIN.COM TO:

☐ Review Key Term Flashcards delivered three ways (print or online)

☐ Complete both Practice Quizzes to prepare for tests

☐ Play Beat the Clock and Quizbowl to master concepts

☐ Complete the Crossword Puzzle to review key terms

☐ Watch the video on Plant Fantasies for a real company example and take the accompanying quiz

☐ Complete the Case Assignment on Dupont

☐ Work through the Management Decision on General Motors's warranties

☐ Work through the Management Team Decision on paying fines

☐ Develop your skills with the Develop Your Career Potential exercise

6 Organizational
Strategy

© Ryan McVay/Photodisc/Getty Images

LEARNING OUTCOMES

6-1 Specify the components of sustainable competitive advantage, and explain why it is important.

6-2 Describe the steps involved in the strategy-making process.

6-3 Explain the different kinds of corporate-level strategies.

6-4 Describe the different kinds of industry-level strategies.

6-5 Explain the components and kinds of firm-level strategies.

CHECK OUT
STUDY TOOLS
AT THE END OF
THIS CHAPTER.

6-1 *Sustainable Competitive Advantage*

Just two years ago, there was no market for tablet computers. A number of computer makers sold touch-screen laptops, but other than some programs that allowed users to handwrite notes, there was little to distinguish these machines from traditional laptops. All of that changed when Apple released its iPad, a tablet computer that is controlled by a multitouch display and can run hundreds and thousands of applications that allow users to read books, watch movies, listen to music, check the weather, or play games. With its innovative product, Apple in effect created a new market for portable, touch-based tablet computers. The iPad is not without its competitors, however. The Amazon Kindle Fire, for example, is a touch-screen tablet that runs on Google's Android system. It features a dual-core processor, a seven-inch screen, and enough capacity to store 10 movies, 800 songs, or 6,000 books. The device also allows users to access Amazon's large collection of e-books. In spite of this competition, Apple dominates the tablet computer market. In 2011, Apple sold 40 million iPads and held a dominant 62 percent market share. To maintain its dominance, Apple recently announced the release of the new iPad, which features a faster processor, 4G network access for faster downloads, and voice dictation that recognizes English, French, German, and Japanese for emails, messaging, and other apps.[1]

How can a company like Apple, which dominates a particular industry, maintain its competitive advantage as strong, well-financed competitors enter the market? What steps can Apple and other companies take to better manage their strategy-making process?

Resources are the assets, capabilities, processes, employee time, information, and knowledge that an organization controls. Firms use their resources to improve organizational effectiveness and efficiency. Resources are critical to organizational strategy because they can help companies create and sustain an advantage over competitors.[2]

Organizations can achieve a **competitive advantage** by using their resources to provide greater value for customers than competitors can. For example, the iPad's competitive advantage came partly from its sleek, attractive design and partly from the reputation of Apple's iPod and iPhone as innovative, easy-to-use products.

The goal of most organizational strategies is to create and then sustain a competitive advantage. A competitive advantage becomes a **sustainable competitive advantage** when other companies cannot duplicate the value a firm is providing to customers. Sustainable competitive advantage is *not* the same as a long-lasting competitive advantage, though companies obviously want a competitive advantage to last a long time. Instead, a competitive advantage is *sustained* if competitors have tried unsuccessfully to duplicate the advantage and have, for the

Resources the assets, capabilities, processes, employee time, information, and knowledge that an organization uses to improve its effectiveness and efficiency and create and sustain competitive advantage

Competitive advantage providing greater value for customers than competitors can

Sustainable competitive advantage a competitive advantage that other companies have tried unsuccessfully to duplicate and have, for the moment, stopped trying to duplicate

Valuable resource a resource that allows companies to improve efficiency and effectiveness

Rare resource a resource that is not controlled or possessed by many competing firms

Imperfectly imitable resource a resource that is impossible or extremely costly or difficult for other firms to duplicate

moment, stopped trying to duplicate it. It's the corporate equivalent of your competitors saying, "We give up. You win. We can't do what you do, and we're not even going to try to do it anymore." Four conditions must be met if a firm's resources are to be used to achieve a sustainable competitive advantage. The resources must be valuable, rare, imperfectly imitable, *and* nonsubstitutable.

Valuable resources allow companies to improve their efficiency and effectiveness. Unfortunately, changes in customer demand and preferences, competitors' actions, and technology can make once-valuable resources much less valuable. Before the iPad was introduced, netbooks appeared to be the next big thing in mobile computing. These laptops were small and light, making them ultra portable, were very affordable, averaging anywhere from $200 to $500, and let users run basic programs like web browsing and word processing on the go. At first sales were brisk—in 2009, 7.5 million netbooks were sold in the United States and more than 34 million worldwide. But all that changed. The iPad had a touch screen, intuitive operating system, and a large selection of app software, while netbooks were often criticized for having small, hard-to-use keyboards, a slow operating system, and a lack of software options. While it took only twenty-eight days for Apple to sell its first one million iPads, netbook sales fell by 40 percent in one year.[3]

For sustained competitive advantage, valuable resources must also be rare resources. Think about it: How can a company sustain a competitive advantage if all of its competitors have similar resources and capabilities? Consequently, **rare resources**, resources that are not controlled or possessed by many competing firms, are necessary to sustain a competitive advantage. One of Apple's truly rare resources is its ability to reconfigure existing technology into a package that is easy to use, elegantly designed, and therefore highly desired by customers. Apple used its wealth of experience from developing the iPod, iPod touch, and iPhone to create an operating system for the iPad that

was easy to use and, more importantly, basically identical to what was found on its other products. In other words, it created a single platform that would give users the same experience across multiple devices. An iPhone user who just purchased an iPad will have little difficulty learning how to use it. This is not the case with the iPad's chief competitors, tablets powered by Google's Android. Because it is open source, meaning that manufacturers can alter the basic operating system in different ways, there is little uniformity across various Android devices. Simply put, one Android tablet might look and work differently than another, and one company might offer an app that will not work on another Android device.[4]

As this example shows, valuable and rare resources can create temporary competitive advantage. For sustained competitive advantage, however, other firms must be unable to imitate or find substitutes for those valuable, rare resources. **Imperfectly imitable resources** are those resources that are impossible or extremely costly or difficult to duplicate. Both Google and Amazon operate online app stores that are in some way similar to Apple's App Store. Users can log on to the sites, browse around for programs, and purchase and download programs to their devices. There is a big difference, however, in security. Apple's App Store is a closed platform, meaning that if a software developer wants to sell an app on Apple's site, the company first puts it through a review process to check for content and security issues. As noted above, however, Android is an open platform, which means that Google does not pre-screen apps before publishing them. This makes it far easier for developers with bad intentions to create and sell applications that can harm devices or steal personal information. According to a study by Juniper Networks, the number of such malware applications for Android climbed to 28,000 in 2011, a 3,325 percent increase from the previous year.[5]

Valuable, rare, imperfectly imitable resources can produce sustainable competitive advantage only if they are also **nonsubstitutable resources**, meaning that no other resources can replace them and produce similar value or competitive advantage. This is most evident in the dominance of Apple's iTunes software. The industry has tried to produce equivalent substitutes for iTunes, but competitors have had to experiment with different business models in order to get customers to accept them. For example, Amazon MP3 not only gives consumers access to 18 million digital songs, it allows consumers to store their files on Amazon's cloud servers. In essence, this means that users can buy a song from Amazon and stream it to any device they own, from their desktop computer to their Android tablet. Google's music service, called appropriately enough Google Music, also allows users to store their music on Google's cloud servers and stream to whatever device they want. The key problem with Google's service, however, is that Google was only able to reach licensing agreements with two record companies, meaning that the selection of songs that Google Music has for sale is quite limited. Apple has responded to these competitors by introducing its own cloud-based service called iCloud. The software essentially provides consumers with an online locker in which they can store music, video, or photo files, as well as apps, to access from multiple devices. In addition, iCloud lets users synchronize other data, like appointments, email, and documents, between their iPhone, iPad, and Mac computers.[6]

In summary, Apple has reaped the rewards of a first-mover advantage when it introduced the iPad. The company's history of developing customer-friendly software, the innovative capabilities of the iPad, the uniformity of experience, and the security of the App Store provide customers with a service that has been valuable, rare, relatively nonsubstitutable, and, in the past, imperfectly imitable. Past success is, however, no guarantee of future success: Apple needs to continually change and develop its offerings or risk being unseated by a more nimble competitor whose products are more relevant and have higher perceived value to the consumer.

6-2 *Strategy-Making Process*

In order to create a sustainable competitive advantage, a company must have a strategy.[7] Exhibit 6.1 displays the three steps of

the strategy-making process: **6-2a assess the need for strategic change, 6-2b conduct a situational analysis,** and then **6-2c choose strategic alternatives.** *Let's examine each of these steps in more detail.*

Nonsubstitutable resource a resource that produces value or competitive advantage and has no equivalent substitutes or replacements

6-2a ASSESSING THE NEED FOR STRATEGIC CHANGE

The external business environment is much more turbulent than it used to be. With customers' needs constantly growing and changing, and with competitors working harder, faster, and smarter to meet those needs, the first step in creating a strategy is determining the need for strategic change. In other words, the company should determine whether it needs to change its strategy to sustain a competitive advantage.[8]

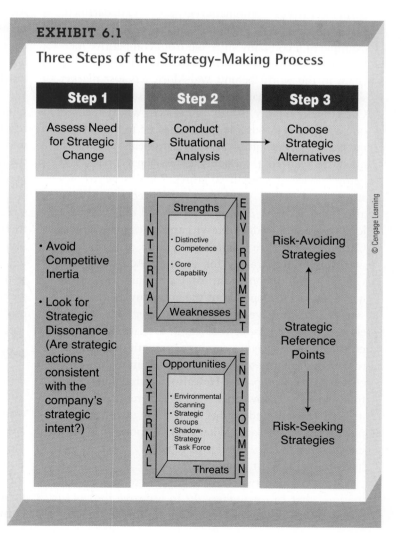

EXHIBIT 6.1

Three Steps of the Strategy-Making Process

© Cengage Learning

Competitive inertia a reluctance to change strategies or competitive practices that have been successful in the past

Strategic dissonance a discrepancy between a company's intended strategy and the strategic actions managers take when implementing that strategy

Situational (SWOT) analysis an assessment of the strengths and weaknesses in an organization's internal environment and the opportunities and threats in its external environment

Determining the need for strategic change might seem easy to do, but it's really not. There's a great deal of uncertainty in strategic business environments. Furthermore, top-level managers are often slow to recognize the need for strategic change, especially at successful companies that have created and sustained competitive advantages. Because they are acutely aware of the strategies that made their companies successful, they continue to rely on those strategies, even as the competition changes. In other words, success often leads to **competitive inertia**—a reluctance to change strategies or competitive practices that have been successful in the past. **Carrefour**, the French retail giant that invented hypermarket stores (combination grocery and department stores under one roof) half a century ago, is a prime example of a company suffering from competitive inertia. Carrefour, which grew to be the second largest retail chain in the world behind Wal-Mart, has lost market share in its hypermarket stores for five straight years.[9] Carrefour's "quality for all" approach, which focused on high-quality goods and food, relied on frequent price increases to keep profits strong. European customers, however, realized they could get cheaper prices and better service at specialized stores, such as electronics stores. And, unlike Carrefour, specialized stores were also quicker to get into and out of and didn't require long drives to the edge of towns and cities (where most Carrefour stores are located). Why did Carrefour stick with this losing strategy for so long? According new CEO Lars Olofsson, none of Carrefour's executives had ever worked outside of the company. Said Olofsson, "Carrefour never had a top manager coming from elsewhere."[10] Olofsson, who came to Carrefour as an outsider, has attacked Carrefour's competitive inertia by replacing the entire top management team with outsiders from other companies. He's also declared that Carrefour will follow a low-price strategy that relies on selling its own house brands rather than those of other companies. Says Olofsson, "What's very important is price image. If I'm the No. 1 preferred retailer . . . I'm the most likely to be the most profitable."[11]

Besides being aware of the dangers of competitive inertia, what can managers do to improve the speed and accuracy with which they determine the need for strategic change? One method is to actively look for signs of strategic dissonance. **Strategic dissonance** is a discrepancy between a company's intended strategy and the strategic actions managers take when actually implementing that strategy.[12] For example, by emphasizing efficiency, lean inventory, and continuous improvement, and even allowing factory workers to stop the assembly line when they spotted problems, Toyota produced the highest-quality cars in the world. But starting in 2008, widespread problems with stuck gas pedals, defective brakes, sludge-ruined engines, and SUVs prone to rolling over led to the recall of eight million Toyotas. How did this happen at a company famed for its quality?[13] Instead of maintaining its focus on quality, which was its long-term strategy, Toyota combined aggressive cost cutting with aggressive expansion, adding seventeen new production plants worldwide, while cutting annual spending by $2.2 billion. These strategic actions were at direct odds with the previous emphasis on quality. CEO Akio Toyoda, grandson of Toyota's founder, agreed, saying, "I fear the pace at which we have grown may be too quick. Priorities became confused, and we were not able to stop, think, and make improvements as much as we were able to before."[14]

Note, however, that strategic dissonance is not the same thing as when a strategy does not produce the results that it's supposed to. While most toy and game makers make big profits during the holidays, Hasbro, the maker of games like Monopoly and Scrabble, saw profits fall 15 percent during a disastrous Christmas season. This sharp decline is due primarily to Hasbro's strategy of focusing on movies and television. Rather than producing innovative board game offerings or investing in the rapidly growing online gaming market, Hasbro has spent most of its resources on trying to develop movies and TV shows based on its toys and games, such as the *Transformers* movie franchise and, most recently, *Battleship*.[15]

6-2b SITUATIONAL ANALYSIS

A situational analysis can also help managers determine the need for strategic change. A **situational analysis**, also called a **SWOT analysis**, for *strengths*, *weaknesses*, *opportunities*, and *threats*, is an assessment of the strengths and weaknesses in an organization's internal environment and the opportunities and threats in its external environment.[16] Ideally, as shown in Step 2 of Exhibit 6.1, a SWOT analysis helps a company determine how to increase internal strengths and minimize internal weaknesses while maximizing external opportunities and minimizing external threats.

An analysis of an organization's internal environment, that is, a company's strengths and weaknesses, often begins with an assessment of its distinctive competencies and core capabilities. A **distinctive competence** is something that a company can make, do, or perform better than its competitors. For example, *Consumer Reports* magazine consistently ranks Honda and Subaru cars as tops in quality and reliability.[17] Similarly, *PC Magazine* readers ranked Apple's desktop and laptop computers best in terms of service and reliability.[18]

Whereas distinctive competencies are tangible—for example, a product or service is faster, cheaper, or better—the core capabilities that produce distinctive competencies are not. **Core capabilities** are the less visible, internal decision-making routines, problem-solving processes, and organizational cultures that determine how efficiently inputs can be turned into outputs. Distinctive competencies cannot be sustained for long without superior core capabilities.

For years, large retail stores like Wal-Mart and Target have been trying to open stores in New York City only to be met with protests. Aldi, however, recently opened two stores in the city, not only with no protests but even with some politicians in attendance. The reason that Aldi faces little opposition as it opens stores in dense, urban settings is that it is able to make money in small, high-rent stores that are dictated by location. It operates with a business model that focuses on selling a limited number of groceries and household items in a small setting; its typical stores are just 16 percent the size of a typical Wal-Mart store and carry just 1,500 or so items, compared to 100,000 items in a superstore. Furthermore, most of its items are private brands, that is, goods that Aldi buys and packages itself. All of this means that Aldi can offer prices that are 20 percent less than Wal-Mart's, making it an attractive place for city dwellers to shop.[19]

After examining internal strengths and weaknesses, the second part of a situational analysis is to look outside the company and assess the opportunities and threats in the external environment. In Chapter 3, you learned that *environmental scanning* involves searching the en-

vironment for important events or issues that might affect the organization, such as pricing trends or new products and technology. In a situational analysis, however, managers use environmental scanning to identify specific opportunities and threats that can either improve or harm the company's ability to sustain its competitive advantage. Identification of strategic groups and formation of shadow-strategy task forces are two ways to do this (see box "Shadow-Strategy Task Force").

Strategic groups are not groups that actually work together. They are companies—usually competitors—that managers closely follow. More specifically, a **strategic group** is a group of other companies within an industry against which top managers compare, evaluate, and benchmark their company's strategic threats and opportunities.[20] (*Benchmarking* involves identifying outstanding practices, processes, and standards at other companies and adapting them to your own company.) Typically, managers include companies as part of their strategic group if they compete directly with those companies for customers or if those companies use strategies similar to theirs. The U.S. home improvement industry has annual sales in excess of $290 billion.[21] It's likely that the managers at Home Depot, the largest U.S. home improvement and hardware retailer, assess strategic threats and opportunities by comparing

Distinctive competence what a company can make, do, or perform better than its competitors

Core capabilities the internal decision-making routines, problem-solving processes, and organizational cultures that determine how efficiently inputs can be turned into outputs

Strategic group a group of companies within an industry against which top managers compare, evaluate, and benchmark strategic threats and opportunities

Core firms the central companies in a strategic group

Secondary firms the firms in a strategic group that follow strategies related to but somewhat different from those of the core firms

Shadow-strategy task force a committee within a company that analyzes the company's own weaknesses to determine how competitors could exploit them for competitive advantage

their company to a strategic group consisting of the other major home improvement supply companies. Exhibit 6.2 shows the number of stores, the size of the typical new store, and the overall geographic distribution (states, countries) of Home Depot stores compared with Lowe's, Ace Hardware, and 84 Lumber.

In fact, when scanning the environment for strategic threats and opportunities, managers tend to categorize the different companies in their industries as core, secondary, and transient firms.[22] **Core firms** are the central companies in a strategic group. Home Depot operates 2,248 stores covering all fifty states, Puerto Rico, the U.S. Virgin Islands, Mexico, Canada, and China. The company has 321,000 employees and annual revenues of over $68 billion. By comparison, Lowe's has more than 1,725 stores and 234,000 employees in fifty states and twelve provinces in Canada, stocks more than 40,000 products in each store, and has annual revenues of more than $48.8 billion.[23] Clearly, Lowe's is the closest competitor to Home Depot and is the core firm in Home Depot's strategic group. Even though Ace Hardware has more stores (4,600) than Home Depot and appears to be a bigger multinational player (seventy different countries), Ace's franchise structure and small, individualized stores (10,000 to 14,000 square feet, with each store laid out differently with a different mix of products) keep it from being a core firm in Home Depot's strategic group.[24] Likewise, Home Depot's management probably doesn't include Aubuchon Hardware in its core strategic group, because Aubuchon has only 125 stores in New England and upstate New York.[25]

When most managers scan their environments for strategic threats and opportunities, they concentrate on the strategic actions of core firms, not unrelated firms like Aubuchon. Where does a firm like Ace Hardware fit in? The company has made significant efforts to position itself as a more helpful version of Home Depot. Ace's Vision 21 strategic plan aims to make franchisees the leaders in Ace's unique convenient-store approach to selling hardware and has moved aggressively over the past decade to improve its supply chain operation.[26]

Secondary firms are firms that use strategies related to but somewhat different from those of core firms. 84 Lumber has 265 stores in thirty-five states, but even though its stores are open to the public, the company focuses on supplying professional contractors, to whom it sells 95 percent of its products. Without the wide variety of products on the shelves or assistance available to the average consumer, people without expertise in building or remodeling probably don't find 84 Lumber stores very accessible. Home Depot would most likely classify 84 Lumber as a secondary firm in its strategic group analysis.[27] Managers need to be aware of the potential threats and oppor-

Shadow-Strategy Task Force

When looking for threats and opportunities, many managers focus on competitors in the external environment. Others, however, prefer to examine the internal environment through a **shadow-strategy task force**. This strategy involves a company actively seeking out its own weaknesses and then thinking like its competitors, trying to determine how they can be exploited for competitive advantage. To make sure that the task force challenges conventional thinking, its members should be independent-minded, come from a variety of company functions and levels, and have the access and authority to question the company's current strategic actions and intent.

Source: W. B. Werther, Jr., and J. L. Kerr, "The Shifting Sands of Competitive Advantage," *Business Horizons* (May–June 1995): 11–17.

EXHIBIT 6.2

Core and Secondary Firms in the Home Improvement Industry

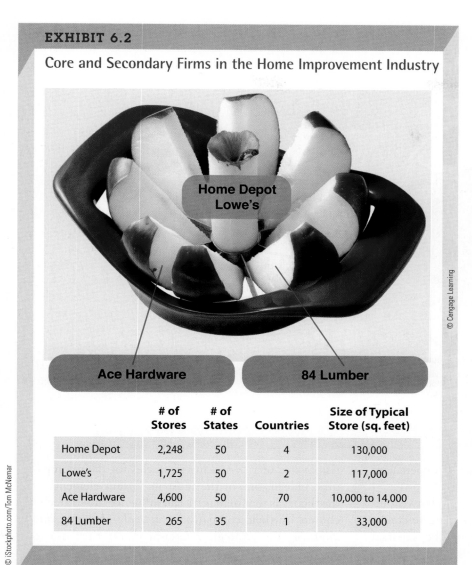

Home Depot
Lowe's

Ace Hardware

84 Lumber

	# of Stores	# of States	Countries	Size of Typical Store (sq. feet)
Home Depot	2,248	50	4	130,000
Lowe's	1,725	50	2	117,000
Ace Hardware	4,600	50	70	10,000 to 14,000
84 Lumber	265	35	1	33,000

© Cengage Learning

© iStockphoto.com/Tom McNemar

tunities posed by secondary firms, but they usually spend more time assessing the threats and opportunities associated with core firms.

6-2c CHOOSING STRATEGIC ALTERNATIVES

After determining the need for strategic change and conducting a situational analysis, the last step in the strategy-making process is to choose strategic alternatives that will help the company create or maintain a sustainable competitive advantage. According to *strategic reference point theory*, managers choose between two basic alternative strategies. They can choose a conservative, *risk-avoiding strategy* that aims to protect an existing competitive advantage. Or

they can choose an aggressive, *risk-seeking strategy* that aims to extend or create a sustainable competitive advantage. Menards is a hardware store chain with 40,000 employees and 210 locations throughout the Midwest.[28] When hardware giant Home Depot entered the Midwest, Menards faced a basic choice: Avoid risk by continuing with the strategy it had in place before Home Depot's arrival or seek risk by trying to further its competitive advantage against Home Depot, which is six times its size. Some of its competitors decided to fold. Kmart closed all of its Builders Square hardware stores when Home Depot came to Minneapolis. Handy Andy liquidated its seventy-four stores when Home Depot came to the Midwest. But Menards decided to fight, spending millions to open thirty-five new stores at the same time that Home Depot was opening forty-four of its own.[29]

The choice to seek risk or avoid risk typically depends on whether top management views the company as falling above or below strategic reference points. **Strategic reference points** are the targets that managers use to measure whether their firm has developed the core competencies that it needs to achieve a sustainable competitive advantage. If a hotel chain decides to compete by providing superior quality and service, then top management will track the success of this strategy through customer surveys or published hotel ratings such as those provided by the prestigious *Mobil Travel Guide*. If a hotel chain decides to compete on price, it will regularly conduct market surveys to check the prices of other hotels. The competitors' prices are the hotel managers' strategic reference points against which to compare their own pricing strategy. If competitors can consistently under-price them, then the managers need to determine whether

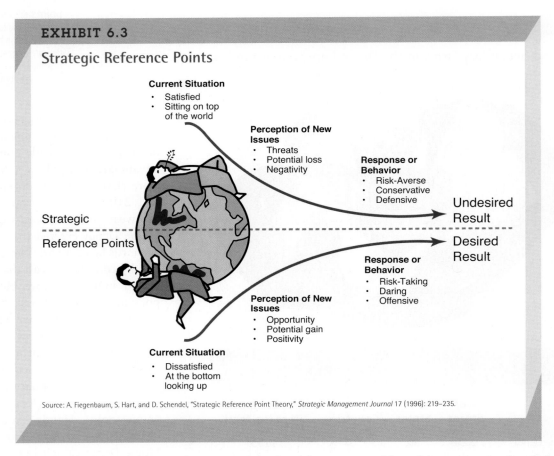

EXHIBIT 6.3

Strategic Reference Points

Current Situation
- Satisfied
- Sitting on top of the world

Perception of New Issues
- Threats
- Potential loss
- Negativity

Response or Behavior
- Risk-Averse
- Conservative
- Defensive

Undesired Result

Strategic

Reference Points

Desired Result

Response or Behavior
- Risk-Taking
- Daring
- Offensive

Perception of New Issues
- Opportunity
- Potential gain
- Positivity

Current Situation
- Dissatisfied
- At the bottom looking up

Source: A. Fiegenbaum, S. Hart, and D. Schendel, "Strategic Reference Point Theory," *Strategic Management Journal* 17 (1996): 219–235.

their staff and resources have the core competencies to compete on price.

As shown in Exhibit 6.3, when a company is performing above or better than its strategic reference points, top management will typically be satisfied with the company's strategy. Ironically, this satisfaction tends to make top management conservative and risk-averse. Since the company already has a sustainable competitive advantage, the worst thing that could happen would be to lose it, so new issues or changes in the company's external environment are viewed as threats. By contrast, when a company is performing below or worse than its strategic reference points, top management will typically be dissatisfied with the company's strategy. In this instance, managers are much more likely to choose a daring, risk-taking strategy. If the current strategy is producing substandard results, the company has nothing to lose by switching to risky new strategies in the hope that it can create a sustainable competitive advantage. Managers of companies in this situation view new issues or changes in the external environment as opportunities for potential gain.

Strategic reference point theory is not deterministic, however. Managers are not predestined to choose

risk-averse or risk-seeking strategies for their companies. Indeed, one of the most important elements of the theory is that managers *can* influence the strategies chosen by their company by *actively changing and adjusting* the strategic reference points they use to judge strategic performance. If a company has become complacent after consistently surpassing its strategic reference points, then top management can change from a risk-averse to a risk-taking orientation by raising the standards of performance (i.e., the strategic reference points). This is just what happened at Menards.

Instead of being satisfied with merely protecting its existing stores (a risk-averse strategy), founder John Menard changed the strategic reference points the company had been using to assess strategic performance. To encourage a daring, offensive-minded strategy that would allow the company to open nearly as many new stores as Home Depot, he determined that Menards would have to beat Home Depot on not one or two, but four strategic reference points: price, products, sales per square foot, and "friendly accessibility." The strategy appears to be succeeding. In terms of price, market research indicates that a 100-item shopping cart of goods is consistently cheaper at

Menards. In terms of products, Menards sells 50,000 products per store, the same as Home Depot. In terms of sales per square foot, Menards ($407 per square foot) outsells Home Depot ($300 per square foot).[30] Finally, unlike Home Depot's warehouse-like stores, Menards's stores are built to resemble grocery stores. Shiny tiled floors, wide aisles, and easy-to-reach products all make Menards a "friendlier" place for shoppers. And now with Lowe's, the second-largest hardware store chain in the nation, also entering its markets, Menards has added a fifth strategic reference point: store size. At 225,000 square feet, most new Menards stores are nearly double the size of Home Depot's stores and 100,000 square feet larger than Lowe's biggest stores.[31] John Caulfield, who wrote a book about Home Depot and the hardware business, says, "Menards is clearly throwing the gauntlet down at Lowe's. They're saying, 'If you come into Chicago, here is what you're going to face.'"[32]

So even when (perhaps *especially* when) companies have achieved a sustainable competitive advantage, top managers must adjust or change strategic reference points to challenge themselves and their employees to develop new core competencies for the future. In the long run, effective organizations will frequently revise their strategic reference points to better focus managers' attention on the new challenges and opportunities that occur in their ever-changing business environments.

6-3 *Corporate-Level Strategies*

To formulate effective strategies, companies must be able to answer these three basic questions:

- What business are we in?
- How should we compete in this industry?
- Who are our competitors, and how should we respond to them?

These simple but powerful questions are at the heart of corporate-, industry-, and firm-level strategies. **Corporate-level strategy** is the overall organizational strategy that addresses the question "What business or businesses are we in or should we be in?"

There are two major approaches to corporate-level strategy that companies use to decide which businesses they should be in: *6-3a portfolio strategy* and *6-3b grand strategies.*

6-3a PORTFOLIO STRATEGY

One of the standard strategies for stock market investors is **diversification**, or owning stocks in a variety of companies in different industries. The purpose of this strategy is to reduce risk in the overall stock portfolio (the entire collection of stocks). The basic idea is simple: If you invest in ten companies in ten different industries, you won't lose your entire investment if one company performs poorly. Furthermore, because they're in different industries, one company's losses are likely to be offset by another company's gains. Portfolio strategy is based on these same ideas. We'll start by taking a look at the theory and ideas behind portfolio strategy and then proceed with a critical review that suggests that some of the key ideas behind portfolio strategy are *not* supported.

Portfolio strategy is a corporate-level strategy that minimizes risk by diversifying investment among various businesses or product lines.[33] Just as a diversification strategy guides an investor who invests in a variety of stocks, portfolio strategy guides the strategic decisions of corporations that compete in a variety of businesses. For example, portfolio strategy could be used to guide the strategy of a company like 3M, which makes 55,000 products for seven different business sectors: consumers and offices (Post-its, Scotch tape); display and graphics (for computers, cell phones, PDAs, TVs); electronics and communications (flexible circuits used in printers and electronic displays); health care (medical, surgical, dental, and personal care products); industrial (tapes, adhesives, supply chain software, products and components for the manufacture, repair, and maintenance of autos, aircraft, boats, and other vehicles); safety, security, and protection services (glass safety, fire protection, respiratory products); and transportation.[34]

Just as investors consider the mix of stocks in their stock portfolio when deciding which stocks to buy or sell, managers following portfolio strategy try to acquire companies that fit well with the rest of their corporate portfolio and to sell those that don't. Procter

Corporate-level strategy the overall organizational strategy that addresses the question "What business or businesses are we in or should we be in?"

Diversification a strategy for reducing risk by buying a variety of items (stocks or, in the case of a corporation, types of businesses) so that the failure of one stock or one business does not doom the entire portfolio

Portfolio strategy a corporate-level strategy that minimizes risk by diversifying investment among various businesses or product lines

& Gamble used to be a big name in the food business, as it sold everything from cake mixes to juice. However, the company decided that it wanted to focus its resources on its core business of household, beauty, and health care items. It thus began selling off products and brands that did not relate to the core business, a process that was completed when P&G sold the Pringles line of potato chips to Kellogg for $2.7 billion.[35]

First, according to portfolio strategy, the more businesses in which a corporation competes, the smaller its overall chances of failing. Think of a corporation as a stool and its businesses as the legs of the stool. The more legs or businesses added to the stool, the less likely it is to tip over. Using this analogy, portfolio strategy reduces 3M's risk of failing because the corporation's survival depends on essentially seven different business sectors. Managers employing portfolio strategy can either develop new businesses internally or look for **acquisitions**, that is, other companies to buy. Either way, the goal is to add legs to the stool.

Second, beyond adding new businesses to the corporate portfolio, portfolio strategy predicts that companies can reduce risk even more through **unrelated diversification**—creating or acquiring companies in completely unrelated businesses (more on the accuracy of this prediction later). According to portfolio strategy, when businesses are unrelated, losses in one business or industry should have minimal effect on the performance of other companies in the corporate portfolio. General Electric, which was founded in part by Thomas Edison, is the largest conglomerate in the world and has a presence in a wide range of businesses. Its appliances division produces refrigerators, ovens, and dishwashers. Its consumer electronics divisions make everything from computer mice to digital cameras to portable generators. Its lighting division, of course, sells light bulbs, as well as traffic signals and specialty lighting. Its aviation division, meanwhile, is one of the world leaders in making jet engines. GE also has divisions in energy distribution, energy, business and consumer finance, health care, oil and gas, rail, software and services, and water.[36]

Because most internally grown businesses tend to be related to existing products or services, portfolio strategy suggests that acquiring new businesses is the preferred method of unrelated diversification.[37]

Third, investing the profits and cash flows from mature, slow-growth businesses into newer, faster-growing businesses can reduce long-term risk. The best-known portfolio strategy for guiding investment in a corporation's businesses is the Boston Consulting Group (BCG) matrix.[38] The **BCG matrix** is a portfolio strategy that managers use to categorize their corporation's businesses by growth rate and relative market share, which helps them decide how to invest corporate funds. The matrix, shown in Exhibit 6.4, separates businesses into four categories based on how fast the market is growing (high-growth or low-growth) and the size of the business's share of that market (small or large). **Stars** are companies that have a large share of a fast-growing market. To take advantage of a star's fast-growing market and its strength in that market (large share), the corporation must invest substantially in it. The investment is usually worthwhile, however, because many stars produce sizable future profits. **Question marks** are companies that have a small share of a fast-growing market. If the corporation invests in these companies, they may eventually become stars, but their relative weakness in the market (small share) makes investing in question marks more risky than investing in stars. **Cash cows** are companies that have a large share of a slow-growing market. Companies in this situation are often highly profitable, hence the name "cash cow." Finally, **dogs** are companies that have a small share of a slow-growing market. As the name suggests, having a small share of a slow-growth market is often not profitable.

Since the idea is to redirect investment from slow-growing to fast-growing companies, the BCG matrix starts by recommending that while the substantial cash flows from cash cows last, they should be reinvested in stars (see 1 in Exhibit 6.4) to help them grow even faster and obtain even more market share. Using this strategy, current profits help produce future profits. Over time, as their market growth slows, some stars may turn into cash cows (see 2). Cash flows should also be directed to some question marks (see 3). Though riskier than stars, question marks have great potential because of their fast-growing market. Managers must decide which question marks are most likely to turn into stars (and therefore warrant further investment) and which ones

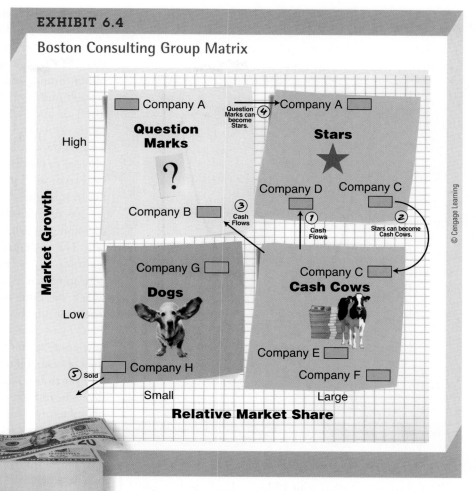

are too risky and should be sold. Over time, managers hope some question marks will become stars as their small markets become large ones (see 4). Finally, because dogs lose money, the corporation should "find them new owners" or "take them to the pound." In other words, dogs should either be sold to other companies or closed down and liquidated for their assets (see 5).

Although the BCG matrix and other forms of portfolio strategy are relatively popular among managers, portfolio strategy has some drawbacks. The most significant? Contrary to the predictions of portfolio strategy, the evidence suggests that acquiring unrelated businesses is *not* useful. As shown in Exhibit 6.5 on page 118, there is a U-shaped relationship between diversification and risk. The left side of the curve shows that single businesses with no diversification are extremely risky (if the single business fails, the entire business fails). So, in part, the portfolio strategy of diversifying is correct—competing in a variety of different businesses can lower risk. However, portfolio strategy is partly wrong, too—the right side of the curve shows that conglomerates composed of completely unrelated businesses are even riskier than single, undiversified businesses.[39]

A second set of problems with portfolio strategy has to do with the dysfunctional consequences that can occur when companies are categorized as stars, cash cows, question marks, or dogs. Contrary to expectations, the BCG matrix often yields incorrect judgments about a company's potential. In other words, managers using the BCG matrix aren't very good at accurately determining which companies should be categorized as stars, cash cows, questions marks, or dogs. The most common mistake is simply miscategorizing highly profitable companies as dogs.[40] In part, this is because the BCG matrix relies on past performance (previous market share and previous market growth), which is a notoriously poor predictor of future company performance. More worrisome, however, is research that

indicates that the BCG matrix actually makes managers worse at judging the future profitability of a business. A study conducted in six countries over five years gave managers and business students clear information about the current and future profits (i.e., slow or fast growth) of three companies and asked them to select the one that would be most successful in the future. Although not labeled this way, one company was clearly a star, another was a dog, and the last was a cash cow. Just exposing people to the ideas in the BCG matrix led them to incorrectly categorize less profitable businesses as the most successful businesses 64 percent of the time, while actually *using* the BCG matrix led to making the same mistake 87 percent of the time.[41]

Furthermore, using the BCG matrix can also weaken the strongest performer in the corporate portfolio, the cash cow. As funds are redirected from cash cows to stars, corporate managers essentially take away the resources needed to take advantage of the cash cow's new business opportunities. As a result, the cash cow becomes less aggressive in seeking new business or in defending its present business. For example,

EXHIBIT 6.5

U-Shaped Relationship between Diversification and Risk

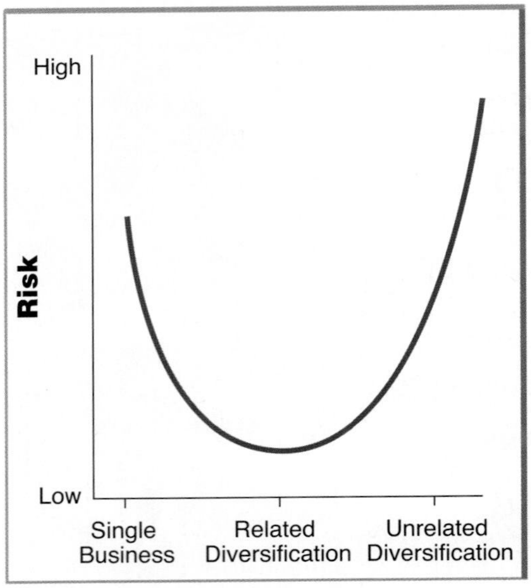

Source: Republished by The Academy of Management, P.O. Box 3020, Briar Cliff Manor, NY, 10510-8020. M. Lubatkin & P.J. Lane, "Psst! . . . The Merger Mavens Still Have It Wrong," *Academy of Management Executive* 10 (1996) 21–39; Reproduced with the permission of the publisher via Copyright Clearance Center, Inc.

Procter & Gamble's Tide, the laundry detergent that P&G brought to market in 1946, is clearly a cash cow, accounting for $3.5 billion in worldwide revenues. In addition to Tide, P&G has twenty-three other brands, such as Bounty paper towels, Crest toothpaste, Gillette razors, and Pampers diapers, each of which exceed $1 billion in annual sales. Out of 250 brands company-wide, those twenty-three $1 billion+ brands account for nearly 70 percent of P&G's sales and 75 percent of its profits.[42] A few years ago, however, in a bid to bring new products to market the company was diverting up to half a billion dollars a year from cash cows like Tide to promote potential product blockbusters (i.e., stars) such as Febreze, a spray that eliminates odors; Dryel, which dry-cleans clothes at home; Fit, a spray that kills bacteria on fruits and vegetables; and Impress, a high-tech plastic wrap.[43] P&G ultimately reversed the diversion of funds when

Related diversification creating or acquiring companies that share similar products, manufacturing, marketing, technology, or cultures

Grand strategy a broad corporate-level strategic plan used to achieve strategic goals and guide the strategic alternatives that managers of individual businesses or subunits may use

the potential blockbusters did not find much success, and the company refocused on its biggest brands (its cash cows).[44] Indeed, of the stars listed above, Febreze, Dryel, Fit, and Impress, only Febreze has become a $1 billion brand, and much of that has been achieved by cross-branding Febreze with existing P&G products, like Tide and Gain detergents and Bounce and Downy fabric softeners.[45] Finally, labeling a top performer as a cash cow can harm employee morale. Cash-cow employees realize that they have inferior status and that instead of working for themselves, they are now working to fund the growth of stars and question marks.

So, what kind of portfolio strategy does the best job of helping managers decide which companies to buy or sell? The U-shaped curve in Exhibit 6.5 indicates that, contrary to the predictions of portfolio strategy, the best approach is probably **related diversification**, in which the different business units share similar products, manufacturing, marketing, technology, or cultures. The key to related diversification is to acquire or create new companies with core capabilities that complement the core capabilities of businesses already in the corporate portfolio. Hormel Foods is an example of related diversification in the food business. The company both manufactures and markets a variety of foods, from deli meats to salsa to the infamous SPAM.

We began this section with the example of 3M and its 55,000 products sold in over seven different business sectors. While seemingly different, most of 3M's product divisions are based in some fashion on its distinctive competencies in adhesives and tape (e.g., wet or dry sandpaper, Post-it notes, Scotchgard fabric protector, transdermal skin patches, and reflective material used in traffic signs). Furthermore, all of 3M's divisions share its strong corporate culture that promotes and encourages risk taking and innovation. In sum, in contrast to a single, undiversified business or unrelated diversification, related diversification reduces risk because the different businesses can work as a team, relying on each other for needed experience, expertise, and support.

6-3b GRAND STRATEGIES

A **grand strategy** is a broad strategic plan used to help an organization achieve its strategic goals.[46] Grand strategies guide the strategic alternatives that managers of individual businesses or subunits may use in deciding what businesses they should be in. There are three kinds of grand strategies: growth, stability, and retrenchment/recovery.

The Shrink-Ray Strategy

Best Buy stands at the top of the consumer electronics market thanks to a strategy that it has used for many years—big stores filled to the brim with a huge selection of products, everything from washers and dryers to laptop computers. Lately, however, it has found success harder to come by. It has seen its shares fall and market share decline, partly because of the global recession, partly because of online competitors, and partly because consumers want a more efficient shopping experience. For those reasons, Best Buy is shifting its strategy to smaller stores. It plans to close some stores, reduce the size of others by 10 percent, and focus on smaller stores that specialize in a particular product, such as Best Buy Mobile, which will emphasize smartphones.

Source: M. Bustillo, "Best Buy to Shrink 'Big-Box' Store Strategy," *Wall Street Journal*, April 15, 2011, B7.

Growth strategy a strategy that focuses on increasing profits, revenues, market share, or the number of places in which the company does business

Stability strategy a strategy that focuses on improving the way in which the company sells the same products or services to the same customers

Retrenchment strategy a strategy that focuses on turning around very poor company performance by shrinking the size or scope of the business

quite helpful at a time of high commodity costs. Thanks to the company's promotional emphasis, sales of Aero increased by 20 percent from the previous year, which helped the company as a whole earn a profit of $10.3 billion and sales growth of 7.5 percent.[47]

The purpose of a **stability strategy** is to continue doing what the company has been doing, just doing it better. Companies following a stability strategy try to improve the way in which they sell the same products or services to the same customers. Since its inception in 1938, **REI** has never strayed from its focus on the outdoors. Its Mountain Safety Research division designs and makes mountaineering equipment, clothing, and camping products. REI Adventures offers adventure travel packages (e.g., kayaking, climbing, and backpacking) with hand-picked local guides on all seven continents. Finally, in addition to its website, REI has eighty stores in twenty-seven states selling high-quality outdoor gear, clothing, and footwear.[48] And today, with 3.5 million members whose membership entitles them to discounts and expert advice, REI is one of the largest retail co-ops in the world. Companies often choose a stability strategy when their external environment doesn't change much or after they have struggled with periods of explosive growth.

The purpose of a **retrenchment strategy** is to turn around very poor company performance by

The purpose of a **growth strategy** is to increase profits, revenues, market share, or the number of places (stores, offices, locations) in which the company does business. Companies can grow in several ways. They can grow externally by merging with or acquiring other companies in the same or different businesses. Some large mergers and acquisitions of recent years include Capital One buying ING Direct (banking), Oracle buying Taleo (software development), and Microsoft buying Skype (Internet communication).

Another way to grow is internally, directly expanding the company's existing business or creating and growing new businesses. Nestlé, the largest food company in the world, faced a serious challenge—it had to find a way to grow while having to deal with record-high prices for cocoa and sugar, two key ingredients for its chocolate products. To boost growth, Nestlé spent $24 million to promote its Aero, a chocolate bar that is filled with bubbles of air. While the bubbles give the chocolate a creamier texture, they also help bulk up the candy bar without adding more ingredients,

Recovery the strategic actions taken after retrenchment to return to a growth strategy

Industry-level strategy a corporate strategy that addresses the question "How should we compete in this industry?"

shrinking the size or scope of the business or, if a company is in multiple businesses, by closing or shutting down different lines of the business (see box "The Shrink-Ray Strategy"). The first step of a typical retrenchment strategy might include making significant cost reductions: laying off employees; closing poorly performing stores, offices, or manufacturing plants; or closing or selling entire lines of products or services.[49] In its most recent financial statement, Delta Air Lines announced that it made a profit of $854 million, an increase of 44 percent from the previous year, making it the first time in more than ten years the airline has been profitable for two straight years. How did it accomplish this when so many other airlines are having difficulty? Delta used a comprehensive plan to raise its profitability by reducing costs in several ways. First, Delta cut back on its flight service. It eliminated service completely to twenty-four midwestern cities in Iowa, Michigan, Minnesota, Mississippi, North Dakota, and South Dakota, where flights averaged just a little above 50 percent occupancy (that is, the average flight was just half full). According to the company, these flights were producing losses of $14 million per year. The airline also reduced the total number of its flights by 7 to 9 percent. By reducing its total number of flights, Delta was able to decrease the supply available to customers and, hence, increase the fares it charged, which resulted in more revenue. Delta also found cost savings through personnel moves, as it offered 2,000 employees voluntary buyouts and early retirement, and eliminated another 200 management positions.[50]

After cutting costs and reducing a business's size or scope, the second step in a retrenchment strategy is recovery. **Recovery** consists of the strategic actions that a company takes to return to a growth strategy. This two-step process of cutting and recovery is analogous to pruning roses. Prior to each growing season, roses should be cut back to two-thirds their normal size. Pruning doesn't damage the roses; it makes them stronger and more likely to produce beautiful, fragrant flowers. The retrenchment-and-recovery process is similar. Cost reductions, layoffs, and plant closings are sometimes necessary to restore companies to good health. In the early days of online shopping, **Priceline.com** started out with a bang, offering a "name your own price" service on everything from airplane tickets to groceries. The business quickly collapsed, however, as consumers realized they didn't want to save $50 by flying from New York to Los Angeles with a five-hour layover in Dallas. The company's stock plummeted from $974 per share to just $7, and it was on the verge of collapse. CEO Jeffrey Boyd has led a dramatic recovery by shifting strategy. Instead of airplane tickets and groceries, Priceline's focus is now on hotels. By partnering with major hotel chains and acquiring discount travel websites in Europe and Asia, Priceline works with 100,000 hotels in ninety countries that appeal to a wide range of consumers. Furthermore, international bookings account for 61 percent of its revenues, nearly twice that of Expedia (34 percent) and 4.4 times Orbitz (14 percent). Thanks to the new emphasis on hotels, the company was recently ranked number one on *Bloomberg Businessweek*'s list of fifty best-performing stocks on the S&P 500 index, its market valuation is estimated at $8.8 billion, and annual growth is estimated to approach 20 percent.[51]

Like pruning, the cuts are made as part of a recovery strategy intended to allow companies to eventually return to a successful growth strategy. When company performance drops significantly, a strategy of retrenchment and recovery may help the company return to a successful growth strategy.

6-4 *Industry-Level Strategies*

Industry-level strategy addresses the question "How should we compete in this industry?"

Let's find out more about industry-level strategies by discussing 6-4a the five industry forces that deter-

© George Frey/Getty Images

*mine overall levels of competition in an industry as well as **6-4b the positioning strategies** and **6-4c adaptive strategies** that companies can use to achieve sustained competitive advantage and above-average profits.*

6-4a FIVE INDUSTRY FORCES

According to Harvard professor Michael Porter, five industry forces determine an industry's overall attractiveness and potential for long-term profitability. These include the character of the rivalry, the threat of new entrants, the threat of substitute products or services, the bargaining power of suppliers, and the bargaining power of buyers. The stronger these forces, the less attractive the industry becomes to corporate investors because it is more difficult for companies to be profitable. Porter's industry forces are illustrated in Exhibit 6.6. Let's examine how these forces are bringing changes to several kinds of industries.

Character of the rivalry is a measure of the intensity of competitive behavior among companies in an industry. Is the competition among firms aggressive and cutthroat, or do competitors focus more on serving customers than on attacking each other? Both industry attractiveness and profitability decrease when rivalry is cutthroat. For example, selling cars is a highly competitive business. Pick up a local newspaper on Friday, Saturday, or Sunday morning, and you'll find dozens of pages of car advertising ("Anniversary Sale-A-Bration," "Ford March Savings!" and "$99 Down, You Choose!"). In fact, competition in new car sales is so intense that if it weren't for used-car sales, repair work, and replacement parts, many auto dealers would actually lose money.

The **threat of new entrants** is a measure of the degree to which barriers to entry make it easy or difficult for new companies to get started in an industry. If new companies can enter the industry easily, then competition will increase and prices and profits will fall. For example, **Unilever PLC** recently introduced its Magnum premium ice cream bars to the United States. Introduced in the United Kingdom in 1987, the Magnum is the top-selling ice cream bar in the world, accounting for 6.8 percent of the global market. While Michael Polk, president of Unilever's global food division, believes that the Magnum bars will double the market for "super-premium ice-cream novelties" in the United States, which accounts for 4 percent of the $9.3 billion U.S. ice cream market, the introduction of Magnum is bad news for Dove and Häagen-Dazs, which have dominated this market in the United States.[52] On the other hand, if there are sufficient barriers to entry, such as large capital requirements to buy expensive equipment or plant facilities or the need for specialized knowledge, then competition will be weaker and prices and profits will generally be higher. For instance, high costs make it very difficult to enter the natural gas business. Anadarko Petroleum has discovered three immense natural gas sites off the coast of Mozambique, which are estimated to yield 6 to 8 trillion cubic feet of gas. At a minimum, it will take $2 billion and six years (two for planning and four for construction) before any gas can be extracted and shipped to customers.[53]

Character of the rivalry a measure of the intensity of competitive behavior between companies in an industry

Threat of new entrants a measure of the degree to which barriers to entry make it easy or difficult for new companies to get started in an industry

Threat of substitute products or services a measure of the ease with which customers can find substitutes for an industry's products or services

EXHIBIT 6.6

Porter's Five Industry Forces

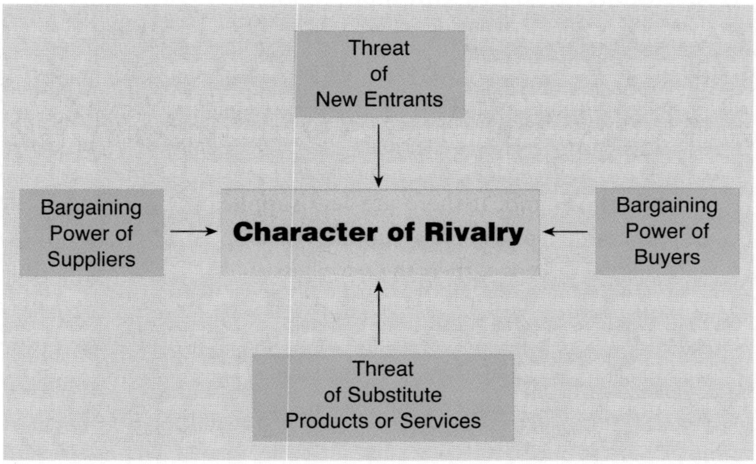

Source: Adapted with permission of the Free Press, a division of Simon & Schuster, Inc. Porter, M. E. *Competitive Strategy: Techniques for Analyzing Industries and Competitors.* New York: Free Press, 1980. © 1980, 1998 by The Free Press. All rights reserved.

The **threat of substitute products or services** is a measure of the ease with which customers can find substitutes for an industry's products or services. If customers can easily find substitute products or services, the competition will be greater and profits will be lower. If there are few or no substitutes, competition will be weaker and profits will be higher. Generic medicines are some of the best-known examples of substitute products. Under U.S. patent law, a company that develops a drug has exclusive rights to produce and market that drug for twenty years. Prices and profits are generally high during this period if the drug sells well. After twenty years, however, the patent will expire, and any pharmaceutical company can manufacture and sell the same drug. When this happens, drug prices drop substantially, and the company that developed the drug typically sees its revenues drop sharply. Over the next few years, AstroZeneca will lose patent protection for Crestor (which lowers cholesterol) and Symbicort (for asthma). Other companies and drugs with expiring patents include Eli Lilly and Zyprexa (for schizophrenia); Forest Laboratories and Lexapro (for depression), and Pfizer and Lipitor (for cholesterol), Aricept (for Alzheimer's disease), and Xalatan (for glaucoma).[54]

Bargaining power of suppliers is a measure of the influence that suppliers of parts, materials, and services to firms in an industry have on the prices of these inputs. When companies can buy parts, materials, and services from numerous suppliers, the companies will be able to bargain with the suppliers to keep prices low. On the other hand, if there are few suppliers, or if a company is dependent on a supplier with specialized skills and knowledge, then the suppliers will have the bargaining power to dictate price levels. In the oil industry, the suppliers have so much power that even the possibility that one of them might reduce production or impose an embargo is enough to send prices skyrocketing. This can be seen clearly in recent developments centered on Iran, the world's third-largest oil producer. For a number of years, several countries have been worried that Iran is trying to develop nuclear weapons. Iran, meanwhile, contends that its nuclear program is intended only for generating electricity and has been uncooperative, if not hostile, to UN inspectors. In an attempt to force Iran to cooperate, the United States and the European Union have threatened to place severe restrictions on Iran's ability to sell oil. Iran, on its part, countered with threats that it would cut Western nations off from the 3.5 million barrels of oil that it produces every day. Just the possibility that oil supplies might be reduced sent prices skyrocketing, with oil reaching $125 per barrel and the price of gas in the United States averaging $3.74 per gallon, the highest since 2008.[55]

Bargaining power of buyers is a measure of the influence that customers have on the firm's prices. If a company sells a popular product or service to multiple buyers, then the company has more power to set prices. By contrast, if a company is dependent on just a few high-volume buyers, those buyers will typically have enough bargaining power to dictate prices. **Costco**, a membership warehouse chain and the third-largest retailer in the United States, focuses on offering extremely low prices. Oftentimes, when it believes that a supplier charges too much for a product, it simply stops carrying it. So when Coca-Cola wanted to aggressively raise prices, Costco stopped selling Coca-Cola products. According to a message on Costco's website, "At this time, Coca-Cola has not provided Costco with competitive pricing so that we may pass along the value our members deserve." After three weeks of negotiations, Coca-Cola lowered its prices and Coca-Cola products were back on Costco shelves.[56]

6-4b POSITIONING STRATEGIES

After analyzing industry forces, the next step in industry-level strategy is to protect your company from the negative effects of industry-wide competition and to create a sustainable competitive advantage. According to Michael Porter, there are three positioning strategies: cost leadership, differentiation, and focus.

Cost leadership means producing a product or service of acceptable quality at consistently lower production costs than competitors so that the firm can offer the product or service at the lowest price in the industry. Cost leadership protects companies from industry forces by deterring new entrants, who will have to match low costs and prices. Cost leadership also forces down the prices of substitute products and services, attracts bargain-seeking buyers, and increases bargaining power with suppliers, who have to keep their prices low if they want to do business with the cost leader. Why do most glasses cost several hundred dollars? It's partly because the cost of each frame includes brand licensing fees and because glasses retailers add their own markup. High prices are also due to the fact that there is one company that dominates the industry. Luxottica, based in Italy, owns LensCrafters, Pearle Vision, and Sunglass Hut, as well as the optical departments of Target and Sears. It also manufactures frames for twenty top brands like Chanel and Prada. Dave Gilboa and Neil Blumenthal decided to do things differently with their company Warby Parker. Rather than paying license fees for brand-name frames, they buy them from the same manufacturer that supplies Luxottica. And because they have no retailers to deal with, there is no huge markup. Thus, Warby Parker charges just $95 for a complete pair of glasses, which are shipped free of charge. Consumers can even get a weeklong free trial of up to five frames to see what fits them the best. In just seventeen months since the company started, Warby Parker sold 50,000 pairs of glasses, turned a profit, and attracted $1.5 million in investments.[57]

Differentiation means making your product or service sufficiently different from competitors' offerings that customers are willing to pay a premium price for the extra value or performance that it provides. Differentiation protects companies from industry forces by reducing the threat of substitute products. It also protects companies by making it easier to retain customers and more difficult for new entrants trying to attract new customers.

With a **focus strategy**, a company uses either cost leadership or differentiation to produce a specialized product or service for a limited, specially targeted group of customers in a particular geographic region or market segment. Focus strategies typically work in market niches that competitors have overlooked or have difficulty serving. From newspapers to magazines to books, the publishing industry is facing falling sales and reduced revenues, and there appear to be no clear ideas of what to do about it. One area in publishing, however, is growing $100 million a year, nearly 8 percent per year on average. It appeals to a small segment of readers and accounts for just 14 percent of all books sold. But, this book segment is the top-performing category on the *New York Times*, *USA Today*, and *Publishers Weekly* best-seller lists. Can you guess what it is? Romance novels. Yes, sales of romance novels are growing for publishers like Avon Romance (owned by HarperCollins Publishers), which are appealing to targeted groups of readers interested in NASCAR, quilting, transgender, knitting, military, and paranormal (think vampires and werewolves). Indeed, on the day

this was written, the Avon Romance website was featuring *Vampire Mine*, by Kerrelyn Sparks, *Sex and the Single Vampire* by Katie MacAlister, *A Tale of Two Vikings* by Sandra Hill, and *How I Met My Countess* by Elizabeth Boyle. One of the most popular subject areas, according to sales figures, is Mennonite and Amish-themed romances. A highly anticipated novel, for example, tells the story of a young woman whose parents have died in a horse-drawn-carriage accident and who meets a suitor who will test the limits of her Amish faith. So, while most people don't read romance novels, catering to those who do with micro-themed books (i.e., a focus strategy) is one of the few successful strategies in publishing today.[58]

6-4c ADAPTIVE STRATEGIES

Adaptive strategies are another set of industry-level strategies. Whereas the aim of positioning strategies is to minimize the effects of industry competition and build a sustainable competitive advantage, the purpose of adaptive strategies is to choose an industry-level strategy that is best suited to changes in the organization's external environment. There are four kinds of adaptive strategies: defenders, prospectors, analyzers, and reactors.[59]

Defenders seek moderate, steady growth by offering a limited range of products and services to a well-defined set of customers. In other words, defenders aggressively "defend" their current strategic position by doing the best job they can to hold on to customers in a particular market segment.

Prospectors seek fast growth by searching for new market opportunities, encouraging risk taking, and being the first to bring innovative new products to market (see box "Beyond Movies"). Prospectors are analogous to gold miners who "prospect" for gold nuggets (i.e., new products) in hope that the nuggets will lead them to a rich deposit of gold (i.e., fast

Differentiation the positioning strategy of providing a product or service that is sufficiently different from competitors' offerings that customers are willing to pay a premium price for it

Focus strategy the positioning strategy of using cost leadership or differentiation to produce a specialized product or service for a limited, specially targeted group of customers in a particular geographic region or market segment

Defenders companies using an adaptive strategy aimed at defending strategic positions by seeking moderate, steady growth and by offering a limited range of high-quality products and services to a well-defined set of customers

Prospectors companies using an adaptive strategy that seeks fast growth by searching for new market opportunities, encouraging risk taking, and being the first to bring innovative new products to market

growth). 3M has long been known for its innovative products, particularly in the area of adhesives. Since 1904, it has invented sandpaper; masking, cellophane, electrical, and Scotch tapes; the first commercially available audio and videotapes; and its most famous invention, Post-it notes. Lately, 3M has invented a film that increases the brightness of LCD displays on laptop computers; developed a digital system for construction companies to detect underground telecommunication, gas, water, sewer, or electrical lines without digging; and created a pheromone spray that, by preventing harmful insects from mating, will protect apple, walnut, tomato, cranberry, and grape crops. For more on 3M's innovative products, see the 3M innovation archive (http://solutions.3mcanada.ca/wps/portal/3M/en_CA/about-3M/information/?WT.mc_id=www.3M.com/cms/CA/en/1-30/cklcFFS/view.html).

Analyzers are a blend of the defender and prospector strategies. They seek moderate, steady growth *and* limited opportunities for fast growth. Analyzers are rarely first to market with new products or services. Instead, they try to simultaneously minimize risk and maximize profits by following or imitating the proven successes of prospectors.

Netflix has achieved growth not only through its mail-order DVD service but also through its video streaming service, which allows users to watch a variety of movies and TV shows almost instantly. In fact, the streaming service has been so successful that Netflix has nearly two times more streaming customers than DVD customers. Motivated by Netflix's success, Verizon, a telecommunications company, and Redbox, operator of DVD rental kiosks, announced that they had formed a joint venture to create a competing video streaming service. Though they did not release information on pricing, the companies did announce that there would be just one subscription package that would include access to physical DVDs from Redbox kiosks as well as movies and TV shows via streaming.[60]

Finally, unlike defenders, prospectors, or analyzers, **reactors** do not follow a consistent strategy. Rather than anticipating and preparing for external opportunities and threats, reactors tend to react to changes in their external environment after they oc-

cur. Not surprisingly, reactors tend to be poorer performers than defenders, prospectors, or analyzers. A reactor approach is inherently unstable, and firms that fall into this mode of operation must change their approach or face almost certain failure.

6-5 *Firm-Level Strategies*

Microsoft brings out its Xbox 360 video-game console; Sony counters with its PlayStation 3. Sprint Nextel drops prices and increases monthly cell phone minutes; Verizon strikes back with better reception and even lower prices and more minutes. FedEx, the overnight delivery company, buys Kinko's copying and printing stores and turns them into FedEx Kinko's Office and Print Centers to provide a convenient place for businesspeople to drop off and pick up packages; UPS buys Mail Boxes, Etc. and turns its outlets into UPS Stores for exactly the same purpose. Starbucks Coffee opens a store, and nearby locally run coffeehouses respond by improving service, increasing portions, and holding the line on prices. Attack and respond, respond and attack. **Firm-level strategy** addresses the question "How should we compete against a particular firm?"

*Let's find out more about the firm-level strategies (direct competition between companies) by reading about **6-5a the basics of direct competition** and **6-5b the strategic moves involved in direct competition between companies**.*

Beyond Movies

Coinstar is the company behind the ubiquitous and successful Redbox DVD kiosks, more than 35,000 of which can be found all over the United States. Its plans for future success, however, are not limited to selling movies, as the company plans to revolutionize vending machines. The company is currently testing a coffee machine that sells Seattle's Best Coffee. In Texas and California, it is testing a vending machine called Gizmo that sells used electronics like video game systems and cell phones. It has also developed a vending machine called ecoATM that allows consumers to deposit old electronics and receive cash.

Source: N. Wingfield, "Thinking Outside the Redbox," *New York Times*, February 17, 2012, accessed March 5, 2012, http://www.nytimes.com/2012/02/18/business/coinstar-ventures-beyond-its-redbox-success.html?pagewanted=all.

Direct competition the rivalry between two companies that offer similar products and services, acknowledge each other as rivals, and act and react to each other's strategic actions

Market commonality the degree to which two companies have overlapping products, services, or customers in multiple markets

Resource similarity the extent to which a competitor has similar amounts and kinds of resources

6-5a DIRECT COMPETITION

Although Porter's five industry forces indicate the overall level of competition in an industry, most companies do not compete directly with all the firms in their industry. For example, McDonald's and Red Lobster are both in the restaurant business, but no one would characterize them as competitors. McDonald's offers low-cost, convenient fast food in a seat-yourself restaurant, while Red Lobster offers mid-priced seafood dinners complete with servers and a bar.

Instead of competing with an entire industry, most firms compete directly with just a few companies within it. **Direct competition** is the rivalry between two companies offering similar products and services that acknowledge each other as rivals and take offensive and defensive positions as they act and react to each other's strategic actions.[61] Two factors determine the extent to which firms will be in direct competition with each other: market commonality and resource similarity. **Market commonality** is the degree to which two companies have overlapping products, services, or customers in multiple markets. The more markets in which there is product, service, or customer overlap, the more intense the direct competition between the two companies. **Resource similarity** is the extent to which a competitor has similar amounts and kinds of resources, that is, similar assets, capabilities, processes, information, and knowledge used to create and sustain an advantage over competitors. From a competitive standpoint, resource similarity means that your direct competitors can probably match the strategic actions that your company takes.

Exhibit 6.7 on the next page shows how market commonality and resource similarity interact to determine when and where companies are in direct competition.[62] The overlapping area in each quadrant (between the triangle and the rectangle, or between the differently colored rectangles) depicts market commonality. The larger the overlap, the greater the market commonality. Shapes depict resource similarity, with rectangles representing one set of competitive resources and triangles representing another. Quadrant I shows two companies in direct competition because they have similar resources at their disposal and a high degree of market commonality. These companies try to sell similar products and services to similar customers. McDonald's and Burger King would clearly fit here as direct competitors.

In Quadrant II, the overlapping parts of the triangle and rectangle show two companies going after similar customers with some similar products or services but doing so with different competitive resources. McDonald's and Wendy's restaurants would fit here. Wendy's is after the same lunchtime and dinner crowds that McDonald's is. Nevertheless, with its more expensive hamburgers, fries, shakes, and salads, Wendy's is less of a direct competitor to McDonald's than Burger King is. For example, Wendy's Garden Sensation salads (using fancy lettuce varieties, grape tomatoes, and mandarin oranges) bring in customers who otherwise would have eaten at more expensive casual dining restaurants like Applebee's.[63] A representative from Wendy's says, "We believe you win customers by consistently offering a better product at a strong, everyday value."[64]

In Quadrant III, the very small overlap shows two companies with different competitive resources and little market commonality. McDonald's and Luby's

A Framework of Direct Competition

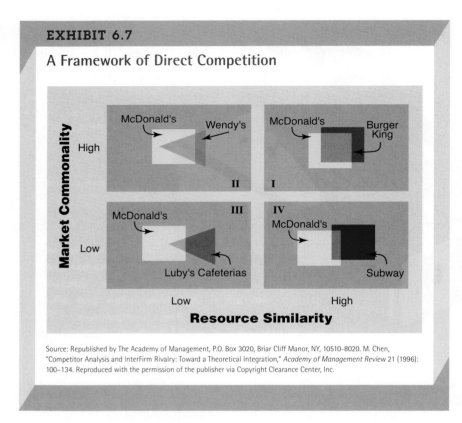

Source: Republished by The Academy of Management, P.O. Box 3020, Briar Cliff Manor, NY, 10510-8020. M. Chen, "Competitor Analysis and InterFirm Rivalry: Toward a Theoretical Integration," *Academy of Management Review* 21 (1996): 100–134. Reproduced with the permission of the publisher via Copyright Clearance Center, Inc.

that McDonald's and Burger King are because Subway, unlike McDonald's, sells itself as a provider of healthy fast food. Thus, the overlap is much smaller in Quadrant IV than in Quadrant I. With its advertising featuring "Jared," who lost 245 pounds eating at Subway, the detailed nutritional information available in its stores, and its close relationship with the American Heart Association, Subway's goal "is to emphasize that the Subway brand represents all that is good about health and well-being."[67] And while fast-food customers tend to eat at both restaurants, Subway's customers are twice as loyal as McDonald's customers, most likely because of Subway's healthier food.[68]

6-5b STRATEGIC MOVES OF DIRECT COMPETITION

cafeterias fit here. Although both are in the fast-food business, there's almost no overlap in terms of products and customers. Luby's sells baked chicken, turkey, roasts, meat loaf, and vegetables, none of which are available at McDonald's. Furthermore, Luby's customers aren't likely to eat at McDonald's. In fact, Luby's is not really competing with other fast-food restaurants, but with eating at home. Company surveys show that close to half of its customers would have eaten at home, not at another restaurant, if they hadn't come to Luby's.[65]

Finally, in Quadrant IV, the small overlap between the two rectangles shows that McDonald's and Subway compete with similar resources but with little market commonality. In terms of resources, sales at McDonald's are much larger, but Subway has grown substantially in the last decade and now has 33,749 stores worldwide, compared to 32,737 worldwide for McDonald's (just 14,027 in the United States).[66] Though Subway and McDonald's compete, they aren't direct competitors in terms of market commonality in the way

Attack a competitive move designed to reduce a rival's market share or profits

Response a competitive countermove, prompted by a rival's attack, to defend or improve a company's market share or profit

While corporate-level strategies help managers decide what business to be in and industry-level strategies help them determine how to compete within an industry, firm-level strategies help managers determine when, where, and what strategic actions should be taken against a direct competitor. Firms in direct competition can make two basic strategic moves: attack and response. These moves occur all the time in virtually every industry, but they are most noticeable in industries where multiple large competitors are pursuing customers in the same market space.

An **attack** is a competitive move designed to reduce a rival's market share or profits. For example, the two leaders in the e-reader market, Amazon and Barnes & Noble, have been engaged in a lengthy battle over prices. In order to reduce sales of Barnes & Noble's Nook readers, Amazon introduced the Kindle with Special Offers model, an e-reader that periodically showed ads and was priced at $114, $35 less than the cheapest Nook model. A few months later, Amazon dropped the price to just $79.[69]

A **response** is a countermove, prompted by a rival's attack, that is designed to defend or improve a company's market share or profit. There are two kinds of responses.[70] The first is to match or mirror your competitor's move. This is what Barnes & Noble did when it lowered the price of its Nook Simple Touch, which had been selling for $139, to $99.[71]

The second kind of response, however, is to respond along a different dimension from your competitor's move or attack. Rather than cutting prices, Amazon responded to Barnes & Noble's moves by letting customers get rid of advertisements. For a fee of $30, users of ad-supported Kindles could use their e-readers without seeing the pop-up advertisements.[72]

Market commonality and resource similarity determine the likelihood of an attack or response, that is, whether a company is likely to attack a direct competitor or to strike back with a strong response when attacked. When market commonality is large and companies have overlapping products, services, or customers in multiple markets, there is less motivation to attack and more motivation to respond to an attack. The reason for this is straightforward: When firms are direct competitors in a large number of markets, they have a great deal at stake. So when Amazon cut prices, Barnes & Noble had no choice but to respond by cutting its own prices. The two market leaders must also react to an outside threat—Apple's iPad. The iPad's threat to Barnes & Noble's Nook and Amazon's Kindle became clear when late Apple CEO Steve Jobs announced that iPad users had purchased over five million e-books in the two months since its release (that's roughly 2.5 books per iPad). Indeed, about one year after the release of the iPad, Amazon launched its Kindle Fire, while Barnes & Noble launched its Nook Tablet. Both devices are tablet computers intended to compete with the iPad. They both offer Internet access, photo and video capabilities, and interactive touch screens, as well as the e-reader experience familiar to Kindle or Nook users.[73]

Whereas market commonality affects the likelihood of an attack or a response to an attack, resource similarity largely affects response capability, that is, how quickly and forcefully a company can respond to an attack. When resource similarity is strong, the responding firm will generally be able to match the strategic moves of the attacking firm. Con-

sequently, a firm is less likely to attack firms with similar levels of resources because it is unlikely to gain any sustained advantage when the responding firms strike back. On the other hand, if one firm is substantially stronger than another (i.e., there is low resource similarity), then a competitive attack is more likely to produce sustained competitive advantage.

In general, the more moves (i.e., attacks) a company initiates against direct competitors, and the greater a company's tendency to respond when attacked, the better its performance. More specifically, attackers and early responders (companies that are quick to launch a retaliatory attack) tend to gain market share and profits at the expense of late responders. This is not to suggest that a full-attack strategy always works best. In fact, attacks can provoke harsh retaliatory responses.

When it first came on the market, Sony's PlayStation 3 (PS3) cost $599, but it came with an 80-GB hard drive and a then-rare Blu-ray disc player. Sales lagged. However, Nintendo's Wii game console cost $249 and Microsoft's Xbox 360 game console cost $400. So Sony cut the price of the 80-GB PS3 to $499 and introduced a 40-GB PS3 for $399.[74] Microsoft responded over the next four years by cutting the price of an Xbox 360 with a 20-GB hard drive from $349 to $299, cutting the price of an Xbox 360 with a 60-GB hard drive from $349 to $299, and cutting a 120-GB Xbox 360 from $399 to $299.[75] Today, with a 320-GB PS3 costing $299 and a 160-GB PS3 costing $249, Sony is now priced more competitively compared to the 250-GB Xbox 360, which costs $299. As a result, global sales of the PS3 now total 43.4 million units compared to

the Xbox 360's 42.9 million.[76] Microsoft responded to the PS3's increased sales with the introduction of the Xbox Kinect, a motion-sensing device that allows you to play games without controllers. With Kinect proving enormously popular—sales of eight million units in the first six months—Microsoft hopes to increase Xbox 360 sales at the expense of the PS3.[77] Consequently, when deciding when, where, and what strategic actions to take against a direct competitor, managers should always consider the possibility of retaliation.

> **In general, the more moves (i.e., attacks) a company initiates against direct competitors, and the greater a company's tendency to respond when attacked, the better its performance.**

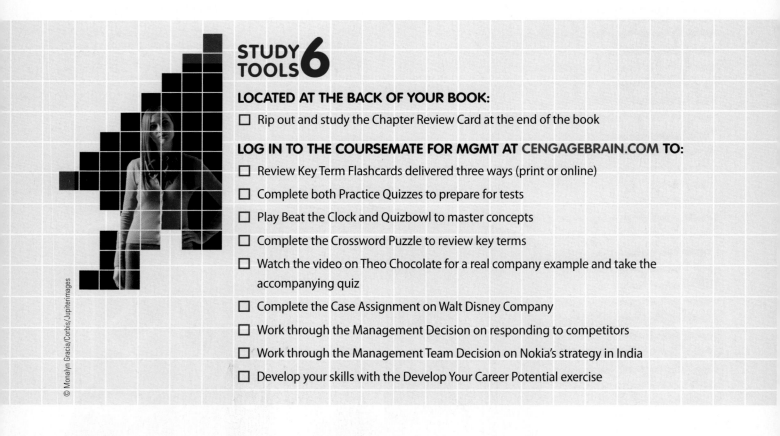

STUDY TOOLS 6

LOCATED AT THE BACK OF YOUR BOOK:

☐ Rip out and study the Chapter Review Card at the end of the book

LOG IN TO THE COURSEMATE FOR MGMT AT CENGAGEBRAIN.COM TO:

☐ Review Key Term Flashcards delivered three ways (print or online)

☐ Complete both Practice Quizzes to prepare for tests

☐ Play Beat the Clock and Quizbowl to master concepts

☐ Complete the Crossword Puzzle to review key terms

☐ Watch the video on Theo Chocolate for a real company example and take the accompanying quiz

☐ Complete the Case Assignment on Walt Disney Company

☐ Work through the Management Decision on responding to competitors

☐ Work through the Management Team Decision on Nokia's strategy in India

☐ Develop your skills with the Develop Your Career Potential exercise

© Monalyn Gracia/Corbis/Jupiterimages

USE THE TOOLS.

- Rip out the Review Cards in the back of your book to study.

Or Visit CourseMate to:

- Read, search, highlight, and take notes in the Interactive eBook
- Review Flashcards (Print or Online) to master key terms
- Test yourself with Auto-Graded Quizzes
- Bring concepts to life with Games, Videos, and Animations!

Go to CourseMate for MGMT to begin using these tools.
Access at **www.cengagebrain.com**

Complete the Speak Up survey in CourseMate at **www.cengagebrain.com**

f Follow us at **www.facebook.com/4ltrpress**

7 Innovation
and Change

© James Porto/Photographer's Choice/Getty Images

LEARNING OUTCOMES

7-1 Explain why innovation matters to companies.

7-2 Discuss the different methods that managers can use to effectively manage innovation in their organizations.

7-3 Discuss why not changing can lead to organizational decline.

7-4 Discuss the different methods that managers can use to better manage change as it occurs.

CHECK OUT
STUDY TOOLS
AT THE END OF
THIS CHAPTER.

© Monalyn Gracia/Corbis/Jupiterimages

7-1 *Why Innovation Matters*

At age 57, composer Richard Einhorn lost his hearing and feared he would never hear music again. So when he went to New York's Metropolitan Opera and was given special headphones to amplify the music, he was hopeful, but the sound quality was poor and filled with background noise, static, and interference. However, when he attended a performance of *Wicked* at the Kennedy Center in Washington, D.C., he said, "For the first time since I lost most of my hearing, live music was perfectly clear, perfectly clean and incredibly rich. There I was at 'Wicked' weeping uncontrollably—and I don't even like musicals." The superb sound at the Kennedy Center was due to a device called a hearing loop, in which a copper wire around the edges of a room broadcasts signals to special receivers built directly into most hearing aids. But unlike other such devices, hearing loops filter background noise and only broadcast sounds coming directly from strategically placed microphones. Janice Schacter Lintz, of the Hearing Access Program, which advocates for the installation of hearing loops in public places, says that with baby boomers turning sixty-five in 2011 and with one-third of people over sixty-five experiencing hearing loss, "This isn't just about disability rights—it's about good customer service. That's a big group of customers who won't go to museums or theaters or restaurants where they can't hear. Put in a loop, and they can hear clearly without any of the bother or embarrassment of wearing a special headset."[1] **Organizational innovation** is the successful implementation of creative ideas, like the hearing loop at the Kennedy Center in Washington, D.C.

We can only guess what changes technological innovations will bring in the next twenty years. Will we carry computers in our pockets? Today's iPhones, BlackBerries, and Android phones are a step in that direction. Will solar power and wind power get cheap and efficient enough so that your home can have a stand-alone power source off the main electrical grid? And will HD TVs, now the standard, be replaced by lifelike HD holographic pictures (think of R2D2 projecting Princess Leia in *Star Wars*)?[2] Who knows? The only thing we do know about the next twenty years is that innovation will continue to change our lives.

*Let's begin our discussion of innovation by learning about **7-1a technology cycles** and **7-2b innovation streams.***

7-1a TECHNOLOGY CYCLES

In Chapter 3, you learned that technology consists of the knowledge, tools, and techniques used to transform inputs (raw materials and information) into outputs (products and services). A **technology cycle** begins with the birth of a new technology and ends when that technology reaches its limits and dies as it is replaced by a newer, substantially better technology.[3] For example, technology cycles occurred when air conditioners supplanted fans, when Henry Ford's Model T replaced horse-drawn carriages, when planes replaced trains as a means of cross-country travel, when vaccines that prevented diseases replaced medicines designed to treat them, and when battery-powered

Organizational innovation the successful implementation of creative ideas in organizations

Technology cycle a cycle that begins with the birth of a new technology and ends when that technology reaches its limits and is replaced by a newer, substantially better technology

wristwatches replaced mechanically powered, stem-wound wristwatches.

From Gutenberg's invention of the printing press in 1448 to the rapid advance of the Internet, studies of hundreds of technological innovations have shown that nearly all technology cycles follow the typical **S-curve pattern of innovation** shown in Exhibit 7.1.[4] Early in a technology cycle, there is still much to learn, so progress is slow, as depicted by point A on the S-curve. The flat slope indicates that increased effort (in terms of money or research and development) brings only small improvements in technological performance.

Fortunately, as the new technology matures, researchers figure out how to get better performance from it. This is represented by point B of the S-curve in Exhibit 7.1. The steeper slope indicates that small amounts of effort will result in significant increases in performance. At point C, the flat slope again indicates that further efforts to develop this particular technology will result in only small increases in performance. More importantly, however, point C indicates that the performance limits of that particular technology are being reached. In other words, additional significant improvements in performance are highly unlikely.

Intel's technology cycles have followed this pattern. Intel spends billions to develop new computer chips and to build new facilities to produce them. Intel has found that the technology cycle for its integrated circuits is about three years. In each three-year cycle, Intel spends billions to introduce a new chip, improves the chip by making it a little bit faster each year, and then replaces that chip at the end of the cycle with a brand new, different chip that is substantially faster than the old chip. At first, though (point A), the billions Intel spends typically produce only small improvements in performance. But after six months to a year

with a new chip design, Intel's engineering and production people typically figure out how to make the new chips much faster than they were initially (point B). Yet, despite impressive gains in performance, Intel is unable to make a particular computer chip run any faster because the chip reaches its design limits.

After a technology has reached its limits at the top of the S-curve, significant improvements in performance usually come from radical new designs or new performance-enhancing materials. In Exhibit 7.1, that new technology is represented by the second S-curve. The changeover or discontinuity between the old and new technologies is represented by the dotted line. At first, the old and new technologies will likely coexist. Eventually, however, the new technology will replace the old technology. When that happens, the old technology cycle will be complete, and a new one will have started. The changeover between newer and older computer chip designs typically takes about one year. Over time, improving existing technology (tweaking the performance of the current technology cycle), combined with replacing old technology with new technology cycles (i.e., new, faster computer chip designs replacing older ones), has increased the speed of Intel's computer processors by a factor of 300. Today's super-powerful 64-bit processors, which provide instantaneous processing and results, have 592 million transistors compared to 3.1 million transistors for 1990s 32-bit processors, 275,000 transistors for the earliest 1980s 32-bit processors, or just 4,500 transistors for the 8-bit processors, which began personal computing in the 1970s.[5]

Though the evolution of Intel's chips has been used to illustrate S-curves and technology cycles, it's important to note that technology cycles and technological innovation don't necessarily involve faster computer chips or cleaner-burning automobile engines. Remember, *technology* is simply the knowledge, tools, and techniques used to transform inputs into outputs. So a

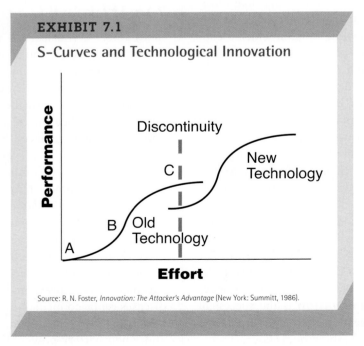

EXHIBIT 7.1

S-Curves and Technological Innovation

Source: R. N. Foster, *Innovation: The Attacker's Advantage* (New York: Summitt, 1986).

technology cycle occurs whenever there are major advances or changes in the *knowledge, tools,* and *techniques* of a field or discipline, whatever they may be.

For example, one of the most important technology cycles in the history of civilization occurred in 1859, when 1,300 miles of central sewer line were constructed throughout London to carry human waste to the sea more than eleven miles away. This extensive sewer system replaced the widespread practice of dumping raw sewage directly into streets, where people walked through it and where it drained into public wells that supplied drinking water. Though the relationship between raw sewage and cholera wasn't known at the time, preventing waste runoff from contaminating water supplies stopped the spread of that disease, which had killed millions of people for centuries in cities throughout the world.[6] Safe water supplies immediately translated into better health and longer life expectancies. Indeed, the water you drink today is safe thanks to this technological breakthrough. So, when you think about technology cycles, don't automatically think "high technology." Instead, broaden your perspective by considering advances or changes in *any* kind of knowledge, tools, and techniques.

7-1b INNOVATION STREAMS

In Chapter 6, you learned that organizations can create *competitive advantage* for themselves if they have a *distinctive competence* that allows them to make, do, or perform something better than their competitors. A competitive advantage becomes sustainable if other companies cannot duplicate the benefits obtained from that distinctive competence. Technological innovation, however, can enable competitors to duplicate the benefits obtained from a company's distinctive advantage. It can also quickly turn a company's competitive advantage into a competitive disadvantage.

In 2006, Pure Digital Technologies released the first version of the Flip, a simple-to-use pocket-sized video camera with two buttons and a d-pad controller. With a built-in hard drive and flip-down USB connector, disks, tapes, memory cards, or USB cables weren't needed to transfer videos to a computer. Users could just turn it on and start shooting incredibly high-quality video. By 2008, the Flip Ultra was the best-selling

video camera on Amazon .com, and Cisco, the largest network company in the world, bought Pure Digital for $590 million. Two years later, however, sales of Flip cameras dropped sharply, and Cisco announced it was shutting down the Flip division. What happened? In a word, smartphones. By the time Cisco had purchased Pure Digital, companies like Samsung, HTC, Apple, and Motorola had released smartphones that could shoot high-definition video and, unlike the Flip, instantly share those videos via social media over wireless or cellular networks.[7]

As the Flip example shows, companies that want to sustain a competitive advantage must understand and protect themselves from the strategic threats of innovation. Over the long run, the best way for a company to do that is to create a stream of its own innovative ideas and products year after year. Consequently, we define **innovation streams** as patterns of innovation over time that can create sustainable competitive advantage.[8] Exhibit 7.2 on the next page shows a typical innovation consisting of a series of technology cycles. Recall that a technology cycle begins with a new technology and ends when that technology is replaced by a newer, substantially better technology. The innovation stream in Exhibit 7.2 shows three such technology cycles.

An innovation stream begins with a **technological discontinuity**, in which a scientific advance or a unique combination of existing technologies creates a significant breakthrough in performance or function. For example, minimally invasive techniques are revolutionizing brain surgery. When Douglas Baptist had a golf ball–sized tumor in his brain, his surgeon cut a tiny opening through his eyebrow, removed the tumor, and sewed up the opening, leaving practically no trace of the operation. Previously, his skull would have been sawed open. Dr. John Mangiardi, who did the procedure, says, "We used to have to shave off half the head. We don't do that anymore."[9] Today, surgeons use endoscopes (tiny cameras with lights attached to mini surgical tools) and MRI and CT scans (which create 3-D maps of the brain) to remove brain tumors with precision and little physical trauma. Further advances in technology are now

Innovation streams patterns of innovation over time that can create sustainable competitive advantage

Technological discontinuity the phase of an innovation stream in which a scientific advance or unique combination of existing technologies creates a significant breakthrough in performance or function

being used to remove brain tumors via an endoscope inserted through the patient's nose. Dr. Carl Snyderman, of the University of Pittsburgh Medical Center, says, "We go into the center of a tumor and take it out in small little pieces and take these little pieces out through the nose one at a time."[10] As a result of these advances, the cost and length of hospital stays associated with these surgeries have been cut in half.

Technological discontinuities are followed by a **discontinuous change**, which is characterized by technological substitution and design competition. **Technological substitution** occurs when customers purchase new technologies to replace older technologies. For example, just twenty years ago nearly all phone calls were made via hardwired landline telephones. Today, with 310 million cell phone subscribers in the United States, more than 25 percent of U.S. homes have no landline service at all.[11]

Discontinuous change is also characterized by **design competition**, the old technology and several different new technologies compete to establish a new technological standard or dominant design (see box "Format War!"). Because of large investments in old technology and because

Discontinuous change the phase of a technology cycle characterized by technological substitution and design competition

Technological substitution the purchase of new technologies to replace older ones

Design competition competition between old and new technologies to establish a new technological standard or dominant design

Dominant design a new technological design or process that becomes the accepted market standard

EXHIBIT 7.2

Innovation Streams: Technology Cycles over Time

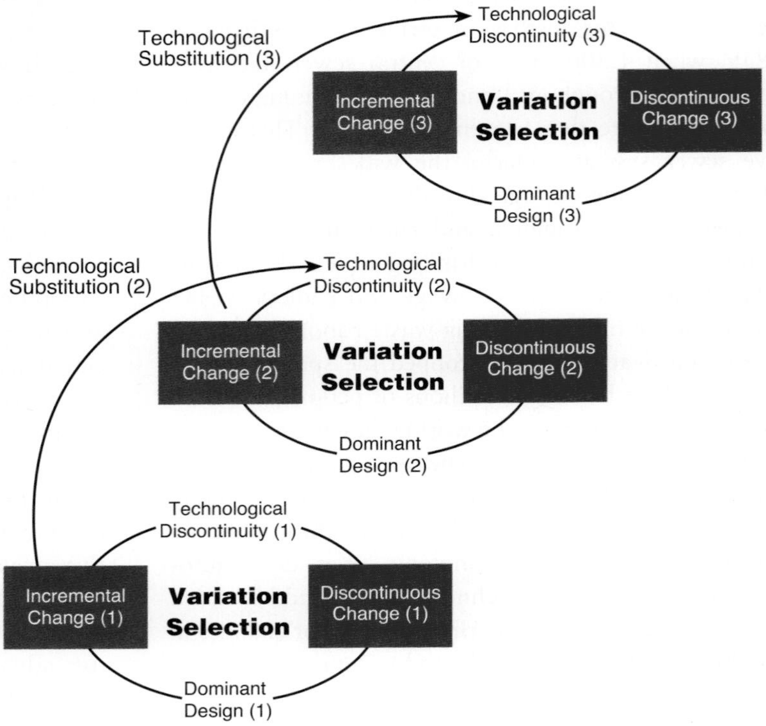

Source: Adapted from M.L. Tushman, P.C. Anderson, and C. O'Reilly, "Technology Cycles, Innovation Streams and Ambidextrous Organizations: Organization Renewal Through Innovation Streams and Strategic Change," *On Managing Strategic Innovation and Change*, eds. M.L. Tushman and P. Anderson (New Oxford Press, 1997) 3–23. Copyright © by Oxford University Press, Inc. Used by permission of Oxford University Press, Inc.

the new and old technologies are often incompatible with each other, companies and consumers are reluctant to switch to a different technology during a design competition. Indeed, the telegraph was so widely used as a means of communication in the late 1800s that at first almost no one understood why telephones would be a better way to communicate. It's hard to envision today, with everyone constantly checking cell phones for email, texts, tweets, and voice mail, but as Edwin Schlossberg explains in his book *Interactive Excellence*: "People could not imagine why they would want or need to talk immediately to someone who was across town or, even more absurdly, in another town. Although people could write letters to one another, and some could send telegraph messages, the idea of sending one's voice to another place and then instantly hearing another voice in return was simply not a model that existed in people's experience. They also did not think it was worth the money to accelerate sending or hearing a message."[12] In addition, during design competition, the older technology usually improves significantly in response to the competitive threat from the new technologies; this response also slows the changeover from older to newer technologies.

Discontinuous change is followed by the emergence of a **dominant design**, which becomes the new accepted market standard for technology.[13] Dominant designs emerge in several ways. One is critical mass, meaning that a particular technology can become the dominant design simply because most people use it.

This happened in the design competition between Toshiba's HD DVD technology and Sony's Blu-ray technology for dominance in establishing a new standard format for high-definition home video. Toshiba lost the design competition because Warner Bros., which had been using both technologies, decided to go exclusively with Blu-ray. At the time of Warner's announcement, Blu-ray held 64 percent of the market, compared to 36 percent for HD DVD.[14] Retailers soon joined Warner Bros. in announcing their intentions to sell only Blu-ray equipment and videos.

The best technology doesn't always become the dominant design because a number of other factors come into play. For instance, a design can become dominant if it solves a practical problem. The QWERTY keyboard (named for the top left line of letters) became the dominant design for typewriters because it slowed typists who, by typing too fast, caused mechanical typewriter keys to jam. Though comput-

ers can easily be switched to the Dvorak keyboard layout, which doubles typing speed and cuts typing errors in half, QWERTY lives on as the standard keyboard. In this instance, the QWERTY keyboard solved a problem that, with computers, is no longer relevant. Yet it remains the dominant design not because it is the best technology, but because most people learned to type that way and continue to use it.

Dominant designs can also emerge through independent standards bodies. The International Telecommunication Union (ITU) (http://www.itu.ch) is an independent organization that establishes standards for the communications industry. The ITU was founded in Paris in 1865 because European countries all had different telegraph systems that could not communicate with each other. Messages crossing borders had to be transcribed from one country's system before they could be coded and delivered on another. After three months of negotiations, twenty countries signed the International Telegraph Convention, which standardized equipment and instructions, enabling telegraph messages to flow seamlessly from country to country. Today, as in 1865, various standards are proposed, discussed, negotiated, and changed until agreement is reached on a final set of standards that communication industries (Internet, telephony, satellites, radio) will follow worldwide.

For example, the ITU has agreed on the new standard for 4G, or fourth-generation, service on mobile phones. "True" 4G, according to the ITU, allows larger amounts of data to be sent over smaller cellular bandwidth and will be much faster than the 4G LTE (or 4G Light) now offered by mobile phone companies. According to Hamadoun Toure, the ITU's Secretary General, true 4G "will make the present day smartphone feel like an old dial-up Internet connection." Francois Rancy, who directs ITU's Radiocommunication Bureau, says that true 4G "would be like putting a fiber optic broadband connection on your mobile phone, making your phone at least 500 times faster than today's 3G smartphones."[15]

No matter how it happens, the emergence of a dominant design is a key event in an innovation stream. First, the emergence of a dominant design indicates that there are winners and losers. Technological innovation is both competence enhancing and competence destroying. Companies that bet on the now-dominant design usually prosper. By contrast, when companies bet on the wrong design or the old technology, they may experience **technological lockout**, which

Format War!

Two television makers, Samsung and LG, are currently engaged in a technological struggle to establish a new standard format for 3-D TVs. LG is using a special type of film technology that creates 3-D images without much of the flicker and blurring that are found on current models. LG's TVs also allow consumers to use light, conventional 3-D glasses. Samsung, meanwhile, is using a stereoscopic technology that requires consumers to wear battery-powered glasses with lenses that rapidly open and close. While the battery-powered glasses might seem cumbersome, Samsung contends that their 3-D technology delivers a higher-definition image than what LG can produce. Thus far, Vizio and a few other Chinese TV makers have aligned with LG, while Panasonic and Sony have followed Samsung's lead.

Source: C. Edwards, "Fighting for 3D Survival," *Bloomberg Businessweek*, April 25–May 1, 2011, 38–40.

© Ethan Miller/Getty Images

Incremental change the phase of a technology cycle in which companies innovate by lowering costs and improving the functioning and performance of the dominant technological design

Creative work environments workplace cultures in which workers perceive that new ideas are welcomed, valued, and encouraged

occurs when a new dominant design (i.e., a significantly better technology) prevents a company from competitively selling its products or makes it difficult to do so.[16] For example, as mentioned above, Toshiba has stopped producing HD DVD players because a critical mass of consumers and technology adopted Blu-ray technology, which became the dominant design. Toshiba will continue to make spare parts for existing machines and may apply the technology to downloading videos online. But it will shift its business strategy to other sectors, such as flash drives, which are beginning to replace hard drives in computers.[17] In fact, more companies are likely to go out of business in a time of discontinuous change and changing standards than in an economic recession or slowdown.

Second, the emergence of a dominant design signals a shift from design experimentation and competition to **incremental change**, a phase in which companies innovate by lowering the cost and improving the functioning and performance of the dominant design. For example, manufacturing efficiencies enable Intel to cut the cost of its chips by one-half to two-thirds during a technology cycle, while doubling or tripling their speed. This focus on improving the dominant design continues until the next technological discontinuity occurs.

7-2 *Managing Innovation*

One consequence of technology cycles and innovation streams is that managers must be equally good at managing innovation in two very different circumstances. First, during discontinuous change, companies must find a way to anticipate and survive the technological changes that can suddenly transform industry leaders into losers and industry unknowns into powerhouses. Companies that can't manage innovation following technological discontinuities risk quick organizational decline and dissolution. Second, after a new dominant design emerges following discontinuous change, companies must manage the very different process of incremental improvement and innovation.

Companies that can't manage incremental innovation slowly deteriorate as they fall further behind industry leaders.

Unfortunately, what works well when managing innovation during discontinuous change doesn't work well when managing innovation during periods of incremental change (and vice versa). *Consequently, to successfully manage innovation streams, companies need to be good at three things: 7-2a managing sources of innovation, 7-2b managing innovation during discontinuous change, and 7-2c managing innovation during incremental change.*

7-2a MANAGING SOURCES OF INNOVATION

Innovation comes from great ideas. So a starting point for managing innovation is to manage the sources of innovation, that is, where new ideas come from. One place that new ideas originate is with brilliant inventors. But only a few companies have the likes of a Thomas Edison or Alexander Graham Bell. Given that great thinkers and inventors are in short supply, what might companies do to ensure a steady flow of good ideas?

Well, when we say that innovation begins with great ideas, we're really saying that innovation begins with creativity. As we defined it at the beginning of this chapter, creativity is the production of novel and useful ideas.[18] Although companies can't command employees to be creative ("You *will* be more creative!"), they can jump-start innovation by building **creative work environments** in which workers perceive that

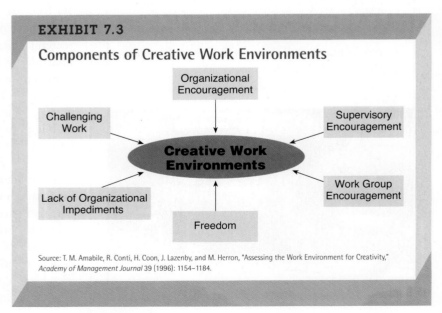

EXHIBIT 7.3

Components of Creative Work Environments

Source: T. M. Amabile, R. Conti, H. Coon, J. Lazenby, and M. Herron, "Assessing the Work Environment for Creativity," *Academy of Management Journal* 39 (1996): 1154–1184.

creative thoughts and ideas are welcomed and valued. As Exhibit 7.3 shows, creative work environments have six components that encourage creativity: challenging work, organizational encouragement, supervisory encouragement, work group encouragement, freedom, and a lack of organizational impediments.[19]

Work is *challenging* when it requires effort, demands attention and focus, and is perceived as important to others in the organization. According to researcher Mihaly Csikszentmihalyi (pronounced ME-high-ee CHICK-sent-me-high-ee), challenging work promotes creativity because it creates a rewarding psychological experience known as "flow." **Flow** is a psychological state of effortlessness, in which you become completely absorbed in what you're doing and time seems to fly. When flow occurs, who you are and what you're doing become one. Csikszentmihalyi first encountered flow when studying artists: "What struck me by looking at artists at work was their tremendous focus on the work, this enormous involvement, this forgetting of time and body. It wasn't justified by expectation of rewards, like, 'Aha, I'm going to sell this painting.'"[20] Csikszentmihalyi has found that chess players, rock climbers, dancers, surgeons, and athletes regularly experience flow, too. A key part of creating flow experiences, and thus creative work environments, is to achieve a balance between skills and task challenge. Workers become bored when they can do more than is required of them and anxious when their skills aren't sufficient to accomplish a task. When skills and task challenge are balanced, however, flow and creativity can occur.

A creative work environment requires three kinds of encouragement: organizational, supervisory, and work group encouragement. *Organizational encouragement* of creativity occurs when management encourages risk taking and new ideas, supports and fairly evaluates new ideas, rewards and recognizes creativity, and encourages the sharing of new ideas throughout different parts of the company. *Supervisory encouragement* of creativity occurs when supervisors provide clear goals, encourage open interaction with subordinates, and actively support development teams' work and ideas. *Work group encouragement* occurs when group members have diverse experience, education, and backgrounds and the group fosters mutual openness to ideas; positive, constructive challenge to ideas; and shared commitment to ideas.

Freedom means having autonomy over one's day-to-day work and a sense of ownership and control over one's ideas. Numerous studies have indicated that creative ideas thrive under conditions of freedom. At Dunkin' Donuts, members of the Culinary Innovation Team are given the freedom to explore new areas, whether it's testing twenty-eight varieties of shortening or spending three months researching new potato products.[21] Likewise, the Tata Group uses IdeaMax, an in-house social media network, to let employees propose, comment, and vote on ideas, some 12,000 of which were proposed in the site's first year.[22]

To foster creativity, companies may also have to *remove impediments* to creativity from their work environments. Internal conflict and power struggles, rigid management structures, and a conservative bias toward the status quo can all discourage creativity. They create the perception that others in the organization will

Flow a psychological state of effortlessness, in which you become completely absorbed in what you're doing and time seems to pass quickly

Have No Fear of Failure

The hard part about encouraging and developing creativity at work is not that people are not creative but that they fear what will happen if they fail. What happens if I, or a colleague, spend a lot of time pursuing a new project, but it doesn't lead to anything productive or marketable? This fear of failure drives many to avoid taking risks—to avoid pursuing the unknown. But what is needed to create an innovative culture is not an avoidance of failure but knowledge of how to manage it. In fact, several innovative companies specifically "reward" failure. The Tata Group, in India, hands out an annual award for the best failed idea, while Intuit and Eli Lilly hold failure parties, where they celebrate the efforts employees make to be creative. By celebrating failure, these companies encourage their employees to keep taking risks for the sake of creativity, thereby fueling innovation.

Source: "Fail Often, Fail Well," *The Economist*, April 16, 2011, 74.

decide which ideas are acceptable and deserve support. In Hollywood, "creative interference," whereby non-creative managers such as marketing, accounting, or financial executives influence key decisions about storylines or actors, is a common impediment to creativity. At Pixar Studios (now owned by Disney), however, creative interference is minimized because each film project is "filmmaker led." In other words, when Pixar's producers and directors made *The Incredibles*, *Finding Nemo*, and the *Toy Story* series of films, they knew that company management, rules, and procedures would not get in the way of producing great films. In fact, at Pixar it's just the opposite. According to Ed Catmull, Pixar cofounder and president of Pixar and Disney Animation Studios, "During production, we leave the operating decisions to the film's leaders, and we don't second-guess or micromanage them. Indeed, even when a production runs into a problem, we do everything possible to provide support without undermining their authority."[23]

7-2b EXPERIENTIAL APPROACH: MANAGING INNOVATION DURING DISCONTINUOUS CHANGE

A study of seventy-two product-development projects (i.e., innovation) in thirty-six computer companies across the United States, Europe, and Asia sheds light on how to manage innovation. Companies that succeeded in periods of discontinuous change (characterized by technological substitution and design competition, as described earlier) typically followed an experiential approach to innovation.[24] The **experiential approach to innovation** assumes that innovation is occurring within a highly uncertain environment and that the key to fast product innovation is to use intuition, flexible options, and hands-on experience to reduce uncertainty and accelerate learning and understanding. The experiential approach to innovation has five aspects: design iterations, testing, milestones, multifunctional teams, and powerful leaders.[25]

An *iteration* is a repetition. So a **design iteration** is a cycle of repetition in which a company tests a prototype of a new product or service, improves on the design, and then builds and tests the improved product or service prototype. A **product prototype** is a full-scale working model that is being tested for design, function, and reliability. **Testing** is a systematic comparison of different product designs or design iterations. Companies that want to create a new dominant design following a technological discontinuity quickly build, test, improve, and retest a series of different product prototypes.

By trying a number of very different designs or making successive improvements and changes in the same design, frequent design iterations reduce uncertainty and improve understanding. Simply put, the more prototypes you build, the more likely you are to learn what works and what doesn't. Also, when designers and engineers build a number of prototypes, they are less likely to fall in love with a particular prototype. Instead, they'll be more concerned with improving the product or technology as much as they can. Testing speeds up and improves the innovation process, too. When two very different design prototypes are tested against each other or the new design iteration is tested against the previous iteration, product design strengths and weaknesses quickly become apparent. Likewise, testing uncovers er-

Experiential approach to innovation an approach to innovation that assumes a highly uncertain environment and uses intuition, flexible options, and hands-on experience to reduce uncertainty and accelerate learning and understanding

Design iteration a cycle of repetition in which a company tests a prototype of a new product or service, improves on that design, and then builds and tests the improved prototype

Product prototype a full-scale, working model that is being tested for design, function, and reliability

Testing the systematic comparison of different product designs or design iterations

Milestones formal project review points used to assess progress and performance

Multifunctional teams work teams composed of people from different departments

rors early in the design process when they are easiest to correct. Finally, testing accelerates learning and understanding by forcing engineers and product designers to examine hard data about product performance. When there's hard evidence that prototypes are testing well, the confidence of the design team grows. Also, personal conflict between design team members is less likely when testing focuses on hard measurements and facts rather than on personal hunches and preferences.

Milestones are formal project review points used to assess progress and performance. For example, a company that has put itself on a twelve-month schedule to complete a project might schedule milestones at the three-month, six-month, and nine-month points on the schedule. At Pixar and Disney Animation Studios, there are fourteen steps involved in creating a full-length animated film, from pitching story ideas, to drawing storyboards, to recording character voices, to using "digital light" (the equivalent of stage lighting) to light each scene in the movie. When it comes time to animate each scene in the movie, Pixar's animation team is always on a short, tight schedule. As a result, the film director uses daily milestones to review progress and keep the film on budget and on schedule. Ed Catmull, president of Pixar and Disney Animation Studios, explains

that at the end of each day's work, the artists performing the computerized animation will "show work in an incomplete state to the whole animation crew, and although the director makes decisions, everyone is encouraged to comment." The benefits from these reviews, what Pixar calls "dailies," are tremendous. Says Catmull, "First, once people get over the embarrassment of showing work still in progress, they become more creative. Second, the director or creative leads guiding the review process can communicate important points to the entire crew at the same time. Third, people learn from and inspire each other; a highly creative piece of animation will spark others to raise their game. Finally, there are no surprises at the end: When you're done, you're done. People's overwhelming desire to make sure their work is 'good' before they show it to others increases the possibility that their finished version won't be what the director wants. The dailies process avoids such wasted efforts."[26]

By making people regularly assess what they're doing, how well they're performing, and whether they need to take corrective action, milestones provide structure to the general chaos that follows technological discontinuities. Milestones also shorten the innovation process by creating a sense of urgency that keeps everyone on task. Finally, milestones are beneficial for innovation because meeting regular milestones builds momentum by giving people a sense of accomplishment.

Multifunctional teams are work teams composed of people from different departments. Multifunctional teams accelerate learning and understanding by mixing and integrating technical, marketing, and manufacturing activities. By involving all key departments in development from the start, multifunctional teams speed innovation through early identification of new ideas or problems that would typically not have been generated or addressed until much later.

After the five-person research and development team at West Paw Design, a manufacturer of pet toys and accessories, struggled to come up with new products, production manager Seth Partain held a company-wide design contest to generate ideas. Partain had two key requirements. First, everyone in the company, from janitors to the president, had to participate. Second, people would be randomly placed in teams by having their names pulled out of a fishbowl. Why randomly? Because company leaders wanted to use multifunctional teams that mixed people and ideas from all areas of the organization. The Eco Bed, which

DOING THE RIGHT THING

Creative Work

Stealing ideas is never a good idea. By taking credit for other people's great work, you're totally disregarding the efforts that they put into thinking of and developing the next great idea that will fuel your company's success. But, did you know that stealing ideas is also bad for the entire organization? When you steal ideas from others, it actually squelches the creative powers in your company. After all, if someone else is just going to take credit for all of your creative work and get all of the benefits, then what's the point? Why even bother thinking of anything innovative? So do the right thing, and don't steal others' ideas; it will help keep the creative juices flowing.

Source: S. Carson, "Plagiarism and Its Effect on Creative Work," *Psychology Today*, October 16, 2010, http://www.psychologytoday.com/blog/life-art/201010/plagiarism-and-its-effect-creative-work.

Compression approach to innovation an approach to innovation that assumes that incremental innovation can be planned using a series of steps and that compressing those steps can speed innovation

Generational change change based on incremental improvements to a dominant technological design such that the improved technology is fully backward compatible with the older technology

won the latest contest, was designed by a salesperson who noticed that retail stores were looking for eco-friendly products, a seamstress who suggested using material made from recycled plastic bottles, and several warehouse workers. The Eco Bed was a hit, and the company now offers it in two designs.[27]

Powerful leaders provide the vision, discipline, and motivation to keep the innovation process focused, on time, and on target. Powerful leaders are able to get resources when they are needed, are typically more experienced, have high status in the company, and are held directly responsible for the products' success or failure. On average, powerful leaders can get innovation-related projects done nine months faster than leaders with little power or influence.

7-2c COMPRESSION APPROACH: MANAGING INNOVATION DURING INCREMENTAL CHANGE

Whereas the experiential approach is used to manage innovation in highly uncertain environments during periods of discontinuous change, the compression approach is used to manage innovation in more certain environments during periods of incremental change. Whereas the goals of the experiential approach are significant improvements in performance and the establishment of a *new* dominant design, the goals of the compression approach are lower costs and incremental improvements in the performance and function of the *existing* dominant design.

The general strategies in each approach are different, too. With the experiential approach, the general strategy is to build something new, different, and substantially better.

Because there's so much uncertainty—no one knows which technology will become the market leader—companies adopt a winner-take-all approach by trying to create the market-leading, dominant design. With the compression approach, the general strategy is to compress the time and steps needed to bring about small, consistent improvements in performance and functionality. Because a dominant technology design already exists, the general strategy is to continue improving the existing technology as rapidly as possible.

In short, a **compression approach to innovation** assumes that innovation is a predictable process, that incremental innovation can be planned using a series of steps, and that compressing the time it takes to complete those steps can speed up innovation. The compression approach to innovation has five aspects: planning, supplier involvement, shortening the time of individual steps, overlapping steps, and multifunctional teams.[28]

In Chapter 5, *planning* was defined as choosing a goal and a method or strategy to achieve that goal. When *planning for incremental innovation*, the goal is to squeeze or compress development time as much as possible, and the general strategy is to create a series of planned steps to accomplish that goal. Planning for incremental innovation helps avoid unnecessary steps and enables developers to sequence steps in the right order to avoid wasted time and delays between steps. Planning also reduces misunderstandings and improves coordination.

Most planning for incremental innovation is based on the idea of generational change. **Generational change** occurs when incremental improvements are made to a dominant technological design such that the improved version of the technology is fully backward compatible with the older version.[29] For example, software is backward compatible if a new version of the software will work with files created by older versions. An expected and important feature of gaming consoles is their ability to play games purchased for earlier machines.

© iStockphoto.com/Joe Belanger

The PlayStation Vita is Sony's latest portable gaming device, featuring a brilliant five-inch screen, excellent battery life, and the ability to act as a portable video player. And after making the mistake of not making its PlayStation 3 console fully backward compatible with PlayStation 2 games, Sony made sure that the PlayStation Vita was fully backward compatible with games for Sony's original portable device, the PlayStation Portable.[30]

Because the compression approach assumes that innovation can follow a series of preplanned steps, one of the ways to shorten development time is *supplier involvement*. Delegating some of the preplanned steps in the innovation process to outside suppliers reduces the amount of work that internal development teams must do. Plus, suppliers provide an alternative source of ideas and expertise that can lead to better designs.

Another way to shorten development time is simply to *shorten the time of individual steps* in the innovation process. A common way to do that is through computer-aided design (CAD). CAD speeds up the design process by allowing designers and engineers to make and test design changes using computer models rather than physically testing expensive prototypes. CAD also speeds innovation by making it easy to see how design changes affect engineering, purchasing, and production. For example, 3-D design software reduces the time and cost involved in creating new products. In the past, when Jeff David, the product manager at **Troy Lee Designs**, wanted to create a new sports helmet, he would have to sketch out a rough concept, mold it in clay, and then ship the mold to a factory in Asia that would produce the prototype. Revisions required physical changes to the prototype, or even a new mold, which would then be sent back to Asia. This process of shipping molds and prototypes slowed development, which could take up to two years before a product was ready for market. After investing in CAD modeling software, David can create digital 3-D models of the helmet on his computer to exact specifications. And, with the click of his mouse, he can instantly send the new design specifications to his Asian factory. By using CAD software, David estimates that production time has been cut by six months while costs have come down 35 percent.[31]

In a sequential design process, each step must be completed before the next step begins. But sometimes multiple development steps can be performed at the same time. *Overlapping steps* shorten the development process by reducing delays or waiting time between steps. Summit Entertainment used overlapping steps to great success in producing the *Twilight* movie franchise. While it used the same actors and screenwriters throughout the series, by using new directors and production crews for each film, Summit was able to begin production on each film while the previous film was in post-production. This allowed the studio to release films at regular intervals in order to capitalize on the surprising success of the first film in a timely manner.[32]

7-3 *Organizational Decline: The Risk of Not Changing*

Five years ago, sales of BlackBerry phones, made by Canadian-based Research in Motion (RIM), dominated corporate and consumer markets and were growing faster than any other cell phone maker. And while RIM still has 12 percent of the world market for smartphones, with the surging sales and growth of Apple's iPhones and Google's Android phones, neither of which was in the market five years ago, no one, based on RIM's recent moves, expects RIM's sales and market share to do anything but continue dropping. Sales of the BlackBerry Torch, RIM's answer to the iPhone and Android phones, have been disappointing. Likewise, so have sales of BlackBerry apps on the online BlackBerry app store. While there are nearly 370,000 apps available for the iPhone and 260,000 available for Android phones, only 26,000 apps are available for the BlackBerry.[33] Also, unlike its competitors' app stores, which are simple to use, buying and installing BlackBerry apps is often cumbersome, requiring multiple

Organizational decline a large decrease in organizational performance that occurs when companies don't anticipate, recognize, neutralize, or adapt to the internal or external pressures that threaten their survival

Change forces forces that produce differences in the form, quality, or condition of an organization over time

Resistance forces forces that support the existing conditions in organizations

download, installation, and payment steps. App developers also find writing apps for BlackBerry phones frustrating. RIM has responded by courting app developers, simplifying its app website, cutting phone prices, and giving away its enterprise server software (needed to link BlackBerry phones to corporate email servers) to small companies. And, since only 16 percent of app developers are interested in writing apps for BlackBerry devices, RIM is now guaranteeing app developers $10,000 for each BlackBerry app they produce, provided the app earns $1,000 in the marketplace.[34]

Some industry analysts are now calling RIM "Research in Slow Motion," because the company has been unable to change its business quickly enough to stop the erosion of its sales and market share. While RIM is financially strong, the fear is that its recent inability to change may eventually lead to its demise.

Businesses operate in a constantly changing environment. Recognizing and adapting to internal and external changes can mean the difference between continued success and going out of business. Companies that fail to change run the risk of organizational decline.[35] **Organizational decline** occurs when companies don't anticipate, recognize, neutralize, or adapt to the internal or external pressures that threaten their survival. In other words, decline occurs when organizations don't recognize the need for change. There are five stages of organizational decline: blinded, inaction, faulty action, crisis, and dissolution.

In the *blinded stage*, decline begins because key managers fail to recognize the internal or external changes that will harm their organizations. This blindness may be due to a simple lack of awareness about changes or an inability to understand their significance. It may also come from the overconfidence that can develop when a company has been successful.

In the *inaction stage*, as organizational performance problems become more visible, management may recognize the need to change but still take no action. The managers may be waiting to see if the problems will correct themselves. Or, they may find it difficult to change the practices and policies that previously led to success. Possibly, too, they wrongly assume that they can easily correct the problems, so they don't feel the situation is urgent.

In the *faulty action stage*, faced with rising costs and decreasing profits and market share, management will announce belt-tightening plans designed to cut costs, increase efficiency, and restore profits. In other words, rather than recognizing the need for fundamental changes, managers assume that if they just run a tighter ship, company performance will return to previous levels.

In the *crisis stage*, bankruptcy or dissolution (breaking up the company and selling its parts) is likely to occur unless the company completely reorganizes the way it does business. At this point, however, companies typically lack the resources to fully change how they run their businesses. Cutbacks and layoffs will have reduced the level of talent among employees. Furthermore, talented managers who were savvy enough to see the crisis coming will have found jobs with other companies, often with competitors.

In the *dissolution stage*, after failing to make the changes needed to sustain the organization, the company is dissolved through bankruptcy proceedings or by selling assets in order to pay suppliers, banks, and creditors. At this point, a new CEO may be brought in to oversee the closing of stores, offices, and manufacturing facilities, the final layoff of managers and employees, and the sale of assets. It is important to note that decline is reversible at each of the first four stages, and that not all companies in decline reach final dissolution. Three years ago, General Motors was on the verge of collapse. It had declared bankruptcy, was forced to shut down two of its historic brands, and had to depend on government bailouts to stay afloat. But after aggressively cutting costs, stabilizing market share, and using innovative production techniques, GM had a record year in 2011, earning $7.6 billion, a 62 percent gain from the previous record set in 2010, and awarding each of its 47,500 union employees a record $7,000 in profit sharing.[36]

7-4 *Managing Change*

According to social psychologist Kurt Lewin, change is a function of the forces that promote change and the opposing forces that slow or resist change.[37] **Change forces** lead to differences in the form, quality, or condition of an organization over time. By contrast, **resistance forces** support the status quo, that is, the existing conditions in an organization. Change is difficult under any circumstances. In a study of heart bypass patients, doctors told participants straightforwardly to change their eating and health habits or they would die. Unbelievably, a full 90 percent of participants did *not* change their habits at all![38] This fierce resistance to change also applies to organizations.

Resistance to change is caused by self-interest, misunderstanding and distrust, and a general intolerance for change.[39] People resist change out of *self-interest* because they fear that change will cost or deprive them of something they value. Resistance might stem from a fear that the changes will result in a loss of pay, power, responsibility or even perhaps one's job. The Mayo Clinic, the world-renowned medical facility in Rochester, Minnesota, announced a new uniform policy for its 900 desk staff and clinical assistants. Rather than wearing scrubs like the doctors and nurses do, they would instead be required to wear black pants and light blue shirts. Because the $400 expense for the new uniforms came out of their paychecks, employees reacted with angry comments on an in-house discussion board, calling themselves "LPEs," or low-paid employees. One wrote, "I think this is an incredible elitist and insensitive decision," while another wrote, "It just seems like none of our opinions matter."[40]

People also resist change because of *misunderstanding and distrust*; they don't understand the change or the reasons for it, or they distrust the people—typically management—behind the change. Resistance isn't always visible at first. In fact, some of the strongest resisters may initially support the changes in public, nodding and smiling their agreement, but then ignore the changes in private and do their jobs as they always have. Management consultant Michael Hammer calls this deadly form of resistance the "Kiss of Yes."[41]

Resistance may also come from a generally low tolerance for change. Some people are simply less capable of handling change than others. People with a *low tolerance for change* feel threatened by the uncertainty associated with change and worry that they won't be able to learn the new skills and behaviors needed to successfully negotiate change in their companies.

Because resistance to change is inevitable, successful change efforts require careful management. *In this section, you will learn about 7-4a managing resistance to change, 7-4b what not to do when leading organi-*

"The Kiss of Yes": Some of the strongest resisters may support the changes in public, but then ignore them in private.

zational change, and 7-4c different change tools and techniques.

7-4a MANAGING RESISTANCE TO CHANGE

According to Kurt Lewin, managing organizational change is a basic process of unfreezing, change intervention, and refreezing. **Unfreezing** is getting the people affected by change to believe that change is needed. During the **change intervention** itself, workers and managers change their behavior and work practices. **Refreezing** is supporting and reinforcing the new changes so that they stick.

Resistance to change is an example of frozen behavior. Given the choice between changing and not changing, most people would rather not change. Because resistance to change is natural and inevitable, managers need to unfreeze resistance to change to create successful change programs. The following methods can be used to manage resistance to change: education and communication, participation, negotiation, top-management support, and coercion.[42]

When resistance to change is based on insufficient, incorrect, or misleading information, managers should *educate* employees about the need for change and *communicate* change-related information to them. Managers must also supply the information and funding, or other support employees need to make changes. For example, resistance to change can be particularly strong when one company buys another company. This is because one company in the merger usually has a higher status due to its size or its higher profitability or the fact that it is the acquiring company. These status differences are important to managers and employees, particularly if they're in the lower-status company, who worry about retaining their jobs or influence after the merger. That fear or concern can greatly increase resistance to change.[43] When PMA Companies, an insurance risk management firm, was acquired by Old

Resistance to change opposition to change resulting from self-interest, misunderstanding and distrust, and a general intolerance for change

Unfreezing getting the people affected by change to believe that change is needed

Change intervention the process used to get workers and managers to change their behaviors and work practices

Refreezing supporting and reinforcing new changes so that they stick

Coercion the use of formal power and authority to force others to change

Republic International, an insurance company, PMA's CEO Vince Donnelly communicated frequently with PMA's employees about the merger. Four months before the acquisition became official, he traveled to each of the company's twenty offices and gave employees a detailed description of how their day-to-day operations would change and why the acquisition was good for everyone involved. He also held quarterly updates with employees via videoconference. Said Donnelly, "It's not just one and done. Communication needs to be continual. You need to continue to reinforce the messages that you want people to internalize. So you need to understand that communication is a continuous process and not something that you do just once." He went on to say, "What you are asking people to do is trust you, [trust] that you have the best interest of everybody in mind, and [trust that] when there is news to tell, you're going to hear it directly from the CEO—good, bad or indifferent."[44]

Another way to reduce resistance to change is to have those affected by the change *participate in planning and implementing the change process*. Employees who participate have a better understanding of the change and the need for it. Furthermore, employee concerns about change can be addressed as they occur if employees participate in the planning and implementation process. When United Airlines and Continental Airlines merged to form the world's largest airline, there were thousands of decisions to be made to integrate the two companies, such as combining websites, ticketing systems, pay and promotion policies, etc. They even had to decide which coffee to serve, as Continental served coffee from Fresh Brew, and United served Starbucks. While seemingly a small decision, United and Continental served a combined 62 million cups of coffee last year. Sandra Pineau-Boddison, the vice president of food services, picked a fourteen-member team consisting of people from flight operations, finance, food service, and marketing to make the decision, even asking them to blindly taste twelve different coffees to identify which tasted best. Then, she took the committee's selection and asked the company's board of directors, as well as 1,100 flight attendants who also tried the new brew, for input.[45]

Employees are also less likely to resist change if they are allowed *to discuss and agree on who will do what* after change occurs. When DEGW, an architectural firm, was working with the Canadian Broadcasting Company to determine how to redesign its 1.5-million-square-foot headquarters in Toronto, it couldn't get company teams, leaders, and real estate managers to agree on what the redesigned space should look like. So, out of frustration, it created a board game called "The Sandbox," in which the goal is to create an ideal work environment within a set space. When playing the game, employees must talk about and make decisions regarding furniture and desk configurations, office privacy, noise, and lounge and public spaces. A finalized design usually emerges after three two-hour game sessions. Game developer Scott Francisco says, "We needed a vehicle to pinpoint the priorities of the company. The Sandbox allowed us to address underperforming space by tapping into the knowledge and skills of staff at all levels, turning an intractable problem into a creative outcome. . . . It's designed to elicit interest and engagement."[46] The Sandbox works so well at generating discussions and leading to consensus that DEGW uses it worldwide with its clients.

Resistance to change also decreases when change efforts receive *significant managerial support*. Managers must do more than talk about the importance of change, though. They must provide the training, resources, and autonomy needed to make change happen. Finally, resistance to change can be managed through **coercion**, or the use of formal power and authority to force others to change. Because of the intense negative reactions it can create (e.g., fear, stress, resentment, sabotage of company products), coercion should be used only when a crisis exists or when all other attempts to reduce resistance to change have failed.

7-4b WHAT NOT TO DO WHEN LEADING CHANGE

So far, you've learned about the basic change process (unfreezing, change intervention, refreezing) and managing resistance to change. Harvard Business School professor John Kotter argues that knowing what *not* to do is just as important as knowing what to do when it comes to achieving successful organizational change.[47]

Managers commonly make certain errors when they lead change. The first two errors occur during the unfreezing phase, when managers try to get the people affected by change to believe that change is really needed. The first and potentially most serious error is *not establishing a great enough sense of urgency*. Indeed, Kotter estimates that more than half of all change efforts fail because the people affected are not convinced that change is necessary. People will feel a greater sense of urgency if a leader in the company makes a public, candid assessment of the company's problems and weaknesses. Celestica, Inc., located in Toronto, Canada, is an electronics manufacturing services company that produces complex printed circuit assemblies, such as PC motherboards and networking cards, flat-screen TVs, and Xbox video game systems for Microsoft. When Craig Muhlhauser took over as president and CEO, Celestica, Inc. was losing money and market share. Muhlhauser went to work right away. He informed employees that the company couldn't survive if it didn't change. Within his first thirty days as CEO, he reduced staff by 35 percent, moved new people into important positions, and had the attention of everyone in the company.[48]

The second mistake that occurs in the unfreezing process is *not creating a powerful enough coalition.* Change often starts with one or two people. But change has to be supported by a critical and growing group of people to build enough momentum to change an entire department, division, or company. Besides top management, Kotter recommends that key employees, managers, board members, customers, and even union leaders be members of a *core change coalition* that guides and supports organizational change. "In a turnaround, there are three kinds of employees," said Celestica's CEO Craig Muhlhauser—those on your side, those on the fence, and those who will never buy in. The lat-

ter have to be let go and those on the fence should be persuaded to contribute or leave. Says Muhlhauser, "We have to make change, change is difficult and as we make change, it is important to realize that there are people who are going to resist that change. In talking to those people, the objective is to move everybody into the column of supporters. But that is probably unachievable."[49] It's also important to strengthen this core change coalition's resolve by periodically bringing its members together for off-site retreats.

The next four errors that managers make occur during the change phase, when a change intervention is used to try to get workers and managers to change their behavior and work practices. *Lacking a vision* for change is a significant error at this point. As you learned in Chapter 5, a *vision* (defined as a *purpose statement* in Chapter 5) is a statement of a company's purpose or reason for existing. A vision for change makes clear where a company or department is headed and why the change is occurring. Change efforts that lack vision tend to be confused, chaotic, and contradictory. By contrast, change efforts guided by visions are clear and easy to understand and can be effectively explained in five minutes or less. As part of his effort to revitalize Ford Motor Company, CEO Alan Mulally is calling for dramatic changes in the Lincoln brand of cars. To restore Lincoln's luxury cachet, Mulally wants to make sweeping changes in nearly

every area—new models, a new naming scheme, new designs, new technologies, and, especially, a new experience at the dealer. And, he doesn't just want dealerships to have nice tile floors and leather couches; he wants dealers to provide high levels of personal service, such as pick-up and delivery service, private spaces where customers can work, or house calls for certain types of repairs, all of which can be found at Lexus dealers. These changes are guided by Mulally's vision that Lincoln competes with established luxury automakers like BMW, Lexus, and Mercedes-Benz.[50]

Undercommunicating the vision by a factor of ten is another mistake in the change phase. According to Kotter, companies mistakenly hold just one meeting to announce the vision. Or, if the new vision receives heavy emphasis in executive speeches or company newsletters, senior management then undercuts the vision by behaving in ways contrary to it. Successful communication of the vision requires that top managers link everything the company does to the new vision and that they "walk the talk" by behaving in ways consistent with the vision. Furthermore, even companies that begin change with a clear vision sometimes make the mistake of *not removing obstacles to the new vision*. They leave formidable barriers to change in place by failing to redesign jobs, pay plans, and technology to support the new way of doing things. One of Celestica's key obstacles was efficiently and effectively managing its supply chain; it worked with 4,000 suppliers around the world. The complexity of this supply chain network and the costs of uncoordinated transportation and shipping reduced the speed with which it could meet customer orders and made it difficult to keep costs low. CEO Craig Muhlhauser and his management team removed this obstacle by implementing Liveshare, an information system that gave it and its suppliers real-time data on sales, production, inventory, and shipping for all of its products. For example, if Best Buy wanted to buy more units of a top-selling video game, it used to have to contact Celestica via phone, email, or fax to see how quickly the order could be delivered. But now with Liveshare, it can see live, up-to-date numbers indicating how many of those video games are rolling off Celestica's production lines or are now on trucks en route to Best Buy trucking depots.[51]

Another error in the change phase is *not systematically planning for and creating short-term wins*. Most people don't have the discipline and patience to wait two years to see if the new change effort works. Change is threatening and uncomfortable, so people need to see an immediate payoff if they are to continue to support it. Kotter recommends that managers create short-term wins by actively picking people and projects that are likely to work extremely well early in the change process. Celestica's Craig Muhlhauser understood the importance of short-term wins. Said Muhlhauser, "My approach was to look at the first thirty days, then at the first three months, then at the first twelve months and then I took a look at the three years. In a turnaround, you have to take hold very quickly. You have to show relatively quick hits [i.e., short-term wins] to show your turnaround strategy is working—and then you deal with a multitude of issues in a very focused way that will allow you to continue to show improvement."[52]

The last two errors that managers make occur during the refreezing phase, when attempts are made to support and reinforce changes so that they stick. *Declaring victory too soon* is a tempting mistake in the refreezing phase. Managers typically declare victory right after the first large-scale success in the change process. Declaring success too early has the same effect as draining the gasoline out of a car: It stops change efforts dead in their tracks. With success declared, supporters of the change process stop pushing to make change happen. After all, why push when success has been achieved? Rather than declaring victory, managers should use the momentum from short-term wins to push for even bigger or faster changes. This maintains urgency and prevents change supporters from slacking off before the changes are frozen into the company's culture.

The last mistake that managers make is *not anchoring changes in the corporation's culture*. An *organization's culture* is the set of key values, beliefs, and attitudes shared by organizational members that determines the accepted way of doing things in a company. As you learned in Chapter 3, changing cultures is extremely difficult and slow. According to Kotter, two things help anchor changes in a corporation's culture. The first is directly showing people that the changes have actually improved performance. At Celestica, this was demonstrated by the quick increase in quarterly profits, which led to a 60 percent increase in its stock price.[53] The second is to make sure that the people who get promoted fit the new culture. If they don't, it's a clear sign that the changes were only temporary. To anchor this change, Muhlhauser created a culture of meritocracy that rewarded managers and employees for their contributions. The rewards have come in the form of promotions, pay increases, and huge bonuses. Customer satisfaction has improved. With the increasing demand for consumer products, such as smartphones, employees are excited about the prospects for Celestica. "We've got some new programs in the pipeline so we're optimistic about our ability to compete in and win in that market," said CEO Muhlhauser.[54]

7-4c CHANGE TOOLS AND TECHNIQUES

Imagine that your boss came to you and said, "All right, genius, you wanted it. You're in charge of turning around the division." Where would you begin? How would you encourage change-resistant managers to change? What would you do to include others in the change process? How would you get the change process off to a quick start? Finally, what approach would you use to promote long-term effectiveness and performance?

Results-driven change, the General Electric workout, and organizational development are different change tools and techniques that can be used to address these issues.

One of the reasons that organizational change efforts fail is that they are activity oriented rather than results oriented. In other words, they focus primarily on changing company procedures, management philosophy, or employee behavior. Typically, there is much buildup and preparation as consultants are brought in, presentations are made, books are read, and employees and managers are trained. There's a tremendous emphasis on doing things the new way. But, with all the focus on "doing," almost no attention is paid to *results*, to seeing if all this activity has actually made a difference.

By contrast, **results-driven change** supplants the emphasis on activity with a laserlike focus on quickly measuring and improving results.[55] Top managers at Hyundai knew that if they were to compete successfully against the likes of Honda and Toyota, they would have to improve the quality of their cars substantially. So top managers guided the company's results-driven change process by,

Results-driven change change created quickly by focusing on the measurement and improvement of results

EXHIBIT 7.4

How to Create a Results-Driven Change Program

1. Set measurable, short-term goals to improve performance.

2. Make sure your action steps are likely to improve measured performance.

3. Stress the importance of immediate improvements.

4. Solicit help from consultants and staffers to achieve quick improvements in performance.

5. Test action steps to see if they actually yield improvements. If they don't, discard them and establish new ones.

6. Use resources you have or that can be easily acquired. It doesn't take much.

Source: R. H. Schaffer and H. A. Thomson, "Successful Change Programs Begin with Results," *Harvard Business Review on Change* (Boston: Harvard Business School Press, 1998), 189–213.

first, increasing the number of quality teams from 100 to 865. Then, all employees were required to attend seminars on quality improvement and use the results of industry quality studies, like those published annually by J. D. Power and Associates, as their benchmark. Hyundai then measured the effects of the focus on quality. Before the change, a new Hyundai averaged 23.4 initial quality problems; after the results-driven change efforts, that number dropped to 9.6.[56] According to J. D. Power, Hyundai ranks twelfth overall out of thirty-three automakers in initial car quality.[57]

Another advantage of results-driven change is that managers introduce changes in procedures, philosophy, or behavior only if they are likely to improve measured performance. In other words, managers and workers actually test to see if changes make a difference. Consistent with this approach, Hyundai invested $30 million in a test center where cars could be subjected to a sequence of extremely harsh conditions for as long as they could withstand them, allowing engineers to pinpoint defects and fix the problems.[58]

A third advantage of results-driven change is that quick, visible improvements motivate employees to continue to make additional changes to improve measured performance. A few years into Hyundai's change process, Chrysler and Mitsubishi Motors announced they would use Hyundai-designed four-cylinder engines in their small and mid-sized cars, reinforcing the quality strides that Hyundai had made.[59] As a result of the superb quality of its cars, Hyundai's global sales actually rose 5 percent during the recession, when nearly every other auto manufacturer, including Toyota and Honda, saw their sales drop 25 to 35 percent.[60] Today, less than a decade after it took steps to address the quality of its cars, Hyundai is the fifth-largest auto manufacturer in the world.[61] As seen at Hyundai, the quick successes associated with results-driven change can be particularly effective at reducing resistance to change. Exhibit 7.4 describes the basic steps of results-driven change.

The **General Electric workout** is a special kind of results-driven change. The "workout" involves a three-day meeting that brings together managers and employees from different levels and parts of an organization to quickly generate and act on solutions to specific business problems.[62] On the first morning, the boss discusses the agenda and targets specific business problems that the group will solve. Then, the boss leaves and an outside facilitator breaks the group (typically thirty to forty people) into five or six teams and helps them spend the next day and a half discussing and debating solutions.

On day three, in what GE calls a "town meeting," the teams present specific solutions to their boss, who has been gone since day one. As each team's spokesperson makes specific suggestions, the boss has only three options: agree on the spot, say no, or ask for more information so that a decision can be made by a specific, agreed-on date. GE boss Armand Lauzon sweated his way through a town meeting. To encourage him to say yes, his workers set up the meeting room to put pressure on Lauzon. He says, "I was wringing wet within half an hour. They had 108 proposals, I had about a minute to say yes or no to each one, and I couldn't make eye

General Electric workout
a three-day meeting in which managers and employees from different levels and parts of an organization quickly generate and act on solutions to specific business problems

contact with my boss without turning around, which would show everyone in the room that I was chicken."[63] In the end, Lauzon agreed to all but eight suggestions. Furthermore, once those decisions were made, no one at GE was allowed to overrule them.

Organizational development is a philosophy and collection of planned change interventions designed to improve an organization's long-term health and performance. Organizational development takes a long-range approach to change; assumes that top-management support is necessary for change to succeed; creates change by educating workers and managers to change ideas, beliefs, and behaviors so that problems can be solved in new ways; and emphasizes employee participation in diagnosing, solving, and evaluating problems.[64] As shown in Exhibit 7.5, organizational development interventions begin with the recognition of a problem. Then, the company designates a **change agent** to be formally in charge of guiding the change effort. This person can be someone from within the company or a professional consultant. The change agent clarifies the problem, gathers information, works with decision makers to create and implement an action plan, helps to evaluate the plan's effectiveness, implements the plan throughout the company, and then leaves (if from outside the company) after making sure the change intervention will continue to work.

Organizational development interventions are aimed at changing large systems, small groups, or people.[65] More specifically, the purpose of *large-system interventions* is to change the character and performance of an organization, business unit, or department. *Small-group intervention* focuses on assessing how a group functions and helping it work more effectively to accomplish its goals. *Person-focused intervention* is intended to increase interpersonal effectiveness by helping people to become aware of their attitudes and behaviors and to acquire new skills and knowledge. Exhibit 7.6 on the following page describes the most frequently used organizational development interventions for large systems, small groups, and people.

Organizational development a philosophy and collection of planned change interventions designed to improve an organization's long-term health and performance

Change agent the person formally in charge of guiding a change effort

EXHIBIT 7.5

General Steps for Organizational Development Interventions

1. Entry	A problem is discovered and the need for change becomes apparent. A search begins for someone to deal with the problem and facilitate change.
2. Startup	A change agent enters the picture and works to clarify the problem and gain commitment to a change effort.
3. Assessment & feedback	The change agent gathers information about the problem and provides feedback about it to decision makers and those affected by it.
4. Action planning	The change agent works with decision makers to develop an action plan.
5. Intervention	The action plan, or organizational development intervention, is carried out.
6. Evaluation	The change agent helps decision makers assess the effectiveness of the intervention.
7. Adoption	Organizational members accept ownership and responsibility for the change, which is then carried out through the entire organization.
8. Separation	The change agent leaves the organization after first ensuring that the change intervention will continue to work.

Source: W. J. Rothwell, R. Sullivan, and G. M. McLean, *Practicing Organizational Development: A Guide for Consultants* (San Diego: Pfeiffer & Co., 1995).

EXHIBIT 7.6

Different Kinds of Organizational Development Interventions

LARGE-SYSTEM INTERVENTIONS

Sociotechnical systems	An intervention designed to improve how well employees use and adjust to the work technology used in an organization.
Survey feedback	An intervention that uses surveys to collect information from the members of the system, reports the results of that survey to the members, and then uses those results to develop action plans for improvement.

SMALL-GROUP INTERVENTIONS

Team building	An intervention designed to increase the cohesion and cooperation of work group members.
Unit goal setting	An intervention designed to help a work group establish short- and long-term goals.

PERSON-FOCUSED INTERVENTIONS

Counseling/ coaching	An intervention designed so that a formal helper or coach listens to managers or employees and advises them on how to deal with work or interpersonal problems.
Training	An intervention designed to provide individuals with the knowledge, skills, or attitudes they need to become more effective at their jobs.

Source: W. J. Rothwell, R. Sullivan, and G. M. McLean, *Practicing Organizational Development: A Guide for Consultants* (San Diego: Pfeiffer & Co., 1995).

© Monalyn Gracia/Corbis/Jupiterimages

STUDY TOOLS 7

LOCATED AT THE BACK OF YOUR BOOK:

☐ Rip out and study the Chapter Review Card at the end of the book

LOG IN TO THE COURSEMATE FOR MGMT AT CENGAGEBRAIN.COM TO:

☐ Review Key Term Flashcards delivered three ways (print or online)

☐ Complete both Practice Quizzes to prepare for tests

☐ Play Beat the Clock and Quizbowl to master concepts

☐ Complete the Crossword Puzzle to review key terms

☐ Watch the video on Holden Outerwear for a real company example and take the accompanying quiz

☐ Complete the case assignment on 3M

☐ Work through the Management Decision on innovation copycats

☐ Work through the Management Team Decision on alternative fuels

☐ Develop your skills with the Develop Your Career Potential exercise

4LTR Press solutions are designed for today's learners through the continuous feedback of students like you. Tell us what you think about MGMT and help us improve the learning experience for future students.

YOUR FEEDBACK MATTERS.

Complete the Speak Up survey in CourseMate at www.cengagebrain.com

 Follow us at www.facebook.com/4ltrpress

8 Global
Management

LEARNING OUTCOMES

8-1 Discuss the impact of global business and the trade rules and agreements that govern it.

8-2 Explain why companies choose to standardize or adapt their business procedures.

8-3 Explain the different ways that companies can organize to do business globally.

8-4 Explain how to find a favorable business climate.

8-5 Discuss the importance of identifying and adapting to cultural differences.

8-6 Explain how to successfully prepare workers for international assignments.

CHECK OUT
STUDY TOOLS
AT THE END OF
THIS CHAPTER.

8-1 Global Business, Trade Rules, and Trade Agreements

Business is the buying and selling of goods or services. Buying this textbook was a business transaction. So was selling your first car. So was getting paid for babysitting or for mowing lawns. **Global business** is the buying and selling of goods and services by people from different countries. The Timex watch that I wore while I was writing this chapter was purchased at a Wal-Mart in Texas. But since it was made in the Philippines, I participated in global business when I wrote Wal-Mart a check. Wal-Mart, for its part, had already paid Timex, which had paid the company that employs the Filipino managers and workers who made my watch. Of course, there is more to global business than buying imported products at Wal-Mart.

Global business presents its own set of challenges for managers. How can you be sure that the way you run your business in one country is the right way to run that business in another? This chapter discusses how organizations answer that question. We will start by examining global business in two ways: first exploring its impact on U.S. businesses and then reviewing the basic rules and agreements that govern global trade. Next, we will examine how and when companies go global by examining the tradeoff between consistency and adaptation and discussing how to organize a global company. Finally, we will look at how companies decide where to expand globally, including finding the best business climate, adapting to cultural differences, and better preparing employees for international assignments.

If you want a simple demonstration of the impact of global business, look at the tag on your shirt, the inside of your shoes, and the inside of your cell phone (take out your battery). Chances are all of these items were made in different places around the world. As I write this, my shirt, shoes, and cell phone were made in Thailand, China, and Korea. Where were yours made?

*Let's learn more about **8-1a the impact of global business, 8-1b how tariff and nontariff trade barriers have historically restricted global business, 8-1c how today global and regional trade agreements are reducing those trade barriers worldwide**, and **8-1d how consumers are responding to those changes in trade rules and agreements.***

8-1a THE IMPACT OF GLOBAL BUSINESS

Multinational corporations are corporations that own businesses in two or more countries. In 1970, more than half of the world's 7,000 multinational corporations were headquartered in just two countries: the United States and the United Kingdom. Today, there are roughly 103,000 multinational corporations, more than fourteen times as many as in 1970, and 9,692, or 9.4 percent, are based in the United States.[1] Today, 73,144 multinationals, or 71 percent, are based in other developed countries (e.g., Germany, Italy, Canada, and Japan), while 30,209, or 29.3 percent, are based in developing countries (e.g., Colombia and South Africa). So, today,

> **Global business** the buying and selling of goods and services by people from different countries
>
> **Multinational corporation** a corporation that owns businesses in two or more countries

multinational companies can be found by the thousands all over the world!

Another way to appreciate the impact of global business is by considering direct foreign investment. **Direct foreign investment** occurs when a company builds a new business or buys an existing business in a foreign country. Royal Dutch Shell, a Netherlands-based oil company, made a direct foreign investment into Africa when it bought Cove Energy, an oil and gas exploration company with assets in Mozambique, Tanzania, and Kenya, for $1.6 billion.[2]

Of course, companies from many other countries also own businesses in the United States. As Exhibit 8.1 shows, companies from the United Kingdom, Japan, Canada, the Netherlands, Germany, France, Switzerland, and Luxembourg have the largest direct foreign investment in the United States. Overall, foreign companies invest more than $2.3 trillion a year to do business in the United States.

But direct foreign investment in the United States is only half the picture. U.S. companies also have made large direct foreign investments in countries throughout the world. Ford Motor Company recently announced that it will build two factories in Chongqing, China, in order to better compete in the world's largest automobile market. A new $350 million factory will supply 400,000 transmission units for Ford's joint venture in China, while a second $500 million factory will produce engines. Joe Hinrichs, Ford's president for Asia Pacific and Africa, said, "Together with prior investments announced in the past few years, this new plant demonstrates Ford's unprecedented commitment to the China market."[3]

As Exhibit 8.2 shows, U.S. companies have made their largest direct foreign investments in the United Kingdom, the Netherlands, and Canada. Overall, U.S. companies invest more than $3.5 trillion a year to do business in other countries.

So, whether foreign companies invest in the United States or U.S. companies invest abroad, direct foreign investment is an increasingly important and common method of conducting global business.

8-1b TRADE BARRIERS

Although today's consumers usually don't care where the products they buy come from (more on this in Section 8-1d), national governments have

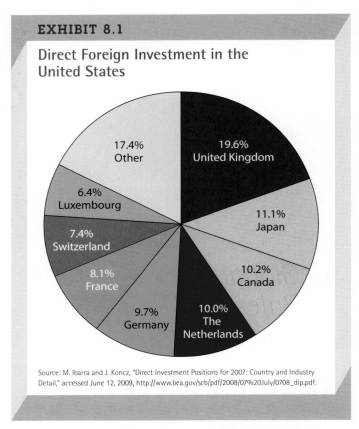

EXHIBIT 8.1

Direct Foreign Investment in the United States

- 19.6% United Kingdom
- 11.1% Japan
- 10.2% Canada
- 10.0% The Netherlands
- 9.7% Germany
- 8.1% France
- 7.4% Switzerland
- 6.4% Luxembourg
- 17.4% Other

Source: M. Ibarra and J. Koncz, "Direct Investment Positions for 2007: Country and Industry Detail," accessed June 12, 2009, http://www.bea.gov/scb/pdf/2008/07%20July/0708_dip.pdf.

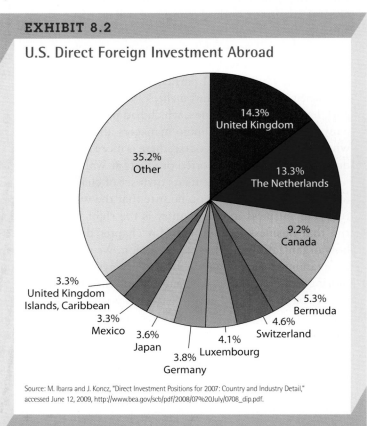

EXHIBIT 8.2

U.S. Direct Foreign Investment Abroad

- 14.3% United Kingdom
- 13.3% The Netherlands
- 9.2% Canada
- 5.3% Bermuda
- 4.6% Switzerland
- 4.1% Luxembourg
- 3.8% Germany
- 3.6% Japan
- 3.3% Mexico
- 3.3% United Kingdom Islands, Caribbean
- 35.2% Other

Source: M. Ibarra and J. Koncz, "Direct Investment Positions for 2007: Country and Industry Detail," accessed June 12, 2009, http://www.bea.gov/scb/pdf/2008/07%20July/0708_dip.pdf.

traditionally preferred that consumers buy domestically made products in hopes that such purchases would increase the number of domestic businesses and workers. Indeed, governments have done much more than hope that you will buy from domestic companies. Historically, governments have actively used **trade barriers** to make it much more expensive or difficult (or sometimes impossible) for consumers to buy or consume imported goods. For example, the Chinese government adds a 105 percent tariff to the price of chickens imported from the United States. The U.S. government, in turn, imposes a 35 percent tariff on tires imported from China.[4] By establishing these restrictions and taxes, the Chinese and U.S. governments are engaging in **protectionism**, which is the use of trade barriers to protect local companies and their workers from foreign competition.

Governments have used two general kinds of trade barriers: tariff and nontariff barriers. A **tariff** is a direct tax on imported goods. Tariffs increase the cost of imported goods relative to that of domestic goods. For example, the U.S. import tax on trucks is 25 percent. This means that U.S. buyers must pay $25,000 for a $20,000 imported truck, with the $5,000 tariff going to the U.S. government. As a result, fewer than 10,000 pickup trucks are imported by the United States each year.[5] **Nontariff barriers** are nontax methods of increasing the cost or reducing the volume of imported goods. There are five types of nontariff barriers: quotas, voluntary export restraints, government import standards, government subsidies, and customs valuation/classification. Because there are so many different kinds of nontariff barriers, they can be an even more potent method of shielding domestic industries from foreign competition.

Quotas are specific limits on the number or volume of imported products. For example, China only allows twenty foreign films to be released in Chinese movie theaters each year.[6] Like quotas, **voluntary export restraints** limit the amount of a product that can be imported annually. The difference is that the exporting country rather than the importing country imposes restraints. Usually, however, the "voluntary" offer to limit exports occurs because the importing country has implicitly threatened to impose quotas. For example, to protect South African textile manufacturers

from cheap and plentiful Chinese textile products, the South African government convinced China to "voluntarily" restrict the textiles it exports to South Africa each year.[7] According to the World Trade Organization (see the discussion in Section 8-1c), however, voluntary export restraints are illegal and should not be used to restrict imports.[8]

In theory, **government import standards** are established to protect the health and safety of citizens. In reality, such standards are often used to restrict or ban imported goods. For example, India bans the importation of chicken, meat, and eggs from the United States, claiming that the ban protects the health of its domestic chicken flocks by preventing the spread of bird flu. U.S. Trade Representative Ron Kirk, however, argues that the ban has no scientific merit and that "India's ban on U.S. Poultry is clearly a case of disguising trade restrictions by invoking unjustified animal health concerns."[9]

Many nations also use **subsidies**, such as long-term, low-interest loans, cash grants, and tax deferments, to develop and protect companies in special industries. Not surprisingly, businesses complain about unfair trade practices when foreign companies receive government subsidies. For nearly six years, jet manufacturers Boeing and Airbus have each filed claims with the World Trade Organization (WTO) claiming the other received billions in illegal subsidies. In 2010, the WTO ruled that Airbus illegally benefitted from $15 billion in low-interest government loans and subsidies from the European Union. In response, the European Union charged that Boeing benefited from $20 billion in tax breaks, military contracts, and subsidies from the U.S. government. In

Trade barriers government-imposed regulations that increase the cost and restrict the number of imported goods

Protectionism a government's use of trade barriers to shield domestic companies and their workers from foreign competition

Tariff a direct tax on imported goods

Nontariff barriers nontax methods of increasing the cost or reducing the volume of imported goods

Quota a limit on the number or volume of imported products

Voluntary export restraints voluntarily imposed limits on the number or volume of products exported to a particular country

Government import standard a standard ostensibly established to protect the health and safety of citizens but, in reality, often used to restrict imports

Subsidies government loans, grants, and tax deferments given to domestic companies to protect them from foreign competition

© iStockphoto.com/ Franck Boston

Customs classification
a classification assigned to imported products by government officials that affects the size of the tariff and the imposition of import quotas

General Agreement on Tariffs and Trade (GATT)
a worldwide trade agreement that reduced and eliminated tariffs, limited government subsidies, and established protections for intellectual property

World Trade Organization (WTO) the successor to GATT; the only international organization dealing with the global rules of trade between nations. Its main function is to ensure that trade flows as smoothly, predictably, and freely as possible

Regional trading zones
areas in which tariff and nontariff barriers on trade between countries are reduced or eliminated

that case, the WTO ruled that Boeing had received $5.3 billion in illegal aid and subsidies from the U.S. government to support the development of its 787 Dreamliner passenger jet.[10]

The last type of nontariff barrier is **customs classification**. As products are imported into a country, they are examined by customs agents, who must decide which of nearly 9,000 categories they should be classified into (see the Official Harmonized Tariff Schedule of the United States at http://www.usitc.gov/tata/hts/index.htm for more information). The category assigned by customs agents can greatly affect the size of the tariff and whether the item is subject to import quotas. For example, the U.S. Customs Service has several customs classifications for imported shoes. Tariffs on imported leather or "nonrubber" shoes are about 10 percent, whereas tariffs on imported rubber shoes, such as athletic footwear, range from 20 to 84 percent. The difference is large enough that some importers try to make their rubber shoes look like leather in hopes of receiving the nonrubber customs classification and lower tariff.

8-1c TRADE AGREEMENTS

Thanks to the trade barriers described above, buying imported goods has often been much more expensive and difficult than buying domestic goods. During the 1990s, however, the regulations governing global trade were transformed. The most significant change was that 124 countries agreed to adopt the **General Agreement on Tariffs and Trade (GATT)**. GATT, which existed from 1947 to 1995, was an agreement to regulate trade among (eventually) more than 120 countries, the purpose of which was "substantial reduction of tariffs and other trade barriers and the elimination of preferences."[11] GATT members engaged in eight rounds of trade negotiations, with the Uruguay Round signed in 1994 and going into effect in 1995. Although GATT itself was replaced by the **World Trade Organization (WTO)** in 1995, the changes that it made continue to encourage international trade. Today, the WTO and its

member countries are negotiating what's known as the Doha Round, which seeks to advance trade opportunities for developing countries in areas ranging from agriculture to services to intellectual property rights. The WTO, headquartered in Geneva, Switzerland, administers trade agreements, provides a forum for trade negotiations, handles trade disputes, monitors national trade policies, and offers technical assistance and training for developing countries for its 157 member countries.

Through tremendous decreases in tariff and nontariff barriers, the Uruguay round of GATT made it much easier and cheaper for consumers in all countries to buy foreign products. First, tariffs were cut 40 percent on average worldwide by 2005. Second, tariffs were eliminated in ten specific industries: beer, alcohol, construction equipment, farm machinery, furniture, medical equipment, paper, pharmaceuticals, steel, and toys. Third, stricter limits were put on government subsidies. For example, the Uruguay round of GATT put limits on how much national governments can subsidize private research in electronic and high-technology industries (see the discussion of subsidies in Section 8-1b). Fourth, the Uruguay round of GATT established protections for intellectual property, such as trademarks, patents, and copyrights.

Protection of intellectual property has become an increasingly important issue in global trade because of widespread product piracy. For example, according to the International Federation of the Phonographic Industry, which represents the global recording industry, 95 percent of all music downloads violate copyrights.[12] Likewise, according to the International Data Corporation, an IT marketing firm, 40 percent of all software used in the world is pirated, costing companies $51 billion in lost sales.[13] Product piracy is also costly to the movie industry, as movie studios, distributors, and theaters, as well as video/DVD distributors, lose $18 billion each year to pirates.[14]

Finally, trade disputes between countries now are fully settled by arbitration panels from the WTO. In the past, countries could use their veto power to cancel a panel's decision. For instance, the French government routinely vetoed rulings that its large cash grants to French farmers constituted unfair subsidies. Now, however, countries that are members of the WTO no longer have veto power. Thus, WTO rulings are complete and final. Exhibit 8.3 provides a brief overview of the WTO and its functions.

The second major development that has reduced trade barriers has been the creation of **regional trading zones**, or zones in which tariff and nontariff barriers are reduced or eliminated for countries within the

Maastricht Treaty of Europe a regional trade agreement between most European countries

North American Free Trade Agreement (NAFTA) a regional trade agreement between the United States, Canada, and Mexico

EXHIBIT 8.3

World Trade Organization

✓ **FACT FILE**

WORLD TRADE ORGANIZATION

Location: Geneva, Switzerland
Established: January 1, 1995
Created by: Uruguay Round negotiations (1986–1994)
Membership: 157 countries (on August 24, 2012)
Budget: 196 million Swiss francs for 2011
Secretariat staff: 640
Head: Pascal Lamy (Director-General)

Functions:
- Administering WTO trade agreements
- Forum for trade negotiations
- Handling trade disputes
- Monitoring national trade policies
- Technical assistance and training for developing countries
- Cooperation with other international organizations

Source: "What Is the WTO?," accessed July 10, 2012, http://www.wto.org/english/thewto_e/whatis_e/whatis_e.htm.

trading zone. The largest and most important trading zones are in Europe (the Maastricht Treaty), North America (the North American Free Trade Agreement, or NAFTA), Central America (Dominican Republic-Central America Free Trade Agreement, or CAFTA-DR), South America (Union of South American Nations, or USAN), and Asia (the Association of Southeast Asian Nations, or ASEAN, and Asia-Pacific Economic Cooperation, or APEC). The map in Exhibit 8.4 on the next page shows the extent to which free-trade agreements govern global trade.

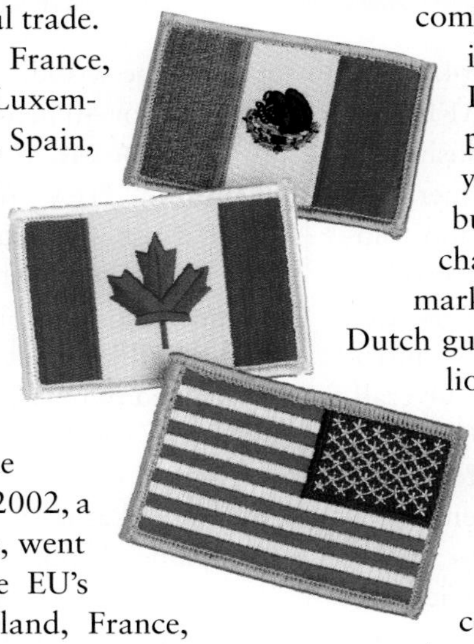

In 1992, Belgium, Denmark, France, Germany, Greece, Ireland, Italy, Luxembourg, the Netherlands, Portugal, Spain, and the United Kingdom adopted the **Maastricht Treaty of Europe**. The purpose of this treaty was to transform their twelve different economies and twelve currencies into one common economic market, called the European Union (EU), with one common currency. On January 1, 2002, a single common currency, the euro, went into circulation in twelve of the EU's members (Austria, Belgium, Finland, France, Germany, Greece, Ireland, Italy, Luxembourg, the Netherlands, Portugal, and Spain). Austria, Finland, and Sweden joined the EU in 1995, followed by Cy-

prus, the Czech Republic, Estonia, Hungary, Latvia, Lithuania, Malta, Poland, Slovakia, and Slovenia in 2004, and Bulgaria and Romania in 2007, bringing the total membership to twenty-seven countries.[15] Croatia, Macedonia, Iceland, Montenegro, and Turkey have applied and are being considered for membership.[16]

Prior to the treaty, trucks carrying products were stopped and inspected by customs agents at each border. Furthermore, since the required paperwork, tariffs, and government product specifications could be radically different in each country, companies often had to file twelve different sets of paperwork, pay twelve different tariffs, produce twelve different versions of their basic product to meet various government specifications, and exchange money in twelve different currencies. Likewise, open business travel, which we take for granted in the United States, was complicated by inspections at each border crossing. If you lived in Germany but worked in Luxembourg, your car was stopped and your passport was inspected twice every day as you traveled to and from work. Also, every business transaction required a currency exchange, for example, from German deutsche marks to Italian lira, or from French francs to Dutch guilders. Imagine all of this happening to millions of trucks, cars, and businesspeople each day, and you can begin to appreciate the difficulty and cost of conducting business across Europe before the Maastricht Treaty. For more information about the Maastricht Treaty, the EU, and Europe's common currency, the euro, see http://europa.eu/index_en.htm.

NAFTA, the **North American Free Trade Agreement** between the United States, Canada, and

© iStockphoto.com/TinaFields

EXHIBIT 8.4

Global Map of Regional Trade Agreements

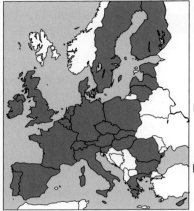

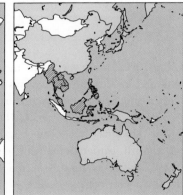

■ **Maastricht Treaty of Europe** Austria, Belgium, Bulgaria, Cyprus, the Czech Republic, Denmark, Estonia, Finland, France, Germany, Greece, Hungary, Ireland, Italy, Latvia, Lithuania, Luxembourg, Malta, the Netherlands, Poland, Portugal, Romania, Slovakia, Slovenia, Spain, Sweden, and the United Kingdom.

▨ **ASEAN (Association of Southeast Asian Nations)** Brunei Darussalam, Cambodia, Indonesia, Lao PDR, Malaysia, Myanmar, the Philippines, Singapore, Thailand, and Vietnam.

☐ **APEC (Asia-Pacific Economic Cooperation)** Australia, Canada, Chile, the People's Republic of China, Hong Kong (China), Japan, Mexico, New Zealand, Papua New Guinea, Peru, Russia, South Korea, Taiwan, the United States, and all members of ASEAN except Cambodia, Lao PDR, and Myanmar.

▨ **NAFTA (North American Free Trade Agreement)** Canada, Mexico, and the United States.

▨ **CAFTA-DR (Dominican Republic-Central American Free Trade Agreement)** Costa Rica, the Dominican Republic, El Salvador, Guatemala, Honduras, Nicaragua, and the United States.

▨ **UNASUR (Union of South American Nations)** Argentina, Bolivia, Brazil, Chile, Colombia, Ecuador, Guyana, Paraguay, Peru, Suriname, Uruguay, and Venezuela.

© Cengage Learning

Mexico, went into effect on January 1, 1994. More than any other regional trade agreement, NAFTA has liberalized trade between countries so that businesses can plan for one market (North America) rather than for three separate markets. One of NAFTA's most important achievements was to eliminate most product tariffs *and* prevent the three countries from increasing existing tariffs or introducing new ones. Overall, Mexican and Canadian exports to the United States are up 247 percent since NAFTA went into effect. U.S. exports to Mexico and Canada are up 171 percent, growing twice as fast as U.S. exports to any other part of the world.[17] In fact, Mexico and Canada now account for 40 percent of all U.S. exports.[18]

CAFTA-DR, the **Dominican Republic-Central America Free Trade Agreement** between the United States, the Dominican Republic, and the Central American countries of Costa Rica, El Salvador, Guatemala, Honduras, Nicaragua, and the Dominican Republic, went into effect in August 2005. With a combined population of 48.2 million, the CAFTA-DR countries together are the seventh-largest U.S. export market in the world and the third-largest U.S. export market in Latin America, after Mexico and Brazil. U.S. companies export more than $26.3 billion in goods each year to the CAFTA-DR countries.[19] Furthermore, U.S. exports to CAFTA-DR countries, which are increasing at 16 percent per year, are by far the fastest-growing export market for U.S. companies.[20]

Dominican Republic-Central America Free Trade Agreement (CAFTA-DR) a regional trade agreement between Costa Rica, the Dominican Republic, El Salvador, Guatemala, Honduras, Nicaragua, and the United States

On May 23, 2008, twelve South American countries signed the **Union of South American Nations (UNASUR)** Constitutive Treaty, which united the countries of the former Mercosur (Argentina, Brazil, Paraguay, Uruguay, and Venezuela) and the countries of the Andean Community (Bolivia, Colombia, Ecuador, and Peru) with Guyana, Suriname, and Chile. UNASUR aims to create a unified South America by permitting free movement between nations, creating a common infrastructure that includes an interoceanic highway, and establishing the region as a single market by eliminating all tariffs by 2019. UNASUR is one of the largest trading zones in the world, encompassing 361 million people in South America with a combined gross domestic product of nearly $973 billion.[21]

ASEAN, the **Association of Southeast Asian Nations**, and **APEC**, the **Asia-Pacific Economic Cooperation**, are the two largest and most important regional trading groups in Asia. ASEAN is a trade agreement between Brunei Darussalam, Cambodia, Indonesia, Lao PDR, Malaysia, Myanmar, the Philippines, Singapore, Thailand, and Vietnam, which form a market of more than 591 million people. U.S. trade with ASEAN countries exceeds $161 billion a year.[22] In fact, the United States is ASEAN's fourth-largest trading partner (China is its largest), and ASEAN'S member nations constitute the fifth-largest trading partner of the United States. An ASEAN free-trade area will be established in 2015 for the six original countries (Brunei Darussalam, Indonesia, Malaysia, the Philippines, Singapore, and Thailand) and in 2018 for the newer member countries (Cambodia, Lao PDR, Myanmar, and Vietnam).[23]

APEC is a broad agreement that includes Australia, Canada, Chile, the People's Republic of China, Hong Kong, Japan, Mexico, New Zealand, Papua New Guinea, Peru, Russia, South Korea, Taiwan, the United States, and all the members of ASEAN except Cambodia, Lao PDR, and Myanmar. APEC's twenty-one member countries contain 2.75 billion people, account for 44 percent of all global trade, and have a combined gross domestic product of over $34 trillion.[24] APEC countries began reducing trade barriers in 2000, though all the reductions will not be completely phased in until 2020.[25]

8-1d CONSUMERS, TRADE BARRIERS, AND TRADE AGREEMENTS

The average worker earns nearly $71,530 a year in Switzerland, $87,350 in Norway, $41,850 in Japan, and $47,340 in the United States.[26] Yet, after adjusting these incomes for how much they can buy, the Swiss income is equivalent to just $49,960, the Norwegian income to $58,570, and the Japanese income to $34,610.[27]

This is the same as saying that $1 of income can buy only $0.70 worth of goods in Switzerland, $0.67 worth in Norway, and $0.83 worth in Japan. In other words, Americans can buy much more with their incomes than those in other countries can.

One reason that Americans get more for their money is that the U.S. marketplace is the most competitive in the world and has been one of the easiest for foreign companies to enter.[28] Although some U.S. industries, such as textiles, have been heavily

Union of South American Nations (UNASUR) a regional trade agreement between Argentina, Brazil, Paraguay, Uruguay, Venezuela, Bolivia, Colombia, Ecuador, Peru, Guyana, Suriname, and Chile

Association of Southeast Asian Nations (ASEAN) a regional trade agreement between Brunei Darussalam, Cambodia, Indonesia, Laos, Malaysia, Myanmar, the Philippines, Singapore, Thailand, and Vietnam

Asia-Pacific Economic Cooperation (APEC) a regional trade agreement between Australia, Canada, Chile, the People's Republic of China, Hong Kong, Japan, Mexico, New Zealand, Papua New Guinea, Peru, Russia, South Korea, Taiwan, the United States, and all the members of ASEAN except Cambodia, Laos, and Myanmar

18th ASEAN Regional Forum
Retreat Session
Bali - Indonesia | 23 July 2011

indonesia 2011

AP Images/Saul Loeb

protected from foreign competition by trade barriers, for the most part, American consumers (and businesses) have had plentiful choices among American-made and foreign-made products. More important, the high level of competition between foreign and domestic companies that creates these choices helps keep prices low in the United States. Furthermore, it is precisely the lack of choice and the low level of competition that keep prices higher in countries that have not been as open to foreign companies and products. For example, Japanese trade barriers are estimated to cost Japanese consumers more than $100 billion a year. In fact, Japanese trade barriers amount to a 51 percent tax on food for the average Japanese family.[29]

So why do trade barriers and free-trade agreements matter to consumers? They're important because free-trade agreements increase choices, competition, and purchasing power and thus decrease what people pay for food, clothing, necessities, and luxuries. Accordingly, today's consumers rarely care where their products and services come from. From seafood to diamonds, people don't care where products are from—they just want to know which brand or kind is cheaper. And why do trade barriers and free-trade agreements matter to managers? The reason, as you're about to read, is that while free-trade agreements create new business opportunities, they also intensify competition, and addressing that competition is a manager's job.

8-2 *Consistency or Adaptation?*

Once a company has decided that it *will* go global, it must decide *how* to go global. For example, if you decide to sell in Singapore, should you try to find a local business partner who speaks the language, knows the laws, and understands the customs and norms of Singapore's culture? Or should you simply export your products from your home country? What do you do if you are also entering Eastern Europe, perhaps starting in Hungary? Should you use the same approach in Hungary that you used in Singapore?

In this section, we return to a key issue: How can you be sure that the way you run your business in one country is the right way to run that business in another? In other words, how can you strike the right balance between global consistency and local adaptation?

Global consistency means that a multinational company with offices, manufacturing plants, and distribution facilities in different countries uses the same rules, guidelines, policies, and procedures to run all of those offices, plants, and facilities. Managers at company headquarters value global consistency because it simplifies decisions. By contrast, a company following a policy of **local adaptation** modifies its standard operating procedures to adapt to differences in foreign customers, governments, and regulatory agencies. Local adaptation is typically preferred by local managers who are charged with making the international business successful in their countries.

If companies lean too much toward global consistency, they run the risk of using management procedures poorly suited to particular countries' markets, cultures, and employees (i.e., a lack of local adaptation). Best Buy became the biggest electronics retailer in the United States thanks to its big-box model featuring huge stores, suburban locations, a vast range of products, and strong customer service. When expanding to China, the world's largest consumer market, it followed the same strategy (i.e., global consistency) but failed, eventually closing all of its Chinese stores. Unlike Americans, Chinese consumers generally prefer small, conveniently located retailers close to their homes that let them avoid China's horrific traffic and shortage of retail parking spots. And, with the Chinese government's recent ban on plastic bags, location matters even more because Chinese consumers must carry everything by hand, necessitating several trips to the store. Likewise, Best Buy stores were not only too far away, their prices were expensive compared to smaller, local stores, which, with lower salaries, rent, and electricity expenses, easily beat Best Buy on price.[30]

If, however, companies focus too much on local adaptation, they run the risk of losing the cost effectiveness and productivity that result from using standardized rules and procedures throughout the world. Once thought to be culturally bound, meaning they could only succeed in domestic markets, Broadway shows from New York and West End shows from London are now routinely exported to other countries. For example, thirteen American or

British musicals now play in Japan. *Legally Blonde: The Musical* plays to large crowds in Manila in the Philippines. And foreign productions of *The Lion King* have earned over $2 billion. In almost all instances, except for some small cultural tweaks, there are few changes in the shows. Fully staged replicas are identical in story, musical score, costumes, and choreography but are performed in native languages. Non-replicas use identical scripts and musical scores but are not allowed to duplicate original sets, costumes, or choreography. Finally, American shows will sometimes take American actors overseas and then project supertitles above the stage so that foreign audiences can follow along.[31]

Rising Costs

For nearly two decades, China has been the go-to spot for companies looking to hire skilled workers at a low wage. It may soon be, however, that companies need to start looking elsewhere. Bolstered by the rapid growth of the Chinese economy and fueled by a shortage of workers, labor costs in China have soared. Twenty-one provinces and municipalities reported increasing their minimum wages by 22 percent, while Shenzhen, in the country's manufacturing center, raised its minimum wage by 15 percent. This has led to higher production costs for companies, which in turn has led to higher costs for consumers. According to the U.S. Department of Labor, the cost of all imports from China rose 3.9 percent from 2010 to 2011. As the demand for higher salaries is unlikely to disappear, manufacturers may need to start looking at countries like India, Vietnam, and Cambodia to keep their labor costs down.

Source: J. Lahart, "U.S. Shoppers Foot Bill for Soaring Pay in China," *Wall Street Journal*, December 15, 2011, accessed March 12, 2012, http://online.wsj.com/article/SB100014240 5297020402680457709877330840020.html.

© iStockphoto.com/samxmeg

8-3 *Forms for Global Business*

Besides determining whether to adapt organizational policies and procedures, a company must also determine how to organize itself for successful entry into foreign markets. *Historically, companies have generally followed the phase model of globalization, in which a company makes the transition from a domestic company to a global company in the following sequential phases:* **8-3a exporting, 8-3b cooperative contracts, 8-3c strategic alliances,** and **8-3d wholly owned affiliates.** At each step, the company grows much larger, uses those resources to enter more global markets, is less dependent on home country sales, and is more committed in its orientation to global business. Some companies, however, do not follow the phase model of globalization.[32] Some skip phases on their way to becoming more global and less domestic. Others don't follow the phase model at all. These are known as **8-3e global new ventures.** This section reviews these forms of global business.[33]

8-3a EXPORTING

When companies produce products in their home countries and sell those products to customers in foreign countries, they are **exporting**. Caterpillar, which makes heavy machinery and engines, opened a $200 million factory with 1,400 employees near Athens, Georgia. Forty percent of the small tractors and mini excavators produced at the plant will be exported to Europe and Asia.[34]

Exporting as a form of global business offers many advantages. It makes the company less dependent on sales in its home market and provides a greater degree of control over research, design, and production decisions. Caterpillar's CEO, Jim Owens, says, "[We try] to educate our employees on the importance of exports to us. We exported $10 billion worth of product last year, and many jobs in our U. S. facilities are very much geared to export markets."[35] Though advantageous in a number of ways, exporting also has its disadvantages. The primary disadvantage is that many exported goods are subject to tariff and nontariff barriers that can substantially increase their final cost to consumers. A second disadvantage is that transportation costs can

Exporting selling domestically produced products to customers in foreign countries

Cooperative contract an agreement in which a foreign business owner pays a company a fee for the right to conduct that business in his or her country

Licensing an agreement in which a domestic company, the licensor, receives royalty payments for allowing another company, the licensee, to produce the licensor's product, sell its service, or use its brand name in a specified foreign market

Franchise a collection of networked firms in which the manufacturer or marketer of a product or service, the franchisor, licenses the entire business to another person or organization, the franchisee

significantly increase the price of an exported product. For example, when the price of crude oil was approaching $150 a barrel, manufacturers who made everything from batteries to sofas to industrial parts started bringing manufacturing production from overseas back to North America. Jeff Rubin, chief economist at CIBC World Markets in Toronto, said, "In a world of triple-digit oil prices, distance costs money."[36] There is a third disadvantage of exporting: Companies that export depend on foreign importers for product distribution. If, for example, the foreign importer makes a mistake on the paperwork that accompanies a shipment of imported goods, those goods can be returned to the foreign manufacturer at the manufacturer's expense.

8-3b COOPERATIVE CONTRACTS

When an organization wants to expand its business globally without making a large financial commitment to do so, it may sign a **cooperative contract** with a foreign business owner who pays the company a fee for the right to conduct that business in his or her country. There are two kinds of cooperative contracts: licensing and franchising.

Under a **licensing** agreement, a domestic company, the *licensor*, receives royalty payments for allowing another company, the *licensee*, to produce its product, sell its service, or use its brand name in a particular foreign market. **BioDelivery Sciences International (BDSI)**, a pharmaceutical company in North Carolina, reached a licensing agreement with TTY Biopharm, a Taiwanese drug company. TTY Biopharm paid BDSI a $1.3 million licensing fee in exchange for the right to manufacture and sell BDSI's Onsolis painkilling drug to cancer patients in Taiwan.[37]

One of the most important advantages of licensing is that it allows companies to earn additional profits without investing more money. As foreign sales increase, the royalties paid to the licensor by the foreign licensee increase. Moreover, the licensee, not the licensor, invests in production equipment and facilities to produce the product. Licensing also helps companies avoid tariff and nontariff barriers. Since the licensee manufactures the product within the foreign country, tariff and nontariff barriers don't apply. **Royal Philips Electronics**, a Dutch consumer electronics company, has signed a licensing agreement with India-based Videocon Industries to make Philips TVs "as per specifications and standards maintained by Philips globally." The agreement gives Philips entry into the growing Indian TV market, which is dominated by Samsung, LG, and Panasonic. Alok Shende, with Ascentius, a technology research firm, commented that "it is a win-win situation for both companies as Videocon, with a low cost base and large manufacturing facilities, gets access to a global brand."[38]

The biggest disadvantage associated with licensing is that the licensor gives up control over the quality of the product or service sold by the foreign licensee. Unless the licensing agreement contains specific restrictions, the licensee controls the entire business from production to marketing to final sales. Many licensors include inspection clauses in their license contracts, but closely monitoring product or service quality from thousands of miles away can be difficult. An additional disadvantage is that licensees can eventually become competitors, especially when a licensing agreement includes access to important technology or proprietary business knowledge.

A **franchise** is a collection of networked firms in which the manufacturer or marketer of a product or service, the *franchisor*, licenses the entire business to another person or organization, the *franchisee*. For the price of an initial franchise fee plus royalties, franchisors provide franchisees with training, assistance with marketing and advertising, and an exclusive right to conduct business in a particular location. Most franchise fees run between $5,000 and $35,000. Franchisees pay McDonald's, one of the largest franchisors in the world, an initial franchise fee of $45,000. Another $950,900 to $1,797,700 is needed beyond that to pay for food inventory, kitchen equipment, construction, landscaping, and other expenses (the cost varies per country). While they typically borrow part of this cost from a bank, McDonald's requires franchisees to put down 40 percent in cash for the initial investment.[39] Since typical royalties range from 2.0 to 12.5 percent of gross sales, franchisors are well rewarded for the help they provide to franchisees. More than four hundred U.S. companies franchise their businesses to foreign franchise partners.

Despite franchising's many advantages, franchisors face a loss of control when they sell businesses to franchisees who are thousands of miles away. Franchising specialist Cheryl Scott says, "One franchisor I know was wondering why the royalties coming from India were so small when he knew the shop was always packed. It was because the franchisee wasn't putting all of the sales through the cash register."[40]

Although there are exceptions, franchising success may be somewhat culture-bound. Because most global franchisors begin by franchising their businesses in similar countries or regions (Canada is by far the first choice for American companies taking their first step into global franchising), and because 65 percent of franchisors make absolutely no change in their business for overseas franchisees, that success may not generalize to cultures with different lifestyles, values, preferences, and technological infrastructures. Customizing menus to local tastes is one of the primary ways that fast-food companies can succeed in international markets. With a 40 percent market share, 3,000 locations in 650 cities, and a new restaurant opening every eighteen hours, U.S.-based KFC, which is part of Yum! Brands, is the most successful foreign restaurant chain in China, even outperforming McDonald's, which has 16 percent of the market. Unlike McDonald's, which largely sells the same food in China that it does in the United States, KFC China, which is run by Chinese managers hired by Yum! Brands, has focused instead on providing Chinese-flavored dishes, such as the Dragon Twister, a chicken wrap with duck sauce and tofu chicken rice, designed to reflect the spicy food found in China's Sichuan province. And, while Chinese customers will find some Western menu items like chicken and corn on the cob, they'll also find Chinese favorites like fried dough sticks, congee (rice porridge), preserved eggs, and other dishes that cater to more local tastes.[41]

© iStockphoto.com/Skip O'Donnell

8-3c STRATEGIC ALLIANCES

Companies forming **strategic alliances** combine key resources, costs, risks, technology, and people. **Garmin**, which produces satellite navigation devices, and Volvo Penta, which makes leisure and commercial boat engines and propulsion systems, have formed a strategic alliance to jointly develop and market marine instrumentation, navigation, and communication equipment.[42] The most common strategic alliance is a **joint venture**, which occurs when two existing companies collaborate to form a third company. The two founding companies remain intact and unchanged, except that together they now own the newly created joint venture.

One of the advantages of global joint ventures is that, like licensing and franchising, they help companies avoid tariff and nontariff barriers to entry. Another advantage is that companies participating in a joint venture bear only part of the costs and the risks of that business. Many companies find this attractive because of the expense of entering foreign markets or developing new products. Starbucks established a fifty-fifty joint venture with Tata Global Beverages, which is part of the Tata Group, the largest conglomerate in India. Starbucks-Tata plans to open fifty stores within a year, eventually establishing 3,000 in India. John Culver, president of Starbucks Asia, said, "We are going to move as fast

Wholly owned affiliates foreign offices, facilities, and manufacturing plants that are 100 percent owned by the parent company

as we possibly can to take advantage of the opportunity that exists in India. It's an economy that is moving very quickly, and the consumer is evolving very quickly."[43]

Global joint ventures can be especially advantageous to smaller local partners who link up with larger, more experienced foreign firms that can bring advanced management, resources, and business skills to the joint venture. For example, Daimler AG, the Germany-based automaker, recently agreed to a joint venture with China-based Beiqi Foton Motor Company to manufacture and sell large trucks in China. While Daimler will benefit from establishing a presence in China's quickly growing market, Beiqi Foton will benefit from having access to Daimler's expertise in diesel engines and exhaust systems.[44]

Global joint ventures are not without problems, though. Because companies share costs and risks with their joint venture partners, they must also share profits. Managing global joint ventures can also be difficult because they represent a merging of four cultures: the country and the organizational culture of the first partner, and the country and the organizational culture of the second partner. Often, to be fair to all in-

volved, each partner in the global joint venture will have equal ownership and power. But this can result in power struggles and a lack of leadership. Because of these problems, companies forming global joint ventures should carefully develop detailed contracts that specify the obligations of each party. Toshiba, which participated in its first global joint ventures in the early 1900s by making light bulb filaments with General Electric, treats joint ventures like a marriage of the two companies and views the contract as a pre-nuptial agreement. The joint venture contract specifies how much each company will invest, what its rights and responsibilities are, and what it is entitled to if the joint venture does not work out. These steps are important because the rate of failure for global joint ventures is estimated to be as high as 70 percent.[45]

8-3d WHOLLY OWNED AFFILIATES (BUILD OR BUY)

Approximately one-third of multinational companies enter foreign markets through wholly owned affiliates. Unlike licensing arrangements, franchises, or joint ventures, **wholly owned affiliates** are 100 percent owned by the parent company. Haier America, which has a refrigerator factory in Camden, South Carolina,

is a wholly owned affiliate of the Haier Group based in Qingdao, China, which sells and markets a wide range of household goods like refrigerators, air conditioners, and MP3 players.[46]

The primary advantage of wholly owned businesses is that the parent company receives all of the profits and has complete control over the foreign facilities. The biggest disadvantage is the expense of building new operations or buying existing businesses. Although the payoff can be enormous if wholly owned affiliates succeed, the losses can be immense if they fail, because the parent company assumes all of the risk. Deutsche Telekom, the largest telecommunications company in Europe, established a presence in the United States through its affiliate T-Mobile USA. Though never a market leader, T-Mobile had decent performance for almost a decade, sometimes even outperforming Deutsche Telekom's other European divisions. More recently, however, T-Mobile has slumped badly. When AT&T, and later Verizon, began selling the extremely popular iPhone, T-Mobile began losing customers almost immediately. In 2010 alone, the company lost 390,000 fixed-contract customers, and it has a churn rate (the percent of customers not renewing their contracts) of 3.2 percent, tops in the industry and more than double the rate of the closest competitor. These struggles in the United States contributed to a 37 percent drop in profits for Deutsche Telekom.[47]

8-3e GLOBAL NEW VENTURES

Companies used to evolve slowly from small operations selling in their home markets to large businesses selling to foreign markets. Furthermore, as companies went global, they usually followed the phase model of globalization. Recently, however, three trends have combined to allow companies to skip the phase model when going global. First, quick, reliable air travel can transport people to nearly any point in the world within one day. Second, low-cost communication technologies such as email, teleconferencing, phone conferencing, and the Internet make it easier to communicate with global customers, suppliers, managers, and employees. Third, there is now a critical mass of businesspeople with extensive personal experience in all aspects of global business.[48] This combination of developments has made it possible to start companies that are global from inception. With sales, employees, and financing in different countries, **global new ventures** are companies that are founded with an active global strategy.[49]

Although there are several different kinds of global new ventures, all share two common factors. First, the company founders successfully develop and communicate the company's global vision from inception. Second, rather than going global one country at a time, new global ventures bring a product or service to market in several foreign markets at the same time. Founded by longtime airline executives Steven Udvar-Hazy and John L. Plueger, **Air Lease Corporation** is a company that provides aircraft to commercial airlines through lease agreements. Although based in Los Angeles, its mission is to provide equipment and financing to airlines all over the world. For example, in April 2012, Air Lease bought eight new Boeing 787-9 jets to lease to Vietnam Airlines in Asia, one Boeing 777-300ER to lease to Emirates in the Middle East, and an Airbus A330-300 to lease to KLM in Europe.[50] CEO Udvar-Hazy says, "We look forward to working with the leading global airlines as they modernize their fleets."[51]

8-4 Finding the Best Business Climate

When deciding where to go global, companies try to find countries or regions with promising business climates.

An attractive global business climate 8-4a positions the company for easy access to growing markets, 8-4b is an effective but cost-efficient place to build an office or manufacturing facility, and 8-4c minimizes the political risk to the company.

8-4a GROWING MARKETS

The most important factor in an attractive business climate is access to a growing market. For example, no product is known and purchased by as many people throughout the world as **Coca-Cola**. Yet even Coke, which is available in over two hundred countries, still has tremendous potential for further global growth. Coca-Cola gets 78 percent of its sales outside of North America, and emerging markets, where it has seen its fastest growth, now account for half of Coke's sales worldwide.[52]

Two factors help companies determine the growth potential of foreign markets: purchasing power and

EXHIBIT 8.5

How Consumption of Coca-Cola Varies with Purchasing Power around the World

Typically, the higher the purchasing power in a country, the better that country will be for doing business. Why? Because higher purchasing power means that consumers have more money to spend on nonessential products, like soft drinks. Coca-Cola has found that per capita consumption of Coca-Cola, that is, the average number of soft drinks a person will drink per year, rises directly with purchasing power (see the solid line).

Per Capita Consumption of Coca-Cola (x-axis)
Purchasing Power (per capita real GDP) (y-axis)

Sources: "Per Capita Consumption of Our Beverages," The Coca-Cola Company, accessed June 14, 2009, http://www.thecoca-colacompany.com/ourcompany /ar/percapitaconsumption.html; "Per Capita Consumption of Our Beverages, 1988, 1998, 2008," The Coca-Cola Company, accessed June 14, 2009, http://www .thecoca-colacompany.com/ourcompany/ar/pdf/perCapitaConsumption2008 .pdf; "Rank Order—GDP—Per Capita (PPP)," *The World Factbook* (September 7, 2008), accessed June 14, 2009, http://www.cia.gov/cia/publications /factbook/rankorder/2004rank.

Even Coca-Cola, which is available in more than 200 countries, still has tremendous potential for further global growth. Currently, the Coca-Cola Company gets about 80 percent of its sales from its sixteen largest markets.

foreign competitors. **Purchasing power** is measured by comparing the relative cost of a standard set of goods and services in different countries. For example, a Coke costs $1.49 in Tokyo. Because a twelve-ounce Coke costs only about 75 cents in the United States, the average American would have more purchasing power than the average Japanese. Purchasing power is growing in countries like India and China, which have low average levels of income. This is because basic living expenses such as food, shelter, and transportation are very inexpensive in those countries, so consumers still have money to spend after paying for necessities, especially as salaries increase thanks to demand from international trade (see box "Paying for a "Mac Attack").

Consequently, countries with high and growing levels of purchasing power are good choices for companies looking for attractive global markets. As Exhibit 8.5 shows, Coke has found that the per capita

Purchasing power the relative cost of a standard set of goods and services in different countries

consumption of Coca-Cola, or the number of Cokes a person drinks per year, rises directly with purchasing power. For example, in China, Brazil, and Australia, where the average person earns, respectively, $7,400, $10,900, and $41,300 annually, the number of Coca-Cola soft drinks consumed per year increases, respectively, from 34 to 229 to 319. The more purchasing power people have, the more likely they are to purchase soft drinks. And the Coca-Cola Company expects strong growth to continue in these markets, stating in its 2010 Annual Report, "To measure our growth potential, we look to our per capita consumption—the average number of eight-ounce servings of our beverages consumed each year in a given market. It is predicted that by the year 2020, the world will have nearly 1 billion more people whose disposable incomes will afford them choices and opportunities unthinkable a generation ago. We must discover innovative ways to connect with our traditional consumer base and this emerging global middle class—by creating new products and packaging formats for all lifestyles and occasions."[53]

Paying for a "Mac Attack"

Every year, *The Economist* magazine produces the Big Mac Index to illustrate differences in purchasing power across countries. By comparing the price of a single item, in this case a Big Mac from McDonald's, the index shows how much (or how little) consumers in each country get for their money. According to the latest index, a Big Mac costs an average of $4.20 in the United States. A Big Mac costs $4.73 in Canada, $5.68 in Brazil, and $6.81 in Switzerland, meaning that residents of those countries get far less for their money than U.S. residents do. Conversely, consumers in Russia only have to pay $2.55 for their Big Mac, while consumers in Turkey pay $3.54 and consumers in India pay only $1.62.

Source: "The Big Mac Index," *The Economist*, January 14, 2012, accessed March 12, 2012, http://www.economist.com/node/21542808.

AP Images/The Tribune Review, Sean Stipp

The second part of assessing the growth potential of global markets involves analyzing the degree of global competition, which is determined by the number and quality of companies that already compete in a foreign market. As the Starbucks-Tata joint venture begins opening stores in India, one of its primary competitors is Café Coffee Day, India's most popular coffee chain, which in the last few years has grown from a dozen stores to more than 1,200 locations in 175 cities. Café Coffee Day, like most of India's coffee shops, charges about $1 for a small cappuccino, which is about one-third the cost of the same drink in U.S. stores. By contrast, Starbucks plans to focus on selling premium coffee, tea, and food.[54]

8-4b CHOOSING AN OFFICE/ MANUFACTURING LOCATION

© iStockphoto.com/Samuel Locke

Companies do not have to establish an office or manufacturing location in each country they en-

ter. They can license, franchise, or export to foreign markets, or they can serve a larger region from one country. But there are many reasons why a company might choose to establish a location in a foreign country. Some foreign offices are established through global mergers and acquisitions, and some are established because of a commitment to grow in a new market. StarChip is a French semiconductor company that makes smart cards—plastic cards with embedded chips that transmit information to devices (like ATM machines), protect the data stored on the card (as with credit cards), or provide extra data storage (on identification cards, for example). StarChip opened a new office in Shanghai as part of its plan to expand its manufacturing and sales network in China. According to COO Christian Dupuy, "Expanding our operation to have engineers based in Shanghai is the logical first step to sustain the growing activity with our manufacturing partners in China."[55]

Other companies choose locations by seeking a tax haven (although this is more difficult for American companies due to legal concerns) or as part of creating a global brand. Although a company must be legally incorporated in one place, some companies have anywhere from nine to twenty-three global hubs and don't regard any one as more central than another.[56]

Brembo SpA, based in Milan, Italy, which makes high-performance brakes for the Cadillac CTS-v and

Corvette ZR1, is opening its U.S. headquarters and research and development facility in Detroit. Brembo Managing Director Alberto Bombassei said, "We want to transfer part of our research and development operations to the United States because we want to invest to boost our market share with new products."[57]

The criteria for choosing an office/manufacturing location are different from the criteria for entering a foreign market. Rather than focusing on costs alone, companies should consider both qualitative and quantitative factors. Two key qualitative factors are work force quality and company strategy. Work force quality is important because it is often difficult to find workers with the specific skills, abilities, and experience that a company needs to run its business. Work force quality is one reason that many companies doing business in Europe locate their customer call centers in the Netherlands. Workers in the Netherlands are the most linguistically gifted in Europe, with 73 percent speaking two languages, 44 percent speaking three languages, and 12 percent speaking more than three. Another advantage of locating a call center in the Netherlands is that 60 percent of call center workers have university or advanced degrees in technology or management.[58]

A company's strategy is also important when choosing a location. For example, a company pursuing a low-cost strategy may need plentiful raw materials, low-cost transportation, and low-cost labor. A company pursuing a differentiation strategy (typically a higher-priced, better product or service) may need access to high-quality materials and a highly skilled and educated work force.

Quantitative factors such as the kind of facility being built, tariff and nontariff barriers, exchange rates, and transportation and labor costs should also be considered when choosing an office/manufacturing location. A real estate specialist in company location decisions explains how things change with different types of facility: "If it's an assembly plant, a company might be inclined to look for incentives that would subsidize its hiring. With a distribution facility, an adequate transportation network will likely be critical. A corporate headquarters will need a good communications network, a multilingual labor force, and easy access by air. On the other hand, a research and development operation will require proximity to a high-tech infrastructure and access to good universities."[59] Companies rely on studies such as Cushman & Wakefield's annually published "European Cities Monitor" to compare business climates throughout Europe.[60] Similar studies are available for other parts of the world. Exhibit 8.6 offers a quick overview of the best cities for business based on a variety of criteria. This information is a good starting point if your company is trying to decide where to put an international office or manufacturing plant.

8-4c MINIMIZING POLITICAL RISK

When managers think about political risk in global business, they envision burning factories and riots in the streets. Although political events such as these receive dramatic and extended coverage from the media, the political risks that most companies face usually are not covered as breaking stories on Fox News or CNN. Nonetheless, the negative consequences of ordinary political risk can be just as devastating to companies that fail to identify and minimize that risk.[61]

When conducting global business, companies should attempt to identify two types of political risk: political uncertainty and policy uncertainty.[62] **Political uncertainty** is associated with the risk of major changes in political regimes that can result from war, revolution, death of political leaders, social unrest, or other influential events. **Policy uncertainty** refers to the risk associated with changes in laws and government policies that directly affect the way foreign companies conduct business.

Policy uncertainty is the most common—and perhaps most frustrating—form of political risk in global business, especially when changes in laws and government policies directly undercut sizable investments made by foreign companies. India is the third-largest retail market in the world behind the United States and China. The Indian government has long protected Indian retail stores by preventing foreign retailers from entering India unless they had a joint venture partner. So when India changed that policy, global retailers like Wal-Mart (United States), Carrefour (France), and Tesco (United Kingdom) began making plans to enter India on their own. The Indian government, however, reversed that decision following large protests from small-business owners and politicians, who feared that huge retail stores would put locally owned, mom-and-pop shops out of business. Kamlesh Gupta and her husband own such a shop, the Radha

EXHIBIT 8.6

World's Best Cities for Business

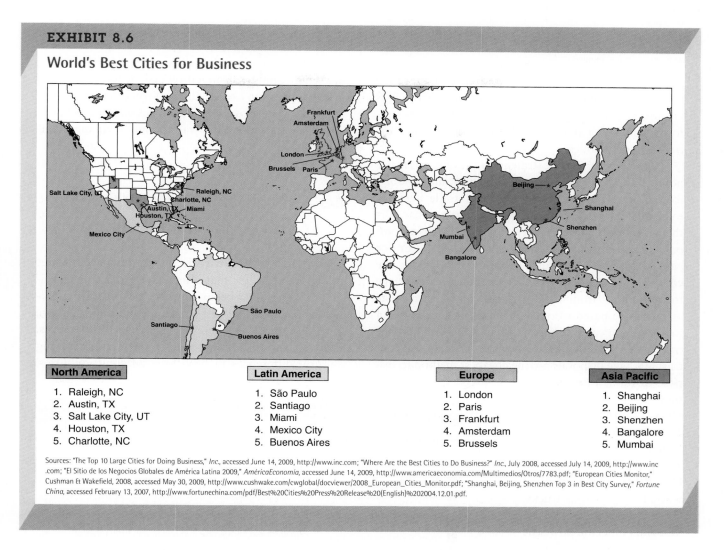

North America	Latin America	Europe	Asia Pacific
1. Raleigh, NC	1. São Paulo	1. London	1. Shanghai
2. Austin, TX	2. Santiago	2. Paris	2. Beijing
3. Salt Lake City, UT	3. Miami	3. Frankfurt	3. Shenzhen
4. Houston, TX	4. Mexico City	4. Amsterdam	4. Bangalore
5. Charlotte, NC	5. Buenos Aires	5. Brussels	5. Mumbai

Sources: "The Top 10 Large Cities for Doing Business," *Inc.*, accessed June 14, 2009, http://www.inc.com; "Where Are the Best Cities to Do Business?" *Inc.*, July 2008, accessed July 14, 2009, http://www.inc.com; "El Sitio de los Negocios Globales de América Latina 2009," *AméricaEconomia*, accessed June 14, 2009, http://www.americaeconomia.com/Multimedios/Otros/7783.pdf; "European Cities Monitor," Cushman & Wakefield, 2008, accessed May 30, 2009, http://www.cushwake.com/cwglobal/docviewer/2008_European_Cities_Monitor.pdf; "Shanghai, Beijing, Shenzhen Top 3 in Best City Survey," *Fortune China*, accessed February 13, 2007, http://www.fortunechina.com/pdf/Best%20Cities%20Press%20Release%20(English)%202004.12.01.pdf.

Krisna Store in Central Delhi. She said that if large retailers are allowed into India, "Everything will be over. If they sell goods cheaper than us, who will come here? Already, we have lost 20 percent of our business since Big Bazaar and Reliance [two other Indian retailers] started operating in the last two years." As a result, the only option for foreign retailers like Wal-Mart, and it's not an attractive one, is to form joint ventures to establish "cash-and-carry" stores that sell to businesses but not consumers.[63]

Several strategies can be used to minimize or adapt to the political risk inherent in global business. An *avoidance strategy* is used when the political risks associated with a foreign country or region are viewed as too great. If firms are already invested in high-risk areas, they may divest or sell their businesses. If they have not yet invested, they will likely postpone their investment until the risk shrinks. For example, fewer companies are investing in Mexico because battles be-

tween drug cartels resulted in over 31,000 murders in the last four years. Ron DeFeo, CEO of Terex, which makes heavy equipment and construction cranes, said, "We won't put a factory in Mexico until some of this violence gets addressed. We just can't put our people at risk."[64]

Exhibit 8.7 on the next page shows the long-term political stability of various countries in the Middle East (higher scores indicate less political risk). The following factors, which were used to compile these ratings, indicate greater political risk: government instability, poor socioeconomic conditions, internal or external conflict, military involvement in politics, religious and ethnic tensions, high foreign debt as a percentage of gross domestic product, exchange rate instability, and high inflation.[65] An avoidance strategy would likely be used for the riskiest countries shown in Exhibit 8.7, such as Iran and Saudi Arabia, but might not be needed for the less risky countries,

National culture the set of shared values and beliefs that affects the perceptions, decisions, and behavior of the people from a particular country

such as Israel or Oman. Risk conditions and factors change, so be sure to make risk decisions with the latest available information from resources such as the PRS Group, http://www.prsgroup.com, which supplies information about political risk to 80 percent of *Fortune* 500 companies.

Control is an active strategy to prevent or reduce political risks. Firms using a control strategy lobby foreign governments or international trade agencies to change laws, regulations, or trade barriers that hurt their business in that country. **Emerson Electric Company** had virtually no business for its InSinkErator garbage disposals in Europe during the 1990s. The company lobbied European governments to convince them of the environmentally friendly impact of a waste disposer compared to other methods of getting rid of food waste, such as composting, which involves garbage trucks, and landfills that emit methane gases. By contrast, garbage disposals are the cheapest method to dispose of food waste because they enable water-treatment plants to turn methane (that comes through the sewer system) into power and decrease the carbon footprint by reducing the amount of waste transported by trucks. Partially as a result of its lobbying, Emerson now sells over 100,000 disposals each year in Europe.[66]

Another method for dealing with political risk is *cooperation*, which involves using joint ventures and collaborative contracts, such as franchising and licensing. Although cooperation does not eliminate the political risk of doing business in a country, it can limit the risk associated with foreign ownership of a business. For example, a German company forming a joint venture with a Chinese company to do business in China may structure the joint venture contract so that the Chinese company owns 51 percent or more of the joint venture. Doing so qualifies the joint venture as a Chinese company and exempts it from Chinese laws that apply to foreign-owned businesses. However, cooperation cannot always protect against *policy risk* if a foreign government changes its laws and policies to directly affect the way foreign companies conduct business.

8-5 Becoming Aware of Cultural Differences

National culture is the set of shared values and beliefs that affects the perceptions, decisions, and behavior of the people from a particular country. The first step in dealing with culture is to recognize that there are meaningful differences. Professor Geert Hofstede spent twenty years studying cultural differences in fifty-three different countries.

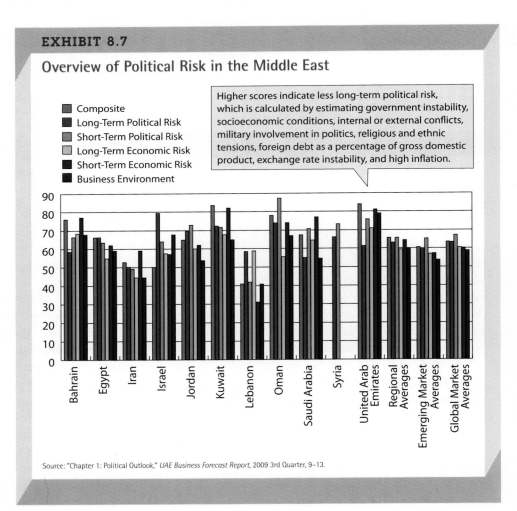

EXHIBIT 8.7

Overview of Political Risk in the Middle East

Legend:
- Composite
- Long-Term Political Risk
- Short-Term Political Risk
- Long-Term Economic Risk
- Short-Term Economic Risk
- Business Environment

Higher scores indicate less long-term political risk, which is calculated by estimating government instability, socioeconomic conditions, internal or external conflicts, military involvement in politics, religious and ethnic tensions, foreign debt as a percentage of gross domestic product, exchange rate instability, and high inflation.

Source: "Chapter 1: Political Outlook," *UAE Business Forecast Report*, 2009 3rd Quarter, 9–13.

His research shows that there are five consistent cultural dimensions across countries: power distance, individualism, masculinity, uncertainty avoidance, and short-term versus long-term orientation.[67]

Power distance is the extent to which people in a country accept that power is distributed unequally in society and organizations. In countries where power distance is weak, such as Denmark and Sweden, employees don't like their organization or their boss to have power over them or tell them what to do. They want to have a say in decisions that affect them. As Exhibit 8.8 shows, Russia and China, with scores of 95 and 80, respectively, are much stronger in power distance than Germany (35), the Netherlands (38), and the United States (40).

Individualism is the degree to which societies believe that individuals should be self-sufficient. In individualistic societies, employees put loyalty to themselves first and loyalty to their company and work group second. In Exhibit 8.8, the United States (91), the Netherlands (80), France (71), and Germany (67) are the strongest in individualism, while Indonesia (14), West Africa (20), and China (20) are the weakest.

Masculinity and *femininity* capture the difference between highly assertive and highly nurturing cultures. Masculine cultures emphasize assertiveness, competition, material success, and achievement, whereas feminine cultures emphasize the importance of relationships, modesty, caring for the weak, and quality of life. In Exhibit 8.8, Japan (95), Germany (66), and the United States (62) have the most masculine orientations, while the Netherlands (14) has the most feminine orientation.

The cultural difference of *uncertainty avoidance* is the degree to which people in a country are uncomfortable with unstructured, ambiguous, unpredictable situations. In countries with strong uncertainty avoidance, like Greece and Portugal, people tend to be aggressive and emotional and seek security rather than uncertainty. In Exhibit 8.8, Japan (92), France (86), West Africa (90), and Russia (90) are strongest in uncertainty avoidance, while Hong Kong (29) is the weakest.

The cultural dimension of *short-term/long-term orientation* addresses whether cultures are oriented to the present and seek immediate gratification or to the future and defer gratification. Not surprisingly,

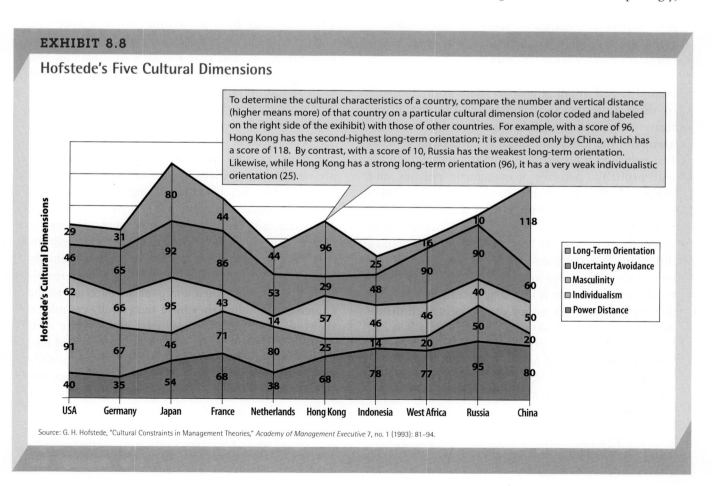

EXHIBIT 8.8

Hofstede's Five Cultural Dimensions

To determine the cultural characteristics of a country, compare the number and vertical distance (higher means more) of that country on a particular cultural dimension (color coded and labeled on the right side of the exihibit) with those of other countries. For example, with a score of 96, Hong Kong has the second-highest long-term orientation; it is exceeded only by China, which has a score of 118. By contrast, with a score of 10, Russia has the weakest long-term orientation. Likewise, while Hong Kong has a strong long-term orientation (96), it has a very weak individualistic orientation (25).

- Long-Term Orientation
- Uncertainty Avoidance
- Masculinity
- Individualism
- Power Distance

Source: G. H. Hofstede, "Cultural Constraints in Management Theories," *Academy of Management Executive* 7, no. 1 (1993): 81–94.

countries with short-term orientations are consumer-driven, whereas countries with long-term orientations are savings-driven. In Exhibit 8.8, China (118) and Hong Kong (96) have very strong long-term orientations, while Russia (10), West Africa (16), Indonesia (25), the United States (29), and Germany (31) have very strong short-term orientations. To generate a graphical comparison of two different countries' cultures, go to http://www.geert-hofstede.com/hofstede_dimensions.php. Select a "country"; then select a "comparison country." A graph comparing the countries on each of Hofstede's five cultural differences will automatically be generated.

Cultural differences affect perceptions, understanding, and behavior. Recognizing cultural differences is critical to succeeding in global business. Nevertheless, as Hofstede pointed out, descriptions of cultural differences are based on averages—the average level of uncertainty avoidance in Portugal, the average level of power distance in Argentina, and so forth. Accordingly, says Hofstede, "If you are going to spend time with a Japanese colleague, you shouldn't assume that overall cultural statements about Japanese society automatically apply to this person."[68] Similarly, cultural beliefs may differ significantly from one part of a country to another.[69]

After becoming aware of cultural differences, the second step is deciding how to adapt your company to those differences. Unfortunately, studies investigating the effects of cultural differences on management practices point more to difficulties than to easy solutions. One problem is that different cultures will probably perceive management policies and practices differently. For example, blue-collar workers in France and Argentina, all of whom performed the same factory jobs for the same multinational company, perceived its company-wide safety policy differently.[70] French workers perceived that safety wasn't very important to the company, but Argentine workers thought that it was. The fact that something as simple as a safety policy can be perceived differently across cultures shows just how difficult it can be to standardize management practices across different countries and cultures.

Another difficulty is that cultural values are changing, albeit slowly, in many parts of the world. The fall of communism in Eastern Europe and the former Soviet Union and the broad economic reforms in China have produced sweeping changes on two continents in the last two decades. Thanks to increased global trade resulting from free-trade agreements, major economic transformations are also under way in India, China, Central America, and South America. Consequently, when trying to adapt management practices to cultural differences, companies must ensure that they are not basing their adaptations on outdated and incorrect assumptions about a country's culture.

8-6 Preparing for an International Assignment

Tom Bonkenburg is director of European operations for St. Onge Company, a supply-chain consulting firm in York, Pennsylvania. Bonkenburg went to Moscow for a first-time meeting with the director of a Russian firm with which his company hoped to do business. He said that when he met the Russian director, "I gave my best smile, handshake and friendly joke . . . only to be met with a dreary and unhappy look." Afterwards, though, he received a friendly email from the Russian director, indicating that the meeting had been very positive. Subsequently, Bonkenburg learned that Russians save smiling and friendliness for personal meetings and are expected to be serious at business meetings. Says Bonkenburg, "He was working as hard to impress me as I was to impress him."[71]

If you become an **expatriate**, someone who lives and works outside his or her native country, chances are you'll run into cultural surprises as Tom Bonkenburg did. The difficulty of adjusting to language, cultural, and social differences is the primary reason for expatriate failure in overseas assignments. For example, although there have recently been disagreements among researchers about these numbers, it is probably safe to say that 5 to 20 percent of American expatriates sent abroad by their companies will return to the United States before they have successfully completed their assignments.[72] Of those who do complete their international assignments, about one-third are judged by their companies to be no better than marginally effective.[73] Since the average cost of sending an employee on a three-year international assignment is $1 million, failure in those assignments can be extraordinarily expensive.[74]

The chances for a successful international assignment can be increased through **8-6a language and** *cross-cultural training* and *8-6b consideration of spouse, family, and dual-career issues.*

8-6a LANGUAGE AND CROSS-CULTURAL TRAINING

Predeparture language and cross-cultural training can reduce the uncertainty that expatriates feel, the misunderstandings that take place between expatriates and natives, and the inappropriate behaviors that expatriates unknowingly commit when they travel to a foreign country. Indeed, simple things like using a phone, locating a public toilet, asking for directions, finding out how much things cost, exchanging greetings, or understanding what people want can become tremendously complex when expatriates don't know a foreign language or a country's customs and cultures. In his book *Blunders in International Business*, David Ricks tells the story of an American manager working in the South Pacific who, by hiring too many local workers from one native group, unknowingly upset the balance of power in the island's traditional status system. The islanders met on their own and quickly worked out a solution to the problem. After concluding their meeting at 3 a.m., they calmly went to the manager's home to discuss their solution with him (time was not important in their culture). But since the American didn't speak their language and didn't understand why they had shown up en masse outside his home at 3 a.m., he called in the Marines, who were stationed nearby, to disperse what he thought was a riot.

Expatriates who receive predeparture language and cross-cultural training make faster adjustments to foreign cultures and perform better on their international assignments.[75] Unfortunately, only a third of the managers who go on international assignments are offered any kind of predeparture training, and only half of those actually participate in the training![76] Suzanne Bernard, director of international mobility at Bombardier Aerospace in Canada, says, "We always offer cross-cultural training, but it's very seldom used by executives leaving in a rush at the last minute."[77] This is somewhat surprising given the failure rates for expatriates and the high cost of those failures. Furthermore, with the exception of some language courses, predeparture training is not particularly expensive or difficult to provide. Three methods can be used to prepare workers for international assignments: documentary training, cultural simulations, and field experiences.

Documentary training focuses on identifying specific critical differences between cultures. For example, when sixty workers at Axcelis Technologies in Beverly, Massachusetts, were preparing to do business in India, they learned that while Americans make eye contact and shake hands firmly when greeting others, Indians, as a sign of respect, do just the opposite, avoiding eye contact and shaking hands limply.[78]

After learning specific critical differences through documentary training, trainees can participate in *cultural simulations*, in which they practice adapting to cultural differences. EMC, a global provider of information storage solutions, uses cultural simulations to train its people. In its early days, EMC was largely based in the United States, but with research labs, offices, and customers on every continent, cross-cultural interactions are a daily part of business. EMC's cultural simulations use photos and audio and video clips to present real-world situations. EMC employees must decide what to do and then learn what happened as a result of their choices. Whether it's interacting with customers or dealing with EMC employees from other countries, at every step they have the opportunity to learn good and bad methods of responding to cultural differences. EMC requires its worldwide work force of 40,500 people to

© iStockphoto.com/Catherine Yeulet

regularly use the cultural simulations. Louise Korver-Swanson, EMC's global head of executive development, said, "This is about ensuring that we're truly a global company. We need everyone in the organization to be tuned in."[79]

Finally, *field simulation* training, a technique made popular by the U.S. Peace Corps, places trainees in an ethnic neighborhood for three to four hours to talk to residents about cultural differences. For example, a U.S. electronics manufacturer prepared workers for assignments in South Korea by having trainees explore a nearby South Korean neighborhood and talk to shopkeepers and people on the street about South Korean politics, family orientation, and day-to-day living.

8-6b SPOUSE, FAMILY, AND DUAL-CAREER ISSUES

Not all international assignments are difficult for expatriates and their families, but the evidence clearly shows that how well an expatriate's spouse and family adjust to the foreign culture is the most important factor in determining the success or failure of an international assignment.[80] Barry Kozloff of Selection Research International says, "The cost of sending a family on a foreign assignment is around $1 million and their failure to adjust is an enormous loss."[81] Unfortunately, despite its importance, there has been little systematic research on what does and does not help expatriates' families successfully adapt. A number of companies, however, have found that adaptability screening and intercultural training for families can lead to more successful overseas adjustment.

Adaptability screening is used to assess how well managers and their families are likely to adjust to foreign cultures. For example, Prudential Relocation Management's international division has developed an "Overseas Assignment Inventory" (**OAI**) to assess a spouse and family's open-mindedness, respect for others' beliefs, sense of humor, and marital communication. The OAI was initially used to help the U.S. Peace Corps, the U.S. Navy, and the Canadian International Development Agency select people who could adapt well in foreign cultures. Success there led to its use in helping companies assess whether managers and their spouses were good candidates for international assignments.[82] Likewise, Pennsylvania-based AMP, a worldwide producer of electrical connectors, conducts extensive psychological screening of expatriates and their spouses when making international assignments. But adaptability screening does not just involve a company assessing an employee; it can also involve an employee screening international assignments for desirability. Since more employees are becoming aware of the costs of international assignments (spouses having to give up or change jobs, children having to change schools, everyone having to learn a new language), some companies are willing to pay for a preassignment trip so the employee and his or her spouse can investigate the country *before* accepting the international assignment.[83]

Only 40 percent of expatriates' families receive language and cross-cultural training, yet such training is just as important for the families of expatriates as for the expatriates themselves.[84] In fact, it may be more important because, unlike expatriates, whose professional jobs often shield them from the full force of a country's culture, spouses and children are fully immersed in foreign neighborhoods and schools. Households must be run, shopping must be done, and bills must be paid. Unfortunately, expatriate spouse Laurel Larsen, despite two hours of Chinese lessons a week, hasn't learned enough of the language to communicate with the family's babysitter. She has to phone her husband, who became fluent in Chinese in his teens, to translate. Expatriates' children must deal with different cultural beliefs and practices, too. While the Larsens' three daughters love the private, international school that they attend, they still have had difficulty adapting to, from their perspective, the incredible differences in inner China. Six-year-old Emma taped this poem to her parents' nightstand: "Amarica is my place! I love Amarica. It was fun. It was so fun. I miss it."[85] In addition to helping families prepare for the cultural differences they will encounter, language and cross-cultural training can help reduce uncertainty about how to act and decrease misunderstandings between expatriates and their families and locals.

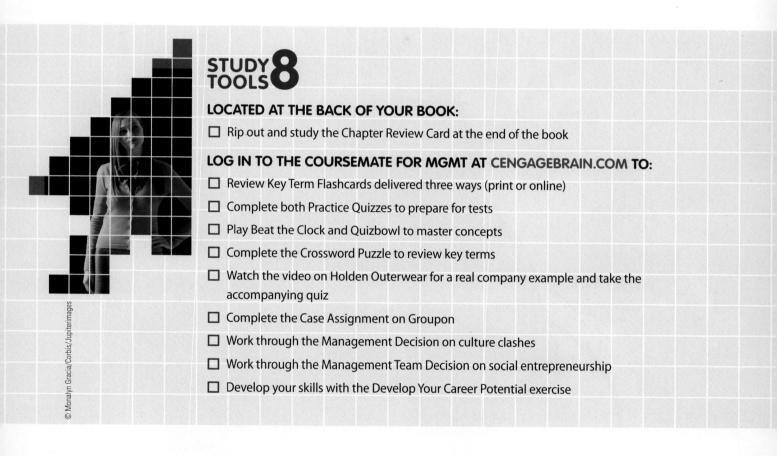

STUDY TOOLS 8

LOCATED AT THE BACK OF YOUR BOOK:

☐ Rip out and study the Chapter Review Card at the end of the book

LOG IN TO THE COURSEMATE FOR MGMT AT CENGAGEBRAIN.COM TO:

☐ Review Key Term Flashcards delivered three ways (print or online)

☐ Complete both Practice Quizzes to prepare for tests

☐ Play Beat the Clock and Quizbowl to master concepts

☐ Complete the Crossword Puzzle to review key terms

☐ Watch the video on Holden Outerwear for a real company example and take the accompanying quiz

☐ Complete the Case Assignment on Groupon

☐ Work through the Management Decision on culture clashes

☐ Work through the Management Team Decision on social entrepreneurship

☐ Develop your skills with the Develop Your Career Potential exercise

9 Designing
Adaptive Organizations

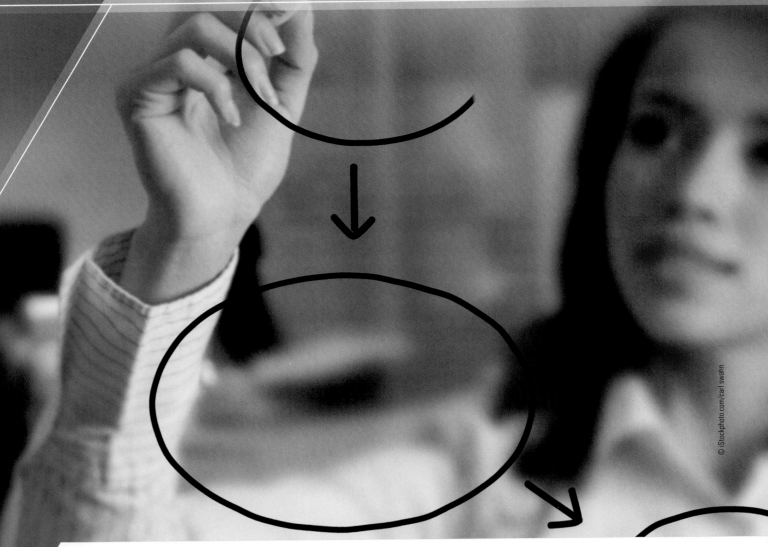

LEARNING OUTCOMES

9-1 Describe the departmentalization approach to organizational structure.

9-2 Explain organizational authority.

9-3 Discuss the different methods for job design.

9-4 Explain the methods that companies are using to redesign internal organizational processes (i.e., intraorganizational processes).

9-5 Describe the methods that companies are using to redesign external organizational processes (i.e., interorganizational processes).

CHECK OUT
STUDY TOOLS
AT THE END OF
THIS CHAPTER.

9-1 *Departmentalization*

Organizational structure is the vertical and horizontal configuration of departments, authority, and jobs within a company. Organizational structure is concerned with questions such as "Who reports to whom?" and "Who does what?" and "Where is the work done?" For example, until April 2012, Sony Corporation of America was headed by Chairman and CEO Howard Stringer, who was based in New York City. But Sony has a number of divisions to handle different sectors of the company's business, each headed by its own president or CEO. PlayStations are developed and managed in Foster City, California,

by Sony Computer Entertainment, which is part of the Consumer Products and Services Group.[1] Sony camcorders, home theater equipment, LCD screens, VAIO computers, Blu-ray players, and the Walkman are handled in San Diego by Sony Electronics. Films like *Men in Black 3* and *21 Jump Street*, and TV shows like *Community*, *The Dr. Oz Show*, and *Damages* are brought to you by Sony Pictures, a division of Sony Entertainment in Culver City, California, while the music of Avril Lavigne, The Fray, One Direction, and Karmin comes courtesy of Sony Music Entertainment in New York City.[2] Companies like Sony use organizational structure to set up departments and relationships among employees in order to make business happen. You can see Sony's organizational structure in Exhibit 9.1.

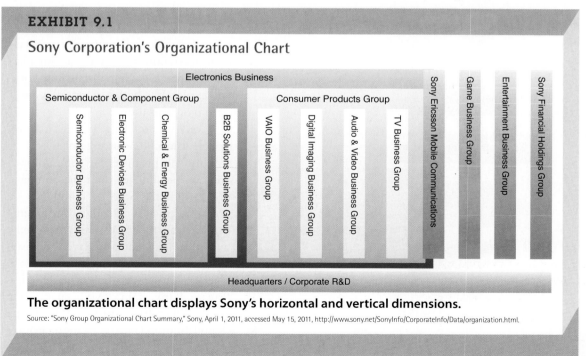

EXHIBIT 9.1

Sony Corporation's Organizational Chart

Electronics Business

Semiconductor & Component Group

Consumer Products Group

Semiconductor Business Group

Electronic Devices Business Group

Chemical & Energy Business Group

B2B Solutions Business Group

VAIO Business Group

Digital Imaging Business Group

Audio & Video Business Group

TV Business Group

Sony Ericsson Mobile Communications

Game Business Group

Entertainment Business Group

Sony Financial Holdings Group

Headquarters / Corporate R&D

The organizational chart displays Sony's horizontal and vertical dimensions.

Source: "Sony Group Organizational Chart Summary," Sony, April 1, 2011, accessed May 15, 2011, http://www.sony.net/SonyInfo/CorporateInfo/Data/organization.html.

Organizational structure the vertical and horizontal configuration of departments, authority, and jobs within a company

Organizational process
the collection of activities that transform inputs into outputs that customers value

In the first half of the chapter, you will learn about the traditional vertical and horizontal approaches to organizational structure, including departmentalization, organizational authority, and job design.

An **organizational process** is the collection of activities that transform inputs into outputs that customers value.[3] Organizational process asks "How do things get done?" For example, **Microsoft** uses basic internal and external processes, shown in Exhibit 9.2, to write computer software. The process starts when Microsoft gets feedback from customers through Internet newsgroups, email, phone calls, or letters. This information helps Microsoft understand customers' needs and problems and identify important software issues and needed changes and functions. Microsoft then rewrites the software, testing it internally at the company and then externally through its beta testing process, in which customers who volunteer or are selected by Microsoft give the company extensive feedback. The feedback is then used to make improvements to the software. Indeed, Microsoft made Windows 8 available for a public beta test before releasing it for sale. Consumers and businesses downloaded the beta, installed it on their computers, and then posted the bugs or errors they found on Microsoft's forums. Microsoft hopes the beta test for Windows 8 goes as well as the beta test for Windows 7, during which users found and reported 2,000 bugs, all of which Microsoft corrected before releasing the software.[4] The beta testing process may take as long as a year and involve thousands of knowledgeable people. After final corrections are made to the software, the company distributes and sells it to customers. They start the process again by giving Microsoft more feedback.

This process view of Microsoft, which focuses on how things get done, is very different from the hierarchical view of Sony, which focuses on accountability, responsibility, and positions within the chain of command. In the second half of the chapter, you will learn how companies use reengineering and empowerment to redesign their internal organizational processes. The chapter ends with a discussion about the ways in which companies are redesigning their external processes, that is, how they are changing to improve their interactions with those outside the company. In that discussion, you will explore the basics of modular and virtual organizations.

Sony was once the premier name in television. Its cutting-edge Trinitron models produced brighter colors and sharper images than the competition, allowing Sony to command a premium price for its TVs. But when cathode-ray tube TVs were replaced by LCD and plasma screens, Sony lost its competitive advantage. Jack Ablin, chief investment officer for Harris Private Bank, said, "My generation was willing to pay a premium for that [Sony] brand. They were innovators. They had quality, and they had con-

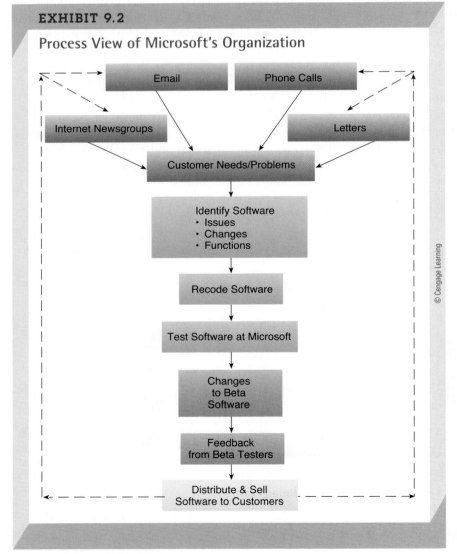

EXHIBIT 9.2

Process View of Microsoft's Organization

Email

Phone Calls

Internet Newsgroups

Letters

Customer Needs/Problems

Identify Software
• Issues
• Changes
• Functions

Recode Software

Test Software at Microsoft

Changes to Beta Software

Feedback from Beta Testers

Distribute & Sell Software to Customers

© Cengage Learning

sumers. But the rest of the world has caught up to them. I'm not sure what their edge is anymore." Looking to maintain its premium brand, Sony focused on selling high-end televisions that had the then unique features of Wi-Fi connectivity and pre-installed hard drives. Consumers, however, flocked to Vizio and Samsung, which produced lower-cost TVs with image quality as good as Sony's. Sony's TV unit, once the flagship of the entire company, lost a billion dollars in 2011 and has not been profitable for seven years. To revitalize the TV division, Sony is restructuring it into three separate divisions, one producing LCD TVs, one responsible for outsourcing, and another charged with designing innovative, next-generation products.[5]

Why would Sony restructure its largest division this way? Will this new organizational design work for Sony? What specifically does it expect to gain from this change?

Traditionally, organizational structures have been based on some form of departmentalization. **Departmentalization** is a method of subdividing work and workers into separate organizational units that take responsibility for completing particular tasks.[6] Bayer, a Germany-based company, has separate departments or divisions for health care, crop science, material science, and services.[7]

Traditionally, organizational structures have been created by departmentalizing work according to five methods: **9-1a functional, 9-1b product, 9-1c customer, 9-1d geographic,** *and* **9-1e matrix.**

9-1a FUNCTIONAL DEPARTMENTALIZATION

The most common organizational structure is functional departmentalization. Companies tend to use this structure when they are small or just starting out. **Functional departmentalization** organizes work and workers into separate units responsible for particular business functions or areas of expertise. A common functional structure might have individuals organized into accounting, sales, marketing, production, and human resources departments.

Not all functionally departmentalized companies have the same functions. The insurance company and the advertising agency shown in Exhibit 9.3 both have sales, accounting, human resources, and information systems departments, as indicated by the pale orange boxes. The purple and green boxes indicate the functions that are different. As would be expected, the insurance company has separate departments for

life, auto, home, and health insurance. The advertising agency has departments for artwork, creative work, print advertising, and Internet advertising. So the functional departments in a company that uses functional structure depend in part on the business or industry a company is in.

Departmentalization subdividing work and workers into separate organizational units responsible for completing particular tasks

Functional departmentalization organizing work and workers into separate units responsible for particular business functions or areas of expertise

Functional departmentalization has some advantages. First, it allows work to be done by highly qualified specialists. While the accountants in the accounting department take responsibility for producing accurate revenue and expense figures, the engineers in research and development can focus their efforts on designing a product that is reliable and simple to manufacture. Second, it lowers costs by reducing duplication. When the engineers in research and development come up with a fantastic new product, they don't have to worry about creating an aggressive advertising campaign to

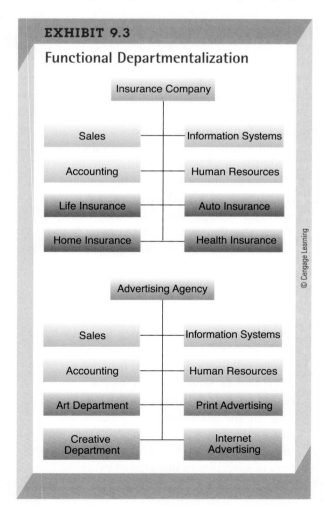

EXHIBIT 9.3

Functional Departmentalization

Insurance Company
- Sales — Information Systems
- Accounting — Human Resources
- Life Insurance — Auto Insurance
- Home Insurance — Health Insurance

Advertising Agency
- Sales — Information Systems
- Accounting — Human Resources
- Art Department — Print Advertising
- Creative Department — Internet Advertising

© Cengage Learning

Product departmentalization organizing work and workers into separate units responsible for producing particular products or services

sell it. That task belongs to the advertising experts and sales representatives in marketing. Third, with everyone in the same department having similar work experience or training, communication and coordination are less problematic for departmental managers.

At the same time, functional departmentalization has a number of disadvantages. To start, cross-department coordination can be difficult. Managers and employees are often more interested in doing what's right for their function than in doing what's right for the entire organization. A good example is the traditional conflict between marketing and manufacturing. Marketing typically pushes for spending more money to make more products with more capabilities to meet customer needs. By contrast, manufacturing pushes for fewer products with simpler designs so that manufacturing facilities can ship finished products on time and keep costs within expense budgets. As companies grow, functional departmentalization may also lead to slower decision making and produce managers and workers with narrow experience and expertise.

9-1b PRODUCT DEPARTMENTALIZATION

Product departmentalization organizes work and workers into separate units responsible for producing particular products or services. Exhibit 9.4 shows the product departmentalization structure used by United Technologies Corporation (UTC), which is organized along six different product lines: Carrier (heating, ventilating, and air-conditioning), Hamilton Sundstrand (aircraft electrical power generation and distribution systems), Otis (design, manufacture, installation, maintenance, and servicing of elevators and escalators), Pratt & Whitney (commercial and military jet aircraft engines), Sikorsky (military and commercial helicopters), and UTC Fire & Security (fire safety and security products and services).[8]

One of the advantages of product departmentalization is that, like functional departmentalization, it allows managers and workers to specialize in one area of expertise. Unlike the narrow expertise and experiences in functional departmentalization, however,

managers and workers develop a broader set of experiences and expertise related to an entire product line. Likewise, product departmentalization makes it easier for top managers to assess work-unit performance. Because of the clear separation of their six different product divisions, UTC's top managers can easily compare the performance of the Otis elevators division and the Pratt & Whitney aircraft engines division. In 2011, Pratt & Whitney had a $1 billion advantage over Otis in net sales ($13.4 billion versus $12.4 billion). However, Otis had a profit of $2.8 billion (a 22.6 percent margin) compared to a profit of $1.9 billion (14.9 percent margin) for Pratt & Whitney.[9]

Finally, decision making should be faster because managers and workers are responsible for the entire product line rather than for separate functional departments; in other words, there are fewer conflicts compared to functional departmentalization.

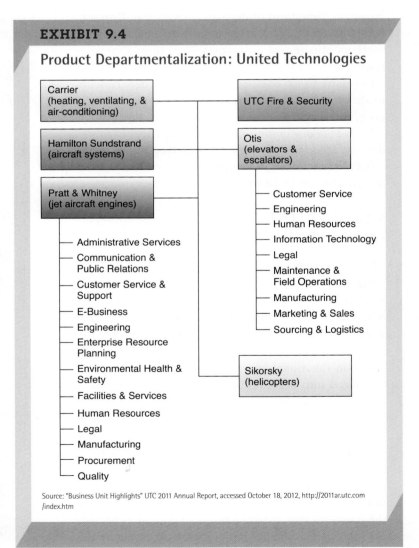

EXHIBIT 9.4

Product Departmentalization: United Technologies

Carrier (heating, ventilating, & air-conditioning)

UTC Fire & Security

Hamilton Sundstrand (aircraft systems)

Otis (elevators & escalators)

Pratt & Whitney (jet aircraft engines)

- Customer Service
- Engineering
- Human Resources
- Information Technology
- Legal
- Maintenance & Field Operations
- Manufacturing
- Marketing & Sales
- Sourcing & Logistics

- Administrative Services
- Communication & Public Relations
- Customer Service & Support
- E-Business
- Engineering
- Enterprise Resource Planning
- Environmental Health & Safety
- Facilities & Services
- Human Resources
- Legal
- Manufacturing
- Procurement
- Quality

Sikorsky (helicopters)

Source: "Business Unit Highlights" UTC 2011 Annual Report, accessed October 18, 2012, http://2011ar.utc.com/index.htm

The primary disadvantage of product departmentalization is duplication. You can see in Exhibit 9.4 that UTC's Otis elevators and Pratt & Whitney divisions both have customer service, engineering, human resources, legal, manufacturing, and procurement (similar to sourcing and logistics) departments. Duplication like this often results in higher costs. If United Technologies were instead organized by function, one lawyer could handle matters related to both elevators and aircraft engines rather than working on only one or the other.

A second disadvantage is the challenge of coordinating across the different product departments. United Technologies would probably have difficulty standardizing its policies and procedures in product departments as different as the Carrier (heating, ventilating, and air-conditioning) and Sikorsky (military and commercial helicopters) divisions.

Customer departmentalization organizing work and workers into separate units responsible for particular kinds of customers

9-1c CUSTOMER DEPARTMENTALIZATION

Customer departmentalization organizes work and workers into separate units responsible for particular kinds of customers. For example, as Exhibit 9.5 shows, **Swisscom AG**, Switzerland's leading telecommunications provider, is organized into departments by type of customer: residential customers (fixed line and voice, mobile and voice, broadband Internet, and digital TV); small- and medium-sized businesses (fixed line and voice, mobile line and voice, Internet and data services, and maintenance and operation of IT

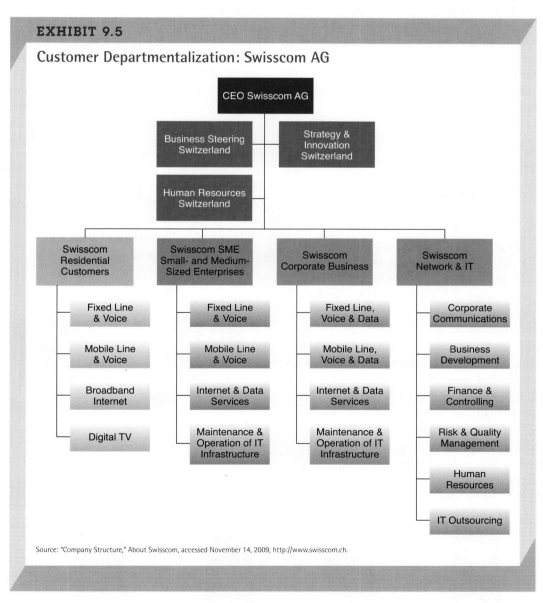

EXHIBIT 9.5

Customer Departmentalization: Swisscom AG

Source: "Company Structure," About Swisscom, accessed November 14, 2009, http://www.swisscom.ch.

infrastructure); larger corporations (fixed line, voice and data, mobile line, voice and data, Internet and data services, and maintenance and operation of IT infrastructure); and network and IT customers (corporate communications, business development, finance and controlling, risk and quality management, human resources, IT outsourcing).[10]

The primary advantage of customer departmentalization is that it focuses the organization on customer needs rather than on products or business functions. Furthermore, creating separate departments to serve specific kinds of customers allows companies to specialize and adapt their products and services to customer needs and problems. The primary disadvantage of customer departmentalization is that, like product departmentalization, it leads to duplication of resources. It can be difficult to achieve coordination across different customer departments, as is also the case with product departmentalization. Finally, the emphasis on meeting customers' needs may lead workers to make decisions that please customers but hurt the business.

9-1d GEOGRAPHIC DEPARTMENTALIZATION

Geographic departmentalization organizes work and workers into separate units responsible for doing business in particular geographic areas. Exhibit 9.6 shows the geographic departmentalization used by **AB InBev**, the largest beer brewer in the world. AB InBev has 133 brewing facilities in twenty-three countries, 114,000 employees, and annual revenue of $36.3 billion.[11]

As shown in Exhibit 9.6, AB InBev has six regional groups: North America, Latin America North, Latin America South, Western Europe, Central and Eastern Europe, and Asia Pacific. Each of these regions would be a sizable company by itself. The smallest region, Asia Pacific, for instance, sold 50.3 million hectoliters of beer for annual revenue of $292 million.

The primary advantage of geographic departmentalization is that it helps companies respond to the demands of different markets. This can be especially important when the company sells in different countries. For example, while AB InBev has three global brands, Budweiser, Stella Artois, and Beck's, sold worldwide, and two, Hoegaarden and Leffe, sold in multiple countries, most of its brands are local. You'll find the Antarctica and Bohemia brands in Brazil, the Belle-Vue and Jupiler brands in Belgium, and the Sibirskaya Korona and Tolstiak brands in Russia.[12]

Another advantage is that geographic departmentalization can reduce costs by locating unique organizational resources closer to customers. For instance, it is cheaper in the long run for AB InBev to build bottling plants in each region than to, for example, transport beer to Belgium, where it has four beverage plants, after it has been brewed and bottled in Russia, where it has ten beverage plants.[13]

The primary disadvantage of geographic departmentalization is that it can lead to duplication of resources. For example, while it may be necessary to adapt products and marketing to different geographic locations, it's doubtful that AB InBev needs significantly different inventory tracking systems from location to location. Also, even more than with the other forms of departmentalization, it can be difficult to coordinate departments that are literally thousands of miles from each other and whose managers have very limited contact with each other.

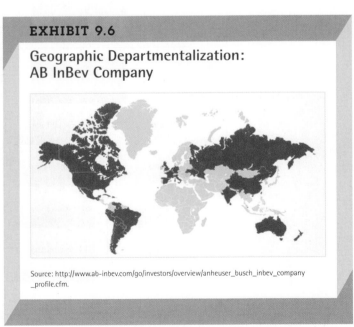

EXHIBIT 9.6

Geographic Departmentalization: AB InBev Company

Source: http://www.ab-inbev.com/go/investors/overview/anheuser_busch_inbev_company_profile.cfm.

9-1e MATRIX DEPARTMENTALIZATION

Matrix departmentalization is a hybrid structure in which two or more forms of departmentalization are used together. The most common matrix combines the product and functional forms of departmentalization, but other forms may also be used. Exhibit 9.7 shows the matrix structure used by Procter & Gamble, which has 127,000 employees working in eighty different countries.[14] Across the top of Exhibit 9.7, you can see that the company uses a product structure where it groups its billion-dollar brands into three global business units, each of which has two segments: beauty care (beauty and grooming), household care (baby care and family care plus fabric care and home care), and health and well-being (health care and pet care). Global business units are responsible for product initiatives or upgrades, which are typically launched simultaneously with a worldwide marketing campaign. The left side of the figure, however, shows that the company is also using a functional structure based on three functions: market development, which makes sure that a product is adapted to and sells well within a particular region of the world (market development regions include North America, Asia/India/

Australia, Northeast Asia, Greater China, Central-Eastern Europe/Middle East Africa, Western Europe, and Latin America); global business services, which enable the company to operate efficiently, work effectively with business partners, and increase employee productivity; and corporate functions, which provide global business units with the functional business assistance (i.e., finance, accounting, human resources, information technology, etc.) they need.[15]

The boxes in the figure represent the matrix structure, created by the combination of the product and functional structures. For example, P&G's Pantene Team (Pantene is a set of hair care products within the beauty segment of the beauty care global business unit) would work with market development to adapt and sell Pantene products worldwide, use global business services to work with suppliers and keep costs down, and then rely on corporate functions for assistance in hiring employees and billing customers and paying suppliers. Similar matrix combinations are shown for P&G's Old Spice, Pampers, Tide, Actonel, and Iams teams within each of the six segments found under its three global business units.

> **Matrix departmentalization** a hybrid organizational structure in which two or more forms of departmentalization, most often product and functional, are used together

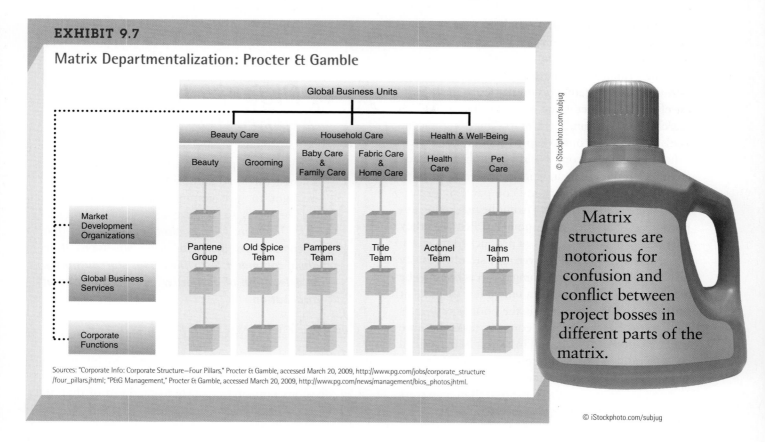

EXHIBIT 9.7

Matrix Departmentalization: Procter & Gamble

Global Business Units

Beauty Care — Household Care — Health & Well-Being

Beauty | Grooming | Baby Care & Family Care | Fabric Care & Home Care | Health Care | Pet Care

Market Development Organizations

Global Business Services

Corporate Functions

Pantene Group | Old Spice Team | Pampers Team | Tide Team | Actonel Team | Iams Team

Matrix structures are notorious for confusion and conflict between project bosses in different parts of the matrix.

© iStockphoto.com/subjug

Sources: "Corporate Info: Corporate Structure—Four Pillars," Procter & Gamble, accessed March 20, 2009, http://www.pg.com/jobs/corporate_structure/four_pillars.jhtml; "P&G Management," Procter & Gamble, accessed March 20, 2009, http://www.pg.com/news/management/bios_photos.jhtml.

© iStockphoto.com/subjug

Simple matrix a form of matrix departmentalization in which managers in different parts of the matrix negotiate conflicts and resources

Complex matrix a form of matrix departmentalization in which managers in different parts of the matrix report to matrix managers, who help them sort out conflicts and problems

Authority the right to give commands, take action, and make decisions to achieve organizational objectives

Several things distinguish matrix departmentalization from the other traditional forms of departmentalization.[16] First, most employees report to two bosses, one from each core part of the matrix. For example, in Exhibit 9.7 a manager on the Pampers team responsible for marketing would report to a boss in the baby care and family care segment of the household care global business unit as well as to a manager in the market development function. Second, by virtue of their hybrid design, matrix structures lead to much more cross-functional interaction than other forms of departmentalization. In fact, while matrix workers are typically members of only one functional department (based on their work experience and expertise), they are also commonly members of several ongoing project, product, or customer groups. Third, because of the high level of cross-functional interaction, matrix departmentalization requires significant coordination between managers in the different parts of the matrix. In particular, managers have the complex job of tracking and managing the multiple demands (project, product, customer, or functional) on employees' time.

The primary advantage of matrix departmentalization is that it allows companies to manage in an efficient manner large, complex tasks like researching, developing, and marketing pharmaceuticals or carrying out complex global businesses. Efficiency comes from avoiding duplication. For example, rather than having an entire marketing function for each project, the company simply assigns and reassigns workers from the marketing department (or market development at P&G) as they are needed at various stages of product completion. More specifically, an employee may simultaneously be part of five different ongoing projects but may be actively completing work on only a few projects at a time. Another advantage is the pool of resources available to carry out large, complex tasks. Because of the ability to quickly pull in expert help from all the functional areas of the company, matrix project managers have a much more diverse set of expertise and experience at their disposal than managers in the other forms of departmentalization.

The primary disadvantage of matrix departmentalization is the high level of coordination required to manage the complexity involved in running large, ongoing projects at various levels of completion. Matrix structures are notorious for confusion and conflict between project bosses in different parts of the matrix. When Yahoo! founder Jerry Yang was trying to convince Carol Bartz, formerly CEO at Autodesk, to become CEO at Yahoo!, she asked him to draw a picture of the organizational structure. Bartz said, "It was like a Catholic school kid diagramming a sentence, where the lines sloppily crisscrossed and it was clear no one was in charge."[17]

Disagreements or misunderstandings about schedules, budgets, available resources, and the availability of employees with particular functional expertise are common in matrix structures. At Yahoo!, this manifested itself in slow decision making because multiple executives and divisions had overlapping responsibility for similar products and services. Because of these problems, many matrix structures evolve from a **simple matrix**, in which managers in different parts of the matrix negotiate conflicts and resources directly, to a **complex matrix**, in which specialized matrix managers and departments are added to the organizational structure. In a complex matrix, managers from different parts of the matrix might report to the same matrix manager, who helps them sort out conflicts and problems.

9-2 *Organizational Authority*

The second part of traditional organizational structures is authority. **Authority** is the right to give commands, take action, and make decisions to achieve organizational objectives.[18] *Traditionally, organizational authority has been characterized by the following dimensions: 9-2a chain of command, 9-2b line versus staff authority, 9-2c delegation of authority, and 9-2d degree of centralization.*

9-2a CHAIN OF COMMAND

Consider again Sony Corporation's organizational structure. A manager in any of the corporation's divisions ultimately reports to the head of that division. That division head, in turn, reports to the corporation's Kazuo Hirai, who took over as CEO when Howard Stringer retired. This line, which vertically connects every job in the company to higher levels of management, represents the chain of command. The **chain of command** is the vertical line of authority that clarifies who reports to whom throughout the organization. People higher in the chain of command have the right, *if they so choose*, to give commands, take action, and make decisions concerning activities occurring anywhere below them in the chain. In the following discussion about delegation and decentralization, you will learn that managers don't always choose to exercise their authority directly.[19]

One of the key assumptions underlying the chain of command is **unity of command**, which means that workers should report to just one boss.[20] In practical terms, this means that only one person can be in charge at a time. Matrix organizations, in which employees have two bosses, automatically violate this principle. This is one of the primary reasons that matrix organizations are difficult to manage. Unity of command serves an important purpose: to prevent the confusion that might arise when an employee receives conflicting commands from two different bosses.

9-2b LINE VERSUS STAFF AUTHORITY

A second dimension of authority is the distinction between line and staff authority. **Line authority** is the right to command immediate subordinates in the chain of command. For example, Sony CEO Kazuo Hirai has line authority over the head of Sony's Professional Device & Solutions Group, which includes Sony's Semiconductor Business Group. Hirai can issue orders to that division president and expect them to be carried out. In turn, the head of Sony Professional Device & Solutions can issue orders to his subordinates and expect them to be carried out. **Staff authority** is the right to *advise* but not command others who are not subordinates in the chain of command. For example, a manager in human resources at Sony might advise the manager in charge of Sony's Home Entertainment Business Group on a hiring decision but cannot order him or her to hire a certain applicant.

The terms *line* and *staff* are also used to describe different functions within the organization. A **line function** is an activity that contributes directly to creating or selling the company's products. So, for example, activities that take place within the manufacturing and marketing departments would be considered

line functions. A **staff function**, such as accounting, human resources, or legal services, does not contribute directly to creating or selling the company's products, but instead supports line activities. For example, marketing managers might consult with the legal staff to make sure the wording of a particular advertisement is legal.

9-2c DELEGATION OF AUTHORITY

Managers can exercise their authority directly by completing tasks themselves, or they can choose to pass on some of their authority to subordinates. **Delegation of authority** is the assignment of direct authority and responsibility to a subordinate to complete tasks for which the manager is normally responsible.

When a manager delegates work, three transfers occur, as illustrated in Exhibit 9.8. First, the manager transfers full responsibility for the assignment to the subordinate. At Apple, when you've been delegated to

Chain of command the vertical line of authority that clarifies who reports to whom throughout the organization

Unity of command a management principle that workers should report to just one boss

Line authority the right to command immediate subordinates in the chain of command

Staff authority the right to advise, but not command, others who are not subordinates in the chain of command

Line function an activity that contributes directly to creating or selling the company's products

Staff function an activity that does not contribute directly to creating or selling the company's products, but instead supports line activities

Delegation of authority the assignment of direct authority and responsibility to a subordinate to complete tasks for which the manager is normally responsible

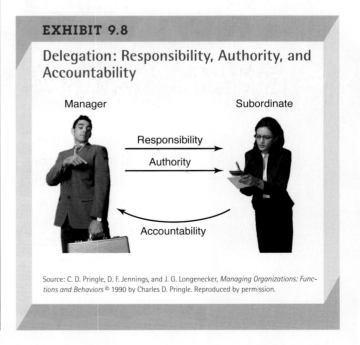

EXHIBIT 9.8

Delegation: Responsibility, Authority, and Accountability

Manager   Subordinate

Responsibility

Authority

Accountability

Source: C. D. Pringle, D. F. Jennings, and J. G. Longenecker, *Managing Organizations: Functions and Behaviors* © 1990 by Charles D. Pringle. Reproduced by permission.

a certain task, you become the DRI, or the "directly responsible individual." As a former Apple employee explains, "Any effective meeting at Apple will have an action list. Next to each action item will be the DRI," who of course, is responsible for completing that delegated responsibility. Furthermore, when you're trying to figure out who to contact to get something done in Apple's corporate structure, people simply ask, "Who's the DRI on that?"[21]

Many managers, however, find giving up full responsibility somewhat difficult. Consultant David Nadler says, "There is a savior complex that says, 'I'm the only one'" who can lead this company effectively.[22] One reason it is difficult for some managers to delegate is that they often fear that the task won't be done as well as if they did it themselves. However, one CEO says, "If you can delegate a task to somebody who can do it 75 percent to 80 percent as well as you can today, you delegate it immediately." Why? Many tasks don't need to be done perfectly; they just need to be *done*. And delegating tasks that someone else can do frees managers to assume other important responsibilities. Delegating authority can generate a related problem: micromanaging. Sometimes managers delegate only to interfere later with how the employee is performing the task. But delegating full responsibility means that

the employee—not the manager—is now completely responsible for task completion. Good managers need to trust their subordinates to do the job.

The second transfer that occurs with delegation is that the manager gives the subordinate full authority over the budget, resources, and personnel needed to do the job. To do the job effectively, subordinates must have the same tools and information at their disposal that managers had when they were responsible for the same task. In other words, for delegation to work, delegated authority must be commensurate with delegated responsibility.

The third transfer that occurs with delegation is the transfer of accountability. The subordinate now has the authority and responsibility to do the job and in return is accountable for getting the job done. In other words, managers delegate their managerial authority and responsibility to subordinates in exchange for results.

9-2d DEGREE OF CENTRALIZATION

If you've ever called a company's toll-free number with a complaint or a special request and been told by the customer-service representative, "I'll have to ask my manager" or "I'm not authorized to do that," you know

Forbes magazine columnist John Rutledge calls delegation "MBB," Managing by Belly Button. He says, "The belly button is the person whose belly you point your finger at when you want to know how the work is proceeding, i.e., the person who will actually be accountable for each step. . . . The belly button is not a scapegoat—a person to blame later when things go wrong. He or she is the person who makes sure that things go right."

Source: J. Rutledge, "Management by Belly Button," *Forbes*, November 4, 1996, 64.

©iStockphoto.com/Christopher Futcher

that centralization of authority exists in that company. **Centralization of authority** is the location of most authority at the upper levels of the organization. In a centralized organization, managers make most decisions, even the relatively small ones. That's why the customer-service representative you called couldn't make a decision without first asking the manager.

If you are lucky, however, you may have talked to a customer-service representative at another company who said, "I can take care of that for you right now." In other words, the person was able to handle your problem without any input from or consultation with company management. **Decentralization** is the location of a significant amount of authority in the lower levels of the organization. An organization is decentralized if it has a high degree of delegation at all levels. In a decentralized organization, workers closest to problems are authorized to make the decisions necessary to solve the problems on their own.

Decentralization has a number of advantages. It develops employee capabilities throughout the company and leads to faster decision making and more satisfied customers and employees. Furthermore, a study of 1,000 large companies found that companies with a high degree of decentralization outperformed those with a low degree of decentralization in terms of return on assets (6.9 percent versus 4.7 percent), return on investment (14.6 percent versus 9.0 percent), return on equity (22.8 percent versus 16.6 percent), and return on sales (10.3 percent versus 6.3 percent). Surprisingly, the same study found that few large companies actually are decentralized. Specifically, only 31 percent of employees in these 1,000 companies were responsible for recommending improvements to management. Overall, just 10 percent of employees received the training and information needed to support a truly decentralized approach to management.[23]

With results like these, the key question is no longer *whether* companies should decentralize, but *where* they should decentralize. One rule of thumb is to stay centralized where standardization is important and to decentralize where standardization is unimportant. **Standardization** is solving problems by consistently applying the same rules, procedures, and processes. Toyota became the largest auto manufacturer in the world by producing highly reliable cars at competitive costs. But as the company grew, it significantly increased the number of kinds of parts used in its cars, for example, using 100 different radiators in the cars it made around the world. Using that many varieties for the same part not only increased costs, it decreased quality, which then reduced Toyota sales. Toyota's leadership addressed this issue by using standardization to significantly reduce the variety of kinds of basic parts. For example, it now uses just 21 different kinds of radiators in its cars rather than 100, as before. This leads to greater volume for each part and thus less cost, higher quality because Toyota awarded increased production to its best suppliers, and fewer suppliers to manage overall, therefore reducing complexity. Standardization has proved so successful that Takeshi Uchiyamada, Toyota's executive vice president of research and development, said, "We won't feel we've succeeded until we raise the use of standardized parts to about 50 percent among similar-size vehicles in our lineup."[24]

9-3 *Job Design*

Could you stand to do the same simple tasks an average of 50 times per hour, 400 times per day, 2,000 times per week, 8,000 times per month? Few can. Fast-food workers rarely stay on the job more than six months. Indeed, McDonald's and other fast-food restaurants have well over 100 percent employee turnover each year.[25]

1. "Welcome to McDonald's. May I have your order please?"
2. Listen to the order. Repeat it for accuracy. State the total cost. "Please drive to the second window."
3. Take the money. Make change.
4. Give customers drinks, straws, and napkins.
5. Give customers food.
6. "Thank you for coming to McDonald's."

In this section, you will learn about **job design**—the number, kind, and variety of tasks that individual workers perform in doing their jobs.

You will learn 9-3a why companies continue to use specialized jobs like the McDonald's drive-through job and 9-3b how job rotation, job enlargement, job enrichment, and 9-3c the job characteristics model are being used to overcome the problems associated with job specialization.

Job specialization a job composed of a small part of a larger task or process

Job rotation periodically moving workers from one specialized job to another to give them more variety and the opportunity to use different skills

Job enlargement increasing the number of different tasks that a worker performs within one particular job

Job enrichment increasing the number of tasks in a particular job and giving workers the authority and control to make meaningful decisions about their work

Job characteristics model (JCM) an approach to job redesign that seeks to formulate jobs in ways that motivate workers and lead to positive work outcomes

9-3a JOB SPECIALIZATION

Job specialization occurs when a job is composed of a small part of a larger task or process. Specialized jobs are characterized by simple, easy-to-learn steps, low variety, and high repetition, like the McDonald's drive-through window job just described. One of the clear disadvantages of specialized jobs is that, being so easy to learn, they quickly become boring. This, in turn, can lead to low job satisfaction and high absenteeism and employee turnover, all of which are very costly to organizations.

Why, then, do companies continue to create and use specialized jobs? The primary reason is that specialized jobs are very economical. As we learned from Frederick W. Taylor and Frank and Lillian Gilbreth in Chapter 2, once a job has been specialized, it takes little time to learn and master. Consequently, when experienced workers quit or are absent, the company can replace them with new employees and lose little productivity. For example, next time you're at McDonald's, notice the pictures of the food on the cash registers. These pictures make it easy for McDonald's trainees to quickly learn to take orders. Likewise, to simplify and speed operations, the drink dispensers behind the counter are set to automatically fill drink cups. Put a medium cup below the dispenser. Punch the medium drink button. The soft-drink machine then fills the cup to within a half-inch of the top, while the worker goes to get your fries. At McDonald's, every task has been simplified in this way. Because the work is designed to be simple, wages can remain low, since it isn't necessary to pay high salaries to attract highly experienced, educated, or trained workers.

9-3b JOB ROTATION, ENLARGEMENT, AND ENRICHMENT

Because of the efficiency of specialized jobs, companies are often reluctant to eliminate them. Consequently, job redesign efforts have focused on modifying jobs to keep the benefits of specialized jobs while reducing their obvious costs and disadvantages. Three methods—job rotation, job enlargement, and job enrichment—have been used to try to improve specialized jobs.[26]

Job rotation attempts to overcome the disadvantages of job specialization by periodically moving workers from one specialized job to another to give them more variety and the opportunity to use different skills. For example, an office receptionist who does nothing but answer phones could be systematically rotated to a different job, such as typing, filing, or data entry, every day or two. Likewise, the "mirror attacher" in an automobile plant might attach mirrors in the first half of the work shift and then install bumpers during the second half. Because employees simply switch from one specialized job to another, job rotation allows companies to retain the economic benefits of specialized work. At the same time, the greater variety of tasks makes the work less boring and more satisfying for workers.

Another way to counter the disadvantages of specialization is to enlarge the job. **Job enlargement** increases the number of different tasks that a worker performs within one particular job. Instead of being assigned just one task, workers with enlarged jobs are given several tasks to perform. For example, an enlarged "mirror attacher" job might include attaching the mirror, checking to see that the mirror's power adjustment controls work, and then cleaning the mirror's surface. Though job enlargement increases variety, many workers report feeling more stress when their jobs are enlarged. Consequently, many workers view enlarged jobs as simply more work, especially if they are not given additional time to complete the additional tasks.

Job enrichment attempts to overcome the deficiencies in specialized work by increasing the number of tasks *and* by giving workers the authority and control to make meaningful decisions about their work.[27]

9-3c JOB CHARACTERISTICS MODEL

In contrast to job rotation, job enlargement, and job enrichment, which focus on providing variety in job tasks, the **job characteristics model (JCM)** is an approach to job redesign that seeks to formulate jobs in ways that motivate workers and lead to positive work outcomes.[28]

As shown in Exhibit 9.9, the primary goal of the model is to create jobs that result in positive personal and work outcomes, such as internal work motivation, satisfaction with one's job, and work effectiveness. Of these, the central concern of the JCM is internal motivation. **Internal motivation** is motivation that comes from the job itself rather than from outside rewards such as a raise or praise from the boss. If workers feel that performing the job well is itself rewarding, then the job has internal motivation. Statements such as "I get a nice sense of accomplishment" or "I feel good about myself and what I'm producing" are examples of internal motivation.

In Exhibit 9.9 you can see that the JCM specifies three critical psychological states that must occur for work to be internally motivating. First, workers must *experience the work as meaningful*; that is, they must view their job as being important. Second, they must *experience responsibility for work outcomes*—they must feel personally responsible for the work being done well. Third, workers must have *knowledge of results*; that is, they must know how well they are performing their jobs. All three critical psychological states must occur for work to be internally motivating.

For example, grocery store cashiers usually have knowledge of results. When you're slow, your checkout line grows long. If you make a mistake, customers point it out: "No, I think that's on sale for $2.99, not $3.99." Likewise, cashiers experience responsibility for work outcomes. At the end of the day, the register is totaled and the money is counted. Ideally, the money matches the total sales in the register. If the money in the till is less than what's recorded in the register, most stores make the cashier pay the difference. Consequently, most cashiers are very careful to avoid being caught short at the end of the day. Nonetheless, despite knowing the results and experiencing responsibility for work outcomes, most grocery store cashiers (at least where I shop) aren't internally motivated, because they don't experience the work as meaningful. With scanners, it takes little skill to learn or do the job. Anyone can do it. In addition, cashiers have few decisions to make, and the job is highly repetitive.

What kinds of jobs produce the three critical psychological states? Moving another step to the left in Exhibit 9.9, you can see that these psychological states arise from jobs that are strong on five core job characteristics: skill variety, task identity, task significance,

Internal motivation motivation that comes from the job itself rather than from outside rewards

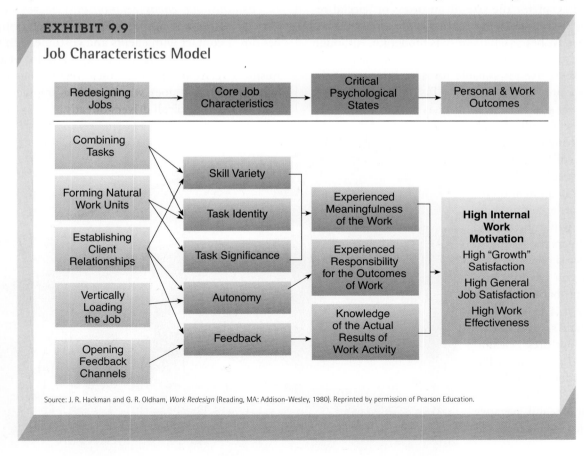

EXHIBIT 9.9

Job Characteristics Model

Source: J. R. Hackman and G. R. Oldham, *Work Redesign* (Reading, MA: Addison-Wesley, 1980). Reprinted by permission of Pearson Education.

autonomy, and feedback. **Skill variety** is the number of different activities performed in a job. **Task identity** is the degree to which a job, from beginning to end, requires completion of a whole and identifiable piece of work. **Task significance** is the degree to which a job is perceived to have a substantial impact on others inside or outside the organization. **Autonomy** is the degree to which a job gives workers the discretion, freedom, and independence to decide how and when to accomplish the work. Finally, **feedback** is the amount of information the job provides to workers about their work performance.

To illustrate how the core job characteristics work together, let's use them to assess more thoroughly why the McDonald's drive-through window job is not particularly satisfying or motivating. To start, skill variety is low. Except for the size of an order or special requests ("no onions"), the process is the same for each customer. At best, task identity is moderate. Although you take the order, handle the money, and deliver the food, others are responsible for a larger part of the process—preparing the food. Task identity will be even lower if the McDonald's has two drive-through windows, because each drive-through window worker will have an even more specialized task. The first is limited to taking the order and making change, while the second just delivers the food.

Task significance, the impact you have on others, is probably low. Autonomy is also very low: McDonald's has strict rules about dress, cleanliness, and procedures. But the job does provide immediate feedback such as positive and negative customer comments, car

horns honking, the amount of time it takes to process orders, and the number of cars in the drive-through. With the exception of feedback, the low levels of the core job characteristics show why the drive-through window job is not internally motivating for many workers.

What can managers do when jobs aren't internally motivating? The far left column of Exhibit 9.9 lists five job redesign techniques that managers can use to strengthen a job's core characteristics. *Combining tasks* increases skill variety and task identity by joining separate, specialized tasks into larger work modules. For example, some trucking firms are now requiring truck drivers to load their rigs as well as drive them. The hope is that involving drivers in loading will ensure that trucks are properly loaded, thus reducing damage claims.

Work can be formed into *natural work units* by arranging tasks according to logical or meaningful groups. Although many trucking companies randomly assign drivers to trucks, some have begun assigning drivers to particular geographic locations (e.g., the Northeast or Southwest) or to truckloads that require special driving skill (e.g., oversized loads or hazardous chemicals). Forming natural work units increases task identity and task significance.

Establishing client relationships increases skill variety, autonomy, and feedback by giving employees direct contact with clients and customers. In some companies, truck drivers are expected to establish business relationships with their regular customers. When something goes wrong with a shipment, customers are told to call drivers directly.

© iStockphoto.com/Steve Debenport

Vertical loading means pushing some managerial authority down to workers. For truck drivers, this means that they have the same authority as managers to resolve customer problems. In some companies, if a late shipment causes problems for a customer, the driver has the authority to fully refund the cost of that shipment without first obtaining management's approval.

The last job redesign technique offered by the model, *opening feedback channels*, means finding additional ways to give employees direct, frequent feedback about their job performance. For example, with advances in electronics, many truck drivers get instantaneous data as to whether they're on schedule and driving their rigs in a fuel-efficient manner. Likewise, the increased contact with customers also means that many drivers now receive monthly data on customer satisfaction.

9-4 *Intraorganizational Processes*

More than forty years ago, Tom Burns and G. M. Stalker described how two kinds of organizational designs, mechanistic and organic, are appropriate for different kinds of organizational environments.[29] **Mechanistic organizations** are characterized by specialized jobs and responsibilities; precisely defined, unchanging roles; and a rigid chain of command based on centralized authority and vertical communication. This type of organization works best in stable, unchanging business environments. By contrast, **organic organizations** are characterized by broadly defined jobs and responsibility; loosely defined, frequently changing roles; and decentralized authority and horizontal communication based on task

knowledge. This type of organization works best in dynamic, changing business environments.

The organizational design techniques described in the first half of this chapter—departmentalization, authority, and job design—are better suited for mechanistic organizations and the stable business environments that were more prevalent before 1980. By contrast, the organizational design techniques discussed next, in the second part of the chapter, are more appropriate for organic organizations and the increasingly dynamic environments in which today's businesses compete. The key difference between these approaches is that mechanistic organizational designs focus on organizational structure, whereas organic organizational designs are concerned with organizational process, or the collection of activities that transform inputs into outputs valued by customers.

An **intraorganizational process** is the collection of activities that take place within an organization to transform inputs into outputs that customers value.

*Let's take a look at how companies are using **9-4a reengineering** and **9-4b empowerment** to redesign intraorganizational processes like these.*

9-4a REENGINEERING

In their best-selling book *Reengineering the Corporation*, Michael Hammer and James Champy define **reengineering** as "the *fundamental* rethinking and *radical* redesign of business *processes* to achieve *dramatic* improvements in critical, contemporary measures of performance, such as cost, quality, service and speed."[30] Hammer and Champy further explained the four key words shown in italics in this definition. The first key word is *fundamental*. When reengineering organizational designs, managers must ask themselves, "Why do we do what we do?" and "Why do we do it the way we do?" The usual answer is "Because that's the way we've always done it." The second key word

Mechanistic organization an organization characterized by specialized jobs and responsibilities; precisely defined, unchanging roles; and a rigid chain of command based on centralized authority and vertical communication

Organic organization an organization characterized by broadly defined jobs and responsibility; loosely defined, frequently changing roles; and decentralized authority and horizontal communication based on task knowledge

Intraorganizational process the collection of activities that take place within an organization to transform inputs into outputs that customers value

Reengineering fundamental rethinking and radical redesign of business processes to achieve dramatic improvements in critical measures of performance, such as cost, quality, service, and speed

is *radical*. Reengineering is about significant change, about starting over by throwing out the old ways of getting work done. The third key word is *processes*. Hammer and Champy noted that "most business people are not process oriented; they are focused on tasks, on jobs, on people, on structures, but not on processes." The fourth key word is *dramatic*. Reengineering is about achieving quantum improvements in company performance.

An example from IBM Credit's operation illustrates how work can be reengineered.[31] IBM Credit lends businesses money to buy IBM computers. Previously, the loan process began when an IBM salesperson called the home office to obtain credit approval for a customer's purchase. The first department involved in the process took the credit information over the phone from the salesperson and recorded it on the credit form. The credit form was sent to the credit checking department, then to the pricing department (where the interest rate was determined), and on through a total of five departments. In all, it took the five departments six days to approve or deny the customer's loan. Of course, this delay cost IBM business. Some customers got their loans elsewhere. Others, frustrated by the wait, simply canceled their orders.

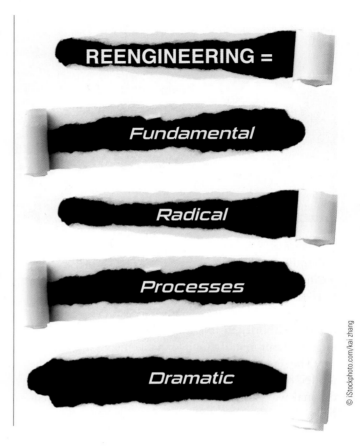

REENGINEERING =

Fundamental

Radical

Processes

Dramatic

© iStockphoto.com/kai zhang

Better Offices for Better Work

Executives at Intel, the leading manufacturer of microprocessors, realized that they needed to take more steps to encourage innovation and collaboration among its employees. For that reason, they converted a million square feet of space in their campus. Gone were the gray cubicles, low ceilings, and endless banks of fluorescent lights, which were replaced with workstations with low partitions, walls painted in vibrant yellow, purple, or white, lounges filled with wide-screen TVs and comfortable sofas, and communal kitchens stocked with the latest and best appliances. According to Neil Tunmore, the changes came because "We realized that we were inefficient and not as collaborative as we would have liked." Sabre Holdings, the company that owns the travel website Travelocity.com, undertook a similar redesign project at its Southlake, Texas, headquarters. It moved all of its offices from five buildings into two, eliminated all private offices, and gave everyone shared cubicles and laptops to increase mobility.

Not only does an open office design spur collaboration within a company, it represents a significant source of cost savings. With its redesigned office, Sabre Holdings will save $10 million per year in mortgage payments, utilities, and other costs.

Source: K. Shevory, "Office Work Space Is Shrinking, but That's Not All Bad," *New York Times*, January 18, 2011, accessed March 13, 2012, http://www.nytimes.com/2011/01/19/realestate/commercial/19space.html?pagewanted=all.

© Justin Sullivan/Getty Images

Finally, two IBM managers decided to walk a loan straight through each of the departments involved in the process. At each step, they asked the workers to stop what they were doing and immediately process their loan application. They were shocked by what they found. From start to finish, the entire process took just ninety minutes! The six-day turnaround time was almost entirely due to delays in handing off the work from one department to another. The solution: IBM redesigned the process so that one person, not five people in five separate departments, now handles the entire loan approval process without any hand-offs. The results were indeed dramatic. Reengineering the credit process reduced approval time from six days to four hours and allowed IBM Credit to increase the number of loans it handled by a factor of 100!

Reengineering changes an organization's orientation from vertical to horizontal. Instead of taking orders from upper management, lower- and middle-level managers and workers take orders from a customer who is at the beginning and end of each process. Instead of running independent functional departments, managers and workers in different departments take ownership of cross-functional processes. Instead of simplifying work so that it becomes increasingly specialized, reengineering complicates work by giving workers increased autonomy and responsibility for complete processes.

In essence, reengineering changes work by changing **task interdependence**, the extent to which collective action is required to complete an entire piece of work. As shown in Exhibit 9.10, there are three kinds of task interdependence.[32] In **pooled interdependence**, each job or department contributes to the whole independently. In **sequential interdependence**, work must be performed in succession, as one group's or job's outputs become the inputs for the next group or job. Finally, in **reciprocal interdependence**, different jobs or groups work together in a back-and-forth manner to complete the process. By reducing the handoffs between different jobs or groups, reengineering decreases sequential interdependence. Likewise, reengineering decreases pooled interdependence by redesigning work so that formerly independent jobs or departments now work together to complete processes. Finally, reengineering increases reciprocal interdependence by making groups or individuals responsible for larger, more complete processes in which several steps may be accomplished at the same time.

As an organizational design tool, reengineering promises big rewards, but it has also come under severe criticism. The most serious complaint is that because it allows a few workers to do the work formerly done by many, reengineering is simply a corporate code word for cost cutting and worker layoffs.[33] For this reason, detractors claim that reengineering hurts morale and performance. Even though ordering times were reduced from three weeks to three days, **Levi Strauss** ended an $850 million reengineering project because of the fear and turmoil it created in the company's work force. One low point occurred when Levi management, encouraged by its reengineering

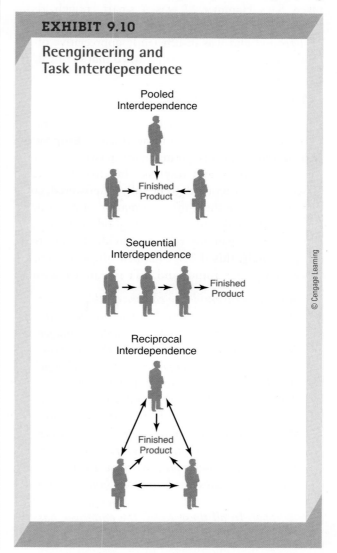

EXHIBIT 9.10

Reengineering and Task Interdependence

Pooled Interdependence

Finished Product

Sequential Interdependence

Finished Product

Reciprocal Interdependence

Finished Product

© Cengage Learning

Empowering workers
permanently passing decision-making authority and responsibility from managers to workers by giving them the information and resources they need to make and carry out good decisions

Empowerment feeling of intrinsic motivation, in which workers perceive their work to have impact and meaning and perceive themselves to be competent and capable of self-determination

Interorganizational process a collection of activities that take place among companies to transform inputs into outputs that customers value

consultants, told 4,000 workers that they would have to "reapply for their jobs" as the company shifted from its traditional vertical structure to a process-based form of organizing. Thomas Kasten, Levi Strauss's vice president for reengineering and customer service, says, "We felt the pressure building up [over reengineering efforts], and we were worried about the business."[34] Today, even reengineering gurus Hammer and Champy admit that roughly 70 percent of all reengineering projects fail because of the effects on people in the workplace. Says Hammer, "I wasn't smart enough about that [the people issues]. I was reflecting my engineering background and was insufficiently appreciative of the human dimension. I've [now] learned that's critical."[35]

9-4b EMPOWERMENT

Another way of redesigning intraorganizational processes is through empowerment. **Empowering workers** means permanently passing decision-making authority and responsibility from managers to workers. For workers to be fully empowered, companies must give them the information and resources they need to make and carry out good decisions and then reward them for taking individual initiative.[36] Unfortunately, this doesn't happen often enough. As Michael Schrage, author and MIT researcher, wrote:

> A warehouse employee can see on the intranet that a shipment is late but has no authority to accelerate its delivery. A project manager knows—and can mathematically demonstrate—that a seemingly minor spec change will bust both her budget and her schedule. The spec must be changed anyway. An airline reservations agent tells the Executive Platinum Premier frequent flier that first class appears wide open for an upgrade. However, the airline's yield management software won't permit any upgrades until just four hours before the flight, frequent fliers (and reservations) be damned. In all these cases, the employee has access to valuable information. Each one possesses the "knowledge" to do the job better.

> But the knowledge and information are irrelevant and useless. Knowledge isn't power; the ability to act on knowledge is power.[37]

When workers are given the proper information and resources and are allowed to make good decisions, they experience strong feelings of empowerment. **Empowerment** is a feeling of intrinsic motivation, in which workers perceive their work to have meaning and perceive themselves to be competent, having an impact, and capable of self-determination.[38] Work has meaning when it is consistent with personal standards and beliefs. Workers feel competent when they believe they can perform an activity with skill. The belief that they are having an impact comes from a feeling that they can affect work outcomes. A feeling of self-determination arises from workers' belief that they have the autonomy to choose how best to do their work.

Empowerment can lead to changes in organizational processes because meaning, competence, impact, and self-determination produce empowered employees who take active rather than passive roles in their work. At **Southwest Airlines**, every employee, from pilots to baggage handlers, is trained to follow a simple philosophy: "Treat others how you'd like to be treated." According to spokeswoman Brandy King, the company deals with customer-relations issues proactively, which means that employees are given freedom to address customers' needs even before they make a complaint. Recently, a man needed to get from Los Angeles to Denver so that he could see his two-year-old grandson who was about to be taken off life support. Though he arrived at the airport two hours early, long lines at security made him late for his flight. He ran through the terminal in his socks, trying to catch his flight, but got to the gate twelve minutes late. At the gate, one of the agents asked him "Are you Mark Dickinson? . . . We're holding the plane for you." As it turns out, the pilot found out about Dickinson's situation from the agent who sold the ticket and decided to hold the plane at the gate until he was ready to go.[39]

9-5 Interorganizational Processes

An **interorganizational process** is a collection of activities that occur *among companies* to transform inputs into outputs that customers value. In other words, many companies work together to create a product or service that

keeps customers happy. *The Artist*, which won the Academy Award for Best Picture, was made by dozens of teams from different companies. It was produced and financed by La Petite Reine, ARP Sélection, Studio 37, France 3 Cinema, Canal+, and CinéCinéma. It was directed by French director Michel Hazanavicius. The costumes were designed by Mark Bridges in New York City. The music was composed by French composer Ludovic Bource but performed by the Brussels Philharmonic Orchestra under the conduction of Ernst Van Tiel. Finally, the film was shot primarily in Los Angeles at several iconic Hollywood locations, such as the Bradbury Building, the American Film Institute, and the Los Angeles Theatre.[40]

*In this section, you'll explore interorganizational processes by learning about **9-5a modular organizations** and **9-5b virtual organizations.***

9-5a MODULAR ORGANIZATIONS

Stephen Roach, chief economist for investment bank Morgan Stanley, says that companies increasingly want to take "functions that aren't central to their core competency" and outsource them.[41] Except for the core business activities that they can perform better, faster, and cheaper than others, **modular organizations** outsource all remaining business activities to outside companies, suppliers, specialists, or consultants. The term *modular* is used because the business activities purchased from outside companies can be added and dropped as needed, much like adding pieces to a three-dimensional puzzle. Exhibit 9.11 depicts a modular organiza-

tion in which the company has chosen to keep training, human resources, sales, product design, manufacturing, customer service, research and development, and information technology as core business activities but has outsourced the noncore activities of product distribution, web page design, advertising, payroll, accounting, and packaging.

Modular organizations have several advantages. First, because modular organizations pay for outsourced labor, expertise, or manufacturing capabilities only when needed, they can cost significantly less to run than traditional organizations. For example, most of the design and marketing work for Apple's new iPad is run out of company headquarters in Cupertino, California. Most of the components for the device, however, are outsourced to other companies. Two South Korean companies, LG and Samsung, make the new iPad's Retina display, while Texas Instruments supplies chips for the touchscreen interface. Broadcom, based

Modular organization an organization that outsources noncore business activities to outside companies, suppliers, specialists, or consultants

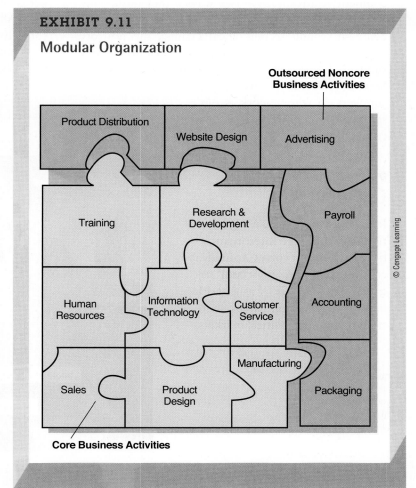

EXHIBIT 9.11

Modular Organization

© Cengage Learning

in Irvine, California, produces the chipsets that control the iPad's wireless connections. Final assembly of the product is handled by Foxconn in China.[42] To obtain these advantages, however, modular organizations need reliable partners—vendors and suppliers with whom they can work closely and can trust.

Modular organizations have disadvantages, too. The primary disadvantage is the loss of control that occurs when key business activities are outsourced to other companies. Also, companies may reduce their competitive advantage in two ways if they mistakenly outsource a core business activity. First, as a result of competitive and technological change, the noncore business activities a company has outsourced may suddenly become the basis for competitive advantage. Second, related to that point, suppliers to whom work is outsourced can sometimes become competitors.

9-5b VIRTUAL ORGANIZATIONS

In contrast to modular organizations in which the interorganizational process revolves around a central company, a **virtual organization** is part of a network in which many companies share skills, costs, capabilities, markets,

and customers with each other. Exhibit 9.12 shows a virtual organization in which, for today, the parts of a virtual company consist of product design, purchasing, manufacturing, advertising, and information technology. Unlike modular organizations, in which the outside organizations are tightly linked to one central company, virtual organizations work with some companies in the network alliance, but not with all. So, whereas a puzzle with various pieces is a fitting metaphor for a modular organization, a potluck dinner is an appropriate metaphor for a virtual organization. All participants bring their finest food dish but eat only what they want.

Another difference is that the working relationships between modular organizations and outside

Virtual organization
an organization that is part of a network in which many companies share skills, costs, capabilities, markets, and customers to collectively solve customer problems or provide specific products or services

EXHIBIT 9.12

Virtual Organizations

Today, I'll have...

Purchasing

Product Design

Information Technology

Manufacturing

Advertising

© Mike Powell/Lifesize/Getty Images

companies tend to be more stable and longer lasting than the shorter, often temporary relationships found among the virtual companies in a network alliance. The composition of a virtual organization is always changing. The combination of network partners that a virtual corporation has at any one time depends on the expertise needed to solve a particular problem or provide a specific product or service. For instance, today the business might need to focus on advertising and product design, as shown in Exhibit 9.12, but tomorrow, the business could want something completely different. In this sense, the term virtual organization means the organization that exists "at the moment."

Virtual organizations have a number of advantages. They let companies share costs, and because members can quickly combine their efforts to meet customers' needs, they are fast and flexible. Finally, because each member of the network alliance is the best at what it does, virtual organizations should in theory provide better products and services in all respects.

As with modular organizations, a disadvantage of virtual organizations is that once work has been outsourced, it can be difficult to control the quality of work done by network partners. The greatest disadvantage, however, is that tremendous managerial skills are required to make a network of independent organizations work well together, especially since their relationships tend to be short and based on a single task or project. Virtual organizations are using two methods to solve this problem. The first is to use a *broker*. In traditional, hierarchical organizations, managers plan, organize, and control. But with the horizontal, interorganizational processes that characterize virtual organizations, the job of a broker is to create and assemble the knowledge, skills, and resources from different companies for outside parties, such as customers.[43] The second way to make networks of virtual organizations more manageable is to use a *virtual organization agreement* that, somewhat like a contract, specifies the schedules, responsibilities, costs, payouts, and liabilities for participating organizations.[44]

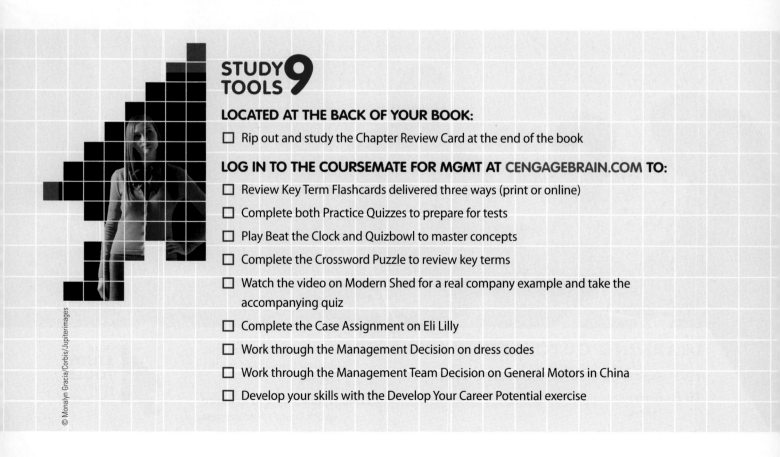

STUDY TOOLS 9

LOCATED AT THE BACK OF YOUR BOOK:

☐ Rip out and study the Chapter Review Card at the end of the book

LOG IN TO THE COURSEMATE FOR MGMT AT CENGAGEBRAIN.COM TO:

☐ Review Key Term Flashcards delivered three ways (print or online)

☐ Complete both Practice Quizzes to prepare for tests

☐ Play Beat the Clock and Quizbowl to master concepts

☐ Complete the Crossword Puzzle to review key terms

☐ Watch the video on Modern Shed for a real company example and take the accompanying quiz

☐ Complete the Case Assignment on Eli Lilly

☐ Work through the Management Decision on dress codes

☐ Work through the Management Team Decision on General Motors in China

☐ Develop your skills with the Develop Your Career Potential exercise

10 Managing
Teams

LEARNING OUTCOMES

10-1 Explain the good and bad of using teams.

10-2 Recognize and understand the different kinds of teams.

10-3 Understand the general characteristics of work teams.

10-4 Explain how to enhance work team effectiveness.

CHECK OUT **STUDY TOOLS** AT THE END OF THIS CHAPTER.

10-1 *The Good and Bad of Using Teams*

Ninety-one percent of organizations are significantly improving their effectiveness by using work teams.[1] Procter & Gamble and Cummins Engine began using teams in 1962 and 1973, respectively. Boeing, Caterpillar, Champion International, Ford Motor Company, 3M, and General Electric established work teams in the mid- to late-1980s. Today, most companies use teams to tackle a variety of issues.[2] "Teams are ubiquitous. Whether we are talking about software development, Olympic hockey, disease outbreak response, or urban warfare, teams represent the critical unit that 'gets things done' in today's world."[3]

Work teams consist of a small number of people with complementary skills who hold themselves mutually accountable for pursuing a common purpose, achieving performance goals, and improving interdependent work processes.[4] By this definition, computer programmers working on separate projects in the same department of a company would not be considered a team. To be a team, the programmers would have to be interdependent and share responsibility and accountability for the quality and amount of computer code they produced.[5] Teams are becoming more important in many industries because they help organizations respond to specific problems and challenges. Though work teams are not the answer for every situation or organization, if the right teams are used properly and in the right settings, teams can dramatically improve company performance over more traditional management approaches while also instilling a sense of vitality in the workplace that is otherwise difficult to achieve.

Let's begin our discussion of teams by learning about **10-1a the advantages of teams, 10-1b the disadvantages of teams,** *and* **10-1c when to use and not use teams.**

10-1a THE ADVANTAGES OF TEAMS

Companies are making greater use of teams because teams have been shown to improve customer satisfaction, product and service quality, speed and efficiency in product development, employee job satisfaction, and decision making.[6] For example, one survey indicated that 80 percent of companies with more than one hundred employees use teams, and 90 percent of all U.S. employees work part of their day in a team.[7]

Teams help businesses increase *customer satisfaction* in several ways. One way is to create work teams that are trained to meet the needs of specific customers. For example, Staff Management, which hires temporary workers for companies, was asked by a leading online retailer to hire 10,000 people for the 2010 holiday season. Joan Davison, chief operating officer for Staff Management says, "Our clients increase their workforce by as much as 100 percent during the holiday season." Staff Management's hiring team used social media such as Facebook, job fairs, and other hiring events to generate the applicants. Jerry Wimer, vice president of operations, said, "Staff Management as an organization is extremely proud of this dedicated team who sacrificed their time with family and friends over the busy holiday season serving our client. Many people, including hard-working recruiters and coaches, supervisors

> **Work team** a small number of people with complementary skills who hold themselves mutually accountable for pursuing a common purpose, achieving performance goals, and improving interdependent work processes

Cross-training training team members to do all or most of the jobs performed by the other team members

and safety managers, data entry clerks and directors from across the country, had a hand in helping this client succeed."[8]

Teams also help firms improve *product and service quality* in several ways.[9] In contrast to traditional organizational structures, in which management is responsible for organizational outcomes and performance, teams take direct responsibility for the quality of the products and service they produce and sell. **Oriental Trading Company** (OTC) sells party supplies, arts and crafts, toys and games, and teaching supplies on the Internet. Like most retail websites, OTC's site allows customers to write comments about the products they buy. When customers complained about the Inflatable Solar System OTC sold, giving it two stars out of five, members of OTC's intradepartmental teams sprang to action. A team member from the quality department worked directly with the manufacturer to improve quality. Another from copy writing worked with a team member from merchandising to post new photos of the improved product along with a more accurate product description. Other members of the team contacted dissatisfied customers to tell them that OTC had listened and had taken steps to address their concerns. Seven weeks after the first negative comment appeared on OTC's website, the improved product was available for sale. Customers consistently rate the new version at four out of five stars.[10]

Another reason for using teams is that teamwork often leads to increased *job satisfaction*.[11] One reason that teamwork can be more satisfying than traditional work is that it gives workers a chance to improve their skills. This is often accomplished through **cross-training**, in which team members are taught how to do all or most of the jobs performed by the other team members. The advantage for the organization is that cross-training allows a team to function normally when one member is absent, quits, or is transferred. The advantage for workers is that cross-training broadens their skills and increases their capabilities while also making their work more varied and interesting.

A second reason that teamwork is satisfying is that work teams often receive proprietary business information that typically is available only to managers. For example, Whole Foods has an "open books, open door, open people" philosophy. Team members are given full access to their store's financial information and everyone's salaries, including those of the store manager and the CEO.[12] Each day, next to the time clock, Whole Foods employees can see the previous day's sales for each team as well as the sales on the same day from the previous year. Each week, team members can examine the same information, broken down by team, for all of the Whole Foods stores in their region. And each month, store managers review information on profitability, including sales, product costs, wages, and operating profits, with each team in the store. Since team members decide how much to spend, what to order, what things should cost, and how many team members should work each day, this information is critical to making teams work at Whole Foods.[13] Whole Foods creates an empowering work environment to honor one of its core values: "supporting team member excellence and happiness."[14]

Team members also gain job satisfaction from unique leadership responsibilities that are not typically available in traditional organizations. Finally, teams share many of the advantages of group decision making discussed in Chapter 5. For instance, because team members possess different knowledge, skills, abilities, and experiences, a team is able to view problems from multiple perspectives. This diversity of viewpoints increases the odds that team decisions will solve the underlying causes of problems and not just address the symptoms. The increased knowledge and information available to teams also make it easier for them to generate more alternative solutions, a critical part of improving the quality of decisions. Because team members are involved in decision-making processes, they are also likely to be more committed to making those decisions work. In short, teams can do a much better job than individuals in two important steps of the decision-making process: defining the problem and generating alternative solutions.

© Hugh Sitton/Photographer's Choice RF/Getty Images

10-1b THE DISADVANTAGES OF TEAMS

Although teams can significantly improve customer satisfaction, product and service quality, speed and efficiency in product development, employee job satisfaction, and decision making, using teams does not

I WANNA HAVE SOME FUN!

Jay Steinfeld, the CEO of Blinds.com, a website that sells window coverings, believes that having fun is key to a healthy work environment. Having fun at work puts people at ease, relieves tension, makes people happier, and helps build better relationships, which leads to better teamwork. Some of his ideas for introducing fun to the workplace include:

- An office decoration contest
- Hanging movie posters
- Holiday parties
- Dress-up days (and not just on Halloween)
- Board games or video games in the break room

Source: J. Steinfeld, "11 Easy Ways to Make Work Fun," *Inc.com*, February 21, 2012, accessed March 13, 2012.

© Katrina Leigh/Shutterstock.com

guarantee these positive outcomes. In fact, if you've ever participated in team projects in your classes, you're probably already aware of some of the problems inherent in work teams. Despite all of their promise, teams and teamwork are also prone to these significant disadvantages: initially high turnover, social loafing, and the problems associated with group decision making.

The first disadvantage of work teams is *initially high turnover*. Teams aren't for everyone, and some workers balk at the responsibility, effort, and learning required in team settings.

Social loafing is another disadvantage of work teams. **Social loafing** occurs when workers withhold their efforts and fail to perform their share of the work.[15] A nineteenth-century French engineer named Maximilian Ringlemann first documented

social loafing when he found that one person pulling on a rope alone exerted an average of 139 pounds of force on the rope. In groups of three, the average force dropped to 117 pounds per person. In groups of eight, the average dropped to just 68 pounds per person. Ringlemann concluded that the larger the team, the smaller the individual effort. In fact, social loafing is more likely to occur in larger groups where identifying and monitoring the efforts of individual team members can be difficult.[16] In other words, social loafers count on being able to blend into the background, where their lack of effort isn't easily spotted. From team-based class projects, most students already know about social loafers or "slackers," who contribute poor, little, or no work whatsoever. Not surprisingly, a study of 250 student teams found that the most talented students are typically the least satisfied with teamwork because of having to carry

Social loafing behavior in which team members withhold their efforts and fail to perform their share of the work

slackers and do a disproportionate share of their team's work.[17] Perceptions of fairness are negatively related to the extent of social loafing within teams.[18]

Finally, teams share many of the *disadvantages of group decision making* discussed in Chapter 5, such as groupthink. In *groupthink*, members of highly cohesive groups feel intense pressure not to disagree with each other so that the group can approve a proposed solution. Because groupthink restricts discussion and leads to consideration of a limited number of alternative solutions, it usually results in poor decisions. Also, team decision making takes considerable time, and team meetings can often be unproductive and inefficient. Another possible pitfall is *minority domination*, where just one or two people dominate team discussions, restricting consideration of different problem definitions and alternative solutions. Scott Jessup, formerly CEO of Marque Inc., an ambulance and hearse manufacturer, explains how his presence would regularly produce minority domination: "I think at times I stifle our best thinking. When a CEO wanders into a team meeting an entirely different dynamic takes place and everybody sits back and waits for the CEO to put forth pearls of wisdom."[19] Finally, team members may not feel accountable for the decisions and actions taken by the team.

10-1c WHEN TO USE TEAMS

As the two previous subsections made clear, teams have significant advantages *and* disadvantages. Therefore, the question is not whether to use teams, but *when* and *where* to use teams for maximum benefit and minimum cost. As Doug Johnson, associate director at the Center for Collaborative Organizations at the University of North Texas, puts it, "Teams are a means to an end, not an end in themselves. You have to ask yourself questions first. Does the work require interdependence? Will the team philosophy fit company strategy? Will management make a long-term commitment to this process?"[20] Exhibit 10.1 provides some additional guidelines on when to use or not use teams.[21]

First, teams should be used when there is a clear, engaging reason or purpose for using them. Too many companies use teams because they're popular or because the companies assume that teams can fix all problems. Teams are much more likely to succeed if they know why they exist and what they are supposed to accomplish, and more likely to fail if they don't.

Second, teams should be used when the job can't be done unless people work together. This typically means that teams are needed when tasks are complex, require multiple perspectives, or require repeated interaction with others to complete. Because of the enormous complexity of today's software, **Microsoft** uses teams to write code, requiring each team to "check in" their computer code every day so the code written by each can be compiled into an updated working build or prototype of the software. The next day, all the teams and their members begin testing and debugging the new build. Over and over again, the computer code is compiled, sent back to

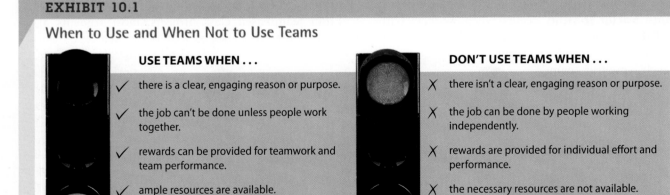

EXHIBIT 10.1

When to Use and When Not to Use Teams

USE TEAMS WHEN . . .

✓ there is a clear, engaging reason or purpose.

✓ the job can't be done unless people work together.

✓ rewards can be provided for teamwork and team performance.

✓ ample resources are available.

DON'T USE TEAMS WHEN . . .

✗ there isn't a clear, engaging reason or purpose.

✗ the job can be done by people working independently.

✗ rewards are provided for individual effort and performance.

✗ the necessary resources are not available.

Source: R. Wageman, "Critical Success Factors for Creating Superb Self-Managing Teams," *Organizational Dynamics* 26, no. 1 (1997): 49–61.

© iStockphoto.com/Serdar Yagci

the teams to be tested and improved, and then compiled and tested again.[22] The mistake that Microsoft made when developing Vista, its widely criticized operating system, was that the different development teams didn't share their code with each other. In other words, the teams didn't interact repeatedly with each other. So, while each team's code tested cleanly on its own, conflicts and failure would occur when the different teams' codes were combined. Microsoft's Julie Larson-Green said, "That's where the conflicts started."[23] So when developing and testing Windows 7, Vista's replacement, Microsoft development teams shared their plans with each other and spent time listening and collaborating with engineers at computer manufacturers like HP and Dell.[24] In the end, the collaboration among teams and with computer manufacturers paid off in Windows 7 being faster, more reliable, and more flexible than Vista. Ian LeGrow, a Microsoft group program manager, said, "Instead of it being a plan owned by one team, our plan was a part of all the teams."[25] Microsoft is using thirty-five feature teams, each with twenty-five to forty software developers, to program and test Windows 8.[26]

Third, teams should be used when rewards can be provided for teamwork and team performance. Rewards that depend on team performance rather than individual performance are the key to rewarding team behaviors and efforts. You'll read more about team rewards later in the chapter, but for now it's enough to know that if the type of reward (individual versus team) is not matched to the type of performance (individual versus team), teams won't work.

10-2 *Kinds of Teams*

Let's continue our discussion of teams by learning about the different kinds of teams that companies like Google and Maytag use to make themselves more competitive. We look first at **10-2a how teams differ in terms of autonomy, which is the key dimension that makes one team different from another**, and then at **10-2b some special kinds of teams**.

10-2a AUTONOMY, THE KEY DIMENSION

Teams can be classified in a number of ways, such as permanent or temporary, or functional or cross-functional. However, studies indicate that the amount of

autonomy possessed by a team is the key difference among teams.[27] *Autonomy* is the degree to which workers have the discretion, freedom, and independence to decide how and when to accomplish their jobs. Exhibit 10.2 on the next page shows how five kinds of teams differ in terms of autonomy. Moving left to right across the autonomy continuum at the top of the exhibit, traditional work groups and employee involvement groups have the least autonomy, semi-autonomous work groups have more autonomy, and, finally, self-managing teams and self-designing teams have the most autonomy. Moving from bottom to top along the left side of the exhibit, note that the number of responsibilities given to each kind of team increases directly with its autonomy. Let's review each of these kinds of teams and their autonomy and responsibilities in more detail.

The smallest amount of autonomy is found in **traditional work groups**, where two or more people work together to achieve a shared goal. In these groups, workers are responsible for doing the work or executing the task, but they do not have direct responsibility or control over their work. Workers report to managers, who are responsible for their performance and have the authority to hire and fire them, make job assignments, and control resources. For instance, suppose that an experienced worker blatantly refuses to do his share of the work, saying, "I've done my time. Let the younger employees do the work." In a team with high autonomy, the responsibility of getting this employee to put forth his fair share of effort would belong to his teammates. But, in a traditional work group, that responsibility belongs to the boss or supervisor. The supervisor in this situation calmly confronted the employee and told him, "We need your talent, [and] your knowledge of these machines. But if you won't work, you'll have to go elsewhere." Within days, the employee's behavior improved.[28]

Employee involvement teams, which have somewhat more autonomy, meet on company time on a weekly or monthly basis to provide advice or make suggestions to management concerning specific issues such as plant safety, customer relations, or product quality.[29] Though they offer advice and suggestions, they do not have the authority to make decisions. Membership on these teams is often voluntary, but members may be selected because of their

Traditional work group a group composed of two or more people who work together to achieve a shared goal

Employee involvement team a team that provides advice or makes suggestions to management concerning specific issues

EXHIBIT 10.2

Team Autonomy Continuum

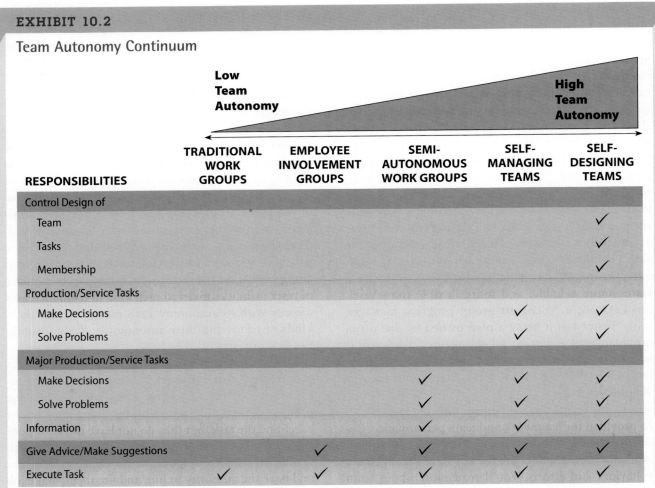

RESPONSIBILITIES	TRADITIONAL WORK GROUPS	EMPLOYEE INVOLVEMENT GROUPS	SEMI-AUTONOMOUS WORK GROUPS	SELF-MANAGING TEAMS	SELF-DESIGNING TEAMS
Control Design of					
Team					✓
Tasks					✓
Membership					✓
Production/Service Tasks					
Make Decisions				✓	✓
Solve Problems				✓	✓
Major Production/Service Tasks					
Make Decisions			✓	✓	✓
Solve Problems			✓	✓	✓
Information			✓	✓	✓
Give Advice/Make Suggestions		✓	✓	✓	✓
Execute Task	✓	✓	✓	✓	✓

Sources: R. D. Banker, J. M. Field, R. G. Schroeder, and K. K. Sinha, "Impact of Work Teams on Manufacturing Performance: A Longitudinal Field Study," *Academy of Management Journal* 39 (1996): 867–890; J. R. Hackman, "The Psychology of Self-Management in Organizations," in *Psychology and Work: Productivity, Change, and Employment*, ed. M. S. Pallak and R. Perlof (Washington, DC: American Psychological Association), 85–136.

expertise. The idea behind employee involvement teams is that the people closest to the problem or situation are best able to recommend solutions. For more than three years, production of Boeing's 787 Dreamliner was delayed by multiple problems—parts shortages, improper installation, failed test flights, and more. Because of production delays, Boeing must build ten planes per month, up from the typical two and a half planes. To meet this aggressive goal, it established nearly 200 employee involvement teams to analyze the way 787s are assembled and make changes to maximize efficiency. For example, one employee involvement team found that ducts already installed in the plane were being dam-

Semi-autonomous work group a group that has the authority to make decisions and solve problems related to the major tasks of producing a product or service

aged because workers were kicking and stepping on them while doing other work. The damaged ducts then had to be removed and replaced. The team recommended that temporary covers be placed over the ducts, thus eliminating delays and increased costs.[30]

Semi-autonomous work groups not only provide advice and suggestions to management but also have the authority to make decisions and solve problems related to the major tasks required to produce a product or service. Semi-autonomous groups regularly receive information about budgets, work quality and performance, and competitors' products. Furthermore, members of semi-autonomous work groups are typically cross-trained in a number of different skills and tasks. In short, semi-autonomous work groups give employees the authority to make decisions that are typically made by supervisors and managers.

That authority is not complete, however. Managers still play a role, though one that is much reduced compared with traditional work groups, in supporting the work of semi-autonomous work groups. The role a manager plays on a team usually evolves over time. "It may start with helping to transition problem-solving responsibilities to the team, filling miscellaneous requests for the team, and doing ad hoc tasks," says Steven Hitchcock, president of Axis Performance Advisors in Portland, Oregon. Later, the team may develop into a mini-enterprise, and the former manager becomes externally focused—sort of an account manager for the customer. Managers have to adjust what they do based on the sophistication of the team.[31] A lot of what managers of semi-autonomous work groups do is ask good questions, provide resources, and facilitate performance of group goals.

Self-managing teams are different from semi-autonomous work groups in that team members manage and control *all* of the major tasks *directly related* to production of a product or service without first getting approval from management. This includes managing and controlling the acquisition of materials, making a product or providing a service, and ensuring timely delivery. At a **Bandag** tire retread factory in Iowa, the self-managing teams in Plant 4 were entirely responsible for decision making, resolving internal and external conflicts, evaluating team member performance and providing feedback, recognizing good performance, running team meetings, deciding who needed what kind of training, and then selecting team members to rotate through three key team leadership roles. Plant 4, which used to lose money, is now solidly profitable thanks to a 50 percent improvement in efficiency produced by its self-managed teams.[32]

The use of self-directed teams has significantly increased productivity at a number of other companies, increasing quality by 12 percent at AT&T, reducing errors by 13 percent at FedEx, and helping 3M increase production by 300 percent at one of its manufacturing plants.[33] Seventy-two percent of *Fortune* 1,000 companies have at least one self-managing team, up from 28 percent in 1987.[34]

Self-designing teams have all the characteristics of self-managing teams, but they can also control and change the design of the teams themselves, the tasks they do and how and when they do them, and the membership of the teams.

10-2b SPECIAL KINDS OF TEAMS

Companies are also increasingly using several other kinds of teams that can't easily be categorized in terms of autonomy: cross-functional teams, virtual teams, and project teams. Depending on how these teams are designed, they can be either low- or high-autonomy teams.

Cross-functional teams are intentionally composed of employees from different functional areas of the organization.[35] Because their members have different functional backgrounds, education, and experience, cross-functional teams usually attack problems from multiple perspectives and generate more ideas and alternative solutions, all of which are especially important when trying to innovate or solve problems creatively.[36] Cross-functional teams can be used almost anywhere in an organization and are often used in conjunction with matrix and product organizational structures (see Chapter 9). They can also be used either with part-time or temporary team assignments or with full-time, long-term teams.

Virtual teams are groups of geographically and/or organizationally dispersed coworkers who use a combination of telecommunications and information technologies to accomplish an organizational task.[37] Members of virtual teams rarely meet face-to-face; instead, they use email, videoconferencing, and group communication software.[38] Virtual teams can be employee involvement teams, self-managing teams, or nearly any kind of team discussed in this chapter. Virtual teams are often (but not necessarily) temporary teams that are set up to accomplish a specific task.[39]

Self-managing team a team that manages and controls all of the major tasks of producing a product or service

Self-designing team a team that has the characteristics of self-managing teams but also controls team design, work tasks, and team membership

Cross-functional team a team composed of employees from different functional areas of the organization

Virtual team a team composed of geographically and/ or organizationally dispersed coworkers who use telecommunication and information technologies to accomplish an organizational task

© iStockphoto.com/iofoto

The principal advantage of virtual teams is their flexibility. Employees can work with each other regardless of physical location, time zone, or organizational affiliation.[40] Because the team members don't meet in a physical location, virtual teams also find it much easier to include other key stakeholders such as suppliers and customers. Plus, virtual teams have certain efficiency advantages over traditional team structures. Because the teammates do not meet face-to-face, a virtual team typically requires a smaller time commitment than a traditional team does. Moreover, employees can fulfill the responsibilities of their virtual team membership from the comfort of their own offices without the travel time or downtime typically required for face-to-face meetings.[41]

A drawback of virtual teams is that the team members must learn to express themselves in new contexts.[42] The give-and-take that naturally occurs in face-to-face meetings is more difficult to achieve through videoconferencing or other methods of virtual teaming. Indeed several studies have shown that physical proximity enhances information processing.[43] Therefore, some companies bring virtual team members together on a regular basis to try to minimize these problems.

Project teams are created to complete specific, one-time projects or tasks within a limited time.[44] Project teams are often used to develop new products, significantly improve existing products, roll out new information systems, or build new factories or offices. The project team is typically led by a project manager who has the overall responsibility for planning, staffing, and managing the team, which usually includes employees from different functional areas. Effective project teams demand both individual and collective responsibility.[45] One advantage of project teams is that drawing employees from different functional areas can reduce or eliminate communication barriers. In turn, as long as team members feel free to express their ideas, thoughts, and concerns, free-flowing communication encourages cooperation among separate departments and typically speeds up the design process.[46] Another advantage of project teams is their flexibility. When projects are finished, project team members either move on to the next project or return to their functional units. For example, publication of this book required designers, editors, page compositors, and Web designers, among others. When the task was finished, these people applied their skills to other textbook projects. Because of this flexibility, project teams are often used with the matrix organizational designs discussed in Chapter 9.

10-3 *Work Team Characteristics*

"Why did I ever let you talk me into teams? They're nothing but trouble."[47] Lots of managers have this reaction after making the move to teams. Many don't realize that this reaction is normal, both for them and for workers. In fact, such a reaction is characteristic of the *storming* stage of team development (discussed in Section 10-3e). Managers who are familiar with these stages and with the other important characteristics of teams will be better prepared to manage the predictable changes that occur when companies make the switch to team-based structures.

Understanding the characteristics of work teams is essential for making teams an effective part of an organization. Therefore, in this section you'll learn about 10-3a team norms, 10-3b team cohesiveness, 10-3c team size, 10-3d team conflict, and 10-3e the stages of team development.

10-3a TEAM NORMS

Over time, teams develop **norms**, which are informally agreed-on standards that regulate team behavior.[48] Norms are valuable because they let team members know what is expected of them. While leading Orbis International, a nonprofit organization in which a DC-10 jet, converted to a "Flying Eye Hospital," transports volunteer doctors and nurses to treat eye disease throughout the world, Jilly Stephens noticed a problem with punctuality. She said, "When I first got to the field, you would have the nurses, engineers, whoever, waiting, and you would maybe have one [person] who just couldn't drag himself out of bed and everybody's waiting." So she simply decided that there would be a new norm for the team: They leave on time. "If they aren't there [on time], the bus leaves. You get to the airport yourself. If we were in Tunisia, that meant finding a bike and cycling across the desert to get to the airport." Says Stephens, "We saw behaviors change fairly rapidly."[49]

Studies indicate that norms are one of the most powerful influences on work behavior because they regulate the everyday actions that allow teams to function effectively. Team norms are often associated with positive outcomes such as stronger organizational commitment, more trust in management, and stronger job and organizational satisfaction.[50] Effective work teams develop norms about the quality and timeliness of job performance, absenteeism, safety, and honest expression of ideas and opinions.

Surgeon Atul Gawande, author of *The Checklist Manifesto*, says that with 6,000 drugs, 4,000 medical procedures, and doctors and nurses specializing in hundreds of medical subfields, "The complexity of what we [in modern medicine] have to deliver on exceeds our abilities as experts partly because the volume of knowledge has exceeded what training can possibly provide."[51] So, in his operating rooms, Gawande and his surgical teams use and review checklists to make sure each small but critical step is completed. Before administering anesthesia, the nurse and anesthetist will determine if the site of the surgery is marked, whether the anesthesia machine and medication check have been completed, and whether the patient has a difficult airway or is at risk of aspiration (vomiting into the airway). Likewise, before the first incision takes place, all team members will be asked to introduce themselves and the roles they'll be performing, and the surgeon will be asked to state where the incision will be made and what kind of critical, nonroutine steps might be taken if things don't go as planned.[52] The review checklists are a powerful way of making sure that all members of the surgical team do what they're supposed to, that is, follow agreed-on standards of behavior or norms.

Norms can also influence team behavior in negative ways. For example, most people would agree that damaging organizational property; saying or doing something to hurt someone at work; intentionally doing one's work badly, incorrectly, or slowly; griping about coworkers; deliberately bending or breaking rules; and doing something to harm the company or boss are negative behaviors. A study of workers from thirty-four teams in twenty different organizations found that teams with negative norms strongly influenced their team members to engage in these negative behaviors. In fact, the longer individuals were members of a team with negative norms and the more frequently they interacted with their teammates, the more likely they were to perform negative behaviors. Since team norms typically develop early in the life of a team, these results indicate how important it is for teams to establish positive norms from the outset.[53]

10-3b TEAM COHESIVENESS

Cohesiveness is another important characteristic of work teams. **Cohesiveness** is the extent to which team members are attracted to a team and motivated to remain in it.[54] Employees at the General Electric Airfoils plant in Greenville, South Carolina, are well paid at $31 an hour, but its cohesive teams are a key reason that employees love their jobs. Teams, not management, screen job applicants in interviews, which include a Lego-based activity that measures the extent to which the applicants work well with others. Teams also have the autonomy to change work on the assembly line—speeding up a certain part or slowing down another—to increase productivity. For example, when two teams created different ways to speed up the washing of jet turbine blades during the manufacturing process, management respected the integrity of the teams so much that it authorized the purchase of different equipment for each team. With that kind of trust, it's little wonder that one employee said, "Out of all the places I've worked, I'd say this is by far the best one."[55]

> **Cohesiveness** the extent to which team members are attracted to a team and motivated to remain in it

© Jim R. Bounds/Bloomberg via Getty Images

What can be done to promote team cohesiveness? First, make sure that all team members are present at team meetings and activities. Team cohesiveness suffers when members are allowed to withdraw from the team and miss team meetings and events.[56] Second, create additional opportunities for teammates to work together by rearranging work schedules and creating common workspaces. When task interdependence is high and team members have lots of chances to work together, team cohesiveness tends to increase.[57] Third, engaging in nonwork activities as a team can help build cohesion. Finally, companies build team cohesiveness by making employees feel that they are part of an organization.

10-3c TEAM SIZE

The relationship between team size and performance appears to be curvilinear. Very small or very large teams may not perform as well as moderately sized teams. For most teams, the right size is somewhere between six and nine members.[58] A team of this size is small enough for the team members to get to know each other and for each member to have an opportunity to contribute in a meaningful way to the success of the team. At the same time, the team is large enough to take advantage of team members' diverse skills, knowledge, and perspectives. It is also easier to instill a sense of responsibility and mutual accountability in teams of this size.[59]

When teams get too large, team members find it difficult to get to know one another, and the team may splinter into smaller subgroups. When this occurs, subgroups sometimes argue and disagree, weakening overall team cohesion. As teams grow, there is also a greater chance of *minority domination*, where just a few team members dominate team discussions. Even if minority domination doesn't occur, larger groups may not have time for all team members to share their input. And when team members feel that their contributions are unimportant or not needed, the result is less involvement, effort, and accountability to the team.[60] Large teams also face logistical problems such as finding an appropriate time or place to meet. Finally, the incidence of social loafing, discussed earlier in the chapter, is much higher in large teams.

Just as team performance can suffer when a team is too large, it can also be negatively affected when a team is too small. Teams with just a few people may lack the diversity of skills and knowledge found in larger teams. Also, teams that are too small are unlikely to gain the advantages of team decision making (multiple perspectives, generating more ideas and alternative solutions, and stronger commitment) found in larger teams.

What signs indicate that a team's size needs to be changed? If decisions are taking too long, if the team has difficulty making decisions or taking action, if a few members dominate the team, or if the commitment or efforts of team members are weak, chances are the team is too big. In contrast, if a team is having difficulty coming up with ideas or generating solutions, or if the team does not have the expertise to address a specific problem, chances are the team is too small.

10-3d TEAM CONFLICT

Conflict and disagreement are inevitable in most teams. But this shouldn't surprise anyone. From time to time, people who work together are going to disagree about what and how things get done. What causes conflict in teams? Although almost anything can lead to conflict—casual remarks that unintentionally offend a team member or fighting over scarce resources—the primary cause of team conflict is disagreement over team goals and priorities.[61] Other common causes of team conflict include disagreements over task-related issues, interpersonal incompatibilities, and simple fatigue.

Though most people view conflict negatively, the key to dealing with team conflict is not avoiding it, but rather making sure that the team experiences the right kind of conflict. In Chapter 5, you learned about *c-type conflict*, or *cognitive conflict*, which focuses on problem-related differences of opinion, and *a-type conflict*, or *affective conflict*, which refers to the emotional reactions that can occur when disagreements become personal rather than professional.[62] Cognitive conflict is strongly associated with improvements in team performance, whereas affective conflict is strongly associated with decreases in team performance.[63] Why does this happen? With cognitive conflict, team members disagree because their different experiences and expertise lead them to different views of the problem and solutions. Indeed, managers who participated on teams that emphasized cognitive conflict described their teammates as "smart," "team players," and "best in the business." They described their teams as "open," "fun," and "productive." One manager summed up the positive attitude that team members had about cognitive conflict by saying, "We scream a lot, then laugh, and then resolve the issue."[64] Thus, cognitive conflict is also characterized by a willingness to examine, compare, and reconcile differences to produce the best possible solution.

By contrast, affective conflict often results in hostility, anger, resentment, distrust, cynicism, and apathy.

Not Like Me, Not Like You

When we are choosing friends or significant others, we are likely to pursue people with whom we have something in common—perhaps a shared hobby, the same favorite football team, or a common love for northern Italian food. When we bring someone new into the workplace, however, it is important that we look for a person that is dissimilar. A new coworker or work team member who is similar will certainly be easier to get along with and make teamwork more comfortable. And while there are benefits of having good relationships, there is also a danger, since conflicts and disagreements among team members can be challenging and productive. Having someone disagree with us teaches us that there is more than one way to solve a problem. And it is that kind of multi-perspective view that helps companies find success.

Source: M. Heffernan, "Danger! Don't Hire People Just Like You," *Inc.*, January 24, 2012, accessed March 13, 2012, http://www.inc.com/margaret-heffernan/danger-dont -hire-people-just-like-you.html.

Managers who participated on teams that experienced affective conflict described their teammates as "manipulative," "secretive," "burned out," and "political."[65] Not surprisingly, affective conflict can make people uncomfortable and cause them to withdraw and decrease their commitment to a team.[66] Affective conflict also lowers the satisfaction of team members, may lead to personal hostility between coworkers, and can decrease team cohesiveness.[67] So, unlike cognitive conflict, affective conflict undermines team performance by preventing teams from engaging in the kinds of activities that are critical to team effectiveness.

So, what can managers do to manage team conflict? First, they need to realize that emphasizing cognitive conflict alone won't be enough. Studies show that cognitive and affective conflicts often occur together in a given team activity! Sincere attempts to reach agreement on a difficult issue can quickly deteriorate from cognitive to affective conflict if the discussion turns personal and tempers and emotions flare. While cognitive conflict is clearly the better approach to take, efforts to engage in cognitive conflict should be managed well and checked before they deteriorate and the team becomes unproductive.

Can teams disagree and still get along? Fortunately, they can. In an attempt to study this issue, researchers examined team conflict in twelve high-tech companies. In four of the companies, work teams used cognitive conflict to address work problems but did so in a way that minimized the occurrence of affective conflict.

There are several ways teams can have a good fight.[68] First, work with more, rather than less, information. If data are plentiful, objective, and up-to-date, teams will focus on issues, not personalities. Second, develop multiple alternatives to enrich debate. Focusing on multiple solutions diffuses conflict by getting the team to keep searching for a better solution. Positions and opinions are naturally more flexible with five alternatives than with just two. Third, establish common goals. Remember, most team conflict arises from disagreements over team goals and priorities. Therefore, common goals encourage collaboration and minimize conflict over a team's purpose. The late Steve Jobs, former CEO of Apple, explained it this way: "It's okay to spend a lot of time arguing about which route to take to San Francisco when everyone wants to end up there, but a lot of time gets wasted in such arguments if one person wants to go to San Francisco and another secretly wants to go to San Diego."[69] Fourth, inject humor into the workplace. Humor relieves tension, builds cohesion, and just makes being in teams fun. Fifth, maintain a balance of power by involving as many people as possible in the decision process. And, sixth, resolve issues without forcing a consensus. Consensus means that everyone must agree before decisions are finalized. Effectively, requiring consensus gives everyone on the team veto power. Nothing gets done until everyone agrees, which, of course, is nearly impossible. As a result, insisting on consensus usually promotes affective rather than cognitive conflict. If team members can't agree after constructively discussing their options, it's better to have the team leader make the final choice. Most team members can accept the team leader's choice if they've been thoroughly involved in the decision process.

10-3e STAGES OF TEAM DEVELOPMENT

As teams develop and grow, they pass through four stages of development. As shown in Exhibit 10.3, those stages are forming, storming, norming, and performing.[70] Although not every team passes through each of these stages, teams that do tend to be better performers.[71] This holds true even for teams composed of seasoned executives. After a period of time, however, if a team is not managed well, its performance may start to deteriorate as the team begins a process of decline and progresses through the stages of de-norming, de-storming, and de-forming.[72]

Forming is the initial stage of team development. This is the getting-acquainted stage in whch team members first meet each other, form initial

impressions, and try to get a sense of what it will be like to be part of the team. Some of the first team norms will be established during this stage as team members begin to find out what behaviors will and won't be accepted by the team. During this stage, team leaders should allow time for team members to get to know each other, set early ground rules, and begin to set up a preliminary team structure.

Conflicts and disagreements often characterize the second stage of team development, **storming**. As team members begin working together, different personalities and work styles may clash. Team members become more assertive at this stage and more willing to state opinions. This is also the stage when team members jockey for position and try to establish a favorable role for themselves on the team. In addition, team members are likely to disagree about what the group should do and how it should do it. Team performance is still relatively low, given that team cohesion is weak and team members are still reluctant to support each other. Since teams that get stuck in the storming stage are almost always ineffective, it is important for team leaders to focus the team on team goals and on improving team performance. Team members need to be particularly patient and tolerant with each other in this stage.

Forming the first stage of team development, in which team members meet each other, form initial impressions, and begin to establish team norms

Storming the second stage of development, characterized by conflict and disagreement, in which team members disagree over what the team should do and how it should do it

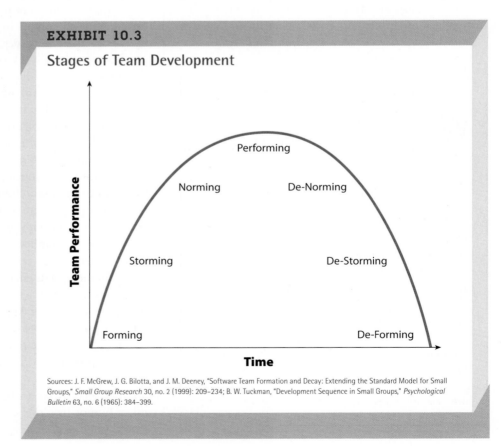

EXHIBIT 10.3

Stages of Team Development

Sources: J. F. McGrew, J. G. Bilotta, and J. M. Deeney, "Software Team Formation and Decay: Extending the Standard Model for Small Groups," *Small Group Research* 30, no. 2 (1999): 209–234; B. W. Tuckman, "Development Sequence in Small Groups," *Psychological Bulletin* 63, no. 6 (1965): 384–399.

During **norming**, the third stage of team development, team members begin to settle into their roles as team members. Positive team norms will have developed by this stage, and teammates should know what to expect from each other. Petty differences should have been resolved, friendships will have developed, and group cohesion will be relatively strong. At this point, team members will have accepted team goals, be operating as a unit, and, as indicated by the increase in performance, be working together effectively. This stage can be very short and is often characterized by someone on the team saying, "I think things are finally coming together." Note, however, that teams may also cycle back and forth between storming and norming several times before finally settling into norming.

In the last stage of team development, **performing**, performance improves because the team has finally matured into an effective, fully functioning team. At this point, members should be fully committed to the team and think of themselves as members of a team and not just employees. Team members often become intensely loyal to one another at this stage and feel mutual accountability for team successes and failures. Trivial disagreements, which can take time and energy away from the work of the team, should be rare. At this stage, teams get a lot of work done, and it is fun to be a team member.

The team should not become complacent, however. Without effective management, its performance may begin to decline as the team passes through the stages of **de-norming**, **de-storming**, and **de-forming**.[73] Indeed, John Puckett, manufacturing vice president for circuit-board manufacturer XEL Communications, says, "The books all say you start in this state of chaos and march through these various stages, and you end up in this state of ultimate self-direction, where everything is going just great. They never tell you it can go back in the other direction, sometimes just as quickly."[74]

10-4 *Enhancing Work Team Effectiveness*

Making teams work is a challenging and difficult process. Nonetheless, companies can increase the likelihood that teams will succeed by carefully managing **10-4a the setting of team goals and priorities** and **10-4b how work team members are selected, 10-4c trained,** and **10-4d compensated.**[75]

10-4a SETTING TEAM GOALS AND PRIORITIES

In Chapter 5, you learned that having specific, measurable, attainable, realistic, and timely (S.M.A.R.T.) goals is one of the most effective means for improving individual job performance. Fortunately, team goals also improve team performance. In fact, team goals lead to much higher team performance 93 percent of the time.[76] For example, Best Buy, the electronics retailer, put together four groups of sales people, all in their twenties and early thirties, and had them live together in a Los Angeles apartment for ten weeks. Jeremy Sevush, a sales floor supervisor, said, "My friends joked and said I was joining 'Real World: Best Buy Edition.'" Their goal—to generate quick, easy-to-start business ideas for Best Buy. Because they had a clear goal and limited time, everyone was focused. Said Sevush, "Living together and knowing we only had ten weeks sped up our team-building process. We voluntarily worked longer hours, talking about business models while making spaghetti." And, it worked. Sevush and his team came up with Best Buy Studio, Web-design consulting for small businesses. It was up and running just a few weeks after the teams moved out of the apartments.[77]

Why is setting *specific* team goals so critical to team success? One reason is that increasing a team's performance is inherently more complex than just increasing one individual's job performance. For instance, consider that any team is likely to involve at least four different kinds of goals: each member's goal for the team, each member's goal for himself or herself on the team, the team's goal for each member, and the team's goal for itself.[78] In other words, without a specific goal for the team itself (the last of the four goals listed), team members may head off in all directions at once pursuing these other goals. Consequently, setting a specific goal *for the team* clarifies team priorities by providing a clear focus and purpose.

Norming the third stage of team development, in which team members begin to settle into their roles, group cohesion grows, and positive team norms develop

Performing the fourth and final stage of team development, in which performance improves because the team has matured into an effective, fully functioning team

De-norming a reversal of the norming stage, in which team performance begins to decline as the size, scope, goal, or members of the team change

De-storming a reversal of the storming phase, in which the team's comfort level decreases, team cohesion weakens, and angry emotions and conflict may flare

De-forming a reversal of the forming stage, in which team members position themselves to control pieces of the team, avoid each other, and isolate themselves from team leaders

Structural accommodation the ability to change organizational structures, policies, and practices in order to meet stretch goals

Bureaucratic immunity the ability to make changes without first getting approval from managers or other parts of an organization

Challenging team goals affect how hard team members work. In particular, they greatly reduce the incidence of social loafing. When faced with difficult goals, team members necessarily expect everyone to contribute. Consequently, they are much more likely to notice and complain if a teammate isn't doing his or her share. In fact, when teammates know each other well, when team goals are specific, when team communication is good, and when teams are rewarded for team performance (discussed later in this section), there is only a one in sixteen chance that teammates will be social loafers.[79]

What can companies and teams do to ensure that team goals lead to superior team performance? One increasingly popular approach is to give teams stretch goals. *Stretch goals* are extremely ambitious goals that workers don't know how to reach.[80] Hyundai recently set a goal of having its entire product line average fifty miles per gallon or better by 2025, an improvement of nearly 60 percent over current

ratings. While John Krafcik, a spokesmen for Hyundai, recognized the difficulty of the goal—"We don't know precisely how to get there right now"—he reaffirmed the company's commitment to setting high ambitions, stating, "We want to help set the trajectory for the industry."[81]

Four things must occur for stretch goals to effectively motivate teams.[82] First, teams must have a high degree of autonomy or control over how they achieve their goals. Second, teams must be empowered with control resources, such as budgets, workspaces, computers, or whatever else they need to do their jobs. Third, teams need structural accommodation. **Structural accommodation** means giving teams the ability to change organizational structures, policies, and practices if doing so helps them meet their stretch goals. Finally, teams need bureaucratic immunity. **Bureaucratic immunity** means that teams no longer have to go through the frustratingly slow process of multilevel reviews and sign-offs to get management approval before making changes. Once granted bureaucratic immunity, teams are immune from the influence of various organizational groups and are ac-

© iStockphoto.com/Branko Habjan

The Rights and Wrongs of Socializing

Looking for a way to bring your team members closer together? There may be nothing better than a team outing. Whether it's dinner on a Friday night or a weekend retreat to Niagara Falls, a group outing is a great way to develop cohesiveness and interpersonal skills within a team. There are, however, certain situations to avoid. For example, you may not want to go to a bar for drinks if a team member is a recovering alcoholic. You may not want to schedule an event too late at night or too far away if some team members have young children at home. So do the right thing—make sure you get to know your team members and their unique circumstances so that you can plan team activities that everyone can participate in and enjoy.

Source: "7 Ways to Socialize with Your Employees (without Getting in Trouble)," *Inc*, August 11, 2010, accessed August 19, 2010, http://www.inc.com/guides/2010/08/7-ways-to-socialize-with-your-employees.html.

countable only to top management. Therefore, teams can act quickly, and even experiment, with little fear of failure.

10-4b SELECTING PEOPLE FOR TEAMWORK

University of Southern California management professor Edward Lawler says, "People are very naive about how easy it is to create a team. Teams are the Ferraris of work design. They're high performance but high maintenance and expensive."[83] It's almost impossible to have an effective work team without carefully selecting people who are suited for teamwork or for working on a particular team. A focus on teamwork (individualism-collectivism), team level, and team diversity can help companies choose the right team members.[84]

Are you more comfortable working alone or with others? If you strongly prefer to work alone, you may not be well suited for teamwork. Indeed, studies show that job satisfaction is higher in teams when team members prefer working with others.[85] An indirect way to measure someone's *preference for teamwork* is to assess the person's degree of individualism or collectivism. **Individualism-collectivism** is the degree to which a person believes that people should be self-sufficient and that loyalty to one's self is more important than loyalty to one's team or company.[86] *Individualists*, who put their own welfare and interests first, generally prefer independent tasks in which they work alone. In contrast, *collectivists*, who put group or team interests ahead of self-interests, generally prefer interdependent tasks in which they work with others. Collectivists would also rather cooperate than compete and are fearful of disappointing team members or of being ostracized from teams. Given these differences, it makes sense to select team members who are collectivists rather than individualists. Indeed, many companies use individualism-collectivism as an initial screening device for team members. If team diversity is desired, however, individualists may also be appropriate, as discussed below. To determine your preference for teamwork, take the Team Player Inventory shown in Exhibit 10.4.

Individualism-collectivism the degree to which a person believes that people should be self-sufficient and that loyalty to one's self is more important than loyalty to team or company

---

EXHIBIT 10.4

The Team Player Inventory

		STRONGLY DISAGREE				STRONGLY AGREE
1.	I enjoy working on team/group projects.	1	2	3	4	5
2.	Team/group project work easily allows others to not pull their weight.	1	2	3	4	5
3.	Work that is done as a team/group is better than work done individually.	1	2	3	4	5
4.	I do my best work alone rather than in a team/group.	1	2	3	4	5
5.	Team/group work is overrated in terms of the actual results produced.	1	2	3	4	5
6.	Working in a team/group gets me to think more creatively.	1	2	3	4	5
7.	Teams/groups are used too often when individual work would be more effective.	1	2	3	4	5
8.	My own work is enhanced when I am in a team/group situation.	1	2	3	4	5
9.	My experiences working in team/group situations have been primarily negative.	1	2	3	4	5
10.	More solutions/ideas are generated when working in a team/group situation than when working alone.	1	2	3	4	5

Reverse score items 2, 4, 5, 7, and 9. Then add the scores for items 1 to 10. Higher scores indicate a preference for teamwork, whereas lower total scores indicate a preference for individual work.

© Cengage Learning

Team level the average level of ability, experience, personality, or any other factor on a team

Team diversity the variances or differences in ability, experience, personality, or any other factor on a team

Team level is the average level of ability, experience, personality, or any other factor on a team. For example, a high level of team experience means that a team has particularly experienced team members. This does not mean that every member of the team has considerable experience, but that enough team members do to significantly raise the average level of experience on the team. Team level is used to guide selection of teammates when teams need a particular set of skills or capabilities to do their jobs well. For example, at GE's Aerospace Engines manufacturing plant in Durham, North Carolina, only applicants who have an FAA-certified mechanic's license are considered for hire. Following that, all applicants are tested in eleven different areas, only one of which involves technical skills. Keith McKee, who works at the plant, says, "You have to be above the bar in all eleven of the areas: helping skills, team skills, communication skills, diversity, flexibility, coaching ability, work ethic, and so forth. Even if just one thing out of the eleven knocks you down, you don't come to work here."[87]

Whereas team level represents the average level or capability on a team, **team diversity** represents the variances or differences in ability, experience, personality, or any other factor on a team.[88] From a practical perspective, why is team diversity important? Professor John Hollenbeck explains, "Imagine if you put all the extroverts together. Everyone is talking, but nobody is listening. [By contrast,] with a team of [nothing but] introverts, you can hear the clock ticking on the wall."[89] Not only do strong teams have talented members (that is, a high team level), but those talented members are also different in terms of ability, experience, or personality.

Once the right team has been put together in terms of individualism-collectivism, team level, and team diversity, it's important to keep the team together as long as practically possible. Interesting research by the National Transportation Safety Board shows that 73 percent of serious mistakes made by jet cockpit crews are made the very first day that a crew flies together as a team and that 44 percent of serious mistakes occur on their very first flight together that day (pilot teams fly two to three flights per day). Moreover, research has shown that fatigued pilot crews who have worked together before make significantly fewer errors than rested crews who have never worked together.[90] Their experience working together helps them overcome their fatigue and outperform new teams that have not worked together before. So, once you've created effective teams, keep them together as long as possible.

10-4c TEAM TRAINING

After selecting the right people for teamwork, you need to train them. To be successful, teams need significant training, particularly in interpersonal skills, decision-making and problem-solving skills, conflict resolution skills, and technical training. Organizations that create

© iStockphoto.com/Robert Churchill

Interpersonal skills skills, such as listening, communicating, questioning, and providing feedback, that enable people to have effective working relationships with others

work teams *often underestimate the amount of training* required to make teams effective. This mistake occurs frequently in successful organizations where managers assume that if employees can work effectively on their own, they can work effectively in teams. In reality, companies that successfully use teams provide thousands of hours of training to make sure that teams work. Stacy Myers, a consultant who helps companies implement teams, says, "When we help companies move to teams, we also require that employees take basic quality and business knowledge classes as well. Teams must know how their work affects the company, and how their success will be measured."[91]

Most commonly, members of work teams receive training in interpersonal skills. **Interpersonal skills** such as listening, communicating, questioning, and providing feedback enable people to have effective working relationships with others. Consultant Peter Grazier, founder of Teambuilding Inc., says, "Teams have told us that if they had to do it over again they would have more of the people skills upfront. They don't struggle with the technical stuff. They tend to struggle with the people skills."[92] Because of teams' autonomy and responsibility, many companies also give team members training in *decision-making and problem-solving skills* to help them do a better job of cutting costs and improving quality and customer service. Many organizations also teach teams *conflict resolution skills*. Teambuilding Inc.'s Grazier explains that "the diversity of values and personalities makes a team powerful, but it can be the greatest source of conflict. If you're a detail person and I'm not, and we get on a team, you might say that we need more analysis on a problem before making a decision, [while I] may want to make a decision [right away]." But, if I've been trained in problem-solving and conflict resolution, "then I look at your detail [focus] as something that is needed in a team because it's a shortcoming of mine."[93] Taine Moufarrige, executive director of Servcorp, a global company hosting serviced and virtual offices for about 12,000 clients, agrees. Says Moufarrige, "It's not just about disagreements, it's about working through problems, managing differences of opinion, and that's vital for moving forward."[94]

Firms must also provide team members with the *technical training* they need to do their jobs, particularly if they are being cross-trained to perform all of the different jobs on the team. Before teams were created at Milwaukee Mutual Insurance, separate employees performed the tasks of rating, underwriting, and processing insurance policies. After extensive cross-training, however, each team member can now do all three jobs.[95] Cross-training is less appropriate for teams of highly skilled workers. For instance, it is unlikely that a group of engineers, computer programmers, and systems analysts would be cross-trained for each other's jobs.

Team leaders need training, too, as they often feel unprepared for their new duties. New team leaders face myriad problems ranging from confusion about their new roles as team leaders (compared with their old jobs as managers or employees) to not knowing where to go for help when their teams have problems. The solution is extensive training. Overall, does team training work? One recent study found that across a wide variety of settings, tasks, team types, and 2,650 teams in different organizations, team training was positively related to team performance outcomes.[96]

10-4d TEAM COMPENSATION AND RECOGNITION

Compensating teams correctly is very difficult. For instance, one survey found that only 37 percent of companies were satisfied with their team compensation plans and even fewer, just 10 percent, reported being "very positive."[97] One of the problems, according to Susan Mohrman of the Center for Effective Organizations at the University of Southern California, is that "there is a very strong set of beliefs in most organizations that people should be paid for how well they do. So when people first get put into team-based organizations, they really balk at being paid for how well the team does. It sounds illogical to them. It sounds like their individuality and

Skill-based pay a compensation system that pays employees for learning additional skills or knowledge

Gainsharing a compensation system in which companies share the financial value of performance gains, such as increased productivity, cost savings, or quality, with their workers

their sense of self-worth are being threatened."[98] Consequently, companies need to carefully choose a team compensation plan and then fully explain how teams will be rewarded. One basic requirement for team compensation to work is that the level of rewards (individual versus team) must match the level of performance (individual versus team).

Employees can be compensated for team participation and accomplishments in three ways: skill-based pay, gainsharing, and nonfinancial rewards. **Skill-based pay** programs pay employees for learning additional skills or knowledge.[99] These programs encourage employees to acquire the additional skills they will need to perform multiple jobs within a team and to share knowledge with others within their work groups.[100] For example, at the **Patience and Nicholson** (P&N) drill bit factory in Kaiapoi, New Zealand, workers produce 50,000 drill bits a day for export to Australia, Taiwan, Thailand, and other locations primarily in Asia. P&N uses a skill-based pay system. As employees learn how to run

the various machines required to produce drill bits, their pay increases. According to operations manager Rick Smith, workers who are dedicated to learning can increase their pay by $6 an hour over the course of three or four years.[101]

In **gainsharing** programs, companies share the financial value of performance gains, such as productivity increases, cost savings, or quality improvements, with their workers.[102] *Nonfinancial rewards* are another way to reward teams for their performance. These rewards, which can range from vacations to T-shirts, plaques, and coffee mugs, are especially effective when coupled with management recognition, such as awards, certificates, and praise.[103] Nonfinancial awards tend to be most effective when teams or team-based interventions, such as total quality management (see Chapter 18), are first introduced.[104]

Which team compensation plan should your company use? In general, skill-based pay is most effective for self-managing and self-directing teams performing complex tasks. In these situations, the more each team member knows and can do, the better the whole team performs. By contrast, gainsharing works best in relatively stable environments where employees can focus on improving productivity, cost savings, or quality.

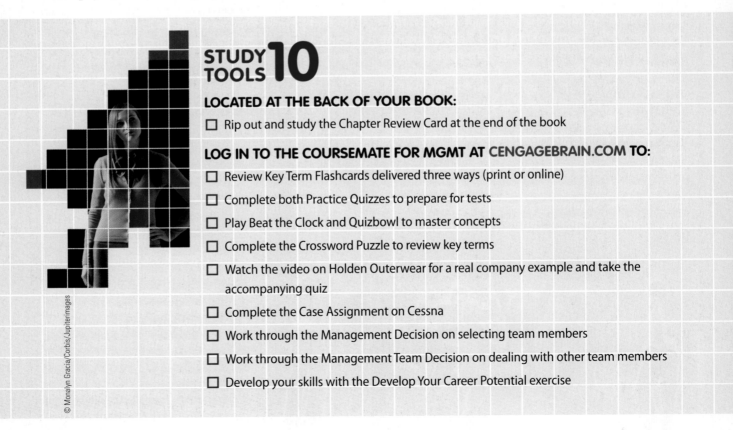

© Monalyn Gracia/Corbis/Jupiterimages

STUDY TOOLS **10**

LOCATED AT THE BACK OF YOUR BOOK:

☐ Rip out and study the Chapter Review Card at the end of the book

LOG IN TO THE COURSEMATE FOR MGMT AT CENGAGEBRAIN.COM TO:

☐ Review Key Term Flashcards delivered three ways (print or online)

☐ Complete both Practice Quizzes to prepare for tests

☐ Play Beat the Clock and Quizbowl to master concepts

☐ Complete the Crossword Puzzle to review key terms

☐ Watch the video on Holden Outerwear for a real company example and take the accompanying quiz

☐ Complete the Case Assignment on Cessna

☐ Work through the Management Decision on selecting team members

☐ Work through the Management Team Decision on dealing with other team members

☐ Develop your skills with the Develop Your Career Potential exercise

THE CR IN-WD

CROWD

Share your 4LTR Press story on Facebook at
www.facebook.com/4ltrpress for a chance to win.

To learn more about the
In-Crowd opportunity 'like'
us on Facebook.

11 Managing
Human Resource Systems

© Chris Whitehead/Cultura/Jupiterimages

Monalyn Gracia/Corbis/Jupiterimages

LEARNING OUTCOMES

11-1 Explain how different employment laws affect human resource practice.

11-2 Explain how companies use recruiting to find qualified job applicants.

11-3 Describe the selection techniques and procedures that companies use when deciding which applicants should receive job offers.

11-4 Describe how to determine training needs and select the appropriate training methods.

11-5 Discuss how to use performance appraisal to give meaningful performance feedback.

11-6 Describe basic compensation strategies and discuss the four kinds of employee separations.

CHECK OUT **STUDY TOOLS** AT THE END OF THIS CHAPTER.

11-1 *Employment Legislation*

Human resource management (HRM), or the process of finding, developing, and keeping the right people to form a qualified work force, is one of the most difficult and important of all management tasks. This chapter is organized around the three parts of the human resource management process shown in Exhibit 11.1: attracting, developing, and keeping a qualified work force.

This chapter will walk you through the steps of the HRM process. We explore how companies use recruiting and selection techniques to attract and hire qualified employees to fulfill human resource needs. The third part of the chapter discusses how training and performance appraisal can develop the knowledge, skills, and abilities of the work force. The chapter concludes with a review of compensation and employee separation; that is, how companies can keep their best workers through effective compensation practices and how they can manage the separation process when employees leave the organization.

Before we explore how human resource systems work, you need to understand better the complex legal environment in which they exist. So we'll begin the chapter by reviewing the federal laws that govern human resource management decisions.

Since their inception, Hooters restaurants have hired only female servers. Moreover, consistent with the company's marketing theme, the servers wear short nylon shorts and cutoff T-shirts that show their midriffs. The Equal Employment Opportunity Commission (EEOC) began an investigation of Hooters when a Chicago man filed a sex-based discrimination

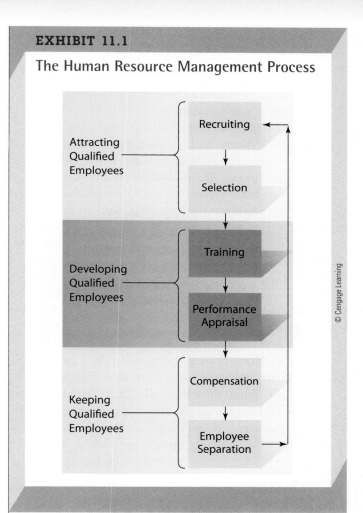

EXHIBIT 11.1

The Human Resource Management Process

© Cengage Learning

charge. The man alleged that he had applied for a server's job at a Hooters restaurant and was rejected because of his sex. The dispute between Hooters and

Human resource management (HRM) the process of finding, developing, and keeping the right people to form a qualified work force

the EEOC quickly gained national attention. One sarcastic letter to the EEOC printed in *Fortune* magazine read as follows:

> *Dear EEOC:*
>
> *Hi! I just wanted to thank you for investigating those Hooters restaurants, where the waitresses wear those shorty shorts and midriffy T-shirts. I think it's a great idea that you have decided to make Hooters hire men as—how do you say it?—waitpersons. Gee, I never knew so many men wanted to be waitpersons at Hooters. No reason to let them sue on their own either. You're right, the government needs to take the lead on this one.*[1]

This letter characterized public sentiment at the time. Given its backlog of 100,000 job discrimination cases, many wondered if the EEOC didn't have better things to do with its scarce resources.

Three years after the initial complaint, the EEOC ruled that Hooters had violated antidiscrimination laws and offered to settle the case if the company would agree to pay $22 million to the EEOC for distribution to male victims of the "Hooters Girl" hiring policy, establish a scholarship fund to enhance opportunities or education for men, and provide sensitivity training to teach Hooters employees how to be more sensitive to men's needs. Hooters responded with a $1 million publicity campaign criticizing the EEOC's investigation. Billboards featuring "Vince," a man dressed in a Hooters Girl uniform and blond wig, sprang up all over the country. Hooters customers were given postcards to send complaints to the EEOC. Of course, Hooters paid the postage. As a result of the publicity campaign, restaurant sales increased by 10 percent. Soon thereafter, the EEOC announced that it would not pursue discriminatory hiring charges against Hooters.[2] Nonetheless, the company ended up paying $3.75 million to settle a class-action suit brought by seven men who claimed that their inability to get a job at Hooters violated federal law.[3] Under the settlement, Hooters maintained its women-only policy for server jobs but had to create additional support jobs, such as hosts and bartenders, that would

Bona fide occupational qualification (BFOQ) an exception in employment law that permits sex, age, religion, and the like to be used when making employment decisions, but only if they are "reasonably necessary to the normal operation of that particular business." BFOQs are strictly monitored by the Equal Employment Opportunity Commission

also be open to men. The story doesn't end there, however, as a male applicant who wants to be a Hooters waitperson has sued Hooters, seeking to overturn the prior settlement, which would allow him to be only a host or bartender.[4]

As the Hooters example illustrates, the human resource planning process occurs in a very complicated legal environment. *Let's explore employment legislation by reviewing* **11-1a the major federal employment laws that affect human resource practice, 11-1b how the concept of adverse impact is related to employment discrimination**, *and* **11-1c the laws regarding sexual harassment in the workplace.**

11-1a FEDERAL EMPLOYMENT LAWS

Exhibit 11.2 lists the major federal employment laws and their websites, where you can find more detailed information. Except for the Family and Medical Leave Act and the Uniformed Services Employment and Reemployment Rights Act, which are administrated by the Department of Labor (http://www.dol.gov), all of these laws are administered by the EEOC (http://www.eeoc.gov). The general effect of this body of law, which is still evolving through court decisions, is that employers may not discriminate in employment decisions on the basis of sex, age, religion, color, national origin, race, or disability. The intent is to make these factors irrelevant in employment decisions. Stated another way, employment decisions should be based on factors that are "job related," "reasonably necessary," or a "business necessity" for successful job performance. The only time that sex, age, religion, and the like can be used to make employment decisions is when they are considered a bona fide occupational qualification.[5] Title VII of the 1964 Civil Rights Act says that it is legal to hire and employ someone on the basis of sex, religion, or national origin when there is a **bona fide occupational qualification (BFOQ)** that is "reasonably necessary to the normal operation of that particular business." A Baptist church hiring a new minister can reasonably specify that being a Baptist rather than a Catholic or Presbyterian is a BFOQ for the position. However, it's unlikely that the church could specify race or national origin as a BFOQ. In general, the courts and the EEOC take a hard look when a business claims that sex, age, religion, color, national origin, race, or disability is a BFOQ. For instance, the EEOC disagreed with Hooters's claim that it was "in the business of providing vicarious sexual recreation" and that "female sexuality is a bona fide occupational qualification."[6]

It is important to understand, however, that these laws apply to the entire HRM process and not just to selection decisions (e.g., hiring or promotion). These laws also cover all training and development activities, performance appraisals, terminations, and compensation decisions. Employers who use sex, age, race, or religion to make employment-related decisions when those factors are unrelated to an applicant's or employee's ability to perform a job may face charges of discrimination from employee lawsuits or the EEOC.

In addition to the laws presented in Exhibit 11.2, there are two other important sets of federal laws: labor laws and laws and regulations governing safety standards. Labor laws regulate the interaction between management and labor unions that represent groups of employees. These laws guarantee employees the right to form and join unions of their own choosing. For more information about labor laws, see the National Labor Relations Board at http://www.nlrb.gov.

The Occupational Safety and Health Act (OSHA) requires that employers provide employees with a workplace that is "free from recognized hazards that are causing or are likely to cause death or serious physical harm." This law is administered by the Occupational Safety and Health Administration (which, like the act, is referred to as OSHA). OSHA sets safety and health standards for employers and conducts inspections to determine whether those standards are being met. Employers who do not meet OSHA standards may be fined.[7] Even though it's well known that asbestos fiber causes cancer, AMD Industries in Cicero, Illinois, used untrained employees to remove asbestos from one of its facilities and did not provide safety training, protective gear, or a vacuum system

EXHIBIT 11.2

Summary of Major Federal Employment Laws

▪ Equal Pay Act of 1963	http://www.eeoc.gov/laws/statutes/epa.cfm	Prohibits unequal pay for males and females doing substantially similar work.
▪ Title VII of the Civil Rights Act of 1964	http://www.eeoc.gov/laws/statutes/titlevii.cfm	Prohibits employment discrimination on the basis of race, color, religion, gender, or national origin.
▪ Age Discrimination in Employment Act of 1967	http://www.eeoc.gov/laws/statutes/adea.cfm	Prohibits discrimination in employment decisions against persons age forty and older.
▪ Pregnancy Discrimination Act of 1978	http://www.eeoc.gov/laws/statutes/pregnancy.cfm	Prohibits discrimination in employment against pregnant women.
▪ Americans with Disabilities Act of 1990	http://www.eeoc.gov/laws/statutes/ada.cfm	Prohibits discrimination on the basis of physical or mental disabilities.
▪ Civil Rights Act of 1991	http://www.eeoc.gov/laws/statutes/cra-1991.cfm	Strengthened the provisions of the Civil Rights Act of 1964 by providing for jury trials and punitive damages.
▪ Family and Medical Leave Act of 1993	http://www.dol.gov/whd/fmla/index.htm	Permits workers to take up to twelve weeks of unpaid leave for pregnancy and/or birth of a new child, adoption or foster care of a new child, illness of an immediate family member, or personal medical leave.
▪ Uniformed Services Employment and Reemployment Rights Act of 1994	http://www.osc.gov/userra.htm	Prohibits discrimination against those serving in the Armed Forces Reserve, the National Guard, or other uniformed services; guarantees that civilian employers will hold and then restore civilian jobs and benefits for those who have completed uniformed service.

Disparate treatment
intentional discrimination that occurs when people are purposely not given the same hiring, promotion, or membership opportunities because of their race, color, sex, age, ethnic group, national origin, or religious beliefs

Adverse impact unintentional discrimination that occurs when members of a particular race, sex, or ethnic group are unintentionally harmed or disadvantaged because they are hired, promoted, or trained (or any other employment decision) at substantially lower rates than others

Four-fifths (or 80 percent) rule a rule of thumb used by the courts and the EEOC to determine whether there is evidence of adverse impact. A violation of this rule occurs when the selection rate for a protected group is less than 80 percent, or four-fifths, of the selection rate for a nonprotected group

Sexual harassment a form of discrimination in which unwelcome sexual advances, requests for sexual favors, or other verbal or physical conduct of a sexual nature occurs while performing one's job

Quid pro quo sexual harassment a form of sexual harassment in which employment outcomes, such as hiring, promotion, or simply keeping one's job, depend on whether an individual submits to sexual harassment

to limit exposure to asbestos dust. Because of these egregious safety violations, OSHA fined the company $1.2 million.[8]

For more information about OSHA, see http://www.osha.gov.

11-1b ADVERSE IMPACT AND EMPLOYMENT DISCRIMINATION

The EEOC has investigatory, enforcement, and informational responsibilities. Therefore, it investigates charges of discrimination, enforces the employment discrimination laws in federal court, and publishes guidelines that organizations can use to ensure they are in compliance with the law. One of the most important guidelines, jointly issued by the EEOC, the Department of Labor, the U.S. Justice Department, and the federal Office of Personnel Management, is the *Uniform Guidelines on Employee Selection Procedures*, which can be read in their entirety at http://www.ipacweb.org/files/ug.pdf. These guidelines define two important criteria, disparate treatment and adverse impact, which are used in determining whether companies have engaged in discriminatory hiring and promotion practices.

Disparate treatment, which is *intentional* discrimination, occurs when people, despite being qualified, are *intentionally* not given the same hiring, promotion, or membership opportunities as other employees because of their race, color, age, sex, ethnic group, national origin, or religious beliefs.[9] 3M reached a $3 million settlement for age discrimination with the EEOC after targeting older employees for layoffs and denying them the chance for leadership training.[10]

Legally, a key element of discrimination lawsuits is establishing motive, meaning that the employer intended to discriminate. If no motive can be established, then a claim of disparate treatment may actually be a case of adverse impact. **Adverse impact**, which is *unintentional* discrimination, occurs when members of a particular race, sex, or ethnic group are *unintentionally* harmed or disadvantaged because they are hired, promoted, or trained (or any other employment decision) at substantially lower rates than others. The courts and federal agencies use the **four-fifths (or 80 percent) rule** to determine if adverse impact has occurred. Adverse impact occurs if the decision rate for a protected group of people is less than four-fifths (or 80 percent) of the decision rate for a nonprotected group (usually white males). So, if one hundred white applicants and one hundred black applicants apply for entry-level jobs, and sixty white applicants are hired (60/100 = 60 percent), but only twenty black applicants are hired (20/100 = 20 percent), adverse impact has occurred (0.20/0.60 = 0.33). The criterion for the four-fifths rule in this situation is 0.48 (0.60 × 0.80 = 0.48). Since 0.33 is less than 0.48, the four-fifths rule has been violated.

Violation of the four-fifths rule is not an automatic indication of discrimination, however. If an employer can demonstrate that a selection procedure or test is valid, meaning that the test accurately predicts job performance or that the test is job related because it assesses applicants on specific tasks actually used in the job, then the organization may continue to use the test. If validity cannot be established, however, then a violation of the four-fifths rule may likely result in a lawsuit brought by employees, job applicants, or the EEOC itself.

11-1c SEXUAL HARASSMENT

According to the EEOC, **sexual harassment** is a form of discrimination in which unwelcome sexual advances, requests for sexual favors, or other verbal or physical conduct of a sexual nature occurs. From a legal perspective, there are two kinds of sexual harassment, quid pro quo and hostile work environment.[11]

Quid pro quo sexual harassment occurs when employment outcomes, such as hiring, promotion, or simply keeping one's job, depend on whether an individual submits to being sexually harassed. For example, in a quid pro quo sexual harassment lawsuit against First Student, a company that provides school bus transportation, four females alleged that a supervisor made explicit comments about their bodies and what he wanted to do to them. He was also alleged to have touched a female worker's breasts, exposed himself, and then rubbed himself against her. When his sexual advances were refused, he punished the women by cutting their work hours, while promising longer hours to the other women if they would do what he asked. This made it a quid pro quo case by linking sexual acts to economic outcomes.[12]

A **hostile work environment** occurs when unwelcome and demeaning sexually related behavior creates an intimidating, hostile, and offensive work environment. In contrast to quid pro quo cases, a hostile work environment may not result in economic injury. However, it can lead to psychological injury when the work environment becomes stressful. ABM Industries, a building maintenance company, agreed to pay $5.8 million for creating a sexually hostile work environment for twenty-one female janitors. The EEOC had charged that male employees exposed themselves and that the women were subject to unwelcome sexual advances. Moreover, when the women complained to management, they were ignored. One of the women said, "I asked for help and they wouldn't help me. Instead my supervisor would laugh at me even more."[13]

Finally, what should companies do to make sure that sexual harassment laws are followed and not violated?[14] First, respond immediately when sexual harassment is reported. A quick response encourages victims of sexual harassment to report problems to management rather than to lawyers or the EEOC. Furthermore, a quick and fair investigation may serve as a deterrent to future ha-

rassment. A lawyer for the EEOC says, "Worse than having no sexual harassment policy is a policy that is not followed. It's merely window dressing. You wind up with destroyed morale when people who come forward are ignored, ridiculed, retaliated against, or nothing happens to the harasser."[15]

Next, take the time to write a clear, understandable sexual harassment policy that is strongly worded, gives specific examples of what constitutes sexual harassment, spells outs sanctions and punishments, and is widely publicized within the company. This lets potential harassers and victims know what will not be tolerated and how the firm will deal with harassment should it occur.

Next, establish clear reporting procedures that indicate how, where, and to whom incidents of sexual harassment can be reported. The best procedures ensure that a complaint will receive a quick response, that impartial parties will handle the complaint, and that the privacy of the accused and accuser will be protected. At DuPont, Avon, and Texas Industries, employees can call a confidential hotline 24 hours a day, 365 days a year.[16]

Finally, managers should also be aware that most states and many cities or local governments have their own employment-related laws and enforcement agencies. So compliance with federal law is often not enough. In fact, organizations can be in full compliance with federal law and at the same time be in violation of state or local sexual harassment laws.

Hostile work environment a form of sexual harassment in which unwelcome and demeaning sexually related behavior creates an intimidating and offensive work environment

Recruiting the process of developing a pool of qualified job applicants

11-2 *Recruiting*

Gail Hyland-Savage, CEO of the real estate and marketing firm Michaelson, Connor & Boul, says, "Staffing is absolutely critical to the success of every company. To be competitive in today's economy, companies need the best people to create ideas and execute them for the organization. Without a competent and talented workforce, organizations will stagnate and eventually perish. The right employees are the most important resources of companies today."[17]

Recruiting is the process of developing a pool of qualified job applicants.

*Let's examine **11-2a what job analysis is and how it is used in recruiting, 11-2b how companies use internal recruiting, and 11-2c external recruiting to find qualified job applicants.***

Job analysis a purposeful, systematic process for collecting information on the important work-related aspects of a job

Job description a written description of the basic tasks, duties, and responsibilities required of an employee holding a particular job

Job specifications a written summary of the qualifications needed to successfully perform a particular job

11-2a JOB ANALYSIS AND RECRUITING

Job analysis is a "purposeful, systematic process for collecting information on the important work-related aspects of a job."[18] A job analysis typically collects four kinds of information:

- Work activities such as what workers do and how, when, and why they do it.
- The tools and equipment used to do the job.
- The context in which the job is performed, such as the actual working conditions or schedule.
- The personnel requirements for performing the job, meaning the knowledge, skills, and abilities needed to do a job well.[19]

Job analysis information can be collected by having job incumbents and/or supervisors complete questionnaires about their jobs, by direct observation, by interviews, or by filming employees as they perform their jobs.

Job descriptions and job specifications are two of the most important results of a job analysis. A **job description** is a written description of the basic tasks, duties, and responsibilities required of an employee holding a particular job. **Job specifications**, which are often included as a separate section of a job description, are a summary of the qualifications needed to successfully perform the job. Exhibit 11.3 shows a job description for a firefighter for the city of Portland, Oregon.

EXHIBIT 11.3

Job Description for a Firefighter for the City of Portland, Oregon

Yes, as a Firefighter you will fight fire and provide emergency medical services to your community. But it doesn't end there: your firefighting career offers you the opportunity to expand your skills to include Hazardous Materials Response, Specialty Response Teams (dive, rope rescue, confined space, etc.), Paramedic Care, Public Education and Information, Fire Investigation, and Fire Code Enforcement.

Teamwork

Professional Firefighters work as a team at emergency scenes. The work day also includes training, fire station and equipment maintenance, fire prevention activities, and public education. As a Firefighter, you must be in excellent physical condition to meet the demands of the job; this means you must work quickly, handling heavy equipment for long periods of time while wearing special protective gear in hot and hazardous environments. If you can meet the challenge of strenuous work and like the idea of helping people, consider applying for the position of Firefighter.

Work Schedule

Portland Fire & Rescue Firefighters work a 24-on/48-off shift. This means that Firefighters report to work at 8:00 a.m. the day of their shift and continue working until 8:00 a.m. the following morning. Our Firefighters then have the following two days (48 hours) off. Firefighters are required to work shifts on holidays and weekends. Portland Fire & Rescue also has 40-hour-a-week firefighters who work in Training, Inspections/Investigations, Public Education, Logistics, and Emergency Management. These positions are usually filled after a Firefighter has met the minimum requirements for these positions.

Source: Portland Fire and Rescue, accessed August 13, 2008, http://www.portlandonline.com/fire/index.cfm?a=haea&c=cgbil.

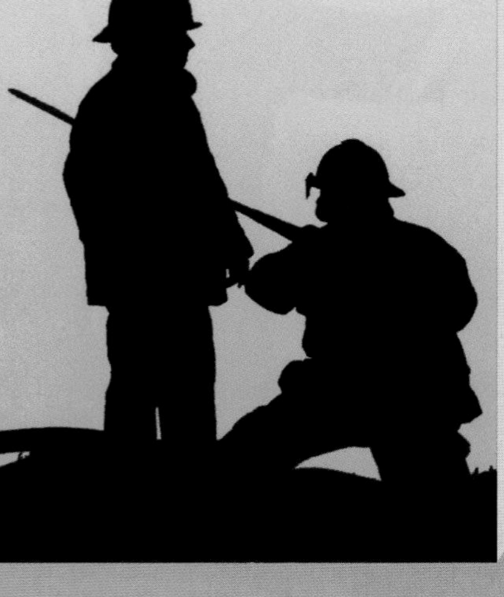

© iStockphoto.com/Kendall Griffin

Because a job analysis specifies what a job entails as well as the knowledge, skills, and abilities that are needed to do the job well, companies must complete a job analysis *before* beginning to recruit job applicants. Job analysis, job descriptions, and job specifications are the foundation on which all critical human resource activities are built. They are used during recruiting and selection to match applicant qualifications with the requirements of the job. Sioux Logan, of RedStream Technology, an IT staffing company, uses job descriptions to sort through the hundreds of applicants she gets for each job. She explains that when she narrows the pool to the best applicants, "I [will] resend the job description first by email [because] a lot of times people apply for many jobs without reading the whole job description." She does this to make sure they really want the job. Then she uses the subsequent email exchanges to judge applicants' professionalism and writing skills. By having applicants read and respond to the job description, Logan is giving them the opportunity to make the case to her that they are a good match for the job. The exchange of emails gives her one more way to make sure she's got the right person for the job.[20]

Job descriptions are also used throughout the staffing process to ensure that selection devices and the decisions based on these devices are job related. For example, the questions asked in an interview should be based on the most important work activities identified by a job analysis. Likewise, during performance appraisals, employees should be evaluated in areas that a job analysis has identified as the most important in a job.

Job analyses, job descriptions, and job specifications also help companies meet the legal requirement that their human resource decisions be job related. To be judged *job related*, recruitment, selection, training, performance appraisals, and employee separations must be valid and be directly related to the important aspects of the job, as identified by a careful job analysis. In fact, in *Griggs v. Duke Power Co.* and *Albemarle Paper Co. v. Moody*, the U.S. Supreme Court stated that companies should use job analyses to help establish the job relatedness of their human resource procedures.[21] The EEOC's *Uniform Guidelines on Employee Selection Procedures* also recommend that companies base their human resource procedures on job analysis.

11-2b INTERNAL RECRUITING

Internal recruiting is the process of developing a pool of qualified job applicants from people who already work in the company. Internal recruiting, sometimes called "promotion from within," improves employee commitment, morale, and motivation. Recruiting current employees also reduces recruitment start-up time and costs, and because employees are already familiar with the company's culture and procedures, they are more likely to succeed in new jobs. Internal recruitment "provides a higher level of employee satisfaction, so certainly it can be a retention driver," says Maureen Henson, vice president of human resources at Henry Ford Bi-County Hospital in Warren, Michigan. Internal applicants represent a "known commodity," relieving some of the risk of making a bad hiring decision.[22] Job posting and career paths are two methods of internal recruiting.

Job posting is a procedure for advertising job openings within the company to existing employees. A job description and requirements are typically posted on a bulletin board, in a company newsletter, or in an internal computerized job bank that is accessible only to employees. Shawna Swanson, an employment litigation partner with Fenwick & West in San Francisco, recommends making the internal and external processes the same, rather than having two separate paths, such as posting internally first for a period of time and then advertising externally.[23] Job posting helps organizations discover hidden talent, allows employees to take responsibility for career planning, and makes it easier for companies to retain talented workers who are dissatisfied in their current jobs and would otherwise leave the company.[24] Tim Reynolds, corporate director of talent and organization development at Whirlpool, the appliance manufacturer, said, "If employees aren't given the opportunity to move within their own company, then they'll get out in the marketplace to get new experiences. As long as they're developing where they are, there's no need to go someplace else."[25] Indeed, a study of seventy large global companies found that organizations that formalize internal recruiting and job posting have a lower average rate of turnover, 11 percent, compared to companies that don't, which average 15 percent turnover.[26]

A *career path* is a planned sequence of jobs through which employees may advance within an organization. Virginia Rometty, IBM's CEO, started as a systems engineer after studying computer science in college, worked in IBM's consulting division, became general manager for IBM's Global Insurance and Financial Services sector, and then became senior vice president of IBM

Internal recruiting the process of developing a pool of qualified job applicants from people who already work in the company

Global Business Services. Immediately prior to being named CEO, she served as the senior vice president of IBM's Global Sales and Distribution division and was responsible for overseeing sales in 170 global markets.[27]

Career paths help employees focus on long-term goals and development while also helping companies increase employee retention. As you can see in Virginia Rometty's case, career paths can also help employees gain a broad range of experience, which is especially useful at higher levels of management.

11-2c EXTERNAL RECRUITING

External recruiting is the process of developing a pool of qualified job applicants from outside the company. For example, Wal-Mart has traditionally promoted from within for store manager jobs. However, the company was unable to keep up with its growth. So Wal-Mart created an external recruiting program to find store managers from the ranks of junior military officers returning from Iraq and Afghanistan who typically led thirty to forty soldiers. According to Jennifer

Seidner, senior recruiting manager at Wal-Mart, this allowed the company to "[b]ring in world-class leadership talent that was already trained and ready to go. And then we could teach them retail, because we know that pretty well." The focus on veterans—company outsiders—is now a critical part of Wal-Mart's recruiting strategy in all parts of the company.[28]

External recruitment methods include advertising (newspapers, magazines, direct mail, radio, or television), employee referrals (asking current employees to recommend possible job applicants), walk-ins (people who apply on their own), outside organizations (universities, technical/trade schools, professional societies), employment services (state or private employment agencies, temporary help agencies, and professional search firms), special events (career conferences or job fairs), and Internet job sites. Which external recruiting method should you use? Studies show that employee referrals, walk-ins, newspaper advertisements, and state employment agencies tend to be used most frequently for office/clerical and production/service employees. By contrast, newspaper advertisements and college/university recruiting are used most frequently for professional/technical employees. When recruiting

© Brendan Hoffman/Getty Images

managers, organizations tend to rely most heavily on newspaper advertisements, employee referrals, and search firms.[29]

In the last decade, the biggest change in external recruiting has been the increased use of the Internet. Some companies now recruit applicants through Internet job sites such as Monster.com, HotJobs.com, Hire.com, and CareerBuilder.com. Companies can post job openings for thirty days on one of these sites for about half the cost of running an advertisement just once in a Sunday newspaper. Plus, Internet job listings generate nine times as many résumés as one ad in the Sunday newspaper.[30] And because these sites attract so many applicants and offer so many services, companies save by finding qualified applicants without having to use more expensive recruitment and search firms, which typically charge one-third or more of a new hire's salary.[31]

Some companies are even hosting virtual job fairs, where job applicants click on recruiting booths to learn about the company, see the kinds of available jobs, and speak with company representatives via video chat or instant message. Because they don't need to send HR representatives on long trips and can interact with potential hires from all over the world, Boeing, Progressive, Citibank, and Amazon.com have found virtual job fairs to be an efficient, cost-effective way to find qualified candidates. When Procter & Gamble conducted a virtual career fair, 900 participants from Eastern Europe, including Turkey, Russia, and Romania, interacted with twenty specialized recruiting booths to learn about jobs in finance, sales, or local P&G offices. Ioannis Boukas learned about the career fair on LinkedIn and logged in from Athens, Greece. His next step was an in-person career fair, which led to three on-site interviews and a job in Geneva, Switzerland as an assistant brand manager.[32]

11-3 *Selection*

Once the recruitment process has produced a pool of qualified applicants, the selection process is used to determine which applicants have the best chance of performing well on the job. At Boston Consulting Group (BCG), one of the world's premier consulting firms, a team of three recruiters examine résumés from thirty universities. Mel Wolfgang, a partner who heads American recruiting for BCG, says, "We look for well-rounded individuals whose interests and life experiences suggest that they would adapt well. We look for evidence that they have led and been em-

pathic with a team or challenging situations." Only six applicants are chosen for a forty-minute interview with two BCG consultants. From there, three applicants go on to second-round interviews with four BCG partners. After consulting with the consultants and partners who conducted interviews, the hiring manager makes the final decision.[33]

As this example illustrates, **selection** is the process of gathering information about job applicants to decide who should be offered a job. To make sure that selection decisions are accurate and legally defensible, the EEOC's *Uniform Guidelines on Employee Selection Procedures* recommend that all selection procedures be validated. **Validation** is the process of determining how well a selection test or procedure predicts future job performance. The better or more accurate the prediction of future job performance, the more valid a test is said to be.

Let's examine common selection procedures such as 11-3a application forms and résumés, 11-3b references and background checks, 11-3c selection tests, and 11-3d interviews.

11-3a APPLICATION FORMS AND RÉSUMÉS

The first selection devices that most job applicants encounter when they seek a job are application forms and résumés. Both contain similar information about an applicant, such as name, address, job and educational history, and so forth. Though an organization's application form often asks for information already provided by the applicant's résumé, most organizations prefer to collect this information in their own format for entry into a **human resource information system (HRIS)**.

Employment laws apply to application forms just as they do to all selection devices. Application forms may ask applicants only for valid, job-related information. Nonetheless, application forms commonly ask applicants for non-job-related information such as marital status, maiden name, age, or date of high school graduation. Indeed, one study found that 73 percent of organizations had application forms that

Selection the process of gathering information about job applicants to decide who should be offered a job

Validation the process of determining how well a selection test or procedure predicts future job performance. The better or more accurate the prediction of future job performance, the more valid a test is said to be

Human resource information system (HRIS) a computerized system for gathering, analyzing, storing, and disseminating information related to the HRM process

Employment references
sources such as previous employers or coworkers who can provide job-related information about job candidates

Background checks
procedures used to verify the truthfulness and accuracy of information that applicants provide about themselves and to uncover negative, job-related background information not provided by applicants

violated at least one federal or state law.[34] Exhibit 11.4 lists the kinds of information that companies may *not* request in application forms, during job interviews, or in any other part of the selection process. Courts will assume that you consider all of the information you request of applicants even if you actually don't. Be sure to ask only those questions that relate directly to the candidate's ability and motivation to perform the job.

Résumés also pose problems for companies, but in a different way. Accu-Screen Inc. has kept records for fourteen years on résumé falsification data and reports that approximately 43 percent of résumés and job applications contain false information. According to a study conducted by J.J. Keller & Associates, Inc., the nation's leading provider of risk and regulatory management solutions, 55 percent of human resource professionals have discovered lies on résumés or applications when conducting pre-employment background or reference checks.[35] Therefore, managers should verify the information collected via résumés and application forms by comparing it with additional information collected during interviews and other stages of the selection process, such as references and background checks, which are discussed next.

11-3b REFERENCES AND BACKGROUND CHECKS

Nearly all companies ask an applicant to provide **employment references**, such as the names of previous employers or coworkers, whom they can contact to learn more about the candidate. **Background checks** are used to verify the truthfulness and accuracy of information that applicants provide about themselves and to uncover negative, job-related background information not provided by applicants. Background checks are conducted by contacting "educational institutions, prior employers, court records, police and governmental agencies, and other informational sources, either by telephone, mail, remote computer access, or through in-person investigations."[36]

Unfortunately, previous employers are increasingly reluctant to provide references or background check information for fear of being sued by previous employees for defamation.[37] If former employers provide potential

EXHIBIT 11.4

Don't Ask! Topics to Avoid in an Interview

1. **Children.** Don't ask applicants if they have children, plan to have them, or have or need child care. Questions about children can unintentionally single out women.

2. **Age.** Because of the Age Discrimination in Employment Act, employers cannot ask job applicants their age during the hiring process. Since most people graduate high school at the age of eighteen, even asking for high school graduation dates could violate the law.

3. **Disabilities.** Don't ask if applicants have physical or mental disabilities. According to the Americans with Disabilities Act, disabilities (and reasonable accommodations for them) cannot be discussed until a job offer has been made.

4. **Physical characteristics.** Don't ask for information about height, weight, or other physical characteristics. Questions about weight could be construed as leading to discrimination toward overweight people, and studies show that they are less likely to be hired in general.

5. **Name.** Yes, you can ask an applicant's name, but you cannot ask a female applicant for her maiden name because it indicates marital status. Asking for a maiden name could also lead to charges that the organization was trying to establish a candidate's ethnic background.

6. **Citizenship.** Asking applicants about citizenship could lead to claims of discrimination on the basis of national origin. However, according to the Immigration Reform and Control Act, companies may ask applicants if they have a legal right to work in the United States.

7. **Lawsuits.** Applicants may not be asked if they have ever filed a lawsuit against an employer. Federal and state laws prevent this to protect whistleblowers from retaliation by future employers.

8. **Arrest records.** Applicants cannot be asked about their arrest records. Arrests don't have legal standing. However, applicants can be asked whether they have been convicted of a crime.

9. **Smoking.** Applicants cannot be asked if they smoke. Smokers might be able to claim that they weren't hired because of fears of higher absenteeism and medical costs. However, they can be asked if they are aware of company policies that restrict smoking at work.

10. **AIDS/HIV.** Applicants can't be asked about AIDS, HIV, or any other medical condition. Questions of this nature would violate the Americans with Disabilities Act, as well as federal and state civil rights laws.

Source: J. S. Pouliot, "Topics to Avoid with Applicants," *Nation's Business* 80, no. 7 (1992): 57.

employers with unsubstantiated information that damages applicants' chances of being hired, applicants can (and do) sue for defamation. As a result, 54 percent of employers will not provide information about previous employees.[38] Many provide only dates of employment, positions held, and date of separation.

When previous employers decline to provide meaningful references or background information, they put other employers at risk of *negligent hiring* lawsuits, in which an employer is held liable for the actions of an employee who would not have been hired if the employer had conducted a thorough reference search and background check.[39] Six people died when a tractor-trailer truck slammed into the side of an Amtrak passenger train in California after the truck's driver jammed on the brakes just 320 feet from the train crossing gates and flashing warning lights. Amtrak sued John Davis Trucking for $10 million for negligent hiring, alleging that it did not conduct a thorough background check, which would have revealed the driver's three speeding tickets in a four-year period along with an arrest for missing a court date for an expired vehicle registration.[40]

With previous employers generally unwilling to give full, candid references and with negligent hiring lawsuits awaiting companies that don't get such references and background information, what can companies do? They can conduct criminal record checks, especially if the job for which the person is applying involves money, drugs, control over valuable goods, or access to the elderly, people with disabilities, or people's homes.[41] According to the Society for Human Resource Management, 96 percent of companies conduct background checks and 80 percent of companies go further and conduct criminal record checks.[42] Now that companies provide criminal record checks

for $10 an applicant, pulling data from 3,100 court systems nationwide, there's no excuse to not check. Louis DeFalco, corporate director of safety, security and investigations at ABC Fine Wine & Spirits, which has 175 stores in Florida, makes the case for criminal record checks: "If I have a guy with four arrests and bad credit versus someone who has never been in trouble in his life, who am I going to hire? It's not rocket science."[43]

Another option is to use public networking sites like www.linkedin.com to identify and contact the colleagues, customers, and suppliers who are linked or connected to job applicants. LinkedIn's former CEO Dan Nye says that the company called twenty-three of his LinkedIn connections without his knowledge before offering him a face-to-face interview. With the growing use and popularity of social networking websites, Nye says such practices are "fair game." One downside to this approach is that it could unintentionally alert an applicant's current employer that the person is seeking another job. As a result, says Chuck Wardell, managing director at Korn/Ferry International, an executive recruitment firm, "You have to be careful referencing people who have jobs because you might blow them out of their jobs."[44]

After doing a background check, dig deeper for more information. Ask references to provide references. Voca Corporation, based in Columbus, Ohio, has 2,500 employees in six states who care for people with mental retardation and developmental disabilities. Hilary Franklin, director of human resources, says she not only checks references but also asks the references to provide references and then asks those references for still others. She says, "As you get two or three times removed, you get more detailed, honest information."[45]

Next, ask applicants to sign a waiver that permits you to check references, run a background check, or contact anyone else with knowledge of their work performance or history. Likewise, ask applicants if there is anything they would like the company to know or if they expect you to hear anything unusual when contacting references.[46] This in itself is often enough to get applicants to share information they typically withhold. When you've

---

What Would You Do?

Google is notorious for its quirky and challenging interview questions. While most companies ask applicants to describe their strengths and weaknesses or to talk about their most enriching work experience, interviewers at Google ask highly unusual questions that seem to have little to do with working for an information technology company. Below is a sample question from a Google interview. How would you answer it?

You are shrunk to the height of a nickel and thrown into a blender. Your mass is reduced so that your density is the same as usual. The blades start moving in sixty seconds. What do you do?

Source: W. Poundstone, "How to Ace a Google Interview," *Wall Street Journal*, December 24, 2011, accessed March 14, 2012, http://online.wsj.com/article/SB10001424052970204552304577112522982505222.html.

finished checking, keep the findings confidential to minimize the chances of a defamation charge. Always document all reference and background checks, noting who was called and what information was obtained. Document everything, not just information you received. To reduce the likelihood that negligent hiring lawsuits will succeed, it's particularly important to document even which companies and people refused to share reference checks and background information.

Finally, consider hiring private investigators to conduct background checks, which can often uncover information missed by traditional background checks. For example, while traditional background checks should be able to verify applicants' academic credentials, a private investigator hired by the *Wall Street Journal* found that seven out of 358 senior executives at publicly traded firms had falsified claims regarding the college degrees they had earned.[47]

11-3c SELECTION TESTS

Selection tests give organizational decision makers a chance to know who will likely do well in a job and who won't. The basic idea behind selection testing is to have applicants take a test that measures something directly or indirectly related to doing well on the job. The selection tests discussed here are specific ability tests, cognitive ability tests, biographical data, personality tests, work sample tests, and assessment centers.

Specific ability tests measure the extent to which an applicant possesses the particular kind of ability needed to do a job well. Specific ability tests are also called **aptitude tests** because they measure aptitude for doing a particular task well. For example, if you took the SAT to get into college, then you've taken the aptly named Scholastic Aptitude Test, which is one of the best predictors of how well students will do in college (i.e., scholastic performance). Specific

ability tests also exist for mechanical, clerical, sales, and physical work. For example, clerical workers have to be good at accurately reading and scanning numbers as they type or enter data. Exhibit 11.5 shows items similar to the Minnesota Clerical Test, in which applicants have only a short time to determine if the two columns of numbers and letters are identical. Applicants who are good at this are likely to do well as clerical or data entry workers.

Cognitive ability tests measure the extent to which applicants have abilities in perceptual speed, verbal comprehension, numerical aptitude, general reasoning, and spatial aptitude. In other words, these tests indicate how quickly and how well people understand words, numbers, logic, and spatial dimensions. Whereas specific ability tests predict job performance in only particular types of jobs, cognitive ability tests accurately predict job performance in almost all kinds of jobs.[48] Why is this so? The reason is that people with strong cognitive or mental abilities are usually good at learning new things, processing complex information, solving problems, and making decisions, and these abilities are important in almost all jobs.[49] In fact, cognitive ability tests are almost always the best predictors of job performance. Consequently, if you were allowed to use just one selection test, a cognitive ability test would be the one to use.[50] (In practice, though, companies use a battery of different tests because doing so leads to much more accurate selection decisions.)

© iStockphoto.com/FineCollection

EXHIBIT 11.5

Clerical Test Items Similar to Those Found on the Minnesota Clerical Test

	NUMBERS/LETTERS		SAME	
1.	3468251	3467251	Yes	No
			O	O
2.	4681371	4681371	Yes	No
			O	O
3.	7218510	7218520	Yes	No
			O	O
4.	ZXYAZAB	ZXYAZAB	Yes	No
			O	O
5.	ALZYXMN	ALZYXNM	Yes	No
			O	O
6.	PRQZYMN	PRQZYMN	Yes	No
			O	O

Source: N. W. Schmitt and R. J. Klimoski, *Research Methods in Human Resource Management* (Mason, OH: South-Western, 1991). Used with permission.

Biographical data, or **biodata**, are extensive surveys that ask applicants questions about their personal backgrounds and life experiences. The basic idea behind biodata is that past behavior (personal background and life experience) is the best predictor of future behavior. For example, during World War II, the U.S. Air Force had to test tens of thousands of men without flying experience to determine who was likely to be a good pilot. Since flight training took several months and was very expensive, quickly selecting the right people for training was important. After examining extensive biodata, it found that one of the best predictors of success in flight school was whether students had ever built model airplanes that actually flew. This one biodata item was almost as good a predictor as the entire set of selection tests that the Air Force was using at the time.[51]

Most biodata questionnaires have over one hundred items that gather information about habits and attitudes, health, interpersonal relations, money, what it was like growing up in your family (parents, siblings, childhood years, teen years), personal habits, current home (spouse, children), hobbies, education

and training, values, preferences, and work.[52] In general, biodata are very good predictors of future job performance, especially in entry-level jobs.

You may have noticed that some of the information requested in biodata surveys is related to those topics employers should avoid in applications, interviews, or other parts of the selection process. This information can be requested in biodata questionnaires provided that the company can demonstrate that the information is job related (i.e., valid) and does not result in adverse impact against protected groups of job applicants. Biodata surveys should be validated and tested for adverse impact before they are used to make selection decisions.[53]

Work sample tests, also called *performance tests*, require applicants to perform tasks that are actually done on the job. So, unlike specific ability tests, cognitive ability tests, biographical data surveys, and personality tests, which are indirect predictors of job performance, work sample tests directly measure job applicants' capability to do the job. For example, a computer-based work sample test for potential real estate agents has applicants assume the role of a real estate agent who must decide how to interact with virtual clients in a game-like scenario. As in real life, the clients can be frustrating, confusing, demanding, or indecisive. In one situation, the wife loves the virtual house, but the husband hates it. The applicants, just like actual real estate agents, must demonstrate what they would do in these realistic situations.[54] This work sample simulation gives real estate companies direct evidence of whether applicants can do the job if they are hired. Work sample tests are generally very good at predicting future job performance; however, they can be expensive to administer and can be used for only one kind of job. For example, an auto dealership could not use a work sample test for mechanics as a selection test for sales representatives.

Assessment centers use a series of job-specific simulations that are graded by multiple trained observers to determine applicants' ability to perform managerial work. Unlike the previously described selection tests that are commonly used for specific jobs

Biographical data (biodata) extensive surveys that ask applicants questions about their personal backgrounds and life experiences

Work sample tests tests that require applicants to perform tasks that are actually done on the job

Assessment centers a series of managerial simulations, graded by trained observers, that are used to determine applicants' capability for managerial work

Interview a selection tool in which company representatives ask job applicants job-related questions to determine whether they are qualified for the job

Unstructured interviews interviews in which interviewers are free to ask the applicants anything they want

or entry-level jobs, assessment centers are most often used to select applicants who have high potential to be good managers. Assessment centers often last two to five days and require participants to complete a number of tests and exercises that simulate managerial work.

Some of the more common assessment center exercises are in-basket exercises, role-plays, small-group presentations, and leaderless group discussions. An *in-basket exercise* is a paper-and-pencil test in which an applicant is given a manager's in-basket containing memos, phone messages, organizational policies, and other communications normally received by and available to managers. Applicants have a limited time to read through the in-basket, prioritize the items, and decide how to deal with each item. Experienced managers then score the applicants' decisions and recommendations. Exhibit 11.6 shows an item that could be used in an assessment center for evaluating applicants for a job as a store manager.

In a *leaderless group discussion*, another common assessment center exercise, a group of six applicants is given approximately two hours to solve a problem, but no one is put in charge (hence the name *leaderless* group discussion). Trained observers watch and score each participant on the extent to which he or she facilitates discussion, listens, leads, persuades, and works well with others.

Are tests perfect predictors of job performance? No, they aren't. Some people who do well on selection tests will do poorly in their jobs. Likewise, some people who do poorly on selection tests (and therefore weren't hired) would have been very good performers. Nonetheless, valid tests will minimize selection errors (hiring people who should not have been hired and not hiring people who should have been hired) while maximizing correct selection decisions (hiring people who should have been hired and not hiring people who should not have been hired). In short, tests increase the chances that you'll hire the right person for the job, that

is, someone who turns out to be a good performer. So, although tests aren't perfect, almost nothing predicts future job performance as well as the selection tests discussed here.

11-3d INTERVIEWS

In **interviews**, company representatives ask job applicants job-related questions to determine whether they are qualified for the job. Interviews are probably the most frequently used and relied on selection device. There are several basic kinds of interviews: unstructured, structured, and semistructured.

In **unstructured interviews**, interviewers are free to ask applicants anything they want, and studies show that they do. Because interviewers often disagree about which questions should be asked during interviews, different interviewers tend to ask applicants very different questions.[55] Furthermore, individual interviewers even seem to have a tough time asking the same questions from one interview to the next. This high level of variety can make things difficult. As a result, while unstructured interviews do predict job performance with some success, they are about half as accurate as structured interviews at predicting which job applicants should be hired.[56]

EXHIBIT 11.6

In-Basket Item for an Assessment Center for Store Managers

```
February 28
Sam & Dave's Discount Warehouse
Orange, California

Dear Store Manager,

Last week, my children and I were shopping in your store.
After doing our grocery shopping, we stopped in the
electronics department and asked the clerk, whose name
is Donald Block, to help us find a copy of the latest
version of the Madden NFL video game. Mr. Block was rude,
unhelpful, and told us to find it for ourselves as he
was busy.

I've been a loyal customer for over six years and expect
you to immediately do something about Mr. Block's
behavior. If you don't, I'll start doing my shopping
somewhere else.

Sincerely,
Margaret Quinlan
```

Source: Adapted from N. W. Schmitt and R. J. Klimoski, *Research Methods in Human Resource Management* (Mason, OH: South-Western 1991).

By contrast, with **structured interviews**, standardized interview questions are prepared ahead of time so that all applicants are asked the same job-related questions.[57] Structuring interviews also ensures that interviewers ask only for important, job-related information. Not only are the accuracy, usefulness, and validity of the interview improved, but the chances that interviewers will ask questions about topics that violate employment laws (see Exhibit 11.4) are reduced.

The primary advantage of structured interviews is that comparing applicants is much easier because they are all asked the same questions. Four kinds of questions are typically asked in structured interviews. Situational questions ask applicants how they would respond in a hypothetical situation ("What would you do if . . .?"). These questions are more appropriate for hiring new graduates, who are unlikely to have encountered real-work situations because of their limited work experience. Behavioral questions ask applicants what they did in previous jobs that were similar to the job for which they are applying ("In your previous jobs, tell me about . . ."). These questions are more appropriate for

hiring experienced individuals. Background questions ask applicants about their work experience, education, and other qualifications ("Tell me about the training you received at . . ."). Job-knowledge questions ask applicants to demonstrate their job knowledge (e.g., nurses might be asked, "Give me an example of a time when one of your patients had a severe reaction to a medication. How did you handle it?").[58]

Semistructured interviews lie between structured and unstructured interviews. A major part of the semi-structured interview (perhaps as much as 80 percent) is based on structured questions, but some time is set aside for unstructured interviewing to allow the interviewer to probe into ambiguous or missing information uncovered during the structured portion of the interview.

How well do interviews predict future job performance? Contrary to what you've probably heard, recent evidence indicates that even unstructured interviews do a fairly good job.[59] When conducted properly, however, structured interviews can lead to much more accurate hiring decisions than unstructured interviews. In some cases, the validity of structured interviews can rival that of cognitive ability tests.

Structured interviews
interviews in which all applicants are asked the same set of standardized questions, usually including situational, behavioral, background, and job-knowledge questions

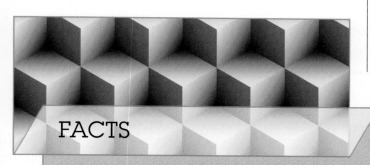

FACTS

Going into a job interview, you might think that your interviewers have done all the necessary prep work. They have a long list of questions that they'll use to find out about your intellect and character. They're willing to give 100 percent of their attention to finding the best person for the job. And, you hope, they are really excited at the chance to have a first meeting with the newest member of their team. You might think all these things, but chances are good that you'll be wrong, because your interviewers may in fact not have done much preparation at all. Here are ten myths that you should know about before heading into a job interview.

1. The interviewer is prepared.
2. Most interviewers have been trained to conduct thorough job interviews.
3. It's only polite to accept an interviewer's offer of a refreshment.
4. Interviewers expect you to hand over references' contact information right away.
5. There is a right answer to every question an interviewer asks.
6. You should always keep your answers short.
7. If you've got great qualifications, your appearance doesn't matter.
8. When asked where you see yourself in five years, you should show tremendous ambition.
9. If the company invites you to an interview, that means the job is still open.
10. The most qualified person gets the job.

Source: A. Fisher, "Top 10 Myths about Job Interviews," *CNNMoney.com*, November 18, 2010, accessed December 21, 2010, http://money.cnn.com/2010/11/18/news/economy/top_10_job_interview_myths.fortune/index.htm.

EXHIBIT 11.7

Guidelines for Conducting Effective Structured Interviews

Interview Stage	What to Do

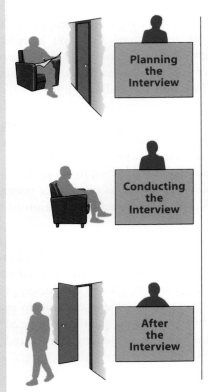

Planning the Interview

- Identify and define the knowledge, skills, abilities, and other (KSAO) characteristics needed for successful job performance.
- For each essential KSAO, develop key behavioral questions that will elicit examples of past accomplishments, activities, and performance.
- For each KSAO, develop a list of things to look for in the applicant's responses to key questions.

Conducting the Interview

- Create a relaxed, nonstressful interview atmosphere.
- Review the applicant's application form, résumé, and other information.
- Allocate enough time to complete the interview without interruption.
- Put the applicant at ease; don't jump right into heavy questioning.
- Tell the applicant what to expect. Explain the interview process.
- Obtain job-related information from the applicant by asking those questions prepared for each KSAO.
- Describe the job and the organization to the applicant. Applicants need adequate information to make a selection decision about the organization.

After the Interview

- Immediately after the interview, review your notes and make sure they are complete.
- Evaluate the applicant on each essential KSAO.
- Determine each applicant's probability of success and make a hiring decision.

Source: B. M. Farrell, "The Art and Science of Employment Interviews," *Personnel Journal* 65 (1986): 91–94.

But even more important, because interviews are especially good at assessing applicants' interpersonal skills, they work particularly well with cognitive ability tests. Combining the two—using structured interviews together with cognitive ability tests to identify smart people who work well with others—leads to even better selection decisions than using either alone.[60] Exhibit 11.7 provides a set of guidelines for conducting effective structured employment interviews.

11-4 *Training*

According to the American Society for Training and Development, a typical in-

vestment in training increases productivity by an average of 17 percent, reduces employee turnover, and makes companies more profitable.[61] Giving employees the knowledge and skills they need to improve their performance is just the first step in developing employees, however. The second step—and not enough companies do this—is giving employees formal feedback about their actual job performance.

Training means providing opportunities for employees to develop the job-specific skills, experience, and knowledge they need to do their jobs or improve their performance. American companies spend more than $60 billion a year on training. *To make sure those training dollars are well spent, companies need to **11-4a determine specific training needs, 11-4b select appropriate training methods**, and **11-4c evaluate training.***

Training developing the skills, experience, and knowledge employees need to perform their jobs or improve their performance

Needs assessment the process of identifying and prioritizing the learning needs of employees

11-4a DETERMINING TRAINING NEEDS

Needs assessment is the process of identifying and prioritizing the learning needs of employees. Needs assessments can be conducted by identifying performance deficiencies, listening to customer complaints, surveying employees and managers, or formally testing employees' skills and knowledge.

Note that training should never be conducted without first performing a needs assessment. Sometimes, training isn't needed at all or isn't needed for all employees. Unfortunately, however, many organizations simply require all employees to attend training whether they need to or not. As a result, employees who are not interested or don't need the training may react negatively during or after training. Likewise, employees who should be sent for training but aren't may also react negatively. Consequently, a needs assessment is an important tool for deciding who should or should not attend training. In fact, employment law restricts employers from discriminating on the basis of age, sex, race, color, religion, national origin, or disability when selecting training participants. Just like hiring decisions, the selection of training participants should be based on job-related information.

11-4b TRAINING METHODS

Assume that you're a training director for a major oil company and that you're in charge of making sure all employees know how to respond effectively in case of an oil spill.[62] Exhibit 11.8 on the next page lists a number of training methods you could use: films and videos, lectures, planned readings, case studies, coaching and mentoring, group discussions, on-the-job training, role-playing, simulations and games, vestibule training, and computer-based learning. Which method would be best?

To choose the best method, you should consider a number of factors, such as the number of people to be trained, the cost of training, and the objectives of the training. For instance, if the training objective is to impart information or knowledge to trainees, then you should use films and videos, lectures, and planned readings. In our example, trainees might read a manual or attend a lecture about how to protect a shoreline to keep it from being affected by the spill.

If developing analytical and problem-solving skills is the objective, then use case studies, coaching and mentoring, and group discussions. In our example, trainees might view a video documenting how a team handled exposure to hazardous substances, talk with first responders, and discuss what they would do in a similar situation.

If practicing, learning, or changing job behaviors is the objective, then use on-the-job training, role-playing, simulations and games, and vestibule training. In our example, trainees might participate in a mock shoreline cleanup to learn what to do in the event oil comes to shore. This simulation could take place on an actual shoreline or on a video game–like virtual shoreline.

If training is supposed to meet more than one of these objectives, then your best choice may be to combine one of the previous methods with computer-based

EXHIBIT 11.8

Training Objectives and Methods

TRAINING OBJECTIVE	TRAINING METHODS
Impart Information and Knowledge	• *Films and videos.* Films and videos present information, illustrate problems and solutions, and effectively hold trainees' attention.
	• *Lectures.* Trainees listen to instructors' oral presentations.
	• *Planned readings.* Trainees read about concepts or ideas before attending training.
Develop Analytical and Problem-Solving Skills	• *Case studies.* Cases are analyzed and discussed in small groups. The cases present a specific problem or decision, and trainees develop methods for solving the problem or making the decision.
	• *Coaching and mentoring.* Coaching and mentoring of trainees by managers involves informal advice, suggestions, and guidance. This method is helpful for reinforcing other kinds of training and for trainees who benefit from support and personal encouragement.
	• *Group discussions.* Small groups of trainees actively discuss specific topics. The instructor may perform the role of discussion leader.
Practice, Learn, or Change Job Behaviors	• *On-the-job training (OJT).* New employees are assigned to experienced employees. The trainee learns by watching the experienced employee perform the job and eventually by working alongside the experienced employee. Gradually, the trainee is left on his or her own to perform the job.
	• *Role-playing.* Trainees assume job-related roles and practice new behaviors by acting out what they would do in job-related situations.
	• *Simulations and games.* Experiential exercises place trainees in realistic job-related situations and give them the opportunity to experience a job-related condition in a relatively low-cost setting. The trainee benefits from hands-on experience before actually performing the job, where mistakes may be more costly.
	• *Vestibule training.* Procedures and equipment similar to those used in the actual job are set up in a special area called a "vestibule." The trainee is then taught how to perform the job at his or her own pace without disrupting the actual flow of work, making costly mistakes, or exposing the trainee and others to dangerous conditions.
Impart Information and Knowledge; Develop Analytical and Problem-Solving Skills; and Practice, Learn, or Change Job Behaviors	• *Computer-based learning.* Interactive videos, software, CD-ROMs, personal computers, teleconferencing, and the Internet may be combined to present multimedia-based training.

Source: A. Fowler, "How to Decide on Training Methods," *People Management* 25, no. 1 (1995): 36.

training. Siemens, which makes everything from power plants to electronic scanners, developed an online video game called Plantville, in which users take on the role of Pete, the plant manager. The goal is to revitalize three old factories by hiring new workers, redesigning fac- tory layouts, and replacing old machines with new ones from Siemens. Raj Batra, president of Siemens's Indus- try Automation division, says, "The virtual activity in Plantville mimics the real-world environment where plant managers continually watch key performance indicators and strive to maximize productivity and efficiency." Plantville's "hands-on" experience helps employees and outsiders better understand the intricacies of running a factory and serves not only as a training tool for employees but also as a recruiting tool for outsiders. Sign up to play and join 21,000 gamers from 160 countries at Plantville.com.[63]

These days, many companies are adopting Internet training, or "computer-based learning." E-learning can offer several advantages. Because employees don't need to leave their jobs, travel costs are greatly reduced. Also, because employees can take training modules when it is convenient (i.e., they don't have to fall behind at their jobs to attend week-long training courses), workplace productivity should increase and employee stress should decrease. And, if a company's technology infrastructure can support it, e-learning can be much faster than traditional training methods.

The training department of Dealer.com, a company that designs and manages car dealer websites to drive customer traffic to auto showrooms, spent fourteen months creating UFuel, the company's online training system. UFuel (for "fuel your own growth") allows employees to become certified on Dealer.com's products and services, and to take more than one hundred other courses from web design to Microsoft Office, all from the comfort of their desks. UFuel also helps new hires learn about the company's history, culture, and policies. And, to make sure that its employees understand their customers, car dealers, UFuel has a dealership simulation that presents its employees with common problems and situations facing dealerships. Matt Murray, the director of training, says, "We want them to see the world through the customer's eyes."[64]

There are, however, several disadvantages to e-learning. First, despite its increasing popularity, it's not always the appropriate training method. E-learning can be a good way to impart information, but it isn't always as effective for changing job behaviors or developing problem-solving and analytical skills. Second, e-learning requires a significant investment in computers and high-speed Internet and network connections for all employees. Finally, though e-learning can be faster, many employees find it so boring and unengaging that they may choose to do their jobs rather than complete e-learning courses when sitting alone at their desks. E-learning may become more interesting, however, as more companies

incorporate gamelike features such as avatars and competition into their e-learning courses.

11-4c EVALUATING TRAINING

After selecting a training method and conducting the training, the last step is to evaluate the training. Training can be evaluated in four ways: on *reactions* (how satisfied trainees were with the program), on *learning* (how much employees improved their knowledge or skills), on *behavior* (how much employees actually changed their on-the-job behavior because of training), or on *results* (how much training improved job performance, such as increased sales or quality, or decreased costs).[65] In general, training provides meaningful benefits for most companies if it is done well. For example, a study by the American Society for Training and Development shows that a training budget as small as $680 per employee can increase a company's total return on investment by 6 percent.[66]

11-5 *Performance Appraisal*

Performance appraisal is the process of assessing how well employees are doing their jobs. Most employees and managers intensely dislike the performance appraisal process. Among them is former Yahoo! CEO Carol Bartz. She says, "If I had

> **Performance appraisal**
> the process of assessing how well employees are doing their jobs

my way, I wouldn't do annual reviews. I think the annual review process is so antiquated. I almost would rather ask each employee to tell us if they've had a meaningful conversation with their manager this quarter. Yes or no. And if they say no, they ought to have one."[67]

Unfortunately, attitudes like this are all too common. In fact, 70 percent of employees are dissatisfied with the performance appraisal process in their companies. Likewise, according to the Society for Human Resource Management, 90 percent of human resource managers are dissatisfied with the performance appraisal systems used by their companies.[68]

Performance appraisals are used for four broad purposes: making administrative decisions (e.g., pay increase, promotion, retention), providing feedback for employee development (e.g., performance, developing career plans), evaluating human resource programs (e.g., validating selection systems), and for documentation purposes (e.g., documenting performance ratings and decisions based on those ratings).[69]

Let's explore how companies can avoid some of these problems with performance appraisals by 11-5a accurately measuring job performance and 11-5b effectively sharing performance feedback with employees.

11-5a ACCURATELY MEASURING JOB PERFORMANCE

Workers often have strong doubts about the accuracy of their performance appraisals—and they may be right. For example, it's widely known that assessors are prone to errors when rating worker performance. Three of the most common rating errors are central tendency, halo, and leniency. *Central tendency error* occurs when assessors rate all workers as average or in the middle of the scale. *Halo error* occurs when assessors rate all workers as performing at the same level (good, bad, or average) in all parts of their jobs. *Leniency error* occurs when assessors rate all workers as performing particularly well. One of the reasons managers make these errors is that they often don't spend enough time gathering or reviewing performance data. Winston Connor, the former vice president of human resources at Huntsman Chemical, says,

"Most of the time, it's just a ritual that managers go through. They pull out last year's review, update it and do it quickly."[70] What can be done to minimize rating errors and improve the accuracy with which job performance is measured? In general, two approaches have been used: improving performance appraisal measures themselves and training performance raters to be more accurate.

One of the ways companies try to improve performance appraisal measures is to use as many objective performance measures as possible. **Objective performance measures** are measures of performance that are easily and directly counted or quantified. Common objective performance measures include output, scrap, waste, sales, customer complaints, and rejection rates.

But when objective performance measures aren't available (and frequently they aren't), subjective performance measures have to be used instead. **Subjective performance measures** require that someone judge or assess a worker's performance. The most common kind of subjective performance measure is the graphic rating scale (GRS) shown in Exhibit 11.9. Graphic rating scales are most widely used because they are easy to construct, but they are very susceptible to rating errors.

A popular alternative to graphic rating scales is the **behavior observation scale (BOS)**. BOS requires raters to rate the frequency with which workers perform specific behaviors representative of the job dimensions that are critical to successful job performance. Exhibit 11.9 shows a BOS for two important job dimensions for a retail salesperson: customer service and money handling. Notice that each dimension lists several specific behaviors characteristic of a worker who excels in that dimension of job performance. (Normally, the scale would list seven to twelve items per dimension, not three, as in the exhibit.) Notice also that the behaviors are good behaviors, meaning they indicate good performance, and the rater is asked to judge how frequently an employee engaged in those good behaviors. The logic behind the BOS is that better performers engage in good behaviors more often.

Not only do BOSs work well for rating critical dimensions of performance, but studies also show that managers strongly prefer BOSs for giving performance feedback; accurately differentiating between poor, average, and good workers; identifying training needs; and accurately measuring performance. And in response to the statement, "If I were defending a company, this rating format would be an asset to my case,"

EXHIBIT 11.9

Subjective Performance Appraisal Scales

	Very poor	Poor	Average	Good	Very good
Graphic Rating Scale					
Example 1: Quality of work performed is	1	2	3	4	5

	Very poor (20% errors)	Poor (15% errors)	Average (10% errors)	Good (5% errors)	Very good (less than 5% errors)
Example 2: Quality of work performed is	1	2	3	4	5

Behavioral Observation Scale

Dimension: Customer Service

	Almost Never				Almost Always
1. Greets customers with a smile and a "hello."	1	2	3	4	5
2. Calls other stores to help customers find merchandise that is not in stock.	1	2	3	4	5
3. Promptly handles customer concerns and complaints.	1	2	3	4	5

Dimension: Money Handling

	Almost Never				Almost Always
1. Accurately makes change from customer transactions.	1	2	3	4	5
2. Accounts balance at the end of the day, no shortages or surpluses.	1	2	3	4	5
3. Accurately records transactions in computer system.	1	2	3	4	5

© Cengage Learning

attorneys strongly preferred BOSs over other kinds of subjective performance appraisal scales.[71]

The second approach to improving the measurement of workers' job performance is **rater training**. The most effective is frame-of-reference training, in which a group of trainees learn how to do performance appraisals by watching a videotape of an employee at work. Next, they evaluate the performance of the person in the videotape. A trainer (an expert in the subject matter) then shares his or her evaluations, and trainees' evaluations are compared with the expert's. The expert then explains the rationales behind his or her evaluations. This process is repeated until the differences in evaluations given by trainees and evaluations by the expert are minimized. The underlying logic behind the frame-of-reference training is that by adopting the frame of reference used by an expert, trainees will be able to accurately observe, judge, and use relevant appraisal scales to evaluate performance of others.[72]

11-5b SHARING PERFORMANCE FEEDBACK

After gathering accurate performance data, the next step is to share performance feedback with employees (see box "Rankings"). Unfortunately, even when performance appraisal ratings are accurate, the appraisal process often breaks down at the feedback stage. Employees become defensive and dislike hearing any

Rater training training performance appraisal raters in how to avoid rating errors and increase rating accuracy

360-degree feedback
a performance appraisal process in which feedback is obtained from the boss, subordinates, peers and coworkers, and the employees themselves

negative assessments of their work, no matter how small. Managers become defensive, too, and dislike giving appraisal feedback as much as employees dislike receiving it. One manager says, "I myself don't go as far as those who say performance reviews are inherently destructive and ought to be abolished, but I agree that the typical annual-review process does nothing but harm. It creates divisions. It undermines morale. It makes people angry, jealous, and cynical. It unleashes a whole lot of negative energy, and the organization gets nothing in return."[73]

What can be done to overcome the inherent difficulties in performance appraisal feedback sessions? Since performance appraisal ratings have traditionally been the judgments of just one person, the boss, one possibility is to use **360-degree feedback**. In this approach, feedback comes from four sources: the boss, subordinates, peers and coworkers, and the employees themselves. The data, which are obtained anonymously (except for the boss's), are compiled into a feedback report comparing the employee's self-ratings with those of the boss, subordinates, and peers and coworkers. Usually, a consultant or human resource specialist discusses the results with the employee. The advantage of 360-degree programs is that negative feedback ("You don't listen") is often more credible when it comes from several people.

Rankings

When it's annual review time at LendingTree, an online mortgage and loan company, all employees are ranked against each other. The top 15 percent of the employees are ranked as 1s, the middle 75 percent are ranked as 2s, and the bottom 10 percent are ranked as 3s. Though the 3s are not automatically fired or disciplined, they are clearly identified as the worst performers and are usually the first to go when downsizing is necessary. Critics of the ranking approach argue that some companies may not have any underperforming employees and that it doesn't make much sense to force people into a bottom tier. Proponents argue, however, that ranking employees helps employees understand that their position in the company is based on hard work and merit, and nothing else.

Source: L. Kwoh, "'Rank and Yank' Retains Vocal Fans," *Wall Street Journal*, January 31, 2012, B6.

Herbert Meyer, who has been studying performance appraisal feedback for more than thirty years, recommends a list of topics to discuss in performance appraisal feedback sessions (see Exhibit 11.10).[74] Furthermore, managers can do three different things to make performance reviews more comfortable and productive. First, they should separate developmental

© iStockphoto.com/iStock inhouse

EXHIBIT 11.10

What to Discuss in a Performance Appraisal Feedback Session

✔ Overall progress—an analysis of accomplishments and shortcomings.

✔ Problems encountered in meeting job requirements.

✔ Opportunities to improve performance.

✔ Long-range plans and opportunities— for the job and for the individual's career.

✔ General discussion of possible plans and goals for the coming year.

Source: H. H. Meyer, "A Solution to the Performance Appraisal Feedback Enigma," *Academy of Management Executive* 5, no. 1 (1991): 68–76.

feedback, which is designed to improve future performance, from administrative feedback, which is used as a reward for past performance, such as for raises. When managers give developmental feedback, they're acting as coaches, but when they give administrative feedback, they're acting as judges. These roles, coaches and judges, are clearly incompatible. As coaches, managers encourage, pointing out opportunities for growth and improvement, and employees are typically open and receptive to feedback. But as judges, managers are evaluative, and employees are typically defensive and closed to feedback.

Second, Meyer suggests that performance appraisal feedback sessions be based on self-appraisals, in which employees carefully assess their own strengths, weaknesses, successes, and failures in writing. Because employees play an active role in the review of their performance, managers can be coaches rather than judges. Also, because the focus is on future goals and development, both employees and managers are likely to be more satisfied with the process and more committed to future plans and changes. And, because the focus is on development and not admin-

istrative assessment, studies show that self-appraisals lead to more candid self-assessments than traditional supervisory reviews.[75]

Finally, what people do with the performance feedback they receive really matters. A study of 1,361 senior managers found that managers who reviewed their 360-degree feedback with an executive coach (hired by the company) were more likely to set specific goals for improvement, ask their bosses for ways to improve, and subsequently improve their performance.[76]

A five-year study of 252 managers found that their performance improved dramatically if they met with their subordinates to discuss their 360-degree feedback ("You don't listen") and how they were going to address it ("I'll restate what others have said before stating my opinion"). Performance was dramatically lower for managers who never discussed their 360-degree feedback with subordinates and for managers who did not routinely do so. Why is discussing 360-degree feedback with subordinates so effective? These discussions help managers understand their weaknesses better, force them to develop a plan to improve, and demonstrate to the subordinates the managers' public commitment to improving.[77] In short, it helps to have people discuss their performance feedback with others, but it particularly helps to have them discuss their feedback with the people who provided it. This is why HCL Technologies, an outsourcer of technology services, not only has employees rate their bosses but also posts each manager's ratings on the company intranet for everyone to see, in order to hold top managers accountable.[78]

11-6 Compensation and Employee Separation

At Penske Automotive Group, which has three hundred car dealerships worldwide, 8 percent of CEO Roger Penske's bonus is tied to keeping employee turnover below 31 percent. Pep Boys, a car parts retail chain, does the same, making 10 percent of its middle managers' pay contingent on low employee turnover. Likewise, ExlService Holdings, an India-based outsourcing company, links 30 percent of its lower-level managers' pay to employee turnover. Why link managers' pay to employee turnover? According to Tony Pordon, senior vice president at Penske Automotive, "We believe that employee turnover is a symptom of bigger problems at the dealership level."[79]

Compensation the financial and nonfinancial rewards that organizations give employees in exchange for their work

Employee separation the voluntary or involuntary loss of an employee

Job evaluation a process that determines the worth of each job in a company by evaluating the market value of the knowledge, skills, and requirements needed to perform it

Piecework a compensation system in which employees are paid a set rate for each item they produce

Commission a compensation system in which employees earn a percentage of each sale they make

Mark Royal, a consultant for the Hay Group, which specializes in employee compensation, further explains that linking managers' pay to turnover "is a recognition, on the one hand, of people as a driver of business success. It also reflects a recognition that turnover is costly."[80]

Compensation includes both the financial and the nonfinancial rewards that organizations give employees in exchange for their work. **Employee separation** is a broad term covering the loss of an employee for any reason. *Involuntary separation* occurs when employers terminate or lay off employees. *Voluntary separation* occurs when employees quit or retire. Because employee separations affect recruiting, selection, training, and compensation, organizations should forecast the number of employees they expect to lose through terminations, layoffs, turnover, or retirements when doing human resource planning.

Let's learn more about compensation by examining the 11-6a compensation decisions that managers must make as well as 11-6b termination, 11-6c downsizing, 11-6d retirement, and 11-6e turnover.

11-6a COMPENSATION DECISIONS

There are three basic kinds of compensation decisions: pay level, pay variability, and pay structure.[81]

Pay-level decisions are decisions about whether to pay workers at a level that is below, above, or at current market wages. Companies use job evaluation to set their pay structures. **Job evaluation** determines the worth of each job by determining the market value of the knowledge, skills, and requirements needed to perform it. After conducting a job evaluation, most companies try to pay the going rate, meaning the current market wage. There are always companies, however, whose financial situation causes them to pay considerably less than current market wages.

Some companies choose to pay above-average wages to attract and keep employees. *Above-market wages* can attract a larger, more qualified pool of job applicants, increase the rate of job acceptance, decrease the time it takes to fill positions, and increase the time that employees stay.[82] One of the best known examples of the power of above-market wages was Henry Ford, founder of Ford Motor, who doubled the pay of his workers in 1914 from $2.50 to $5 a day. Ford did this to combat an astronomical 380 percent rate of turnover, which forced him to hire 52,000 people a year to staff the company's 13,600 assembly jobs. But after he doubled wages, Ford was able to attract a much more qualified, reliable pool of job applicants. Employee turnover fell to 16 percent, and despite higher wages, Ford saw overall costs drop dramatically. With productivity skyrocketing, he was able to cut the price of Ford's Model T car by 10 percent a year for three straight years. And with more people able to buy Model Ts, Ford's profit doubled. Ford concluded that doubling wages "was one of the finest cost-cutting moves we ever made."[83]

Pay-variability decisions concern the extent to which employees' pay varies with individual and organizational performance. Linking pay to performance is intended to increase employee motivation, effort, and job performance. Piecework, sales commissions, profit sharing, employee stock ownership plans, and stock options are common pay-variability options. For instance, under **piecework** pay plans, employees are paid a set rate for each item produced up to some standard (e.g., thirty-five cents per item produced for output up to one hundred units per day). Once productivity exceeds the standard, employees are paid a set amount for each unit of output over the standard (e.g., forty-five cents for each unit above one hundred units). Under a sales **commission** plan, salespeople are paid a percentage of the purchase price of items they sell. The more they sell, the more they earn. At **Installation & Service Technologies**, which sells point-of-sales (high-tech cash registers) systems, a salespeople's pay is determined in large part by how much they sell. All members of the sales staff receive a small base salary (about 35 percent of total pay) and a commission based on how much gross profit they make on sales—17 percent for $1 to $50,000, 24 percent for $50,001 to $100,000, and 30 percent over $100,000. Plus, every time salespersons reach a new profit level, they receive an extra $1,000.[84]

Because pay plans such as piecework and commissions are based on individual performance, they can reduce the incentive that people have to work together. Therefore, companies also use group incentives (discussed in Chapter 10) and organizational incentives, such as profit sharing, employee stock ownership plans, and stock options, to encourage teamwork and cooperation.

With **profit sharing**, employees receive a portion of the organization's profits over and above their regular compensation. Chrysler posted a profit of $183 million in 2011—the first time that the company turned a profit since 1997. As a result, all hourly employees received profit sharing checks, on average, of $1,500.[85]

Employee stock ownership plans (ESOPs) compensate employees by awarding them shares of the company stock in addition to their regular compensation. Flynn Canada, a Toronto-based construction company, has grown from a small, family-owned, local roofing company in Winnipeg, Canada to a multimillion-dollar company with 3,000 employees across seventeen Canadian locations. Today, the company is owned by fifty-seven key managers. Doug Flynn, president and CEO, says, "If you had told me 10 years ago that Flynn would have 57 owners some day, I would have said, 'No way.' But now, looking over the last 10 years, I'm thoroughly convinced that we couldn't have grown the way we have if we didn't have our [ESOP] equity program."[86]

Stock options give employees the right to purchase shares of stock at a set price. Options work like this. Let's say you are awarded the right (or option) to buy one hundred shares of stock from the company for $5 a share. If the company's stock price rises to $15 a share, you can exercise your options, sell the stock for $15 a share, come out with $1,000. When you exercise your options, you pay the company $500 (one hundred shares at $5 a share), but, because the stock is selling for $15 in the stock market, you can sell your one hundred shares for $1,500 and make $1,000. Of course, as the company's profits and share values increase, stock options become even more valuable to employees. Stock options have no value, however, if the company's stock falls below the option

"grant price," the price at which the options have been issued to you. The options you have on one hundred shares of stock with a grant price of $5 aren't going to do you a lot of good if the company's stock is worth $2.50. Proponents of stock options argue that this gives employees and managers a strong incentive to work hard to make the company successful. If they do, the company's profits and stock price increase, and their stock options increase in value. If they don't, profits stagnate or turn into losses, and their stock options decrease in value or become worthless. To learn more about ESOPs and stock options, see the National Center for Employee Ownership (http://www.nceo.org).

The incentive has to be more than just a piece of paper, however. At Van Meter Industrial, based in Cedar Rapids, Iowa, some employees didn't know what stock was, let alone care about their ESOP program. One even said, "Why don't you just give me a couple hundred bucks for beer and cigarettes [instead]?"[87] So the company created an employee committee to educate their coworkers about how the ESOP program works, meeting with workers in small groups where it's safe to ask questions, and emphasizing, for example, that the company contributes the equivalent of nine and a half weeks of their pay into each employee ESOP each year. Also, employees reaching their six-month anniversary are given a jacket with the words "I am in" written on it to emphasize that they're now part of the ESOP. As a result of these efforts, Van Meter Industrial's workers now take a strong interest in what they can do to

© iStockphoto.com/Valentin Mosichev

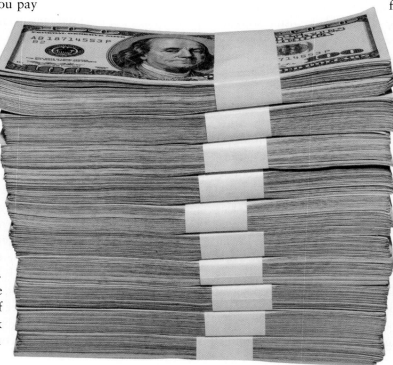

Profit sharing a compensation system in which a company pays a percentage of its profits to employees in addition to their regular compensation

Employee stock ownership plan (ESOP) a compensation system that awards employees shares of company stock in addition to their regular compensation

Stock options a compensation system that gives employees the right to purchase shares of stock at a set price, even if the value of the stock increases above that price save the company money on a daily basis because, as the company becomes more profitable, the value of their ESOP shares rises. Although Van Meter's stock value was barely keeping up with inflation before this program, it increased 78 percent after the program was implemented.[88]

Pay-structure decisions are concerned with internal pay distributions, meaning the extent to which people in the company receive very different levels of pay.[89] With *hierarchical pay structures,* there are big differences from one pay level to another. The highest pay levels are for people near the top of the pay distribution. The basic idea behind hierarchical pay structures is that large differences in pay between jobs or organizational levels should motivate people to work harder to obtain those higher-paying jobs. Many publicly owned companies have hierarchical pay structures, paying huge salaries to their top managers and CEOs. For example, the average CEO now makes $1.4 million per year, which is 343 times the average employee salary of $33,190. This huge difference can have a significant detrimental impact on employee morale.[90]

By contrast, *compressed pay structures* typically have fewer pay levels and smaller differences in pay between levels. Pay is less dispersed and more similar across jobs in the company. The basic idea behind compressed pay structures is that similar pay levels should lead to higher levels of cooperation, feelings of fairness and a common purpose, and better group and team performance.

So should companies choose hierarchical or compressed pay structures? The evidence isn't straightforward, but studies seem to indicate that there are significant problems with the hierarchical approach. The most damaging finding is that there appears to be little link between organizational performance and the pay of top managers.[91] Furthermore, studies of professional athletes indicate that hierarchical pay structures (e.g., paying superstars forty to fifty times as much as the lowest-paid athlete on the team) hurt the performance of teams and individual players.[92] Likewise, managers are twice as likely to quit their jobs when their companies have very strong hierarchical pay structures (i.e., when they're paid dramatically less than the people above them).[93] For now, it seems that hierarchical pay structures work best for independent work, where it's easy to determine the contributions of individual performers and little coordination with others is needed to get the job done. In other words, hierarchical pay structures work best when clear links can be drawn between individual performance and individual rewards. By contrast, compressed pay structures, in which everyone receives similar pay, seem to work best for interdependent work, which requires employees to work together. Some companies are pursuing a middle ground: combining hierarchical and compressed pay structures by giving ordinary workers the chance to earn more through ESOPs, stock options, and profit sharing.

11-6b TERMINATING EMPLOYEES

The words "You're fired!" may have never been directed at you, but lots of people hear them, as more than 400,000 people a year get fired from their jobs. Getting fired is a terrible thing, but many managers make it even worse by bungling the firing process, needlessly provoking the person who was fired and unintentionally inviting lawsuits. Manager Craig Silverman had to fire the head of a company whom his organization had just acquired. He was specifically instructed to invite her to a meeting, which would require her to travel halfway across the country, and then fire her immediately on arrival. He said, "I literally had to tell the car service to wait. I don't think it ever entered [her] mind that [she] would be terminated."[94] A computer systems engineer was fired on "Take Your Daughter to Work Day," with his eight-year-old daughter sitting next to him in the human resource manager's office. He and his daughter were both escorted from the building.[95] Four hundred employees at the Fort Worth headquarters of RadioShack got the following email message: "The work force reduction notification is currently in progress. Unfortunately your position is one that has been eliminated."[96] How would you feel if you had been fired in one of these ways? Though firing is never pleasant (and managers hate firings nearly as much as employees do), managers can do several things to minimize the problems inherent in firing employees.

To start, in most situations, firing should not be the first option. Instead, employees should be given a chance to change their behavior. When problems arise, employees should have ample warning and must be specifically informed as to the nature and seriousness of the trouble they're in. After being notified, they should be given sufficient time to change their behavior. Mitch McLeod, owner of Arcos Inc., a software company based in Columbus, Ohio, was frustrated with his best software engineer, who always showed up late to work with bizarre excuses, such as that his cat hid his car keys. McLeod could have fired him but instead decided to switch his schedule so that he could start later in the day. With the later start time, the engineer was never late again. And, because McLeod worked with him and gave him the chance to change, he was able to keep a top performer.[97]

If problems continue, the employees should again be counseled about their job performance, what could be done to improve it, and the possible consequences if things don't change (such as a written reprimand, suspension without pay, or firing). Sometimes this is enough to solve the problem. If the problem isn't corrected after several rounds of warnings and discussions, however, the employee may be terminated.[98]

Second, employees should be fired only for a good reason. Employers used to hire and fire employees under the legal principle of employment at will, which allowed them to fire employees for a good reason, a bad reason, or no reason at all. (Employees could also quit for a good reason, a bad reason, or no reason whenever they desired.) As employees began contesting their firings in court, however, the principle of wrongful discharge emerged. **Wrongful discharge** is a legal doctrine that requires employers to have a job-related reason to terminate employees. In other words, like other major human resource decisions, termination decisions should be made on the basis of job-related factors such as violating company rules or consistently poor performance. And with former employees winning 68 percent of wrongful discharge cases and the average wrongful termination award at $532,000 and climbing, managers should record the job-related reasons for the termination, document specific instances of rule violations or continued poor performance, and keep notes and documents from the counseling sessions held with employees.[99]

11-6c DOWNSIZING

Downsizing is the planned elimination of jobs in a company (see box "How to Conduct Layoffs"). Whether it's because of cost cutting, declining market share, previous overaggressive hiring and growth, or outsourcing, companies typically eliminate 1 million to 1.9 million jobs a year.[100] Two-thirds of companies that downsize will downsize a second time within a year. In 2010, Hewlett-Packard laid off 9,000 employees in its enterprise service division, which provided consulting, outsourcing, and technology services. Just a year later, HP announced another round of layoffs, this time eliminating 500 jobs at its webOS mobile computing division after deciding to close its personal computer tablet division following poor sales.[101]

Does downsizing work? In theory, downsizing is supposed to lead to higher productivity and profits, better stock performance, and increased organizational flexibility. However, numerous studies demonstrate that it doesn't. For instance, a fifteen-year study of downsizing found that downsizing 10 percent of a company's work force produced only a 1.5 percent

How to Conduct Layoffs

1. Provide clear reasons and explanations for the layoffs.
2. To avoid laying off employees with critical or irreplaceable skills, knowledge, and expertise, get input from human resources, the legal department, and several levels of management.
3. Train managers in how to tell employees that they are being laid off (i.e., stay calm; make the meeting short; explain why but don't be personal; and provide information about immediate concerns such as benefits, finding a new job, and collecting personal goods).
4. Give employees the bad news early in the day, and try to avoid laying off employees before holidays.
5. Provide outplacement services and counseling to help laid-off employees find new jobs.
6. Communicate with employees who have not been laid off to explain how the company and their jobs will change.

Source: M. Boyle, "The Not-So-Fine Art of the Layoff," *Fortune*, March 19, 2001, 209.

decrease in costs; that firms that downsized increased their stock price by only 4.7 percent over three years, compared with 34.3 percent for firms that didn't; and that profitability and productivity were generally not improved by downsizing.[102] Downsizing can also result in the loss of skilled workers who would be expensive to replace when the company grows again.[103] These results make it clear that the best strategy is to conduct effective human resource planning and avoid downsizing altogether. Indeed, downsizing should always be a last resort.

If companies do find themselves in financial or strategic situations where downsizing is required for survival, however, they should train managers in how to break the news to downsized employees, have senior managers explain in detail why downsizing is necessary, and time the announcement so that employees hear it from the company and not from other sources, such as TV or newspaper reports.[104] Finally, companies should do everything they can to help downsized employees find other jobs. One of the best ways to do this is to use **outplacement services** that provide employment counseling for employees faced with downsizing. Outplacement services often include advice and training in preparing résumés, getting ready for job interviews, and even identifying job opportunities in other companies. Fifty-five percent of companies provide outplacement services for laid-off employees, 76 percent provide extended health coverage, and 45 percent offer extended access to employee assistance programs.[105]

Companies also need to pay attention to the survivors, the employees remaining after layoffs have occurred. University of Pennsylvania management professor Peter Cappelli says that survivors "may feel like they could just as easily be the next person laid off."[106] Lori Stewart Coletti, director of client services at Elaine Construction, a Newton, Massachusetts–based firm, said, "The general feeling is, 'Could I be next?' That's the level of uncertainty that you really have to combat."[107] The key to working with layoff survivors, according to Barry Nickerson, president of Dallas-based Marlow Industries, which downsized from 800 to 200 employees, is "Communicate. Communicate. Communicate." Nickerson says, "Every time we had a change we had a meeting to explain exactly what we were doing. We were very open with our employees about where we were financially. We would explain exactly the current status and where we were."[108]

11-6d RETIREMENT

Early retirement incentive programs (ERIPs) offer financial benefits to employees to encourage them to retire early. Companies use ERIPs to reduce the number of employees in the organization, to lower costs by eliminating positions after employees retire, to lower costs by replacing high-paid retirees with lower-paid, less-experienced employees, or to create openings and job opportunities for people inside the company. For example, the state of Wyoming offered its employees a lump-sum bonus, additional insurance benefits, and increased monthly retirement payments to encourage early retirement. Its ERIP must have been fairly attractive, because 56 percent of the state employees eligible for early retirement accepted. Thirty percent of the 437 positions vacated by the early retirees remained empty, saving the state $23.2 million over the first forty-six months of the program and a projected $65 million over eight years. After accounting for the costs of the increased early retirement benefits, the predicted savings came to more than $148,000 per retiree.[109]

Although ERIPs can save companies money, they can pose a big problem for managers if they fail to accurately predict which employees—the good performers or the poor performers—and how many will retire early. Consultant Ron Nicol says, "The thing that doesn't work is just asking for volunteers. You get the wrong volunteers. Some of your best people will feel they can get a job anywhere. Or you have people who are close to retirement and are a real asset to the company."[110] When Progress Energy, in Raleigh, North Carolina, identified 450 jobs it wanted to eliminate with an ERIP, it carefully shared the list of jobs with employees, indicated that layoffs would follow if not enough people took early retirement, and then held eighty meetings with employees to answer questions. Despite this care, an extra 1,000 employees, for a total of 1,450, took the ERIP offer and applied for early retirement![111]

Because of the problems associated with ERIPs, many companies are now offering **phased retirement**, in which employees transition to retirement by working reduced hours over a period of time before completely retiring. The advantage for employees is that they have more free time but continue to earn salaries and benefits without changing companies or careers. The advantage for companies is that it allows them to reduce salaries and hiring and training costs and retain experienced, valuable workers.[112]

11-6e EMPLOYEE TURNOVER

Employee turnover is the loss of employees who voluntarily choose to leave the company. In general, most companies try to keep the rate of employee turnover low to reduce recruiting, hiring, training, and replacement costs. Not all kinds of employee turnover are bad for organizations, however. In fact, some turnover can actually be good. **Functional turnover** is the loss of poor-performing employees who choose to leave the organization.[113] Functional turnover gives the organization a chance to replace poor performers with better workers. In fact, one study found that simply replacing poor-performing workers with average workers would increase the revenues produced by retail salespeople in an upscale department store by $112,000 per person per year.[114] By contrast, **dysfunctional turnover**, the loss of high performers who choose to leave, is a costly loss to the organization.

Employee turnover should be carefully analyzed to determine whether good or poor performers are choosing to leave the organization. If the company is losing too many high performers, managers should determine the reasons and find ways to reduce the loss of valuable employees. The company may have to raise salary levels, offer enhanced benefits, or improve working conditions to retain skilled workers. One of the best ways to influence functional and dysfunctional turnover is to link pay directly to performance. A study of four sales forces found that when pay was strongly linked to performance via sales commissions and bonuses, poor performers were much more likely to leave (that is, functional turnover). By contrast, poor performers were much more likely to stay when paid large, guaranteed monthly salaries and small sales commissions and bonuses.[115]

Employee turnover loss of employees who voluntarily choose to leave the company

Functional turnover loss of poor-performing employees who voluntarily choose to leave a company

Dysfunctional turnover loss of high-performing employees who voluntarily choose to leave a company

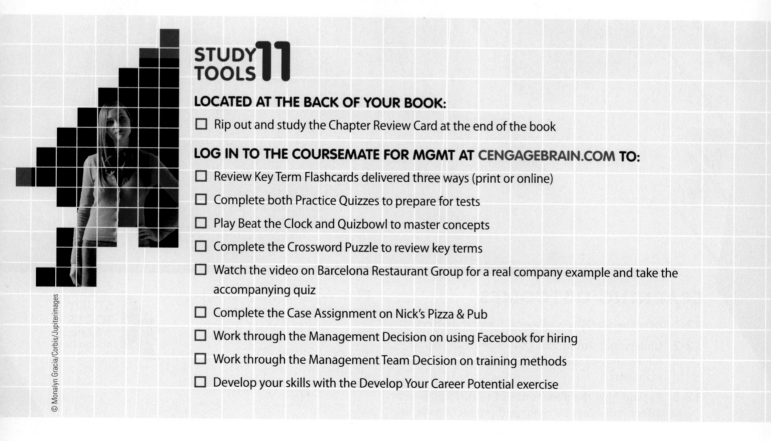

© Monalyn Gracia/Corbis/Jupiterimages

STUDY TOOLS 11

LOCATED AT THE BACK OF YOUR BOOK:

☐ Rip out and study the Chapter Review Card at the end of the book

LOG IN TO THE COURSEMATE FOR MGMT AT CENGAGEBRAIN.COM TO:

☐ Review Key Term Flashcards delivered three ways (print or online)

☐ Complete both Practice Quizzes to prepare for tests

☐ Play Beat the Clock and Quizbowl to master concepts

☐ Complete the Crossword Puzzle to review key terms

☐ Watch the video on Barcelona Restaurant Group for a real company example and take the accompanying quiz

☐ Complete the Case Assignment on Nick's Pizza & Pub

☐ Work through the Management Decision on using Facebook for hiring

☐ Work through the Management Team Decision on training methods

☐ Develop your skills with the Develop Your Career Potential exercise

12 Managing
Individuals and a Diverse Work Force

© Adrian Weinbrecht/Cultura/Jupiterimages

LEARNING OUTCOMES

12-1 Describe diversity and explain why it matters.

12-2 Understand the special challenges that the dimensions of surface-level diversity pose for managers.

12-3 Explain how the dimensions of deep-level diversity affect individual behavior and interactions in the workplace.

12-4 Explain the basic principles and practices that can be used to manage diversity.

CHECK OUT
STUDY TOOLS
AT THE END OF
THIS CHAPTER.

12-1 *Diversity: Differences That Matter*

Workplace diversity as we know it is changing. Exhibit 12.1 shows predictions from the U.S. Bureau of the Census of how the U.S. population will change over the next forty years. The percentage of white, non-Hispanic Americans in the general population is expected to decline from 64.7 percent in 2010 to 46.3 percent by 2050. Similarly, the percentage of black Americans will decrease (from 12.2 percent to 11.8 percent). By contrast, the percentage of Asian Americans will increase (from 4.5 percent to 7.6 percent). Meanwhile, the proportion of Native Americans will hold steady at 0.8 percent. The fastest-growing group by far, though, will be Hispanics, who are expected to increase from 16 percent of the total population in 2010 to 30.3 percent by 2050. Other significant changes have already occurred. For example, today women hold

EXHIBIT 12.1

Percent of the Projected Population by Race and Hispanic Origin for the United States: 2010 to 2050

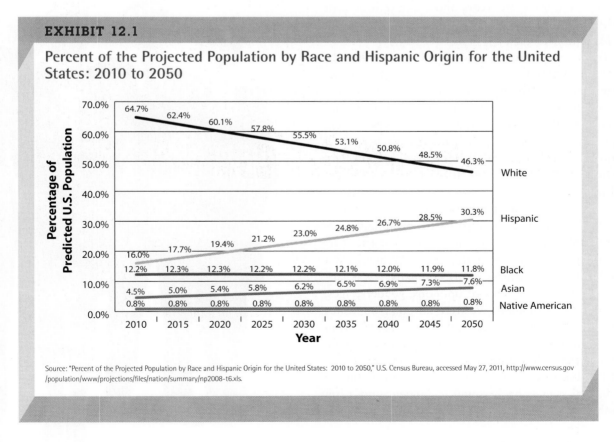

Source: "Percent of the Projected Population by Race and Hispanic Origin for the United States: 2010 to 2050," U.S. Census Bureau, accessed May 27, 2011, http://www.census.gov /population/www/projections/files/nation/summary/np2008-t6.xls.

Diversity a variety of demographic, cultural, and personal differences among an organization's employees and customers

Affirmative action purposeful steps taken by an organization to create employment opportunities for minorities and women

46.5 percent of the jobs in the United States, up from 38.2 percent in 1970.[1] Furthermore, white males, who composed 63.9 percent of the work force in 1950, hold just 38.2 percent of today's jobs.[2]

These rather dramatic changes have taken place in a relatively short time. And, as these trends clearly show, the work force of the near future will be increasingly Hispanic, Asian American, and female. It will also be older, as the average Baby Boomer approaches the age of seventy around 2020. Since many Boomers are likely to postpone retirement and work well into their seventies to offset predicted reductions in Social Security and Medicare benefits, the work force may become even older than expected. For instance, between 1984 and 2014, sixteen- to twenty-four-year-olds (21.1 percent to 13.7 percent), twenty-five- to thirty-four-year-olds (28.8 percent to 22.7 percent), and thirty-five- to forty-four-year-olds (22 percent to 20.6 percent) will have become a smaller part of the U.S. labor force. By contrast, those forty-five years and older (28.1 percent to 43.1 percent), fifty-five years and older (13.1 percent to 21.2 percent), and sixty-five years and older (2.6 percent to 5.4 percent) will all have become larger parts of the U.S. labor force.[3]

Diversity means variety. Therefore, **diversity** exists in organizations when there is a variety of demographic, cultural, and personal differences among the people who work there and the customers who do business there. For example, because Kayak.com, a travel search engine, works with airlines, car rental companies, and hotels all over the world, CEO Paul English hired German, Greek, Russian, Italian, French, and Indian employees to address the different needs, cultures, and languages represented in its customer base.[4] Likewise, diversity also means personality differences. Sharon Nunes, vice president of Smarter Cities Strategy & Solutions at IBM, says, "When I led a new health-care business at my company, I was surrounded by a crazy quilt of opinions, genders, ages, and schools of thought. We were all polar opposites and strongly opinionated, and styles ranged from those of a 'show me' marketing exec to a pragmatic mathematician. It was a living lab of personality types, and I had to force myself outside the comfort zone of my logical science background to influence my team members, when to speak up or push back, and to use our time together more for working and less for sparring."[5]

You'll begin your exploration of diversity by learning **12-1a** *that diversity is not affirmative action and* **12-1b** *that diversity makes good business sense.*

12-1a DIVERSITY IS NOT AFFIRMATIVE ACTION

A common misconception is that workplace diversity and affirmative action are the same, yet these concepts differ in several critical ways, including their purpose, how they are practiced, and the reactions they produce. To start, **affirmative action** refers to purposeful steps taken by an organization to create employment opportunities for minorities and women.[6] By contrast, diversity has a broader focus that includes demographic, cultural, and personal differences.

A second difference is that affirmative action is a policy for actively creating diversity, but diversity can exist even if organizations don't take purposeful steps to create it. A local restaurant located near a university in a major city is likely to have a more diverse

© iStockphoto.com/Lise Gagne

group of employees than one located in a small town. So, organizations can achieve diversity without affirmative action. Conversely, affirmative action does not guarantee diversity. An organization can create employment opportunities for women and minorities yet not have a diverse work force.

A third important difference is that affirmative action is required by law for private employers with fifty or more employees, whereas diversity is not. Affirmative action originated with Executive Order 11246 (http://www.dol.gov/ofccp/regs/compliance/fs11246 .htm) but is also related to the 1964 Civil Rights Act, which bans discrimination in voting, public places, federal government programs, federally supported public education, and employment. Title VII of the Civil Rights Act (http://www.eeoc.gov/policy/vii .html) requires that workers have equal employment opportunities when being hired or promoted. More specifically, Title VII prohibits companies from discriminating on the basis of race, color, religion, sex, or national origin. Title VII also created the Equal Employment Opportunity Commission, or EEOC (http:// www.eeoc.gov), to administer these laws. By contrast, there is no federal law or agency to oversee diversity. Organizations that pursue diversity goals and programs do so voluntarily. "Until recently, the commitment many companies had to diversity was fundamentally based on moral, ethical and compliance reasons," says Rudy Mendez, vice president for diversity and inclusion at McDonald's. "But now that we can add business impact, diversity executives are being given a much bigger role."[7]

Fourth, affirmative action programs and diversity programs have different purposes. The purpose of affirmative action programs is to compensate for past discrimination, which was widespread when legislation was introduced in the 1960s; to prevent ongoing discrimination; and to provide equal opportunities to all, regardless of race, color, religion, sex, or national origin. Organizations that fail to uphold affirmative action laws may be required to

- hire, promote, or give back pay to those not hired or promoted;
- reinstate those who were wrongly terminated;
- pay attorneys' fees and court costs for those who bring charges against them; or
- take other actions that make individuals whole by returning them to the condition or place they would have been had it not been for discrimination.[8]

Consequently, affirmative action is basically a punitive approach.[9] By contrast, the general purpose of diversity programs is to create a positive work environment where no one is advantaged or disadvantaged, where "we" is everyone, where everyone can do his or her best work, where differences are respected and not ignored, and where everyone feels comfortable.[10] So, unlike affirmative action, which punishes companies for not achieving specific sex and race ratios in their work forces, diversity programs seek to benefit both organizations and their employees by encouraging organizations to value all kinds of differences.

Despite the overall success of affirmative action in making workplaces much fairer than they used to be, many people argue that some affirmative action programs unconstitutionally offer preferential treatment to females and minorities at the expense of other employees, a view accepted by some courts.[11] The American Civil Rights Institute successfully campaigned to ban race- and sex-based affirmative action in college admissions, government hiring, and government contracting programs in California (1996), Washington (1998), and Michigan (2006). Led by Ward Connerly, the Institute backed similar efforts in Arizona, Colorado, Missouri, Nebraska, and Oklahoma in 2008. Opponents of affirmative action, like Connerly, believe that affirmative action policies establish only surface-level diversity and, ironically, promote preferential treatment.[12]

Furthermore, research shows that people who have gotten a job or promotion as a result of affirmative action are frequently viewed as unqualified, even when clear evidence of their qualifications exists.[13] One woman said, "I won a major prize [in my field], and some of the guys in my lab said it was because I was a woman. I'm certain they didn't choose me because I was a woman. But it gave some disgruntled guys who didn't get the prize a convenient excuse."[14] So, while affirmative action programs have created opportunities for minorities and women, those same minorities and women are frequently presumed to be unqualified when others believe they obtained their jobs as a result of affirmative action.

12-1b DIVERSITY MAKES GOOD BUSINESS SENSE

Those who support the idea of diversity in organizations often ignore its business aspects altogether, claiming instead that diversity is simply the right thing to do. Yet diversity actually makes good business sense in several ways: cost savings, attracting and retaining talent, and driving business growth.[15]

Diversity helps companies with *cost savings* by reducing turnover, decreasing absenteeism, and avoiding expensive lawsuits.[16] Because of lost productivity and the cost of recruiting and selecting new workers, companies lose substantial amounts of money when employees quit their jobs. In fact, turnover costs typically amount to more than 90 percent of employees' salaries. By this estimate, if an executive who makes $200,000 leaves, the organization will have to spend approximately $180,000 to find a replacement; even the lowest-paid hourly workers can cost the company as much as $10,000 when they quit. Since turnover rates for African Americans average 40 percent higher than for whites, and since women quit their jobs at twice the rate men do, companies that manage diverse work forces well can cut costs by reducing the turnover rates of these employees.[17] And, with women absent from work 60 percent more often than men, primarily because of family responsibilities, diversity programs that address the needs of female workers can also reduce the substantial costs of absenteeism.

Diversity programs also save companies money by helping them avoid discrimination lawsuits, which have increased by a factor of twenty since 1970 and quadrupled just since 1995. In one survey conducted by the Society for Human Resource Management, 78 percent of respondents reported that diversity efforts helped them avoid lawsuits and litigation costs.[18] Indeed, because companies lose two-thirds of all discrimination cases that go to trial, the best strategy from a business perspective is not to be sued for discrimination at all. When companies lose, the average individual settlement amounts to more than $600,000.[19] And settlement costs can be substantially higher in class-action lawsuits, in which individuals join together to sue a company as a group. Electronics retailer Best Buy faced a class-action lawsuit alleging it discriminated against female, African American, and Latino employees, denying them desirable job assignments and promotions and thus keeping them in relatively low-paying positions because of their gender or race. Best Buy settled the case for $10.3 million and committed to changing its personnel policies and procedures "to enhance the equal employment opportunities of the thousands of women, African Americans and Latinos employed by Best Buy nationwide."[20]

Diversity also makes business sense by helping companies *attract and retain talented workers*.[21] Indeed, diversity-friendly companies tend to attract better *and* more diverse job applicants. Very simply, diversity begets more diversity. Companies that make *Fortune* magazine's list of the fifty best companies for minorities or are recognized by *Working Women* and *Diversity Inc.* magazine have already attracted a diverse and talented pool of job applicants. But, after being recognized for their efforts, they subsequently experience big increases in both the quality and the diversity of people who apply for jobs. Research shows that companies with acclaimed diversity programs not only attract more talented workers but also have higher performance in the stock market.[22]

The third way that diversity makes business sense is by *driving business growth*. In the United States today, there are 40.5 million African Americans, 47.7 million Hispanic Americans, and 14.2 million Asian Americans with, respectively, $1.1 trillion, $1.2 trillion, and $459 billion in purchasing power.[23] Given the size of those markets, it shouldn't be surprising that a survey conducted by the Society for Human Resource Management found that tapping into "diverse customers and markets" was the number-one reason managers gave for implementing diversity programs.[24] Diversity, therefore, can help companies grow by improving their understanding of the marketplace. When companies have diverse work forces, they are better able to understand the needs of their increasingly diverse customer bases.

Macy's is an upscale department store, and more than half of its urban customers are African American, Hispanic, or Asian. To serve those customers better and drive business growth, Macy's is building a network of minority retailers who already do business with those customers. Because most of these businesses are small and lack the resources to supply a nationwide department store, Macy's started a training program to help them "learn the basics of big-time retail," such as managing supply and inventory, and retail financing. Recent graduates of the program, whose products can be found in Macy's stores, include Lamik Beauty, a cosmetics line geared toward

African Americans, Monif C., specializing in plus-size clothing, and Big Girl Cosmetics, which targets "poly-ethnic" women. Macy's CEO Terry Lundgren says, "We are not doing this not just as a nice thing, but as a business proposition." Macy's expects sales from minority- and women-owned businesses, which were at $683 million in 2011, to rise to $1 billion within two years.[25]

Diversity also helps companies grow through higher-quality problem solving. Though diverse groups initially have more difficulty working together than homogeneous groups, diverse groups eventually establish a rapport and do a better job of identifying problems and generating alternative solutions, the two most important steps in problem solving.[26] Ernest Drew, former CEO of Hoechst Celanese, a chemical company, recalls a company conference in which the top 125 managers, mostly white males, were joined by fifty lower-level employees, mostly minorities and women. Problem-solving teams were formed to discuss how the company's corporate culture affected business and how it could be changed. Half the teams were composed of white males, while the other half were of mixed sex and race. Drew says, "It was so obvious that the diverse teams had the broader solutions. They had ideas I hadn't even thought of. For the first time, we realized that diversity is a strength as it relates to problem solving. Before, we just thought of diversity as the total number of minorities and women in the company, like affirmative action. Now we knew we needed diversity at every level of the company where decisions are made."[27]

In short, "diversity is no longer about counting heads; it's about making heads count," says Amy George, vice president of diversity and inclusion at PepsiCo.[28] Harvard Business School professor David Thomas agrees, "Where ten or twenty years ago, companies were asking, 'Will we be diverse?' today they

must ask, 'How should we use diversity as a resource to be more effective as a business?'"[29] Ernest Hicks, who directs Xerox's corporate diversity office, says, "Because we gain a competitive advantage by drawing on the experience, insight and creativity of a well-balanced, diverse workforce, diversity enables Xerox to attract talent from the broadest possible pool of candidates. It creates more diverse work teams—facilitating diversity of thought and more innovative ideas—and it positions Xerox to attract a wider customer base and to address the needs of diverse customers."[30]

12-2 Surface-Level Diversity

A survey that asked managers "What is meant by diversity to decision-makers in your organization?" found that they most frequently mentioned race, culture, sex, national origin, age, religion, and regional origin.[31] When managers describe workers this way, they are focusing on surface-level diversity. **Surface-level diversity** consists of differences that are immediately observable, typically unchangeable, and easy to measure.[32] In other words, independent observers can usually agree on dimensions of surface-level diversity, such as another person's age, sex, race/ethnicity, or physical capabilities.

Most people start by using surface-level diversity to categorize or stereotype other people. But those initial categorizations typically give way to deeper impressions formed from knowledge of others' behavior and psychological characteristics such as personality and attitudes.[33] When you think of others this way, you are focusing on deep-level diversity. **Deep-level diversity** consists of differences that are communicated through verbal and nonverbal behaviors and are learned only through extended interaction with others.[34] Examples of deep-level diversity include personality differences, attitudes, beliefs, and values. In other words, as people in diverse workplaces get to know each other, the initial focus on surface-level differences such as age, race/ethnicity, sex, and physical capabilities is replaced by deeper, more complex knowledge of coworkers.

Surface-level diversity differences such as age, sex, race/ethnicity, and physical disabilities that are observable, typically unchangeable, and easy to measure

Deep-level diversity differences such as personality and attitudes that are communicated through verbal and nonverbal behaviors and are learned only through extended interaction with others

© iStockphoto.com/Alexey Fiodorov

Social integration the degree to which group members are psychologically attracted to working with each other to accomplish a common objective

Age discrimination treating people differently (e.g., in hiring and firing, promotion, and compensation decisions) because of their age

If managed properly, the shift from surface- to deep-level diversity can accomplish two things.[35] First, coming to know and understand each other better can result in reduced prejudice and conflict. Second, it can lead to stronger social integration. **Social integration** is the degree to which group members are psychologically attracted to working with each other to accomplish a common objective, or, as one manager put it, "working together to get the job done."

Because age, sex, race/ethnicity, and disabilities are usually immediately observable, many managers and workers use these dimensions of surface-level diversity to form initial impressions and categorizations of coworkers, bosses, customers, or job applicants. Whether intentionally or not, sometimes those initial categorizations and impressions lead to decisions or behaviors that discriminate. Consequently, these dimensions of surface-level diversity pose special challenges for managers who are trying to create positive work environments where everyone feels comfortable and no one is advantaged or disadvantaged.

*Let's learn more about those challenges and the ways that **12-2a age, 12-2b sex, 12-2c race/ethnicity,** and **12-2d mental or physical disabilities can affect decisions and behaviors in organizations.***

12-2a AGE

Age discrimination is treating people differently (e.g., in hiring and firing, promotion, and compensation decisions) because of their age. The victims of age discrimination are almost always older workers, and the discrimination is based on the assumption that "you can't teach an old dog new tricks." It's commonly believed that older workers can't learn how to use computers and technology, won't adapt to change, are sick more often, and, in general, are much more expensive to employ than younger workers (see box "Facts"). One manager explains his preference for younger workers

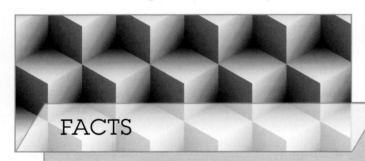

FACTS

Eighty percent of human resource managers surveyed by *Personnel Management* magazine said that age discrimination was a major problem in their organizations and, moreover, that older employees were not receiving the same training and promotional opportunities as younger workers. Likewise, two-thirds of 10,000 people surveyed by AARP (American Association of Retired Persons) felt that they had been wrongly discharged from a job because of their age. In fact, a study by the Society for Human Resource Management found that 20 percent of all companies had been sued for age discrimination in the preceding five years.

Sources: S. E. Sullivan and E. A. Duplaga, "Recruiting and Retaining Older Workers for the Millennium," *Business Horizons* 40 (November 12, 1997): 65; N. Munk, "Finished at Forty: In the New Economy, the Skills That Come with Age Count for Less and Less," *Fortune*, February 1, 1999, 50.

over older workers this way: "The way I look at it, for $40,000 or $50,000, I can get a smart, raw kid right out of undergrad who's going to work seven days a week for me for the next two years. I'll train him the way I want him, he'll grow with me, and I'll pay him long-term options so I own him, for lack of a better word. He'll do exactly what I want—and if he doesn't, I'll fire him. . . . The alternative is to pay twice as much for some forty-year-old who does half the amount of work, has been trained improperly, and doesn't listen to what I say."[36] Unfortunately, attitudes like this are all too common.[37] According to the Society for Human Resource Management, 53 percent of 428 surveyed managers believed that older workers "didn't keep up with technology," and 28 percent said that older workers were "less flexible."[38] It is also commonly assumed that older workers cost more, and some companies fear that older workers will require higher salaries and more health care benefits.[39]

So, what's reality and what's myth? Do older employees actually cost more? In some ways, they do. The older people are and the longer they stay with a company, the more the company pays for salaries, pension plans, and vacation time. But older workers cost companies less, too, because they show better judgment, care more about the quality of their work, and are less likely to quit, show up late, or be absent, the cost of which can be substantial.[40] A survey by Chicago outplacement firm Challenger, Gray & Christmas found that only 3 percent of employees age fifty and over changed jobs in any given year, compared with 10 percent of the entire work force and 12 percent of workers ages twenty-five to thirty-four. The study also found that while older workers make up about 14 percent of the work force, they suffer only 10 percent of all workplace injuries and use fewer health care benefits than younger workers with school-age children.[41] As for the widespread belief that job performance declines with age, the scientific evidence clearly refutes this stereotype. Performance does not decline with age, regardless of the type of job.[42]

What can companies do to reduce age discrimination?[43] To start, managers need to recognize that age discrimination is much more pervasive than they probably think. Whereas "old" used to mean mid-fifties, in today's workplace, "old" is closer to forty. When 773 CEOs were asked, "At what age does a worker's productivity peak?" the average age they gave was forty-three. Thus, age discrimination may be affecting more workers because perceptions about age have changed.

In addition, with the aging of the Baby Boomers, age discrimination is more likely to occur simply because there are millions more older workers than there used to be. And, because studies show that interviewers rate younger job candidates as more qualified (even when they aren't), companies need to train managers and recruiters to make hiring and promotion decisions on the basis of qualifications, not age.

Companies also need to monitor the extent to which older workers receive training. The Bureau of Labor Statistics found that the number of training courses and number of hours spent in training drop dramatically after employees reach the age of forty-four.[44] Finally, companies need to ensure that younger and older workers interact with each other. One study found that younger workers generally hold positive views of older workers and that the more time they spent working with older coworkers, the more positive their attitudes became.[45]

DOING THE RIGHT THING

Helping Women Stay on the Job in India

Women make up 42 percent of the college graduates in India, and yet they account for just 34 percent of the country's work force, largely because Indian women often put their careers on hold to take on family responsibilities. A number of companies are taking action to help women meet responsibilities at home and at work. Google, for example, has taxis available for workers who might need to rush home to take care of family members. The pharmaceutical company Boehringer Ingelheim allows employees to travel with their mothers, since the Indian culture looks negatively on young women traveling alone. The accounting firm Ernst & Young not only gives female employees flexible schedules and on-site child care, but also regularly schedules times when employees' families can visit the office, meet executives, and find out more about what their daughters do at work.

Source: M. Srivastava, "Keeping Women on the Job in India," *Bloomberg Businessweek*, March 3, 2011, accessed March 15, 2012, http://www.businessweek.com/magazine/content/11_11/b4219010769063.htm.

Sex discrimination treating people differently because of their sex

Glass ceiling the invisible barrier that prevents women and minorities from advancing to the top jobs in organizations

12-2b SEX

Sex discrimination occurs when people are treated differently because of their sex. Sex discrimination and racial/ethnic discrimination (discussed in the next section) are often associated with the so-called **glass ceiling**, the invisible barrier that prevents women and minorities from advancing to the top jobs in organizations.

To what extent do women face sex discrimination in the workplace? Almost every year, the EEOC receives between 23,000 and 28,000 charges of sex-based discrimination.[46] In some ways, there is much less sex discrimination than there used to be. For example, whereas women held only 17 percent of managerial jobs in 1972, today they hold 40 percent of managerial jobs, 51.5 percent of managerial and professional jobs, and 46.8 percent of all jobs in the workplace.[47] Likewise, women own 40 percent of all U.S. businesses. Whereas women owned 700,000 businesses in 1977 and 4.1 million businesses in 1987, today they own 10.1 million businesses generating $1.9 trillion in sales![48] Finally, though women still earn less than men on average, the differential is narrowing, as Exhibit 12.2 shows. Women earned 81.2 percent of what men did in 2010, up from 63 percent in 1979.[49]

Although progress is being made, sex discrimination continues to operate via the glass ceiling at higher levels in organizations, as shown in Exhibit 12.3. For instance, while the trends are going upward, women were the top earners in just 7.6 percent of companies in 2010.[50] Likewise, only 14.4 percent of corporate officers (i.e., top management) were women, and the numbers were even lower for women of color. Indra K. Nooyi, PepsiCo's CEO, and Ursula Burns, Xerox's CEO, are the only women of color heading *Fortune* 500 companies.[51] Indeed, only seventeen of the 500 largest companies in the United States have women CEOs.[52] Similarly, only 15.72 percent of the members of corporate boards of directors are women.[53]

Is sex discrimination the sole reason for the slow rate at which women have been promoted to middle and upper levels of management and corporate boards? Some studies indicate that it's not.[54] In some instances, the slow progress appears to be due to career and job choices. Whereas men's career and job choices are often driven by the search for higher pay and advancement, women are more likely to choose jobs or careers that also give them a greater sense of accomplishment, more control over their work schedules, and easier movement in and out of the workplace.[55] For instance, 82 percent of women without children are interested in being promoted to the next level compared to 73 percent of women with two or more children.[56] As those numbers suggest, women are historically much more likely than men to prioritize family over work at some time in their careers. For example, 96 percent of 600 female Harvard MBAs held jobs while they were in their twenties. That dropped to 71 percent in their late thirties when they had chil-

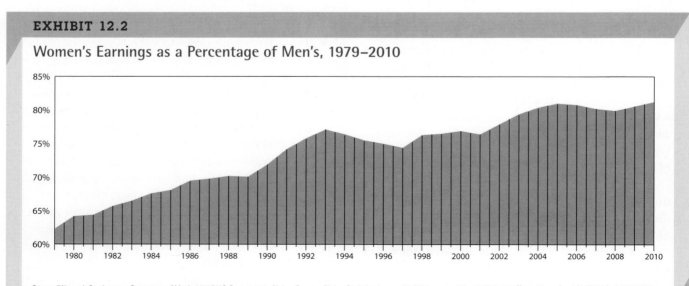

EXHIBIT 12.2

Women's Earnings as a Percentage of Men's, 1979–2010

Source: "Women's Earnings as a Percentage of Men's, 2010," U.S. Department of Labor, Bureau of Labor Statistics, January 10, 2012, accessed May 9, 2012, http://www.bls.gov/opub/ted/2012/ted_20120110.htm.

EXHIBIT 12.3

Women at *Fortune* 500 and 1000 Companies

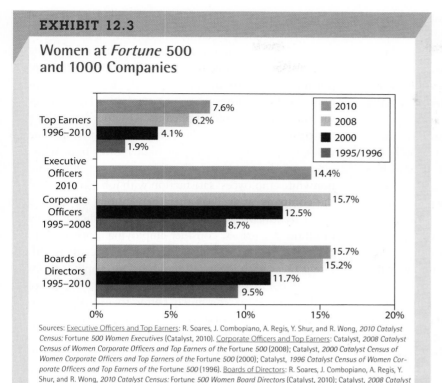

Sources: <u>Executive Officers and Top Earners</u>: R. Soares, J. Combopiano, A. Regis, Y. Shur, and R. Wong, *2010 Catalyst Census: Fortune 500 Women Executives* (Catalyst, 2010). <u>Corporate Officers and Top Earners</u>: Catalyst, *2008 Catalyst Census of Women Corporate Officers and Top Earners of the Fortune 500* (2008); Catalyst, *2000 Catalyst Census of Women Corporate Officers and Top Earners of the Fortune 500* (2000); Catalyst, *1996 Catalyst Census of Women Corporate Officers and Top Earners of the Fortune 500* (1996). <u>Boards of Directors</u>: R. Soares, J. Combopiano, A. Regis, Y. Shur, and R. Wong, *2010 Catalyst Census: Fortune 500 Women Board Directors* (Catalyst, 2010); Catalyst, *2008 Catalyst Census of Women Board Directors of the Fortune 500* (2009); Catalyst, *2000 Catalyst Census of Women Board Directors of the Fortune 500* (2000); Catalyst, *1995 Catalyst Census of Women Board Directors of the Fortune 500* (1995).

dren but then increased to 82.5 percent in their late forties as their children became older.[57]

Beyond these reasons, however, it's likely that sex discrimination does play a role in women's slow progress into the higher levels of management. And even if you don't think so, many of the women you work with probably do. Indeed, one study found that more than 90 percent of executive women believed that the glass ceiling had hurt their careers.[58] In another study, 80 percent of women said they left their last organization because the glass ceiling had limited their chances for advancement.[59] A third study indicated that the glass ceiling is prompting more and more women to leave companies to start their own businesses.[60] In fact, discrimination is believed to be the most significant factor behind the lack of women at top levels of management.[61]

So, what can companies do to make sure that women have the same opportunities for development and advancement as men? (see box "Doing the Right Thing") One strategy is mentoring, or pairing promising female executives with senior executives from whom they can seek advice and support. A vice president at a utility company says, "I think it's the single most critical piece to women advancing career-wise.

In my experience you need somebody to help guide you and . . . go to bat for you."[62] In fact, 91 percent of female executives had a mentor at some point and feel their mentor was critical to their advancement.

Another strategy is to make sure that male-dominated social activities don't unintentionally exclude women. Nearly half (47 percent) of women in the work force believe that "exclusion from informal networks" makes it more difficult to advance their careers. By contrast, just 18 percent of male CEOs thought this was a problem.[63] One final strategy is to designate a go-to person other than their supervisors that women can talk to if they believe that they are being held back or discriminated against because of their sex. Make sure this person has the knowledge and authority to conduct a fair, confidential internal investigation.[64]

12-2c RACE/ETHNICITY

Racial and ethnic discrimination occurs when people are treated differently because of their race or ethnicity. To what extent is racial and ethnic discrimination a factor in the workplace? Every year, the EEOC receives between 26,000 and 35,000 charges of race discrimination, which is more than any other type of charge of discrimination.[65] However, it is true that since the passage of the 1964 Civil Rights Act and Title VII, there is much less racial and ethnic discrimination than there used to be. For example, nineteen *Fortune* 500 firms had an African American, Hispanic, or Asian CEO in 2011, whereas none did in 1988.[66] Nonetheless, strong racial and ethnic disparities still exist. For instance, whereas 12.2 percent of Americans are black, only 6.4 percent of managers and 2.8 percent of CEOs are black. Similarly, 16 percent of Americans are Hispanic, but only 7.6 percent are managers and 4.8 percent are CEOs. By contrast, Asians, who constitute 4.5 percent of the population, are better represented, holding 4.8 percent of management jobs and 4.4 percent of CEO jobs.[67]

What accounts for the disparities between the percentages of minority groups in the general population

Racial and ethnic discrimination treating people differently because of their race or ethnicity

and their smaller representation in management positions? Some studies have found that the disparities are due to preexisting differences in training, education, and skills. When African Americans, Hispanics, Asian Americans, and whites have similar skills, training, and education, they are much more likely to have similar jobs and salaries.[68]

Other studies, however, provide increasingly strong direct evidence of racial or ethnic discrimination in the workplace. For example, one study directly tested hiring discrimination by sending pairs of black and white males and pairs of Hispanic and non-Hispanic males to apply for the same jobs. Each pair had résumés with identical qualifications, and all were trained to present themselves in similar ways to minimize differences during interviews. The researchers found that the white males got three times as many job offers as the black males, and that the non-Hispanic males got three times as many offers as the Hispanic males.[69] Another study, which used similar methods to test hiring procedures at 149 different companies, found that whites received 10 percent more interviews than blacks. Half of the whites interviewed then received job offers, but only 11 percent of the blacks. And when job offers were made, blacks were much more likely to be offered lower-level positions, while whites were more likely to be offered jobs at higher levels than the jobs they had applied for.[70]

Critics of these studies point out that it's nearly impossible to train different applicants to give identical responses in job interviews and that differences in interviewing skills may have somehow accounted for the results. However, British researchers found similar kinds of discrimination just by sending letters of inquiry to prospective employers. As in the other studies, the letters were identical except for the applicant's race. Employers frequently responded to letters from Afro-Caribbean, Indian, or Pakistani applicants by indicating that the positions had been filled. By contrast, they often responded to white, Anglo-Saxon applicants by inviting them to face-to-face interviews. Similar results were found with Vietnamese and Greek applicants in Australia.[71] In short, the evidence indicates that there is strong and persistent racial and ethnic discrimination in the hiring processes of many organizations.

What can companies do to make sure that people of all racial and ethnic backgrounds have the same opportunities?[72] Start by looking at the numbers. Compare the hiring rates of whites with the hiring rates for racial and ethnic applicants. Do the same thing for promotions within the company. See if nonwhite workers quit the company at higher rates than white workers. Also, survey employees to compare white and nonwhite employees' satisfaction with jobs, bosses, and the company as well as their perceptions concerning equal treatment. Next, if the numbers indicate racial or ethnic disparities, consider employing a private firm to test your hiring system by having applicants of different races with identical qualifications apply for jobs in your company.[73] Although disparities aren't proof of discrimination, it's much better to investigate hiring and promotion disparities yourself than to have the EEOC or a plaintiff's lawyer do it for you.

Another step companies can take is to eliminate unclear selection and promotion criteria. Vague criteria allow decision makers to focus on non-job-related characteristics that may unintentionally lead to employment discrimination. Instead, selection and promotion criteria should spell out the specific knowledge, skills, abilities, education, and experience needed to perform a job well. Finally, as explained in Chapter 11, "Managing Human Resource Systems,"

© Goodluz/Shutterstock.com

it is also important to train managers and others who make hiring and promotion decisions.

12-2d MENTAL OR PHYSICAL DISABILITIES

According to the Americans with Disabilities Act (http://www.ada.gov), a **disability** is a mental or physical impairment that substantially limits one or more major life activities.[74] One in every five Americans, or more than 54 million people, has a disability.[75] **Disability discrimination** occurs when people are treated differently because of their disabilities. To what extent is disability discrimination a factor in the workplace? Although 79.7 percent of the overall U.S. population was employed in 2006, just 36.9 percent of people with disabilities had jobs. Individuals with sensory disabilities (46.4 percent), such as blindness or deafness, had the highest employment rates; those with self-care disabilities (16.7 percent), which inhibit their motor skills and their ability to care for their grooming needs, were the least represented in the work force.[76] Furthermore, people with disabilities are disproportionately employed in low-status or part-time jobs, have little chance for advancement, and, on average, are twice as likely to live in poverty as people without disabilities.[77] Numerous studies also indicate that managers and the general public believe that discrimination against people with disabilities is common and widespread.[78]

What accounts for the disparities between the employment and income levels of people with and without disabilities? Contrary to popular opinion, it has nothing to do with how well people with disabilities can do their jobs. Studies show that as long as companies make reasonable accommodations for disabilities (e.g., changing procedures or equipment), people with disabilities perform their jobs just as well as people without disabilities. Furthermore, they have better safety records and are not any more likely to be absent or quit their jobs.[79]

What can companies do to make sure that people with disabilities have the same opportunities as everyone else? Beyond educational efforts to address incorrect stereotypes and expectations, a good place to start is to commit to reasonable workplace accommodations such as changing work schedules, reassigning jobs, acquiring or modifying equipment, or providing assistance when needed. Accommodations for disabilities needn't be expensive. According to the Job Accommodation Network, 56 percent of accommo-

dations don't cost anything at all, while those with costs are typically just $600.[80]

At Laser Soft Info Systems, an India-based software developer, 15 percent of the staff has some disability, with causes ranging from hearing, speech, and sight impairment to cerebral palsy, polio, or accidents, and work throughout the company. "We don't have any rule that teams must take a minimum or maximum number of people with disabilities in their roles. They are recruited like any other associate," says Suresh Kamath, Laser Soft's founder and president. Laser Soft's accommodations include wheelchair ramps, wider office aisles, elevators with audio controls for the blind, and facilitators to provide physical assistance when an employee asks for it. The company also allows employees to work from home should it become difficult to make into the office.[81]

Some of the accommodations just described involve *assistive technology* that gives workers with disabilities the tools they need to overcome their disabilities. Providing workers with assistive technology is also an effective strategy to recruit, retain, and enhance the productivity of people with disabilities. According to the National Council on Disability, 92 percent of workers with disabilities who use assistive technology report that it helps them work faster and better, 81 percent indicate that it helps them work longer hours, and 67 percent say that it is critical to getting a job.[82] To learn about assistive technologies that can help workers with disabilities, see Abledata (http://www.abledata.com), which lists 25,000 products from 3,000 organizations, or the National Rehabilitation Information Center (http://www.naric.com), which provides information for specific disabilities.

Finally, companies should actively recruit qualified workers with disabilities. Numerous organizations, such as Mainstream, Kidder Resources, the American Council of the Blind (http://www.acb.org), the National Federation of the Blind (http://www.nfb.org), the National Association of the Deaf (http://www.nad.org), the Epilepsy Foundation (http://www.epilepsyfoundation.org), and the National Amputation Foundation (http://www.nationalamputation.org), actively work with employers to find jobs for qualified people with disabilities. Companies can also place advertisements in publications, such as *Careers and the Disabled*, that specifically target workers with disabilities.[83]

Disability a mental or physical impairment that substantially limits one or more major life activities

Disability discrimination treating people differently because of their disabilities

12-3 Deep-Level Diversity

As you learned in Section 12-2, people often use the dimensions of surface-level diversity to form initial impressions about others. Over time, however, as people have a chance to get to know each other, initial impressions based on age, sex, race/ethnicity, and mental or physical disabilities give way to deeper impressions based on behavior and psychological characteristics. When we think of others this way, we are focusing on deep-level diversity. *Deep-level diversity* represents differences that can be learned only through extended interaction with others. Examples of deep-level diversity include differences in personality, attitudes, beliefs, and values. In short, recognizing deep-level diversity requires getting to know and understand one another better. And that matters, because it can result in less prejudice, discrimination, and conflict in the workplace. These changes can then lead to better *social integration*, the degree to which organizational or group members are psychologically attracted to working with each other to accomplish a common objective.

Stop for a second and think about your boss (or the boss you had in your last job). What words would you use to describe him or her? Is your boss introverted or extraverted? Emotionally stable or unstable? Agreeable or disagreeable? Organized or disorganized? Open or closed to new experiences? When you describe your boss or others in this way, what you're really doing is describing dispositions and personality.

A **disposition** is the tendency to respond to situations and events in a predetermined manner. **Personality** is the relatively stable set of behaviors, attitudes, and emotions displayed over time that makes people different from each other.[84] For example, which of your aunts or uncles is a little offbeat, a little out of the ordinary? What was that aunt or uncle like when you were small? What is she or he like now? Chances are that she or he is pretty much the same wacky person. In other words, the person's core personality hasn't changed. For years, personality researchers studied hundreds of different ways to describe people's personalities. In the last decade, however, personality research conducted in different cultures, different settings, and different languages has shown that five basic dimensions of personality account for most of the differences in peoples' behaviors, attitudes, and emotions (or for why your boss is the way he or she is!). The *Big Five Personality Dimensions* are extraversion, emotional stability, agreeableness, conscientiousness, and openness to experience.[85]

Extraversion is the degree to which someone is active, assertive, gregarious, sociable, talkative, and energized by others. In contrast to extraverts, introverts are less active, prefer to be alone, and are shy, quiet, and reserved. For the best results in the workplace, introverts and extraverts should be correctly matched to their jobs.

Emotional stability is the degree to which someone is not angry, depressed, anxious, emotional, insecure, or excitable. People who are emotionally stable respond well to stress. In other words, they can maintain a calm, problem-solving attitude in even the toughest situations (e.g., conflict, hostility, dangerous conditions, or extreme time pressures). By contrast, emotionally unstable people find it difficult to handle the most basic demands of their jobs under only moderately stressful situations and become distraught, tearful, self-doubting, and anxious. Emotional stability is particularly important for high-stress jobs such as police work, fire fighting, emergency medical treatment, piloting planes, or commanding rockets.

Agreeableness is the degree to which someone is cooperative, polite, flexible, forgiving, good-natured, tolerant, and trusting. Basically, agreeable people are

Disposition the tendency to respond to situations and events in a predetermined manner

Personality the relatively stable set of behaviors, attitudes, and emotions displayed over time that makes people different from each other

Extraversion the degree to which someone is active, assertive, gregarious, sociable, talkative, and energized by others

Emotional stability the degree to which someone is not angry, depressed, anxious, emotional, insecure, and excitable

Agreeableness the degree to which someone is cooperative, polite, flexible, forgiving, good-natured, tolerant, and trusting

The Big Five Personality Dimensions:

- Extraversion
- Emotional stability
- Agreeableness
- Conscientiousness
- Openness to experience

Can introverts be effective managers? Sixty-five percent of senior managers believe that introversion prevents people from being promoted to higher management levels. But research shows that both introverts and extraverts can be successful managers. While extraverts may be more effective (and comfortable) in public roles, introverts are effective in one-on-one interactions and in involving others in decision making. Colgate-Palmolive CEO Ian Cook says his listening skills helped him advance in the company. Says Cook, "I listen intently. I am extremely attentive to language and body cues." Subordinates can mistakenly view their boss's introversion as aloofness, particularly if they're quiet during meetings. Douglas Conant, former CEO of Campbell Soup Company, notes that when he was president of a division at Nabisco, "People were drawing [inaccurate] conclusions about my behavior." So, he shared with his coworkers and subordinates that it takes him time to formulate his thoughts and responses. Conant says that helped, and "the more transparent I became, the more engaged people became."

Source: J. Lublin, "Introverted Execs Find Ways to Shine," *Wall Street Journal*, April 14, 2011, accessed May 29, 2011, http://online.wsj.com/article/SB10001424052748703983104576263053775879800.html.

easy to work with and be around, whereas disagreeable people are distrusting and difficult to work with and be around. A number of companies have made general attitude or agreeableness the most important factor in their hiring decisions. Small-business owner Roger Cook says, "Hire nice people. I'm looking for personal—not professional—traits. I want a good or nice person. I can teach the skills. I call their references and ask, 'Is he or she a nice person?' I take a close look at how applicants answer questions and carry themselves. Why nice people? Because they're trustworthy; they get along with other crew members: they are good with customers and they are usually hard workers."[86]

Conscientiousness is the degree to which someone is organized, hardworking, responsible, persevering, thorough, and achievement oriented. One management consultant wrote about his experiences with a conscientious employee: "He arrived at our first meeting with a typed copy of his daily schedule, a sheet bearing his home and office phone numbers, addresses, and his email address. At his request, we established a timetable for meetings for the next four months. He showed up on time every time, day planner in hand, and carefully listed tasks and due dates. He questioned me exhaustively if he didn't understand an assignment and returned on schedule with the completed work or with a clear explanation as to why it wasn't done."[87] Conscientious employees are also more likely to engage in positive behaviors, such as helping new employees, coworkers, and supervisors and are less likely to engage in negative behaviors, such as verbally or physically abusing coworkers or stealing.[88]

Openness to experience is the degree to which someone is curious, broadminded, and open to new ideas, things, and experiences; is spontaneous; and has a high tolerance for ambiguity. Most companies need people who are strong in terms of openness to experience to fill certain positions, but for other positions, this dimension is less important. People in marketing, advertising, research, or other creative jobs need to be curious, open to new ideas, and spontaneous. By contrast, openness to experience is not particularly important to accountants, who need to apply stringent rules and formulas consistently to make sense out of complex financial information.

Which of the Big Five Personality Dimensions has the largest impact on behavior in organizations? The cumulative results of multiple studies indicate that conscientiousness is related to job performance across five different occupational groups (professionals, police, managers, salespeople, and skilled or semiskilled workers).[89] In short, people "who are dependable, persistent, goal directed, and organized tend to be higher performers on virtually any job; viewed negatively, those who are careless, irresponsible, low achievement striving, and impulsive tend to be lower performers on virtually any job."[90] The results also indicate that extraversion is related to performance in jobs, such as sales and management, that involve significant interaction with others. In people-intensive jobs like these, it helps to be sociable, assertive, and talkative and to have energy and be able to energize others. Finally,

people who are extraverted and open to experience seem to do much better in training. Being curious and open to new experiences as well as sociable, assertive, talkative, and full of energy helps people perform better in learning situations.[91]

12-4 *Managing Diversity*

How much should companies change their standard business practices to accommodate the diversity of their workers? What do you do when a talented top executive has a drinking problem that seems to affect his behavior only at company business parties (for entertaining clients), where he has made inappropriate advances toward female employees? What do you do when, despite aggressive company policies against racial discrimination, employees continue to tell racist jokes and publicly post cartoons displaying racist humor? And, since many people confuse diversity with affirmative action, what do you do to make sure that your company's diversity practices and policies are viewed as benefiting all workers and not just some workers?

No doubt about it, questions like these make managing diversity one of the toughest challenges that managers face.[92] Nonetheless, there are steps companies can take to begin to address these issues.

As discussed earlier, diversity programs try to create a positive work environment where no one is ad-vantaged or disadvantaged, where "we" is everyone, where everyone can do his or her best work, where differences are respected and not ignored, and where everyone feels comfortable.

Let's begin to address those goals by learning about **12-4a different diversity paradigms, 12-4b diversity principles,** *and* **12-4c diversity training and practices.**

12-4a DIVERSITY PARADIGMS

There are several different methods or paradigms for managing diversity: the discrimination and fairness paradigm, the access and legitimacy paradigm, and the learning and effectiveness paradigm.[93]

The *discrimination and fairness paradigm*, which is the most common method of approaching diversity, focuses on equal opportunity, fair treatment, recruitment of minorities, and strict compliance with the equal employment opportunity laws. Under this approach, success is usually measured by how well companies achieve recruitment, promotion, and retention goals for women, people of different racial/ethnic backgrounds, or other underrepresented groups. According to a recent workplace diversity practices survey conducted by the Society for Human Resource Management, 66 percent to 91 percent of companies use specialized strategies to recruit, retain, and promote talented women and minorities. The percentages increase with company size, and companies of more than 500 employees are the most likely to use

© iStockphoto.com/Robert Churchill

"We are all on the same team,

these strategies. Seventy-seven percent of companies with more than 500 employees systematically collect measurements on diversity-related practices.[94] One manager says, "If you don't measure something, it doesn't count. You measure your market share. You measure your profitability. The same should be true for diversity. There has to be some way of measuring whether you did, in fact, cast your net widely and whether the company is better off today in terms of the experience of people of color than it was a few years ago. I measure my market share and my profitability. Why not this?"[95] The primary benefit of the discrimination and fairness paradigm is that it generally brings about fairer treatment of employees and increases demographic diversity. The primary limitation is that the focus of diversity remains on the surface-level diversity dimensions of sex, race, and ethnicity.[96]

The *access and legitimacy paradigm* focuses on the acceptance and celebration of differences to ensure that the diversity within the company matches the diversity found among primary stakeholders, such as customers, suppliers, and local communities. This is similar to the *business growth* advantage of diversity discussed earlier in the chapter. The basic idea behind this approach is to create a demographically diverse work force that attracts a broader customer base. Consistent with this goal, Ed Adams, vice president of human resources for Enterprise Rent-a-Car, says, "We want people who speak the same language, literally

and figuratively, as our customers. We don't set quotas. We say [to our managers], 'Reflect your local market.'"[97] The primary benefit of this approach is that it establishes a clear business reason for diversity. Like the discrimination and fairness paradigm, however, it focuses only on the surface-level diversity dimensions of sex, race, and ethnicity. Furthermore, employees who are assigned responsibility for customers and stakeholders on the basis of their sex, race, or ethnicity may eventually feel frustrated and exploited.

Whereas the discrimination and fairness paradigm focuses on assimilation (having a demographically representative work force) and the access and legitimacy paradigm focuses on differentiation (having demographic differences inside the company match those of key customers and stakeholders), the *learning and effectiveness paradigm* focuses on integrating deep-level diversity differences, such as personality, attitudes, beliefs, and values, into the actual work of the organization. One sign that a company hasn't yet created a learning and effectiveness paradigm is that people withhold their opinions for fear of being seen as different. For example, while Helena Morrissey is the CEO of New Investment Management, a London firm that invests $71 billion for its clients, she admits to sometimes keeping her business opinions to herself for fear of being seen as "the annoying" woman at the table. She says, "At a recent meeting I wasn't comfortable with a controversial point and I spoke up, but I also had a different view on the next item

with our differences—not despite them."
D. A. Thomas and R. J. Ely

Organizational plurality
a work environment where (1) all members are empowered to contribute in a way that maximizes the benefits to the organization, customers, and themselves, and (2) the individuality of each member is respected by not segmenting or polarizing people on the basis of their membership in a particular group

on the agenda but instead of speaking up I held back." Says Morrissey, "I have been conscious of feeling that where I did have different views from the rest of the [all-male] group, I may be being perceived as the 'difficult woman' rather than being listened to for what I was saying." She felt this way despite there being, "no evidence that the men were actually feeling that."[98]

The learning and effectiveness paradigm is consistent with achieving organizational plurality. **Organizational plurality** is a work environment where (1) all members are empowered to contribute in a way that maximizes the benefits to the organization, customers, and themselves and (2) the individuality of each member is respected by not segmenting or polarizing people on the basis of their membership in a particular group.[99]

The learning and effectiveness diversity paradigm offers four benefits.[100] First, it values common ground. David Thomas of the Harvard Business School explains, "Like the fairness paradigm, it promotes equal opportunity for all individuals. And like the access paradigm, it acknowledges cultural differences among people and recognizes the value in those differences. Yet this new model for managing diversity lets the organization internalize differences among employees so that it learns and grows because of them. Indeed, with the model fully in place, members of the organization can say, 'We are all on the same team, with our differences—not despite them.'"[101]

Second, this paradigm makes a distinction between individual and group differences. When diversity focuses only on differences between groups, such as females versus males, large differences within groups are ignored.[102] For example, think of the women you know at work. Now, think for a second about what they have in common. After that, think about how they're different. If your situation is typical, the list of differences should be just as long as the list of commonalties, if not longer. In short, managers can achieve a greater understanding of diversity and their employees by treating them as individuals and by realizing that not all African Americans, Hispanics, women, or white males want the same things at work.[103]

Third, because the focus is on individual differences, the learning and effectiveness paradigm is less likely to encounter the conflict, backlash, and divisiveness sometimes associated with diversity programs that focus only on group differences. Taylor Cox, one of the leading management writers on diversity, says, "We are concerned here with these more destructive forms of conflict which may be present with diverse work forces due to language barriers, cultural clash, or resentment by majority-group members of what they may perceive as preferential and unwarranted treatment of minority-group members."[104] And Ray Haines, a consultant who has helped companies deal with the aftermath of diversity programs that became divisive, says, "There's a large amount of backlash related to diversity training. It stirs up a lot of hostility, anguish, and resentment but doesn't give people tools to deal with [the backlash]. You have people come in and talk about their specific ax to grind."[105] Not all diversity programs are divisive or lead to conflict. But by focusing on individual rather than group differences, the learning and effectiveness paradigm helps to minimize these potential problems.

Finally, unlike the other diversity paradigms that simply focus on surface-level diversity, the learning and effectiveness paradigm focuses on bringing different talents and perspectives (i.e., deep-level diversity) *together* to make the best organizational decisions and to produce innovative, competitive products and services.

12-4b DIVERSITY PRINCIPLES

Diversity paradigms are general approaches or strategies for managing diversity. Whatever diversity paradigm a manager chooses, diversity principles will help

---

Swift Punishment

When two Asian men ordered meals at their local Chick-fil-A, the cashier did not ask for their names, which are usually printed on the receipts. Instead, she typed in two derogatory words about the customers' Asian heritage, which then showed up on the receipts. When the restaurant manager found out what happened, he acted quickly by firing the employee. What's more, the company rushed to issue a detailed apology in which it fully admitted to what the employee had done and pledged to serve all customers with respect.

Source: "Chick-fil-A Cashier Fired for Racist Receipts Mocking Asians," *MSNBC.com*, December 14, 2011, accessed March 15, 2012, http://usnews.msnbc.msn.com/_news/2011/12/14/9444087-chick-fil-a-cashier-fired-for-racist-receipts-mocking-asians.

managers do a better job of *managing company diversity programs.*[106]

Begin by *carefully and faithfully following and enforcing federal and state laws regarding equal opportunity employment.* Diversity programs can't and won't succeed if the company is being sued for discriminatory actions and behavior. Faithfully following the law will also reduce the time and expense associated with EEOC investigations or lawsuits. Start by learning more at the EEOC website (http://www.eeoc.gov). Following the law also means strictly and fairly enforcing company policies.

Treat group differences as important but not special. Surface-level diversity dimensions such as age, sex, and race/ethnicity should be respected but should not be treated as more important than other kinds of differences (i.e., deep-level diversity). Remember, the shift in focus from surface- to deep-level diversity helps people know and understand each other better, reduces prejudice and conflict, and leads to stronger social integration with people wanting to work together and get the job done. Also, *find the common ground.* Although respecting differences is important, it's just as important, especially with diverse work forces, to actively find ways for employees to see and share commonalties.

Tailor opportunities to individuals, not groups. Special programs for training, development, mentoring, or promotions should be based on individual strengths and weaknesses, not on group status. Instead of making mentoring available for just one group of workers, create mentoring opportunities for everyone who wants to be mentored. All programs at Pacific Enterprises, including Career Conversations forums, in which upper-level managers are publicly interviewed about themselves and how they got their jobs, are open to all employees.[107]

Maintain high standards. Companies have a legal and moral obligation to make sure that their hiring and promotion procedures and standards are fair to all. At the same time, in today's competitive markets, companies should not lower standards to promote diversity. This not only hurts the organizations but also feeds the stereotype that applicants who are hired or promoted in the name of affirmative action or diversity are less qualified. Chrysler's executive director of diversity, Monica Emerson, says, "As a diversity executive, I not only have to have solid business capabilities, I need to be very knowledgeable of the different businesses in my organization to align diversity initiatives to support the needs of the businesses. Maintaining high standards when making employment decisions

and involving the top management and the board in diversity initiatives is critical to the success of workplace diversity practices."[108]

Solicit negative as well as positive feedback. Diversity is one of the most difficult management issues. No company or manager gets it right from the start. Consequently, companies should aggressively seek positive and negative feedback about their diversity programs. One way to do that is to use a series of measurements to see if progress is being made. Jaya Bohlmann, a vice president at Sodexo, a food services and facilities management company, says, "We measure our progress systematically, using an objective scorecard that ties 15 percent of managers' compensation and 25 percent of our executives' compensation to their success [to ensure that] we continue to attract, develop and retain a diverse and highly skilled workforce. We report on our diversity progress annually, posting the reports on our website."[109]

Set high but realistic goals. Just because diversity is difficult doesn't mean that organizations shouldn't try to accomplish as much as possible. The general purpose of diversity programs is to try to create a positive work environment where no one is advantaged or disadvantaged, where "we" is everyone, where everyone can do his or her best work, where differences are respected and not ignored, and where everyone feels comfortable. Even if progress is slow, companies should not shrink from these goals.

12-4c DIVERSITY TRAINING AND PRACTICES

Organizations use diversity training and several common diversity practices to manage diversity. There are two basic types of diversity training programs. **Awareness training** is designed to raise employees' awareness of diversity issues, such as those discussed in this chapter, and to get employees to challenge underlying assumptions or stereotypes they may have about others. As a starting point in awareness training, some companies have begun using the Implicit Association Test (IAT), which measures the extent to which people associate positive or negative thoughts (i.e., underlying assumptions or stereotypes) with blacks or whites, men or women, homosexuals or heterosexuals, young or old, or other groups. For example, test takers are shown black or white faces that they must instantly pair with

Awareness training training that is designed to raise employees' awareness of diversity issues and to challenge the underlying assumptions or stereotypes they may have about others

Skills-based diversity training training that teaches employees the practical skills they need for managing a diverse work force, such as flexibility and adaptability, negotiation, problem solving, and conflict resolution

Diversity audits formal assessments that measure employee and management attitudes, investigate the extent to which people are advantaged or disadvantaged with respect to hiring and promotions, and review companies' diversity-related policies and procedures

Diversity pairing a mentoring program in which people of different cultural backgrounds, sexes, or races/ethnicities are paired together to get to know each other and change stereotypical beliefs and attitudes

various words. Response times (shorter responses generally indicate stronger associations) and the pattern of associations indicate the extent to which people are biased. Most people are, and strongly so. For example, 88 percent of whites have a more positive mental association toward whites than toward blacks, but, surprisingly, 48 percent of blacks show the same bias. Taking the IAT is a good way to increase awareness of diversity issues. To take the IAT and to learn more about the decade of research behind it, go to https://implicit.harvard.edu /implicit/demo.[110] By contrast, **skills-based diversity training** teaches employees the practical skills they need for managing a diverse work force, skills such as flexibility and adaptability, negotiation, problem solving, and conflict resolution.[111]

Companies also use diversity audits, diversity pairing, and minority experiences for top executives to better manage diversity. **Diversity audits** are formal assessments that measure employee and management attitudes, investigate the extent to which people are advantaged or disadvantaged with respect to hir-

ing and promotions, and review companies' diversity-related policies and procedures. At Intel, the world's leading computer chip manufacturer, diversity is a key part of its competitive strategy and vision. Accordingly, Intel's managers develop annual diversity action plans with specific measures and indicators that are reviewed every three months. For example, since the creation of Intel's Women's Initiative in 2004, the percentage of women in technical middle-level and senior-level jobs has increased by 24 percent.[112]

Intel also assesses its diversity practices through an annual survey about the company's policies and their effectiveness at creating a supportive environment. The survey results are shared with all employees and used to create or revise action plans consistent with its annual diversity action plans.[113]

Earlier in the chapter you learned that *mentoring*, pairing a junior employee with a senior employee, is a common strategy for creating learning and promotional opportunities for women. Diversity pairing is a special kind of mentoring. In **diversity pairing**, people of different cultural backgrounds, sexes, or races/ethnicities are paired for mentoring. The hope is that stereotypical beliefs and attitudes will change as people get to know each other as individuals.[114] Consultant Tom McGee, who has set up mentoring programs for numerous companies, supports diversity pairing, saying, "The assumption that people participating in diversity mentoring programs are looking for someone of the same race or gender has been proved wrong in many cases."[115]

© iStockphoto.com/nicole waring

For more than twenty years, Xerox has been fostering a culture where women and minorities are prepared and considered for top positions. CEO Ursula Burns, the first African American woman to lead a major U.S. company, worked as special assistant to Xerox's president of marketing and customer operations, Wayland Hicks. Reginald Brown, Jr., CEO of Brown Technology Group, who worked with Burns at Xerox, said, "These [appointments as special assistants] were jobs in the company that division presidents put their best people in. Most of them were white males, so to have an African American female in such a position of power, you knew early on she had great potential." Burns was then given a similar role with former Xerox CEO Paul A. Allaire. When Anne Mulcahy became CEO in 2001, Burns was gradually given control of day-to-day operations while Mulcahy repaired Xerox's financial position and customer service. David Thomas, a Harvard Business School professor, says that because of steps (such as diversity pairing) to promote diversity at Xerox, "You have a culture where having women and people of color as candidates for powerful jobs has been going on for two decades."[116]

Finally, because top managers are still overwhelmingly white and male, a number of companies believe that it is worthwhile to *have top executives experience what it is like to be in the minority*. This can be done by having top managers go to places or events where nearly everyone else is of a different sex or racial/ethnic background. For example, managers at Raytheon are required to spend an entire day in the office in a wheelchair so that they have a better understanding of the challenges faced by their disabled colleagues. Managers and executives at Sodexho Alliance are asked to spend time working with organizations that represent minorities. One male manager became the sponsor of a women employees group at Sodexho and accompanied a female colleague to a meeting of the Women's Food Service Forum. The manager called the experience, in which he was at a conference with 1,500 women, "profound" and said that it taught him what it feels like to be different. He also describes how his experiences working with women made him more sensitive to women's feelings and even led him to change the social activities that he plans with co-workers from golf to dinner cruises. Rohini Anand, Sodexho's chief diversity officer, endorses this experiential approach, saying, "To really engage people, you have to create a series of epiphanies and take leaders through those epiphanies."[117]

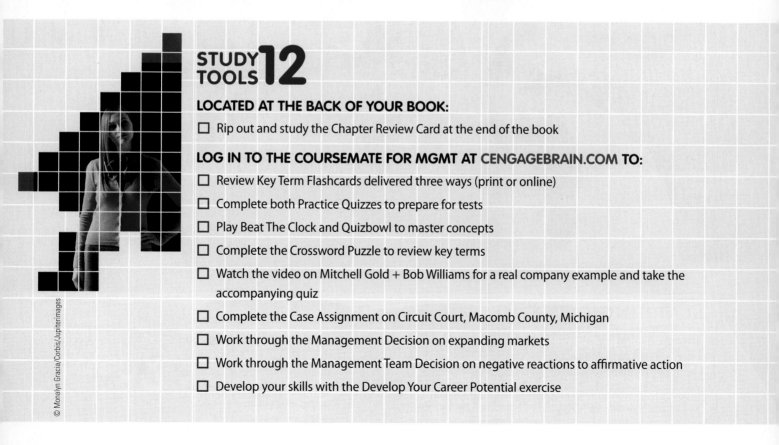

STUDY TOOLS 12

© Monalyn Gracia/Corbis/Jupiterimages

LOCATED AT THE BACK OF YOUR BOOK:

☐ Rip out and study the Chapter Review Card at the end of the book

LOG IN TO THE COURSEMATE FOR MGMT AT CENGAGEBRAIN.COM TO:

☐ Review Key Term Flashcards delivered three ways (print or online)

☐ Complete both Practice Quizzes to prepare for tests

☐ Play Beat The Clock and Quizbowl to master concepts

☐ Complete the Crossword Puzzle to review key terms

☐ Watch the video on Mitchell Gold + Bob Williams for a real company example and take the accompanying quiz

☐ Complete the Case Assignment on Circuit Court, Macomb County, Michigan

☐ Work through the Management Decision on expanding markets

☐ Work through the Management Team Decision on negative reactions to affirmative action

☐ Develop your skills with the Develop Your Career Potential exercise

13 Motivation

LEARNING OUTCOMES

13-1 Explain the basics of motivation.

13-2 Use equity theory to explain how employees' perceptions of fairness affect motivation.

13-3 Use expectancy theory to describe how workers' expectations about rewards, effort, and the link between rewards and performance influence motivation.

13-4 Explain how reinforcement theory works and how it can be used to motivate.

13-5 Describe the components of goal-setting theory and how managers can use them to motivate workers.

13-6 Discuss how the entire motivation model can be used to motivate workers.

CHECK OUT
STUDY TOOLS
AT THE END OF THIS CHAPTER.

13-1 *Basics of Motivation*

What makes people happiest and most productive at work? Is it money, benefits, opportunities for growth, interesting work, or something else altogether? And if people desire different things, how can a company keep everyone motivated? It takes insight and hard work to motivate workers to join the company, perform well, and then stay with the company. Indeed, when asked to name their biggest management challenge, nearly one-third of executives polled by Creative Group, a specialized staffing service in Menlo Park, California, cited "motivating employees."[1]

So what is motivation? **Motivation** is the set of forces that initiates, directs, and makes people persist in their efforts to accomplish a goal.[2] *Initiation of effort* is concerned with the choices that people make about how much effort to put forth in their jobs. ("Do I really knock myself out for these performance appraisals or just do a decent job?") *Direction of effort* is concerned with the choices that people make in deciding where to put forth effort in their jobs. ("I should be spending time with my high-dollar accounts instead of learning this new computer system!") *Persistence of effort* is concerned with the choices that people make about how long they will put forth effort in their jobs before reducing or eliminating those efforts. ("I'm only halfway through the project, and I'm exhausted. Do I plow through to the end, or just call it quits?") Initiation, direction, and persistence are at the heart of motivation.

Jenny Miller manages 170 engineers who design and build computer systems for aircraft carrier flight decks. Despite long hours each week, they were at risk of not meeting a December 1st deadline for their project. So, with the overtime budget already spent, she asked for volunteers to work Friday, Saturday, or Sunday of Thanksgiving weekend without pay or compensatory time off. Still, twenty engineers showed up, the deadline was met, and Miller thanked those who volunteered with $100 gift cards.[3]

At **37signals.com**, a Chicago software company, founder Jason Fried has avoided using promotions to reward his thirty employees. Says Fried, "We revere 'horizontal' ambition—in which employees who love what they do are encouraged to dig deeper, expand their knowledge, and become better at it. We always try to hire people who yearn to be master craftspeople, that is, designers who want to be great designers, not managers of designers; developers who want to master the art of programming, not management."[4]

Would you be motivated to volunteer to work over a holiday weekend if it helped your company meet a key deadline? Which would motivate you more, the chance to become a master craftsperson or the opportunity for promotion and management responsibilities? Answering questions like these is at the heart of figuring out how best to motivate people at work.

Let's learn more about motivation by building a basic model of motivation out of **13-1a effort and performance,** **13-1b need satisfaction,** *and* **13-1c extrinsic and intrinsic rewards** *and then discussing* **13-1d how to motivate people with this basic model of motivation.**

13-1a EFFORT AND PERFORMANCE

When most people think of work motivation, they think that working hard

Motivation the set of forces that initiates, directs, and makes people persist in their efforts to accomplish a goal

Needs the physical or psychological requirements that must be met to ensure survival and well-being

(effort) should lead to a good job (performance). Exhibit 13.1 shows a basic model of work motivation and performance, displaying this process. The first thing to notice about Exhibit 13.1 is that this is a basic model of work motivation *and* performance. In practice, it's almost impossible to talk about one without mentioning the other. Not surprisingly, managers often assume motivation to be the only determinant of performance, saying things such as "Your performance was really terrible last quarter. What's the matter? Aren't you as motivated as you used to be?" In fact, motivation is just one of three primary determinants of job performance. In industrial psychology, job performance is frequently represented by this equation:

Job Performance =
Motivation × Ability × Situational Constraints

In this formula, *job performance* is how well someone performs the requirements of the job. *Motivation*, as defined above, is effort, the degree to which someone works hard to do the job well. *Ability* is the degree to which workers possess the knowledge, skills, and talent needed to do a job well. And *situational constraints* are factors beyond the control of individual employees, such as tools, policies, and resources that have an effect on job performance.

Since job performance is a multiplicative function of motivation times ability times situational constraints, job performance will suffer if any one of these components is weak. Does this mean that motivation doesn't matter? No, not at all. It just means that all the motivation in the world won't translate into high performance when an employee has little ability and high situational constraints. So, even though we will spend this chapter developing a model of work motivation, it is important to remember that ability and situational constraints affect job performance as well.

13-1b NEED SATISFACTION

In Exhibit 13.1, we started with a very basic model of motivation in which effort leads to job performance. But managers want to know, "What leads to effort?" Determining employee needs is the first step to answering that questions.

Needs are the physical or psychological requirements that must be met to ensure survival and well-being.[5] As shown on the left side of Exhibit 13.2, a person's unmet need creates an uncomfortable, internal state of tension that must be resolved. For exam-

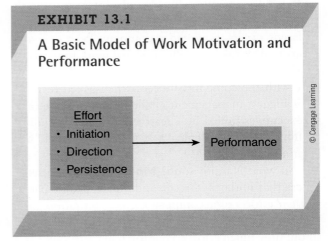

EXHIBIT 13.1

A Basic Model of Work Motivation and Performance

© Cengage Learning

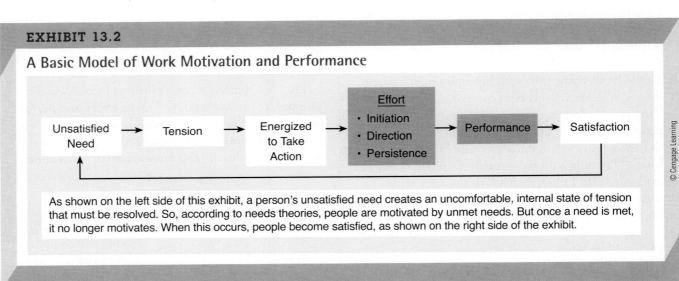

EXHIBIT 13.2

A Basic Model of Work Motivation and Performance

As shown on the left side of this exhibit, a person's unsatisfied need creates an uncomfortable, internal state of tension that must be resolved. So, according to needs theories, people are motivated by unmet needs. But once a need is met, it no longer motivates. When this occurs, people become satisfied, as shown on the right side of the exhibit.

© Cengage Learning

ple, if you normally skip breakfast but then have to work through lunch, chances are you'll be so hungry by late afternoon that the only thing you'll be motivated to do is find something to eat. So, according to needs theories, people are motivated by unmet needs. But a need no longer motivates once it is met. When this occurs, people become satisfied, as shown on the right side of Exhibit 13.2.

Note: Throughout the chapter, as we build on this basic model, the parts of the model that we've already discussed will appear shaded in color. For example, since we've already discussed the effort → performance part of the model, those components are shown with a colored background. When we add new parts to the model, they will have a white background. Since we're adding need satisfaction to the model at this step, the need-satisfaction components of unsatisfied need, tension, energized to take action, and satisfaction are shown with a white background. This shading convention should make it easier to understand the work motivation model as we add to it in each section of the chapter.

Since people are motivated by unmet needs, managers must learn what those unmet needs are and address them. This is not always a straightforward task, however, because different needs theories suggest different needs categories. Consider three well-known needs theories. Maslow's Hierarchy of Needs suggests that people are motivated by *physiological* (food and water), *safety* (physical and economic), *belongingness* (friendship, love, social interaction), *esteem* (achievement and recognition), and *self-actualization* (realizing your full potential) needs.[6] Alderfer's ERG Theory collapses Maslow's five needs into three: *existence* (safety and physiological needs), *relatedness* (belongingness), and *growth* (esteem and self-actualization).[7] McClelland's Learned Needs Theory suggests that people are motivated by the need for *affiliation* (to be liked and accepted), the need for *achievement* (to accomplish challenging goals), or the need for *power* (to influence others).[8]

Things become even more complicated when we consider the different predictions made by these theories. According to Maslow, needs are arranged in a hierarchy from low (physiological) to high (self-actualization). Within this hierarchy, people are motivated by their lowest unsatisfied need. As each need is met, they work their way up the hierarchy from physiological to self-actualization needs. By contrast, Alderfer says that people can be motivated by more

than one need at a time. Furthermore, he suggests that people are just as likely to move down the needs hierarchy as up, particularly when they are unable to achieve satisfaction at the next higher need level. McClelland argues that the degree to which particular needs motivate varies tremendously from person to person, with some people being motivated primarily by achievement and others by power or affiliation. Moreover, McClelland says that needs are learned, not innate. For instance, studies show that children whose parents own a small business or hold a managerial position are much more likely to have a high need for achievement.[9]

So, with three different sets of needs and three very different ideas about how needs motivate, how do we provide a practical answer to managers who just want to know "What leads to effort?" Fortunately, the research evidence simplifies things a bit. To start, studies indicate that there are two basic kinds of needs categories.[10] *Lower-order needs* are concerned with safety and with physiological and existence requirements, whereas *higher-order needs* are concerned with relationships (belongingness, relatedness, and affiliation); challenges and accomplishments (esteem, self-actualization, growth, and achievement); and influence (power). Studies generally show that higher-order needs will not motivate people as long as lower-order needs remain unsatisfied.[11]

For example, imagine that you graduated from college six months ago and are still looking for your first job. With money running short (you're probably living on your credit cards) and the possibility of having to move back in with your parents looming (if this doesn't motivate you, what will?), your basic needs for food, shelter, and security drive your thoughts, behavior, and choices at this point. But once you land that job, find a great place (of your own!) to live, and put some money in the bank, these basic needs should decrease in importance as you begin to think about making new friends and taking on challenging work assignments. In fact, once lower-order needs are satisfied, it's difficult for managers to predict which higher-order needs will motivate behavior.[12] Some people will be motivated by affiliation, while others will be motivated by growth or esteem. Also, the relative importance of the various needs may change over time but not necessarily in any predictable pattern. So, what leads to effort? In part, needs do. After we discuss rewards in Subsection 13-1c, in Subsection 13-1d we discuss how managers can use what we know from need-satisfaction theories to motivate workers.

Extrinsic reward a reward that is tangible, visible to others, and given to employees contingent on the performance of specific tasks or behaviors

Intrinsic reward a natural reward associated with performing a task or activity for its own sake

13-1c EXTRINSIC AND INTRINSIC REWARDS

No discussion of motivation would be complete without considering rewards. Let's add two kinds of rewards, extrinsic and intrinsic, to the model in Exhibit 13.3.[13]

Extrinsic rewards are tangible and visible to others and are given to employees contingent on the performance of specific tasks or behaviors.[14] External agents (managers, for example) determine and control the distribution, frequency, and amount of extrinsic rewards, such as pay, company stock, benefits, and promotions. (see box "The Benefits of Working Here") For example, 80 percent of 1,000 large and medium-sized U.S. companies surveyed by Hewitt Associates, a consulting company based in Lincolnshire, Illinois, offer incentives or bonuses to reward employees.[15]

After exceeding operational and financial goals, Alaska Air Group awarded $58.3 million in bonuses to 12,800 employees. This was in addition to a $1,000 bonus that all employees received earlier in the year for meeting goals related to customer satisfaction and on-time arrivals and departures (Alaska Air was number one in both categories). CEO Brad Tilden said, "We earned these awards because of the hard work and dedication of our people. I want to thank them for their

focus on running a safe and on-time operation, and for their commitment to our customers."[16]

Why do companies need extrinsic rewards? To get people to do things they wouldn't otherwise do. Companies use extrinsic rewards to motivate people to perform four basic behaviors: join the organization, regularly attend their jobs, perform their jobs well, and stay with the organization.[17] Think about it. Would you show up at work every day to do the best possible job that you could just out of the goodness of your heart? Very few people would.

Intrinsic rewards are the natural rewards associated with performing a task or activity for its own sake. For example, aside from the external rewards management offers for doing something well, employees often find the activities or tasks they perform interesting and enjoyable. Examples of intrinsic rewards include a sense of accomplishment or achievement, a feeling of responsibility, the chance to learn something new or interact

EXHIBIT 13.3

Adding Rewards to the Model

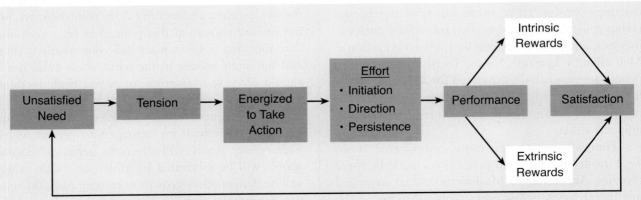

Performing a job well can be rewarding intrinsically (the job itself is fun, challenging, or interesting) or extrinsically (as you receive better pay, promotions, etc.). Intrinsic and extrinsic rewards lead to satisfaction of various needs.

with others, or simply the fun that comes from performing an interesting, challenging, and engaging task.

Atlassian, an Australian software company that develops collaboration tools for teams, uses intrinsic rewards during its quarterly "FedEx Days." Atlassian's Jesse Gibbs says, "During FedEx days, Atlassian developers have twenty-four hours to build and deliver a working software prototype. They've produced a ton of cool features that eventually made it into shipping products (as well as producing a lot of empty beer bottles and pizza cartons). At the end, everyone presents their software in front of the company, and Atlassians vote for their favorite FedEx 'delivery.'"[18] The program produced so many valuable innovations that Atlassian expanded the policy, allowing employees to use 20 percent of the workweek on projects of their choice. A company spokesperson says, "Our hope is that 20 percent time gives engineers back dedicated slack time—of their own direction—to spend on product innovation, features, plugins, fixes or additions that *they* think are the most important."[19]

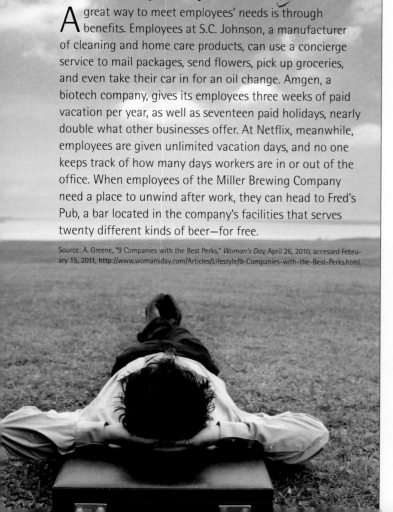

The Benefits of Working Here

A great way to meet employees' needs is through benefits. Employees at S.C. Johnson, a manufacturer of cleaning and home care products, can use a concierge service to mail packages, send flowers, pick up groceries, and even take their car in for an oil change. Amgen, a biotech company, gives its employees three weeks of paid vacation per year, as well as seventeen paid holidays, nearly double what other businesses offer. At Netflix, meanwhile, employees are given unlimited vacation days, and no one keeps track of how many days workers are in or out of the office. When employees of the Miller Brewing Company need a place to unwind after work, they can head to Fred's Pub, a bar located in the company's facilities that serves twenty different kinds of beer—for free.

Source: A. Greene, "9 Companies with the Best Perks," *Woman's Day*, April 26, 2010, accessed February 15, 2011, http://www.womansday.com/Articles/Lifestyle/9-Companies-with-the-Best-Perks.html.

Which types of rewards are most important to workers in general? A number of surveys suggest that both extrinsic and intrinsic rewards are important. One survey found that the most important rewards were good benefits and health insurance, job security, a week or more of vacation (all extrinsic rewards), interesting work, the opportunity to learn new skills, and independent work situations (all intrinsic rewards). And employee preferences for intrinsic and extrinsic rewards appear to be relatively stable. Studies conducted over the last three decades have consistently found that employees are twice as likely to indicate that important and meaningful work matters more to them than what they are paid.[20] Indeed, when asked, "If you were to get enough money to live as comfortably as you would like for the rest of your life, would you continue to work or would you stop working?" Sixty-nine percent of American workers said they would keep working. Clearly, intrinsic rewards matter.[21]

13-1d MOTIVATING WITH THE BASICS

So, given the basic model of work motivation in Exhibit 13.3, what practical steps can managers take to motivate employees to increase their effort?

The first step is to *start by asking people what their needs are*. Dan Amos, the CEO of **Aflac**, which sells supplemental insurance, wanted to find out what could be done to prevent talented people from leaving the company for other jobs. So two decades ago, when he became CEO he asked—and that process of asking created Aflac's annual employee companywide survey. What he found was that instead of just more money, Aflac's employees, nearly 70 percent of whom are women, wanted more recognition for their work and on-site daycare. The survey also revealed that many women in the company struggled with balancing work and home responsibilities, so Amos set up a flexible scheduling program. By asking employees what they needed, Aflac has been able to keep its employee turnover rate close to zero. As Amos says, if you listen, "the survey never lies."[22] So, if you want to meet employees' needs, just ask.

Next, *satisfy lower-order needs first*. Since higher-order needs will not motivate people as long as lower-order needs remain unsatisfied, companies should satisfy lower-order needs first. In practice, this means providing the equipment, training, and knowledge to create a safe workplace free of physical risks, paying employees well enough to provide financial security,

Equity theory a theory that states that people will be motivated when they perceive that they are being treated fairly

Inputs in equity theory, the contributions employees make to the organization

Outcomes in equity theory, the rewards employees receive for their contributions to the organization

and offering a benefits package that will protect employees and their families through good medical coverage and health and disability insurance. Indeed, a survey based on a representative sample of Americans found that when people choose jobs or organizations, three of the four most important factors—starting pay/salary (62 percent), employee benefits (57 percent), and job security (47 percent)—are lower-order needs.[23] Consistent with the idea of satisfying lower-order needs first, a survey of 12,000 employees found that inadequate compensation is the number-one reason employees leave organizations.[24]

Third, managers should *expect people's needs to change.* As some needs are satisfied or situations change, what motivated people before may not motivate them now. Likewise, what motivates people to accept a job may not necessarily motivate them once they have the job. For instance, David Stum, president of the Loyalty Institute, says, "The [attractive] power of pay and benefits is only [strong] during the recruitment stage. After employees take the job, pay and benefits become entitlements to them. They think: 'Now that I work here, you owe me that.'"[25] Managers should also expect needs to change as people mature. For older employees, benefits are as important as pay, which is always ranked as more important by younger employees. Older employees also rank job security as more important than personal and family time, which is more important to younger employees.[26]

Finally, *as needs change and lower-order needs are satisfied, create opportunities for employees to satisfy higher-order needs.* Recall that intrinsic rewards such as accomplishment, achievement, learning something new, and interacting with others are the natural rewards associated with performing a task or activity for its own sake. And, with the exception of influence (power), intrinsic rewards correspond very closely to higher-order needs that are concerned with relationships (belongingness, relatedness, and affiliation) and challenges and accomplishments (esteem, self-actualization, growth, and achievement). Therefore, one way for managers to meet employees' higher-order needs is to create opportunities for employees to experience intrinsic rewards by providing challenging work, encouraging employees to take greater responsibility for their work, and giving employees the freedom to pursue tasks and projects they find naturally interesting.

13-2 *Equity Theory*

We've seen that people are motivated to achieve intrinsic and extrinsic rewards. However, if employees don't believe that rewards are fairly awarded or don't believe that they can achieve the performance goals the company has set for them, they won't be very motivated.

Fairness, or what people perceive to be fair, is also a critical issue in organizations. **Equity theory** says that people will be motivated at work when they *perceive* that they are being treated fairly. In particular, equity theory stresses the importance of perceptions. So, regardless of the actual level of rewards people receive, they must also perceive that, relative to others, they are being treated fairly. For example, you learned in Chapter 11 that the average CEO now makes 343 times more than the average worker.[27] Furthermore, CEOs of companies listed in the Standard & Poor's 500 make an average of $11.4 million a year.[28] The ten highest-paid CEOs received an average of $76 million in compensation, led by John Hammergren, the CEO of McKesson Corporation, who made $145 million.[29]

Many people believe that CEO pay is obscenely high and unfair. Others believe that CEO pay is fair because the supply and demand for executive talent largely determine what CEOs are paid. They argue that if it were easier to find good CEOs, then CEOs would be paid much less. Equity theory doesn't focus on objective equity (that is, that CEOs make 343 times more than blue-collar workers). Instead, equity theory says that equity, like beauty, is in the eye of the beholder.

Let's learn more about equity theory by examining **13-2a the components of equity theory, 13-2b how people react to perceived inequity,** *and* **13-2c how to motivate people using equity theory.**

13-2a COMPONENTS OF EQUITY THEORY

The basic components of equity theory are inputs, outcomes, and referents. **Inputs** are the contributions employees make to the organization. They include education and training, intelligence, experience, effort, number of hours worked, and ability. **Outcomes** are what employees receive in exchange for their contributions to the organization. They include

REFERENT'S OUTCOME/INPUT RATIO

MY OUTCOME/INPUT RATIO

pay, fringe benefits, status symbols, and job titles and assignments. And, since perceptions of equity depend on comparisons, **referents** are other people with whom people compare themselves to determine if they have been treated fairly. The referent can be a single person (comparing yourself with a coworker), a generalized other (comparing yourself with "students in general," for example), or even yourself over time ("I was better off last year than I am this year"). Usually, people choose to compare themselves with referents who hold the same or similar jobs or who are otherwise similar in gender, race, age, tenure, or other characteristics.[30] For instance, by any objective measure, it's hard to argue that the best professional athletes, who make as much as $30 million a year (and no doubt more by the time you read this), are treated unfairly, given that the typical American earns $46,040 a year.[31] Nonetheless, most top athletes' contracts include escalator clauses specifying that if another top player at the same position (i.e., their referent) receives a larger contract, then their contract will automatically be increased to that amount.

According to equity theory, employees compare their outcomes (the rewards they receive from the organization) with their inputs (their contributions to the organization). This comparison of outcomes with inputs is called the **outcome/input (O/I) ratio**. After an internal comparison in which they compare their outcomes with their inputs, employees then make an external comparison in which they compare their O/I ratio with the O/I ratio of a referent.[32]

When people perceive that their O/I ratio is equal to the referent's O/I ratio, they conclude that they are being treated fairly. But when people perceive that their O/I ratio is different from their referent's O/I ratio, they conclude that they have been treated inequitably or unfairly.

Inequity can take two forms, underreward and overreward. **Underreward** occurs when a referent's O/I ratio is better than your O/I ratio. In other words, you are getting fewer outcomes relative to your inputs than the referent you compare yourself with is getting. When people perceive that they have been underrewarded, they tend to experience anger or frustration. For example, when a manufacturing company received notice that some important contracts had been canceled, management cut employees' pay by 15 percent in one plant but not in another. Just as equity theory predicts, theft doubled in the plant that received the pay cut. Likewise, employee turnover increased from 5 percent to 23 percent.[33]

By contrast, **overreward** occurs when a referent's O/I ratio is worse than your O/I ratio. In this case, you are getting more outcomes relative to your inputs than your referent is. In theory, when people perceive that they have been overrewarded, they experience guilt. But, not surprisingly, people have a very high tolerance for overreward. It takes a tremendous amount of overpayment before people decide that their pay or benefits are more than they deserve.

13-2b HOW PEOPLE REACT TO PERCEIVED INEQUITY

So what happens when people perceive that they have been treated inequitably at work? Exhibit 13.4 on the next page shows that perceived inequity affects satisfaction. In the case of underreward, this usually translates into frustration or anger; with overreward, the reaction is guilt. These reactions lead to tension and a strong need to take action to restore equity in some way. At first, a slight inequity may not be strong enough to motivate an employee to take immediate action. If the inequity continues or there are multiple inequities,

Referents in equity theory, others with whom people compare themselves to determine if they have been treated fairly

Outcome/input (O/I) ratio in equity theory, an employee's perception of how the rewards received from an organization compare with the employee's contributions to that organization

Underreward a form of inequity in which you are getting fewer outcomes relative to inputs than your referent is getting

Overreward a form of inequity in which you are getting more outcomes relative to inputs than your referent

EXHIBIT 13.4

Adding Equity Theory to the Model

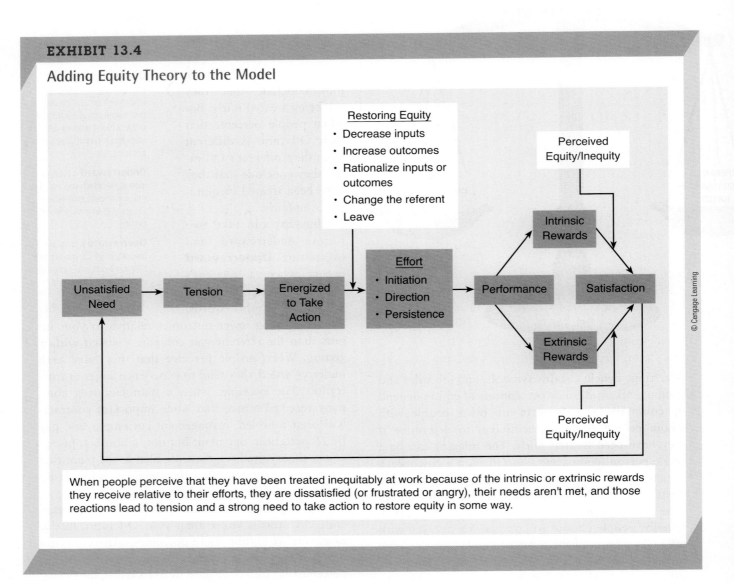

Restoring Equity
- Decrease inputs
- Increase outcomes
- Rationalize inputs or outcomes
- Change the referent
- Leave

When people perceive that they have been treated inequitably at work because of the intrinsic or extrinsic rewards they receive relative to their efforts, they are dissatisfied (or frustrated or angry), their needs aren't met, and those reactions lead to tension and a strong need to take action to restore equity in some way.

© Cengage Learning

however, tension may build over time until a point of intolerance is reached, and the person is energized to take action.[34]

Dejan Karabasevic, a programmer at American Superconductor, an energy technologies company, had access to the company's proprietary computer code that provided its key competitive advantage. After the company demoted him, Karabasevic sold the code to Sinovel, a Chinese power company and key customer. After Sinovel received the proprietary computer code, it canceled all of its orders, refusing to pay American Superconductor for products it had already received. Because of Karabasevic's actions, which he took in response to being demoted, American Superconductor lost $6.5 million and saw its stock price drop a staggering 86 percent.[35]

When people perceive that they have been treated unfairly, they may try to restore equity by reducing inputs, increasing outcomes, rationalizing inputs or outcomes, changing the referent, or simply leaving. We will discuss these possible responses in terms of the inequity associated with underreward, which is much more common than the inequity associated with overreward.

People who perceive that they have been underrewarded may try to restore equity by *decreasing or withholding their inputs (that is, effort)*. Workers at an LG flat panel display factory in Nanjing, China, went on strike after receiving a bonus equal to one month's pay. Workers felt underrewarded in two ways. To start, the previous year's bonus was equal to three months' pay. Second, LG's employees in a South Korean factory doing identical work received a bonus equal to six months' pay. When LG's 8,000 Nanjing employees discovered that they were receiving bonuses one-sixth the size of their South Korean counterparts, they

immediately called a strike, despite risking arrest by the Chinese government.[36]

Increasing outcomes is another way people try to restore equity. This might include asking for a raise or pointing out the inequity to the boss and hoping that he or she takes care of it. Sometimes, however, employees may go to external organizations such as labor unions, federal agencies, or the courts for help in increasing outcomes to restore equity. For instance, the U.S. Department of Labor estimates that 10 percent of workers are not getting the extra overtime pay they deserve when they work more than forty hours a week.[37] These are known as Fair Labor Standards Act (FLSA) violations. In fact, more than 30,000 such cases are brought each year, and employees win two-thirds of them.[38] Edward Harold, a partner with the law firm of Fisher & Phillips in New Orleans, says, "There has been an explosion of Fair Labor Standards Act litigation since 2002."[39]

Federal air marshals, who are employed by the U.S. Department of Homeland Security (DHS), provide security on airline flights by posing as passengers and taking action if threatening behavior occurs. Although marshals frequently work sixteen- to twenty-hour days, DHS denied them overtime pay, contending they were exempt from the FLSA and that their "availability pay," a 25 percent increase in pay for being available twenty-four hours a day, compensated them for their long hours. A federal judge ruled, however, that the marshals were not exempt from the FLSA, that availability pay was not intended as overtime pay, and that the DHS owed the marshals $106 million in unpaid overtime.[40]

Another method of restoring equity is to *rationalize or distort inputs or outcomes*. Instead of decreasing inputs or increasing outcomes, employees restore equity by making mental or emotional adjustments in

their O/I ratios or the O/I ratios of their referents. For example, suppose that a company downsizes 10 percent of its work force. It's likely that the people who still have jobs will be angry or frustrated with company management because of the layoffs. If alternative jobs are difficult to find, however, these survivors may rationalize or distort their O/I ratios and conclude, "Well, things could be worse. At least I still have my job." Rationalizing or distorting outcomes may be used when other ways to restore equity aren't available.

Changing the referent is another way of restoring equity. In this case, people compare themselves with someone other than the referent they had been using for previous O/I ratio comparisons. Since people usually choose to compare themselves with others who hold the same or similar jobs or who are otherwise similar (i.e., friends, family members, neighbors who work at other companies), they may change referents to restore equity when their personal situations change, such as a decrease in job status or pay.[41]

13-2c MOTIVATING WITH EQUITY THEORY

What practical steps can managers take to use equity theory to motivate employees? They can *start by looking for and correcting major inequities*. Among other things, equity theory makes us aware that an employee's sense of fairness is based on subjective perceptions. What one employee considers grossly unfair may not affect another employee's perceptions of equity at all. Although these different perceptions make it difficult for managers to create conditions that satisfy all employees, it's critical that they do their best to take care of major inequities that can energize employees to take disruptive, costly, or harmful actions such as decreasing inputs or leaving. So, whenever possible, managers should look for and correct major inequities.

At Burgerville, a thirty-nine–restaurant fast-food chain in Vancouver, Washington, annual employee turnover was 128 percent per year. The key inequity? Employees making $9 an hour couldn't afford health insurance for themselves and their families. Indeed, while Burgerville's health plan was cheap at $42 a month for employees and $105 a month for families, it provided limited benefits and came with a $1,000 deductible. As a result, only 3 percent of employees were enrolled in it. Under Burgerville's revised health plan, employees who work at least twenty hours a week get full health insurance at a cost of just $15 a month for themselves and $90 a month for their

Distributive justice the perceived degree to which outcomes and rewards are fairly distributed or allocated

Procedural justice the perceived fairness of the process used to make reward allocation decisions

families—in both instances, there's no deductible. Although the new plan was expensive, nearly doubling the company's health care costs from $2.1 million to $4.1 million, the cost was easily offset by lower employee turnover, which dropped from 128 percent per year to 54 percent per year, and higher sales, which were up 11 percent. Furthermore, 98 percent of Burgerville's hourly employees and 97 percent of its salaried employees enrolled in the new health plan, compared to just 3 percent before.[42]

Second, managers can *reduce employees' inputs*. Increasing outcomes is often the first and only strategy that companies use to restore equity, yet reducing employee inputs is just as viable a strategy. In fact, with dual-career couples working fifty-hour weeks, more and more employees are looking for ways to

reduce stress and restore a balance between work and family. Consequently, it may make sense to ask employees to do less, not more; to have them identify and eliminate the 20 percent of their jobs that doesn't increase productivity or add value for customers; and to eliminate company-imposed requirements that really aren't critical to the performance of managers, employees, or the company (for example, unnecessary meetings and reports). According to Chinese labor laws, employees may not work more than thirty-six hours of overtime per month, or no more than nine overtime hours per week. However, after a catastrophic plant explosion and a series of employee suicides disrupted production at a Foxconn factory in China, factory workers, who assemble everything from iPads to laptop computers, worked 80 to 100 overtime hours each month on top of their 174 regular hours to make up for the production shortfalls. During this time, employees regularly worked twelve-hour shifts, six days a week, or sixty hours a month over the legal limit. As a result of pressure from Apple and from international workers' rights groups, Foxconn has agreed to immediately increase pay as much as 25 percent and limit the number of hours an employee works to forty-nine per week.[43]

Finally, managers should *make sure decision-making processes are fair*. Equity theory focuses on **distributive justice**, the perceived degree to which outcomes and rewards are fairly distributed or allocated. However, **procedural justice**, the perceived fairness of the procedures used to make reward allocation decisions, is just as important.[44] Procedural justice matters because even when employees are unhappy with their outcomes (that is, low pay), they're much less likely to be unhappy with company management if they believe that the procedures used to allocate outcomes were fair. For example, employees who are laid off tend to be hostile toward their employer when they perceive that the procedures leading to the layoffs were unfair. By contrast, employees who perceive layoff procedures to be

Game On

LiveOps, which provides call center services to various companies, uses games to motivate employees to improve their performance. The company tracks every call that their employees take and awards badges and points based on how long the calls last (shorter is best) and how effective employees are at closing sales. A company-wide leaderboard helps employees see where they rank compared to everyone else. Since it has started using this system, call times have decreased by 15 percent, and sales rates have increased 8–12 percent.

Source: R. E. Silverman, "Latest Game Theory: Mixing Work and Play," *Wall Street Journal*, October 10, 2011, accessed March 21, 2012, http://online.wsj.com/article/SB10001424052970204294504576615371783795248.html?mod=WSJ_business_LeftSecondHighlights.

© Flying Colours Ltd/Photodisc/Jupiterimages

fair tend to continue to support and trust their employers.[45] Also, if employees perceive that their outcomes are unfair (that is, distributive injustice), but that the decisions and procedures leading to those outcomes were fair (that is, procedural justice), they are much more likely to seek constructive ways of restoring equity, such as discussing these matters with their manager. By contrast, if employees perceive both distributive and procedural injustice, they may resort to more destructive tactics, such as withholding effort, absenteeism, tardiness, or even sabotage and theft.[46]

13-3 *Expectancy Theory*

One of the hardest things about motivating people is that not everyone is attracted to the same rewards. **Expectancy theory** says that people will be motivated to the extent to which they believe that their efforts will lead to good performance, that good performance will be rewarded, and that they will be offered attractive rewards (see box "What Employees Want").[47]

Let's learn more about expectancy theory by examining **13-3a the components of expectancy theory** *and* **13-3b how to use expectancy theory as a motivational tool.**

13-3a COMPONENTS OF EXPECTANCY THEORY

Expectancy theory holds that people make conscious choices about their motivation. The three factors that affect those choices are valence, expectancy, and instrumentality.

Valence is simply the attractiveness or desirability of various rewards or outcomes. Expectancy theory recognizes that the same reward or outcome— say, a promotion—will be highly attractive to some people, will be highly disliked by others, and will not make much difference one way or the other to still others. Accordingly, when people are deciding how much effort to put forth, expectancy theory says that they will consider the valence of all possible rewards and outcomes that they can receive from their jobs. The greater the sum of those valences, each of which can be positive, negative, or neutral, the more effort people will choose to put forth on the job.

CrowdFlower, an employment agency based in San Francisco that breaks big projects into smaller tasks that can be completed by individual workers (i.e., "crowdsourcing"), understands that different people are motivated by different rewards. So, when it assigns someone to a task, which can range from verifying search engine links to categorizing Twitter posts, it gives them the option of receiving payment in cash or virtual cash. Some employees choose real money, while others choose virtual money that can be spent in online games like FarmVille, Mafia Wars, or Tinier Me. Though the idea of working for virtual money may sound strange, Amanda Dorsey, one of CrowdFlower's workers, says, "Doing work for virtual currency is pretty much like any other form of

Expectancy theory the theory that people will be motivated to the extent to which they believe that their efforts will lead to good performance, that good performance will be rewarded, and that they will be offered attractive rewards

Valence the attractiveness or desirability of a reward or outcome

What Employees Want

A bonus or a rewards program is only good if employees get what they want. If most of the employees of a company are motivated by extra days off, a $100 gift certificate to a local restaurant is unlikely to be effective motivation. So what do employees want? In a survey of 2,574 U.S. workers, almost 75 percent said that they preferred receiving cash bonuses, 62 percent reported that they would prefer a salary increase, and 32 percent responded that they wanted more paid time off.

Source: "Forget the Christmas Parties, Employees Want Cash," Reuters, December 6, 2011, accessed March 21, 2012, http://www.reuters.com/article/2011/12/06/us-holidays-wishlist -idUSTRE7B520920111206.

putting forth an effort for a reward."[48]

Expectancy is the perceived relationship between effort and performance. When expectancies are strong, employees believe that their hard work and efforts will result in good performance, so they work harder. By contrast, when expectancies are weak, employees figure that no matter what they do or how hard they work, they won't be able to perform their jobs successfully, so they don't work as hard.

Instrumentality is the perceived relationship between performance and rewards. When instrumentality is strong, employees believe that improved performance will lead to better and more rewards, so they choose to work harder. When instrumentality is weak,

employees don't believe that better performance will result in more or better rewards, so they choose not to work as hard.

Expectancy theory holds that for people to be highly motivated, all three variables—valence, expectancy, and instrumentality—must be high. Thus, expectancy theory can be represented by the following simple equation:

Motivation =
Valence x Expectancy x Instrumentality

If any one of these variables (valence, expectancy, or instrumentality) declines, overall motivation will decline, too.

Exhibit 13.5 incorporates the expectancy theory variables into our motivation model. Valence and instrumentality combine to affect employees' will-

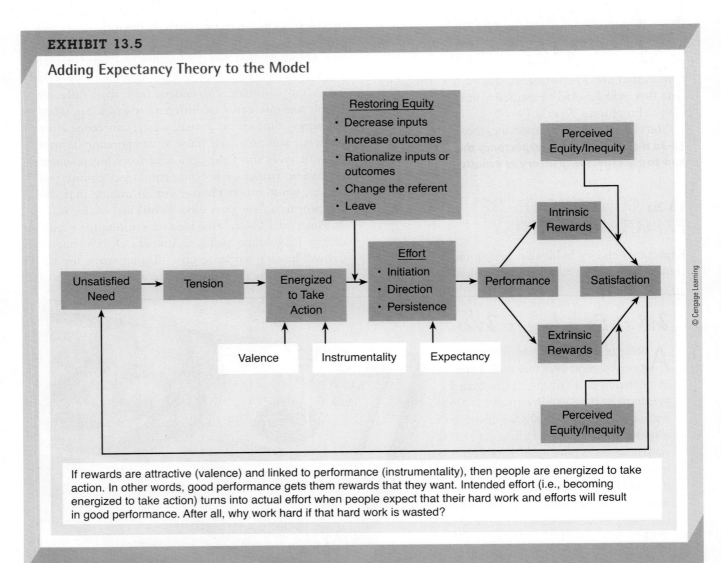

EXHIBIT 13.5

Adding Expectancy Theory to the Model

If rewards are attractive (valence) and linked to performance (instrumentality), then people are energized to take action. In other words, good performance gets them rewards that they want. Intended effort (i.e., becoming energized to take action) turns into actual effort when people expect that their hard work and efforts will result in good performance. After all, why work hard if that hard work is wasted?

© Cengage Learning

ingness to put forth effort (i.e., the degree to which they are energized to take action), while expectancy transforms intended effort ("I'm really going to work hard in this job") into actual effort. If you're offered rewards that you desire and you believe that you will in fact receive these rewards for good performance, you're highly likely to be energized to take action. However, you're not likely to actually exert effort unless you also believe that you can do the job (i.e., that your efforts will lead to successful performance).

13-3b MOTIVATING WITH EXPECTANCY THEORY

What practical steps can managers take to use expectancy theory to motivate employees? First, they can *systematically gather information to find out what employees want from their jobs*. In addition to individual managers directly asking employees what they want from their jobs (see Subsection 13-1d, "Motivating with the Basics"), companies need to survey their employees regularly to determine their wants, needs, and dissatisfactions. Since people consider the valence of all the possible rewards and outcomes that they can receive from their jobs, regular identification of wants, needs, and dissatisfactions gives companies the chance to turn negatively valent rewards and outcomes into positively valent rewards and outcomes, thus raising overall motivation and effort. Mark Peterman, vice president of client solutions at Maritz Incentives, says that individual employees are motivated in vastly different ways: "For some, being honored in front of one's peers is a great award, but for others, the thought of being put on display in front of peers embarrasses them." And companies have a long way to go to ensure that their employees feel valued, Peterman says. A Maritz survey found that only 27 percent of employees who want to be recognized by nonmonetary incentives are recognized that way.[49] Such findings suggest that employers should routinely survey employees to identify not only the range of rewards that are valued by most employees but also to understand the preferences of specific employees.

Second, managers can *take specific steps to link rewards to individual performance in a way that is clear and understandable to employees*. Unfortunately, most employees are extremely dissatisfied with the link between pay and performance in their organizations. In one study, based on a representative sample, 80 percent of the employees surveyed wanted to be paid according to a different kind of pay system! Moreover, only 32 percent of employees were satisfied with how

Use Expectancy Theory to Motivate by:
☐ surveying employees to identify preferred rewards
☐ ensuring that employees see the connection between pay and performance
☐ motivating employees to take active rather than passive roles

their annual pay raises were determined, and only 22 percent were happy with the way the starting salaries for their jobs were determined.[50]

One way to make sure that employees see the connection between pay and performance (see Chapter 11 for a discussion of compensation strategies) is for managers to publicize the way in which pay decisions are made. This is especially important given that only 41 percent of employees know how their pay increases are determined.[51] At Fog Creek Software, founder Joel Spolsky addresses this issue by using experience (years of full-time experience in your area), scope of responsibilities (Do you manage others, a department, a product or product line?), and programming skills (from new programmer to an expert critical to project success) to categorize each employee into one of nine different levels. Then, to make sure that the connection between pay and performance is clear, Fog Creek does two things. People with higher levels get more pay. And, everyone at the same level gets the same pay. Spolsky says, "Once a year, my management team sits down, reviews every employee's work, and recalculates every employee's level." And, if your responsibilities and experience and programming skills increase, your level and your pay do, too.[52]

Finally, managers should *empower employees to make decisions if management really wants them to believe that their hard work and effort will lead to good performance*. If valent rewards are linked to good performance, people should be energized to take action. However, this works only if they also believe that their efforts will lead to good performance. One of the ways that managers destroy the expectancy that hard work and effort will lead to good performance is by restricting what employees can do or by ignoring employees' ideas. In Chapter 9, you learned that *empowerment* is a feeling of intrinsic motivation, in which workers perceive their work to have meaning and perceive themselves to be competent, to have an impact, and to be capable of self-determination.[53] So, if managers want workers to have strong expectancies, they should empower them to make decisions. Doing so will motivate employees to take active rather than passive roles in their work.

13-4 *Reinforcement Theory*

When used properly, rewards motivate and energize employees. But when used incorrectly, they can demotivate, baffle, and even anger them. Goals are supposed to motivate employees. But leaders who focus blindly on meeting goals at all costs often find that they destroy motivation.

Reinforcement theory says that behavior is a function of its consequences, that behaviors followed by positive consequences (i.e., reinforced) will occur more frequently, and that behaviors either followed by negative consequences or not followed by positive consequences will occur less frequently.[54] In an effort to reduce health care costs, many companies now require employees who smoke, have high cholesterol, or are overweight to pay significantly more for health insurance. Wal-Mart, for example, requires smoking employees to pay $2,000 per year more for health insurance than nonsmokers. Similarly, Home Depot charges smokers $20 more each month, while PepsiCo requires smokers to pay $600 more per year. Clearly, companies hope that more expensive health insurance premiums penalize unhealthy lifestyles, thereby encouraging employees to take steps to improve their health. Jerome Allen, who works part time at a Wal-Mart in Texas, did just that by quitting smoking after he saw how much the higher insurance premiums reduced his take-home pay.[55] More specifically, **reinforcement** is the process of changing behavior by changing the consequences that follow behavior.[56]

Reinforcement has two parts: reinforcement contingencies and schedules of reinforcement. **Reinforcement contingencies** are the cause-and-effect relationships between the performance of specific behaviors and specific consequences. For example, if you get docked an hour's pay for being late to work, then a reinforcement contingency exists between a behavior (being late to work) and a consequence (losing an hour's pay). A **schedule of reinforcement** is the set of rules regarding reinforcement contingencies such as which behaviors will be reinforced, which consequences will follow those behaviors, and the schedule by which those consequences will be delivered.[57]

Exhibit 13.6 incorporates reinforcement contingencies and reinforcement schedules into our motivation model. First, notice that extrinsic rewards and the schedules of reinforcement used to deliver them are the primary method for creating reinforcement contingencies in organizations. In turn, those reinforcement contingencies directly affect valences (the attractiveness of rewards), instrumentality (the perceived link between rewards and performance), and effort (how hard employees will work).

*Let's learn more about reinforcement theory by examining **13-4a the components of reinforcement theory, 13-4b the different schedules for delivering reinforcement**, and **13-4c how to motivate with reinforcement theory**.*

13-4a COMPONENTS OF REINFORCEMENT THEORY

As just described, *reinforcement contingencies* are the cause-and-effect relationships between the performance of specific behaviors and specific consequences. There are four kinds of reinforcement contingencies: positive reinforcement, negative reinforcement, punishment, and extinction.

Positive reinforcement strengthens behavior (i.e., increases its frequency) by following behaviors with desirable consequences. While some companies are penalizing unhealthy behaviors, others have chosen to reward employees who practice healthy behaviors. At Whole Foods, for example, nonsmoking employees receive larger discounts on merchandise than smoking employees. Humana, a health insurance provider, has a program called HumanaVitality, in

Reinforcement theory the theory that behavior is a function of its consequences, that behaviors followed by positive consequences will occur more frequently, and that behaviors followed by negative consequences, or not followed by positive consequences, will occur less frequently

Reinforcement the process of changing behavior by changing the consequences that follow behavior

Reinforcement contingencies cause-and-effect relationships between the performance of specific behaviors and specific consequences

Schedule of reinforcement rules that specify which behaviors will be reinforced, which consequences will follow those behaviors, and the schedule by which those consequences will be delivered

Positive reinforcement reinforcement that strengthens behavior by following behaviors with desirable consequences

which people with Humana-provided health care coverage earn points for things ranging from exercising regularly, reaching and maintaining a healthy weight, giving up smoking, and getting annual checkups and preventive care screenings to taking health education classes. Those points, in turn, can be used to buy electronics and hotel stays or used toward discounts on over 600,000 items. As part of that program, Humana has partnered with game developer Ubisoft on an Xbox 360 game, *Your Shape: Fitness Evolved 2012*. HumanaVitality members can earn fifteen Vitality points each day they play and burn 200 calories.[58]

Negative reinforcement strengthens behavior by withholding an unpleasant consequence when employees perform a specific behavior. Negative reinforcement is also called *avoidance learning* because workers perform a behavior to *avoid* a negative consequence. Paul English, the co-founder of travel website Kayak.com, which searches hundreds of travel websites, is obsessed with customer service. He even handles calls himself and gives out his cell phone number to customers. English, however, uses a negative reinforcement strategy to get his sixty software engineers to write better code for Kayak's website—he makes them answer phones and talk to customers—something they'd rather avoid doing. He says, "Anytime anyone contacts us with a question, whether it's by e-mail or telephone, they get a personal

Negative reinforcement
reinforcement that strengthens behavior by withholding an unpleasant consequence when employees perform a specific behavior

---

EXHIBIT 13.6

Adding Reinforcement Theory to the Model

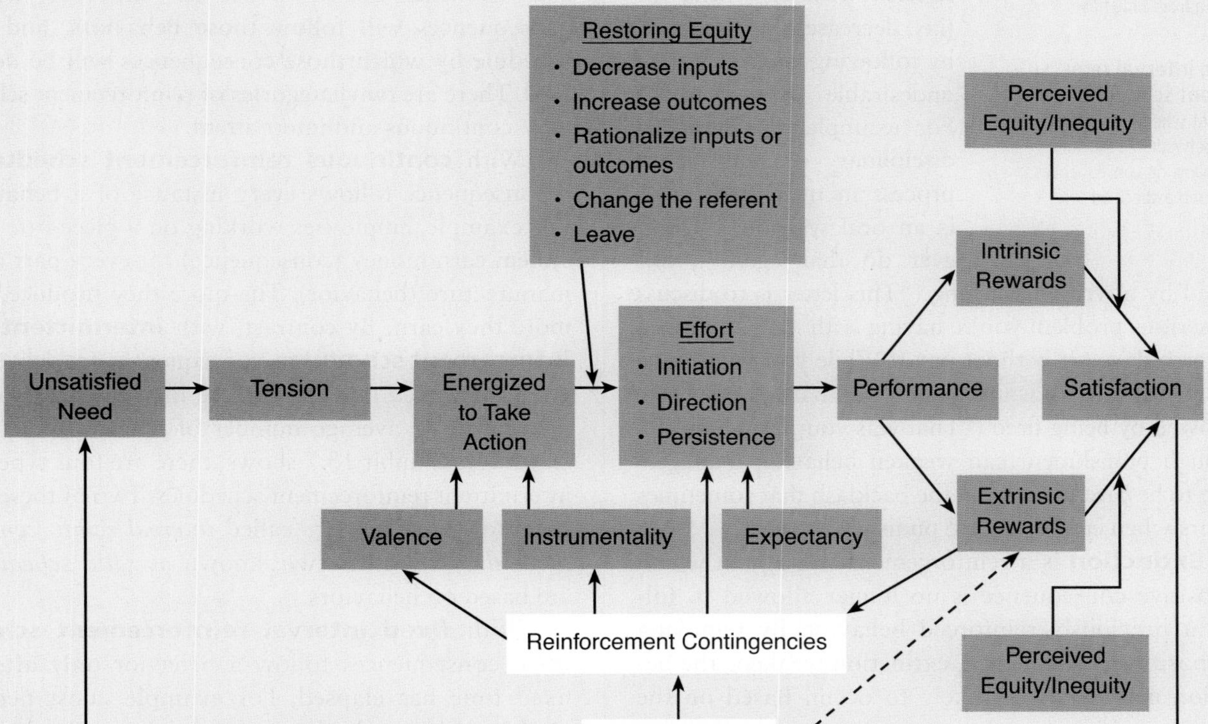

© Cengage Learning

Extrinsic rewards and the schedules of reinforcement used to deliver them are the primary methods for creating reinforcement contingencies in organizations. In turn, those reinforcement contingencies directly affect valence (the attractiveness of rewards), instrumentality (the perceived link between rewards and performance), and effort (how hard employees will work).

Punishment reinforcement that weakens behavior by following behaviors with undesirable consequences

Extinction reinforcement in which a positive consequence is no longer allowed to follow a previously reinforced behavior, thus weakening the behavior

Continuous reinforcement schedule a schedule that requires a consequence to be administered following every instance of a behavior

Intermittent reinforcement schedule a schedule in which consequences are delivered after a specified or average time has elapsed or after a specified or average number of behaviors has occurred

Fixed interval reinforcement schedule an intermittent schedule in which consequences follow a behavior only after a fixed time has elapsed

Variable interval reinforcement schedule an intermittent schedule in which the time between a behavior and the following consequences varies around a specified average

reply. The engineers and I handle customer support. When I tell people that, they look at me like I'm smoking crack. They say, 'Why would you pay an engineer $150,000 to answer phones when you could pay someone in Arizona $8 an hour?' If you make the engineers answer e-mails and phone calls from the customers, the second or third time they get the same question, they'll actually stop what they're doing and fix the code. Then we don't have those questions anymore."[59]

By contrast, **punishment** weakens behavior (i.e., decreases its frequency) by following behaviors with undesirable consequences. For example, the standard disciplinary or punishment process in most companies is an oral warning ("Don't ever do that again"), followed by a written warning ("This letter is to discuss the serious problem you're having with . . ."), followed by three days off without pay ("While you're at home not being paid, we want you to think hard about . . ."), followed by being fired ("That was your last chance"). Though punishment can weaken behavior, managers have to be careful to avoid the backlash that sometimes occurs when employees are punished at work.

Extinction is a reinforcement strategy in which a positive consequence is no longer allowed to follow a previously reinforced behavior. By removing the positive consequence, extinction weakens the behavior, making it less likely to occur. Based on the idea of positive reinforcement, most companies give company leaders and managers substantial financial rewards when the company performs well. Based on the idea of extinction, you would then expect that leaders and managers would not be rewarded (i.e., the positive consequence would be removed) when companies perform poorly. If companies really want pay to reinforce the right kinds of behaviors, then rewards have to be removed when company management doesn't produce successful performance. In an

attempt to overtake its largest competitor, Verizon, and become the largest wireless phone service provider in the United States, AT&T submitted plans to government regulators to buy T-Mobile for $39 billion. Antitrust regulators, however, rejected the deal, saying that it would hurt consumers by limiting the number of companies that competed for their business. Even though the deal was not approved, AT&T was still contractually obliged to pay T-Mobile a $4.2 billion "break-up fee," which led to a quarterly loss of $6.7 billion. Because of the enormous cost of the failed merger, AT&T's board cut CEO Randall Stephenson's compensation by $2.08 million.[60]

13-4b SCHEDULES FOR DELIVERING REINFORCEMENT

As mentioned earlier, a *schedule of reinforcement* is the set of rules regarding reinforcement contingencies, such as which behaviors will be reinforced, which consequences will follow those behaviors, and the schedule by which those consequences will be delivered. There are two categories of reinforcement schedules: continuous and intermittent.

With **continuous reinforcement schedules**, a consequence follows every instance of a behavior. For example, employees working on a piece-rate pay system earn money (consequence) for every part they manufacture (behavior). The more they produce, the more they earn. By contrast, with **intermittent reinforcement schedules**, consequences are delivered after a specified or average time has elapsed or after a specified or average number of behaviors has occurred. As Exhibit 13.7 shows, there are four types of intermittent reinforcement schedules. Two of these are based on time and are called *interval reinforcement schedules*; the other two, known as *ratio schedules*, are based on behaviors.

With **fixed interval reinforcement schedules**, consequences follow a behavior only after a fixed time has elapsed. For example, most people receive their paychecks on a fixed interval schedule (e.g., once or twice per month). As long as they work (behavior) during a specified pay period (interval), they get a paycheck (consequence). With **variable interval reinforcement schedules**, consequences follow a behavior after different times, some shorter and some longer, that vary around a specified average time. On a ninety-day variable interval reinforcement schedule, you might receive a bonus after eighty days or perhaps after 100 days, but the average inter-

EXHIBIT 13.7

Intermittent Reinforcement Schedules

INTERMITTENT REINFORCEMENT SCHEDULES

	FIXED	VARIABLE
INTERVAL (TIME)	Consequences follow behavior after a fixed time has elapsed.	Consequences follow behavior after different times, some shorter and some longer, that vary around a specific average time.
RATIO (BEHAVIOR)	Consequences follow a specific number of behaviors.	Consequences follow a different number of behaviors, sometimes more and sometimes less, that vary around a specified average number of behaviors.

val between performing your job well (behavior) and receiving your bonus (consequence) would be ninety days.

With **fixed ratio reinforcement schedules**, consequences are delivered following a specific number of behaviors. For example, a car salesperson might receive a $1,000 bonus after every ten sales. Therefore, a salesperson with only nine sales would not receive the bonus until he or she finally sold a tenth car.

With **variable ratio reinforcement schedules**, consequences are delivered following a different number of behaviors, sometimes more and sometimes less, that vary around a specified average number of behaviors. With a ten-car variable ratio reinforcement schedule, a salesperson might receive the bonus after seven car sales, or after twelve, eleven, or nine sales, but the average number of cars sold before receiving the bonus would be ten cars.

Which reinforcement schedules work best? In the past, the standard advice was to use continuous reinforcement when employees were learning new behaviors because reinforcement after each success leads to faster learning. Likewise, the standard advice was to use intermittent reinforcement schedules to maintain behavior after it is learned because intermittent rewards are supposed to make behavior much less subject to extinction.[61] Research shows, however, that except for interval-based systems, which usually produce weak results, the effectiveness of continuous reinforcement, fixed ratio, and variable ratio schedules differs very little.[62] In organizational settings, all three consistently produce large increases over noncontingent reward schedules. So managers should choose whichever of these three is easiest to use in their companies.

13-4c MOTIVATING WITH REINFORCEMENT THEORY

What practical steps can managers take to use reinforcement theory to motivate employees? University of Nebraska business professor Fred Luthans, who has been studying the effects of reinforcement theory in organizations for more than a quarter of a century, says that there are five steps to motivating workers with reinforcement theory: *identify*, *measure*, *analyze*, *intervene*, and *evaluate* critical performance-related behaviors.[63]

Identify means singling out critical, observable, performance-related behaviors. These are the behaviors that are most important to successful job performance. In addition, they must also be easily observed so that they can be accurately measured. *Measure* means determining the baseline frequencies of these behaviors. In other words, find out how often workers perform them. *Analyze* means studying the causes and consequences of these behaviors. Analyzing the causes helps managers create the conditions that produce these critical behaviors, and analyzing the consequences helps them determine if these behaviors produce the results that they want. *Intervene* means changing the organization by using positive and negative reinforcement to increase the frequency of these critical behaviors. *Evaluate* means assessing

Fixed ratio reinforcement schedule an intermittent schedule in which consequences are delivered following a specific number of behaviors

Variable ratio reinforcement schedule an intermittent schedule in which consequences are delivered following a different number of behaviors, sometimes more and sometimes less, that vary around a specified average number of behaviors

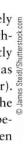

the extent to which the intervention actually changed workers' behavior. This is done by comparing behavior after the intervention to the original baseline of behavior before the intervention.

In addition to these five steps, managers should remember three other key things when motivating with reinforcement theory. First, *Don't reinforce the wrong behaviors*. Although reinforcement theory sounds simple, it's actually very difficult to put into practice. One of the most common mistakes is accidentally reinforcing the wrong behaviors. Sometimes managers reinforce behaviors that they don't want! If you want to become a merit-based company, stop rewarding behavior that is not exceptional, says Dave Anderson, a management consultant. According to him, "the average car salesperson in the United States sells ten cars per month, but many pay plans begin to pay bonuses at seven, eight, nine, or ten cars. Under a typical plan, an employee who sells eight cars gets a $200 bonus, another $250 for selling two additional cars, and $300 for selling two more cars. The total bonus for selling twelve cars in a month is $750." Anderson notes, "Based on national averages, such a pay plan financially rewards average and below-average results." Many of his clients have revised their system and only pay an $800 bonus to an employee *after* he or she has sold twelve cars, thus ending bonus payments for employees who sell fewer than the target amount of cars.[64] In this system, you pay more for better performance but don't fall into the trap of rewarding and endorsing the wrong things—that is, rewarding below-average performance.

Managers should also *correctly administer punishment at the appropriate time*. Many managers believe that punishment can change workers' behavior and help them improve their job performance. Furthermore, managers believe that fairly punishing workers also lets other workers know what is or isn't acceptable.[65] A danger of using punishment is that it can produce a backlash against managers and companies. But, if administered properly, punishment can weaken the frequency of undesirable behaviors without creating a backlash.[66] To be effective, the punishment must be strong enough to stop the unde-

sired behavior and must be administered objectively (same rules applied to everyone), impersonally (without emotion or anger), consistently and contingently (each time improper behavior occurs), and quickly (as soon as possible following the undesirable behavior). In addition, managers should clearly explain what the appropriate behavior is and why the employee is being punished. Employees typically respond well when punishment is administered this way.[67]

Finally, managers should *choose the simplest and most effective schedule of reinforcement*. When choosing a schedule of reinforcement, managers need to balance effectiveness against simplicity. In fact, the more complex the schedule of reinforcement, the more likely it is to be misunderstood and resisted by managers and employees. For example, a forestry and logging company experimented with a unique variable ratio schedule. When tree-planters finished planting a bag of seedlings (about 1,000 seedlings per bag), they got to flip a coin. If they called the coin flip correctly (heads or tails), they were paid $4, double the regular rate of $2 per bag. If they called the coin flip incorrectly, they got nothing. The company began having problems when several workers and a manager, who was a part-time minister, claimed that the coin flip was a form of gambling. Then another worker found that the company was taking out too much money for taxes from workers' paychecks. Since the workers didn't really understand the reinforcement schedule, they blamed the payment plan associated with it and accused the company of trying to cheat them out of their money. After all of these problems, the researchers who implemented the variable ratio schedule concluded that "the results of this study may not be so much an indication of the relative effectiveness of different schedules of reinforcement as they are an indication of the types of problems that one encounters when applying these concepts in an industrial setting."[68] In short, choose the simplest, most effective schedule of reinforcement. Since continuous reinforcement, fixed ratio, and variable ratio schedules are about equally effective, continuous reinforcement schedules may be the best choice in many instances by virtue of their simplicity.

13-5 *Goal-Setting Theory*

The basic model of motivation with which we began this chapter showed that individuals feel tension after becoming aware of an unfulfilled need. Once they experience tension, they search for and select courses of action that they believe will eliminate this tension. In other words, they direct their behavior toward something. This something is a goal. A **goal** is a target, objective, or result that someone tries to accomplish. **Goal-setting theory** says that people will be motivated to the extent to which they accept specific, challenging goals and receive feedback that indicates their progress toward goal achievement.

Let's learn more about goal setting by examining **13-5a the components of goal-setting theory** *and* **13-5b how to motivate with goal-setting theory.**

13-5a COMPONENTS OF GOAL-SETTING THEORY

The basic components of goal-setting theory are goal specificity, goal difficulty, goal acceptance, and performance feedback.[69] **Goal specificity** is the extent to which goals are detailed, exact, and unambiguous. Specific goals, such as "I'm going to have a 3.0 average this semester," are more motivating than general goals, such as "I'm going to get better grades this semester."

Goal difficulty is the extent to which a goal is hard or challenging to accomplish. Difficult goals, such as "I'm going to have a 3.5 average and make the dean's list this semester," are more motivating than easy goals, such as "I'm going to have a 2.0 average this semester."

Goal acceptance, which is similar to the idea of goal commitment discussed in Chapter 5, is the extent to which people consciously understand and agree to goals. Accepted goals, such as "I really want to get a 3.5 average this semester to show my parents how much I've improved," are more motivating than unaccepted goals, such as "My parents really want me to get a 3.5 average this semester, but there's so much more I'd rather do on campus than study!"

Performance feedback is information about the quality or quantity of past performance and indicates whether progress is being made toward the accomplishment of a goal. Performance feedback, such as "My prof said I need a 92 on the final to get an A in that class," is more motivating than no feedback, as in "I have no idea what my grade is in that class." In short, goal-setting theory says that people will be motivated to the extent to which they accept specific, challenging goals and receive feedback that indicates their progress toward goal achievement.

Goal a target, objective, or result that someone tries to accomplish

Goal-setting theory the theory that people will be motivated to the extent to which they accept specific, challenging goals and receive feedback that indicates their progress toward goal achievement

Goal specificity the extent to which goals are detailed, exact, and unambiguous

Goal difficulty the extent to which a goal is hard or challenging to accomplish

Goal acceptance the extent to which people consciously understand and agree to goals

Performance feedback information about the quality or quantity of past performance that indicates whether progress is being made toward the accomplishment of a goal

© Morgan Lane Photography/Shutterstock.com

How does goal setting work? To start, challenging goals focus employees' attention (i.e., direction of effort) on the critical aspects of their jobs and away from unimportant areas. Goals also energize behavior. When faced with unaccomplished goals, employees typically develop plans and strategies to reach those goals. Goals also create tension between the goal, which is the desired future state of affairs, and where the employee or company is now, meaning the current state of affairs. This tension can be satisfied only by achieving or abandoning the goal. Finally, goals influence persistence. Since goals only go away when they are accomplished, employees are more likely to persist in their efforts in the presence of goals. Exhibit 13.8 incorporates goals into the motivation model by showing how goals directly affect tension, effort, and the extent to which employees are energized to take action.

13-5b MOTIVATING WITH GOAL-SETTING THEORY

What practical steps can managers take to use goal-setting theory to motivate employees? Managers can do three things, beginning with *assign specific, challenging goals*. One of the simplest, most effective ways to motivate workers is to give them specific, challenging goals.

For example, Valpak Direct Marketing Systems is a direct-mailing company that awards regional franchises to people with enough business experience and cash ($43,000 is usually enough for a small region). However, if you work for Valpak and meet the goal of $1.1 million in sales over three years, putting you among the top third of its best salespeople, the company lets you choose your reward: $50,000 toward the purchase of a small regional territory or $10,000

EXHIBIT 13.8

Adding Goal-Setting Theory to the Model

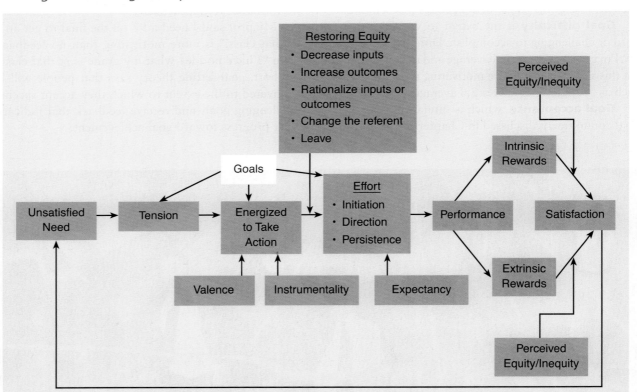

Goals create tension between the goal, which is the desired future state of affairs, and where the employee or company is now, meaning the current state of affairs. This tension can be satisfied only by achieving or abandoning the goal. Goals also energize behavior. When faced with unaccomplished goals, employees typically develop plans and strategies to reach those goals. Finally, goals influence persistence.

© Cengage Learning

toward getting your MBA. Commenting on this system, Valpak's president said, "Sharp people coming out of school have choices, and so we're trying to give them a reason to at least consider us."[70]

Second, managers should *make sure workers truly accept organizational goals*. Specific, challenging goals won't motivate workers unless they really accept, understand, and agree to the organization's goals. For this to occur, people must see the goals as fair and reasonable. Employees must also trust management and believe that managers are using goals to clarify what is expected from them rather than to exploit or threaten them ("If you don't achieve these goals . . ."). Participative goal setting, in which managers and employees generate goals together, can help increase trust and understanding and thus acceptance of goals. Furthermore, providing workers with training can help increase goal acceptance, particularly when workers don't believe they are capable of reaching the organization's goals.[71]

Finally, managers should *provide frequent, specific, performance-related feedback*. Once employees have accepted specific, challenging goals, they should receive frequent performance-related feedback so that they can track their progress toward goal completion. Feedback leads to stronger motivation and effort in three ways.[72]

Receiving specific feedback about the quality of their performance can encourage employees who don't have specific, challenging goals to set goals to improve their performance. Once people meet goals, performance feedback often encourages them to set higher, more difficult goals. And feedback lets people know whether they need to increase their efforts or change strategies in order to accomplish their goals.

13-6 Motivating with the Integrated Model

We began this chapter by defining motivation as the set of forces that initiates, directs, and makes people persist in their efforts to accomplish a goal. We also asked the basic question that managers ask when they try to figure out how to motivate their workers: "What leads to effort?" The answer to that question is likely to be somewhat different for each employee. So, if you're having difficulty figuring out why people aren't motivated where you work, check your Review Card for a useful, theory-based starting point.

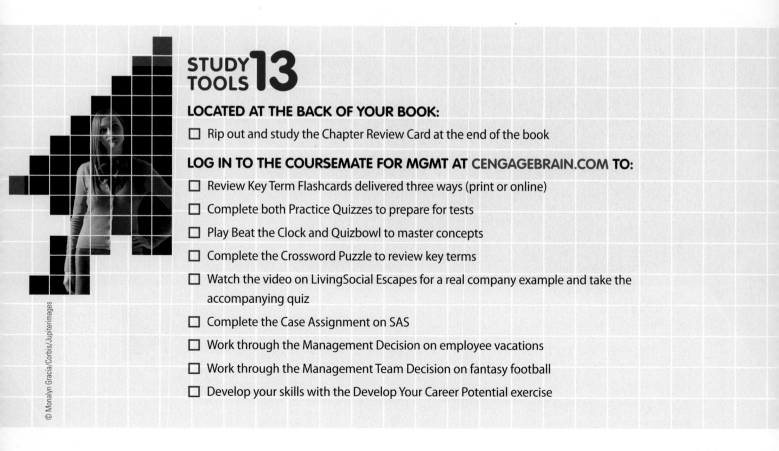

STUDY TOOLS 13

LOCATED AT THE BACK OF YOUR BOOK:

☐ Rip out and study the Chapter Review Card at the end of the book

LOG IN TO THE COURSEMATE FOR MGMT AT CENGAGEBRAIN.COM TO:

☐ Review Key Term Flashcards delivered three ways (print or online)

☐ Complete both Practice Quizzes to prepare for tests

☐ Play Beat the Clock and Quizbowl to master concepts

☐ Complete the Crossword Puzzle to review key terms

☐ Watch the video on LivingSocial Escapes for a real company example and take the accompanying quiz

☐ Complete the Case Assignment on SAS

☐ Work through the Management Decision on employee vacations

☐ Work through the Management Team Decision on fantasy football

☐ Develop your skills with the Develop Your Career Potential exercise

© Monalyn Gracia/Corbis/Jupiterimages

14 Leadership

LEARNING OUTCOMES

14-1 Explain what leadership is.

14-2 Describe who leaders are and what effective leaders do.

14-3 Explain Fiedler's contingency theory.

14-4 Describe how path-goal theory works.

14-5 Explain the normative decision theory.

14-6 Explain how visionary leadership (i.e., charismatic and transformational leadership) helps leaders achieve strategic leadership.

CHECK OUT
STUDY TOOLS
AT THE END OF THIS CHAPTER.

© Dave & Les Jacobs/Blend Images/Jupiterimages

© Monalyn Gracia/Corbis/Jupiterimages

14-1 *Leaders versus Managers*

If you've ever been in charge, or even just thought about it, chances are you've considered questions like: Do I have what it takes to lead? What are the most important things leaders do? How can I transform a poorly performing department, division, or company? Do I need to adjust my leadership depending on the situation and the employee? Why doesn't my leadership inspire people? If you feel overwhelmed at the prospect of being a leader, you're not alone—millions of leaders in organizations across the world struggle with these fundamental leadership issues on a daily basis.

How does an ensemble of one hundred or more musicians, all playing different parts at different times on different instruments, manage to produce something as beautiful as Beethoven's Fifth Symphony? (Or, if Gustav Mahler's "Symphony of a Thousand" is on the program, a lot more people might be involved!) The con-ductor, like a CEO, is responsible for managing all of this complexity and ensuring a great performance. But conductors do much more than just keep the beat with a baton. According to Ramona Wis, author of *The Conductor as Leader: Principles of Leadership Applied to Life on the Podium*, conductors must also build connections between people, inspire them with vision, command their trust, and persuade them to participate in the ensemble at their very best.

Whether the end result is a stirring musical performance, innovation of new products, or increased profits, **leadership** is the process of influencing others to achieve group or organizational goals. The knowledge and skills you'll learn in this chapter won't make the task of leadership less daunting, but they will help you navigate it.

According to University of Southern California business professor Warren Bennis, the primary difference between leaders and managers is that leaders are concerned with doing the right thing, while managers are concerned with doing things right.[1] In other words, leaders begin with the question, "What should we be doing?" while managers start with "How can we do what we're already doing better?" Leaders focus on vision, mission, goals, and objectives, while managers focus on productivity and efficiency. Managers see themselves as preservers of the status quo, while leaders see themselves as promoters of change and challengers of the status quo in that they encourage creativity and risk taking. Virginia Rometty, IBM's new CEO, plans to keep

Leadership the process of influencing others to achieve group or organizational goals

© iStockphoto.com/Suprijono Suharjoto

Trait theory a leadership theory that holds that effective leaders possess a similar set of traits or characteristics

Traits relatively stable characteristics, such as abilities, psychological motives, or consistent patterns of behavior

her $100 billion company growing and innovating by doing one thing—pressing managers and employees to take risks and embrace change. Rometty believes that risk-taking and change will provide the fuel for future growth, just like fifteen years ago when IBM changed from manufacturing and selling mainframe and personal computers to providing technology services and consulting. Rometty says, "I don't believe in the inevitable, or in thinking that things have to and will turn out in a certain way. Whatever business you're in, it's going to commoditize over time, so you have to keep moving it to a higher value and change. . . . Growth and comfort do not coexist."[2]

Another difference is that managers have a relatively short-term perspective, while leaders take a long-term view. Managers are concerned with control and limiting the choices of others, while leaders are more concerned with expanding people's choices and options.[3] Managers also solve problems so that others can do their work, while leaders inspire and motivate others to find their own solutions.

Finally, managers are also more concerned with *means*, how to get things done, while leaders are more concerned with *ends*, what gets done. Prior to its bankruptcy several years ago, General Motors designed and produced cars based on the capabilities of its manufacturing plants—for example, if it had excess truck capacity, it built more trucks. Management consultant James Hall says, "Before, marketing was not involved in product decisions. It was 'here's your car, go and sell it.'" Never mind whether customers wanted those cars. Now, several years after GM's government bailout and emergence from bankruptcy, CEO Dan Akerson is fundamentally altering how GM gets things done, by putting the company's focus squarely on customers, and that means building and designing cars customers clearly want. One sign of that focus is the hiring of Joel Ewanick as global chief marketing officer, a position that the 102-year-old company has never had. Ewanick's charge is to gather feedback from consumers and then share it with GM's engineers and designers. Ewanick says, "Dan finds it very important that we become consumer-centric and make the company more of a marketing organization."[4]

Although leaders are different from managers, organizations need them both. Managers are critical to getting out the day-to-day work, and leaders are critical to inspiring employees and setting the organization's long-term direction. The key issue for any organization is the extent to which it is properly led and properly managed. As Warren Bennis said in summing up the difference between leaders and managers, "American organizations (and probably those in much of the rest of the industrialized world) are underled and overmanaged. They do not pay enough attention to doing the right thing, while they pay too much attention to doing things right."[5]

14-2 *Who Leaders Are and What Leaders Do*

Indra Nooyi, PepsiCo's CEO, talks straight, has a sharp sense of humor, and sings in the hallways wherever she is. Nooyi is an extrovert. By contrast, Douglas Conant, former CEO of Campbell Soup Company, is an introvert who says that he feels exhausted after spending time in large groups of people he doesn't know.[6]

Which one is likely to be successful as a CEO? According to a survey of 1,542 senior managers, it's the extrovert. Forty-seven percent of those 1,542 senior managers felt that extroverts make better CEOs, while 65 percent said that being an introvert hurts a CEO's chances of success.[7] So clearly, senior managers believe that extroverted CEOs are better leaders. But are they? Not necessarily. In fact, a relatively high percentage of CEOs, 40 percent, are introverts. Former Sara Lee CEO Brenda Barnes said, "I've always been shy. . . . People wouldn't call me that [an introvert], but I am."[8] Indeed, Barnes turned down all speaking requests and rarely gave interviews.

So, what makes a good leader? Does leadership success depend on who leaders are, such as introverts or extroverts, or on what leaders do and how they behave?

Let's learn more about who leaders are by investigating **14-2a leadership traits** *and* **14-2b leadership behaviors.**

14-2a LEADERSHIP TRAITS

Trait theory is one way to describe who leaders are. **Trait theory** says that effective leaders possess a similar set of traits or characteristics. **Traits** are relatively stable characteristics such as abilities, psychological motives, or consistent patterns of behavior. For exam-

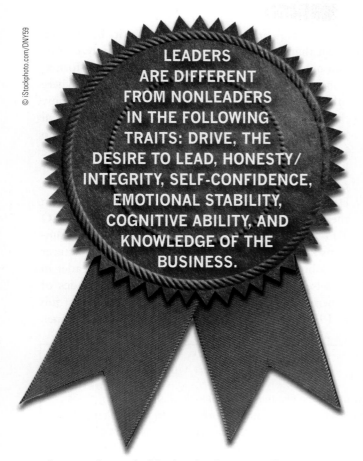

LEADERS ARE DIFFERENT FROM NONLEADERS IN THE FOLLOWING TRAITS: DRIVE, THE DESIRE TO LEAD, HONESTY/INTEGRITY, SELF-CONFIDENCE, EMOTIONAL STABILITY, COGNITIVE ABILITY, AND KNOWLEDGE OF THE BUSINESS.

ple, trait theory holds that leaders are taller and more confident and have greater physical stamina (i.e., higher energy levels) than nonleaders. Indeed, while just 14.5 percent of men are six feet tall, 58 percent of *Fortune* 500 CEOs are six feet or taller.[9] Author Malcolm Gladwell says, "We have this sense of what a leader is supposed to look like. And that stereotype is so powerful that when someone fits it, we simply become blind to other considerations."[10] Trait theory is also known as the "great person" theory because early versions of the theory stated that leaders are born, not made. In other words, you either have the right stuff to be a leader, or you don't. And if you don't, there is no way to get it.

For some time, it was thought that trait theory was wrong and that there are no consistent trait differences between leaders and nonleaders, or between effective and ineffective leaders. However, more recent evidence shows that "successful leaders are not like other people," that successful leaders are indeed different from the rest of us.[11] More specifically, leaders are different from nonleaders in the following traits: drive, the desire to lead, honesty/integrity, self-confidence, emotional stability, cognitive ability, and knowledge of the business.[12]

Drive refers to high levels of effort and is characterized by achievement, motivation, initiative, energy, and tenacity. In terms of achievement and ambition, leaders always try to make improvements or achieve success in what they're doing. Because of their initiative, they have strong desires to promote change or solve problems. Leaders typically have more energy—they have to, given the long hours they put in and followers' expectations that they be positive and upbeat. Thus, leaders must have physical, mental, and emotional vitality. Leaders are also more tenacious than nonleaders and are better at overcoming obstacles and problems that would deter most of us.

Successful leaders also have a stronger *desire to lead*. They want to be in charge and think about ways to influence or convince others about what should or shouldn't be done. *Honesty/integrity* is also important to leaders. *Honesty*, being truthful with others, is a cornerstone of leadership. Without it, leaders won't be trusted. When leaders are honest, subordinates are willing to overlook other flaws. For example, one follower said this about the leadership qualities of his manager: "I don't like a lot of the things he does, but he's basically honest. He's a genuine article, and you'll forgive a lot of things because of that. That goes a long way in how much I trust him."[13] *Integrity* is the extent to which leaders do what they say they will do. Leaders may be honest and have good intentions, but if they don't consistently deliver on what they promise, they won't be trusted.

Self-confidence, or believing in one's abilities, also distinguishes leaders from nonleaders. Self-confident leaders are more decisive and assertive and are more likely to gain others' confidence. Moreover, self-confident leaders will admit mistakes because they view them as learning opportunities rather than as refutations of their leadership capabilities. When Netflix was getting ready to split into two companies (Netflix for streaming services and Qwikster for DVDs by mail), CEO Reed Hastings shared the news with a friend, who happened to be a Netflix subscriber. Hastings believed the split was necessary, since DVD by mail, the foundation of Netflix's success, was in decline, while streaming services were growing exponentially. His friend, however, told him, "That is awful. I don't want to deal with two accounts."[14]

Hastings noted his friend's objection but went ahead with the plan, which was followed, as his friend's reaction foretold, by 800,000 outraged customers canceling their subscriptions. Hastings soon admitted his mistake in his blog, writing, "Consumers value the simplicity Netflix has always offered and we respect that. There is a difference between moving quickly—which Netflix has done very well for years—and moving too fast, which is what we did in this case." He went on to say, "It is clear that for many of our members two websites would make things more difficult, so we are going to keep Netflix as one place to go for streaming and DVDs. This means no change: one website, one account, one password . . . in other words, no Qwikster."[15]

Leaders also have *emotional stability*. Even when things go wrong, they remain even-tempered and consistent in their outlook and in the way they treat others. Leaders who can't control their emotions, who anger quickly or attack and blame others for mistakes, are unlikely to be trusted.

Leaders are also smart—they typically have strong *cognitive abilities*. This doesn't mean that leaders are necessarily geniuses—far from it. But it does mean that leaders have the capacity to analyze large amounts of seemingly unrelated, complex information and see patterns, opportunities, or threats where others might not see them. Finally, leaders also know their stuff, which means they have superior technical knowledge about the businesses they run. Leaders who have a good *knowledge of the business* understand the key technological decisions and concerns facing their companies. More often than not, studies indicate that effective leaders have long, extensive experience in their industries. For example, thanks to former CEO Tim Solso's leadership over the last decade, Cummins Inc., an engine and power systems manufacturer in Columbus, Indiana, has become a world leader in diesel-engine technology. Solso had four decades of experience with Cummins, starting with his first job in 1971 as assistant to the vice president of personnel.

Get It Done

When Ben Verwaayen took over as the CEO of Alcatel-Lucent, one of the first things he had to do was to get rid of chaos that ran throughout the organization. There were multiple managers and executives overseeing even the simplest of projects, making efficient, innovative work virtually impossible. One day early in his tenure, he received an email from one of his managers, who was asking Verwaayen to approve the hiring of a secretary for another office—and this was after sixteen other company executives had already approved the hiring. Verwaayen was absolutely perplexed at how a seemingly simple decision had to go through so many people. So he forward the email to all employees and let them know that from that point on, hiring decisions would be made by the office manager and his or her supervisor.

Source: P. Burrows and M. Campbell, "Alcatel-Lucent Chops Away at Years of Failure," *Bloomberg Businessweek*, April 28, 2011, accessed March 23, 2012, http://www.businessweek.com/magazine/content/11_19/b4227029794705.htm.

MEIGNEUX/SIPA via AP Images

Later in his career, he became director of development and training, executive director of personnel, and executive vice president of operations before being appointed CEO in 2000.[16]

14-2b LEADERSHIP BEHAVIORS

Thus far, you've read about who leaders *are*. But traits alone are not enough to make a successful leader. They are, however, a precondition for success. After all, it's hard to imagine a truly successful leader who lacks most of these qualities. Leaders who have these traits (or many of them) must then take actions that encourage people to achieve group or organizational goals.[17] Accordingly, we now examine what leaders *do*, meaning the behaviors they perform or the actions they take to influence others to achieve group or organizational goals.

Researchers at the University of Michigan, Ohio State University, and the University of Texas examined the specific behaviors that leaders use to improve subordinate satisfaction and performance. Hundreds of studies were conducted and hundreds of leader behaviors were examined. At all three universities, two basic leader behaviors emerged as central to successful leadership: initiating structure (called *job-centered leadership* at the University of Michigan and *concern for production* at the University of Texas) and considerate leader behavior (called *employee-centered leadership* at the University of Michigan and *concern for people* at the University of Texas).[18] These two leader behaviors form the basis for many of the leadership theories discussed in this chapter.

Initiating structure is the degree to which a leader structures the roles of followers by setting goals, giving directions, setting deadlines, and assigning tasks. A leader's ability to initiate structure primarily affects subordinates' job performance. With intense competition from the web, Taiwanese newspaper and magazine publisher Jimmy Lai decided that his stories would be more compelling if accompanied by visuals. Says Lai, "Images can transmit information so much faster." So he started Next Media Animation, a media company that produces computer animations of news events. When his animation team told him that it would take two weeks to produce an animated video of a new story, Lai told them they would have to figure out how to do it in two hours. They spent several months experimenting with stock digital faces and motion-capture technology and can now animate any news story in less than two hours.[19]

Consideration is the extent to which a leader is friendly, approachable, and supportive and shows concern for employees. Consideration primarily affects subordinates' job satisfaction. Specific leader consideration behaviors include listening to employees' problems and concerns, consulting with employees before making decisions, and treating employees as equals. Marian Salzman, the CEO of Euro RSCG Worldwide PR, a New York City–based public relations firm with 233 offices worldwide, spends a lot of time listening to her staff, most of whom are millennials (i.e., born after 1980). While she hasn't provided them free food, a juice bar, or reimbursement for using personal trainers, all of which they've asked for, she allows casual dress in the office—even flip-flops!—hosts happy hours on the roof of the building three times a week, and allows employees to take time off to do volunteer work. Why? Because, she says, "They want the workplace to recognize that they're not 9 to 5 people. They're not people [who are] ever going to wear gray flannel suits." It makes sense, she believes, to not play the "boss card" with millennials. Salzman says, "You're not the smartest person in the room anymore. You may be the most experienced, you may be the wisest. You're not the smartest." The payoff? Euro RSCG Worldwide PR attracts and keeps a highly motivated staff that is propelling its work in digital communications and social media.[20]

Although researchers at all three universities generally agreed that initiating structure and consideration were basic leader behaviors, their interpretation differed on how these two behaviors are related to one another and which are necessary for effective leadership. The University of Michigan studies indicated that initiating structure and consideration were mutually exclusive behaviors on opposite ends of the same continuum. In other words, leaders who wanted to be more considerate would have to do less initiating of structure (and vice versa). The University of Michigan studies also indicated that only considerate leader behaviors (i.e., employee-centered behaviors) were associated with successful leadership. By contrast, researchers at Ohio State University and the University of Texas found that initiating structure and consideration were independent behaviors, meaning that leaders can be considerate and initiate structure at the same time. Additional evidence confirms this finding.[21]

Initiating structure the degree to which a leader structures the roles of followers by setting goals, giving directions, setting deadlines, and assigning tasks

Consideration the extent to which a leader is friendly, approachable, and supportive and shows concern for employees

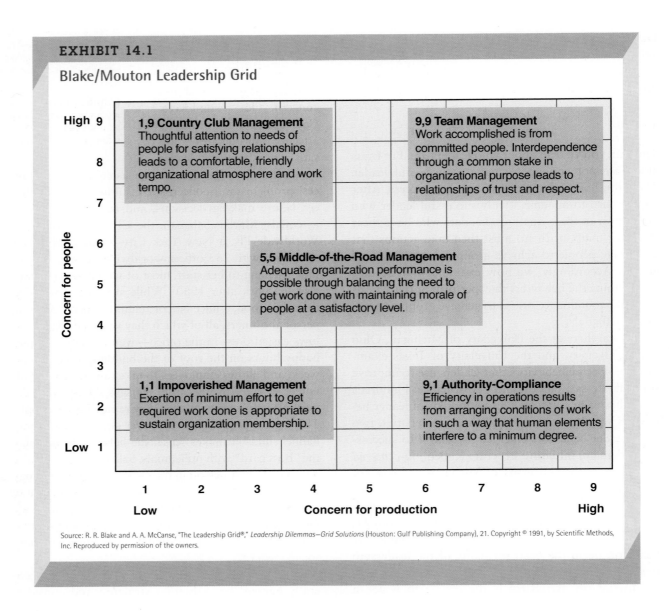

EXHIBIT 14.1

Blake/Mouton Leadership Grid

1,9 Country Club Management
Thoughtful attention to needs of people for satisfying relationships leads to a comfortable, friendly organizational atmosphere and work tempo.

9,9 Team Management
Work accomplished is from committed people. Interdependence through a common stake in organizational purpose leads to relationships of trust and respect.

5,5 Middle-of-the-Road Management
Adequate organization performance is possible through balancing the need to get work done with maintaining morale of people at a satisfactory level.

1,1 Impoverished Management
Exertion of minimum effort to get required work done is appropriate to sustain organization membership.

9,1 Authority-Compliance
Efficiency in operations results from arranging conditions of work in such a way that human elements interfere to a minimum degree.

Concern for people — High 9, 8, 7, 6, 5, 4, 3, 2, Low 1

Concern for production — 1 Low, 2, 3, 4, 5, 6, 7, 8, 9 High

Source: R. R. Blake and A. A. McCanse, "The Leadership Grid®," *Leadership Dilemmas—Grid Solutions* (Houston: Gulf Publishing Company), 21. Copyright © 1991, by Scientific Methods, Inc. Reproduced by permission of the owners.

The same researchers also concluded that the most effective leaders were strong on both initiating structure and considerate leader behaviors.

This "high-high" approach can be seen in the upper right corner of the Blake/Mouton leadership grid, shown in Exhibit 14.1. Blake and Mouton used two leadership behaviors, concern for people (i.e., consideration) and concern for production (i.e., initiating structure), to categorize five different leadership styles. Both behaviors are rated on a 9-point scale, with 1 representing "low" and 9 representing "high." Blake and Mouton suggest that a "high-high," or 9,9, leadership style is the best. They call this style *team management* because leaders who use it display a high concern for people (9) and a high concern for production (9).

By contrast, leaders use a 9,1 *authority-compliance* leadership style when they have a high concern for production and a low concern for people. A 1,9 *country club* style occurs when leaders care about having a friendly, enjoyable work environment but don't really pay much attention to production or performance. The worst leadership style, according to the grid, is the 1,1 *impoverished* leader, who shows little concern for people or production and does the bare minimum needed to keep his or her job. Finally, the 5,5 *middle-of-the-road* style occurs when leaders show a moderate amount of concern for both people and production.

Is the team management style, with a high concern for production and a high concern for people, the best leadership style? Logically, it would seem so. Why wouldn't you want to show high concern for both people and production? Nonetheless, nearly fifty years of research indicates that there isn't one best leadership style. The best leadership style depends on the situation. In other words, no one leadership behavior by itself and no one combination of leadership behaviors works well across all situations and employees.

14-3 *Putting Leaders in the Right Situation: Fiedler's Contingency Theory*

After leader traits and behaviors, the situational approach to leadership is the third major method used in the study of leadership. We'll review three major situational approaches to leadership—Fiedler's contingency theory, path-goal theory, and Vroom, Yetton, and Jago's normative decision model. All assume that the effectiveness of any **leadership style**, the way a leader generally behaves toward followers, depends on the situation.[22] Stanford Business School professor Jeffrey Pfeffer agrees: "Situations differ, often wildly, in the extent to which one individual can make a difference and in the set of attributes required to be successful. . . . But utopia is impossible, which is why management consultants and authors should stop talking so much about how to find an ideal leader and instead focus on placing people into jobs that play to their strengths—and where their flaws won't be fatal."[23]

According to situational leadership theories, there is no one best leadership style. But one of these situational theories differs from the other three in one significant way. Fiedler's contingency theory assumes that leadership styles are consistent and difficult to change. Therefore, leaders must be placed in or matched to a situation that fits their leadership style. By contrast, the other three situational theories all assume that leaders are capable of adapting and adjusting their leadership styles to fit the demands of different situations.

Fiedler's **contingency theory** states that in order to maximize work group performance, leaders must be matched to the right leadership situation.[24] More specifically, the first basic assumption of Fiedler's theory is that leaders are effective when the work groups they lead perform well. So, instead of judging leaders' effectiveness by what they do (i.e., initiating structure and consideration) or who they are (i.e., trait theory), Fiedler assesses leaders by the conduct and performance of the people they supervise. Second, Fiedler assumes that leaders are generally unable to change their leadership styles and that they will be more effective when their styles are matched to the proper situation. Ken Ottenbourg, former managing editor of the *Winston-Salem Journal*, agrees. After attending a week-long course at the Center for Creative Leadership, a world-leading leadership institute, he struggled to implement the leadership ideas he learned. Says Ottenbourg, "It's easier to talk about changing behavior, and a lot harder to do it in the real world."[25]

Third, Fiedler assumes that the favorableness of a situation for a leader depends on the degree to which the situation permits the leader to influence the behavior of group members. Fiedler's third assumption is consistent with our definition of leadership as the process of influencing others to achieve group or organizational goals. In other words, in addition to traits, behaviors, and a favorable situation to match, leaders have to be allowed to lead.

Let's learn more about Fiedler's contingency theory by examining **14-3a the least preferred coworker and leadership styles,** *14-3b situational favorableness,* **and** **14-3c how to match leadership styles to situations.**

14-3a LEADERSHIP STYLE: LEAST PREFERRED COWORKER

When Fiedler refers to *leadership style*, he means the way that leaders generally behave toward their followers. Do the leaders yell and scream and blame others when things go wrong? Or do they correct mistakes by listening and then quietly but directly make their point? Do they take credit for others' work when things go right? Or do they make sure that those who did the work receive the credit they rightfully deserve? Do they let others make their own decisions and hold them accountable for the results? Or do they micromanage, insisting that all decisions be approved first by them? Fiedler also assumes that leadership styles are tied to leaders' underlying needs and personalities. Since personalities and needs are relatively stable, he assumes that leaders are generally incapable of changing their leadership styles. In other words, the way that leaders treat people now is probably the way they've

Leadership style the way a leader generally behaves toward followers

Contingency theory a leadership theory that states that in order to maximize work group performance, leaders must be matched to the situation that best fits their leadership style

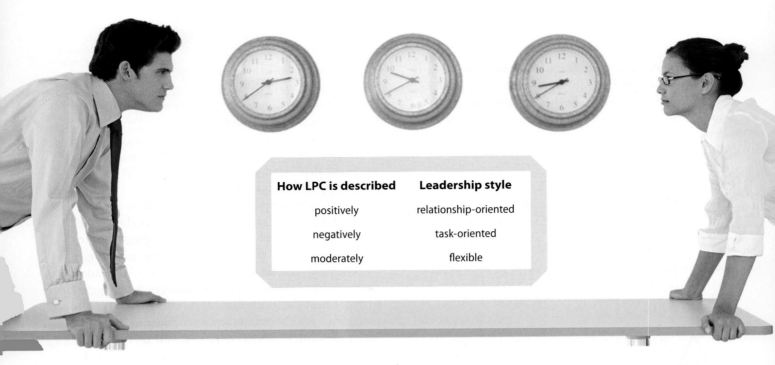

How LPC is described	Leadership style
positively	relationship-oriented
negatively	task-oriented
moderately	flexible

always treated others. So, according to Fiedler, if your boss's first instinct is to yell and scream and blame others, chances are he or she has always done that.

Fiedler uses a questionnaire called the Least Preferred Coworker (LPC) scale to measure leadership style. When completing the LPC scale, people are instructed to consider all of the people with whom they have ever worked and then to choose the one person with whom they have worked *least* well. Fiedler explains, "This does not have to be the person you liked least well, but should be the one person with whom you have the most trouble getting the job done."[26]

Would you describe your LPC as pleasant, friendly, supportive, interesting, cheerful, and sincere? Or would you describe the person as unpleasant, unfriendly, hostile, boring, gloomy, and insincere? People who describe their LPC in a positive way (scoring 64 and above) have *relationship-oriented* leadership styles. After all, if they can still be positive about their least preferred coworker, they must be people-oriented. By contrast, people who describe their LPC in a negative way (scoring 57 or below) have *task-oriented* leadership styles. Given a choice, they'll focus first on getting the job done and second on

Situational favorableness the degree to which a particular situation either permits or denies a leader the chance to influence the behavior of group members

Leader-member relations the degree to which followers respect, trust, and like their leaders

Task structure the degree to which the requirements of a subordinate's tasks are clearly specified

Position power the degree to which leaders are able to hire, fire, reward, and punish workers

making sure everyone gets along. Finally, those with moderate scores (from 58 to 63) have a more flexible leadership style and can be somewhat relationship-oriented or somewhat task-oriented.

14-3b SITUATIONAL FAVORABLENESS

Fiedler assumes that leaders will be more effective when their leadership styles are matched to the proper situation. More specifically, Fiedler defines **situational favorableness** as the degree to which a particular situation either permits or denies a leader the chance to influence the behavior of group members.[27] In highly favorable situations, leaders find that their actions influence followers. But in highly unfavorable situations, leaders have little or no success influencing the people they are trying to lead.

Three situational factors determine the favorability of a situation: leader-member relations, task structure, and position power. The most important situational factor is **leader-member relations**, which refers to how well followers respect, trust, and like their leaders. When leader-member relations are good, followers trust the leader and there is a friendly work atmosphere. **Task structure** is the degree to which the requirements of a subordinate's tasks are clearly specified. With highly structured tasks, employees have clear job responsibilities, goals, and procedures. **Position power** is the degree to which leaders are able to hire, fire, reward, and punish workers. The more influence leaders have over hiring, firing, rewards, and punishments, the greater their power.

Exhibit 14.2 shows how leader-member relations, task structure, and position power can be combined into eight situations that differ in their favorability to leaders. In general, Situation I, on the left side of Exhibit 14.2, is the most favorable leader situation. Followers like and trust their leaders and know what to do because their tasks are highly structured. Also, the leaders have the formal power to influence workers through hiring, firing, rewarding, and punishing them. Therefore, it's relatively easy for a leader to influence followers in Situation I. By contrast, Situation VIII, on the right side of Exhibit 14.2, is the least favorable situation for leaders. Followers don't like or trust their leaders. Plus, followers are not sure what they're supposed to be doing, given that their tasks or jobs are highly unstructured. Finally, leaders find it difficult to influence followers because they don't have the ability to hire, fire, reward, or punish the people who work for them. In short, it's very difficult to influence followers given the conditions found in Situation VIII.

14-3c MATCHING LEADERSHIP STYLES TO SITUATIONS

After studying thousands of leaders and followers in hundreds of different situations, Fiedler found that the performance of relationship- and task-oriented leaders followed the pattern displayed in Exhibit 14.3.

Relationship-oriented leaders with high LPC scores were better leaders (i.e., their groups performed more effectively) under moderately favorable situations. In moderately favorable situations, the leader may be liked somewhat, tasks may be somewhat structured, and the leader may have some position power. In this situation, a relationship-oriented leader improves leader-member relations, which is the most important of the three situational factors. In turn, morale and performance improve. How did Gordon Bethune turn around Continental Airlines and its previously poisonous labor-management relations? He explains it this way: "When I was a mechanic, I knew how much faster I could fix an airplane when I

EXHIBIT 14.2

Situational Favorableness

Leader-Member Relations	Good	Good	Good	Good	Poor	Poor	Poor	Poor
Task Structure	High	High	Low	Low	High	High	Low	Low
Position Power	Strong	Weak	Strong	Weak	Strong	Weak	Strong	Weak
Situation	I	II	III	IV	V	VI	VII	VIII
	Favorable			**Moderately Favorable**			**Unfavorable**	

© Cengage Learning

EXHIBIT 14.3

Matching Leadership Styles to Situations

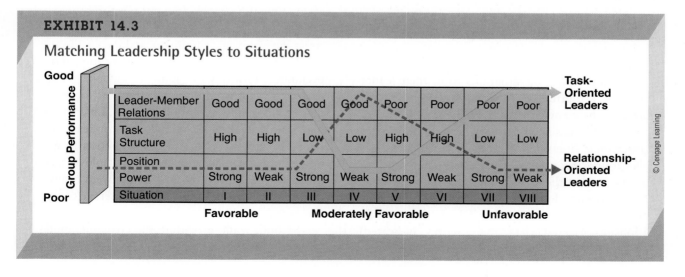

© Cengage Learning

wanted to fix it than when I didn't. I've tried to make it so our guys want to do it."[28]

By contrast, as Exhibit 14.3 shows, task-oriented leaders with low LPC scores are better leaders in highly favorable and unfavorable situations. Task-oriented leaders do well in favorable situations where leaders are liked, tasks are structured, and the leader has the power to hire, fire, reward, and punish. In these favorable situations, task-oriented leaders effectively step on the gas of a well-tuned car. Their focus on performance sets the goal for the group, which then charges forward to meet it. But task-oriented leaders also do well in unfavorable situations where leaders are disliked, tasks are unstructured, and the leader doesn't have the power to hire, fire, reward, and punish. In these unfavorable situations, the task-oriented leader sets goals, which focus attention on performance and clarify what needs to be done, thus overcoming low task structure. This is enough to jump-start performance even if workers don't like or trust the leader.

Finally, though not shown in Exhibit 14.3, people with moderate LPC scores, who can be somewhat relationship-oriented or somewhat task-oriented, tend to do fairly well in all situations because they can adapt their behavior. Typically, though, they don't perform quite as well as relationship-oriented or task-oriented leaders whose leadership styles are well matched to the situation.

Recall, however, that Fiedler assumes leaders to be incapable of changing their leadership styles. Accordingly, the key to applying Fiedler's contingency theory in the workplace is to accurately measure and match leaders to situations or to teach leaders how to change situational favorableness by changing leader-member relations, task structure, or position power. Though matching or placing leaders in appropriate situations works particularly well, practicing managers have had little luck reengineering situations to fit their leadership styles. The primary problem, as you've no doubt realized, is the complexity of the theory.

In a study designed to teach leaders how to reengineer their situations to fit their leadership styles, Fiedler found that most of the leaders simply did not understand what they were supposed to do to change their situations. Furthermore, if they didn't like their LPC profile (perhaps they felt they were more relationship-oriented than their scores indicated), they arbitrarily changed it to better suit their view of

themselves. Of course, the theory won't work as well if leaders are attempting to change situational factors to fit their perceived leadership style rather than their real leadership style.[29]

14-4 Adapting Leader Behavior: Path-Goal Theory

Just as its name suggests, **path-goal theory** states that leaders can increase subordinate satisfaction and performance by clarifying and clearing the paths to goals and by increasing the number and kinds of rewards available for goal attainment. Said another way, leaders need to clarify how followers can achieve organizational goals, take care of problems that prevent followers from achieving goals, and then find more and varied rewards to motivate followers to achieve those goals.[30]

Leaders must meet two conditions for path clarification, path clearing, and rewards to increase followers' motivation and effort. First, leader behavior must be a source of immediate or future satisfaction for followers. The things you do as a leader must either please your followers today or lead to activities or rewards that will satisfy them in the future. Employees at Lincoln Electric, a manufacturer of industrial equipment based in Cleveland, Ohio, are expected to meet high standards. They are not paid an hourly wage. Instead, they are paid according to how much they produce on the line. The rate that an employee receives per piece produced can fluctuate, and all employees are required to work overtime. Further, an employee can be let go of at any time if he or she does not meet rigorous performance standards. Even though this seems like a high-stress environment, employees at Lincoln Electric are quite happy, because in return for meeting those expectations, former CEO John M. Stropki guaranteed that employees would never be laid off for economic reasons. Indeed, in seventy-four years, Lincoln Electric has never laid off even one worker for reasons other than performance deficiencies. In addition to guaranteed employment, Stropki gave each employee a sizable profit-sharing bonus—in 2011, employees received an average bonus of $30,775, and the average compensation was $79,050.[31]

Second, while providing the coaching, guidance, support, and rewards necessary for effective work per-

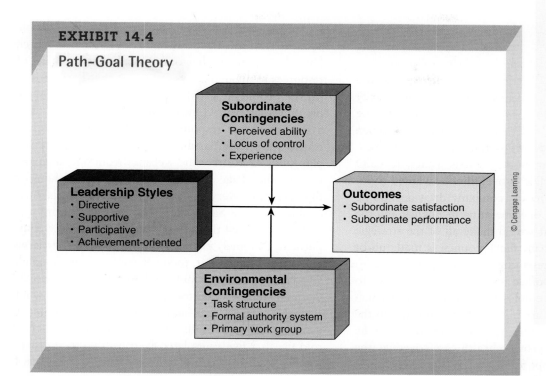

EXHIBIT 14.4

Path–Goal Theory

Subordinate Contingencies
• Perceived ability
• Locus of control
• Experience

Leadership Styles
• Directive
• Supportive
• Participative
• Achievement-oriented

Outcomes
• Subordinate satisfaction
• Subordinate performance

Environmental Contingencies
• Task structure
• Formal authority system
• Primary work group

© Cengage Learning

formance, leader behaviors must complement and not duplicate the characteristics of followers' work environments. Thus, leader behaviors must offer something unique and valuable to followers beyond what they're already experiencing as they do their jobs or what they can already do for themselves.

In contrast to Fiedler's contingency theory, path-goal theory assumes that leaders *can* change and adapt their leadership styles. Exhibit 14.4 illustrates this process, showing that leaders change and adapt their leadership styles contingent on their subordinates or the environment in which those subordinates work.

Let's learn more about path-goal theory by examining *14-4a the four kinds of leadership styles that leaders use, 14-4b the subordinate and environmental contingency factors that determine when different leader styles are effective,* and *14-4c the outcomes of path-goal theory in improving employee satisfaction and performance.*

14-4a LEADERSHIP STYLES

As illustrated in Exhibit 14.4, the four leadership styles in path-goal theory are directive, supportive, participative, and achievement oriented.[32] **Directive leadership** involves letting employees know precisely what is expected of them, giving them specific guidelines for performing tasks, scheduling work, set-

ting standards of performance, and making sure that people follow standard rules and regulations.

Supportive leadership involves being approachable and friendly to employees, showing concern for them and their welfare, treating them as equals, and creating a friendly climate. Supportive leadership is very similar to considerate leader behavior. Supportive leadership often results in employee satisfaction with the job and with leaders. This leadership style may also result in improved performance when it increases employee confidence, lowers employee job stress, or improves relations and trust between employees and leaders.[33]

Participative leadership involves consulting employees for their suggestions and input before

Achievement-Oriented Leadership
"Let's go and make big things happen."

—*Google CEO Larry Page*

Directive leadership a leadership style in which the leader lets employees know precisely what is expected of them, gives them specific guidelines for performing tasks, schedules work, sets standards of performance, and makes sure that people follow standard rules and regulations

Supportive leadership a leadership style in which the leader is friendly and approachable to employees, shows concern for employees and their welfare, treats them as equals, and creates a friendly climate

Participative leadership a leadership style in which the leader consults employees for their suggestions and input before making decisions

making decisions. Participation in decision making should help followers understand which goals are most important and clarify the paths to accomplishing them. Furthermore, when people participate in decisions, they become more committed to making them work. Thomas Walter, the CEO of Tasty Catering in Elk Grove, Illinois, wanted to involve his employees in key company decisions. So he started two councils, one operating in English and the other in Spanish, that would make all of the strategic choices for the company. Each council is made up of eight employees representing the entire work force—cooks, accountants, office staff, and drivers. And to make sure that every employee has a chance to participate, two employees are picked at random to join the councils for one-month terms. When the owners of the company wanted to provide health care coverage, the councils decided to opt for a less-costly package, since most employees already had coverage through spouses. Anna Wollin, an account executive, says the councils "[put] us all on an even playing field. I have been with the company for less than a year, and my opinion was as important as an owner's opinion."[34]

Achievement-oriented leadership means setting challenging goals, having high expectations of employees, and displaying confidence that employees will assume responsibility and put forth extraordinary effort. Though he's an introvert, Google co-founder and CEO Larry Page is clearly an achievement-oriented

leader. A former Google executive says, "When people come to Larry with ideas, he always wants it bigger. His whole point is that only Google has the kind of resources to make big bets. The asset that Larry brings [to the people he leads] is to say, 'Let's go and make big things happen.'" One example involves Franz Och, a top researcher responsible for Google's "machine-translation system," artificial intelligence that uses complex statistics to translate websites from one language into another. Page spent a year trying to hire him for this task, and every time Och would tell Page that it couldn't be done. Says Och, "They were very optimistic, and I tried to tell them to be cautious. It's really complicated, extremely expensive, and you need very large amounts of data." But, today, if you're using Google's Chrome web browser and you happen on a Chinese or German website, a button appears asking if you want the website translated—and it works for fifty-eight languages. Och says, "When I started at Google, if you told me that five years later we'd be able to translate Yiddish, Maltese, Icelandic, Azerbaijani, and Basque, I would have said, 'That's just not going to happen.' But [co-founders Larry Page and Sergey Brin] didn't believe me. And I guess they were more right than I was."[35]

14-4b SUBORDINATE AND ENVIRONMENTAL CONTINGENCIES

As shown in Exhibit 14.4, path-goal theory specifies that leader behaviors should be adapted to subordi-

DOING THE RIGHT THING

A Leadership Gap

The shift from one leader to another is one of the most crucial times for a company, yet very few organizations have planned for the process. A smooth transition to a successor can help a company maintain, and even expand, the company's success. A rough transition, however, can throw the company into chaos as it struggles to find a coherent vision and strategy. This is the reason why 98 percent of global companies recently surveyed believed that a CEO succession plan was critically important to the organization. However, only 35 percent of responding companies actually have a plan set in place. It may sound strange, of course, to think about how you're going to find a new leader when you already have one. But CEOs don't just retire or leave when you're ready for them to; they can resign suddenly, fall ill, or even be fired. So do the right thing, plan for the future, and set up a solid succession plan so that your company's stability isn't jeopardized.

Source: "Korn/Ferry Survey Reveals More Interest Than Action in CEO Succession Planning among Top Companies," *Korn/Ferry International*, December 21, 2010, http://www.kornferry.com/PressRelease/11916.

© iStockphoto.com/fredfroese

nate characteristics. The theory identifies three kinds of subordinate contingencies: perceived ability, experience, and locus of control. *Perceived ability* is simply how much ability subordinates believe they have for doing their jobs well. Subordinates who perceive that they have a great deal of ability will be dissatisfied with directive leader behaviors. Experienced employees are likely to react in a similar way. Since they already know how to do their jobs (or perceive that they do), they don't need or want close supervision. By contrast, subordinates with little experience or little perceived ability will welcome directive leadership.

Locus of control is a personality measure that indicates the extent to which people believe that they have control over what happens to them in life. *Internals* believe that what happens to them, good or bad, is largely a result of their choices and actions. *Externals*, on the other hand, believe that what happens to them is caused by external forces beyond their control. Accordingly, externals are much more comfortable with a directive leadership style, whereas internals greatly prefer a participative leadership style because they like to have a say in what goes on at work.

Path-goal theory specifies that leader behaviors should complement rather than duplicate the characteristics of followers' work environments. There are three kinds of environmental contingencies: task structure, the formal authority system, and the primary work group. As in Fiedler's contingency theory, *task structure*

is the degree to which the requirements of a subordinate's tasks are clearly specified. When task structure is low and tasks are unclear, directive leadership should be used because it complements the work environment. When task structure is high and tasks are clear, however, directive leadership is not needed because it duplicates what task structure provides. Alternatively, when tasks are stressful, frustrating, or dissatisfying, leaders should respond with supportive leadership.

The *formal authority system* is an organization's set of procedures, rules, and policies. When the formal authority system is unclear, directive leadership complements the situation by reducing uncertainty and increasing clarity. But when the formal authority system is clear, directive leadership is redundant and should not be used.

Primary work group refers to the amount of work-oriented participation or emotional support that is provided by an employee's immediate work group. Participative leadership should be used when tasks are complex and there is little existing work-oriented participation in the primary work group. When tasks are stressful, frustrating, or repetitive, supportive leadership is called for.

Finally, since keeping track of all of these subordinate and environmental contingencies can get a bit confusing, Exhibit 14.5 provides a summary of when directive, supportive, participative, and achievement-oriented leadership styles should be used.

EXHIBIT 14.5

Path-Goal Theory: When to Use Directive, Supportive, Participative, or Achievement-Oriented Leadership

DIRECTIVE LEADERSHIP	SUPPORTIVE LEADERSHIP	PARTICIPATIVE LEADERSHIP	ACHIEVEMENT-ORIENTED LEADERSHIP
Unstructured tasks	Structured, simple, repetitive tasks; Stressful, frustrating tasks	Complex tasks	Unchallenging tasks
Workers with external locus of control	Workers lack confidence	Workers with internal locus of control	
Unclear formal authority system	Clear formal authority system	Workers not satisfied with rewards	
Inexperienced workers		Experienced workers	
Workers with low perceived ability		Workers with high perceived ability	

© Cengage Learning

14-4c OUTCOMES

Does following path-goal theory improve subordinate satisfaction and performance? Preliminary evidence suggests that it does.[36] In particular, people who work for supportive leaders are much more satisfied with their jobs and their bosses. Likewise, people who work for directive leaders are more satisfied with their jobs and bosses (but not quite as much as when their bosses are supportive) and perform their jobs better, too. Does adapting one's leadership style to subordinate and environmental characteristics improve subordinate satisfaction and performance? At this point, because it is difficult to completely test this complex theory, it's too early to tell.[37] However, since the data clearly show that it makes sense for leaders to be both supportive *and* directive, it also makes sense that leaders could improve subordinate satisfaction and performance by adding participative and achievement-oriented leadership styles to their capabilities as leaders.

14-5 *Adapting Leader Behavior: Normative Decision Theory*

Many people believe that making tough decisions is at the heart of leadership. Yet experienced leaders will tell you that deciding *how* to make decisions is just as important. The **normative decision theory** (also known as the *Vroom-Yetton-Jago model*) helps leaders decide how much employee participation (from none to letting employees make the entire decision) should be used when making decisions.[38]

Let's learn more about normative decision theory by investigating **14-5a decision styles** and **14-5b decision quality and acceptance.**

14-5a DECISION STYLES

Unlike nearly all of the other leadership theories discussed in this chapter, which have specified *leadership* styles, that is, the way a leader generally behaves toward followers, the normative decision theory specifies five different *decision* styles, or ways of making decisions. (See Chapter 5 for a more complete review of decision making in organizations.) As shown in Exhibit 14.6, those styles vary from *autocratic decisions* (AI or AII) on the left, in which leaders make the decisions by themselves, to *consultative decisions* (CI or CII), in which leaders share problems with subordinates but still make the decisions themselves, to *group decisions* (GII) on the right, in which leaders share the problems with subordinates and then have the group make the decisions.

GE Aircraft Engines in Durham, North Carolina, uses a similar approach when making decisions. According to *Fast Company* magazine, "At GE/Durham, every decision is either an 'A' decision, a 'B' decision, or a 'C' decision. An 'A' decision is one that the plant manager makes herself, without consulting anyone."[39] Plant manager Paula Sims says, "I don't make very many of those, and when I do make one, everyone at the plant knows it. I make maybe ten or twelve a year."[40] "B" decisions are also made by the plant manager but with input from the people affected. "C" decisions, the most common type, are made by consensus, by the people directly involved, with plenty of discussion. With "C" decisions, the view of the plant manager doesn't necessarily carry more weight than the views of those affected.[41]

14-5b DECISION QUALITY AND ACCEPTANCE

According to the normative decision theory, using the right degree of employee participation improves the quality of decisions and the extent to which employees accept and are committed to decisions. Exhibit 14.7 lists the decision rules that normative decision theory uses to increase the quality of a decision and the degree to which employees accept and commit to it.

The quality, leader information, subordinate information, goal congruence, and problem structure rules are used to increase decision quality. For example, the leader information rule states that if a leader doesn't have enough information to make a decision on his or her own, then the leader should not use an autocratic decision style. The commitment probability, subordinate conflict, and commitment requirement rules shown in Exhibit 14.7 are used to increase employee acceptance and commitment to decisions. For example, the commitment requirement rule says that if decision acceptance and commitment are important and the subordinates share the organization's goals, then you shouldn't use an autocratic or consultative

EXHIBIT 14.6

Normative Theory, Decision Styles, and Levels of Employee Participation

Leader solves the problem or makes the decision

Leader is willing to accept any decision supported by the entire group

AI	AII	CI	CII	GII
Using information available at the time, the leader solves the problem or makes the decision.	The leader obtains necessary information from employees and then selects a solution to the problem. When asked to share information, employees may or may not be told what the problem is.	The leader shares the problem and gets ideas and suggestions from relevant employees on an individual basis. Individuals are not brought together as a group. Then the leader makes the decision, which may or may not reflect their input.	The leader shares the problem with employees as a group, obtains their ideas and suggestions, and then makes the decision, which may or may not reflect their input.	The leader shares the problem with employees as a group. Together, the leader and employees generate and evaluate alternatives and try to reach an agreement on a solution. The leader acts as a facilitator and does not try to influence the group. The leader is willing to accept and implement any solution that has the support of the entire group.

Source: Table 2.1, Decision Methods for Group and Individual Problems, from *Leadership and Decision-Making*, by V. H. Vroom and P. W. Yetton, © 1973. Reprinted by permission of the University of Pittsburgh Press.

EXHIBIT 14.7

Normative Theory Decision Rules

DECISION RULES TO INCREASE DECISION QUALITY

Quality Rule. If the quality of the decision is important, then don't use an autocratic decision style.

Leader Information Rule. If the quality of the decision is important, and if the leader doesn't have enough information to make the decision on his or her own, then don't use an autocratic decision style.

Subordinate Information Rule. If the quality of the decision is important, and if the subordinates don't have enough information to make the decision themselves, then don't use a group decision style.

Goal Congruence Rule. If the quality of the decision is important, and subordinates' goals are different from the organization's goals, then don't use a group decision style.

Problem Structure Rule. If the quality of the decision is important, the leader doesn't have enough information to make the decision on his or her own, and the problem is unstructured, then don't use an autocratic decision style.

DECISION RULES TO INCREASE DECISION ACCEPTANCE

Commitment Probability Rule. If having subordinates accept and commit to the decision is important, then don't use an autocratic decision style.

Subordinate Conflict Rule. If having subordinates accept the decision is important and critical to successful implementation and subordinates are likely to disagree or end up in conflict over the decision, then don't use an autocratic or consultative decision style.

Commitment Requirement Rule. If having subordinates accept the decision is absolutely required for successful implementation and subordinates share the organization's goals, then don't use an autocratic or consultative style.

Sources: Adapted from V. H. Vroom, "Leadership," in *Handbook of Industrial and Organizational Psychology*, ed. M. D. Dunnette (Chicago: Rand McNally, 1976); V. H. Vroom and A. G. Jago, *The New Leadership: Managing Participation in Organizations* (Englewood Cliffs, NJ: Prentice Hall, 1988).

Strategic leadership the ability to anticipate, envision, maintain flexibility, think strategically, and work with others to initiate changes that will create a positive future for an organization

style. In other words, if followers want to do what's best for the company and you need their acceptance and commitment to make a decision work, then use a group decision style and let them make the decision. As you can see, these decision rules help leaders improve decision quality and follower acceptance and commitment by eliminating decision styles that don't fit the particular decision or situation they're facing. Normative decision theory, like path-goal theory, is situational in nature. The abstract decision rules in Exhibit 14.7 are framed as yes/no questions, which makes the process of applying these rules more concrete. These questions are shown in the decision tree displayed in Exhibit 14.8. You start at the left side of the tree and answer the first question, "How important is the technical quality of this decision?" by choosing "high" or "low." Then you continue by answering each question as you proceed along the decision tree until you get to a recommended decision style.

Let's use the model to make the decision of whether to change from a formal business attire policy to a casual wear policy. The problem sounds simple, but it is actually more complex than you might think. Follow the yellow line in Exhibit 14.8 as we work through the decision in the following discussion.

Problem: Change to Casual Wear?

1. *Quality requirement: How important is the technical quality of this decision?* High. This question has to do with whether there are quality differences in the alternatives and whether those quality differences matter. In other words: Is there a lot at stake in this decision? Although most people would assume that quality isn't an issue here, it really is, given the incredibly strong reactions that people have regarding the rules for casual wear at their companies.

2. *Commitment requirement: How important is subordinate commitment to the decision?* High. Changes in culture, like dress codes, require subordinate commitment or they fail.

3. *Leader's information: Do you have sufficient information to make a high-quality decision?* Yes. Let's assume that you've done your homework. Much has been written about casual wear, from how to make the change to the effects it has in companies (almost all positive).

4. *Commitment probability: If you were to make the decision by yourself, is it reasonably certain that your subordinate(s) would be committed to the decision?* No. Studies of casual wear find that employees' reactions are almost uniformly positive. Nonetheless, employees are likely to be angry if you change something as personal as clothing policies without consulting them.

5. *Goal congruence: Do subordinates share the organizational goals to be attained in solving this problem?* Yes. The goals that usually accompany a change to casual dress policies are a more informal culture, better communication, and less money spent on business attire.

6. *Subordinate information: Do subordinates have sufficient information to make a high-quality decision?* No. Most employees know little about casual wear policies or even what constitutes casual wear in most companies. Consequently, most companies have to educate employees about casual wear practices and policies before making a decision.

7. *CII is the answer:* With a CII, or consultative decision process, the leader shares the problem with employees as a group, obtains their ideas and suggestions, and then makes the decision, which may or may not reflect their input. So, given the answers to these questions (remember, different managers won't necessarily answer these questions the same way), the normative decision theory recommends that leaders consult with their subordinates before deciding whether to change to a casual wear policy.

How well does the normative decision theory work? A prominent leadership scholar has described it as the best supported of all leadership theories.[42] In general, the more managers violate the decision rules in Exhibit 14.7, the less effective their decisions are, especially with respect to subordinate acceptance and commitment.[43]

14-6 *Visionary Leadership*

Strategic leadership is the ability to anticipate, envision, maintain flexibility, think strategically, and work with others to initiate changes that will create a positive future for an organization.[44] Heidrick & Struggles (H&S), one of the world's largest executive

EXHIBIT 14.8

Normative Decision Theory Tree for Determining the Level of Participation in Decision Making

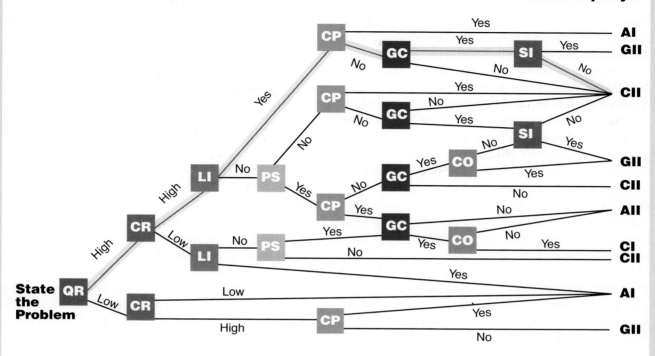

Problem Attributes

QR	Quality requirement:	How important is the technical quality of this decision?	
CR	Commitment requirement:	How important is subordinate commitment to the decision?	
LI	Leader's information:	Do you have sufficient information to make a high-quality decision?	
PS	Problem structure:	Is the problem well structured?	
CP	Commitment probability:	If you were to make the decision by yourself, are you reasonably certain that your subordinate(s) would be committed to the decision?	
GC	Goal congruence:	Do subordinates share the organizational goals to be attained in solving this problem?	
CO	Subordinate conflict:	Is conflict among subordinates over preferred solutions likely?	
SI	Subordinate information:	Do subordinates have sufficient information to make a high-quality decision?	

Source: Figure 9.3, Decision-Process Flow Chart for Both Individual and Group Problems, from *Leadership and Decision-Making*, by V. H. Vroom and P. W. Yetton, © 1973. Reprinted by permission of the University of Pittsburgh Press.

search firms, helps companies find CEOs, board members, and senior executives. When the economy turned down, CEO Kevin Kelly realized it was time to dramatically change the company's strategy. Currently, 95 percent of its business is executive search. But with online resources like LinkedIn .com making it easier to find and identify talent, and NASDAQ's website boardrecruiting.com charging just $350 per candidate to help companies find board members, Kelly wants to shrink search to just 50 percent of the business. In its place, he wants to grow leadership advisory services, such as executive retention and succession, to 40 percent. Says Kelly, "You can't pick up a newspaper today without seeing organizations that don't have proper succession planning in place. It's a major issue. What we're trying to become over the next three to five years is more of a leadership advisory firm, not only focusing on the acquisition of talent at the senior level, but also focusing on helping them develop their own employees and retention [strategies]. Forty percent of executives who join firms from the outside last only eighteen months. How do we as a firm help reduce that and help them with that turnover?"[45]

Thus, strategic leadership captures how leaders inspire their companies to change and their followers to give extraordinary effort to accomplish organizational goals.

In Chapter 5, we defined a purpose statement, which is often referred to as an organizational mission or vision, as a statement of a company's purpose or reason for existing. Similarly, **visionary leadership** creates a positive image of the future that motivates organizational members and provides direction for future planning and goal setting.[46]

*Two kinds of visionary leadership are **14-6a charismatic leadership** and **14-6b transformational leadership**.*

14-6a CHARISMATIC LEADERSHIP

Charisma is a Greek word meaning "divine gift." The ancient Greeks saw people with charisma as inspired by the gods and capable of incredible accomplishments. German sociologist Max Weber viewed charisma as a special bond between leaders and followers.[47] Weber wrote that the special qualities of charismatic leaders enable them to strongly influence followers. Weber also noted that charismatic leaders tend to emerge in times of crisis and that the radical solutions they propose enhance the admiration that followers feel for them. Indeed, charismatic leaders tend to have incredible influence over followers who may be inspired by their leaders and become fanatically devoted to them. From this perspective, charismatic leaders are often seen as larger-than-life or more special than other employees of the company.

Charismatic leaders have strong, confident, dynamic personalities that attract followers and enable the leaders to create strong bonds with their followers. Followers trust charismatic leaders, are loyal to them, and are inspired to work toward the accomplishment of the leader's vision. Followers who become devoted

The ancient Greeks saw people with charisma as inspired by the gods and capable of incredible accomplishments.

to charismatic leaders may go to extraordinary lengths to please them. Therefore, we can define **charismatic leadership** as the behavioral tendencies and personal characteristics of leaders that create an exceptionally strong relationship between them and their followers. Charismatic leaders also

- Articulate a clear vision for the future that is based on strongly held values or morals;
- Model those values by acting in a way consistent with the vision;
- Communicate high performance expectations to followers; and
- Display confidence in followers' abilities to achieve the vision.[48]

Does charismatic leadership work? Studies indicate that it often does. In general, the followers of charismatic leaders are more committed and satisfied, are better performers, are more likely to trust their leaders, and simply work harder.[49] Nonetheless, charismatic leadership also has risks that are at least as large as its benefits. The problems are likely to occur with ego-driven charismatic leaders who take advantage of fanatical followers.

In general, there are two kinds of charismatic leaders, ethical charismatics and unethical charismatics.[50] **Ethical charismatics** provide developmental opportunities for followers, are open to positive and negative feedback, recognize others' contributions, share information, and have moral standards that emphasize the larger interests of the group, organization, or society. Jim McNerney, Boeing's CEO, believes that providing development opportunities for followers should be a leader's highest priority. Says McNerney, "I don't start with the company's strategy or products. I start with people's growth because I believe that if the people who are running and participating in a company grow, then the company's growth will in many respects take care of itself. I have this idea in my mind—all of us get 15 percent better every year. . . . Usually that means your ability to lead, and that's all about your ability to chart the course for [your employees], to inspire them to reach for performance— the values you bring to the job, with a focus on the courage to do the right thing. I tend to think about this in terms of helping others get better."[51] As you would expect, ethical charismatics produce stronger commitment, higher satisfaction, more effort, better performance, and greater trust.

By contrast, **unethical charismatics** control and manipulate followers, do what is best for themselves in-

stead of their organizations, want to hear only positive feedback, share information that is only beneficial to themselves, and have moral standards that put their interests before everyone else's. Because followers can become just as committed to unethical charismatics as to ethical charismatics, unethical characteristics pose a tremendous risk for companies. John Thompson, a management consultant, warns, "Often what begins as a mission becomes an obsession. Leaders can cut corners on values and become driven by self-interest. Then they may abuse anyone who makes a mistake."[52]

After an eight-month trial, David H. Brooks, the former CEO of DHB Industries, a military contractor that makes body armor, was found guilty of seventeen counts of fraud and of stealing nearly $190 million from the company. According to prosecutors, Brooks repeatedly used company funds to buy luxury items for himself and his family, including a Bentley, a Ferrari, purebred horses, family vacations, his wife's facelift, and a jewel-encrusted belt buckle worth more than $100,000. Along with chief operating officer Sandra Hatfield, Brooks also falsely inflated the value of inventory, lied about the number of body armor units that were being shipped to the U.S. Army, ordered company accountants to produce false reports about the company's performance, and committed insider trading through an illegal sale of stock.[53]

Exhibit 14.9 on the next page shows the stark differences between ethical and unethical charismatics on several leader behaviors: exercising power, creating the vision, communicating with followers, accepting feedback, stimulating followers intellectually, developing followers, and living by moral standards. For example, ethical charismatics account for the concerns and wishes of their followers when creating a vision by having followers participate in the development of the company vision. By contrast, unethical charismatics develop a vision by themselves solely to meet their personal agendas. One unethical charismatic said, "The key thing is that it is my idea; and I am going to win with it at all costs."[54]

Charismatic leadership the behavioral tendencies and personal characteristics of leaders that create an exceptionally strong relationship between them and their followers

Ethical charismatics charismatic leaders who provide developmental opportunities for followers, are open to positive and negative feedback, recognize others' contributions, share information, and have moral standards that emphasize the larger interests of the group, organization, or society

Unethical charismatics charismatic leaders who control and manipulate followers, do what is best for themselves instead of their organizations, want to hear only positive feedback, share only information that is beneficial to themselves, and have moral standards that put their interests before everyone else's

EXHIBIT 14.9

Ethical and Unethical Charismatics

CHARISMATIC LEADER BEHAVIORS	ETHICAL Charismatics . . .	UNETHICAL Charismatics . . .
Exercising power	. . . use power to serve others.	. . . use power to dominate or manipulate others for personal gain.
Creating the vision	. . . allow followers to help develop the vision.	. . . are the sole source of vision, which they use to serve their personal agendas.
Communicating with followers	. . . engage in two-way communication and seek out viewpoints on critical issues.	. . . engage in one-way communication and are not open to suggestions from others.
Accepting feedback	. . . are open to feedback and willing to learn from criticism.	. . . have inflated egos, thrive on attention and admiration of sycophants, and avoid candid feedback.
Stimulating followers intellectually	. . . want followers to think and question status quo as well as leader's views.	. . . don't want followers to think but instead want uncritical acceptance of leader's ideas.
Developing followers	. . . focus on developing people with whom they interact, express confidence in them, and share recognition with others.	. . . are insensitive and unresponsive to followers' needs and aspirations.
Living by moral standards	. . . follow self-guided principles that may go against popular opinion and have three virtues: courage, a sense of fairness or justice, and integrity.	. . . follow standards only if they satisfy immediate self-interests, manipulate impressions so that others think they are doing the right thing, and use communication skills to manipulate others to support their personal agendas.

Source: J. M. Howell and B. J. Avolio, "The Ethics of Charismatic Leadership: Submission or Liberation?" *Academy of Management Executive* 6, no. 2 (1992): 43–54.

14-6b TRANSFORMATIONAL LEADERSHIP

While charismatic leadership involves articulating a clear vision, modeling values consistent with that vision, communicating high performance expectations, and establishing very strong relationships with followers, **transformational leadership** goes further by generating awareness and acceptance of a group's purpose and mission and by getting employees to see beyond their own needs and self-interest for the good of the group.[55] Like charismatic leaders, transformational leaders are visionary, but they transform their organizations by getting their followers to accomplish more than they intended and even more than they thought possible.

Transformational leaders are able to make their followers feel that they are a vital part of the organization and help them see how their jobs fit with the organization's vision. By linking individual and organizational interests, transformational leaders encourage followers to make sacrifices for the organization because they know that they will prosper when the organization prospers. Transformational leadership has four components: charismatic leadership or idealized influence, inspirational motivation, intellectual stimulation, and individualized consideration.[56]

Charismatic leadership or idealized influence means that transformational leaders act as role models for their followers. Because transformational leaders put others' needs ahead of their own and share risks with their followers, they are admired, respected, and trusted,

Transformational leadership leadership that generates awareness and acceptance of a group's purpose and mission and gets employees to see beyond their own needs and self-interests for the good of the group

and followers want to emulate them. Thus, in contrast to purely charismatic leaders (especially unethical charismatics), transformational leaders can be counted on to do the right thing and maintain high standards for ethical and personal conduct. After Jim McNerney became Boeing's third CEO in three years, he pushed company lawyers to settle ethics violations that occurred under his predecessors. Under the settlement with the U.S. Justice Department, Boeing agreed to pay a $615 million penalty. But that wasn't enough for McNerney. He apologized before a Senate committee and refused to take a $200 million tax deduction to which Boeing was entitled for its costs in obtaining the settlement. Critics charge that McNerney's decision to not take the tax deduction wrongly cost Boeing shareholders $200 million. McNerney, who was responsible for restoring the company's commitment to ethical behavior, said, "I thought it was the right thing to do."[57] McNerney also instituted a new organization-wide ethics program and has linked bonuses and promotion to ethical behavior.

Inspirational motivation means that transformational leaders motivate and inspire followers by providing meaning and challenge to their work. By clearly communicating expectations and demonstrating commitment to goals, transformational leaders help followers envision future states, such as the organizational vision or mission. In turn, this leads to greater enthusiasm and optimism about the future.

Intellectual stimulation means that transformational leaders encourage followers to be creative and innovative, to question assumptions, and to look at problems and situations in new ways even if their ideas are different from those of leaders.

Individualized consideration means that transformational leaders pay special attention to followers' individual needs by creating learning opportunities, accepting and tolerating individual differences, encouraging two-way communication, and being good listeners. At the Sky Factory, an Iowa company that installs ocean- and sky-scape ceilings and walls in hospitals, restaurants, and spas, founder Bill Witherspoon makes sure there is no hierarchy. He gives everyone the option to buy shares in the company. Every Friday, a companywide meeting is held, during which financial numbers, quality issues, and the number of clients that visited is shared with everyone. Says Witherspoon, "Everyone is trained in financial literacy so he or she can make the best use of the information." Witherspoon is so committed to empowering his workers that when he wanted to expand to Europe but the group decided against it, he accepted their decision. "I argued my case for fifteen minutes and then

Honesty Is the Best Policy

Under Alan Mulally's leadership, Ford Motor Company went through an incredible revival. After nearly a decade of losses, the company had a profit of $10.5 billion and was able to cut its debt by more than a third. And unlike its competitors GM or Chrysler, it was able to do so without declaring bankruptcy or taking government bailout money. One of the keys to this revival was how Mulally emphasized finding solutions to problems rather than self-preservation. During one of his first meetings with executives, Mulally asked how things were going. He got just about the same response from everyone—"Fine . . ." He then wondered aloud how they could answer "Fine" when the company was looking at a loss of $17 billion. At the next meeting, Mulally again asked how things were, but this time, the head of North American operations took a risk and announced that a part defect threatened the launch of a new model. Formerly, this executive might have been chastised for letting such a major problem occur under his watch. Mulally, however, clapped his hands and praised the manager for bringing attention to the problem. His response then encouraged other managers to focus on solving problems rather than looking out for their own interest.

Source: "Epiphany at Ford," *The Economist*, December 11–17, 2010, 83–85.

Transactional leadership leadership based on an exchange process, in which followers are rewarded for good performance and punished for poor performance

said, 'Clearly we don't have consensus, so we'll forget about it.' And we have."[58]

Finally, a distinction needs to be drawn between transformational leadership and transactional leadership. While transformational leaders use visionary and inspirational appeals to influence followers, **transactional leadership** is based on an exchange process in which followers are rewarded for good performance and punished for poor performance. When leaders administer rewards fairly and offer followers the rewards that they want, followers will often reciprocate with effort. A problem, however, is that transactional leaders often rely too heavily on discipline or threats to bring performance up to standards. This may work in the short run, but it's much less effective in the long run. Also, as discussed in Chapters 11 and 13, many leaders and organizations have difficulty successfully linking pay practices to individual performance. As a result, studies consistently show that transformational leadership is much more effective on average than transactional leadership. In the United States, Canada, Japan, and India and at all organizational levels, from first-level supervisors to upper-level executives, followers view transformational leaders as much better leaders and are much more satisfied when working for them. Furthermore, companies with transformational leaders have significantly better financial performance.[59]

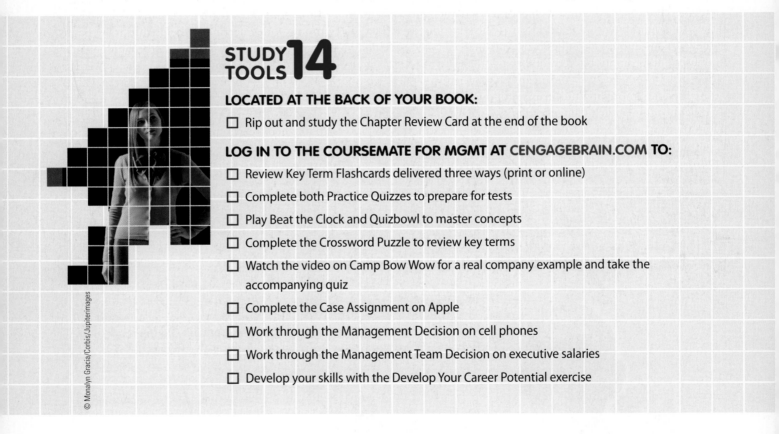

© Monalyn Gracia/Corbis/Jupiterimages

STUDY TOOLS 14

LOCATED AT THE BACK OF YOUR BOOK:

☐ Rip out and study the Chapter Review Card at the end of the book

LOG IN TO THE COURSEMATE FOR MGMT AT CENGAGEBRAIN.COM TO:

☐ Review Key Term Flashcards delivered three ways (print or online)

☐ Complete both Practice Quizzes to prepare for tests

☐ Play Beat the Clock and Quizbowl to master concepts

☐ Complete the Crossword Puzzle to review key terms

☐ Watch the video on Camp Bow Wow for a real company example and take the accompanying quiz

☐ Complete the Case Assignment on Apple

☐ Work through the Management Decision on cell phones

☐ Work through the Management Team Decision on executive salaries

☐ Develop your skills with the Develop Your Career Potential exercise

USE THE TOOLS.

- Rip out the Review Cards in the back of your book to study.

Or Visit CourseMate to:

- Read, search, highlight, and take notes in the Interactive eBook
- Review Flashcards (Print or Online) to master key terms
- Test yourself with Auto-Graded Quizzes
- Bring concepts to life with Games, Videos, and Animations!

Go to CourseMate for MGMT to begin using these tools.
Access at **www.cengagebrain.com**

Complete the Speak Up survey in CourseMate at
www.cengagebrain.com

f **Follow us at**
www.facebook.com/4ltrpress

15 Managing
Communication

© Thomas Jackson/Stone+/Getty Images

LEARNING OUTCOMES

15-1 Explain the role that perception plays in communication and communication problems.

15-2 Describe the communication process and the various kinds of communication in organizations.

15-3 Explain how managers can manage effective one-on-one communication.

15-4 Describe how managers can manage effective organization-wide communication.

CHECK OUT **STUDY TOOLS** AT THE END OF THIS CHAPTER.

© Monalyn Gracia/Corbis/Jupiterimages

15-1 *Perception and Communication Problems*

It's estimated that managers spend over 80 percent of their day communicating with others.[1] Indeed, much of the basic management process—planning, organizing, leading, and controlling—cannot be performed without effective communication. If this weren't reason enough to study communication, consider that effective oral communication—achieved by listening, following instructions, conversing, and giving feedback—is the most important skill for college graduates who are entering the work force.[2] **Communication** is the process of transmitting information from one person or place to another. While some bosses sugarcoat bad news, smart managers understand that effective, straightforward communication between managers and employees is essential for success.

One study found that when *employees* were asked whether their supervisor gave recognition for good work, only 13 percent said their supervisor gave a pat on the back, and a mere 14 percent said their supervisor gave sincere and thorough praise. But when the *supervisors* of these employees were asked if they gave recognition for good work, 82 percent said they gave pats on the back, while 80 percent said that they gave sincere and thorough praise.[3] Given that these managers and employees worked closely together, how could they have had such different perceptions of something as simple as praise?

*Let's learn more about perception and communication problems by examining **15-1a the basic perception process, 15-1b perception problems, 15-1c how we***

*perceive others, and **15-1d how we perceive ourselves**. We'll also consider how all of these factors make it difficult for managers to communicate effectively.*

15-1a BASIC PERCEPTION PROCESS

As shown in Exhibit 15.1 on the next page, **perception** is the process by which individuals attend to, organize, interpret, and retain information from their environments. And since communication is the process of transmitting information from one person or place to another, perception is obviously a key part of communication. Yet perception can also be a key obstacle to communication.

As people perform their jobs, they are exposed to a wide variety of informational stimuli such as emails, direct conversations with the boss or coworkers, rumors heard over lunch, stories about the company in the press, or a video broadcast of a speech from the CEO to all employees. Just being exposed to an informational stimulus, however, is no guarantee that an individual will pay attention or attend to that stimulus. People experience stimuli through their own **perceptual filters**—the personality-, psychology-, or experience-based differences that influence them to ignore or pay attention to particular stimuli. Because of filtering, people exposed to the same information will often disagree about what they saw or heard. As shown in Exhibit 15.1, perceptual

Communication the process of transmitting information from one person or place to another

Perception the process by which individuals attend to, organize, interpret, and retain information from their environments

Perceptual filters the personality-, psychology-, or experience-based differences that influence people to ignore or pay attention to particular stimuli

filters affect each part of the *perception process*: attention, organization, interpretation, and retention.

Attention is the process of noticing, or becoming aware of, particular stimuli. Because of perceptual filters, we attend to some stimuli and not others. For instance, a study at the University of Illinois asked viewers to watch people in black shirts and white shirts toss a basketball back and forth and to count the number of times someone in a black shirt tossed the basketball. Because their perceptual filters had narrowed to track the activities of people in black shirts, half of the viewers did not notice when the experimenters had someone in a gorilla suit walk through the midst of the people tossing the basketball back and forth.[4] *Organization* is the process of incorporating new information (from the stimuli that you notice) into your existing knowledge. Because of perceptual filters, we are more likely to incorporate new knowledge that is consistent with what we already know or believe. *Interpretation* is the process of attaching meaning to new knowledge. Because of perceptual filters, our preferences and beliefs strongly influence the meaning we attach to new information (e.g., "This decision must mean that top management supports our project"). Finally, *retention* is the process of remembering interpreted information. Retention affects what we recall and commit to memory after we have perceived something. Of course, perceptual filters affect retention as much as they do organization and interpretation.

For instance, imagine that you miss the first ten minutes of a TV show and turn on your TV to see two people talking to each other in a living room. As they talk, they walk around the room, picking up and putting down various items. Some items, such as a ring, watch, and credit card, appear to be valuable, while others appear to be drug-related, such as a water pipe for smoking marijuana. In fact, this situation was depicted on videotape in a well-known study that manipulated people's perceptual filters.[5] Before watching the video, one-third of the study participants were told that the people were there to rob the apartment. Another third of the participants were told that police were on their way to conduct a drug raid and that the people in the apartment were getting rid of incriminating evidence. The remaining third of the participants were told that the people were simply waiting for a friend.

After watching the video, participants were asked to list all of the objects from the video that they could remember. Not surprisingly, the different perceptual filters (theft, drug raid, and waiting for a friend) affected what the participants attended to, how they organized the information, how they interpreted it, and ultimately which objects they remembered. Participants who thought a theft was in progress were more likely to remember the valuable objects in the video. Those who thought a drug raid was imminent were more likely to remember the drug-related objects. There was no discernible pattern to the items remembered by those who thought that the people in the video were simply waiting for a friend.

In short, because of perception and perceptual filters, people are likely to pay attention to different things, organize and interpret what they pay attention to differently, and, finally, remember things differently. Consequently, even when people are exposed to the same communications (e.g., organizational memos, discussions with managers or customers), they can end up with very different perceptions and understandings. This is why communication can be so difficult and frustrating for managers. Let's review some

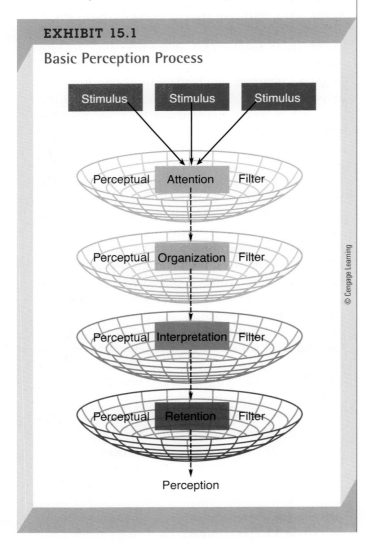

EXHIBIT 15.1

Basic Perception Process

Stimulus   Stimulus   Stimulus

Perceptual   Attention   Filter

Perceptual   Organization   Filter

Perceptual   Interpretation   Filter

Perceptual   Retention   Filter

Perception

© Cengage Learning

of the communication problems created by perception and perceptual filters.

15-1b PERCEPTION PROBLEMS

Perception creates communication problems for organizations because people exposed to the same communication and information can end up with completely different ideas and understandings. Two of the most common perception problems in organizations are selective perception and closure.

At work, we are constantly bombarded with sensory stimuli: phones ringing, people talking in the background, computers dinging as new email arrives, people calling our names, and so forth. As limited processors of information, we cannot possibly notice, receive, and interpret all of this information. As a result, we attend to and accept some stimuli but screen out and reject others. This isn't a random process.

Selective perception is the tendency to notice and accept objects and information consistent with our values, beliefs, and expectations, while ignoring or screening out inconsistent information. Apple products are acclaimed for their innovative styling and design, but when consumers point out flaws in its products, often Apple's first response is to discount the complaints. For example, touching any antenna reduces signal reception, and the iPhone 4 had a metal antenna encircling its edge. So when consumers complained that the iPhone 4 frequently dropped calls, then CEO Steve Jobs, who didn't think there was an issue (i.e., selective perception), emailed customers who contacted him about the issue, suggesting they "avoid gripping it in the lower left corner in a way that covers both sides of the black strip in the metal [antenna] band, or simply use one of many available cases."[6] Within ten days, though, Apple offered each of its iPhone 4 customers a free "bumper," or case, that solved the problem by preventing contact with the antenna. Likewise, consumers also posted numerous complaints about the iPhone 4S. Tens of thousands of iPhone 4S owners contacted Apple customer service and posted complaints to Apple's website, saying that their phones didn't have incoming audio during outgoing calls when using hands-free microphones—the person they called could hear them, but they could not hear the person they called. The Apple Support Communities forum that described this problem was 108 pages long, but Apple did not issue an official response or solution for the problem other than to have its Apple Genius Bar employees offer free replacement phones, which sometimes had the same problem.[7]

Once we have initial information about a person, event, or process, **closure** is the tendency to fill in the gaps where information is missing, that is, to assume that what we don't know is consistent with what we already do know. If employees are told that budgets must be cut by 10 percent, they may automatically assume that 10 percent of employees will lose their jobs, too, even if that isn't the case. Not surprisingly, when closure occurs, people sometimes fill in the gaps with inaccurate information, which can create problems for organizations.

15-1c PERCEPTIONS OF OTHERS

Attribution theory says that we all have a basic need to understand and explain the causes of other people's behavior.[8] In other words, we need to know why people do what they do. According to attribution theory, we use two general reasons or attributions to explain people's behavior: an *internal attribution*, in which behavior is thought to be voluntary or under the control of the individual; and an *external attribution*, in which behavior is thought to be involuntary and outside of the control of the individual.

Have you ever seen someone changing a flat tire on the side of the road and thought to yourself, "What rotten luck—somebody's having a bad day"?

Selective perception the tendency to notice and accept objects and information consistent with our values, beliefs, and expectations, while ignoring or screening out inconsistent information

Closure the tendency to fill in gaps of missing information by assuming that what we don't know is consistent with what we already know

Attribution theory the theory that we all have a basic need to understand and explain the causes of other people's behavior

© iStockphoto.com/Chris Schmelke

Defensive bias the tendency for people to perceive themselves as personally and situationally similar to someone who is having difficulty or trouble

Fundamental attribution error the tendency to ignore external causes of behavior and to attribute other people's actions to internal causes

If you did, you perceived the person through an external attribution known as the defensive bias. The **defensive bias** is the tendency for people to perceive themselves as personally and situationally similar to someone who is having difficulty or trouble.[9] When we identify with the person in a situation, we tend to use external attributions (i.e., features related to the situation) to explain the person's behavior. For instance, since flat tires are common, it's easy to perceive ourselves in that same situation and put the blame on external causes such as running over a nail.

Now, let's assume a different situation, this time in the workplace:

> A *utility company worker puts a ladder on a utility pole and then climbs up to do his work. As he's doing his work, he falls from the ladder and seriously injures himself.*[10]

Answer this question: Who or what caused the accident? If you thought, "It's not the worker's fault. Anybody could fall from a tall ladder," then you interpreted the incident with a defensive bias in which you saw yourself as personally and situationally similar to someone who is having difficulty or trouble. In other words, you made an external attribution by attributing the accident to an external cause or some feature of the situation.

Most accident investigations, however, initially blame the worker (i.e., an internal attribution) and not the situation (i.e., an external attribution). Typically, 60 to 80 percent of workplace accidents each year are blamed on "operator error," that is, on the employees themselves. In reality, more complete investigations usually show that workers are responsible for only 30 to 40 percent of all workplace accidents.[11] Why are accident investigators so quick to blame workers? The reason is that they are committing the **fundamental attribution error**, which is the tendency to ignore external causes of behavior and to attribute other people's actions to internal causes.[12] In other words, when investigators examine the possible causes of an accident, they're much more likely to assume that the accident is a function of the person and not the situation.

Which attribution—the defensive bias or the fundamental attribution error—are workers likely to make when something goes wrong? In general, as shown in Exhibit 15.2, employees and coworkers are more likely to perceive events and explain behavior from a defensive bias. Because they do the work

EXHIBIT 15.2

Defensive Bias and Fundamental Attribution Error

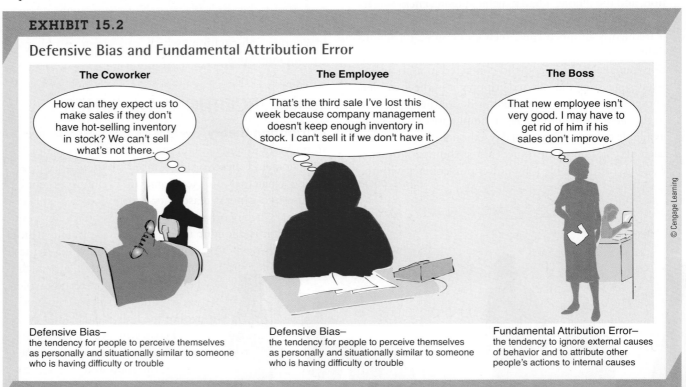

The Coworker

How can they expect us to make sales if they don't have hot-selling inventory in stock? We can't sell what's not there.

The Employee

That's the third sale I've lost this week because company management doesn't keep enough inventory in stock. I can't sell it if we don't have it.

The Boss

That new employee isn't very good. I may have to get rid of him if his sales don't improve.

Defensive Bias—
the tendency for people to perceive themselves as personally and situationally similar to someone who is having difficulty or trouble

Defensive Bias—
the tendency for people to perceive themselves as personally and situationally similar to someone who is having difficulty or trouble

Fundamental Attribution Error—
the tendency to ignore external causes of behavior and to attribute other people's actions to internal causes

© Cengage Learning

themselves and see themselves as similar to others who make mistakes, have accidents, or are otherwise held responsible for things that go wrong at work, employees and coworkers are likely to attribute problems to external causes such as failed machinery, poor support, or inadequate training. By contrast, because they are typically observers (who don't do the work themselves) and see themselves as situationally and personally different from workers, managers tend to commit the fundamental attribution error and blame mistakes, accidents, and other things that go wrong on workers (i.e., an internal attribution).

Consequently, workers and managers in most workplaces can be expected to take opposite views when things go wrong. Therefore, the defensive bias, which is typically used by workers, and the fundamental attribution error, which is typically made by managers, together present a significant challenge to effective communication and understanding in organizations.

15-1d SELF-PERCEPTION

The **self-serving bias** is the tendency to overestimate our value by attributing successes to ourselves (internal causes) and attributing failures to others or the environment (external causes).[13] The self-serving bias can make it especially difficult for managers to talk to employees about performance problems. In general, people have a need to maintain a positive self-image. This need is so strong that when people seek feedback at work, they typically want verification of their worth (rather than information about performance deficiencies) or assurance that mistakes or problems weren't their fault.[14] People can become defensive and emotional when managerial communication threatens their positive self-image. They quit listening, and communication becomes ineffective. In the second half of the chapter, which focuses on improving communication, we'll explain ways in which managers can minimize this self-serving bias and improve effective one-on-one communication with employees.

15-2 *Kinds of Communication*

There are many kinds of communication—formal, informal, coaching/counseling, and nonverbal—but they all follow the same fundamental process.

Let's learn more about the different kinds of communication by examining **15-2a the communication process, 15-2b formal communication channels, 15-2c informal communication channels, 15-2d coaching and counseling, or one-on-one communication,** *and* **15-2e nonverbal communication.**

15-2a THE COMMUNICATION PROCESS

At the beginning of this chapter, we defined *communication* as the process of transmitting information from one person or place to another. Exhibit 15.3 on the next page displays a model of the communication process and its major components: the sender (message to be conveyed, encoding the message, transmitting the message); the receiver (receiving message, decoding the message, and the message that was understood); and noise, which interferes with the communication process.

The communication process begins when a *sender* thinks of a message he or she wants to convey to another person. Throughout the world, customers expect to find lower prices when they shop at Wal-Mart. Following the example of founder Sam Walton, Wal-Mart's top executives, including the CEO, shop competitors to make sure Wal-Mart's prices really are lower. So, when on a business trip to China, CEO Mike Duke shopped his Chinese competitors and noticed that they carried bananas from China, as well imported bananas (which cost about 20 percent more). Wal-Mart's Wanda supercenter in Beijing, however, carried only the more expensive imported bananas (but at a cheaper price than the competition). So, Duke wondered why they weren't carrying the cheaper Chinese-grown bananas.

The next step is to encode the message. **Encoding** means putting a message into a verbal (written or spoken) or symbolic form that can be recognized and understood by the receiver. The sender then *transmits the message* via *communication channels*. Duke asked the store manager and the head of Wal-Mart's China division why they sold only the more expensive imported bananas and not the less expensive bananas from China. With some communication channels such as the telephone and face-to-face communication, the sender receives immediate feedback, whereas with others such as email (or text messages and file attachments), fax,

Decoding the process by which the receiver translates the written, verbal, or symbolic form of a message into an understood message

Feedback to sender in the communication process, a return message to the sender that indicates the receiver's understanding of the message

Noise anything that interferes with the transmission of the intended message

Jargon vocabulary particular to a profession or group that interferes with communication in the workplace

beepers, voice mail, memos, and letters, the sender must wait for the receiver to respond.

Unfortunately, because of technical difficulties (e.g., fax down, dead battery on the mobile phone, inability to read email attachments) or people-based transmission problems (e.g., forgetting to pass on the message), messages aren't always transmitted. If the message is transmitted and received, however, the next step is for the receiver to decode it. **Decoding** is the process by which the receiver translates the verbal or symbolic form of the message into an understood message. In Duke's case, the message was decoded accurately, and the Beijing Wanda store had the cheaper bananas in stock within twenty-four hours. Within a week, all of Wal-Mart's forty-nine northern China stores carried them. Within a month, shoppers could find the cheaper Chinese bananas in Wal-Mart's three hundred Wanda stores.[15]

The last step of the communication process occurs when the receiver gives the sender feedback. **Feedback to sender** is a return message to the sender that

indicates the receiver's understanding of the message (of what the receiver was supposed to know, to do, or not to do). Feedback makes senders aware of possible miscommunications and enables them to continue communicating until the receiver understands the intended message.

Unfortunately, feedback doesn't always occur in the communication process. Complacency and overconfidence about the ease and simplicity of communication can lead senders and receivers to simply assume that they share a common understanding of the message and, consequently, to not use feedback to improve the effectiveness of their communication. This is a serious mistake, especially since messages and feedback are always transmitted with and against a background of noise. **Noise** is anything that interferes with the transmission of the intended message. Noise can occur in any of the following situations:

- The sender isn't sure what message to communicate.
- The message is not clearly encoded.
- The wrong communication channel is chosen.
- The message is not received or decoded properly.
- The receiver doesn't have the experience or time to understand the message.

Jargon, which is vocabulary particular to a profession or group,

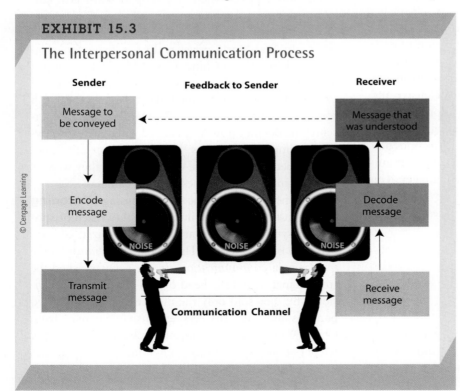

EXHIBIT 15.3

The Interpersonal Communication Process

Sender · Feedback to Sender · Receiver

Message to be conveyed → Message that was understood

Encode message · NOISE · NOISE · NOISE · Decode message

Transmit message · Communication Channel · Receive message

© Cengage Learning

© Burke/Triolo Productions/Brand X Pictures/Jupiterimages / © TongRo Image Stock/Jupiterimages

is another form of noise that interferes with communication in the workplace (see box "No More Jargon!"). Any idea what "rightsizing," "delayering," "unsiloing," and "knowledge acquisition" mean? Rightsizing means laying off workers. Delayering means firing managers, or getting rid of layers of management. Unsiloing means getting workers in different parts of the company (i.e., different vertical silos) to work with others outside their own areas. Knowledge acquisition means teaching workers new knowledge or skills. Unfortunately, the business world is rife with jargon. Carol Hymowitz of the *Wall Street Journal* points out, "A new crop of buzzwords usually sprouts every three to five years, or about the same length of time many top executives have to prove themselves. Some can be useful in swiftly communicating, and spreading, new business concepts. Others are less useful, even devious."[16]

15-2b FORMAL COMMUNICATION CHANNELS

An organization's **formal communication channel** is the system of official channels that carry organizationally approved messages and information. Organizational objectives, rules, policies, procedures, instructions, commands, and requests for information are all transmitted via the formal communication system or channel. There are three formal communication channels: downward communication, upward communication, and horizontal communication.[17]

Downward communication flows from higher to lower levels in an organization. Downward communication is used to issue orders down the organizational hierarchy, to give organizational members job-related information, to give managers and workers performance reviews from upper managers, and to clarify organizational objectives and goals.[18] Michael Beer, professor emeritus at Harvard Business School, says, "You can never over communicate. When you think you've communicated well, go out three or four more times and communicate again." Beer's consulting firm TruePoint studied forty CEOs whose companies have been above-average performers for over a decade. He found that those remarkable leaders spend an enormous amount of time in communicating downward. They have a simple story, and that story gets out every place they go."[19]

Upward communication flows from lower levels to higher levels in an organization. Upward communication is used to give higher-level managers feedback about operations, issues, and problems; to help higher-level managers assess organizational performance and effectiveness; to encourage lower-level managers and employees to participate in organizational decision making; and to give those at lower levels the chance to share their concerns with higher-level authorities. Barry Salzberg, the CEO of Big Four accounting firm Deloitte & Touche USA, facilitates upward communication through a series of regular town hall meetings in different locations. Says Salzberg, "I hold town hall meetings in which no question is out of bounds. I

Formal communication channel the system of official channels that carry organizationally approved messages and information

Downward communication communication that flows from higher to lower levels in an organization

Upward communication communication that flows from lower to higher levels in an organization

Huh?

Technology provides a lot of tools for communication, but it can also contribute to misunderstood, or improperly decoded, messages. Nordstrom's customer Dan Sheeran had a tailor make some changes to pants he had purchased. When the pants were ready, the tailor left this hard-to-understand message on Sheeran's voice mail in a thick accent, "Just wanted to let you know that your pants is already done and ready for pickup. Ok, then you can pick up your pants at Nordstrom." Google Voice, which automatically turns voice messages into text, translated that as "Just wanted to know that your punches ordered the done in the Dipper pickup. Ok. Then you can pick up the French abortion." Sheeran says, "It sounded like a coded message for a drug deal." He didn't understand what the message was about until he clicked the link that played the voice message aloud.

Source: N. Wingfield, "Say What? High-Tech Messages Can Get Lost in Translation: Devices Make Communicating Easier—Or Incomprehensible; Phone Doesn't Swear," *Wall Street Journal*, May 4, 2011, accessed June 17, 2011, http://online.wsj.com /article/SB10001424052748703841904576256851860269320.html.

© iStockphoto.com/David Meharey

Horizontal communication communication that flows among managers and workers who are at the same organizational level

Informal communication channel (grapevine) the transmission of messages from employee to employee outside of formal communication channels

24/7." So far, Salzberg has conducted a dozen meetings with more than half of the firm's employees participating. Why take the time to hold these meetings? Say Salzberg, "[People] want to feel part of a caring community with leaders who, when making the hard choices, will balance the health of the organization with the best long-term interests of the workforce."[20]

Horizontal communication flows among managers and workers who are at the same organizational level, such as when a day shift nurse comes in at 7:30 a.m. for a half-hour discussion with the midnight nurse supervisor who leaves at 8:00 a.m. Horizontal communication helps facilitate coordination and cooperation between different parts of a company and allows coworkers to share relevant information. It also helps people at the same level resolve conflicts and solve problems without involving high levels of management.

In general, what can managers do to improve formal communication? First, decrease reliance on downward communication. Second, increase chances for upward communication by increasing personal contact with lower-level managers and workers. Third, encourage much better use of horizontal communication.

15-2c INFORMAL COMMUNICATION CHANNELS

An organization's **informal communication channel**, sometimes called the **grapevine**, is the transmission of messages from employee to employee outside of formal communication channels. The grapevine arises out of curiosity, that is, the need to know what is going on in an organization and how it might affect you or others. To satisfy this curiosity, employees need a consistent supply of relevant, accurate, in-depth information about "who is doing what and what changes are occurring within the organization."[21] For example, at the University of Texas Medical Branch (part of the UT system), any of the 13,000 employees wanting to know the truth about rumors working their way through the campus grapevine can log on to the school's website and click on "Rumors or Trumors." Campus administrators comment on each posted rumor and rate it using the "kernel of truth" system. One kernel of corn indicates a little bit of truth. Two kernels indicate that more of the rumor is accurate, but it's still not entirely true. Three kernels indicate that the rumor is accurate. Wildly inaccurate rumors are rated with a spaceship, indicating that they're too far out to be believed. Reaction thus far has been positive. Lecturer Sheryl Prather says, "It looks sincere. I've found that everything thus far has been pretty factual. It at least shows that somebody's listening to some of the talk that goes on around here and [is] putting it down on the computer where we can all see it."[22]

Grapevines arise out of informal communication networks such as the gossip or cluster chains shown in Exhibit 15.4. In a *gossip chain*, one highly connected individual shares information with many other managers and workers. By contrast, in a *cluster chain*, numerous people simply tell a few of their friends. The result in both cases is that information flows freely and quickly through the organization. Some believe that grapevines are a waste of employees' time, that they promote gossip and rumors that fuel political speculation, and that they are sources of highly unreliable, inaccurate information. Yet studies clearly show that grapevines are

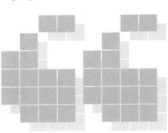

© John Lund/Blend Images/Jupiterimages

The main focus of rumor is to figure out the truth. It's the group trying to make sense of something that's important to them.

EXHIBIT 15.4

Grapevine Communication Networks

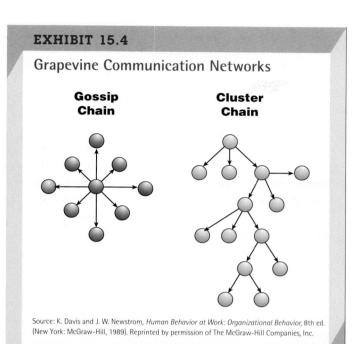

Gossip Chain

Cluster Chain

Source: K. Davis and J. W. Newstrom, *Human Behavior at Work: Organizational Behavior*, 8th ed. (New York: McGraw-Hill, 1989). Reprinted by permission of The McGraw-Hill Companies, Inc.

highly accurate sources of information for a number of reasons.[23] First, because grapevines typically carry "juicy" information that is interesting and timely, information spreads rapidly. During Allstate's annual Leaders Forum, a gathering of 2,000 agents and employees, CEO Thomas Wilson announced plans for reducing the company's sales force and changing sales commission rates. Later that evening, a group of employees were at the hotel bar, complaining about the changes and about Wilson, when Joseph Lacher, the president of Allstate's home and auto insurance division was allegedly overheard using two expletives in reference to CEO Wilson. By the next day, nearly all conference attendees had heard about Lacher's critical remarks. Lacher was abruptly let go just a few weeks later.[24]

Second, since information is typically spread by face-to-face conversation, receivers can send feedback to make sure they understand the message that is being communicated. This reduces misunderstandings and increases accuracy. Third, since most of the information in a company moves along the grapevine rather than formal communication channels, people can usually verify the accuracy of information by checking it out with others.

What can managers do to manage organizational grapevines? The very worst thing they can do is withhold information or try to punish those who share information with others. The grapevine abhors a vacuum, so rumors and anxiety will flourish in the absence of information from company management. Why does this occur? According to workplace psychologist Nicholas DiFonzo, "The main focus of rumor is to figure out the truth. It's the group trying to make sense of something that's important to them."[25] A better strategy is to embrace the grapevine and keep employees informed about possible changes and strategies. Failure to do so will just make things worse. And, in addition to using the grapevine to communicate with others, managers should not overlook the grapevine as a tremendous source of valuable information and feedback. In fact, information flowing through organizational grapevines is estimated to be 75 to 95 percent accurate.[26]

15-2d COACHING AND COUNSELING: ONE-ON-ONE COMMUNICATION

When the Wyatt Company surveyed 531 U.S. companies undergoing major changes and restructuring, it asked the CEOs, "If you could go back and change one thing, what would it be?" The answer: "The way we communicated with our employees." The CEOs said that instead of flashy videos, printed materials, or formal meetings, they would make greater use of one-on-one communication, especially with employees' immediate supervisors instead of with higher-level executives whom employees didn't know.[27]

Coaching and counseling are two kinds of one-on-one communication. **Coaching** is communicating with someone for the direct purpose of improving the person's on-the-job performance or behavior.[28] George Parsons, chief learning officer for Goldman Sachs says, "As soon as people become good managers, we want them to be good coaches too. You have to be good at getting and giving feedback so you can help individuals fully contribute."[29]

Managers tend to make several mistakes when coaching employees. First, they wait for a problem to arise before coaching. Jim Concelman, manager for leadership development at Development Dimensions International, says, "Of course, a boss has to coach an employee if a mistake has been made, but they shouldn't be waiting for the error. While it is a lot easier to see a mistake and correct it, people learn more through success than through failure, so bosses should ensure that employees are experiencing as many successes as possible. Successful employees lead

Counseling communicating with someone about non-job-related issues that may be affecting or interfering with the person's performance

Nonverbal communication any communication that doesn't involve words

Kinesics movements of the body and face

to a more successful organization."[30] Second, when mistakes *are* made, managers wait much too long before talking to the employee about the problem. Management professor Ray Hilgert says, "A manager must respond as soon as possible after an incident of poor performance. Don't bury your head. . . . When employees are told nothing, they assume everything is okay."[31]

In contrast to coaching, **counseling** is communicating with someone about non-job-related issues such as stress, child care, health issues, retirement planning, or legal issues that may be affecting or interfering with the person's performance. But counseling does not mean that managers should try to be clinicians, even though an estimated 20 percent of employees are dealing with personal problems at any one time. Dana Kiel, who works for Cigna Behavioral Health, says, "We call it the quicksand. If you're a good supervisor, you do care about your employees, but it's not your job to be a therapist."[32] Instead, managers should discuss specific performance problems, listen if the employee chooses to share personal issues, and then recommend that the employee call the company's *Employee Assistance Program (EAP)*. EAPs are typically free when provided as part of a company's benefit package. In emergencies or times of crisis, EAPs can offer immediate counseling and support; they can also provide referrals to organizations and professionals that can help employees and their family members address personal issues. Apparel maker Levi Strauss, for example, established an EAP called HIV Connect, which aims to improve employees' access to HIV/AIDS education, testing, treatment, and care. Paurvi Bhatt, senior director of strategic health initiatives and the Employee HIV/AIDS Program at Levi Strauss, says, "How we make [HIV] relevant is [by] understanding the importance of prevention and how

it affects people at work. Addressing HIV isn't just addressing the health side, but learning how to manage the issue at work. This, like a lot of issues, can affect teamwork and collaboration." HIV Connect is a part of Levi Strauss's larger EAP program.[33]

15-2e NONVERBAL COMMUNICATION

Nonverbal communication is any communication that doesn't involve words. Nonverbal communication almost always accompanies verbal communication and may either support and reinforce the verbal message or contradict it. The importance of nonverbal communication is well established. Researchers have estimated that as much as 93 percent of any message is transmitted nonverbally, with 55 percent coming from body language and facial expressions and 38 percent coming from the tone and pitch of the voice.[34] Since many nonverbal cues are unintentional, receivers often consider nonverbal communication to be a more accurate representation of what senders are thinking and feeling than the words they use. If you have ever asked someone out on a date and been told "yes," but realized that the real answer was "no," then you understand the importance of paying attention to nonverbal communication.

Kinesics and paralanguage are two kinds of nonverbal communication.[35] **Kinesics** (from the Greek word *kinesis*, meaning "movement") are movements of the body and face.[36] These movements include arm and hand gestures, facial expressions, eye contact, folding arms, crossing legs, and leaning toward or away from another person. For example, people tend to avoid eye contact when they are embarrassed or unsure of the message they are sending. Crossed arms or legs usually indicate defensiveness or that the person is not receptive to the message or the sender. Also, people tend to smile frequently when they are seeking someone's approval.

It turns out that kinesics play an incredibly important role in communication. Studies of married couples'

© iStockphoto.com/4x6

kinesic interactions can predict whether they will stay married with 93 percent accuracy.[37] The key is the ratio of positive to negative kinesic interactions between husbands and wives as they communicate. Negative kinesic expressions such as eye rolling suggest contempt, whereas positive kinesic expressions such as maintaining eye contact and nodding suggest listening and caring. When the ratio of positive to negative interactions drops below 5 to 1, the chances for divorce quickly increase. Kinesics operate similarly in the workplace, providing clues about people's true feelings, over and above what they say (or don't say). For instance, Louis Giuliano, former CEO of ITT (which makes heavy use of teams), says, "When you get a team together and say to them we're going to change a process, you always have people who say, 'No, we're not.'" They usually don't say it out loud, but "the body language is there," making it clear that their real answer is "no."[38]

Paralanguage includes the pitch, rate, tone, volume, and speaking pattern (use of silences, pauses, or hesitations) of one's voice. For example, when people are unsure what to say, they tend to decrease their communication effectiveness by speaking softly. When people are nervous, they tend to talk faster and louder. These characteristics have a tremendous influence on whether listeners are receptive to what speakers are saying.

In short, because nonverbal communication is so informative, especially when it contradicts verbal communication, managers need to learn how to monitor and control their nonverbal behaviors.

15-3 *Managing One-on-One Communication*

When it comes to improving communication, managers face two primary tasks, managing one-on-one communication and managing organization-wide communication.

On average, first-line managers spend 57 percent of their time with people, middle managers spend 63 percent of their time directly with people, and top managers spend as much as 78 percent of their time dealing with people.[39] These numbers make it clear that managers spend a great deal of time in one-on-one communication with others.

*Let's learn more about managing one-on-one communication by reading how to **15-3a choose the right com-***

munication medium, 15-3b be a good listener, and *15-3c give effective feedback.*

15-3a CHOOSING THE RIGHT COMMUNICATION MEDIUM

Sometimes messages are poorly communicated simply because they are delivered using the wrong **communication medium**, which is the method used to deliver a message. For example, the wrong communication medium is being used when an employee returns from lunch, picks up the note left on her office chair, and learns she has been fired. The wrong communication medium is also being used when an employee pops into your office every ten minutes with a simple request. (An email would be better.)

There are two general kinds of communication media: oral and written communication. *Oral communication* includes face-to-face interactions and group meetings through telephone calls, videoconferencing, or any other means of sending and receiving spoken messages. Studies show that managers generally prefer oral communication over written because it provides the opportunity to ask questions about parts of the message that they don't understand. Oral communication is also a rich communication medium because it allows managers to receive and assess the nonverbal communication that accompanies spoken messages (i.e., body language, facial expressions, and the voice characteristics associated with paralanguage).

Furthermore, you don't need a personal computer and an Internet connection to conduct oral communication. Simply schedule an appointment, track someone down in the hall, or catch someone on the phone. In fact, *Wall Street Journal* columnist Jason Fry worries that voice mail and email have made managers less willing to engage in meaningful, face-to-face oral communication than before. In fact, 67 percent of managers admit to using email as a substitute for face-to-face conversations. While there are advantages to email (e.g., it creates a record of what's been said), it's often better to talk to people instead of just emailing them. Jason Fry writes, "If you're close enough that the person you're emailing uses the plonk of your return key as a cue to look for the little Outlook envelope, [it's] best [to] think carefully about whether you should be typing instead of talking."[40] But the oral medium should not be used for *all* communication. In general, when the message is simple, such as a quick

Paralanguage the pitch, rate, tone, volume, and speaking pattern (i.e., use of silences, pauses, or hesitations) of one's voice

Communication medium the method used to deliver an oral or written message

request or a presentation of straightforward information, a memo or email is often the better communication medium.

Written communication includes letters, email, and memos. Although most managers still like and use oral communication, email in particular is changing how they communicate with workers, customers, and each other. Email is the fastest-growing form of communication in organizations primarily because of its convenience and speed. For instance, because people read six times faster than they can listen, they usually can read thirty email messages in ten to fifteen minutes.[41] By contrast, dealing with voice messages can take a considerable amount of time.

Written communication such as email is well suited for delivering straightforward messages and information. Furthermore, with email accessible at the office, at home, and on the road (by laptop computer, cell phone, or web-based email), managers can use email to stay in touch from anywhere at almost any time. And, since email and other written communications don't have to be sent and received simultaneously, messages can be sent and stored for reading at any time. Consequently, managers can send and receive many more messages using email than by using oral communication, which requires people to get together in person or by phone or videoconference.

Email has its own drawbacks, however. One is that it lacks the formality of paper memos and letters. It is easy to fire off a rushed email that is not well written or fully thought through. Another drawback to email is that it lacks nonverbal cues, making emails very easy to misinterpret. Kristin Byron, assistant professor of management at **Syracuse University**, says, "People perceive emails as more negative than they are intended to be, and even emails that are intended to be positive can be misinterpreted as more neutral. You get an email that's really short, with no greeting, no closing; it's probably because they were very rushed, or maybe they're not very good typists. But because of those things, people have a tendency to perceive the message as negative."[42]

Although written communication is well suited for delivering straightforward messages and information, it is not well suited to complex, ambiguous, or emotionally laden messages, which are better delivered through oral communication.

15-3b LISTENING

Are you a good listener? You probably think so. In fact, most people, including managers, are terrible listeners, retaining only about 25 percent of what they hear. You qualify as a poor listener if you frequently interrupt others, jump to conclusions about what people will say before they've said it, hurry the speaker to finish his or her point, are a passive listener (not actively working at your listening), or simply don't pay attention to what people are saying.[43] On this last point—attentiveness—college students were periodically asked to record their thoughts during a psychology course. On average, 20 percent of the students

DOING THE RIGHT THING
One Thing at a Time

It's easier than ever for people to multitask. With blazing-fast computers and software, and the wealth of information from the Internet, we can work on lots of things at one time—writing a memo, checking email, following stock prices, or doing research, all while talking on the phone or meeting with colleagues. It seems like a great, efficient use of time and a way to get employees to do more during the workday. But as efficient as all of this might seem, multitasking may actually be unethical. According to a study by a scholar at Stanford University, while people who multitask can do many things at once, they don't do any of them well. In short, multitasking reduces the quality of our work. And sometimes, multitasking can even be dangerous. The Virginia Tech Transportation Institute found that truck drivers who multitask by texting on their phones were twenty-three times more likely to have an accident than those who just drove. So as a manger, you should do the right thing—set a good example by focusing on one task at a time, so that you (and your employees) will be better at what you're doing.

Source: B. Weinstein, "The Ethics of Multitasking," *Bloomberg Businessweek*, September 4, 2009, accessed October 10, 2010, http://www.businessweek.com/managing/content/sep2009/ca20094_935233.htm.

were paying attention (only 12 percent were actively working at being good listeners), 20 percent were thinking about sex, 20 percent were thinking about things they had done before, and the remaining 40 percent were thinking about other things unrelated to the class (e.g., worries, religion, lunch, daydreaming).[44]

How important is it to be a good listener? In general, about 45 percent of the total time you spend communicating with others is spent listening. Furthermore, listening is important for managerial and business success, even for those at the top of an organization. Curt Anastasio, the CEO of NuStar Energy LP, says, "We had a rough patch in our asphalt business. One reaction could have been to lay off 10 percent of the workforce. Instead, I said we had a problem and asked [employees] for suggestions [on] how to solve it." The response was an employee-driven efficiency drive focused on wringing costs out of power consumption, purchasing, travel, and overtime hours. The next year, profits increased $25 million. Anastasio said, "If you're not supportive of employees and their families, where do you think they'll be when the company has a downturn?" Not surprisingly, NuStar has never had a layoff. Says Anastasio, "If you take care of the employees, they'll take care of their communities and the investors."[45]

Listening is a more important skill for managers than ever, since Generation X employees tend to expect a high level of interaction with their supervisors. They want feedback on their performance, but they also want to offer feedback and know that it is heard. In fact, managers with better listening skills are rated more highly by their employees and are much more likely to be promoted.[46]

So, what can you do to improve your listening ability? First, understand the difference between hearing and listening. According to *Webster's New World Dictionary*, **hearing** is the "act or process of perceiving sounds," whereas **listening** is "making a conscious effort to hear." In other words, we react to sounds, such as bottles breaking or music being played too loud, because hearing is an involuntary physiological process. By contrast, listening is a voluntary behavior. So, if you want to be a good listener, you have to choose to be a good listener. Typically, that means choosing to be an active, empathetic listener.[47]

Active listening means assuming half the responsibility for successful communication by actively giving the speaker nonjudgmental feedback that shows you've accurately heard what he or she said. Active listeners make it clear from their behavior

that they are listening carefully to what the speaker has to say. Active listeners put the speaker at ease, maintain eye contact, and show the speaker that they are attentively listening by nodding and making short statements.

Several specific strategies can help you be a better active listener. First, *clarify responses* by asking the speaker to explain confusing or ambiguous statements. Second, when there are natural breaks in the speaker's delivery, use this time to paraphrase or summarize what has been said. *Paraphrasing* is restating what has been said in your own words. *Summarizing* is reviewing the speaker's main points or emotions. Paraphrasing and summarizing give the speaker the chance to correct the message if the active listener has attached the wrong meaning to it. Paraphrasing and summarizing also show the speaker that the active listener is interested in the speaker's message. Exhibit 15.5 on the next page lists specific statements that listeners can use to clarify responses, paraphrase, or summarize what has been said.

Active listeners also avoid evaluating the message or being critical until the message is complete. They recognize that their only responsibility during the transmission of a message is to receive it accurately and derive the intended meaning from it. Evaluation and criticism can take place after the message is accurately received. Finally, active listeners recognize that a large portion of any message is transmitted nonverbally and thus pay very careful attention to the nonverbal cues transmitted by the speaker.

> **Hearing** the act or process of perceiving sounds
>
> **Listening** making a conscious effort to hear
>
> **Active listening** assuming half the responsibility for successful communication by actively giving the speaker nonjudgmental feedback that shows you've accurately heard what he or she said

Empathetic listening understanding the speaker's perspective and personal frame of reference and giving feedback that conveys that understanding to the speaker

Empathetic listening means understanding the speaker's perspective and personal frame of reference and giving feedback that conveys that understanding to the speaker. Empathetic listening goes beyond active listening because it depends on our ability to set aside our own attitudes or relationships to be able to see and understand things through someone else's eyes. Empathetic listening is just as important as active listening, especially for managers, because it helps build rapport and trust with others.

The key to being a more empathetic listener is to show your desire to understand and to reflect people's feelings. You can *show your desire to understand* by listening, that is, asking people to talk about what's most important to them and then by giving them sufficient time to talk before responding or interrupting. Altera Corporation, which makes computer chips, uses empathetic listening as the key sales tool for its sales force. When salesperson Mike Dionne first met with an information technology manager from a medical company, he told the manager he was there to find out how Altera could expand its business in the medical field. During the ninety-minute meeting, Dionne rarely spoke and never said that Altera wanted to sell computer chips. Instead, Dionne listened quietly and didn't interrupt as the manager described the kinds of technology (using computer chips) that his company wanted to buy. Dionne says, "You could tell [he] was jazzed. He was comfortable, leaning back in his chair and talking freely."[48]

Reflecting feelings is also an important part of empathetic listening because it demonstrates that you understand the speaker's emotions. Unlike active listening, in which you restate or summarize the informational content of what has been said, the focus is on the affective part of the message. As an empathetic listener, you can use the following statements to *reflect the speaker's emotions*:

- So, right now it sounds like you're feeling . . . .
- You seem as if you're . . . .
- Do you feel a bit . . . ?
- I could be wrong, but I'm sensing that you're feeling . . . .

In the end, says management consultant Terry Pearce, empathetic listening can be boiled down to these three steps. First, wait ten seconds before you respond. It will seem an eternity, but waiting prevents you from interrupting others and rushing your response. Second, to be sure you understand what the speaker wants, ask questions to clarify the speaker's intent. Third, only then should you respond first with feelings and then facts (notice that facts *follow* feelings).[49]

A word of caution, however: not everyone appreciates having what they said repeated back to them. Manager Candy Friesen says that whenever she did that, "I seemed to engender animosity or hostility. . . . the person to whom you're speaking may not appreciate having his thoughts paraphrased one little bit."[50] So, when applying these listening techniques, pay attention to the body language and tone of voice of the person you're communicating with to make sure they appreciate your attempts to be a better listener.

EXHIBIT 15.5

Clarifying, Paraphrasing, and Summarizing Responses for Active Listeners

CLARIFYING RESPONSES	PARAPHRASING RESPONSES	SUMMARIZING RESPONSES
Could you explain that again?	What you're really saying is	Let me summarize . . . .
I don't understand what you mean.	If I understand you correctly	Okay, your main concerns are . . . .
I'm not sure how	In other words	To recap what you've said . . . .
I'm confused. Would you run through that again?	So your perspective is that	Thus far, you've discussed . . . .
	Tell me if I'm wrong, but what you seem to be saying is	

Source: E. Atwater, *I Hear You*, rev. ed. (New York: Walker, 1992).

15-3c GIVING FEEDBACK

In Chapter 11, you learned that performance appraisal feedback (i.e., judging) should be separated from developmental feedback (i.e., coaching).[51] We can now focus on the steps needed to communicate feedback one-on-one to employees.

To start, managers need to recognize that feedback can be constructive or destructive. **Destructive feedback** is disapproving without any intention of being helpful and almost always causes a negative or defensive reaction in the recipient. By contrast, **constructive feedback** is intended to be helpful, corrective, and/or encouraging. It is aimed at correcting performance deficiencies and motivating employees.

Michael Flatt, CEO of First General Services North America, a construction company, says the problem with workplace feedback is that it's given like a sandwich—something nice to start with, some criticism in the middle, and then something nice again at the end. The problem, says Flatt, is that employees only remember the negative stuff in the middle. So instead, Flatt prefers just to get straight to the point. He delivers feedback in two sessions—one focused on the positive, and the other focusing on where the employee needs to improve. Says Flatt, "I prefer to deliver positive and negative feedback as separate courses, while maintaining that everyone can stomach some extra dessert. In other words, if you acknowledge good performance as often as possible, the occasional constructive feedback you offer will go down easier and will more likely be acted on."[52]

For feedback to be constructive rather than destructive, it must be immediate, focused on specific behaviors, and problem-oriented. *Immediate feedback* is much more effective than delayed feedback because manager and worker can recall the mistake or incident more accurately and discuss it in detail. For example, if a worker is rude to a customer and the customer immediately reports the incident to management, and if the manager, in turn, immediately discusses the incident with the employee, there should be little disagreement over what was said or done. By contrast, it's unlikely that either the manager or the worker will be able to accurately remember the specifics of what occurred if the manager waits several weeks to discuss the incident. When that happens, it's usually too late to have a meaningful conversation.

Specific feedback focuses on particular acts or incidents that are clearly under the control of the employee. For instance, instead of telling an employee that he or she is "always late for work," it's much more constructive to say, "In the last three weeks, you have been thirty minutes late on four occasions and more than an hour late on two others." Furthermore, specific feedback isn't very helpful unless employees have control over the problems that the feedback addresses. Giving negative feedback about behaviors beyond someone's control is likely to be seen as unfair. Similarly, giving positive feedback about behaviors beyond someone's control may be viewed as insincere.

Last, *problem-oriented feedback* focuses on the problems or incidents associated with the poor performance rather than on the worker or the worker's personality. Giving feedback does not give managers the right to personally attack workers. Although managers may be frustrated by a worker's poor performance, the point of problem-oriented feedback is to draw attention to the problem in a nonjudgmental way so that the employee has enough information to correct it. For example, if an employee has body odor, a surprisingly common workplace problem, don't leave deodorant, soap, or shampoo on the person's desk (for all to see) or say, "You stink." *HR Magazine* advises handling the problem this way: "Because this is a sensitive issue and the employee will likely be uncomfortable and embarrassed in discussing it, keep the meeting private and confidential. Be compassionate but direct. Treat it as you would handle any other job-related performance issue. Explain the problem and the need to correct it. Be specific about expectations. . . . If the employer has a dress and grooming policy, refer to the policy and provide the employee with a copy."[53]

15-4 *Managing Organization-Wide Communication*

Although managing one-on-one communication is important, managers must also know how to communicate effectively with a larger number of people throughout an organization.

*Learn more about organization-wide communication by reading the following sections about **15-4a improving***

Destructive feedback feedback that disapproves without any intention of being helpful and almost always causes a negative or defensive reaction in the recipient

Constructive feedback feedback intended to be helpful, corrective, and/or encouraging

transmission by getting the message out and 15-4b *improving reception by finding ways to hear what others feel and think.*

15-4a IMPROVING TRANSMISSION: GETTING THE MESSAGE OUT

Several methods of electronic communication—email, collaborative discussion sites, televised/videotaped speeches and conferences, and broadcast voice mail—now make it easier for managers to communicate with people throughout the organization and get the message out.

Although we normally think of email, the transmission of messages via computers, as a means of one-on-one communication, it also plays an important role in organization-wide communication. With the click of a button, managers can send email to everyone in the company via distribution lists. After two quarters of poor financial performance, including an 18 percent drop in the company's stock, CEO John Chambers sent a company-wide email to Cisco's managers and employees, saying, "As I've said, our strategy is sound. It is aspects of our operational execution that are not. We have been slow to make decisions, we have had surprises where we should not, and we have lost the accountability that has been a hallmark of our ability to execute consistently for our customers and our shareholders. That is unacceptable. And it is exactly what we will attack. That said, today we face a simple truth: we have disappointed our investors and we have confused our employees. Bottom line, we have lost some of the credibility that is foundational to Cisco's success—and we must earn it back."[54]

Collaborative websites are another means of electronically promoting organization-wide communication. **Online discussion forums** use web- or software-based discussion tools to allow employees across the company to easily ask questions and share knowledge with each other. The point is to share expertise and not du-

plicate solutions already discovered by others in the company. Furthermore, because collaborative discussion sites remain online, they provide a historical database for people who are dealing with particular problems for the first time.

Collaborative discussion sites are typically organized by topic, project, or person and can take the shape of blogs that allow readers to post comments, wikis to allow collaborative discussions, document sharing and editing, or traditional discussion forums (see Chapter 17 on managing information for further explanation). Red Hat is the leading provider of Linux operating systems. CEO and President Jim Whitehurst says, "Your most creative ideas are going to come from people on the front lines who see a different way of doing the jobs they do every day. You have to create vehicles for those ideas to be heard. So the question is, how do you make that happen? How do you engage your employees?" One way in which Red Hat does that is through an internal collaborative discussion site called the Memo List. Says Whitehurst, "We have about 4,000 employees, but on average you'll see a couple hundred posts a day. And I go through it every single day. I would say probably three-quarters of the people are on it every day, either reading or posting." What's the value of the Memo List to Red Hat? Whitehurst argues, "Engaging people in how decisions are getting made means it can take forever to get decisions made. But once you make a decision, you get flawless execution because everybody's engaged. They know what you're doing and they know why you're doing it."[55]

Exhibit 15.6 lists the steps companies need to take to establish successful collaborative discussion sites.

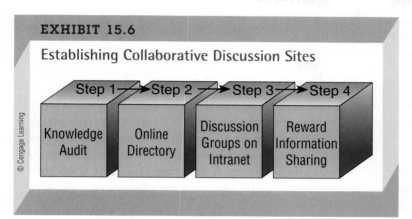

EXHIBIT 15.6

Establishing Collaborative Discussion Sites

Step 1 → Step 2 → Step 3 → Step 4

| Knowledge Audit | Online Directory | Discussion Groups on Intranet | Reward Information Sharing |

© Cengage Learning

First, pinpoint your company's top intellectual assets through a knowledge audit and spread that knowledge throughout the organization. Second, create an online directory detailing the expertise of individual workers and make it available to all employees. Third, set up collaborative discussion sites on the intranet so that managers and workers can collaborate on problem solving. Finally, reward information sharing by making the online sharing of knowledge a key part of performance ratings.

Televised/videotaped speeches and meetings are a third electronic method of organization-wide communication. **Televised/videotaped speeches and meetings** are simply speeches and meetings originally made to a small audience that are either simultaneously broadcast to other locations in the company or videotaped for subsequent distribution and viewing by a broader audience.

Voice messaging, or voice mail, is a telephone answering system that records audio messages. In one survey, 89 percent of respondents said that voice messaging is critical to business communication, 78 percent said that it improves productivity, and 58 percent said they would rather leave a message on a voice messaging system than with a receptionist.[56] Nonetheless, most people are unfamiliar with the ability to *broadcast voice mail* by sending a recorded message to everyone in the company. Broadcast voice mail gives top managers a quick, convenient way to address their work forces via oral communication—but only if people actually listen to the message, and that turns out to be a challenge with Generation Y workers. Jeff Schwarz, global talent leader at Deloitte & Touche, says, "If you send a message on voicemail or send an email, they are likely to ignore it. It's very frustrating to our leaders, most of whom are boomers [and] some of whom are Gen X'ers. When they broadcast voicemail messages, big swaths of their organization are not hearing it. They're not even

listening to it and they're not even sure it's directed to them because they don't think about being communicated with in that way. CEOs or HR leaders or business leaders think they're sending a direct message, but that is not the most effective way to communicate across the generations." Deloitte's solution—imbed the broadcast voice mail in an email.[57]

15-4b IMPROVING RECEPTION: HEARING WHAT OTHERS FEEL AND THINK

When people think of "organization-wide" communication, they think of the CEO and top managers getting their message out to people in the company. But organization-wide communication also means finding ways to hear what people throughout the organization are thinking and feeling. This is important because most employees and managers are reluctant to share their thoughts and feelings with top managers. Surveys indicate that only 29 percent of first-level managers feel that their companies encourage employees to express their opinions openly. Another study of twenty-two companies found that 70 percent of the people surveyed were afraid to speak up about problems they knew existed at work.

Withholding information about organizational problems or issues is called **organizational silence**. Organizational silence occurs when employees believe that telling management about problems won't make a difference or that they'll be punished or hurt in some way for sharing such information.[58] At Jetstar Airways, an Australia-based airline, pilots were afraid to speak up about fatigue from flying too many hours. Captain Richard Woodward, vice president of the Australian and International Pilots Association, said that his organization had received dozens of complaints from Jetstar pilots, but that the pilots were afraid to complain to Jetstar management because "there was a culture of fear and intimidation at that airline."[59] One pilot scheduler told his pilots, "Toughen up princesses! You aren't fatigued, you are tired and can't be bothered to go into work." A report from Australia's

Televised/videotaped speeches and meetings speeches and meetings originally made to a smaller audience that are either simultaneously broadcast to other locations in the company or videotaped for subsequent distribution and viewing

Organizational silence when employees withhold information about organizational problems or issues

Company hotlines phone numbers that anyone in the company can call anonymously to leave information for upper management

Survey feedback information that is collected by surveys from organizational members and then compiled, disseminated, and used to develop action plans for improvement

Civil Aviation Safety Authority concluded, "'There remains reluctance from a number of flight crew to report fatigue risk and/or to say no to an extension of duty based on the perceived punitive nature of taking such actions."[60]

Company hotlines, survey feedback, frequent informal meetings, surprise visits, and blogs are additional ways of overcoming organizational silence. **Company hotlines** are phone numbers that anyone in the company can call anonymously to leave information for upper management. Company hotlines are incredibly useful, as 47 percent of the calls placed to them result in an investigation and some form of corrective action within the organization. Anonymity is critical, too, because as those investigations proceeded, 54 percent of the callers did not want their identities revealed.[61]

Survey feedback is information that is collected by survey from organization members and then compiled, disseminated, and used to develop action plans for improvement. Many organizations make use of survey feedback by surveying their managers and employees several times a year.

Guardian News and Media, the publisher of the British newspaper *The Guardian*, conducts an annual survey of its employees to gauge their satisfaction and confidence in the company. After a recent restructuring, during which more than one hundred journalists, editors, and editorial staff lost their jobs, the survey showed *Guardian* employees still had confidence in the company. Eighty-six percent of respondents reported that they were still proud to work at *The Guardian*, while 93 percent reported that they did extra work beyond what was required of them. And perhaps most importantly, 86 percent stated that they understood the need for cost-cutting measures and layoffs given the declining readership challenges facing the newspaper and the news industry. Managing director Tim Brooks said, "Some people—among them, friends of mine who do similar jobs to me in other media companies—thought we were bonkers to be conducting the staff survey at a time of major reorganization, cuts and redundancies. But why take someone's temperature when they are feeling fine? Taking it when they are stressed tells you much more. And actually what this survey tells us—both from the scores themselves, many of which are as high or higher than in previous surveys—and from the participation rate, which is only one percentage point below last time (and much higher than the rate in most organizations)—is that although we are an organization under stress, we are fundamentally in very good health."[62]

Frequent *informal meetings* between top managers and lower-level employees are one of the best ways for top managers to hear what others think and feel. Many people assume that top managers are at the center of everything that goes on in organizations, but top managers commonly feel isolated from most of their lower-level managers and employees.[63] Consequently, more and more top managers are scheduling frequent informal meetings with people throughout their companies.

Yogesh Gupta, CEO of **FatWire**, which makes software to manage business websites, says that managers must not get defensive during informal meetings. Says Gupta, "I've heard so many executives tell employees to be candid and then jump down their throats if they bring up a problem or ask a critical question."[64] Gupta has spent hundreds of hours in informal meetings with his two hundred managers and nine executives. He meets with each privately because he believes that it encourages people to be

---

Let's Talk

HCL Technologies, an IT services firm located in Noida, India, encourages collaboration through a site it calls U&I. The online forum allows employees to post questions and complaints, and to respond to others' posts. The forum is completely uncensored, and many of the first postings were variants of "Why do you guys [management] suck?" "Why does your strategy suck?" "Why aren't you living up to your ideals?" Though some managers were tempted to censor posts, employees saw U&I as a commitment to communication transparency and a way to hold management accountable. CEO Vineet Nayar also hosts a "My Problems" section on the U&I site, in which he describes various issues that company leaders are dealing with and asks employees at all levels to give him advice on how to handle them.

Source: G. Hamel, "HCL: Extreme Management Makeover," *Wall Street Journal*, July 6, 2010, accessed August 20, 2010, http://blogs.wsj.com/management/2010/07/06/hcl-extreme-management-makeover.

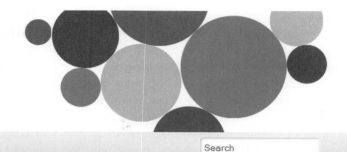

Introducing the Knowledge Graph: things, not strings

May 16, 2012 at 1:00 PM

g +1 695

Cross-posted on the Inside Search Blog

Search is a lot about discovery—the basic human need to learn and broaden your horizons. But searching still requires a lot of hard work by you, the user. So today I'm really excited to launch the Knowledge Graph, which will help you discover new information quickly and easily.

Take a query like [taj mahal]. For more than four decades, search has essentially been about matching keywords to queries. To a search engine the words [taj mahal] have been just that—two words.

But we all know that [taj mahal] has a much richer meaning. You might think of one of the world's most beautiful monuments, or a Grammy Award-winning musician, or possibly even a casino in Atlantic City, NJ. Or, depending on when you last ate, the nearest Indian restaurant. It's why we've been working on an intelligent model—in geek-speak, a "graph"—that understands real-world entities and their relationships to one another: things, not strings.

The Knowledge Graph enables you to search for things, people or places that Google knows about—landmarks, celebrities, cities, sports teams, buildings, geographical features, movies, celestial objects, works of art and more—and instantly get information that's relevant to your query. This is a critical first step towards building the next generation of search, which taps into the collective intelligence of the web and understands the world a bit more like people do.

Google's Knowledge Graph isn't just rooted in public sources such as Freebase, Wikipedia and the CIA World Factbook. It's also augmented at a much larger scale—because we're focused on comprehensive breadth and depth. It currently contains more than 500 million objects, as well as more than 3.5 billion facts about and relationships between these different objects. And it's tuned based on what people search for, and what we find out on the web.

The Knowledge Graph enhances Google Search in three main ways to start:

1. Find the right thing

More blogs from Google

© Google

Connect with us
Subscribe to this blog:

FeedBurner

RSS Feed

Browse all of Google's blogs for specific interests & topics:

Blog Directory

Follow Google alerts and news on Twitter:

@Google

We'd love to hear your feedback — discuss Google's products with others:

Product Forums

g+ Follow

Search

---

candid. And, he asks each these questions: What am I doing wrong? What would you do differently if you were running the company? What's the biggest thing getting in the way of you doing your job well? As a result of these meetings, Gupta learned that FatWire was understaffed in marketing and product development.

Have you ever been around when a supervisor learns that upper management is going to be paying a visit? First, there's shock. Next, there's anxiety. And then there's panic, as everyone is told to drop what he or she is doing to polish, shine, and spruce up the workplace so that it looks perfect for the visit. Of course, when visits are conducted under these conditions, top managers don't get a realistic look at what's going on in the company. Consequently, one of the ways to get an accurate picture is to pay *surprise visits* to various parts of the organization. These visits should not just be surprise inspections, but should also be used as opportunities to encourage meaningful upward communication from those who normally don't get a chance to communicate with upper management.

Blogs are another way to hear what people are thinking and saying, both inside and outside the organization. A **blog** is a personal website that provides personal opinions or recommendations, news summaries, and reader comments. At Google, which owns the blog-hosting service Blogger, hundreds of employees are writing *internal blogs*. One employee even wrote a blog that posted all the notes from the brainstorming sessions used to redesign the search page used by millions each day. Marissa Mayer, now vice president of search products and user experience, said, "Our legal department loves the blogs, because it basically is a written-down, backed-up, permanent time-stamped version of the scientist's notebook. When you want to file a patent, you can now show in blogs where this idea happened."[65]

External blogs and *Twitter sites* (micro blogs where entries are limited to 140 characters), written by people outside the company, can be a good way to find out what others are saying or thinking about your organization or its products or actions. But keeping up with these communication media requires someone in the firm to actively monitor what is being said on web, blog, and Twitter sites. At its Texas headquarters, Dell operates a Social Media Listening Command Center, where staff members track what is being said about Dell on a variety of social media sites like Facebook, Twitter, and YouTube, as well as blogs. When they see that a Dell customer posts a problem with a Dell product, they quickly contact the customer and take steps to address the issue. Nearly two-thirds of Dell consumers contacted through the Social Media Listening Command Center report positive service experiences. Manish Mehta, Dell's then–vice president for social media and community, says, "Customers were thrilled and elated that Dell was reaching out to them. It changed their perception of the company."[66]

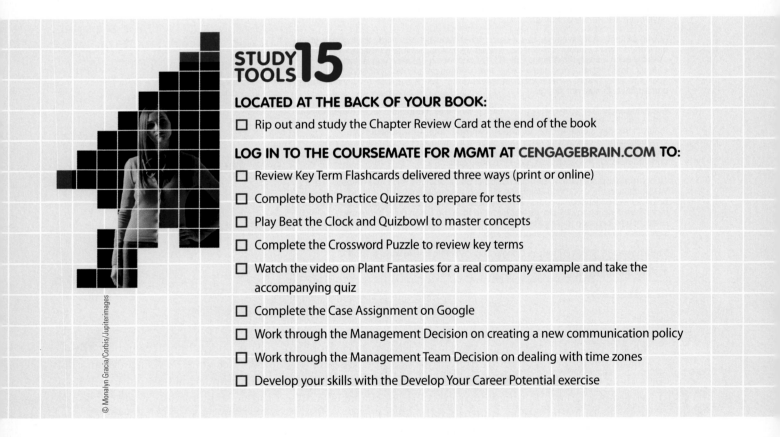

STUDY TOOLS 15

LOCATED AT THE BACK OF YOUR BOOK:

☐ Rip out and study the Chapter Review Card at the end of the book

LOG IN TO THE COURSEMATE FOR MGMT AT CENGAGEBRAIN.COM TO:

☐ Review Key Term Flashcards delivered three ways (print or online)

☐ Complete both Practice Quizzes to prepare for tests

☐ Play Beat the Clock and Quizbowl to master concepts

☐ Complete the Crossword Puzzle to review key terms

☐ Watch the video on Plant Fantasies for a real company example and take the accompanying quiz

☐ Complete the Case Assignment on Google

☐ Work through the Management Decision on creating a new communication policy

☐ Work through the Management Team Decision on dealing with time zones

☐ Develop your skills with the Develop Your Career Potential exercise

© Monalyn Gracia/Corbis/Jupiterimages

ONE APPROACH.
70 UNIQUE SOLUTIONS.

CENGAGE
Learning™

www.cengage.com/4ltrpress

16 / Control

LEARNING OUTCOMES

16-1 Describe the basic control process.

16-2 Discuss the various methods that managers can use to maintain control.

16-3 Describe the behaviors, processes, and outcomes that today's managers are choosing to control in their organizations.

CHECK OUT
STUDY TOOLS
AT THE END OF
THIS CHAPTER.

16-1 *The Control Process*

For all companies, past success is no guarantee of future success. Even successful companies fall short or face challenges and thus have to make changes. **Control** is a regulatory process of establishing standards to achieve organizational goals, comparing actual performance to the standards, and taking corrective action when necessary to restore performance to those standards. Control is achieved when behavior and work procedures conform to standards and when company goals are accomplished.[1] Control is not just an after-the-fact process, however. Preventive measures are also a form of control.

A thief robbed the **Bellagio** casino in Las Vegas at gunpoint, speeding off with $1.5 million in casino chips that he thought could be cashed in at a later date. But, thanks to the Bellagio's security procedures (i.e., control), the chips that the thief stole were made worthless when the casino's stock of chips was completely replaced. According to Alan Feldman, spokesperson for MGM Resorts International, which owns the Bellagio resort, "The new set was put out probably a half an hour after the robbery took place."[2]

The basic control process 16-1a begins with the establishment of clear standards of performance; 16-1b involves a comparison of performance to those standards; 16-1c takes corrective action, if needed, to repair performance deficiencies; 16-1d is a dynamic, cybernetic process; and 16-1e consists of three basic methods: feedback control, concurrent control, and feedforward control. However, as much as managers would like, *16-1f control isn't always worthwhile or possible.*

16-1a STANDARDS

The control process begins when managers set goals such as satisfying 90 percent of customers or increasing sales by 5 percent. Companies then specify the performance standards that must be met to accomplish those goals. **Standards** are a basis of comparison for measuring the extent to which organizational performance is satisfactory or unsatisfactory. For example, many pizzerias use thirty to forty minutes as the standard for delivery times. Since anything longer is viewed as unsatisfactory, they'll typically reduce the price if they can't deliver a hot pizza to you within that time period.

So how do managers set standards? How do they decide which levels of performance are satisfactory and which are unsatisfactory? The first criterion for a good standard is that it must enable goal achievement. If you're meeting the standard but still not achieving company goals, then the standard may have to be changed. In the salmon industry, to maximize productivity, it was standard procedure to grow as many fish as possible in fish farms and then deal with diseases (that spread as a result of the fish being in close proximity) through liberal use of antibiotics in fish food. This was effective until a few years ago, when the new ISA (infectious salmon anemia) virus, which is resistant to antibiotics, developed. Norwegian salmon farms, the largest in the world, sharply reduced the incidence of ISA by developing new production standards that involved

Control a regulatory process of establishing standards to achieve organizational goals, comparing actual performance against the standards, and taking corrective action when necessary

Standards a basis of comparison for measuring the extent to which various kinds of organizational performance are satisfactory or unsatisfactory

the use of anti-viral vaccines and no longer allowing overcrowded fish pens.[3]

Companies also determine standards by listening to customers' comments, complaints, and suggestions or by observing competitors. Walk into a busy Starbucks and you can generally count on a fast-moving line. The focus on speed, however, has also led to customer complaints about "average" quality and inconsistently prepared drinks, for example, a latte tasting differently from barista to barista or store to store. Starbucks is now addressing those concerns. Instead of grinding a day's worth of coffee beans first thing in the morning, baristas will grind fresh beans for each batch of coffee. Rather than steaming a pitcher of milk to be used in several drinks, baristas will steam just enough fresh milk for the drink they're preparing. Finally, baristas are to prepare only two drinks at a time—and even then, they're to only start the second drink while finishing the first. Starbucks believes these steps will address customers' concerns about quality. However, Starbucks baristas are worried that customers will begin to complain about long lines. Erik Forman, a Starbucks barista in Bloomington, Minnesota, says these new procedures have "doubled the amount of time it takes to make drinks in some cases," and lines have gotten longer. If customers complain about long waits, Starbucks may have to reconsider some of these changes and change its standards accordingly.[4]

Standards can also be determined by benchmarking other companies. **Benchmarking** is the process of determining how well other companies (though not just competitors) perform business functions or tasks. In other words, benchmarking is the process of determining other companies' standards. When setting standards by benchmarking, the first step is to determine what to benchmark. Companies can benchmark anything from cycle time (how fast) to quality (how well) to price (how much). For example, based on national benchmarking studies of thousands of fire departments, many firefighters are expected to respond to an alarm within fifteen seconds 95 percent of the time. Additionally, 90 percent of the time it should take no more than sixty seconds to leave the firehouse, and then no more than four minutes to arrive at the scene.[5]

The next step is to identify the companies against which to benchmark your standards. The last step is to collect data to determine other companies' performance standards. When Brad Smith became CEO of Intuit, maker of financial software and websites such as QuickBooks, Pay Employees, TurboTax, and Quicken, a dinner with Hewlett-Packard's then-CEO Mark Hurd and Intuit's founder Scott Cook gave him the idea to benchmark Intuit's performance against other companies, particularly in Silicon Valley where the top web and software companies are located. After learning how Google gave its engineers time each week to work on whatever they wanted, Smith created a similar program where Intuit's software engineers could spend 10 percent of their time, about half a day each week, working on experimental projects. Smith spent time with Facebook's chief operating officer Sheryl Sandberg to learn how Intuit could build online communities for each of its products. In the end, Intuit benchmarked its spending and performance against hundreds of companies in procurement, marketing, legal services, information technology, and human resources.[6]

© iStockphoto.com/nicolas hansen

Gone Rogue

UBS, the Swiss banking giant, learned the perils of not having enough control over its employees. In certain types of trades, payment is made to the seller before the buyer can make final confirmation of the sale. While this doesn't mean that sellers can simply take the cash and run, it does allow for the sellers to show in their books that they have the cash and to use it in future transactions. A trader at UBS tried to use this loophole to make a series of transactions. But instead of making money, either for himself or the bank, he lost, and lost, and lost, to the tune of $2 billion when everything was said and done. This financial disaster forced the resignation of CEO Oswald Gruebel, as well as other top executives.

Sources: G. Broom, "UBS in 'Disarray' as Gruebel Quits, Ermotti Named Interim Chief Executive," *Bloomberg Businessweek*, September 26, 2011, accessed March 29, 2012, http://www.bloomberg.com/news/2011-09-25/ubs-in-disarray-as-gruebel-quits-ermotti-named-interim-chief.html; "UBS Says Rogue Trader Caused $2-Billion Loss," *Los Angeles Times*, September 16, 2011, accessed March 29, 2012, http://articles.latimes.com/2011/sep/16/business/la-fi-ubs-rogue-20110915.

16-1b COMPARISON TO STANDARDS

The next step in the control process is to compare actual performance to performance standards. Although this sounds straightforward, the quality of the comparison depends largely on the measurement and information systems a company uses to keep track of performance. The better the system, the easier it is for companies to track their progress and identify problems that need to be fixed.

On average, 5 percent of hospital patients catch an infection at the hospital. It costs an average of $15,000 per incident to treat such infections, and one hundred thousand patients will die each year from them. Why? Because in most hospitals, health care workers wash their hands only 40 percent of the time before examining or touching a patient. So, how can a hospital measure the rate at which its employees wash their hands so it can compare the actual rate of hand washing to its goal for hand washing? Some hospitals measure how much soap and alcohol are used in each hospital area. Of course, that's not very accurate. By contrast, at North Shore University Hospital in Manhasset, New York, cameras in the ceiling pointing toward sinks and hand sanitizer dispensers are activated by an electronic door monitor each time someone enters a room. Employees then have ten seconds to wash their hands. Arrowsight Medical, which runs the monitoring system, calculates hand washing rates by having employees in India observe video snippets to determine whether hands were washed or not. Unfortunately, using this video system, North Shore found out that intensive care unit (ICU) workers were washing their hands only an abysmally low 6.5 percent of the time![7]

16-1c CORRECTIVE ACTION

The next step in the control process is to identify performance deviations, analyze those deviations, and then develop and implement programs to correct them. This is similar to the planning process discussed in Chapter 5. Regular, frequent performance feedback allows workers and managers to track their performance and make adjustments in effort, direction, and strategies.

After discovering that its ICU staff were washing their hands only 6.5 percent of the time, North Shore University Hospital decided that frequent feedback was the best way to change its health care workers'

hand washing behavior. So, it provided feedback in two ways. First, an L.E.D display by the nurses' station shows that shift's hand washing percentage and an evaluation, such as "Great Shift!!" Second, the nursing shift manager receives an email with the shift's hand washing rates three hours into the shift and then again at the shift's conclusion. Since this system was installed, hand washing rates at North Shore's ICU have risen from 6.5 percent to 81 percent.[8]

16-1d DYNAMIC, CYBERNETIC PROCESS

As shown in Exhibit 16.1, control is a continuous, dynamic, cybernetic process. Control begins by setting standards, measuring performance, and then comparing performance to the standards. If the performance deviates from the standards, then managers and employees analyze the deviations and develop and implement corrective programs that (they hope) achieve the desired performance by meeting the standards. Managers must repeat the entire process again and again in an endless feedback loop (a continuous process). Thus, control is not a one-time achievement or result. It continues over time (i.e., it is dynamic) and requires daily, weekly, and monthly attention from managers

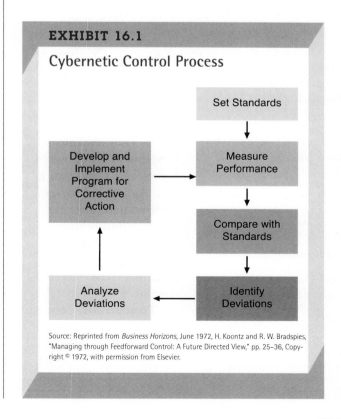

EXHIBIT 16.1

Cybernetic Control Process

Source: Reprinted from *Business Horizons*, June 1972, H. Koontz and R. W. Bradspies, "Managing through Feedforward Control: A Future Directed View," pp. 25–36, Copyright © 1972, with permission from Elsevier.

to maintain performance levels at the standard (i.e., it is cybernetic). **Cybernetic** derives from the Greek word *kubernetes*, meaning "steersman," that is, one who steers or keeps on course.[9] The control process shown in Exhibit 16.1 is cybernetic because constant attention to the feedback loop is necessary to keep the company's activity on course.

16-1e FEEDBACK, CONCURRENT, AND FEEDFORWARD CONTROL

The three basic control methods are feedback control, concurrent control, and feedforward control. **Feedback control** is a mechanism for gathering information about performance deficiencies *after* they occur. This information is then used to correct or prevent performance deficiencies. Study after study has clearly shown that feedback improves both individual and organizational performance. In most instances, any feedback is better than no feedback.

If feedback has a downside, it's that feedback always comes after the fact. For example, when an electrical transformer malfunctions on a neighborhood utility pole, 90 percent of the time, the cause of the problem is a squirrel. Paul Gogan of **We Energies,** an energy provider in Wisconsin and Michigan's upper peninsula, says, "Trying to keep squirrels off poles is like trying to herd cats. We insulate the wires and put protective covers over the grounded equipment." Brian Manthey, a spokesperson for We Energies, says, "If they are on a wire and touch a piece of equipment that's grounded, the current flows through them. They're killed and sometimes the power to homes and businesses goes out." And, there's never any warning until after the fact and usually nothing left of the squirrel because of the electrical surge or because predators have taken the remains.[10]

Concurrent control addresses the problems inherent in feedback control by gathering information about performance deficiencies *as* they occur. Thus, it is an improvement over feedback because it attempts to eliminate or shorten the delay between performance and feedback about the performance. Concussions represent one of the biggest health concerns for football players. Sometimes, however, it can be difficult to tell whether a player has suffered a concussion. And, because they don't want to come out of the game, players won't always be honest with doctors about their symptoms. Other times, teams, especially high school and small college teams, don't have staff who have been properly trained to diagnose concussions. To address this problem, Battle Sports Science created the Impact Indicator, a helmet chin strap equipped with an accelerometer that instantly measures the force that a player experiences when hit. When sensors detect a hit so hard that there is a 50 percent chance or better of injury, an indicator light flashes, letting sideline medical personnel know that they should further examine the player for possible signs of a concussion.[11]

Feedforward control is a mechanism for gathering information about performance deficiencies *before* they occur. In contrast to feedback and concurrent control, which provide feedback on the basis of outcomes and results, feedforward control provides information about performance deficiencies by monitoring inputs rather than outputs. Thus, feedforward control seeks to prevent or minimize performance deficiencies before they happen.

16-1f CONTROL ISN'T ALWAYS WORTHWHILE OR POSSIBLE

Control is achieved when behavior and work procedures conform to standards and goals are accomplished. By contrast, **control loss** occurs when behavior and work procedures do not conform to standards.[12] At an egg production facility run by Michael Foods, repairs to machinery in a packaging room accidentally contaminated eggs with listeria, bacteria that can cause fever, muscle aches, nausea, abdominal pain, and sometimes death. As a result, Michael Foods was forced to recall more than a million eggs sold in thirty-four states.[13]

Maintaining control is important because control loss prevents organizations from achieving their goals. When control loss occurs, managers need to find out what, if anything, they could have done to prevent it. Usually, that means identifying deviations from standard performance, analyzing the causes of those deviations, and taking corrective action. Even so, implementing controls isn't always worthwhile or

Cybernetic the process of steering or keeping on course

Feedback control a mechanism for gathering information about performance deficiencies after they occur

Concurrent control a mechanism for gathering information about performance deficiencies as they occur, thereby eliminating or shortening the delay between performance and feedback

Feedforward control a mechanism for monitoring performance inputs rather than outputs to prevent or minimize performance deficiencies before they occur

Control loss the situation in which behavior and work procedures do not conform to standards

possible. Let's look at regulation costs and cybernetic feasibility to see why this is so.

To determine whether control is worthwhile, managers need to carefully assess **regulation costs**, that is, whether the costs and unintended consequences of control exceed its benefits. If a control process costs more than it benefits, it may not be worthwhile. During the U.S. Open golf tournament held at Congressional Country Club in Montgomery County, Maryland, two children decided to open a lemonade stand nearby to raise money for pediatric cancer. But because they had not applied for a permit, county officials fined each child $500 for operating an illegal business. Parent Carrie Marriott asked the county inspector, "Does every kid who sells lemonade now have to register with the county?" The inspector replied, "Cute little kids making five or ten dollars is a little bit different than making hundreds. You've got coolers and coolers here."[14] But, after receiving enormous negative publicity, the county decided that it was not worth the trouble to pursue the matter and rescinded the fines.[15]

Another factor to consider is **cybernetic feasibility**, the extent to which it is possible to implement each of the three steps in the control process. If one or more steps cannot be implemented, then maintaining effective control may be difficult or impossible.

16-2 *Control Methods*

In January 2010, a gallon of diesel fuel was $2.95. By March 2012, the price had climbed 40 percent to $4.12. Consequently, companies with truck fleets have become much more aggressive in exploring ways to reduce fuel costs and increase gas mileage. For example, Coca-Cola added to its fleet of 650 hybrid trucks by purchasing the all-electric Navistar International eStar truck that can go one hundred miles per charge and has battery packs that can be swapped out in as little as twenty minutes. UPS, on the other hand, is controlling fuel costs by using composite materials in trucks that are one thousand pounds lighter than the steel and aluminum trucks it currently uses.

Combined with 13 percent better aerodynamics, UPS's composite trucks use 40 percent less diesel fuel. Dale Spencer, director of engineering for UPS, said, "This technology is available to us today. We don't have to worry about plugging it in or getting propane or CNG (compressed natural gas)."[16]

Managers can use five different methods to achieve control in their organizations: 16-2a bureaucratic, 16-2b objective, 16-2c normative, 16-2d concertive, and 16-2e self-control.

16-2a BUREAUCRATIC CONTROL

When most people think of managerial control, what they have in mind is bureaucratic control. **Bureaucratic control** is top-down control, in which managers try to influence employee behavior by rewarding or punishing employees for compliance or noncompliance with organizational policies, rules, and procedures. Most employees, however, would argue that bureaucratic managers emphasize punishment for noncompliance much more than rewards for compliance.

As you learned in Chapter 2, bureaucratic management and control were created to prevent just this type of managerial behavior. By encouraging managers to apply well-thought-out rules, policies, and procedures in an impartial, consistent manner to everyone in the organization, bureaucratic control is supposed to make companies more efficient, effective, and fair. Ironically, it frequently has just the opposite effect. Managers who use bureaucratic control often emphasize following the rules above all else.

Another characteristic of bureaucratically controlled companies is that, due to their rule- and policy-driven decision making, they are highly resistant to change and slow to respond to customers and competitors. Recall from Chapter 2 that even Max Weber, the German philosopher who is largely credited with popularizing bureaucratic ideals in the late nineteenth century, referred to bureaucracy as the "iron cage." He said, "Once fully established, bureaucracy is among those social structures which are the hardest to destroy."[17] Of course, the national government, with hundreds of bureaus, agencies, and departments, is typically the largest bureaucracy in most countries. In

Regulation costs the costs associated with implementing or maintaining control

Cybernetic feasibility the extent to which it is possible to implement each step in the control process

Bureaucratic control the use of hierarchical authority to influence employee behavior by rewarding or punishing employees for compliance or noncompliance with organizational policies, rules, and procedures

the United States, because of the thousands of career bureaucrats who staff the offices of the federal government, even presidents and Congress have difficulty making changes. When General Dwight Eisenhower became president, his predecessor, Harry Truman, quipped: "Poor Ike. It won't be a bit like the army. He'll sit here and he'll say, 'Do this, do that,' and nothing will happen."[18]

16-2b OBJECTIVE CONTROL

In many companies, bureaucratic control has evolved into **objective control**, which is the use of observable measures of employee behavior or output to assess performance and influence behavior. Whereas bureaucratic control focuses on whether policies and rules are followed, objective control focuses on observing and measuring worker behavior or output. The Angus Barn, a steakhouse in Raleigh, North Carolina, has a strict privacy policy because it is visited by numerous celebrities—employees and managers are to keep all guests' dining experiences private. A waiter was fired for violating the policy after uploading a copy of NFL quarterback Peyton Manning's dinner receipt, following Manning's dinner at the restaurant. The picture, which quickly went viral, showed that Manning had left a generous tip of $200, on top of an 18 percent gratuity that the restaurant had already added to the bill. Speaking about the incident and the firing, Van Eure, the owner of the Angus Barn, said, "This goes against every policy we have. It's just horrible."[19]

There are two kinds of objective control: behavior control and output control. **Behavior control** is regulating behaviors and actions that workers perform on the job. The basic assumption of behavior control is that if you do the right things (i.e., the right behaviors) every day, then those things should lead to goal achievement. Behavior control is still management-based, however, which means that managers are re-

sponsible for monitoring and rewarding or punishing workers for exhibiting desired or undesired behaviors.

Instead of measuring what managers and workers do, **output control** measures the results of their efforts. Whereas behavior control regulates, guides, and measures how workers behave on the job, output control gives managers and workers the freedom to behave as they see fit as long as they accomplish prespecified, measurable results. Output control is often coupled with rewards and incentives.

Three things must occur for output control to lead to improved business results. First, output control measures must be reliable, fair, and accurate. Second, employees and managers must believe that they can produce the desired results. If they don't, then the output controls won't affect their behavior. Third, the rewards or incentives tied to output control measures must truly be dependent on achieving established standards of performance. For example, University of Hawaii football coach Norm Chow will earn a base salary of $392,142 per year. The more successful the team is in any one year, the more money he'll make. Chow will receive a $25,000 to $40,000 bonus for each nationally televised victory, $25,000 if his team appears in a non-Bowl Championship Series (BCS) bowl, and $100,000 for a BCS bowl.[20]

16-2c NORMATIVE CONTROL

Rather than monitoring rules, behavior, or output, another way to control what goes on in organizations is to use normative control to shape the beliefs and values of the people who work there. With **normative controls**, a company's widely shared values and beliefs guide workers' behavior and decisions.

Philip Rosedale, the founder and CEO of LoveMachine, an information technology firm, runs his company entirely on one value—transparency. He applies transparency to everything at the company. Every employee, contractor, and freelancer who works for the company has access to information about everything that others are working on, what others are earning, or what other freelancers are charging and how many hours it took them to complete a project. Even Rosedale's salary and benefits are

AP Images/Eric Risberg

openly available to everyone. Rosedale believes that this extreme level of transparency is vital for creating an open, collaborative environment in which there is a free exchange of information from one person to another.[21]

Normative controls are created in two ways. First, companies that use normative controls are very careful about who they hire. While many companies screen potential applicants on the basis of their abilities, normatively controlled companies are just as likely to screen potential applicants based on their attitudes and values. Billionaire Richard Branson, founder of Virgin, which has three hundred branded companies (Virgin Airways, Virgin Mobile, Virgin Megastore, etc.) employing 50,000 people in thirty countries, hires entrepreneurial people with positive attitudes. He says, "We stumbled on this formula when we were launching our record store business in the late 1960s. We decided to look for employees who were passionate about music, because we thought their enthusiasm and knowledge would be as important a draw as the beanbag chairs, coffee and listening posts we planned to feature in our first stores and that turned out to be correct." Branson says, "When we launched Virgin Records a couple of years later . . . we put a lot of effort into finding and hiring the right people and then we made sure that they felt empowered to run the business as they saw fit that's what we had hired them for. This approach helped us to attract and keep great talent . . . Virgin has launched 400 businesses in more than forty years of expansion; our focus on employees is one of the main reasons for our success."[22]

Second, with normative controls, managers and employees learn what they should and should not do by observing experienced employees and by listening to the stories they tell about the company. Ed Fuller, the head of international lodging at Marriott International, loves to tell stories to illustrate Marriott's commitment to customer service. One of his favorites is about when he was a general manager at a Marriott in Boston. A senior executive told him that Bill Marriott, the chairman of the company, was upset about something at his hotel. Fuller was positive that he was going to be fired for being $300,000 behind his catering sales goal. But when Marriott met with Fuller, he wasn't upset about the sales, he was upset that a member of the Marriott family had been served cold clam chowder and that the restaurant manager handled the complaint poorly. Fuller says that the moral of the story is, "If [the family] is treated badly, we assume the customer is treated worse."[23]

This story makes clear the attitude that drives employee performance at Marriott in ways that rules, behavioral guidelines, or output controls could not.

AP Images/The Decatur Daily, Gary Cosby Jr.

Concertive control the regulation of workers' behavior and decisions through work group values and beliefs

16-2d CONCERTIVE CONTROL

Whereas normative controls are based on beliefs that are strongly held and widely shared throughout a company, **concertive controls** are based on beliefs that are shaped and negotiated by work groups.[24] Whereas normative controls are driven by strong organizational cultures, concertive controls usually arise when companies give work groups complete autonomy and responsibility for task completion (see Chapter 10, "Managing Teams," for a complete discussion of the role of autonomy in teams and groups). The most autonomous groups operate without managers and are completely responsible for controlling work group processes, outputs, and behavior. Such groups do their own hiring, firing, worker discipline, scheduling, materials ordering, budget making and meeting, and decision making.

Self-control (self-management) a control system in which managers and workers control their own behavior by setting their own goals, monitoring their own progress, and rewarding themselves for goal achievement

Concertive control is not established overnight. Highly autonomous work groups evolve through two phases as they develop concertive control. In phase one, group members learn to work with each other, supervise each other's work, and develop the values and beliefs that will guide and control their behavior. And because they develop these values and beliefs themselves, work group members feel strongly about following them.

In the steel industry, Nucor was long considered an upstart compared with the "biggies," U.S. Steel and Bethlehem Steel. Today, however, not only has Nucor managed to outlast many other mills, the company has bought out thirteen other mills in the past five years. Nucor has a unique culture that gives real power to employees on the line and fosters teamwork throughout the organization. This type of teamwork can be a difficult thing for a newly acquired group of employees to get used to. For example, at Nucor's first big acquisition in Auburn, New York, David Hutchins is a frontline supervisor or "lead man" in the rolling mill, where steel from the furnace is spread thin enough to be cut into sheets. When the plant was under the previous ownership, if the guys doing the cutting got backed up, the guys doing the rolling—including Hutchins—would just take a break. He says, "We'd sit back, have a cup of coffee, and complain: 'Those guys stink.'" It took six months to convince the employees at the Auburn plant that the Nucor teamwork way was better than the old way. Now, Hutchins says: "At Nucor, we're not 'you guys' and 'us guys.' It's all of us guys. Wherever the bottleneck is, we go there, and everyone works on it."[25]

The second phase in the development of concertive control is the emergence and formalization of objective rules to guide and control behavior. The beliefs and values developed in phase one usually develop into more objective rules as new members join teams. The clearer those rules, the easier it becomes for new members to figure out how and how not to behave.

Ironically, concertive control may lead to even more stress for workers to conform to expectations than bureaucratic control. Under bureaucratic control, most workers only have to worry about pleasing the boss. But with concertive control, their behavior has to satisfy the rest of their team members. For example, one team member says, "I don't have to sit there and look for the boss to be around; and if the boss is not around, I can sit there and talk to my neighbor or do what I want. Now the whole team is around me and the whole team is observing what I'm doing."[26] Plus, with concertive control, team members have a second, much more stressful role to perform: that of making sure that their team members adhere to team values and rules.

16-2e SELF-CONTROL

Self-control, also known as **self-management**, is a control system in which managers and workers control their own behavior.[27] Self-control does not result in anarchy, in which everyone gets to do whatever he or she wants. In self-control or self-management, leaders and managers provide workers

A Job for You?

Need a job? Maybe you can apply to be the new product security manager at Apple. The job description is fairly simple—keep Apple's unreleased products (i.e., demos and prototypes) out of the public eye. Apple's motivation for creating this position was quite simple. While it was still testing the iPhone 4, an Apple engineer accidentally left a prototype at a bar, where it was found by another patron and eventually sold to the technology blog Gizmodo, which quickly published all the details surrounding the anxiously awaited phone. A similar incident happened during testing of the iPhone 4S. An Apple employee left a prototype at a Mexican restaurant, where another patron found it and sold it on Craigslist.

Source: N. Bilton, "Apple Seeking Product Security Manager," *New York Times*, September 6, 2011, accessed March 29, 2012, http://bits.blogs.nytimes.com/2011/09/06/apple-seeking-new-product-security-manager/.

with clear boundaries within which they may guide and control their own goals and behaviors.[28] Leaders and managers also contribute to self-control by teaching others the skills they need to maximize and monitor their own work effectiveness. In turn, individuals who manage and lead themselves establish self-control by setting their own goals, monitoring their own progress, rewarding or punishing themselves for achieving or for not achieving their self-set goals, and constructing positive thought patterns that remind them of the importance of their goals and their ability to accomplish them.[29]

For example, let's assume you need to do a better job of praising and recognizing the good work that your staff does for you. You can use goal setting, self-observation, and self-reward to manage this behavior on your own. For self-observation, write "praise/recognition" on a three-by-five-inch card. Put the card in your pocket. Put a check on the card each time you praise or recognize someone. (Wait until the person has left before you do this.) Keep track for a week. This serves as your baseline or starting point. Simply keeping track will probably increase how often you do this. After a week, assess your baseline or starting point and then set a specific goal. For instance, if your baseline was twice a day, you might set a specific goal to praise or recognize others' work five times a day. Continue monitoring your performance with your cards. Once you've achieved your goal every day for a week, give yourself a reward (perhaps a movie or lunch with a friend at a new restaurant) for achieving your goal.[30]

As you can see, the components of self-management, self-set goals, self-observation, and self-reward have their roots in the motivation theories you read about in Chapter 13. The key difference, though, is that the goals, feedback, and rewards originate from employees themselves and not from their managers or organizations.

16-3 *What to Control?*

In the first section of this chapter, we discussed the basics of the control process and the fact that control isn't always worthwhile or possible. In the second section, we looked at the various ways in which control can be achieved. In this third and final section, we address an equally important issue: What should managers control? Costs? Quality? Customer satisfaction? The way managers answer this question has critical implications for most businesses.

If you control for just one thing, such as costs, as many grocers have done in their meat departments, then other dimensions like marketing, customer service, and quality are likely to suffer. But if you try to control for too many things, then managers and employees become confused about what's really important. In the end, successful companies find a balance that comes from doing three or four things right, like managing costs, providing value, and keeping customers and employees satisfied.

After reading this section, you should be able to explain **16-3a the balanced scorecard approach to control** *and how companies can achieve balanced control of company performance by choosing to control* **16-3b budgets, cash flows, and economic value added; 16-3c customer defections; 16-3d quality;** *and* **16-3e waste and pollution.**

16-3a THE BALANCED SCORECARD

Most companies measure performance using standard financial and accounting measures such as return on capital, return on assets, return on investments, cash flow, net income, and net margins. The **balanced scorecard** encourages managers to look beyond such traditional financial measures to four different perspectives on company performance. How do customers see us (the customer perspective)? At what must we excel (the internal perspective)? Can we continue to improve and create value (the innovation and learning perspective)? How do we look to shareholders (the financial perspective)?[31]

The balanced scorecard has several advantages over traditional control processes that rely solely on financial measures. First, it forces managers at each level of the company to set specific goals and measure performance in each of the four areas. For example, Exhibit 16.2 on the next page shows that Southwest Airlines uses nine different measures in its balanced scorecard in order to determine whether it is meeting the standards it has set for itself in the control process. Of those, only three—market value, seat revenue, and plane lease costs (at various compounded annual growth rates, or CAGR)—are standard financial measures of performance. In addition, Southwest measures its Federal Aviation Administration (FAA) on-time arrival rating and the cost of its airfares compared with those of competitors (customer perspective);

Suboptimization performance improvement in one part of an organization but only at the expense of decreased performance in another part

how much time each plane spends on the ground after landing and the percentage of planes that depart on time (internal business perspective); and the percentage of its ground crew workers, such as mechanics and luggage handlers, who own company stock and have received job training (learning perspective).

The second major advantage of the balanced scorecard approach to control is that it minimizes the chances of **suboptimization**, which occurs when performance improves in one area at the expense of decreased performance in others. Jon Meliones, chief medical director at Duke Children's Hospital, says, "We explained the [balanced scorecard] theory to clinicians and administrators like this: if you sacrifice too much in one quadrant to satisfy another, your organization as a whole is thrown out of balance. We could, for example, cut costs to improve the financial quadrant by firing half the staff, but that would hurt quality of service, and the customer quadrant would fall out of balance. Or we could increase productivity in the internal business quadrant by assigning more patients to a nurse, but doing so would raise the likelihood of errors—an unacceptable trade-off."[32]

Let's examine some of the ways in which companies are controlling the four basic parts of the balanced scorecard: the financial perspective (budgets, cash flows, and economic value added), the customer perspective (customer defections), the internal perspective (total quality management), and the innovation and learning perspective (waste and pollution).

EXHIBIT 16.2

Southwest Airlines's Balanced Scorecard

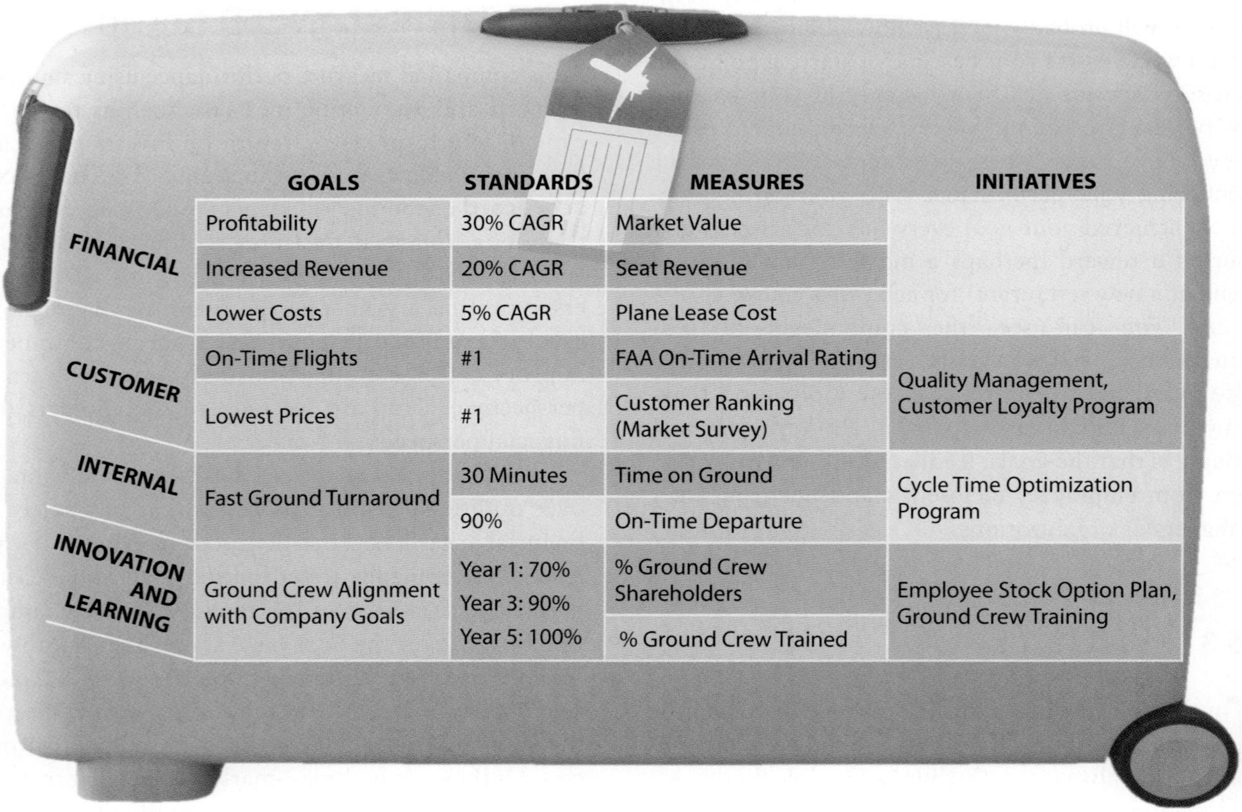

	GOALS	STANDARDS	MEASURES	INITIATIVES
FINANCIAL	Profitability	30% CAGR	Market Value	
	Increased Revenue	20% CAGR	Seat Revenue	
	Lower Costs	5% CAGR	Plane Lease Cost	
CUSTOMER	On-Time Flights	#1	FAA On-Time Arrival Rating	Quality Management, Customer Loyalty Program
	Lowest Prices	#1	Customer Ranking (Market Survey)	
INTERNAL	Fast Ground Turnaround	30 Minutes	Time on Ground	Cycle Time Optimization Program
		90%	On-Time Departure	
INNOVATION AND LEARNING	Ground Crew Alignment with Company Goals	Year 1: 70% Year 3: 90% Year 5: 100%	% Ground Crew Shareholders	Employee Stock Option Plan, Ground Crew Training
			% Ground Crew Trained	

© Image100/Jupiterimages

Source: G. Anthes, "ROI Guide: Balanced Scorecard," *Computer World*, February 17, 2003, accessed September 5, 2008, http://www.computerworld.com/action/article.do?command=viewArticleBasic&articleId=78512&intsrc=article_pots_bot.

16-3b THE FINANCIAL PERSPECTIVE: CONTROLLING BUDGETS, CASH FLOWS, AND ECONOMIC VALUE ADDED

The traditional approach to controlling financial performance focuses on accounting tools such as cash flow analysis, balance sheets, income statements, financial ratios, and budgets. **Cash flow analysis** predicts how changes in a business will affect its ability to take in more cash than it pays out. **Balance sheets** provide a snapshot of a company's financial position at a particular time (but not the future). **Income statements**, also called profit and loss statements, show what has happened to an organization's income, expenses, and net profit (income less expenses) over a period of time. **Financial ratios** are typically used to track a business's liquidity (cash), efficiency, and profitability over time compared with other businesses in its industry. Finally, **budgets** are used to project costs and revenues, prioritize and control spending, and ensure that expenses don't exceed available funds and revenues.

By themselves, none of these tools—cash flow analyses, balance sheets, income statements, financial ratios, or budgets—tell the whole financial story of a business. They must be used together when assessing a company's financial performance. Since these tools are reviewed in detail in your accounting and finance classes, only a brief overview is provided here. Still, these are necessary tools for controlling organizational finances and expenses, and they should be part of your business toolbox. Unfortunately, most managers don't have a good understanding of these accounting tools even though they should.[33] When Boeing's new chief financial officer attended her first company retreat with other Boeing executives, she assumed that her discussion of financial ratios would be a boring review for everyone present. Afterward, she was shocked when dozens of the 280 executives attending the retreat told her that for the very first time they finally understood what the formulas meant.[34]

Though no one would dispute the importance of cash flow analyses, balance sheets, income statements, financial ratios, or budgets for determining the financial health of a business, accounting research also indicates that the complexity and sheer amount of information contained in these accounting tools can shut down the brain and glaze over the eyes of even the most experienced manager.[35] Sometimes there's simply too much information to make sense of. The balanced scorecard simplifies things by focusing on one simple question when it comes to finances: How do we look to shareholders? One way to answer that question is through something called economic value added.

Conceptually, **economic value added (EVA)** is not the same thing as profits. It is the amount by which profits exceed the cost of capital in a given year. It is based on the simple idea that capital is necessary to run a business and that capital comes at a cost. Although most people think of capital as cash, once it is invested (i.e., spent), capital is more likely to be found in a business in the form of computers, manufacturing plants, employees, raw materials, and so forth. And just like the interest that a homeowner pays on a mortgage or that a college student pays on a student loan, there is a cost to that capital.

The most common costs of capital are the interest paid on long-term bank loans used to buy all those resources, the interest paid to bondholders (who lend organizations their money), and the dividends (cash payments) and growth in stock value that accrue to shareholders. EVA is positive when company profits (revenues minus expenses minus taxes) exceed the cost of capital in a given year. In other words, if a business is to truly grow, its revenues must be large enough to cover both short-term costs (annual expenses and taxes) and long-term costs (the cost of borrowing capital from bondholders and shareholders). If you're a bit confused, the late Roberto Goizueta, the former CEO of Coca-Cola, explained it this way: "You borrow money at a certain rate and invest it at a higher rate and pocket the difference. It is simple. It is the essence of banking."[36]

Exhibit 16.3 on the next page shows how to calculate EVA. First, starting with a company's income statement, you calculate the net operating profit after taxes (NOPAT) by subtracting taxes owed from

Cash flow analysis a type of analysis that predicts how changes in a business will affect its ability to take in more cash than it pays out

Balance sheets accounting statements that provide a snapshot of a company's financial position at a particular time

Income statements accounting statements, also called "profit and loss statements," that show what has happened to an organization's income, expenses, and net profit over a period of time

Financial ratios calculations typically used to track a business's liquidity (cash), efficiency, and profitability over time compared to other businesses in its industry

Budgets quantitative plans through which managers decide how to allocate available money to best accomplish company goals

Economic value added (EVA) the amount by which company profits (revenues, minus expenses, minus taxes) exceed the cost of capital in a given year

EXHIBIT 16.3

Calculating Economic Value Added (EVA)

1.	Calculate net operating profit after taxes (NOPAT).	$3,500,000
2.	Identify how much capital the company has invested (i.e., spent).	$16,800,000
3.	Determine the cost (i.e., rate) paid for capital (usually between 5 percent and 13 percent).	10%
4.	Multiply capital used (Step 2) times cost of capital (Step 3).	(10% × $16,800,000) = $1,680,000
5.	Subtract the total dollar cost of capital from net profit after taxes.	$3,500,000 NOPAT − $1,680,000 Total cost of capital $1,820,000 Economic value added

© Cengage Learning

© iStockphoto.com/Morgan Lane Studios

income from operations. (Remember, a quick review of an income statement is on the Financial Review Card found at the back of your book.) The NOPAT shown in Exhibit 16.3 is $3,500,000. Second, identify how much capital the company has invested (i.e., spent). Total liabilities (what the company owes) less accounts payable and less accrued expenses, neither of which you pay interest on, provides a rough approximation of this amount. In Exhibit 16.3, total capital invested is $16,800,000. Third, calculate the cost (i.e., rate) paid for capital by determining the interest paid to bondholders (who lend organizations their money), which is usually somewhere between 5 and 8 percent, and the return that stockholders want in terms of dividends and stock price appreciation, which is historically about 13 percent. Take a weighted average of the two to determine the overall cost of capital. In Exhibit 16.3, the cost of capital is 10 percent. Fourth, multiply the total capital ($16,800,000) from Step 2 by the cost of capital (10 percent) from Step 3. In Exhibit 16.3, this amount is $1,680,000. Fifth, subtract the total dollar cost of capital in Step 4 from the NOPAT in Step 1. In Exhibit 16.3, this value is $1,820,000, which means that our example company has created economic value or wealth this year. If our EVA number had been negative, meaning that the company didn't make enough profit to cover the cost of capital from bondholders and shareholders, then the company would have destroyed economic value or wealth by taking in more money than it returned.[37]

Why is EVA so important? First and most importantly, because it includes the cost of capital, it shows whether a business, division, department, profit cen-

ter, or product is really paying for itself. The key is to make sure that managers and employees can see how their choices and behavior affect the company's EVA. For example, because of EVA training and information systems, factory workers at Herman Miller, a leading office furniture manufacturer, understand that using more efficient materials, such as less expensive wood-dust board instead of real wood sheeting, contributes an extra dollar of EVA from each desk the company makes. On its website, Herman Miller explains that, "Under the terms of the EVA plan, we shifted our focus from budget performance to long-term continuous improvements and the creation of economic value. When we make plans for improvements around here, we include an EVA analysis. When we make decisions to add or cut programs, we look at the impact on EVA. Every month we study our performance in terms of EVA, and this measurement system is one of the first things new recruits to the company learn."[38] "The result is a highly motivated and business-literate workforce that challenges convention and strives to create increasingly greater value for both customers and owners. Every month the company and all employees review performance in terms of EVA, which has proven to be a strong corollary to shareholder value."[39]

Second, because EVA can easily be determined for subsets of a company such as divisions, regional offices, manufacturing plants, and sometimes even departments, it makes managers and workers at all levels pay much closer attention to their segment of the business. In other words, EVA motivates managers and workers to think like small-business owners who must scramble to contain costs and generate enough business to meet their bills each month. And, unlike many kinds of financial controls, EVA doesn't specify what should or should not be done to improve performance. Thus, it encourages managers and workers to be creative in looking for ways to improve EVA performance.

Remember that EVA is the amount by which profits exceed the cost of capital in a given year. So the more that EVA exceeds the total dollar cost of capital, the better a company has used investors' money that year. For example, Apple had an EVA of $10.03 billion in 2010, by far the largest EVA in the world. The next closest company was Google at $5.28 billion. To put Apple's 2010 EVA performance in perspective, note that Apple had an average EVA of $1.7 billion a year from 2005 to 2009, and that was 2.5 times more than what investors were expecting. Apple's EVA financial performance in 2010 was truly extraordinary.[40]

16-3c THE CUSTOMER PERSPECTIVE: CONTROLLING CUSTOMER DEFECTIONS

The second aspect of organizational performance that the balanced scorecard helps managers monitor is customers. It does so by forcing managers to address the question, "How do customers see us?" Unfortunately, most companies try to answer this question through customer satisfaction surveys, but these are often misleadingly positive. Most customers are reluctant to talk about their problems because they don't know who to complain to or think that complaining will not do any good. Indeed, a study by the federal Office of Consumer Affairs found that 96 percent of unhappy customers never complain to anyone in the company.[41]

One reason that customer satisfaction surveys can be misleading is that sometimes even very satisfied customers will leave to do business with competitors. Rather than poring over customer satisfaction surveys from current customers, studies indicate that companies may do a better job of answering the question "How do customers see us?" by closely monitoring **customer defections**, that is, by identifying which customers are leaving the company and measuring the rate at which they are leaving. Unlike the results of customer satisfaction surveys, customer defections and retention do have a great effect on profits.

For example, very few managers realize that obtaining a new customer costs ten times as much as keeping a current one. In fact, the cost of replacing old customers with new ones is so great that most companies could double their profits by increasing the rate of customer retention by just 5 to 10 percent per year.[42] Retaining customers obviously means having more customers, but how many more? Consider two companies starting with a customer base of 100,000 customers and an acquisition rate of 20 percent (i.e., yearly each company's customer base grows by 20 percent). Assuming company B has a higher retention rate of just 5 percent (90 percent retention rate for company B versus an 85 percent retention rate for company A), company B will double its customer base around the ninth year, while it will take company A slightly more than fifteen years to double its

customer base. On average, this means company B also profited by a higher percentage.[43] And if a company can keep a customer for life, the benefits are even larger. According to Stew Leonard, owner of the Connecticut-based Stew Leonard's grocery store chain: "The lifetime value of a customer in a supermarket is about $246,000. Every time a customer comes through our front door I see, stamped on their forehead in big red numbers, '$246,000.' I'm never going to make that person unhappy with me. Or lose her to the competition."[44]

Beyond the clear benefits to the bottom line, the second reason to study customer defections is that customers who have left are much more likely than current customers to tell you what you are doing wrong. Perhaps the best way to tap into this source of good feedback is to have top-level managers from various departments talk directly to customers who have left. It's also worthwhile to have top managers talk to dissatisfied customers who are still with the company. Finally, companies that understand why customers leave can not only take steps to fix ongoing problems but also identify which customers are likely to leave and can make changes to prevent them from leaving.

16-3d THE INTERNAL PERSPECTIVE: CONTROLLING QUALITY

The third part of the balanced scorecard, the internal perspective, consists of the processes, decisions, and actions that managers and workers make within the organization. In contrast to the financial perspective of EVA and the outward-looking customer perspective, the internal perspective focuses on internal processes and systems that add value to the organization. For McDonald's, it could be processes and systems that enable the company to provide consistent, quick, low-cost food. For Toyota, it could be reliability—when you turn on your car it starts, no matter whether the car has 20,000 or 200,000 miles on it. Yet no matter what area a company chooses, the key is to excel in that area. Consequently, the internal perspective of the balanced scorecard usually leads managers to a focus on quality.

Quality is typically defined and measured in three ways: excellence, value, and conformance to expectations.[45] When the company defines its quality goal as *excellence*, managers must try to produce a product or service of unsurpassed performance and features. *Conde Nast Traveler* magazine has been ranking global airlines for twenty-three years. For twenty-two of those years, Singapore Airlines was named the best airline in the world.[46] Whereas many airlines try to cram passengers into every available inch on a plane, Singapore Airlines delivers creature comforts to encourage repeat business and customers willing to pay premium prices. On its newer planes, the first-class cabin is divided into eight private mini-rooms, each with an unusually wide leather seat that folds down flat for sleeping, a twenty-three-inch LCD TV that doubles as a computer monitor, and an adjustable table.

These amenities and services are common for private jets but truly unique in the commercial airline industry.[47] Singapore Airlines was the first airline, in the 1970s, to introduce a choice of meals, complimentary drinks, and earphones in coach class. It was the first to introduce worldwide video, news, telephone, and fax services and the first to feature personal video monitors for movies, news, documentaries, and games. Singapore Airlines has had AC power for laptop computers for some time, and recently it became the first airline to introduce on-board high-speed Internet access.

Value is the customer perception that the product quality is excellent for the price offered. At a higher price, for example, customers may perceive the product to be less of a value. When a company emphasizes value as its quality goal, managers must simultaneously control excellence, price, durability, and any other features of a product or service that customers strongly associate with value. The Kia Optima was recently recognized by *Kiplinger's Personal Finance* as a Best New Car Value. It has a turbocharged engine with not only the highest horsepower in its class but also the highest fuel efficiency as well. Standard equipment includes Bluetooth connectivity, power seats, satellite radio, a cooled glove box, and a voice-controlled entertainment system. The car is also backed by a five-year warranty, as well as a five-year roadside assistance program. With all these features and a $25,000 to $30,000 price that is several thousand dollars cheaper than the Toyota Camry and Honda Accord, sales have jumped 131 percent.[48]

When a company defines its quality goal as conformance to specifications, employees must base decisions and actions on whether services and products measure up to the standard. In contrast to excellence and value-based definitions of quality that can be somewhat ambiguous, measuring whether products and services are "in spec" is relatively easy. Furthermore, while conformance to specifications (e.g., precise tolerances for a part's weight or thickness) is usually associated with manufacturing, it can be used equally well to control quality in nonmanufacturing jobs. Exhibit 16.4 shows a checklist that a cook or restaurant owner would use to ensure quality when buying fresh fish.

The way in which a company defines quality affects the methods and measures that workers use to control quality. Accordingly, Exhibit 16.5 shows the advantages and disadvantages associated with the excellence, value, and conformance to specification definitions of quality.

EXHIBIT 16.4

Conformance to Specifications Checklist for Buying Fresh Fish

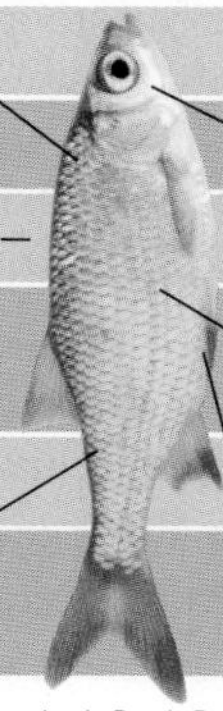

FRESH WHOLE FISH	ACCEPTABLE	NOT ACCEPTABLE
Gills	bright red, free of slime, clear mucus	brown to grayish, thick, yellow mucus
Eyes	clear, bright, bulging, black pupils	dull, sunken, cloudy, gray pupils
Smell	inoffensive, slight ocean smell	ammonia, putrid smell
Skin	opalescent sheen, scales adhere tightly to skin	dull or faded color, scales missing or easily removed
Flesh	firm and elastic to touch, tight to the bone	soft and flabby, separating from the bone
Belly cavity	no viscera or blood visible, lining intact, no bone protruding	incomplete evisceration, cuts or protruding bones, off-odor

Sources: "A Closer Look: Buy It Fresh, Keep It Fresh," *Consumer Reports Online*, accessed June 20, 2005, http://www.seagrant.sunysb.edu/SeafoodTechnology/SeafoodMedia/CR02-2001/CR-SeafoodII020101.htm; "How to Purchase: Buying Fish," *AboutSeaFood*, accessed June 20, 2005, http://www.aboutseafood.com/faqs/purchase1.html.

EXHIBIT 16.5

Advantages and Disadvantages of Different Measures of Quality

QUALITY MEASURE	ADVANTAGES	DISADVANTAGES
Excellence	Promotes clear organizational vision.	Provides little practical guidance for managers.
	Being/providing the "best" motivates and inspires managers and employees.	Excellence is ambiguous. What is it? Who defines it?
Value	Appeals to customers who know excellence "when they see it."	Difficult to measure and control.
	Customers recognize differences in value.	Can be difficult to determine what factors influence whether a product/service is seen as having value.
	Easier to measure and compare whether products/services differ in value.	Controlling the balance between excellence and cost (i.e., affordable excellence) can be difficult.
Conformance to Specifications	If specifications can be written, conformance to specifications is usually measurable.	Many products/services cannot be easily evaluated in terms of conformance to specifications.
	Should lead to increased efficiency.	Promotes standardization, so may hurt performance when adapting to changes is more important.
	Promotes consistency in quality.	May be less appropriate for services, which are dependent on a high degree of human contact.

Source: Republished by The Academy of Management, P.O. Box 3020, Briar Cliff Manor, NY, 10510-8020; C. A. Reeves and D. A. Bednar, "Defining Quality: Alternatives and Implications," *Academy of Management Review* 19 (1994): 419–445. Reproduced by permission of the publisher via Copyright Clearance Center, Inc.

16-3e THE INNOVATION AND LEARNING PERSPECTIVE: CONTROLLING WASTE AND POLLUTION

The last part of the balanced scorecard, the innovation and learning perspective, addresses the question "Can we continue to improve and create value?" Thus, the innovation and learning perspective involves continuous improvement in ongoing products and services (discussed in Chapter 18), as well as relearning and redesigning the processes by which products and services are created (discussed in Chapter 7). Since these are discussed in more detail elsewhere in the text, this section reviews an increasingly important topic, waste and pollution minimization. Exhibit 16.6 shows the four levels of waste minimization, ranging from waste disposal, which produces the smallest minimization of waste, to waste prevention and reduction, which produces the greatest minimization.[49]

The goals of the top level, *waste prevention and reduction*, are to prevent waste and pollution before they occur or to reduce them when they do occur. For example, A. P. Moller-Maersk A/S, the world's largest shipping container company, recently placed an order for ten of the biggest container ships in the world. At 1,312 feet long and 193.5 feet wide, these ships can carry 18,000 twenty-foot containers, or 2,500 more than the largest ships currently in service. Thanks to an innovative hull design, as well as a heat-recovery system that reuses energy from engine exhaust, the ships produce 50 percent less carbon dioxide and consume 35 percent less fuel than the average ship, despite their massive size. Maersk has even drawn up detailed plans for how the ships will be recycled when they are decommissioned.[50]

There are three strategies for waste prevention and reduction:

1. *Good housekeeping*—performing regularly scheduled preventive maintenance for offices, plants, and equipment. Examples of good housekeeping include fixing leaky valves quickly to prevent wasted water and making sure machines are running properly so that they don't use more fuel than necessary. UPS uses GPS and telematic tracking systems to improve the efficiency of its fleet of delivery trucks. While the GPS tracker helps drivers find the most fuel-efficient route for deliveries, the telematic device monitors more than two hundred elements of a truck's condition, such as oil pressure, idling time, acceleration, and gas mileage. Routine maintenance used to be done based on fixed intervals (say, every 7,500 miles). But thanks to telematics information, maintenance is performed when needed and needed repair work is detected and carried out much earlier, thus reducing downtime and repair expenses. Because of these steps, UPS reduced the amount of time that its U.S. trucks spend idling by fifteen minutes per day, saving 1.4 million gallons of fuel per year. Donna Longina, a UPS spokesperson, said, "Multiply results like that by more than 90,000 drivers worldwide, and you can see the potential."[51]

2. *Material/product substitution*—replacing toxic or hazardous materials with less harmful materials.

3. *Process modification*—changing steps or procedures to eliminate or reduce waste.

EXHIBIT 16.6 Four Levels of Waste Minimization

- Waste Prevention & Reduction
- Recycle & Reuse
- Waste Treatment
- Waste Disposal

Source: Reprinted from *Business Horizons*, September–October 1995, D. R. May and B. L. Flannery, "Cutting Waste with Employee Involvement Teams," pp. 28–38, Copyright © 1995, with permission from Elsevier.

© iStockphoto.com/Olga Lyubkina

At the second level of waste minimization, *recycle and reuse*, wastes are reduced by reusing materials as long as possible or by collecting materials for on- or off-site recycling. For example, Ford Motor Company uses recycled tires and soy-based plastics to make engine gaskets and seals for its Ford F-150, Escape, Mustang, Focus, and Fiesta. According to the company, "The gaskets and seals are derived from 25 percent post-consumer, recycled-tire particulate and 17 percent biorenewable content from soy." By doing so, Ford reused 2.2 million pounds of tires, which would have otherwise ended up in landfills. Likewise, Ford recycled 4.1 million pounds of carpet to create cylinder head covers for the engines in its Mustang, Fusion, and Escape vehicles.[52]

A growing trend in recycling is *design for disassembly*, where products are designed from the start for easy disassembly, recycling, and reuse once they are no longer usable. Herman Miller, a manufacturer of office equipment, not only uses recycled material in its award-winning office chairs, it makes it easy to recycle them once they're no longer usable. It clearly labels which parts are recyclable, identifies the type of plastic used in each part, and then minimizes the different types of plastics used. Finally, it designs its chairs so that they are easy to take apart and includes detailed disassembly instructions. As a result, Herman Miller has won a number of Cradle-to-Cradle (C2C) certifications for its chairs, storage systems, and office systems.[53] While Herman Miller is doing this voluntarily, the European Union requires companies to make most of their products and packaging recyclable. And since companies, not consumers, are held responsible for recycling the products they manufacture, they must design their products from the start with recycling in mind.[54] Under the EU's end-of-life vehicle program, companies have to be able to recover and recycle 80 percent of parts from cars built in Europe since January 2002. The requirement rises to 85 percent for cars made since 2006, and will be 95 percent for cars made after 2015. Moreover, since 2007, the EU has required auto manufacturers to recycle all the cars that they made between 1989 and 2002.[55]

At the third level of waste minimization, waste treatment, companies use biological, chemical, or other processes to turn potentially harmful waste into harmless compounds or useful by-products. Cow manure is a concern for cattle and dairy farmers, especially since it can pollute water supplies, spread disease, and contribute to global warming through carbon dioxide and methane. One solution, however, is to use "biodigester" technology to capture methane gas and use it to power electricity-generating turbines. A farm of 750 cows, for example, can generate enough methane each year to power 300 houses. Another benefit is that the process creates an odorless, harmless by-product that can be used to fertilize and enhance soil on farms.[56]

The fourth and lowest level of waste minimization is *waste disposal*. Wastes that cannot be prevented, reduced, recycled, reused, or treated should be safely disposed of in processing plants or in environmentally secure landfills that prevent leakage and contamination of soil and underground water supplies. Contrary to common belief, all businesses, not just manufacturing firms, have waste disposal problems. For example, with the average computer lasting just three years, approximately 60 million computers come out of service each year, creating disposal problems for offices all over the world. But organizations can't just throw old computers away, since they have lead-containing cathode ray tubes in the

Dell's Three C's

When Dell Inc. set out to reduce the environmental impact of its packaging, it undertook a strategy focused on three Cs. The first *C* stands for cube, which meant using a smaller box with more efficient packaging and less unnecessary material. By switching to smaller boxes, Dell was able to fit 17 percent more notebook computers per shipping pallet. The second *C* is content—Dell increased the amount of recycled and sustainable material that it used to produce its packaging material. So, for example, it used recycled foam; products derived from bamboo, which is a fast-growing, sustainable plant; and recycled milk jugs (over 9 million of them, actually). The third *C* stands for curbside recyclability. Dell committed to educating both consumers and recycling companies about how to recycle the packaging material that the company uses. Dell also set a goal of making sure that 75 percent of its packaging can be recycled. In all, Dell's efforts to reduce waste have reduced the amount of packaging it uses by 18 million pounds in just two years.

Source: H. Clancy, "In Green Packaging, Little Things Mean a Lot," *ZDNet*, August 25, 2010, http://www.zdnet.com/blog/green/in-green-packaging-little-things-mean-a-lot/13757; L. Kaye, "Dell Reduced Packaging by 18 Million Pounds since 2008," *Triple Pundit*, August 26, 2010, http://www.triplepundit.com/2010/08/dell-reduced-packaging-by-18-million-pounds-since-2008/.

monitors, toxic metals in the circuit boards, paint-coated plastic, and metal coatings that can contaminate groundwater.[57] Many companies give old computers and computer equipment to local computer recycling centers that distribute usable computers to nonprofit organizations or safely dispose of lead and other toxic materials. A number of retailers and electronics manufacturers operate recycling programs to keep electronics out of landfills. For example, customers can drop off computers, TVs, DVD players, batteries, and other items at Best Buy stores. There is a $10 recycling fee for anything with a screen, but Best Buy offsets that with a $10 gift card. Best Buy will recycle 80 million pounds of electronics this year. But for those items that still function, Costco and Newegg .com work with Gazelle.com, which buys, refurbishes, and resells 250,000 items overseas and on eBay. College student Bobby Lozano sold his used iPod Nano and LG EnV Touch phone to Gazelle, because he says, "I got an iPhone, so I no longer needed the other two." Gazelle wiped the devices of personal information and put $70 into his PayPal account.[58]

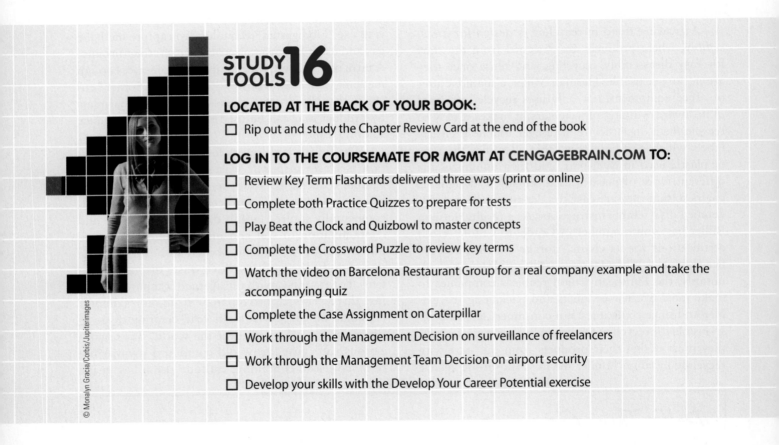

STUDY TOOLS 16

LOCATED AT THE BACK OF YOUR BOOK:

☐ Rip out and study the Chapter Review Card at the end of the book

LOG IN TO THE COURSEMATE FOR MGMT AT CENGAGEBRAIN.COM TO:

☐ Review Key Term Flashcards delivered three ways (print or online)

☐ Complete both Practice Quizzes to prepare for tests

☐ Play Beat the Clock and Quizbowl to master concepts

☐ Complete the Crossword Puzzle to review key terms

☐ Watch the video on Barcelona Restaurant Group for a real company example and take the accompanying quiz

☐ Complete the Case Assignment on Caterpillar

☐ Work through the Management Decision on surveillance of freelancers

☐ Work through the Management Team Decision on airport security

☐ Develop your skills with the Develop Your Career Potential exercise

© Monalyn Gracia/Corbis/Jupiterimages

WHY CHOOSE?

Every 4LTR Press solution comes complete with a visually engaging textbook in addition to an interactive eBook. Go to CourseMate for MGMT to begin using the eBook. Access at **www.cengagebrain.com**

Complete the Speak Up survey in CourseMate at **www.cengagebrain.com**

 Follow us at **www.facebook.com/4ltrpress**

17 Managing
Information

LEARNING OUTCOMES

17-1 Explain the strategic importance of information.

17-2 Describe the characteristics of useful information (i.e., its value and costs).

17-3 Explain the basics of capturing, processing, and protecting information.

17-4 Describe how companies can access and share information and knowledge.

CHECK OUT **STUDY TOOLS** AT THE END OF THIS CHAPTER.

17-1 *Strategic Importance of Information*

A generation ago, computer hardware and software had little to do with managing business information. Rather than storing information on hard drives, managers stored it in filing cabinets. Instead of uploading daily sales and inventory levels by satellite to corporate headquarters, they mailed hard-copy summaries to headquarters at the end of each month. Instead of word processors, reports were typed on electric typewriters. Instead of spreadsheets, calculations were made on adding machines. Managers communicated by sticky notes, not email. Phone messages were written down by assistants and coworkers, not forwarded in your email as a sound file with the message converted to text. Workers did not use desktop or laptop computers as daily tools to get work done. Instead, they scheduled limited access time to run batch jobs on the mainframe computer (and prayed that the batch job computer code they wrote would work).

Today, a generation later, computer hardware and software are an integral part of managing business information. This is due mainly to something called **Moore's law**. Gordon Moore is one of the founders of Intel Corporation, which makes 75 percent of the integrated processors used in personal computers. In 1965, Moore predicted that computer-processing power would double and that its cost would drop by 50 percent every two years.[1] As Exhibit 17.1 on the next page shows, Moore was right. Computer power, as measured by the number of transistors per computer chip, *has* more than doubled every few years. Consequently, the computer sitting in your lap or on your desk is not only smaller but also much cheaper and more powerful than the large mainframe computers used by *Fortune* 500 companies fifteen years ago. In fact, if car manufacturers had achieved the same power increases and cost decreases attained by computer manufacturers, a fully outfitted Lexus or Mercedes sedan would cost less than $1,000!

Raw data are facts and figures. For example, 11, $452, 32, and 26,100 are some data that I used the day I wrote this section of the chapter. However, facts and figures aren't particularly useful unless they have meaning. For example, you probably can't guess what these four pieces of raw data represent, can you? If you can't, these data are useless. That's why researchers make the distinction between raw data and information. Whereas raw data consist of facts and figures, **information** is useful data that can influence someone's choices and behavior. One way to think about the difference between data and information is that information has context.

So what did those four pieces of data mean to me? Well, 11 stands for Channel 11, the local CBS affiliate on which I watched part of the men's PGA golf tournament; $452 is how much it would cost me to rent a minivan for a week if I go skiing over spring break; 32 is for the 32-gigabyte storage card that I want to add to my digital camera (prices are low, so I'll probably buy it); and 26,100 means that it's time to get the oil changed in my car.

In today's hypercompetitive business environments, information is as important as capital (i.e., money) for business success, whether it's about product

Moore's law the prediction that about every two years, computer processing power would double and its cost would drop by 50 percent

Raw data facts and figures

Information useful data that can influence people's choices and behavior

EXHIBIT 17.1

Moore's Law

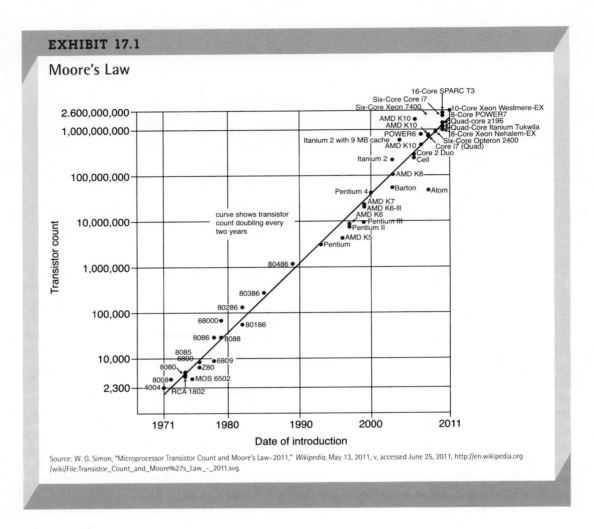

Source: W. G. Simon, "Microprocessor Transistor Count and Moore's Law–2011," *Wikipedia*, May 13, 2011, v, accessed June 25, 2011, http://en.wikipedia.org/wiki/File:Transistor_Count_and_Moore%27s_Law_-_2011.svg.

inventory, pricing, or costs. It takes money to get businesses started, but businesses can't survive and grow without the right information. *Information has strategic importance for organizations because it can be used to 17-1a obtain first-mover advantage and 17-1b sustain competitive advantage once it has been created.*

17-1a FIRST–MOVER ADVANTAGE

First-mover advantage is the strategic advantage that companies earn by being the first in an industry to use new information technology to substantially lower costs or to differentiate a product or service from that of competitors. In a time of rising fuel costs, U.S. Xpress, one of the largest trucking companies in the United States, has managed to save millions each year by installing a monitoring device in its

First-mover advantage
the strategic advantage that companies earn by being the first to use new information technology to substantially lower costs or to make a product or service different from that of competitors

trucks that records the speed and location of each truck in addition to how hard the brakes are applied. And since truck drivers idle their engines while sleeping (for heating and cooling the truck cabin), the system also monitors and controls cabin temperatures. Chief technology officer Timothy Leonard says, "If you have a 10-hour break, we want your AC going for the first two hours at 70 degrees so you can go to sleep. After that, we want it back up to 78 or 79 degrees." That saves an average of sixty-two gallons of fuel per truck, which comes to $24 million per year.[2] First-mover advantages like those established by U.S. Xpress can be sizable.[3]

17-1b SUSTAINING COMPETITIVE ADVANTAGE

As described, companies that use information technology to establish first-mover advantage usually have higher market shares and profits. According to the resource-based view of information technology shown in Exhibit 17.2, companies need to address three criti-

EXHIBIT 17.2

Using Information Technology to Sustain a Competitive Advantage

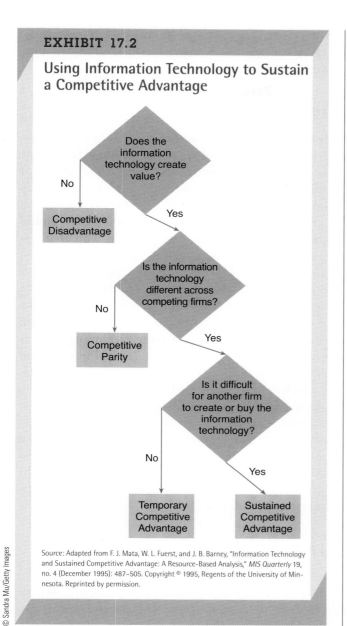

Does the information technology create value?

No → **Competitive Disadvantage**

Yes ↓

Is the information technology different across competing firms?

No → **Competitive Parity**

Yes ↓

Is it difficult for another firm to create or buy the information technology?

No → **Temporary Competitive Advantage**

Yes → **Sustained Competitive Advantage**

Source: Adapted from F. J. Mata, W. L. Fuerst, and J. B. Barney, "Information Technology and Sustained Competitive Advantage: A Resource-Based Analysis," *MIS Quarterly* 19, no. 4 (December 1995): 487–505. Copyright © 1995, Regents of the University of Minnesota. Reprinted by permission.

cal questions in order to sustain a competitive advantage through information technology. First, does the information technology create value for the firm by lowering costs or providing a better product or service? If an information technology doesn't add value, then investing in it would put the firm at a competitive disadvantage relative to companies that choose information technologies that do add value.

Second, is the information technology the same or different across competing firms? If all the firms have access to the same information technology and use it in the same way, then no firm has an advantage over another (i.e., there is competitive parity).

Third, is it difficult for another company to create or buy the information technology used by the firm? If so, then the firm has established a sustainable competitive advantage over competitors through information technology. If not, then the competitive advantage is just temporary, and competitors should eventually be able to duplicate the advantages the leading firm has gained from information technology.

In short, the key to sustaining a competitive advantage is not faster computers, more memory, or larger hard drives. The key is using information technology to continuously improve and support the core functions of a business. While American Airlines was the first airline to issue tablet computers to pilots to replace manuals and navigation charts (previously held in binders in forty-pound carry-on bags), British Airways is using iPads to improve a core part of its business—the level of customer service flight attendants deliver to high-value business- and first-class travelers. Previously, prior to each departure, flight attendants read through stacks of printouts to memorize key passengers' preferences. Now, however, with the iPads automatically updated hours before flights depart and available discreetly in the

THE KEY TO SUSTAINING A COMPETITIVE ADVANTAGE IS USING INFORMATION TECHNOLOGY TO CONTINUOUSLY IMPROVE AND SUPPORT THE CORE FUNCTIONS OF A BUSINESS.

cabin throughout the flight, attendants have immediate access to passengers' likes and dislikes, special meal requests, and even medical needs. Furthermore, the iPads contain seating charts showing where loyalty club members are seated, so attendants can greet them personally when they board. Flight attendant Daljit Kaur says, "I'm ahead of myself in knowing where our corporate and high-value customers are sitting, and who needs help." Because we can attend to them so well, "They look at you and say 'have you been on a special course?'" Finally, flight attendants use the iPads to submit customer complaints. Pippa Grech, who manages British Airways' iPad program, says, "The crew does it so that passengers don't have to run around on holiday trying to do it themselves. Otherwise, by the time they get off the plane, they think 'oh, I won't bother about it.'"[4]

17-2 *Characteristics and Costs of Useful Information*

Komatsu, the second largest producer of heavy machinery (bulldozers, dump trucks, and backhoes), couples a GPS device and a web-application, KOMTRAX, to provide real-time information on every machine it sells. KOMTRAX measures fuel consumption, gauges the load that each machine bears, provides maintenance alerts, and even reports how many hours a machine was working, idling, or in transport. Jeff Davis, president of Edge Contracting Inc., keeps track of whether his workers are needlessly letting big machines idle in place too long, thus wasting fuel. Davis, who tells his workers, "if you're not using the machine, turn it off," says, "When I can actually show them what it cost the company, it starts to sink in." Davis estimates that reducing idling time will save between $50,000 and $100,000 a year.[5] The KOMTRAX information also benefits Komatsu by providing a detailed real-time snapshot of worldwide construction activity. As spokeswoman Natsuko Usami says, "If mines and construction sites are operating the equipment full-time, we know there's a chance that market demand will go up, and we can order our factories to ramp up production."[6]

As Komatsu's KOMTRAX system demonstrates, information is useful when it is 17-2a accurate, 17-2b complete, 17-2c relevant, and 17-2d timely. However, there can be significant *17-2e acquisition, 17-2f processing, 17-2g storage, 17-2h retrieval, and 17-2i communication costs associated with useful information.*

17-2a ACCURATE INFORMATION

Information is useful when it is accurate. Before relying on information to make decisions, you must know that the information is correct. But what if it isn't? For example, in Japan, 7-Eleven used to rely on centralized sales data to determine the kind and quantity of products that its 13,000 stores should stock on their shelves. The problem with that approach, however, is that a 7-Eleven in downtown Tokyo next to skyscrapers filled with office workers doesn't sell the same kind and number of products as a 7-Eleven in suburban Sapporo, which is one-tenth the size of Tokyo. So, to provide more accurate sales information to each store, 7-Eleven Japan is giving its 200,000 sales clerks detailed information about what sells in *their* stores. Based on those data, each clerk makes educated hypotheses each morning about what will sell that day and receives feedback on what sold by the end of the day. Twice a week, data analysts work with the clerks at each store to help improve their sales predictions. Thanks to more accurate information, 7-Eleven Japan's 13,000 stores are now filled with the products that their local customers desire.[7]

17-2b COMPLETE INFORMATION

Information is useful when it is complete. Incomplete or missing information makes it difficult to recognize problems and identify potential solutions. For example, doctors hate learning new technology, but they hate inaccurate and incomplete information even more, since it makes treatment less efficient and possibly even dangerous. This led the University of California San Francisco Medical Center to invest $150 million to switch to an electronic medical records system known as APeX. The system allows any doctor in the medical center and its associated clinics to look at a patient's complete medical record and update it as needed, at the touch of a button. Using APeX will enable the hospital to avoid problems with illegible notes, missing or misfiled paperwork, or delays in receiving files from other care providers. As Ken Jones, the chief operating officer of the medical center, describes it, "Whether a doctor took care of you ten minutes ago in the hospital, two weeks ago at a clinic or this second in the ER, they'll have up-to-date information." Says Jones, "It's more efficient and less room for error."[8]

17-2c RELEVANT INFORMATION

You can have accurate, complete information, but it's not very useful if it doesn't pertain to the problems you're facing. Imagine that an earthquake destroys a large city in Japan or that a hurricane destroys cities and towns in a five-state area in the southeastern part of the United States. Usually, when disaster strikes, the power goes out, and the authorities, first responders, and people affected lose access to what they need most, relevant information. Microsoft's Claire Bonilla is a senior director of field operations who coordinates Microsoft's resources to help people affected by disasters around the world (this is part of Microsoft's corporate social responsibility efforts). Bonilla says, "The core to the effectiveness of any disaster response is the ability to share information and coordinate the effort between the many organizations involved. Software can play a huge role in doing that. Whenever we hear about a disaster, the first step is to establish a connection with the lead response organization locally. Then we help with real-time communication and use mapping software to provide partners with situational awareness so that, for example, relief agencies can see the location of a shelter in need of medical supplies. We also give data-sharing capability to first responders and government agencies so they can share relevant information with outside organizations without compromising security."[9]

In the aftermath of the devastating earthquake and tsunami in Japan in March 2011, Microsoft partnered with a number of Japanese companies to set up a communications infrastructure to coordinate relief organizations and bring much-needed aid to survivors. Working with Aidmatrix and Slalom Consulting, Microsoft created a communication portal for Second Harvest Japan, a network of food banks that collected food from throughout the country and distributed it to victims. Second Harvest used Microsoft services to coordinate its collection, transportation, and distribution activities and to set up a website showing where food was available. Microsoft also partnered with software company Digital Office to create a mobile app called JResQ, which let people record a voice message and send it to friends and family to let them know their condition. JResQ messages were also embedded with GPS information to make it easier for family and friends who had been separated to find each other. Finally, Toyota and Microsoft created a virtual map showing which roads were passable and the locations where water, gas, and medical care were accessible. Microsoft offers these services at no charge.[10]

17-2d TIMELY INFORMATION

Finally, information is useful when it is timely. To be timely, the information must be available when needed to define a problem or to begin to identify possible solutions. If you've ever thought, "I wish I had known that earlier," then you understand the importance of timely information and the opportunity cost of not having it. Several years ago, the I-35 bridge in Minneapolis collapsed during rush hour, killing thirteen people and injuring hundreds. The collapse was caused by extra layers of concrete used to resurface the bridge over the years. In catastrophic accidents like this, investigators can usually determine the cause by gathering and analyzing information. But they rarely have timely information that could have prevented the disaster. That, however, is changing as researchers

© iStockphoto.com/Lawrence Sawyer

create smart structures—buildings, bridges, and tunnels equipped with wireless sensors that provide real-time information. For example, researchers from the University of California at Berkeley have installed sensors on the Golden Gate Bridge to monitor vibrations and analyze structural integrity. Humidity sensors installed on the Humber Bridge in East Yorkshire, England, now monitor the threat to its steel struts, which are susceptible to moisture. And, to monitor future problems, the St. Anthony Falls Bridge, which replaced the fallen bridge in Minneapolis, is now equipped with temperature sensors that control antifreeze systems that prevent the bridge surface from freezing.[11]

17-2e ACQUISITION COSTS

Acquisition cost is the cost of obtaining data that you don't have. Acxiom, a billion-dollar company, gathers and processes data for direct-mail marketing companies. If you've received an unsolicited, "preapproved" credit card application recently (and who hasn't?), chances are Acxiom helped the credit card company gather information about you. Where does Acxiom get that information? The first place it turns is to companies that sell consumer credit reports at a wholesale cost of $1 each. Acxiom also obtains information from retailers. Each time you use your credit card, websites and retailers' checkout scanners gather information about your spending habits and product preferences. Acxiom also uses publicly available information such as motor vehicle and real estate records, as well as website traffic.

So why pay for this information? Acquiring it can help credit card companies better identify who will mail back a signed credit card application and who will rip the credit card application in half and toss it in the trash. Likewise, Acxiom's information helps retailers by categorizing consumers into seventy demographic groups. For example, Nordstrom, an upscale department store, would find it worthwhile to advertise to "Apple Pie Families," married homeowners between the ages of forty-six and sixty-five who live in urban areas, earn $100,000 to $500,000, and have school-age children. Likewise, Wal-Mart is better off advertising to "Trucks and Trailers," people between the ages of thirty and forty-five who earn less than $100,000 and live in rural areas. Paying Acxiom to acquire this kind of data significantly increases the return that retailers and credit card companies get from advertising and direct marketing.

17-2f PROCESSING COSTS

Companies often have massive amounts of data, but not in the form or combination they need. **Processing cost** is the cost of turning raw data into usable information. While Google offers a wide range of online services, most of its revenues come from search-related ads. But those ads are effective only when Google serves up accurate searches that help people find what they're looking for. In an effort to provide more precise searches, Google is now connecting and linking the information that users "leave behind" as they use Google search, YouTube, Gmail, other Google services, and their Android phones. For example, Google says that these additional data can help it determine if a user searching for "jaguar" is looking for a cat or a car. Of course, turning all of that data into meaningful information to improve search accuracy requires massive computing power. Thus, Google operates ten ex-

jaguar OR jaguar

traordinarily expensive data centers around the world. Google's data center in Finland, for example, cost $273 million; the one in Hong Kong, $300 million; and the one in Singapore, $120 million. And that is just the up-front cost; the cost of staffing and maintaining the centers for years to come will be millions more.[12]

17-2g STORAGE COSTS

Storage cost is the cost of physically or electronically archiving information for later retrieval and use. For consumers who want to make sure they never lose their computer data, Carbonite offers an online-backup service. For an annual fee, Carbonite gives users unlimited storage space on its servers so that they can back up critical files they can't afford to lose. Over 100 million data files are added to Carbonite's servers each day. To make room for them, Carbonite opened a new server facility in Boston at a cost of more than $46 million. The facility features multiple air-conditioning feeds (necessary for preventing the servers from over-heating), an uninterruptable diesel generator in case the electricity ever goes out, and twenty-four-hour security (complete with fingerprint scanners).[13]

17-2h RETRIEVAL COSTS

Retrieval cost is the cost of accessing already-stored and processed information. One of the most common misunderstandings about information is that it is easy and cheap to retrieve once the company has it. Not so. First, you have to find the information. Then, you've got to convince whoever has it to share it with you. Then the information has to be processed into a form that is useful for you. By the time you get the information you need, it may not be timely anymore.

For example, as companies move toward paper-less office systems, how will employees quickly and easily retrieve archived emails, file records, website information, word processing documents, or images? One solution is Enterprise Content Management (ECM), which is a way of storing and providing access to unstructured information wherever it exists.

Ulrich Kampffmeyer, former member of the board of directors of the Association for Information and Image Management, summed up the challenge of retrieval costs well when he said, "The most important job is to keep in-house information under control. The questions add up: where to put the thousands and thousands of emails, what to do with the electronically signed business correspondence, where to put taxation-relevant data, how to transfer information from the disorganized file system, how to consolidate information in a repository that everybody can use, how to get a single login for all the systems, how to create a uniform in-basket for all incoming information, how to make sure that no information is lost or ignored, etc. etc."[14]

17-2i COMMUNICATION COSTS

Communication cost is the cost of transmitting information from one place to another. Flight data recorders, also called "black boxes," are used to investigate accidents because they record flight data such as altitude, speed, and climb rate. Sometimes the black box can't be found, leaving investigators little information about what caused the accident. To solve this problem, Star Aviation and AeroMechanical Services market a next-generation "black box" that provides airlines real-time flight data. However, at a cost of $3 to $5 per minute via satellite, this information doesn't come cheap. An airline operating hundreds of flights per day would spend several hundred million dollars to obtain real-time data.[15]

17-3 *Capturing, Processing, and Protecting Information*

In 1907, Metropolitan Life Insurance built a huge office building in New York City for its brand-new, state-of-the-art information technology system. What was this great breakthrough in information management? Card files. That's right, the same card file system that every library in America used before computers. Metropolitan Life's information technology consisted of 20,000 separate file drawers that sat in hundreds of file cabinets more than fifteen feet tall. This filing system held 20 million insurance applications, 700,000 accounting books, and 500,000 death certificates. Metropolitan Life employed sixty-one workers who did nothing but sort, file, and climb ladders to pull files as needed.[16]

Storage cost the cost of physically or electronically archiving information for later retrieval and use

Retrieval cost the cost of accessing already-stored and processed information

Communication cost the cost of transmitting information from one place to another

How we get and share information has clearly changed. The cost, inefficiency, and ineffectiveness of using this formerly state-of-the-art system would put an insurance company out of business within months. Today, if storms, fire, or accidents damage policyholders' property, insurance companies write checks on the spot to cover the losses. When policyholders buy a car, they call their insurance agent from the dealership to activate their insurance before driving off in their new cars. And now, insurance companies are marketing their products and services to customers directly from the Internet. From card files to Internet files in just under a century, the rate of change in information technology is spectacular.

*In this section, you will learn about the information technologies that companies use to **17-3a capture, 17-3b process,** and **17-3c protect information.***

17-3a CAPTURING INFORMATION

There are two basic methods of capturing information: manual and electronic. Manual capture of information is a slow, costly, labor-intensive, and often inaccurate process, which entails recording and entering data by hand into a data storage device. For example, when you applied for a driver's license, you probably recorded personal information about yourself by filling out a form. Then, after you passed your driver's test, someone typed your handwritten information into the department of motor vehicles' computer database so that local and state police could access it from their patrol cars in the event they pulled you over for speeding. (Isn't information great?) To avoid the problems inherent in such a system, companies are relying more on electronic capture. They use electronic storage devices such as bar codes, radio frequency identification tags, and document scanners to capture and record data electronically.

Bar codes represent numerical data by varying the thickness and pattern of vertical bars. The primary advantage of bar codes is that the data they represent can be read and recorded in an instant with a handheld or pen-type scanner. One pass of the scanner (okay, sometimes several) and "beep!" the information has been captured. Bar codes cut checkout times in half, reduce data entry errors by 75 percent, and save stores money

because stockers don't have to go through the labor-intensive process of putting a price tag on each item in the store.[17] All airlines use bar codes on boarding passes, either printed from your home computer or from the check-in kiosk at the airport. An increasing number of airlines, however, now send paperless bar codes to smartphones to be scanned in place of bar codes on printed boarding passes. The U.S. Transportation Security Administration says that paperless boarding passes are more secure "and will prevent fraudulent paper boarding passes that could be created and printed at home."[18] Besides saving time and the cost of printing and paper, paperless boarding passes are likely to be popular with frequent travelers. Dan Green, a frequent business traveler who lives in Burlington, Vermont, says, "It's easier. I like to use my laptop, but I don't have a printer. Especially in hotels, where sometimes you don't have access to a printer, it makes not having a printer easier for those of us on the go."[19]

Radio frequency identification (RFID) tags contain minuscule microchips and antennas that transmit information via radio waves.[20] Unlike bar codes, which require direct line-of-sight scanning, RFID tags

are read by turning on an RFID reader that, like a radio, tunes into a specific frequency to determine the number *and* location of products, parts, or anything else to which the RFID tags are attached. Turn on an RFID reader, and every RFID tag within the reader's range (from several hundred to several thousand feet) is accounted for.

Because they are now so inexpensive, RFID tags and readers are being put to thousands of uses in all kinds of businesses. Coca-Cola is slowly introducing a soft drink vending machine, the Freestyle, which has thirty different flavor cartridges that can be used to make one hundred different Coca-Cola brand drinks. A Coke, for example, is made by dispensing flavor concentrate from the cartridge into a cup, and then mixing it with a sweetener, water, and carbonation. Ice can be added if wanted. What makes this machine unique, however, is the use of RFID chips attached to each flavor cartridge. Thanks to RFID, Coca-Cola can track which drinks are selling, how many are being sold, and when. The RFID tags also indicate when cartridges are running low and need to be replaced. Furthermore, RFID enhances functionality and security by showing whether a cartridge has been installed correctly or whether it is a genuine Coca-Cola product. In the case of a product recall, Coca-Cola can even stop particular cartridges from dispensing drinks until they can be pulled from the machines. Ray Crockett, Coca-Cola's director of communications, says, "We consider Freestyle nothing short of a revolution in the fountain dispenser business."[21] The Freestyle is in 1,800 locations and has just been added to 850 of Burger King's company-owned restaurants. Restaurants that install the Freestyle typically see double-digit increases in soft drink sales, counter to the 6 percent decrease observed over the last five years.[22]

Electronic scanners, which convert printed text and pictures into digital images, have become an increasingly popular method of capturing data electronically because they are inexpensive and easy to use. The first requirement for a good scanner is a document feeder that automatically feeds document pages into the scanner or turns the pages (often with a puff of air) when scanning books or bound documents. Text that has been digitized cannot be searched or edited like the regular text in your word processing software, however, so the second requirement for a good scanner is **optical character recognition** software to scan and convert original or digitized documents into ASCII (American Standard Code for Information Interchange) text or Adobe PDF documents. ASCII text can be searched, read, and edited with standard word processing, email, desktop publishing, database management, and spreadsheet software, and PDF documents can be searched and edited with Adobe's Acrobat software.

17-3b PROCESSING INFORMATION

Processing information means transforming raw data into meaningful information that can be applied to business decision making. Evaluating sales data to determine the best- and worst-selling products, examining repair records to determine product reliability, and monitoring the cost of long-distance phone calls are all examples of processing raw data into meaningful information. And with automated, electronic capture of data, increased processing power, and cheaper and more plentiful ways to store data, managers no longer worry about getting data. Instead, they scratch their heads about how to use the overwhelming amount of data that pours into their businesses every day. Furthermore, most managers know little about statistics and have neither the time nor the inclination to learn how to use them to analyze data.

Electronic scanner an electronic device that converts printed text and pictures into digital images

Optical character recognition the ability of software to convert digitized documents into ASCII (American Standard Code for Information Interchange) text that can be searched, read, and edited by word processing and other kinds of software

Processing information transforming raw data into meaningful information

---

Smart Parking Meters

The city of San Francisco recently introduced "smart" parking meters that are equipped with sensors that can sense when a car is parked in a designated spot and communicate with other meters within a certain distance. Other cities have used similar systems to charge different rates at different hours, but San Francisco is the first city to use the real-time information from meters in an effort to reduce traffic congestion and pollution from emissions. Instead of endlessly circling around a block looking for an open parking space, drivers are able to use an application on their smartphones or laptops that shows the precise location of empty parking spots. They can even use the application to "feed the meter" digitally.

Source: B. Worthen, "New Meters Aim to Cure Parking Headaches," *Wall Street Journal*, January 27, 2011, http://online.wsj.com/article/SB10001424052748703555804576102090737327466.html.

Data mining the process of discovering unknown patterns and relationships in large amounts of data

Data warehouse stores huge amounts of data that have been prepared for data mining analysis by being cleaned of errors and redundancy

Supervised data mining the process when the user tells the data mining software to look and test for specific patterns and relationships in a data set

Unsupervised data mining the process when the user simply tells the data mining software to uncover whatever patterns and relationships it can find in a data set

One promising tool to help managers dig out from under the avalanche of data is data mining. **Data mining** is the process of discovering patterns and relationships in large amounts of data.[23] Data mining is carried out using complex algorithms such as neural networks, rule induction, and decision trees. If you don't know what those are, that's okay. With data mining, you don't have to. Most managers only need to know that data mining looks for patterns that are already in the data but are too complex for them to spot on their own. Surprisingly, Osco Drug, based in Chicago, found that beer and diapers tended to be bought together between 5 and 7 p.m. The question, of course, was: Why? The answer, on further review, was fairly straightforward. Fathers, who were told by their wives to buy some diapers on their way home, decided to pick up a six-pack for themselves, too.[24]

Data mining typically splits a data set in half, finds patterns in one half, and then tests the validity of those patterns by trying to find them again in the second half of the data set. The data typically come from a **data warehouse** that stores huge amounts of data

that have been prepared for data mining analysis by being cleaned of errors and redundancy. The data in a data warehouse can then be analyzed using two kinds of data mining. **Supervised data mining** usually begins with the user telling the data mining software to look and test for specific patterns and relationships in a data set. Typically, this is done through a series of "what-if?" questions or statements. For instance, a grocery store manager might instruct the data mining software to determine if coupons placed in the Sunday paper increase or decrease sales. By contrast, with **unsupervised data mining**, the user simply tells the data mining software to uncover whatever patterns and relationships it can find in a data set. For example, State Farm Insurance used to have three pricing categories for car insurance depending on your driving record: preferred for the best drivers, standard for typical drivers, and nonstandard for the worst drivers. Now, however, it has moved to tiered pricing based on the three hundred different kinds of driving records that its data mining software was able to discover. This allows State Farm to be much more precise in matching three hundred different price levels to three hundred different kinds of driving records.[25]

Unsupervised data mining is particularly good at identifying association or affinity patterns, sequence patterns, and predictive patterns. It can also identify what data mining technicians call data clusters.[26]

© iStockphoto.com/Alvin Burrows

Association or affinity patterns occur when two or more database elements tend to occur together in a significant way. Most retailers send flyers and coupons about baby products after a woman has given birth (after the birth announcement is made public), but Target wanted to act earlier, sometime around the first twenty weeks of pregnancy, when mothers-to-be start buying items to get ready for their new baby. So it turned to association and affinity patterns to see if there was a way to identify through purchasing patterns when a woman was pregnant. Target's Guest Marketing Analytics department analyzed consumer data from Target's baby registry and found that around the beginning of their second trimester, pregnant women often bought lotion, mineral and vitamin supplements, unscented soap, hand sanitizer, and washcloths. Target found a pattern of twenty-five products that identified pregnant customers with such accuracy that the company could even estimate a due date. For example, if you're female, are twenty-three years old, and have bought cocoa-butter lotion, a large purse that doubles as a diaper bag, zinc and magnesium supplements (taken by pregnant women), and a blue or pink throw rug, there's an 87 percent chance that you are pregnant. Why? Because those purchases are almost always associated with being pregnant.[27]

Sequence patterns appear when two or more database elements occur together in a significant pattern in which one of the elements precedes the other. The newest trend among baseball teams is dynamic ticket pricing. The San Francisco Giants pioneered the practice of charging different prices for the same seat, depending on the game. Using data mining, the Giants re-priced tickets on a daily basis by calculating the impact of various factors (i.e., database elements) that only become clear a few days before a game, such as the weather, winning streaks, and pitching matchups, all of which influence how many people will want to attend. During the 2009 season, the Giants lowered and raised prices in a small section of seats using such data and were able to sell an extra 25,000 tickets, which increased revenue by $500,000. And, for the 2010 season, when the Giants switched to dynamic pricing for all single-game seats, ticket revenues were up by 6 percent.[28] Other teams that have adopted dynamic pricing include the Atlanta Braves, the Minnesota Twins, the Chicago Cubs, the San Diego Padres, and the Pittsburgh Pirates. According to economist Barry Kahn, teams that have used dynamic pricing have been able to raise attendance by 15 percent and

revenue from ticket sales by 30 percent.[29]

Predictive patterns are just the opposite of association or affinity patterns. Whereas association or affinity patterns look for database elements that seem to go together, **predictive patterns** help identify database elements that are different. Banks and credit card companies use data mining to find predictive patterns that distinguish customers who are good credit risks from those who are poor credit risks and less likely to pay their loans and monthly bills. J. P. Martin, an executive at Canadian Tire, pioneered the use of purchase data to predict consumer behavior. By analyzing what customers were buying, he identified predictive patterns that accurately forecast whether consumers would pay their debts. For example, he found that people who bought generic motor oil were more likely to miss payments than those who bought more expensive, name-brand oil. People who bought felt furniture pads, which protect wood floors from scratches, were very unlikely to miss payments. And, he found that 47 percent of the Canadian Tire customers who frequented the Sharx Pool Bar in Montreal missed an average of four credit card payments per year.[30]

Data clusters are the last kind of pattern found by data mining. **Data clusters** occur when three or more database elements occur together (i.e., cluster) in a significant way. For example, after analyzing several years' worth of repair and warranty claims, Ford Motor Company might find that, compared with cars built in its Chicago plant, the cars it builds in Kansas City (first element) are more likely to have problems with over-tightened fan belts (second element) that break (third element) and result in overheated engines (fourth element), ruined radiators (fifth element), and payments for tow trucks (sixth element), which are paid for by Ford's five-year, 60,000-mile power train warranty.

Traditionally, data mining has been very expensive and very complex. Today, however, data mining services and analysis are much more affordable and within reach of most companies' budgets. And, if it follows the path of most technologies, data mining will become even easier and cheaper to use in the future.

Association or affinity patterns when two or more database elements tend to occur together in a significant way

Sequence patterns when two or more database elements occur together in a significant pattern in which one of the elements precedes the other

Predictive patterns patterns that help identify database elements that are different

Data clusters when three or more database elements occur together (i.e., cluster) in a significant way

17-3c PROTECTING INFORMATION

Protecting information is the process of ensuring that data are reliably and consistently retrievable in a usable format for authorized users but no one else. For instance, when customers purchase prescription medicine at Drugstore.com, an online drugstore and health-aid retailer, they want to be confident that their medical and credit card information is available only to them, the pharmacists at Drugstore.com, and their doctors. So Drugstore.com has an extensive privacy policy (click "Privacy Policy" at http://www.drugstore.com to read details of the policy).[31]

Companies like Drugstore.com find it necessary to protect information because of the numerous security threats to data and data networks listed in Exhibit 17.3. People inside and outside companies can steal or destroy company data in various ways, including denial-of-service web server attacks that can bring down some of the busiest and best-run sites on the Internet; viruses and spyware/adware that spread quickly and can result in data loss and business disruption; keystroke monitoring, in which every mouse click and keystroke you make is monitored, stored, and sent to unauthorized users; password-cracking software that steals supposedly secure passwords; and phishing, where fake but real-looking emails and websites trick users into sharing personal information (user names, passwords, account numbers) leading to unauthorized account access. On average, 19 percent of computers are infected with viruses, 80 percent have spyware, and only one-third are running behind a protected firewall (discussed shortly). Studies show that the threats listed in Exhibit 17.3 are so widespread that automatic attacks will begin on an unprotected computer just fifteen seconds after it connects to the Internet.[32]

As shown in the right-hand column of Exhibit 17.3, numerous steps can be taken to secure data and data networks. Some of the most important are authentication and authorization, firewalls, antivirus software for PCs and email servers, data encryption, and virtual private networks.[33] We will review those steps and then finish this section with a brief review of the dangers of wireless networks.

Two critical steps are required to make sure that data can be accessed by authorized users and no one else. One is **authentication**, that is, making sure users are who they claim to be.[34] The other is **authorization**, that is, granting authenticated users approved access to data, software, and systems.[35] When an ATM prompts

No More Passwords?

Passwords are one of the biggest inconveniences when going online. If you pick a password that's too simple, you might get hacked. If you pick a complicated password, it can be too hard to remember. And then there's the question of how many passwords you should have. Should you make a different password for email, Twitter, Facebook, Amazon.com, Tumblr, and so on? This might soon be a problem of the past. The U.S. Department of Commerce recently proposed replacing all passwords with a digital ID, a system where every person would have a digital profile stored on an app or a flash drive, and which would give password-free access to email, social media, and other online accounts. While some critics are concerned that this would give government too much power over privacy, government officials counter that they ultimately want big business, rather than the government itself, to create the password-free system.

Source: J. Valentino-DeVries, "A Government Plan for IDs to Replace Online Passwords," *Wall Street Journal*, April 15, 2011, accessed April 2, 2012, http://blogs.wsj.com/digits/2011/04/15/a-government-plan-for-ids-to-replace-online-passwords/.

EXHIBIT 17.3

Security Threats to Data and Data Networks

Security Problem	Source	Affects	Severity	The Threat	The Solution
Denial of service; web server attacks and corporate network attacks	Internet hackers	All servers	High	Loss of data, disruption of service, and theft of service.	Implement firewall, password control, server-side review, threat monitoring, and bug fixes; turn PCs off when not in use.
Password cracking software and unauthorized access to PCs	Local area network, Internet	All users, especially digital subscriber line and cable Internet users	High	Hackers take over PCs. Privacy can be invaded. Corporate users' systems are exposed to other machines on the network.	Close ports and firewalls, disable file and print sharing, and use strong passwords.
Viruses, worms, Trojan horses, and rootkits	Email, downloaded and distributed software	All users	Moderate to high	Monitor activities and cause data loss and file deletion; compromise security by sometimes concealing their presence.	Use antivirus software and firewalls; control Internet access.
Spyware, adware, malicious scripts and applets	Rogue web pages	All users	Moderate to high	Invade privacy, intercept passwords, and damage files or file system.	Disable browser script support; use security, blocking, and spyware/adware software.
Email snooping	Hackers on your network and the Internet	All users	Moderate to high	People read your email from intermediate servers or packets, or they physically access your machine.	Encrypt messages, ensure strong password protection, and limit physical access to machines.
Keystroke monitoring	Trojan horses, people with direct access to PCs	All users	High	Records everything typed at the keyboard and intercepts keystrokes before password masking or encryption occurs.	Use antivirus software to catch Trojan horses, control Internet access to transmission, and implement system monitoring and physical access control.
Phishing	Hackers on your network and the Internet	All users, including customers	High	Fake but real-looking emails and websites that trick users into sharing personal information on what they wrongly think is a company's website. This leads to unauthorized account access.	Educate and warn users and customers about the dangers. Encourage both not to click on potentially fake URLs, which might take them to phishing websites. Instead, have them type your company's URL into the web browser.
Spam	Email	All users and corporations	Mild to high	Clogs and overloads email servers and inboxes with junk mail. HTML-based spam may be used for profiling and identifying users.	Filter known spam sources and senders on email servers; have users create further lists of approved and unapproved senders on their personal computers.
Cookies	Websites you visit	Individual users	Mild to moderate	Trace web usage and permit the creation of personalized web pages that track behavior and interest profiles.	Use cookie managers to control and edit cookies, and use ad blockers.

Sources: K. Bannan, "Look Out: Watching You, Watching Me," *PC Magazine*, July 2002, 99; A. Dragoon, "Fighting Phish, Fakes, and Frauds," *CIO*, September 1, 2004, 33; B. Glass, "Are You Being Watched?" *PC Magazine*, April 23, 2002, 54; K. Karagiannis, "DDoS: Are You Next?" *PC Magazine*, January 2003, 79; B. Machrone, "Protect & Defend," *PC Magazine*, June 27, 2000, 168–181; "Top 10 Security Threats," *PC Magazine*, April 10, 2007, 66; M. Sarrel, "Master End-User Security," *PC Magazine*," May 2008, 101.

you to enter your personal identification number (PIN), the bank is authenticating that you are you. Once you've been authenticated, you are authorized to access your funds and no one else's. Of course, as anyone who has lost a PIN or password or had one stolen knows, user authentication systems are not foolproof. In particular, users create security risks by not changing their default account passwords (such as birth dates) or by using weak passwords such as names ("Larry") or complete words ("football") that are quickly guessed by password-cracker software.[36]

This is why many companies are now turning to **two-factor authentication**, which is based on what users know, such as a password, and what they have, such as a secure ID card.[37] To provide increased security for its users, for example, Yahoo! recently introduced two-factor authentication for its Yahoo! Mail service. When logging in, users are first asked for their passwords, as is done with most email accounts. But then they must provide a second authentication factor, such as an answer to a security question or a validation code that has been sent to their mobile phone.[38]

Unfortunately, stolen or cracked passwords are not the only way for hackers and electronic thieves to gain access to an organization's computer resources. Unless special safeguards are put in place, every time corporate users are online there's literally nothing between their personal computers and the Internet (home users with high-speed DSL or cable Internet access face the same risks). Hackers can access files, run programs, and control key parts of computers if precautions aren't taken. To reduce these risks, companies use **firewalls**, hardware or software devices that sit between the computers in an internal organizational network and outside networks such as the Internet. Firewalls filter and check incoming and outgoing data. They prevent company insiders from accessing unauthorized sites or from sending confidential company information to people outside the company. Firewalls also prevent outsiders from identifying and gaining access to company computers and data. Indeed, if a firewall is working properly, the computers behind the company firewall literally cannot be seen or accessed by outsiders.

A **virus** is a program or piece of code that, without your knowledge, attaches itself to other programs on your computer and can trigger anything from a harmless flashing message to the reformatting of your hard drive to a system-wide network shutdown. You used to have to do something or run something to get a virus, such as double-clicking an infected email attachment. Today's viruses are much more threatening. In fact, with some viruses, just being connected to a network can infect your computer. *Antivirus software for personal computers* scans email, downloaded files, and computer hard drives, disk drives, and memory to detect and stop computer viruses from doing damage. However, this software is effective only to the extent that users of individual computers have and use up-to-date versions. With new viruses appearing all the time, users should update their antivirus software weekly or, even better, configure their virus software to automatically check for, download, and install updates. By contrast, *corporate antivirus software* automatically scans email attachments such as Microsoft Word documents, graphics, or text files as they come across the company email server. It also monitors and scans all file downloads across company databases and network servers. So, while antivirus software for personal computers prevents individual computers from being infected, corporate antivirus software for email servers, databases, and network servers adds another layer of protection by preventing infected files from multiplying and being sent to others.

Another way of protecting information is to encrypt sensitive data. **Data encryption** transforms data into complex, scrambled digital codes that can be decrypted only by authorized users who possess unique decryption keys. One method of data encryption is to use products by PGP (Pretty Good Privacy) (http://www.symantec.com) to encrypt the files stored on personal computers or network servers and databases. This is especially important with laptop computers, which are easily stolen. After a Boeing employee's laptop PC was stolen from his hotel room, the company implemented a training program that requires managers and employees to have data encryption software installed on their laptops and become certified in using it. Those not following the encryption procedures can be reprimanded and even fired.[39]

With people increasingly gaining unauthorized access to email messages—email snooping—it's also important to encrypt sensitive email messages and file attachments. You can use a system called "public key encryption" to do so. First, give copies of your "public key" to anyone who sends you files or email. Have the sender use the public key, which is actually a piece of software, to encrypt files before sending them to you. The only way to decrypt the files is with a companion "private key" that you keep to yourself.

Although firewalls can protect personal computers and network servers connected to the corporate network, people away from their offices (e.g., salespeople, business travelers, telecommuters) who interact with their company networks via the Internet face a security risk. Because Internet data are not encrypted, "packet sniffer" software easily allows hackers to read everything sent or received except files that have been encrypted before sending. Previously, the only practical solution was to have employees dial in to secure company phone lines for direct access to the company network. Of course, with international and long-distance phone calls, the costs quickly added up. Now, **virtual private networks (VPNs)** have solved this problem by using software to encrypt all Internet data at both ends of the transmission process. Instead of making long-distance calls, employees connect to the Internet. But, unlike typical Internet connections in which data packets are decrypted, the VPN encrypts the data sent by employees outside the company computer network, decrypts the data when they arrive within the company network, and does the same when data are sent back to the computer outside the network. VPN connections provide secure access to everything on a company's network.

Alternatively, many companies are now adopting web-based **secure sockets layer (SSL) encryption** to provide secure off-site access to data and programs. If you've ever entered your credit card in a web browser to make an online purchase, you've used SSL technology to encrypt and protect that information.

You can tell if SSL encryption is being used on a website if you see a padlock icon (gold in Internet Explorer or Firefox; green in Google Chrome, silver in Safari) or if the URL begins with "https." SSL encryption works the same way in the workplace. Managers and employees who aren't at the office simply connect to the Internet, open a web browser, and then enter a user name and password to gain access to SSL-encrypted data and programs.

Finally, many companies now have wireless networks, which make it possible for anybody with a laptop and a wireless card to access the company network from anywhere in the office. Though wireless networks come equipped with security and encryption capabilities that, in theory, permit only authorized users to access the wireless network, those capabilities are easily bypassed with the right tools. Compounding the problem, many wireless networks are shipped with their security and encryption capabilities turned off for ease of installation.[40] Caution is important even when encryption is turned on, because the WEP (Wired Equivalent Privacy) security protocol is easily compromised. If you work at home or are working on the go, extra care is critical because Wi-Fi networks in homes and public places like hotel lobbies are among the most targeted by hackers.[41] See the Wi-Fi Alliance site at http://www.wi-fi.org for the latest information on wireless security and encryption protocols that provide much stronger protection for your company's wireless network.

Virtual private network (VPN) software that securely encrypts data sent by employees outside the company network, decrypts the data when they arrive within the company computer network, and does the same when data are sent back to employees outside the network

Secure sockets layer (SSL) encryption Internet browser–based encryption that provides secure off-site web access to some data and programs

Skimming Information

There's a way that thieves can steal all of the information on your debit or ATM card, including the PIN, without ever getting hold of your card. It's called skimming, and it works like this. Thieves go into a store and attach a small device to the store's credit card scanning machines. The device copies all of the information contained on a debit/ATM card as it is swiped, and the thieves use a small camera or a clear plastic sheet to record the PIN associated with the card. Once they have this information, they can quickly make a duplicate of the card and start spending away. Recently, the hobby and art supply retailer Michael's discovered that skimmers had manipulated ninety of its credit card scanners, and hundreds of customers reported that their bank accounts had been drained.

Source: A. Zimmerman and M. Bustillo, "Thieves Swipe Debit Card Data," *Wall Street Journal*, May 13, 2011, B1–B2.

17-4 Accessing and Sharing Information and Knowledge

Today, information technologies are letting companies communicate data, share data, and provide data access to workers, managers, suppliers, and customers in ways that were unthinkable just a few years ago.

After reading this section, you should be able to explain how companies use information technology to improve **17-4a internal access and sharing of information, 17-4b external access and sharing of information,** *and* **17-4c the sharing of knowledge and expertise.**

17-4a INTERNAL ACCESS AND SHARING

Executives, managers, and workers inside the company use three kinds of information technology to access and share information: executive information systems, intranets, and portals. An **executive information system (EIS)** uses internal and external sources of data to provide managers and executives the information they need to monitor and analyze organizational performance.[42] The goal of an EIS is to provide accurate, complete, relevant, and timely information to managers. With just a few mouse clicks and basic commands such as *find*, *compare*, and *show*, the EIS displays costs, sales revenues, and other kinds of data in color-coded charts and graphs. Managers can drill down to view and compare data by global region, country, state, time period, and product. Managers at Colgate-Palmolive, which makes dental (Colgate toothpastes), personal (Irish Spring soap and Speed Stick antiperspirants), and home care (Palmolive dish soaps) products, as well as pet nutrition (Hill's Science Diet), use their EIS, which they call their "dashboard," to see how well the company is running. Ruben Panizza, Colgate's global IT director of business intelligence, says, "These real-time dashboards are a change for people who are used to seeing a lot of numbers with their data. But they quickly realize they can use the information as it's presented in the dashboards to make faster decisions. In the past, executives relied on other people to get custom reports and data. Now, they can look at the information themselves. They see the real data as it is in the system much more easily and quickly. For the first time, many of the company's business leaders are running BI [business intelligence] tools—in this case, dashboards—to monitor the business to see what's going on at a high level."[43]

Intranets are private company networks that allow employees to easily access, share, and publish information using Internet software. Intranet websites are just like external websites, but the firewall separating the internal company network from the Internet permits only authorized internal access.[44] Companies typically use intranets to share information (e.g., about benefits) and to replace paper forms with online forms. Many company intranets are built on the web model as it existed a decade ago. Intranets are evolving to include:

- collaboration tools, such as wikis, where team members can post all relevant information for a project they're working on together
- customizable email accounts
- presence awareness (information on whether someone you are looking for on the network is in the office, in a meeting, working from home, etc.)
- instant messaging
- simultaneous access to files for virtual team members

Duke Energy's intranet, which it calls "The Portal," was recently named one of the ten best corporate intranets by the Nielsen Norman Group. The Portal not only provides the documents, forms, and information needed to get your work done at Duke, it also incorporates social media to help employees communicate with each other and management. A key feature is "My Site," a Facebook-like function that employees can use to share information. The Portal also allows employees to comment and communicate on nearly every part of the site. If management posts an article about a new work process, The Portal not only gives employees the article, but allows them to respond to the article, so that an interactive conversation can take place. Tom Shiel, from Duke's corporate communications department, said, "Our old system concentrated on top-down communication. Now when we have an article from senior management, employees can respond on the site. It is much more a tool for conversation back and forth."[45]

Executive information system (EIS) a data processing system that uses internal and external data sources to provide the information needed to monitor and analyze organizational performance

Intranets private company networks that allow employees to easily access, share, and publish information using Internet software

Finally, **corporate portals** are a hybrid of executive information systems and intranets. While an EIS provides managers and executives with the information they need to monitor and analyze organizational performance, and intranets help companies distribute and publish information and forms within the company, corporate portals allow company managers and employees to access customized information *and* complete specialized transactions using a web browser.

17-4b EXTERNAL ACCESS AND SHARING

Historically, companies have been unable or reluctant to let outside groups have access to corporate information. Now, however, a number of information technologies—electronic data interchange, extranets, web services, and the Internet—are making it easier to share company data with external groups like suppliers and customers. They're also reducing costs, increasing productivity by eliminating manual information processing (70 percent of the data output from one company, like a purchase order, ends up as data input at another company, such as a sales invoice or shipping order), reducing data entry errors, improving customer service, and speeding communications.

As a result, managers are scrambling to adopt these technologies.

With **electronic data interchange, or EDI**, two companies convert purchase and ordering information to a standardized format to enable direct electronic transmission of that information from one company's computer system to the other company's system. For example, when a Wal-Mart checkout clerk drags an Apple iPod across the checkout scanner, Wal-Mart's computerized inventory system automatically reorders another iPod through the direct EDI connection that its computer has with Apple's manufacturing and shipping computer. No one at Wal-Mart or Apple fills out paperwork. No one makes phone calls. There are no delays to wait to find out whether Apple has the iPod in stock. The transaction takes place instantly and automatically because the data from both companies were translated into a standardized, shareable, compatible format.

Corporate portal a hybrid of executive information systems and intranets that allows managers and employees to use a web browser to gain access to customized company information and to complete specialized transactions

Electronic data interchange (EDI) when two companies convert their purchase and ordering information to a standardized format to enable the direct electronic transmission of that information from one company's computer system to the other company's computer system

Web services are another way for companies to directly and automatically transmit purchase and ordering information from one company's computer system to another company's computer system. **Web services** use standardized protocols to describe and transfer data from one company in such a way that those data can automatically be read, understood, transcribed, and processed by different computer systems in another company.[46] Route One, which helps automobile dealers process loans for car buyers, was started by the financing companies of DaimlerChrysler, Ford, General Motors, and Toyota. Not surprisingly, each auto company had a different computer system with different operating systems, different programs, and different data structures. Route One relies on web services to connect these different computer systems to the wide variety of different databases and software used by various auto dealers, credit bureaus, banks, and other auto financing companies. Without web services, there's no way these different companies and systems could share information.[47]

Now, what's the difference between web services and EDI? For EDI to work, the data in different companies' computer, database, and network systems must adhere to a particular set of standards for data structure and processing. For example, company X, which has a seven-digit parts numbering system, and company Y, which has an eight-digit parts numbering system, would agree to convert their internal parts numbering systems to identical ten-digit parts numbers when their computer systems talk to each other. By contrast, the tools underlying web services such as extensible markup language (or XML) automatically do the describing and transcribing so that data with different structures can be shared across very different computer systems in different companies. (Don't worry if you don't understand how this works, just appreciate what it does.) As a result, by automatically handling those differences, web services allow organizations to communicate data without special knowledge of each other's computer information systems.

In EDI and web services, the different purchasing and ordering applications in each company interact automatically without any human input. No one has to lift a finger to click a mouse, enter data, or hit the return key. An **extranet**, by contrast, allows companies to exchange information and conduct transactions by purposely providing outsiders with direct, web browser–based access to authorized parts of a company's intranet or information system. Typically, user names and passwords are required to access an extranet.[48]

In an attempt to improve the marketing efforts of the contractors that it works with, Mitsubishi Electric Cooling & Heating developed its Creative Center extranet. The site provides a host of tools that contractors can use to grow their business. These include a range of company-approved marketing tools like newspaper ads, posters, and banners that each contractor can customize to his or her preference and use to promote both the contractor's business and the Mitsubishi electric brand.[49]

Finally, companies are reducing paperwork and manual information processing by using the Internet to electronically automate transactions with customers; this is similar to the way in which extranets are used to handle transactions with suppliers and distributors. For example, most airlines have automated the ticketing process by eliminating paper tickets altogether. Simply buy an e-ticket via the Internet, and then check yourself in online by printing your boarding pass from your personal computer or from a kiosk at the airport. Internet purchases, ticketless travel, and automated check-ins have together fully automated the purchase of airline tickets. Use of self-service kiosks is expanding, too.

Grocery store shoppers in Houston and San Antonio, Texas, can use Chirp automated kiosks to buy designer handbags from Coach, Michael Kors, or DKNY. Other Chirp machines display high-def scenes from recent movies while offering shoppers items like jewelry, perfume, or accessories inspired by the films. To buy, customers swipe a credit card, and as with a typical vending machine, out comes your purchase. Typically, the prices are 30 percent to 75 percent below retail because Chirp avoids the cost of retail employees or stores and buys discounted goods in small lots from designers like Gucci, Prada, and others. Returning goods is just as easy. Customers call a toll-free number and Chirp sends them a box with pre-paid postage to mail the goods back.[50]

In the long run, the goal is to link customer Internet sites with company intranets (or EDI) and extranets so that everyone—all the employees and managers within a company as well as the suppliers and distributors outside the company—involved in providing a service or making a product for a customer is automatically notified when a purchase is made. Companies that use EDI, web services, extranets, and the Internet to share data with customers and suppliers achieve increases in productivity 2.7 times larger than those that don't.[51]

17-4c SHARING KNOWLEDGE AND EXPERTISE

At the beginning of the chapter, we distinguished between raw data, which consist of facts and figures, and information, which consists of useful data that influence someone's choices and behavior. One more im-

MGMT TRENDS

Many retailers use information technology to make shopping more convenient and increase sales. At Walmart.com you can buy an item online and have it shipped, at no cost, for pickup at your local store. At Target.com, customers can see if local stores carry items from the website, but they can't buy them until they get to the store. Nordstrom department stores take information technology one step further by offering nationwide real-time inventory information. At Nordstrom.com, customers not only can see whether an item is in stock at their local store, they can see how many are in Nordstrom's warehouses and how many can be found at Nordstrom's 115 stores nationwide. Jamie Nordstrom, president of Nordstrom Direct, said, "We have 115 full-line stores out there—chances are one of them has it." And, because people can see that the items they want are in stock somewhere in a Nordstrom store, the percentage of people who buy an item after searching for it at Nordstrom.com has doubled. The advantage for customers is that they get what they were looking for. The advantage for Nordstrom is that it reduces store inventory at regular prices. Said Jamie Nordstrom, "By pulling merchandise from the store, you've now dramatically lessened the likelihood that you'll take a markdown." By giving customers real-time information, Nordstrom increased same-store sales by 8 percent.

Source: S. Clifford, "Nordstrom Links Online Inventory to Real World," *New York Times*, August 23, 2010, accessed October 10, 2010, http://www.nytimes.com/2010/08/24/business/24shop.html.

portant distinction needs to be made, namely, that data and information are not the same as knowledge. **Knowledge** is the understanding that one gains from information. Importantly, knowledge does not reside in information. Knowledge resides in people. That's why companies hire consultants and why family doctors refer patients to specialists. Unfortunately, it can be quite expensive to employ consultants, specialists, and experts. So companies have begun using two information technologies to capture and share the knowledge of consultants, specialists, and experts with other managers and workers: decision support systems and expert systems.

Whereas an executive information system speeds up and simplifies the acquisition of information, a **decision support system (DSS)** helps managers understand problems and potential solutions by acquiring and analyzing information with sophisticated models and tools.[52] Furthermore, whereas EIS programs are broad in scope and permit managers to retrieve all kinds of information about a company, DSS programs are usually narrow in scope and targeted toward helping managers solve specific kinds of problems. DSS programs have been developed to help managers pick the shortest and most efficient routes for delivery trucks, select the best combination of stocks for investors, and schedule the flow of inventory through complex manufacturing facilities.

It's important to understand that DSS programs don't replace managerial decision making; they *improve* it by furthering managers' and workers' understanding of the problems they face and the solutions that might work. Though used by just 2 percent of physicians, medical DSS programs hold the promise of helping doctors make more accurate patient diagnoses. A British study of eighty-eight cases misdiagnosed or initially misdiagnosed (to be correctly diagnosed much later) found that a medical DSS made the right diagnosis 69 percent of the time.[53] With a medical DSS, doctors enter patient data such as age, gender, weight, and medical symptoms. The medical DSS then produces a list of diseases and conditions, ranked by probability, low or high, or by medical specialty, such as cardiology or oncology. For instance, when emergency room physician Dr. Harold Cross treated a ten-year-old boy who had been ill with nausea and dizziness for two weeks, he wasn't sure what was wrong because the boy had a healthy appetite, no abdominal

Knowledge the understanding that one gains from information

Decision support system (DSS) an information system that helps managers understand specific kinds of problems and potential solutions

Expert system an information system that contains the specialized knowledge and decision rules used by experts and experienced decision makers so that nonexperts can draw on this knowledge base to make decisions

pain, and just one brief headache. However, when the medical DSS that Dr. Cross used suggested a possible problem in the back of the boy's brain, Cross ordered an MRI scan that revealed a tumor, which was successfully removed two days later. Says Dr. Cross, "My personal knowledge of the literature and physical findings would not have prompted me to suspect a brain tumor."[54]

Expert systems are created by capturing the specialized knowledge and decision rules used by experts and experienced decision makers. They permit nonexpert employees to draw on this expert knowledge base to make decisions. Most expert systems work by using a collection of "if–then" rules to sort through information and recommend a course of action. For example, let's say that you're using your American Express card to help your spouse celebrate a promotion. After dinner and a movie, the two of you stroll by a travel office with a Las Vegas poster in its window. Thirty minutes later, caught up in the moment, you find yourselves at the airport ticket counter trying to purchase last-minute tickets to Vegas. But there's just one problem. American Express didn't approve your purchase. In fact, the ticket counter agent is now on the phone with an American Express customer service agent. So what put a temporary halt to your weekend escape to Vegas? An expert system that American Express calls "Authorizer's Assistant."[55]

The first "if–then" rule that prevented your purchase was the rule "*if* a purchase is much larger than the cardholder's regular spending habits, *then* deny approval of the purchase." This if–then rule, just one of 3,000, is built into American Express's transaction-processing system that handles thousands of purchase requests per second. Now that the American Express customer service agent is on the line, he or she is prompted by the Authorizer's Assistant to ask the ticket counter agent to examine your identification. You hand over your driver's license and another credit card to prove you're you. Then the ticket agent asks for your address, phone number, Social Security number, and your mother's maiden name and relays the information to American Express. Finally, your ticket purchase is approved. Why? Because you met the last series of "if–then" rules. *If* the purchaser can provide proof of identity and *if* the purchaser can provide personal information that isn't common knowledge, *then* approve the purchase.

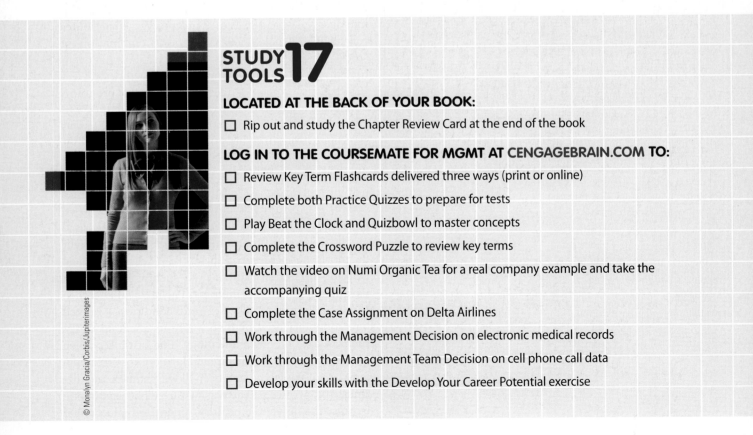

© Monalyn Gracia/Corbis/Jupiterimages

STUDY TOOLS 17

LOCATED AT THE BACK OF YOUR BOOK:

☐ Rip out and study the Chapter Review Card at the end of the book

LOG IN TO THE COURSEMATE FOR MGMT AT CENGAGEBRAIN.COM TO:

☐ Review Key Term Flashcards delivered three ways (print or online)

☐ Complete both Practice Quizzes to prepare for tests

☐ Play Beat the Clock and Quizbowl to master concepts

☐ Complete the Crossword Puzzle to review key terms

☐ Watch the video on Numi Organic Tea for a real company example and take the accompanying quiz

☐ Complete the Case Assignment on Delta Airlines

☐ Work through the Management Decision on electronic medical records

☐ Work through the Management Team Decision on cell phone call data

☐ Develop your skills with the Develop Your Career Potential exercise

4LTR Press solutions are designed for today's learners through the continuous feedback of students like you. Tell us what you think about MGMT and help us improve the learning experience for future students.

YOUR FEEDBACK MATTERS.

Complete the Speak Up
survey in CourseMate at
www.cengagebrain.com

 Follow us at
www.facebook.com/4ltrpress

18 Managing Service
and Manufacturing Operations

© Steve Cole/The Image Bank/Getty Images

© Menalyn Gracia Corbis/Jupiterimages

LEARNING OUTCOMES

18-1 Discuss the kinds of productivity and their importance in managing operations.

18-2 Explain the role that quality plays in managing operations.

18-3 Explain the essentials of managing a service business.

18-4 Describe the different kinds of manufacturing operations.

18-5 Explain why and how companies should manage inventory levels.

CHECK OUT
STUDY TOOLS
AT THE END OF THIS CHAPTER.

18-1 *Productivity*

Furniture manufacturers, hospitals, restaurants, automakers, airlines, and many other kinds of businesses struggle to find ways to produce quality products and services efficiently and then deliver them in a timely manner. Managing the daily production of goods and services, or **operations management**, is a key part of a manager's job. But an organization depends on the quality of its products and services as well as its productivity.

At 18.6 million cars and trucks per year, 50 percent more than in the United States, China is the largest and fastest-growing auto market in the world, with huge potential for even more growth as hundreds of millions of new middle-class Chinese families want to buy a car. But since Chinese consumers earn only about $7,500 a year, auto manufacturers will have to significantly cut development costs, which normally run about $1 billion per car model. Since that's far too expensive for a $7,500 car, automakers are slashing development costs and time by reusing designs from previously built cars. General Motors' Chinese brand, Baojun, is built on platform designs that GM had already used in other countries. Likewise, Honda's Chinese brand, Linian, is based on a previous generation of Honda's City model, while Nissan uses a recently retired car, the Tiida, for its new Chinese brand, Qichen. Reusing older designs cuts development time, largely eliminates development costs, and enables automakers to sell cars at prices that middle-class Chinese families can afford.[1]

At their core, organizations are production systems. Companies combine inputs such as labor, raw materials, capital, and knowledge to produce outputs in the form of finished products or services. **Produc-tivity** is a measure of performance that indicates how many inputs it takes to produce or create an output.

$$\text{Productivity} = \frac{\text{Outputs}}{\text{Inputs}}$$

The fewer inputs it takes to create an output (or the greater the output from one input), the higher the productivity. For example, a car's gas mileage is a common measure of productivity. A car that gets thirty-five miles (output) per gallon (input) is more productive and fuel efficient than a car that gets eighteen miles per gallon.

Let's examine **18-1a why productivity matters** and **18-1b the different kinds of productivity.**

18-1a WHY PRODUCTIVITY MATTERS

Why does productivity matter? For companies, higher productivity—that is, doing more with less—results in lower costs for the company, lower prices, faster service, higher market share, and higher profits. For example, every second saved in the drive-through lane at a fast-food restaurant increases sales by 1 percent. Furthermore, increasing the efficiency of drive-through service by 10 percent adds nearly 10 percent to a fast-food restaurant's sales. And with up to 75 percent of all fast-food restaurant sales coming from the drive-through window, it's no wonder that Wendy's (average drive-through time of 131 seconds per vehicle), Burger King (average time of 153 seconds per vehicle), and McDonald's (average

Operations management managing the daily production of goods and services

Productivity a measure of performance that indicates how many inputs it takes to produce or create an output

time of 167.1 seconds per vehicle) continue to look for ways to shorten the time it takes to process a drive-through order.[2]

Productivity matters so much at the drive-through that McDonald's is experimenting with outsourcing. At roughly fifty McDonald's franchises around the country, drive-through orders are taken by someone at a California call center. An operator can take orders from customers at restaurants in Honolulu one minute and in Gulfport, Mississippi, the next. Although it seems counterintuitive, initial results show the system has improved order-taking accuracy and improved productivity. During the ten seconds it takes for a car to pull away from the microphone at the drive-through, a call center operator can take the order of a different customer who has pulled up to the microphone at another restaurant, even if it's thousands of miles away. According to Jon Anton, cofounder of Bronco Communications, which operates the call center for McDonald's, the goal is "saving seconds to make millions," because more efficient service can lead to more sales and lower labor costs.[3]

The productivity of businesses within a country matters to that country because it results in a higher standard of living. One way productivity leads to a higher standard of living is through increased wages. When companies can do more with less, they can raise employee wages without increasing prices or sacrificing normal profits. For instance, recent government economic data indicated that U.S. companies were paying workers 2 percent more than in the previous year. But since workers were producing 1.8 percent more than they had the year before, real labor costs actually rose by 0.2 percent.[4] The average American family earned approximately $60,395 in 2010. If productivity grows 1 percent per year, that family's income will increase to $77,452 in 2035. But if productivity grows 2 percent per year, their income in 2035 will be $99,084, an increase of more than $21,000, and that's without working longer hours.[5]

Thanks to long-term increases in business productivity, the average American family today earns 19 percent more than the average family in 1980 and 40 percent more than the average family in 1967—and that's after accounting for inflation.[6] Rising income stemming from increased productivity creates other benefits as well. Productivity increased an average of 2.3 percent between 1995 and 2005, and then slowed to an average of 1.2 percent from 2005 to 2009.[7] And, from 1998 to 2008, the U.S. economy created nearly 16.6 million new jobs.[8]

And when more people have jobs that pay more, they give more to charity. For example, in 2007, Americans donated over $306 billion to charities, 3.9 percent more than they gave in 2006. Did Americans become more thoughtful, caring, conscientious, and giving? Probably not. Yet, because of strong increases in productivity during this time, the average American income increased by 30 percent, from $35,190 in 2000 to $45,840 in 2007.[9] Because more people earned more money, they were able to share their good fortune with others by giving more to charity.[10] Likewise, charitable giving fell slightly from $306 billion in 2007 to $291 billion in 2010, as average income was essentially unchanged from $46,240 in 2006 to $47,153 in 2010, while unemployment rose dramatically from 4.6 percent in 2006 to 9.7 percent in 2010.[11]

Another benefit of productivity is that it makes products more affordable or better. For example, while inflation has pushed the average cost of a new car to $27,950, increases in manufacturing productivity have actually made cars cheaper. In 1960, the average family needed 26 weeks of income to pay for an average car. Today, the average family needs just 23.2 weeks of income—and today's car is loaded with accessories that weren't available in the sixties, including air bags, power steering and brakes, CD and DVD players, seat warmers, air conditioning, and satellite navigation. So, in terms of real purchasing power, productivity gains have actually

made today's $27,950 car cheaper than the sixties car that sold for $2,000.[12]

18-1b KINDS OF PRODUCTIVITY

Two common measures of productivity are partial productivity and multifactor productivity. **Partial productivity** indicates how much of a particular kind of input it takes to produce an output.

$$\text{Partial Productivity} = \frac{\text{Outputs}}{\text{Single Kind of Input}}$$

Labor is one kind of input that is frequently used when determining partial productivity. *Labor productivity* typically indicates the cost or number of hours of labor it takes to produce an output. In other words, the lower the cost of the labor to produce a unit of output, or the less time it takes to produce a unit of output, the higher the labor productivity. For example, the automobile industry often measures labor productivity by determining the average number of hours of labor needed to completely assemble a car. According to the most recent *Harbour Report*, the three Detroit-based automakers have reached near parity with their Japanese rivals in manufacturing efficiency. Toyota and Chrysler assemble a car in 30.37 hours, Honda in 31.33 hours, GM in 32.29 hours, Nissan in 32.96 hours, and Ford in 33.88 hours. The gap between the most and least productive automakers narrowed from 10.51 labor hours in 2003 to just 3.5 labor hours in 2008.[13]

Partial productivity assesses how efficiently companies use only one input, such as labor, when creating outputs. Multifactor productivity is an overall measure of productivity that assesses how efficiently companies use all the inputs it takes to make outputs. More specifically, **multifactor productivity** indicates how much labor, capital, materials, and energy it takes to produce an output.[14]

$$\frac{\text{Multifactor}}{\text{Productivity}} = \frac{\text{Outputs}}{(\text{Labor} + \text{Capital} + \text{Materials} + \text{Energy})}$$

Exhibit 18.1 shows the trends in multifactor productivity across a number of U.S. industries since 1987.

With a 268 percent increase between 2002 (scaled at 100) and 2008 (when it reached a level of 368) and a thirtyfold increase since 1987, the growth in multifactor productivity in the computer and electronic products industry far exceeded the productivity growth in retail stores, auto manufacturing, mining,

Partial productivity a measure of performance that indicates how much of a particular kind of input it takes to produce an output

Multifactor productivity an overall measure of performance that indicates how much labor, capital, materials, and energy it takes to produce an output

EXHIBIT 18.1

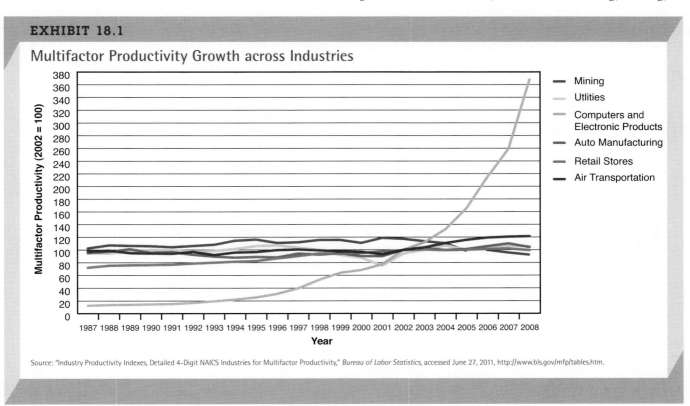

Multifactor Productivity Growth across Industries

Source: "Industry Productivity Indexes, Detailed 4-Digit NAICS Industries for Multifactor Productivity," *Bureau of Labor Statistics*, accessed June 27, 2011, http://www.bls.gov/mfp/tables.htm.

When Prices Rise

For apparel maker Hanes, a rise in the price of cotton is a huge problem. About two-thirds of the company's products consist of at least 90 percent cotton, meaning that any sharp rise in cotton prices will have a hugely adverse effect on the bottom line. This is exactly what happened in 2011, as cotton prices doubled, leading Hanesbrands CEO Richard Noll to announce that product prices would rise by as much as 30 percent. In order to bring some stability to its costs, Hanes is using flax as a substitute for cotton. The fiber is supplied by Oregon-based Naturally Advanced Technologies, which uses a special enzyme treatment to break down flax fiber, which is naturally quite tough, to make it soft like cotton.

Source: R. Dodes, "Hemmed in by Cotton, Hanes Eases into Flax," *Wall Street Journal*, April 12, 2011, accessed April 9, 2012, http://online.wsj.com/article /SB10001424052748703696704576222800474866630.html.

utilities, and air transportation as well as most other industries tracked by the U.S. government.

Should managers use multiple or partial productivity measures? In general, they should use both. Multifactor productivity indicates a company's overall level of productivity relative to its competitors. In the end, that's what counts most. However, multifactor productivity measures don't indicate the specific contributions that labor, capital, materials, or energy make to overall productivity. To analyze the contributions of these individual components, managers need to use partial productivity measures. Doing so can help them determine what factors need to be adjusted or in what areas adjustment can make the most difference in overall productivity.

18-2 *Quality*

With the average car costing $27,950, car buyers want to make sure that they're getting good quality for their money.[15] Fortunately, as indicated by the number of problems per 100 cars (PP100), today's cars are of much higher quality than earlier models. In 1981, Japanese cars averaged 240 PP100. General Motors' cars averaged 670, Ford's averaged 740, and Chrysler's averaged 870 PP100!

Quality a product or service free of deficiencies, or the characterics of a product or service that satisfies customer needs

In other words, as measured by PP100, the quality of American cars was two to three times worse than that of Japanese cars. By 1992, however, U.S. carmakers had made great strides, significantly reducing the number of problems to an average of 155 PP100. Japanese vehicles had improved, too, averaging just 125 PP100. According to the 2011 J. D. Power and Associates survey of initial car quality, however, overall quality improved to 107 problems per 100 vehicles, and even the worst rated cars beat the scores of the Japanese cars of decades ago. Category leaders like Porsche, Acura, Mercedes-Benz, Lexus, Ford, and Honda came in with scores under 100. That means there's fewer than one problem per car![16]

The American Society for Quality gives two meanings for **quality**. It can mean a product or service free of deficiencies, such as the number of problems per 100 cars, or it can mean the characteristics of a product or service that satisfy customer needs.[17] Today's cars are of higher quality than those produced twenty years ago in both senses. Not only do they have fewer problems per 100 cars, they also have a number of additional standard features (power brakes and steering, stereo/CD/MP3 player, power windows and locks, air bags, cruise control).

In this part of the chapter, you will learn about 18-2a quality-related characteristics for products and services, 18-2b ISO 9000 and 14000, 18-2c the Baldrige National Quality Award, and 18-2d total quality management.

18-2a QUALITY-RELATED CHARACTERISTICS FOR PRODUCTS AND SERVICES

Quality products usually possess three characteristics: reliability, serviceability, and durability.[18] A breakdown occurs when a product quits working or doesn't do what it was designed to do. The longer it takes for a product to break down, or the longer the time between breakdowns, the more reliable the product. Consequently, many companies define *product reliability* in terms of the average time between breakdowns. *Serviceability* refers to how easy or difficult it is to fix a product. The easier it is to maintain a working product or fix a broken product, the more serviceable that product is.

A product breakdown assumes that a product can be repaired. However, some products don't break down; they fail. *Product failure* means products can't be repaired. They can only be replaced. *Durability* is defined as the mean time to failure. Typically, for example, when an LCD screen quits working, it "dies" and can't be repaired. Consequently, durability, or the average time before failure, is a key part of LCD quality. Why buy a great-looking LCD if it's only going to last a few years? Indeed, Toshiba is now producing thin-film transistor LCDs with a mean time between failures of 100,000 hours, or 11.4 years.[19]

While high-quality products are characterized by reliability, serviceability, and durability, services are different. There's no point in assessing the durability of a service because services don't last but are consumed the minute they're performed. For example, once a lawn service has mowed your lawn, the job is done until the mowers come back next week to do it again. Services also don't have serviceability. You can't maintain or fix a service. If a service wasn't performed correctly, all you can do is perform it again. Rather than serviceability and durability, the quality of service interactions often depends on how the service provider interacts with the customer. Was the service provider friendly, rude, or helpful? Five characteristics typically distinguish a quality service: reliability, tangibles, responsiveness, assurance, and empathy.[20]

Service reliability is the ability to consistently perform a service well. Studies clearly show that reliability matters more to customers than anything else when buying services. When you take your clothes to the dry cleaner, you don't want them returned with cracked buttons or wrinkles down the front. If your dry cleaner gives you back perfectly clean and pressed clothes every time, it's providing a reliable service.

Also, although services themselves are not tangible (you can't see or touch them), services are provided in tangible places. Thus, *tangibles* refer to the appearance of the offices, equipment, and personnel involved with the delivery of a service. One of the best examples of the effect of tangibles on the perception of quality is the restroom. When you eat at a fancy restaurant, you expect clean, upscale, restrooms. How different is your perception of a business, say a gas station, if it has clean restrooms rather than filthy ones?

Responsiveness is the promptness and willingness with which service providers give good service. *Assurance* is the confidence that service providers are knowledgeable, courteous, and trustworthy. *Empathy* is the extent to which service providers give individual attention and care to customers' concerns and problems.

When Apple first launched its retail stores, they were widely predicted to fail given all of the locations already available where consumers could buy computer and electronics equipment. Those predictions were wrong, however, as over a quarter billion people visited Apple's 326 stores in 2012. Why? Because the stores are great at delivering responsiveness, assurance, and empathy.

At Apple stores, responsiveness manifests itself in a sales philosophy of not selling. Instead, Apple store employees are trained to help customers solve problems. An Apple training manual says, "Your job is to understand all of your customers' needs—some of which they may not even realize they have." David Ambrose, a former Apple store employee, says, "You were never trying to close a sale. It was about finding solutions for a customer and finding their pain points."

Apple store employees demonstrate assurance through the high level of training that they receive. Apple "geniuses," who staff the "Genius Bar" in each Apple store, are trained at Apple headquarters and, according to Apple's website, "can take care of everything from troubleshooting your problems to actual repairs." Geniuses are regularly tested on their knowledge and problem-solving skills to maintain their certification. Other Apple store employees are highly trained, too, and are not allowed to help customers until they've spent two to four weeks shadowing experienced store employees.

The acronym, APPLE, instructs employees on how to empathetically engage with customers: "Approach customers with a personalized warm welcome," "Probe politely to understand all the customer's needs," "Present a solution for the customer to take home today," "Listen for and resolve any issues or concerns," and "End with a fond farewell and an invitation to return." And when customers are frustrated and become emotional, the advice is to "listen and limit your responses to simple reassurances that you are doing so. 'Uh-huh' 'I understand,' etc."

The results from Apple's retail approach speak for themselves, as Apple retail sales average $4,406 per square foot, higher than Tiffany & Co. jewelry stores ($3,070), Coach luxury retail ($1,776), or Best Buy ($880), a full-service computer and electronics store.[21]

18-2b ISO 9000 AND 14000

ISO, pronounced *eye-so*, comes from the Greek word *isos*, meaning "equal, similar, alike, or identical" and is also an acronym for the International Organization for Standardization, which helps set standards for 162 countries. The purpose of this agency is to develop and publish standards that facilitate the international exchange of goods and services.[22] **ISO 9000** is a series of five international standards, from ISO 9000 to ISO 9004, for achieving consistency in quality management and quality assurance in companies throughout the world. **ISO 14000** is a series of international standards for managing, monitoring, and minimizing an organization's harmful effects on the environment.[23] (For more on environmental quality and issues, see subsection 16-3e of Chapter 16 on controlling waste and pollution.)

The ISO 9000 and 14000 standards publications, which are available from the American National Standards Institute (see the end of this section), are general and can be used for manufacturing any kind of product or delivering any kind of service. Importantly, the ISO 9000 standards don't describe how to make a better-quality car, computer, or widget. Instead, they describe how companies can extensively document (and thus standardize) the steps they take to create and improve the quality of their products. Why should companies go to the trouble to achieve ISO 9000 certification? Because their customers increasingly want them to. In fact, studies show that customers clearly prefer to buy from companies that are ISO 9000 certi-

fied. Companies, in turn, believe that being ISO 9000 certified helps them keep customers who might otherwise switch to an ISO 9000–certified competitor.[24]

To become ISO certified, a process that can take months, a company must show that it is following its own procedures for improving production, updating design plans and specifications, keeping machinery in top condition, educating and training workers, and satisfactorily dealing with customer complaints.[25] An accredited third party oversees the ISO certification process, just as a certified public accountant verifies that a company's financial accounts are up-to-date and accurate. Once a company has been certified as ISO 9000 compliant, the accredited third party will issue an ISO 9000 certificate that the company can use in its advertising and publications. This is the quality equivalent of the *Good Housekeeping* Seal of Approval. But continued ISO 9000 certification is not guaranteed. Accredited third parties typically conduct periodic audits to make sure the company is still following quality procedures. If it is not, its certification is suspended or canceled.

To get additional information on ISO 9000 guidelines and procedures, see the American National Standards Institute (http://www.webstore.ansi.org; the ISO 9000 and ISO 14000 standards publications are available here for about $400 and $300, respectively), the American Society for Quality (http://www.asq.org), and the International Organization for Standardization (http://www.iso.org).

18-2c BALDRIGE NATIONAL QUALITY AWARD

The Baldrige National Quality Award, which is administered by the U.S. government's National Institute for Standards and Technology, is given "to recognize U.S. companies for their achievements in quality and business performance and to raise awareness about the importance of quality and performance excellence as a competitive edge."[26] Each year, up to three awards may be given in the categories of manufacturing, education, health care, service, small business, and nonprofit.

The cost of applying for the Baldrige Award includes a $150 eligibility fee, an application fee of $7,000 for manufacturing firms and $3,500 for small businesses, and a site visitation fee of $20,000 to $35,000 for manufacturing firms and $10,000 to $17,000 for small businesses.[27] Why does it cost so much? Because you get a great deal of useful information about your business even if you don't win. At a minimum, each company that applies receives an extensive report based on 300 hours of assessment from at least eight business and quality experts. At $10 an hour for small businesses and about $20 an hour for manufacturing and service businesses, the *Journal for Quality and Participation* called the Baldrige feedback report "the best bargain in consulting in America."[28] Arnold Weimerskirch, former chair of the Baldrige Award panel of judges and vice president of quality at Honeywell, says, "The application and review process for the Baldrige Award is the best, most cost-effective and comprehensive business health audit you can get."[29]

Businesses that apply for the Baldrige Award are judged on a 1,000-point scale based on the seven criteria shown in Exhibit 18.2: leadership; strategic planning; customer focus; measurement, analysis, and knowledge management; workforce focus; process management; and results.[30] Results are clearly the most important category, as it takes up 450 out of 1,000 points. In other words, in addition to the six other criteria, companies must show that they have achieved superior quality when it comes to products and services, customers, financial performance and market share, treatment of employees, work systems

and processes, and leadership and social responsibility. This emphasis on results is what differentiates the Baldrige Award from the ISO 9000 standards. The Baldrige Award indicates the extent to which companies have actually achieved world-class quality. The ISO 9000 standards simply indicate whether a company is following the management system it put into place to improve quality. In fact, ISO 9000 certification

The National Institute of Standards and Technology (NIST) is an agency of the U.S. Commerce Department.

EXHIBIT 18.2

Criteria for the Baldrige National Quality Award

2007 Categories/Items	Point Values
1 LEADERSHIP	**120**
1.1 Senior Leadership	70
1.2 Governance and Social Responsibilities	50
2 STRATEGIC PLANNING	**85**
2.1 Strategy Development	40
2.2 Strategy Deployment	45
3 CUSTOMER FOCUS	**85**
3.1 Customer Engagement	40
3.2 Voice of the Customer	45
4 MEASUREMENT, ANALYSIS, AND KNOWLEDGE MANAGEMENT	**90**
4.1 Measurement, Analysis, and Improvement of Organizational Performance	45
4.2 Management of Information, Information Technology, and Knowledge	45
5 WORKFORCE FOCUS	**85**
5.1 Workforce Engagement	45
5.2 Workforce Environment	40
6 PROCESS MANAGEMENT	**85**
6.1 Work Systems	35
6.2 Work Processes	50
7 RESULTS	**450**
7.1 Product Outcomes	100
7.2 Customer-Focused Outcomes	70
7.3 Financial and Market Outcomes	70
7.4 Workforce-Focused Outcomes	70
7.5 Process Effectiveness Outcomes	70
7.6 Leadership Outcomes	70
TOTAL POINTS 1,000	

Source: "Criteria for Performance Excellence," *Baldrige National Quality Program 2007*, accessed September 15, 2008, http://www.quality.nist.gov/PDF_files/2008_Business_Nonprofit_Criteria.pdf.

You're the Best!

Today's savvy consumer is likely to seek out advice before buying anything, and of course quality and reliability ratings are available for almost any product from dozens of sources, such as the U.S. Consumer Product Safety Commission's reports on batteries, Edmunds.com's car-buying guides, and any number of magazines that cover the latest high-tech gadgets. For example, *PCWorld* magazine annually surveys its approximately 60,000 readers on which tech brands they consider most trustworthy. In the smartphones category for 2011, the iPhone was the clear winner for reliability, ease of use, and features; Verizon scored best of the national cell phone carriers for wireless service reliability, data speed, call quality, and customer service.

Source: M. Sullivan, "Smartphone Reliability and Satisfaction: iPhone Tops the List," *PCWorld*, December, 5, 2011, accessed April 5, 2012, http://www.pcworld.com/article/244607/smartphone_reliability_and_satisfaction_iphone_tops_the_list.html.

covers less than 10 percent of the requirements for the Baldrige Award.[31]

Why should companies go to the trouble of applying for the Baldrige Award? Earnest Deavenport, CEO of Eastman Chemical, explains, "Eastman, like other Baldrige Award winners, didn't apply the concepts of total quality management to win an award. We did it to win customers. We did it to grow. We did it to prosper and to remain competitive in a world marketplace."[32] Furthermore, the companies that have won the Baldrige Award have achieved superior financial returns. Since 1988, an investment in Baldrige Award winners would have outperformed the Standard & Poor's 500 stock index 80 percent of the time.[33]

18-2d TOTAL QUALITY MANAGEMENT

Total quality management (TQM) is an integrated, organization-wide strategy for improving product and service quality.[34] TQM is not a specific tool or technique. Rather, TQM is a philosophy or overall approach to management that is characterized by three principles: customer focus and satisfaction, continuous improvement, and teamwork.[35]

Although most economists, accountants, and financiers argue that companies exist to earn profits for shareholders, TQM suggests that customer focus and customer satisfaction should be a company's primary goals. **Customer focus** means that the entire organization, from top to bottom, should be focused on meeting customers' needs. The result of that customer focus should be **customer satisfaction**, which occurs when the company's products or services meet or exceed customers' expectations.

At companies where TQM is taken seriously, such as Enterprise Rent-A-Car, paychecks and promotions depend on keeping customers satisfied.[36] Enterprise measures customer satisfaction with a detailed survey called the Enterprise Service Quality index. Enterprise not only ranks each branch office by operating profits and customer satisfaction but also makes promotions to higher-paying jobs contingent on above-average customer satisfaction scores. According to Andy Taylor, Enterprise's CEO, "Once we showed we were serious—a couple of star performers who had achieved good growth and profit numbers but had generated below-average satisfaction scores were passed over for promotions—all doubt about the importance of the scores vanished."[37] Not surprisingly, this emphasis on quality increased the number of completely satisfied Enterprise Rent-A-Car customers from the high 60 percent range to the high 70 percent range in just five years. As a result, Enterprise customers are three times more likely to rent an Enterprise car again than are customers of other car rental companies, and Enterprise has topped J. D. Power and Associates's rental car satisfaction ratings for five straight years.[38]

Continuous improvement is an ongoing commitment to increase product and service quality by constantly assessing and improving the processes and procedures used to create those products and services. How do companies know whether they're achieving continuous improvement? Besides higher customer satisfaction, continuous improvement is usually associated with a reduction in variation. **Variation** is a deviation in the form, condition, or appearance of a product from the quality standard for that product. The less a product varies from the quality standard, or the more consistently a company's products meet a quality standard, the higher the quality. At Freudenberg-NOK, a manufacturer of seals and gaskets for the automotive industry, continuous improvement means shooting for a goal of Six Sigma quality, meaning just 3.4 defective or nonstandard parts per million (ppm). Achieving this goal would eliminate almost all product variation. In a recent year, Freudenberg-NOK made over 200 million seals and gaskets with a defect rate of 9 ppm.[39] This represents a significant improvement from seven years before, when Freudenberg-NOK was averaging a defect rate of 650 ppm. General manager Gary VanWambeke says, "The whole goal is variation reduction," so Freudenberg-NOK expects the quality of its products to continue to improve.[40]

The third principle of TQM is teamwork. **Teamwork** means collaboration between managers and nonmanagers, across business functions, and between the company and its customers and suppliers. In short, quality improves when everyone in the company is given the incentive to work together and the responsibility and authority to make improvements and solve problems. Reid Carr, the president of Red Door Interactive, an Internet presence management firm, believes that teamwork is critical to his company's success. Therefore, his employees work collaboratively on multiple account teams made up of people from throughout the company. He says, "Forming teams made up of employees that perform different job functions allows staff to better understand how their colleagues contribute. Combining different skills sets and allowing staff members to work together to complete a client project that will produce better outcomes and allow individuals to recognize and appreciate what each person brings to the table." Furthermore, he says, "it's the formation of internal teams that yields ultimate results and leads to increased productivity among employees."[41]

Customer focus and satisfaction, continuous improvement, and teamwork mutually reinforce each other to improve quality throughout a company. Customer-focused, continuous improvement is necessary to increase customer satisfaction. At the same time, continuous improvement depends on teamwork from different functional and hierarchical parts of the company.

18-3 *Service Operations*

At the start of this chapter, you learned that operations management means managing the daily production of goods and services. Then you learned that to manage production, you must oversee the factors that affect productivity and quality. In this half of the chapter, you will learn about managing operations in service and manufacturing businesses.

The chapter ends with a discussion of inventory management, a key factor in a company's profitability.

Imagine that your trusty TIVO digital video recorder (DVR) breaks down as you try to record your favorite TV show. You've got two choices. You can run to Wal-Mart and spend $250 to purchase a new DVR, or you can spend less (you hope) to have it fixed at a repair shop. Either way, you end up with the same thing, a working DVR. However, the first choice, getting a new DVR, involves buying a physical product (a good), while the second, dealing with a repair shop, involves buying a service.

Services differ from goods in several ways. First, goods are produced or made, but services are performed. In other words, services are almost always labor-intensive: Someone typically has to perform the service for you. A repair shop could give you the parts needed to repair your old DVR, but you're still going to have a broken DVR without the technician to perform the repairs. Second, goods are tangible, but services are intangible. You can touch and see that new DVR, but you can't touch or see the service provided by the technician who fixed your old DVR. All you can "see" is that the DVR works. Third, services are perishable and unstorable. If you don't use them when they're available, they're wasted. For example, if your DVR repair shop is backlogged on repair jobs, then you'll just have to wait until next week to get your DVR repaired. You can't store an unused service and use it when you like. By contrast, you can purchase a good, such as motor oil, and store it until you're ready to use it. Finally, services account for 59 percent of gross national product, whereas manufacturing accounts for only 30.8 percent.[42]

Because services are different from goods, managing a service operation is different from managing a manufacturing or production operation. *Let's look at **18-3a the service-profit chain** and **18-3b service recovery and empowerment.***

18-3a THE SERVICE-PROFIT CHAIN

One of the key assumptions in the service business is that success depends on how well employees—that is, service providers—deliver their services to customers. But success actually begins with how well management treats service employees, as the service-profit chain, depicted in Exhibit 18.3 on the next page, demonstrates.[43]

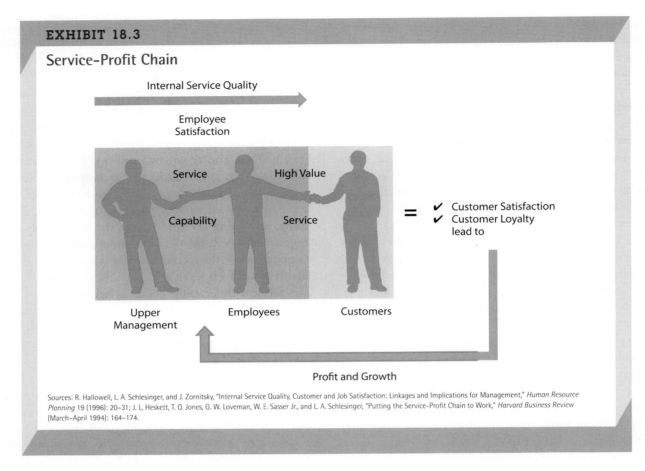

EXHIBIT 18.3

Service–Profit Chain

Internal Service Quality

Employee Satisfaction

Service

Capability

High Value

Service

Upper Management

Employees

Customers

= ✔ Customer Satisfaction
✔ Customer Loyalty lead to

Profit and Growth

Sources: R. Hallowell, L. A. Schlesinger, and J. Zornitsky, "Internal Service Quality, Customer and Job Satisfaction: Linkages and Implications for Management," *Human Resource Planning* 19 (1996): 20–31; J. L. Heskett, T. O. Jones, G. W. Loveman, W. E. Sasser Jr., and L. A. Schlesinger, "Putting the Service-Profit Chain to Work," *Harvard Business Review* (March–April 1994): 164–174.

The key concept behind the service-profit chain is **internal service quality**, meaning the quality of treatment that employees receive from a company's internal service providers, such as management, payroll and benefits, human resources, and so forth. For example, employees at Clif Bar, a maker of organic energy bars and drinks, get 2.5 hours a week to work out at the company's fitness center, which is equipped with a climbing wall and everything from yoga to spin classes to free sessions with trainers and nutritionists; have a concierge that provides car washes, laundry, dry cleaning and other services; are eligible for incentives for car pools (up to $960 a year), buying a biodiesel car ($6,500) or a commuter bike ($500), or making eco-improvements in their homes ($1,000); and are enrolled in the employee stock ownership plan, which vests after three years, at which point the employee receives full ownership shares of the company. These extraordinary benefits are clearly a sign of a company with an internal service quality orientation.[44]

As depicted in Exhibit 18.3, good internal service leads to employee satisfac-

Internal service quality
the quality of treatment employees receive from management and other divisions of a company

tion and service capability. *Employee satisfaction* occurs when companies treat employees in a way that meets or exceeds their expectations. In other words, the better employees are treated, the more satisfied they are, and the more likely they are to give high-value service that satisfies customers. How employers treat employees is important because it affects service capability. *Service capability* is an employee's perception of his or her ability to serve customers well. When an organization serves its employees in ways that help them to do their jobs well, employees, in turn, are more likely to believe that they can and ought to provide high-value service to customers.

Finally, according to the service-profit chain shown in Exhibit 18.3, *high-value service* leads to *customer satisfaction* and *customer loyalty*, which, in turn, lead to *long-term profits and growth* (see box "Not Just An Average Joe").[45] What's the link between customer satisfaction and loyalty and profits? To start, the average business keeps only 70 to 90 percent of its existing customers each year. No big deal, you say? Just replace leaving customers with new customers. Well, there's one significant problem with that solution. It costs ten times as much to find a new customer

Not Just an Average Joe

I'm just 75¢!

One company that understands the relationship between high-value service, customer loyalty, and profits is Trader Joe's, a California-based chain of grocery stores, where everything employees do is focused on the customer. Perishable items, such as apples or bananas, are sold by the unit (for example, $0.75 per apple) rather than by the pound, so that customers know how much they are spending before checking out. When employees put products on the floor, they aren't told what the margin is on the products. So instead of stocking items according to what makes the most money, employees stock what's popular with customers. Refunds are made cheerfully—employees are encouraged to give full refunds on any and all products, no questions asked. Thanks to this great level of customer service, Trader Joe's is one of the hottest retail chains in the United States, with sales of $8 billion.

Source: B. Kowitt, "Inside the Secret World of Trader Joe's," *Fortune*, August 23, 2010, http://money.cnn.com/2010/08/20/news/companies/inside_trader_joes_full_version.fortune/index.htm.

as it does to keep an existing customer. Also, new customers typically buy only 20 percent as much as established customers. In fact, keeping existing customers is so cost-effective that most businesses could double their profits by simply keeping 5 percent more customers per year![46] How does this work? Imagine that keeping more of your customers turns some of those customers into customers for life. How much of a difference would that make to company profits? Consider that just one lifetime customer spends $8,000 on pizza and over $330,000 on luxury cars![47]

18-3b SERVICE RECOVERY AND EMPOWERMENT

When mistakes are made, when problems occur, and when customers become dissatisfied with the service they've received, service businesses must switch from the process of service delivery to the process of **service recovery**, or restoring customer satisfaction to strongly dissatisfied customers.[48] Service recovery sometimes requires service employees to not only fix whatever mistake was made but also perform heroic service acts that delight highly dissatisfied customers by far surpassing their expectations of fair treatment. Jason Friend, co-founder of 37signals.com, which provides web-based collaboration software such as Basecamp and Campfire, bought a custom bike via the web from Mission Bicycle Company in San Francisco. When the bike arrived, he found a large gash on the side of the bike's frame. He described what happened when he contacted Mission: "They said sending the whole bike back would be overkill since the only thing

that was damaged was the frame. Further, the bike was rideable—it was just a paint problem—so sending the bike back would mean I didn't have a bike for a week or so. They didn't feel good about that. So here's what they did: They called up a local shop (On The Route) and arranged to ship a new frame to them. Then one of their bike techs would drive down to my office and swap the frames and reassemble the bike for me while I waited. All of this at Mission's expense." He concluded by saying, "That's incredible customer service. I'm a happy customer for life. If you're in the market for a great custom bike, check out the good people and products at Mission Bicycle Company."[49]

Unfortunately, when mistakes occur, service employees often don't have the discretion to resolve customer complaints. Customers who want service employees to correct or make up for poor service are frequently told, "I'm not allowed to do that," "I'm just following company rules," or "I'm sorry, only managers are allowed to make changes of any kind." In other words, company rules prevent them from engaging in acts of service recovery meant to turn dissatisfied customers back into satisfied customers. The result is frustration for customers and service employees and lost customers for the company.

Now, however, many companies are empowering their service employees.[50] In Chapter 9, you learned that *empowering workers* means permanently passing decision-making author-ity and responsibility from managers to workers. With respect to service recovery, empowering workers means

Service recovery restoring customer satisfaction to strongly dissatisfied customers

Make-to-order operation
a manufacturing operation that does not start processing or assembling products until a customer order is received

giving service employees the authority and responsibility to make decisions that immediately solve customer problems.[51] For example, when customers call into Nicor National, an energy utility, to ask for credits to their accounts, they are not transferred to a billing department. They are not put on hold while the operator looks for a supervisor or manager. Instead, the operator, who is empowered to make this decision, simply awards the credit without having to check with anyone else. According to Barbara Porter, the company's vice president of business development and customer service, empowering the call centers in this way is a quick, easy resolution. "They're professionals and we trust them to make the right decisions," says Porter.[52]

18-4 *Manufacturing Operations*

Ford makes cars and Dell does computers. BP produces gasoline, whereas Sherwin-Williams makes paint. Boeing makes jet planes, but Budweiser makes beer. Maxtor makes hard drives, and Maytag makes appliances. The *manufacturing operations* of

these companies all produce physical goods. But not all manufacturing operations, especially these, are the same. *Let's learn how various manufacturing operations differ in terms of* **18-4a the amount of processing that is done to produce and assemble a product** *and* **18-4b the flexibility to change the number, kind, and characteristics of products that are produced.**

18-4a AMOUNT OF PROCESSING IN MANUFACTURING OPERATIONS

Manufacturing operations can be classified according to the amount of processing or assembly that occurs after a customer order is received. The highest degree of processing occurs in **make-to-order operations**. A make-to-order operation does not start processing or assembling products until it receives a customer order. In fact, some make-to-order operations may not even order parts until a customer order is received. Not surprisingly, make-to-order operations produce or assemble highly specialized or customized products for customers (see box "Electric Cars, Made to Order").

For example, **Dell** has one of the most advanced make-to-order operations in the computer business. Because Dell has no finished goods inventory and no component parts inventory, its computers always have the latest, most advanced components, and Dell can

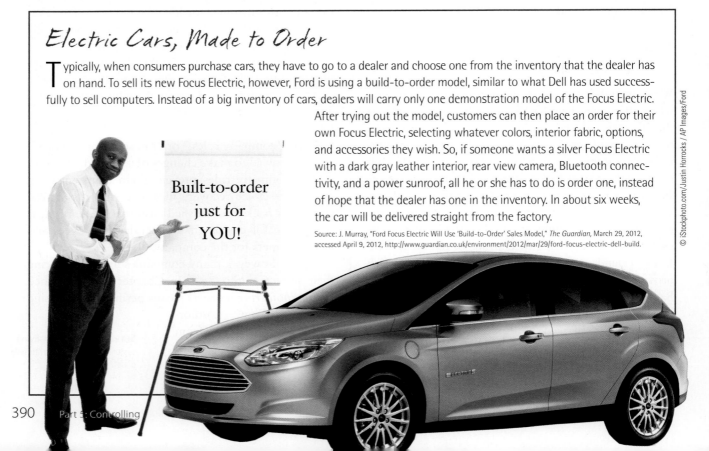

Electric Cars, Made to Order

Typically, when consumers purchase cars, they have to go to a dealer and choose one from the inventory that the dealer has on hand. To sell its new Focus Electric, however, Ford is using a build-to-order model, similar to what Dell has used successfully to sell computers. Instead of a big inventory of cars, dealers will carry only one demonstration model of the Focus Electric.

After trying out the model, customers can then place an order for their own Focus Electric, selecting whatever colors, interior fabric, options, and accessories they wish. So, if someone wants a silver Focus Electric with a dark gray leather interior, rear view camera, Bluetooth connectivity, and a power sunroof, all he or she has to do is order one, instead of hope that the dealer has one in the inventory. In about six weeks, the car will be delivered straight from the factory.

Source: J. Murray, "Ford Focus Electric Will Use 'Build-to-Order' Sales Model," *The Guardian*, March 29, 2012, accessed April 9, 2012, http://www.guardian.co.uk/environment/2012/mar/29/ford-focus-electric-dell-build.

Built-to-order just for YOU!

© iStockphoto.com/Justin Horrocks / AP Images/Ford

pass on price cuts to customers. Plus, Dell can customize all of its orders, big and small. So whether you're ordering five thousand personal computers for your company or just one personal computer for your home, Dell doesn't make the computers until you order them.

A moderate degree of processing occurs in **assemble-to-order operations**. A company using an assemble-to-order operation divides its manufacturing or assembly process into separate parts or modules. The company orders parts and assembles modules ahead of customer orders. Then, based on actual customer orders or on research forecasting what customers will want, those modules are combined to create semi-customized products. For example, when a customer orders a new car, General Motors may have already ordered the basic parts or modules it needs from suppliers. In other words, based on sales forecasts, GM may already have ordered enough tires, air-conditioning compressors, brake systems, and seats from suppliers to accommodate nearly all customer orders on a particular day. Special orders from customers and car dealers are then used to determine the final assembly checklist for particular cars as they move down the assembly line.

The lowest degree of processing occurs in **make-to-stock operations** (also called build-to-stock). Because the products are standardized, meaning each product is exactly the same as the next, a company using a make-to-stock operation starts ordering parts and assembling finished products before receiving customer orders. Customers then purchase these standardized products—such as Rubbermaid storage containers, microwave ovens, and vacuum cleaners—at retail stores or directly from the manufacturer. Because parts are ordered and products are assembled before customers order the products, make-to-stock operations are highly dependent on the accuracy of sales forecasts. If sales forecasts are incorrect, make-to-stock operations may end up building too many or too few products, or they may make products with the wrong features or without the features that customers want.

18-4b FLEXIBILITY OF MANUFACTURING OPERATIONS

A second way to categorize manufacturing operations is by **manufacturing flexibility**, meaning the degree to which manufacturing operations can easily and quickly change the number, kind, and characteristics of products they produce. Flexibility allows companies to respond quickly to changes in the marketplace (i.e., respond to competitors and customers) and to reduce the lead time between ordering and final delivery of products. There is often a trade-off between flexibility and cost, however, with the most flexible manufacturing operations frequently having higher costs per unit and the least flexible operations having lower costs per unit. Some common manufacturing operations, arranged in order from the least flexible to the most flexible, are continuous-flow production, line-flow production, batch production, and job shops.

Most production processes generate finished products at a discrete rate. A product is completed, and then—perhaps a few seconds, minutes, or hours later—another is completed, and so on. For instance, if you stood at the end of an automobile assembly line, nothing much would seem to be happening for fifty-five seconds of every minute. In that last five seconds, however, a new car would be started and driven off the assembly line, ready for its new owner. By contrast, in **continuous-flow production**, products are produced continuously rather than at a discrete rate. Like a water hose that is never turned off and just keeps on flowing, production of the final product never stops. Liquid chemicals and petroleum products are examples of continuous-flow production. If you're still struggling with this concept, think of Play-Doh. Continuous-flow production is similar to squeezing Play-Doh into a toy press and watching the various shapes ooze out of the Play-Doh machine. With continuous-flow production, the Play-Doh machine would never stop oozing or producing rectangle- or triangle-shaped Play-Doh. Because of their complexity, continuous-flow production processes are the most standardized and least flexible manufacturing operations.

Line-flow production processes are preestablished, occur in a serial or linear manner, and are dedicated to making one type of product. In this way, the ten different steps required to make product X can be completed in a separate manufacturing process (with separate machines, parts, treatments, locations, and workers) from the twelve different steps required to

Assemble-to-order operation a manufacturing operation that divides manufacturing processes into separate parts or modules that are combined to create semicustomized products

Make-to-stock operation a manufacturing operation that orders parts and assembles standardized products before receiving customer orders

Manufacturing flexibility the degree to which manufacturing operations can easily and quickly change the number, kind, and characteristics of products they produce

Continuous-flow production a manufacturing operation that produces goods at a continuous, rather than a discrete, rate

Line-flow production manufacturing processes that are preestablished, occur in a serial or linear manner, and are dedicated to making one type of product

make product Y. Line-flow production processes are inflexible because they are typically dedicated to manufacturing one kind of product. For example, nearly every city has a local bottling plant for soft drinks or beer. The processes or steps in bottling plants are serial, meaning they must occur in a particular order. After empty bottles are sterilized, they are filled with soft drinks or beer using a special dispenser that distributes the liquid down the inside walls of the bottle. This fills the bottle from the bottom up and displaces the air that was in the bottle. The bottles are then crowned or capped, checked for underfilling and missing caps, labeled, inspected a final time for fill levels and missing labels, and then placed in cases that are shrink-wrapped on pallets and put on trucks for delivery.[53]

The next most flexible manufacturing operation is **batch production**, which involves the manufacture of large batches of different products in standard lot sizes. A worker in a batch production operation will perform the same manufacturing process on one hundred copies of product X, followed by two hundred copies of product Y, and then fifty copies of product Z. Furthermore, these batches move through each manufacturing department or process in identical order. So, if the paint department follows chemical treatment, and chemical treatment is now processing a batch of fifty copies of product Z, then the paint department's next task will be to paint fifty copies of product Z. Batch production is finding increasing use among restaurant chains. To ensure consistency in the taste and quality of their products, many restaurant chains have central kitchens, or commissaries, that produce batches of food such as mashed potatoes, stuffing, macaroni and cheese, rice, quiche filling, and chili, in volumes ranging from 10 to 200 gallons. These batches are then delivered to the individual restaurant locations, which in turn serve the food to customers.

Next in terms of flexibility is the job shop. **Job shops** are typically small manufacturing operations that handle special manufacturing processes or jobs. In contrast to batch production, which handles large batches of different products, job shops typically handle very small batches, some as small as one product or process per batch. Basically, each job in a job shop is different, and once a job is done, the job shop

moves on to a completely different job or manufacturing process for, most likely, a different customer. For example, **Grauch Enterprises** in Philipsburg, Pennsylvania, is a job shop that mills, turns, drills, paints, and finishes everything from plastics, such as nylon, polycarbonates, and laminates, to metals, such as brass, aluminum, stainless and alloy steels, titanium, and cast iron. It made 650 different parts for one customer alone and received one order to make 5,000 units out of 20,000 individual parts. When it comes to making different parts for different customers, owner Fred Grauch says, "There's very little we won't try."[54]

18-5 *Inventory*

Inventory is the amount and number of raw materials, parts, and finished products that a company has in its possession. When a devastating earthquake and an accompanying tsunami damaged factories throughout the eastern coast of Japan, inventory shortages, arising from destroyed or damaged Japanese factories, disrupted production around the world. Xirallic, for example, is a shiny pigment with coated glass flakes used in automotive paint by nearly all car companies worldwide. It also happens to be made in just one factory, located in Onahama, Japan, which was damaged and without power following the devastating earthquake and tsunami of March 2011. Consequently, auto manufacturers, who were suddenly short of Xirallic, had little choice but to begin rationing the inventory they had in stock. Ford, for example, stopped taking orders for red cars and for "Tuxedo Black" F-150 trucks, all of which used Xirallic. Likewise, because it didn't have enough Xirallic inventory on hand to fill demand, Chrysler immediately reduced the number of orders it would take for ten different car colors.[55]

*In this section, you will learn about **18-5a the different types of inventory, 18-5b how to measure inventory levels, 18-5c the costs of maintaining an inventory,** and **18-5d the different systems for managing inventory.***

18-5a TYPES OF INVENTORY

Exhibit 18.4 shows the four kinds of inventory a manufacturer stores: raw materials, component parts, work-in-process, and finished goods. The flow of inventory through a manufacturing plant begins when the purchasing department buys raw materials from vendors. **Raw material inventories** are the basic inputs in the manufacturing process. For example, to

EXHIBIT 18.4

Types of Inventory

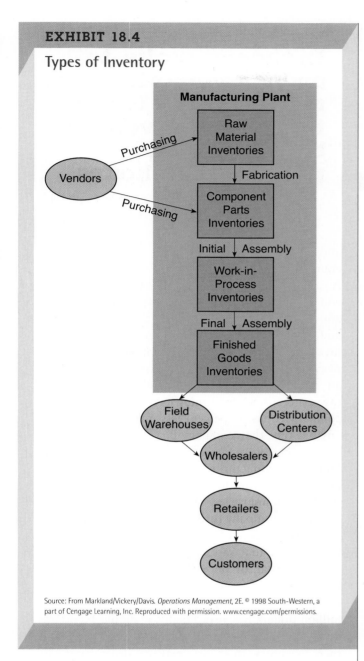

Source: From Markland/Vickery/Davis. *Operations Management*, 2E. © 1998 South-Western, a part of Cengage Learning, Inc. Reproduced with permission. www.cengage.com/permissions.

begin making a car, automobile manufacturers purchase raw materials like steel, iron, aluminum, copper, rubber, and unprocessed plastic.

Next, raw materials are fabricated or processed into **component parts inventories**, meaning the basic parts used in manufacturing a product. For example, in an automobile plant, steel is fabricated or processed into a car's body panels, and steel and iron are melted and shaped into engine parts like pistons or engine blocks. Some component parts are purchased from vendors rather than fabricated in-house.

The component parts are then assembled to make unfinished **work-in-process inventories**, which are

also known as partially finished goods. This process is also called *initial assembly*. For example, steel body panels are welded to each other and to the frame of the car to make a "unibody," which comprises the unpainted interior frame and exterior structure of the car. Likewise, pistons, camshafts, and other engine parts are inserted into the engine block to create a working engine.

Next, all the work-in-process inventories are assembled to create **finished goods inventories**, which are the final outputs of the manufacturing process. This process is also called *final assembly*. For a car, the engine, wheels, brake system, suspension, interior, and electrical system are assembled into a car's painted unibody to make the working automobile, which is the factory's finished product. In the last step in the process, the finished goods are sent to field warehouses, distribution centers, or wholesalers, and then to retailers for final sale to customers.

18-5b MEASURING INVENTORY

As you'll learn next, uncontrolled inventory can lead to huge costs for a manufacturing operation. Consequently, managers need good measures of inventory to prevent inventory costs from becoming too large. Three basic measures of inventory are average aggregate inventory, weeks of supply, and inventory turnover.

If you've ever worked in a retail store and had to take inventory, you probably weren't too excited about the process of counting every item in the store and storeroom. It's an extensive task that's a bit easier today because of bar codes that mark items and computers that can count and track them. Nonetheless, inventories still differ from day to day. An inventory count taken at the beginning of the month will likely be different from a count taken at the end of the month. Similarly, an inventory count taken on a Friday will differ from a count taken on a Monday. Because of such differences, companies often measure **average aggregate inventory**, which is the average overall inventory during a particular time period. Average aggregate inventory for a month can be determined by simply averaging

Component parts inventories the basic parts used in manufacturing that are fabricated from raw materials

Work-in-process inventories partially finished goods consisting of assembled component parts

Finished goods inventories the final outputs of manufacturing operations

Average aggregate inventory average overall inventory during a particular time period

In theory, make-to-order companies have no inventory. In fact, they've got inventory, but you have to measure it in hours.

© iStockphoto.com/Pablo Eder

Stockout the point when a company runs out of finished product

Inventory turnover the number of times per year that a company sells, or "turns over," its average inventory

Ordering cost the cost associated with ordering inventory, including the cost of data entry, phone calls, obtaining bids, correcting mistakes, and determining when and how much inventory to order

the inventory counts at the end of each business day for that month. One way companies know whether they're carrying too much or too little inventory is to compare their average aggregate inventory with the industry average for aggregate inventory. For example, seventy-two days of inventory is the average for the automobile industry.

The automobile industry records inventory in terms of days of supply, but most other industries measure inventory in terms of *weeks of supply*, meaning the number of weeks it would take for a company to run out of its current supply of inventory. In general, there is an acceptable number of weeks of inventory for a particular kind of business. Too few weeks of inventory on hand, and a company risks a **stockout**—running out of inventory. For more than a decade, Lowe's significantly outperformed its key rival Home Depot, posting higher sales and larger profits and opening more stores. Home Depot, however, is catching up because, unlike Lowe's, it has done a better job of avoiding stockouts. After a particularly stormy winter across the country, Home Depot's profits rose twice as fast as Lowe's, and its same-store sales rose four times as fast. The key was Home Depot's strong sales of snow blowers, shovels, salt, and other winter-weather items that were in high demand. Lowe's, meanwhile, ran out of these products and lost sales.[56]

Another common inventory measure, **inventory turnover**, is the number of times per year that a company sells, or "turns over," its average inventory. For example, if a company keeps an average of one hundred finished widgets in inventory each month, and it sold one thousand widgets this year, then it turned its inventory ten times this year.

In general, the higher the number of inventory turns, the better. In practice, a high turnover means that a company can continue its daily operations with just a small amount of inventory on hand. For example, let's take two companies, A and B, which have identical inventory levels (520,000 widget parts

and raw materials) over the course of a year. If company A turns its inventories twenty-six times a year, it will completely replenish its inventory every two weeks and have an average inventory of 20,000 widget parts and raw materials. By contrast, if company B turns its inventories only two times a year, it will completely replenish its inventory every twenty-six weeks and have an average inventory of 260,000 widget parts and raw materials. So, by turning its inventory more often, company A has 92 percent less inventory on hand at any one time than company B.

The average number of inventory turns across all kinds of manufacturing plants is approximately eight per year, although the average can be higher or lower for different industries.[57] For example, whereas the average auto company turns its entire inventory thirteen times per year, some of the best auto companies more than double that rate, turning their inventory 27.8 times per year, or once every two weeks.[58] Turning inventory more frequently than the industry average can cut an auto company's costs by several hundred million dollars per year. Finally, it should be pointed out that even make-to-order companies like Dell turn their inventory. In theory, make-to-order companies have no inventory. In fact, they've got inventory, but you have to measure it in hours. For example, Dell turns the inventory in its faculties 500 times a year, which means that on average it has seventeen hours—that's *hours* and not days—of inventory on hand in its factories.[59]

18-5c COSTS OF MAINTAINING AN INVENTORY

Maintaining an inventory incurs four kinds of costs: ordering, setup, holding, and stockout. **Ordering cost** is not the cost of the inventory itself but the costs associated with ordering the inventory. It includes the costs of completing paperwork, manually entering data into a computer, making phone calls, getting competing bids, correcting mistakes, and simply determining when and how much new inventory should be reordered. For example, ordering costs are relatively high in the restaurant business because 80 percent of foodservice orders (in which restaurants reorder food supplies) are processed manually. A report, *Enabling Profitable Growth in the Food-Prepared-Away-From-Home Industries*, estimated that the food industry could save $14.3 billion if all restaurants converted to electronic data interchange (see Chapter 17), in which purchase and ordering information from one company's computer system is automatically relayed to another company's computer system. Toward that end, an industry-wide effort, Efficient Foodservice Response (EFR), is underway to improve efficiencies in the foodservice supply chain.[60]

Setup cost is the cost of changing or adjusting a machine so that it can produce a different kind of inventory.[61] For example, 3M uses the same production machinery to make several kinds of industrial tape, but it must adjust the machines whenever it switches from one kind of tape to another. There are two kinds of setup costs: downtime and lost efficiency. *Downtime* occurs whenever a machine is not being used to process inventory. If it takes five hours to switch a machine from processing one kind of inventory to another, then five hours of downtime have occurred. Downtime is costly because companies earn an economic return only when machines are actively turning raw materials into parts or parts into finished products. The second setup cost is *lost efficiency*. Recalibrating a machine to its optimal settings after a switchover typically takes some time. It may take several days of fine-tuning before a machine finally produces the number of high-quality parts that it is supposed to. So, each time a machine has to be changed to handle a different kind of inventory, setup costs (downtime and lost efficiency) rise.

Holding cost, also known as *carrying* or *storage cost*, is the cost of keeping inventory until it is used or sold. Holding cost includes the cost of storage facilities, insurance to protect inventory from damage or theft, inventory taxes, the cost of obsolescence (holding inventory that is no longer useful to the company), and the opportunity cost of spending money on inventory that could have been spent elsewhere in the company. For example, it's estimated that U.S. airlines have a total of $44 billion worth of airplane parts in stock at any one time for maintenance, repair, and overhauling of their planes. The holding cost for managing, storing, and purchasing these parts is nearly $11 billion—or roughly one-fourth of the cost of the parts themselves.[62]

Stockout cost is the cost incurred when a company runs out of a product. There are two basic kinds of stockout costs. First, the company incurs the transaction costs of overtime work, shipping, and the like in trying to quickly replace out-of-stock inventories with new inventories. The second and perhaps more damaging cost is the loss of customers' goodwill when a company cannot deliver the products it promised. Stockouts occur more often than you might think. In the United States, the supermarket industry's average out-of-stock rate (the percentage of items that are unavailable at a given time) is 7.9 percent, according to research firm Market6. Highly promoted items have, as would be expected, a higher average out-of-stock rate of 13.1 percent. How costly is it for stores to run out of stock? Market6 estimates that running out of stock on the twenty-five best-selling product categories reduces a grocery store's revenue by an average of $200,000 per year, per store.[63] In general, retailers can increase sales 4 percent if they never run out of stock.

18-5d MANAGING INVENTORY

Inventory management has two basic goals. The first is to avoid running out of stock and thus angering and dissatisfying customers. This goal seeks to increase inventory to a safe level that won't risk stockouts. The second is to efficiently reduce inventory levels and costs as much as possible without impairing daily operations. This goal seeks a minimum level of inventory. The following inventory management techniques—economic order quantity (EOQ), just-in-time inventory (JIT), and materials requirement planning (MRP)—are different ways of balancing these competing goals.

Setup cost the cost of downtime and lost efficiency that occurs when a machine is changed or adjusted to produce a different kind of inventory

Holding cost the cost of keeping inventory until it is used or sold, including storage, insurance, taxes, obsolescence, and opportunity costs

Stockout cost the cost incurred when a company runs out of a product, including the transaction cost to replace inventory and the loss of customers' goodwill

© iStockphoto.com/Luis Carlos Torres

Economic order quantity (EOQ) is a system of formulas that helps determine how much and how often inventory should be ordered. EOQ takes into account the overall demand (D) for a product while trying to minimize ordering costs (O) and holding costs (H). The formula for EOQ is

$$EOQ = \sqrt{\frac{2DO}{H}}$$

For example, if a factory uses 40,000 gallons of paint a year (D), ordering costs (O) are $75 per order, and holding costs (H) are $4 per gallon, then the optimal quantity to order is 1,225 gallons:

$$EOQ = \sqrt{\frac{2(40,000)(75)}{4}} = 1,225$$

With 40,000 gallons of paint being used per year, the factory uses approximately 110 gallons per day:

$$\frac{40,000 \text{ gallons}}{365 \text{ days}} = 110$$

Consequently, the factory would order 1,225 new gallons of paint approximately every eleven days:

$$\frac{1,225 \text{ gallons}}{110 \text{ gallons per day}} = 11.1 \text{ days}$$

In general, EOQ formulas do a good job of letting managers know what size or amount of inventory they should reorder to minimize ordering and holding costs. Mark Lore, CEO of Diapers.com, explains how his company uses EOQ formulas to decide precisely how much inventory to keep on hand. He says, "We built software with computational algorithms to determine what the optimal number of boxes to have in the warehouse is and what the sizes of those boxes should be. Should we stock five different kinds of boxes to ship product in? Twenty kinds? Fifty kinds? And what size should those boxes be? Right now, it's twenty-three box sizes, given what we sell, in order to minimize the cost of dunnage (those little plastic air-filled bags or peanuts), the cost of corrugated boxes, and the cost of shipping. We rerun the simulation every quarter."[64] As this example makes clear, EOQ formulas and models can become much more complex as adjustments are made for price changes, quantity discounts, setup costs, and many other factors.[65]

While EOQ formulas try to minimize holding and ordering costs, the just-in-time (JIT) approach to inventory management attempts to eliminate holding costs by reducing inventory levels to near zero. With a **just-in-time (JIT) inventory** system, component parts arrive from suppliers just as they are needed at each stage of production. By having parts arrive just in time, the manufacturer has little inventory on hand and thus avoids the costs associated with holding inventory. By combining a JIT inventory system with its make-to-order production system, Dell turns its inventory more than five hundred times a year, as mentioned earlier. John Egan heads Dell's inventory fulfillment center in Austin, Texas, and has this to say about Dell's JIT inventory system: "We used to measure our factory inventory in days; but now we manage it in hours. Our suppliers see demand changes every two hours. We try to achieve a perfect balance between the parts that are needed and what's already in the factory."[66]

To have just the right amount of inventory arrive at just the right time requires a tremendous amount of coordination between manufacturing operations and suppliers. One way to promote tight coordination under JIT is close proximity. Most parts suppliers for Toyota's JIT system at its Georgetown, Kentucky, plant are located within two hundred miles of the plant. Furthermore, parts are picked up from suppliers and delivered to Toyota as often as sixteen times a day.[67] A second way to promote close coordination under JIT is to have a shared information system that allows a manufacturer and its suppliers to know the quantity and kinds of parts inventory the other has in stock. Generally, factories and suppliers facilitate information sharing by using the same part numbers and names. Ford's seat supplier accomplishes this by sticking a bar code on each seat, and Ford then uses the sticker to route the seat through its factory.

Manufacturing operations and their parts suppliers can also facilitate close coordination by using the system of kanban. **Kanban**, which is Japanese for "sign," is a simple ticket-based system that indicates when it is time to reorder inventory. Suppliers attach kanban cards to batches of parts. Then, when an assembly-line worker uses the first part out of a batch, the kanban card is removed. The cards are then collected, sorted, and quickly returned to the supplier, who begins resupplying the factory with parts that match the order information on the kanban cards. Glenn Uminger, manager of production control and logistics at Toyota's Georgetown, Kentucky, plant, says, "We are placing orders for new parts as the first part is used out of a box." Because prices and batch sizes are typically agreed to ahead of time, kanban tickets greatly reduce paperwork and ordering costs.[68]

A third method for managing inventory is **materials requirement planning (MRP)**. MRP is a production and inventory system that, from beginning to end, precisely determines the production schedule, production batch sizes, and inventories needed to complete final products. The three key parts of MRP systems are the master production schedule, the bill of materials, and inventory records. The *master production schedule* is a detailed schedule that indicates the quantity of each item to be produced, the planned delivery dates for those items, and the time by which each step of the production process must be completed in order to meet those delivery dates. Based on the quantity and kind of products set forth in the master production schedule, the *bill of materials* identifies all the necessary parts and inventory, the quantity or volume of inventory to be ordered, and the order in which the parts and inventory should be assembled. *Inventory records* indicate the kind, quantity, and location of inventory that is on hand or that has been ordered. When inventory records are combined with the bill of materials, the resulting report indicates what to buy, when to buy it, and what it will cost to order. Today, nearly all MRP systems are available in the form of powerful, flexible computer software.[69]

Which inventory management system should you use? Economic order quantity (EOQ) formulas are intended for use with **independent demand systems**, in which the level of one kind of inventory does not depend on another. For example, because inventory levels for automobile tires are unrelated to the inventory levels of women's dresses, Sears could use EOQ formulas to calculate separate optimal order quantities for dresses and tires. By contrast, JIT and MRP are used with **dependent demand systems**, in which the level of inventory depends on the number of finished units to be produced. For example, if Yamaha makes one thousand motorcycles a day, then it will need one thousand seats, one thousand gas tanks, and two thousand wheels and tires each day. So, when optimal inventory levels depend on the number of products to be produced, use a JIT or MRP management system.

Materials requirement planning (MRP) a production and inventory system that determines the production schedule, production batch sizes, and inventory needed to complete final products

Independent demand system an inventory system in which the level of one kind of inventory does not depend on another

Dependent demand system an inventory system in which the level of inventory depends on the number of finished units to be produced

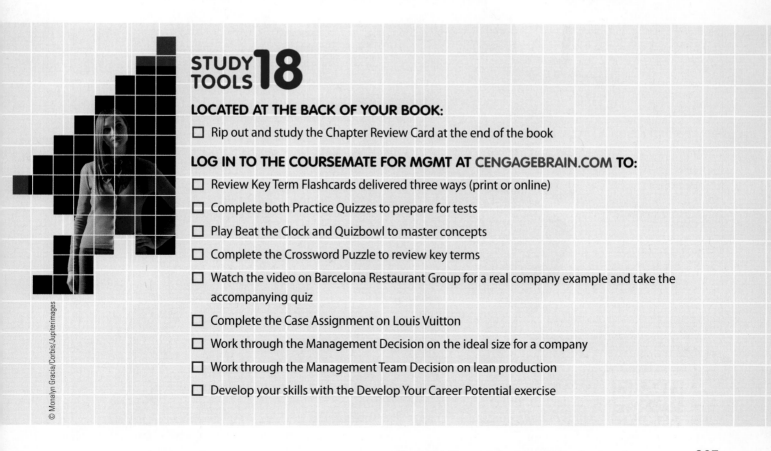

© Monalyn Gracia/Corbis/Jupiterimages

STUDY TOOLS 18

LOCATED AT THE BACK OF YOUR BOOK:

☐ Rip out and study the Chapter Review Card at the end of the book

LOG IN TO THE COURSEMATE FOR MGMT AT CENGAGEBRAIN.COM TO:

☐ Review Key Term Flashcards delivered three ways (print or online)

☐ Complete both Practice Quizzes to prepare for tests

☐ Play Beat the Clock and Quizbowl to master concepts

☐ Complete the Crossword Puzzle to review key terms

☐ Watch the video on Barcelona Restaurant Group for a real company example and take the accompanying quiz

☐ Complete the Case Assignment on Louis Vuitton

☐ Work through the Management Decision on the ideal size for a company

☐ Work through the Management Team Decision on lean production

☐ Develop your skills with the Develop Your Career Potential exercise

USE THE TOOLS.

- Rip out the Review Cards in the back of your book to study.

Or Visit CourseMate to:

- Read, search, highlight, and take notes in the Interactive eBook
- Review Flashcards (Print or Online) to master key terms
- Test yourself with Auto-Graded Quizzes
- Bring concepts to life with Games, Videos, and Animations!

Go to CourseMate for MGMT to begin using these tools.
Access at **www.cengagebrain.com**

Complete the Speak Up
survey in CourseMate at
www.cengagebrain.com

f **Follow us at**
www.facebook.com/4ltrpress

Endnotes

Chapter 1

1 Y. Q. Mui, "Bank of America Scraps Debit Card Fee after Consumer Backlash," *Washington Post*, November 1, 2011, accessed February 22 2012, http://www.washingtonpost.com /business/economy/bank-of-american -drops-debit-card-fee/2011/11/01 /gIQADvugcM_story.html; M. C. White, "Bank of America Backlash: Consumers React to Debit Card Fee," *Time*, October 3, 2011, accessed February 22, 2012, http://moneyland .time.com/2011/10/03/bank-of -america-backlash-consumers-react -to-debit-card-fee/.

2 "Business Services: Global Industry Guide," *Data Monitor*, January 21, 2010, accessed April 18, 2009, http:// www.marketresearch.com.

3 V. Nayar, "Corner Office: He's Not Bill Gates, or Fred Astaire," interview by A. Bryant, *New York Times*, February 13, 2010, accessed June 22, 2010, http://www.nytimes.com/2010/02/14 /business/14cornerweb.html.

4 J. Levitz, "Delivery Drivers to Pick Up Pace by Surrendering Keys," *Wall Street Journal*, September 16, 2011, accessed February 23, 2012, http:// online.wsj.com/article/SB1000142405 31119040606045765728910408953 66.html.

5 S. McCartney, "At JFK, More Flying, Less Waiting on the Tarmac," *Wall Street Journal*, July 29, 2010, D3.

6 D. A. Wren, A. G. Bedeian, and J. D. Breeze, "The Foundations of Henri Fayol's Administrative Theory," *Management Decision* 40 (2002): 906–918.

7 A. Bryant, "Google's Quest to Build a Better Boss," *New York Times*, March 12, 2011, accessed February 23, 2012, http://www.nytimes .com/2011/03/13/business/13hire .html?adxnnl=1&adxnnlx =1330002058-Rqx1lDmdrAh0+ +W48oHbRA#.

8 H. Fayol, *General and Industrial Management* (London: Pittman & Sons, 1949).

9 R. Stagner, "Corporate Decision Making," *Journal of Applied Psychology* 53 (1969): 1–13.

10 D. W. Bray, R. J. Campbell, and D. L. Grant, *Formative Years in Business: A Long-Term AT&T Study of Managerial Lives* (New York: Wiley, 1993).

11 J. Duffy, "Cisco's Umi Still Dead. As a Doornail. Really, Really Dead," *Network World*, January 4, 2012, http://www.networkworld.com /news/2012/010412-cisco-umi-254517 .html; P. Martin, "How a Once-Smart Cisco Temporarily Lost Its Mind," The Motley Fool.com, June 17, 2011, http://www.fool.com/investing /general/2011/06/17/how-a-once -smart-cisco-temporarily-lost-its -mind.aspx.

12 M. J. Credeur, "Making United and Continental Fly in Formation," *Bloomberg Business Week*, June 30, 2011, accessed February 23, 2012, http://www.businessweek.com /magazine/making-united-and -continental-fly-information -07012011.html.

13 N. Bunkley, "For Ford, Three Years of Profit in a Row," *New York Times*, January 27, 2012, accessed February 23, 2012, http://www .nytimes.com/2012/01/28/business /fords-posts-third-straight-annual -profit.html; A. Taylor III, "Fixing Up Ford," *Fortune*, May 25, 2009, 44–51 (para 1, para 2); N. Bunkley, "Ford Profit Comes as Toyota Hits a Bump," *New York Times*, January 28, 2010, accessed June 23, 2010, http://www.nytimes.com/2010/01/29 /business/29ford.html.

14 B. O'Keefe and D. Burke, "Meet the CEO of the Biggest Company on Earth," *Fortune*, September 27, 2010, 80–94.

15 H. S. Jonas III, R. E. Fry, and S. Srivastva, "The Office of the CEO: Understanding the Executive Experience," *Academy of Management Executive* 4 (1990): 36–47.

16 D. Goldman, "HP CEO Apotheker Fired, Replaced by Meg Whitman," CNN Money, September 22, 2011, accessed April 9, 2012, http://money.cnn .com/2011/09/22/technology/hp_ceo

_fired/index.htm; V. G. Kopytoff and C. C. Miller, "Yahoo Board Fired Chief Executive," *New York Times*, September 6, 2011, accessed April 9, 2012, http://www.nytimes .com/2011/09/07/technology/carol -bartz-yahoos-chief-executive-is-fired .html.

17 Jonas et al., "The Office of the CEO."

18 Ibid.

19 M. Porter, J. Lorsch, and N. Nohria, "Seven Surprises for New CEOs," *Harvard Business Review* (October 2004): 62.

20 M. Murray, "As Huge Firms Keep Growing, CEOs Struggle to Keep Pace," *Wall Street Journal*, February 8, 2001, A1.

21 T. Gutner, "Career Journal—90 Days: Plotting a Smooth Course When You Take the Helm," *Wall Street Journal*, March 24, 2009, D5.

22 E. Byron, "P & G's Lafley Sees CEOs As Link to World," *Wall Street Journal*, March 23, 2009, B6.

23 Q. Huy, "In Praise of Middle Managers," *Harvard Business Review* (September 2001): 72–79.

24 I. Barat, "Rebuilding after a Catastrophe: How Caterpillar Is Responding to Tornado's Lesson," *Wall Street Journal*, May 19, 2008, B1–2.

25 T. Demos, "Motivate without Spending Millions," *Fortune*, April 12, 2010, 37–38.

26 S. Tully, "What Team Leaders Need to Know," *Fortune*, February 20, 1995, 93.

27 B. Francella, "In a Day's Work," *Convenience Store News*, September 25, 2001, 7.

28 L. Liu and A. McMurray, "Frontline Leaders: The Entry Point for Leadership Development in the Manufacturing Industry," *Journal of European Industrial Training* 28, no. 2–4 (2004): 339–352.

29 "What Makes Teams Work?" *Fast Company*, November 1, 2000, 109.

30 K. Hultman, "The 10 Commandments of Team Leadership," *Training & Development*, February 1, 1998, 12–13.

31 A. Bryant, "The Trust That Makes a Team Click," *New York Times*, July 30, 2011, accessed February 23, 2012, http://www.nytimes.com/2011/07/31/business/siemens-ceo-on-building-trust-and-teamwork.html.

32 N. Steckler and N. Fondas, "Building Team Leader Effectiveness: A Diagnostic Tool," *Organizational Dynamics*, (Winter 1995): 20–34.

33 Tully, "What Team Leaders Need to Know."

34 Ibid.

35 H. Mintzberg, *The Nature of Managerial Work* (New York: Harper & Row, 1973).

36 C. P. Hales, "What Do Managers Do? A Critical Review of the Evidence," *Journal of Management Studies* 23, no. 1 (1986): 88–115.

37 S. Hendren, "NetJets Holds Headquarters Groundbreaking," WOSU, April 5, 2011, accessed February 23, 2012, http://beta.wosu.org/news/2011/04/05/netjets-holds-headquarters-groundbreaking/.

38 C. Penttila, "Employee Benefits in Today's Economy," *Entrepreneur* 37, no. 1 (January 2009): 51–55.

39 K. Clark and R. Sidel, "Gang Green Meets Wall Street," *Wall Street Journal*, May 5, 2010, accessed June 22, 2010, http://online.wsj.com/article/SB10001424052748703866704575224480779342098.html?mod=WSJ_hpp_MIDDLENexttoWhatsNewsForth.

40 "News by Industry," *Business Wire*, accessed March 11, 2009, http://www.businesswire.com/portal/site/home/news/industries/.

41 "Media Monitoring," *CyberAlert*, accessed March 11, 2009, http://www.cyberalert.com.

42 "What Is FNS News Clips Online?" *FNS NewsClips*, accessed March 11, 2009, http://www.news-clips.com.

43 "100 Best Companies to Work for 2009," *Sunday Times* (London), March 8, 2009, 20.

44 S. Humphries, "Grapevine Goes High-Tech," *The Courier Mail*, January 10, 2009.

45 "Maserati SUV to Be Built in Detroit, Unveiled in Frankfurt," *Detroit Free Press*, September 13, 2011, accessed February 23, 2012, http://www.freep.com/article/20110913/BUSINESS0103/110913037/Maserati-SUV-built-Detroit-unveiled-Frankfurt.

46 R. Weis and B. Kammel, "How Siemens Got Its Mojo Back," *Bloomberg BusinessWeek*, January 27, 2011, accessed February 25, 2012, http://www.businessweek.com/magazine/content/11_06/b4214018593359.htm.

47 "Sony CEO Apologizes for PlayStation Network Hack, Announces ID-Theft Insurance," *Los Angeles Times*, May 6, 2011, accessed February 23, 2012, http://latimesblogs.latimes.com/technology/2011/05/sony-ceo-stringer-apologizes-for-playstation-network-hack-outage-announces-1-million-identity-theft.html.

48 J. Lendino "Adobe Flash Meets Its End," *PC Magazine*, November 9, 2011, accessed February 25, 2012, http://www.pcmag.com/article2/0,2817,2396094,00.asp.

49 N. Bilton, "Adobe to Kill Mobile Flash, Focus on HTML5," *New York Times*, November 9, 2011, http://bits.blogs.nytimes.com/2011/11/09/adobe-to-kill-mobile-flash-focus-on-html5/.

50 L. Greenblatt, "Beatles Sales on iTunes Hit New Milestone," *Music-Mix*, January 14, 2011, accessed January 17, 2011, http://music-mix.ew.com/2011/01/14/beatles-sales-itunes/; E. Smith, "A Day in the Life of a Deal—How EMI's New CEO Helped Beatles Clear iTunes Hurdles," *Wall Street Journal*, November 17, 2010, B12.

51 L. A. Hill, *Becoming a Manager: Mastery of a New Identity* (Boston: Harvard Business School Press, 1992).

52 R. L. Katz, "Skills of an Effective Administrator," *Harvard Business Review* (September–October 1974): 90–102.

53 C. A. Bartlett and S. Ghoshal, "Changing the Role of Top Management: Beyond Systems to People," *Harvard Business Review* (May–June 1995): 132–142.

54 F. L. Schmidt and J. E. Hunter, "Development of a Causal Model of Process Determining Job Performance," *Current Directions in Psychological Science* 1 (1992): 89–92.

55 J. B. Miner, "Sentence Completion Measures in Personnel Research: The Development and Validation of the Miner Sentence Completion Scales," in *Personality Assessment in Organizations*, ed. H. J. Bernardin and D. A. Bownas (New York: Praeger, 1986), 145–176.

56 M. W. McCall, Jr., and M. M. Lombardo, "What Makes a Top Executive?" *Psychology Today*, February 1983, 26–31; E. van Velsor and J. Brittain, "Why Executives Derail: Perspectives across Time and Cultures," *Academy of Management Executive* (November 1995): 62–72.

57 McCall and Lombardo, "What Makes a Top Executive?"

58 A. K. Naj, "Corporate Therapy: The Latest Addition to Executive Suite Is Psychologist's Couch," *Wall Street Journal*, August 29, 1994, A1.

59 Ibid.

60 P. Wallington, "Management2 Toxic!" *Financial Mail*, July 28, 2006, 48.

61 J. Sandberg, "Overcontrolling Bosses Aren't Just Annoying; They're Also Inefficient," *Wall Street Journal*, March 30, 2005, B1.

62 Hill, *Becoming a Manager*, p. 17.

63 Ibid., p. 55.

64 Ibid., p. 57.

65 Ibid., p. 64.

66 Ibid., p. 67.

67 Ibid., p. 161.

68 J. Pfeffer, *The Human Equation: Building Profits by Putting People First* (Boston: Harvard Business School Press, 1996); *Competitive Advantage through People: Unleashing the Power of the Work Force* (Boston: Harvard Business School Press, 1994).

69 M. A. Huselid, "The Impact of Human Resource Management Practices on Turnover, Productivity, and Corporate Financial Performance," *Academy of Management Journal* 38 (1995): 635–672.

70 D. McDonald and A. Smith, "A Proven Connection: Performance Management and Business Results," *Compensation & Benefits Review* 27, no. 6 (January 1, 1995): 59.

71 I. Fulmer, B. Gerhart, and K. Scott, "Are the 100 Best Better? An Empirical Investigation of the Relationship between Being a 'Great Place to Work' and Firm Performance," *Personnel Psychology* (Winter 2003): 965–993.

72 B. Schneider and D. E. Bowen, "Employee and Customer Perceptions of Service in Banks: Replication and Extension," *Journal of Applied Psychology* 70 (1985): 423–433; B. Schneider, J. J. Parkington, and V. M. Buxton, "Employee and Customer Perceptions of Service in Banks," *Administrative Science Quarterly* 25 (1980): 252–267.

73 "How Investing in Intangibles—Like Employee Satisfaction—Translates into Financial Returns," *Knowledge@Wharton*, January 9, 2008, accessed January 24, 2010, http://knowledge.wharton.upenn.edu/article.cfm?articleid=1873.

Chapter 2

1 C. S. George, Jr., *The History of Management Thought* (Englewood Cliffs, NJ: Prentice-Hall, 1972).

2 D. Schmandt-Besserat, *How Writing Came About* (Austin: University of Texas Press, 1997).

3 A. Erman, *Life in Ancient Egypt* (London: Macmillan & Co., 1984).

4 J. Burke, *The Day the Universe Changed* (Boston: Little, Brown, 1985).

5 S. A. Epstein, *Wage Labor and Guilds in Medieval Europe* (Chapel Hill: University of North Carolina Press, 1991).

6 R. Braun, *Industrialization and Everyday Life*, trans. S. Hanbury-Tenison (Cambridge: Cambridge University Press, 1990).

7 J. B. White, "The Line Starts Here: Mass-Production Techniques Changed the Way People Work and Live throughout the World," *Wall Street Journal*, January 11, 1999, R25.

8 R. B. Reich, *The Next American Frontier* (New York: Time Books, 1983).

9 J. Mickelwait and A. Wooldridge, *The Company: A Short History of a Revolutionary Idea* (New York: Modern Library, 2003).

10 H. Kendall, "Unsystematized, Systematized, and Scientific Management," in *Scientific Management: A Collection of the More Significant Articles Describing the Taylor System of Management*, ed. C. Thompson (Easton, PA: Hive Publishing, 1972), 103–131.

11 United States Congress, House, Special Committee, *Hearings to Investigate the Taylor and Other Systems of Shop Management*, vol. 3. (Washington, DC: Government Printing Office, 1912).

12 Ibid.

13 Ibid.

14 A. Derickson, "Physiological Science and Scientific Management in the Progressive Era: Frederic S. Lee and the Committee on Industrial Fatigue," *Business History Review* 68 (1994): 483–514.

15 United States Congress, House, Special Committee, 1912.

16 Taylor, *The Principles of Scientific Management*.

17 C. D. Wrege, and R. M. Hodgetts, "Frederick W. Taylor's 1899 Pig Iron Observations: Examining Fact, Fiction, and Lessons for the New Millennium, *Academy of Manage-* ment *Journal*, 43 (December 2000): 1283; J. R. Hough and M. A. White, "Using Stories to Create Change: The Object Lesson of Frederick Taylor's 'Pig-tale,'" *Journal of Management*, 27, no. 5 (October 2001): 585–601; E. A. Locke, "The Ideas of Frederick W. Taylor: An Evaluation," *Academy of Management Review* 7, no. 1(1982) 14–24.

18 Locke, "The Ideas of Frederick W. Taylor."

19 George, *The History of Management Thought.*

20 F. Gilbreth and L. Gilbreth, "Applied Motion Study," in *The Writings of the Gilbreths*, ed. W. R. Spriegel and C. E. Myers (1917; reprint, Homewood, IL: Irwin, 1953), 207–274.

21 Ibid.

22 D. Ferguson, "Don't Call It 'Time and Motion Study,'" *IIE Solutions* 29, no. 5 (1997): 22–23.

23 H. Gantt, "A Graphical Daily Balance in Manufacture," *Transactions of the American Society of Mechanical Engineers* 24 (1903): 1325.

24 P. Peterson, "Training and Development: The View of Henry L. Gantt (1861–1919)," *SAM Advanced Management Journal* (Winter 1987): 20–23.

25 H. Gantt, "Industrial Efficiency," *National Civic Federation Report of the 11th Annual Meeting*, New York, January 12, 1991, 103.

26 Ibid.

27 M. Weber, *The Theory of Social and Economic Organization*, trans. A. Henderson and T. Parsons (New York: Free Press, 1947).

28 M. Weber, *The Protestant Ethic and the Spirit of Capitalism* (New York: Scribner's, 1958).

29 George, *The History of Management Thought.*

30 D. A. Wren, "Henri Fayol as Strategist: A Nineteenth Century Corporate Turnaround," *Management Decision*, 39, no. 6 (2001): 475–487; D. Reid, "Fayol: From Experience to Theory," *Journal of Management History* (Archive) 1, no. 3 (1995): 21–36.

31 Ibid.

32 Ibid.

33 Ibid.

34 F. Blancpain, "Les cahiers inédits d'Henri Fayol," trans. D. Wren, *Extrait du bulletin de l'institut international d'administration publique* 28–29 (1974): 1–48.

35 D. A. Wren, A. G. Bedeian, and J. D. Breeze, "The Foundations of Henri Fayol's Administrative Theory," *Management Decision* 40 (2002): 906–918.

36 H. Fayol, *General and Industrial Management* (London: Pittman & Sons, 1949); Wren, Bedeian, and Breeze, "Foundations."

37 P. Graham, ed., *Mary Parker Follett— Prophet of Management: A Celebration of Writings from the 1920s* (Boston: Harvard Business School Press, 1995).

38 D. Linden, "The Mother of Them All," *Forbes,* January 16, 1995, 75.

39 J. H. Smith, "The Enduring Legacy of Elton Mayo," *Human Relations* 51, no. 3 (1998): 221–249.

40 E. Mayo, *The Human Problems of an Industrial Civilization* (New York: Macmillan, 1933).

41 Ibid.

42 "Hawthorne Revisited: The Legend and the Legacy," *Organizational Dynamics* (Winter 1975): 66–80.

43 E. Mayo, *The Social Problems of an Industrial Civilization* (Boston: Harvard Graduate School of Business Administration, 1945).

44 "Hawthorne Revisited: The Legend and the Legacy."

45 Mayo, *The Social Problems of an Industrial Civilization*, 45.

46 George, *The History of Management Thought.*

47 C. I. Barnard, *The Functions of the Executive* (Cambridge, MA: Harvard University Press, 1938), 4.

48 C. I. Barnard, *The Functions of the Executive: 30th Anniversary Edition* (Cambridge, MA: Harvard University Press, 1968), 5.

49 J. Fuller and A. Mansour, "Operations Management and Operations Research: A Historical and Relational Perspective," *Management Decision* 41 (2003): 422–426.

50 D. Wren and R. Greenwood, "Business Leaders: A Historical Sketch of Eli Whitney," *Journal of Leadership & Organizational Studies* 6 (1999): 131.

51 "Monge, Gaspard, comte de Péluse," *Britannica Online*, accessed January 9, 2005, http://www.eb.com.

52 M. Schwartz and A. Fish, "Just-in-Time Inventories in Old Detroit," *Business History* 40, no. 3 (July 1998): 48.

53 D. Ashmos and G. Huber, "The Systems Paradigm in Organization

Theory: Correcting the Record and Suggesting the Future," *Academy of Management Review* 12 (1987): 607–621; F. Kast and J. Rosenzweig, "General Systems Theory: Applications for Organizations and Management," *Academy of Management Journal* 15 (1972): 447–465; D. Katz and R. Kahn, *The Social Psychology of Organizations* (New York: Wiley, 1966).

54 R. Mockler, "The Systems Approach to Business Organization and Decision Making," *California Management Review* 11, no. 2 (1968): 53–58.

55 F. Luthans and T. Stewart, "A General Contingency Theory of Management," *Academy of Management Review* 2, no. 2 (1977): 181–195.

Chapter 3

1 Associated Press, "Thai Flooding Impact on Tech Companies, Suppliers," Yahoo! News, March 29, 2012, http://news.yahoo.com/thai-flooding-impact-tech-companies-suppliers-004001255.html; J. Ribeiro, "Hard Drive Shortages Continue to Bite Tech Industry," *InfoWorld*, January 25, 2012, accessed February 25, 2012, http://www.infoworld.com/d/the-industry-standard/hard-drive-shortages-continue-bite-tech-industry-184973.

2 "Industry Profile: Food Distributors," *First Research*, January 24, 2011, accessed February 2, 2011, http://www.firstresearch.com/Focus-Research/Food-Distributors.html.

3 P. Burrows and H. Miller, "Research in Motion: The Living Dead?" *Bloomberg Businessweek*, January 30–February 2012, 36–37.

4 E. Romanelli and M. L. Tushman, "Organizational Transformation as Punctuated Equilibrium: An Empirical Test," *Academy of Management Journal* 37 (1994): 1141–1166.

5 H. Banks, "A Sixties Industry in a Nineties Economy," *Forbes*, May 9, 1994, 107–112.

6 L. Cowan, "Cheap Fuel Should Carry Many Airlines to More Record Profits for 1st Quarter," *Wall Street Journal*, April 4, 1998, B17A.

7 "Annual Revenues and Earnings: U.S. Airlines—All Services," *Air Transport Association*, accessed January 15, 2005, http://www.airlines.org; S. Carey, "Carrier Makes Deeper Cuts as It Seeks Federal Backing Needed to Exit Chapter 11," *Wall Street Journal*, November 27, 2002, A3; S. Carey, "UAL Will Lay Off 1,500 Workers As Part of Cost-Cutting Strategy,"

Wall Street Journal, January 6, 2003, A3; D. Carty, "Oral Testimony of Mr. Donald J. Carty, Chairman and CEO, American Airlines: United States Senate, Committee on Commerce, Science, and Transportation," accessed January 9, 2003, http://www.amrcorp.com; S. McCartney, M. Trottman, and S. Carey, "Northwest, Continental, America West Post Losses as Delta Cuts Jobs," *Wall Street Journal*, November 18, 2002, B4.

8 "Airlines Still in Upheaval, 5 Years after 9/11," *CNNMoney.com*, September 8, 2006, accessed July 25, 2008, http://money.cnn.com/2006/09/08/news/companies/airlines_sept11/?postversion=2006090813&eref=yahoo.

9 B. Jones, "The Changing Dairy Industry," Department of Agricultural & Applied Economics & Center for Dairy Profitability, accessed July 25, 2008, http://www.aae.wisc.edu/jones/Presentations/Wisc&TotalDairyTrends.pdf.

10 E. Sass, "Newspaper Ad Spending Now Half What It Was in 2005," *Media DailyNews*, March 26, 2012, http://www.mediapost.com/publications/article/171052/newspaper-ad-spending-now-half-what-it-was-in-2005.html.

11 A. Chozick, "Fourth-Quarter Profit and Revenue Decline at the New York Times Company," *New York Times*, February 2, 2012, accessed February 25, 2012, http://www.nytimes.com/2012/02/03/business/media/quarterly-profit-falls-12-2-at-times-co.html; "The Washington Post Company Newspaper Division Reports $18.2M Loss for 2011," *Citybizlist*, February 24, 2012, accessed February 25, 2012, http://dc.citybizlist.com/5/2012/2/24/The-Washington-Post-Company-Newspaper-Division-Reports-18.2M-Loss-for-2011.aspx.

12 K. Bradsher, "China Consolidates Grip on Rare Earths," *New York Times*, September 15, 2011, accessed February 25, 2012, http://www.nytimes.com/2011/09/16/business/global/china-consolidates-control-of-rare-earth-industry.html?pagewanted=1; "China Cuts Rare Earth Export Quota 72%, May Spark Trade Dispute with U.S.," *Bloomberg Businessweek*, July 9, 2010, accessed February 25, 2012, http://www.bloomberg.com/news/2010-07-09/china-reduces-rare-earth-export-quota-by-72-in-second-half-lynas-says.html.

13 M. C. Jalonick, "FDA Proposes Calorie Counts on Menus," *MSNBC*

.com, April 1, 2011, accessed February 25, 2012, http://www.msnbc.msn.com/id/42381553/ns/health-diet_and_nutrition/t/fda-proposes-calorie-counts-menus/#.T0mT_fGPU2w.

14 R. Norton, "Where Is This Economy Really Heading?" *Fortune*, August 7, 1995, 54–56.

15 "CEO Confidence Survey," *The Conference Board*, April 9, 2009, accessed April 27, 2009, http://www.conference-board.org.

16 "Despite Recession, U.S. Small Business Confidence Index Increases Six Points; Small Business Research Board Study Finds Increase in Key Indicators," *U.S. Business Confidence*, February 23, 2009, accessed April 27, 2009, http://www.ipasbrb.net.

17 J. Cuneo, "10 Perks We Love," *Inc.*, June 2010, 94–95.

18 "The Civil Rights Act of 1991," U.S. Equal Employment Opportunity Commission, accessed July 25, 2008, http://www.eeoc.gov/policy/cra91.html.

19 "Compliance Assistance—Family and Medical Leave Act (FMLA)," U.S. Department of Labor: Employment Standards Administration, Wage and Hour Division, accessed July 25, 2005, http://www.dol.gov/.

20 R. J. Bies and T. R. Tyler, "The Litigation Mentality in Organizations: A Test of Alternative Psychological Explanations," *Organization Science* 4 (1993): 352–366.

21 M. Orey, "Fear of Firing," *BusinessWeek*, April 23, 2007, 52–62.

22 S. Gardner, G. Gomes, and J. Morgan, "Wrongful Termination and the Expanding Public Policy Exception: Implications and Advice," *SAM Advanced Management Journal* 65 (2000): 38.

23 Orey, "Fear of Firing."

24 Ibid.

25 C. Morris, "Activision Battles 'Trolls', Backs Down on Privacy Fears," *CNBC.com*, July 9, 2010, accessed July 10, 2010, http://www.cnbc.com/id/38171990/.

26 R. Johnston and S. Mehra, "Best-Practice Complaint Management," *Academy of Management Experience* 16 (November 2002): 145–154.

27 D. Smart and C. Martin, "Manufacturer Responsiveness to Consumer Correspondence: An Empirical Investigation of Consumer Perceptions," *Journal of Consumer Affairs* 26 (1992): 104.

28 C. Binkley, "Lucky Numbers: Casino Chain Mines Data on Its Gamblers, and Strikes Pay Dirt—'Secret Recipe' Lets Harrah's Target Its Low-Rollers at the Individual Level—A Free-Meal 'Intervention,'" *Wall Street Journal*, May 4, 2000, A1; "Harrah's Hits Customer Loyalty Jackpot: SAS Identifies Customers with Highest Potential to Return," *SAS Customer Success*, accessed February 4, 2011, http://www.sas.com.

29 T. Mullaney, "Harrah's," *BusinessWeek*, November 24, 2003, 94.

30 S. A. Zahra and S. S. Chaples, "Blind Spots in Competitive Analysis," *Academy of Management Executive* 7 (1993): 7–28.

31 J. M. Moran, "Getting Closer Together—Videophones Don't Deliver TV Quality Sound, Visuals, but They're Improving," *Seattle Times*, March 15, 1998.

32 R. Broida, "Replace Your Landline with $199 Ooma Telo," *The Cheapskate*, July 12, 2010, accessed February 5, 2011, http://www.cnet.com.

33 K. G. Provan, "Embeddedness, Interdependence, and Opportunism in Organizational Supplier-Buyer Networks," *Journal of Management* 19 (1993): 841–856.

34 B. Berger and D. Leone, "Sources: United Space Alliance Directed to Stop Pursuing New Business," *Space News*, January 6, 2012, accessed February 26, 2012, http://www.spacenews.com/civil/120106-usa-stop-pursuing-business.html\; C. Moskowitz, "Space Shuttle Contractor Announces Layoffs for 2800 workers," Space.com, April 15, 2011, accessed February 26, 2012, http://www.space.com/11408-nasa-space-shuttle-contractor-layoffs-usa.html.

35 D. Birch, "Staying on Good Terms," *Supply Management*, April 12, 2001, 36.

36 S. Parker and C. Axtell, "Seeing Another Viewpoint: Antecedents and Outcomes of Employee Perspective Taking," *Academy of Management Journal* 44 (2001): 1085–1100; B. K. Pilling, L. A. Crosby, and D. W. Jackson, "Relational Bonds in Industrial Exchange: An Experimental Test of the Transaction Cost Economic Framework," *Journal of Business Research* 30 (1994): 237–251.

37 "Carmakers Eye Economy with Unease," *USA Today*, May 24, 2004, B.06.

38 B. McKay and D. Kesmodel, "Labels Give Cigarette Packs a Ghoulish Makeover," *Wall Street Journal*, June 22, 2011, accessed February 26, 2012, http://online.wsj.com/article/SB10001424052702303936704576399320327189158.html.

39 "Seafood HACCP," U.S. Food and Drug Administration Center for Food Safety & Applied Nutrition, accessed March 12, 2009, http://www.cfsan.fda.gov/~comm/haccpsea.html.

40 S. Armour, "FDA Suspends Orange Juice Imports to Examine for Fungicide," *Bloomberg Businessweek*, January 11, 2012, accessed February 26, 2012, http://www.bloomberg.com/news/2012-01-11/fda-halts-orange-juice-imports-to-check-for-banned-fungicide-carpendazim.html.

41 "EU's Aggressive Anti-Smoking Campaign," *Creative Bits*, January 17, 2005, http://creativebits.org/eus_agressive_anti-smoking_campaign.

42 R. Blake, "Boycotting BP: Who Gets Hurt?" *ABCNews.com*, June 2, 2010, accessed February 5, 2011, http://abcnews.go.com/Business/bp-boycotts-spreading-frustration-oil-spill-boils/story?id=10800309.

43 "AHA Environmental Scan 2012," *American Hospital Association*, accessed February 26, 2012, http://www.hhnmag.com/hhnmag_app/gateFold/pages/SEPTEMBER11.jsp.

44 N. Ungerleider, "Super Bowl Command Center Monitors Parking Gripes, Terrorist Threats," *Fast Company*, February 3, 2012, accessed February 26, 2012, http://www.fastcompany.com/1813684/inside-super-bowl-social-media-command.

45 D. F. Jennings and J. R. Lumpkin, "Insights between Environmental Scanning Activities and Porter's Generic Strategies: An Empirical Analysis," *Journal of Management* 4 (1992): 791–803.

46 S. Greenhouse, "Factory Defines Sweatshop Label, but Can It Thrive?" *New York Times*, July 18, 2010, BU1.

47 Ibid.

48 E. Jackson and J. E. Dutton, "Discerning Threats and Opportunities," *Administrative Science Quarterly* 33 (1988): 370–387.

49 B. Thomas, S. M. Clark, and D. A. Gioia, "Strategic Sensemaking and Organizational Performance: Linkages among Scanning, Interpretation, Action, and Outcomes," *Academy of Management Journal* 36 (1993): 239–270.

50 R. Daft, J. Sormunen, and D. Parks, "Chief Executive Scanning, Environmental Characteristics, and Company Performance: An Empirical Study," *Strategic Management Journal* 9 (1988): 123–139; V. Garg, B. Walters, and R. Priem, "Chief Executive Scanning Emphases, Environmental Dynamism, and Manufacturing Firm Performance," *Strategic Management Journal* 24 (2003): 725–744; D. Miller and P. H. Friesen, "Strategy-Making and Environment: The Third Link," *Strategic Management Journal* 4 (1983): 221–235.

51 P. Burrows, "Stephen Elop's Nokia Adventure," *Bloomberg Businessweek*, June 2, 2011, accessed February 26, 2012, http://www.businessweek.com/magazine/content/11_24/b4232056703101.htm; L. Dignan "Nokia to rely on Micro-soft's Windows Phone 7: 'This is now a three horse race,'" ZDnet, February 11, 2011, accessed February 26, 2012, http://www.zdnet.com/blog/btl/nokia-to-rely-on-microsofts-windows-phone-7-this-is-now-a-three-horse-race/44725?tag=content;siu-container.

52 P. Elmer-DeWitt, "How Many iPhones Did Apple Sell Last Quarter?" *CNNMoney*, July 13, 2011, accessed February 26, 2012, http://tech.fortune.cnn.com/2011/07/13/how-many-iphones-did-apple-sell-last-quarter-2/; K. Eaton, "Apple Just Sold Its 15 Billionth App," *Fast Company*, July 7, 2011, accessed February 26, 2012, http://www.fastcompany.com/1765528/apple-just-sold-its-15-billionth-app-and-shifted-one-billion-of-them-last-month.

53 R. Feitelberg, "Building a Winning Culture," *WWD*, December 1, 2011, SR12.

54 P. Elmer-DeWitt, "Mine, All Mine; Bill Gates Wants a Piece of Everybody's Action, but Can He Get It?" *Time*, June 5, 1995.

55 D. M. Boje, "The Storytelling Organization: A Study of Story Performance in an Office-Supply Firm," *Administrative Science Quarterly* 36 (1991): 106–126.

56 S. Walton and J. Huey, *Sam Walton: Made in America* (New York: Doubleday, 1992).

57 D. Rushe, "Wal-Martians," *Sunday Times* (London), June 10, 2001, 5.

58 C. Morran, "Home Depot Staff Makes 8-Hour Trip To Find Me a Snow Blower," *The Consumerist*, December 2, 2011, accessed February 26, 2012, http://consumerist.com/2011/12/home-depot-staff-makes-8-hour-trip-to-find-me-a-snow-blower.html.

59 D. R. Denison and A. K. Mishra, "Toward a Theory of Organizational Culture and Effectiveness," *Organization Science* 6 (1995): 204–223.

60 F. Haley, "Mutual Benefit: How Does Genencor Maintain Its Incredibly Loyal Workforce? By Involving Its Employees in Almost Everything," *Fast Company*, October 2004, 98–100.

61 "Changing Diabetes," Norvo Nordisk, accessed August 4, 2010, http://changingdiabetes.novonordisk.com/.

62 T. Hsieh, "Corner Office: On a Scale of 1 to 10, How Weird Are You?" interview by A. Bryant, *New York Times*, January 9, 2010, accessed June 1, 2010, http://www.nytimes.com/2010/01/10/business/10corner.html.

63 A. Zuckerman, "Strong Corporate Cultures and Firm Performance: Are There Tradeoffs?" *Academy of Management Executive*, November 2002, 158–160.

64 E. Schein, *Organizational Culture and Leadership*, 2nd ed. (San Francisco: Jossey-Bass, 1992).

65 E. Byron, "'Call Me Mike!'—To Attract and Keep Talent, JCPenney CEO Loosens Up Once-Formal Workplace," *Wall Street Journal*, March 27, 2006, B1.

66 D. MacMillan, "AOL Tries for Some Silicon Valley Cred," *Bloomberg Businessweek*, March 24, 2011, accessed February 26, 2012, http://www.businessweek.com/magazine/content/11_14/b4222043205512.htm.

67 C. Daniels, "Does This Man Need a Shrink? Companies Are Using Psychological Testing to Screen Candidates for Top Jobs," *Fortune*, February 5, 2001, 205.

68 A. Bryant, "On Her Team, It's All About Bench Strength," *New York Times*, May 8, 2010, accessed November 11, 2011, http://www.nytimes.com/2010/05/09/business/09corner.html.

69 L. Buchanan, "You'll Never Work Alone," Inc.com, June 2011, accessed April 15, 2012, http://www.inc.com/winning-workplaces/magazine/201106/youll-never-work-alone.html.

Chapter 4

1 J. Schramm, "Perceptions on Ethics," *HR Magazine* 49 (November 2004): 176.

2 M. Jackson, "Workplace Cheating Rampant, Half of Employees Surveyed Admit They Take Unethical Actions," *Peoria Journal Star*, April 5, 1997.

3 C. Smith, "The Ethical Workplace," *Association Management* 52 (2000): 70–73.

4 D. Jones, "More Workers Do Now Than Before Recent Big Scandals," *USA Today*, February 12, 2003, B7.

5 A. Bryant, "In a Word, He Wants Simplicity," *New York Times*, May 23, 2009, accessed August 15, 2010, http://www.nytimes.com/2009/05/24/business/24corner.html?_r=2&pagewanted=1.

6 "2008 Report to the Nation on Occupational Fraud and Abuse," *Association of Certified Fraud Examiners*, accessed July 15, 2008, http://www.acfe.com/resources/publications.asp?copy=rttn; K. Gibson, "Excuses, Excuses: Moral Slippage in the Workplace," *Business Horizons* 43, no. 6 (2000): 65; S. L. Robinson and R. J. Bennett, "A Typology of Deviant Workplace Behaviors: A Multidimensional Scaling Study," *Academy of Management Journal* 38 (1995): 555–572.

7 Harvard Management Update, "Learn by 'Failing Forward,'" *Globe & Mail*, October 31, 2000, B17.

8 "March Madness Costs Offices $192 Million," *MSN Money*, March 15, 2011, accessed February 26, 2012, http://money.msn.com/saving-money-tips/post.aspx?post=87aa1afb-e29c-41ce-ac80-49cae0cc9a60.

9 C. Dufresne, "Work Farce: Distracted Employees, Absenteeism, Lost Profit and Productivity—March Madness is Bad for Business," *Los Angeles Times*, March 13, 2012, C1.

10 S. Needleman, "Businesses Say Theft by Their Workers Is Up—Companies Find That Trusted Employees Often Commit the Crimes, and They Believe the Recession Is to Blame," *Wall Street Journal*, December 11, 2008, B8.

11 J. Norman, "Cultivating a Culture of Honesty," *The Orange County [California] Register*, October 23, 2006.

12 K. Grannis, "Retail Losses Hit $41.6 Billion Last Year, According to National Retail Security Survey," *National Retail Federation*, June 11, 2007, accessed July 12, 2010, http://www.nrf.com/modules.php?name=News&op=viewlive&sp_id=318.

13 M. Pressler, "Cost and Robbers; Shoplifting and Employee Thievery Add Dollars to Price Tag," *Washington Post*, February 16, 2003, H05.

14 L. Middlebrooks and P. C. Vreeland, "Many U.S. Employers Aren't Doing Enough to Address Workplace Violence," *Alabama Employment Law Letter*, December 2006.

15 J. Merchant and J. Lundell, "Workplace Violence: A Report to the Nation," University of Iowa Injury Prevention Center, accessed July 15, 2008, http://www.public-health.uiowa.edu/iprc/NATION.PDF.

16 D. Palmer and A. Zakhem, "Bridging the Gap between Theory and Practice: Using the 1991 Federal Sentencing Guidelines as a Paradigm for Ethics Training," *Journal of Business Ethics* 29, no. 1/2 (2001): 77–84.

17 K. Tyler, "Do the Right Thing: Ethics Training Programs Help Employees Deal with Ethical Dilemmas," *HR Magazine*, February 2005, accessed March 13, 2009, http://moss07.shrm.org/Publications/hrmagazine/EditorialContent/Pages/0205tyler.aspx.

18 D. R. Dalton, M. B. Metzger, and J. W. Hill, "The 'New' U.S. Sentencing Commission Guidelines: A Wake-Up Call for Corporate America," *Academy of Management Executive* 8 (1994): 7–16.

19 B. Ettore, "Crime and Punishment: A Hard Look at White-Collar Crime," *Management Review* 83 (1994): 10–16.

20 F. Robinson and C. C. Pauze, "What Is a Board's Liability for Not Adopting a Compliance Program?" *Healthcare Financial Management* 51, no. 9 (1997): 64.

21 D. Murphy, "The Federal Sentencing Guidelines for Organizations: A Decade of Promoting Compliance and Ethics," *Iowa Law Review* 87 (2002): 697–719.

22 Robinson and Pauze, "What Is a Board's Liability?"

23 B. Schwartz, "The Nuts and Bolts of an Effective Compliance Program," *HR Focus* 74, no. 8 (1997): 13–15.

24 L. A. Hays, "A Matter of Time: Widow Sues IBM over Death Benefits," *Wall Street Journal*, July 6, 1995.

25 S. Morris and R. McDonald, "The Role of Moral Intensity in Moral Judgments: An Empirical Investigation," *Journal of Business Ethics* 14 (1995): 715–726; B. Flannery and D. May, "Environmental Ethical Decision Making in the U.S. Metal-Finishing Industry," *Academy of Management Journal* 43 (2000): 642–662.

26 L. Chao, "China Court Issues Rare Piracy Penalty to Windows Copycats,"

Wall Street Journal, August 22, 2009, A9.

27 L. Kohlberg, "Stage and Sequence: The Cognitive-Developmental Approach to Socialization," in *Handbook of Socialization Theory and Research*, ed. D. A. Goslin (Chicago: Rand McNally, 1969); L. Trevino, "Moral Reasoning and Business Ethics: Implications for Research, Education, and Management," *Journal of Business Ethics* 11 (1992): 445–459.

28 L. Trevino and M. Brown, "Managing to be Ethical: Debunking Five Business Ethics Myths," *Academy of Management Executive* 18 (May 2004): 69–81.

29 L. T. Hosmer, "Trust: The Connecting Link between Organizational Theory and Philosophical Ethics," *Academy of Management Review* 20 (1995): 379–403.

30 M. R. Cunningham, D. T. Wong, and A. P. Barbee, "Self-Presentation Dynamics on Overt Integrity Tests: Experimental Studies of the Reid Report," *Journal of Applied Psychology* 79 (1994): 643–658; J. Wanek, P. Sackett, and D. Ones, "Toward an Understanding of Integrity Test Similarities and Differences: An Item-Level Analysis of Seven Tests," *Personnel Psychology* 56 (Winter 2003): 873–894.

31 H. J. Bernardin, "Validity of an Honesty Test in Predicting Theft among Convenience Store Employees," *Academy of Management Journal* 36 (1993): 1097–1108.

32 J. M. Collins and F. L. Schmidt, "Personality, Integrity, and White Collar Crime: A Construct Validity Study," *Personnel Psychology* (1993): 295–311.

33 W. C. Borman, M. A. Hanson, and J. W. Hedge, "Personnel Selection," *Annual Review of Psychology* 48 (1997).

34 P. E. Murphy, "Corporate Ethics Statements: Current Status and Future Prospects," *Journal of Business Ethics* 14 (1995): 727–740.

35 "Code of Ethical Business Conduct," The Hershey Company, no date, accessed February 26, 2012, http://www.thehersheycompany.com/investors/corporate-governance/code-of-conduct.aspx.

36 "More Corporate Boards Involved in Ethics Programs; Ethics Training Becoming Standard Practice," *PR Newswire*, October 16, 2006.

37 S. J. Harrington, "What Corporate America Is Teaching about Ethics,"

Academy of Management Executive 5 (1991): 21–30.

38 L. A. Berger, "Train All Employees to Solve Ethical Dilemmas," *Best's Review–Life-Health Insurance Edition* 95 (1995): 70–80.

39 D. Schmidt, "Ethics Can Be Taught," *Inc.*, June 24, 2008, accessed July 10, 2010, http://www.inc.com/leadership-blog/2008/06/ethics_can_be_taught1.html.

40 L. Trevino, G. Weaver, D. Gibson, and B. Toffler, "Managing Ethics and Legal Compliance: What Works and What Hurts," *California Management Review* 41, no. 2 (1999): 131–151.

41 M. Swanton, "Compliance Comedy," *Inside Counsel* 22 (2011): 56.

42 "Leader's Guide: A Culture of Trust 2008," Lockheed Martin, accessed July 17, 2008, http://www.lockheedmartin.com/data/assets/corporate/documents/ethics/2008_EAT_Leaders_Guide.pdf.

43 E. White, "Theory & Practice: What Would You Do? Ethics Courses Get Context; Beyond Checking Boxes, Some Firms Start Talking about Handling Gray Areas," *Wall Street Journal*, June 12, 2006, B3.

44 A. Countryman, "Leadership Key Ingredient in Ethics Recipe, Experts Say," *Chicago Tribune*, December 1, 2002, Business 1.

45 "More Corporate Boards Involved in Ethics Programs," *PR Newswire*.

46 Supplemental Research Brief, "2009 National Business Ethics Survey: The Importance of Ethical Culture," Ethics Resource Center, June 2010, accessed February 25, 2011, http://www.ethics.org/files/u5/CultureSup4.pdf.

47 G. Weaver and L. Trevino, "Integrated and Decoupled Corporate Social Performance: Management Commitments, External Pressures, and Corporate Ethics Practices," *Academy of Management Journal* 42 (1999): 539–552; Trevino, Weaver, Gibson, and Toffler, "Managing Ethics and Legal Compliance.

48 J. Salopek, "Do the Right Thing," *Training & Development* 55 (July 2001): 38–44.

49 M. Gundlach, S. Douglas, and M. Martinko, "The Decision to Blow the Whistle: A Social Information Processing Framework," *Academy of Management Executive* 17 (2003): 107–123.

50 M. Schwartz, "Business Ethics: Time to Blow the Whistle?" *Globe & Mail*, March 5, 1998, B2.

51 H. Son, "BofA Ordered to Pay $930,000 to Fired Whistleblower," *Bloomberg*, September 14, 2011, accessed February 26, 2012, http://www.bloomberg.com/news/2011-09-14/bofa-ordered-to-pay-930-000-to-whistleblower.html.

52 M. P. Miceli and J. P. Near, "Whistleblowing: Reaping the Benefits," *Academy of Management Executive* 8 (1994): 65–72.

53 R. McMillan, "Netflix Fires Call Center Worker for Stealing Data," *Computerworld*, May 4, 2011, accessed February 27, 2011, http://www.computerworld.com/s/article/9216429/Netflix_fires_call_center_worker_for_stealing_data.

54 M. Master and E. Heresniak, "The Disconnect in Ethics Training," *Across the Board* 39 (September 2002): 51–52.

55 H. R. Bower, *Social Responsibilities of the Businessman* (New York: Harper & Row, 1953).

56 "Beyond the Green Corporation," *BusinessWeek*, January 29, 2007.

57 S. L. Wartick and P. L. Cochran, "The Evolution of the Corporate Social Performance Model," *Academy of Management Review* 10 (1985): 758–769.

58 J. Nocera, "The Paradox of Businesses as Do-Gooders," *New York Times*, November 11, 2006, C1.

59 S. Waddock, C. Bodwell, and S. Graves, "Responsibility: The New Business Imperative," *Academy of Management Executive* 16 (2002): 132–148.

60 T. Donaldson and L. E. Preston, "The Stakeholder Theory of the Corporation: Concepts, Evidence, and Implications," *Academy of Management Review* 20 (1995): 65–91.

61 "PepsiCo CEO: Redefine Profit and Loss" *Marketplace*, January 29, 2010, accessed February 25, 2010, http://marketplace.publicradio.org/display/web/2010/01/29/pm-davos-pepsi-ceo-q/.

62 M. B. E. Clarkson, "A Stakeholder Framework for Analyzing and Evaluating Corporate Social Performance," *Academy of Management Review* 20 (1995): 92–117.

63 B. Agle, R. Mitchell, and J. Sonnenfeld, "Who Matters to CEOs? An Investigation of Stakeholder Attributes and Salience, Corporate Performance, and CEO Values," *Academy of Management Journal* 42 (1999): 507–525.

64 K. Capell, "The Wool Industry Gets Bloodied," *BusinessWeek*, July 14, 2008, 40.

65 S. Williams and J. Melocco, "Telling the Real Yarn," *The Daily Telegraph* (Australia), June 14, 2008, 115.

66 "Australian Wool Innovation's Road Map for Flystrike Control and Prevention," *Australian Wool Innovation*, accessed February 26, 2011, http://images.wool.com/pub/AWI0595_Flystrike_Road_Map_Leaflet_271109.pdf.

67 E. W. Orts, "Beyond Shareholders: Interpreting Corporate Constituency Statutes," *George Washington Law Review* 61 (1992): 14–135.

68 A. B. Carroll, "A Three-Dimensional Conceptual Model of Corporate Performance," *Academy of Management Review* 4 (1979): 497–505.

69 Ibid.

70 M. Bunz, "What Ended Owen Van Natta's Short Reign at MySpace?" *The Guardian*, February 11, 2010, accessed August 12, 2010, http://www.guardian.co.uk/media/pda/2010/feb/11/myspace-murdoch.

71 J. Lublin and M. Murray, "CEOs Leave Faster Than Ever Before as Boards, Investors Lose Patience," *Wall Street Journal Interactive*, October 27, 2000.

72 J. Lublin, "CEO Firings On the Rise as Downturn Gains Steam," *Wall Street Journal*, January 13, 2009, B1.

73 D. Woodruff, "Europe Shows More CEOs the Door," *Wall Street Journal*, July 1, 2002.

74 C. Bray, "Ex-Monster President Found Guilty in Backdating Case," *Wall Street Journal*, May 13, 2009, C4.

75 J. Bandler, "McKelvey Admits Monster Backdating; Ex-CEO to Repay Millions but Avoids Jail Due to Illness," *Wall Street Journal*, January 24, 2008, B4.

76 P. Sonne, C. Bryan-Low, and R. Adams, "Tabloid to Close amid Scandal," *Wall Street Journal*, July 8, 2011, A1.

77 "About the Major Earthquake in Northeastern Japan," Honda, March 14, 2011, accessed February 26, 2012, http://world.honda.com/news/2011/c110314Earthquake-Northeastern-Japan/index.html; "Ikea Japan to Give Home Products to Evacuees in Quake-Hit Miyagi, Iwate," *Breitbart*, May 12, 2011, accessed February 26, 2012, http://www.breitbart.com/article.php?id=D9N6BKO00; "Softbank CEO to Donate $120M to Tsunami Victims," *ABC News*, April 4, 2011, accessed February 26, 2012, http://abcnews.go.com/Technology/wireStory?id=13289484#.T0xFT_GPU2w.

78 C. Duhigg, "In China, Human Costs Are Built into an iPad," *New York Times*, January 25, 2012, accessed February 28, 2012, http://www.nytimes.com/2012/01/26/business/ieconomy-apples-ipad-and-the-human-costs-for-workers-in-china.html?pagewanted=all; H. Perlberg and T. Culpan, "Apple Says Fair Labor Association Began Foxconn Inspection," *Bloomberg Businessweek*, February 14, 2012, accessed February 28, 2012, http://www.bloomberg.com/news/2012-02-13/apple-says-fair-labor-association-will-inspect-suppliers-including-foxconn.html; J. Stern, "Foxconn, Apple, and the Fair Labor Association Respond to ABC News' Exclusive Report," *ABCNews*, February 22, 2012, accessed February 28, 2012, http://abcnews.go.com/blogs/technology/2012/02/foxconn-apple-and-the-fair-labor-association-respond-to-abc-news-exclusive-report/.

79 A. Patrick, "After Protests, Unilever Does About-Face on Palm Oil," *Wall Street Journal*, May 2, 2008, B1.

80 "Sustainable Palm Oil," Unilever, accessed August 30, 2009, http://www.unilever.com.

81 "FACT Sheet—Merck Mectizan® Donation Program—River Blindness (Onchocerciasis)," Merck, accessed February 26, 2011, http://www.merck.com/cr/docs/River%20Blindness%20Fact%20Sheet.pdf.

82 A. Weintraub, "Will Pfizer's Giveaway Drugs Polish Its Public Image?" *BusinessWeek*, August 3, 2009, 13.

83 A. McWilliams and D. Siegel, "Corporate Social Responsibility: A Theory of the Firm Perspective," *Academy of Management Review* 26, no.1 (2001): 117–127; H. Haines, "Noah Joins Ranks of Socially Responsible Funds," *Dow Jones News Service*, October 13, 1995. A meta-analysis of 41 different studies also found no relationship between corporate social responsibility and profitability. Though not reported in the meta-analysis, when confidence intervals are placed around its average sample-weighted correlation of.06, the lower confidence interval includes zero, leading to the conclusion that there is no relationship between corporate social responsibility and profitability. See M. Orlitzky, "Does Firm Size Confound the Relationship between Corporate Social Responsibility and Firm Performance?" *Journal of Business Ethics* 33 (2001): 167–180; S. Ambec and P. Lanoie, "Does It Pay to Be Green? A Systematic Overview," *Academy of Management Perspectives*, 22 (2008): 45–62.

84 M. Orlitzky, "Payoffs to Social and Environmental Performance," *Journal of Investing* 14 (2005): 48–51.

85 M. Orlitzky, F. Schmidt, and S. Rynes, "Corporate Social and Financial Performance: A Meta-analysis," *Organization Studies* 24 (2003): 403–441.

86 Orlitzky, "Payoffs to Social and Environmental Performance."

87 G. Reynolds, "Can Honda Bring Corporate-Style Jet Travel to the Masses?" *Popular Mechanics*, March 4, 2010, accessed September 5, 2010, http://www.popularmechanics.com/technology/aviation/news/hondajet_air_travel.

88 Orlitzky, Schmidt, and Rynes, "Corporate Social and Financial Performance."

89 A. Murray and A. Strassel, "Environment (A Special Report); Ahead of the Pack: GE's Jeffrey Immelt on Why It's Business, Not Personal," *Wall Street Journal*, March 24, 2008, R3.

90 K. Kranhold, "Greener Postures: GE's Environment Push Hits Business Realities; CEO's Quest to Reduce Emissions Irks Clients; The Battle of the Bulbs," *Wall Street Journal*, September 14, 2007, A1.

91 "Ecoimagination Is GE," 2008 Ecoimagination Annual Report, accessed August 30, 2009, http://ge.ecoimagination.com.

92 D. Kadlec and B. Van Voorst, "The New World of Giving: Companies Are Doing More Good, and Demanding More Back," *Time*, May 5, 1997, 62.

93 P. Carlin, "Will Rapid Growth Stunt Corporate Do-Gooders?" *Business & Society Review* (Spring 1995), 36–43.

94 K. Brown, "Chilling at Ben & Jerry's: Cleaner, Greener," *Wall Street Journal*, April 15, 2004, B1.

Chapter 5

1 L. A. Hill, *Becoming a Manager: Master a New Identity* (Boston: Harvard Business School Press, 1992).

2 C. Reiter, "Having Thrived in America, Hyundai Takes On Europe," *Bloomberg Businessweek*, January 26, 2012, accessed February 28, 2012, http://www.businessweek.com/magazine/having-thrived-in-america-hyundai-takes-on-europe-01262012.html.

3 E. A. Locke and G. P. Latham, *A Theory of Goal Setting & Task Performance* (Englewood Cliffs, NJ: Prentice Hall, 1990).

4 M. E. Tubbs, "Goal-Setting: A Meta-Analytic Examination of the Empirical Evidence," *Journal of Applied Psychology* 71 (1986): 474–483.

5 J. Bavelas and E. S. Lee, "Effect of Goal Level on Performance: A Trade-Off of Quantity and Quality," *Canadian Journal of Psychology* 32 (1978): 219–240.

6 D. Turner, "Ability, Aspirations Fine, but Persistence Is What Gets Results," *Seattle Times*, February 13, 2005, http://community.seattletimes.nwsource.com/archive/?date=20030215&slug=dale15m.

7 Harvard Management Update, "Learn by 'Failing Forward,'" *Globe & Mail*, October 31, 2000, B17.

8 C. C. Miller, "Strategic Planning and Firm Performance: A Synthesis of More Than Two Decades of Research," *Academy of Management Performance* 37 (1994): 1649–1665.

9 H. Mintzberg, "Rethinking Strategic Planning: Part I: Pitfalls and Fallacies," *Long Range Planning* 27 (1994): 12–21, and "Part II: New Roles for Planners," 22–30; H. Mintzberg, "The Pitfalls of Strategic Planning," *California Management Review* 36 (1993): 32–47.

10 D. McCarty and B. Jinks, "Kodak Files for Bankruptcy as Digital Era Spells End to Film," *Bloomberg Businessweek*, January 25, 2012, accessed February 28, 2012, http://www.businessweek.com/news/2012-01-25/kodak-files-for-bankruptcy-as-digital-era-spells-end-to-film.html.

11 Mintzberg, "The Pitfalls of Strategic Planning."

12 A. Cosslett, "Corner Office: Where Are You When the Going Gets Tough?" interview by A. Bryant, *New York Times*, April 2, 2010, accessed August 11, 2010, http://www.nytimes.com/2010/04/04/business/04corner.html?_r=1.

13 Locke and Latham, *A Theory of Goal Setting & Task Performance*.

14 A. King, B. Oliver, B. Sloop, and K. Vaverek, *Planning & Goal Setting for Improved Performance: Participant's Guide* (Cincinnati, OH: Thomson Executive Press, 1995).

15 J. Korzeniewski, "Honda Plan Calls for Best Fuel Economy in Every Segment within Three Years," *Autoblog*, December 5, 2011, accessed February 28, 2012, http://www.autoblog.com/2011/12/05/honda-plan-calls-for-best-fuel-economy-in-every-segment-within-t/.

16 C. Loomis, J. Schlosser, J. Sung, M. Boyle, and P. Neering, "The 15% Delusion: Brash Predictions about Earnings Growth Often Lead to Missed Targets, Battered Stock, and Creative Accounting—And That's When Times Are Good," *Fortune*, February 5, 2001, 102; H. Paster, "Manager's Journal: Be Prepared," *Wall Street Journal*, September 24, 2001, A24; P. Sellers, "The New Breed: The Latest Crop of CEOs Is Disciplined, Deferential, Even a Bit Dull," *Fortune*, November 18, 2002, 66; H. Klein and M. Wesson, "Goal and Commitment and the Goal-Setting Process: Conceptual Clarification and Empirical Synthesis," *Journal of Applied Psychology* 84 (1999): 885–896.

17 Locke and Latham, *A Theory of Goal Setting & Task Performance*.

18 S. Frier, "Mozilla's Catch-Up Strategy for Mobile," *Bloomberg Businessweek*, December 5–December 12, 2011, 48–49.

19 A. Bandura and D. H. Schunk, "Cultivating Competence, Self-Efficacy, and Intrinsic Interest through Proximal Self-Motivation," *Journal of Personality & Social Psychology* 41 (1981): 586–598.

20 Locke and Latham, *A Theory of Goal Setting & Task Performance*.

21 M. J. Neubert, "The Value of Feedback and Goal Setting over Goal Setting Alone and Potential Moderators of This Effect: A Meta-Analysis," *Human Performance* 11 (1998): 321–335.

22 E. H. Bowman and D. Hurry, "Strategy through the Option Lens: An Integrated View of Resource Investments and the Incremental-Choice Process," *Academy of Management Review* 18 (1993): 760–782.

23 M. Lawson, "In Praise of Slack: Time Is of the Essence," *Academy of Management Executive* 15 (2000): 125–135.

24 A. Efrati and S. E. Ante, "Google's $12.5 Billion Gamble," *Wall Street Journal*, August 16, 2011, accessed February 26, 2012, http://online.wsj.com/article/SB10001424053111903392904576509953821437960.html; "Financial Statement for Google Inc.," Google, accessed February 26 2012, http://www.google.com/finance?q=NASDAQ:GOOG&fstype=ii; B. Womack, "Google Discloses $151 Million Price Tag for Acquisition of Zagat Service," *Bloomberg Businessweek*, October 26, 2011, http://www.bloomberg.com/news/2011-10-27/google-spent-151-million-on-zagat-review-service-last-quarter.html; R. Singel, "Feds Clear Google to Buy ITA Travel Search Company, Conditions Apply," Wired.com, April 8, 2011, accessed February 26, 2012, http://www.wired.com/epicenter/2011/04/google-ita/.

25 O. Kinnander and K. McLaughlin, "Electrolux Takes Aim at Whirlpool," *Bloomberg Businessweek*, March 24, 2011, accessed February 26 2012, http://www.businessweek.com/magazine/content/11_14/b4222033381179.htm.

26 J. C. Collins and J. I. Porras, "Organizational Vision and Visionary Organizations," *California Management Review* (Fall 1991): 30–52.

27 Ibid.

28 Collins and Porras, "Organizational Vision and Visionary Organizations"; J. A. Pearce II, "The Company Mission as a Strategic Goal," *Sloan Management Review* (Spring 1982): 15–24. Collins and Porras define an organization's mission: "A mission is a clear and compelling goal that serves to unify an organization's efforts. An effective mission must stretch and challenge the organization, yet be achievable." However, many others define mission as an organization's purpose. In this edition, to be more specific and avoid confusion, we used Collins and Porras's term "purpose statement," meaning a clear statement of an organization's purpose or reason for existence. Furthermore, we continued to use Collins and Porras's definition of a mission (i.e., "a clear and compelling goal...") but instead call it "the strategic objective."

29 "President Bush Announces New Vision for Space Exploration Program," The White House, accessed April 17, 2005, http://www.whitehouse.gov/news/releases/2004/01/20040114-1.html.

30 "NASA's Exploration Systems Mission Directorate," Exploration: NASA's Plans to Explore the Moon, Mars, and Beyond, accessed May 29, 2009, http://www.nasa.gov.

31 J. Mouawad, "American Airlines Seeks 13,000 Job Cuts," *New York Times*, February 1, 2012, accessed April 23, 2012, http://www.nytimes.com/2012/02/02/business/american-airlines-seeks-job-cuts.html?_r=1.

32 L. Lorberf, "Running the Show—An Open Book: When Companies Share

Their Financial Data with Employees, the Results Can Be Dramatic," *Wall Street Journal*, February 23, 2009, R8.

33 Y. Okada and M. Suga, "Sony, Toyota Cut Electricity Usage as Mandatory Savings Start," *Bloomberg Business-week*, June 30, 2011, accessed February 26, 2012, http://www.bloomberg.com/news/2011-07-01/sony-toyota-cut-electricity-usage-as-mandatory-savings-start.html.

34 "2011 Working Mother 100 Best Companies," *Working Mother*, accessed February 26, 2012, http://www.workingmother.com/best-company-list/116542.

35 Adapted from quality procedure at G & G Manufacturing, Cincinnati, Ohio.

36 N. Humphrey, "References a Tricky Issue for Both Sides," *Nashville Business Journal* 11 (May 8, 1995): 1A.

37 K. R. MacCrimmon, R. N. Taylor, and E. A. Locke, "Decision Making and Problem Solving," in *Handbook of Industrial & Organizational Psychology*, ed. M. D. Dunnette (Chicago: Rand McNally, 1976), 1397–1453.

38 A. Zimmerman, "Cricket Lee Takes on the Fashion Industry," *Wall Street Journal,* March 17, 2008, R1.

39 MacCrimmon, Taylor, and Locke, "Decision Making and Problem Solving."

40 G. Kress, "The Role of Interpretation in the Decision Process," *Industrial Management* 37 (1995): 10–14.

41 A. Lowrey, "Readers without Borders," July 20, 2011, *Slate Magazine*, accessed February 29, 2012, http://www.slate.com/articles/business/moneybox/2011/07/readers_without_borders.html.

42 "Notebook Shipments Surpass Desktops in the U.S. Market for the First Time, according to IDC," *IDC*, October 28, 2008, accessed May 30, 2009, http://www.idc.com.

43 *Consumer Reports Buying Guide 2006*, 129–131.

44 "New-Vehicle Ratings Comparison by Car Category," *ConsumerReports.org*, February 19, 2005, http://www.consumerreports.org/cro/cars/index.htm.

45 P. Djang, "Selecting Personal Computers," *Journal of Research on Computing in Education* 25 (1993): 327.

46 "European Cities Monitor," *Cushman & Wakefield*, 2010, http://www.europeancitiesmonitor.eu/wp-content/uploads/2010/10/ECM-2010-Full-Version.pdf.

47 B. Dumaine, "The Trouble with Teams," *Fortune*, September 5, 1994, 86–92.

48 I. L. Janis, *Groupthink* (Boston: Houghton Mifflin, 1983).

49 C. P. Neck and C. C. Manz, "From Groupthink to Teamthink: Toward the Creation of Constructive Thought Patterns in Self-Managing Work Teams," *Human Relations* 47 (1994): 929–952; J. Schwartz and M. L. Wald, "'Groupthink' Is 30 Years Old, and Still Going Strong," *New York Times*, March 9, 2003, 5.

50 "Everything on One Calendar, Please," *New York Times*, December 26, 2009, accessed January 2, 2010, http://www.nytimes.com/2009/12/27/business/27corner.html?pagewanted=all.

51 A. Mason, W. A. Hochwarter, and K. R. Thompson, "Conflict: An Important Dimension in Successful Management Teams," *Organizational Dynamics* 24 (1995): 20.

52 C. Olofson, "So Many Decisions, So Little Time: What's Your Problem?" *Fast Company*, October 1, 1999, 62.

53 Ibid.

54 R. Cosier and C. R. Schwenk, "Agreement and Thinking Alike: Ingredients for Poor Decisions," *Academy of Management Executive* 4 (1990): 69–74.

55 K. Jenn and E. Mannix, "The Dynamic Nature of Conflict: A Longitudinal Study of Intragroup Conflict and Group Performance," *Academy of Management Journal* 44, no. 2 (2001): 238–251; R. L. Priem, D. A. Harrison, and N. K. Muir, "Structured Conflict and Consensus Outcomes in Group Decision Making," *Journal of Management* 21 (1995): 691–710.

56 A. Van De Ven and A. L. Delbecq, "Nominal versus Interacting Group Processes for Committee Decision Making Effectiveness," *Academy of Management Journal* 14 (1971): 203–212.

57 A. R. Dennis and J. S. Valicich, "Group, Sub-Group, and Nominal Group Idea Generation: New Rules for a New Media?" *Journal of Management* 20 (1994): 723–736.

58 R. B. Gallupe, W. H. Cooper, M. L. Grise, and L. M. Bastianutti, "Blocking Electronic Brainstorms," *Journal of Applied Psychology* 79 (1994): 77–86.

59 R. B. Gallupe and W. H. Cooper, "Brainstorming Electronically," *Sloan Management Review*, Fall 1993, 27–36.

60 Ibid.

61 G. Kay, "Effective Meetings through Electronic Brainstorming," *Management Quarterly* 35 (1995): 15.

62 A. LaPlante, "90s Style Brainstorming," *Forbes ASAP*, October 25, 1993, 44.

Chapter 6

1 C. Albanesius, "iPhone 4S Impacted iPad Market Share More than Kindle Fire," *PC Magazine*, February 16, 2012, accessed April 10 2012, http://www.pcmag.com/article2/0,2817,2400378,00.asp; R. Alexander, "Apple's Toughest Competition in the Fourth-Quarter Tablet Market Was...Apple," *iSupplie*, February 16, 2012, accessed April 10, 2012, http://www.isuppli.com/Display-Materials-and-Systems/News/Pages/Apples-Toughest-Competition-in-the-Fourth-Quarter-Tablet-Market-Was-Apple.aspx; T. Claburn, "Apple's New iPad: 6 Key Features," *InformationWeek*, March 7, 2012, accessed April 10, 2012, http://www.informationweek.com/news/hardware/mac/232602197; H. Tsukayama, "Apple's 'iPad3' Faces Stiffer Competition than iPad2," *Washington Post*, March 1, 2012, accessed April 10, 2012, http://www.washingtonpost.com/business/technology/apples-ipad-3-faces-stiffer-competition-than-ipad-2/2012/02/29/gIQAGhzKkR_story.html.

2 J. Barney, "Firm Resources and Sustained Competitive Advantage," *Journal of Management* 17 (1991): 99–120; J. Barney, "Looking Inside for Competitive Advantage," *Academy of Management Executive* 9 (1995): 49–61.

3 D. Bailey, "Is It Time to Say Goodbye to Netbooks?" *The Motley Fool*, April 30, 2011, accessed March 1, 2012, http://www.fool.com/investing/general/2011/04/30/is-it-time-to-say-goodbye-to-netbooks.aspx; S. Lohr, "Netbooks Lose Status as Tablets Like the iPad Rise," *New York Times*, February 13, 2011, accessed March 1, 2012, http://www.nytimes.com/2011/02/14/technology/14netbook.html?pagewanted=all.

4 D. Pogue, "Just How Many Android Tablet Apps Are There?" *New York Times*, July 1, 2011, accessed March 2, 2012, http://pogue.blogs.nytimes.com/2011/07/01/mystery-how-many-android-tablet-apps/.

5 Juniper Networks, "2011 Mobile Threats Report," accessed March 1, 2012, http://www.juniper.net/us/en/local/pdf/additional-resources

/jnpr-2011-mobile-threats-report
.pdf?utm_source=promo&utm
_medium=right_promo&utm
_campaign=mobile_threat_report
_0212.

6 J. Newman, "In Defense of Google Music," *Time*, February 24, 2012, accessed March 1, 2012, http://techland .time.com/2012/02/24/in-defense-of -google-music/; D. Pogue, "A Look at Apple's iCloud," *New York Times*, October 13, 2011, accessed March 1, 2012, http://pogue.blogs.nytimes .com/2011/10/13/a-look-at-icloud/; B. Stone, "Will Amazon's Cloud Music Service Fly?" *Bloomberg Businessweek*, March 31, 2011, accessed March 1, 2012, http://www .businessweek.com/magazine/content /11_15/b4223043644684.htm.

7 S. Hart and C. Banbury, "How Strategy-Making Processes Can Make a Difference," *Strategic Management Journal* 15 (1994): 251–269.

8 R. A. Burgelman, "Fading Memories: A Process Theory of Strategic Business Exit in Dynamic Environments," *Administrative Science Quarterly* 39 (1994): 24–56; R. A. Burgelman and A. S. Grove, "Strategic Dissonance," *California Management Review* 38 (Winter 1996): 8–28.

9 C. Passariello, "Carrefour's Makeover Plan: Become IKEA of Groceries," *Wall Street Journal*, September 16, 2010, B1.

10 C. Passariello, "Olofsson's Fight against the Status Quo at Carrefour," *Wall Street Journal*, September 16, 2010, accessed online March 29, 2011.

11 Passariello, "Carrefour's Makeover Plan."

12 Burgelman and Grove, "Strategic Dissonance."

13 B. Saporito, "Behind the Troubles at Toyota," *Time*, February 11, 2010, accessed September 23, 2010, http:// www.time.com/time/business/article /0,8599,1963595-2,00.html.

14 A. Ohnsman, J. Green, and K. Inoue, "Toyota Recall Crisis Said to Lie in Cost Cuts, Growth Ambitions," *Bloomberg*, February 26, 2010, accessed March 30, 2011, http:// www.bloomberg.com/apps/news?pid =newsarchive&sid=aF0aX8t0Q6lk.

15 A. Zimmerman, "Hasbro Falls Prey to 'Angry Birds,'" *Wall Street Journal*, December 15, 2011, accessed March 1, 2012, http://online.wsj.com/article /SB1000142405297020484450457700 98780656830196.html.

16 A. Fiegenbaum, S. Hart, and D. Schendel, "Strategic Reference Point Theory," *Strategic Management Journal* 17 (1996): 219–235.

17 "Consumer Reports Automaker Report Cards 2012: Subaru Drives into Top Spot as Honda Slips," *Sacramento Bee*, March 1, 2012, accessed March 1, 2012, http://www.sacbee .com/2012/02/28/4297509/consumer -reports-automaker-report.html.

18 B. Gottesman, "The Tech Brands You Trust Most," *PC Magazine*, October 2011, 30–43.

19 S. Clifford, "Where Wal-Mart Failed, Aldi Succeeds," *New York Times*, March 29, 2011, accessed March 1, 2012, http://www.nytimes .com/2011/03/30/business/30aldi .html?pagewanted =all.

20 A. Fiegenbaum and H. Thomas, "Strategic Groups as Reference Groups: Theory, Modeling and Empirical Examination of Industry and Competitive Strategy," *Strategic Management Journal* 16 (1995): 461–476.

21 "Continued Weaknesses in Housing and the Overall Economy Are Now Foreseen to Result in Three Consecutive Years of Market Declines," *Home Improvement Research Institute*, accessed June 5, 2009, http:// www.hiri.org.

22 R. K. Reger and A. S. Huff, "Strategic Groups: A Cognitive Perspective," *Strategic Management Journal* 14 (1993): 103–124.

23 "U.S. Store Count by State," Home Depot, accessed April 5, 2011, http:// ir.homedepot.com/phoenix.zhtml?c =63646&p=irol-factsFaq; "Frequently Asked Questions," Lowes, accessed April 5, 2011, http://media.lowes.com.

24 "Frequently Asked Questions," Ace Hardware, accessed April 6, 2011, http://www.acehardware.com/corp /index.jsp?page=faq.

25 "About Aubuchon Hardware," Aubuchon Hardware, accessed April 6, 2011, http://www.hardwarestore.com /about-aubuchon-hardware.aspx.

26 "Frequently Asked Questions," Ace Hardware, accessed July 29, 2008, http://www.acehardware.com/corp /index.jsp?page=faq.

27 84 Lumber, accessed July 29, 2008, http://www.84lumber.com.

28 "Menard, Inc.," *Hoover's Company Profiles*, May 8, 2003.

29 J. Samuelson, "Tough Guy Billionaire," *Forbes*, February 24, 1997, 64–66.

30 S. Bucksot, C. Jensen, and D. Tratensek, "Where Are We Headed?" *2005 Market Measure: The Industry's Annual Report*, March 6, 2005, http:// www.nrha.org/MM2004.pdf.

31 H. Murphy, "Menard's Tool in Retail Battle: Gigantic Stores," *Crain's Chicago Business*, August 12, 2002, 3.

32 Ibid.

33 M. Lubatkin, "Value-Creating Mergers: Fact or Folklore?" *Academy of Management Executive* 2 (1988): 295–302; M. Lubatkin and S. Chatterjee, "Extending Modern Portfolio Theory into the Domain of Corporate Diversification: Does It Apply?" *Academy of Management Journal* 37 (1994): 109–136; M. H. Lubatkin and P. J. Lane, "Psst... The Merger Mavens Still Have It Wrong!" *Academy of Management Executive* 10 (1996): 21–39.

34 "Who We Are," 3M, accessed April 7, 2009, http://solutions.3m.com /wps/portal/3M/en_US/about-3M /information/about/us/.

35 D. Holthaus, "Pringles Sale Allows Procter & Gamble to keep Its Focus," *Cincinnati.com*, April 5, 2011, accessed March 1, 2012, http://news .cincinnati.com/article/20110405 /BIZ/304050039/Pringles-sale-allows -Procter-Gamble-keep-its-focus; M. Geller and J. Wohl, "Kellogg to Buy Pringles for $2.7 Billion," *Reuters*, February 15, 2012, accessed March 1, 2012, http://www.reuters.com/article /2012/02/15/us-kellogg-pringles -idUSTRE81E0S620120215.

36 "Products & Services," General Electric, no date, accessed March 1, 2012, http://www.ge.com/products_services /index.html.

37 "Affiliated Companies," Samsung, accessed April 7, 2011, http://www .samsung.com/hk_en/aboutsamsung /samsunggroup/affiliatedcompanies /SAMSUNGGroup _AffiliatedCompanies.html.

38 Http://www.bcg.com/this_is_BCG /bcg_history/bcg_history_2005.html; http:www.wikipedia.org.

39 D. Hambrick, I. MacMillan, and D. Day, "Strategic Attributes and Performance in the BCG Matrix—A PIMS-based Analysis of Industrial Product Businesses," *Academy of Management Journal* 25 (1982): 510–531.

40 J. Armstrong and R. Brodie, "Effects of Portfolio Planning Methods on Decision Making: Experimental Results," *International Journal of Research in Marketing* 11 (1994): 73–84.

41 K. Brooker, "Plugging the Leaks at P&G: A First-Year Report Card for

CEO Durk Jager," *Fortune*, February 21, 2000, 44; "R&D's Formula for Success," Procter & Gamble, accessed March 17, 2009, http://www.pg.com /science/rd_formula_success.jhtml.

42 J. McCracken and E. Byron, "P&G Considers Booting Some Brands," *Wall Street Journal*, October 29, 2009, B1.

43 P. Sellers, "P&G: Teaching an Old Dog New Tricks," *Fortune*, May 31, 2004, 166.

44 E. Byron, "P&G Rekindles an Old Flame; New Febreze Candles Aim to Extend Product Line; Is Growth a Burning Issue?" *Wall Street Journal*, June 5, 2007, B6.

45 E. Byron, "Febreze Joins P&G's $1 Billion Club," *Wall Street Journal*, March 9, 2011, B1.

46 J. A. Pearce II, "Selecting among Alternative Grand Strategies," *California Management Review* (Spring 1982): 23–31.

47 M. Laycock, "Aero Sales Help York Nestle Factory in Tough Year," *The Press*, December 31, 2011, accessed March 2, 2012, http://www.yorkpress .co.uk/news/9446032.Aero_sales _help_York_factory_in_tough_year/; T. Mulier, "Breathing More Profit into Chocolate Bars," *Bloomberg Businessweek*, February 24, 2011, accessed March 2, 2012, http:// www.businessweek.com/magazine /content/11_10/b4218021563564 .htm; "Nestle Reports £6.5bn Annual Profit," *The Independent*, February 16, 2012, accessed March 2, 2012, http:// www.independent.co.uk/news/business /news/nestle-reports-65bn-annual -profit-6977817.html.

48 "About REI," *REI*, accessed June 7, 2009, http://www.rei.com/aboutrei /about_rei.html; "Recreational Equipment, Inc.," *Hoover*, accessed June 7, 2009, http://www.hoovers.com.

49 J. A. Pearce II, "Retrenchment Remains the Foundation of Business Turnaround," *Strategic Management Journal* 15 (1994): 407–417.

50 Associated Press, "Delta Cuts Number of Flights to Small Cities in the Midwest," *New York Times*, July 15, 2011, accessed March 2, 2012, http://www .nytimes.com/2011/07/16/business /delta-cuts-flights-to-small-cities-in -midwest.html; B. Murtzabaugh, "Buyouts Not Enough to Prevent Lay-offs at Delta," *USA Today*, September 9, 2011, accessed March 2, 2012, http://travel.usatoday.com/flights /post/2011/09/delta-lay-offs/546536/1.

51 "50 Top Performers," *Bloomberg Businessweek*, June 21–27, 2010, 56–58.

52 P. Sonne, "Unilever Brings Out Its Magnum, Escalating a U.S. Ice Cream War," *Wall Street Journal*, March 18, 2011, B5.

53 D. Winning, "Anadarko Considers Mozambique Gas Site," *Wall Street Journal*, November 30, 2010, April 7, 2008, accessed April 8, 2011, http:// online.wsj.com/article/SB1000142405 2748704584804575645190168232 732.html.

54 "10 Pharmaceutical Stocks and Their Patent Expiration Drugs," *Seeking Alpha*, accessed June 7, 2009, http:// www.seekingalpha.com.

55 Associated Press, "Gasoline Pump Price in US Climbs for 24 Straight Days to $3.74 per Gallon," *Washington Post*, March 2, 2012, accessed March 2, 2012, http://www .washingtonpost.com/business /industries/gasoline-pump-price -in-us-climbs-for-24-straight-days-to -374-per-gallon/2012/03/02 /gIQAzpnnmR_story.html.

56 E. Fredrix and S. Skidmore, "Costco Nixes Coke Products over Pricing Dispute," *ABCNews.com*, November 17, 2009, http://abcnews.go.com/Business /wireStory?id=9103485; "Update1— Costco to Resume Stocking Coca-Cola Drinks," *Reuters*, December 10, 2009, http://www.reuters.com/article /idUSN1020190520091210.

57 S. Berfield, "A Startup's New Prescription for Eyewear" *Bloomberg Businessweek*, June 30, 2011, accessed March 2, 2012, http://www .businessweek.com/magazine/hip -eyewear-warby-parkers-new -spectacles-07012011.html.

58 S. Morgan, "Getting Dirty in Dutch Country," *Bloomberg Businessweek*, July 26–August 1, 2010, 69–71.

59 R. E. Miles and C. C. Snow, *Organizational Strategy, Structure, & Process* (New York: McGraw-Hill, 1978); S. Zahra and J. A. Pearce, "Research Evidence on the Miles-Snow Typology," *Journal of Management* 16 (1990): 751–768; W. L. James and K. J. Hatten, "Further Evidence on the Validity of the Self Typing Paragraph Approach: Miles and Snow Strategic Archetypes in Banking," *Strategic Management Journal* 16 (1995): 161–168.

60 B. Fritz, "Redbox and Verizon to Create Streaming Movie Service," *Los Angeles Times*, February 7, 2012, accessed March 2, 2012, http://articles .latimes.com/2012/feb/07/business /la-fi-ct-verizon-redbox-20120207.

61 M. Chen, "Competitor Analysis and Interfirm Rivalry: Toward a Theoretical Integration," *Academy of Management Review* 21 (1996): 100–134; J. C. Baum and H. J. Korn, "Competitive Dynamics of Interfirm Rivalry," *Academy of Management Journal* 39 (1996): 255–291.

62 M. Chen, "Competitor Analysis and Interfirm Rivalry: Toward a Theoretical Integration," *Academy of Management Review* 21 (1996): 100–134.

63 S. Leung, "Wendy's Sees Green in Salad Offerings—More Sophistication, Ethnic Flavors Appeal to Women, Crucial to Building Market Share," *Wall Street Journal*, April 24, 2003, B2.

64 M. Stopa, "Wendy's New-Fashioned Growth: Buy Hardee's," *Crain's Detroit Business*, October 21, 1996.

65 L. Lavelle, "The Chickens Come Home to Roost, and Boston Market Is Prepared to Expand," *The Record*, October 6, 1996.

66 J. Jargon, "Subway Runs Past McDonald's Chain," *Wall Street Journal (Online)*, March 8, 2011, accessed April 9, 2011; "2010 Annual Report," McDonald's, accessed April 9, 2011, http://www.aboutmcdonalds.com/etc /medialib/aboutMcDonalds/investor _relations3.Par.56096.File.dat/2010.

67 "Frequently Asked Questions," Subway Restaurants, accessed March 18, 2009, http://www.subway.com /subwayroot/AboutSubway /subwayFaqs.aspx.

68 S. Leung, "Fast-Food Firms' Big Budgets Don't Buy Consumer Loyalty," *Wall Street Journal*, July 24, 2003, B4.

69 C. Cain Miller, "Amazon to Sell the Kindle Reader at a Lower Price, but with Advertising Added," *New York Times*, April 11, 2011, accessed March 5, 2012, http://www.nytimes .com/2011/04/12/technology /12amazon.html; J. Pepitone, "Amazon Pushes Hard on Ad-Supported Kindle Line," *CNNMoney*, October 3, 2011, accessed March 5, 2012, http://money .cnn.com/2011/10/03/technology /amazon_kindle_ads/index.htm.

70 D. Ketchen, Jr., C. Snow, and V. Street, "Improving Firm Performance by Matching Strategic Decision-Making Processes to Competitive Dynamics," *Academy of Management Executive* 18 (2004): 29–43.

71 N. Olivarez-Giles, "Barnes & Noble Nook Simple Touch E-reader Drops to $99," *Los Angeles Times*, Novem-

ber 7, 2011, accessed March 5, 2012, http://latimesblogs.latimes.com /technology/2011/11/barnes-noble -drops-nook-simple-touch-ereader-to -99-dollars.html.

72 C. Sorrel, "Remove Ads from 'Special Offers' Kindle for $30," *Wired.com*, October 7, 2011, accessed March 5, 2012, http://www.wired.com /gadgetlab/2011/10/remove-ads -from-special-offers-kindle-for-30/.

73 M. J. Perenson, "Kindle Fire vs. Nook Tablet: Which Should You Buy?" *PC World*, November 18, 2011, accessed March 10, 2012, http://www.pcworld .com/article/244282/kindle_fire_vs _nook_tablet_which_should_you_buy .html.

74 Y. Kane, "Sony Price Cut Helps Its PS3 Gain Traction; Move Boosts Sales of Game Consoles in Time for Holidays," *Wall Street Journal*, November 26, 2007, B4.

75 D. Wakabayashi, "Hope Fades for PS3 as a Comeback Player—In Battle of the Game Consoles, Nintendo Wii and Microsoft Xbox Widen Leads over Sony's PlayStation," *Wall Street Journal*, December 29, 2008, B1; N. Wingfield, "Microsoft Cuts Xbox to $199," *Wall Street Journal*, September 4, 2008, B9; N. Wingfield, "Microsoft to Cut Xbox 360 Pro Price," *Wall Street Journal*, July 11, 2008, B6.

76 B. Strauss, "PS3 Surpasses Xbox 360 in Worldwide Sales," *Business Insider*, March 31, 2011, accessed April 9, 2011, http://www.businessinsider.com /ps3-surpasses-xbox-360-in-worldwide -sales-2011-3.

77 A. Ostrow, "Microsoft Kinect Sales Surpass 8 Million," *Mashable.com*, January 5, 2011, accessed April 9, 2011, http://mashable.com/2011 /01/05/kinect-sales/.

Chapter 7

1 J. Tierney, "A Hearing Aid That Cuts Out All the Clatter," *New York Times*, October 23, 2011, http://www.nytimes .com/2011/10/24/science/24loops .html, accessed May 2, 2012.

2 S. McBride, "Thinking about Tomorrow: How We Watch Movies and TV," *Wall Street Journal*, January 28, 2008, R1.

3 P. Anderson and M. L. Tushman, "Managing through Cycles of Technological Change," *Research/Technology Management*, May–June 1991, 26–31.

4 R. N. Foster, *Innovation: The Attacker's Advantage* (New York: Summit, 1986).

5 "The Silicon Engine: A Timeline of Semiconductors in Computers," Computer History Museum, accessed April 22, 2001, http://www.computerhistory .org/semiconductor/.

6 J. Burke, *The Day the Universe Changed* (Boston: Little, Brown, 1985).

7 B. X. Chen, "Why Cisco's Flip Flopped in the Camera Business," Wired.com, April 12, 2011, accessed March 6, 2012, http://www.wired.com /gadgetlab/2011/04/flip-camera-rip/; D. Pogue, "Camcorder Brings Zen to the Shoot," *New York Times*, March 20, 2008, accessed March 6, 2012, http://www.nytimes.com/2008/03/20 /technology/personaltech/20pogue .html?pagewanted=all.

8 M. L. Tushman, P. C. Anderson, and C. O'Reilly, "Technology Cycles, Innovation Streams, and Ambidextrous Organizations: Organization Renewal Through Innovation Streams and Strategic Change," in *Managing Strategic Innovation and Change*, ed. M. L. Tushman and P. Anderson (New York: Oxford Press, 1997), 3–23.

9 P. Landers, "Brain Surgery Made Simple—New Less-Invasive Procedures Reduce Pain, Recovery Time; Sending in the Tiny Robots," *Wall Street Journal*, October 31, 2002, D1.

10 "Breakthrough Brain Surgery: Neurosurgeons Can Now Remove Brain Cancer Endoscopically," *ScienceDaily*, August 1, 2005, accessed November 8, 2009, http://www.sciencedaily.com.

11 "Percentage of Cell Phone-Only U.S. Homes Doubles," CBSNews.com, April 23, 2011, accessed March 6, 2012, http://www.cbsnews.com/2100 -3480_162-20056730.html; "U.S. Wireless Quick Facts," no date, accessed March 6, 2012, http://www .ctia.org/advocacy/research/index.cfm /aid/10323.

12 E. Schlossberg, *Interactive Excellence: Defining and Developing New Standards for the Twenty-First Century* (New York: Ballantine, 1998).

13 W. Abernathy and J. Utterback, "Patterns of Industrial Innovation," *Technology Review* 2 (1978): 40–47.

14 "Blu Capabilities Still up in the Air," *Home Media Magazine*, accessed September 17, 2008, http://www .nxtbook.com/nxtbooks/questex /hom041308/#/2.

15 M. Ramsay, "'Real' 4G Standards Ratified by ITU," *Wireless Week*, January 19, 2012, http://wirelessweek.com /News/2012/01/Technologies-Real-4G -Standards-Ratified-ITU-Wireless -Networks/.

16 M. Schilling, "Technological Lockout: An Integrative Model of the Economic and Strategic Factors Driving Technology Success and Failure," *Academy of Management Review* 23 (1998): 267–284; M. Schilling, "Technology Success and Failure in Winner-Take-All Markets: The Impact of Learning Orientation, Timing, and Network Externalities," *Academy of Management Journal* 45 (2002): 387–398.

17 S. McBride and Y. I. Kane, "As Toshiba Surrenders: What's Next for DVDs?" *Wall Street Journal*, February 18, 2008, accessed October 2, 2008, http://online.wsj.com/article /SB120321618700574049.html?mod =MKTW; Y. I. Kane, "Toshiba Regroups after Losing DVD War," *Wall Street Journal*, February 20, 2008, accessed October 2, 2008, http://online.wsj.com/article /SB120342115442976687 .html?mod=googlenews.

18 T. M. Amabile, R. Conti, H. Coon, J. Lazenby, and M. Herron, "Assessing the Work Environment for Creativity," *Academy of Management Journal* 39 (1996): 1154–1184.

19 Ibid.

20 M. Csikszentmihalyi, *Flow: The Psychology of Optimal Experience* (New York: Harper & Row, 1990).

21 B. Kowitt, "Dunkin' Brands' Kitchen Crew," *Fortune*, May 24, 2010, 72–74.

22 J. Scanlon, "How to Build a Culture of Innovation," *BloombergBusinessweek*, August 19, 2009, accessed August 9, 2010, http://www.businessweek.com /innovate/content/aug20.

23 E. Catmull, "How Pixar Fosters Collective Creativity," *Harvard Business Review*, September 2008, 64–72.

24 K. M. Eisenhardt, "Accelerating Adaptive Processes: Product Innovation in the Global Computer Industry," *Administrative Science Quarterly* 40 (1995): 84–110.

25 Ibid.

26 Catmull, "How Pixar Fosters Collective Creativity."

27 N. Heintz, "Managing: Unleashing Employee Creativity," *Inc.*, June 1, 2009, http://www.inc.com/magazine /20090601/managing-unleashing -employee-creativity.html.

28 L. Kraar, "25 Who Help the U.S. Win: Innovators Everywhere Are Generating Ideas to Make America a Stronger Competitor. They Range from a Boss Who Demands the Impossible to a

Mathematician with a Mop," *Fortune*, March 22, 1991.

29 M. W. Lawless and P. C. Anderson, "Generational Technological Change: Effects of Innovation and Local Rivalry on Performance," *Academy of Management Journal* 39 (1996): 1185–1217.

30 D. Daw, "PlayStation Vita Hands-On Report," *PCWorld*, February 9, 2012, accessed March 7, 2012, http://www.pcworld.com/article/249677/playstation_vita_handson_report.html.

31 E. Maltby, "Affordable 3-D Arrives," *Wall Street Journal*, July 29, 2010, B7.

32 J. Rich, "Twilight Exclusive: Chris Weitz Will Not Direct Third Film, 'Eclipse,'" *Hollywood Insider*, February 21, 2009, accessed July 23, 2010, http://hollywoodinsider.ew.com/2009/02/21/twilight-chris/; G. McIntyre, "On the Set: 'New Moon' on the Rise," *Los Angeles Times*, July 19, 2009, accessed July 23, 2010, http://www.latimes.com/entertainment/news/la-ca-newmoon19-2009jul19,0,3312678,full.story; N. Sperling, "It's Official: Bill Condon Will Direct Twilight's Final Chapter 'Breaking Dawn,'" *Hollywood Insider*, April 28, 2010, accessed July 23, 2010, http://hollywoodinsider.ew.com/2010/04/28/bill-condon-will-direct-twilights-final-chapter-breaking-dawn/.

33 "No. of Apps: Apple vs. Blackberry vs. Windows!" *Gadget Fan Site*, April 4, 2011, accessed April 23, 2011, http://gadgetfansite.com/no-of-apps-apple-vs-android-vs-blackberry-vs-windows/.

34 W. Connors, "RIM Offers Peek at Its Next Phone," *Wall Street Journal*, May 2, 2012, B1.

35 P. Strebel, "Choosing the Right Change Path," *California Management Review* (Winter 1994): 29–51.

36 J. Hirsch, "Resurgent General Motors Posts Record Profit for 2011," *Los Angeles Times*, February 16, 2012, accessed March 7, 2012, http://www.latimes.com/business/money/la-fi-mo-general-motors-profits-20120215,0,1837452.story.

37 K. Lewin, *Field Theory in Social Science: Selected Theoretical Papers* (New York: Harper & Brothers, 1951).

38 A. Deutschman, "Making Change: Why Is It So Darn Hard to Change Our Ways?" *Fast Company*, May 2005, 52–62.

39 Lewin, *Field Theory in Social Science*.

40 J. Hansel, "Pulse on Health: A Uniform Policy," PostBulletin.com, March 5, 2012, accessed March 7, 2012, http://www.postbulletin.com/news/stories/display.php?id=1488969.

41 A. B. Fisher, "Making Change Stick," *Fortune*, April 17, 1995, 121.

42 J. P. Kotter and L. A. Schlesinger, "Choosing Strategies for Change," *Harvard Business Review* (March–April 1979): 106–114.

43 S. Giessner, G. Viki, T. Otten, S. Terry, and D. Tauber, "The Challenge of Merging: Merger Patterns, Premerger Status, and Merger Support," *Personality and Social Psychology Bulletin* 32, no. 3 (2006): 339–352.

44 E. Cassano, "How Vince Donnelly Led PMA Companies through an Acquisition by Involving Everyone," *Smart Business*, February 1, 2012, accessed March 7, 2012, http://www.sbnonline.com/2012/02/how-vince-donnelly-led-pma-companies-through-an-acquisition-by-involving-everyone/.

45 D. Bennett, "Marriage at 30,000 Feet," *Bloomberg Businessweek*, February 6–12, 2012, 58–63.

46 H. Schwarz, "A Game Can Change the Office," *TFM Facility Blog*, July 16, 2008, accessed April 23, 2011, http://www.todaysfacilitymanager.com/facilityblog/2008/07/a-game-can-change-the-office.html.

47 J. P. Kotter, "Leading Change: Why Transformation Efforts Fail," *Harvard Business Review* 73, no. 2 (March–April 1995): 59.

48 G. Pitts, "A Classic Turnaround—With Some Twists," *The Globe and Mail*, July 7, 2008, B1.

49 Ibid.

50 D. Choy, "Ford Gets Serious about Re-Inventing Lincoln," Autoguide.com, February 2, 2012, accessed March 7, 2012, http://www.autoguide.com/auto-news/2012/02/ford-gets-more-serious-about-lincoln.html; C. Woodyard, "Ford: Saving Lincoln Will Take 'Every Ounce of Our Energy,'" *USA Today*, January 17, 2012, accessed March 7, 2012, http://content.usatoday.com/communities/driveon/post/2012/01/ford-saving-lincoln-will-take-every-ounce-of-our-energy/1#.T1f8AzGPU2w.

51 P. Engardio and J. McGregor, "Lean and Mean Gets Extreme," *BusinessWeek*, March 23, 2009, 60.

52 Pitts, "A Classic Turnaround."

53 R. Carrick, "Rising from the Stock Market Rubble," *The Globe and Mail (Canada)*, June 21, 2008, B15;

W. Dabrowski, "Celestica Buoyed by Smartphone Market Potential: Electronics Maker's CEO Optimistic about Ability to 'Compete and Win' Despite Fall in Profit, Revenue," *Toronto Star*, April 24, 2009, B04.

54 W. Dabrowski, "Celestica Buoyed by Smartphone Market Potential."

55 S. Cramm, "A Change of Hearts," *CIO*, April 1, 2003, May 20, 2003, http://www.cio.com/archive/040103/hsleadership.html.

56 M. Ihlwan, L. Armstrong, and M. Eidam, "Hyundai: Kissing Clunkers Goodbye," *BusinessWeek*, May 17, 2004, 46.

57 C. Woodyard, "Lexus, Honda Top J.D. Power Initial Quality Survey, Ford Plummets," *USA Today*, June 23, 2011, accessed March 7, 2012, http://content.usatoday.com/communities/driveon/post/2011/06/lexus-toyota-gm-ford-jd-power-initial-quality-survey/1#.T1gA9jGPU2w.

58 P. Ingrassia, "Why Hyundai Is an American Hit," *Wall Street Journal*, September 14, 2009, A13.

59 Ibid.

60 Ihlwan, Armstrong, and Eidam, "Hyundai: Kissing Clunkers Goodbye."

61 K. Choi, "Hyundai Targets 10% Growth in Auto Sales," *Wall Street Journal* (Online), January 3, 2011, no page number available.

62 R. N. Ashkenas and T. D. Jick, "From Dialogue to Action in GE WorkOut: Developmental Learning in a Change Process," in *Research in Organizational Change and Development*, vol. 6, ed. W. A. Pasmore and R. W. Woodman (Greenwich, CT: JAI Press, 1992), 267–287.

63 T. Stewart, "GE Keeps Those Ideas Coming," *Fortune*, August 12, 1991, 40.

64 W. J. Rothwell, R. Sullivan, and G. M. McLean, *Practicing Organizational Development: A Guide for Consultants* (San Diego, CA: Pfeiffer & Co., 1995).

65 Ibid.

Chapter 8

1 "Annex Table A.I.8. Number of Parent Corporations and Foreign Affiliates, by Region and Economy, Latest Available Year (Number)," *World Investment Report 2011*, United Nations Conference on Trade & Development, accessed May 4, 2012, http://www

.unctad.org/sections/dite_dir/docs /WIR11_web%20tab%2034.pdf.

2 M. Scott, "Shell to Buy Cove Energy for $1.6 Billion," *New York Times*, February 22, 2012, accessed March 8, 2012, http://dealbook.nytimes .com/2012/02/22/shell-to-buy-cove -energy-for-1-6-billion/.

3 "Ford to Build First Transmission Plant in China," Boston.com, May 19, 2011, accessed March 8, 2012, http:// articles.boston.com/2011-05-19 /business/29561203_1_chongqing -joint-venture-china-association.

4 E. L. Andrews, "U.S. Adds Tariffs on Chinese Tires," *Wall Street Journal*, September 11, 2009, accessed June 9, 2010, http://www .nytimes.com/2009/09/12/business /global/12tires.html?_r=1&scp=1&sq =tariff&st=cse; M. Kitchen, "China to Set Anti-Dumping Measures on U.S. Chicken," *Market Watch*, February 5, 2010, accessed August 3, 2010, http:// www.marketwatch.com/story/china -to-set-anti-dumping-measures-on-us -chicken-2010-02-05.

5 G. Williams III, "News on the Road Column," *San Antonio Express–News*, March 3, 2006.

6 K. Bradsher, "W.T.O. Rules against China's Limits on Imports," *New York Times*, August 12, 2009, accessed June 9, 2009, http://www.nytimes.com /2009/08/13/business/global/13trade .html?scp=3&sq=trade%20quota&st =cse.

7 R. Geldenhuys, "China Import Quotas Illegal under WTO Law?" Floor, Inc. Attorneys, September 18, 2006, http:// www.tradelaw.co.za/news/article .asp?newsID_101.

8 "Understanding the WTO," *World Trade Organization,* accessed August 5, 2008, http://www.wto.org/english /thewto_e/whatis_e/tif_e/agrm9_e.htm.

9 "US Seeks Talks with India over Poultry Imports Ban," Yahoo! News, March 6, 2012, accessed March 9, 2012, http://news.yahoo.com/us-seeks -talks-india-over-poultry-imports -ban-164750391.html.

10 T. Hepher and A. Callus, "WTO Raps U.S. Subsidies to Boeing," Reuters, March 31, 2011, accessed March 9, 2012, http://www.reuters.com /article/2011/03/31/us-boeing-airbus -wto-idUSTRE72U40Z20110331.

11 "GATT/WTO," *Duke Law: Library & Technology,* accessed June 12, 2009, http://www.law.duke.edu/libtech.

12 P. Sonne and M. Colchester, "France, the U.K. Take Aim at Digital Pirates," *Wall Street Journal*, April 15, 2010, accessed June 9, 2010, http://online .wsj.com/article/SB100014240527023 046042045751818207550614 94 .html.

13 J. E. Dunn, "Pirate Software Costs $51 Billion, Says Survey," *ComputerworldUK*, September 16, 2010, accessed October 6, 2010, http:// www.computerworlduk.com/news /it-business/3239830/pirate-software -costs-51-billion-says-survey/.

14 G. Fowler, "Estimates of Copyright Piracy Losses Vary Widely," *Wall Street Journal*, June 2, 2006, A13.

15 "The History of the European Union," *Europa—The European Union Online*, accessed August 6, 2008, http://europa.eu.int/abc/history /index_en.htm; http://europa.eu/abc /european_countries/index_en.htm; "Member States of the EU," *Europa: The EU at a Glance*, accessed May 8, 2011, http://europa.eu/abc/european _countries/candidate_countries/index _en.htm.

16 "Candidate Countries," *Europa: The EU at a Glance*, accessed May 8, 2011, http://europa.eu/abc/european _countries/candidate_countries /index_en.htm.

17 "Testimony of Under Secretary of Commerce for International Trade Grant D. Aldona: The Impact of NAFTA on the United States Economy," Senate Foreign Relations Committee, Subcommittee on International Economic Policy, Export & Trade Promotion, February 7, 2007.

18 "Top U.S. Export Markets: Free Trade Agreement and Country Fact Sheets," International Trade Administration, U.S. Department of Commerce, 2009, accessed May 8, 2011, http://trade .gov/publications/pdfs/top-us-export -markets-2009.pdf.

19 "CAFTA-DR (Dominican Republic-Central America FTA)," Office of the United States Trade Representative, June 13, 2009, http://www.ustr.gov.

20 "US Trade with the CAFTA-DR Countries," Office of the United States Trade Representative (July 2007), accessed August 6, 2008, http://www .ustr.gov/assets/Trade_Agreements /Bilateral/CAFTA/Briefing_Book /asset_upload_file601_13191.pdf.

21 "UNASUR," *Union of South American Nations*, accessed May 8, 2011, http://www.comunidadandina.org /ingles/sudamerican.htm.

22 "Selected Basic ASEAN Indicators, 2011," *Association of Southeast Asian Nations*, February 15, 2011, accessed May 8, 2011, http://www.aseansec.org /stat/Table1.pdf.

23 "Selected Basic ASEAN Indicators, 2005," *Association of Southeast Asian Nations*, accessed August 6, 2008, http://www.aseansec.org/stat/Table1 .pdf; "Top Ten ASEAN Trade Partner Countries/Regions, 2005," *Association of Southeast Asian Nations*, accessed August 6, 2008, http://www.aseansec .org/Stat/Table20.pdf; "ASEAN Free Trade Area (AFTA)," *Association of Southeast Asian Nations*, accessed August 6, 2008, http://www.aseansec .org/12021.htm.

24 "Frequently Asked Questions (FAQs)," *Asia-Pacific Economic Cooperation,* accessed May 8, 2011, http://www .apec.org/FAQ.aspx.

25 "Member Economies," *Asia Pacific Economic Cooperation,* accessed August 6, 2008, http://www.apec.org /apec/member_economies/key _websites.html; "Frequently Asked Questions (FAQs)," *Asia-Pacific Economic Cooperation,* accessed August 6, 2008, http://www.apec.org/apec /tools/faqs.html.

26 "The Big Mac Index: An Indigestible Problem," *The Economist*, October 14, 2010, accessed May 8, 2011, http://www.economist.com/node /17257797?story_id=17257797.

27 "GNI per Capita, PPP (Current International $)," The World Bank, accessed May 3, 2012, http://data .worldbank.org/indicator/NY.GNP .PCAP.PP.CD; "GNI per Capita, Atlas Method (Current US $)," The World Bank, accessed May 3, 2012, http:// data.worldbank.org/indicator /NY.GNP.PCAP.CD.

28 "The Global Competitiveness Report: 2008–2009," *World Economic Forum*, accessed June 14, 2009, http://www .weforum.org/documents/GCR0809 /index.html.

29 "Freer Trade Cuts the Cost of Living," *World Trade Organization,* accessed August 6, 2008, http://www.wto.org /english/thewto_e/whatis_e/10ben_e /10b04_e.htm.

30 S. Rein, "Why Best Buy Failed in China," CNBC, March 7, 2011, accessed March 9, 2012, http:// www.cnbc.com/id/41882157 /Why_Best_Buy_Failed_in_China.

31 E. Gamerman, "Exporting Broadway; The Business of Sending Musicals Abroad Has Never Been Bigger," *Wall Street Journal*, July 15, 2010, W1.

32 A. Sundaram and J. S. Black, "The Environment and Internal Organization of Multinational Enterprises,"

Academy of Management Review 17 (1992): 729–757.

33 H. S. James, Jr., and M. Weidenbaum, *When Businesses Cross International Borders: Strategic Alliances & Their Alternatives* (Westport, CT: Praeger Publishers, 1993).

34 J. R. Hagerty, "Caterpillar Strikes Deal to Build Georgia Plant," *Wall Street Journal*, February 18, 2012, accessed March 9, 2012, http://online .wsj.com/article/SB10001424052970 2048804045772292521692606 94 .html.

35 I. Brat and B. Gruley, "Boss Talk: Global Trade Galvanizes Caterpillar; Maker of Heavy Equipment Thrives under CEO Owens, Fervent Free-Trade Advocate," *Wall Street Journal*, February 26, 2007, B1.

36 T. Aeppel, "Oil Shocker: Stung by Soaring Transportation Cost, Factories Bring Jobs Home Again," *Wall Street Journal*, June 13, 2008, A1.

37 F. Vinulan "BDSI Strikes $1.3 Million Licensing Deal for Onsolis Cancer Patch in Taiwan," *Triangle Business Journal*, October 7, 2010, accessed October 7, 2010, http://www .bizjournals.com/triangle/stories/2010 /10/04/daily41.html?q=licensing.

38 K. Machado, "Videocon to Make, Sell Philips' TV Sets in India," *Wall Street Journal (Online)*, April 19, 2010, accessed May 9, 2011, http://online.wsj .com/article/SB100014240527487046 71904575193670822088824.html.

39 "New Restaurants," McDonald's, accessed March 18, 2009, http:// www.mcdonalds.com/corp/franchise /purchasingYourFranchise/new Restaurants.html.

40 K. Le Mesurier, "Overseas and Over-whelmed," *BRW*, January 25, 2007, 51.

41 W. Mellor, "McDonald's No Match for KFC in China as Colonel Rules Fast Food," *Bloomberg Businessweek*, January 26, 2011, accessed March 9, 2012, http://www.bloomberg.com /news/2011-01-26/mcdonald-s-no -match-for-kfc-in-china-where-colonel -sanders-rules-fast-food.html.

42 Press Release, "Garmin and Volvo Penta Form Strategic Alliance to Create Marine Instrumentation, Navigation and Communication Equipment," *Garmin*, February 18, 2011, accessed May 9, 2011, http://garmin.blogs .com/my_weblog/2011/02/garmin -and-volvo-penta-form-strategic -alliance-to-create-marine -instrumentation-navigation-and -commu.html.

43 V. Bajaj, "After a Year of Delays, the First Starbucks Is to Open in Tea-Loving India This Fall," *New York Times*, January 30, 2012, accessed March 9, 2012, http://www.nytimes .com/2012/01/31/business/global /starbucks-to-open-first-indian-store -this-autumn.html.

44 C. Rauwald, "Daimler, Beiqi Foton Ink Deal on China Truck Joint Venture," *Wall Street Journal*, July 16, 2010, accessed September 10, 2010, http:// online.wsj.com/article/SB100014240 52748704682604575370061075262 570.html.

45 B. R. Schlender, "How Toshiba Makes Alliances Work," *Fortune*, October 4, 1993, 116–120; "Joint Ventures," *Encyclopedia of Business*, 2nd ed., accessed August 6, 2008, http:// www.referenceforbusiness.com /encyclopedia/Int-Jun/Joint-Ventures .html#WHY_JOINT_VENTURES _FAIL.

46 S. Prasso, "American Made...Chinese Owned," *Fortune*, May 24, 2010, 87; "About Haier," Haier.com, accessed August 8, 2010, http://www .haieramerica.com/en/aboutus/ ?sessid=6bad9187383748176bddd8a 3e6cf55c9.

47 "Deutsche Telekom Profit Down 37 Percent to $696 Mln," *Yahoo! News*, May 6, 2011, accessed May 14, 2011, http://news.yahoo.com/s/ap/20110506 /ap_on_bi_ge/eu_germany_earns _deutsche_telekom_1; K. J. O'Brien, "How the iPhone Led to the Sale of T-Mobile USA," *New York Times*, March 21, 2011, accessed May 14, 2011, http://dealbook.nytimes .com/2011/03/21/how-the-iphone-led -to-the-sale-of-t-mobile-usa/.

48 W. Hordes, J. A. Clancy, and J. Bad-daley, "A Primer for Global Start-Ups," *Academy of Management Executive*, May 1995, 7–11.

49 P. Dimitratos, J. Johnson, J. Slow, and S. Young, "Micromultinationals: New Types of Firms for the Global Competitive Landscape," *European Management Journal* 21, no. 2 (April 2003): 164; B. M. Oviatt and P. P. McDougall, "Toward a Theory of International New Ventures," *Journal of International Business Studies* (Spring 1994): 45–64; S. Zahra, "A Theory of International New Ventures: A Decade of Research," *Journal of International Business Studies* (January 2005): 20–28.

50 Press Release, "Air Lease Corporation Announces Additional Aircraft Purchases and Lease Placements Including its First Boeing 787-9 Lease Transac-tion," Air Lease Corporation, April 30, 2012, http://www.airleasecorp.com /index.php?option=com_pressarchives &Itemid=16.

51 "Air Lease Corporation, the New Global Aviation Venture, Is Ready for Take-Off with Substantial Financing and a Top-Flight Senior Management Team," *PR Newswire*, July 15, 2010, accessed July 23, 2010, http://www .prnewswire.com/news-releases/air -lease-corporation-the-new-global -aviation-venture-is-ready-for-take -off-with-substantial-financing-and -a-top-flight-senior-management -team-98529409.html.

52 "2010 Annual Report," The Coca-Cola Company, accessed May 11, 2011, http://www.thecoca -colacompany.com/ourcompany/ar /pdf/TCCC_2010_Annual_Review.pdf.

53 Ibid.

54 "After a Year of Delays."

55 "StarChip Opens New Office in Shanghai, China," *Asia Today*, March 6, 2012, accessed March 9, 2012, http://www.asiatoday.com/pressrelease /starchip-opens-new-office-shanghai -china.

56 P. Dvorak, "Why Multiple Headquarters Multiply," *Wall Street Journal*, November 19, 2007, B1; J. L. Yang, "Making Mergers Work," *Fortune*, November 26, 2007, 42.

57 J. Clark, "Italy's Brembo Looks to Increase U.S. Market Share," *Wall Street Journal*, June 24, 2010, accessed May 11, 2011, http://online.wsj.com/article /SB10001424052748704904911704575 326590322494762.html.

58 "Customer Care in the Netherlands," *The Netherlands Foreign Investment Agency*, accessed February 13, 2007, http://www.nfia.com/solutions .php?pageid=11 (content no longer available online).

59 "Foreign Corrupt Business Practices Act," U.S. Department of Justice, May 10, 2003, http://www.usdoj.gov /criminal/fraud/.

60 A. Snyder, "European Expansion: How to Shop Around," *Management Review*, November 1, 1993, 16.

61 J. Oetzel, R. Bettis, and M. Zenner, "How Risky Are They?" *Journal of World Business* 36, no. 2 (Summer 2001): 128–145.

62 K. D. Miller, "A Framework for Integrated Risk Management in International Business," *Journal of International Business Studies*, 2nd Quarter 1992, 311.

63 M. Bahree, "Foreign Retailers Regroup in India," *Wall Street Journal*, December 12, 2011, B3.

64 N. Casey and J. Hagerty, "Companies Shun Violent Mexico," *Wall Street Journal*, December 17, 2010, B1.

65 "Chapter 1: Political Outlook," *UAE Business Forecast Report*, 2007, 1st Quarter, 5–10.

66 I. Brat, "Going Global by Going Green," *Wall Street Journal*, February 26, 2008, B1.

67 G. Hofstede, "The Cultural Relativity of the Quality of Life Concept," *Academy of Management Review* 9 (1984): 389–398; G. Hofstede, "The Cultural Relativity of Organizational Practices and Theories," *Journal of International Business Studies*, Fall 1983, 75–89; G. Hofstede, "The Interaction between National and Organizational Value Systems," *Journal of Management Studies*, July 1985, 347–357; M. Hoppe, "An Interview with Geert Hofstede," *Academy of Management Executive*, February 2004, 75–79.

68 R. Hodgetts, "A Conversation with Geert Hofstede," *Organizational Dynamics*, Spring 1993, 53–61.

69 T. Lenartowicz and K. Roth, "Does Subculture within a Country Matter? A Cross-Cultural Study of Motivational Domains and Business Performance in Brazil," *Journal of International Business Studies* 32 (2001): 305–325.

70 M. Janssens, J. M. Brett, and F. J. Smith, "Confirmatory Cross-Cultural Research: Testing the Viability of a Corporation-Wide Safety Policy," *Academy of Management Journal* 38 (1995): 364–382.

71 E. Maltby, "Expanding Abroad? Avoid Cultural Gaffes—Entrepreneurs Looking Overseas Often Neglect to Learn Local Business Etiquette; In Britain, a 'Scheme' Carries No Taint," *Wall Street Journal*, January 19, 2010, B5.

72 J. S. Black, M. Mendenhall, and G. Oddou, "Toward a Comprehensive Model of International Adjustment: An Integration of Multiple Theoretical Perspectives," *Academy of Management Review* 16 (1991): 291–317; R. L. Tung, "American Expatriates Abroad: From Neophytes to Cosmopolitans," *Columbia Journal of World Business*, June 22, 1998, 125; A. Harzing, "The Persistent Myth of High Expatriate Failure Rates," *International Journal of Human Resource Management* 6 (1995): 457–475; A. Harzing, "Are Our Referencing Errors Undermining Our Scholarship and Credibility? The Case of Expatriate Failure Rates," *Journal of Organizational Behavior* 23 (2002): 127–148; N. Forster, "The Persistent Myth of High Expatriate Failure Rates: A Reappraisal," *International Journal of Human Resource Management* 8 (1997): 414–433.

73 J. Black, "The Right Way to Manage Expats," *Harvard Business Review* 77 (March–April 1999): 52; C. Joinson, "No Returns," *HR Magazine*, November 1, 2002, 70.

74 Joinson, "No Returns."

75 J. S. Black and M. Mendenhall, "Cross-Cultural Training Effectiveness: A Review and Theoretical Framework for Future Research," *Academy of Management Review* 15 (1990): 113–136.

76 K. Essick, "Executive Education: Transferees Prep for Life, Work in Far-Flung Lands," *Wall Street Journal*, November 12, 2004, A6.

77 Ibid.

78 P. W. Tam, "Culture Course—'Awareness Training' Helps U.S. Workers Better Know Their Counterparts in India," *Wall Street Journal*, May 25, 2004, B1.

79 S. Hamm, "Aperian: Helping Companies Bridge Cultures," *Business Week*, September 8, 2008, 16.

80 W. Arthur, Jr., and W. Bennett, Jr., "The International Assignee: The Relative Importance of Factors Perceived to Contribute to Success," *Personnel Psychology* 48 (1995): 99–114; B. Cheng, "Home Truths about Foreign Postings; To Make an Overseas Assignment Work, Employers Need More Than an Eager Exec with a Suitcase. They Must Also Motivate the Staffer's Spouse," *BusinessWeek Online*, accessed March 20, 2009, http://www.businessweek.com/careers/content/jul2002/ca20020715_9110.htm.

81 M. Netz, "It's Not Judging—It's Assessing: The Truth about Candidate Assessments," *NRRE Magazine*, March 2004, August 8, 2008, http://rismedia.com/wp/2004-03-03/its-not-judging-its-assessing.

82 "OAI: Overseas Assignment Inventory," *Prudential Real Estate and Relocation Services Intercultural Group*, May 11, 2011, http://www.performanceprograms.com/userfiles/image/Cross%20Culture/OAI_Fact_Sheet.pdf.

83 S. P. Deshpande and C. Visweswaran, "Is Cross-Cultural Training of Expatriate Managers Effective? A Meta-Analysis," *International Journal of Intercultural Relations* 16, no. 3 (1992): 295–310.

84 D. M. Eschbach, G. Parker, and P. Stoeberl, "American Repatriate Employees' Retrospective Assessments of the Effects of Cross-Cultural Training on Their Adaptation to International Assignments," *International Journal of Human Resource Management* 12 (2001): 270–287; "Culture Training: How to Prepare Your Expatriate Employees for Cross- Cultural Work Environments," *Managing Training & Development*, February 1, 2005.

85 J. Areddy, "Deep Inside China, American Family Struggles to Cope," *Wall Street Journal*, August 2, 2005, A1.

Chapter 9

1 "Sony Group Organizational Chart Summary," *Sony*, April 1, 2011, accessed May 15, 2011, http://www.sony.net/SonyInfo/CorporateInfo/Data/organization.html.

2 "Corporate Fact Sheet," *Sony Pictures*, accessed May 15, 2011, http://www.sonypictures.com/corp/corporatefact.html; "Facts and Figures," *Sony Music*, accessed May 15, 2011, http://www.sonymusic.com/page/facts-and-figures.

3 M. Hammer and J. Champy, *Reengineering the Corporation: A Manifesto for Business Revolution* (New York: Harper & Row, 1993).

4 J. Mick, "Windows 8 Public 'Consumer Preview' Beta Is Live," *Daily Tech*, February 29, 2012, accessed March 11, 2012, http://www.dailytech.com/Windows+8+Public+Consumer+Preview+Beta+is+Live/article24123.htm.

5 C. Edwards, "Sony's TV Business Keeps Fading to Red," *Bloomberg Businessweek*, August 3, 2011, accessed March 11, 2012, http://www.businessweek.com/magazine/sonys-tv-business-keeps-fading-to-red-08042011.html.

6 J. G. March and H. A. Simon, *Organizations* (New York: John Wiley & Sons, 1958).

7 "Bayer Group: Profile and Organization," Bayer AG, accessed March 20, 2009, http://www.bayer.com/bayer-group/profile-and-organization/page2351.htm.

8 "Company Overview: 2010" *UTC*, accessed May 15, 2010, http://www.utc.com/StaticFiles/UTC/StaticFiles/utc_overview.pdf.

9 "2011 Annual Report," United Technologies, http://2011ar.utc.com/pdfs/UT_2011_Financials.pdf.

10 "Company Structure," *Swisscom AG*, accessed May 15, 2011, http://www.swisscom.ch/GHQ/content/Portraet/Unternehmen/Unternehmensstruktur/?lang=en.

11 "About AB InBev: In a Few Facts," *AB InBev*, accessed May 16, 2011, http://www.ab-inbev.com/go/about_abinbev/our_company/in_a_few_facts.cfm.

12 "Our Top 10 Markets," *AB InBev*, accessed May 16, 2011, http://www.ab-inbev.com/pdf/AB_InBev_AR10_OurTopTenMarkets.pdf.

13 "Anheuser Busch InBev in Russia Key Facts & Figures," *AB InBev*, accessed May 16, 2011, http://www.ab-inbev.com/pdf/factsheets/Russia2010.pdf; "Anheuser Busch InBev in Belgium Key Facts & Figures," *AB InBev*, http://www.ab-inbev.com/pdf/factsheets/Belgium2010.pdf.

14 "Who We Are," *Procter & Gamble*, accessed November 14, 2009, http://www.pg.com.

15 "Corporate Info: Corporate Structure—Four Pillars," *Procter & Gamble*, accessed March 20, 2009, http://www.pg.com/jobs/corporate_structure/four_pillars.jhtml; "P&G Management," accessed March 20, 2009, http://www.pg.com/news/management/bios_photos.jhtml.

16 L. R. Burns, "Adoption and Abandonment of Matrix Management Programs: Effects of Organizational Characteristics and Interorganizational Networks," *Academy of Management Journal* 36 (1993): 106–138.

17 J. Fortt, "Yahoo's Taskmaster," *Fortune* April 27, 2009, 80–84, http://money.cnn.com/2009/04/15/technology/fortt_yahoo.fortune/index.htm.

18 H. Fayol, *General and Industrial Management*, trans. C. Storrs (London: Pitman Publishing, 1949).

19 M. Weber, *The Theory of Social and Economic Organization*, trans. and ed. A. M. Henderson and T. Parsons (New York: Free Press, 1947).

20 Fayol, *General and Industrial Management*.

21 A. Lashinsky, "Inside Apple, From Steve Jobs Down to the Janitor: How America's Most Successful—And Most Secretive—Big Company Really Works," *Fortune*, May 23, 2011, 125–134.

22 R. Guth, "Gates–Ballmer Clash Shaped Microsoft's Coming Hando-ver," *Wall Street Journal*, June 5, 2008, A1.

23 E. E. Lawler, S. A. Mohrman, and G. E. Ledford, *Creating High Performance Organizations: Practices and Results of Employee Involvement and Quality Management in Fortune 1000 Companies* (San Francisco: Jossey-Bass, 1995).

24 C. Dawson, "Toyota Overhauls Its R&D Efforts; Japan's Biggest Car Maker Aims for Quicker Decisions, Lower Costs," *Wall Street Journal*, April 9, 2012, http://online.wsj.com/article/SB10001424052702304587704577333522051377812.html.

25 S. Curry, "Retention Getters," *Incentive*, April 1, 2005.

26 R. W. Griffin, *Task Design* (Glenview, IL: Scott, Foresman, 1982).

27 F. Herzberg, *Work and the Nature of Man* (Cleveland, OH: World Press, 1966).

28 R. Hackman and G. R. Oldham, *Work Redesign* (Reading, MA: Addison-Wesley, 1980).

29 T. Burns and G. M. Stalker, *The Management of Innovation* (London: Tavistock, 1961).

30 Hammer and Champy, *Reengineering the Corporation*.

31 Ibid.

32 J. D. Thompson, *Organizations in Action* (New York: McGraw-Hill, 1967).

33 D. Pink, "Who Has the Next Big Idea?" *Fast Company*, September 1, 2001, 108.

34 J. B. White, "'Next Big Thing': Re-Engineering Gurus Take Steps to Remodel Their Stalling Vehicles," *Wall Street Journal Interactive*, November 26, 1996.

35 C. Tuna, "Remembrances: Champion of 'Re-Engineering' Saved Companies, Challenged Thinking," *Wall Street Journal*, September 6, 2008, A12.

36 G. M. Spreitzer, "Individual Empowerment in the Workplace: Dimensions, Measurement, and Validation," *Academy of Management Journal* 38 (1995): 1442–1465.

37 M. Schrage, "I Know What You Mean. And I Can't Do Anything about It," *Fortune*, April 2, 2001, 186.

38 K. W. Thomas and B. A. Velthouse, "Cognitive Elements of Empowerment," *Academy of Management Review* 15 (1990): 666–681.

39 D. Stanley, "Southwest Holds Plane for Grandfather of Slain Boy," *The Denver Channel.com*, January 13, 2011, accessed February 3, 2011, http://www.thedenverchannel.com/news/26483696/detail.html.

40 "The Artist," *Wikipedia*, no date, accessed March 12, 2012, http://en.wikipedia.org/wiki/The_Artist_(film).

41 W. Bulkeley, "New IBM Jobs Can Mean Fewer Jobs Elsewhere," *Wall Street Journal*, March 8, 2004, B1.

42 B. Crothers, "iPad 3's Dense Display a Challenge for Manufacturers," CNET, October 26, 2011, accessed March 12, 2012, http://news.cnet.com/8301-13924_3-20125504-64/ipad-3s-dense-display-a-challenge-for-manufacturers/; P. B. Lusk, "Apple iPad Suppliers to Watch," CBOE Communities, March 8, 2012, accessed March 12, 2012, http://communities.cboe.com/t5/What-s-On-Our-Minds/Apple-iPad-Suppliers-to-Watch-By-Peter-B-Lusk/ba-p/2349; D. E. Diliger, "Report Details iPad 2 Components, 5 Million Unit Supply," *Apple Insider*, http://www.appleinsider.com/articles/11/01/30/report_details_ipad_2_components_5_million_unit_supply.html.

43 C. C. Snow, R. E. Miles, and H. J. Coleman, Jr., "Managing 21st Century Network Organizations," *Organizational Dynamics*, Winter 1992, 5–20.

44 J. H. Sheridan, "The Agile Web: A Model for the Future?" *Industry Week*, March 4, 1996, 31.

Chapter 10

1 B. Dumaine, "The Trouble with Teams," *Fortune*, September 5, 1994, 86–92.

2 K. C. Stag, E. Salas, and S. M. Fiore, "Best Practices in Cross Training Teams," in *Workforce Cross Training Handbook*, ed. D. A. Nembhard (Boca Raton, FL: CRC Press), 156–175.

3 M. Marks, "The Science of Team Effectiveness," *Psychological Science in the Public Interest* (December 2006): pi–i.

4 J. R. Katzenbach and D. K. Smith, *The Wisdom of Teams* (Boston: Harvard Business School Press, 1993).

5 S. G. Cohen and D. E. Bailey, "What Makes Teams Work: Group Effectiveness Research from the Shop Floor to the Executive Suite," *Journal of Management* 23, no. 3 (1997): 239–290.

6 S. E. Gross, *Compensation for Teams* (New York: American Management Association, 1995); B. L. Kirkman and B. Rosen, "Beyond Self- Management: Antecedents and Consequences of Team Empowerment," *Academy of Management Journal* 42 (1999):

58–74; G. Stalk and T. M. Hout, *Competing against Time: How Time-Based Competition Is Reshaping Global Markets* (New York: Free Press, 1990); S. C. Wheelwright and K. B. Clark, *Revolutionizing New Product Development* (New York: Free Press, 1992).

7 D. A. Harrison, S. Mohamed, J. E. McGrath, A. T. Florey, and S. W. Vanderstoep, "Time Matters in Team Performance: Effects of Member Familiarity, Entrainment, and Task Discontinuity on Speed and Quality," *Personnel Psychology* 56, no. 3 (August 2003): 633–669.

8 PRWeb, "Staff Management | SMX Named a Finalist in the 2011 American Business Awards," *Yahoo! News*, May 18, 2011, accessed May 21, 2011, http://news.yahoo .com/s/prweb/20110518/bs_prweb /prweb8455166_2; "Staff Management's Expertise in Large-Scale Seasonal Hiring Projects Featured in Several Major Online Publications," *Staff Management*, December 10, 2010, accessed May 21, 2011, http:// www.staffmanagement.com/News -Story/Staff-Management-Expertise -Large-Scale-Hiring.aspx.

9 R. D. Banker, J. M. Field, R. G. Schroeder, and K. K. Sinha, "Impact of Work Teams on Manufacturing Performance: A Longitudinal Field Study," *Academy of Management Journal* 39 (1996): 867–890.

10 "Entire Organization Rallies to Improve Product Ratings, Sales," *Bazaarvoice*, accessed May 21, 2011, http://www.bazaarvoice.com /resources/case-studies/entire -organization-rallies-improve-product -ratings-sales.

11 J. L. Cordery, W. S. Mueller, and L. M. Smith, "Attitudinal and Behavioral Effects of Autonomous Group Working: A Longitudinal Field Study," *Academy of Management Journal* 34 (1991): 464–476; T. D. Wall, N. J. Kemp, P. R. Jackson, and C. W. Clegg, "Outcomes of Autonomous Workgroups: A Long-Term Field Experiment," *Academy of Management Journal* 29 (1986): 280–304.

12 "Declaration of Interdependence," *Whole Foods Market*, accessed August 12, 2008, http://www .wholefoodsmarket.com/mission -values/core-values/declaration -interdependence

13 C. Fishman, "The Anarchist's Cookbook," *Fast Company*, July 1, 2004, http://www.fastcompany.com /magazine/84/wholefoods.html.

14 "Whole Foods Market Soars to Number 5 Spot on *Fortune*'s '100 Best Companies to Work For' List," *Whole Foods*, accessed March 20, 2009, http://www.wholefoodsmarket.com /pressroom/2007/01/09/whole-foods -market-soars-to-number-5-spot-on -fortunes-100-best-companies-to -work-for-list/.

15 R. Liden, S. Wayne, R. Jaworski, and N. Bennett, "Social Loafing: A Field Investigation," *Journal of Management* 30 (2004): 285–304.

16 J. George, "Extrinsic and Intrinsic Origins of Perceived Social Loafing in Organizations," *Academy of Management Journal* 35 (1992): 191–202.

17 T. T. Baldwin, M. D. Bedell, and J. L. Johnson, "The Social Fabric of a Team-Based M.B.A. Program: Network Effects on Student Satisfaction and Performance," *Academy of Management Journal* 40 (1997): 1369–1397.

18 K. H. Price, D. A. Harrison, and J. H. Gavin, "Withholding Inputs in Team Contexts: Member Composition, Interaction Processes, Evaluation Structure and Social Loafing," *Journal of Applied Psychology* 91(6) (2006): 1375–1384.

19 P. Strozniak, "Teams at Work," *Industry Week*, accessed May 21, 2011, http://www.teambuildinginc.com /article_teamsatwork.htm.

20 C. Joinson, "Teams at Work," *HR Magazine*, May 1, 1999, 30.

21 R. Wageman, "Critical Success Factors for Creating Superb Self- Managing Teams," *Organizational Dynamics* 26, no. 1 (1997): 49–61.

22 M. A. Cusumano, "How Microsoft Makes Large Teams Work Like Small Teams," *Sloan Management Review* 39, no. 1 (Fall 1997): 9–20.

23 N. Wingfield, "Tech Journal: To Rebuild Windows, Microsoft Razed Walls; Three-Year Effort to Create Latest Version Meant Close Collaboration among Workers to Avoid Vista's Woes," *Wall Street Journal*, October 20, 2009, B9.

24 Ibid.

25 Ibid.

26 "Microsoft Presents the Development Team of Windows 8," *Wicked Sago*, November 2011, accessed June 14, 2011, http://wickedsago.blogspot .com/2011/08/microsoft-presents -development-team-of.html.

27 Kirkman and Rosen, "Beyond Self-Management: Antecedents and Consequences of Team Empowerment."

28 K. Kelly, "Managing Workers Is Tough Enough in Theory. When Human Nature Enters the Picture, It's Worse," *BusinessWeek*, October 21, 1996, 32.

29 S. Easton and G. Porter, "Selecting the Right Team Structure to Work in Your Organization," in *Handbook of Best Practices for Teams*, vol. 1, ed. G. M. Parker (Amherst, MA: Irwin, 1996).

30 S. Wilhelm, "Quadrupling 787 Production Won't Be Easy for Boeing, Just Necessary," *Puget Sound Business Journal*, February 10, 2012, accessed March 12, 2012, http://www .bizjournals.com/seattle/print-edition /2012/02/10/quadrupling-787 -production-wont-be.html?page=all.

31 R. M. Yandrick, "A Team Effort: The Promise of Teams Isn't Achieved without Attention to Skills and Training," *HR Magazine*, June 2001, 46(6), 136–144.

32 D. O'Connell and D. Heriein, "The Marvel of Plant 4: Bandag's Journey of Self-Direction," *People & Strategy* 32 (2009): 34–41.

33 R. Williams, "Self-Directed Work Teams: A Competitive Advantage," *Quality Digest*, accessed November 18, 2009, http://www.qualitydigest .com.

34 Yandrick, "A Team Effort."

35 R. J. Recardo, D. Wade, C. A. Mention, and J. Jolly, *Teams* (Houston: Gulf Publishing Co., 1996).

36 D. R. Denison, S. L. Hart, and J. A. Kahn, "From Chimneys to Cross-Functional Teams: Developing and Validating a Diagnostic Model," *Academy of Management Journal* 39, no. 4 (1996): 1005–1023.

37 A. M. Townsend, S. M. DeMarie, and A. R. Hendrickson, "Virtual Teams: Technology and the Workplace of the Future," *Academy of Management Executive* 13, no. 3 (1998): 17–29.

38 J. Hyatt, "MySQL: Workers in 25 Countries with No HQ," *Fortune*, June 1, 2006, accessed August 12, 2008, http://money.cnn.com/2006 /05/31/magazines/fortune/mysql _greatteams_fortune/index.htm.

39 A. M. Townsend, S. M. DeMarie, and A. R. Hendrickson, "Are You Ready for Virtual Teams?" *HR Magazine* 41, no. 9 (1996): 122–126.

40 R. S. Wellins, W. C. Byham, and G. R. Dixon, *Inside Teams: How 20 World-Class Organizations Are Winning through Teamwork* (Jossey-Bass, 1996).

41 Townsend, DeMarie, and Hendrickson, "Virtual Teams."

42 W. F. Cascio, "Managing a Virtual Workplace," *Academy of Management Executive* 14 (2000): 81–90.

43 R. Katz, "The Effects of Group Longevity on Project Communication and Performance," *Administrative Science Quarterly* 27 (1982): 245–282.

44 D. Mankin, S. G. Cohen, and T. K. Bikson, *Teams and Technology: Fulfilling the Promise of the New Organization* (Boston: Harvard Business School Press, 1996).

45 A. P. Ammeter and J. M. Dukerich, "Leadership, Team Building, and Team Member Characteristics in High Performance Project Teams," *Engineering Management* 14, no. 4 (2002, December): 3–11.

46 K. Lovelace, D. Shapiro, and L. Weingart, "Maximizing Cross-Functional New Product Teams' Innovativeness and Constraint Adherence: A Conflict Communications Perspective," *Academy of Management Journal* 44 (2001): 779–793.

47 L. Holpp and H. P. Phillips, "When Is a Team Its Own Worst Enemy?" *Training*, September 1, 1995, 71.

48 S. Asche, "Opinions and Social Pressure," *Scientific American* 193 (1995): 31–35.

49 J. Stephens, "Corner Office: Rah-Rah Isn't for Everyone," interview by A. Bryant, *New York Times*, April 9, 2010, accessed June 11, 2010, http://www.nytimes.com/2010/04/11/business/11corner.html?pagewanted=.

50 S. G. Cohen, G. E. Ledford, and G. M. Spreitzer, "A Predictive Model of Self-Managing Work Team Effectiveness," *Human Relations* 49, no. 5 (1996): 643–676.

51 R. Collett, "How to Improve Product Development Productivity—Lessons from the Checklist Manifesto," *The EE Compendium: The Home of Electronic Engineering and Embedded Systems Programming*, accessed May 22, 2011, http://ee.cleversoul.com/news/lessons-from-the-checklist-manifesto.html.

52 "Surgical Safety Checklist," *World Health Organization*, accessed May 22, 2011, http://www.projectcheck.org/uploads/1/0/9/0/1090835/surgical_safety_checklist_production.pdf. While this seems simple, checklists are remarkably effective in reducing surgical errors. M. Semel, S. Resch, A. Haynes, L. Funk, A. Bader, W. Berry, T. Weiser, and A. Gawande, "Adopting a Surgical Safety Checklist Could Save Money and Improve the Quality of Care in US Hospitals," *Health Affairs* 29, no. 9 (2010): 1593–1599.

53 M. Fischetti, "'Team Doctors, Report to ER': Is Your Team Headed for Intensive Care? Our Specialists Offer Prescriptions for the Five Illnesses That Can Afflict Even the Best Teams," *Fast Company*, February 1, 1998, 170.

54 K. Bettenhausen and J. K. Murnighan, "The Emergence of Norms in Competitive Decision-Making Groups," *Administrative Science Quarterly* 30 (1985): 350–372.

55 P. Coy, "The Case for Making It in the USA," *BloombergBusinessweek*, May 5, 2011, accessed March 13, 2012, http://www.businessweek.com/magazine/content/11_20/b4228011719321.htm.

56 E. Levenson, "The Power of an Idea," *Fortune*, June 12, 2006, 131.

57 S. M. Gully, D. S. Devine, and D. J. Whitney, "A Meta-Analysis of Cohesion and Performance: Effects of Level of Analysis and Task Interdependence," *Small Group Research* 26, no. 4 (1995): 497–520.

58 Ibid.

59 F. Tschan and M. V. Cranach, "Group Task Structure, Processes and Outcomes," in *Handbook of Work Group Psychology*, ed. M. A. West (Chichester, UK: Wiley, 1996).

60 D. E. Yeatts and C. Hyten, *High-Performing Self-Managed Work Teams* (Thousand Oaks, CA: Sage Publications, 1998); H. M. Guttman and R. S. Hawkes, "New Rules for Strategic Development," *Journal of Business Strategy* 25, no. 1 (2004): 34–39.

61 Yeatts and Hyten, *High-Performing Self-Managed Work Teams*; J. Colquitt, R. Noe, and C. Jackson, "Justice in Teams: Antecedents and Consequences of Procedural Justice Climate," *Personnel Psychology*, April 1, 2002, 83.

62 D. S. Kezsbom, "Re-Opening Pandora's Box: Sources of Project Team Conflict in the '90s," *Industrial Engineering* 24, no. 5 (1992): 54–59.

63 A. C. Amason, W. A. Hochwarter, and K. R. Thompson, "Conflict: An Important Dimension in Successful Management Teams," *Organizational Dynamics* 24 (1995): 20.

64 A. C. Amason, "Distinguishing the Effects of Functional and Dysfunctional Conflict on Strategic Decision Making: Resolving a Paradox for Top Management Teams," *Academy of Management Journal* 39, no. 1 (1996): 123–148.

65 K. M. Eisenhardt, J. L. Kahwajy, and L. J. Bourgeois III, "How Management Teams Can Have a Good Fight," *Harvard Business Review* 75, no. 4 (July–August 1997): 77–85.

66 Ibid.

67 C. Nemeth and P. Owens, "Making Work Groups More Effective: The Value of Minority Dissent," in *Handbook of Work Group Psychology*, ed. M. A. West (Chichester, UK: Wiley, 1996).

68 J. M. Levin and R. L. Moreland, "Progress in Small Group Research," *Annual Review of Psychology* 9 (1990): 72–78; S. E. Jackson, "Team Composition in Organizational Settings: Issues in Managing a Diverse Work Force," in *Group Processes and Productivity*, ed. S. Worchel, W. Wood, and J. Simpson (Beverly Hills, CA: Sage, 1992).

69 Eisenhardt, Kahwajy, and Bourgeois, "How Management Teams Can Have a Good Fight."

70 Ibid.

71 B. W. Tuckman, "Development Sequence in Small Groups," *Psychological Bulletin* 63, no. 6 (1965): 384–399.

72 Gross, *Compensation for Teams*.

73 J. F. McGrew, J. G. Bilotta, and J. M. Deeney, "Software Team Formation and Decay: Extending the Standard Model for Small Groups," *Small Group Research* 30, no. 2 (1999): 209–234.

74 J. Case, "What the Experts Forgot to Mention: Management Teams Create New Difficulties, but Succeed for XEL Communication," *Inc.*, September 1, 1993, 66.

75 J. R. Hackman, "The Psychology of Self-Management in Organizations," in *Psychology and Work: Productivity, Change, and Employment*, ed. M. S. Pallak and R. Perloff (Washington, DC: American Psychological Association, 1986), 85–136.

76 A. O'Leary-Kelly, J. J. Martocchio, and D. D. Frink, "A Review of the Influence of Group Goals on Group Performance," *Academy of Management Journal* 37, no. 5 (1994): 1285–1301.

77 R. Jana, "Real Life Imitates Real World," *BusinessWeek*, March 23, 2009, 42.

78 A. Zander, "The Origins and Consequences of Group Goals," in *Retrospections on Social Psychology*, ed. L. Festinger (New York: Oxford University Press, 1980), 205–235.

79 M. Erez and A. Somech, "Is Group Productivity Loss the Rule or the Exception? Effects of Culture and Group-Based Motivation," *Academy of Management Journal* 39, no. 6 (1996): 1513–1537.

80 S. Sherman, "Stretch Goals: The Dark Side of Asking for Miracles," *Fortune*, November 13, 1995.

81 N. Bunkley, "Hyundai Says Its Cars Will Average 50 M.P.G. by 2025," *New York Times Wheels Blog*, August 4, 2010, http://wheels.blogs.nytimes .com/2010/08/04/hyundai-says-its -cars-will-average-50-m-p-g-by-2025/.

82 K. R. Thompson, W. A. Hochwarter, and N. J. Mathys, "Stretch Targets: What Makes Them Effective?" *Academy of Management Executive* 11, no. 3 (1997): 48–60.

83 Dumaine, "The Trouble with Teams."

84 G. A. Neuman, S. H. Wagner, and N. D. Christiansen, "The Relationship between Work-Team Personality Composition and the Job Performance of Teams," *Group & Organization Management* 24, no. 1 (1999): 28–45.

85 M. A. Campion, G. J. Medsker, and A. C. Higgs, "Relations between Work Group Characteristics and Effectiveness: Implications for Designing Effective Work Groups," *Personnel Psychology* 46, no. 4 (1993): 823–850.

86 B. L. Kirkman and D. L. Shapiro, "The Impact of Cultural Values on Employee Resistance to Teams: Toward a Model of Globalized Self-Managing Work Team Effectiveness," *Academy of Management Review* 22, no. 3 (1997): 730–757.

87 C. Fishman, "Engines of Democracy: The General Electric Plant in Durham, North Carolina Builds Some of the World's Most Powerful Jet Engines. But the Plant's Real Power Lies in the Lessons That It Teaches about the Future of Work and about Workplace Democracy," *Fast Company*, October 1, 1999, 174.

88 J. Bunderson and K. Sutcliffe, "Comparing Alternative Conceptualizations of Functional Diversity in Management Teams: Process and Performance Effects," *Academy of Management Journal* 45 (2002): 875–893.

89 J. Barbian, "Getting to Know You," *Training*, June 2001, 60–63.

90 J. Hackman, "New Rules for Team Building—The Times Are Changing—And So Are the Guidelines for Maximizing Team Performance," *Optimize*, July 1, 2002, 50.

91 Joinson, "Teams at Work."

92 Strozniak, "Teams at Work."

93 Ibid.

94 P. Nicholas, "It's All about Flight or Fight," *Weekend Australian*, March 14, 2009, 1.

95 Wellins, Byham, and Dixon, *Inside Teams*.

96 E. Salas, D. DiazGranados, C. Klein, C. Burke, K. Stagl, G. Goodwin, and S. Halpin, "Does Team Training Improve Team Performance? A Meta-Analysis," *Human Factors* 50, no. 6 (2008): 903–933.

97 S. Caudron, "Tie Individual Pay to Team Success," *Personnel Journal* 73, no. 10 (October 1994): 40.

98 Ibid.

99 Gross, *Compensation for Teams*.

100 G. Ledford, "Three Case Studies on Skill-Based Pay: An Overview," *Compensation & Benefits Review* 23, no. 2 (1991): 11–24.

101 T. Law, "Where Loyalty Is Rewarded," *The Press*, September 29, 2008, Business Day 4.

102 J. R. Schuster and P. K. Zingheim, *The New Pay: Linking Employee and Organizational Performance* (New York: Lexington Books, 1992).

103 Cohen and Bailey, "What Makes Teams Work."

104 R. Allen and R. Kilmann, "Aligning Reward Practices in Support of Total Quality Management," *Business Horizons* 44 (May 2001): 77–85.

Chapter 11

1 S. Bing, "The Feds Make a Pass at Hooters," *Fortune*, January 15, 1996, 82.

2 J. Helyar, "Hooters: A Case Study," *Fortune*, September 1, 2003, 140.

3 A. Samuels, "Pushing Hot Buttons and Wings," *St. Petersburg (FL) Times*, March 10, 2003, 1A.

4 J. Casale, R. Ceniceros, and M. Hofmann, "Hooters Wannabe Resists Girls-Only Policy," *Business Insurance* 43, no. 4 (2009): 23.

5 Ibid.

6 Associated Press, "Hooters Settles Suit, Won't Hire Waiters," *Denver Post*, October 1, 1997, A11.

7 P. S. Greenlaw and J. P. Kohl, "Employer 'Business' and 'Job' Defenses in Civil Rights Actions," *Public Personnel Management* 23, no. 4 (1994): 573.

8 F. Hosier, "OSHA Slaps Company with $1.2M Fine for Training, PPE Violations," *Safety News Alert*, May 31, 2011, accessed March 14, 2012, http://www.safetynewsalert.com/osha -slaps-company-with-1-2m-fine-for -asbestos-violations/.

9 Greenlaw and Kohl, "Employer 'Business' and 'Job' Defenses in Civil Rights Actions."

10 J. Crosby, "3M Will Pay $3 Million to Settle Age-Bias Suit," *Minneapolis Star Tribune*, August 22, 2011, accessed March 14, 2012, http://www .startribune.com/business/128179578 .html.

11 W. Peirce, C. A. Smolinski, and B. Rosen, "Why Sexual Harassment Complaints Fall on Deaf Ears," *Academy of Management Executive* 12, no. 3 (1998): 41–54.

12 R. Gray, "First Student to Pay $150K to Settle Sexual Harassment, Retaliation Suit," *School Transportation News*, February 4, 2011, accessed May 23, 2011, http://www.stnonline .com/home/latest-news/3104-eeoc -orders-first-student-to-pay-150k-to -settle-sexual-harassment-retaliation -suit.

13 B. Watt, "ABM Industries Settles Sexual Harassment Suit with Female Janitorial Workers," *SCPR.org*, September 2, 2010, accessed September 11, 2010, http://www.scpr.org/news/2010/09/02 /abm-industries-agrees-settle-sexual -harassment-sui/.

14 Peirce, Smolinski, and Rosen, "Why Sexual Harassment Complaints Fall on Deaf Ears."

15 Ibid.

16 E. Larson, "The Economic Costs of Sexual Harassment," *The Freeman* 46, August 1996, accessed August 13, 2008, http://www.thefreemanonline .org/featured/the-economic-costs-of -sexual-harassment/.

17 G. Hyland-Savage, "General Management Perspective on Staffing: The Staffing Commandments," in *On Staffing*, eds. N. C. Bukholder, P. J. Edwards, Jr., and L. Sartain (Hoboken, NJ: Wiley, 2004), 280.

18 R. D. Gatewood and H. S. Field, *Human Resource Selection* (Fort Worth, TX: Dryden Press, 1998).

19 Ibid.

20 G. Marks, "How to Surf the Resume Tsunami," *Forbes*, July 16, 2010, accessed August 23, 2010, http://www .forbes.com/2010/07/16/hiring-jobs -small-business-entrepreneurs-human -resources-gene-marks.html.

21 *Griggs v. Duke Power Co.*, 401 U.S. 424, 436 (1971); *Albemarle Paper Co. v. Moody*, 422 U.S. 405 (1975).

22 L. Grensing-Pophal, "Internal Selections," *HR Magazine* 51, no. 12 (2006), http://www.shrm.org/publications/hrmagazine.

23 Ibid.

24 J. A. Breaugh, *Recruitment: Science and Practice* (Boston: PWSKent, 1992).

25 L. Klaff, "New Internal Hiring Systems Reduce Cost and Boost Morale," *Workforce Management* 83 (March 2004): 76–79.

26 Ibid.

27 "Virginia M. Rometty," Forbes.com, no date, accessed March 14, 2012, http://people.forbes.com/profile/virginia-m-rometty/4788.

28 B. O'Keefe, "Battle-Tested: How a Decade of War Has Created…A New Generation of Elite Business Leaders," *Fortune*, March 22, 2010, 108–111.

29 J. Breaugh and M. Starke, "Research on Employee Recruitment: So Many Studies, So Many Remaining Questions," *Journal of Management* 26 (2000): 405–434.

30 "Internet Recruitment Report," *NAS Insights*, accessed August 14, 2008, http://www.nasrecruitment.com/talenttips/NASinsights/InternetRecruitingReport06.pdf.

31 K. Maher, "Corporations Cut Middlemen and Do Their Own Recruiting," *Wall Street Journal*, January 14, 2003, B10.

32 E. Glazer, "Virtual Fairs Offer Real Jobs," *Wall Street Journal*, October 31, 2011, B9.

33 S. E. Needleman, "Lifting the Curtain on the Hiring Process," *Wall Street Journal*, January 26, 2010, accessed March 4, 2011, http://online.wsj.com/article/SB10001424052748703808904575025250789355156.html.

34 C. Camden and B. Wallace, "Job Application Forms: A Hazardous Employment Practice," *Personnel Administrator* 28 (1983): 31–32.

35 T. Minton-Eversole, "Background Screens Even More Crucial during Economic Slump," *Society of Human Resource Management*, July 30, 2008, http://www.shrm.org/hrdisciplines/staffingmanagement/articles.

36 S. Adler, "Verifying a Job Candidate's Background: The State of Practice in a Vital Human Resources Activity," *Review of Business* 15, no. 2 (1993/1994): 3–8.

37 W. Woska, "Legal Issues for HR Professionals: Reference Checking/Background Investigations," *Public Personnel Management* 36 (Spring 2007): 79–89.

38 "More Than 70 Percent of HR Professionals Say Reference Checking Is Effective in Identifying Poor Performers," *Society for Human Resource Management*, accessed February 3, 2005, http://www.shrm.org/press_published/CMS_011240.asp.

39 P. Babcock, "Spotting Lies: The High Cost of Careless Hiring," *HR Magazine* 48, no. 10 (October 2003), accessed November 5, 2009, http://findarticles.com/p/articles/mi_m3495/is_10_48/ai_109136217/.

40 S. Sonner and G. Burke, "Amtrak Sues Nevada Truck Company over Fatal Crash," *U-T San Diego*, June 30, 2011, accessed March 14, 2012, http://www.utsandiego.com/news/2011/jun/30/amtrak-sues-nevada-truck-company-over-fatal-crash/?page=1#article.

41 M. Le, T. Nguyen, and B. Kleiner, "Legal Counsel: Don't Be Sued for Negligent Hiring," *Nonprofit World*, May 1, 2003, 14–15.

42 "Why It's Critical to Set a Policy on Background Checks for New Hires," *Managing Accounts Payable*, September 2004, 6; J. Schramm, "Future Focus: Background Checking," *HR Magazine* (January 2005), page not available.

43 D. Belkin, "More Job Seekers Scramble to Erase Their Criminal Past," *Wall Street Journal*, November 11, 2009, A1.

44 A. Athavaley, "Job References You Can't Control," *Wall Street Journal*, September 27, 2007, D1.

45 M. P. Cronin, "This Is a Test," *Inc.*, August 1993, 64–69.

46 C. Cohen, "Reference Checks," *CA Magazine*, November 2004, 41.

47 Keith J. Winstein, "Inflated Credentials Surface in Executive Suite," *Wall Street Journal*, November 13, 2008, accessed May 30, 2011, http://online.wsj.com/article/SB122652836844922165.html.

48 J. Hunter, "Cognitive Ability, Cognitive Aptitudes, Job Knowledge, and Job Performance," *Journal of Vocational Behavior* 29 (1986): 340–362.

49 F. L. Schmidt, "The Role of General Cognitive Ability and Job Performance: Why There Cannot Be a Debate," *Human Performance* 15 (2002): 187–210.

50 K. Murphy, "Can Conflicting Perspectives on the Role of *g* in Personnel Selection Be Resolved?" *Human Performance* 15 (2002): 173–186.

51 E. E. Cureton, "Comment," in *Research Conference on the Use of Autobiographical Data as Psychological Predictors*, ed. E. R. Henry (Greensboro, NC: The Richardson Foundation, 1965), 13.

52 J. R. Glennon, L. E. Albright, and W. A. Owens, *A Catalog of Life History Items* (Greensboro, NC: The Richardson Foundation, 1966).

53 Gatewood and Field, *Human Resource Selection*.

54 I. Kotlyar and K. Ades, "HR Technology: Assessment Technology Can Help Match the Best Applicant to the Right Job," *HR Magazine* (May 1, 2002): 97.

55 M. S. Taylor and J. A. Sniezek, "The College Recruitment Interview: Topical Content and Applicant Reactions," *Journal of Occupational Psychology* 57 (1984): 157–168.

56 M. Harris, "Reconsidering the Employment Interview: A Review of Recent Literature and Suggestions for Future Research," *Personnel Psychology* (Winter 1989): 691–726.

57 Taylor and Sniezek, "The College Recruitment Interview."

58 R. Burnett, C. Fan, S. J. Motowidlo, and T. DeGroot, "Interview Notes and Validity," *Personnel Psychology* 51, (1998): 375–396; M. A. Campion, D. K. Palmer, and J. E. Campion, "A Review of Structure in the Selection Interview," *Personnel Psychology* 50, no. 3 (1997): 655–702.

59 T. Judge, "The Employment Interview: A Review of Recent Research and Recommendations for Future Research," *Human Resource Management Review* 10, no. 4 (2000): 383–406.

60 J. Cortina, N. Goldstein, S. Payne, K. Davison, and S. Gilliland, "The Incremental Validity of Interview Scores Over and Above Cognitive Ability and Conscientiousness Scores," *Personnel Psychology* 53, no. 2 (2000): 325–351; F. L. Schmidt and J. E. Hunter, "The Validity and Utility of Selection Methods in Personnel Psychology: Practical and Theoretical Implications of 85 Years of Research Findings," *Psychological Bulletin* 124, no. 2 (1998): 262–274.

61 K. Tyler, "Training Revs Up," *HR Magazine* (April 2005), *Society for Human Resource Management*, accessed March 23, 2009, http://www.shrm.org.

62 The Oil Spill Training Company, accessed August 14, 2008, http://oilspilltraining.com/home/index.asp.

63 R. King, "The Games Companies Play," *BloombergBusinessweek*, April 4, 2011, accessed March 14, 2012, http://www.businessweek.com/technology/content/apr2011/tc2011044_943586.htm; "Siemens' Plantville Celebrates One Year, Announces New Site Features," Siemens, March 30, 2012, http://www.industry.usa.siemens.com/topics/us/en/pressarchive/2012/pressreleases/Pages/SiemensPlantvilleCelebratesOneYearAnnouncesNewSiteFeatures.aspx

64 L. Buchanan, "Training: Auto Didacts," *Inc.*, June 8, 2010, accessed August 12, 2010, http://www.inc.com/top-workplaces/2010/articles/online-employee-training.html.

65 D. L. Kirkpatrick, "Four Steps to Measuring Training Effectiveness," *Personnel Administrator* 28 (1983): 19–25.

66 L. Bassi, J. Ludwig, D. McMurrer, and M. Van Buren, "Profiting from Learning: Do Firms' Investments in Education and Training Pay Off?" *American Society for Training and Development*, accessed August 14, 2008, http://www.astd.org/NR/rdonlyres/91956A5E-6E57-44DDAE5D-FCFFCDC11C3F/0/ASTD_Profiting_From_Learning.pdf.

67 C. Bartz, "Corner Office: Imagining a World of No Annual Reviews," interview by A. Bryant, *New York Times*, October 17, 2009, accessed July 30, 2010, http://www.nytimes.com/2009/10/18/business/18corner.html?_r=1.

68 D. Murphy, "Are Performance Appraisals Worse Than a Waste of Time? Book Derides Unintended Consequences," *San Francisco Chronicle*, September 9, 2001, W1.

69 K. R. Murphy and J. N. Cleveland, *Understanding Performance Appraisal: Social, Organizational and Goal-Based Perspectives* (Thousand Oaks, CA: Sage, 1995).

70 T. D. Schellhardt, "Annual Agony: It's Time to Evaluate Your Work, and All Involved Are Groaning," *Wall Street Journal*, November 19, 1996, A1.

71 U. J. Wiersma and G. P. Latham, "The Practicality of Behavioral Observation Scales, Behavioral Expectation Scales, and Trait Scales," *Personnel Psychology* 39 (1986): 619–628; U. J. Wiersma, P. T. Van Den Berg, and G. P. Latham, "Dutch Reactions to Behavioral Observation, Behavioral Expectation, and Trait Scales," *Group & Organization Management* 20 (1995): 297–309.

72 D. J. Schleicher, D. V. Day, B. T. Mayes, and R. E. Riggio, "A New Frame for Frame-of-Reference Training: Enhancing the Construct Validity of Assessment Centers," *Journal of Applied Psychology* (August 2002): 735–746.

73 J. Stack, "The Curse of the Annual Performance Review," *Inc.*, March 1, 1997, 39.

74 H. H. Meyer, "A Solution to the Performance Appraisal Feedback Enigma," *Academy of Management Executive* 5, no. 1 (1991): 68–76; G. C. Thornton, "Psychometric Properties of Self-Appraisals of Job Performance," *Personnel Psychology* 33 (1980): 263–271.

75 Thornton, "Psychometric Properties of Self-Appraisals of Job Performance."

76 J. Smither, M. London, R. Flautt, Y. Vargas, and I. Kucine, "Can Working with an Executive Coach Improve Multisource Feedback Ratings over Time? A Quasi-Experimental Field Study," *Personnel Psychology* (Spring 2003): 21–43.

77 A. Walker and J. Smither, "A Five-Year Study of Upward Feedback: What Managers Do with Their Results Matters," *Personnel Psychology* (Summer 1999): 393–422.

78 J. McGregor, "The Employee Is Always Right," *Business Week*, November 8, 2007, accessed August 14, 2008, http://www.businessweek.com/globalbiz/content/nov2007/gb2007118_541063.htm.

79 C. Tuna, "In Some Offices, Keeping Workers Earns a Bonus; More Firms Like Penske Tie Top Managers' Pay to Employee Retention," *Wall Street Journal*, June 30, 2008, B6.

80 Ibid.

81 G. T. Milkovich and J. M. Newman, *Compensation*, 4th ed. (Homewood, IL: Irwin, 1993).

82 M. L. Williams and G. F. Dreher, "Compensation System Attributes and Applicant Pool Characteristics," *Academy of Management Journal* 35, no. 3 (1992): 571–595.

83 D. Lee, "The Supply-Side Lesson of Henry Ford," *Investors.com*, September 20, 2010, accessed May 24, 2011, http://www.investors.com/NewsAndAnalysis/Article/547855/201009201845/The-Supply-Side-Lesson-Of-Henry-Ford.aspx.

84 S. Cooper and C. Debaise, "Best Ways to Pay Your Sales Staff," *Bloomberg Business Week*, June 5, 2009, accessed September 6, 2010, http://www.businessweek.com/magazine/content/09_66/s0906028668952.htm.

85 P. A. Eisenstein, "Chrysler Profit Triggers First Profit-Sharing Checks Since 2005," MSNBC.com, February 2, 2012, accessed March 14, 2012, http://bottomline.msnbc.msn.com/_news/2012/02/02/10300845-chrysler-profit-triggers-first-profit-sharing-checks-since-2005.

86 M. Johne, "When Employees Have Skin in the Game," *The Globe and Mail*, March 22, 2012, B16.

87 L. S. Covel, "How to Get Workers to Think and Act Like Owners," *Wall Street Journal*, February 7, 2008, B6.

88 Ibid.

89 M. Bloom, "The Performance Effects of Pay Dispersion on Individuals and Organizations," *Academy of Management Journal* 42, no. 1 (1999): 25–40.

90 J. Liberto, "CEOs Earn 343 Times More than Typical Workers," CNNMoney, April 20, 2011, accessed March 14, 2012, http://money.cnn.com/2011/04/19/news/economy/ceo_pay/index.htm.

91 W. Grossman and R. E. Hoskisson, "CEO Pay at the Crossroads of Wall Street and Main: Toward the Strategic Design of Executive Compensation," *Academy of Management Executive* 12, no. 1 (1998): 43–57.

92 Bloom, "The Performance Effects of Pay Dispersion."

93 M. Bloom and J. Michel, "The Relationships among Organizational Context, Pay Dispersion, and Managerial Turnover," *Academy of Management Journal* 45 (2002): 33–42.

94 S. Needleman, "Bad Firings Can Hurt Firm's Reputation," *Wall Street Journal*, July 8, 2008, D4.

95 A. Rupe, "Horrors from the Bad-Firing File," *Workforce Management*, November 2003, 16.

96 "400 at RadioShack Are Told by E-mail: You're Outta Here," *Associated Press*, August 31, 2006, http://seattletimes.nwsource.com/html/businesstechnology/2003236874_radioshack31.html.

97 S. E. Needleman, "'The Cat Hid My Car Keys'—Excuses Workers Make," *Wall Street Journal*, May 14, 2010, accessed September 5, 2010, http://online.wsj.com/article/NA_WSJ_PUB:SB10001424052748703339304575240770333031744.html.

98 P. Michal-Johnson, *Saying Good-Bye: A Manager's Guide to Employee*

Dismissal (Glenview, IL: Scott, Foresman & Co., 1985).

99 M. Bordwin, "Employment Law: Beware of Time Bombs and Shark-Infested Waters," *HR Focus*, April 1, 1995, 19; D. Jones, "Fired Workers Fight Back… and Win; Laws, Juries Shift Protection to Terminated Employees," *USA Today*, April 2, 1998, 01B.

100 "Mass Layoffs in December 2007 and Annual Totals for 2007," *Bureau of Labor Statistics News*, January 24, 2008, accessed August 15, 2008, http://www.bls.gov/news.release /archives/mmls_01242008.pdf.

101 D. McIntyre, "HP to Lay Off 9,000 in Enterprise Services Revamp," *Daily Finance*, June 1, 2010, accessed March 14, 2012, http://www.dailyfinance .com/2010/06/01/hp-layoffs-enterprise -services/; Z. Whittaker, "HP Confirms Layoffs; Cutting 500 Jobs at WebOS Division," *ZDNet*, September 20, 2011, accessed March 14, 2012, http://www.zdnet.com/blog/btl/hp -confirms-layoffs-cutting-500-jobs-at -webos-division/58413.

102 J. R. Morris, W. F. Cascio, and C. E. Young, "Downsizing after All These Years: Questions and Answers about Who Did It, How Many Did It, and Who Benefited from It," *Organizational Dynamics* 27, no. 3 (1999): 78–87.

103 K. Maher, "Hiring Freezes Cushion New Layoffs," *Wall Street Journal,* January 24, 2008, A13.

104 K. E. Mishra, G. M. Spreitzer, and A. K. Mishra, "Preserving Employee Morale during Downsizing," *Sloan Management Review* 39, no. 2 (1998): 83–95.

105 K. Frieswick, "Until We Meet Again?" *CFO*, October 1, 2001, 41.

106 J. Hilsenrath, "Adventures in Cost Cutting," *Wall Street Journal*, May 10, 2004, R1.

107 M. Jackson, "Downsized, but Still in the Game: Keeping up Morale Crucial after Job Cuts," *Boston Globe*, January 11, 2009, G1.

108 J. Ackerman, "Helping Layoff Survivors Cope: Companies Strive to Keep Morale High," *Boston Globe*, December 30, 2001, H1.

109 D. Ferrari, "Designing and Evaluating Early Retirement Programs: The State of Wyoming Experience," *Government Finance Review* 15, no. 1 (1999): 29–31.

110 Hilsenrath, "Adventures in Cost Cutting."

111 J. Lublin and S. Thurm, "How Companies Calculate Odds in Buyout Offers," *Wall Street Journal*, March 27, 2009, B1.

112 M. Willett, "Early Retirement and Phased Retirement Programs for the Public Sector," *Benefits & Compensation Digest*, April 2005, 31.

113 D. R. Dalton, W. D. Todor, and D. M. Krackhardt, "Turnover Overstated: The Functional Taxonomy," *Academy of Management Review* 7 (1982): 117–123.

114 J. R. Hollenbeck and C. R. Williams, "Turnover Functionality versus Turnover Frequency: A Note on Work Attitudes and Organizational Effectiveness," *Journal of Applied Psychology* 71 (1986): 606–611.

115 C. R. Williams, "Reward Contingency, Unemployment, and Functional Turnover," *Human Resource Management Review* 9 (1999): 549–576.

Chapter 12

1 J. H. Boyett and J. T. Boyett, *Beyond Workforce 2000* (New York: Dutton, 1995); "Quick Stats on Women Workers, 2008," *U.S. Department of Labor*," accessed November 4, 2009, http://www.dol.gov/wb/stats/main .htm.

2 Ibid.

3 M. Toossi, "Labor Force Projections to 2014: Retiring Boomers," *Monthly Labor Review* (November 2005): 25–44.

4 P. English, "The Way I Work: Paul English of Kayak," interview by L. Welch, *Inc.*, February 1, 2010, accessed July 27, 2010, http://www.inc .com/magazine/20100201/the-way-i -work-paul-english-of-kayak.html.

5 S. Nunes, "How to Work Outside Your Comfort Zone," *Bloomberg Businessweek*, July 7, 2010, http:// www.businessweek.com/managing /content/jul2010/ca2010071_670440 .htm.

6 Equal Employment Opportunity Commission, "Affirmative Action Appropriate under Title VII of the Civil Rights Act of 1964, As Amended. Chapter XIV—Equal Employment Opportunity Commission, Part 1608," accessed November 5, 2009, http:// www.access.gpo.gov/nara/cfr /waisidx_04/29cfr1608_04.html.

7 R. Rodriguez, "Diversity Finds Its Place: More Organizations Are Dedicating Senior-Level Executives to Drive Diversity Initiatives for Bottom-Line Effect," *HR Magazine*, August

2006, Society for Human Resource Management, accessed March 24, 2009, http://www.shrm.org.

8 Equal Employment Opportunity Commission, "Federal Laws Prohibiting Job Discrimination: Questions and Answers," accessed August 21, 2008, http://www.eeoc.gov/facts/qanda.html.

9 A. P. Carnevale and S. C. Stone, *The American Mosaic: An In-Depth Report on the Future of Diversity at Work* (New York: McGraw-Hill, 1995).

10 T. Roosevelt, "From Affirmative Action to Affirming Diversity," *Harvard Business Review* 68, no. 2 (1990): 107–117.

11 A. M. Konrad and F. Linnehan, "Formalized HRM Structures: Coordinating Equal Employment Opportunity or Concealing Organizational Practices?" *Academy of Management Journal* 38, no. 3 (1995): 787–820; see, for example, *Hopwood v. Texas*, 78 F.3d 932 (5th Cir., March 18, 1996). The U.S. Supreme Court has upheld the principle of affirmative action but has struck down some specific programs.

12 P. Schmidt, "5 More States May Curtail Affirmative Action," *The Chronicle of Higher Education*, October 19, 2007, A1.

13 M. E. Heilman, C. J. Block, and P. Stathatos, "The Affirmative Action Stigma of Incompetence: Effects of Performance Information Ambiguity," *Academy of Management Journal* 40, no. 3 (1997): 603–625.

14 K. C. Cole, "Jury Out on Whether Affirmative Action Beneficiaries Face Stigma: Research Studies Arrive at Conflicting Conclusions," *Los Angeles Times*, May 1, 1995, 18.

15 E. Orenstein, "The Business Case for Diversity," *Financial Executive*, May 2005, 22–25; G. Robinson and K. Dechant, "Building a Business Case for Diversity," *Academy of Management Executive* 11, no. 3 (1997): 21–31.

16 E. Esen, "2005 Workplace Diversity Practices: Survey Report," *Society for Human Resource Management*, accessed March 24, 2009, http://www .shrm.org/research.

17 Orenstein, "Business Case for Diversity."

18 Esen, "2005 Workplace Diversity Practices: Survey Report."

19 Orenstein, "Business Case for Diversity."

20 "Best Buy Settles Discrimination Lawsuit," MarketWatch, June 17, 2011, accessed March 15, 2012, http://

articles.marketwatch.com/2011-06 -17/industries/30754842_1 _discrimination-lawsuit-plaintiffs -individual-claims.

21 P. Wright and S. P. Ferris, "Competitiveness through Management of Diversity: Effects on Stock Price Valuation," *Academy of Management Journal* 38 (1995): 272–285.

22 Ibid.

23 D. Dodson, "Minority Groups' Share of $10 Trillion U.S. Consumer Market Is Growing Steadily, According to Annual Buying Power Study from Terry College's Selig Center for Economic Growth," *Selig Center for Economic Growth*, accessed November 6, 2009, http://www.terry.uga.edu.

24 Esen, "2005 Workplace Diversity Practices: Survey Report"; L. E. Wynter, "Business & Race: Advocates Try to Tie Diversity to Profit," *Wall Street Journal*, February 7, 1996, B1.

25 C. Timberlake, "Macy's Mentors Minority Vendors," *Bloomberg Businessweek*, January 12, 2012, accessed March 15, 2012, http://www .businessweek.com/magazine/macys -mentors-minority-vendors-01122012 .html.

26 W. W. Watson, K. Kumar, and L. K. Michaelsen, "Cultural Diversity's Impact on Interaction Process and Performance: Comparing Homogeneous and Diverse Task Groups," *Academy of Management Journal* 36 (1993): 590–602; K. A. Jehn, G. B. Northcraft, and M. A. Neale, "Why Differences Make a Difference: A Field Study of Diversity, Conflict, and Performance in Workgroups," *Administrative Science Quarterly* 44 (1999): 741–763; E. Kearney, D. Gebert, and S. Voelpel, "When and How Diversity Benefits Teams: The Importance of Team Members' Need for Cognition," *Academy of Management Journal* 52 (2009): 581–598.

27 F. Rice, "How to Make Diversity Pay," *Fortune*, August 8, 1994, 78.

28 Rodriguez, "Diversity Finds Its Place."

29 C. Hymowitz, "The New Diversity: In a Global Economy, It's No Longer about How Many Employees You Have in This Group and That Group; It's a Lot More Complicated—And if You Do It Right, a Lot More Effective," *Wall Street Journal*, November 14, 2005, R1.

30 "Diversity at Work: Public Relations Make a Difference for Global Giants," *Public Relations Society of America*, October 1, 2010, accessed June 1, 2011, http://www.prsa.org/Intelligence /Tactics/Articles/view/8828/1021 /Diversity_at_work_Public_relations _makes_a_differe.

31 M. R. Carrell and E. E. Mann, "Defining Workplace Diversity Programs and Practices in Organizations," *Labor Law Journal* 44 (1993): 743–764.

32 D. A. Harrison, K. H. Price, and M. P. Bell, "Beyond Relational Demography: Time and the Effects of Surface- and Deep-Level Diversity on Work Group Cohesion," *Academy of Management Journal* 41 (1998): 96–107.

33 D. Harrison, K. Price, J. Gavin, and A. Florey, "Time, Teams, and Task Performance: Changing Effects of Surface- and Deep-Level Diversity on Group Functioning," *Academy of Management Journal* 45 (2002): 1029–1045.

34 Harrison, Price, and Bell, "Beyond Relational Demography."

35 Ibid.

36 N. Munk, "Finished at Forty: In the New Economy, the Skills That Come with Age Count for Less and Less," *Fortune*, February 1, 1999, 50.

37 K. Wrenn and T. Maurer, "Beliefs about Older Workers' Learning and Development Behavior in Relation to Beliefs about Malleability of Skills, Age-Related Decline, and Control," *Journal of Applied Social Psychology* 34 (February 2004): 223–242.

38 J. Helyar and B. Cherry, "50 and Fired," *Fortune*, May 16, 2005, 78.

39 E. White, "The New Recruits: Older Workers," *Wall Street Journal,* January 14, 2008, B3.

40 S. R. Rhodes, "Age-Related Differences in Work Attitudes and Behavior," *Psychological Bulletin* 92 (1983): 328–367.

41 A. Fisher, "Wanted: Aging Baby-Boomers," *Fortune*, September 30, 1996, 204.

42 G. M. McEvoy and W. F. Cascio, "Cumulative Evidence of the Relationship between Employee Age and Job Performance," *Journal of Applied Psychology* 74 (1989): 11–17.

43 S. E. Sullivan and E. A. Duplaga, "Recruiting and Retaining Older Workers for the Millennium," *Business Horizons* 40 (November 12, 1997): 65.

44 T. Maurer and N. Rafuse, "Learning, Not Litigating: Managing Employee Development and Avoiding Claims of Age Discrimination," *Academy of Management Executive* 15, no. 4 (2001): 110–121.

45 B. L. Hassell and P. L. Perrewe, "An Examination of Beliefs about Older Workers: Do Stereotypes Still Exist?" *Journal of Organizational Behavior* 16 (1995): 457–468.

46 "Charge Statistics: FY 1997 through FY 2010," *U.S. Equal Employment Opportunity Commission*, accessed May 28, 2011, http://eeoc.gov/eeoc/ statistics/enforcement/charges.cfm.

47 "Statistics & Data: Quick Stats on Women Workers, 2009," *U.S. Department of Labor*, accessed May 28, 2011, http://www.dol.gov/wb/stats /main.htm; "Employment Status of the Civilian Noninstitutional Population by Age, Sex, and Race," 2010 Current Population Survey, *Bureau of Labor Statistics*, accessed May 28, 2011, http://www.bls.gov/cps/cpsaat3.pdf.

48 "Key Facts about Women-Owned Businesses, The Overall Picture: 2008–2009," *Center for Women's Business Research*, accessed May 28, 2011, http://www.womensbusiness researchcenter.org/research/keyfacts/.

49 "Women's Earnings as a Percentage of Men's, 2010," *U.S. Department of Labor, Bureau of Labor Statistics*, January 10, 2012, accessed May 9, 2012, http://www.bls.gov/opub/ted/2012 /ted_20120110.htm.

50 "U.S. Women in Business," *Catalyst*, accessed May 28, 2011, http:// www.catalyst.org/publication/132 /us-women-in-business.

51 "Catalyst 2008: Census of the *Fortune* 500 Reveals Women Gained Little Ground Advancing to Business Leadership Positions," *Catalyst*, December 10, 2008, accessed November 7, 2009, http://www.catalyst.org; A. Joyce, "They Open More Doors for Women," *Washington Post,* February 4, 2007, F4; "The 2007 *Fortune* 500: Women CEOs," *Fortune*, accessed August 21, 2008, http://money.cnn.com/galleries /2007/fortune/0704/gallery.F500 _womenCEOs.fortune/index.html.

52 "Women CEOs," CNNMoney, no date, accessed March 14, 2012, http:// money.cnn.com/magazines/fortune /fortune500/2011/womenceos/; "Meet the 18 *Fortune* 500 Female CEOs," CNNMoney, October 26, 2011, accessed March 16, 2012, http://money .cnn.com/galleries/2011/news /companies/1110/gallery.18_female _fortune_500_ceos.fortune/index .html.

53 "Women on Boards: Global Board Seats Held by Women," *Catalyst*, May 2011, accessed May 28, 2011, http:// www.catalyst.org/publication/433 /women-on-boards.

54 M. Bertrand and K. Hallock, "The Gender Gap in Top Corporate Jobs," *Industrial & Labor Relations Review* 55 (2001): 3–21.

55 J. R. Hollenbeck, D. R. Ilgen, C. Ostroff, and J. B. Vancouver, "Sex Differences in Occupational Choice, Pay, and Worth: A Supply-Side Approach to Understanding the Male-Female Wage Gap," *Personnel Psychology* 40 (1987): 715–744.

56 S. Shellenbarger, "Does Having Kids Dull Career Opportunities?" *WSJ Blogs: The Juggle, Wall Street Journal*, April 6, 2011, accessed May 28, 2011, http://blogs.wsj.com /juggle/2011/04/06/does-having -kids-dull-job-ambition/.

57 A. Chaker and H. Stout, "Second Chances: After Years Off, Women Struggle to Revive Careers," *Wall Street Journal*, May 6, 2004, A1.

58 Korn-Ferry International, 1993.

59 Department of Industry, Labor and Human Relations, *Report of the Governor's Task Force on the Glass Ceiling Commission* (Madison, WI: State of Wisconsin, 1993).

60 M. Fix, G. C. Galster, and R. J. Struyk, "An Overview of Auditing for Discrimination," in *Clear and Convincing Evidence: Measurement of Discrimination in America*, ed. M. Fix and R. Struyk (Washington, DC: Urban Institute Press, 1993), 1–68.

61 E. O. Wright and J. Baxter, "The Glass Ceiling Hypothesis: A Reply to Critics," *Gender & Society* 14 (2000): 814–821.

62 B. R. Ragins, B. Townsend, and M. Mattis, "Gender Gap in the Executive Suite: CEOs and Female Executives Report on Breaking the Glass Ceiling," *Academy of Management Executive* 12 (1998): 28–42.

63 N. Lockwood, "The Glass Ceiling: Domestic and International Perspectives," *HRMagazine* (2004 Research Quarterly): 2–10.

64 T. B. Foley, "Discrimination Lawsuits Are a Small-Business Nightmare: A Guide to Minimizing the Potential Damage," *Wall Street Journal*, September 28, 1998, 15.

65 "Charge Statistics FY 1997 through FY 2008," *U.S. Equal Employment Opportunity Commission*, accessed November 7, 2008, http://www.eeoc .gov.

66 "African American CEOs of *Fortune* 500 Companies," *Black-EntrepreneurProfile.com*, May 29, 2011, accessed May 29, 2011, http:// www.blackentrepreneurprofile.com /fortune-500-ceos/; R. Fortner, "Cracking the Plexi Glass Ceiling: 2010 *Fortune* 500 CEOs of Color," *USA Rise Up*, February 9, 2011, accessed May 29, 2011, http://www.usariseup.com /eyes-enterprise/cracking-plexi-glass -ceiling-2010-fortune-500-ceos-color.

67 "*Fortune* 500 Black, Latino, Asian CEOs," *DiversityInc*, no date, accessed March 15, 2012, http://diversityinc .com/leadership/fortune-500-black -latino-asian-ceos/.

68 D. A. Neal and W. R. Johnson, "The Role of Premarket Factors in Black-White Wage Differences," *Journal of Political Economy* 104, no. 5 (1996): 869–895.

69 Fix, Galster, and Struyk, "An Overview of Auditing for Discrimination."

70 M. Bendick, Jr., C. W. Jackson, and V. A. Reinoso, "Measuring Employment Discrimination through Controlled Experiments," in *African-Americans and Post-Industrial Labor Markets*, ed. James B. Stewart (New Brunswick, NJ: Transaction Publishers, 1997), 77–100.

71 P. B. Riach and J. Rich, "Measuring Discrimination by Direct Experimental Methods: Seeking Gunsmoke," *Journal of Post Keynesian Economics* 14, no. 2 (Winter 1991–1992): 143–150.

72 A. P. Brief, R. T. Buttram, R. M. Reizenstein, and S. D. Pugh, "Beyond Good Intentions: The Next Steps toward Racial Equality in the American Workplace," *Academy of Management Executive* 11 (1997): 59–72.

73 L. E. Wynter, "Business & Race: Federal Agencies, Spurred on by Nonprofit Groups, Are Increasingly Embracing the Use of Undercover Investigators to Identify Discrimination in the Marketplace," *Wall Street Journal*, July 1, 1998, B1.

74 "ADA Questions and Answers," *U.S. Department of Justice*, May 2002, accessed March 24, 2009, http://www .ada.gov.

75 "Frequently Asked Questions," *Disability Statistics: Online Resource for U.S. Disability Statistics*, accessed August 21, 2008, http://www.ilr.cornell .edu/edi/disabilitystatistics.

76 "2007 Disability Status Report: United States," *Rehabilitation Research and Training Center on Disability Demographics and Statistics*, accessed November 7, 2009, http://www.ilr.cornell.edu/edi /disabilitystatistics/statusreports.

77 F. Bowe, "Adults with Disabilities: A Portrait," *President's Committee on Employment of People with Disabilities* (Washington, DC: GPO, 1992); D. Braddock and L. Bachelder, *The Glass Ceiling and Persons with Disabilities*, Glass Ceiling Commission, U.S. Department of Labor (Washington, DC: GPO, 1994).

78 Louis Harris & Associates, Inc., *Public Attitudes toward People with Disabilities* (Washington, DC: National Organization on Disability, 1991); Louis Harris & Associates, Inc., *The ICD Survey II: Employing Disabled Americans* (New York: Louis Harris & Associates, Inc., 1987).

79 R. Greenwood and V. A. Johnson, "Employer Perspectives on Workers with Disabilities," *Journal of Rehabilitation* 53 (1987): 37–45.

80 "Work Accommodations: Low Cost, High Impact," *U.S. Department of Labor's Office of Disability Employment Policy*, accessed November 7, 2009, http://www.jan.wvu.edu/media /LowCostHighImpact.doc.

81 T. E. Narashimhan and G. Babu, "The Chosen Ones," *Business Standard*, March 11, 2012, accessed March 16, 2012, http://www.business-standard .com/india/news/the-chosen-ones /467290/.

82 "Study on the Financing of Assistive Technology Devices and Services for Individuals with Disabilities: A Report to the President and the Congress of the United States," *National Council on Disability*, accessed August 21, 2008, http://www.ncd.gov/newsroom /publications/assistive.html.

83 Ibid.

84 R. B. Cattell, "Personality Pinned Down," *Psychology Today* 7 (1973): 40–46; C. S. Carver and M. F. Scheier, *Perspectives on Personality* (Boston: Allyn & Bacon, 1992).

85 J. M. Digman, "Personality Structure: Emergence of the Five-Factor Model," *Annual Review of Psychology* 41 (1990): 417–440; M. R. Barrick and M. K. Mount, "The Big Five Personality Dimensions and Job Performance: A Meta-Analysis," *Personnel Psychology* 44 (1991): 1–26.

86 R. Cook, "The Changing 'Face' of Your Business: Finding Good People... and Keeping Them Motivated," *PRO Magazine*, March 2005, 43.

87 O. Behling, "Employee Selection: Will Intelligence and Conscientiousness Do the Job?" *Academy of Management Executive* 12 (1998): 77–86.

88 R. S. Dalal, "A Meta-Analysis of the Relationship between Organizational Citizenship Behavior and Counter-productive Work Behavior," *Journal of Applied Psychology* 90 (2005): 1241–1255.

89 Barrick and Mount, "The Big Five Personality Dimensions and Job Performance"; M. K. Mount and M. R. Barrick, "The Big Five Personality Dimensions: Implications for Research and Practice in Human Resource Management," *Research in Personnel & Human Resources Management* 13 (1995): 153–200; M. K. Mount and M. R. Barrick, "Five Reasons Why the 'Big Five' Article Has Been Frequently Cited," *Personnel Psychology* 51 (1998): 849–857; D. S. Ones, M. K. Mount, M. R. Barrick, and J. E. Hunter, "Personality and Job Performance: A Critique of the Tett, Jackson, and Rothstein (1991) Meta-Analysis," *Personnel Psychology* 47 (1994): 147–156.

90 Mount and Barrick, "Five Reasons Why the 'Big Five' Article Has Been Frequently Cited."

91 J. A. Lopez, "Talking Desks: Personality Types Revealed in State Workstations," *Arizona Republic*, January 7, 1996, D1.

92 "The Diverse Work Force," *Inc.*, January 1993, 33.

93 D. A. Thomas and R. J. Ely, "Making Differences Matter: A New Paradigm for Managing Diversity," *Harvard Business Review* 74 (September–October 1996): 79–90.

94 Esen, "2005 Workplace Diversity Practices: Survey Report."

95 D. A. Thomas and S. Wetlaufer, "A Question of Color: A Debate on Race in the U.S. Workplace," *Harvard Business Review* 75 (September–October 1997): 118–132.

96 E. Esen, "2007 State of Workplace Diversity Management. A Survey Report by the Society for Human Resource Management," 2008.

97 A. Fisher, "How You Can Do Better on Diversity," *Fortune*, November 15, 2004, 60.

98 J. Espinoza, "Working to Prove Benefits of More Women at the Top," *Wall Street Journal*, February 27, 2011, accessed March 15, 2011, http://online.wsj.com/article/SB1000142405274 870415060457616648301282135 2.html.

99 J. R. Norton and R. E. Fox, *The Change Equation: Capitalizing on Diversity for Effective Organizational Change* (Washington, DC: American Psychological Association, 1997).

100 Ibid.

101 Thomas and Ely, "Making Differences Matter."

102 R. R. Thomas, Jr., *Beyond Race and Gender: Unleashing the Power of Your Total Workforce by Managing Diversity* (New York: AMACOM, 1991).

103 Ibid.

104 T. Cox, Jr., "The Multicultural Organization," *Academy of Management Executive* 5 (1991): 34–47.

105 S. Lubove, "Damned If You Do, Damned If You Don't: Preference Programs Are on the Defensive in the Public Sector, but Plaintiffs' Attorneys and Bureaucrats Keep Diversity Inc. Thriving in Corporate America," *Forbes*, December 15, 1997, 122.

106 L. S. Gottfredson, "Dilemmas in Developing Diversity Programs," in *Diversity in the Workplace*, ed. S. E. Jackson & Associates (New York: Guilford Press, 1992).

107 R. B. Lieber and L. Urresta, "Pacific Enterprises Keeping Talent: After Being Encouraged to Explore Jobs Elsewhere, Most Employees Stay Put," *Fortune*, August 3, 1998, 96.

108 Rodriguez, "Diversity Finds Its Place."

109 "Diversity at Work: Public Relations Makes a Difference for Global Giants".

110 A. Greenwald, B. Nosek, and M. Banaji, "Understanding and Using the Implicit Association Test: I. An Improved Scoring Algorithm," *Journal of Personality & Social Psychology* (August 2003): 197–206; S. Vedantam, "See No Bias; Many Americans Believe They Are Not Prejudiced," *Washington Post*, January 23, 2005, W12.

111 Carnevale and Stone, *The American Mosaic*.

112 "2010 Corporate Responsibility Report," Intel, accessed May 5, 2012, http://csrreportbuilder.intel.com/PDFFiles/CSR_2010_Full-Report.pdf.

113 "Intel Corp.—2012 50 Out Front #16," *Diversity MBA Magazine*, September 16, 2011, accessed March 16, 2012, http://diversitymbamagazine.com/tag/intel.

114 R. Joplin and C. S. Daus, "Challenges of Leading a Diverse Workforce," *Academy of Management Executive* 11 (1997): 32–47.

115 A. Fisher, "Should People Choose Their Own Mentors?" *Fortune*, November 29, 2004, 72.

116 N. Byrnes and R. O. Crocket, "An Historic Succession at Xerox," *Business Week*, June 8, 2009, 18–22.

117 P. Dvorak, "How Executives Are Pushed to Foster Diversity," *Wall Street Journal*, December 18, 2006, accessed March 16, 2012, http://online.wsj.com/article/SB1166407 64543853102.html?mod=rss_build _workplace_cul.

Chapter 13

1 T. Daniel and G. Metcalf, "Motivation: A Management Challenge," *T+D* 60 (November 2006): 11.

2 P. Campbell and R. D. Pritchard, "Motivation Theory in Industrial and Organizational Psychology," in *Handbook of Industrial and Organizational Psychology*, ed. M. D. Dunnette (Chicago: Rand McNally, 1976).

3 D. Mattioli, "Rewards for Extra Work Come Cheap in Lean Times—With Raises and Promotions Scarce, Managers Are Generous with Low-Cost Incentives Like Thank-You Notes, Gift Cards," *Wall Street Journal*, January 4, 2010, B7.

4 J. Fried, "When the Only Way Up Is Out," *Inc.*, April 2011, 35–36.

5 A. Locke, "The Nature and Causes of Job Satisfaction," in *Handbook of Industrial and Organizational Psychology*, ed. M. D. Dunnette (Chicago: Rand McNally, 1976).

6 H. Maslow, "A Theory of Human Motivation," *Psychological Review* 50 (1943): 370–396.

7 P. Alderfer, *Existence, Relatedness, and Growth: Human Needs in Organizational Settings* (New York: Free Press, 1972).

8 C. McClelland, "Toward a Theory of Motive Acquisition," *American Psychologist* 20 (1965): 321–333; D. C. McClelland and D. H. Burnham, "Power Is the Great Motivator," *Harvard Business Review* 54, no. 2 (1976): 100–110.

9 J. H. Turner, "Entrepreneurial Environments and the Emergence of Achievement Motivation in Adolescent Males," *Sociometry* 33 (1970): 147–165.

10 L. W. Porter, E. E. Lawler III, and J. R. Hackman, *Behavior in Organizations* (New York: McGraw-Hill, 1975).

11 C. Ajila, "Maslow's Hierarchy of Needs Theory: Applicability to the Nigerian Industrial Setting," *IFE Psychology* (1997): 162–174.

12 M. A. Wahba and L. B. Birdwell, "Maslow Reconsidered: A Review of Research on the Need Hierarchy Theory," *Organizational Behavior & Human Performance* 15 (1976): 212–240; J. Rauschenberger, N. Schmitt, and J. E. Hunter, "A Test of the Need Hierarchy Concept by a Markov Model of Change in Need Strength," *Administrative Science Quarterly* 25 (1980): 654–670.

13 E. E. Lawler III and L. W. Porter, "The Effect of Performance on Job Satisfaction," *Industrial Relations* 7 (1967): 20–28.

14 Porter, Lawler, and Hackman, *Behavior in Organizations.*

15 E. White, "Employers Increasingly Favor Bonuses to Raises," *Wall Street Journal*, August 28, 2006, B3.

16 D. Gates, "Alaska Air Pays Average $5200 Annual Bonus to Local Employees," *Seattle Times*, February 29, 2012, accessed March 21, 2012, http://seattletimes.nwsource.com/html/businesstechnology/2017625974_alaska01.html.

17 Porter, Lawler, and Hackman, *Behavior in Organizations.*

18 J. Gibbs, "Atlassian Summit 2010 Highlights—FedEx Champions," *Atlassian Blogs*, accessed May 31, 2011, http://blogs.atlassian.com/developer/fedex/.

19 M. Cannon-Brookes, "Atlassian's 20% Time Experiment," *Atlassian Blogs*, March 10, 2008, accessed May 31, 2011, http://blogs.atlassian.com/developer/2008/03/20_time_experiment.html; RSA Vision, *Dan Pink: Drive*, video of a lecture by Daniel Pink at the Royal Society for the Encouragement of Arts, Manufacture, & Commerce, London, England, January 27, 2010, accessed July 29, 2010, http://www.thersa.org/events/vision/vision-videos/dan-pink-drive.

20 C. Caggiano, "What Do Workers Want?" *Inc.*, November 1992, 101–104; "National Study of the Changing Workforce," *Families & Work Institute*, accessed May 31, 2005, http://www.familiesandwork.org/summary/nscw.pdf.

21 A. Brooks, "I LOVE my WORK," *American: A Magazine of Ideas* 6 (September/October 2007), 20–28.

22 A. Fisher, "To Keep Employees Loyal, Try Asking What They Want," *Fortune*, January 27, 2011, accessed March 16, 2012, http://management.fortune.cnn.com/2011/01/27/to-keep-employees-loyal-try-asking-what-they-want/.

23 "America@Work: A Focus on Benefits and Compensation," *Aon Consulting*, http://www.aon.com/pdf/america/awork2.pdf [content no longer available online].

24 H. Dolezalek, "Good Job! Recognition Training," *Training*, July 28, 2008.

25 J. Laabs, "Satisfy Them with More Than Money," *Personnel Journal* 77, no. 11 (1998): 40.

26 R. Kanfer and P. Ackerman, "Aging, Adult Development, and Work Motivation," *Academy of Management Review* (2004): 440–458.

27 E. White, "The New Recruits: Older Workers," *Wall Street Journal*, January 14, 2008, B3.

28 "CEO Pay: Feeding the 1%," *AFL-CIO Executive Paywatch*, no date, accessed March 16, 2012, http://archive.aflcio.org/corporatewatch/paywatch/paywatch2011_indexmore.cfm.

29 "Highest Paid CEOs," *Yahoo! Finance*, February 17, 2012, accessed March 16, 2012, http://finance.yahoo.com/news/highest-paid-ceos-174613134.html.

30 C. T. Kulik and M. L. Ambrose, "Personal and Situational Determinants of Referent Choice," *Academy of Management Review* 17 (1992): 212–237.

31 World Bank, "GNI per Capita 2007, Atlas Method and PPP," accessed September 17, 2009, http://siteresources.worldbank.org.

32 J. S. Adams, "Toward an Understanding of Inequity," *Journal of Abnormal Social Psychology* 67 (1963): 422–436.

33 J. Greenberg, "Employee Theft as a Reaction to Underpayment Inequity: The Hidden Costs of Pay Cuts," *Journal of Applied Psychology* 75 (1990): 561–568.

34 R. A. Cosier and D. R. Dalton, "Equity Theory and Time: A Reformulation," *Academy of Management Review* 8 (1983): 311–319; M. R. Carrell and J. E. Dittrich, "Equity Theory: The Recent Literature, Methodological Considerations, and New Directions," *Academy of Management Review* 3 (1978): 202–209.

35 J. Doom, "American Superconductor Drops on Wider Loss, Lower Forecast," *Bloomberg Businessweek*, February 9, 2012, accessed March 21, 2012, http://www.bloomberg.com/news/2012-02-09/american-superconductor-s-loss-widens-as-sales-fall-43-percent.html; T. Hoium, "American Superconductor: A Disastrous Year in Review," *The Motley Fool*, December 14, 2011, accessed March 21, 2012, http://www.fool.com/investing/general/2011/12/14/american-superconductor-a-disastrous-year-in-revi.aspx; T. Hoium, "Sinovel Drops the Hammer on American Superconductor," *The Motley Fool*, April 6, 2011, accessed March 21, 2012, http://www.fool.com/investing/general/2011/04/06/sinovel-drops-the-hammer-on-american-superconducto.aspx.

36 "LG Display China Factory Workers Strike on Strike, QQ, Sina Websites Say," *Bloomberg Businessweek*, December 27, 2011, accessed March 21, 2012, http://www.bloomberg.com/news/2011-12-28/lg-display-china-factory-workers-strike-on-strike-qq-sina-websites-say.html; "LG Factory Strike in China Caused by Disagreements over Year-End Bonuses," *Huffington Post*, December 28, 2011, accessed March 21, 2012, http://www.huffingtonpost.com/2011/12/28/lg-factory-strike-china_n_1172431.html.

37 J. Bendich, "When Is a Temp Not a Temp?" *Trial Magazine*, October 1, 2001, 42.

38 U.S. Department of Labor, "2002 Statistics Fact Sheet: Back Wages for Fair Labor Standards Act Violations Increased by 29%," accessed March 25, 2009, http://www.dol.gov/esa/whd/statistics/200212.htm; M. Orey, "Lawsuits Abound from Workers Seeking Overtime Pay," *Wall Street Journal*, May 30, 2002, B1.

39 K. Maher, "Workers Are Filing More Lawsuits against Employers over Wages," *Wall Street Journal*, June 5, 2006, A2.

40 M. B. Ahlers, "Government Finally Doles out $106 Million Settlement to Air Marshals," *CNN*, January 17, 2011, accessed March 21, 2012, http://articles.cnn.com/2011-06-17/travel/air.marshals.pay_1_air-marshals-fair-labor-standards-act-million-settlement?_s=PM:TRAVEL.

41 C. Chen, J. Choi, and S. Chi, "Making Justice Sense of Local-Expatriate Compensation Disparity: Mitigation by Local Referents, Ideological Explanations, and Interpersonal Sensitivity in China-Foreign Joint Ventures," *Academy of Management Journal* (2002): 807–817.

42 S. Needleman, "Burger Chain's Health-Care Recipe—Paying More for Insurance Cuts Turnover, Boosts Sales and Productivity," *Wall Street Journal*, August 31, 2009, B4.

43 "Apple Supplier Foxconn Cuts Working Hours, Workers Ask Why," *Reuters*, March 30, 2012, accessed May 8, 2012, http://www.reuters.com /article/2012/03/30/us-apple-foxconn -workers-idUSBRE82T0FC20120330; D. Barboza, "Foxconn Plant to Lift Pay Sharply at Factories in China," *New York Times*, February 18, 2012, accessed March 21, 2012, http:// www.nytimes.com/2012/02/19 /technology/foxconn-to-raise-salaries -for-workers-by-up-to-25.html; M. Brown, "New Report Details Oner- ous, Illegal Working Conditions at Foxconn," *Wired.com*, May 6, 2011, accessed March 21, 2012, http:// www.wired.com/epicenter/2011/05 /foxconn-no-suicide-pledge/; H. Koch, "We Were Not a Very Open Com- pany Before," *Spiegel Online*, May 11, 2011, accessed March 21, 2012, http://www.spiegel.de/international /world/0,1518,761934,00.html.

44 R. Folger and M. A. Konovsky, "Ef- fects of Procedural and Distributive Justice on Reactions to Pay Raise Decisions," *Academy of Management Journal* 32 (1989): 115–130; M. A. Konovsky, "Understanding Procedural Justice and Its Impact on Business Or- ganizations," *Journal of Management* 26 (2000): 489–512.

45 E. Barret-Howard and T. R. Tyler, "Procedural Justice as a Criterion in Allocation Decisions," *Journal of Personality & Social Psychology* 50 (1986): 296–305; Folger and Konovsky, "Effects of Procedural and Distributive Justice on Reactions to Pay Raise Decisions."

46 R. Folger and J. Greenberg, "Proce- dural Justice: An Interpretive Analysis of Personnel Systems," in *Research in Personnel and Human Resources Management*, vol. 3, ed. K. Row- land and G. Ferris (Greenwich, CT: JAI, 1985); R. Folger, D. Rosenfield, J. Grove, and L. Corkran, "Effects of 'Voice' and Peer Opinions on Responses to Inequity," *Journal of Personality & Social Psychology* 37 (1979): 2253–2261; E. A. Lind and T. R. Tyler, *The Social Psychology of Pro- cedural Justice* (New York: Plenum, 1988); Konovsky, "Understanding Procedural Justice and Its Impact on Business Organizations."

47 V. H. Vroom, *Work and Motivation* (New York: John Wiley & Sons, 1964); L. W. Porter and E. E. Lawler III, *Managerial Attitudes and Perfor- mance* (Homewood, IL: Dorsey & Richard D. Irwin, 1968).

48 J. Galante, "Another Day, Another Vir- tual Dollar," *Bloomberg Businessweek*, June 21–June 27, 2010, 43–44.

49 S. Miller, "Countering the Employee Recognition Gap," SHRM Library, *Society for Human Resource Manage- ment*, February 2006, accessed March 25, 2009, http://www.shrm.org.

50 P. V. LeBlanc and P. W. Mulvey, "How American Workers See the Rewards of Work," *Compensation & Benefits Review* 30 (February 1998): 24–28.

51 A. Fox, "Companies Can Benefit When They Disclose Pay Processes to Employees," *HR Magazine*, July 2002, 25.

52 J. Spolsky, "Why I Never Let Employees Negotiate a Raise," *Inc .com*, April 1, 2009, accessed February 15, 2010, http://www.inc .com/magazine/20090401/how-hard -could-it-be-employees-negotiate-pay -raises.html.

53 K. W. Thomas and B. A. Velthouse, "Cognitive Elements of Empower- ment," *Academy of Management Review* 15 (1990): 666–681.

54 E. L. Thorndike, *Animal Intelligence* (New York: Macmillan, 1911).

55 R. Ableson, "The Smokers' Sur- charge," *New York Times*, November 16, 2011, accessed March 21, 2012, http://www.nytimes.com/2011/11/17 /health/policy/smokers-penalized -with-health-insurance-premiums .html?pagewanted=all.

56 B. F. Skinner, *Science and Human Behavior* (New York: Macmillan, 1954); B. F. Skinner, *Beyond Freedom and Dignity* (New York: Bantam, 1971); B. F. Skinner, *A Matter of Consequences* (New York: New York University Press, 1984).

57 A. M. Dickinson and A. D. Poling, "Schedules of Monetary Reinforce- ment in Organizational Behavior Management: Latham and Huber Revisited," *Journal of Organizational Behavior Management* 16, no. 1 (1992): 71–91.

58 B. Dolan, "Humana Launches Well- ness Platform Vitality," *MobiHealth- News*, July 6, 2011, accessed March 21, 2012, http://mobihealthnews .com/11675/humana-launches -wellness-platform-vitality/; J. McGregor, "Should Companies Penalize Employees Who Smoke?" *Washington Post*, July 7, 2011, accessed March 21, 2012, http:// www.washingtonpost.com/blogs /post-leadership/post/should -companies-penalize-employees-who -smoke/2011/04/01/gIQAENh71H_

blog.html; M. Raby, "Humana Offers Incentives for Playing Ubisoft Fitness Games," *Slashgear*, March 14, 2012, accessed March 21, 2012, http:// www.slashgear.com/humana-offers -incentives-for-playing-ubisoft-fitness -games-14218455/.

59 L. Welch, "The Way I Work: Paul English of Kayak," *Inc.*, February 1, 2010, accessed June 2, 2011, http:// www.inc.com/magazine/20100201 /the-way-i-work-paul-english-of -kayak.html.

60 P. Svensson, "Randall Stephenson, AT&T CEO, Takes $2 Million Pay Cut over Failed T-Mobile Deal," *Huffington Post*, February 21, 2012, accessed March 21, 2012, http:// www.huffingtonpost.com/2012/02/21 /randall-stephenson-att-ceo-pay-cut -tmobile_n_1292231.html; J. Wortham, "AT&T in $6.7 Billion Loss on Failure of T-Mobile Deal," *New York Times*, January 26, 2012, accessed March 21, 2012, http://www .nytimes.com/2012/01/27/technology /atts-net-loss-tied-to-t-mobile-merger -fees.html.

61 J. B. Miner, *Theories of Organiza- tional Behavior* (Hinsdale, IL: Dryden, 1980).

62 Dickinson and Poling, "Schedules of Monetary Reinforcement in Organiza- tional Behavior Management."

63 F. Luthans and A. D. Stajkovic, "Re- inforce for Performance: The Need to Go beyond Pay and Even Rewards," *Academy of Management Executive* 13, no. 2 (1999): 49–57.

64 D. Anderson, *Up Your Business! 7 Steps to Fix, Build or Stretch Your Or- ganization* (New York: Wiley, 2003).

65 K. D. Butterfield, L. K. Trevino, and G. A. Ball, "Punishment from the Manager's Perspective: A Grounded Investigation and Inductive Model," *Academy of Management Journal* 39 (1996): 1479–1512.

66 R. D. Arvey and J. M. Ivancevich, "Punishment in Organizations: A Review, Propositions, and Research Suggestions," *Academy of Manage- ment Review* 5 (1980): 123–132.

67 R. D. Arvey, G. A. Davis, and S. M. Nelson, "Use of Discipline in an Organization: A Field Study," *Journal of Applied Psychology* 69 (1984): 448–460; M. E. Schnake, "Vicarious Punishment in a Work Setting," *Jour- nal of Applied Psychology* 71 (1986): 343–345.

68 G. A. Yukl and G. P. Latham, "Consequences of Reinforcement Schedules and Incentive Magnitudes

for Employee Performance: Problems Encountered in a Field Setting," *Journal of Applied Psychology* 60 (1975): 294–298.

69 E. A. Locke and G. P. Latham, *Goal Setting: A Motivational Technique That Works* (Englewood Cliffs, NJ: Prentice-Hall, 1984); E. A. Locke and G. P. Latham, *A Theory of Goal Setting and Task Performance* (Englewood Cliffs, NJ: Prentice-Hall, 1990).

70 "Franchising—In with the New: As More Boomers Retire, Franchisers Set Their Sights on a Much Younger Crowd," *Wall Street Journal*, September 28, 2009, R9.

71 G. P. Latham and E. A. Locke, "Goal Setting—A Motivational Technique That Works," *Organizational Dynamics* 8, no. 2 (1979): 68.

72 Ibid.

Chapter 14

1 W. Bennis, "Why Leaders Can't Lead," *Training & Development Journal* 43, no. 4 (1989).

2 C. Hymnowitz and S. Frier, "Can This IBMer Keep Big Blue's Edge?" *Bloomberg Businessweek*, October 6–November 31, 2011, 31–32.

3 A. Zaleznik, "Managers and Leaders: Are They Different?" *Harvard Business Review* 55 (1977): 76–78; A. Zaleznik, "The Leadership Gap," *Washington Quarterly* 6 (1983): 32–39.

4 D. Welch, "For Dan Akerson, a Magic Moment to Remake GM," *Bloomberg Businessweek*, January 24–January 30, 2011, 21–22.

5 Bennis, "Why Leaders Can't Lead."

6 J. S. Lublin, "Introverted Execs Find Ways to Shine," *Wall Street Journal*, April 14, 2011, accessed March 21, 2012, http://online.wsj.com/article /SB1000142405274870398310457 6263053775879800.html.

7 D. Jones, "Not All Successful CEOs Are Extroverts," *USA Today*, June 7, 2006, B.1.

8 Ibid.

9 M. Gladwell, "Why Do We Love Tall Men?" *Gladwell.com*, accessed August 27, 2008, http://www.gladwell.com /blink/blink_excerpt2.html.

10 D. Sacks, "The Accidental Guru," *Fast Company*, January 1, 2005, 64.

11 R. J. House and R. M Aditya, "The Social Scientific Study of Leadership: Quo Vadis?" *Journal of Management* 23 (1997): 409–473; T. Judge, R. Illies, J. Bono, and M. Gerhardt, "Personal-ity and Leadership: A Qualitative and Quantitative Review," *Journal of Applied Psychology* (August 2002): 765–782; S. A. Kirkpatrick and E. A. Locke, "Leadership: Do Traits Matter?" *Academy of Management Executive* 5, no. 2 (1991): 48–60.

12 House and Aditya, "The Social Scientific Study of Leadership"; Kirkpatrick and Locke, "Leadership: Do Traits Matter?"

13 J. J. Gabarro, *The Dynamics of Taking Charge* (Boston: Harvard Business School Press, 1987).

14 N. Wingfield and B. Stelter, "How Netflix Lost 800,000 Members, and Good Will," *New York Times*, October 25, 2011, accessed March 22, 2012, http://www.nytimes.com/2011/10/25 /technology/netflix-lost-800000 -members-with-price-rise-and-split -plan.html?pagewanted=all.

15 B. Stelter, "Netflix, in Reversal, Will Keep Its Services Together," *New York Times*, October 10, 2011, accessed March 22, 2012, http://mediadecoder .blogs.nytimes.com/2011/10/10 /netflix-abandons-plan-to-rent-dvds -on-qwikster/; J. Voorhees, "Netflix Stock Plunges as Subscribers Flee," *Slate.com*, October 25, 2011, accessed March 22, 2012, http:// slatest.slate.com/posts/2011/10/10 /netflix_ qwikster_reed_hastings _drops_plan_to_split_dvd_streaming .html; Wingfield and Stelter, "How Netflix Lost 800,000 Members, and Good Will."

16 A. Bary, "The Best CEOs," *Barron's*, March 29, 2010, accessed August 30, 2010, http://online.barrons.com /article/SB126964409156568321 .html; "Cummins Inc," *Bloomberg Businessweek*, no date, accessed August 30, 2010, http://investing .businessweek.com/research/stocks /people/person.asp?personId=265255 &ticker=CMI:US.

17 Kirkpatrick and Locke, "Leadership: Do Traits Matter?"

18 E. A. Fleishman, "The Description of Supervisory Behavior," *Journal of Applied Psychology* 37 (1953): 1–6; L. R. Katz, *New Patterns of Management* (New York: McGraw-Hill, 1961).

19 B. Einhorn, "Innovator: Jimmy Lai," *Bloomberg Businessweek*, August 26, 2010, accessed September 9, 2010, http://www.businessweek.com /magazine/content/10_36 /b4193038847783.htm.

20 A. Chernoff, "Bosses Listening to Millennial Workers," *CNN*, July 22, 2011, accessed March 22, 2012, http:// articles.cnn.com/2011-07-22/living /managing.millennials_1_millennials -social-media-volunteer-work/2? _s=PM:LIVING.

21 P. Weissenberg and M. H. Kavanagh, "The Independence of Initiating Structure and Consideration: A Review of the Evidence," *Personnel Psychology* 25 (1972): 119–130.

22 R. J. House and T. R. Mitchell, "Path-Goal Theory of Leadership," *Journal of Contemporary Business* 3 (1974): 81–97; F. E. Fiedler, "A Contingency Model of Leadership Effectiveness," in *Advances in Experimental Social Psychology*, ed. L. Berkowitz (New York: Academic Press, 1964); V. H. Vroom and P. W. Yetton, *Leadership and Decision Making* (Pittsburgh: University of Pittsburgh Press, 1973); P. Hersey and K. H. Blanchard, The *Management of Organizational Behavior*, 4th ed. (Englewood Cliffs, NJ: Prentice Hall, 1984); S. Kerr and J. M. Jermier, "Substitutes for Leadership: Their Meaning and Measurement," *Organizational Behavior & Human Performance* 22 (1978): 375–403.

23 J. Pfeffer, "In Defense of the Boss from Hell," *Business 2.0*, March 1, 2007, 70.

24 F. E. Fiedler and M. M. Chemers, *Leadership and Effective Management* (Glenview, IL: Scott, Foresman, 1974); F. E. Fiedler and M. M. Chemers, *Improving Leadership Effectiveness: The Leader Match Concept*, 2nd ed. (New York: Wiley, 1984).

25 J. Walker, "Executives Learn New Skills to Improve Their Communication," *Wall Street Journal*, May 6, 2010, accessed June 5, 2011, http:// online.wsj.com/article/SB1000142405 2748704342604575222701379951106.html.

26 Fiedler and Chemers, *Improving Leadership Effectiveness*.

27 F. E. Fiedler, "The Effects of Leadership Training and Experience: A Contingency Model Interpretation," *Administrative Science Quarterly* 17, no. 4 (1972): 455; F. E. Fiedler, *A Theory of Leadership Effectiveness* (New York: McGraw-Hill, 1967).

28 J. Helyar, "Why Is This Man Smiling?" *Fortune,* October 18, 2004, 130.

29 L. S. Csoka and F. E. Fiedler, "The Effect of Military Leadership Training: A Test of the Contingency Model," *Organizational Behavior & Human Performance* 8 (1972): 395–407.

30 House and Mitchell, "Path-Goal Theory of Leadership."

31 B. Richards, "For the 63rd Straight Year (at Least), This Remarkable Company Says 'No' to Layoffs," *DailyFinance*, December 13, 2011, accessed March 23, 2012, http://www.dailyfinance.com/2011/12/13/for-the-63rd-straight-year-at-least-this-remarkabl/; B. Richards, "The Remarkable True Story of the Company That Doesn't Lay Off Its Employees," *The Motley Fool*, June 23, 2011, accessed March 23, 2012, http://www.fool.com/investing/general/2011/06/23/the-remarkable-true-story-of-the-company-that-does.aspx.

32 House and Mitchell, "Path-Goal Theory of Leadership."

33 B. M. Fisher and J. E. Edwards, "Consideration and Initiating Structure and Their Relationships with Leader Effectiveness: A Meta-Analysis," *Proceedings of the Academy of Management*, August 1988, 201–205.

34 L. Buchanan, "Letting Employees Run the Company," *Inc.*, June 8, 2010, accessed August 30, 2010, http://www.inc.com/top-workplaces/2010/letting-employees-run-the-company.html.

35 F. Manjoo, "Google: The Quest," *Fast Company*, April 2011, 68–75.

36 J. C. Wofford and L. Z. Liska, "Path-Goal Theories of Leadership: A Meta-Analysis," *Journal of Management* 19 (1993): 857–876.

37 House and Aditya, "The Social Scientific Study of Leadership."

38 V. H. Vroom and A. G. Jago, *The New Leadership: Managing Participation in Organizations* (Englewood Cliffs, NJ: Prentice Hall, 1988).

39 C. Fishman, "How Teamwork Took Flight: This Team Built a Commercial Engine—and Self-Managing GE Plant—from Scratch," *Fast Company*, October 1, 1999, 188.

40 Ibid.

41 Ibid.

42 G. A. Yukl, *Leadership in Organizations*, 3rd ed. (Englewood Cliffs, NJ: Prentice Hall, 1995).

43 B. M. Bass, *Bass & Stogdill's Handbook of Leadership: Theory, Research, and Managerial Applications* (New York: Free Press, 1990).

44 R. D. Ireland and M. A. Hitt, "Achieving and Maintaining Strategic Competitiveness in the 21st Century: The Role of Strategic Leadership," *Academy of Management Executive* 13, no. 1 (1999): 43–57.

45 CEO Insight: Kevin Kelly, "An Executive Recruiter's New Strategy," *Bloomberg Businessweek*, January 15, 2009, accessed June 6, 2011, http://www.businessweek.com/managing/content/jan2009/ca20090115_508822.htm.

46 P. Thoms and D. B. Greenberger, "Training Business Leaders to Create Positive Organizational Visions of the Future: Is It Successful?" *Academy of Management Journal* (Best Papers & Proceedings 1995): 212–216.

47 M. Weber, *The Theory of Social and Economic Organizations*, trans. R. A. Henderson and T. Parsons (New York: Free Press, 1947).

48 D. A. Waldman and F. J. Yammarino, "CEO Charismatic Leadership: Levels-of-Management and Levels-of-Analysis Effects," *Academy of Management Review* 24, no. 2 (1999): 266–285.

49 K. B. Lowe, K. G. Kroeck, and N. Sivasubramaniam, "Effectiveness Correlates of Transformational and Transactional Leadership: A Meta-Analytic Review of the MLQ Literature," *Leadership Quarterly* 7 (1996): 385–425.

50 J. M. Howell and B. J. Avolio, "The Ethics of Charismatic Leadership: Submission or Liberation?" *Academy of Management Executive* 6, no. 2 (1992): 43–54.

51 M. Adams, "Boeing Bounces Back against Odds," *USA Today*, January 11, 2007, B.1.

52 P. Sellers, "What Exactly Is Charisma?" *Fortune*, January 15, 1996, 68.

53 S. Gardiner and P. Hurtado, "DHB Industries Ex-Chief David Brooks Looted Company, Jury Told," *Bloomberg Businessweek*, January 26, 2010, accessed February 24, 2011, http://www.bloomberg.com/apps/news?pid=newsarchive&sid=; A. G. Sulzberger, "Military Contractor with $100,000 Belt Buckle Is Found Guilty," *New York Times*, September 14, 2010, accessed February 22, 2011, http://www.nytimes.com/2010/09/15/nyregion/15brooks.html.

54 Howell and Avolio, "The Ethics of Charismatic Leadership."

55 B. M. Bass, "From Transactional to Transformational Leadership: Learning to Share the Vision," *Organizational Dynamics* 18 (1990): 19–36.

56 B. M. Bass, *A New Paradigm of Leadership: An Inquiry into Transformational Leadership* (Alexandra, VA: U.S. Army Research Institute for the Behavioral and Social Sciences, 1996).

57 Adams, "Boeing Bounces Back against Odds."

58 L. Buchanan, "How to Build a Beautiful Company," *Inc.*, June 8, 2010, accessed July 30, 2010, http://www.inc.com/top-workplaces/2010/how-to-build-a-beautiful-company.html.

59 Bass, "From Transactional to Transformational Leadership."

Chapter 15

1 E. E. Lawler III, L. W. Porter, and A. Tannenbaum, "Manager's Attitudes toward Interaction Episodes," *Journal of Applied Psychology* 52 (1968): 423–439; H. Mintzberg, *The Nature of Managerial Work* (New York: Harper & Row, 1973).

2 J. D. Maes, T. G. Weldy, and M. L. Icenogle, "A Managerial Perspective: Oral Communication Competency Is Most Important for Business Students in the Workplace," *Journal of Business Communication* 34 (1997): 67–80.

3 E. E. Jones and K. E. Davis, "From Acts to Dispositions: The Attribution Process in Person Perception," in *Advances in Experimental and Social Psychology*, vol. 2, ed. L. Berkowitz (New York: Academic Press, 1965), 219–266; R. G. Lord and J. E. Smith, "Theoretical, Information-Processing, and Situational Factors Affecting Attribution Theory Models of Organizational Behavior," *Academy of Management Review* 8 (1983): 50–60.

4 D. Simons and C. Chabris, "Gorillas in Our Midst: Sustained Inattentional Blindness for Dynamic Events," *Perception* 28 (1999): 1059–1074.

5 J. Zadney and H. B. Gerard, "Attributed Intentions and Informational Selectivity," *Journal of Experimental Social Psychology* 10 (1974): 34–52.

6 J. Topolsky, "Apple Responds to iPhone 4 Reception Issues: You're Holding the Phone the Wrong Way," *Engadget.com*, June 24, 2010, accessed June 12, 2011, http://www.engadget.com/2010/06/24/apple-responds-over-iphone-4-reception-issues-youre-holding-th/.

7 V. Blue, "Apple Ignores iPhone 4S Audio Problem, Faces Backlash," *ZDNet*, January 2, 2012, accessed March 27, 2012, http://www.zdnet.com/blog/violetblue/apple-ignores-iphone-4s-audio-problem-faces-backlash/932.

8 H. H. Kelly, *Attribution in Social Interaction* (Morristown, NJ: General Learning Press, 1971).

9 J. M. Burger, "Motivational Biases in the Attribution of Responsibility for an Accident: A Meta-Analysis of the Defensive-Attribution Hypothesis,"

Psychological Bulletin 90 (1981): 496–512.

10 D. A. Hofmann and A. Stetzer, "The Role of Safety Climate and Communication in Accident Interpretation: Implications for Learning from Negative Events," *Academy of Management Journal* 41, no. 6 (1998): 644–657.

11 C. Perrow, *Normal Accidents: Living with High-Risk Technologies* (New York: Basic Books, 1984).

12 A. G. Miller and T. Lawson, "The Effect of an Informational Opinion on the Fundamental Attribution Error," *Journal of Personality & Social Psychology* 47 (1989): 873–896; J. M. Burger, "Changes in Attribution Errors over Time: The Ephemeral Fundamental Attribution Error," *Social Cognition* 9 (1991): 182–193.

13 F. Heider, *The Psychology of Interpersonal Relations* (New York: Wiley, 1958); D. T. Miller and M. Ross, "Self-Serving Biases in Attribution of Causality: Fact or Fiction?" *Psychological Bulletin* 82 (1975): 213–225.

14 J. R. Larson, Jr., "The Dynamic Interplay between Employees' Feedback-Seeking Strategies and Supervisors' Delivery of Performance Feedback," *Academy of Management Review* 14, no. 3 (1989): 408–422.

15 B. O'Keefe, "Meet the CEO of the Biggest Company on Earth," *Fortune*, September 9, 2010, accessed February 25, 2011, http://money.cnn.com/2010/09/07/news/companies/mike_duke_walmart_full.fortune/.

16 C. Hymowitz, "Mind Your Language: To Do Business Today, Consider Delayering," *Wall Street Journal*, March 27, 2006, B1.

17 G. L. Kreps, *Organizational Communication: Theory and Practice* (New York: Longman, 1990).

18 Ibid.

19 J. Jusko, "A Little More Communication," *Industry Week*, March 1, 2010, 19.

20 B. Salzberg, "Trusting a CEO in the Twitter Age," *Businessweek*, August 7, 2009, accessed August 10, 2010, http://www.businessweek.com/managing/content/aug2009/ca2009087_680028.htm?chan=careers_managing+your+company+page_top+stories.

21 J. Sandberg, "Ruthless Rumors and the Managers Who Enable Them," *Wall Street Journal*, October 29, 2003, B1.

22 W. Davis and J. R. O'Connor, "Serial Transmission of Information: A Study of the Grapevine," *Journal of Applied Communication Research* 5 (1977): 61–72.

23 Sandberg, "Ruthless Rumors and the Managers Who Enable Them."

24 E. Holm and J. S. Lublin, "Loose Lips Trip Up a Good Hands Executive," *Wall Street Journal*, August 1, 2011, C1.

25 K. Voight, "Office Intelligence," *Asian Wall Street Journal*, January 21, 2005, P1.

26 Davis and O'Connor, "Serial Transmission of Information: A Study of the Grapevine"; C. Hymowitz, "Managing: Spread the Word, Gossip Is Good," *Wall Street Journal*, October 4, 1988, online, page number not available.

27 W. C. Redding, *Communication within the Organization: An Interpretive View of Theory and Research* (New York: Industrial Communication Council, 1972).

28 D. T. Hall, K. L. Otazo, and G. P. Hollenbeck, "Behind Closed Doors: What Really Happens in Executive Coaching," *Organizational Dynamics* 27, no. 3 (1999): 39–53.

29 P. O'Connell, "Goldman Sachs: Committed to the Next Generation," *Bloomberg Businessweek*, February 17, 2010, 12.

30 J. Kelly, "Blowing the Whistle on the Boss," *PR Newswire*, November 15, 2004, http://www.prnewswire.com [content no longer available online].

31 R. McGarvey, "Lords of Discipline," *Entrepreneur Magazine*, January 1, 2000, page number not available.

32 C. Hirschman, "Firm Ground: EAP Training for HR and Managers Improves Supervisor-Employee Communication and Helps Organizations Avoid Legal Quagmires," *Employee Benefit News*, June 13, 2005, http://www.benefitnews.com [content no longer available online].

33 L. V. Gillespie, "Raising A-wear-ness," *Employee Benefit News*, December 1, 2011, accessed March 27, 2012, http://ebn.benefitnews.com/news/hiv-aids-levi-strauss-eap-disease-management-2720149-1.html.

34 A. Mehrabian, "Communication without Words," *Psychology Today* 3 (1968): 53; A. Mehrabian, *Silent Messages* (Belmont, CA: Wadsworth, 1971); R. Harrison, *Beyond Words: An Introduction to Nonverbal Communication* (Upper Saddle River, NJ: Prentice Hall, 1974); A. Mehrabian, *Non-Verbal Communication* (Chicago: Aldine, 1972).

35 M. L. Knapp, *Nonverbal Communication in Human Interaction*, 2nd ed. (New York: Holt, Rinehart & Winston, 1978).

36 H. M. Rosenfeld, "Instrumental Affiliative Functions of Facial and Gestural Expressions," *Journal of Personality & Social Psychology* 24 (1966): 65–72; P. Ekman, "Differential Communication of Affect by Head and Body Cues," *Journal of Personality & Social Psychology* 23 (1965): 726–735; A. Mehrabian, "Significance of Posture and Position in the Communication of Attitude and Status Relationships," *Psychological Bulletin* 71 (1969): 359–372.

37 J. Gottman and R. Levenson, "The Timing of Divorce: Predicting When a Couple Will Divorce over a 14-Year Period," *Journal of Marriage & the Family* 62 (August 2000): 737–745; J. Gottman, R. Levenson, and E. Woodin, "Facial Expressions during Marital Conflict," *Journal of Family Communication* 1, no. 1 (2001): 37–57.

38 T. Aeppel, "Career Journal: Nicknamed 'Nag,' She's Just Doing Her Job," *Wall Street Journal*, May 14, 2002, B1.

39 A. Joyce, "Confidentiality as a Valued Benefit; Loose Lips Can Defeat the Purpose of an Employee Assistance Program," *Washington Post*, May 11, 2003, F05.

40 C. A. Bartlett and S. Ghoshal, "Changing the Role of Top Management: Beyond Systems to People," *Harvard Business Review*, May–June 1995, 132–142.

41 E. Spragins, "Sending the Wrong Message," *Fortune Small Business*, July 1, 2003, 32.

42 J. Fry, "When Talk Isn't Cheap: Is Emailing Colleagues Who Sit Feet Away a Sign of Office Dysfunction, or a Wise Move?" *Wall Street Journal*, November 28, 2005, http://online.wsj.com [content no longer available online].

43 "The Joys of Voice Mail," *Inc.*, November 1995, 102.

44 R. G. Nichols, "Do We Know How to Listen? Practical Helps in a Modern Age," in *Communication Concepts and Processes*, ed. J. DeVitor (Englewood Cliffs, NJ: Prentice Hall, 1971); P. V. Lewis, *Organizational Communication: The Essence of Effective*

Management (Columbus, OH: Grid Publishing Company, 1975).

45 E. Atwater, *I Hear You*, rev. ed. (New York: Walker, 1992).

46 D. A. Kaplan, "Undercover Employee: A Day on the Job at Three Best Companies," *CNNMoney*, January 20, 2011, accessed March 27, 2012, http://features.blogs.fortune.cnn.com/2011/01/20/undercover-employee-a-day-on-the-job-at-three-best-companies/.

47 C. Gallo, "Why Leadership Means Listening," *BusinessWeek Online*, January 31, 2007, accessed September 3, 2008, http://www.businessweek.com.

48 B. D. Seyber, R. N. Bostrom, and J. H. Seibert, "Listening, Communication Abilities, and Success at Work," *Journal of Business Communication* 26 (1989): 293–303.

49 Atwater, *I Hear You*.

50 C. Edwards, "Death of a Pushy Salesman," *BusinessWeek*, July 3, 2006, 108.

51 J. Sandberg, "Not Communicating with Your Boss? Count Your Blessings," *Wall Street Journal*, May 22, 2007, B1.

52 P. Sellers, A. Diba, and E. Florian, "Get Over Yourself—Your Ego Is Out of Control. You're Screwing Up Your Career," *Fortune*, April 30, 2001, 76.

53 M. Flatt, "How to Give Feedback That Works," *Inc.com*, December 21, 2011, accessed March 27, 2012, http://www.inc.com/michael-flatt/how-to-give-feedback-that-works.html.

54 L. Anguish, N. Cossack, and A. Maingault, "Payroll Cuts, Personal Hygiene, Extra Leave," *HR Magazine*, June 1, 2003, 41.

55 C. Tuna, "Corporate News: Chambers Vows 'Fix' as Cisco Stumbles," *Wall Street Journal*, April 6, 2011, B2.

56 A. Bryant, "The Memo List: Where Everyone Has an Opinion," *New York Times*, March 10, 2012, accessed March 27, 2012, http://www.nytimes.com/2012/03/11/business/jim-whitehurst-of-red-hat-on-merits-of-an-open-culture.html

57 M. Campanelli and N. Friedman, "Welcome to Voice Mail Hell: The New Technology Has Become a Barrier between Salespeople and Customers," *Sales & Marketing Management* 147 (May 1995): 98–101.

58 S. Ali, "Why No One under 30 Answers Your Voicemail," *DiversityInc*, February 3, 2011, accessed February 22, 2011, http://www.diversityinc.com/article/7967/Why-No-One-Under-30-Answers-Your-Voicemail/.

59 E. W. Morrison, "Organizational Silence: A Barrier to Change and Development in a Pluralistic World," *Academy of Management Review* 25 (2000): 706–725.

60 R. Willingham, "Jetstar Pilots 'Afraid to Report Risks,'" *The Age*, March 19, 2011, accessed June 17, 2011, http://www.theage.com.au/travel/travel-news/jetstar-pilots-afraid-to-report-risks-20110318-1c0mi.html.

61 A. Heasley, "Tired Jetstar Pilots Told to 'Toughen up Princesses,'" *The Age*, March 31, 2011, accessed June 17, 2011, http://www.theage.com.au/travel/travel-news/tired-jetstar-pilots-told-to-toughen-up-princesses-20110331-1chh1.html.

62 "An Inside Look at Corporate Hotlines," *Security Director's Report*, February 2007, 8.

63 J. Confino, "Guardian Employee Survey Maintains High Scores Despite Radical Restructuring," *Guardian.co.uk*, January 11, 2010, accessed July 15, 2010, http://www.guardian.co.uk/sustainability/corporate-social-responsibility-employee-survey-employee-engagement-sustainability.

64 C. Hymowitz, "Sometimes, Moving up Makes It Harder to See What Goes on Below," *Wall Street Journal*, October 15, 2007, B1.

65 Ibid.

66 D. Kirkpatrick and D. Roth, "Why There's No Escaping the Blog," *Fortune* (Europe), January 24, 2005, 64.

67 J. Bertolucci, "Tech Support Goes Social," *PCWorld*, April 5, 2011, accessed March 27, 2012, http://www.pcworld.com/article/224336/tech_support_goes_social.html.

Chapter 16

1 R. Leifer and P. K. Mills, "An Information Processing Approach for Deciding upon Control Strategies and Reducing Control Loss in Emerging Organizations," *Journal of Management* 22 (1996): 113–137.

2 S. Mayerowitz, "Casinos Always Win, Even When Robbed," *ABC News*, January 4, 2011, accessed June 13, 2011, http://abcnews.go.com/m/story?id=12531632.

3 R. Grais-Targow, "Big Salmon Exporter Fights Virus—Chile's Share of Global Output Expected to Fall; Pickup Unlikely until 2011," *Wall Street Journal*, July 7, 2009, B6.

4 J. Jargon, "At Starbucks, Baristas Told No More Than Two Drinks," *Wall Street Journal*, October 13, 2010, accessed April 5, 2011, http://online.wsj.com/article/SB10001424052748704164004575548403514060736.html.

5 P. Bryan and P. Pane, "Evaluating Fire Service Delivery," *Fire Engineering*, April 2008, 207–210.

6 A. Ricadela, "Intuit Taps Hewlett-Packard and Google for Advice," *BusinessWeek*, October 1, 2008, 15.

7 T. Rosenberg, "An Electronic Eye on Hospital Hand-Washing," *New York Times*, November 24, 2011, http://opinionator.blogs.nytimes.com/2011/11/24/an-electronic-eye-on-hospital-hand-washing.

8 Ibid.

9 N. Wiener, *Cybernetics; Or Control and Communication in the Animal and the Machine* (New York: Wiley, 1948).

10 M. Rohde, "Squirrelly Behavior: Critters Shock the System," *Daily Reporter*, January 4, 2011, accessed June 20, 2011, http://dailyreporter.com/2011/01/04/squirrely-behavior-critters-shock-the-system/.

11 K. Stack, "Concussion-Sensing Chin Strap Raises Questions," *Wired.com*, March 26, 2012, accessed March 28, 2012 , http://www.wired.com/playbook/2012/03/battle-sports-science-impact-indicator/.

12 Leifer and Mills, "An Information Processing Approach."

13 "Minn. Food Company Recalls about 1 Million Eggs in 34 States," *USA Today*, February 3, 2012, accessed March 28, 2012, http://yourlife.usatoday.com/fitness-food/safety/story/2012-02-03/Minn-food-company-recalls-eggs-in-34-states/52951110/1.

14 B. Leshan, "Montgomery County Changes Stance on Lemonade Stand; $500 Fine Waived," *9NewsNow*, June 17, 2011, accessed September 10, 2011, http://www.wusa9.com/news/article/155167/158/County-Shuts-Down-Kids-Lemonade-Stand-500-Fine.

15 H. Bradford, "Children's Families Fined $500 for Operating Illegal Lemonade Stand," *Huffington Post*, June 17, 2011, accessed March 28, 2012, http://www.huffingtonpost.com/2011/06/17/us-open-lemonade-fine-neighbors-parking_n_878949.html.

16 C. Woodyard, "UPS Tries to Save Fuel by Cutting Weight," *USA Today*, June 9, 2011, accessed March 28, 2012, http://www.usatoday.com/money /autos/environment/2011-06-09-ups -vans-save-energy_n.htm; S. McGlaun, "Coca-Cola Company to Deploy Electric Delivery Trucks to Save Fuel and Go Greener," *Slashgear.com*, September 9, 2011, accessed March 28, 2012, http://www.slashgear.com /coca-cola-company-to-deploy-electric -delivery-trucks-to-save-fuel-and-go -greener-09178333/; C. Michelsen, "Smith Electric Vehicles Delivers New Electric Truck to FedEx," *CleanTechnica.com*, March 8, 2012, accessed March 28, 2012, http:// cleantechnica.com/2012/03/08/smith -electric-vehicles-delivers-new-electric -truck-to-fedex/.

17 M. Weber, *The Protestant Ethic and the Spirit of Capitalism* (New York: Scribner's, 1958).

18 L. Criner, "Politicians Come and Go, Bureaucracies Stay and Grow," *Washington Times*, March 11, 1996, 33.

19 D. Gibson, "Angus Barn's Eure: Peyton Manning Check Posting 'Horrible,'" *Triangle Business Journal*, March 7, 2012, accessed March 29, 2012, http://www.bizjournals.com/triangle /blog/2012/03/peyton-leaves-whopper -tip-at-angus-barn.html.

20 Chow's Contract Offers Incentives for Ticket Sales, Bowl Games," Honolulu Star-Adviser, January 3, 2012, accessed July 17, 2012, http://www .staradvertiser.com/news/breaking /136635633.html?id=136635633.

21 D. Dahl, "Breaking 3 Workplace Taboos," *Inc.*, March 1, 2011, accessed April 5, 2011, http://www.inc .com/magazine/20110301/breaking -3-workplace-taboos.html; D. Dahl, "A Radical Take on the Virtual Company," *Inc.*, March 1, 2011, accessed April 5, 2011, http://www.inc.com /magazine/20110301/philip-rosedale -on-freelancing-business-processes .html?nav=related.

22 R. Branson, "Motivated Employees Are Your Greatest Asset," *The West Australian*, May 26, 2011, 38.

23 V. Elmer, "How Storytelling Spurs Success," *Fortune*, December 3, 2010, accessed April 5, 2011, http:// management.fortune.cnn.com/2010 /12/03/how-storytelling-spurs-success/.

24 J. R. Barker, "Tightening the Iron Cage: Concertive Control in Self-Managing Teams," *Administrative Science Quarterly* 38 (1993): 408–437.

25 N. Byrnes, "The Art of Motivation," *BusinessWeek*, May 1, 2006, 56–62.

26 Barker, "Tightening the Iron Cage."

27 C. Manz and H. Sims, "Leading Workers to Lead Themselves: The External Leadership of Self-Managed Work Teams," *Administrative Science Quarterly* 32 (1987): 106–128.

28 J. Slocum and H. A. Sims, "Typology for Integrating Technology, Organization and Job Design," *Human Relations* 33 (1980): 193–212.

29 C. C. Manz and H. P. Sims, Jr., "Self-Management as a Substitute for Leadership: A Social Learning Perspective," *Academy of Management Review* 5 (1980): 361–367.

30 C. Manz and C. Neck, *Mastering Self-Leadership*, 3rd ed. (Upper Saddle River, NJ: Pearson, Prentice Hall, 2004).

31 R. S. Kaplan and D. P. Norton, "Using the Balanced Scorecard as a Strategic Management System," *Harvard Business Review* (January–February 1996): 75–85; R. S. Kaplan and D. P. Norton, "The Balanced Scorecard: Measures That Drive Performance," *Harvard Business Review* (January–February 1992): 71–79.

32 J. Meliones, "Saving Money, Saving Lives," *Harvard Business Review* (November–December 2000): 57–65.

33 S. L. Fawcett, "Fear of Accounts: Improving Managers' Competence and Confidence through Simulation Exercises," *Journal of European Industrial Training* (February 1996): 17.

34 J. Cole, "New Boeing CFO's Assignment: Signal a Turnaround Quickly," *Wall Street Journal*, January 26, 1999, B1.

35 M. H. Stocks and A. Harrell, "The Impact of an Increase in Accounting Information Level on the Judgment Quality of Individuals and Groups," *Accounting, Organizations & Society* (October–November 1995): 685–700.

36 B. Morris, "Roberto Goizueta and Jack Welch: The Wealth Builders," *Fortune*, December 11, 1995, 80–94.

37 G. Colvin, "America's Best & Worst Wealth Creators: The Real Champions Aren't Always Who You Think. Here's an Eye-Opening Look at Which Companies Produce and Destroy the Most Money for Investors—Plus a New Tool for Spotting Future Winners," *Fortune*, December 18, 2000, 207.

38 "About Herman Miller: Operational Excellence," *Herman Miller*, accessed June 20, 2011, http://www .hermanmiller.com/About-Us/About -Herman-Miller/Operational -Excellence.

39 M. Schurman, "A Herman Miller Primer," *Herman Miller*, accessed June 20, 2011, http://www .hermanmiller.com/MarketFacingTech /hmc/about_us/News_Events_Media /Corporate_Backgrounder.pdf.

40 "EVA Momentum Ranking for S&P 500," *EVA Dimensions*, December 15, 2010, accessed June 20, 2011, http:// evadimensions.com/wp-content /rankings/ForbesEVAMomentum Rank12142010_website.pdf; S. Cendrowski, "Buying Apple Stock? Think Twice," *CNNMoney*, September 28, 2010, accessed June 20, 2011, http:// money.cnn.com/2010/09/09/pf /apple_stock.fortune/index.htm.

41 "Welcome Complaints," Office of Consumer and Business Affairs, Government of South Australia, accessed June 20, 2005, http://www .ocba.sa.gov.au/businessadvice /complaints/03_welcome.html.

42 C. B. Furlong, "12 Rules for Customer Retention," *Bank Marketing* 5 (January 1993): 14.

43 Customer retention graphs, *Vox, Inc.*, accessed August 1, 2009, http://www .voxinc.com/customer-experience -graphs/impact-customer-retention .htm.

44 M. Raphel, "Vanished Customers Are Valuable Customers," *Art Business News*, June 2002, 46.

45 C. A. Reeves and D. A. Bednar, "Defining Quality: Alternatives and Implications," *Academy of Management Review* 19 (1994): 419–445.

46 B. Mutzabaugh, "Virgin America Named USA's Top Airline; Singapore Tops Global Ratings," *USA Today*, October 15, 2010, accessed April 4, 2011, http://travel.usatoday.com /flights/post/2010/10/virgin-america -singapore-top-airline-/127567/1.

47 S. Holmes, "Creature Comforts at 30,000 Feet," *BusinessWeek*, December 18, 2006, 138.

48 C. Krome, "Kia Optima Earns 'Best Value' Award, Debuts SX Limited," *Autobytel*, February 13, 2012, accessed March 29, 2012, http://www .autobytel.com/kia/optima/2012/news /kia-optima-earns-best-value-award -debuts-sx-limited-109911/.

49 D. R. May and B. L. Flannery, "Cutting Waste with Employee Involvement Teams," *Business Horizons*, September–October 1995, 28–38.

50 J. W. Miller, "Maersk Orders 10 Huge Ships from Daewoo," *Wall Street Jour-*

nal, February 22, 2011, accessed April 5, 2011, http://online.wsj.com/article /SB10001424052748704476604576 157871902178028.html.

51 S. Mika, "Telematics Sensor-Equipped Trucks Help UPS Control Costs," *Automotive Fleet*, July 2010, accessed April 5, 2011, http://www.automotive -fleet.com/Channel/GPS-Telematics /Article/Story/2010/07/GREEN -FLEET-Telematics-Sensor-Equipped -Trucks-Help-UPS-Control-Costs .aspx.

52 S. Ashe, "Ford Practices Reduce, Reuse, Recycle by Turning Carpet into Car Parts," *CNET*, April 8, 2011, accessed March 29, 2012, http://reviews .cnet.com/8301-13746_7-20052213 -48.html?tag=mncol;txt; S. Ashe, "Ford Uses Recycled Tires, Soy for Seals and Gaskets in Several 2011MY Vehicles," *CNET*, July 12, 2011, accessed March 29, 2012, http://reviews .cnet.com/8301-13746_7-20078866 -48/ford-uses-recycled-tires-soy-for -seals-and-gaskets-in-several-2011my -vehicles/.

53 "Herman Miller Earns Design for Recycling Award," *GreenerDesign*, May 12, 2009, accessed July 23, 2010, http://www.greenbiz.com/news/2009 /05/12/herman-miller-earns-design -recycling-award.

54 M. Conlin and P. Raeburn, "Industrial Evolution: Bill McDonough Has the Wild Idea He Can Eliminate Waste. Surprise! Business Is Listening," *BusinessWeek*, April 8, 2002, 70.

55 B. Byrne, "EU Says Makers Must Destroy Their Own Brand End-of-Life Cars," *Irish Times*, April 23, 2003, 52.

56 S. B. McDonald, "Oregon Farmer Turns Cow Pies into Kilowatts," *KATU*, April 29, 2011, accessed March 29, 2012, http://www.katu .com/news/business/120968354.html.

57 "The End of the Road: Schools and Computer Recycling," *Intel*, accessed September 5, 2008, http://www.intel .com/education/recycling_computers /recycling.htm.

58 M. Meece, "Giving Those Old Gadgets a Proper Green Burial," *New York Times*, January 6, 2011, accessed March 5, 2011, http://www.nytimes .com/2011/01/06/technology /personaltech/06basics.html?ref =recyclingofwastematerials.

Chapter 17

1 R. Lenzner, "The Reluctant Entrepreneur," *Forbes*, September 11, 1995, 162–166.

2 A. Vance, "The Data Knows," *Bloomberg Businessweek*, September 12–18, 2011, 71–74.

3 R. McGill Murphy, "Rising Stars," *Fortune*, September 6, 2010, 110–116.

4 S. Rothwell, "British Airways Crews Read Up on VIPs on iPads," *Bloomberg Businessweek*, February 15, 2012, accessed April 2, 2012, http:// www.bloomberg.com/news/2012-02 -16/british-airways-crews-tap-into -ipads-for-lowdown-on-vip-flyers .html.

5 J. Hagerty, "'Big Brother' Keeps as Eye on Fleet of Heavy Equipment," *Wall Street Journal*, June 1, 2011, B1.

6 K. Hall, "How Komatsu Innovations Keep Its Machinery Selling," *Bloomberg Businessweek*, October 1, 2009, accessed July 10, 2010, http://www .businessweek.com/globalbiz/content /sep2009/gb20090930_232338.htm ?campaign_id=alerts.

7 J. Ross and P. Weill, "Four Questions Every CEO Should Ask about IT," *Wall Street Journal*, April 25, 2011, R3.

8 A. Koskey, "UC San Francisco Moving to Electronic Medical Records," *SF Examiner*, June 9, 2011, accessed April 2, 2012, http://www.sfexaminer .com/local/2011/06/uc-san-francisco -moving-electronic-medical-records.

9 A. Palanjian, "Career Journal: Disasters Are Her Specialty," *Wall Street Journal*, April 7, 2009, B12.

10 S. Bekker, "Earthquake Aftermath: How Microsoft, Partners Are Rebuilding in Japan," *Redmond Channel Partner*, May 24, 2011, accessed April 2, 2012, http://rcpmag.com/blogs /scott-bekker/2011/05/how-microsoft -partners-are-rebuilding-in-japan.aspx; Microsoft Citizenship Team, "How Technology Is Helping Distribute Food in Japan," *Microsoft Corporate Citizenship Blog*, March 18, 2011, accessed April 2, 2012, http://blogs .technet.com/b/microsoftupblog /archive/2011/03/18/how-technology -is-helping-distribute-food-in-japan .aspx.

11 "Superstructures," *The Economist*, December 11, 2010, 17–19.

12 C. Kang, "Experts: Google Privacy Shift Will Have Greater Impact on Android Users," *Washington Post*, January 25, 2012, accessed April 2, 2012, http://www.washingtonpost .com/business/technology/google-sees -profit-in-tracking-users/2012/01/25 /gIQAfDJVRQ_story.html; "Google Invests $300 Million in Hong Kong Datacenter," *PCWorld*, December 11, 2011, accessed April 2, 2012, http:// www.pcworld.com/article/245982 /google_invests_300_million_in_hong _kong_datacenter.html; S. Grundberg and N. Rolander, "For Data Center, Google Goes for the Cold," *Wall Street Journal*, September 12, 2011, accessed April 2, 2012, http://online .wsj.com/article/SB1000142405311 19048361045765605510055570810 .html; S. Mahtani, "Google to Invest $120 Million in Singapore Data Center," *Wall Street Journal*, December 15, 2011, accessed April 2, 2012, http:// online.wsj.com/article/SB100014240 52970204026804577099453458240 254.html.

13 "Carbonite Expands Boston Data Center," *PressReleasePoint*, November 2, 2009, accessed September 16, 2010, http://www.pressreleasepoint.com /carbonite-expands-boston-data -center-0.

14 M. Santosus, "Procter & Gamble's Enterprise Content Management (ECM) System," *CIO*, May 15, 2003, accessed September 12, 2008, http:// www.cio.com/article/31920/Procter _Gamble_s_Enterprise_Content _Management_ECM_System; U. Kampffmeyer, "Trends in Records, Document and Enterprise Content Management," *Whitepaper*, S.E.R. conference, Visegrád, September 28, 2004.

15 N. Clark, "Crash Spurs Interest in Real-Time Flight Data," *New York Times*, July 21, 2010, accessed July 29, 2010, http://www.nytimes.com /2010/07/22/business/global /22blackbox.html?_r=1&hp.

16 S. Lubar, *Infoculture: The Smithsonian Book of Information Age Inventions* (Boston: Houghton Mifflin, 1993).

17 Ibid.

18 A. Pawlowski, "Paperless Boarding Takes Off at United," *CNN.com*, March 15, 2010, accessed March 10, 2011, http://articles.cnn.com/2010 -03-15/travel/mobile.boarding .passes_1_boarding-airport-gates -passes?_s=PM:TRAVEL.

19 L. Loyd, "US Airways Introduces Paperless Boarding Passes in Philadelphia," *Philly.com*, March 9, 2011, accessed June 25, 2011, http://www .philly.com/philly/business/20110309 _US_Airways_introduces_paperless _boarding_passes_in_Philadelphia .html?c=r.

20 B. Worthen, "Bar Codes on Steroids," *CIO*, December 15, 2002, 53.

21 C. Swedberg, "RFID to Revolutionize Coca-Cola's Dispensers," *RFID Journal,* June 10, 2009, accessed June 25, 2011, http://www.rfidjournal.com /article/view/4967.

22 P. Ziobro, "Burger King Putting Coke Freestyle Machine at All Company Stores," *Wall Street Journal,* December 7, 2011, http://online.wsj.com/article /SB100014240529702047704045770 83002945187794.html.

23 N. Rubenking, "Hidden Messages," *PC Magazine,* May 22, 2001, 86.

24 G. Saitz, "Naked Truth—Data Miners, Who Taught Retailers to Stock Beer Near Diapers, Find Hidden Sales Trends, a Science That's Becoming Big Business," *Newark (NJ) Star-Ledger,* August 1, 2002, 41.

25 A. Carter and D. Beucke, "A Good Neighbor Gets Better," *Business Week,* June 20, 2005, 16.

26 Rubenking, "Hidden Messages."

27 C. Duhigg, "How Companies Learn Your Secrets," *New York Times,* February 16, 2012, accessed April 3, 2012, http://www.nytimes .com/2012/02/19/magazine/shopping -habits.html?pagewanted=all.

28 Joshua Brustein "Star Pitchers in a Duel? Tickets Will Cost More" *New York Times,* June 27, 2010, accessed July 10, 2010, http://www.nytimes .com/2010/06/28/technology/28tickets .html.

29 "The Price Is Right," *The Economist,* January 9, 2012, accessed April 2, 2012, http://www.economist.com /blogs/gametheory/2012/01/sports -ticketing.

30 C. Duhigg, "What Does Your Credit-Card Company Know About You?" *New York Times Magazine,* May 12, 2009, accessed June 16, 2010, http:// www.nytimes.com/2009/05/17 /magazine/17credit-t.html ?pagewanted=1.

31 "Privacy Policy," accessed June 26, 2011, http://www.drugstore.com.

32 B. Gottesman and K. Karagiannis, "A False Sense of Security," *PC Magazine,* February 22, 2005, 72.

33 F. J. Derfler, Jr., "Secure Your Network," *PC Magazine,* June 27, 2000, 183–200.

34 "Authentication," *Webopedia,* accessed September 12, 2008, http:// www.webopedia.com/TERM/a /authentication.html.

35 "Authorization," *Webopedia,* accessed September 12, 2008, http://www .webopedia.com/TERM/a /authorization.html.

36 L. Seltzer, "Password Crackers," *PC Magazine,* February 12, 2002, 68.

37 "Two-Factor Authentication," *Information Security Glossary,* accessed June 28, 2009, http://www.rsa.com.

38 D. Danchev, "Yahoo! Mail Introduces Two Factor Authentication," *ZDNet,* December 19, 2011, accessed April 3, 2012, http://www.zdnet.com/blog /security/yahoo-mail-introduces-two -factor-authentication/9846.

39 M. McQueen, "Laptop Lockdown," *Wall Street Journal,* June 28, 2006, D1.

40 C. Metz, "Total Security," *PC Magazine,* October 1, 2003, 83.

41 J. DeAvila, "Wi-Fi Users, Beware: Hot Spots Are Weak Spots," *Wall Street Journal,* January 16, 2008, D1.

42 J. van den Hoven, "Executive Support Systems & Decision Making," *Journal of Systems Management* 47, no. 8 (March–April 1996): 48.

43 D. Hannon, "Colgate-Palmolive Empowers Senior Leaders with Executive Dashboards," *InsiderProfiles,* April 1, 2011, accessed June 26, 2011, http:// insiderprofiles.wispubs.com/article .aspx?iArticleId=5720.

44 "Intranet," *Webopedia,* accessed August 26, 2001, http://www.webopedia .com/TERM/i/intranet.html.

45 "Duke Energy Gives Its Employees a Portal on Company News," *Charlotte Business Journal,* January 21, 2011, accessed March 11, 2011, http:// www.bizjournals.com/charlotte/print -edition/2011/01/21/Duke-gives-its -employees-a-news-Portal.html.

46 "Web Services," *Webopedia,* accessed April 16, 2009, http://www.webopedia .com/TERM/W/Web_Services.html.

47 S. Overby, "This Could Be the Start of Something Small," *CIO,* February 15, 2003, 54.

48 "Extranet," *Webopedia,* accessed September 12, 2008, http://www .webopedia.com/TERM/E/extranet .html.

49 "Mitsubishi Opens Sales/Training Center; Establishes Online Creative Centers," *ContractingBusiness.com,* March 27, 2012, accessed April 3, 2012, http://contractingbusiness.com /news/Mitsubishi-training-creative -centers-0328/.

50 V. Vaughan, "Smart Little Retail Shops," *Houston Chronicle,* August 17, 2010, accessed March 11, 2011, http://www.chron.com/disp/story.mpl /business/7157804.html.

51 S. Hamm, D. Welch, W. Zellner, F. Keenan, and F. Engardio, "Down But Hardly Out: Downturn Be Damned, Companies Are Still Anxious to Expand Online," *Business Week,* March 26, 2001, 126.

52 K. C. Laudon and J. P. Laudon, *Management Information Systems: Organization and Technology* (Upper Saddle River, NJ: Prentice Hall, 1996).

53 J. Borzo, "Software for Symptoms," *Wall Street Journal,* May 23, 2005, R10.

54 Ibid.

55 R. Hernandez, "American Express Authorizer's Assistant," *Business Rules Journal,* August 2001, accessed June 26, 2011, http://bizrules.info/page /art_amexaa.htm.

Chapter 18

1 N. Shirouzu, "In China, Making Cars on a Budget," *Wall Street Journal,* December 20, 2012, accessed April 9, 2012, http://online.wsj.com/article /SB1000142405274870461090457603 1293046766076.html?mod=WSJ _business_whatsNews; "Table— China 2011 Car Sales up 5.2 Percent," *Reuters,* January 16, 2012, accessed April 9, 2012, http://www.reuters .com/article/2012/01/17/autos-china -idUSL3E8CH0V920120117.

2 B. Baker, "America's Best Drive-Thru 2008 Is... Chick-fil-A! (Again)," *QRS Magazine,* accessed August 2, 2009, http://www.qsrmagazine.com/reports.

3 M. Richtel, "The Long-Distance Journey of a Fast-Food Order," *New York Times,* April 11, 2006, accessed September 12, 2008, http:// www.nytimes.com/2006/04/11 /technology/11fast.html?pagewanted =all&_r=0&gwh=540D1ECDA0B 5FAE2B7ADF4FCEFE8A7E6.

4 "Employment Cost Index News Release Text," *Bureau of Labor Statistics,* April 29, 2011, accessed June 27, 2011, http://www.bls.gov/news .release/eci.nr0.htm; "Productivity and Costs, First Quarter 2011, Revised," *Bureau of Labor Statistics,* June 2, 2011, accessed June 27, 2011, http:// www.bls.gov/news.release/prod2.nr0 .htm.

5 "Historical Income Tables—Families: Table F-23—Families by Total Money Income, Race, and Hispanic Origin of Householder: 1967 to 2010," *U.S. Census Bureau,* accessed April 4, 2012, http://www.census.gov/hhes

/www/income/data/historical/families /2010/F23_2010.xls.

6 "Historical Income Tables—Families: Table F-23—Families by Total Money Income, Race, and Hispanic Origin of Householder: 1967 to 2009," *U.S. Census Bureau*, accessed June 27, 2011, http://www.census.gov/hhes /www/income/data/historical/families /f23.xls.

7 The Conference Board Total Economy Data Base, Summary Statistics 1995–2010, "Table 3: Growth of Labor Productivity, Real GDP and Total Hours Worked by Region for Advanced Countries, 1995–2010," *The Conference Board*, September 2010, accessed June 27, 2011, http:// www.conference-board.org/retrievefile .cfm?filename=SummaryTables _Sep20101.pdf&type=subsite.

8 "Employment Projections, Table 1: Civilian Labor Force by Sex, Age, Race, and Hispanic Origin, 1988, 1998, 2008, and Projected 2018," in Employment Outlook: 2008–18; "Labor Force Projections to 2018: Older Workers Staying More Active," *Monthly Labor Review*, November 2008, 30–51, accessed June 27, 2011, http://www.bls.gov/opub/mlr/2009/11 /art3full.pdf.

9 "Key Development Data & Statistics: United States Data Profile," *World Bank*, accessed September 9, 2009, http://web.worldbank.org.

10 "Philanthropy in the American Economy," *Council of Economic Advisers*, February 19, 2002, accessed April 13, 2009, http://clinton4.nara.gov/media /pdf/philanthropy.pdf.

11 "Unemployment," *U.S. News & World Report*, accessed May 7, 2012, http://www.usnews.com/topics /subjects/unemployment; "U.S. Charitable Giving Shows Modest Uptick in 2010 Following Two Years of Declines," *The Center on Philanthropy at Indiana University*, June 20, 2011, http://www.philanthropy.iupui.edu /news/2011/06/pr-GUSA.aspx.

12 "Are Cars Becoming Less Affordable for the Average American Family?" *Cars.com*, accessed March 23, 2010, http://blogs.cars.com/kickingtires/2010 /08/are-cars-becoming-less-affordable -for-the-average-american-family.html; "Auto Affordability Flat in First Quarter of 2011, Comerica Bank Reports," *Comerica*, May 12, 2011, accessed June 27, 2011, http://www.comerica .com/Comerica_Content/Corporate _Communications/Docs/Auto%20

Affordability%20Index/Auto _Affordability_Index_Q12011.pdf.

13 R. Harbour and M. Hill, "Productivity Gap Narrows across North America and Europe," *The Harbour Report*, accessed August 2, 2009, http://www .theharbourreport.com/index2.jsp (also see http://www.oliverwyman .com/automotive).

14 "Profiles International's America's Most Productive Companies," *Drug Week*, May 15, 2009, 265; "America's Most Productive Companies," accessed August 2, 2009, http://www .americasmostproductive.com.

15 "Study: Automakers Initial Quality Improves Considerably," *Quality Digest*, accessed August 2, 2009, http:// www.qualitydigest.com; "2008 Initial Quality Study Results," accessed August 2, 2009, http://www.jdpower .com/autos/articles/2008-Initial -Quality-Study-Results.

16 "2011 Initial Quality Study Results (IQS)," *JD Power and Associates*, June 23, 2011; "2008 Initial Quality Study Results," accessed June 27, 2011, http://www.jdpower.com/autos /articles/2008-Initial-Quality-Study -Results.

17 "Basic Quality Concepts," *American Society for Quality*, accessed August 2, 2009, http://www.asq.org/learn-about -quality/basic-concepts.html.

18 R. E. Markland, S. K. Vickery, and R. A. Davis, "Managing Quality" (Chapter 7), in *Operations Management: Concepts in Manufacturing and Services* (Cincinnati, OH: South-Western College Publishing, 1998).

19 "New Industrial LCD Panels with 100,000 Hour MTBF LED Backlight Systems from Toshiba America Electronic Components," *Your Industry News*, August 26, 2009, accessed September 12, 2009, http://www .yourindustrynews.com.

20 L. L. Berry and A. Parasuraman, *Marketing Services* (New York: Free Press, 1991).

21 Y. Kane and I. Sherr, "Penney Picks Boss from Apple—Secrets from Genius Bar: Full Loyalty, No Negativity," *Wall Street Journal*, June 25, 2011, A1.

22 "FAQs—General Information on ISO," *International Organization for Standardization*, accessed September 12, 2009, http://www.iso.org/iso /support/faqs/faqs_general _information_on_iso.htm.

23 "ISO 9000 Essentials," and "ISO 14000 Essentials," *International Organization for Standardization*, accessed

September 12, 2009, http://www.iso .org/iso/iso_catalogue/management _standards/iso_9000_iso_14000.htm.

24 J. Briscoe, S. Fawcett, and R. Todd, "The Implementation and Impact of ISO 9000 among Small Manufacturing Enterprises," *Journal of Small Business Management* 43 (July 1, 2005): 309.

25 R. Henkoff, "The Hot New Seal of Quality (ISO 9000 Standard of Quality Management)," *Fortune*, June 28, 1993, 116.

26 "Frequently Asked Questions about the Malcolm Baldrige National Quality Award," *National Institute of Standards and Technology*, accessed September 12, 2009, http://www.nist .gov/public_affairs/factsheet/baldfaqs .htm.

27 "Baldrige Award Application Forms," *National Institute of Standards and Technology*, accessed September 12, 2009, http://www.quality.nist.gov /PDF_files/2009_Award_Application _Forms.pdf.

28 "Frequently Asked Questions about the Malcolm Baldrige National Quality Award."

29 Ibid.

30 "Criteria for Performance Excellence," *Baldrige National Quality Program 2008*, accessed September 15, 2008, http://www.quality.nist.gov/PDF _files/2008_Business_Criteria.pdf.

31 Ibid.

32 Ibid.

33 "Baldrige Index Beaten by S&P 500 for Second Year," *NIST Tech Beat*, accessed September 12, 2009, http:// www.quality.nist.gov/Stock_Studies .htm.

34 J. W. Dean, Jr., and J. Evans, *Total Quality: Management, Organization, and Strategy* (St. Paul, MN: West, 1994).

35 J. W. Dean, Jr., and D. E. Bowen, "Management Theory and Total Quality: Improving Research and Practice through Theory Development," *Academy of Management Review* 19 (1994): 392–418.

36 R. Allen and R. Kilmann, "Aligning Reward Practices in Support of Total Quality Management," *Business Horizons*, May 1, 2001, 77; F. Reichheld and P. Rogers, "Motivating Through Metrics," *Harvard Business Review* (September 2005): 20–24.

37 A. Taylor, "Driving Customer Satisfaction," *Harvard Business Review* (July 2002): 24.

38 "J. D. Power and Associates Reports: Customer Satisfaction with Rental Cars Continues to Decline," *J. D. Power and Associates*, November 11, 2008, accessed September 12, 2009, http://www.jdpower.com.

39 R. Carter, "Best Practices: Freudenberg-NOK/Cleveland, GA: Continuous Kaizens," *Industrial Maintenance & Plant Operations*, June 1, 2004, 10.

40 Ibid.

41 R. Carr, "Teamwork at Its Best," *Fast Company*, May 16, 2010, accessed March 23, 2011, http://www.fastcompany.com/1648449/teamwork-at-its-best.

42 "Table 647, Gross Domestic Product in Current and Real (2000) Dollars by Type of Product and Sector; 1990 to 2007," *The 2009 Statistical Abstract*, U.S. Census Bureau, accessed September 12, 2009, http://www.census.gov.

43 R. Hallowell, L. A. Schlesinger, and J. Zornitsky, "Internal Service Quality, Customer and Job Satisfaction: Linkages and Implications for Management," *Human Resource Planning* 19 (1996): 20–31; J. L. Heskett, T. O. Jones, G. W. Loveman, W. E. Sasser, Jr., and L. A. Schlesinger, "Putting the Service-Profit Chain to Work," *Harvard Business Review* (March–April 1994): 164–174.

44 L. Drell, "6 Companies with Awesome Employee Perks," *Mashable Business*, August 7, 2011, accessed April 9, 2012, http://mashable.com/2011/08/07/startup-employee-perks/.

45 J. Paravantis, N. Bouranta, and L. Chitiris, "The Relationship between Internal and External Service Quality," *International Journal of Contemporary Hospital Management* 21 (2009): 275–293.

46 G. Brewer, "The Ultimate Guide to Winning Customers: The Customer Stops Here," *Sales & Marketing Management* 150 (March 1998): 30; F. F. Reichheld, *The Loyalty Effect: The Hidden Force behind Growth, Profits, and Lasting Value* (Cambridge, MA: Harvard Business School Press, 2001).

47 J. Heskett, T. Jones, G. Loveman, E. Sasser, and L. Schlesinger, "Putting the Service-Profit Chain to Work," *Harvard Business Review* 86 (July–August 2008): 118–129.

48 L. L. Berry and A. Parasuraman, "Listening to the Customer—The Concept of a Service-Quality Information System," *Sloan Management Review* 38, no. 3 (Spring 1997): 65; C. W. L. Hart, J. L. Heskett, and W. E. Sasser, Jr., "The Profitable Art of Service Recovery," *Harvard Business Review* (July–August 1990): 148–156.

49 "Great Customer Service from the Mission Bicycle Company," *37signals.com*, August 16, 2011, accessed April 9, 2012, http://37signals.com/svn/posts/2989-great-customer-service-from-the-mission-bicycle.com.

50 D. E. Bowen and E. E. Lawler III, "The Empowerment of Service Workers: What, Why, How, and When," *Sloan Management Review* 33 (Spring 1992): 31–39; D. E. Bowen and E. E. Lawler III, "Empowering Service Employees," *Sloan Management Review* 36 (Summer 1995): 73–84.

51 Bowen and Lawler, "The Empowerment of Service Workers: What, Why, How, and When."

52 J. Shelly, "Empowering Employees," *Human Resource Executive*, October 2, 2011, accessed April 9, 2012, http://www.hreonline.com/HRE/story.jsp?storyId=533341639.

53 "The Top 100 Beverage Companies: The List," *Beverage Industry*, July 2001, 30.

54 "Job Shop Hits Bull's Eye with Multitasking," *Manufacturing Engineering* (November 2008): 43–105.

55 N. E. Boudette and J. Bennett, "Pigment Shortage Hits Auto Makers," *Wall Street Journal*, May 25, 2011, accessed April 9, 2012, http://online.wsj.com/article/SB10001424052748703696704576222990521120106.html.

56 M. Bustillo, "For Lowe's, Landscape Begins to Shift," *Wall Street Journal*, February 24, 2011, B3.

57 D. Drickhamer, "Reality Check," *Industry Week*, November 2001, 29.

58 D. Drickhamer, "Zeroing In on World-Class," *Industry Week*, November 2001, 36.

59 J. Zeiler, "The Need for Speed," *Operations & Fulfillment*, April 1, 2004, 38.

60 "Efficient Foodservice Response (EFR)," accessed August 3, 2009, http://www.ifdaonline.org/webarticles.

61 J. R. Henry, "Minimized Setup Will Make Your Packaging Line S.M.I.L.E.," *Packaging Technology & Engineering*, February 1, 1998, 24.

62 J. Donoghue, "The Future Is Now," *Air Transport World*, April 1, 2001, 78; D. Evans, "Aftermarket Outlook," *Aviation Maintenance Magazine*, May 1, 2006, accessed September 13, 2004, http://www.aviationtoday.com.

63 K. Clark, "An Eagle Eye for Inventory," *Chain Store Age*, May 2005, Supplement, 8A.

64 "The Way I Work: Marc Lore of Diapers.com." *Inc.*, September 1, 2009, accessed March 15, 2010, http://www.inc.com/magazine/20090901/the-way-i-work-marc-lore-of-diaperscom.html.

65 E. Powell, Jr., and F. Sahin, "Economic Production Lot Sizing with Periodic Costs and Overtime," *Decision Sciences* 32 (2001): 423–452.

66 J. Bonasia, "Just-in-Time Cuts Costs, but Has Risks," *Investor's Business Daily*, October 3, 2002, 4.

67 N. Shirouzu, "Why Toyota Wins Such High Marks on Quality Surveys," *Wall Street Journal*, March 15, 2001, A1.

68 Ibid.

69 G. Gruman, "Supply on Demand; Manufacturers Need to Know What's Selling before They Can Produce and Deliver Their Wares in the Right Quantities," *Info World*, April 18, 2005, accessed April 15, 2009, http://www.infoworld.com.

Index

Hong Kong (China), 158, 159, 171, 172
Hooters, 219, 220
Horizontal communication, 322
Hormel Foods, 118
Hosmer, LaRue, 72
Hostile work environment, 223
HotJobs.com, 227
Hotlines, 332
   company, 332
Hourly wages, 53
Housekeeping, good, 352
How I Met My Countess, 123
HP, *see* Hewlett Packard
HR Magazine, 329
Hsieh, Tony, 60
HTC, 44, 133
HTML5, 13
Hugo Boss, 79
Human Equation: Building Profits by Putting People First, The, 18
Human Problems of an Industrial Civilization, The, 36
Human relations management, 34–37
Human resource information system (HRIS), 227
Human resource management (HRM), 219
Human resource management process, 219
Human skills, 14
Humana, 282, 283
Humana Vitality, 282, 283
Humber Bridge in East Yorkshire, England, 362
Humor, 209
Hungary, 157, 158
Huntsman Chemical, 238
Hurd, Mark, 338
Hutchins, David, 344
Hybrid, 90
Hybrid vehicle, 83
Hyland-Savage, Gail, 223
Hymowitz, Carol, 321
Hyundai, 51, 87, 147, 148, 212

I

IAT, 266
IBM, 52, 58, 70, 72, 193, 225, 250, 291, 292
   Credit, 192, 193
   Global Business Services, 225
   Global Insurance and Financial Services, 225
   Global Sales and Distribution, 226
Iceland, 157
iCloud, 109
Ideas, stealing, 139
Identity decision criteria, 97
If-then rule, 376

IKEA Japan, 81
Immediate feedback, 329
Immelt, Jeffrey, 83
Immunity, bureaucratic, 212
Impact Indicator, 340
Impediments to creativity, removing, 137
Imperfectly imitable resource, 108
Implicit Association Teat (IAT), 265
Import standard, government, 155
Impoverished management, 296
Improvement, continuous, 386
Improvements, 140
Improving transmission, 330
Inactive stage of organizational decline, 142
In-basket exercises, 232
In-basket item for store managers, 232
Incentives, financial, 36
Income, 159, 380
Income statements, 347
Incorporated organizations, 67
Incremental change, 136
   managing innovation during, 140–141
Independent demand system, 397
India, 155, 161, 162, 163, 164, 166, 167, 168, 169, 172, 173, 183, 255
Indifference, zone of, 37
Individual rights, 72
   principle of, 73
Individualism, 171
Individualism-collectivism, 213, 214
Individualists, 213
Individualized consideration, 311
Indonesia Lao PDR, 158, 159, 171, 172
Industrial revolution, 25
Industry forces, 121–122
   Porter's five, 121, 125
Industry-level strategy, 120–124
Industry regulation, 52
   of specific external environment, 52–53
Inequity, perceived, 275–277
Inertia, competitive, 110
Informal communication channel (grapevine), 322–323
Information, 357, 360, 361, 362, 363, 372
   accurate, 360
   and knowledge, assessing and sharing, 372–376
   capturing, 364–365
   processing and protecting, 363–371

characteristics and costs of useful, 360–363
   complete, 360–361
   management, 39
   managing, 357–376
   processing, 365–367
   protecting, 368–371
   relevant, 361
   sharing, 19
   sharing and external access, 373–376
   sharing and internal access, 372–373
   strategic importance of, 357–360
   timely, 361–362
Information technologies, 39, 359
   to sustain a competitive advantage, 359
Informational roles, 10–12
   of managers, 11–12
Infringements, copyright, 67
ING Direct, 119
Initial assembly, 393
Initiating structure, 295
Initiation of effort, 269
Initiative, 33
Innovation, 136, 192
   and change, 131–150
   and learning perspective, 345, 352–354
   compression approach to, 140
   experiential approach to, 138
   managing, 136–141
   managing during discontinuous change, 138–140
   managing during incremental change, 140–141
   managing sources of, 136–138
   organizational, 131
   S-curve pattern of, 132
   technological, 131, 135
   why it matters, 131–136
Innovation streams, 133–136
Innovative culture, 137
Inputs, 274, 379, 381
Inspirational motivation, 311
Installation & Service Technologies, 242
Instrumentality, 280
Integrated circuits, 132
Integrated model, motivating with, 289
Integrative conflict resolution, 34
Integrity, 293
   and ethics, 65
   personal-based, 74
Integrity test, overt, 74
Intel Corporation, 132, 136, 192, 266, 357
   Women's Initiative, 266

Intellectual property, protection of, 156
Intellectual stimulation, 311
Intentional discrimination, 222
Interactive Excellence, 134
Interchangeable parts, 38
InterContinental Hotels, 88
Interdependence,
   pooled, 193
   reciprocal, 193
   sequential, 193
   task, 193
Interference, creative, 138
Intermittent reinforcement schedule, 284, 285
Internal access and sharing information, 372–373
Internal attribution, 317, 318
Internal blogs, 334
Internal business perspective, 346
Internal environment, 58
Internal motivation, 189
Internal perspective, 345, 350–351
Internal recruiting, 225–226
Internal service quality, 388
Internals, 303
International assignment, preparing for, 172–175
International Data Corporation, 156
International Federation of the Phonographic Industry, 156
International Harvester, 25
International Organization, 384
International Pilots Association, 331
International Telecommunications (ITU), 135
International Telegraph Convention, 135
Internet, 39, 132, 227
   phone, 51
   service and content providers, 62
   training, 237
Internet Explorer, 371
Interorganizational process, 194–197
Interpersonal roles of managers, 10–11
Interpersonal skills, 215
Interpretation, 316
Interval reinforcement, 284
Interventions,
   change, 143
   large-system, 150
   organization development, 149
   person-focused, 150
   small-group, 150
Interview(s), 232
   effective structured, 234
   job, 233
   questions, 229
   semistructured, 233
   structured, 233

REVIEW 1

Each Review Card contains summaries for the Learning Outcomes in order by chapter section.

LEARNING OUTCOMES

1-1 (p. 3) Describe what management is.

Good management is working through others to accomplish tasks that help fulfill organizational objectives as efficiently as possible.

1-2 (p. 4) Explain the four functions of management.

Henri Fayol's classic management functions are known today as planning, organizing, leading, and controlling. Planning is determining organizational goals and a means for achieving them. Organizing is deciding where decisions will [be made,] what jobs and tasks, and who will work for whom. Leading is in[spiring and motivating] workers to work hard to achieve organizational goals. Controlli[ng is monitoring progress] toward goal achievement and taking corrective action when n[eeded.] [. . .] performing the management functions well leads to better ma[nagement.]

1-3 (p. 6) Describe different kinds of manag[ers.]

There are four different kinds of managers. Top managers are r[esponsible for creating] a context for change, developing attitudes of commitment an[d . . . creating] a positive organizational culture through words and actions, and monitoring their companies' business environments. Middle managers are responsible for planning and allocating resources, coordinating and linking groups and departments, monitoring and managing the performance of subunits and managers, and implementing the changes or strategies generated by top managers. First-line managers are responsible for managing the performance of nonmanagerial employees, teaching entry-level employees how to do the[ir jobs, and making] operating plans based on middle manag[ers' plans.] [. . . team leaders] are responsible for facilitating team per[formance . . .] team members, and managing extern[al] [relationships.]

Key Terms from the chapter's margins appear in this column (and continue on the back of the card) in the same order in which they appear in the chapter.

Graphics from the chapter are often used as memory prompts to help you recall the information in the written summary.

EXHIBIT 1.2

What the Four Kinds of Managers Do

Jobs		Responsibilities
Top Managers		
CEO	CIO	Change
COO	Vice president	Commitment
CFO	Corporate heads	Culture
		Environment
Middle Managers		
General manager		Resources
Plant manager		Objectives
Regional manager		Coordination
Divisional manager		Subunit performance
		Strategy implementation
First-Line Managers		
Office manager		Nonmanagerial worker supervision
Shift supervisor		Teaching and training
Department manager		Scheduling
		Facilitation
Team Leaders		
Team leader		Facilitation
Team contact		External relationships
Group facilitator		Internal relationships

© iStockphoto.com/Cliff Parnell / © Will Woods/Digital Vision/Getty Images / © ColorBlind Images/Blend Images/Getty Images / © Eric Audras/PhotoAlto Agency RF Collections/Getty Images

KEY TERMS

Management getting work done through others

Efficiency getting work done with a minimum of effort, expense, or waste

Effectiveness accomplishing tasks that help fulfill organizational objectives

Planning determining organizational goals and a means for achieving them

Organizing deciding where decisions will be made, who will do what jobs and tasks, and who will work for whom

Leading inspiring and motivating workers to work hard to achieve organizational goals

Controlling monitoring progress toward goal achievement and taking corrective action when needed

Top managers executives responsible for the overall direction of the organization

Middle managers responsible for setting objectives consistent with top management's goals and for planning and implementing subunit strategies for achieving these objectives

First-line managers train and supervise the performance of nonmanagerial employees who are directly responsible for producing the company's products or services

Team leaders managers responsible for facilitating team activities toward goal accomplishment

Figurehead role the interpersonal role managers play when they perform ceremonial duties

Leader role the interpersonal role managers play when they motivate and encourage workers to accomplish organizational objectives

Liaison role the interpersonal role managers play when they deal with people outside their units

Monitor role the informational role managers play when they scan their environment for information

Disseminator role the informational role managers play when they share information with others in their departments or companies

Spokesperson role the informational role managers play when they share information with people outside their departments or companies

Entrepreneur role the decisional role managers play when they adapt themselves, their subordinates, and their units to change

Disturbance handler role the decisional role managers play when they respond to severe problems that demand immediate action

1-4 (p. 10) Explain the major roles and subroles that managers perform in their jobs.

Managers perform interpersonal, informational, and decisional roles in their jobs. In fulfilling interpersonal roles, managers act as figureheads by performing ceremonial duties, as leaders by motivating and encouraging workers, and as liaisons by dealing with people outside their units. In performing informational roles, managers act as monitors by scanning their environment for information, as disseminators by sharing information with others in their companies, and as spokespeople by sharing information with people outside their departments or companies. In fulfilling decisional roles, managers act as entrepreneurs by adapting their units to change, as disturbance handlers by responding to larger problems that demand immediate action, as resource allocators by deciding resource recipients and amounts, and as negotiators by bargaining with others about schedules, projects, goals, outcomes, and resources.

1-5 (p. 13) Explain what companies look for in managers.

Companies do not want one-dimensional managers. They want managers with a balance of skills. Managers need to have the knowledge and abilities to get the job done (technical skills), must be able to work effectively in groups and be good listeners and communicators (human skills), must be able to assess the relationships between the different parts of their companies and the external environment and position their companies for success (conceptual skills), and should want to assume positions of leadership and power (motivation to manage). Technical skills are most important for team leaders and lower-level managers, human skills are equally important at all levels of management, and conceptual skills and motivation to manage increase in importance as managers rise through the managerial ranks.

EXHIBIT 1.4

Management Skills

Top Managers · First-Line Managers · Middle Managers · Team Leaders

© Cengage Learning

1-6 (p. 15) Discuss the top mistakes that managers make in their jobs.

Another way to understand what it takes to be a manager is to look at the top mistakes managers make. Five of the most important mistakes made by managers are being abrasive and intimidating; being cold, aloof, or arrogant; betraying trust; being overly ambitious; and being unable to ...

How to Use this Card:

1. Look over the card to preview the new concepts you'll be introduced to in the chapter.

2. Read the chapter to fully understand the material.

3. Go to class (and pay attention).

4. Review the card one more time to make sure you've registered the key concepts.

5. Don't forget, this card is only one of many MGMT learning tools available to help you succeed in your management course.

... sition that employees go through when they are promoted to

... ore formal authority and less people management skill. However, most managers find that ...ng" their subordinates. According to a study of managers in their first year, after six months ... the fast pace and heavy workload and by the fact that "helping" their subordinates was ...ob, most of the managers had come to think of themselves not as doers but as managers ... because they finally realized that people management was the most important part ...heir authoritarian approach for one based on communication, listening, and positive

... why companies can create competitive advantage through people.

...aged companies are competitive because their work forces are smarter, better trained, more ...ore, companies that practice good management consistently have greater sales revenues, ... companies that don't. Finally, good management matters because good management ...rovide better service to customers. Because employees tend to treat customers the same ...management can improve customer satisfaction.

Resource allocator role the decisional role managers play when they decide who gets what resources and in what amounts

Negotiator role the decisional role managers play when they negotiate schedules, projects, goals, outcomes, resources, and employee raises

Technical skills the specialized procedures, techniques, and knowledge required to get the job done

Human skills the ability to work well with others

Conceptual skills the ability to see the organization as a whole, understand how the different parts affect each other, and recog-

nize how the company fits into or is affected by its environment

Motivation to manage an assessment of how enthusiastic employees are about managing the work of others

LEARNING OUTCOMES

1-1 (p. 3) Describe what management is.

Good management is working through others to accomplish tasks that help fulfill organizational objectives as efficiently as possible.

1-2 (p. 4) Explain the four functions of management.

Henri Fayol's classic management functions are known today as planning, organizing, leading, and controlling. Planning is determining organizational goals and a means for achieving them. Organizing is deciding where decisions will be made, who will do what jobs and tasks, and who will work for whom. Leading is inspiring and motivating workers to work hard to achieve organizational goals. Controlling is monitoring progress toward goal achievement and taking corrective action when needed. Studies show that performing the management functions well leads to better managerial performance.

1-3 (p. 6) Describe different kinds of managers.

There are four different kinds of managers. Top managers are responsible for creating a context for change, developing attitudes of commitment and ownership, creating a positive organizational culture through words and actions, and monitoring their companies' business environments. Middle managers are responsible for planning and allocating resources, coordinating and linking groups and departments, monitoring and managing the performance of subunits and managers, and implementing the changes or strategies generated by top managers. First-line managers are responsible for managing the performance of nonmanagerial employees, teaching entry-level employees how to do their jobs, and making detailed schedules and operating plans based on middle management's intermediate-range plans. Team leaders are responsible for facilitating team performance, fostering good relationships among team members, and managing external relationships.

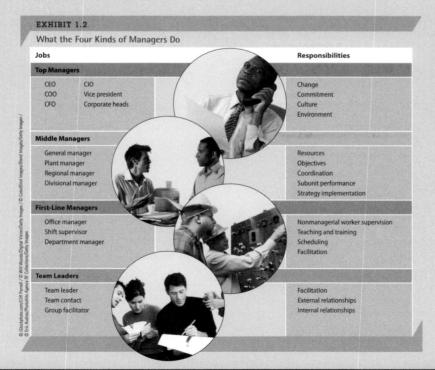

EXHIBIT 1.2

What the Four Kinds of Managers Do

Jobs		Responsibilities
Top Managers		
CEO	CIO	Change
COO	Vice president	Commitment
CFO	Corporate heads	Culture
		Environment
Middle Managers		
General manager		Resources
Plant manager		Objectives
Regional manager		Coordination
Divisional manager		Subunit performance
		Strategy implementation
First-Line Managers		
Office manager		Nonmanagerial worker supervision
Shift supervisor		Teaching and training
Department manager		Scheduling
		Facilitation
Team Leaders		
Team leader		Facilitation
Team contact		External relationships
Group facilitator		Internal relationships

© iStockphoto.com/Cliff Parnell / © Will Woods/Digital Vision/Getty Images / © ColorBlind Images/Blend Images/Getty Images / © Eric Audras/PhotoAlto Agency RF Collections/Getty Images

KEY TERMS

Management getting work done through others

Efficiency getting work done with a minimum of effort, expense, or waste

Effectiveness accomplishing tasks that help fulfill organizational objectives

Planning determining organizational goals and a means for achieving them

Organizing deciding where decisions will be made, who will do what jobs and tasks, and who will work for whom

Leading inspiring and motivating workers to work hard to achieve organizational goals

Controlling monitoring progress toward goal achievement and taking corrective action when needed

Top managers executives responsible for the overall direction of the organization

Middle managers responsible for setting objectives consistent with top management's goals and for planning and implementing subunit strategies for achieving these objectives

First-line managers train and supervise the performance of nonmanagerial employees who are directly responsible for producing the company's products or services

Team leaders managers responsible for facilitating team activities toward goal accomplishment

Figurehead role the interpersonal role managers play when they perform ceremonial duties

Leader role the interpersonal role managers play when they motivate and encourage workers to accomplish organizational objectives

Liaison role the interpersonal role managers play when they deal with people outside their units

Monitor role the informational role managers play when they scan their environment for information

Disseminator role the informational role managers play when they share information with others in their departments or companies

Spokesperson role the informational role managers play when they share information with people outside their departments or companies

Entrepreneur role the decisional role managers play when they adapt themselves, their subordinates, and their units to change

Disturbance handler role the decisional role managers play when they respond to severe problems that demand immediate action

1-4 (p. 10) Explain the major roles and subroles that managers perform in their jobs.

Managers perform interpersonal, informational, and decisional roles in their jobs. In fulfilling interpersonal roles, managers act as figureheads by performing ceremonial duties, as leaders by motivating and encouraging workers, and as liaisons by dealing with people outside their units. In performing informational roles, managers act as monitors by scanning their environment for information, as disseminators by sharing information with others in their companies, and as spokespeople by sharing information with people outside their departments or companies. In fulfilling decisional roles, managers act as entrepreneurs by adapting their units to change, as disturbance handlers by responding to larger problems that demand immediate action, as resource allocators by deciding resource recipients and amounts, and as negotiators by bargaining with others about schedules, projects, goals, outcomes, and resources.

1-5 (p. 13) Explain what companies look for in managers.

Companies do not want one-dimensional managers. They want managers with a balance of skills. Managers need to have the knowledge and abilities to get the job done (technical skills), must be able to work effectively in groups and be good listeners and communicators (human skills), must be able to assess the relationships between the different parts of their companies and the external environment and position their companies for success (conceptual skills), and should want to assume positions of leadership and power (motivation to manage). Technical skills are most important for team leaders and lower-level managers, human skills are equally important at all levels of management, and conceptual skills and motivation to manage increase in importance as managers rise through the managerial ranks.

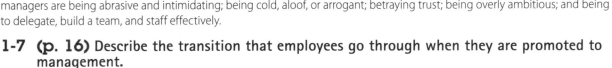

EXHIBIT 1.4

Management Skills

1-6 (p. 15) Discuss the top mistakes that managers make in their jobs.

Another way to understand what it takes to be a manager is to look at the top mistakes managers make. Five of the most important mistakes made by managers are being abrasive and intimidating; being cold, aloof, or arrogant; betraying trust; being overly ambitious; and being unable to delegate, build a team, and staff effectively.

1-7 (p. 16) Describe the transition that employees go through when they are promoted to management.

Managers often begin their jobs by using more formal authority and less people management skill. However, most managers find that being a manager has little to do with "bossing" their subordinates. According to a study of managers in their first year, after six months on the job, the managers were surprised by the fast pace and heavy workload and by the fact that "helping" their subordinates was viewed as interference. After a year on the job, most of the managers had come to think of themselves not as doers but as managers who get things done through others. And, because they finally realized that people management was the most important part of their job, most of them had abandoned their authoritarian approach for one based on communication, listening, and positive reinforcement.

1-8 (p. 18) Explain how and why companies can create competitive advantage through people.

Why does management matter? Well-managed companies are competitive because their work forces are smarter, better trained, more motivated, and more committed. Furthermore, companies that practice good management consistently have greater sales revenues, profits, and stock market performance than companies that don't. Finally, good management matters because good management leads to satisfied employees who, in turn, provide better service to customers. Because employees tend to treat customers the same way that their managers treat them, good management can improve customer satisfaction.

Resource allocator role the decisional role managers play when they decide who gets what resources and in what amounts

Negotiator role the decisional role managers play when they negotiate schedules, projects, goals, outcomes, resources, and employee raises

Technical skills the specialized procedures, techniques, and knowledge required to get the job done

Human skills the ability to work well with others

Conceptual skills the ability to see the organization as a whole, understand how the different parts affect each other, and recog-

nize how the company fits into or is affected by its environment

Motivation to manage an assessment of how enthusiastic employees are about managing the work of others

REVIEW 2

LEARNING OUTCOMES

2-1 (p. 23) Explain the origins of management.

Management as a field of study is just 125 years old, but management ideas and practices have actually been used since 5000 BCE. From ancient Sumer to 16th-century Europe, there are historical antecedents for each of the functions of management discussed in this textbook: planning, organizing, leading, and controlling. However, there was no compelling need for managers until systematic changes in the nature of work and organizations occurred during the last two centuries. As work shifted from families to factories; from skilled laborers to specialized, unskilled laborers; from small, self-organized groups to large factories employing thousands under one roof; and from unique, small batches of production to standardized mass production; managers were needed to impose order and structure, to motivate and direct large groups of workers, and to plan and make decisions that optimized overall performance by effectively coordinating the different parts of an organizational system.

2-2 (p. 25) Explain the history of scientific management.

Scientific management involves studying and testing different work methods to identify the best, most efficient way to complete a job. According to Frederick W. Taylor, the father of scientific management, managers should follow four scientific management principles. First, study each element of work to determine the one best way to do it. Second, scientifically select, train, teach, and develop workers to reach their full potential. Third, cooperate with employees to ensure that the scientific principles are implemented. Fourth, divide the work and the responsibility equally between management and workers. Above all, Taylor believed these principles could be used to align managers and employees by determining a fair day's work (what an average worker could produce at a reasonable pace) and a fair day's pay (what management should pay workers for that effort). Taylor believed that incentives were one of the best ways to align management and employees.

Frank and Lillian Gilbreth are best known for their use of motion studies to simplify work. Whereas Taylor used time study to determine a fair day's work based on how long it took a "first-class man" to complete each part of his job, Frank Gilbreth used motion-picture films and micro chronometers to conduct motion studies to improve efficiency by eliminating unnecessary or repetitive motions. Henry Gantt is best known for the Gantt chart, which graphically indicates when a series of tasks must be completed in order to complete a job or project, but he also developed ideas regarding worker training specifically, that all workers should be trained and their managers should be rewarded for training them.

2-3 (p. 30) Discuss the history of bureaucratic and administrative management.

Today, we associate bureaucracy with inefficiency and red tape. Yet German sociologist Max Weber thought that bureaucracy—that is, running organizations on the basis of knowledge, fairness, and logical rules and procedures—would accomplish organizational goals much more efficiently than monarchies and patriarchies, where decisions were based on personal or family connections, personal gain, and arbitrary decision making. Bureaucracies are characterized by seven elements: qualification-based hiring; merit-based promotion; chain of command; division of labor; impartial application of rules and procedures; recording rules, procedures, and decisions in writing; and separating managers from owners. Nonetheless, bureaucracies are often inefficient and can be highly resistant to change.

KEY TERMS

Scientific management thoroughly studying and testing different work methods to identify the best, most efficient way to complete a job

Soldiering when workers deliberately slow their pace or restrict their work output

Rate buster a group member whose work pace is significantly faster than the normal pace in his or her group

Motion study breaking each task or job into its separate motions and then eliminating those that are unnecessary or repetitive

Time study timing how long it takes good workers to complete each part of their jobs

Gantt chart a graphical chart that shows which tasks must be completed at which times in order to complete a project or task

Bureaucracy the exercise of control on the basis of knowledge, expertise, or experience

Domination an approach to dealing with conflict in which one party satisfies its desires and objectives at the expense of the other party's desires and objectives

Compromise an approach to dealing with conflict in which both parties give up some of what they want in order to reach agreement on a plan to reduce or settle the conflict

Integrative conflict resolution an approach to dealing with conflict in which both parties indicate their preferences and then work together to find an alternative that meets the needs of both

Organization a system of consciously coordinated activities or forces created by two or more people

System a set of interrelated elements or parts that function as a whole

Subsystems smaller systems that operate within the context of a larger system

Synergy when two or more subsystems working together can produce more than they can working apart

Closed systems systems that can sustain themselves without interacting with their environments

Open systems systems that can sustain themselves only by interacting with their environments, on which they depend for their survival

Contingency approach holds that there are no universal management theories and that the most effective management theory or idea depends on the kinds of problems or situations that managers are facing at a particular time and place

The Frenchman Henri Fayol, whose ideas were shaped by his more than twenty years of experience as a CEO, is best known for developing five management functions (planning, organizing, coordinating, commanding, and controlling) and fourteen principles of management (division of work, authority and responsibility, discipline, unity of command, unity of direction, subordination of individual interests to the general interest, remuneration, centralization, scalar chain, order, equity, stability of tenure of personnel, initiative, and *esprit de corps*).

2-4 (p. 34) Explain the history of human relations management.

Unlike most people who view conflict as bad, Mary Parker Follett believed that it should be embraced rather than avoided. Of the three ways of dealing with conflict—domination, compromise, and integration—she argued that the latter was the best because it focuses on developing creative methods for meeting conflicting parties' needs.

Elton Mayo is best known for his role in the Hawthorne Studies at the Western Electric Company. In the first stage of the Hawthorne Studies, production went up because both the increased attention paid to the workers in the study and their development into a cohesive work group led to significantly higher levels of job satisfaction and productivity. In the second stage, productivity dropped because the workers had already developed strong negative norms. The Hawthorne Studies demonstrated that workers' feelings and attitudes affect their work, that financial incentives aren't necessarily the most important motivator for workers, and that group norms and behavior play a critical role in behavior at work.

Chester Barnard, president of New Jersey Bell Telephone, emphasized the critical importance of willing cooperation in organizations. In general, Barnard argued that people will be indifferent to managerial directives or orders if they (1) are understood, (2) are consistent with the purpose of the organization, (3) are compatible with the people's personal interests, and (4) can actually be carried out by those people. Acceptance of managerial authority (i.e., cooperation) is not automatic, however.

2-5 (p. 38) Discuss the history of operations, information, systems, and contingency management.

Operations management uses a quantitative or mathematical approach to find ways to increase productivity, improve quality, and manage or reduce costly inventories. The manufacture of standardized, interchangeable parts, the graphical and computerized design of parts, and the accidental discovery of just-in-time inventory systems were some of the most important historical events in operations management.

Throughout history, organizations have pushed for and quickly adopted new information technologies that reduce the cost or increase the speed with which they can acquire, store, retrieve, or communicate information. Historically, some of the most important technologies that have revolutionized information management were the invention of machines to produce pulp for paper and the printing press in the 14th and 15th centuries, the manual typewriter in 1850, the telephone in the 1880s, the personal computer in the 1980s, and the Internet in the 1990s.

A system is a set of interrelated elements or parts (subsystems) that function as a whole. Organizational systems obtain inputs from both general and specific environments. Managers and workers then use their management knowledge and manufacturing techniques to transform those inputs into outputs, which, in turn, provide feedback to the organization. Organizational systems must also address the issues of synergy and open versus closed systems.

Finally, the contingency approach to management clearly states that there are no universal management theories. The most effective management theory or idea depends on the kinds of problems or situations that managers or organizations are facing at a particular time. This means that management is much harder than it looks.

LEARNING OUTCOMES

3-1 (p. 43) Discuss how changing environments affect organizations.

Environmental change, environmental complexity, and resource scarcity are the basic components of external environments. Environmental change is the rate of variation in a company's general and specific environments. Environmental complexity is the number and intensity of factors in the external environment. Resource scarcity is the abundance or shortage of critical resources in the external environment. As the rate of environmental change increases, as the environment becomes more complex, and as resources become more scarce, managers become less confident that they can understand, predict, and effectively react to the trends affecting their businesses. According to punctuated equilibrium theory, companies experience long periods of stability followed by short periods of dynamic, fundamental change, followed by a return to stability.

3-2 (p. 46) Describe the four components of the general environment.

The general environment consists of trends that affect all organizations. Because the economy influences basic business decisions, managers often use economic statistics and business confidence indices to predict future economic activity. Changes in technology, which transforms inputs into outputs, can be a benefit or a threat to a business. Sociocultural trends, such as changing demographic characteristics, affect how companies staff their businesses. Similarly, sociocultural changes in behavior, attitudes, and beliefs affect the demand for businesses' products and services. Court decisions and new federal and state laws have imposed much greater political/legal responsibility on companies. The best way to manage legal responsibilities is to educate managers and employees about laws and regulations as well as potential lawsuits that could affect a business.

3-3 (p. 50) Explain the five components of the specific environment.

The specific environment is made up of five components: customers, competitors, suppliers, industry regulations, and advocacy groups. Companies can monitor customers' needs by identifying customer problems after they occur or by anticipating problems before they occur. Because they tend to focus on well-known competitors, managers often underestimate their competition or do a poor job of identifying future competitors. Suppliers and buyers are very dependent on each other, and that dependence sometimes leads to opportunistic behavior, in which one party benefits at the expense of the other. Regulatory agencies affect businesses by creating rules and then enforcing them. Advocacy groups cannot regulate organizations' practices. Nevertheless, through public communications, media advocacy, and product boycotts, they try to convince companies to change their practices.

3-4 (p. 55) Describe the process that companies use to make sense of their changing environments.

Managers use a three-step process to make sense of external environments: environmental scanning, interpreting information, and acting on threats and opportunities. Managers scan their environments in order to keep up to date on factors influencing their industries, to reduce uncertainty, and to detect potential problems.

KEY TERMS

External environments all events outside a company that have the potential to influence or affect it

Environmental change the rate at which a company's general and specific environments change

Stable environment an environment in which the rate of change is slow

Dynamic environment an environment in which the rate of change is fast

Punctuated equilibrium theory the theory that companies go through long periods of stability (equilibrium), followed by short periods of dynamic, fundamental change (revolutionary periods), and then a new equilibrium

Environmental complexity the number and the intensity of external factors in the environment that affect organizations

Simple environment an environment with few environmental factors

Complex environment an environment with many environmental factors

Resource scarcity the abundance or shortage of critical organizational resources in an organization's external environment

Uncertainty extent to which managers can understand or predict which environmental changes and trends will affect their businesses

General environment the economic, technological, sociocultural, and political trends that indirectly affect all organizations

Specific environment the customers, competitors, suppliers, industry regulations, and advocacy groups that are unique to an industry and directly affect how a company does business

Business confidence indices indices that show managers' level of confidence about future business growth

Technology the knowledge, tools, and techniques used to transform input into output

Competitors companies in the same industry that sell similar products or services to customers

Competitive analysis a process for monitoring the competition that involves identifying competition, anticipating their moves, and determining their strengths and weaknesses

Suppliers companies that provide material, human, financial, and informational resources to other companies

When managers identify environmental events as threats, they take steps to protect their companies from harm. When managers identify environmental events as opportunities, they formulate alternatives for taking advantage of them to improve company performance. Using cognitive maps can help managers visually summarize the relationships between environmental factors and the actions they might take to deal with them.

3-5 (p. 58) Explain how organizational cultures are created and how they can help companies be successful.

Organizational culture is the set of key values, beliefs, and attitudes shared by members of an organization. Organizational cultures are often created by company founders and then sustained through repetition of organizational stories and recognition of organizational heroes. Companies with adaptable cultures that promote employee involvement, make clear the organization's strategic purpose and direction, and actively define and teach organizational values and beliefs can achieve higher sales growth, return on assets, profits, quality, and employee satisfaction. Organizational cultures exist on three levels: the surface level, where visible artifacts and behaviors can be observed; just below the surface, where values and beliefs are expressed; and deep below the surface, where unconsciously held assumptions and beliefs exist. Managers can begin to change company cultures by focusing on the top two levels. Techniques for changing organizational cultures include using behavioral substitution and behavioral addition, changing visible artifacts, and selecting job applicants who have values and beliefs consistent with the desired company culture.

Supplier dependence the degree to which a company relies on a supplier because of the importance of the supplier's product to the company and the difficulty of finding other sources of that product

Buyer dependence the degree to which a supplier relies on a buyer because of the importance of that buyer to the supplier and the difficulty of finding other buyers for its products

Opportunistic behavior a transaction in which one party in the relationship benefits at the expense of the other

Relationship behavior the establishment of mutually beneficial, long-term exchanges between buyers and suppliers

Industry regulation regulations and rules that govern the business practices and procedures of specific industries, businesses, and professions

Advocacy groups concerned citizens who band together to try to influence the business practices of specific industries, businesses, and professions

Public communications an advocacy group tactic that relies on voluntary participation by the news media and the advertising industry to get the advocacy group's message out

Media advocacy an advocacy group tactic that involves framing issues as public issues; exposing questionable, exploitative, or unethical practices; and forcing media coverage by buying media time or creating controversy that is likely to receive extensive news coverage

Product boycott an advocacy group tactic that involves protesting a company's actions by persuading consumers not to purchase its product or service

Environmental scanning searching the environment for important events or issues that might affect an organization

Cognitive maps graphic depictions of how managers believe environmental factors relate to possible organizational actions

Internal environment the events and trends inside an organization that affect management, employees, and organizational culture

Organizational culture the values, beliefs, and attitudes shared by organizational members

Organizational stories stories told by organizational members to make sense of organizational events and changes and to emphasize culturally consistent assumptions, decisions, and actions

Organizational heroes people celebrated for their qualities and achievements within an organization

Company mission a company's purpose or reason for existing

Consistent organizational culture a company culture in which the company actively defines and teaches organizational values, beliefs, and attitudes

Behavioral addition the process of having managers and employees perform new behaviors that are central to and symbolic of the new organizational culture that a company wants to create

Behavioral substitution the process of having managers and employees perform new behaviors central to the new organizational culture in place of behaviors that were central to the old organizational culture

Visible artifacts visible signs of an organization's culture, such as the office design and layout, company dress code, and company benefits and perks, like stock options, personal parking spaces, or the private company dining room

LEARNING OUTCOMES

4-1 (p. 65) Identify common kinds of workplace deviance.

Ethics is the set of moral principles or values that define right and wrong. Workplace deviance is behavior that violates organizational norms about right and wrong and harms the organization or its workers. There are four different types of workplace deviance. Production deviance and property deviance harm the company, whereas political deviance and personal aggression harm individuals within the company.

4-2 (p. 67) Describe the U.S. Sentencing Commission Guidelines for Organizations and explain how they both encourage ethical behavior and punish unethical behavior by businesses.

Under the U.S. Sentencing Commission Guidelines, companies can be prosecuted and fined up to $300 million for employees' illegal actions. Fines are computed by multiplying the base fine by a culpability score. Companies that establish compliance programs to encourage ethical behavior can reduce their culpability scores and their fines.

4-3 (p. 69) Describe what influences ethical decision making.

Three factors influence ethical decisions: the ethical intensity of the decision, the moral development of the manager, and the ethical principles used to solve the problem. Ethical intensity is high when decisions have large, certain, immediate consequences and when the decision maker is physically or psychologically close to those affected by the decision. There are three levels of moral development. At the preconventional level, decisions are made for selfish reasons. At the conventional level, decisions conform to societal expectations. At the postconventional level, internalized principles are used to make ethical decisions. Each of these levels has two stages within it. Managers can use a number of different principles when making ethical decisions: long-term self-interest, personal virtue, religious injunctions, government requirements, utilitarian benefits, individual rights, and distributive justice.

4-4 (p. 74) Explain what practical steps managers can take to improve ethical decision making.

Employers can increase their chances of hiring ethical employees by testing all job applicants. Most large companies now have corporate codes of ethics. In addition to offering general rules, ethics codes must also provide specific, practical advice. Ethics training seeks to increase employees' awareness of ethical issues; make ethics a serious, credible factor in organizational decisions; and teach employees a practical model of ethical decision making. The most important factors in creating an ethical business climate are the personal examples set by company managers, the involvement of management in the company ethics program, a reporting system that encourages whistleblowers to report potential ethics violations, and fair but consistent punishment of violators.

4-5 (p. 77) Explain to whom organizations are socially responsible.

Social responsibility is a business's obligation to benefit society. According to the shareholder model, a company's only social responsibility is to maximize shareholder wealth by maximizing company profits. According to the stakeholder model, companies must satisfy the needs and interests of multiple corporate stakeholders, not just

KEY TERMS

Ethics the set of moral principles or values that defines right and wrong for a person or group

Ethical behavior behavior that conforms to a society's accepted principles of right and wrong

Workplace deviance unethical behavior that violates organizational norms about right and wrong

Production deviance unethical behavior that hurts the quality and quantity of work produced

Property deviance unethical behavior aimed at the organization's property or products

Employee shrinkage employee theft of company merchandise

Political deviance using one's influence to harm others in the company

Personal aggression hostile or aggressive behavior toward others

Ethical intensity the degree of concern people have about an ethical issue

Magnitude of consequences the total harm or benefit derived from an ethical decision

Social consensus agreement on whether behavior is bad or good

Probability of effect the chance that something will happen that results in harm to others

Temporal immediacy the time between an act and the consequences the act produces

Proximity of effect the social, psychological, cultural, or physical distance between a decision maker and those affected by his or her decisions

Concentration of effect the total harm or benefit that an act produces on the average person

Preconventional level of moral development the first level of moral development, in which people make decisions based on selfish reasons

Conventional level of moral development the second level of moral development, in which people make decisions that conform to societal expectations

Postconventional level of moral development the third level of moral development, in which people make decisions based on internalized principles

Principle of long-term self-interest an ethical principle that holds that you should never take any action that is not in your or your organization's long-term self-interest

Principle of personal virtue an ethical principle that holds that you should never do anything

shareholders. The needs of primary stakeholders, on which the organization relies for its existence, take precedence over those of secondary stakeholders.

4-6 (p. 79) Explain for what organizations are socially responsible.

Companies can best benefit their stakeholders by fulfilling their economic, legal, ethical, and discretionary responsibilities. Being profitable, or meeting its economic responsibility, is a business's most basic social responsibility. Legal responsibility consists of following a society's laws and regulations. Ethical responsibility means not violating accepted principles of right and wrong when doing business. Discretionary responsibilities are social responsibilities beyond basic economic, legal, and ethical responsibilities.

4-7 (p. 81) Explain how organizations can choose to respond to societal demands for social responsibility.

Social responsiveness is a company's response to stakeholders' expectations concerning socially responsible behavior. There are four social responsiveness strategies. When a company uses a reactive strategy, it denies responsibility for a problem. When it uses a defensive strategy, a company takes responsibility for a problem but does the minimum required to solve it. When a company uses an accommodative strategy, it accepts responsibility for problems and does all that society expects to solve them. Finally, when a company uses a proactive strategy, it does much more than expected to solve social responsibility problems.

4-8 (p. 82) Explain whether social responsibility hurts or helps an organization's economic performance.

Does it pay to be socially responsible? Studies show that there is generally no trade-off between social responsibility and economic performance. In most circumstances, there is generally a small positive relationship between social responsibility and economic performance that becomes stronger when a company or its products have a positive reputation. Social responsibility, however, does not guarantee profitability, as socially responsible companies experience the same ups and downs as other companies.

that is not honest, open, and truthful and that you would not be glad to see reported in the newspapers or on TV

Principle of religious injunctions an ethical principle that holds that you should never take any action that is not kind and that does not build a sense of community

Principle of government requirements an ethical principle that holds that you should never take any action that violates the law, for the law represents the minimal moral standard

Principle of utilitarian benefits an ethical principle that holds that you should never take any action that does not result in greater good for society

Principle of individual rights an ethical principle that holds that you should never take any action that infringes on others' agreed-upon rights

Principle of distributive justice an ethical principle that holds that you should never take any action that harms the least fortunate among us: the poor, the uneducated, the unemployed

Overt integrity test a written test that estimates job applicants' honesty by directly asking them what they think or feel about theft or about punishment of unethical behaviors

Personality-based integrity test a written test that indirectly estimates job applicants' honesty by measuring psycho-

logical traits, such as dependability and conscientiousness

Whistleblowing reporting others' ethics violations to management or legal authorities

Social responsibility a business's obligation to pursue policies, make decisions, and take actions that benefit society

Shareholder model a view of social responsibility that holds that an organization's overriding goal should be profit maximization for the benefit of shareholders

Stakeholder model a theory of corporate responsibility that holds that management's most important responsibility, long-term survival, is achieved by satisfying the interests of multiple corporate stakeholders

Stakeholders persons or groups with a "stake," or legitimate interest, in a company's actions

Primary stakeholder any group on which an organization relies for its long-term survival

Secondary stakeholder any group that can influence or be influenced by a company and can affect public perceptions about the company's socially responsible behavior

Economic responsibility a company's social responsibility to make a profit by producing a valued product or service

Legal responsibility a company's social responsibility to obey society's laws and regulations

Ethical responsibility a company's social responsibility not to violate accepted principles of right and wrong when conducting its business

Discretionary responsibilities the social roles that a company fulfills beyond its economic, legal, and ethical responsibilities

Social responsiveness refers to a company's strategy to respond to stakeholders' economic, legal, ethical, or discretionary expectations concerning social responsibility

Reactive strategy a social responsiveness strategy in which a company does less than society expects

Defensive strategy a social responsiveness strategy in which a company admits responsibility for a problem but does the least required to meet societal expectations

Accommodative strategy a social responsiveness strategy in which a company accepts responsibility for a problem and does all that society expects to solve that problem

Proactive strategy a social responsiveness strategy in which a company anticipates a problem before it occurs and does more than society expects to take responsibility for and address the problem

LEARNING OUTCOMES

5-1 (p. 87) Discuss the benefits and pitfalls of planning.

Planning is choosing a goal and developing a method or strategy for achieving it. Planning is one of the best ways to improve organizational and individual performance. It encourages people to work harder (intensified effort), to work hard for extended periods (persistence), to engage in behaviors directly related to goal accomplishment (directed behavior), and to think of better ways to do their jobs (task strategies). However, planning also has three potential pitfalls. Companies that are overly committed to their plans may be slow to adapt to environmental changes. Planning can create a false sense of security: Planning is based on assumptions about the future, and when those assumptions are wrong, plans can fail. Finally, planning can fail when planners are detached from the implementation of their plans.

5-2 (p. 89) Describe how to make a plan that works.

There are five steps to making a plan that works: (1) Set S.M.A.R.T. goals—goals that are Specific, Measurable, Attainable, Realistic, and Timely. (2) Develop commitment to the goals. Managers can increase workers' goal commitment by encouraging their participation in goal setting, making goals public, and getting top management to show support for goals. (3) Develop action plans for goal accomplishment. (4) Track progress toward goal achievement by setting both proximal and distal goals and by providing workers with regular performance feedback. (5) Maintain flexibility by keeping options open.

5-3 (p. 92) Discuss how companies can use plans at all management levels, from top to bottom.

Proper planning requires that the goals at the bottom and middle of the organization support the objectives at the top of the organization. The goals at the top will be longer range than those at the bottom, as shown in the exhibit on the reverse. Top management develops strategic plans, which start with the creation of an organizational purpose statement and strategic objectives. Middle managers use techniques such as management by objectives (MBO) to develop tactical plans that direct behavior,

EXHIBIT 5.3

Planning from Top to Bottom

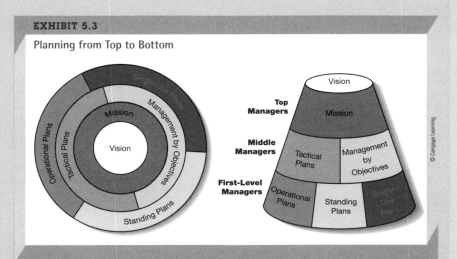

KEY TERMS

Planning choosing a goal and developing a strategy to achieve that goal

S.M.A.R.T. goals goals that are specific, measurable, attainable, realistic, and timely

Goal commitment the determination to achieve a goal

Action plan a plan that lists the specific steps, people, resources, and time period needed to attain a goal

Proximal goals short-term goals or subgoals

Distal goals long-term or primary goals

Options-based planning maintaining planning flexibility by making small, simultaneous investments in many alternative plans

Slack resources a cushion of extra resources that can be used with options-based planning to adapt to unanticipated changes, problems, or opportunities

Strategic plans overall company plans that clarify how the company will serve customers and position itself against competitors over the next two to five years

Purpose statement a statement of a company's purpose or reason for existing

Strategic objective a more specific goal that unifies company-wide efforts, stretches and challenges the organization, and possesses a finish line and a time frame

Tactical plans plans created and implemented by middle managers that specify how the company will use resources, budgets, and people over the next six months to two years to accomplish specific goals within its mission

Management by objectives (MBO) a four-step process in which managers and employees discuss and select goals, develop tactical plans, and meet regularly to review progress toward goal accomplishment

Operational plans day-to-day plans, developed and implemented by lower-level managers, for producing or delivering the organization's products and services over a thirty-day to six-month period

Single-use plans plans that cover unique, one-time-only events

Standing plans plans used repeatedly to handle frequently recurring events

Policies standing plans that indicate the general course of action that should be taken in response to a particular event or situation

efforts, and priorities. Finally, lower-level managers develop operational plans that guide daily activities in producing or delivering an organization's products and services. There are three kinds of operational plans: single-use plans, standing plans (policies, procedures, and rules and regulations), and budgets.

5-4 (p. 96) Explain the steps and limits to rational decision making.

Rational decision making is a six-step process in which managers define problems, evaluate alternatives, and compute optimal solutions. Step 1 is identifying and defining the problem. Problems are gaps between desired and existing states. Managers won't begin the decision-making process unless they are aware of a gap, are motivated to reduce it, and possess the necessary resources to fix it. Step 2 is defining the decision criteria used to judge alternatives. In Step 3, an absolute or relative comparison process is used to rate the importance of the decision criteria. Step 4 involves generating many alternative courses of action (i.e., solutions). Potential solutions are assessed in Step 5 by systematically gathering information and evaluating each alternative against each criterion. In Step 6, criterion ratings and weights are used to compute the weighted average for each alternative course of action. Rational managers then choose the alternative with the highest value.

The rational decision-making model describes how decisions should be made in an ideal world without constraints. However, managers' limited resources, incomplete and imperfect information, and limited decision-making capabilities restrict their decision-making processes in the real world.

5-5 (p. 100) Explain how group decisions and group decision-making techniques can improve decision making.

When groups view problems from multiple perspectives, use more information, have a diversity of knowledge and experience, and become committed to solutions they help choose, they can produce better solutions than do individual decision makers. However, group decisions can suffer from several disadvantages: groupthink, slowness, discussions dominated by just a few individuals, and unfelt responsibility for decisions. Group decision making works best when group members encourage c-type (cognitive) conflict. Group decision making doesn't work as well when groups become mired in a-type (affective) conflict. The devil's advocacy approach improves group decisions because it brings structured c-type conflict into the decision-making process. By contrast, the nominal group technique improves decision making by reducing a-type conflict. Because it overcomes the problems of production blocking and evaluation apprehension, electronic brainstorming is more effective than face-to-face brainstorming.

Procedures standing plans that indicate the specific steps that should be taken in response to a particular event

Rules and regulations standing plans that describe how a particular action should be performed, or what must happen or not happen in response to a particular event

Budgeting quantitative planning through which managers decide how to allocate available money to best accomplish company goals

Decision making the process of choosing a solution from available alternatives

Rational decision making a systematic process of defining problems, evaluating alternatives, and choosing optimal solutions

Problem a gap between a desired state and an existing state

Decision criteria the standards used to guide judgments and decisions

Absolute comparisons a process in which each decision criterion is compared to a standard or ranked on its own merits

Relative comparisons a process in which each decision criterion is compared directly with every other criterion

Maximize choosing the best alternative

Satisficing choosing a "good-enough" alternative

Groupthink a barrier to good decision making caused by pressure within the group for members to agree with each other

C-type conflict (cognitive conflict) disagreement that focuses on problem- and issue-related differences of opinion

A-type conflict (affective conflict) disagreement that focuses on individuals or personal issues

Devil's advocacy a decision-making method in which an individual or a subgroup is assigned the role of critic

Dialectical inquiry a decision-making method in which decision makers state the assumptions of a proposed solution (a thesis) and generate a solution that is the opposite (antithesis) of that solution

Nominal group technique a decision-making method that begins and ends by having group members quietly write down and evaluate ideas to be shared with the group

Delphi technique a decision-making method in which members of a panel of experts respond to questions and to each other until reaching agreement on an issue

Brainstorming a decision-making method in which group members build on each others' ideas to generate as many alternative solutions as possible

Electronic brainstorming a decision-making method in which group members use computers to build on each others' ideas and generate as many alternative solutions as possible

Production blocking a disadvantage of face-to-face brainstorming in which a group member must wait to share an idea because another member is presenting an idea

Evaluation apprehension fear of what others will think of your ideas

REVIEW 6

LEARNING OUTCOMES

6-1 (p. 107) Specify the components of sustainable competitive advantage, and explain why it is important.

Firms can use their resources to create and sustain a competitive advantage, that is, to provide greater value for customers than competitors can. A competitive advantage becomes sustainable when other companies cannot duplicate the benefits it provides and have, for now, stopped trying. Four conditions must be met if a firm's resources are to be used to achieve a sustainable competitive advantage. The resources must be valuable, rare, imperfectly imitable, and nonsubstitutable.

6-2 (p. 109) Describe the steps involved in the strategy-making process.

The first step in strategy making is determining whether a strategy needs to be changed to sustain a competitive advantage. The second step is to conduct a situational (SWOT) analysis that examines internal strengths and weaknesses as well as external threats and opportunities. The third step involves choosing a strategy. Strategic reference point theory suggests that when companies are performing better than their strategic reference points, top management will typically choose a risk-averse strategy. When performance is below strategic reference points, risk-seeking strategies are more likely to be chosen.

6-3 (p. 115) Explain the different kinds of corporate-level strategies.

Corporate-level strategies, consisting of portfolio strategies and grand strategies, help managers determine what businesses they should be in. Portfolio strategy focuses on lowering business risk by being in multiple, unrelated businesses and by investing the cash flows from slow-growing businesses into faster-growing businesses. One portfolio strategy is based on the BCG matrix. The most successful way to use the portfolio approach to corporate strategy is to reduce risk through related diversification.

The three kinds of grand strategies are growth, stability, and retrenchment/recovery. Companies can grow externally by merging with or acquiring other companies, or they can grow internally through direct expansion or creating new businesses. Companies choose a stability strategy when their external environment changes very little or after they have dealt with periods of explosive growth. Retrenchment strategy, shrinking the size or scope of a business, is used to turn around poor performance. If retrenchment works, it is often followed by a recovery strategy that focuses on growing the business again.

6-4 (p. 120) Describe the different kinds of industry-level strategies.

The five industry forces determine an industry's overall attractiveness to corporate investors and its potential for long-term profitability. Together, a high level of these elements combine to increase competition and decrease profits. Industry-level strategies focus on how companies choose to compete in their industries. The three positioning strategies can help companies protect themselves from the negative effects of industry-wide competition. The four adaptive strategies help companies adapt to changes in the external environment. Defenders want to defend their current strategic positions. Prospectors look for new market opportunities to bring innovative new products to

KEY TERMS

Resources the assets, capabilities, processes, employee time, information, and knowledge that an organization uses to improve its effectiveness and efficiency and create and sustain competitive advantage

Competitive advantage providing greater value for customers than competitors can

Sustainable competitive advantage a competitive advantage that other companies have tried unsuccessfully to duplicate and have, for the moment, stopped trying to duplicate

Valuable resource a resource that allows companies to improve efficiency and effectiveness

Rare resource a resource that is not controlled or possessed by many competing firms

Imperfectly imitable resource a resource that is impossible or extremely costly or difficult for other firms to duplicate

Nonsubstitutable resource a resource that produces value or competitive advantage and has no equivalent substitutes or replacements

Competitive inertia a reluctance to change strategies or competitive practices that have been successful in the past

Strategic dissonance a discrepancy between a company's intended strategy and the strategic actions managers take when implementing that strategy

Situational (SWOT) analysis an assessment of the strengths and weaknesses in an organization's internal environment and the opportunities and threats in its external environment

Distinctive competence what a company can make, do, or perform better than its competitors

Core capabilities the internal decision-making routines, problem-solving processes, and organizational cultures that determine how efficiently inputs can be turned into outputs

Strategic group a group of companies within an industry against which top managers compare, evaluate, and benchmark strategic threats and opportunities

Core firms the central companies in a strategic group

Secondary firms the firms in a strategic group that follow strategies related to but somewhat different from those of the core firms

Shadow-strategy task force a committee within a company that analyzes the company's own weaknesses to determine how competitors could exploit them for competitive advantage

market. Analyzers minimize risk by following the proven successes of prospectors. Reactors do not follow a consistent adaptive strategy but instead react to changes in the external environment after they occur.

6-5 (p. 124) Explain the components and kinds of firm-level strategies.

Firm-level strategies are concerned with direct competition between firms. Market commonality and resource similarity determine whether firms are in direct competition and thus likely to attack each other and respond to each other's attacks. In general, the more markets in which there is product, service, or customer overlap and the greater the resource similarity between two firms, the more intense the direct competition between them.

Strategic reference points the strategic targets managers use to measure whether a firm has developed the core competencies it needs to achieve a sustainable competitive advantage

Corporate-level strategy the overall organizational strategy that addresses the question "What business or businesses are we in or should we be in?"

Diversification a strategy for reducing risk by buying a variety of items (stocks or, in the case of a corporation, types of businesses) so that the failure of one stock or one business does not doom the entire portfolio

Portfolio strategy a corporate-level strategy that minimizes risk by diversifying investment among various businesses or product lines

Acquisition the purchase of a company by another company

Unrelated diversification creating or acquiring companies in completely unrelated businesses

BCG matrix a portfolio strategy, developed by the Boston Consulting Group, that categorizes a corporation's businesses by growth rate and relative market share and helps managers decide how to invest corporate funds

Star a company with a large share of a fast-growing market

Question mark a company with a small share of a fast-growing market

Cash cow a company with a large share of a slow-growing market

Dog a company with a small share of a slow-growing market

Related diversification creating or acquiring companies that share similar products, manufacturing, marketing, technology, or cultures

Grand strategy a broad corporate-level strategic plan used to achieve strategic goals and guide the strategic alternatives that managers of individual businesses or subunits may use

Growth strategy a strategy that focuses on increasing profits, revenues, market share, or the number of places in which the company does business

Stability strategy a strategy that focuses on improving the way in which the company sells the same products or services to the same customers

Retrenchment strategy a strategy that focuses on turning around very poor company performance by shrinking the size or scope of the business

Recovery the strategic actions taken after retrenchment to return to a growth strategy

Industry-level strategy a corporate strategy that addresses the question "How should we compete in this industry?"

Character of the rivalry a measure of the intensity of competitive behavior between companies in an industry

Threat of new entrants a measure of the degree to which barriers to entry make it easy or difficult for new companies to get started in an industry

Threat of substitute products or services a measure of the ease with which customers can find substitutes for an industry's products or services

Bargaining power of suppliers a measure of the influence that suppliers of parts, materials, and services to firms in an industry have on the prices of these inputs

Bargaining power of buyers a measure of the influence that customers have on a firm's prices

Cost leadership the positioning strategy of producing a product or service of acceptable quality at consistently lower production costs than competitors can, so that the firm can offer the product or service at the lowest price in the industry

Differentiation the positioning strategy of providing a product or service that is sufficiently different from competitors' offerings that customers are willing to pay a premium price for it

Focus strategy the positioning strategy of using cost leadership or differentiation to produce a specialized product or service for a limited, specially targeted group of customers in a particular geographic region or market segment

Defenders companies using an adaptive strategy aimed at defending strategic positions by seeking moderate, steady growth and by offering a limited range of high-quality products and services to a well-defined set of customers

Prospectors companies using an adaptive strategy that seeks fast growth by searching for new market opportunities, encouraging risk taking, and being the first to bring innovative new products to market

Analyzers companies using an adaptive strategy that seeks to minimize risk and maximize profits by following or imitating the proven successes of prospectors

Reactors companies that do not follow a consistent adaptive strategy, but instead react to changes in the external environment after they occur

Firm-level strategy a corporate strategy that addresses the question "How should we compete against a particular firm?"

Direct competition the rivalry between two companies that offer similar products and services, acknowledge each other as rivals, and act and react to each other's strategic actions

Market commonality the degree to which two companies have overlapping products, services, or customers in multiple markets

Resource similarity the extent to which a competitor has similar amounts and kinds of resources

Attack a competitive move designed to reduce a rival's market share or profits

Response a competitive countermove, prompted by a rival's attack, to defend or improve a company's market share or profit

LEARNING OUTCOMES

7-1 (p. 131) Explain why innovation matters to companies.

Technology cycles typically follow an S-curve pattern of innovation. Early in the cycle, technological progress is slow, and improvements in technological performance are small. As a technology matures, however, performance improves quickly. Finally, as the limits of a technology are reached, only small improvements occur. At this point, significant improvements in performance must come from new technologies. The best way to protect a competitive advantage is to create a stream of innovative ideas and products. Innovation streams begin with technological discontinuities that create significant breakthroughs in performance or function. Technological discontinuities are followed by discontinuous change, in which customers purchase new technologies and companies compete to establish the new dominant design. Dominant designs emerge because of critical mass, because they solve a practical problem, or because of the negotiations of independent standards bodies. Because technological innovation both enhances and destroys competence, companies that bet on the wrong design often struggle, while companies that bet on the eventual dominant design usually prosper. When a dominant design emerges, companies focus on incremental change, lowering costs and making small but steady improvements in the dominant design. This focus continues until the next technological discontinuity occurs.

7-2 (p. 136) Discuss the different methods that managers can use to effectively manage innovation in their organizations.

To successfully manage innovation streams, companies must manage the sources of innovation and learn to manage innovation during both discontinuous and incremental change. Since innovation begins with creativity, companies can manage the sources of innovation by supporting a work environment in which creative thoughts and ideas are welcomed, valued, and encouraged. Creative work environments provide challenging work; offer organizational, supervisory, and work group encouragement; allow significant freedom; and remove organizational impediments to creativity.

Discontinuous and incremental change require different strategies. Companies that succeed in periods of discontinuous change typically follow an experiential approach to innovation. The experiential approach assumes that intuition, flexible options, and hands-on experience can reduce uncertainty and accelerate learning and understanding. A compression approach to innovation works best during periods of incremental change. This approach assumes that innovation can be planned using a series of steps and that compressing the time it takes to complete those steps can speed up innovation.

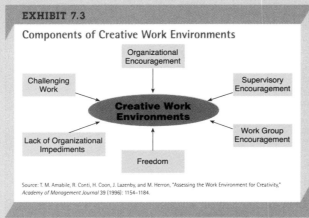

EXHIBIT 7.3

Components of Creative Work Environments

Organizational Encouragement

Challenging Work

Supervisory Encouragement

Creative Work Environments

Lack of Organizational Impediments

Work Group Encouragement

Freedom

Source: T. M. Amabile, R. Conti, H. Coon, J. Lazenby, and M. Herron, "Assessing the Work Environment for Creativity," *Academy of Management Journal* 39 (1996): 1154–1184.

KEY TERMS

Organizational innovation the successful implementation of creative ideas in organizations

Technology cycle a cycle that begins with the birth of a new technology and ends when that technology reaches its limits and is replaced by a newer, substantially better technology

S-curve pattern of innovation a pattern of technological innovation characterized by slow initial progress, then rapid progress, and then slow progress again as a technology matures and reaches its limits

Innovation streams patterns of innovation over time that can create sustainable competitive advantage

Technological discontinuity the phase of an innovation stream in which a scientific advance or unique combination of existing technologies creates a significant breakthrough in performance or function

Discontinuous change the phase of a technology cycle characterized by technological substitution and design competition

Technological substitution the purchase of new technologies to replace older ones

Design competition competition between old and new technologies to establish a new technological standard or dominant design

Dominant design a new technological design or process that becomes the accepted market standard

Technological lockout the inability of a company to competitively sell its products because it relied on old technology or a nondominant design

Incremental change the phase of a technology cycle in which companies innovate by lowering costs and improving the functioning and performance of the dominant technological design

Creative work environments workplace cultures in which workers perceive that new ideas are welcomed, valued, and encouraged

Flow a psychological state of effortlessness, in which you become completely absorbed in what you're doing and time seems to pass quickly

Experiential approach to innovation an approach to innovation that assumes a highly uncertain environment and uses intuition, flexible options, and hands-on experience to reduce uncertainty and accelerate learning and understanding

7-3 (p. 141) Discuss why not changing can lead to organizational decline.

The five-stage process of organizational decline begins when organizations don't recognize the need for change. In the blinded stage, managers fail to recognize the changes that threaten their organization's survival. In the inaction stage, management recognizes the need to change but doesn't act, hoping that the problems will correct themselves. In the faulty action stage, management focuses on cost cutting and efficiency rather than facing up to the fundamental changes needed to ensure survival. In the crisis stage, failure is likely unless fundamental reorganization occurs. Finally, in the dissolution stage, the company is dissolved through bankruptcy proceedings; by selling assets to pay creditors; or through the closing of stores, offices, and facilities. If companies recognize the need to change early enough, however, dissolution may be avoided.

7-4 (p. 142) Discuss the different methods that managers can use to better manage change as it occurs.

The basic change process involves unfreezing, change intervention, and refreezing. Resistance to change stems from self-interest, misunderstanding, and distrust as well as a general intolerance for change. Resistance can be managed through education and communication, participation, negotiation, top-management support, and coercion. Knowing what *not* to do is as important as knowing what to do to achieve successful change. Managers should avoid these errors when leading change: not establishing a sense of urgency, not creating a guiding coalition, lacking a vision, undercommunicating the vision, not removing obstacles to the vision, not creating short-term wins, declaring victory too soon, and not anchoring changes in the corporation's culture. Finally, managers can use a number of change techniques. Results-driven change and the General Electric workout reduce resistance to change by getting change efforts off to a fast start. Organizational development is a collection of planned change interventions (large-system, small-group, person-focused), guided by a change agent, that are designed to improve an organization's long-term health and performance.

EXHIBIT 7.6

Different Kinds of Organizational Development Interventions

LARGE-SYSTEM INTERVENTIONS

Sociotechnical systems	An intervention designed to improve how well employees use and adjust to the work technology used in an organization.
Survey feedback	An intervention that uses surveys to collect information from the members of the system, reports the results of that survey to the members, and then uses those results to develop action plans for improvement.

SMALL-GROUP INTERVENTIONS

Team building	An intervention designed to increase the cohesion and cooperation of work group members.
Unit goal setting	An intervention designed to help a work group establish short- and long-term goals.

PERSON-FOCUSED INTERVENTIONS

Counseling/ coaching	An intervention designed so that a formal helper or coach listens to managers or employees and advises them on how to deal with work or interpersonal problems.
Training	An intervention designed to provide individuals with the knowledge, skills, or attitudes they need to become more effective at their jobs.

Source: W. J. Rothwell, R. Sullivan, and G. M. McLean, *Practicing Organizational Development: A Guide for Consultants* (San Diego: Pfeiffer & Co., 1995).

Design iteration a cycle of repetition in which a company tests a prototype of a new product or service, improves on that design, and then builds and tests the improved prototype

Product prototype a full-scale, working model that is being tested for design, function, and reliability

Testing the systematic comparison of different product designs or design iterations

Milestones formal project review points used to assess progress and performance

Multifunctional teams work teams composed of people from different departments

Compression approach to innovation an approach to innovation that assumes that incremental innovation can be planned using a series of steps and that compressing those steps can speed innovation

Generational change change based on incremental improvements to a dominant technological design such that the improved technology is fully backward compatible with the older technology

Organizational decline a large decrease in organizational performance that occurs when companies don't anticipate, recognize, neutralize, or adapt to the internal or external pressures that threaten their survival

Change forces forces that produce differences in the form, quality, or condition of an organization over time

Resistance forces forces that support the existing conditions in organizations

Resistance to change opposition to change resulting from self-interest, misunderstanding and distrust, and a general intolerance for change

Unfreezing getting the people affected by change to believe that change is needed

Change intervention the process used to get workers and managers to change their behaviors and work practices

Refreezing supporting and reinforcing new changes so that they stick

Coercion the use of formal power and authority to force others to change

Results-driven change change created quickly by focusing on the measurement and improvement of results

General Electric workout a three-day meeting in which managers and employees from different levels and parts of an organization quickly generate and act on solutions to specific business problems

Organizational development a philosophy and collection of planned change interventions designed to improve an organization's long-term health and performance

Change agent the person formally in charge of guiding a change effort

REVIEW 8

LEARNING OUTCOMES

8-1 (p. 153) Discuss the impact of global business and the trade rules and agreements that govern it.

Today, there are 103,000 multinational corporations worldwide; just 9.4 percent are based in the United States. Global business affects the United States in two ways: through direct foreign investment in the United States by foreign companies, and through U.S. companies' investment in businesses in other countries. U.S. direct foreign investment throughout the world amounts to more than $3.5 trillion per year, whereas direct foreign investment by foreign companies in the United States amounts to more than $2.3 trillion per year. Historically, tariffs and nontariff trade barriers such as quotas, voluntary export restraints, government import standards, government subsidies, and customs classifications have made buying foreign goods much harder or more expensive than buying domestically produced products. In recent years, however, worldwide trade agreements such as GATT and the WTO, along with regional trading agreements like the Maastricht Treaty of Europe, NAFTA, CAFTA-DR, UNASUR, ASEAN, and APEC, have substantially reduced tariffs and nontariff barriers to international trade. Consumers have responded by purchasing products based on value rather than geography.

8-2 (p. 160) Explain why companies choose to standardize or adapt their business procedures.

Global business requires a balance between global consistency and local adaptation. Global consistency means using the same rules, guidelines, policies, and procedures in each location. Managers at company headquarters like global consistency because it simplifies decisions. Local adaptation means adapting standard procedures to differences in markets. Local managers prefer a policy of local adaptation because it gives them more control. Not all businesses need the same combination of global consistency and local adaptation. Some thrive by emphasizing global consistency and ignoring local adaptation. Others succeed by ignoring global consistency and emphasizing local adaptation.

8-3 (p. 161) Explain the different ways that companies can organize to do business globally.

The phase model of globalization says that, as companies move from a domestic to a global orientation, they use these organizational forms in sequence: exporting, cooperative contracts (licensing and franchising), strategic alliances, and wholly owned affiliates. Yet not all companies follow the phase model. For example, global new ventures are global from their inception.

8-4 (p. 165) Explain how to find a favorable business climate.

The first step in deciding where to take your company global is finding an attractive business climate. Be sure to look for a growing market where consumers have strong purchasing power and foreign competitors are weak. When locating an office or manufacturing facility, consider both qualitative and quantitative factors. In assessing political risk, be sure to examine both political uncertainty and policy uncertainty. If the location you choose has considerable political risk, you can avoid it, try to control the risk, or use a cooperation strategy.

KEY TERMS

Global business the buying and selling of goods and services by people from different countries

Multinational corporation a corporation that owns businesses in two or more countries

Direct foreign investment a method of investment in which a company builds a new business or buys an existing business in a foreign country

Trade barriers government-imposed regulations that increase the cost and restrict the number of imported goods

Protectionism a government's use of trade barriers to shield domestic companies and their workers from foreign competition

Tariff a direct tax on imported goods

Nontariff barriers nontax methods of increasing the cost or reducing the volume of imported goods

Quota a limit on the number or volume of imported products

Voluntary export restraints voluntarily imposed limits on the number or volume of products exported to a particular country

Government import standard a standard ostensibly established to protect the health and safety of citizens but, in reality, often used to restrict imports

Subsidies government loans, grants, and tax deferments given to domestic companies to protect them from foreign competition

Customs classification a classification assigned to imported products by government officials that affects the size of the tariff and the imposition of import quotas

General Agreement on Tariffs and Trade (GATT) a worldwide trade agreement that reduced and eliminated tariffs, limited government subsidies, and established protections for intellectual property

World Trade Organization (WTO) the successor to GATT; the only international organization dealing with the global rules of trade between nations. Its main function is to ensure that trade flows as smoothly, predictably, and freely as possible

Regional trading zones areas in which tariff and nontariff barriers on trade between countries are reduced or eliminated

Maastricht Treaty of Europe a regional trade agreement between most European countries

8-5 (p. 170) Discuss the importance of identifying and adapting to cultural differences.

National culture is the set of shared values and beliefs that affects the perceptions, decisions, and behavior of the people from a particular country. The first step in dealing with culture is to recognize meaningful differences such as power distance, individualism, masculinity, uncertainty avoidance, and short-term/long-term orientation. Cultural differences should be interpreted carefully because they are based on generalizations rather than specific individuals. Adapting managerial practices to cultural differences is difficult, because policies and practices can be perceived differently in different cultures.

8-6 (p. 172) Explain how to successfully prepare workers for international assignments.

Many expatriates return prematurely from international assignments because of poor performance. This is much less likely to happen if employees receive language and cross-cultural training, such as documentary training, cultural simulations, or field experiences, before going on assignment. Adjustment of expatriates' spouses and families, which is the most important determinant of success in international assignments, can be improved through adaptability screening and language and cross-cultural training.

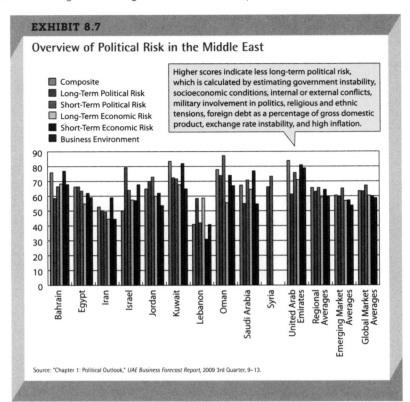

EXHIBIT 8.7

Overview of Political Risk in the Middle East

Legend:
- Composite
- Long-Term Political Risk
- Short-Term Political Risk
- Long-Term Economic Risk
- Short-Term Economic Risk
- Business Environment

Higher scores indicate less long-term political risk, which is calculated by estimating government instability, socioeconomic conditions, internal or external conflicts, military involvement in politics, religious and ethnic tensions, foreign debt as a percentage of gross domestic product, exchange rate instability, and high inflation.

Countries: Bahrain, Egypt, Iran, Israel, Jordan, Kuwait, Lebanon, Oman, Saudi Arabia, Syria, United Arab Emirates, Regional Averages, Emerging Market Averages, Global Market Averages

Source: "Chapter 1: Political Outlook," *UAE Business Forecast Report*, 2009 3rd Quarter, 9–13.

North American Free Trade Agreement (NAFTA) a regional trade agreement between the United States, Canada, and Mexico

Dominican Republic-Central America Free Trade Agreement (CAFTA-DR) a regional trade agreement between Costa Rica, the Dominican Republic, El Salvador, Guatemala, Honduras, Nicaragua, and the United States

Union of South American Nations (UN-ASUR) a regional trade agreement between Argentina, Brazil, Paraguay, Uruguay, Venezuela, Bolivia, Colombia, Ecuador, Peru, Guyana, Suriname, and Chile

Association of Southeast Asian Nations (ASEAN) a regional trade agreement between Brunei Darussalam, Cambodia, Indonesia, Laos, Malaysia, Myanmar, the Philippines, Singapore, Thailand, and Vietnam

Asia-Pacific Economic Cooperation (APEC) a regional trade agreement between Australia, Canada, Chile, the People's Republic of China, Hong Kong, Japan, Mexico, New Zealand, Papua New Guinea, Peru, Russia, South Korea, Taiwan, the United States, and all the members of ASEAN except Cambodia, Laos, and Myanmar

Global consistency when a multinational company has offices, manufacturing plants,

and distribution facilities in different countries and runs them all using the same rules, guidelines, policies, and procedures

Local adaptation modifying rules, guidelines, policies, and procedures to adapt to differences in foreign customers, governments, and regulatory agencies

Exporting selling domestically produced products to customers in foreign countries

Cooperative contract an agreement in which a foreign business owner pays a company a fee for the right to conduct that business in his or her country

Licensing an agreement in which a domestic company, the licensor, receives royalty payments for allowing another company, the licensee, to produce the licensor's product, sell its service, or use its brand name in a specified foreign market

Franchise a collection of networked firms in which the manufacturer or marketer of a product or service, the franchisor, licenses the entire business to another person or organization, the franchisee

Strategic alliance an agreement in which companies combine key resources, costs, risk, technology, and people

Joint venture a strategic alliance in which two existing companies collaborate to form a third, independent company

Wholly owned affiliates foreign offices, facilities, and manufacturing plants that are 100 percent owned by the parent company

Global new ventures new companies that are founded with an active global strategy and have sales, employees, and financing in different countries

Purchasing power the relative cost of a standard set of goods and services in different countries

Political uncertainty the risk of major changes in political regimes that can result from war, revolution, death of political leaders, social unrest, or other influential events

Policy uncertainty the risk associated with changes in laws and government policies that directly affect the way foreign companies conduct business

National culture the set of shared values and beliefs that affects the perceptions, decisions, and behavior of the people from a particular country

Expatriate someone who lives and works outside his or her native country

LEARNING OUTCOMES

9-1 (p. 177) Describe the departmentalization approach to organizational structure.

There are five traditional departmental structures: functional, product, customer, geographic, and matrix. Functional departmentalization is based on the different business functions or types of expertise used to run a business. Product departmentalization is organized according to the different products or services a company sells. Customer departmentalization focuses its divisions on the different kinds of customers a company has. Geographic departmentalization is based on the different geographic areas or markets in which the company does business. Matrix departmentalization is a hybrid form that combines two or more forms of departmentalization, the most common being the product and functional forms. There is no single best departmental structure. Each structure has advantages and disadvantages.

9-2 (p. 184) Explain organizational authority.

Organizational authority is determined by the chain of command, line versus staff authority, delegation, and the degree of centralization in a company. The chain of command vertically connects every job in the company to higher levels of management and makes clear who reports to whom. Managers have line authority to command employees below them in the chain of command but have only staff, or advisory, authority over employees not below them in the chain of command. Managers delegate authority by transferring to subordinates the authority and responsibility needed to do a task; in exchange, subordinates become accountable for task completion. In centralized companies, most authority to make decisions lies with managers in the upper levels of the company. In decentralized companies, much of the authority is delegated to the workers closest to the problems, who can then make the decisions necessary for solving the problems themselves.

9-3 (p. 187) Discuss the different methods for job design.

Companies use specialized jobs because they are economical and easy to learn and don't require highly paid workers. However, specialized jobs aren't motivating or particularly satisfying for employees. Companies have used job rotation, job enlargement, job enrichment, and the job characteristics model to make specialized jobs more interesting and motivating. The goal of the job characteristics model is to make jobs intrinsically motivating. For this to happen, jobs must be strong on five core job characteristics (skill variety, task identity, task significance, autonomy, and feedback), and workers must experience three critical psychological states (knowledge of results, responsibility for work outcomes, and meaningful work). If jobs aren't internally motivating, they can be redesigned by combining tasks, forming natural work units, establishing client relationships, vertical loading, and opening feedback channels.

9-4 (p. 191) Explain the methods that companies are using to redesign internal organizational processes (i.e., intraorganizational processes).

Today, companies are using reengineering and empowerment to change their intraorganizational processes. Reengineering changes an organization's orientation from vertical to horizontal and its work processes by decreasing sequential and pooled interdependence and by increasing reciprocal interdependence. Reengineering promises

KEY TERMS

Organizational structure the vertical and horizontal configuration of departments, authority, and jobs within a company

Organizational process the collection of activities that transform inputs into outputs that customers value

Departmentalization subdividing work and workers into separate organizational units responsible for completing particular tasks

Functional departmentalization organizing work and workers into separate units responsible for particular business functions or areas of expertise

Product departmentalization organizing work and workers into separate units responsible for producing particular products or services

Customer departmentalization organizing work and workers into separate units responsible for particular kinds of customers

Geographic departmentalization organizing work and workers into separate units responsible for doing business in particular geographic areas

Matrix departmentalization a hybrid organizational structure in which two or more forms of departmentalization, most often product and functional, are used together

Simple matrix a form of matrix departmentalization in which managers in different parts of the matrix negotiate conflicts and resources

Complex matrix a form of matrix departmentalization in which managers in different parts of the matrix report to matrix managers, who help them sort out conflicts and problems

Authority the right to give commands, take action, and make decisions to achieve organizational objectives

Chain of command the vertical line of authority that clarifies who reports to whom throughout the organization

Unity of command a management principle that workers should report to just one boss

Line authority the right to command immediate subordinates in the chain of command

Staff authority the right to advise, but not command, others who are not subordinates in the chain of command

Line function an activity that contributes directly to creating or selling the company's products

dramatic increases in productivity and customer satisfaction, but it has been criticized as simply an excuse to cut costs and lay off workers. Empowering workers means taking decision-making authority and responsibility from managers and giving it to workers. Empowered workers develop feelings of competence and self-determination and believe that their work has meaning and impact.

9-5 (p. 194) Describe the methods that companies are using to redesign external organizational processes (i.e., interorganizational processes).

Organizations are using modular and virtual organizations to change interorganizational processes. Because modular organizations outsource all noncore activities to other businesses, they are less expensive to run than traditional companies. However, modular organizations require extremely close relationships with suppliers, may result in a loss of control, and could create new competitors if the wrong business activities are outsourced. Virtual organizations participate in a network in which they share skills, costs, capabilities, markets, and customers. Virtual organizations can reduce costs, respond quickly, and, if they can successfully coordinate their efforts, produce outstanding products and services.

Staff function an activity that does not contribute directly to creating or selling the company's products, but instead supports line activities

Delegation of authority the assignment of direct authority and responsibility to a subordinate to complete tasks for which the manager is normally responsible

Centralization of authority the location of most authority at the upper levels of the organization

Decentralization the location of a significant amount of authority in the lower levels of the organization

Standardization solving problems by consistently applying the same rules, procedures, and processes

Job design the number, kind, and variety of tasks that individual workers perform in doing their jobs

Job specialization a job composed of a small part of a larger task or process

Job rotation periodically moving workers from one specialized job to another to give them more variety and the opportunity to use different skills

Job enlargement increasing the number of different tasks that a worker performs within one particular job

Job enrichment increasing the number of tasks in a particular job and giving workers the authority and control to make meaningful decisions about their work

Job characteristics model (JCM) an approach to job redesign that seeks to formulate jobs in ways that motivate workers and lead to positive work outcomes

Internal motivation motivation that comes from the job itself rather than from outside rewards

Skill variety the number of different activities performed in a job

Task identity the degree to which a job, from beginning to end, requires the completion of a whole and identifiable piece of work

Task significance the degree to which a job is perceived to have a substantial impact on others inside or outside the organization

Autonomy the degree to which a job gives workers the discretion, freedom, and independence to decide how and when to accomplish the job

Feedback the amount of information the job provides to workers about their work performance

Mechanistic organization an organization characterized by specialized jobs and responsibilities; precisely defined, unchanging roles; and a rigid chain of command based on centralized authority and vertical communication

Organic organization an organization characterized by broadly defined jobs and responsibility; loosely defined, frequently changing roles; and decentralized authority and horizontal communication based on task knowledge

Intraorganizational process the collection of activities that take place within an organization to transform inputs into outputs that customers value

Reengineering fundamental rethinking and radical redesign of business processes to achieve dramatic improvements in critical measures of performance, such as cost, quality, service, and speed

Task interdependence the extent to which collective action is required to complete an entire piece of work

Pooled interdependence work completed by having each job or department independently contribute to the whole

Sequential interdependence work completed in succession, with one group's or job's outputs becoming the inputs for the next group or job

Reciprocal interdependence work completed by different jobs or groups working together in a back-and-forth manner

Empowering workers permanently passing decision-making authority and responsibility from managers to workers by giving them the information and resources they need to make and carry out good decisions

Empowerment feelings of intrinsic motivation, in which workers perceive their work to have impact and meaning and perceive themselves to be competent and capable of self-determination

Interorganizational process a collection of activities that take place among companies to transform inputs into outputs that customers value

Modular organization an organization that outsources noncore business activities to outside companies, suppliers, specialists, or consultants

Virtual organization an organization that is part of a network in which many companies share skills, costs, capabilities, markets, and customers to collectively solve customer problems or provide specific products or services

LEARNING OUTCOMES

10-1 (p. 199) Explain the good and bad of using teams.

In many industries, teams are growing in importance because they help organizations respond to specific problems and challenges. Teams have been shown to increase customer satisfaction (specific customer teams), product and service quality (direct responsibility), and employee job satisfaction (cross-training, unique opportunities, and leadership responsibilities). Although teams can produce significant improvements in these areas, using teams does not guarantee these positive outcomes. Teams and teamwork have the disadvantages of initially high turnover and social loafing (especially in large groups). Teams also share many of the advantages (multiple perspectives, generation of more alternatives, and more commitment) and disadvantages (groupthink, time, poorly run meetings, domination by a few team members, and weak accountability) of group decision making. Teams should be used for a clear purpose, when the work requires that people work together, when rewards can be provided for both teamwork and team performance, and when ample resources can be provided.

10-2 (p. 203) Recognize and understand the different kinds of teams.

Companies use different kinds of teams to make themselves more competitive. Autonomy is the key dimension that makes teams different. Traditional work groups (which execute tasks) and employee involvement groups (which make suggestions) have the lowest levels of autonomy. Semi-autonomous work groups (which control major direct tasks) have more autonomy, while self-managing teams (which control all direct tasks) and self-designing teams (which control membership and how tasks are done) have the highest levels of autonomy. Cross-functional, virtual, and project teams are common but are not easily categorized in terms of autonomy. Cross-functional teams combine employees from different functional areas to help teams attack problems from multiple perspectives and generate more ideas and solutions. Virtual teams use telecommunications and information technologies to bring coworkers together, regardless of physical location or time zone. Virtual teams reduce travel and work time, but communication may suffer since team members don't work face-to-face. Finally, project teams are used for specific, one-time projects or tasks that must be completed within a limited time. Project teams reduce communication barriers and promote flexibility; teams and team members are reassigned to their departments or to new projects as their current projects are completed.

10-3 (p. 206) Understand the general characteristics of work teams.

The most important characteristics of work teams are team norms, cohesiveness, size, conflict, and development. Norms let team members know what is expected of them and can influence team behavior in positive and negative ways. Positive team norms are associated with organizational commitment, trust, and job satisfaction. Team cohesiveness helps teams retain members, promotes cooperative behavior, increases motivation, and facilitates team performance. Attending team meetings and activities, creating opportunities to work together, and engaging in nonwork activities can increase cohesiveness. Team size has a curvilinear relationship with team performance: teams that are very small or very large do not perform as well as moderate-sized teams of six to nine members. Teams of this size are cohesive and small enough for team members to

KEY TERMS

Work team a small number of people with complementary skills who hold themselves mutually accountable for pursuing a common purpose, achieving performance goals, and improving interdependent work processes

Cross-training training team members to do all or most of the jobs performed by the other team members

Social loafing behavior in which team members withhold their efforts and fail to perform their share of the work

Traditional work group a group composed of two or more people who work together to achieve a shared goal

Employee involvement team a team that provides advice or makes suggestions to management concerning specific issues

Semi-autonomous work group a group that has the authority to make decisions and solve problems related to the major tasks of producing a product or service

Self-managing team a team that manages and controls all of the major tasks of producing a product or service

Self-designing team a team that has the characteristics of self-managing teams but also controls team design, work tasks, and team membership

Cross-functional team a team composed of employees from different functional areas of the organization

Virtual team a team composed of geographically and/or organizationally dispersed coworkers who use telecommunication and information technologies to accomplish an organizational task

Project team a team created to complete specific, one-time projects or tasks within a limited time

Norms informally agreed-on standards that regulate team behavior

Cohesiveness the extent to which team members are attracted to a team and motivated to remain in it

Forming the first stage of team development, in which team members meet each other, form initial impressions, and begin to establish team norms

Storming the second stage of development, characterized by conflict and disagreement, in which team members disagree over what the team should do and how it should do it

get to know each other and contribute in a meaningful way but are large enough to take advantage of team members' diverse skills, knowledge, and perspectives. Conflict and disagreement are inevitable in most teams. The key to dealing with team conflict is to maximize cognitive conflict, which focuses on issue-related differences, and minimize affective conflict, the emotional reactions that occur when disagreements become personal rather than professional. As teams develop and grow, they pass through four stages of development: forming, storming, norming, and performing. If a team is not managed well, its performance may decline after a period of time as the team regresses through the stages of de-norming, de-storming, and de-forming.

10-4 (p. 211) Explain how to enhance work team effectiveness.

Companies can make teams more effective by setting team goals and managing how team members are selected, trained, and compensated. Team goals provide a clear focus and purpose, reduce the incidence of social loafing, and lead to higher team performance 93 percent of the time.

Extremely difficult stretch goals can be used to motivate teams as long as teams have autonomy, control over resources, structural accommodation, and bureaucratic immunity. Not everyone is suited for teamwork. When selecting team members, companies should select people who have a preference for teamwork (that is, are more collectivists than individualists) and should consider team level (average ability of a team) and team diversity (different abilities of a team). Organizations that use teams successfully provide thousands of hours of training to make sure that teams work. The most common types of team training are for interpersonal skills, decision-making and problem-solving skills, conflict resolution, technical training to help team members learn multiple jobs (i.e., cross-training), and training for team leaders. Employees can be compensated for team participation and accomplishments in three ways: skill-based pay, gainsharing, and nonfinancial rewards.

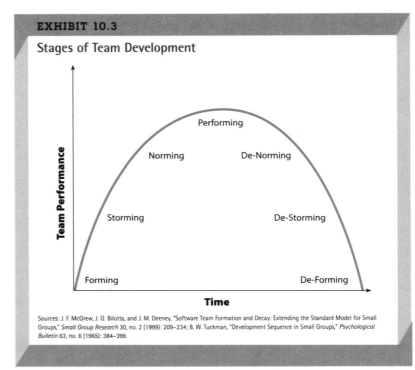

EXHIBIT 10.3

Stages of Team Development

Sources: J. F. McGrew, J. G. Bilotta, and J. M. Deeney, "Software Team Formation and Decay: Extending the Standard Model for Small Groups," *Small Group Research* 30, no. 2 (1999): 209–234; B. W. Tuckman, "Development Sequence in Small Groups," *Psychological Bulletin* 63, no. 6 (1965): 384–399.

Norming the third stage of team development, in which team members begin to settle into their roles, group cohesion grows, and positive team norms develop

Performing the fourth and final stage of team development, in which performance improves because the team has matured into an effective, fully functioning team

De-norming a reversal of the norming stage, in which team performance begins to decline as the size, scope, goal, or members of the team change

De-storming a reversal of the storming phase, in which the team's comfort level decreases, team cohesion weakens, and angry emotions and conflict may flare

De-forming a reversal of the forming stage, in which team members position themselves to control pieces of the team, avoid each other, and isolate themselves from team leaders

Structural accommodation the ability to change organizational structures, policies, and practices in order to meet stretch goals

Bureaucratic immunity the ability to make changes without first getting approval from managers or other parts of an organization

Individualism-collectivism the degree to which a person believes that people should be self-sufficient and that loyalty to one's self is more important than loyalty to team or company

Team level the average level of ability, experience, personality, or any other factor on a team

Team diversity the variances or differences in ability, experience, personality, or any other factor on a team

Interpersonal skills skills, such as listening, communicating, questioning, and providing feedback, that enable people to have effective working relationships with others

Skill-based pay a compensation system that pays employees for learning additional skills or knowledge

Gainsharing a compensation system in which companies share the financial value of performance gains, such as increased productivity, cost savings, or quality, with their workers

1	Chapter 9
	1 Functional Departmentalization
	2 Matrix
	3 Authority
	4 Line vs Staff Authority
	5 Centralization vs Decentralization of authority
	6 Job Design – Job Characteristics Model (JCM)
7	7 Autonomy and Feedback
2	Chapter 10
	1 Work Team
	2 Cross-training
	3 Self-managing Team
	4 Cross-functional Team
	5 Norms
	6 Cohesiveness
	7 Skill-based Pay
15	8 Gain-sharing
3	Chapter 11
	1 Define - Human Resource Management
	2 BFPQ
	3 Disparate Treatment
	4 Adverse Impact
	5 Sexual Harassment
	6 Quid Pro Quo
	7 Hostile Work Environment
	8 Job Analysis – Job description – Job specification
	9 Selection - Validation of Selection Process and Tools
	10 Performance Appraisal – Behavior Observation Scales (BOSs) 238
26	11 360 degree feedback
4	Chapter 12
	1 Diversity
	2 Workplace Diversity and Affirmative Action are not the same
	3 Age, sex, racial, ethnic, disability discrimination
	4 Five factors in Personality…
	• Extraversion
	• Emotional Stability
	• Agreeableness
	• Conscientiousness
30	• Openness to experience

5	Chapter 13

38	1 Motivation and Needs
	3 Extrinsic vs Intrinsic Rewards
	4 Equity Theory
	5 Distributive vs Procedural Justice
	6 Expectancy Theory - valence, expectancy, instrumentality
	7 Reinforcement Theory – Positive and Negative Reinforcement, Punishment, Extinction,
	8 Goal Setting Theory
	    • Goal Specificity
	    • Goal Difficulty
	    • Goal Acceptance

6	Chapter 14
43	1 Leadership and Leadership Style 2 Path-goal theory - Directive, Supportive, Participative, Achievement-oriented 3 Normative Decision Theory 4 Decision Quality and Acceptance 304 to 307 5 Differences between: Visionary, Charismatic, Transformational Leadership
7	Chapter 15
48	1 Communication 2 Perception and Selective Perception 3 Attribution Theory and Fundamental Attribution Error 4 Active and empathetic listening 5 Destructive and constructive feedback
8	Chapter 16
55	1 Control 2 Standards 3 Benchmarking 4 Feedback, Concurrent, Feed-forward Control 5 Financial Statements: Cash Flow, Balance Sheet, Income Statement 6 Financial Ratios 7 Economic Value Added

LEARNING OUTCOMES

11-1 (p. 219) Explain how different employment laws affect human resource practice.

Human resource management is subject to numerous major federal employment laws and subject to review by several federal agencies. In general, these laws indicate that sex, age, religion, color, national origin, race, disability, and pregnancy may not be considered in employment decisions unless these factors reasonably qualify as BFOQs. Two important criteria, disparate treatment (intentional discrimination) and adverse impact (unintentional discrimination), are used to decide whether companies have wrongly discriminated against someone. The two kinds of sexual harassment are quid pro quo sexual harassment and hostile work environment.

11-2 (p. 223) Explain how companies use recruiting to find qualified job applicants.

Recruiting is the process of finding qualified job applicants. The first step in recruiting is to conduct a job analysis, which is used to write a job description of basic tasks, duties, and responsibilities and to write job specifications indicating the knowledge, skills, and abilities needed to perform the job. Whereas internal recruiting involves finding qualified job applicants from inside the company, external recruiting involves finding qualified job applicants from outside the company.

11-3 (p. 227) Describe the selection techniques and procedures that companies use when deciding which applicants should receive job offers.

Selection is the process of gathering information about job applicants to decide who should be offered a job. Accurate selection procedures are valid, are legally defendable, and improve organizational performance. Application forms and résumés are the most common selection devices. Managers should check references and conduct background checks even though previous employers are often reluctant to provide such information for fear of being sued for defamation. Unfortunately, without this information, other employers are at risk of negligent hiring lawsuits. Selection tests generally do the best job of predicting applicants' future job performance. The three kinds of job interviews are unstructured, structured, and semistructured interviews.

11-4 (p. 234) Describe how to determine training needs and select the appropriate training methods.

Training is used to give employees the job-specific skills, experience, and knowledge they need to do their jobs or improve their job performance. To make sure training dollars are well spent, companies need to determine specific training needs, select appropriate training methods, and then evaluate the training.

11-5 (p. 237) Discuss how to use performance appraisal to give meaningful performance feedback.

The keys to successful performance appraisal are accurately measuring job performance and effectively sharing performance feedback with employees. Organizations should develop good performance appraisal scales; train raters how to accurately evaluate performance; and impress upon managers the value of providing feedback in a clear, consistent, and fair manner, as well as setting goals and monitoring progress toward those goals.

KEY TERMS

Human resource management (HRM) the process of finding, developing, and keeping the right people to form a qualified work force

Bona fide occupational qualification (BFOQ) an exception in employment law that permits sex, age, religion, and the like to be used when making employment decisions, but only if they are "reasonably necessary to the normal operation of that particular business." BFOQs are strictly monitored by the Equal Employment Opportunity Commission

Disparate treatment intentional discrimination that occurs when people are purposely not given the same hiring, promotion, or membership opportunities because of their race, color, sex, age, ethnic group, national origin, or religious beliefs

Adverse impact unintentional discrimination that occurs when members of a particular race, sex, or ethnic group are unintentionally harmed or disadvantaged because they are hired, promoted, or trained (or any other employment decision) at substantially lower rates than others

Four-fifths (or 80 percent) rule a rule of thumb used by the courts and the EEOC to determine whether there is evidence of adverse impact. A violation of this rule occurs when the selection rate for a protected group is less than 80 percent, or four-fifths, of the selection rate for a nonprotected group

Sexual harassment a form of discrimination in which unwelcome sexual advances, requests for sexual favors, or other verbal or physical conduct of a sexual nature occurs while performing one's job

Quid pro quo sexual harassment a form of sexual harassment in which employment outcomes, such as hiring, promotion, or simply keeping one's job, depend on whether an individual submits to sexual harassment

Hostile work environment a form of sexual harassment in which unwelcome and demeaning sexually related behavior creates an intimidating and offensive work environment

Recruiting the process of developing a pool of qualified job applicants

Job analysis a purposeful, systematic process for collecting information on the important work-related aspects of a job

Job description a written description of the basic tasks, duties, and responsibilities required of an employee holding a particular job

Job specifications a written summary of the qualifications needed to successfully perform a particular job

11-6 (p. 241) Describe basic compensation strategies and discuss the four kinds of employee separations.

Compensation includes both the financial and the nonfinancial rewards that organizations give employees in exchange for their work. There are three basic kinds of compensation decisions: pay level, pay variability, and pay structure. Employee separation is the loss of an employee, which can occur voluntarily or involuntarily. Companies use downsizing and early retirement incentive programs (ERIPs) to reduce the number of employees in the organization and lower costs. However, companies generally try to keep the rate of employee turnover low to reduce costs associated with finding and developing new employees. Functional turnover, on the other hand, can be good for organizations.

Internal recruiting the process of developing a pool of qualified job applicants from people who already work in the company

External recruiting the process of developing a pool of qualified job applicants from outside the company

Selection the process of gathering information about job applicants to decide who should be offered a job

Validation the process of determining how well a selection test or procedure predicts future job performance. The better or more accurate the prediction of future job performance, the more valid a test is said to be

Human resource information system (HRIS) a computerized system for gathering, analyzing, storing, and disseminating information related to the HRM process

Employment references sources such as previous employers or coworkers who can provide job-related information about job candidates

Background checks procedures used to verify the truthfulness and accuracy of information that applicants provide about themselves and to uncover negative, job-related background information not provided by applicants

Specific ability tests (aptitude tests) tests that measure the extent to which an applicant possesses the particular kind of ability needed to do a job well

Cognitive ability tests tests that measure the extent to which applicants have abilities in perceptual speed, verbal comprehension, numerical aptitude, general reasoning, and spatial aptitude

Biographical data (biodata) extensive surveys that ask applicants questions about their personal backgrounds and life experiences

Work sample tests tests that require applicants to perform tasks that are actually done on the job

Assessment centers a series of managerial simulations, graded by trained observers, that are used to determine applicants' capability for managerial work

Interview a selection tool in which company representatives ask job applicants job-related questions to determine whether they are qualified for the job

Unstructured interviews interviews in which interviewers are free to ask the applicants anything they want

Structured interviews interviews in which all applicants are asked the same set of standardized questions, usually including situational, behavioral, background, and job-knowledge questions

Training developing the skills, experience, and knowledge employees need to perform their jobs or improve their performance

Needs assessment the process of identifying and prioritizing the learning needs of employees

Performance appraisal the process of assessing how well employees are doing their jobs

Objective performance measures measures of job performance that are easily and directly counted or quantified

Subjective performance measures measures of job performance that require someone to judge or assess a worker's performance

Behavior observation scales (BOSs) rating scales that indicate the frequency with which workers perform specific behaviors that are representative of the job dimensions critical to successful job performance

Rater training training performance appraisal raters in how to avoid rating errors and increase rating accuracy

360-degree feedback a performance appraisal process in which feedback is obtained from the boss, subordinates, peers and coworkers, and the employees themselves

Compensation the financial and nonfinancial rewards that organizations give employees in exchange for their work

Employee separation the voluntary or involuntary loss of an employee

Job evaluation a process that determines the worth of each job in a company by evaluating the market value of the knowledge, skills, and requirements needed to perform it

Piecework a compensation system in which employees are paid a set rate for each item they produce

Commission a compensation system in which employees earn a percentage of each sale they make

Profit sharing a compensation system in which a company pays a percentage of its profits to employees in addition to their regular compensation

Employee stock ownership plan (ESOP) a compensation system that awards employees shares of company stock in addition to their regular compensation

Stock options a compensation system that gives employees the right to purchase shares of stock at a set price, even if the value of the stock increases above that price

Wrongful discharge a legal doctrine that requires employers to have a job-related reason to terminate employees

Downsizing the planned elimination of jobs in a company

Outplacement services employment-counseling services offered to employees who are losing their jobs because of downsizing

Early retirement incentive programs (ERIPs) programs that offer financial benefits to employees to encourage them to retire early

Phased retirement employees transition to retirement by working reduced hours over a period of time before completely retiring

Employee turnover loss of employees who voluntarily choose to leave the company

Functional turnover loss of poor-performing employees who voluntarily choose to leave a company

Dysfunctional turnover loss of high-performing employees who voluntarily choose to leave a company

LEARNING OUTCOMES

12-1 (p. 249) Describe diversity and explain why it matters.

Diversity exists in organizations when there are demographic, cultural, and personal differences among the employees and the customers. A common misconception is that workplace diversity and affirmative action are the same. However, affirmative action is more narrowly focused on demographics; is required by law; and is used to punish companies that discriminate on the basis of race/ethnicity, religion, sex, or national origin. By contrast, diversity is broader in focus (going beyond demographics); voluntary; more positive in that it encourages companies to value all kinds of differences; and, at this time, substantially less controversial than affirmative action. Affirmative action and diversity thus differ in purpose, practice, and the reactions they produce. Diversity also makes good business sense in terms of reducing costs (decreasing turnover and absenteeism and avoiding lawsuits), attracting and retaining talent, and driving business growth (improving marketplace understanding and promoting higher-quality problem solving).

12-2 (p. 253) Understand the special challenges that the dimensions of surface-level diversity pose for managers.

Age, sex, race/ethnicity, and physical and mental disabilities are dimensions of surface-level diversity. Because those dimensions are (usually) easily observed, managers and workers tend to rely on them to form initial impressions and stereotypes. Sometimes this can lead to age, sex, racial/ethnic, or disability discrimination (i.e., treating people differently) in the workplace. In general, older workers, women, people of color or different national origins, and people with disabilities are much less likely to be hired or promoted than are white males. This disparity is often due to incorrect beliefs or stereotypes such as "job performance declines with age," or "women aren't willing to travel on business," or "workers with disabilities aren't as competent as able workers." To reduce discrimination, companies can determine the hiring and promotion rates for different groups, train managers to make hiring and promotion decisions on the basis of specific criteria, and make sure that everyone has equal access to training, mentors, reasonable work accommodations, and assistive technology. Finally, companies need to designate a go-to person to whom employees can talk if they believe they have suffered discrimination.

12-3 (p. 260) Explain how the dimensions of deep-level diversity affect individual behavior and interactions in the workplace.

Deep-level diversity matters because it can reduce prejudice, discrimination, and conflict while increasing social integration. It consists of dispositional and personality differences that can be recognized only through extended interaction with others. Research conducted in different cultures, settings, and languages indicates that there are five basic dimensions of personality: extraversion, emotional stability, agreeableness, conscientiousness, and openness to experience. Of these, conscientiousness is perhaps the most important because conscientious workers tend to be better performers on virtually any job. Extraversion is also related to performance in jobs that require significant interaction with others.

KEY TERMS

Diversity a variety of demographic, cultural, and personal differences among an organization's employees and customers

Affirmative action purposeful steps taken by an organization to create employment opportunities for minorities and women

Surface-level diversity differences such as age, sex, race/ethnicity, and physical disabilities that are observable, typically unchangeable, and easy to measure

Deep-level diversity differences such as personality and attitudes that are communicated through verbal and nonverbal behaviors and are learned only through extended interaction with others

Social integration the degree to which group members are psychologically attracted to working with each other to accomplish a common objective

Age discrimination treating people differently (e.g., in hiring and firing, promotion, and compensation decisions) because of their age

Sex discrimination treating people differently because of their sex

Glass ceiling the invisible barrier that prevents women and minorities from advancing to the top jobs in organizations

Racial and ethnic discrimination treating people differently because of their race or ethnicity

Disability a mental or physical impairment that substantially limits one or more major life activities

Disability discrimination treating people differently because of their disabilities

Disposition the tendency to respond to situations and events in a predetermined manner

Personality the relatively stable set of behaviors, attitudes, and emotions displayed over time that makes people different from each other

Extraversion the degree to which someone is active, assertive, gregarious, sociable, talkative, and energized by others

Emotional stability the degree to which someone is not angry, depressed, anxious, emotional, insecure, and excitable

Agreeableness the degree to which someone is cooperative, polite, flexible, forgiving, good-natured, tolerant, and trusting

12-4 (p. 262) Explain the basic principles and practices that can be used to manage diversity.

The three paradigms for managing diversity are the discrimination and fairness paradigm (equal opportunity, fair treatment, strict compliance with the law), the access and legitimacy paradigm (matching internal diversity to external diversity), and the learning and effectiveness paradigm (achieving organizational plurality by integrating deep-level diversity into the work of the organization). Unlike the other paradigms that focus on surface-level differences, the learning and effectiveness paradigm values common ground, distinguishes between individual and group differences, minimizes conflict and divisiveness, and focuses on bringing different talents and perspectives together. What principles can companies use when managing diversity? Follow and enforce federal and state laws regarding equal employment opportunity. Treat group differences as important but not special. Find the common ground. Tailor opportunities to individuals, not groups. Solicit negative as well as positive feedback. Set high but realistic goals. The two types of diversity training are awareness training and skills-based diversity training. Companies also manage diversity through diversity audits and diversity pairing and by having top executives experience what it is like to be in the minority.

Paradigms for Managing Diversity

DIVERSITY PARADIGM	FOCUS	SUCCESS MEASURED BY	BENEFITS	LIMITATIONS
Discrimination & Fairness	Equal opportunity Fair treatment Recruitment of minorities Strict compliance with laws	Recruitment, promotion, and retention goals for underrepresented group	Fairer treatment Increased demographic diversity	Focus on surface-level diversity
Access & Legitimacy	Acceptance and celebration of differences	Diversity in company matches diversity of primary stakeholders	Establishes a clear business reason for diversity	Focus on surface-level diversity
Learning & Effectiveness	Integrating deep-level differences into organization	Valuing people on the basis of individual knowledge, skills, and abilities	Values common ground Distinction between individual and group differences Less conflict, backlash, and divisiveness Bringing different talents and perspectives together	Focus on deep-level diversity, which is more difficult to measure and quantify

© Cengage Learning

Conscientiousness the degree to which someone is organized, hardworking, responsible, persevering, thorough, and achievement oriented

Openness to experience the degree to which someone is curious, broad-minded, and open to new ideas, things, and experiences; is spontaneous; and has a high tolerance for ambiguity

Organizational plurality a work environment where (1) all members are empowered to contribute in a way that maximizes the benefits to the organization, customers, and themselves, and (2) the individuality of each member is respected by not segmenting or polarizing people on the basis of their membership in a particular group

Awareness training training that is designed to raise employees' awareness of diversity issues and to challenge the underlying assumptions or stereotypes they may have about others

Skills-based diversity training training that teaches employees the practical skills they need for managing a diverse work force, such as flexibility and adaptability, negotiation, problem solving, and conflict resolution

Diversity audits formal assessments that measure employee and management attitudes, investigate the extent to which people are advantaged or disadvantaged with respect to hiring and promotions, and review companies' diversity-related policies and procedures

Diversity pairing a mentoring program in which people of different cultural backgrounds, sexes, or races/ethnicities are paired together to get to know each other and change stereotypical beliefs and attitudes

REVIEW 13

LEARNING OUTCOMES

13-1 (p. 269) Explain the basics of motivation.

Motivation is the set of forces that initiates, directs, and makes people persist in their efforts over time to accomplish a goal. Managers often confuse motivation and performance, but job performance is a multiplicative function of motivation times ability times situational constraints. Needs are the physical or psychological requirements that must be met to ensure survival and well-being. Different motivational theories (Maslow's Hierarchy of Needs, Alderfer's ERG Theory, and McClelland's Learned Needs Theory) specify a number of different needs. However, studies show that there are only two general kinds of needs: lower-order needs and higher-order needs. Both extrinsic and intrinsic rewards motivate people.

13-2 (p. 274) Use equity theory to explain how employees' perceptions of fairness affect motivation.

The basic components of equity theory are inputs, outcomes, and referents. After an internal comparison in which employees compare their outcomes to their inputs, they then make an external comparison in which they compare their O/I ratio with the O/I ratio of a referent, a person who works in a similar job or is otherwise similar. When their O/I ratio is equal to the referent's O/I ratio, employees perceive that they are being treated fairly. But, when their O/I ratio is lower than or higher than their referent's O/I ratio, they perceive that they have been treated inequitably or unfairly. There are two kinds of inequity: underreward and overreward. Underreward, which occurs when a referent's O/I ratio is higher than the employee's O/I ratio, leads to anger or frustration. Overreward, which occurs when a referent's O/I ratio is lower than the employee's O/I ratio, can lead to guilt but only when the level of overreward is extreme.

13-3 (p. 279) Use expectancy theory to describe how workers' expectations about rewards, effort, and the link between rewards and performance influence motivation.

Expectancy theory holds that three factors affect the conscious choices people make about their motivation: valence, expectancy, and instrumentality. Expectancy theory holds that all three factors must be high for people to be highly motivated. If any one of these factors declines, overall motivation will decline, too.

13-4 (p. 282) Explain how reinforcement theory works and how it can be used to motivate.

Reinforcement theory says that behavior is a function of its consequences. Reinforcement has two parts: reinforcement contingencies and schedules of reinforcement. The four kinds of reinforcement contingencies are positive reinforcement and negative reinforcement, which strengthen behavior, and punishment and extinction, which weaken behavior. There are two kinds of reinforcement schedules, continuous and intermittent; intermittent schedules, in turn, can be divided into fixed and variable interval schedules and fixed and variable ratio schedules.

13-5 (p. 286) Describe the components of goal-setting theory and how managers can use them to motivate workers.

A goal is a target, objective, or result that someone tries to accomplish. Goal-setting theory says that people will be motivated to the extent to which they accept specific,

KEY TERMS

Motivation the set of forces that initiates, directs, and makes people persist in their efforts to accomplish a goal

Needs the physical or psychological requirements that must be met to ensure survival and well-being

Extrinsic reward a reward that is tangible, visible to others, and given to employees contingent on the performance of specific tasks or behaviors

Intrinsic reward a natural reward associated with performing a task or activity for its own sake

Equity theory a theory that states that people will be motivated when they perceive that they are being treated fairly

Inputs in equity theory, the contributions employees make to the organization

Outcomes in equity theory, the rewards employees receive for their contributions to the organization

Referents in equity theory, others with whom people compare themselves to determine if they have been treated fairly

Outcome/input (O/I) ratio in equity theory, an employee's perception of how the rewards received from an organization compare with the employee's contributions to that organization

Underreward a form of inequity in which you are getting fewer outcomes relative to inputs than your referent is getting

Overreward a form of inequity in which you are getting more outcomes relative to inputs than your referent

Distributive justice the perceived degree to which outcomes and rewards are fairly distributed or allocated

Procedural justice the perceived fairness of the process used to make reward allocation decisions

Expectancy theory the theory that people will be motivated to the extent to which they believe that their efforts will lead to good performance, that good performance will be rewarded, and that they will be offered attractive rewards

Valence the attractiveness or desirability of a reward or outcome

Expectancy the perceived relationship between effort and performance

Instrumentality the perceived relationship between performance and rewards

Reinforcement theory the theory that behavior is a function of its consequences, that behaviors followed by positive consequences will occur more frequently, and that behaviors followed by negative consequences, or not followed by positive consequences, will occur less frequently

challenging goals and receive feedback that indicates their progress toward goal achievement. The basic components of goal-setting theory are goal specificity, goal difficulty, goal acceptance, and performance feedback. Goal specificity is the extent to which goals are detailed, exact, and unambiguous. Goal difficulty is the extent to which a goal is hard or challenging to accomplish. Goal acceptance is the extent to which people consciously understand and agree to goals. Performance feedback is information about the quality or quantity of past performance and indicates whether progress is being made toward the accomplishment of a goal.

13-6 (p. 289) Discuss how the entire motivation model can be used to motivate workers.

Motivating with the Integrated Model

MOTIVATING WITH	MANAGERS SHOULD . . .
THE BASICS	• Ask people what their needs are. • Satisfy lower-order needs first. • Expect people's needs to change. • As needs change and lower-order needs are satisfied, satisfy higher-order needs by looking for ways to allow employees to experience intrinsic rewards.
EQUITY THEORY	• Look for and correct major inequities. • Reduce employees' inputs. • Make sure decision-making processes are fair.
EXPECTANCY THEORY	• Systematically gather information to find out what employees want from their jobs. • Take specific steps to link rewards to individual performance in a way that is clear and understandable to employees. • Empower employees to make decisions if management really wants them to believe that their hard work and efforts will lead to good performance.
REINFORCEMENT THEORY	• Identify, measure, analyze, intervene, and evaluate critical performance-related behaviors. • Don't reinforce the wrong behaviors. • Correctly administer punishment at the appropriate time. • Choose the simplest and most effective schedules of reinforcement.
GOAL-SETTING THEORY	• Assign specific, challenging goals. • Make sure workers truly accept organizational goals. • Provide frequent, specific, performance-related feedback.

© Cengage Learning

Reinforcement the process of changing behavior by changing the consequences that follow behavior

Reinforcement contingencies cause-and-effect relationships between the performance of specific behaviors and specific consequences

Schedule of reinforcement rules that specify which behaviors will be reinforced, which consequences will follow those behaviors, and the schedule by which those consequences will be delivered

Positive reinforcement reinforcement that strengthens behavior by following behaviors with desirable consequences

Negative reinforcement reinforcement that strengthens behavior by withholding an unpleasant consequence when employees perform a specific behavior

Punishment reinforcement that weakens behavior by following behaviors with undesirable consequences

Extinction reinforcement in which a positive consequence is no longer allowed to follow a previously reinforced behavior, thus weakening the behavior

Continuous reinforcement schedule a schedule that requires a consequence to be administered following every instance of a behavior

Intermittent reinforcement schedule a schedule in which consequences are delivered after a specified or average time has elapsed or after a specified or average number of behaviors has occurred

Fixed interval reinforcement schedule an intermittent schedule in which consequences follow a behavior only after a fixed time has elapsed

Variable interval reinforcement schedule an intermittent schedule in which the time between a behavior and the following consequences varies around a specified average

Fixed ratio reinforcement schedule an intermittent schedule in which consequences are delivered following a specific number of behaviors

Variable ratio reinforcement schedule an intermittent schedule in which consequences are delivered following a different number of behaviors, sometimes more and sometimes less, that vary around a specified average number of behaviors

Goal a target, objective, or result that someone tries to accomplish

Goal-setting theory the theory that people will be motivated to the extent to which they accept specific, challenging goals and receive feedback that indicates their progress toward goal achievement

Goal specificity the extent to which goals are detailed, exact, and unambiguous

Goal difficulty the extent to which a goal is hard or challenging to accomplish

Goal acceptance the extent to which people consciously understand and agree to goals

Performance feedback information about the quality or quantity of past performance that indicates whether progress is being made toward the accomplishment of a goal

REVIEW 14

LEARNING OUTCOMES

14-1 (p. 291) Explain what leadership is.

Management is getting work done through others; leadership is the process of influencing others to achieve group or organizational goals. Leaders are different from managers. The primary difference is that leaders are concerned with doing the right thing, while managers are concerned with doing things right. Organizations need both managers and leaders. But, in general, companies are overmanaged and underled.

14-2 (p. 292) Describe who leaders are and what effective leaders do.

Trait theory says that effective leaders possess traits or characteristics that differentiate them from nonleaders. Those traits are drive, the desire to lead, honesty/integrity, self-confidence, emotional stability, cognitive ability, and knowledge of the business. These traits alone aren't enough for successful leadership; leaders who have many or all of them must also behave in ways that encourage people to achieve group or organizational goals. Two key leader behaviors are initiating structure, which improves subordinate performance, and consideration, which improves subordinate satisfaction. There is no ideal combination of these behaviors. The best leadership style depends on the situation.

14-3 (p. 297) Explain Fiedler's contingency theory.

Fiedler's contingency theory assumes that leaders are effective when their work groups perform well, that leaders are unable to change their leadership styles, that leadership styles must be matched to the proper situations, and that favorable situations permit leaders to influence group members. According to the Least Preferred Coworker (LPC) scale, there are two basic leadership styles. People who describe their LPC in a positive way have a relationship-oriented leadership style. By contrast, people who describe their LPC in a negative way have a task-oriented leadership style. Situational favorableness, which occurs when leaders can influence followers, is determined by leader-member relations, task structure, and position power. In general, relationship-oriented leaders with high LPC scores are better leaders under moderately favorable situations, whereas task-oriented leaders with low LPC scores are better leaders in highly favorable and highly unfavorable situations. Since Fiedler assumes that leaders are incapable of changing their leadership styles, the key is to accurately measure and match leaders to situations or to teach leaders how to change situational factors. Though matching or placing leaders in appropriate situations works well, reengineering situations to fit leadership styles doesn't, because the complexity of the model makes it difficult for people to understand.

14-4 (p. 300) Describe how path–goal theory works.

Path-goal theory states that leaders can increase subordinate satisfaction and performance by clarifying and clearing the paths to goals and by increasing the number and kinds of rewards available for goal attainment. For this to work, however, leader behavior must be a source of immediate or future satisfaction for followers and must complement and not duplicate the characteristics of followers' work environments. In contrast to Fiedler's contingency theory, path-goal theory assumes that leaders can and do change their leadership styles (directive, supportive, participative, and achievement-oriented), depending on their subordinates (experience, perceived ability, and internal or external locus of control) and the environment in which those subordinates work (task structure, formal authority system, and primary work group).

KEY TERMS

Leadership the process of influencing others to achieve group or organizational goals

Trait theory a leadership theory that holds that effective leaders possess a similar set of traits or characteristics

Traits relatively stable characteristics, such as abilities, psychological motives, or consistent patterns of behavior

Initiating structure the degree to which a leader structures the roles of followers by setting goals, giving directions, setting deadlines, and assigning tasks

Consideration the extent to which a leader is friendly, approachable, and supportive and shows concern for employees

Leadership style the way a leader generally behaves toward followers

Contingency theory a leadership theory that states that in order to maximize work group performance, leaders must be matched to the situation that best fits their leadership style

Situational favorableness the degree to which a particular situation either permits or denies a leader the chance to influence the behavior of group members

Leader-member relations the degree to which followers respect, trust, and like their leaders

Task structure the degree to which the requirements of a subordinate's tasks are clearly specified

Position power the degree to which leaders are able to hire, fire, reward, and punish workers

Path-goal theory a leadership theory that states that leaders can increase subordinate satisfaction and performance by clarifying and clearing the paths to goals and by increasing the number and kinds of rewards available for goal attainment

Directive leadership a leadership style in which the leader lets employees know precisely what is expected of them, gives them specific guidelines for performing tasks, schedules work, sets standards of performance, and makes sure that people follow standard rules and regulations

Supportive leadership a leadership style in which the leader is friendly and approachable to employees, shows concern for employees and their welfare, treats them as equals, and creates a friendly climate

Participative leadership a leadership style in which the leader consults employees for their suggestions and input before making decisions

14-5 (p. 304) Explain the normative decision theory.

The normative decision theory helps leaders decide how much employee participation should be used when making decisions. Using the right degree of employee participation improves the quality of decisions and the extent to which employees accept and are committed to decisions. The theory specifies five different decision styles or ways of making decisions: autocratic decisions (AI or AII), consultative decisions (CI or CII), and group decisions (GII). The theory improves decision quality via decision rules concerning quality, leader information, subordinate information, goal congruence, and problem structure. The theory improves employee commitment and acceptance via decision rules related to commitment probability, subordinate conflict, and commitment requirement. These decision rules help leaders improve decision quality and follower acceptance and commitment by eliminating decision styles that don't fit the decision or situation the group or organization is facing. Normative decision theory operationalizes these decision rules in the form of yes/no questions, as shown in the decision tree displayed in Exhibit 14.8.

14-6 (p. 306) Explain how visionary leadership (i.e., charismatic and transformational leadership) helps leaders achieve strategic leadership.

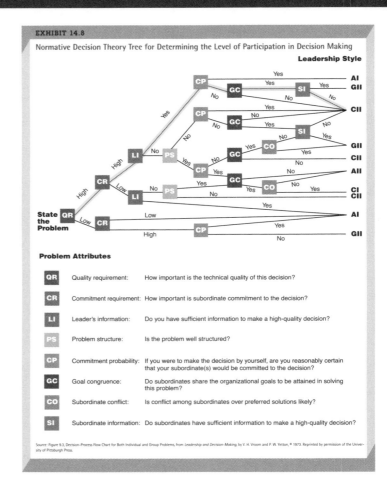

EXHIBIT 14.8

Normative Decision Theory Tree for Determining the Level of Participation in Decision Making

Problem Attributes

QR	Quality requirement:	How important is the technical quality of this decision?
CR	Commitment requirement:	How important is subordinate commitment to the decision?
LI	Leader's information:	Do you have sufficient information to make a high-quality decision?
PS	Problem structure:	Is the problem well structured?
CP	Commitment probability:	If you were to make the decision by yourself, are you reasonably certain that your subordinate(s) would be committed to the decision?
GC	Goal congruence:	Do subordinates share the organizational goals to be attained in solving this problem?
CO	Subordinate conflict:	Is conflict among subordinates over preferred solutions likely?
SI	Subordinate information:	Do subordinates have sufficient information to make a high-quality decision?

Source: Figure 9.3, Decision-Process Flow Chart for Both Individual and Group Problems, from *Leadership and Decision-Making*, by V. H. Vroom and P. W. Yetton, © 1973. Reprinted by permission of the University of Pittsburgh Press.

Strategic leadership requires visionary leadership, which can be charismatic and transformational. Visionary leadership creates a positive image of the future that motivates organizational members and provides direction for future planning and goal setting. Charismatic leaders have strong, confident, dynamic personalities that attract followers, enable the leader to create strong bonds, and inspire followers to accomplish the leader's vision. Followers of ethical charismatic leaders work harder, are more committed and satisfied, are better performers, and are more likely to trust their leaders. Followers can be just as supportive and committed to unethical charismatics, but these leaders can pose a tremendous risk for companies. Unethical charismatics control and manipulate followers and do what is best for themselves instead of their organizations. Transformational leadership goes beyond charismatic leadership by generating awareness and acceptance of a group's purpose and mission and by getting employees to see beyond their own needs and self-interests for the good of the group. The four components of transformational leadership are charismatic leadership or idealized influence, inspirational motivation, intellectual stimulation, and individualized consideration.

Achievement-oriented leadership a leadership style in which the leader sets challenging goals, has high expectations of employees, and displays confidence that employees will assume responsibility and put forth extraordinary effort

Normative decision theory a theory that suggests how leaders can determine an appropriate amount of employee participation when making decisions

Strategic leadership the ability to anticipate, envision, maintain flexibility, think strategically, and work with others to initiate changes that will create a positive future for an organization

Visionary leadership leadership that creates a positive image of the future that motivates organizational members and provides direction for future planning and goal setting

Charismatic leadership the behavioral tendencies and personal characteristics of leaders that create an exceptionally strong relationship between them and their followers

Ethical charismatics charismatic leaders who provide developmental opportunities for followers, are open to positive and negative feedback, recognize others' contributions, share information, and have moral standards that emphasize the larger interests of the group, organization, or society

Unethical charismatics charismatic leaders who control and manipulate followers, do what is best for themselves instead of their organizations, want to hear only positive feedback, share only information that is beneficial to themselves, and have moral standards that put their interests before everyone else's

Transformational leadership leadership that generates awareness and acceptance of a group's purpose and mission and gets employees to see beyond their own needs and self-interests for the good of the group

Transactional leadership leadership based on an exchange process, in which followers are rewarded for good performance and punished for poor performance

REVIEW 15

LEARNING OUTCOMES

15-1 (p. 315) Explain the role that perception plays in communication and communication problems.

Perception is the process by which people attend to, organize, interpret, and retain information from their environments. Perception is not a straightforward process. Because of perceptual filters such as selective perception and closure, people exposed to the same information or stimuli often end up with very different perceptions and understandings. Perception-based differences can also lead to differences in the attributions (internal or external) that managers and workers make when explaining workplace behavior. In general, workers are more likely to explain behavior from a

defensive bias, in which they attribute problems to external causes (i.e., the situation). Managers, on the other hand, tend to commit the fundamental attribution error, attributing problems to internal causes (i.e., the worker made a mistake or error). Consequently, when things go wrong, it's common for managers to blame workers and for workers to blame the situation or context in which they do their jobs. Finally, this problem is compounded by a self-serving bias that leads people to attribute successes to internal causes and failures to external causes. So, when workers receive negative feedback from managers, they may become defensive and emotional and not hear what their managers have to say. In short, perceptions and attributions represent a significant challenge to effective communication and understanding in organizations.

EXHIBIT 15.1

Basic Perception Process

Stimulus | Stimulus | Stimulus

Perceptual **Attention** Filter

Perceptual **Organization** Filter

Perceptual **Interpretation** Filter

Perceptual **Retention** Filter

Perception

© Cengage Learning

15-2 (p. 319) Describe the communication process and the various kinds of communication in organizations.

Organizational communication depends on the communication process, formal and informal communication channels, one-on-one communication, and nonverbal communication. The major components of the communication process are the sender, the receiver, noise, and feedback. Senders often mistakenly assume that they can pipe their intended messages directly into receivers' heads with perfect clarity. Formal communication channels such as downward, upward, and horizontal communication

KEY TERMS

Communication the process of transmitting information from one person or place to another

Perception the process by which individuals attend to, organize, interpret, and retain information from their environments

Perceptual filters the personality-, psychology-, or experience-based differences that influence people to ignore or pay attention to particular stimuli

Selective perception the tendency to notice and accept objects and information consistent with our values, beliefs, and expectations, while ignoring or screening out inconsistent information

Closure the tendency to fill in gaps of missing information by assuming that what we don't know is consistent with what we already know

Attribution theory the theory that we all have a basic need to understand and explain the causes of other people's behavior

Defensive bias the tendency for people to perceive themselves as personally and situationally similar to someone who is having difficulty or trouble

Fundamental attribution error the tendency to ignore external causes of behavior and to attribute other people's actions to internal causes

Self-serving bias the tendency to overestimate our value by attributing successes to ourselves (internal causes) and attributing failures to others or the environment (external causes)

Encoding putting a message into a written, verbal, or symbolic form that can be recognized and understood by the receiver

Decoding the process by which the receiver translates the written, verbal, or symbolic form of a message into an understood message

Feedback to sender in the communication process, a return message to the sender that indicates the receiver's understanding of the message

Noise anything that interferes with the transmission of the intended message

Jargon vocabulary particular to a profession or group that interferes with communication in the workplace

Formal communication channel the system of official channels that carry organizationally approved messages and information

carry organizationally approved messages and information. By contrast, the informal communication channel, called the *grapevine*, arises out of curiosity and is carried out through gossip or cluster chains. There are two kinds of one-on-one communication. Coaching is used to improve on-the-job performance, while counseling is used to communicate about non-job-related issues affecting job performance. Nonverbal communication, such as kinesics and paralanguage, accounts for as much as 93 percent of the transmission of a message's content.

15-3 (p. 325) Explain how managers can manage effective one-on-one communication.

One-on-one communication can be managed by choosing the right communication medium, being a good listener, and giving effective feedback. Managers generally prefer oral communication because it provides the opportunity to ask questions and assess nonverbal communication. Oral communication is best suited to complex, ambiguous, or emotionally laden topics. Written communication is best suited for delivering straightforward messages and information. Listening is important for managerial success, but most people are terrible listeners. To improve your listening skills, choose to be an active listener (clarify responses, paraphrase, and summarize) and an empathetic listener (show your desire to understand, reflect feelings). Feedback can be constructive or destructive. To be constructive, feedback must be immediate, focused on specific behaviors, and problem-oriented.

EXHIBIT 15.3
The Interpersonal Communication Process

© Burke/Triolo Productions/Brand X Pictures/Jupiterimages / © TongRo Image Stock/Jupiterimages

15-4 (p. 329) Describe how managers can manage effective organization-wide communication.

Managers need methods for managing organization-wide communication and for making themselves accessible so that they can hear what employees throughout their organizations are feeling and thinking. Email, collaborative discussion sites, televised/videotaped speeches and conferences, and broadcast voice mail make it much easier for managers to improve message transmission and get the message out. By contrast, anonymous company hotlines, survey feedback, frequent informal meetings, and surprise visits help managers avoid organizational silence and improve reception by giving them the opportunity to hear what others in the organization think and feel. Monitoring internal and external blogs is another way to find out what people are saying and thinking about your organization.

Downward communication communication that flows from higher to lower levels in an organization

Upward communication communication that flows from lower to higher levels in an organization

Horizontal communication communication that flows among managers and workers who are at the same organizational level

Informal communication channel (grapevine) the transmission of messages from employee to employee outside of formal communication channels

Coaching communicating with someone for the direct purpose of improving the person's on-the-job performance or behavior

Counseling communicating with someone about non-job-related issues that may be affecting or interfering with the person's performance

Nonverbal communication any communication that doesn't involve words

Kinesics movements of the body and face

Paralanguage the pitch, rate, tone, volume, and speaking pattern (i.e., use of silences, pauses, or hesitations) of one's voice

Communication medium the method used to deliver an oral or written message

Hearing the act or process of perceiving sounds

Listening making a conscious effort to hear

Active listening assuming half the responsibility for successful communication by actively giving the speaker nonjudgmental feedback that shows you've accurately heard what he or she said

Empathetic listening understanding the speaker's perspective and personal frame of reference and giving feedback that conveys that understanding to the speaker

Destructive feedback feedback that disapproves without any intention of being helpful and almost always causes a negative or defensive reaction in the recipient

Constructive feedback feedback intended to be helpful, corrective, and/or encouraging

Online discussion forums the in-house equivalent of Internet newsgroups. By using web- or software-based discussion tools that are available across the company, employees can easily ask questions and share knowledge with each other

Televised/videotaped speeches and meetings speeches and meetings originally made to a smaller audience that are either simultaneously broadcast to other locations in the company or videotaped for subsequent distribution and viewing

Organizational silence when employees withhold information about organizational problems or issues

Company hotlines phone numbers that anyone in the company can call anonymously to leave information for upper management

Survey feedback information that is collected by surveys from organizational members and then compiled, disseminated, and used to develop action plans for improvement

Blog a personal website that provides personal opinions or recommendations, news summaries, and reader comments

REVIEW 16

LEARNING OUTCOMES

16-1 (p. 337) Describe the basic control process.

The control process begins by setting standards and then measuring performance and comparing performance to the standards. The better a company's information and measurement systems, the easier it is to make these comparisons. The control process continues by identifying and analyzing performance deviations and then developing and implementing programs for corrective action. Control is a continuous, dynamic, cybernetic process, not a one-time achievement or result. Control requires frequent managerial attention. The three basic control methods are feedback control (after-the-fact performance information), concurrent control (simultaneous performance information), and feedforward control (preventive performance information). Control has regulation costs and unanticipated consequences and therefore isn't always worthwhile or possible.

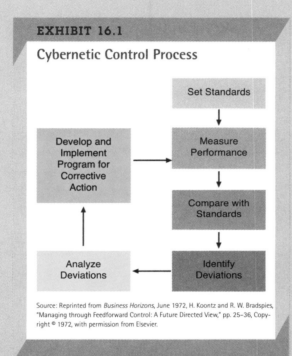

EXHIBIT 16.1

Cybernetic Control Process

Set Standards → Measure Performance → Compare with Standards → Identify Deviations → Analyze Deviations → Develop and Implement Program for Corrective Action → (back to Measure Performance)

Source: Reprinted from *Business Horizons*, June 1972, H. Koontz and R. W. Bradspies, "Managing through Feedforward Control: A Future Directed View," pp. 25–36, Copyright © 1972, with permission from Elsevier.

16-2 (p. 341) Discuss the various methods that managers can use to maintain control.

There are five methods of control: bureaucratic, objective, normative, concertive, and self-control (self-management). Bureaucratic and objective controls are top-down, management-based, and measurement-based. Normative and concertive controls represent shared forms of control because they evolve from company-wide or team-based beliefs and values. Self-control, or self-management, is a control system in which managers and workers control their own behavior.

Bureaucratic control is based on organizational policies, rules, and procedures. Objective control is based on reliable measures of behavior or outputs. Normative control is based on strong corporate beliefs and careful hiring practices. Concertive control is based on the development of values, beliefs, and rules in autonomous work groups. Self-control is based on individuals setting their own goals, monitoring themselves, and rewarding or punishing themselves with respect to goal achievement.

Each of these control methods may be more or less appropriate depending on the circumstances.

KEY TERMS

Control a regulatory process of establishing standards to achieve organizational goals, comparing actual performance against the standards, and taking corrective action when necessary

Standards a basis of comparison for measuring the extent to which various kinds of organizational performance are satisfactory or unsatisfactory

Benchmarking the process of identifying outstanding practices, processes, and standards in other companies and adapting them to your company

Cybernetic the process of steering or keeping on course

Feedback control a mechanism for gathering information about performance deficiencies after they occur

Concurrent control a mechanism for gathering information about performance deficiencies as they occur, thereby eliminating or shortening the delay between performance and feedback

Feedforward control a mechanism for monitoring performance inputs rather than outputs to prevent or minimize performance deficiencies before they occur

Control loss the situation in which behavior and work procedures do not conform to standards

Regulation costs the costs associated with implementing or maintaining control

Cybernetic feasibility the extent to which it is possible to implement each step in the control process

Bureaucratic control the use of hierarchical authority to influence employee behavior by rewarding or punishing employees for compliance or noncompliance with organizational policies, rules, and procedures

Objective control the use of observable measures of worker behavior or outputs to assess performance and influence behavior

Behavior control the regulation of the behaviors and actions that workers perform on the job

Output control the regulation of workers' results or outputs through rewards and incentives

Normative control the regulation of workers' behavior and decisions through widely shared organizational values and beliefs

Concertive control the regulation of workers' behavior and decisions through work group values and beliefs

16-3 (p. 345) Describe the behaviors, processes, and outcomes that today's managers are choosing to control in their organizations.

Deciding what to control is just as important as deciding whether to control or how to control. In most companies, performance is measured using financial measures alone. However, the balanced scorecard encourages managers to measure and control company performance from four perspectives: financial, customer, internal, and innovation and learning. Traditionally, financial control has been achieved through cash flow analysis, balance sheets, income statements, financial ratios, and budgets. (For a refresher on these traditional financial control tools, see the Financial Review Card.) Another way to measure and control financial performance is to evaluate economic value added (EVA). Unlike traditional financial measures, EVA helps managers assess whether they are performing well enough to pay the cost of the capital needed to run the business. Instead of using customer satisfaction surveys to measure performance, companies should pay attention to customer defections, as customers who leave are more likely to speak up about what the company is doing wrong. From the internal perspective, performance is often measured in terms of quality, which is defined in three ways: excellence, value, and conformance to specifications. Minimizing waste has become an important part of innovation and learning in companies. The four levels of waste minimization are waste prevention and reduction, recycling and reuse, waste treatment, and waste disposal.

EXHIBIT 16.5

Advantages and Disadvantages of Different Measures of Quality

QUALITY MEASURE	ADVANTAGES	DISADVANTAGES
Excellence	Promotes clear organizational vision.	Provides little practical guidance for managers.
Excellence	Being/providing the "best" motivates and inspires managers and employees.	Excellence is ambiguous. What is it? Who defines it?
Value	Appeals to customers who know excellence "when they see it."	Difficult to measure and control.
Value	Customers recognize differences in value.	Can be difficult to determine what factors influence whether a product/service is seen as having value.
Value	Easier to measure and compare whether products/services differ in value.	Controlling the balance between excellence and cost (i.e., affordable excellence) can be difficult.
Conformance to Specifications	If specifications can be written, conformance to specifications is usually measurable.	Many products/services cannot be easily evaluated in terms of conformance to specifications.
Conformance to Specifications	Should lead to increased efficiency.	Promotes standardization, so may hurt performance when adapting to changes is more important.
Conformance to Specifications	Promotes consistency in quality.	May be less appropriate for services, which are dependent on a high degree of human contact.

Source: Republished by The Academy of Management, P.O. Box 3020, Briar Cliff Manor, NY, 10510-8020; C. A. Reeves and D. A. Bednar, "Defining Quality: Alternatives and Implications," *Academy of Management Review* 19 (1994): 419–445. Reproduced by permission of the publisher via Copyright Clearance Center, Inc.

Self-control (self-management) a control system in which managers and workers control their own behavior by setting their own goals, monitoring their own progress, and rewarding themselves for goal achievement

Balanced scorecard measurement of organizational performance in four equally important areas: finances, customers, internal operations, and innovation and learning

Suboptimization performance improvement in one part of an organization but only at the expense of decreased performance in another part

Cash flow analysis a type of analysis that predicts how changes in a business will affect its ability to take in more cash than it pays out

Balance sheets accounting statements that provide a snapshot of a company's financial position at a particular time

Income statements accounting statements, also called "profit and loss statements," that show what has happened to an organization's income, expenses, and net profit over a period of time

Financial ratios calculations typically used to track a business's liquidity (cash), efficiency, and profitability over time compared to other businesses in its industry

Budgets quantitative plans through which managers decide how to allocate available money to best accomplish company goals

Economic value added (EVA) the amount by which company profits (revenues, minus expenses, minus taxes) exceed the cost of capital in a given year

Customer defections a performance assessment in which companies identify which customers are leaving and measure the rate at which they are leaving

Value customer perception that the product quality is excellent for the price offered

Basic Accounting Tools for Controlling Financial Performance

STEPS FOR A BASIC CASH FLOW ANALYSIS

1. Forecast sales (steady, up, or down).
2. Project changes in anticipated cash inflows (as a result of changes).
3. Project anticipated cash outflows (as a result of changes).
4. Project net cash flows by combining anticipated cash inflows and outflows.

PARTS OF A BASIC BALANCE SHEET (ASSETS = LIABILITIES + OWNER'S EQUITY)

1. Assets
   a. Current assets (cash, short-term investment, marketable securities, accounts receivable, etc.)
   b. Fixed assets (land, buildings, machinery, equipment, etc.)
2. Liabilities
   a. Current liabilities (accounts payable, notes payable, taxes payable, etc.)
   b. Long-term liabilities (long-term debt, deferred income taxes, etc.)
3. Owner's Equity
   a. Preferred stock and common stock
   b. Additional paid-in capital
   c. Retained earnings

BASIC INCOME STATEMENT

SALES REVENUE
− sales returns and allowances
+ other income
= NET REVENUE
− cost of goods sold (beginning inventory, costs of goods purchased, ending inventory)
= GROSS PROFIT
− total operating expenses (selling, general, and administrative expenses)
= INCOME FROM OPERATIONS
− interest expense
= PRETAX INCOME
− income taxes
= NET INCOME

Common Kinds of Budgets

Revenue Budgets—used to project or forecast future sales.	• Accuracy of projection depends on economy, competitors, sales force estimates, etc. • Determined by estimating future sales volume and sales prices for all products and services.
Expense Budgets—used within departments and divisions to determine how much will be spent on various supplies, projects, or activities.	• One of the first places that companies look for cuts when trying to lower expenses.
Profit Budgets—used by profit centers, which have "profit and loss" responsibility.	• Profit budgets combine revenue and expense budgets into one budget. • Typically used in large businesses with multiple plants and divisions.
Cash Budgets—used to forecast how much cash a company will have on hand to meet expenses.	• Similar to cash-flow analyses. • Used to identify cash shortfalls, which must be covered to pay bills, or cash excesses, which should be invested for a higher return.
Capital Expenditure Budgets—used to forecast large, long-lasting investments in equipment, buildings, and property.	• Help managers identify funding that will be needed to pay for future expansion or strategic moves designed to increase competitive advantage.
Variable Budgets—used to project costs across varying levels of sales and revenues.	• Important because it is difficult to accurately predict sales revenue and volume. • Lead to more accurate budgeting with respect to labor, materials, and administrative expenses, which vary with sales volume and revenues. • Build flexibility into the budgeting process.

Common Financial Ratios

RATIOS	FORMULA	WHAT IT MEANS	WHEN TO USE
LIQUIDITY RATIOS			
Current Ratio	$\dfrac{\text{Current Assets}}{\text{Current Liabilities}}$	• Whether you have enough assets on hand to pay for short-term bills and obligations. • Higher is better. • Recommended level is two times as many current assets as current liabilities.	• Track monthly and quarterly. • Basic measure of your company's health.
Quick (Acid Test) Ratio	$\dfrac{(\text{Current Assets} - \text{Inventories})}{\text{Current Liabilities}}$	• Stricter than current ratio. • Whether you have enough (i.e., cash) to pay short-term bills and obligations. • Higher is better. • Recommended level is one or higher.	• Track monthly. • Also calculate quick ratio with potential customers to evaluate whether they're likely to pay you in a timely manner.
LEVERAGE RATIOS			
Debt to Equity	$\dfrac{\text{Total Liabilities}}{\text{Total Equity}}$	• Indicates how much the company is leveraged (in debt) by comparing what is owed (liabilities) to what is owned (equity). • Lower is better. A high debt-to-equity ratio could indicate that the company has too much debt. • Recommended level depends on industry.	• Track monthly. • Lenders often use this to determine the creditworthiness of a business (i.e., whether to approve additional loans).
Debt Coverage	$\dfrac{(\text{Net Profit} + \text{Noncash Expense})}{\text{Debt}}$	• Indicates how well cash flow covers debt payments. • Higher is better.	• Track monthly. • Lenders look at this ratio to determine if there is adequate cash to make loan payments.
EFFICIENCY RATIOS			
Inventory Turnover	$\dfrac{\text{Cost of Goods Sold}}{\text{Average Value of Inventory}}$	• Whether you're making efficient use of inventory. • Higher is better, indicating that inventory (dollars) isn't purchased (spent) until needed. • Recommended level depends on industry.	• Track monthly by using a twelve-month rolling average.
Average Collections Period	$\dfrac{\text{Accounts Receivable}}{(\text{Annual Net Credit Sales} \div 365)}$	• Shows on average how quickly your customers are paying their bills. • Recommended level is no more than fifteen days longer than credit terms. If credit is net thirty days, then average should not be longer than forty-five days.	• Track monthly. • Use to determine how long company's money is being tied up in customer credit.
PROFITABILITY RATIOS			
Gross Profit Margin	$\dfrac{\text{Gross Profit}}{\text{Total Sales}}$	• Shows how efficiently a business is using its materials and labor in the production process. • Higher is better, indicating that a profit can be made if fixed costs are controlled.	• Track monthly. • Analyze when unsure about product or service pricing. • Low margin compared to competitors means you're underpricing.
Return on Equity	$\dfrac{\text{Net Income}}{\text{Owner's Equity}}$	• Shows what was earned on your investment in the business during a particular period. Often called "return on investment." • Higher is better.	• Track quarterly and annually. • Use to compare to what you might have earned on the stock market, bonds, or government Treasury bills during the same period.

REVIEW 17

LEARNING OUTCOMES

17-1 (p. 357) Explain the strategic importance of information.

The first company to use new information technology to substantially lower costs or differentiate products or services often gains a first-mover advantage, higher profits, and a larger market share. According to the resource-based view of information technology, sustainable competitive advantage occurs when information technology adds value, is different across firms, and is difficult to create or acquire.

17-2 (p. 360) Describe the characteristics of useful information (i.e., its value and costs).

Raw data are facts and figures. Raw data do not become information until they are in a form that can affect decisions and behavior. For information to be useful, it has to be reliable and valid (accurate), of sufficient quantity (complete), pertinent to the problems you're facing (relevant), and available when you need it (timely). Useful information is not cheap. The five costs of obtaining good information are the costs of acquiring, processing, storing, retrieving, and communicating information.

17-3 (p. 363) Explain the basics of capturing, processing, and protecting information.

Electronic data capture (using bar codes, radio frequency identification [RFID] tags, scanners, or optical character recognition), is much faster, easier, and cheaper than manual data capture. Processing information means transforming raw data into meaningful information that can be applied to business decision making. Data mining helps managers with this transformation by discovering unknown patterns and relationships in data. Supervised data mining looks for patterns specified by managers, while unsupervised data mining looks for four general kinds of data patterns: association or affinity patterns, sequence patterns, predictive patterns, and data clusters. Protecting information ensures that data are reliably and consistently retrievable in a usable format by authorized users but no one else. Authentication and authorization, firewalls, antivirus software for PCs and corporate email and network servers, data encryption, virtual private networks (VPNs), and web-based secure sockets layer (SSL) encryption are some of the best ways to protect information. Be careful when using wireless networks, which are easily compromised even when security and encryption protocols are in place.

17-4 (p. 372) Describe how companies can access and share information and knowledge.

Executive information systems, intranets, and corporate portals facilitate internal sharing and access to company information and transactions. Electronic data interchange and the Internet allow external groups like suppliers and customers to easily access company information. Both decrease costs by reducing or eliminating data entry, data errors, and paperwork and by speeding up communication. Organizations use decision support systems and expert systems to capture and share specialized knowledge with nonexpert employees.

KEY TERMS

Moore's law the prediction that about every two years, computer processing power would double and its cost would drop by 50 percent

Raw data facts and figures

Information useful data that can influence people's choices and behavior

First-mover advantage the strategic advantage that companies earn by being the first to use new information technology to substantially lower costs or to make a product or service different from that of competitors

Acquisition cost the cost of obtaining data that you don't have

Processing cost the cost of turning raw data into usable information

Storage cost the cost of physically or electronically archiving information for later retrieval and use

Retrieval cost the cost of accessing already-stored and processed information

Communication cost the cost of transmitting information from one place to another

Bar code a visual pattern that represents numerical data by varying the thickness and pattern of vertical bars

Radio frequency identification (RFID) tags tags containing minuscule microchips that transmit information via radio waves and can be used to track the number and location of the objects into which the tags have been inserted

Electronic scanner an electronic device that converts printed text and pictures into digital images

Optical character recognition the ability of software to convert digitized documents into ASCII (American Standard Code for Information Interchange) text that can be searched, read, and edited by word processing and other kinds of software

Processing information transforming raw data into meaningful information

Data mining the process of discovering unknown patterns and relationships in large amounts of data

Data warehouse stores huge amounts of data that have been prepared for data mining analysis by being cleaned of errors and redundancy

Supervised data mining the process when the user tells the data mining software to look and test for specific patterns and relationships in a data set

Unsupervised data mining the process when the user simply tells the data mining software to uncover whatever patterns and relationships it can find in a data set

Association or affinity patterns when two or more database elements tend to occur together in a significant way

Sequence patterns when two or more database elements occur together in a significant pattern in which one of the elements precedes the other

Predictive patterns patterns that help identify database elements that are different

Data clusters when three or more database elements occur together (i.e., cluster) in a significant way

Protecting information the process of ensuring that data are reliably and consistently retrievable in a usable format for authorized users but no one else

Authentication making sure potential users are who they claim to be

Authorization granting authenticated users approved access to data, software, and systems

Two-factor authentication authentication based on what users know, such as a password and what they have in their possession, such as a secure ID card or key

Biometrics identifying users by unique, measurable body features, such as fingerprint recognition or iris scanning

Firewall a protective hardware or software device that sits between the computers in an internal organizational network and outside networks, such as the Internet

Virus a program or piece of code that, without your knowledge, attaches itself to other programs on your computer and can trigger anything from a harmless flashing message to the reformatting of your hard drive to a systemwide network shutdown

Data encryption the transformation of data into complex, scrambled digital codes that can be decrypted only by authorized users who possess unique decryption keys

Virtual private network (VPN) software that securely encrypts data sent by employees outside the company network, decrypts the data when they arrive within the company computer network, and does the same when data are sent back to employees outside the network

Secure sockets layer (SSL) encryption Internet browser–based encryption that provides secure off-site web access to some data and programs

Executive information system (EIS) a data processing system that uses internal and external data sources to provide the information needed to monitor and analyze organizational performance

Intranets private company networks that allow employees to easily access, share, and publish information using Internet software

Corporate portal a hybrid of executive information systems and intranets that allows managers and employees to use a web browser to gain access to customized company information and to complete specialized transactions

Electronic data interchange (EDI) when two companies convert their purchase and ordering information to a standardized format to enable the direct electronic transmission of that information from one company's computer system to the other company's computer system

Web services software that uses standardized protocols to describe data from one company in such a way that those data can automatically be read, understood, transcribed, and processed by different computer systems in another company

Extranets networks that allow companies to exchange information and conduct transactions with outsiders by providing them direct, web-based access to authorized parts of a company's intranet or information system

Knowledge the understanding that one gains from information

Decision support system (DSS) an information system that helps managers understand specific kinds of problems and potential solutions

Expert system an information system that contains the specialized knowledge and decision rules used by experts and experienced decision makers so that nonexperts can draw on this knowledge base to make decisions

EXHIBIT 17.3

Security Threats to Data and Data Networks

Security Problem	Source	Affects	Severity	The Threat	The Solution
Denial of service; web server attacks and corporate network attacks	Internet hackers	All servers	High	Loss of data, disruption of service, and theft of service.	Implement firewall, password control, server-side review, threat monitoring, and bug fixes; turn PCs off when not in use.
Password cracking software and unauthorized access to PCs	Local area network, Internet	All users, especially digital subscriber line and cable Internet users	High	Hackers take over PCs. Privacy can be invaded. Corporate users' systems are exposed to other machines on the network.	Close ports and firewalls, disable file and print sharing, and use strong passwords.
Viruses, worms, Trojan horses, and rootkits	Email, downloaded and distributed software	All users	Moderate to high	Monitor activities and cause data loss and file deletion; compromise security by sometimes concealing their presence.	Use antivirus software and firewalls; control internet access.
Spyware, adware, malicious scripts and applets	Rogue web pages	All users	Moderate to high	Invade privacy, intercept passwords, and damage files or file system.	Disable browser script support; use security, blocking, and spyware/adware software.
Email snooping	Hackers on your network and the Internet	All users	Moderate to high	People read your email from intermediate servers or packets, or they physically access your machine.	Encrypt messages, ensure strong password protection, and limit physical access to machines.
Keystroke monitoring	Trojan horses, people with direct access to PCs	All users	High	Records everything typed at the keyboard and intercepts keystrokes before password masking or encryption occurs.	Use antivirus software to catch Trojan horses, control Internet access to transmission, and implement system monitoring and physical access control.
Phishing	Hackers on your network and the internet	All users, including customers	High	Fake but real-looking emails and websites that trick users into sharing personal information on what they wrongly think is a company's website. This leads to unauthorized account access.	Educate and warn users and customers about the dangers. Encourage both not to click on potentially fake URLs, which might take them to phishing websites. Instead, have them type your company's URL into the web browser.
Spam	Email	All users and corporations	Mild to high	Clogs and overloads email servers and inboxes with junk mail. HTML-based spam may be used for profiling and identifying users.	Filter known spam sources and senders on email servers; have users create further lists of approved and unapproved senders on their personal computers.
Cookies	Websites you visit	Individual users	Mild to moderate	Trace web usage and permit the creation of personalized web pages that track behavior and interest profiles.	Use cookie managers to control and edit cookies, and use ad blockers.

Sources: K. Bannan, "Look Out: Watching You, Watching Me," *PC Magazine*, July 2002, 99; A. Dragoon, "Fighting Phish, Fakes, and Frauds," *CIO*, September 1, 2004, 33; B. Glass, "Are You Being Watched?" *PC Magazine*, April 23, 2002, 54; K. Karagiannis, "DDoS: Are You Next?" *PC Magazine*, January 2003, 79; B. Machrone, "Protect & Defend," *PC Magazine*, June 27, 2000, 168–181; "Top 10 Security Threats," *PC Magazine*, April 10, 2007, 66; M. Sarrel, "Master End-User Security," *PC Magazine*, May 2008, 101.

LEARNING OUTCOMES

18-1 (p. 379) Discuss the kinds of productivity and their importance in managing operations.

Productivity is a measure of how many inputs it takes to produce or create an output. The greater the output from one input, or the fewer inputs it takes to create an output, the higher the productivity. Partial productivity measures how much of a single kind of input, such as labor, is needed to produce an output. Multifactor productivity is an overall measure of productivity that indicates how much labor, capital, materials, and energy are needed to produce an output.

$$\text{Partial Productivity} = \frac{\text{Outputs}}{\text{Single Kind of Input}}$$

$$\frac{\text{Multifactor}}{\text{Productivity}} = \frac{\text{Outputs}}{(\text{Labor} + \text{Capital} + \text{Materials} + \text{Energy})}$$

18-2 (p. 382) Explain the role that quality plays in managing operations.

Quality can mean that a product or service is practically free of deficiencies or has characteristics that satisfy customer needs. Quality products usually possess three characteristics: reliability, serviceability, and durability. Quality service includes reliability, tangibles, responsiveness, assurance, and empathy. ISO 9000 is a series of five international standards for achieving consistency in quality management and quality assurance, while ISO 14000 is a set of standards for minimizing an organization's harmful effects on the environment. The Baldrige National Quality Award recognizes U.S. companies for their achievements in quality and business performance. Each year, up to three Baldrige Awards may be given in the categories of manufacturing, service, small business, education, nonprofit, and health care. Total quality management (TQM) is an integrated organization-wide strategy for improving product and service quality. TQM is based on three mutually reinforcing principles: customer focus and satisfaction, continuous improvement, and teamwork.

18-3 (p. 387) Explain the essentials of managing a service business.

Services are different from goods. Goods are produced, tangible, and storable. Services are performed, intangible, and perishable. Likewise, managing service operations is different from managing production operations. The service-profit chain indicates that success begins with internal service quality, meaning how well management treats employees. Internal service quality leads to employee satisfaction and service capability, which, in turn, lead to high-value service to customers, customer satisfaction,

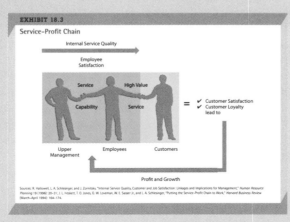

EXHIBIT 18.3

Service–Profit Chain

Internal Service Quality

Employee Satisfaction

Service   High Value

Capability   Service

= ✔ Customer Satisfaction
  ✔ Customer Loyalty
  lead to

Upper Management   Employees   Customers

Profit and Growth

Sources: R. Hallowell, L. A. Schlesinger, and J. Zornitsky, "Internal Service Quality, Customer and Job Satisfaction: Linkages and Implications for Management," *Human Resource Planning* 19 (1996): 20–31; J. L. Heskett, T. O. Jones, G. W. Loveman, W. E. Sasser Jr., and L. A. Schlesinger, "Putting the Service–Profit Chain to Work," *Harvard Business Review* (March–April 1994): 164–174.

KEY TERMS

Operations management managing the daily production of goods and services

Productivity a measure of performance that indicates how many inputs it takes to produce or create an output

Partial productivity a measure of performance that indicates how much of a particular kind of input it takes to produce an output

Multifactor productivity an overall measure of performance that indicates how much labor, capital, materials, and energy it takes to produce an output

Quality a product or service free of deficiencies, or the characteristics of a product or service that satisfies customer needs

ISO 9000 a series of five international standards, from ISO 9000 to ISO 9004, for achieving consistency in quality management and quality assurance in companies throughout the world

ISO 14000 a series of international standards for managing, monitoring, and minimizing an organization's harmful effects on the environment

Total quality management (TQM) an integrated, principle-based, organization-wide strategy for improving product and service quality

Customer focus an organizational goal to concentrate on meeting customers' needs at all levels of the organization

Customer satisfaction an organizational goal to provide products or services that meet or exceed customers' expectations

Continuous improvement an organization's ongoing commitment to constantly assess and improve the processes and procedures used to create products and services

Variation a deviation in the form, condition, or appearance of a product from the quality standard for that product

Teamwork collaboration between managers and nonmanagers, across business functions, and between companies, customers, and suppliers

Internal service quality the quality of treatment employees receive from management and other divisions of a company

Service recovery restoring customer satisfaction to strongly dissatisfied customers

Make-to-order operation a manufacturing operation that does not start processing or assembling products until a customer order is received

customer loyalty, and long-term profits and growth. Keeping existing customers is far more cost-effective than finding new ones. Consequently, to prevent disgruntled customers from leaving, some companies are empowering service employees to perform service recovery—restoring customer satisfaction to strongly dissatisfied customers—by giving employees the authority and responsibility to immediately solve customer problems. The hope is that empowered service recovery will prevent customer defections.

18-4 (p. 390) Describe the different kinds of manufacturing operations.

Manufacturing operations produce physical goods. Manufacturing operations can be classified according to the amount of processing or assembly that occurs after receiving an order from a customer.

Manufacturing operations can also be classified in terms of flexibility, the degree to which the number, kind, and characteristics of products can easily and quickly be changed. Flexibility allows companies to respond quickly to competitors and customers and to reduce order lead times, but it can also lead to higher unit costs.

18-5 (p. 392) Explain why and how companies should manage inventory levels.

There are four kinds of inventory: raw materials, component parts, work-in-process, and finished goods. Because companies incur ordering, setup, holding, and stockout costs when handling inventory, inventory costs can be enormous. To control those costs, companies measure and track inventory in three ways: average aggregate inventory, weeks of supply, and turnover. Companies meet the basic goals of inventory management (avoiding stockouts and reducing inventory without hurting daily operations) through economic order quantity (EOQ) formulas, just-in-time (JIT) inventory systems, and materials requirement planning (MRP). The formula for EOQ is

$$EOQ = \sqrt{\frac{2DO}{H}}$$

Use EOQ formulas when inventory levels are independent, and use JIT and MRP when inventory levels are dependent on the number of products to be produced.

Assemble-to-order operation a manufacturing operation that divides manufacturing processes into separate parts or modules that are combined to create semicustomized products

Make-to-stock operation a manufacturing operation that orders parts and assembles standardized products before receiving customer orders

Manufacturing flexibility the degree to which manufacturing operations can easily and quickly change the number, kind, and characteristics of products they produce

Continuous-flow production a manufacturing operation that produces goods at a continuous, rather than a discrete, rate

Line-flow production manufacturing processes that are preestablished, occur in a serial or linear manner, and are dedicated to making one type of product

Batch production a manufacturing operation that produces goods in large batches in standard lot sizes

Job shops manufacturing operations that handle custom orders or small batch jobs

Inventory the amount and number of raw materials, parts, and finished products that a company has in its possession

Raw material inventories the basic inputs in a manufacturing process

Component parts inventories the basic parts used in manufacturing that are fabricated from raw materials

Work-in-process inventories partially finished goods consisting of assembled component parts

Finished goods inventories the final outputs of manufacturing operations

Average aggregate inventory average overall inventory during a particular time period

Stockout the point when a company runs out of finished product

Inventory turnover the number of times per year that a company sells, or "turns over," its average inventory

Ordering cost the cost associated with ordering inventory, including the cost of data entry, phone calls, obtaining bids, correcting mistakes, and determining when and how much inventory to order

Setup cost the cost of downtime and lost efficiency that occurs when a machine is changed or adjusted to produce a different kind of inventory

Holding cost the cost of keeping inventory until it is used or sold, including storage, insur-

ance, taxes, obsolescence, and opportunity costs

Stockout cost the cost incurred when a company runs out of a product, including the transaction cost to replace inventory and the loss of customers' goodwill

Economic order quantity (EOQ) a system of formulas that minimizes ordering and holding costs and helps determine how much and how often inventory should be ordered

Just-in-time (JIT) inventory system an inventory system in which component parts arrive from suppliers just as they are needed at each stage of production

Kanban a ticket-based JIT system that indicates when to reorder inventory

Materials requirement planning (MRP) a production and inventory system that determines the production schedule, production batch sizes, and inventory needed to complete final products

Independent demand system an inventory system in which the level of one kind of inventory does not depend on another

Dependent demand system an inventory system in which the level of inventory depends on the number of finished units to be produced